INJUNCTIONS

SECOND EDITION

By

OWEN M. FISS
Alexander M. Bickel Professor of Public Law,
Yale University

and

DOUG RENDLEMAN
Godwin Professor of Law,
College of William and Mary

Mineola, New York
THE FOUNDATION PRESS, INC.
1984

395 Hudson Street
New York, N.Y. 10014
Phone Toll Free 1–877–888–1330
Fax (212) 367–6799
fdpress.com

Library of Congress Cataloging in Publication Data

Fiss, Owen M.
Injunctions.
(University casebook series)
Includes index.
1. Injunctions—United States—Cases. I. Rendleman, Doug. II. Title. III. Series.
KF9014.A7F58 1983 347.73'77 83–20573

ISBN 0–88277–151–5 347.30777

TEXT IS PRINTED ON 10% POST CONSUMER RECYCLED PAPER

1st Reprint — 2002

PREFACE TO THE SECOND EDITION

The first edition was a child of the sixties. The first word was written in 1968 and the last in 1972. Its overriding purpose was to bring into the classroom the many remarkable developments that had occurred to the injunction in the civil rights era. The first edition sought to develop new categories of injunctions, and drawing from the school desegregation experience, introduced the idea of the structural injunction. It examined the traditional remedial hierarchy, which made the injunction the remedy of last resort, and identified the circumstances that made the injunction the preferred remedy in constitutional litigation. The first edition also asked whether the injunction could be made to serve group, rather than individual, rights, and sought to identify the changes occurring in the remedy because of this group focus. And the first edition depicted many of the truly dramatic and now historic struggles of the era—the integration of Ole Miss in 1962 was one and Martin Luther King's campaign in Birmingham in the spring of 1963 was another. These struggles tested the modern-day chancellors' coercive imagination and revealed all that was involved in enforcing an injunction.

The civil rights era was one of the most extraordinary periods of American law. It closed in the early seventies, but its lessons are indelible. The idealism it engendered, not just in the judiciary but for an entire generation of lawyers, did not die, and has been transferred to new domains. The structural injunction now copes with the dangers posed to public values by a wide variety of bureaucratic organizations, including prisons, mental hospitals, public housing authorities, and institutions for the mentally retarded. The injunction is now often used to protect the environment, preserve the public order, and strike a balance between fair trial and free press. These developments are an important part of the last decade and are analyzed in this edition. Another side of the seventies, however, accounts for the special flavor of what follows. The seventies were a period of reaction.

Dissenting voices to the civil rights injunction have always existed. In the sixties they were small and feeble, often associated with people who had no, or little, credibility in the profession or in the academy. But in the seventies the dissenting voices grew and we listened. New questions were raised about judicial activism and the use of the injunction to reform existing social structures. Some attribute this change to the fortuities of politics—the election of Richard Nixon and his appointments to the Department of Justice and the Supreme Court. Others attribute it to the decline in the American economy or to the energy crisis, asserting that justice was a luxury we could no longer afford. And still others emphasize the violence and social dislocation that marred the close of the civil rights era and the protests against the war in Vietnam. We think, however, that the reaction can be explained in terms intrinsic to the law: Society finally understood all that the injunction had done and all that had happened to it. Some of these legal changes were to be marvelled at, even with the perspective that comes from the passage of time, but others seemed more problematic.

We are no friends of the reaction, as these pages and our earlier writing make evident, but as editors of a casebook and as teachers, it has been a joy. The reaction has brought into sharp focus what we had dimly seen before or what, in the late sixties, appeared as bizarre hypotheticals. The reaction has forced us to reexamine our fundamental premises and to defend those parts of the legacy of the civil rights injunction that we regard as most durable and inspiring. The reaction has generated a rich body of literature that either condemns the civil rights injunction or alternatively seeks to reconcile it with traditional conceptions of the judicial process. The reaction added a new dimension to the ongoing debate about the legitimacy of judicial power and created a new phase in the history of equity. It has given us something to talk about (as though that were really necessary).

The injunction represents the most visible and perhaps the most ambitious exercise of judicial power-at times it tries to reconstruct the world. The reaction of the seventies brought a course on injunctions to the forefront of public law, poised between memory and imagination, demanding a mastery of technical doctrine and intricate procedural details, and yet raising some of the most perplexing jurisprudential issues of our day.

OWEN M. FISS
DOUG RENDLEMAN

November, 1983

SUMMARY OF CONTENTS

TABLE OF CONTENTS

CHAPTER 14. WHO IS BOUND BY AN INJUNCTION—Continued

INJUNCTIONS

*

Chapter One

GOVERNMENT BY INJUNCTION?

I. History's Legacy

IN RE DEBS

158 U.S. 564, 15 S.Ct. 900, 39 L.Ed. 1092 (1895).

On July 2, 1894, the United States, by Thomas E. Milchrist, district attorney for the Northern District of Illinois, under the direction of Richard Olney, Attorney General, filed their bill of complaint in the Circuit Court of the United States for the Northern District of Illinois against these petitioners and others. This bill set forth, among other things, the following facts: It named twenty-two railroad companies, and it alleged that they were engaged in the business of interstate commerce and subject to the provisions of the act of Congress of February 4, 1887, known as "the Interstate Commerce Act," and all other laws of the United States relating to interstate transportation of passengers and freight; that the number of passengers annually carried by them into the city of Chicago from other States than Illinois, and out of Chicago into other States than Illinois, was more than twelve million, and in like manner that the freight so carried into and out of the city of Chicago, from and into other States than Illinois, amounted to many millions of tons; that each of the roads was under contract to carry, and in fact carrying, the mails of the United States; that all were by statute declared post roads of the government; that many were by special acts of Congress required at any and all times to carry the troops and military forces of the United States, and provisions, munitions, and general supplies therefor; and that two of them were in the hands of receivers appointed by the courts of the United States. It stated at some length the necessity of the continued and uninterrupted running of such interstate railroads for the bringing into the city of Chicago supplies for its citizens and for the carrying on of the varied industries of that city.

The bill further averred that four of the defendants, naming them, were officers of an association known as the American Railway Union; that in the month of May 1894, there arose a difference or dispute between the Pullman Palace Car Company and its employés, as the result of which a considerable portion of the latter left the service of the car company; that thereafter the four officers of the railway union combined together, and with others, to compel an adjustment of such dispute, by creating a boycott against the cars of the car company; that, to make such boycott effective, they had already prevented certain of the railroads running out of Chicago from operating their trains, and were combining to extend such boycott against Pullman sleeping cars by causing strikes among employés of all railroads attempting to haul the same. It charged knowledge on the part of the defendants of the necessity of the use of sleeping cars in the operation of the business of the railroads as common carriers, of the contracts for such use between the railroad companies and the car company, of the contracts, laws, and regulations binding the railway companies and the receivers to the carrying of the mails; also of the fact that sleeping cars were and of necessity must be carried upon the trains of said carriers with cars containing the mails; that with this knowledge they entered into a combination and conspiracy to prevent the railroad companies and the receivers, and each of them, from performing their duties as common carriers of interstate commerce, and in carrying into execution that conspiracy did induce various employés of the railway companies to leave the service of the companies, and prevent such companies and the receivers from securing other persons to take their places; that they issued orders, notifications, etc., to the members of the railway union to leave the service of the companies and receivers, and to prevent the companies and receivers from operating their trains; that they had asserted that they could and would tie up, paralyze, and break down any and every of said railway companies and receivers which did not accede to their demands; that in pursuance of the instructions, commands and requests of said officers large numbers of the employés of the railway companies and receivers left their service.

Then followed these allegations:

"And your orator further charges that said defendants aimed and intended and do now aim and intend in and by the said conspiracy and combination, to secure unto themselves the entire control of the interstate industrial and commercial business in which the population of the city of Chicago and of the other communities along the lines of road of said railways are engaged with each other, and to restrain any and all other persons from any independent control or management of such interstate industrial or commercial enterprises save according to the will and with the consent of the defendants.

"Your orator further avers that in pursuance of said combination and conspiracy and to accomplish the purpose thereof as hereinbefore set forth, the said defendants Debs, Howard, Rodgers, Keliher and others, officers of said American Railway Union, issued or caused to be issued the orders and directions as above set forth, and that in obedience of such orders and in pursuance of said conspiracy and combination, numerous employés of said railroad companies and receivers unitedly refused to obey the orders of said employers or to perform the usual duties of such service, and many others of such employés quit such service with the common purpose, and with the result of preventing said railroad companies and receivers from operating their said railroads and from transporting the United States mails, and from carrying on or conducting their duties as common carriers of interstate traffic.

"Your orator further avers that, pursuant to said combination and conspiracy, and under the direction as aforesaid of said officers and directors of said American Railway Union, said other defendants and other persons whose names are to your orator unknown, proceeded by collecting together in large numbers, by threats, intimidation, force and violence at the station grounds, yards and right of way of said railroad companies, respectively, in the State of Illinois, to prevent said railroad companies from employing other persons to fill the vacancies aforesaid; to compel others still employés of said railroad companies to quit such employment and to refuse to perform the duties of their service, and to prevent the persons remaining in such service and ready and willing to perform the duties of the same from doing so.

"Your orator further avers that said defendants, in pursuance of said combination and conspiracy, acting under the direction of said officers and directors of said American Railway Union, did with force and violence at divers times and places within said State of Illinois and elsewhere, stop, obstruct and derail and wreck the engines and trains of said railroad companies, both passenger and freight, then and there engaged in interstate commerce and in transporting United States mails, by locking the switches of the railroad of said railroad companies, by removing the spikes and rails from the track thereof, by turning switches and displacing and destroying signals, by assaulting and interfering with and disabling the switchmen and other employés of said railroad companies having charge of the signals, switches and tracks of said companies, and the movement of trains thereon, and in other manners by force and violence, depriving the employés of said railroad companies in charge of such trains of the control and management of the same, and by these and other unlawful means attempted to obtain and exercise absolute control and domination over the entire operations of said railroads."

The bill further set forth that there had become established in the city of Chicago a business conducted under the name of the Union Stock Yards, at which for many years immense numbers of live stock from States and Territories beyond the State of Illinois had been received, slaughtered, and converted into food products, and distributed to all quarters of the globe, and that all the large centres of population in the United States were in a great degree dependent upon those stock yards for their food supply of that character; that for the purpose of handling such live stock and the products thereof the company conducting such business operated certain railroad tracks, and that in pursuance of the combination and conspiracy aforesaid the four defendants, officers of the railway union, issued orders directing all the employés handling such railroad tracks to abandon such service.

To this was added the following:

"And your orator further alleges that in pursuance of the like combination and unlawful conspiracy, the said defendants and others combining and conspiring with them for the purpose of still further restraining and preventing the conduct of such business, have by menaces, threats and intimidation prevented the employment of other persons to take the place of the employés quitting the service of said company so operating said Union Stock Yards.

"And your orator further charges that by reason of said unlawful combination and conspiracy and the acts and doings aforesaid thereunder, the supply of coal and fuel for consumption throughout the different States of the Union and of grain, breadstuffs, vegetables, fruits, meats and other necessaries of life, has been cut off, interrupted and interfered with, and the market therefor made largely unavailable, and dealers in all of said various products and the consumers thereof have been greatly injured, and trade and commerce therein among the States has been restrained, obstructed and largely destroyed."

The bill alleged that the defendants threatened and declared that they would continue to restrain, obstruct, and interfere with interstate commerce, as above set forth, and that they "will if necessary to carry out the said unlawful combination and conspiracy above set forth tie up and paralyze the operations of every railway in the United States, and the business and industries dependent thereon." Following these allegations was a prayer for an injunction. The bill was verified.

On presentation of it to the court an injunction was ordered commanding the defendants "and all persons combining and conspiring with them, and all other persons whomsoever, absolutely to desist and refrain from in any way or manner interfering with, hindering, obstructing or stopping any of the business of any of the following named railroads," (specifically naming the various roads named in the bill,) "as common carriers of passengers and freight between or among any States of the United States, and from in any way or manner interfering with, hindering, obstructing or stopping any mail trains, express trains or other trains, whether freight or passenger, engaged in interstate commerce, or carrying passengers or freight between or among the States; and from in any manner interfering with, hindering or stopping any trains carrying the mail; and from in any manner interfering with, hindering, obstructing or stopping any engines, cars, or rolling stock of any of said companies engaged in interstate commerce, or in connection with the carriage of passengers or freight between or among the States; and from in any manner interfering with, injuring or destroying any of the property of any of said railroads engaged in or for the purpose of or in connection with, interstate commerce or the carriage of the mails of the United States or the transportation of passengers or freight between or among the States; and from entering upon the grounds or premises of any of said railroads for the purpose of interfering with, hindering, obstructing, or stopping any of said mail trains, passenger or freight trains engaged in interstate commerce, or in the transportation of passengers or freight between or among the States, or for the purpose of interfering with, injuring, or destroying any of said property so engaged in or used in connection with interstate commerce or the transportation of passengers or property between or among the States; and from injuring or destroying any part of the tracks, roadbed, or road, or permanent structures of said railroads; and from injuring, destroying, or in any way interfering with any of the signals or switches of any of said railroads; and from displacing or extinguishing any of the signals of any of said railroads, and from spiking, locking, or in any manner fastening any of the switches of any of said railroads, and from uncoupling or in any way hampering or obstructing the control by any of said railroads of any of the cars, engines, or parts of trains of any of said railroads engaged in interstate commerce or in the transportation of passengers or freight between or among the States, or engaged in carrying any of the mails of the United States; and from compelling or inducing or attempting to compel or induce, by threats, intimidation, persuasion, force, or violence, any of the employés of any of said railroads to refuse or fail to perform any of their duties as employés of any of said railroads in connection with the interstate business or commerce of such railroads or the carriage of the United States mail by such railroads, or the transportation of passengers or property between or among the States; and from compelling or inducing or attempting to compel or induce by threats, intimidation, force, or violence any of the employés of any said railroads who are employed by such railroads, and engaged in its service in the conduct of interstate business or in the operation of any of its trains carrying the mail of the United States, or doing interstate business, or the transportation of passengers and freight between and among the States, to leave the service of such railroads; and from preventing any person whatever, by threats, intimidation, force, or violence from entering the service of any of said railroads and doing the work thereof, in the carrying of the mails of the United States, or the transportation of passengers and freight between or among the States; and from doing any act whatever in furtherance of any conspiracy or combination to restrain either of said railroad companies or receivers in the free and unhindered control and handling of interstate commerce over the lines of said railroads, and of transportation of persons and freight between and among the States; and from ordering, directing, aiding, assisting, or abetting in any manner whatever, any person or persons to commit any or either of the acts aforesaid.

"And it is further ordered that the aforesaid injunction and writ of injunction shall be in force and binding upon such of said defendants as are named in said bill from and after the service upon them severally of said writ by delivering to them severally a copy of said writ or by reading the same to them and the service upon them respectively of the writ of subpoena herein, and shall be binding upon said defendants, whose names are alleged to be unknown, from and after the service of such writ upon them respectively by the reading of the same to them or by the publication thereof by posting or printing, and after service of subpoena upon any of said defendants named herein shall be binding upon said defendants and upon all other persons whatsoever who are not named herein from and after the time when they shall severally have knowledge of the entry of such order and the existence of said injunction."

This injunction was served upon the defendants—at least upon those who are here as petitioners. On July 17 the district attorney filed in the office of the clerk of said court an information for an attachment against the four defendants, officers of the railway union, and on August 1 a similar information against the other petitioners. A hearing was had before the Circuit Court, and on December 14 these petitioners were found guilty of contempt, and sentenced to imprisonment in the county jail for terms varying from three to six months. 64 Fed.Rep. 724. Having been committed to jail in pursuance of this order they, on January 14, 1895, applied to this court for a writ of error and also one of *habeas corpus.* The former was, on January 17, denied, on the ground that the order of the Circuit Court was not a final judgment or decree. The latter is now to be considered. [Decision was rendered on May 27, 1895.]

Justice BREWER, after stating the case, delivered the opinion of the court.

The case presented by the bill is this: The United States, finding that the interstate transportation of persons and property, as well as the carriage of the mails, is forcibly obstructed, and that a combination and conspiracy exists to subject the control of such transportation to the will of the conspirators, applied to one of their courts, sitting as a court of equity, for an injunction to restrain such obstruction and prevent carrying into effect such conspiracy. Two questions of importance are presented: First. Are the relations of the general government to interstate commerce and the transportation of the mails such as authorize a direct interference to prevent a forcible obstruction thereof? Second. If authority exists, as authority in governmental affairs implies both power and duty, has a court of equity jurisdiction to issue an injunction in aid of the performance of such duty?

First. What are the relations of the general government to interstate commerce and the transportation of the mails? They are those of direct supervision, control, and management. While under the dual system which prevails with us the powers of government are distributed between the State and the Nation, and while the latter is properly styled a government of enumerated powers, yet within the limits of such enumeration it has all the attributes of sovereignty, and, in the exercise of those enumerated powers, acts directly upon the citizen, and not through the intermediate agency of the State.

"The government of the Union, then, is emphatically and truly, a government of the people. In form and in substance it emanates from them. Its powers are granted by them, and are to be exercised directly on them, and for their benefit.

"No trace is to be found in the Constitution of an intention to create a dependence of the government of the Union on those of the States, for the execution of the great powers assigned to it. Its means are adequate to its ends; and on those means alone was it expected to rely for the accomplishment of its ends. To impose on it the necessity of resorting to means which it cannot control, which another government may furnish or withhold, would render its course precarious, the result of its measures uncertain, and create a dependence on other governments, which might disappoint its most important designs, and is incompatible with the language of the Constitution." Chief Justice Marshall in McCulloch v. Maryland, 4 Wheat. 316, 405, 424.

. . .

Among the powers expressly given to the national government are the control of interstate commerce and the creation and management of a post office system for the nation. Article I, section 8, of the Constitution provides that "the Congress shall have power. . . . Third, to regulate commerce with foreign nations and among the several States, and with the Indian tribes. . . . Seventh, to establish post offices and post roads."

Congress has exercised the power granted in respect to interstate commerce in a variety of legislative acts. Passing by for the present all that legislation in respect to commerce by water, and considering only that which bears upon railroad interstate transportation, (for this is the specific matter involved in this case,) these acts may be noticed: First, that of June 15, 1866, c. 124, 14 Stat. 66, carried into the Revised Statutes as section 5258, which provides:

"Whereas the Constitution of the United States confers upon Congress, in express terms, the power to regulate commerce among the several States, to establish post roads, and to raise and support armies: Therefore, *Be it enacted by the Senate and House of Representatives of the United States of America in Congress assembled,* That every railroad company in the United States whose road is operated by steam, its successors and assigns, be, and is hereby, authorized to carry upon and over its road, boats, bridges, and ferries all passengers, troops, government supplies, mails, freight, and property on their way from any State to another State, and to receive compensation therefor, and to connect with roads of other States so as to form continuous lines for the transportation of the same to the place of destination."

Second. That of March 3, 1873, c. 252, 17 Stat. 584, (Rev.Stat. §§ 4386 to 4389,) which regulates the transportation of live stock over interstate railroads. Third. That of May 29, 1884, c. 60, § 6, 23 Stat. 31, 32, prohibiting interstate transportation by railroads of live stock affected with any contagious or infectious disease. Fourth. That of February 4, 1887, c. 104, 24 Stat. 379, with its amendments of March 2, 1889, c. 382, 25 Stat. 855, and February 10, 1891, c. 128, 26 Stat. 743, known as the "interstate commerce act," by which a commission was created with large powers of regulation and control of interstate commerce by railroads, and the sixteenth section of which act gives to the courts of the United States power to enforce the orders of the commission. Fifth. That of October 1, 1888, c. 1063, 25 Stat. 501, providing for arbitration between railroad interstate companies and their employés; and sixth, the act of March 2, 1893, c. 196, 27 Stat. 531, requiring the use of automatic couplers on interstate trains, and empowering the Interstate Commerce Commission to enforce its provisions.

Under the power vested in Congress to establish post offices and post roads, Congress has, by a mass of legislation, established the great post office system of the country, with all its detail of organization, its machinery for the transaction of business, defining what shall be carried and what not, and the prices of carriage, and also prescribing penalties for all offences against it.

Obviously these powers given to the national government over interstate commerce and in respect to the transportation of the mails were not dormant and unused. Congress had taken hold of these two matters, and by various and specific acts had assumed and exercised the powers given to it, and was in the full discharge of its duty to regulate interstate commerce and carry the mails. The validity of such exercise and the exclusiveness of its control had been again and again presented to this court for consideration. It is curious to note the fact that in a large proportion of the cases in respect to interstate commerce brought to this court the question presented was of the validity of state legislation in its bearings upon interstate commerce, and the uniform course of decision has been to declare that it is not within the competency of a State to legislate in such a manner as to obstruct interstate commerce. If a State with its recognized powers of sovereignty is impotent to obstruct interstate commerce, can it be that any mere voluntary association of individuals within the limits of that State has a power which the State itself does not possess?

As, under the Constitution, power over interstate commerce and the transportation of the mails is vested in the national government, and Congress by virtue of such grant has assumed actual and direct control, it follows that the national government may prevent any unlawful and forcible interference therewith. But how shall this be accomplished? Doubtless, it is within the competency of Congress to prescribe by legislation that any interference with these matters shall be offences against the United States, and prosecuted and punished by indictment in the proper courts. But is that the only remedy? Have the vast interests of the nation in interstate commerce, and in the transportation of the mails, no other protection than lies in the possible punishment of those who interfere with it? To ask the question is to answer it. By article 3, section 2, clause 3 of the Federal Constitution it is provided: "The trial of all crimes except in cases of impeachment shall be by jury; and such trial shall be held in the State where the said crime shall have been committed." If all the inhabitants of a State, or even a great body of them, should combine to obstruct interstate commerce or the transportation of the mails, prosecutions for such offences had in such a community would be doomed in advance to failure. And if the certainty of such failure was known, and the national government had no other way to enforce the freedom of interstate commerce and the transportation of the mails than by prosecution and punishment for interference therewith, the whole interest of the nation in these respects would be at the absolute mercy of a portion of the inhabitants of that single State.

But there is no such impotency in the national government. The entire strength of the nation may be used to enforce in any part of the land the full and free exercise of all national powers and the security of all rights entrusted by the Constitution to its care. The strong arm of the national government may be put forth to brush away all obstructions to the freedom of interstate commerce or the transportation of the mails. If the emergency arises, the army of the Nation, and all its militia, are at the service of the Nation to compel obedience to its laws.

But passing to the second question, is there no other alternative than the use of force on the part of the executive authorities whenever obstructions arise to the freedom of interstate commerce or the transportation of the mails? Is the army the only instrument by which rights of the public can be enforced and the peace of the nation preserved? Grant that any public nuisance may be forcibly abated either at the instance of the authorities, or by any individual suffering private damage therefrom, the existence of this right of forcible abatement is not inconsistent with nor does it destroy the right of appeal in an orderly way to the courts for a judicial determination, and an exercise of their powers by writ of injunction and otherwise to accomplish the same result. In Borough of Stamford v. Stamford Horse R. Co., 56 Conn. 381, 15 Atl. 749, an injunction was asked by the borough to restrain the company from laying down its track in a street of the borough. The right of the borough to forcibly remove the track was insisted upon as a ground for questioning the jurisdiction of a court of equity, but the court sustained the injunction, adding: "And none the less so because of its right to remove the track by force. As a rule, injunctions are denied to those who have adequate remedy at law. Where the choice is between the ordinary and the extraordinary processes of law, and the former are sufficient, the rule will not permit the use of the latter. In some cases of nuisance and in some cases of trespass the law permits an individual to abate the one and prevent the other by force, because such permission is necessary to the complete protection of property and person. When the choice is between redress or prevention of injury by force and by peaceful process, the law is well pleased if the individual will consent to waive his right to the use of force and await its action. Therefore, as between force and the extraordinary writ of injunction, the rule will permit the latter."

So, in the case before us, the right to use force does not exclude the right of appeal to the courts for a judicial determination and for the exercise of all their powers of prevention. Indeed, it is more to the praise than to the blame of the government, that, instead of determining for itself questions of right and wrong on the part of these petitioners and their associates and enforcing that determination by the club of the policeman and the bayonet of the soldier, it submitted all those questions to the peaceful determination of judicial tribunals, and invoked their consideration and judgment as to the measure of its rights and powers and the correlative obligations of those against whom it made complaint. And it is equally to the credit of the latter that the judgment of those tribunals was by the great body of them respected, and the troubles which threatened so much disaster terminated.

Neither can it be doubted that the government has such an interest in the subject-matter as enables it to appear as party plaintiff in this suit. It is said that equity only interferes for the protection of property, and that the government has no property interest. A sufficient reply is that the United States have a property in the mails, the protection of which was one of the purposes of this bill. Searight v. Stokes, 3 How. 151, arose upon a compact between the United States and the State of Pennsylvania in respect to the Cumberland Road, which provided, among other things, "that no toll shall be received or collected for the passage of any wagon or carriage laden with the property of the United States;" the question being whether a carriage employed in transporting the mails of the United States was one "laden with the property of the United States," and it was held that it was, the court, by Chief Justice Taney, saying: "The United States have unquestionably a property in the mails. They are not mere common carriers, but a government, performing a high official duty in holding and guarding its own property as well as that of its citizens committed to its care; for a very large portion of the letters and packages conveyed on this road, especially during the session of Congress, consists of communications to or from the officers of the executive departments, or members of the legislature, on public service, or in relation to matters of public concern. . . . We think that a carriage, whenever it is carrying the mail, is laden with the property of the United States within the true meaning of the compact."

We do not care to place our decision upon this ground alone. Every government, entrusted, by the very terms of its being, with powers and duties to be exercised and discharged for the general welfare, has a right to apply to its own courts for any proper assistance in the exercise of the one and the discharge of the other, and it is no sufficient answer to its appeal to one of those courts that it has no pecuniary interest in the matter. The obligations which it is under to promote the interest of all, and to prevent the wrongdoing of one resulting in injury to the general welfare, is often of itself sufficient to give it a standing in court. . . .

It is obvious from these decisions that while it is not the province of the government to interfere in any mere matter of private controversy between individuals, or to use its great powers to enforce the rights of one against another, yet, whenever the wrongs complained of are such as affect the public at large, and are in respect of matters which by the Constitution are entrusted to the care of the Nation, and concerning which the Nation owes the duty to all the citizens of securing to them their common rights, then the mere fact that the government has no pecuniary interest in the controversy is not sufficient to exclude it from the courts, or prevent it from taking measures therein to fully discharge those constitutional duties.

The national government, given by the Constitution power to regulate interstate commerce, has by express statute assumed jurisdiction over such commerce when carried upon railroads. It is charged, therefore, with the duty of keeping those highways of interstate commerce free from obstruction, for it has always been recognized as one of the powers and duties of a government to remove obstructions from the highways under its control.

. . . Indeed, the obstruction of a highway is a public nuisance . . . , and a public nuisance has always been held subject to abatement at the instance of the government. . . .

State of Pennsylvania v. Wheeling, etc., Bridge Co., 13 How. 518, was a bill filed by the State of Pennsylvania to enjoin the erection of a bridge over the Ohio River within the limits of the State of Virginia. As the alleged obstruction was not within the State of Pennsylvania, its right to relief was only that of an individual in case of a private nuisance, and it was said, on page 564:

"The injury makes the obstruction a private nuisance to the injured party; and the doctrine of nuisance applies to the case where the jurisdiction is made out, the same as in a public prosecution. If the obstruction be unlawful, and the injury irreparable by a suit at common law, the injured party may claim the extraordinary protection of a court of chancery.

"Such a proceeding is as common and as free from difficulty as an ordinary injunction bill, against a proceeding at law, or to stay waste or trespass. The powers of a court of chancery are as well adapted, and as effectual for relief in the case of a private nuisance, as in either of the cases named. And, in regard to the exercise of these powers, it is of no importance whether the eastern channel, over which the bridge is thrown, is wholly within the limits of the State of Virginia. The Ohio being a navigable stream, subject to the commercial power of Congress, and over which that power has been exerted, if the river be within the State of Virginia, the commerce upon it, which extends to other States, is not within its jurisdiction; consequently, if the act of Virginia authorized the structure of the bridge, so as to obstruct navigation, it could afford no justification to the bridge company." . . .

It is said that the jurisdiction heretofore exercised by the national government over highways has been in respect to waterways—the natural highways of the country—and not over artificial highways such as railroads; but the occasion for the exercise by Congress of its jurisdiction over the latter is of recent date. Perhaps, the first act in the course of such legislation is that heretofore referred to, of June 14, 1866, but the basis upon which rests its jurisdiction over artificial highways is the same as that which supports it over the natural highways. Both spring from the power to regulate commerce. The national government has no separate dominion over a river within the limits of a State; its jurisdiction there is like that over land within the same State. Its control over the river is simply by virtue of the fact that it is one of the highways of interstate and international commerce. . . .

Up to a recent date commerce, both interstate and international, was mainly by water, and it is not strange that both the legislation of Congress and the cases in the courts have been principally concerned therewith. The fact that in recent years interstate commerce has come mainly to be carried on by railroads and over artificial highways has in no manner narrowed the scope of the constitutional provision or abridged the power of Congress over such commerce. On the contrary, the same fulness of control exists in the one case as in the other, and the same power to remove obstructions from the one as from the other.

Constitutional provisions do not change, but their operation extends to new matters as the modes of business and the habits of life of the people vary with each succeeding generation. The law of the common carrier is the same to-day as when transportation on land was by coach and wagon, and on water by canal boat and sailing vessel, yet in its actual operation it touches and regulates transportation by modes then unknown, the railroad train and the steamship. Just so is it with the grant to the national government of power over interstate commerce. The Constitution has not changed. The power is the same. But it operates to-day upon modes of interstate commerce unknown to the fathers, and it will operate with equal force upon any new modes of such commerce which the future may develop.

It is said that seldom have the courts assumed jurisdiction to restrain by injunction in suits brought by the government, either state or national, obstructions to highways, either artificial or natural. This is undoubtedly true, but the reason is that the necessity for such interference has only been occassional. Ordinarily the local authorities have taken full control over the matter, and by indictment for misdemeanor, or in some kindred way, have secured the removal of the obstruction and the cessation of the nuisance. As said in Attorney General v. Brown, 24 N.J.Eq. 89, 91: "The jurisdiction of courts of equity to redress the grievance of public nuisances by injunction is undoubted and clearly established; but it is well settled that, as a general rule, equity will not interfere, where the object sought can be as well attained in the ordinary tribunals. . . . And because the remedy by indictment is so efficacious, courts of equity entertain jurisdiction in such cases with great reluctance, whether their intervention is invoked at the instance of the attorney general, or of a private individual who suffers some injury therefrom distinct from that of the public, and they will only do so where there appears to be a necessity for their interference. . . . The jurisdiction of the court of chancery with regard to public nuisances is founded on the irreparable damage to individuals, or the great public injury which is likely to ensue. . . ." Indeed, it may be affirmed that in no well-considered case has the power of a court of equity to interfere by injunction in cases of public nuisance been denied, the only denial ever being that of a necessity for the exercise of that jurisdiction under the circumstances of the particular case. Story's Eq.Jur. §§ 921, 923, 924; Pomeroy's Eq.Jur. § 1349; High on Injunctions, §§ 745 and 1554; 2 Daniell's Ch.Pl. and Pr. 4th ed. p. 1636.

That the bill filed in this case alleged special facts calling for the exercise of all the powers of the court is not open to question. The picture drawn in it of the vast interests involved, not merely of the city of Chicago and the State of Illinois, but of all the States, and the general confusion into which the interstate commerce of the country was thrown; the forcible interference with that commerce; the attempted exercise by individuals of powers belonging only to government, and the threatened continuance of such invasions of public right, presented a condition of affairs which called for the fullest exercise of all the powers of the courts. If ever there was a special exigency, one which demanded that the court should do all that courts can do, it was disclosed by this bill, and we need not turn to the public history of the day, which only reaffirms with clearest emphasis all its allegations.

The difference between a public nuisance and a private nuisance is that the one affects the people at large and the other simply the individual. The quality of the wrong is the same, and the jurisdiction of the courts over them rests upon the same principles and goes to the same extent. Of course, circumstances may exist in one case, which do not in another, to induce the court to interfere or to refuse to interfere by injunction, but the jurisdiction, the power to interfere, exists in all cases of nuisance. True many more suits are brought by individuals than by the public to enjoin nuisances, but there are two reasons for this. First, the instances are more numerous of private than of public nuisances; and, second, often that which is in fact a public nuisance is restrained at the suit of a private individual, whose right to relief arises because of a special injury resulting therefrom.

Again, it is objected that it is outside of the jurisdiction of a court of equity to enjoin the commission of crimes. This, as a general proposition, is unquestioned. A chancellor has no criminal jurisdiction. Something more than the threatened commission of an offence against the laws of the land is necessary to call into exercise the injunctive powers of the court. There must be some interferences, actual or threatened, with property or rights of a pecuniary nature, but when such interferences appear the jurisdiction of a court of equity arises, and is not destroyed by the fact that they are accompanied by or are themselves violations of the criminal law. Thus, in Cranford v. Tyrrell, 128 N.Y. 341, 28 N.E. 514, an injunction to restrain the defendant from keeping a house of ill-fame was sustained, the court saying, on page 344: "That the perpetrator of the nuisance is amenable to the provisions and penalties of the criminal law is not an answer to an action against him by a private person to recover for injury sustained, and for an injunction against the continued use of his premises in such a manner." And in Port of Mobile v. Louisville & N.R. Co., 84 Ala. 115, 126, 4 South. 106, is a similar declaration in these words: "The mere fact that an act is criminal does not divest the jurisdiction of equity to prevent it by injunction, if it be also a violation of property rights, and the party aggrieved has no other adequate remedy for the prevention of the irreparable injury which will result from the failure or inability of a court of law to redress such rights."

The law is full of instances in which the same act may give rise to a civil action and a criminal prosecution. An assault with intent to kill may be punished criminally, under an indictment therefor, or will support a civil action for damages, and the same is true of all other offences which cause injury to person or property. In such cases the jurisdiction of the civil court is invoked, not to enforce the criminal law and punish the wrongdoer, but to compensate the injured party for the damages which he or his property has suffered, and it is no defence to the civil action that the same act by the defendant exposes him also to indictment and punishment in a court of criminal jurisdiction. So here, the acts of the defendants may or may not have been violations of the criminal law. If they were, that matter is for inquiry in other proceedings. The complaint made against them in this is of disobedience to an order of a civil court, made for the protection of property and the security of rights. If any criminal prosecution be brought against them for the criminal offences alleged in the bill of complaint, of derailing and wrecking engines and trains, assaulting and disabling employés of the railroad companies, it will be no defence to such prosecution that they disobeyed the orders of injunction served upon them and have been punished for such disobedience.

Nor is there in this any invasion of the constitutional right of trial by jury. We fully agree with counsel that "it matters not what form the attempt to deny constitutional right may take. It is vain and ineffectual, and must be so declared by the courts," and we reaffirm the declaration made for the court by Mr. Justice Bradley in Boyd v. U.S., 116 U.S. 616, 635, that "it is the duty of courts to be watchful for the constitutional rights of the citizen, and against any stealthy encroachments thereon. Their motto should be *obsta principiis.*" But the power of a court to make an order carries with it the equal power to punish for a disobedience of that order, and the inquiry as to the question of disobedience has been, from time immemorial, the special function of the court. And this is no technical rule. In order that a court may compel obedience to its orders it must have the right to inquire whether there has been any disobedience thereof. To submit the question of disobedience to another tribunal, be it a jury or another court, would operate to deprive the proceedings of half its efficiency. . . . In Watson v. Williams, 36 Miss. 331, 341, it was said: "The power to fine and imprison for contempt, from the earliest history of jurisprudence, has been regarded as a necessary incident and attribute of a court, without which it could no more exist than without a judge. It is a power inherent in all courts of record, and coexisting with them by the wise provisions of the common law. A court without the power effectually to protect itself against the assaults of the lawless, or to enforce its orders, judgments, or decrees against the recusant parties before it, would be a disgrace to the legislation, and a stigma upon the age which invented it." . . .

In brief, a court, enforcing obedience to its orders by proceedings for contempt, is not executing the criminal laws of the land, but only securing to suitors the rights which it has adjudged them entitled to.

Further, it is said by counsel in their brief:

"No case can be cited where such a bill in behalf of the sovereign has been entertained against riot and mob violence, though occurring on the highway. It is not such fitful and temporary obstruction that constitutes a nuisance. The strong hand of executive power is required to deal with such lawless demonstrations.

"The courts should stand aloof from them and not invade executive prerogative, nor even at the behest or request of the executive travel out of the beaten path of well-settled judicial authority. A mob cannot be suppressed by injunction; nor can its leaders be tried, convicted, and sentenced in equity.

"It is too great a strain upon the judicial branch of the government to impose this essentially executive and military power upon courts of chancery."

We do not perceive that this argument questions the jurisdiction of the court, but only the expediency of the action of the government in applying for its process. It surely cannot be seriously contended that the court has jurisdiction to enjoin the obstruction of a highway by one person, but that its jurisdiction ceases when the obstruction is by a hundred persons. It may be true, as suggested, that in the excitement of passion a mob will pay little heed to processes issued from the courts, and it may be, as said by counsel in argument, that it would savor somewhat of the puerile and ridiculous to have read a writ of injunction to Lee's army during the late civil war. It is doubtless true that *inter arma leges silent,* and in the throes of rebellion or revolution the processes of civil courts are of little avail for the power of the courts rests on the general support of the people and their recognition of the fact that peaceful remedies are the true resort for the correction of wrongs. But does not counsel's argument imply too much? Is it to be assumed that these defendants were conducting a rebellion or inaugurating a revolution, and that they and their associates were thus placing themselves beyond the reach of the civil process of the courts? We find in the opinion of the Circuit Court a quotation from the testimony given by one of the defendants before the United States Strike Commission, which is sufficient answer to this suggestion.

"As soon as the employés found that we were arrested, and taken from the scene of action, they became demoralized, and that ended the strike. It was not the soldiers that ended the strike. It was not the old brotherhoods that ended the strike. It was simply the United States courts that ended the strike. Our men were in a position that never would have been shaken, under any circumstances, if we had been permitted to remain upon the field among them. Once we were taken from the scene of action, and restrained from sending telegrams or issuing orders or answering questions, then the minions of the corporations would be put to work. . . . Our headquarters were temporarily demoralized and abandoned, and we could not answer any messages. The men went back to work, and the ranks were broken, and the strike was broken up, . . . not by the army, and not by any other power, but simply and solely by the action of the United States courts in restraining us from discharging our duties as officers and representatives of our employés."

Whatever any single individual may have thought or planned, the great body of those who were engaged in these transactions contemplated neither rebellion nor revolution, and when in the due order of legal proceedings the question of right and wrong was submitted to the courts, and by them decided, they unhesitatingly yielded to their decisions. The outcome, by the very testimony of the defendants, attests the wisdom of the course pursued by the government, and that it was well not to oppose force simply by force, but to invoke the jurisdiction and judgment of those tribunals to whom by the Constitution and in accordance with the settled conviction of all citizens is committed the determination of questions of right and wrong between individuals, masses, and States.

It must be borne in mind that this bill was not simply to enjoin a mob and mob violence. It was not a bill to command a keeping of the peace; much less was its purport to restrain the defendants from abandoning whatever employment they were engaged in. The right of any laborer, or any number of laborers, to quit work was not challenged. The scope and purpose of the bill was only to restrain forcible obstructions of the highways along which interstate commerce travels and the mails are carried. And the facts set forth at length are only those facts which tended to show that the defendants were engaged in such obstructions.

A most earnest and eloquent appeal was made to us in eulogy of the heroic spirit of those who threw up their employment, and gave up their means of earning a livelihood, not in defence of their own rights, but in sympathy for and to assist others whom they believed to be wronged. We yield to none in our admiration of any act of heroism or self-sacrifice, but we may be permitted to add that it is a lesson which cannot be learned too soon or too thoroughly that under this government of and by the people the means of redress of all wrongs are through the courts and at the ballot-box, and that no wrong, real or fancied, carries with it legal warrant to invite as a means of redress the coöperation of a mob, with its accompanying acts of violence.

We have given to this case the most careful and anxious attention, for we realize that it touches closely questions of supreme importance to the people of this country. Summing up our conclusions, we hold that the government of the United States is one having jurisdiction over every foot of soil within its territory, and acting directly upon each citizen; that while it is a government of enumerated powers, it has within the limits of those powers all the attributes of sovereignty; that to it is committed power over interstate commerce and the transmission of the mail; that the powers thus conferred upon the national government are not dormant, but have been assumed and put into practical exercise by the legislation of Congress; that in the exercise of those powers it is competent for the nation to remove all obstructions upon highways, natural or artificial, to the passage of interstate commerce or the carrying of the mail; that while it may be competent for the government (through the executive branch and in the use of the entire executive power of the nation) to forcibly remove all such obstructions, it is equally within its competency to appeal to the civil courts for an inquiry and determination as to the existence and character of any alleged obstructions, and if such are found to exist, or threaten to occur, to invoke the powers of those courts to remove or restrain such obstructions; that the jurisdiction of courts to interfere in such matters by injunction is one recognized from ancient times and by indubitable authority; that such jurisdiction is not ousted by the fact that the obstructions are accompanied by or consist of acts in themselves violations of the criminal law; that the proceeding by injunction is of a civil character, and may be enforced by proceedings in contempt; that such proceedings are not in execution of the criminal laws of the land; that the penalty for a violation of injunction is no substitute for and no defence to a prosecution for any criminal offences committed in the course of such violation; that the complaint filed in this case clearly showed an existing obstruction of artificial highways for the passage of interstate commerce and the transmission of the mail—an obstruction not only temporarily existing, but threatening to continue; that under such complaint the Circuit Court had power to issue its process of injunction; that it having been issued and served on these defendants, the Circuit Court had authority to inquire whether its orders had been disobeyed, and when it found that they had been, then to proceed under section 725, Revised Statutes, which grants power "to punish, by fine or imprisonment, . . . disobedience, . . . by any party . . . or other person, to any lawful writ, process, order, rule, decree or command," and enter the order of punishment complained of; and, finally, that, the Circuit Court, having full jurisdiction in the premises, its finding of the fact of disobedience is not open to review on *habeas corpus* in this or any other court. . . .

We enter into no examination of the act of July 2, 1890, c. 647, 26 Stat. 209, upon which the Circuit Court relied mainly to sustain its jurisdiction. It must not be understood from this that we dissent from the conclusions of that court in reference to the scope of the act, but simply that we prefer to rest our judgment on the broader ground which has been discussed in this opinion, believing it of importance that the principles underlying it should be fully stated and affirmed.

The petition for a writ of *habeas corpus* is *denied.*

---

1) Two contemporary accounts are Dunbar, Government by Injunction, 13 L.Q.Rev. 347 (1897), and Gregory, Government by Injunction, 11 Harv. L.Rev. 487 (1898). When reading injunction opinions, observe Mr. Dunbar's caution: "A looseness of thought is apparent in the decisions discussing the use of injunctions which has tended to conceal the principles involved." Dunbar, 13 L.Q.Rev. at 358. Professor Gregory tells us that Mr. Debs's counsel, Clarence Darrow, quoted the following witticism in the Supreme Court brief "but without naming its author": "The present Chief Justice of the United States, before he became a head of the bench, remarked of a reforming member of the Chicago bar, 'Brother B. would codify all laws in an act of two sections: 1st, All people must be good; 2d, Courts of equity are hereby given full power and authority to enforce the provisions of this act.' " 11 Harv.L.Rev. at 510.

2) Many generations of students at the Harvard Law School heard Professor Ernest Brown comment that *Debs* was the darkest day in Supreme Court history. This comment seems particularly intriguing since Professor Brown thought that the Court had many dark days, and yet few have had the courage to ask him why he thought *Debs* was *that* bad. He was known for refusing to answer "obvious" questions.

Was Professor Brown concerned about the substantive law that allowed the government to take one side of an industrial dispute? Was he, on the other hand, disturbed with the equitable remedy as distinguished from the substantive law? Would he have been as concerned if the Court had held, in an action brought by the railroads, that Debs's conduct was a tort that led to a suit for damages? What if the trial judge had held that the strike was a crime and sentenced all the strikers to prison terms? Professor Joseph H. Beale, Jr., said that in *Debs* "the requirements of the private suit would be met by simple restraint of the person until the danger of violation of the injunction had passed, or until security was given that the injunction would not be violated; but in addition a punitive sentence is called for on account of the contemptuous nature of the act of violation." Beale, Contempt of Court, Criminal and Civil, 21 Harv.L.Rev. 161, 171 (1908).

3) Did the procedure followed in obtaining the injunction correspond with that you normally expect a court to observe before granting relief? Was the procedure necessary under the circumstances? Did the defendants have an opportunity to defend? Could the government have supplied more procedural amenities to defendants before adjudication? What were the reasons for attenuated procedure? Might notice to defendants have spurred them to frustrate the judge's opportunity to grant relief to plaintiff? Did the judge find the facts or apply the law incorrectly? Will expedited procedure increase the risk of factual or legal error? Will it lead the losers to feel that they have been treated unfairly?

4) Who had to comply with the injunction? Which branch of government usually makes rules everyone must obey? Should injunctions only govern the conduct of people who have an opportunity to defend? Does the judge have any other way to stop mob action? Would it be preferable, instead of enjoining, for the executive to send in the police, marshals, or the militia? Dunbar, 13 L.Q.Rev. at 353–54, 362–65.

5) To address Professor Brown's comment further, think about the conduct enjoined. Does the injunction simply restate the criminal law? If the conduct was already illegal, how did the injunction prejudice the defendants? Mr. Dunbar remonstrated, "Learned judges have spoken as if courts of equity could prevent acts in some manner other than by fear of the penalties attending the violation of an injunction." Dunbar, 13 L.Q.Rev. at 358. Does the Court think that the government can punish Debs for the criminal offense in addition to the punishment for contempt? Had Debs as contemnor received the procedural advantages that would have been available if he had been a criminal defendant? Did the plaintiff resort to equity "because of the prejudices of juries"? Dunbar at 360. Why didn't the idea that "equity will not enjoin a crime" protect Debs's right to criminal procedure? Professor Beale said, "If the court limits itself to its proper action in such cases, namely, process of imprisonment merely to prevent the violation of the decree, and if the imprisonment is to cease as soon as the danger of disobedience has ceased, the jury which is thought necessary to pass upon the desert of a defendant to suffer punishment is not required." Beale, 21 Harv.L.Rev. at 173. Did Beale mean that some substantive law is too important to be entrusted to juries?

6) Examine the paragraph below p. 21 that the Supreme Court omitted from its statement of the injunction. How did Debs feel about the effectiveness of that part of the injunction? Did the enjoined conduct include protected speech? Could Congress or the Illinois legislature have passed that paragraph as a criminal statute? Would a present day court think the injunction a prior restraint?

7) Congress enacted a number of statutes which addressed injunctions. The Clayton Act of 1914 is now partially codified as Rule 65. Read Rule 65 and Title 18 sections 3691 and 3692 in the Appendix. (The *Debs* Court based contempt on Section 725 which is present 18 U.S.C. § 401 and also in the Appendix.) The Norris-LaGuardia Act, 29 U.S.C. §§ 101–115, was the second wave of reform; it bans injunctions against strikes in all but very lim-

ited circumstances. Sections 101, 104, 107 are in the Appendix. Taken together do these corrections and improvements mollify the concern expressed by Professor Brown? Some historical perspective may be necessary to help you to evaluate *Debs;* for that purpose we have excerpted the following material. We also urge you to look at F. Frankfurter & N. Greene, The Labor Injunction (1930).

UNITED STATES STRIKE COMMISSION, REPORT ON THE CHICAGO STRIKE OF JUNE–JULY, 1894

S.Exec.Doc.No.7, 53rd Cong. 3rd Sess. (1895).

[This report (at XXXIX–XL) contains the following chronology of the strike and comment on the role of the injunction:]

Between June 9 and June 26 a regular convention of the American Railway Union was held with open doors at Chicago, representing 465 local unions and about 150,000 members, as claimed. The Pullman matter was publicly discussed at these meetings before and after its committees above mentioned reported their interviews with the Pullman company. On June 21 the delegates, under instructions from their local unions, unanimously voted that the members of the union should stop handling Pullman cars on June 26 unless the Pullman company would consent to arbitration. On June 26 the boycott and strike began. The strike on the part of the railroad employees was a sympathetic one. No grievances against the railroads had been presented by their employees, nor did the American Railway Union declare any such grievances to be any cause whatever of the strike. To simply boycott Pullman cars would have been an incongruous step for the remedy of complaints of railroad employees. Throughout the strike the strife was simply over handling Pullman cars, the men being ready to do their duty otherwise. The contracts between the railroads and the Pullman company as to Pullman cars created such close relations between them as to increase the natural sympathy of organization between the members of the American Railway Union upon railroads and their brothers at Pullman. It is also apparent that the readiness to strike sympathetically was promoted by the disturbed and apprehensive condition of railroad employees resulting from wage reductions on different lines, blacklisting, etc., and from the recent growth and development of the General Managers' Association, which seemed to them a menace. Hence the railroad employees were ripe to espouse the cause of the Pullman strikers. In some instances they struck in disregard of existing contracts between their different organizations and the railroads, notably upon the Illinois Central. They evaded the responsibility of their organizations for this conduct by claiming to act as individuals. They justified themselves under the idea of balancing wrongs.

After June 26 the officers and agents of the union managed and urged on the strike at every available point upon the railroads centering at Chicago until it reached proportions far in excess of their original anticipations, and led to disorders beyond even their control. Urgent solicitations and appeals to strike and to stand firm continued in the many public meetings held each day in and about Chicago, and appear in the telegrams sent about the country.

On July 7 the principal officers of the American Railway Union were indicted, arrested, and held under $10,000 bail. Upon July 13 they were attached for contempt of the United States court in disobeying an injunction issued on July 2 and served on the 3d and 4th, enjoining them, among other things, from compelling, or inducing by threats, intimidation, persuasion, force, or violence, railroad employees to refuse or fail to perform their duties. It is seriously questioned, and with much force, whether courts have jurisdiction to enjoin citizens from "persuading" each other in industrial or other matters of common interest. However, it is generally recognized among good citizens that a mandate of a court is to be obeyed until it is modified and corrected by the court that issued it.

[In its opinion the Supreme Court quoted certain excerpts from Eugene Debs's testimony before the Strike Commission; the following exchange puts those excerpts in context, and sheds some light on why the injunction was effective in this instance.]

76 (Commissioner Wright). It is the facts we are after, and then your conclusions by and by.—Ans. Very well. On the 2d day of July I was served with a very sweeping injunction that restrained me, as president of the union, from sending out any telegram or any letter or issuing any order that would have the effect of inducing or persuading men to withdraw from the service of the company, or that would in any manner whatsoever, according to the language of the injunction, interfere with the operation.

77 (Commissioner Worthington). Will you attach a copy of the injunction to your testimony?—Ans. It is in the hands of my attorney, and I will secure a copy of it and introduce it as part of the testimony. That injunction was served simultaneously, or practically so, by all of the courts embracing or having jurisdiction in the territory in which the trouble existed. From Michigan to California there seemed to be concerted action on the part of the courts in restraining us from exercising any of the functions of our offices. That resulted practically in the demoralization of our ranks. Not only this, but we were organized in a way that this was the center, of course, of operations. It is understood that a strike is war; not necessarily a war of blood and bullets, but a war in the sense that it is a conflict between two contending interests or classes of interests. There is more or less strategy resorted to in war, and this was the center in our operations. Orders were issued from here, questions were answered, and our men were kept in line from here.

At the time I was served with this injunction all of the officers at all of the points at the headquarters or terminals of all of these roads were served with a similar injunction restraining them all from sending any telegrams or from discharging the functions attached to their several offices. Following the issuance of that injunction a few days, I have forgotten the exact date, a special grand jury was convened for the purpose of examining into my conduct as president of the American Railway Union in connection with this trouble. The grand jury was in session very briefly, but found a bill upon an information that was filed, and I was ordered to be arrested. A warrant was issued and placed in the hands of a United States marshal for that purpose. On the 7th day of July, if I am not mistaken, I was arrested and brought before the court, and my bond was fixed, with my three official associates, Mr. Howard, vice-president; Mr. Rodgers, editor of the Times, and Mr. Keliher, our secretary, we were simultaneously arrested and we were placed under a joint bond of $10,000. Very shortly after this there was an attachment issued for an alleged contempt of court, upon information that I had, as president, violated the injunction issued by Judges Woods and Grosscup.

78 (Commissioner Wright). That is, the injunction served on you on the 2d day of July?—Ans. Yes. As soon as the employees found that we were arrested and taken from the scene of action, they became demoralized, and that ended the strike. It was not the soldiers that ended the strike; it was not the old brotherhoods that ended the strike; it was simply the United States courts that ended the strike. Our men were in a position that never would have been shaken under any circumstances if we had been permitted to remain upon the field, remain among them; but once that we were taken from the scene of action and restrained from sending telegrams or issuing the orders necessary, or answering questions; when the minions of the corporations would be put to work at such a place, for instance, as Nickerson, Kans., where they would go and say to the men that the men at Newton had gone back to work, and Nickerson would wire me to ask if that were true; no answer would come to the message, because I was under arrest, and we were all under arrest. The headquarters were demoralized and abandoned, and we could not answer any telegrams or questions that would come in. Our headquarters were temporarily demoralized and abandoned, and we could not answer any messages. The men went back to work, and the ranks were broken, and the strike was broken up by the Federal courts of the United States, and not by the Army, and not by any other power, but simply and solely by the action of the United States courts in restraining us from discharging our duties as officers and representatives of the employees. . . .

[Subsequently, Debs gave the requested decree to the Commission. That decree is substantially quoted and paraphrased in the Supreme Court opinion. The following paragraph in the decree, which appears in the Strike Commission's report at 180 seems to have been omitted by the Supreme Court:

And Eugene V. Debs and all other persons are hereby enjoined and restrained from sending out any letters, messages, or communications directing, inciting, encouraging, or instructing any persons whatsoever to interfere with the business or affairs, directly or indirectly, of any of the railway companies hereinabove named, or from persuading any of the employees of said railway companies while in the employment of their respective companies to fail or refuse to perform the duties of their employment.]

A. LINDSEY, THE PULLMAN STRIKE

(Copyright 1942 The University of Chicago).

. . . One of the most incredible and perhaps least justifiable things which Olney [the Attorney General] did was to appoint on June 30 Edwin Walker as special attorney for the federal government at Chicago. The general managers were committed to the belief that one of their own lawyers, as special United States counsel, would give them a decisive advantage in suppressing the stike, and so they advised Olney that it was not only desirable but necessary to have the district attorney reinforced by expert counsel. Their nominee for this position was a very clever corporation lawyer, who since 1870 had been general counsel for the Chicago, Milwaukee, and St. Paul Railroad. At the first outbreak of trouble, he was invited with others to serve the General Managers' Association in a legal advisory capacity. . . . Somewhat ironically, Clarence Darrow observed that the federal government "might with as good grace have appointed the attorney for the American Railway Union to represent the United States." To the corporation-minded Olney, such a choice was not in bad taste, and so he hastily carried out the recommendation of the general managers without even consulting Thomas Milchrist.

The appointment of Walker was in no wise a reflection on the ability of Milchrist to perform the duties of his office, but was due to a firm conviction on the part of Olney that the exigencies of the situation demanded the selection of a highly resourceful lawyer who, as assistant to the United States attorney, would help to wage a more effective campaign against the strikers. To Olney, Chicago represented the heart of the union's cause, from which radiated all the impulses that kept the morale of the strikers intact. Convinced that the most adequate precaution should be taken here, he appointed Edwin Walker several days before the occurrence of any serious disorder in that city. As special counsel, Walker proved more than just an assistant to Milchrist; in a sense he became the director of affairs in Chicago for the Department of Justice. . . .

By July 1 the boycott was becoming increasingly effective in this city, but neither then nor for several days subsequently did any rioting or serious disturbance develop there. Unfortunately for the cause of labor, the same could not be said for the outlying village of Blue Island, where disorders were inspired by a riotous element. Reports transmitted to the Department of Justice were anything but reassuring. The United States marshal on July 1 telegraphed to the attorney-general: "The situation here tonight is desperate. I have sworn in over 400 deputies, and many more will be needed to protect the mail trains. I expect great trouble. Shall I purchase 100 riot guns? . . . ." The dispatch of Milchrist on the same day, no less disconcerting, revealed his determination to meet the situation by applying for an injunction. "The general paralysis," he announced, "warrants this course. Very little mail and no freight moving. Marshal is using all his force now owing to mob and obstruction of tracks, especially at Blue Island, Riverdale and other points. His force is clearly inadequate." . . .

The bill for this injunction was largely the handiwork of Thomas Milchrist, who labored on its preparation all night of July 1. When submitted the following morning to Circuit Judge Woods and District Judge Grosscup, certain recommended changes were made. Present at this discussion was Edwin Walker, who protested that the complaint should be given a broader basis. Apparently, Milchrist had endeavored to establish the need for a restraining order almost exclusively upon the dangers, threatened and real, which confronted interstate commerce; but, upon the suggestion of Walker, it was decided that interference with mail trains should likewise become a prominent feature of the complaint. . . .

In serving the writ, various means were employed by the federal marshal and his deputy. Eugene Debs and some of the directors of the union were presented personally with copies, but general notice to all strikers was achieved through publication of the injunction in the newspapers of Chicago on July 3. Copies were also posted in public places and read to demonstrative crowds whenever the situation warranted.

. . . Marshal Arnold, accompanied by some public officials, railroad attorneys, and deputy marshals, went to the scene of disturbance [at Blue Island] on the afternoon of July 2 and read the injunction to a milling boisterous throng of two thousand people. Jibes, cheers, and groans greeted the reading, and when it was finished, the crowd seemed unwilling or unable to grasp the meaning of the order. John Arnold called on them in the name of the President of the United States to disperse and to resist no more the movement of trains. The injunction was read a second time but, as before, without results. The attorney for the Rock Island Road and the deputy sheriff of Cook County each, in turn, tried to explain the full meaning of the writ. In a parting speech Arnold issued a warning that sufficient force would be secured and that all trains would be moved regardless of consequences. He again urged them to avert trouble by retiring to their homes.

So hopeless did conditions appear that on July 2 the marshal telegraphed to the attorney-general about his failure to disperse the rioters. "We have had a desperate time with them here all day," he professed, "and our force is inadequate, and in my judgment it is impossible to move trains here without having the Fifteenth Infantry from Fort Sheridan ordered here now." This situation played directly into the hands of Olney and afforded him the opportunity to have federal troops rushed to Chicago. The avidity with which he favored this policy, without first seeking to exhaust all other means in suppressing disorders at Blue Island, including recourse to the state militia, raises the question as to Olney's basic motive for having the injunction issued. Did he entertain the belief or hope that the enforcement of the writ would involve difficulties sufficient to furnish an excuse for military intervention? The *Chicago Times* seemed to think so. On July 2 the editor observed that "the object of the injunction is not so much to prevent interference with trains as to lay a foundation for calling out the United States troops. . . . Declaration by the United States marshal that he is unable to execute the orders of the court might be alleged as the basis of a call for troops." . . .

The first occurrence of trouble in the strike was met by a rapid increase in the number of deputy marshals wherever conditions seemed to indicate any need. United States marshals were granted unrestricted freedom to recruit men, and many thousands of deputies were thus sworn in as temporary law-enforcing agents. This policy did not necessarily mean that Richard Olney was willing to repose much confidence in this arm of the government. The ineffectualness of federal deputies in suppressing the Coxeyite disturbances was still vivid in his memory and doubtless shook his faith in this force as a means of adequately protecting mail and interstate commerce. Precisely what he expected from these deputies is not known, but on June 30, when the first group in Chicago was being commissioned for service, he disclosed to Edwin Walker a complete absence of faith in the capacity of these men to cope with the situation. Perhaps he never intended that they should suppress the strike but that by their inadequacy they should demonstrate the need for federal troops.

In Chicago—hub of the strike—a total of about five thousand deputy marshals were recruited, by far the greatest force of United States deputies anywhere assembled during the struggle. From the last day of June until July 5, John Arnold and his chief deputy, John Donnelly, swore in a continuous stream of these special officers, each of whom received a star as his insignia of authority. As to how many and what disposition should be made of them, Arnold was advised to consult with Milchrist and Walker. As quickly as the deputies received their commissions, they were taken in groups to whatever railroad area seemed to require their services. They were orally instructed to guard and protect interstate freight and passenger trains, as well as the movement of mail.

This large aggregation of civil officers, fell into two broad classifications: the regular force and those who were armed and paid by the railroads. The latter group, representing over two-thirds of all deputy marshals in Chicago, comprised those who were chosen by the railroad corporations and directly responsible to them. Any road desiring to have its own corps of deputy marshals would designate one of its officials as a sort of captain, to whom was intrusted the duty of choosing the men and directing their activities. The names of those selected for deputy service were submitted to the General Managers' Association, which in turn promptly transmitted them to the federal marshal with the recommendation that they be accepted. The men were then sent over to the marshal's office and commissioned without even the most superficial examination into their qualifications. Badges, but not guns, were supplied to these men by this office, which exercised no control over them and received no reports on their performance of duty. No effort was made to ascertain whether or not they were citizens. Many were regular employees of the railroad, and it was not unusual for the same hand that held the throttle of a locomotive to use a revolver in the name of the federal government. The engineers, firemen, and others, thus cloaked with this special authority, were in no wise relieved of their customary duties but were allowed to serve in a double capacity. . . . Concerning the propriety of all this, the Strike Commission commented: "It is placing officers of the Government under control of a combination of railroads. It is bad precedent, that might well lead to serious consequences."

The indiscriminate method of choosing deputy marshals may largely explain the unhappy record of these federal agents. Even the regular force of deputies was organized in a haphazard manner, many of whom were at first picked up off the streets. In the rush of rapid recruiting, applicants were accepted on their appearance, with the result that thugs, drunkards, and other disreputable individuals were placed in the role of maintaining law and order. Some did not know how to carry their authority and became extremely aggressive and provocative. Needless arrests were made and unnecessary trouble precipitated by a few of the more swaggering and arrogant of the deputy marshals. In certain cases freight cars were plundered and other railroad property destroyed by the very men employed to help prevent depredations.

. . . Although the more objectionable deputy marshals were weeded out and the quality of men somewhat improved as the strike continued, the general character of the force remained poor. The performance of these men must have sorely tried the patience of Walker, who on July 9 sent the following telegram to Olney: "At the risk of being thought meddlesome, I suggest that the marshal is appointing a mob of deputies that are worse than useless." On the following day, the attorney-general wired Marshal Arnold: "Under the circumstances what is the use of the great mob of deputies which you seem to be employing? Are not a large proportion wholly unreliable? Do Messrs. Walker and Milchrist approve your action?" In reply John Arnold explained that what he did was done with the approval of Milchrist but that he had already ceased swearing in deputies. . . .

Although the maximum pay allowed to deputy marshals was $2.50 per day, with expenses not to exceed an additional $1.50, the cost to the federal government of this great army of civil officers during the Pullman strike was $375,000. In Chicago alone the outlay was $125,000. Because this money was not immediately forthcoming, since it had to await appropriation by Congress, the marshals were placed in an embarrassing position when their deputies clamored for compensation. None found this situation more trying than John Arnold, whose force was extremely large and crowded with many in desperate need of money. The attorney-general advised him, as he did others, to borrow from a railroad or some other source until money was available from Congress. This course Arnold seemed reluctant to follow, apparently because he did not wish to assume personal responsibility for such a large loan. He nevertheless believed that, since the deputies had been employed almost exclusively in defense of railroad property, the companies should at least pay the boarding and lodging bills of these men. The General Managers' Association, to whom he made this recommendation, took the position, shared by Richard Olney, that such expenses were incurred by the government for the "maintenance of Federal law and the authority of Federal Courts, and therefore ought no more to be paid by the railroads than by any individual citizen." . . .

From the very beginning of the struggle it appears that the attorney-general pondered the advisability of using federal troops. He realized that sweeping injunctions and the resulting difficulties of enforcement by federal marshals would create the proper conditions for an appeal to the military. The disorders at Blue Island, therefore, must have come to him as a welcome opportunity for immediate action. On July 3 he wired Edwin Walker that, whenever in his opinion the need for federal soldiers arose, they would be used "promptly and decisively." In demanding troops, Walker was urged to do so in co-operation with the United States judge, marshal, and district attorney. The special district attorney immediately replied that it was of "utmost importance that soldiers should be distributed at certain points within the city. . . ."

Moving with alacrity and supported by the signatures of Judge Grosscup, Edwin Walker, and Thomas Milchrist, the United States marshal promptly sent a dispatch to the attorney-general stressing the urgency of the situation and asking for the aid of federal troops. He pointed out that the mob at Blue Island had ditched a mail train and upset several baggage cars, thereby blocking the movement of all trains, and that he had met with complete failure in trying to enforce the orders of the court. To Richard Olney this communication was merely the final proof that the time for military intervention had arrived.

During the two or three preceding days, the attorney-general had done much to impress the President and his closest advisers with the seriousness of the situation and the need for drastic action. Telegrams and other pertinent dispatches, some rather alarming, had been submitted by Olney at the daily meetings of the Cabinet. All those in close touch with Grover Cleveland were genuinely disturbed over the alleged gravity of the situation. Precautionary steps were quickly taken to meet the emergency. On July 2 confidential instructions were issued to the commanding officer at Fort Sheridan to make the necessary arrangements to move his men to Chicago at a moment's notice. A special train was sent to the fort and held in readiness. During the evening of July 2 and the morning of July 3 the expediency of using federal troops was weighed at the White House. . . .

When on July 3 Olney drew his trump card—the urgent request for troops by the federal marshal at Chicago—Cleveland decided to delay no longer. At four o'clock in the afternoon Colonel Crofton, in charge at Fort Sheridan, was ordered to move his entire command to Chicago for the purpose of enforcing the processes of the federal court, protecting the transportation of mail, and otherwise helping to execute the laws of the government. Jubilantly the attorney-general announced: "The subject has now passed out of my hands. The filing of the injunction practically concluded my work, and it is for other branches to execute such action as the courts take." . . .

Chicago at this time was still free from riots. The confidential records of the General Managers' Association as well as the report of the Chicago superintendent of police show that prior to the arrival of troops the city was orderly, except for a few isolated and relatively unimportant acts of sabotage. Many trains did not move, but this was in no way due to threatening mobs but to insufficient crews. Blue Island experienced disorders, to be sure, but this locality was beyond the farthest limits of Chicago. Nevertheless, what happened in this suburb served as the basis for greatly exaggerated fears and the immediate concentration of troops in the great metropolis nearby. The impressive display of the military could hardly have been made because of what had actually transpired but because of forebodings and expectations of what might occur. . . .

Within five hours after he received orders to move, Colonel Crofton and his troops were en route to Chicago. They arrived at 12:30 A.M. on July 4, and immediately the Colonel entered into a conference with Thomas Milchrist, John Egan, and Assistant United States Marshal Donnelly as to how the soldiers should be distributed. The attorney-general intended that Walker, Milchrist, and Arnold should advise the military in such matters; but none of these men proved more active in this respect than John Egan, strike manager of the General Managers' Association. As a result of this first conference, it was decided to concentrate the infantry at Blue Island and Grand Crossing and the artillery and cavalry at the Stock Yards. Before dawn all contingents, except those assigned to the Stock Yards, were at their posts;

and after the break of day, the remaining ones were moved quickly to their new positions.

. . . When the omnibus injunction was issued at Chicago, General Miles was in the East, apparently not much disturbed about developments. He was promptly summoned to Washington, where on July 3 he took part in discussions relative to the need for military intervention. In his opinion such a course was not necessary then, but the President preferred to disregard this advice. Under orders, Miles left at once for his command and reached Chicago shortly before noon on July 4, many hours after Colonel Crofton had completed the arrangement of his troops.

In a rapid survey of conditions, Miles had occasion to reverse his earlier judgment and even decided that the eleven companies already on duty were inadequate. To Major General Schofield he expressed a desire for more troops and alluded to what he believed would be the salutary effect at this time of moving additional soldiers to Chicago. The government was not adverse to such a suggestion and proceeded to rush new reserves to Chicago from Leavenworth, Kansas, and Fort Brady, Michigan. Subsequently, troops were also ordered from Madison Barracks, New York; Fort Riley, Kansas; and Fort Niobrara, Nebraska. The last of these contingents reached Chicago on July 10, increasing the total of federal troops there to 1,936 men. For fifteen days they remained on duty and were recalled only after the strike had been broken and all resistance had virtually disappeared. . . .

The American Railway Union protested against military intervention, particularly because conditions in Chicago at that time did not in any way seem to justify such drastic measures. The appearance of regular soldiers served to arouse the anger of labor and, in the opinion of union officials, greatly to aggravate the situation. At first Eugene Debs seemed to take the position that the use of troops would not jeopardize the cause of labor since soldiers could not themselves run trains and since they did not dare molest the strikers in their lawful and orderly conduct. He even indicated that soldiers might prove helpful to the cause of labor by preventing rioters from "destroying property, the stigma of which is placed by capital on labor." On further reflection, however, he realized that these troops, under the guise of protecting interstate commerce and the processes of the courts, would be used in a manner highly prejudicial to the strikers. It was this unhappy contemplation that must have furnished the impetus for his extravagant statement to a United Press reporter:

"The first shot fired by the regular soldiers at the mobs here will be the signal for a civil war. I believe this as firmly as I believe in the ultimate success of our course. Bloodshed will follow, and 90 per cent of the people of the United States will be arrayed against the other 10 per cent. And I would not care to be arrayed against the laboring people in the contest, or find myself out of the ranks of labor when the struggle ended. I do not say this as an alarmist, but calmly and thoughtfully."

. . . On July 3 Edwin Walker outlined his plan of action to the attorney-general. Equity proceedings would have to await the gathering of further evidence; but, as was confidently expected, sufficient proof of contempt would be assembled within a few days, and then Debs and his associates would be sent to jail. It was further indicated that in one week a grand jury would be summoned to indict the strike leaders for conspiracy. Walker was careful, however, to emphasize the dangers of precipitate action but explained that, since he had a thorough understanding with Judge Grosscup, everything would proceed as rapidly and effectively as circumstances warranted. To Richard Olney this strategy seemed agreeable, although he was becoming impatient for action, and in reply he instructed the special assistant district attorney not to lose any time in calling a special session of the grand jury.

On July 6 Walker informed the attorney-general that sufficient evidence had now been gathered for presentation to the grand jury which was scheduled to meet on July 10. He expressed the belief that the bail would be so large in the aggregate that Debs and his associates would have to go to jail and remain there until their cases were called up for trial. . . .

When Milchrist and Walker met the special grand jury on July 10, they asked for indictments against Eugene Debs and his co-officials on the grounds of conspiracy. Composed of out-of-town residents, the jury proved extremely amenable. In his instructions to this group Judge Grosscup smoothed the way for prompt action by leaving virtually no course open but the one demanded by the government. He pointed out that an agreement on the part of two or more individuals to stop trains unlawfully would have the effect of halting mail trains and interstate commerce, and this should be proof of the existence of a conspiracy. The railroads, he explained, have a right to the service of each employee until he lawfully decides to quit and that concerted action to induce men to strike "under any effective penalty or threat . . . to the injury of the mail service or the prompt transportation of interstate commerce" might be classified as conspiracy.

With such advice the grand jury retired to hear evidence, which consisted principally of telegrams dispatched from the headquarters of the American Railway Union. The only witness was Edward M. Mulford, manager of the Western Union office in Chicago, who was subpoenaed to produce copies of these messages. At first he refused to make them available, on the grounds that, being "privileged communications," they should remain in the custody of his company. When Grosscup, however, threatened him with a jail sentence, he decided to yield to the will of the court.

Only the telegrams that seemed most incriminating were submitted to the jury. None advocated violence while some advised against it, but there were many which counseled the railroad workers to support the boycott. In view of what Judge Grosscup had said, such urgings were construed as evidence of conspiracy, and without delay the grand jury voted true bills for the four highest officials of the American Railway Union: President Eugene Debs, Vice-President George W. Howard, Secretary Sylvester Keliher, and Lewis W. Rodgers, editor of the *Railway Times.* The jury was in session not more than two hours when this action was taken, and ten minutes later bench warrants were issued. With a speed that must have gladdened the hearts of Walker and Olney, the accused were quickly apprehended and brought into court. After a few hours of detention, they were released on bail, the bonds required for each being ten thousand dollars.

While Debs and his associates were in the custody of the court, the union headquarters were raided by a squad of deputy marshals and deputy post-office inspectors. Every room was completely ransacked; and all books, papers, records, and correspondence, including the unopened personal mail of Eugene Debs, were seized and transferred to the office of the United States district attorney. Although conducted according to instructions from Thomas Milchrist, the raid was in complete violation of the subpoena issued for the occasion—a court order which merely required that the private secretary of Debs and certain other persons appear before the grand jury with the books and papers of the union. There was no authority to make any arrests or seizures. Realizing the illegality of the action, Judge Grosscup quickly repudiated it and ordered all private papers returned. At a special session of the court on July 11, he explained to Milchrist that Debs was charged with a serious crime but possessed the same rights as any other accused citizen and that his private papers could not be confiscated and used as evidence against him, any more than he could be incriminated by his own testimony extracted under compulsion.

The attorney-general viewed this raid as embarrassing to the government. On July 11 he bluntly reminded Walker that the seizure of Debs's papers was unlawful and that they should be returned and the affair publicly disavowed. Olney was careful to explain that, in enforcing the law, the government could not itself afford to be lawless by violating personal rights. "The government is too strong," he admonished, "and its cause too righteous to warrant or require anything of that nature." . . .

Convinced that the strike leaders feared the grand jury more than the presence of troops, the prosecution made the greatest possible use of this jury. Numerous arrests were made during the rioting in Chicago, and those who could not furnish bail were committed to jail. The grand jury indicted many of these and in all named sixty-nine persons in the omnibus indictments for conspiracy. Seven indictments were voted against Debs, Howard, and Rodgers, but only three each against the full board of directors. . . . On July 19 the jury completed its investigation and was discharged. . . .

Before the special grand jury in Chicago had completed its work, contempt proceedings were commenced. On July 17 two informations were filed in the federal district court against Debs, Howard, Keliher, and Rodgers: one by George R. Peck in behalf of the receivers of the Santa Fe Road, and the other by Milchrist and Walker in behalf of the United States government. The defendants were charged with contempt and their immediate arrest demanded. The prosecution declared that the injunction of Judges Grosscup and Woods had been wilfully and deliberately violated by Debs and his co-officials, not once, but on numerous occasions. It was alleged that in open disregard of the writ, the defendants by telegram had continued to urge railroad employees on various lines to quit work. Hundreds of such messages were dispatched and many employees were induced to strike, often in a body, thus causing serious interference to the movement of interstate commerce. The government further charged that the strikers seized railroad property, fostered violence, and by physical force obstructed mail and interstate trains. Workers who refused to join the strike were intimidated. By this and other means the union was charged with seeking to establish unlawfully a boycott of Pullman sleepers. The prosecution contended that the directors of the American Railway Union possessed full authority to call the workers out on a strike and by the exercise of this power had flagrantly violated the injunction.

In seeking to prove contempt the government submitted some telegrams to the court. When only a few had been read, the judge announced that sufficient evidence had been presented to indicate a deliberate violation of the injunction. The attorney for the American Railway Union, S. S. Gregory, vainly protested that the information failed to charge the defendants with personal participation in any violence and that the case as presented did not warrant jurisdiction by a court of equity. The government, he announced, was really using its power and authority to vindicate the property rights of the railroads. The judge, however, could see no need for further discussion at this time and ordered the arrest of the defendants but suspended service of the writs when assured that the accused would voluntarily surrender themselves. This Debs and his three associates did at the afternoon session of the court. Again Gregory endeavored to save his clients by declaring that if time permitted he could prove that the information failed to show any violation of the injunction and that until contempt had been proved there could be no punishment. He explained it was no offense for workers to quit work peacefully; and as for the allegation that threats and intimidation had been used by the accused—there was nothing in the information to bear this out.

Although unimpressed by these arguments, the court was willing to grant the defense sufficient time to answer the informations and accordingly deferred the hearing until July 23. This was done over the strenuous objections of Edwin Walker, who, being anxious to get away for his summer vacation, demanded an immediate hearing. The bail was fixed at three thousand dollars for each defendant; and, although there were several bondsmen present, Debs and his colleagues waived bail and were committed to jail. When interrogated about this, Debs explained that it was a matter of principle. "The poor striker who is arrested," he averred, "would be thrown in jail. We are no better than he." The refusal of these men to accept bail came as a surprise to Walker, who was hardly prepared for such as extraordinary gesture. In explaining the matter to Richard Olney, he was at first inclined to characterize it as an act to arouse sympathy but later expressed the belief that it was done because Debs, confronted by defeat, felt the need for rest and seclusion from the excitement of office. . . .

As scheduled, the hearing for contempt began on July 23, with Judges Grosscup and Woods presiding. The four defendants, each wearing a new white ribbon, appeared without showing any trace of their imprisonment. Gregory, who was now assisted by another attorney, W. W. Erwin, filed a joint answer to the contempt charges. All the allegations set forth by Milchrist and Walker were categorically denied. The defendants disclaimed any intention of violating the restraining order and emphatically declared that they had not done so. It was pointed out that the workers on each railroad, by a majority vote, alone possessed the power to call a strike and that the high officials of the union might advise but could exercise no authority in the matter. Those who struck, it was claimed, did so on their own accord and not because of any control or direction from the American Railway Union.

Did the accused interfere with the operation of trains carrying mail and interstate commerce or in any way seek to induce others to do so? Were the defendants or the members of the union involved in the violence and disorders? To every charge of this sort the defendants issued a flat denial, while emphasizing the fact that they had strongly urged the strikers to abstain from intimidation and other forms of lawlessness. It was even affirmed that in seeking not to violate the injunction, Eugene Debs had sought and scrupulously followed the advice of competent lawyers.

The defense took the position that contempt and conspiracy would involve punishment for the same acts and that the prosecution should decide which of the two proceedings to abandon, since it would be illegal to punish a man twice for the same offense. Gregory asked the court to quash the equity charges and, should this be denied, at least to grant the defendants the benefit of a jury trial. The United States attorney vigorously opposed the suggestion by announcing that he had never known of a contempt case being tried by a jury and that just because the defendants had been indicted for the same acts which constituted contempt was their misfortune. The court sustained the prosecution by refusing to dismiss contempt proceedings or to permit a jury to hear the case. Before the hearing could progress further, however, Edwin Walker became ill, and the court decided on July 25 to postpone the case until September 5. The defendants were each required to post an additional bond of seven thousand dollars, which increased the aggregate amount of their guaranty for the contempt hearing to forty thousand dollars. This time Debs and his associates preferred not to waive bail and were released from custody.

In the judgment of Richard Olney this delay in equity proceedings was extremely unfortunate since, as he believed, it would give the American Railway Union the opportunity to start another strike. He felt that freedom for Debs and his co-officials at this juncture would tend to create apprehension and alarm among the business classes. Edwin Walker did not think so and at some length explained to the perturbed attorney-general why postponement was necessary and in what respects the government would benefit from this course. It was quite apparent that Walker's illness was not serious and nothing more than a case of mild indisposition. "The heat was really stifling," he wrote, "and the crowd of strikers present at the hearing made the air of the room intolerable." Overwhelmed by fatigue, he felt an impelling need for an immediate vacation at the seashore; but there were other reasons why he wanted the hearing deferred.

In a lengthy conference with Judge Woods the special district attorney was advised that the best interests of the government would be served by the proposed delay. Woods had to leave Chicago within a few days and could not possibly conclude the hearing before his departure; and so there seemed to remain no other course open to the prosecution, unless it had been willing to refer the matter to the master for proof—a procedure that would have kept all parties in the city during the entire summer. Walker could see no reason for doing this, particularly since the situation did not require haste. He believed the strike was already broken and the American Railway Union so badly demoralized that by September there would be little left of the organization. In seeking to quiet Olney's fears, he explained that until the hearing was held, contempt proceedings would hang over the heads of the accused, and, as Judge Woods had warned, any repetition of the acts complained of would only aggravate the contempt.

Walker felt certain that labor considered the contempt proceedings as a test case involving the effectiveness of equity in controlling unions. In view of this he believed that the defendants would contest the case, if possible, even more strenuously than the indictments for conspiracy. The need for a government victory in the matter seemed imperative to him; and to Olney he explained: "If the courts sustain the position of the government, that equity has jurisdiction to restrain such confederations, and enforce the rule of non-interference with the transportation of the mails and interstate commerce, there would be no more boycotting, and no further violence, in aid of strikes." While impressed with the importance of equity in prosecuting the union leaders, Walker was just as anxious to secure convictions under the indictments and for this reason believed that the contempt case should be delayed until fall since the same evidence would be used in both proceedings. He was inclined to believe that the government would commit a strategical blunder by showing its full hand in the civil case in advance of criminal proceedings.

Among other reasons for the delay in contempt proceedings was the belief that by waiting a few weeks some very damaging evidence would be made available by the *Chicago Herald.* This publication had agreed to aid in the prosecution of both the civil and criminal cases and had already furnished some evidence, the rest of which was expected by the first of September. With this proof Walker seemed confident that he would have "no trouble whatever in connecting the directors of the American Railway Union with all the violence and intimidation that was exercised over the employees that remained in the service of the different railway companies, as well as over new employees that were called to take the place of strikers." . . .

In the federal court at Chicago on September 5 William A. Woods, as presiding judge, began the hearing on contempt. The defense was represented by Erwin, Darrow, and Gregory, and the government by Walker and Milchrist. . . .

As the hearing progressed, it became apparent that the defense was pursuing a course at variance with what the government expected. Not only did the defendants avail themselves of the privilege not to testify, but they called no witnesses and offered no evidence in their behalf except parts of certain documents which were offered in connection with other parts presented by the prosecution. Such a policy was doubtless dictated by the belief that it would be better strategy to save their witnesses and most of their evidence for the conspiracy trial, considered much more crucial. The counsel for the defense also may have questioned the wisdom of revealing their full case in a court where there was no jury and before a judge whose lack of sympathy for labor was mirrored in the injunction which he had helped to issue.

The defense was, nevertheless, emphatic in denying that there had been any violation of the injunction. It was contended that the defendants did not favor interference with the movement of mail or interstate commerce, nor did they at any time urge the strikers to engage in lawlessness. The right of the court to issue the writ and to hear and determine the contempt case was seriously questioned. The court, it was held, had no authority under the

Sherman Anti-trust Act to issue the injunction. The denial of trial by jury and the punishment of the accused for conspiracy and contempt—thus twice for the same offense—were declared to be unconstitutional.

In seeking to prove guilt the prosecution called numerous witnesses, most of whom were furnished by the railroads; and in addition submitted much documentary material, principally telegrams. As the hearing proceeded, Walker kept Olney well informed of developments and was in turn advised by the attorney-general. Walker acknowledged to Olney on the fourteenth of September that the defendants "did not personally or physically interfere with the movement of trains" and that they did "expressly warn all persons against violence and interference with the transportation of the mails." In the opinion of Walker, however, this fact did not lessen their guilt. As the railroads were being paralyzed and as disorders were spreading, he explained, the accused continued to dispatch orders "calling the men out and urging those who were not members of the union to join the strike." Walker confided to Olney the belief that, if the court should deny the legality of the injunction under the Sherman Anti-trust Act, the government could still invoke the writ to prevent unlawful interference with the transportation of the mail.

In the judgment of Richard Olney, the Sherman Anti-trust Law furnished the necessary authority for the writ; but, even without resort to this measure, the government was still able to protect the mail by equity proceedings. He believed, however, that the injunction could be sustained on broader grounds—the right of a court of equity to render protection against a public nuisance. In clarifying this point Olney explained to Walker that a railroad was nothing but "a peculiar species of a public highway" and that, if the courts could enjoin any obstruction or obstacle on a public highway, they could do the same for any railroad. By virtue of the Interstate Commerce Act, declared the attorney-general, all interstate railroads were subject to the jurisdiction of the United States, and any obstruction thereon could be enjoined by the federal government as a public nuisance. Nor did the obstruction necessarily have to be some physical obstacle; it could be a strike. By uniting the workers and simultaneously withdrawing them from an interstate railroad, the defendants obstructed the operation of the road and were guilty of creating a public nuisance. Such an action, averred Olney, was illegal and could be restrained by a court of equity. Realizing the effectiveness of this contention, Walker gave it considerable emphasis in his closing arguments, without, however, overlooking the Sherman Anti-trust Act as a source of authority for the writ.

Since Judge Woods viewed the Debs contempt case as a real opportunity, he was in no hurry to hand down the decision, which he desired to be an extremely able piece of work. Although the final arguments were heard during the latter part of September, it was not until December 14 that the decision was rendered. In all respects it was a sweeping victory for the government. . . .

Eugene Debs was sentenced by Judge Woods to six months' confinement, while the other defendants were given only three. Because of crowded conditions at the Cook County jail it was decided to commit the prisoners to the

McHenry County jail at Woodstock, Illinois, where on January 8, 1895, they began serving their sentences for contempt. . . .

[S]ixteen days after the defendants started serving their sentence for contempt, the trial for conspiracy began in the federal court of Judge Grosscup. From the Woodstock jail, some fifty miles northwest of Chicago, Debs and his fellow-prisoners were taken daily to that city for the trial which opened on January 24. The directors of the American Railway Union were not the only ones accused of conspiracy to obstruct and retard the mails. Originally sixty-nine had been indicted for this offense by the federal grand jury in Chicago, but the government decided, prior to the commencement of the trial, to proceed against only forty-five—a number which was shortly reduced to twenty.

The attorneys for the defense consisted of Clarence Darrow and S. S. Gregory, while the prosecution comprised Edwin Walker, Thomas Milchrist, and the new federal district attorney, John C. Black. As the trial got under way, it became apparent to all that this was no ordinary case but one having far-reaching significance to labor. In the opinion of Darrow, it was a historical case—one which would count much for liberty or against liberty. The punishment for conspiracy carried a maximum penalty of two years' imprisonment or a fine of ten thousand dollars or both; but to Darrow it was not just a question of securing an acquittal for the defendants but of safeguarding the rights of labor. . . .

The progress of the trial was suddenly halted on February 8 by the illness of one of the jury. Being satisfied with developments, the defense was eager that some arrangement be made to resume the trial. It was proposed that a new jury be immediately impaneled, consisting of the eleven old jurors and one other, and that the evidence already taken be read to them. The judge, however, was inclined to question the legality of such procedure and accordingly dismissed the jury on February 12. This was done over the strenuous objections of the defense, which was convinced that the jury was growing more and more sympathetic to their side. According to Darrow, the jury, when discharged, stood eleven to one for acquittal. Convinced of the futility of prosecuting the accused, the district attorney continued the case for a year and then quietly entered nolle prosequi on the records, thus indicating that no further action would be taken. . . .

II. A Modern Crucible: Suits by the Attorney General

The historical reaction to *Debs* and the injunction was in part colored by the nature of the substantive claim and a doubt as to its legitimacy. Many believed that the injunction was being used to interfere with the organization of labor. Then in 1954 the Supreme Court altered the substantive premises. In Brown v. Board of Education, 347 U.S. 483 (1954); 349 U.S. 294 (1955), the Court declared the dual school system unconstitutional. It turned to the injunction as the instrument of reform. As the following excerpts describe, this brought the legacy of *Debs* back into prominence.

"*Brown* gave the injunction a special prominence. School desegregation became one of the prime litigative chores of the courts in the period of

1954–74, and in these cases the typical remedy was the injunction. School desegregation not only gave the injunction a greater currency, it also presented the injunction with new challenges, in terms of both the enormity and the kinds of tasks it was assigned. The injunction was to be used to restructure educational systems throughout the nation.

"The impact of *Brown* on our remedial jurisprudence—giving a primacy to the injunction—was not confined to school desegregation. It also extended to civil rights cases in general, and beyond civil rights to litigation involving electoral reapportionment, mental hospitals, prisons, trade practices, and the environment. Having desegregated the schools of Alabama, it was only natural for Judge Johnson to try to reform the mental hospitals and then the prisons of the state in the name of human rights—the right to treatment or to be free from cruel and unusual punishment—and to attempt this Herculean feat through the injunction.[9] And he was not alone. The same logic was manifest in the action of other judges, North and South.

"These developments rested in part on certain normative premises, especially ones concerning the legitimacy of *Brown* and the exercise of the injunctive power implied in that case. At the outset, *Brown* met with a hostile reception, but over time it was generally viewed as legitimate. Indeed, by the late 1960s, *Brown* was viewed as so legitimate that it commonly functioned as an *axiom*—a decision of unquestioned correctness, a starting point for normative reasoning in domains far removed from schools and race. It was the foundation for arguments of the form, 'If this use of the injunction is denied, *Brown* is being denied, and therefore, this use cannot be denied.' "[10] O. Fiss, The Civil Rights Injunction 4–5 (1978).

The Attorney General brought *Debs*. *Brown* and the early school cases were brought by private parties and organizations; the United States participated now and then as an amicus. In the years following *Brown*, however, the pressure grew for the United States to play a prominent role in civil rights litigation. Many demanded that the special resources and standing of the Attorney General be put to the cause of racial equality, and as a consequence the similarity between civil rights litigation and *Debs* became more pronounced.

The Sherman Act of 1890 authorized injunctive suits by the Attorney General to prevent restraints of trade. The lower court had based the *Debs* injunction on the Sherman Act; however, for reasons not entirely clear, the Supreme Court found the injunction to be authorized by the Commerce

9. Wyatt v. Stickney, 344 F.Supp. 373 (M.D.Ala.1972), aff'd in part and rev'd in part sub nom. Wyatt v. Aderholt, 503 F.2d 1305 (5th Cir. 1974) (mental hospital); and Pugh v. Locke, 406 F.Supp. 318 (M.D.Ala.1976), aff'd in part and rev'd in part sub nom. Newman v. Alabama, 559 F.2d 283 (5th Cir. 1977) (prison case). On these cases, see Note, The Wyatt Case: Implementation of a Judicial Decree Ordering Institutional Change, 84 Yale L.J. 1338 (1975); Robbins & Buster, Punitive Conditions of Prison Confinement: An Analysis of Pugh v. Locke and Federal Court Supervision of State Penal Administration Under the Eighth Amendment, 29 Stan.L.Rev. 893 (1977).

10. Also, because of the collapse of the common law writs and a failure to exploit the full potential of the new declaratory judgment provisions, the injunction became the primary means for obtaining the more standard form of judicial review of administrative action. This development also increased the prominence of the injunction, for during the 1950s and 1960s judicial review of administrative action became more common.

Clause. The Court also decided that it was not necessary for Congress to specifically authorize the suit by the Attorney General; it viewed the government's power to initiate the injunctive suit as an integral part of the executive function. The civil rights era forced the Attorney General and the courts to reexamine the nonstatutory power of the United States to sue to enforce the Constitution. In the context of that narrow legal question, the courts struggled with the ghost of *Debs* and the cry of government by injunction.

The legal system conspired against a neat answer to the question. In 1957, Congress established the Civil Rights Division of the Department of Justice and authorized suits by the Attorney General to protect the right to vote. During the Eisenhower years, the Attorney General was content with this statute. But in the early 1960s, once Kennedy took control of the White House and the civil rights movement gained momentum, people pressed the Attorney General to move to public accommodations and education. The Department responded to this pressure, but in a narrow and highly constrained fashion; and before the courts confronted the *Debs* question head on, Congress intervened again. In 1964, Congress passed a statute allowing the Attorney General to bring civil rights cases in the areas of public accommodations, state facilities, public education, and employment, 42 U.S.C. § 2000e–5(a). The statute also authorized the United States to intervene in all cases brought by private parties alleging a denial of equal protection. 42 U.S.C. § 2000h–2. In 1968 Congress authorized suits by the Attorney General to prevent discrimination in housing. 42 U.S.C. § 3613.

Although this statutory framework included all the traditional civil rights claims, by the late 1960s, new claims were developing. For example, people in prisons or mental hospitals sued, asserting that their treatment was grossly inadequate. Despite the lack of statutory authorization the Attorney General sought to participate in a number of lawsuits in the late 1960s. This pattern continued throughout the 1970s in institutional litigation. Some lower courts cooperated; others resisted. The issue finally found its way to the Supreme Court in the Texas prison case, Estelle v. Justice, 426 U.S. 925 (1976).

Following a practice that was first initiated by Judge Johnson in the 1960s, the trial judge in *Estelle* invited the Attorney General to participate as a "litigating amicus": the Attorney General was to be denominated an amicus but with the rights normally associated with party status, e.g., the right to present evidence and to cross-examine witnesses. The Department responded to this invitation by moving to intervene, and when that motion was granted, the state sought a writ of mandamus from the Fifth Circuit. The mandamus was denied, and the Supreme Court also denied the writ of certiorari. Justice Rehnquist wrote a dissent, joined by Chief Justice Burger and Justice Powell: "If *Debs*, which held a federal court has authority to issue an injunction against an armed conspiracy that threatened the interstate transportation of the mails, is to be extended to the situation presented by this case, I think the decision to do so should be made by this Court." 426 U.S. at 929 (1976).

Once again, however, events prevented a definite resolution. In 1980 Congress passed a statute that mooted the question Justice Rehnquist sought to reach. The statute authorized suits by the Attorney General to protect the constitutional rights of institutionalized persons. 42 U.S.C. § 1997. But in the closing days of President Jimmy Carter's administration, the Department of Justice brought a suit that fell into one of the gaps in the statutory scheme.

UNITED STATES v. CITY OF PHILADELPHIA

644 F.2d 187 (3d Cir. 1980).

Before ALDISERT, VAN DUSEN and GARTH, Circuit Judges.

ALDISERT, Circuit Judge.

The primary question in this appeal is whether the United States has implied authority to sue a city and its officials for an injunction against violations of the fourteenth amendment rights of individuals. The government argues that both the criminal provisions of the Civil Rights Acts of 1866 and 1870, 18 U.S.C. §§ 242 and 241, and the fourteenth amendment itself give rise to an implied right of action. We also must decide whether the government has stated a claim for relief under the Omnibus Crime Control and Safe Streets Act of 1968, 42 U.S.C. § 3789d, or the State and Local Fiscal Assistance Act of 1972 (the "Revenue Sharing Act"), 31 U.S.C. § 1242. In a pair of published opinions, the district court held that the Attorney General has no standing to advance the civil rights of third persons absent an express statutory grant of the necessary authority and that the complaint did not allege claims under the two funding statutes with sufficient specificity; and accordingly it dismissed the complaint. United States v. City of Philadelphia, 482 F.Supp. 1248 and 1274 (E.D.Pa.1979). We affirm.

Because the case comes before this court on appeal from orders of the district court dismissing the complaint, we assume that all well-pleaded allegations of the complaint are true, and we set out the facts alleged in the light most favorable to the appellant.

The government's theory is that the appellees, the City of Philadelphia and numerous high-ranking officials of the City and its Police Department, have engaged in a pattern or practice of depriving persons of rights protected by the due process clause of the fourteenth amendment. The allegations of the complaint can be conveniently divided into two categories. First, it alleges that Philadelphia police officers have engaged in a widespread practice of violating the rights of persons they encounter on the streets and elsewhere in the city. In particular, it charges that officers have stopped automobiles and pedestrians without probable cause and physically abused or illegally arrested those who protested, arbitrarily closed public areas and responded to protests or resistance with physical abuse and unwarranted arrests, conducted illegal searches and seizures, detained persons without probable cause or for excessive periods, denied them access to counsel or to medical care while detained, physically abused arrested persons, extracted information and confessions by means of physical brutality, subjected individuals to verbal abuse (including racial slurs), filed unwarranted criminal charges, and engaged in unnecessary use of deadly force, such as shooting criminal suspects who offer no realistic threat to the safety of police officers or other persons.

Second, the United States alleges that the appellees have deliberately encouraged these illegal practices through the policies and procedures they have established for investigating complaints of illegal police activity. It charges that the appellees discourage victims of abuse from complaining, suppress evidence that inculpates police officers, accept implausible explanations of abusive conduct, harass complainants and witnesses, prematurely terminate investigations, compile reports that justify policy officers' conduct regardless of actual circumstances, refuse to discipline police officers for known violations, and protect officers from outside investigations. It also charges various appellees with pursuing inadequate training practices, resulting in a pattern of police abuses, and with engaging in surveillance and harassment of critics of the police department.

The United States also alleges generally that some or all of the appellees have deliberately endeavored to encourage police violations of civil rights. It charges that these practices have been implemented with the intent and the effect of inflicting abuse disproportionately on black and Hispanic persons. And finally, it alleges that the foregoing practices have been implemented by police department personnel whose activities are funded in part by federal grants dispensed for the purpose of improving police procedures.

In its prayer for relief, the government asks for a declaration "that the acts, practices, policies and procedures alleged herein violate the Constitution and laws of the United States." It also asks the court to enjoin "the defendants, their agents, employees, successors in office, and all those acting in concert or participation with them" from engaging in the conduct alleged, "from failing or refusing to correct the effects" of that conduct, "from failing or refusing to ensure" that such conduct will not recur, "and from receiving, expending, or failing to make restitution for previously expended federal funds, unless and until defendants cease such acts, policies, practices, and procedures and correct their effects." . . .

[The court held that 18 U.S.C. §§ 241 and 242 neither expressly nor by implication granted the United States the right to sue for an injunction.]

The Attorney General's second theory for maintaining this lawsuit rests on the fourteenth amendment itself and on the President's duty under Article II, § 3 to "take Care that the Laws be faithfully executed." His premise is that because the national government is the "guarantor" of the rights of individuals, we must provide him with a remedy under the Constitution. Relying on Carlson v. Green, 446 U.S. 14 (1980), Davis v. Passman, 442 U.S. 228 (1979), and Bivens v. Six Unknown Federal Narcotics Agents, 403 U.S. 388 (1971), he argues that he has a right of action even though Congress has not exercised its power under § 5 of the fourteenth amendment to create one.

Carlson, Davis, and *Bivens* do not support the government's case. Those decisions rest on the principle that "the class of those litigants who allege that their own constitutional rights have been violated, and who at the same time have no effective means other than the judiciary to enforce these rights, must be able to invoke the existing jurisdiction of the courts for the protection of their justiciable constitutional rights."

That principle does not apply to the government's action in this case. The appellant is not a member of the class whose rights have been violated, but an officer of the federal government seeking to vindicate the constitutional rights of citizens. To allow this action to proceed under the "constitutional tort" theory of *Bivens* and its progeny would be to ignore, not merely to extend, the ratio decidendi of those decisions.

In addition, we note that the Supreme Court has held that a cause of action that otherwise would be recognized under the *Bivens* theory "may be defeated . . . in two situations."

"The first is when defendants demonstrate 'special factors counselling hesitation in the absence of affirmative action by Congress.' The second is when defendants show that Congress has provided an alternative remedy which it explicitly declared to be a *substitute* for recovery directly under the Constitution and viewed as equally effective. . . ."

The second test cannot be applied literally in this case, but we think it weighs against the government's action because Congress has enacted a comprehensive remedial scheme while deliberately refusing to create the right of action asserted here. More important, however, and by itself sufficient to require rejection of the government's *Bivens* theory if it were valid otherwise, this case involves important "special factors counselling hesitation in the absence of affirmative action by Congress." Recognition of the asserted right of action would violate the constitutional scheme of separation of powers as exemplified and embodied in § 5 of the fourteenth amendment and would trample on important constitutional principles that underlie and give life to our federal system.

Section 5 of the fourteenth amendment confers on Congress, not on the Executive or the Judiciary, the "power to enforce, by appropriate legislation, the provisions of this article." The Supreme Court has repeatedly recognized the central role of Congress in establishing appropriate mechanisms to enforce the fourteenth amendment. See e.g., Fitzpatrick v. Bitzer, 427 U.S. 445 (1976); Katzenbach v. Morgan, 384 U.S. 641 (1966); cf. South Carolina v. Katzenbach, 383 U.S. 301 (1966) (§ 2 of the fifteenth amendment). "It is not said the *judicial power* of the general government shall extend to enforcing the prohibitions and to protecting the rights and immunities guaranteed . . . . It is the power of Congress which has been enlarged." Ex parte Virginia, 100 U.S. 339, 345 (1879). Congress has exercised its power to "enforc[e] the prohibitions" on many occasions, but it has refused to grant the Executive and the Judiciary the authority that now is asserted. . . . In our view, it would be entirely inappropriate for a federal court to overrule the explicit decisions of Congress not to increase federal executive and judicial authority over state and local governments in this manner.

In addition, the Supreme Court in the last decade has repeatedly recognized the importance of a proper respect for the independent roles of state and local governments in our federal system. See e.g., Juidice v. Vail, 430 U.S. 327 (1977); National League of Cities v. Usery, 426 U.S. 833 (1976); Rizzo v. Goode, 423 U.S. 362 (1976); Huffman v. Pursue, Ltd., 420 U.S. 592 (1975); Younger v. Harris, 401 U.S. 37 (1971); Oregon v. Mitchell, 400 U.S. 112 (1970). Judge Ditter wrote eloquently and persuasively for the court below that to permit this action to proceed "would be to vest an excessive and dangerous degree of power in the hands of the Attorney General":

"The point is that the power which the Attorney General claims in this case is simply not compatible with the federal system of government envisioned by the Constitution. This power, in essence, would permit the Justice Department to bring a civil suit against any state or local administrative body merely because the Attorney General and his subordinates have determined that the defendant's operating policies and procedures violate any one of the civil rights guaranteed to citizens by the Constitution and laws of the United States. The purpose of such a lawsuit would be to obtain an injunction altering the challenged procedures. Quite literally, there would be no end to the local and state agencies, bureaus, offices, departments, or divisions whose day-to-day operating procedures could be challenged by suit, and changed by injunction.

"It is well to remember that this case does not present an attack on brutality, *per se.* Rather, the challenge here is to policies, practices and procedures of the police department that are said to violate constitutional rights because they *foster* brutality. The conceivable variations on this lawsuit are practically infinite." We agree that judicial recognition of the asserted right of action would violate important principles of federalism and separation of powers.

The Attorney General's apparent (albeit oblique) response is that the asserted right of action will be limited to "exceptional" cases involving "widespread and continuing" violations, for which the remedies expressly provided are not "adequate." There are several problems with this argument. First, the asserted standards are so vague as to lack real content. Second, the fundamental objection is to permitting the federal executive to assume authority over state and local governments. If that power is once granted, it will take an active judiciary indeed to confine it within principled limits. Third, even if the government's authority could be confined to "exceptional" cases, judicial assertion of the power to compel drastic and far-reaching changes in local governments would be inconsistent with a proper division of power in a federal system.

We hold, therefore, that the fourteenth amendment does not implicitly authorize the United States to sue to enjoin violations of its substantive prohibitions. . . .

Our conclusion, that neither §§ 241 and 242 nor the fourteenth amendment create in the government a right to maintain this action for an injunction, is bolstered by an additional consideration: the longstanding and uniform agreement of all concerned that no such right of action has ever existed. . . . [N]either Attorneys General nor Congress between 1956 and 1964 believed that either Congress or the Constitution had created this power *sub silentio.* Those officials did not act out a meaningless charade, debating whether to create what they believed already existed, but in a serious and responsible manner decided for reasons of constitutional principle and sound public policy not to create new federal authority over state and local governments.

The same understanding, that the United States may not sue to enjoin violations of individuals' fourteenth amendment rights without specific statutory authority, has been shared by almost every court that has had the opportunity to pass on the question. In United States v. Mattson, 600 F.2d 1295 (9th Cir. 1979), and in United States v. Solomon, 563 F.2d 1121 (4th Cir. 1977), the courts of appeals affirmed district court decisions and held that the Attorney General may not sue to vindicate the constitutional rights of institutionalized mentally retarded citizens without express statutory authority. In United States v. Elrod, No. 76–C–4768 (N.D.Ill. May 16, 1978), rev'd on other grounds, 627 F.2d 813 (7th Cir. 1980), the district court held that the Attorney General had no standing to sue to protect the constitutional rights of local prisoners. The Court of Appeals reversed and remanded because intervening legislation, the Civil Rights of Institutionalized Persons Act, Pub. L. No. 96–247, § 3, 94 Stat. 350 (1980), provided *explicit* statutory authority for the action.[22] Three Justices of the Supreme Court have expressed their opinion that the United States does not have authority under either the fourteenth amendment or §§ 241 and 242 to seek an injunction against state corrections officials. Estelle v. Justice, 426 U.S. 925, 928–29 (1976) (Rehnquist, J., joined by Burger, C.J., and Powell, J., dissenting from denial of petition for certiorari). To our knowledge, the only decision that has held squarely that the United States may sue to enjoin "large-scale denials of due process" is a much criticized district court decision, United States v. Brand Jewelers, Inc., 318 F.Supp. 1293, 1299–1300 (S.D.N.Y.1970). We agree with the numerous critics of that decision,[23] and we think it is significant that the United States does not rely on it here.

We note also that as recently as two years ago, only eight months before the complaint initiating this action was filed, Assistant Attorney General Drew S. Days, III, head of the Civil Rights Division, who argued for the government in this case, publicly stated his opinion that §§ 241 and 242 do not give the Justice Department authority to seek injunctions against violations of civil rights. Addressing the shortcomings of criminal prosecutions under §§ 241 and 242 as a means of deterring police brutality, Mr. Days stated:

"A prosecution for police misconduct does not address itself to the activities of a police department as such or of a city administration per se, but only to the actions of one or more officers in a given circumstance, framed by and limited to the wording of the criminal indictment. Moreover, criminal prosecutions are reactive litigations involving only the calling to account of individuals who have already engaged in acts of misconduct. Any conscious effort to anticipate instances of police misconduct and head them off before they occur must arise from *some other source than the Federal criminal code.*"

22. The same Attorney General who filed this civil action, speaking through Assistant Attorney General Days, advocated passage of the Civil Rights of Institutionalized Persons Act. See Civil Rights for Institutionalized Persons: Hearings on H.R. 2439 and H.R. 5791 Before the Subcomm. on Courts, Civil Liberties, and the Administration of Justice of the House Comm. on the Judiciary, 95th Cong., 1st Sess. 3 (1977) (testimony of Hon. Drew S. Days, III). The act authorizes the Attorney General to institute civil actions to redress systematic deprivations of the rights of institutionalized persons. The history of this legislation both demonstrates that no member of Congress believed that the Justice Department already possessed the broad implied authority that it now claims and emphasizes the fact that Congress frequently has acted to give the Department explicit authority to engage in limited areas of civil rights litigation: . . .

23. See, e.g., United States v. City of Philadelphia, 482 F.Supp. 1248, 1265–66 (E.D.Pa.1979); United States v. Solomon, 419 F.Supp. 358, 365–68 (D.Md.1976), aff'd, 563 F.2d 1121 (4th Cir. 1977); id., 563 F.2d at 1128; United States v. School District of Ferndale, Michigan, 400 F.Supp. 1122, 1129–30 (E.D.Mich.1975), aff'd, in pertinent part, 577 F.2d 1339 (6th Cir. 1978). See also 85 Harv.L.Rev. 1566, 1576–79 (1972); 84 Harv.L.Rev. 1930 (1971); 37 Brooklyn L.Rev. 426 (1971); 17 Wayne L.Rev. 1287 (1971).

Police Practices and the Preservation of Civil Rights, A Consultation Sponsored by the United States Commission on Civil Rights, Washington, D.C., December 12–13, 1978, at 141 (emphasis added). We agree with Mr. Days' 1978 statement that the criminal code does not authorize the Justice Department to seek prospective relief. . . .

In sum, the Attorney General argues that he possesses implied authority under the Civil Rights Acts and under the fourteenth amendment to request far-reaching mandatory injunctions, notwithstanding three separate refusals of Congress to grant him this authority and a widely-shared understanding that the authority does not exist. He also has looked to the courts, and applications similar to this have been rejected in the fourth, seventh, and ninth circuits. Unabashed, he has continued to shop for a forum that will lend its ear. He will not find it here.

We think that what he asks is unnecessary, because other avenues of relief are available. What he seeks is a grant of unbridled authority that does violence to the delicate balance of power among the legislative, executive, and judicial branches of government. What he requests strikes at the heart of fundamental comity between federal and state governments. Finally, what is sought—government by injunction—is anathematic to the American judicial tradition, succinctly and eloquently described by Justice Marshall:

"The Constitution provides that Congress shall make laws, the President execute laws, and courts interpret laws. . . . It [does] not provide for government by injunction in which the courts and the Executive Branch can 'make law' without regard to the action of Congress. It may be more convenient for the Executive Branch if it need only convince a judge to prohibit conduct rather than ask the Congress to pass a law, and it may be more convenient to enforce a contempt order than to seek a criminal conviction in a jury trial. Moreover, it may be considered politically wise to get a court to share the responsibility for arresting those who the Executive Branch has probable cause to believe are violating the law. But convenience and political considerations of the moment do not justify a basic departure from the principles of our system of government."

New York Times Co. v. United States, (Marshall, J., concurring) (citation omitted). . . .

[The court also held that the United States had failed to plead with sufficient specificity claims that defendants had administered federal funds in a discriminatory fashion.]

The judgment of the district court will be affirmed in all respects. . . .

GIBBONS, Circuit Judge, dissenting from an order denying rehearing.

Rule 35 of the Federal Rules of Appellate Procedure provides that rehearing by the court in banc "will not be ordered except (1) when consideration by the full court is necessary to secure or maintain uniformity of its decisions, or (2) when the proceedings involve a question of exceptional importance." This case, in which the United States petitions for rehearing of a panel decision affirming the dismissal of its complaint, more clearly meets both criteria of Rule 35 than any of those which we have heard in banc in the eleven years of my service on this court. The panel decision is plainly inconsistent with an in banc opinion of this court filed little over a year ago, and with two prior panel opinions, one of them written by the very author of the opinion of which the United States seeks reconsideration. . . .

This suit grows out of an eight-month Justice Department investigation into police brutality in Philadelphia. Following the failure of private plaintiffs in Rizzo v. Goode, 423 U.S. 362 (1976), to convince the Supreme Court of a sufficient factual nexus between particular acts of brutality and official collusion in condoning the conduct of or obstructing the disciplining of police officers, and system-wide deprivations of civil rights, the Justice Department undertook to establish that connection. Its investigations into police files of citizen complaints, and review of internal police department training and disciplinary procedures revealed a pervasive pattern or practice of verbal abuse (often involving racial epithets), physical abuse, false arrests, compounding of charges to cover up false arrests or to discourage the filing of complaints, illegal searches and seizures, and unlawful detainments.

As detailed in the government's complaint and replies to defendants' interrogatories, the investigation also discovered inadequate training in the use of firearms. The training did not attempt to discourage officers from using deadly force, with the result that innocent bystanders and fleeing persons were too often shot, 29 of them in the back. The government's investigation uncovered 290 complaints by citizens that they had been shot. The police department did not afford adequate psychological training to help officers deal with stress situations and to screen out officers with abusive tendencies. Officers were also inadequately trained to recognize victims of diabetic, epileptic and other disease-related seizures, with the result that persons in need of medical care were often locked up without medication and sometimes physically abused.

The internal investigative and disciplinary procedures, or rather lack of them, were an especial subject of investigation. The Justice Department found that the police department pressured citizen complainants and witnesses to take lie detector tests, but did not impose the tests on police officers. Statements from witnesses would often be taken in the presence of the allegedly abusive officer. Police officers would offer to drop charges if the arrestee withdrew or agreed not to file a complaint. The police department would often accept the officer's explanation of his conduct, and would compile reports justifying the officer's conduct. Compilers of these reports would discuss them with the directors of the police department internal affairs bureau, and would often alter the reports to suit the protective views of the directors. Moreover, despite complaints of brutality filed against police officers, who may or may not have been internally investigated, these officers would nonetheless receive commendations and promotions. The Justice Department further found that the police department harassed citizen critics of the police by surveillance and false arrests. Police officers critical of department practices would also be harassed.

The district court issued two opinions, one dismissing the bulk of the government's claims for lack of standing, the other dismissing the remainder of the complaint for failure to plead discrimination in the administration of federally funded programs with sufficient factual specificity.

In its first opinion, the district court concluded the Attorney General lacked authority, express or implied, statutory or constitutional, to initiate the greater part of its suit seeking declaratory and injunctive relief against a pattern or practice of civil rights violations. The court reviewed the legislative history of the Civil Rights Acts of 1957, 1960 and 1964, in which amendments explicitly authorizing the Attorney General to initiate suits for injunctions were proposed but never incorporated in the bills' final versions. Relying, in the absence of direction from the Third Circuit, on decisions from the Fourth and Ninth Circuits, the court concluded that congressional failure explicitly to authorize executive branch suits for injunctions meant Congress intended to prohibit the suit.

The district court rejected the Attorney General's argument that 28 U.S.C. § 518(b), authorizing his Department to conduct in federal court any case in which the United States is interested, afforded explicit statutory authority for this suit. The court found that statute a "mere housekeeping provision," that could not have been intended to confer broad power to vindicate the United States' interests. . . .

The district court also rejected the Attorney General's claim of inherent executive authority to bring the suit. The court found unpersuasive the government's analogy of an implied constitutional right of action by the government from Supreme Court decisions affording private litigants an implied constitutional claim. It also dismissed the Attorney General's contention that he has inherent constitutional authority to sue to protect the United States' interests, including power to remove burdens on interstate commerce and to protect constitutional and statutory rights. The court found no authority in In re Debs, for the government's arguments. That case, in which the Supreme Court announced a broad Executive Branch right and duty to sue to protect the public interest, was, according to the court, limited to its facts of dire nationwide emergency. The government's allegations of burdens on interstate commerce in Philadelphia were said to be of much less magnitude than the burdens proved in *Debs*. The court declined to follow the ruling of the Southern District of New York in United States v. Brand Jewelers, 318 F.Supp. 1293 (S.D.N.Y.1970). . . . which had upheld the Attorney General's standing to sue to enjoin wide-spread deprivations of due process.

The court also rejected the government's argument that it had standing to sue as *parens patriae* to protect the health and welfare of its citizens. It held that remedy to be available only when no private alternative existed. Because private enforcement alternatives were available, the court found no merit in this last argument.

The district judge then embarked on a policy discussion of the impropriety, and indeed, danger of the government's suit. In a discussion reminiscent of South Carolina's attitude toward federal revenue officers,[2] he stated that "the power which the Attorney General claims in this case simply is not compatible with the federal system of government envisioned by the Constitution." He envisioned "legions of lawyer-bureaucrats," dispatched to reconnoiter and to rampage "the policy making machinery at every level of government from the village hall to the governor's mansion." He suggested that permitting the government's suit would encourage the Executive to take

2. On November 24, 1832, South Carolina passed a statute making it a state crime for a federal official to take steps to enforce the Federal Tariff Law. 1 Statutes at Large of South Carolina 329 et seq.

the law into its own hands, and in effect, to rewrite congressional enactments to satisfy its power-hungry tastes. Finally, the district judge argued that not only did the government's suit threaten potential executive abuse, it had in fact already resulted in abuse. The judge believed the Justice Department's tactics of investigation and prosecution of the suit catered to the press and jeopardized the reputations of former Mayor Rizzo and several high police department officials. It did not seem to occur to the court that a trial on the merits might vindicate the ex-mayor's and the police officials' reputations. . . .

Article II section 3 of the Constitution charges the Executive to "take care that the Laws be faithfully executed." Independent of any explicit statutory grant of authority, provided Congress has not expressly limited its authority, the Executive has the inherent constitutional power and duty to enforce constitutional and statutory rights by resort to the courts. When Federal courts have upheld executive standing without explicit congressional authority, they have looked to other provisions of the Constitution, such as the commerce clause and the fourteenth amendment, and to a general statutory scheme defining federal rights but lacking the specific remedy of executive suit. In addition, 28 U.S.C. § 518(b) affords the Attorney General statutory authority to "conduct and argue any case in a court of the United States in which the United States is interested." The Supreme Court has held that this statute confers on the Executive general authority to initiate suits "to safeguard national interests." Moreover, the Supreme Court has [in *Debs*] held that the Executive's general constitutional duty to protect the public welfare "is often of itself sufficient to give it standing in court."

A review of the caselaw construing executive authority to bring suit helps set this suit in context. Prior cases show that the district court's arguments for denying standing because of congressional inaction to afford explicit standing or because of a threat of abuse of executive power have already been rehearsed and rejected.

From the beginning of the nineteenth century, the Supreme Court has recognized the nonstatutory authority of the executive to sue to protect the United States' contractual and proprietary interests. . . .

After the civil war, with the creation of the Justice Department, An Act to Establish the Department of Justice, 16 Stat. 162 ch. 150 (June 22, 1870), the scope of the Attorney General's statutory and nonstatutory authority to conduct litigation in which the United States had an interest expanded. The 1870 Justice Department Act, part of the Reconstruction Congress' efforts to implement and to secure enforcement of the 13th, 14th and 15th amendments, see generally, H. Cummings & C. McFarland, Federal Justice, 218–249 (1937), broadened the Attorney General's authority to appear in federal court to present the interests of the United States.

The 1870 Justice Department Act added the provision now found at 28 U.S.C. § 518(b).

"When the Attorney General considers it in the interests of the United States, he may personally conduct and argue any case in a court of the United States in which the United States is interested, or he may direct the Solicitor General or any officer of the Department of Justice to do so."

Whether this statute, along with other Reconstruction Era enactments, see, e.g., 17 Stat. 13 ch. 22 § 3 (1871), now at 10 U.S.C. 333 (part of the Ku Klux Klan Act, authorizing the executive to use military or "any other means" to enforce federal law), in effect creates explicit congressional authority for the executive to seek declaratory or injunctive relief in civil rights cases, is perhaps debatable. . . . Nonetheless, in the vast expansion of federal law and of the activities of federal lawyers that occurred after the Civil War, the nature of suits brought by the Attorney General without explicit statutory authority also widened. The Justice Department Act, if it did not automatically grant standing (a latter-day concept with which the legislators of 1870, accustomed to practice under the Process Act, would hardly be familiar), did authorize the Attorney General, or his designees, to sue in the lower federal courts. See United States v. San Jacinto Tin Co., 125 U.S. 273, 278–79 (1888).

In United States v. San Jacinto Tin Co., the Attorney General sued to revoke a fraudulently obtained land patent. Although the United States had a proprietary interest in the action, for if the patent were revoked the land would have reverted to the United States, the Court's concerns focused more on protecting the integrity of the land patents scheme than on any pecuniary interest of the United States. Thus, although the Court spoke of the rights of the United States as analogous to those of a private litigant interested in the suit's subject matter, it also declared:

"[I]n short, if there does not appear any obligation on the part of the United States to the public, or to any individual, or any interest of its own, it can no more sustain such an action than any private person could under similar circumstances."

The analogy to private litigants is in fact imperfect, for as the Court recognized, and was to elaborate further in *Bell Telephone*, the Executive has a duty to the public, which no private litigant suing to enforce his property interests has.

It is important to note that this early non-statutory action afforded the Supreme Court the opportunity to reflect on, and to reject, the argument that executive resort to the courts without congressional authority threatened the balance of power among the coordinate branches of the federal government.

"We are not insensible to the enormous power and its capacity for evil thus reposed in that department of the government. Since the title to all of the land in more than half of the States and Territories of the Union depends upon patents from the government of the United States, it is to be seen what a vast power is confided to the officer who may order the institution of suits to set aside every one of these patents; and if the doctrine that the United States in bringing such actions is not controlled by any statute of limitations, or governed by the rule concerning laches be sound, of which we express no opinion at present, then the evil which may result would seem to be endless as well as enormous. But it has often been said that the fact that the exercise of power may be abused is no sufficient reason for denying its existence, and if restrictions are to be placed upon the exercise of this authority by the Attorney General, it is for the legislative body which created the office to enact them."

In United States v. American Bell Telephone Co., 128 U.S. 315 (1888), the Supreme Court expanded on the public protection theme announced in *San Jacinto*. In this case, the United States had no pecuniary interest, for the Attorney General was suing, without Congressional authority, to revoke a fraudulently obtained inventor's patent. Unlike revocation of a land patent, revocation of an inventor's patent would not return property to the United States. Nonetheless the Court held,

"The essence of the right of the United States to interfere in the present case is its obligation to protect the public from the monopoly of the patent which was procured by fraud, and it would be difficult to find language more aptly used to include this in the class of cases which are not excluded from the jurisdiction of the court by want of interest in the government of the United States."

One commentator has suggested that the Executive's obligation to protect the public interest in the abstract did not itself afford the Attorney General standing:

"But in concluding that there was a public interest at stake entitling the Executive to bring suit, the Court did not rely on a mere assertion that such was the case. Rather, it inferred the existence of an interest from the extensive congressional activity in the patent area; and it permitted the Executive to bring suit to protect that public interest—despite the absence of express statutory authority to do so—because of the constitutional responsibility of the Executive to effectuate a congressionally established scheme."

Note, Nonstatutory Executive Authority to Bring Suit, 85 Harv.L.Rev. 1566, 1568 (1972). In effect, the Executive was filling in the interstices of a statutory scheme whose policy was clear. Congress' failure specifically to provide for this mode of enforcing patent policy did not prevent the Executive from taking its own steps to effect the general statutory goal of awarding a monopoly only to those inventions meeting the statutory criteria of unique originality. Even accepting this more narrow reading of United States v. American Bell Telephone, this case falls within it, for there is a pervasive federal statutory policy protecting civil rights.

In In re Debs, the Attorney General sought an injunction against the activities of Eugene V. Debs and other leaders of the Pullman railway workers. Several grounds were available to confirm the Executive's nonstatutory right to bring the suit. The Pullman strike prevented the passage of the mails through Chicago. The unanimous Court observed that the United States' proprietary interest in the mails would afford a nonstatutory right of action. The Court continued, however:

"We do not care to place our decision upon this ground alone. Every government, entrusted, by the very terms of its being, with powers and duties to be exercised and discharged for the general welfare, has a right to apply to its own courts for any proper assistance in the exercise of the one and the discharge of the other, and it is no sufficient answer to its appeal to one of those courts that it has no pecuniary interest in the matter. The obligations which it is under to promote the interest of all, and to prevent the wrongdoing of one resulting in injury to the general welfare, is often of itself sufficient to give it a standing in court."

The Court reviewed its decisions in *San Jacinto* and *Bell Telephone*, concluding:

"It is obvious from these decisions that while it is not the province of the government to interfere in any mere matter of private controversy between individuals, or to use its great powers to enforce the rights of one against another, yet, whenever the wrongs complained of are such as affect the public at large, and are in respect of matters which by the Constitution are entrusted to the care of the Nation, and concerning which the Nation owes the duty to all the citizens of securing to them their common rights, then the mere fact that the government has no pecuniary interest in the controversy is not sufficient to exclude it from the courts, or prevent it from taking measures therein to fully discharge those constitutional duties."

Thus, the Attorney General's nonstatutory right of action derived from the constitutional duty to protect the public from injury to the general welfare. The Pullman strike impeded commerce, obstructed the highways, and in effect, represented a nuisance whose removal the executive was obliged to effect.[15] While one might attempt to limit *Debs* to its facts of extreme crisis, or to suggest that extensive congressional regulation of interstate commerce made *Debs*, like *Bell Telephone*, an example of filling in remedial interstices, see Note, Nonstatutory Executive Authority to Bring Suit, 85 Harv.L.Rev. at 1569–70, the Court's express language goes well beyond these interpretations. While in 1895 there might have been differences in the Court as to the appropriate standard of conduct, even then the Court would not have suggested that the interests protected by the thirteenth, fourteenth and fifteenth amendments were less "entrusted to the care of the nation" than were those protected by the commerce clause.

In United States v. California, 332 U.S. 19 (1946), the dispute concerned legal title to oil-rich land under three-mile belt off the California shore. California maintained the Attorney General had no standing to assert the United States' claim. Invoking the inertia-as-law principle on which the district court in this case relied, California argued

"that Congress has for a long period of years acted in such a way as to manifest a clear policy that the states, not the Federal Government, have legal title to the land under the three-mile belt. Although Congress has not expressly declared such a policy, [the Court] is asked to imply it from certain conduct of Congress and other governmental agencies charged with responsibilities concerning the national domain. And, in effect, [the Court is] asked to infer that Congress has by implication amended its long-existing statutes which grant the Attorney General broad powers to institute and maintain court proceedings in order to safeguard national interests."

The "long-existing statutes" to which the Court referred are the portions of the 1870 Justice Department Act creating the Department, and authorizing

15. The court observed that the executive might call out the army forcibly to abate the public nuisance, but concluded that this extreme prerogative comprehended lesser measures.

"[T]he existence of this right of forcible abatement is not inconsistent with nor does it destroy the right of appeal in an orderly way to the courts for a judicial determination and an exercise of their power by a writ of injunction and otherwise to accomplish the same result. . . . So, in the case before us, the right to use force does not exclude the right of appeal to the courts for a judicial determination and for the exercise of all their powers of prevention."

the Attorney General to assert the United States' interests in federal court, now at 28 U.S.C. §§ 501, 503 & 518. United States v. California thus found clear statutory authority for the government's suit, despite the absence of more explicit authority to institute the particular suit at hand. In reply to California's standing contentions, the Court held:

"[N]o act of Congress has amended the statutes which impose on the Attorney General the authority and the duty to protect the Government's interests through the courts. That Congress twice failed to grant the Attorney General specific authority to file suit against California, is not a sufficient basis upon which to rest a restriction of the Attorney General's statutory authority."

The Court's examination of the legislative history of Congress' two failures to grant express standing to the Executive to initiate a suit to confirm the United States' title, did not lead the Court to conclude that Congressional failure to authorize the suit therefore meant Congress forbade the action. The broad statutory authority invested in the Attorney General to argue the interests of the United States supplied ample standing.[17]

The Supreme Court's treatment of Executive standing thus outlines four grounds of the Attorney General's authority to initiate suit despite the absence of express congressional directive to bring particular kinds of actions. 28 U.S.C. § 518 affords a general statutory source of standing when the United States' interests, and particularly its federal sovereign interests, are at stake. Moreover, without referring to that statute, the Court has declared a general federal right to protect Government property, and to supply an additional remedy to effect a general statutory scheme, as well as a constitutional obligation to protect the public welfare.

More recently, the civil rights movement of the late fifties and early sixties also occasioned nonstatutory executive resort to the federal courts. Courts in the Fifth Circuit, addressing the activities of the Ku Klux Klan against the "freedom riders," and segregation in bus and airline terminals, applied the *Debs* precedent to hold that the Executive had a nonstatutory right of action to sue to enjoin burdens on interstate commerce. See, e.g., United States v. U. S. Klans, 194 F.Supp. 897 (M.D.Ala.1961) (Johnson, J.); United States v. City of Montgomery, 201 F.Supp. 590 (M.D.Ala.1962) (Johnson, J.); United States v. Lassiter, 203 F.Supp. 20 (W.D.La.) (3 judge court), aff'd per curiam, 371 U.S. 10 (1962); United States v. City of Shreveport, 210 F.Supp. 36 (W.D.La.1962); United States v. City of Jackson, 318 F.2d 1 (5th Cir. 1963) (Wisdom, J.); United States v. Original Knights of the KKK, 250 F.Supp. 330 (E.D.La.1965) (3 judge court) (Wisdom, J.); Fla. East Coast Ry. v. United States, 348 F.2d 682 (5th Cir. 1965). . . . While some of these decisions find statutory standing under interstate commerce acts and under the Federal Aviation Act, all explicitly also ground the Attorney General's right of action in the duty to enforce the commerce clause of

17. United States v. California, incidentally, involved a far more direct threat to state interests than this case, for here the governing standards of state conduct have long been established, while in the offshore oil case the substantive issue was a matter of warm debate in Congress; a debate which eventually resulted in legislation. Submerged Lands Act of 1953, 67 Stat. 29, 43 U.S.C. § 1301. See Alabama v. Texas, 347 U.S. 272 (1954).

the Constitution.[19] It must be acknowledged that between 1877 and the late fifties, instances of Executive Branch civil actions to enforcement of rights protected by the post Civil War amendments cannot be found. The reason, however, is not lack of standing. Any kind of Executive Branch enforcement of those amendments was almost non-existent. The question was not lack of standing, but lack of initiative.

In United States v. Brand Jewelers, Inc., 318 F.Supp. 1293 (S.D.N.Y. 1970), Judge Marvin Frankel, relying on *Debs* and its Fifth Circuit progeny, held that the Attorney General had nonstatutory authority to sue to enjoin the New York "sewer service" practice. Brand Jewelers and similar operations sold on credit to impecunious customers, then filed a suit to collect, employing process servers who never delivered the summons but filed an affidavit of service. Armed with the affidavit, Brand would obtain a state court default judgment, and would garnish the wages of the hapless and unnotified defendants. In addition to the burden on interstate commerce this practice engendered, Judge Frankel found the practice resulted in "large-scale denials of due process." The court held "the United States may maintain this action because it has standing to sue to end widespread deprivation (i.e. deprivation affecting many people) of property through 'state action' without due process of law." The court found the *Debs* principle provided

"no acceptable basis in principle for distinguishing today the authority of the Attorney General to protect against large-scale burdens on interstate commerce from his authority to protect against large-scale denials of due process."

Judge Frankel reviewed and rejected defendants' argument that the Executive's nonstatutory suit threatened abuse, and that Congress' failure to confer standing meant Congress intended to deny the Attorney General a right of action.

"Defendants warn that the power claimed by the Government in this case is 'overwhelming' and 'awesome'—a power that 'can readily become a terri-

19. See generally Dixon, Civil Rights in Transportation and Government Initiative, 49 U.Va.L.Rev. 205, 224–27 (1963).

In United States v. City of Jackson, Judge Wisdom found it unnecessary to hold that the United States also had direct standing under the fourteenth amendment. Judge Wisdom wrote:

"When a State, not by some sporadic act against a particular individual but by a law or pattern of conduct, takes action motivated by a policy which collides with national policy as embodied in the Constitution, the interest of the United States 'to promote the interest of all' gives it standing to challenge the State in the courts. When the action of a State violative of the Fourteenth Amendment conflicts with the Commerce Clause and casts more than a shadow on the Supremacy Clause, the United States has a duty to protect the 'interests of all.' The courts offer the first avenue for counteraction by the Nation. Such thinking may take us down the road to recognition of Government standing to sue under the Fourteenth Amendment or under any clause of the Constitution. But this case is only a way station. The issue here is framed by the Commerce Clause. Under that clause there is authority for the United States to sue without specific congressional authorization."

318 F.2d at 14. Two lower court decisions, United States v. Biloxi Municipal School District, 219 F.Supp. 691 (S.D. Miss.1963), and United States v. Madison County Bd. of Ed., 219 F.Supp. 60 (N.D. Ala.1963), explicitly rejected fourteenth amendment standing. The Fifth Circuit affirmed these decisions on other grounds, 326 F.2d 237 (5th Cir.), cert. denied, 379 U.S. 929 (1964).

ble engine of oppression.' This is a little hyperbolic to describe the peaceable submission of the United States that it should be permitted to sue in court and pray for judgment on behalf of thousands of people alleged to have been cheated in ways that deny their constitutional rights and burden the nation's commerce. At the same time, defendants have a point when they urge that it is no small matter for anyone to have the resources of the Federal Government drawn up against him in a lawsuit. In the end, however, the potential of imaginable horrors is not a pointedly useful test. Possible abuses by the Attorney General are subject to the control of Congress. See United States v. San Jacinto Tin Co., supra, 125 U.S. 273 at 284. Still more immediately, the whole matter is in court, where the Attorney General submits for judicial judgment all questions of propriety, possible excess, scope and limit."

Judge Frankel continued:

"It is said that Congress has on occasion given to the Attorney General power to sue for enforcement of individual rights, but has declined to grant by statute the standing now claimed: expressio unius, as the saying runs, est exclusio alterius. But the range and effectiveness of that canon are in general somewhat limited. It was available, mutatis mutandis, in *Debs* and other cases in the line. The failure of Congress to take positive action, sometimes a matter of moment, is hardly the equivalent of a negation. It seems especially dubious to fashion a prohibition from Congressional inaction in a case like this one, where both Congress and the courts are conceded by the executive to have veto powers, on the issue of standing as well as on the merits. . . ." [21]

The following year, in New York Times Co. v. United States, the Supreme Court heard and ruled on the Executive's nonstatutory action seeking an injunction against publication of the "Pentagon Papers." In his dissent, Justice Harlan argued the Court should have faced the question whether "the Attorney General is authorized to bring these suits in the name of the United States." The rest of the court assumed the United States could sue.

In addition to initiating suits to protect the public from "large-scale deprivation of due process," burdens on interstate commerce, and fraud, and to assert its federal sovereign interests, the Executive has successfully intervened in civil rights actions. In Faubus v. United States, 254 F.2d 797 (8th Cir. 1958), the court invited the United States' nonstatutorily authorized intervention to secure the enforcement of school desegregation orders in Little Rock, Arkansas, when the governor of that state had called out the local national guard to prevent the attendance of black children in white schools. In Bush v. Orleans Parish School Bd., 191 F.Supp. 871 (E.D.La.) (3 judge court), aff'd per curiam, 367 U.S. 908 (1961), the Court invited the Attorney General's participation as *amicus curiae*. The court had already declared plaintiffs' right to attend desegregated schools, but the injunction had yet to be en-

21. *Brand Jewelers* has not gone uncriticized. See, e.g., Comment, 84 Harv. L.Rev. 1930 (1971). In some respects, *Brand Jewelers* may go beyond its precedent, for Judge Frankel was arguably entertaining not merely a new remedy through executive suit. Because the closest applicable statute The Consumer Credit Protection Act of 1968, governed deceptive and credit practices in general, but did not address the sewer service procedure, commentators charge Judge Frankel with having created a new right. In this case, 42 U.S.C. §§ 1983 and 1985 and 18 U.S.C. §§ 241 and 242 confer a clear right to be free from police abuse. In that respect, therefore, this case is less controversial than *Brand Jewelers*.

forced. The court rejected defendants' argument that congressional failure, in the Civil Rights Acts of 1957 and 1960, expressly to permit the United States to initiate civil rights actions, denied the Attorney General standing to intervene.

In footnote the court further observed:

"There is some doubt whether the mere failure of Congress to expressly authorize the Attorney General to prosecute desegregation suits strips him of that power, if the United States has an interest in the matter. See United States v. State of California, 332 U.S. 19, 28, in which the Supreme Court rejected a similar argument saying: 'That Congress twice failed to grant the Attorney General specific authority to file suit against California, is not a sufficient basis upon which to rest a restriction of the Attorney General's statutory authority.' "

Moreover, the Court held:

"The absence of specific statutory authority is of itself no obstacle, for it is well settled that there is no such prerequisite to the appearance of the United States before its own courts. United States v. San Jacinto Tin Co., 125 U.S. 273; Kern River Co. v. United States, 257 U.S. 147; Sanitary Dist. of Chicago v. United States, 266 U.S. 405. Nor do the statutes governing the Attorney General's participation in court proceedings contain a prohibition. See 5 U.S.C.A. §§ 309, 316 [now 28 U.S.C. §§ 501, 503, 518]."

This circuit, en banc, has recently affirmed the Attorney General's nonstatutory right of intervention in civil rights cases. In Halderman v. Pennhurst State School and Hospital, 612 F.2d 84 (3d Cir. 1979), cert. granted, 449 U.S. 814 (1980), this court reviewed and rejected the Fourth Circuit's decision in United States v. Solomon, which had denied the Attorney General standing to initiate an action to enjoin civil rights violations in a state hospital for the mentally retarded. The Fourth Circuit had held that Congress' failure to afford the executive an express right of action, and the Supreme Court's decision in Youngstown Sheet & Tube Co. v. Sawyer, 343 U.S. 579 (1952), compelled a refusal to permit the Attorney General's suit. This court held:

> We do not find persuasive the *Solomon* court's analogy between President Truman's nonjudicial seizure of the steel mills by military force and a judicial proceeding to obtain injunctive relief enforcing legislative policies in aid of the mentally retarded. There is all the difference in the world for separation of powers purposes between a naked exercise of executive power and executive branch resort to the judicial branch for relief which Congress has not expressly prohibited. The President is, after all, charged with the responsibility to "take Care that the Laws be faithfully executed . . . " U.S.Const. art. II, § 3. When, in an effort to do so, he resorts to an Article III court under a recognized grant of federal jurisdiction such as 28 U.S.C. § 1345, and that court finds no legislative prohibition against that resort, the lawsuit cannot reasonably be seen as an invasion of the powers of Congress. Before relief can be given in such a suit, one branch, the judiciary, must agree that it is authorized by the law promulgated by a third branch. If the judiciary has, in an individual case, misconstrued the law, Congress can, constitutional pronouncements aside, change the rule for the future. If Congress wishes to withhold from the

> executive branch the civil remedies available under the Federal Rules of Civil Procedure, it can by specific legislation say so. Thus, we find unconvincing the separation of powers argument invoked by the *Solomon* court to reject executive branch enforcement of federal law.

Six members of the court joined in the *Halderman* opinion, including one who now joins in the panel opinion expressly approving the *Solomon* case, which little more than a year ago we expressly disapproved! Even the dissenters in *Halderman* did not dissent from that part of the opinion. Although this court suggested the rationale for permitting executive intervention and the rationale for permitting executive initiation of a civil rights action might be the same, in *Halderman* we were not called upon to decide the latter question. . . .

Thus statutory and Third Circuit case law authority present the following picture: when a private action implicates the United States' interests, the Attorney General may 1) intervene; and 2) take over the conduct of the litigation with respect to issues involving the United States' interests. It is difficult to perceive a qualitatively different "threat" to separation of powers, or to local autonomy, when the Attorney General intervenes and conducts the injunctive action, and when he initiates the action. Clearly, had the United States joined a class or even individual private plaintiffs in this action, the Attorney General's standing would be indisputable. To hold the absence of private plaintiffs denies the Attorney General standing seems an exercise in piercing the substance to uncover the form.

The district court did not hold that the United States lacked the requisite "interest" under 28 U.S.C. § 518. Rather, it construed the statute as "merely a housekeeping provision which pertains to the internal organization of the federal government." The district judge felt "such an innocuous statute," could not confer general statutory authority to sue to protect the United States' interests. This court's construction of § 518 in Brawer v. Horowitz, however, controverts the district court's "mere housekeeping" interpretation. This circuit has explicitly followed *Debs* in construing that provision. The United States' "interest" comprehends "matters . . . 'affect[ing] the public at large' and . . . 'entrusted to the care of the nation.'" Had this court found section 518 merely concerned internal Justice Department organization, it could not have advanced its broad reading of the Attorney General's statutory authority, nor sustained its holding in *Brawer*. Because the United States clearly has the requisite "interest" in preventing the wide-scale deprivation of due process and burdens on interstate commerce the government's complaint, alleges, it certainly has standing to bring this action.[24]

24. Cf. Pasadena City Bd. of Ed. v. Spangler, in which the Supreme Court held the United States, permitted by statute to intervene in a school desegregation action, was an adequate class representative for the plaintiffs, even though the individual plaintiffs had not, in fact, been certified under Rule 23, and by the time the suit reached the Supreme Court, lacked standing because all had graduated. "Except for the intervention of the United States . . . [the] case would clearly be moot." Justice Rehnquist held the statute authorizing the United States' intervention implicitly permitted the United States "to continue as a party plaintiff . . . despite the disappearance of the original plaintiffs and the absence of any class certification . . . ." Id. at 431.

While the *Spangler* Court rested its holding that the United States was an adequate class representative for the plaintiffs' civil rights action on an interpretation of the statute permitting intervention, *Spangler* may also afford

The district court went on at some fulminating length about federal interference in local government.[25] The district judge found it most unseemly that the United States would seek by injunction to enforce the civil rights of residents of Philadelphia. In what might be termed an expression of the "dog pound theory," the judge envisioned massive and unwarranted federal infiltration into every level of local authority, even down to canine administration, and concluded that the "very threat" of executive action to enforce the civil rights laws "could alter the conduct of local policy makers." The Court did not consider whether the fourteenth amendment itself was not designed to affect local policy. Instead, the court seemed to assume that local policy should be insulated from federal law, at least when that arm of the federal government constitutionally charged with enforcing the law in fact seeks to enforce it.

There is, however, no authority for the district court's dire pronouncements. Even in its most solicitous affirmance of local autonomy, the Supreme Court, in National League of Cities v. Usery, 426 U.S. 833 (1976), did not rule that state and local insulation from federal law extended to freedom from the application of the fourteenth amendment. Subsequently, in Fitzpatrick v. Bitzer, 427 U.S. 445, 453 n.9, a unanimous Supreme Court made clear that *National League of Cities* did not insulate local government from the fourteenth amendment. This court in Usery v. Allegheny County Institution Dist., 544 F.2d 148 (3d Cir. 1976), held that under no construction does the 10th amendment limit the fourteenth.

The fourteenth amendment and the civil rights statutes present the threat to local authority. The Executive's injunctive action merely compounds, or perhaps makes good, that threat. It should, moreover, be emphasized that the district court's federalism discussion was, by that court's admission, dicta. The court based its *holding* that the executive lacked standing on the 4th circuit's *Solomon* decision, and on the 9th circuit's parallel holding in United States v. Mattson, 600 F.2d 1295 (9th Cir. 1979). The district court ren-

authority for the proposition that once the United States may intervene, it may also continue the suit as an effective class representative inasmuch as the United States' intervention serves the public interest and fosters the general statutory or constitutional objective of enforcing the fourteenth amendment and congressional enactments based on it.

25. The district judge combined his discussion of federalism with his treatment of separation of powers, collapsing and confusing the two. The two concerns are, however, quite distinct. The subordination of state to federal sovereignty has nothing to do with the allocation of power among coordinate branches of the federal government. As Thayer's seminal article, The Origin and Scope of the American Doctrine of Constitutional Law, 7 Harv.L.Rev. 129 (1893), points out, in one of its less-quoted passages:

"But at last the convention, rejecting all these, settled down upon the common expedients of two legislative houses, to be a check upon each other, and of an executive revision and veto, qualified by the legislative power of reconsideration and enactment by a majority of two-thirds;— upon these expedients, and upon the declaration that the constitution, and constitutional laws and treaties, shall be the supreme law of the land, and shall bind the judges of the several States. This provision, as the phrasing of it indicates, was inserted with an eye to secure the authority of the general government as against the States, i.e., as an essential feature of any efficient Federal system, and not with direct reference to the other departments of the government of the United States itself. The first form of it was that 'legislative Acts of the United States, and treaties, are the supreme law of the respective States, and bind the judges there as against their own laws.'"

Id. at 137 n. 1.

dered its decision almost two months before this circuit announced its en banc decision in *Halderman*. The district judge recognized the decisions of other circuits did not bind him. "Nevertheless, in the absence of contrary authority from the Supreme Court or from the Court of Appeals for the Third Circuit, the decisions of other courts of appeals are entitled to careful consideration, and are not to be lightly ignored." That contrary authority was forthcoming in *Halderman*, in which this court unequivocally rejected *Solomon*.[26] The very basis of the district court's holding on this issue is therefore undercut by a subsequent en banc decision of this court, which the panel members have brazenly ignored.

Separation of powers afforded a second ground for the district court's bewailing of nonstatutory executive activity. Because Congress had thrice declined to grant the Attorney General explicit authority to seek an injunction, the district court concluded it must therefore have meant to prohibit such an action. For the Executive nonetheless to resort to the courts would thus represent an abuse of executive power. There are several flaws in this argument. First, as Judge Frankel observed in *Brand Jewelers*, and as the Supreme Court held in United States v. California, congressional failure explicitly to approve executive action does not equal congressional prohibition.[27]

Second, Supreme Court precedent provides that the Executive has implicit statutory authority to seek an injunction to fill in the remedial interstices of a general statutory scheme. Moreover, 28 U.S.C. § 518 has been construed to confer explicit statutory authority, in the absence of a clear congressional prohibition, to initiate suits.

Third, in this Circuit, the United States would have standing to participate in this action as plaintiff-intervenor. See Halderman v. Pennhurst. The United States would also have authority fully to conduct the suit, so long as the Attorney General's discretion did not prejudice the interests of the private plaintiffs—an unlikely circumstance in this case. Any greater "threat" executive initiation of suits poses to congressional prerogative is therefore rather ethereal.

Fourth, while neither the Supreme Court nor, with the exception of the Southern District of New York in *Brand Jewelers*, the lower federal courts, have squarely held the fourteenth amendment affords the Executive nonstatutory standing, all courts which have considered the question have held the commerce clause confers nonstatutory authority to sue to remove obstructions and burdens on interstate commerce. Neither the Supreme Court nor the federal courts perceived a threat to separation of powers in the Attorney

26. Moreover, Congress has since overruled *Solomon*. Civil Rights of Institutionalized Persons Act, Pub.L.No. 96–247, § 3, 94 Stat. 350 (1980).

27. See also United States v. Marion County School Dist., 625 F.2d 607, 611 (5th Cir. 1980). Defendants had argued the United States had no standing to sue a racially discriminatory school for a breach of a federal funding contract because Congress had "deliberately nullified" a statutory contract claim. The unanimous panel rejected this contention, holding "it is well established that the government's right to sue to enforce its contracts exists as a matter of federal common law, without necessity of a statute. E.g., United States v. Tingey, 30 U.S. [5 Pet.] 113, 127–28 (Story, J.) (calling the right 'an incident to the general right of sovereignty') . . . . Congress may nullify the right, but as the Supreme Court has repeatedly emphasized, courts are entitled to conclude that Congress has done so only if the evidence of Congress' intent is extremely, even unmistakably, clear."

General's suit to enforce the commerce clause. To the contrary, they saw the suit as implementing the constitutional scheme that the Executive enforce the laws. The government has alleged in its complaint in this case that the practices of Philadelphia police and city officials impose burdens on interstate commerce. The government has had no opportunity to demonstrate the interstate commerce impact, and while a trial on the merits may fail to substantiate that claim, the claim itself afforded standing to the Attorney General.

Fifth, as this court recognized in *Halderman*, executive action to secure an injunction is by its nature not an overweening exercise of power. A suit for an injunction is not a naked exercise of executive authority. Unlike the steel seizure in *Youngstown Sheet & Tube*, the Executive can do nothing here without the concurrence of the federal judiciary. And, because the United States is in effect suing as class representative for the citizens of Philadelphia, the Executive is entitled to no more relief than would be accorded the class members. Cf. Pasadena City Bd. of Ed. v. Spangler.

Sixth, despite its fear that this action would violate separation of powers, the district court failed to articulate a congressional purpose or intent that the Executive's nonstatutory action would undermine. What are the identifiable congressional interests this action threatens? Congress cannot intend to insulate defendants from enforcement of the fourteenth amendment. At most, Congress might prefer that Justice Department energies and resources be expended in some other way. Congress has not so declared, however, and were it to announce such an intent, an attempt to enforce it might itself implicate separation of powers. Cf. Myers v. United States, 272 U.S. 52 (1926). While the Executive may not decline to follow a congressional mandate within its proper legislative competence, see National Treasury Employees v. Nixon, 492 F.2d 587 (D.C.Cir.1974) (writ of mandamus lies for Executive's failure to grant pay adjustments required by act of Congress), it is questionable, to say the least, whether Congress may compel the Executive not to enforce the fourteenth amendment or the commerce clause. The Executive's Article II § 3 duty to enforce the laws may override certain congressionally imposed limitations on executive authority. But in any event, because Congress has not here attempted to forbid the Executive from carrying out its constitutional obligations, the question whether such an endeavor would violate separation of powers need not be reached.

Finally, the general problem of suits by the Executive to protect the public welfare should be confronted. While the potential of unbridled executive initiation of suits in the "national interest" understandably may evoke visceral fears of executive power run rampant, careful analysis of the Attorney General's action in this case reveals those fears to be baseless. It is true that phrases like "the public welfare," "the national interest," and "cases in which the United States is interested," can have a formless, and perhaps dangerously expansive quality.[30] Before any court upholds the exercise of executive re-

30. Is the "national interest" any policy the incumbent Executive seeks to promote? And if so, may the Attorney General attempt to enforce it by resort to the courts despite the absence of any supporting legislation or judicial decision? If, for example, the Executive interprets the fourteenth amendment to prohibit racial quotas, may the Attorney General sue to enjoin a municipality's minority set-aside program for civil service employees? Or if the Executive concludes that trenchant media critiques of foreign policy undermine national security, may the Attorney General sue to enjoin publication of such unflattering commentaries?

sort to it without explicit statutory standing, however, the court should determine what kind of right the Executive is seeking to enforce. Is the Executive endeavoring to protect its contractual and proprietary rights? To fill in the remedial interstices of a statutory scheme? To enforce a judicially recognized constitutional right? [31] Or is the Executive instead attempting to create a new right that may conflict with statutory or judicial precedent? When, as here, the Attorney General can substantiate the "national interest" and "public welfare" by reference to clearly articulated legislative policies or judicial precedent, the danger of untoward exercise of executive power is fanciful. Thus viewed, this case does not pose a threat of limitless definition of executive authority to bring suit. In this action, the Attorney General seeks to enjoin the pattern or practice of police brutality in Philadelphia. The Attorney General can point to at least four statutes specifically enacted to prohibit concerted and official deprivations of civil rights by physical abuse, 42 U.S.C. §§ 1983 and 1985 and 18 U.S.C. §§ 241 and 242. In addition, the Attorney General has invoked a host of other statutes guaranteeing civil rights, as well as the fourteenth amendment. Thus, this action does not involve the creation of new rights conflicting with legislative and judicial precedent in the "national interest." Rather, it falls comfortably into the category of decisions upholding nonspecific statutory authority to supply a new remedy for an established scheme of rights.

[Judge Gibbons also said that the way the panel rejected a right of action implied from statute "is an elaborate straw man, designed to divert attention from the real issue of executive authority to act as an effective class representative" and reveals "most clearly" the panel opinion's "essential Calhounism."]

I would grant the petition for rehearing.

---

1) Outgoing Solicitor General Wade McCree decided not to seek certiorari. Two reasons were articulated. First, a new mayor had eliminated many of the abusive police practices that provoked the litigation. The lawsuit was not, therefore, an appropriate vehicle to test nonstatutory authority to sue. Second, no one anticipated that the Reagan administration would utilize the authority to sue extensively. National Law Journal, August 3, 1981, 5. Could it be that Justice Rehnquist's opinion in Estelle v. Justice foreshadowed an affirmance?

2) Is the problem the Attorney General sought to correct in United States v. Philadelphia too large, too complex, and too deeply entrenched to be amenable to judicial remedies? Is the majority's holding a way to limit structural injunctions without facing the merits?

31. Or to protect the integrity of the judiciary, see United States v. Shipp, 203 U.S. 563 (1906); 214 U.S. 386 (1909); 215 U.S. 580 (1909) (upholding nonstatutory information filed against defendants for criminal contempt of the Supreme Court when the Court was considering habeas corpus petition of state prisoner and defendants instigated prisoner's lynching). See also In re Neagle, 135 U.S. 1 (1890) (upholding nonstatutory exercise of executive power without contemporaneous judicial approval to dispatch federal marshall to protect federal judge riding circuit).

3) What remains of the broad view of the executive's power to sue absent statute? A useful Note suggests several ways to read *Debs*. Nonstatutory Executive Authority to Bring Suit, 85 Harv.L.Rev. 1566, 1569–70 (1972). See also Oakley, The United States as Participant in Public Law Litigation: Recent Developments, 13 U.C.D.L.Rev. 247 (1980); Note, Protecting the Public Interest: Nonstatutory Suits by the United States, 89 Yale L.J. 118 (1979). Did the Supreme Court in *Pentagon Papers*, p. 217 allow the executive to sue to protect the national security and perhaps some other vital interests? May the United States sue under the commerce clause? Does it matter whether an emergency will allow the harm to occur before Congress can act? Is United States v. Philadelphia limited to suits by the Attorney General against state and local officials? May the Attorney General sue private corporations or individuals as in *Pentagon Papers* and United States v. United States Klans, 194 F.Supp. 897 (M.D.Ala.1961)?

4) Is the "standing" doctrine at once too amorphous and too focused on private litigation to provide a frame of reference when the government sues? Is the majority's major concern to prevent a) the executive and judicial branches from overreaching Congress? b) the federal government from overreaching the state and local government? c) both forms of overreaching? Do executive suits to enforce constitutional rights threaten Congress's sphere? Does an executive action against state or local government defendants to enforce a constitutional right threaten federalism interests more than an action brought by the aggrieved citizen? Should we distinguish between the executive initiating an action, intervening, or appearing as amicus curiae in a private plaintiff's action? Does the definition of "public interest" affect the answers to the preceding questions? Has the modern era of comprehensive statutes influenced the courts to refuse to allow suit if statutory authority is lacking? Does the absence of affirmative authority to sue evidence that Congress intends to bar an executive action for an injunction to enforce constitutional rights? Juries are available in criminal prosecutions and most tort actions for damages. Does refusing to allow the executive to seek injunctions protect defendants' rights to jury trials? Will robust concern to limit the federal executive coddle lawbreakers of a different sort?

Chapter Two

THE UNIQUENESS OF THE INJUNCTION

The legal system possesses three remedial tools to protect interests defined by common and statutory substantive law. Criminal statutes define forbidden conduct and threaten punishment. Liability rules tell the offending defendant to pay the wronged person money. Finally, judges may enjoin, tell a defendant to do or not to do something. The risk that judges will employ these remedial tools structures conduct and advances the protected interests. And if a wrongdoer thwarts or threatens a protected interest, the judge employs the tools to repair or prevent the harm and to deter the wrongdoer from repeating it.

The remedies for antisocial conduct overlap. For example, under the copyright statutes an infringement may lead to a criminal prosecution, a damage judgment, and an injunction. 17 U.S.C. §§ 101–12. The remedies overlap because they advance different interests. Criminal liability protects the public from serious antisocial conduct. The decision that conduct is sufficiently serious to merit a criminal sanction is the highest order of political choice. Judges use liability rules and injunctions to assist litigants. Damage awards share with criminal sanctions the characteristic of retrospectivity; both refer to past conduct. Injunctions look to the future; judges enjoin to prevent expected harm.

Does comparing injunctions to damage awards and criminal convictions overstate the uniqueness of injunctions? Should we compare injunctions to rules of conduct in liability rules and criminal statutes? Do all three address the future and deter wrongdoing by threatening damage awards or punishment? Should we compare contempt, the remedy for breach of an injunction, to damage awards and criminal convictions? Do courts enjoin simply to express the substantive law specifically and address it to identified individual defendants? See O. Fiss, The Civil Rights Injunction 8–12 (1978).

In this Chapter we explore these questions and the claim of uniqueness for the injunction. We also examine form doctrines that especially limit the issuance of the injunction and are said to arise from its unique quality: the inadequacy prerequisite, balancing the equities, clean hands, and laches. Remember how difficult it is for courts to place plaintiffs in the position they would have occupied but for defendants' improper conduct. Leubsdorf, Remedies for Uncertainty, 61 B.U.L.Rev. 132 (1981). After defendant's wrong, the judge must construct a world that never was. "What would have happened had the defendant not misbehaved?" 61 B.U.L.Rev. at 134. How would plaintiff be situated if defendant had performed the contract or avoided negligence? How much money will it take to bring plaintiff to the point where she will be indifferent whether she had that amount of money or the unimpaired substantive interest? Administrative feasibility leads to artificial concepts like value to measure loss. Judges also limit plaintiff's recovery to results within the scope of defendant's risk. An injunction, in contrast, orders defendant to allow plaintiff to enjoy her substantive rights and avoids the foregoing problems. Why don't judges enjoin more to prevent harm and to avoid damage computations?

I. The Inadequacy Prerequisite

A plaintiff seeking an injunction must show that there is an imminent threat of harm and that the threatened harm is "irreparable." In this section we will explore two interrelated questions: (1) Why must the harm have this special quality? (2) What factors are to be considered in deciding whether the harm is, in fact, irreparable?

One of the central limiting principles of equity is that equity will act only when there is no adequate remedy at law. The injunction is an equitable remedy; and it, like all other equitable remedies, is available only after the applicant shows that the legal remedies are inadequate. Legal remedies embrace any alternate remedy, including an action for damages, a criminal prosecution, or perhaps even a defense in a civil or criminal proceeding. In *Debs*, the question was whether a criminal prosecution was adequate. "Irreparable injury" is defined as harm that cannot be (fully? adequately?) repaired by the remedies available in the common law courts. If the threatened harm is one that can be rectified by a legal remedy, then the judge will refuse to enjoin. We are more concerned here with the choice between money and an injunction; we return to the choice between an injunction and a criminal prosecution in the chapter on prior restraints.

First a word about terminology. Courts use the term "irreparable injury" to describe two discrete but obviously related inquiries: whether to grant interlocutory relief and whether to issue an injunction at all. We attempt to limit "irreparable" to interlocutory relief, which we deal with later, and to employ the term "inadequacy" to describe the present issue: whether to grant plaintiff an injunction because damages are inadequate.

The inadequacy prerequisite raises two general problems. One concerns what factors render the alternative remedies inadequate. Is it the seriousness of the harm or the importance or uniqueness of the interests threatened? Is it the mere fact that injunctive relief is preventive and thus eliminates the need to wait for the harm to occur? Is it that if damages were sought, many actions would have to be brought? Is it that the defendant is financially unable to respond to damages? A second problem is more normative: Why should the injunction—or any other equitable remedy—be available only when the legal remedy is inadequate? Why should our legal system subordinate the equitable remedy to remedies traditionally provided by the law courts, or to any other alternative remedy?

Professor Fiss's answer is clear: "It shouldn't." He has argued that courts should abandon doctrines that subordinate injunctions to other remedies and adopt a nonhierarchical approach to choosing remedies. The choice of remedy should hinge on "the technical advantages of each remedy" and the way each remedy allocates power. "[T]he rules governing the choice of remedy . . . should not be fashioned apart from and independent of one's belief about the nature and justice of the underlying claim." O. Fiss, The Civil Rights Injunction 91 (1978). On the other hand, Professor Rendleman suggested that the inadequacy prerequisite serves important contemporary purposes. The Inadequate Remedy at Law Prerequisite for an Injunction, 33 U.Fla.L.Rev. 346 (1981).

Evolution of Chancery: History will not resolve normative questions. It explains but does not justify. It tells us why something was done but not why it should have been done. Yet it often puts the normative question in perspective. Regardless of whether there is an analytically sound justification for the no-adequate-remedy-at-law prerequisite it does have deep historical roots. The ancient rule reflects the way that the English Court of Chancery in fact arose. As T.F.T. Plucknett put it, "the rules [of equity] were a product of the institution, and so partook of the external accidents which often mould the history of institutions." A Concise History of the Common Law 677 (5th ed. 1956).

S.F.C. Milsom commented that on the history of the English Court of Chancery "[m]uch has been written but little is known." Historical Foundations of the Common Law, 74 (1969). Both parts of that statement seem to be true. In addition to Plucknett and Milsom, the following are most useful in gaining an understanding of this history: 1 W.S. Holdsworth, A History of English Law 395–476 (7th ed. 1956), which is a more detailed and thorough account of the same story that Plucknett tells; two essays by D.E.C. Yale that appeared as introductions to volumes he has edited on the work of a seventeenth-century chancellor, Lord Nottingham—Lord Nottingham's 'Manual of Chancery Practice' and 'Prolegomena of Chancery and Equity' (1965) and 1 Nottingham's Chancery Cases, 73 Selden Society (1957); J. H. Baker, An Introduction to English Legal History (1971); J. P. Dawson, A History of Lay Judges 145–172 (1960), primarily on the history of equity procedure; and on the American reception, see S. N. Katz, The Politics of Law in Colonial America: Controversies over Chancery Courts and Equity Law in the Eighteenth Century, in 5 Perspectives in American History 257 (Fleming & Baylin, eds. 1971). Of lesser value have been the following: F. W. Maitland, Equity: A Course of Lectures, first printed in 1909 and revised, reissued and reprinted numerous times; D. M. Kerly, An Historical Sketch of the Equitable Jurisdiction of the Court of Chancery (1890); G. Spence, The Equitable Jurisdiction of the Court of Chancery (1846), consists of two volumes and is the classic on which the later scholarship is built.

The Court of Chancery originated in the thirteenth century in petitions addressed to the King asking for special relief. The theory underlying these petitions was that adequate relief could not be obtained in the usual courts. Historians dispute the type of defects in the common law that triggered these petitions. Some have stressed substantive or doctrinal shortcomings of the common law—for example, the rigidity of the writ system. See, e.g., W. W. Cook, "Equity," in Encyclopedia of the Social Sciences 582–588 (1931). Others have stressed the procedural shortcomings of the common law system—slowness, formality, failure to admit the evidence of parties and witnesses, and reliance on the jury, which, among other things, might be corrupted or partial. See, e.g., Plucknett at 177–178. And still others have stressed the fact that special treatment is often sought because "the petitioner is too poor to sue, or his adversary so powerful that sheriffs will not do their duty or jurors tell the truth." Milsom, Historical Foundation of the Common Law

83 (1981). But this dispute among historians as to the precise grounds of the early petitions should not obscure a consensus on the more general point: the petitions were addressed to the King—as the fountain of justice—to provide justice in the face of some defect, shortcoming or inadequacy in the common law system.

The second part of the story is one of successive delegations of authority. Who was to deal with these petitions? By the fourteenth century the number of petitions increases and the King delegates the task to the Council—like today's cabinet, a small group of officials and advisers of the King. Then, starting in the latter part of the fourteenth century, the Council begins to delegate this to one of its members, the Chancellor. Why the Chancellor? This too is one of the questions on which historians disagree. On one view, the Chancellor was chosen because he was thought to be "the keeper of the King's conscience"—whatever that meant. But that view has lost favor. As Plucknett writes, "At a later date, it is true, Chancery became a court of conscience, with a jurisprudence deliberately based on that idea, but that was a later development and will not account for the earliest period of Chancery history" (at 180). Plucknett's view, and perhaps the more widely accepted one today, is that the choice of the Chancellor lacked any *a priori* or theoretical basis. It just turned out that, given his other jobs and his prominence in the Council, the Chancellor was the natural choice.

He was the one who was most constantly in attendance and was often the King's principal adviser in political matters. In addition, he had certain law-oriented duties. He was the keeper of the great seal of England, which was used to authenticate the common law writs. The writs issued from his department, the Chancery. (According to Baker at 39, the word "chancellor" stems from the latticed screen or chancel behind which the Chancellor's staff, the clerks, worked.) At one time his department drew up the writs and was able to exercise some creative influence over them. By the end of the thirteenth century, chancery played only a ministerial role—engrossing and sealing the common law writs—for it became clear that the common law judges were the ones to pass on the validity of the writs. Holdsworth at 398. But the common law writs still issued from Chancery. Moreover, in another and narrower range of writs, namely, those directly affecting the King, the Chancellor had significant adjudicative responsibilities. Plucknett insists that it is these factors which account for the choice of the Chancellor as the one to pass on the petitions. As he put it, "[N]othing could be simpler than for the Council to transmit the petitions addressed to it to the Chancellor, sometimes (but not always) endorsing them with a brief instruction what to do" (at 180–81).

The third part of the story is one of an increase in the number of petitions and more frequent delegation to the Chancellor. One effect was to increasingly differentiate the Chancellor from the other members of the Council. The petitions became his responsibility. They were addressed directly to the Chancellor, rather than to the Council. Another effect was the gradual transformation of Chancery. It ceased to be an "office" (with its administrative connotations) and began to act like a "court" (with its judicial connotations). The facts stated in the petition had to be sifted; the parties had to be summoned; opportunity had to be made for a defense; a decision had to be announced. The performance of these tasks judicialized the Chancery, although it also continued to perform secretarial functions. These changes start to occur in the fourteenth century. By the end of the fifteenth century an independent Court of Chancery emerges—a court with one judge, the Chancellor. He did have the assistance of a staff, including officials called Masters in Chancery; and he sometimes delegated various functions to his deputy, the Master of the Rolls. Holdsworth at 403–04; Dawson at 157–163. From that time on, actually starting with Sir Thomas More, the Chancellor is usually a lawyer rather than a bishop or archbishop, as had been the medieval practice.

The next chapter is one of coexistence of two independent court systems—the Court of Chancery and the common law courts. At some point, probably in the sixteenth century, Chancery identifies with a jurisprudence of equity—not just a system correcting the defects of the common law system but also a flexible one, able to account for individual hardships—to rationalize its continued separate existence. Yet even this distinctive jurisprudence overlaps with the law courts—neither sphere is sharply defined; but, by and large, the coexistence seems to be friendly for some time. By the beginning of the seventeenth century, however, the situation sharpens and deteriorates. The relationship between the two systems is marred by jurisdictional jealousies and increasing interferences. The greatest friction is caused when Chancery grants injunctions to stop proceedings in the common law courts. The common law courts were not powerless to retaliate; they had the writs of prohibition and habeas corpus. This leads up to the famous Coke-Ellsmore dispute. In 1616 the issue of the survival of the Court of Chancery is put to King James I. Chancery survives—but presumably only on the terms for which it was created and upon which it existed up to that time—to supplement the common law system and to correct its defects.

At the founding of the nation the distinction between law and equity was recognized, and indeed became the touchstone for the right to trial by jury guaranteed by the seventh amendment. Reflecting the general practice that prevailed in England in the late eighteenth century, the jury trial right was assured in suits at law but not in equitable proceedings. This quirk of history has given us reasons to emphasize the distinction between law and equity, understood as two separate court systems. But with only minor exceptions, the courts of equity and law have merged. The injunction is the remedy of a single, unified court system, and one may be left to wonder why the inadequacy prerequisite persists. Is it only to protect the jury trial right? Or are there other values that are served by it? For two contemporary and general treatments of this issue, see O. Fiss, The Civil Rights Injunction (1978), and Rendleman, The Inadequate Remedy at Law Prerequisite for an Injunction, 33 U.Fla.L.Rev. 346 (1981).

Much of the language in American sources about inadequacy can be traced to Chancellor Kent's opinion in Jerome v. Ross, one of the classic expressions of the traditional formula. Focus not on the verbal formula—the black-letter rule—but rather on the application of the formula and the prevailing doctrine to the specific situation facing the court. Ask: (1) Did Chancellor Kent successfully distinguish the precedents—particularly those of Lord Eldon—which suggested that the English Chancellor was beginning to take a more relaxed view of the requirement? (2) Did Chancellor Kent's view about this prerequisite to injunctive relief merely reflect his views as to the merits of the underlying dispute—that the Erie Canal was "good for the country" and private interests should not stand in the way of "progress?"

JEROME v. ROSS

7 John.Ch.R. 315 (1823).

. . . The bill, filed by Ross (appellee) in the Court below, against Jerome and others, stated, that the plaintiff was seised and possessed of two certain lots of land in Troy, and of an undivided fifth part, as tenant in common, of two other lots, &c., on which there is an extensive ledge of stone and mass of rock, &c. That on the 23d of May last, and divers times between that time and the filing of the bill, the defendants, without the consent and against the will of the plaintiff, entered upon the said lots, and with cattle, implements, powder, &c., dug up, &c., and removed large parcels of stone, and applied the same for building a dam in the Hudson river, near to the north line of the city of Troy. That the plaintiff has commenced several actions at law, in a Court of record, to recover damages for the injuries, &c. That he brought a suit before a justice of the peace against J. R. V. and N. C., two persons employed in digging and carrying away stone, for four or five days, &c.; and a verdict and judgment were given for the plaintiff, on the 28th of June last, for 25 dollars, being about half of the value of the stone, &c. That L., one of the defendants, appeared and pleaded for the defendants in that suit, who proved on the trial, that they acted under the direction of the defendants in this suit, or some of them; and that the defendants K. B. and L. had entered into a contract to build the dam; and that the defendant Jerome assumed to act as engineer, and had taken possession of the ledge of rocks, and directed the others to take the stone for building the dam, &c.; and more than twenty teams, and a great number of men, were employed in digging up and carrying away stone, &c. That after the verdict and judgment, to wit, on the 30th of June last, the plaintiff found the defendant L. on the ground, with a great many laborers, taking and removing stone, &c.; and though prohibited by the plaintiff and the other tenants in common, he refused to desist; and the defendants still continue, with their teams and servants, to dig, take and carry away the stone, declaring that they will not desist, nor pay for the stone, &c. That suits at law are an inadequate remedy for the irreparable injuries of which the plaintiff complains, in the wrongful taking and destruction of his property, which cannot be replaced or restored. That the lots of land, from which the stone is taken, are not contiguous to the Hudson river, but are more than sixty rods from the bank, between which and the lots there is a public highway, besides several building lots intervening. That the defendants intend to use the stone, without leave, in completing the dam, for which more than a thousand loads are requisite; and it would involve the plaintiff in great peril and trouble, if he should pursue his legal remedies. That the defendants pretend, that they are acting on behalf of the state of New York, and by authority of the statutes relative to canals, whereas their acts are wholly unauthorized. . . .

The defendants, in their answer, admitted the seisin of the plaintiff, and of the other tenants in common, as charged in the bill. They stated, that, on the third of May last, eight persons (named) entered into a contract with Samuel Young, one of the canal commissioners, to complete the lock and dam on the Hudson river, &c. That it was expressly understood between the contractors and the canal commissioners, that the materials for filling in the dam should be furnished to the contractors from the rocky hill near the dam; and from which materials for that purpose had been previously obtained, without objection on the part of the owners, under the direction of the engineer, and by virtue of several statutes; and it was covenanted by the contractors, that the lock and dam should be completed, in a permanent and substantial manner, by the 1st day of October next. That on the 20th of May last, the contractors entered into a sub-contract with the defendants L. B. and R. K., for the completion of the dam, &c., under the direction of the engineer, by the 1st day of September next. That the erection and construction of the dam are absolutely necessary for the completion of the Champlain canal, inasmuch as part of the canal, adopted by the canal commissioners, can be supplied with the necessary quantity of water in no other way; and the commissioners have taken the possession and control of the dam, and the lock connected with it, upon the terms and under the provisions of the act of the legislature, entitled, "An act respecting the navigation of the Hudson river between Troy and Waterford," passed March 9, 1821; and the works mentioned are an essential part of the canal. That the defendant Jerome, by the appointment of the canal commissioners, is, and from the 1st of May, 1823, has been, the principal engineer on the Champlain canal, and in the employment of the canal commissioners; and as such engineer, and by the authority of the statutes, &c., he entered upon, and located a sufficient quantity of a certain rocky hill near the dam, for the purpose of getting good and substantial materials, &c., to be used in the erection and completion of the dam, and directed the defendants, the subcontractors, to enter upon, break up, and take away the rock for these purposes; and which location was seen and approved of by S. Y., the acting canal commissioner on the Champlain canal. The defendants admitted the entry on the plaintiff's land, and the digging, &c., without any other license than that received from the public agents. That the stones have been taken along the foot of the east side of the hill, for about ten rods in length, and penetrating into the side of the hill about thirty feet; and that the foot of the hill crosses the lots of the plaintiff, &c. They admitted the suit and judgment stated in the bill; but, being advised that the judgment was erroneous, they had brought a certiorari to reverse it. They alleged, that the stone and rock broken up and taken away are of no use, except for some such purpose as that to which they have been applied; and are of no use for buildings or inclosures; and that the injury to the plaintiff is merely nominal. They admitted that they told the plaintiff that they would not pay for the stone. That it will take above 5000 loads of stone to complete the work, and there was nearly a sufficient quantity broken up and lying on the premises, for the completion of the dam, &c., and that the expense of breaking them up had been above 800 dollars. That if the work should be delayed until a freshet in the river, before the timber curbs, which had been sunk, were filled in, the work would be endangered, and the canal could not be completed this season, to the great damage of the contractors, and serious detriment of the public, as the free use of the canal depends on the completion of the work. They admitted that the injury, if any, was irreparable, because the stones could not be restored to their former place; but they denied that the rocks, in the situation in which they were, being broken up, were of any great value; and alleged that the laws have provided sufficient means of compensation, without troublesome litigation. . . .

[On July 15 an injunction was issued. On July 21 a motion to dissolve was filed, and that was denied by the trial judge, who issued this opinion:]

1. The grounds laid for the injunction in the bill are, that the defendants are committing irreparable waste, without any pretence of title or right to the occupation of the soil; and that the plaintiff has no adequate remedy at law, without bringing a multiplicity of suits; or, at all events, that the mischief may be completely effected before their termination. Since the disuse of the common law actions of waste and estrepement, the more easy and complete mode of proceeding by bill in equity, to stay waste, either threatened, or which the party is in the act of committing, and for an account of such as may have already been done, has been particularly favored by the Courts, both in England and in this country. And it is laid down, by the present chancellor, in one of the earliest cases before him, (Kane v. Vandenburgh, 1 Johns.Ch. Rep. 12.) "that it is a wholesome jurisdiction, to be liberally exercised in the prevention of irreparable injury, and depends on much latitude of discretion in the Court."

The Courts in England were, however, for a long time, extremely strict in confining the relief in equity to cases of tenancy, founding their interference in restraint of waste on the privity of title between the parties. The first instance of relaxation was in a case where an injunction was granted, upon a forcible entry, against the commissioners of a turnpike for digging gravel on land of the plaintiff; but this seems to have been grounded on the equity of *quieting possession* merely. (Hughes v. Merton College, 1 Ves. 188.) The rigor of the ancient rule was at length further relaxed, upon the avowed principle of enjoining in matters of *trespass, where irreparable injury is the consequence*; and upon the authority of this case, Lord Eldon granted an injunction to restrain a trespasser from digging coal upon the premises of another. (Mitchell v. Dors, 6 Ves. 147.) . . .

Had the right of the plaintiff in this case to the premises appeared doubtful from the bill, or had the bill disclosed an adverse *claim* to the land, I should have refused the injunction, unless it had been alleged, that the injury would have been complete before the right could have been settled at law; in which case I should have directed notice of the application to have been given, before ordering the writ. But I consider the bill as presenting a clear case of irreparable injury, without pretence or claim of title to the premises; a case in which it is evident, from the nature of the injury, that the remedy at law must be inadequate, not merely from the necessity of resorting to a multiplicity of suits, but from the ineffectual nature of those suits in preventing a continuance or repetition of the injury. . . .

[The judge went on to consider the merits of the claim, that is, the lawfulness of the entry. On that score the judge ruled:]

If the words of the statute warrant the taking of the stone under these circumstances, I can imagine no possible limit to the authority or discretion of the commissioners. If they have power to take from land, not appropriated as necessary to the prosecution of their works, materials which they conceive *suitable* in their nature, and *convenient*, in point of situation, at the distance of 60 rods, I see nothing to prevent their taking from the lands and inclosures of individuals, any other materials they may fancy, in any situation, or at any distance. Such a construction, therefore, is unreasonable and dangerous; and, if adopted, would give sanction to a stretch of power never contemplated by the act. . . .

The CHANCELLOR. [July 28] This is the case of an appeal from an interlocutory decree of the circuit judge, for the third circuit, sitting in equity, pronounced on the 21st of July instant, and by which decree, the injunction, allowed on the 15th instant, is continued until the hearing. The reasons assigned in the order for the continuance of the injunction, are, that the injury complained of in the bill is irreparable in its nature, and the matter set up in the answer insufficient for the justification of the defendants. . . .

1. I have not been able to satisfy myself that the bill contains sufficient equity to warrant the injunction.

The bill contains a charge of trespass, by entering upon the land of the plaintiff, and digging, throwing up, and carrying away, large parcels of stone, from a ledge of stone and mass of rock on the premises. Several actions have been commenced in a Court of record to recover damages for this trespass; but it is not stated that any of these actions have been brought to trial. One action has likewise been instituted before a justice of the peace, and that action has been tried, and the plaintiff recovered damages to the amount of 25 dollars. The plaintiff has his complete and perfect remedy at law for the trespass, as often as it may be repeated; and the only question is, whether the injury be so ruinous and irreparable as to call for the extraordinary interposition of a Court of equity. The bill does not pretend that the ledge of rock, upon which the trespass was committed, was of any particular use or value to the plaintiff, or that he ever did or ever intended to apply it to any valuable purpose. The plaintiff speaks of the injury as irreparable, because the loads of stone, taken from the mass of rock, cannot be replaced or restored; but as he does not state that the rock was of any use to him, as proper or fit for building, fencing, &c., or that it was even desirable as an object of ornament or taste, there was no need of having the same identical fragments of stone replaced, and the injury was not, in the sense of the law, irreparable. It was susceptible of a perfect pecuniary compensation. The case, therefore, seems to resolve itself into this single point, whether a Court of equity ought to interpose, by injunction, to restrain a trespass, when the injury does not appear to be irremediable and destructive to the estate, and when the ordinary legal remedy in the Courts of law can afford adequate satisfaction.

The English Court of Chancery is now in the habit of granting injunctions in trespass, when the case is peculiar and special; and even this practice came into use long subsequent to the date of our revolution. As late as 1786, (Mogg v. Mogg, Dickens, 670.) Lord Thurlow directed a search to be made, to see if ever there was an instance of an injunction, where a mere trespasser entered upon land and cut timber; and as no such precedent could be found, he denied it even in a case of trespass in cutting down timber. But since that time, the practice has been introduced, and justly and reasonably applied to special cases, where irreparable ruin would have followed the refusal to enjoin the trespass. It was allowed by Lord Thurlow, in *Fleming's* case, (cited 6 Vesey, 147.) where the defendant had worked from his own land into the coal mine of the plaintiff; and that case was followed by Lord Eldon, (6 Vesey, 147. 7 Ves. 307.) on the principle that irreparable mischief and ruin of the property, as a mine, would be the consequence, if the party was not stopped. On the same ground, the injunction is granted against diverting a water-course from a mill; (1 Bro. 588.) against the destruction of timber; (10 Vesey, 290.) against the taking of stones of a peculiar value; (17 Vesey, 128.) or stones from a quarry. (18 Vesey, 184.) But all these are cases of great and irremediable mischief, which damages could not compensate, because the mischief reaches to the very substance and value of the estate, and goes to the destruction of it in the character in which it is enjoyed. The present case is, in no reasonable sense, analogous to those cases. The plaintiff does not aver, or show, that the "ledge of stone and mass of rock," on which the trespass is committed, is of any essential use, or that he does or can apply it to any valuable purpose. It is very possible that this "ledge of rock" may be some precipitous, naked, barren hill, absolutely worthless for any other purpose than that to which the defendants apply it. Is the case, then, to be compared to that of a lead or coal mine, or a quarry of marble, or a fine building, or precious stone, or a grove of timber, or a mill establishment, which the Court of Chancery has thought proper to protect from trespass and ruin, by the strong and menacing hand of an injunction? Certainly not; and if the plaintiff is entitled to an injunction in this case, I do not see why every man, in possession of land, may not call for an injunction to protect him from his neighbor's trespasses in every possible case.

The objection to the injunction, in cases of private trespass, except under very special circumstances, is, that it would be productive of public inconvenience, by drawing cases of ordinary trespass within the cognizance of equity, and by calling forth, upon all occasions, its power to punish by attachment, fine and imprisonment, for a further commission of trespass, instead of the more gentle common law remedy by action, and the assessment of damages by a jury. In ordinary cases, this latter remedy has been found amply sufficient for the protection of property; and I do not think it advisable, upon any principle of justice or policy, to introduce the chancery remedy as its substitute, except in strong and aggravated instances of trespass, which go to the destruction of the inheritance or where the mischief is remediless. . . . I do not know a case in which an injunction has been granted to restrain a trespasser, *merely because he was a trespasser*, without showing that the property itself was of peculiar value, and could not well admit of due recompense, and would be destroyed by repeated acts of trespass. In ordinary cases, the damages to be assessed by a jury will be adequate for a check and for a recompense. Every man is undoubtedly entitled to be protected in the possession and enjoyment of his property, though it may be of no intrinsic value. He may have on his land a large mound of useless stone or sand, which he may not deem worth the expense of inclosing, and yet it would be a trespass for any person to remove any portion of the stone or sand without his consent; and he would be entitled to his action, even though the damages were nominal. But would it be proper for this Court to assume cognizance of such a trespass, and lay the interdict of an injunction upon it? I apprehend not.

The bill, to which I am still confining myself, does not, except in a very imperfect manner, disclose the pretences or claim of right under which the trespass has been committed. It only states, that the defendants are engaged in building a dam in Hudson's river, near the north line of the city of Troy, and that the materials taken from the ledge of rock are applied to the dam; that one of the defendants acts as engineer in that operation, and that the defendants pretend that they are acting on behalf of this state, and by authority of the statutes relative to canals. But admitting that the defendants do pretend to act by public authority in their commission of the trespass, it does not alter the principle; and the trespass itself must be of the character I have described, before a Court of equity can be called upon to interfere by injunction. All the cases referred to, were those in which the trespass went to the destruction of the property, as it had been held and enjoyed. In the case of Agar v. The Regent's Canal Company, (Cooper's Eq.Rep. 77.) the defendants were empowered by a private act of parliament to cut a canal; the line of the canal had been prescribed, and they departed from that line, and were carrying the canal through a garden and brickyard; and Lord Eldon allowed an injunction. So, in the case of Shand v. Henderson, (2 Dow, 519.) the Aberdeen Canal Navigation Company were charged with having taken and appropriated lands to their use, by unwarrantably deviating from the line particularly prescribed by statute, and an injunction to restrain the Canal Company within their limits, was admitted to be proper. But in both these cases, the companies were making a permanent appropriation of the land, and destroying the inheritance; and upon the acknowledged principle, in all the cases, it was necessary to restrain them. In the case, also, of Hughes v. The Trustees of Merton College, (1 Vesey, 188. and Belt's Supp.) the commissioners of a turnpike company entered, took possession of, and were destroying, by digging for gravel, large garden grounds of the plaintiff, who was a gardener by trade. The turnpike act had specially accepted gardens, as well as orchards, planted walks, &c.; and Lord Hardwicke thought it a clear case of trespass, and of such a nature, that the plaintiff was entitled to seek his remedy by injunction, though he had his remedy at law. But he admitted, that if there had been any ground for doubt, whether or not the commissioners had authority, he would not have interposed until the doubt had been removed, and the matter finally determined at law. And it is to be observed, that here was the destruction of what a man was using *as his trade or livelihood.*

Several cases have occurred in this Court, in which public trustees have been restrained by injunction from acts of trespass; but the acts were such as went to destroy the enjoyment of valuable property and privileges.

Thus, in the case of Gardner v. The Trustees of Newburgh, (2 Johns.Ch. Rep. 162.) the trustees were going to divert a stream of water that had flowed immemorially, and had supplied the brickyard, the distillery, and mill erections of the plaintiff; and the case not being deemed within the provisions of the act in favor of those trustees, an injunction was granted. Afterwards, in Belknap v. Belknap, (2 Johns.Ch.Rep. 463.) an injunction was allowed upon the same principle, of preventing a great and irreparable mischief. In that case, inspectors under an act of the legislature for draining certain swamps and bog meadows, for the benefit of some individuals, undertook to lower a large pond of 400 acres, by cutting down the outlet, which would destroy the value of the pond and outlet as a source of water for the use of mills established on the outlet. It was considered to be an interference not warranted by the statute, and to be a great and special trespass, leading to lasting mischief, and the destruction of the estate. It was further observed, that it was not a case which concerned the public, but one of mere private convenience and profit, and the act ought to be strictly construed.

These cases all show, that, in respect to acts of trespass committed upon land, even by persons in a public trust, under color of law, the Court has not interfered by injunction, unless where the trespass was permanent, as well as grievous, or went to destroy the value of the property to the owner. It is not sufficient that the act be simply, per se, a trespass; but it must be a case of mischief and of irreparable ruin to the property, in the character in which it has been enjoyed. In all other cases, the common law remedy is deemed to be adequate, and perfectly competent to give compensation, as well as to deter and prevent the repetition of the trespass, by the exemplary damages which it will inflict.

A Court of equity will sometimes interfere to prevent a multiplicity of suits, by a bill of peace. . . . But that is only in cases where the right is controverted by numerous persons, each standing on his own pretensions; and it has no application to the case of one or more persons choosing to persevere in acts of trespass, in despite of suits and recoveries against them. A troublesome man may vex and harass his neighbor, by throwing down his fences, and turning cattle upon his grounds, or by passing over them, or otherwise annoying him; but it is to be presumed, that repeated recoveries for damages, with the punishment of costs, and such smart money as a jury would naturally give, would soon effectually correct any such disposition. At any rate, I do not know that a Court of equity has ever interfered merely to correct such a practice; and it would certainly require very strong evidence of the inefficacy of the ordinary legal remedies for compensation, as well as for correction, before this Court would venture to assume a jurisdiction hitherto unknown.

For these reasons, I am of opinion, that the bill itself does not contain matter sufficient to warrant or sustain the injunction; and that the plaintiff ought to have been left to his remedy at law.

2. But, admitting that the injunction was warranted by the bill, the next question is, whether the answer does not contain a sufficient justification. . . .

After the opinion which has been expressed upon the first point, it is not necessary, for the present disposition of the case, to give any decided opinion on the validity of the matter alluded to in the bill, and expressly set up in the answer by way of justification. It might, perhaps, be as well to avoid it altogether, inasmuch as the justification under the canal acts is a legal question, and which appears from the pleadings to be pending at law. But as this second point was discussed and passed upon by the Court below, and as it has been raised and discussed before me, without objection, and is involved in the decree appealed from, and as the essential facts leading to that justification are founded on statute powers, and are not controverted, it cannot be improper to take it into consideration; and it would be required, if I am to pass in review the whole merits of the decree.

The canal commissioners, in the erection of the lock and dam in question have the same powers that are conferred upon them in respect to the Champlain canal. By the act referred to in the answer, (sess. 44. c. 78.) the canal commissioners were authorized to complete the lock and dam, "in order to connect the Champlain canal with sloop navigation," if they should deem it advisable, and should signify in writing their intention to do the same. The answer avers that they have done so. It becomes, therefore, essentially part and parcel of the Champlain canal, and the real property appropriated for the site of the lock and its appendages, vests in the people of this state, on the completion of the lock and dam, and the canal commissioners are authorized to establish and collect tolls at the lock.

Assuming, then, as a clear and plain proposition, that the canal commissioners are vested with the same powers in the erection of this dam, as in the construction of works on any part of the line of the canals, they had a right to take possession of, and use the ledge of rock in question, for the construction of the dam. The 3d section of the act of the 15th of April, 1817, "respecting navigable communications between the great western and northern lakes and the Atlantic ocean," (sess. 40. c. 262.) declared, that it should be "lawful for the canal commissioners, and each of them, by themselves, and by any and every superintendent, agent, and engineer, employed by them, to enter upon, take possession of, and use, all and singular any lands, waters and streams, necessary for the prosecution of the improvements intended by this act; and to make all such canals, feeders, dikes, locks, dams, and other works and devices, as they may think proper for making said improvements, doing, nevertheless, no unnecessary damage."

The case before us falls precisely within the words of this provision. The commissioners, and those under them, may *enter upon and use any lands necessary for the prosecution of the improvements intended by the act.* The dam in question, being connected with the Champlain canal, is an improvement within the meaning of the act. What lands are necessary to be entered upon, and used, must rest in the judgment of the commissioners, and all that can be required is, that they act with good faith, and with sound discretion. The word "*necessary*" does not mean absolute and indispensable, or that without the use of the land, in the given case, the work could not possibly go on. That would be the same as extreme necessity. The legislature used the word in a more reasonable and popular sense. It is sufficient that the land used, and the materials taken from it, are needful and conducive to the object, and more convenient in the application, and less valuable, and the use of them less injurious to the owner, than any that might readily be selected. There must, from the reason of the thing, and the nature of the case, be great latitude of discretion in the selection of the land and the materials; and, in the present case, it is perfectly apparent, that the canal commissioner located the ground from which the materials for filling in the dam were to be taken, with judgment, and according to the spirit and letter of the act. He did take care, as the act required, to do *no unnecessary damage.* The materials must have been taken from some adjoining land; and from whence could they have been taken with more discretion?

I cannot perceive any room for doubt, as to the power of the commissioners to *enter upon and use* the ledge of rock in question, for the purpose of making the dam. There is no avoiding this conclusion, unless we can maintain the construction, that the act only intended that the commissioners might enter, use, and take possession of land, for *permanent appropriation* of the whole fee of the land, and not for temporary use. According to this construction, if they wanted room adjoining the canal, for a temporary deposit of materials for locks and dams, or a right of way or passage to the canal, or the materials of stone, gravel, clay, &c. from the adjoining lands, they could not use them, without at the same time appropriating the fee of the land. But why should the commissioners be obliged to appropriate a greater interest in the adjoining land than is requisite for the public object? and what possible objection can there be to the construction, allowing them to make as much use of the adjoining grounds as should be necessary for the prosecution of the improvements, *and no more*? The precaution enjoined upon them, to do *no unnecessary damage*, seems to imply, that they were authorized to make a temporary use of the lands. The act of 1816 authorized the commissioners to explore and examine the lands contiguous to the probable course of the canal, and to cause surveys and levels to be taken. This necessarily implied a right of entry upon lands for these purposes. The act of 1820 (sess. 43. c. 202. s. 3.) also authorized them to enter upon any lands contiguous to the canals, or the works connected therewith, "and to dig for, work, get, and carry away, and use, all such stone, gravel, clay, timber, and other materials, as might be necessary or proper, in their opinion, for *the reparation of the canals*, or the works connected therewith, doing as little damage thereby as the nature of the case would permit." The commissioners would then be authorized to take the stone from the ledge of rock in question to repair this dam in the Hudson; and can it be reasonably supposed, that the legislature did not intend they should have this power for the necessary construction of the dam in the first instance? The public utility is as much concerned in the exercise of the one power as of the other, and these several canal acts constitute a distinct code of statute law, and are to be taken and construed together, as being made in furtherance of one great, useful, and splendid public object, and which, in the language of the legislature, in their act of 1817, will "promote agriculture, manufactures, and commerce, mitigate the calamities of war, and enhance the blessings of peace, consolidate the union, and advance the prosperity and elevate the character of the *United States*." Statutes made for the public good, and for general and beneficent national purposes, are to receive a very liberal construction, and to be expounded in such a manner, as that they may, as far as possible, attain the end. The rule is, that they are to be so construed, as not to advance a private and destroy the public interest, but always to advance the public interest, doing as little damage as possible to the private interest. So, it is a general rule of interpretation, that a greater will include a less interest; and a provision as to more objects than one, includes a provision for one of those objects.

I have no doubt, therefore, that under the general authority to *enter upon and use any lands necessary for the prosecution of the improvements, doing no unnecessary damage*, the commissioners, and the defendants, by their authority, might lawfully enter upon and use the ledge of rock in question for the building of the dam; and that a contrary construction is not only against the words, but is too narrow and too rigid for the liberal spirit and enlarged policy of the act, and the immense pressure of the public interest. If there was ever a case in the ordinary pacific operations of government, in which all petty private interests should be made subservient to the interest of an entire people, this is one. The canals were undertaken "in full confidence that the congress of the *United States*, and the states equally interested with this state in the commencement, prosecution, and completion of these important works, would contribute their full proportion of the expense." We have not, as yet, realized the fruits of that confidence, and we are left to bear singly the whole expense, as well as to enjoy all the honor and glory of this stupendous undertaking. We have advanced too far to recede. The whole entire plan must and will be completed. All little impediments must be surmounted; and the powers of the commissioners must be taken to be, as they were certainly intended to be, commensurate with the duties to be performed. . . .

There is an additional provision in the 3d section of the act of 1817, which declares that "in case any lands, waters, or streams, taken and appropriated for any of the purposes aforesaid, shall not be given or granted to the people of this state, it shall be the duty of the canal commissioners to cause the loss and damage, if any, over and above the benefit and advantage to the owner, to be certified in the way pointed out, and the damages to be paid, and the fee simple of the premises so appropriated shall vest in the people of this state."

This provision applies only to lands taken *and appropriated*, and which, I should rather think, means lands permanently applied, so as to be entirely lost to the owner, and not lands affording a temporary use for passage and deposit, or for procuring materials for the locks, dams, &c. But there is no sufficient reason to consider this latter part of the section as qualifying and controlling the general powers given in the former part of it. The general power is, to *enter upon and use all lands necessary for the prosecution of the improvements, and to make canals, feeders, locks, dams, &c., doing, nevertheless, no unnecessary damage*; and then comes the provision, that any lands taken *and appropriated* for any of the purposes aforesaid, shall be paid for and vest in the state. There was no need that the fee of lands used only for a temporary purpose, should be vested in the public. If the owner is paid for the damage occasioned by the temporary use of his lands, it is all that he can justly require, and this compensation the state is bound to give him. If the act we are examining has omitted to make any provision for the assessment and payment of damages for such temporary use, it may have escaped the attention of the legislature, or the case may have been deemed, at the time, immaterial and unimportant. The omission, however, if it be one, does not prevent the right of the commissioners to enter and use the land; nor prevent the just claim of the owner upon the commissioners or the legislature for his reasonable compensation. The commissioners are not trespassers, when the act authorizes them to enter, if they enter before the damages are paid for. . . . The claim for compensation arises after the use has been had; and the damages cannot well be assessed before they have arisen. Whatever, therefore, may be the better construction as to the mode of ascertaining and enforcing the compensation, it does not affect the right of the commissioners to enter, nor justify the interference of a Court of equity to interdict their entry.

It is probable the legislature considered that the canal commissioners had sufficient discretionary power to pay for all damages arising from the temporary use of lands, upon which they might enter for the prosecution of the improvements, and the appropriation of materials, which they might derive from such use. Their discretion, in the expenditure of the canal moneys, is very large. They are "to cause the same to be expended in the most prudent and economical manner, in all such works as may be proper to make the canals." And as they are to do no unnecessary damage, it was doubtless intended that all *necessary damage* should be paid for by them. The only difficulty in the case is, how to assess the damages when the parties cannot agree. If the lands are *appropriated* permanently by the transfer of the fee, or if materials are taken from adjoining lands for *reparations* of injuries to the canals, or the works connected therewith, the statute points out a specific mode of assessment. As all these canal statutes are to be taken and construed together, as being made *in pari materia*, the damages resulting from a temporary use of the land fall within the equity of these provisions; and the commissioners would be justified in adopting one of them, or the owner might, perhaps, by application to the Supreme Court, or to a Court of equity, enforce an assessment and payment, in the mode provided for in other cases.

But the question of compensation is distinct from the right of entry to take and use the land necessary for the purpose of the improvements; and that right I hold to be unquestionable, provided it be not abused in the exercise, through the want of good faith or due discretion. If the commissioners enter to procure necessary materials, and they keep within the limits of a reasonable discretion, and do no unnecessary damage, they come within the range of the strong powers conferred upon them, and their entry is justified by the statute.

I am of opinion, therefore, on this second point, as well as on the other, that the injunction ought to be dissolved.

STORY ON INADEQUACY

Trespass is one area in which the inadequacy prerequisite proves particularly troublesome for the plaintiff. In other types of injunctive litigation, nuisance, copyright and patents, where injunctions are more commonly granted, the inadequacy prerequisite seems to be easily satisfied. And we thought it may be useful, in order to get a fuller perspective to see how another great of the formative period of our jurisprudence—this time Justice Story—deals with the issue in these contexts as well as trespass. The excerpts are from volume 2 of the 1843 edition of his famous treatise, Commentaries on Equity Jurisprudence as Administered in England and America; and he acknowledges that his section on injunctions draws heavily on what may be considered the first treatise on injunctions—that of Robert Henley Eden, first published in England around 1822.

"§ 924. The ground of this jurisdiction of Courts of Equity in cases of . . . public nuisances [that is, ones injurious to the public at large] undoubtedly is, their ability to give a more complete and perfect remedy, than is attainable at law, in order to prevent irreparable mischief, and also to suppress oppressive and vexatious litigations. In the first place, they can interpose, where the Courts of Law cannot, to restrain and prevent such nuisances, which are threatened, or are in progress, as well as to abate those already existing. In the next place, by a perpetual injunction, the remedy is made complete through all future time; whereas, an information or indictment at the Common Law can only dispose of the present nuisance; and for future acts new prosecutions must be brought. In the next place, the remedial justice in Equity may be prompt and immediate, before irreparable mischief is done; whereas, at law, nothing can be done, except after a trial, and upon the award of judgment. In the next place, a Court of Equity will not only interfere upon the information of the Attorney-General, but also upon the application of private parties, directly affected by the nuisance; whereas, at law, in many cases the remedy is, or may be, solely through the instrumentality of the Attorney-General. . . .

"§ 925. In regard to private nuisances, the interference of Courts of Equity by way of injunction is undoubtedly founded upon the ground of restraining irreparable mischief, or of suppressing oppressive and interminable litigation, or of preventing multiplicity of suits. It is not every case, which will furnish a right of action against a party for a nuisance, which will justify the interposition of Courts of Equity to redress the injury, or to remove the annoyance. But there must be such an injury, as from its nature is not susceptible of being adequately compensated by damages at law, or such as, from its continuance or permanent mischief, must occasion a constantly recurring grievance, which cannot be otherwise prevented, but by an injunction. . . . [A] mere diminution of the value of property by the nuisance, without irreparable mischief, will not furnish any foundation for equitable relief.

"§ 926. On the other hand, where the injury is irreparable, as, where loss of health, loss of trade, destruction of the means of subsistence, or permanent ruin to property, may or will ensue from the wrongful act or erection; in every such case Courts of Equity will interfere by injunction, in furtherance of justice and the violated rights of the party. Thus, for example, where a party builds so near the house of another party, as to darken his windows, against the clear rights of the latter, either by contract, or by ancient possession, Courts of Equity will interfere by injunction to prevent the nuisance, as well as to remedy it, if already done, although an action for damages would lie at law; for the latter can in no just sense be deemed an adequate relief in such a case. The injury is material, and operates daily to destroy or diminish the comfort and use of the neighbouring house; and the remedy by a multiplicity of actions, for the continuance of it, would furnish no substantial compensation.

"§ 926. a. The same rule will apply to cases, where blocks of buildings have been erected, with particular covenants respecting the enjoyment thereof, and the erection of livery stables, slaughter houses, glue factories, and other special privileges or inconveniences; for in such cases, each purchaser or owner of one of the block will be entitled to an injunction to prevent the breach, and to enforce the observance of such covenants, since they are for the mutual benefit and protection of all the owners and purchasers in the block.

"§ 927. Cases of a nature, calling for the like remedial interposition of Courts of Equity are, the obstruction of water-courses, the diversion of streams from mills, the back flowage on mills, and the pulling down of the banks of rivers, and thereby exposing adjacent lands to inundation, or adjacent mills to destruction. . . .

"§ 928. It is upon similar grounds, that Courts of Equity interfere in cases of trespasses, that is to say, to prevent irreparable mischiefs, or to suppress multiplicity of suits and oppressive litigation. For if the trespass be fugitive and temporary, and adequate compensation can be obtained in an action at law, there is no ground to justify the interposition of Courts of Equity. Formerly, indeed, Courts of Equity were extremely reluctant to interfere, at all, even in regard to cases of repeated trespasses. But, now, there is not the slightest hesitation, if the acts done, or threatened to be done, to the property would be ruinous or irreparable, or would impair the just enjoyment of the property in future. If, indeed, Courts of Equity did not interfere in cases of this sort, there would (as has been truly said) be a great failure of justice in the country.

"§ 929. Thus, for instance, where a mere trespasser digs into, and works a mine, to the injury of the owner, an injunction will be granted, because it operates a permanent injury to the property, as a mine. So, where timber is attempted to be cut down by a trespasser in collusion with the tenant of the land. So, where there is a dispute respecting the boundaries of estates, and one of the claimants is about to cut down ornamental or timber trees in the disputed territory. So, where a party, who is in possession under articles, is proceeding to cut down timber trees. So, where lessees are taking away from a manor, bordering on the sea, stones of a peculiar value. In short, it is now granted in all cases of timber, coals, ores, and quarries, where the party is a mere trespasser; or, where he exceeds the limited rights, with which he is clothed; upon the ground, that the acts are, or may be an irreparable damage to the particular species of property.

"§ 930. It is upon similar principles, to prevent irreparable mischiefs, or to suppress multiplicity of suits and vexatious litigation, that Courts of Equity interfere in cases of Patents for inventions, and in cases of Copyrights, to secure the rights of the inventor, or author, and his assignees and representatives. It is wholly beside the purpose of the present Commentaries to enter upon the subject of the general rights of inventors and authors, or to state the circumstances, under which an exclusive property, in virtue of those rights, may be acquired or lost. Our observations will rather be limited to the consideration of the cases, in which Courts of Equity will interfere to protect those rights, when acquired, by granting injunctions.

"§ 931. It is quite plain, that, if no other remedy could be given in cases of patents and copyrights, than an action at law for damages, the inventor or author might be ruined by the necessity of perpetual litigation, without ever being able to have a final establishment of his rights.

"§ 932. Indeed, in cases of this nature, it is almost impossible to know the extent of the injury done to the party, without a discovery from the party, guilty of the infringement of the patent or copyright; and if it were otherwise, mere damages would give no adequate relief. For example, in the case of a copyright, the sale of copies by the defendant is not only, in each instance, taking from the author the profit upon the individual book, which he might otherwise have sold; but it may also be injuring him, to an incalculable extent, in regard to the value and disposition of his copyright, which no inquiry for the purpose of damages could fully ascertain.

"§ 933. In addition to this consideration, the plaintiff could at law have no preventive remedy, which should restrain the future use of his invention, or the future publication of his work, injuriously to his title and interests. And it is this preventive remedy, which constitutes the peculiar feature of Equity Jurisprudence, and enables it to accomplish the great purposes of justice. Besides, in most cases of this sort, the bill usually seeks an account, in one case of the books printed, and in the other of the profits, which have arisen from the use of the invention, from the persons, who have pirated the same. And this account will, in all cases, where the right has been already established, or is established under direction of the Court, be decreed as incidental, in addition to the other relief by a perpetual injunction."

---

1) "It is clear that [Jerome v. Ross was] decided before the jurisdiction of equity in trespass had developed, and that [it] would be decided otherwise today." W. Walsh, A Treatise on Equity, 51 n. 18 (1930). "Though the acts of trespass are not in the nature of waste in that they are not destructive of the property, nevertheless an injunction will be made against continuous trespasses, or a succession of trespasses which threaten to be continued indefinitely in order to prevent multiplicity of suits. The remedy at law is clearly inadequate; the plaintiff may recover damages at law only up to the time of the trial, and he will therefore be forced to sue at reasonable intervals indefinitely to get such remedy as the law gives him, or in the alternative to forego his relief until shortly before his action would be barred by the statute of limitations." Id. at 151–52. See also Boerner v. McCallister, 197 Va. 169, 89 S.E.2d 23 (1955); D. Dobbs, Handbook on the Law of Remedies § 5.6 (1973).

Looking at *Jerome* another way, a modern court might refuse to enjoin on the ground that condemnation procedure is an adequate remedy at law. Compare Goadby v. Philadelphia Electric Co., 639 F.2d 117 (3d Cir.1981). If the conflict between the landowner and the engineer is purely economic, why should the judge enjoin?

2) Is the conflict in *Jerome* between two views of property? The engineer, Jerome, takes a development perspective and views lands as merely another economic resource. Ross, the landowner, stands for a feudal, exclusionary view of property. Hasn't history vindicated Jerome? See M. Horwitz, The Transformation of American Law 31, 63–66, 69 (1977). If land is simply an economic resource, is there some point at which, if Jerome augments his offer, Ross will be indifferent to whether he has the money or the land? Does an injunction unbalance negotiation by allowing Ross to hold out until Jerome's offer is far larger than it would otherwise be? If you favor an injunction is it because you think Ross's interest is 1) too hard to value, 2) noneconomic, or 3) too important for damages?

3) The verbal formula has been unchanged for over 150 years, but contemporary courts administer the inadequacy prerequisite in a vastly different way. What accounts for the changes? See O. Fiss, The Civil Rights Injunction 50–51 (1978). Law and equity are merged into a unified civil action.

But, on one account, law-equity differences persist because a right to a jury trial is guaranteed in suits at law, generally for damages, and in criminal prosecutions but not in equitable proceedings for injunctions. Courts subordinate injunctions to damages because treating the injunction as equal or preferred might curtail the right to a jury trial. This theory requires courts to define the scope of the jury trial right with great precision and also tests their commitment to the right.

Society is more complex than it was in the early 19th century when *Jerome* was decided, and interests too fine-tuned for money are recognized. Judges possess more self-confidence. In particular, the lessons learned in school desegregation have been applied to protect other interests. Judges realize that they possess no other appropriate tools to protect social, political, and constitutional rights. Imagine a money judgment for a malapportioned legislature. Who would be defendants? Plaintiffs? Who would pay? And how much? A primary office of the injunction today is to protect citizens against government interference with the free exercise of their constitutional rights.

Certainly the decision whether to enjoin or grant damages is a policy choice of the first magnitude. The Inadequate Remedy at Law Prerequisite for an Injunction, 33 U.Fla.L.Rev. 346 (1981). Judges prefer to recognize most substantive rights with money, but they want people to enjoy other rights in fact. They seem to draw the line for economic, moral, and administrative reasons. Valuation is an imperfect art. Money damages omit important subjective impairments that are important enough to protect. When objective damages fail to compensate for the legally recognized impairment, judges enjoin to recognize that uncompensated, but legally recognized, impairment. Two recent articles on the related equitable subject of specific performance advance our understanding. Kronman, Specific Performance, 45 U.Chi.L.Rev. 351 (1978); Schwartz, The Case for Specific Performance, 89 Yale L.J. 271 (1979). See also Leubsdorf, Remedies for Uncertainty, 61 B.U.L.Rev. 132 (1981); Linzer, On the Amorality of Contract Remedies—Efficiency, Equity, and the Second Restatement, 81 Colum.L.Rev. 111 (1981). Chapter 48 of the Restatement of Torts (Second) is a useful and comprehensive survey.

Some substantive interests are so basic that courts think people deserve to enjoy them in fact. In Kenyon v. City of Chicopee, 320 Mass. 528, 533–34, 70 N.E.2d 241, 244 (1946), some Jehovah's Witnesses sought and obtained injunctive relief against repeated arrests and prosecution for distributing handbills. The court said "[I]f equity would safeguard their right to sell bananas, it ought to be at least equally solicitous of their personal liberties guaranteed by the Constitution." Compensation tolerates the wrong and allows the perpetrator to buy injustice. In Civil Liberties and Injunctive Protection, Moscovitz said,

"Committed, as we are, to the *effective* protection of civil liberties, we must label insufficient the action for damages. If the damages are to be compensatory, we are defeated before we start, due to the impossibility of computing in terms of money the loss occasioned by a violation of such rights as the right to worship, or to speak freely. Were punitive damages allowed, the verdicts would vary with the varying political and social convictions of the respective juries. This objection to punitive damages cannot be made with equal force in the cases in which they are at present allowed. Community disapproval of assault or battery, for example, is fairly uniform compared to the sharply divergent reactions to the issues raised by civil liberties cases. Furthermore, the insolvency of the defendant destroys whatever remedial value the action for damages may have. All of these difficulties are avoided by the use of the equitable remedy of injunction which has, in addition, two great advantages. First, its unique flexibility, the power to 'custom tailor' the decree to fit the situation, is of exceptional utility where, as in the civil liberties field, the problem is apt to be both complex and non-standardized; secondly, adjudication prior to action eliminates the risks involved in acting first and defending a prosecution later. Our most treasured rights deserve our most effective remedies." 39 Ill.L.Rev. 144 (1944). Do all constitutional rights fit this category? The first amendment? Equal protection? Due process? What about environmental harm?

4) Administrative considerations often militate against an injunction. The decision that damages are inadequate is a decision to dispense with a jury. Remember that in *Debs,* p. 1 the United States chose juryless equity over a criminal prosecution to deal with the Pullman strike. Is the choice of equity an elitist, antimajoritarian decision? Would juries have desegregated schools as well as judges have? Would lay juries be compatible with structural litigation in prisons and residential institutions?

A damage judgment may be easier to enforce than an injunction. Money judgments are enforced impersonally by the sheriff who seizes and sells defendant's property. An injunction is a personal command, enforced by contempt. Should the judge consider breach and enforcement before enjoining? Does considering defendant's possible disobedience reduce plaintiff's substantive right to a hostage to a wrongdoer's obduracy? Does an injunction resemble a stop sign: to succeed the defendant must put on the brakes and obey?

5) The eleventh amendment and official immunity doctrine create some puzzling law/equity questions for federal district courts in Civil Rights actions against nonlegislative state or local government defendants. The judge may grant prospective equitable, injunctive or declaratory relief. Ex parte Young, 209 U.S. 123 (1908). Different rules govern for officials exercising legislative authority. Supreme Court of Virginia v. Consumers Union of United States, 446 U.S. 719 (1980). Prospective relief may have an ancillary effect on the state treasury. Quern v. Jordan, 440 U.S. 332, 337 (1979). But official defendants are immune from retrospective equitable relief in the form of back pay or damages that will cause the state to pay money. Quern v. Jordan, 440 U.S. at 332 (1979); Edelman v. Jordan, 415 U.S. 651 (1974). The judge, however, may award plaintiff damages or back pay against the officials as individuals. Scheuer v. Rhodes, 416 U.S. 232 (1974). Under Hutto v. Finney, 437 U.S. 678 (1978), the state may be charged with plaintiffs' attorney fees. Moreover, under Wood v. Strickland, 420 U.S. 308 (1975), an official acting in good faith possesses a good faith defense in a money damage action. Equitable relief may be available, however, against supervisors and official defendants acting in good faith. Isaac v. Jones, 529 F.Supp. 175, 182 (N.D.Ill.1981). Have these federal decisions created a

modest but real preference for suits to enjoin and recover attorneys fees? Does this reverse the "traditional hierarchy?"

6) One line of cases infused the inadequacy prerequisite with new vitality and made it serve the interests of federalism to structure the relationships between state courts and federal courts. The first was Douglas v. City of Jeannette, 319 U.S. 157 (1943). Jehovah Witnesses sought a federal injunction against a state criminal proceeding. Concerned with the impact of such an injunction on the relationship between the two courts, the Supreme Court said that the federal judge should withhold an injunction unless the plaintiffs demonstrated the inadequacy of the legal remedies. These legal remedies were not actions for damages, but defenses in the state criminal proceedings.

The rule of Douglas v. City of Jeannette took on an increasing urgency in the early 1960's. Civil rights activists were harassed with groundless state criminal prosecutions and turned to the federal courts for protection. They claimed injury from the prosecution itself, regardless of outcome; thus the legal remedy—the defense in the prosecution—was inadequate. At the height of the civil rights era this claim was honored, and the inadequacy prerequisite was deprived of much its restrictive force. Dombrowski v. Pfister, 380 U.S. 479 (1965). See Laycock, Federal Interference with State Prosecutions: The Cases Dombrowski Forgot, 46 U.Chi.L.Rev. 636 (1979). In the early 1970's the civil rights movement faded, public protest took an increasingly violent turn, and the personnel of the Supreme Court began to shift. The Court limited the conditions that rendered the legal remedy inadequate. Younger v. Harris, 401 U.S. 37 (1971). Under the banner of "Our Federalism," the inadequacy prerequisite once again emerged, as it had in Douglas v. City of Jeannette, as a vital limitation on injunctions. In the 1970s the Supreme Court created a preference for the state criminal defense to preserve state autonomy. The inadequacy prerequisite assumed a new prominence because it subordinated the federal injunction. In some instances, the Court discarded the language of equity and freely substituted "comity" for the "inadequacy" of the legal remedy. Fiss, Dombrowski, 86 Yale L.J. 1103 (1977). Do these developments vindicate the "traditional hierarchy?"

7) John Frank wrote in 1975: "In the past twenty years the courts finally have dropped that obsolete bit of wisdom [the inadequacy prerequisite] down a deep well. It lives only as a kind of verbal echo, faintly repeated but largely ignored." Bringing Equity Up to Date, 61 A.B.A.J. 91 (1975). Is the funeral premature?

II. Balancing the Equities

BOOMER v. ATLANTIC CEMENT CO.

26 N.Y.2d 219, 309 N.Y.S.2d 312, 257 N.E.2d 870 (1970).

BERGAN, Judge. Defendant operates a large cement plant near Albany. These are actions for injunction and damages by neighboring land owners alleging injury to property from dirt, smoke and vibration emanating from the plant. A nuisance has been found after trial, temporary damages have been allowed; but an injunction has been denied.

The public concern with air pollution arising from many sources in industry and in transportation is currently accorded ever wider recognition accompanied by a growing sense of responsibility in State and Federal Governments to control it. Cement plants are obvious sources of air pollution in the neighborhoods where they operate.

But there is now before the court private litigation in which individual property owners have sought specific relief from a single plant operation. The threshold question raised by the division of view on this appeal is whether the court should resolve the litigation between the parties now before it as equitably as seems possible; or whether, seeking promotion of the general public welfare, it should channel private litigation into broad public objectives.

A court performs its essential function when it decides the rights of parties before it. Its decision of private controversies may sometimes greatly affect public issues. Large questions of law are often resolved by the manner in which private litigation is decided. But this is normally an incident to the court's main function to settle controversy. It is a rare exercise of judicial power to use a decision in private litigation as a purposeful mechanism to achieve direct public objectives greatly beyond the rights and interests before the court.

Effective control of air pollution is a problem presently far from solution even with the full public and financial powers of government. In large measure adequate technical procedures are yet to be developed and some that appear possible may be economically impracticable.

It seems apparent that the amelioration of air pollution will depend on technical research in great depth; on a carefully balanced consideration of the economic impact of close regulation; and of the actual effect on public health. It is likely to require massive public expenditure and to demand more than any local community can accomplish and to depend on regional and interstate controls.

A court should not try to do this on its own as a by-product of private litigation and it seems manifest that the judicial establishment is neither equipped in the limited nature of any judgment it can pronounce nor prepared to lay down and implement an effective policy for the elimination of air pollution. This is an area beyond the circumference of one private lawsuit. It is a direct responsibility for government and should not thus be undertaken as an incident to solving a dispute between property owners and a single cement plant—one of many—in the Hudson River valley.

The cement making operations of defendant have been found by the court at Special Term to have damaged the nearby properties of plaintiffs in these two actions. That court, as it has been noted, accordingly found defendant maintained a nuisance and this has been affirmed at the Appellate Division. The total damage to plaintiffs' properties is, however, relatively small in comparison with the value of defendant's operation and with the consequences of the injunction which plaintiffs seek.

The ground for the denial of injunction, notwithstanding the finding both that there is a nuisance and that plaintiffs have been damaged substantially, is the large disparity in economic consequences of the nuisance and of the injunction. This theory cannot, however, be sustained without overruling a doctrine which has been consistently reaffirmed in several leading cases in this court and which has never been disavowed here, namely that where a nuisance has been found and where there has been any substantial damage shown by the party complaining an injunction will be granted.

The rule in New York has been that such a nuisance will be enjoined although marked disparity be shown in economic consequence between the effect of the injunction and the effect of the nuisance.

The problem of disparity in economic consequence was sharply in focus in Whalen v. Union Bag & Paper Co., 208 N.Y. 1, 101 N.E. 805. A pulp mill entailing an investment of more than a million dollars polluted a stream in which plaintiff, who owned a farm, was "a lower riparian owner." The economic loss to plaintiff from this pollution was small. This court, reversing the Appellate Division, reinstated the injunction granted by the Special Term against the argument of the mill owner that in view of "the slight advantage to plaintiff and the great loss that will be inflicted on defendant" an injunction should not be granted. "Such a balancing of injuries cannot be justified by the circumstances of this case," Judge Werner noted. He continued: "Although the damage to the plaintiff may be slight as compared with the defendant's expense of abating the condition, that is not a good reason for refusing an injunction."

Thus the unconditional injunction granted at Special Term was reinstated. The rule laid down in that case, then, is that whenever the damage resulting from a nuisance is found not "unsubstantial," viz., $100 a year, injunction would follow. This states a rule that had been followed in this court with marked consistency. . . .

Although the court at Special Term and the Appellate Division held that injunction should be denied, it was found that plaintiffs had been damaged in various specific amounts up to the time of the trial and damages to the respective plaintiffs were awarded for those amounts. The effect of this was, injunction having been denied, plaintiffs could maintain successive actions at law for damages thereafter as further damage was incurred.

The court at Special Term also found the amount of permanent damage attributable to each plaintiff, for the guidance of the parties in the event both sides stipulated to the payment and acceptance of such permanent damage as a settlement of all the controversies among the parties. The total of permanent damages to all plaintiffs thus found was $185,000. This basis of adjustment has not resulted in any stipulation by the parties.

This result at Special Term and at the Appellate Division is a departure from a rule that has become settled; but to follow the rule literally in these cases would be to close down the plant at once. This court is fully agreed to avoid that immediately drastic remedy; the difference in view is how best to avoid it.*

One alternative is to grant the injunction but postpone its effect to a specified future date to give opportunity for technical advances to permit defend-

* Respondent's investment in the plant is in excess of $45,000,000. There are over 300 people employed there.

ant to eliminate the nuisance; another is to grant the injunction conditioned on the payment of permanent damages to plaintiffs which would compensate them for the total economic loss to their property present and future caused by defendant's operations. For reasons which will be developed the court chooses the latter alternative.

If the injunction were to be granted unless within a short period—e.g., 18 months—the nuisance be abated by improved methods, there would be no assurance that any significant technical improvement would occur.

The parties could settle this private litigation at any time if defendant paid enough money and the imminent threat of closing the plant would build up the pressure on defendant. If there were no improved techniques found, there would inevitably be applications to the court at Special Term for extensions of time to perform on showing of good faith efforts to find such techniques.

Moreover, techniques to eliminate dust and other annoying by-products of cement making are unlikely to be developed by any research the defendant can undertake within any short period, but will depend on the total resources of the cement industry nationwide and throughout the world. The problem is universal wherever cement is made.

For obvious reasons the rate of the research is beyond control of defendant. If at the end of 18 months the whole industry has not found a technical solution a court would be hard put to close down this one cement plant if due regard be given to equitable principles.

On the other hand, to grant the injunction unless defendant pays plaintiffs such permanent damages as may be fixed by the court seems to do justice between the contending parties. All of the attributions of economic loss to the properties on which plaintiffs' complaints are based will have been redressed.

The nuisance complained of by these plaintiffs may have other public or private consequences, but these particular parties are the only ones who have sought remedies and the judgment proposed will fully redress them. The limitation of relief granted is a limitation only within the four corners of these actions and does not foreclose public health or other public agencies from seeking proper relief in a proper court.

It seems reasonable to think that the risk of being required to pay permanent damages to injured property owners by cement plant owners would itself be a reasonable effective spur to research for improved techniques to minimize nuisance.

The power of the court to condition on equitable grounds the continuance of an injunction on the payment of permanent damages seems undoubted. . . .

The damage base here suggested is consistent with the general rule in those nuisance cases where damages are allowed. "Where a nuisance is of such a permanent and unabatable character that a single recovery can be had, including the whole damage past and future resulting therefrom, there can be but one recovery" (66 C.J.S. Nuisances § 140, p. 947). It has been said that permanent damages are allowed where the loss recoverable would obviously be small as compared with the cost of removal of the nuisance (Kentucky-Ohio Gas Co. v. Bowling, 264 Ky. 470, 477, 95 S.W.2d 1).

The present cases and the remedy here proposed are in a number of other respects rather similar to Northern Indiana Public Service Co. v. W.J. & M.S. Vesey, 210 Ind. 338, 200 N.E. 620 decided by the Supreme Court of Indiana. The gases, odors, ammonia and smoke from the Northern Indiana company's gas plant damaged the nearby Vesey greenhouse operation. An injunction and damages were sought, but an injunction was denied and the relief granted was limited to permanent damages "present, past and future." . . .

Denial of injunction was grounded on a public interest in the operation of the gas plant and on the court's conclusion "that less injury would be occasioned by requiring the appellant [Public Service] to pay the appellee [Vesey] all damages suffered by it . . . than by enjoining the operation of the gas plant; and that the maintenance and operation of the gas plant should not be enjoined." . . .

The Indiana Supreme Court opinion continued: "When the trial court refused injunctive relief to the appellee upon the ground of public interest in the continuance of the gas plant, it properly retained jurisdiction of the case and awarded full compensation to the appellee. This is upon the general equitable principle that equity will give full relief in one action and prevent a multiplicity of suits." . . .

It was held that in this type of continuing and recurrent nuisance permanent damages were appropriate. See, also, City of Amarillo v. Ware, 120 Tex. 456, 40 S.W.2d 57 where recurring overflows from a system of storm sewers were treated as the kind of nuisance for which permanent depreciation of value of affected property would be recoverable.

There is some parallel to the conditioning of an injunction on the payment of permanent damages in the noted "elevated railway cases" (Pappenheim v. Metropolitan El. Ry. Co., 128 N.Y. 436, 28 N.E. 518 and others which followed). Decisions in these cases were based on the finding that the railways created a nuisance as to adjacent property owners, but in lieu of enjoining their operation, the court allowed permanent damages.

Judge Finch, reviewing these cases in Ferguson v. Village of Hamburg, 272 N.Y. 234, 239–240, 5 N.E.2d 801, 803, said: "The courts decided that the plaintiffs had a valuable right which was being impaired, but did not grant an absolute injunction or require the railway companies to resort to separate condemnation proceedings. Instead they held that a court of equity could ascertain the damages and grant an injunction which was not to be effective unless the defendant failed to pay the amount fixed as damages for the past and permanent injury inflicted." . . .

Thus it seems fair to both sides to grant permanent damages to plaintiffs which will terminate this private litigation. The theory of damage is the "servitude on land" of plaintiffs imposed by defendant's nuisance. (See United States v. Causby, 328 U.S. 256, 261, 262, 267, where the term "servitude" addressed to the land was used by Justice Douglas relating to the effect of airplane noise on property near an airport.)

The judgment, by allowance of permanent damages imposing a servitude on land, which is the basis of the actions, would preclude future recovery by plaintiffs or their grantees . . . .

This should be placed beyond debate by a provision of the judgment that the payment by defendant and the acceptance by plaintiffs of permanent damages found by the court shall be in compensation for a servitude on the land.

Although the Trial Term has found permanent damages as a possible basis of settlement of the litigation, on remission the court should be entirely free to re-examine this subject. It may again find the permanent damage already found; or make new findings.

The orders should be reversed, without costs, and the cases remitted to Supreme Court, Albany County to grant an injunction which shall be vacated upon payment by defendant of such amounts of permanent damage to the respective plaintiffs as shall for this purpose be determined by the court.

JASEN, Judge (dissenting). I agree with the majority that a reversal is required here, but I do not subscribe to the newly enunciated doctrine of assessment of permanent damages, in lieu of an injunction, where substantial property rights have been impaired by the creation of a nuisance.

It has long been the rule in this State, as the majority acknowledges, that a nuisance which results in substantial continuing damage to neighbors must be enjoined. . . . To now change the rule to permit the cement company to continue polluting the air indefinitely upon the payment of permanent damages is, in my opinion, compounding the magnitude of a very serious problem in our State and Nation today.

In recognition of this problem, the Legislature of this State has enacted the Air Pollution Control Act (Public Health Law, Consol.Laws, c. 45, §§ 1264 to 1299–m) declaring that it is the State policy to require the use of all available and reasonable methods to prevent and control air pollution (Public Health Law § 1265).

The harmful nature and widespread occurrence of air pollution have been extensively documented. Congressional hearings have revealed that air pollution causes substantial property damage, as well as being a contributing factor to a rising incidence of lung cancer, emphysema, bronchitis and asthma.

The specific problem faced here is known as particulate contamination because of the fine dust particles emanating from defendant's cement plant. The particular type of nuisance is not new, having appeared in many cases for at least the past 60 years. . . . It is interesting to note that cement production has recently been identified as a significant source of particulate contamination in the Hudson Valley. This type of pollution, wherein very small particles escape and stay in the atmosphere, has been denominated as the type of air pollution which produces the greatest hazard to human health. We have thus a nuisance which not only is damaging to the plaintiffs,[5] but also is decidedly harmful to the general public.

I see grave dangers in overruling our long-established rule of granting an injunction where a nuisance results in substantial continuing damage. In per-

5. There are seven plaintiffs here who have been substantially damaged by the maintenance of this nuisance. The trial court found their total permanent damages to equal $185,000.

mitting the injunction to become inoperative upon the payment of permanent damages, the majority is, in effect, licensing a continuing wrong. It is the same as saying to the cement company, you may continue to do harm to your neighbors so long as you pay a fee for it. Furthermore, once such permanent damages are assessed and paid, the incentive to alleviate the wrong would be eliminated, thereby continuing air pollution of an area without abatement.

It is true that some courts have sanctioned the remedy here proposed by the majority in a number of cases, but none of the authorities relied upon by the majority are analogous to the situation before us. In those cases, the courts, in denying an injunction and awarding money damages, grounded their decision on a showing that the use to which the property was intended to be put was primarily for the public benefit. Here, on the other hand, it is clearly established that the cement company is creating a continuing air pollution nuisance primarily for its own private interest with no public benefit.

This kind of inverse condemnation . . . may not be invoked by a private person or corporation for private gain or advantage. Inverse condemnation should only be permitted when the public is primarily served in the taking or impairment of property. . . . The promotion of the interests of the polluting cement company has, in my opinion, no public use or benefit.

Nor is it constitutionally permissible to impose servitude on land, without consent of the owner, by payment of permanent damages where the continuing impairment of the land is for a private use. . . . This is made clear by the State Constitution (art. I, § 7, subd. [a]) which provides that "[p]rivate property shall not be taken for *public use* without just compensation" (emphasis added). It is, of course, significant that the section makes no mention of taking for a *private* use.

In sum, then, by constitutional mandate as well as by judicial pronouncement, the permanent impairment of private property for private purposes is not authorized in the absence of clearly demonstrated public benefit and use.

I would enjoin the defendant cement company from continuing the discharge of dust particles upon its neighbors' properties unless, within 18 months, the cement company abated this nuisance.[7]

It is not my intention to cause the removal of the cement plant from the Albany area, but to recognize the urgency of the problem stemming from this stationary source of air pollution, and to allow the company a specified period of time to develop a means to alleviate this nuisance.

I am aware that the trial court found that the most modern dust control devices available have been installed in defendant's plant, but, I submit, this does not mean that *better* and more effective dust control devices could not be developed within the time allowed to abate the pollution.

Moreover, I believe it is incumbent upon the defendant to develop such devices, since the cement company, at the time the plant commenced production (1962), was well aware of the plaintiffs' presence in the area, as well as

7. The issuance of an injunction to become effective in the future is not an entirely new concept. For instance, in Schwarzenbach v. Oneonta Light & Power Co., 207 N.Y. 671, 100 N.E. 1134, an injunction against the maintenance of a dam spilling water on plaintiff's property was issued to become effective one year hence.

the probable consequences of its contemplated operation. Yet it still chose to build and operate the plant at this site.

In a day when there is a growing concern for clean air, highly developed industry should not expect acquiescence by the courts, but should, instead, plan its operations to eliminate contamination of our air and damage to its neighbors.

Accordingly, the orders of the Appellate Division, insofar as they denied the injunction, should be reversed, and the actions remitted to Supreme Court, Albany County to grant an injunction to take effect 18 months hence, unless the nuisance is abated by improved techniques prior to said date.

---

1) Consider the following standard justification for the balancing-the-equities defense. "[P]ractical experience has shown that in the administration of specific relief there must be more discretion vested in the judge than in the allowance of money damages for the injury suffered. In the latter there can never be any greater injury inflicted on defendant by allowing recovery than would be inflicted on plaintiff by denying it. But it very often happens that the award of specific relief would inflict a hardship on the defendant which is out of all proportion to the injury its refusal would cause to plaintiff. In these cases, by the great weight of authority equity still has discretion in adjusting the relief to be awarded to the needs of the fact situation." H.L. McClintock, Equity 51–52 (2d ed. 1948). Ask while reading the following notes whether this rationale has stood the test of time.

2) Several excellent articles have been written about the problems raised in *Boomer*. They include: Keeton and Morris, Notes on "Balancing the Equities," 18 Tex.L.Rev. 412 (1940); McLaren, The Common Law Nuisance Actions and the Environmental Battle—Well-Tempered Swords or Broken Reeds?, 10 Osgoode Hall L.J. 505 (1972); Polinsky, Resolving Nuisance Disputes: The Simple Economics of Injunctive and Damage Remedies, 32 Stan.L.Rev. 1075 (1980); Wade, Environmental Protection, The Common Law of Nuisance and the Restatement of Torts, 8 The Forum 165 (1972); Note, Injunction Negotiations: An Economic, Moral, and Legal Analysis, 27 Stan.L.Rev. 1563 (1975); Comment, Internalizing Externalities: Nuisance Law and Economic Efficiency, 53 N.Y.U.L.Rev. 219 (1978).

3) The judge has three options: a) no nuisance, b) nuisance and damages, c) nuisance and an injunction.

a) The defendant's conduct may not amount to a nuisance. Nuisance doctrine is "markedly open-ended." In 1942, Dean William Prosser called nuisance a "legal garbage can." Prosser, Nuisance Without Fault, 20 Tex.L.Rev. 399, 410 (1942). In the fourth edition of his Torts treatise, mellowed by the intervening years, Prosser said that nuisance was an "impenetrable jungle." W. Prosser, Law of Torts 571 (1971). Confirmation for these conclusions will be found in Wade, 8 The Forum 165 (1972) and the Restatement (Second) of Torts § 40 (1977). This state of the law may provide an opportunity for a creative judge to mold nuisance doctrine to meet changed conditions. McLaren, 10 Osgoode Hall L.J. at 506. "Whatever the legitimacy of the oft-voiced fear of judicial activism in other areas, in the environmental field a complex of political, legal, and social factors makes judicial sensitivity and creativity pivotally important to the way in which all of us work, play, eat, sleep, and die." Oakes, The Judicial Role in Environmental Law, 52 N.Y.U.L.Rev. 498, 499 (1977).

Could a judge find that where the defendant's activity is useful to the community, no nuisance exists? What are the proper "costs" or "expenses" of an enterprise? Is particulate pollution from a cement plant a homeowner's cost? Who bears the burden of the defendant's pollution? If a cement plant need not bear the expense of its particulate pollution, are resources allocated efficiently? Will this keep the price of cement lower than otherwise? Lead to overconsumption of cement?

The New York courts may have retreated from *Boomer* in Copart Industries v. Consolidated Edison Co., 41 N.Y.2d 564, 394 N.Y.S.2d 169, 362 N.E.2d 968 (1977). Copart prepared and stored new automobiles next to Con Ed's generating plant. Fly ash containing acid allegedly from the plant marred new car finishes, and Copart went out of business. Copart sued Con Ed for damages. The jury found for Con Ed. The court of appeals in affirming approved instructions that required Copart to have shown that Con Ed had negligently or intentionally harmed Copart. Did the court of appeals find the flexibility of adjusting to be too much and retreat to a rigid and absolutist nuisance-no nuisance approach? Will this inadequately protect those affected by pollution and restrict nuisance as a method of environmental control? See Comment, 53 N.Y.U.L.Rev. 219.

b) The judge may follow *Boomer,* find a nuisance, and impose money damages. If the utility of defendant's alleged nuisance exceeds the harm it causes, shouldn't the judge avoid an all or nothing approach and force the defendant to compensate those injured? While we usually think of equity as flexible, isn't payment a more flexible remedy than either enjoining the plant or allowing it to continue to pollute the neighborhood? Will damages 1) distribute the cost of making cement or generating electricity? 2) maximize the combined value of both tracts of land? 3) allow defendant to save the expense of anti-pollution devices if paying damages is cheaper?

Nevertheless, the candid observer must register a few doubts about the money remedy. Does it violate the notion that real property is unique and that damages are inadequate to protect real property? Does money tell the property owners that their interest is merely economic? Chancellor Kent allowed the contractor, Jerome, to buy a right to trespass on Ross's property and sever stone. p. 63. Does *Boomer* similarly allow the cement company to buy a license to pollute? Are the courts granting an eminent domain power to private interests? Do the courts believe in commercial progress even if it exacts a toll on residents and property owners?

The Arizona Supreme Court employed a "compensated injunction" in Spur Industries, Inc. v. Del E. Webb Development Co., 108 Ariz. 178, 494 P.2d 700 (1972). The plaintiff, a developer, expanded toward an existing cattle feedlot. The court held that the feedlot was an enjoinable nuisance but manipulated the "coming to the nuisance" defense to require the developer to pay the cost of moving the feedlot away from residential areas. Not even in a classroom hypothetical could we expect the homeowners in *Boomer* or the insolvent Copart company to move a cement plant or a generating facility. Does the *Spur* approach consider proportion, fairness, and the utility of defendant's activity? Will it maximize the combined value of both cattle feeding and residential development?

c) The judge may enjoin. Will the plant close? Or will the parties negotiate? Does the *Boomer* court fear that if the judge enjoins, the homeowners will exchange their rights to enforce the injunction for valuable consideration? Do economic rules as strong as self-interest teach us that the *Boomer* plaintiffs would relinquish their injunction for more than their loss but less than Atlantic Cement's $45,000,000 investment? If the homeowners' interest is money, then why not limit them to damages set by a judge instead of a coerced settlement from the cement company?

An injunction allows the homeowners to negotiate from a position of strength. Would this better recognize the unique features of plaintiff's property interest? It can be argued that in Jerome v. Ross the chancellor ignored the subjective aspect of the landowner's interest. Does the *Boomer* court's fear that the homeowners may use an injunction to extract excessive settlements also ignore that subjective aspect? Does the equitable hardship doctrine prove that the court is ignoring the inadequacy prerequisite? If a judge cannot consider fully the subjective value of sentiment, attachment, discomfort and annoyance in setting damages, then isn't an injunction a better assurance of full compensation?

Will homeowners employ injunctions to punish defendants or to achieve overcompensation? Is equitable hardship too strong a medicine? Is the risk of a plaintiff either closing a valuable enterprise or being overcompensated worth denying an injunction and risking judicial undercompensation? Could the judge prevent overcompensation by supervising negotiations and approving settlements? Should courts expand equitable estoppel and laches to bar plaintiffs who led defendants on or waited too long to sue? What about situations as in *Boomer,* where defendant does a little harm to a lot of people and it will be hard to locate all affected people as well as to calculate and distribute damages. Is the *Boomer* rationale valid where there are too many parties to negotiate after the injunction? "In conflicting-use situations in which transaction costs are high, the allocation of resources to their most valuable uses is facilitated by denying property right holders an injunctive remedy against invasion of their rights and instead limiting them to a remedy in damages (why?). Where transaction costs are low, injunctive relief should normally be allowed as a matter of course (why?) . . . " R. Posner, Economic Analysis of Law § 3.7 at 51 (2d ed. 1977). See also section 4.12.

These questions as well as other refinements not herein encountered are pursued in Polinsky, 32 Stan.L.Rev. 1075 (1980); and Note, 27 Stan.L.Rev. 1563 (1975).

III. Clean Hands

MITCHELL BROTHERS FILM GROUP v. CINEMA ADULT THEATER

604 F.2d 852 (5th Cir. 1979), certiorari denied 445 U.S. 917 (1980).

Before GODBOLD, SIMPSON and MORGAN, Circuit Judges.

GODBOLD, Circuit Judge:

This is a copyright infringement suit, arising under the now-superseded Copyright Act of 1909. But it is more than the usual commercial contest between copyright holder and alleged infringer. The infringers asserted as an affirmative defense that the copyrighted material—a movie—was obscene, and that, therefore, under the equitable rubric of "unclean hands" plaintiffs were barred from relief. After viewing the film the court found it obscene, adopted the unclean hands rationale, and denied relief to the copyright owners. Review of this holding requires us to consider the constitutional limits upon the power granted to Congress to issue copyrights, the manner in which Congress had chosen to exercise that power, and the applicability of the unclean hands doctrine.

Plaintiffs-appellants owned a properly registered copyright on a motion picture titled "Behind the Green Door." . . . Two groups of defendants, each group consisting of a theater and several individuals, obtained copies of the movie without plaintiffs' permission and infringed the copyright by exhibiting the film at the theaters. The Lido Art Theater group did not appear for trial, default judgment was entered against it and a statutory penalty awarded to plaintiffs. . . . The Cinema Adult Theater group appeared for trial, and after a bench trial the court found in its favor. On appeal the Cinema Adult group has not appeared.

We hold that the district court erred in permitting the assertion of obscenity as an affirmative defense to the claim of infringement, and, accordingly, reverse without reaching the question whether the film is obscene.

I. The statutory language

The statutory provision that controls in this case reads:

"The works for which copyright may be secured under this title shall include all the writings of an author."

17 U.S.C. § 4 (1970) (repealed). Motion pictures are unquestionably "writings" under the Copyright Act.

The district court did not base its decision on standards found within the Act, which it described as "silent as to works which are subject to registration and copyright." The Act is not "silent." Rather, the statutory language "all the writings of an author" is facially all-inclusive, within itself admitting of no exceptions. There is not even a hint in the language of § 4 that the obscene nature of a work renders it any less a copyrightable "writing." There is no other statutory language from which it can be inferred that Congress intended that obscene materials could not be copyrighted.[3]

Moreover, there is good reason not to read an implied exception for obscenity into the copyright statutes. The history of content-based restrictions on copyrights, trademarks, and patents suggests that the absence of such limitations in the Copyright Act of 1909 is the result of an intentional policy choice and not simply an omission. See generally 74 Colum.L.Rev. 1351, 1354 n.27 (1974). From the first copyright act in 1790, Congress has seldom added restrictions on copyright based on the subject matter of the work, and in each instance has later removed the content restriction.[4] These congressional additions and subsequent deletions, though certainly not conclusive, suggest that Congress has been hostile to content-based restrictions on copyrightability.[5] In contrast Congress has placed explicit content-related restrictions in the current statutes governing the related areas of trademarks and patents. The Lanham Act prohibits registration of any trademark that "[c]onsists of or comprises immoral, deceptive, or scandalous matter," 15 U.S.C. § 1052(a), and inventions must be shown to be "useful" before a patent is issued. See 35 U.S.C. § 101.

The legislative history of the 1976 Act reveals that Congress intends to continue the policy of the 1909 Act of avoiding content restrictions on copyrightability. In recommending passage of the 1976 Act, the House Judiciary Committee stated:

"The phrase 'original works of authorship,' [§ 102] which is purposely left undefined, is intended to incorporate without change the standard of originality established by the courts under the present copyright statute. This standard does not include requirements of novelty, ingenuity, or *esthetic merit*, and

3. See 1 M. Nimmer, On Copyright § 2.17, at 2–193 (1978); Chafee, Coming into Equity with Clean Hands, 47 Mich.L.Rev. 1065, 1068 (1947); Schneider, Authority of the Register of Copyrights to Deny Registration of a Claim to Copyright on the Ground of Obscenity, 51 Chi.-Kent L.Rev. 691, 692–93 (1975); Note, Immorality, Obscenity and the Law of Copyright, 6 S.Dakota L.Rev. 109, 111 (1961); 74 Colum.L.Rev. 1351, 1354 (1974); 46 Fordham L.Rev. 1037, 1038 (1978).

4. Congress has enacted two statutory copyright restrictions that were arguably content based, but afterwards repealed them. After the language "composition designed or suited for public representation," which was contained in the 1856 version of the Copyright Act, Act of August 18, 1856, 11 Stat. 138, was construed in Martinetti v. Maguire, 16 Fed.Cas. p. 920 (No. 9173) (C.C.Cal.1867) to mean that the moral content of the work had to be suitable for public consumption (rather than the more natural meaning of "suited" by form. i.e., capable of being performed on the stage), Congress deleted the "suited" language from the next version of the Act. See Act of July 8, 1870, 16 Stat. 198. A later version, Act of June 18, 1874, ch. 301, § 3, 18 Stat. 78, 79, contained language arguably placing content restrictions on the copyrightability of engravings, cuts and prints. (The Act provided that such works were copyrightable only if "connected with the fine arts.") After this language was narrowly construed by the Supreme Court, see Bleistein v. Donaldson Lithograph Co., 188 U.S. 239 (1903), the language was deleted from the 1909 version of the Act, which is controlling in this case, leaving no content-based restrictions in the Act.

5. See, e.g., 17 U.S.C. § 8 (1970) (repealed) (copyright not available for works in public domain or for government publications); cf. 17 U.S.C.A. § 101 (1977 Supp.) (works not " 'fixed' in a tangible medium of expression" uncopyrightable under 1976 Act); Schneider, supra note 3, at 693 (regulations promulgated by Register of Copyrights under 1909 Act barred only material "deficient in quantity, originality or formal concreteness while obscenity suffers from lack of literary, social or artistic quality.")

there is no intention to enlarge the standard of copyright protection to require them."

H.R.Rep. No. 1476, 94th Cong., 2d Sess. 51. . . .

It appears to us that Congress has concluded that the constitutional purpose of its copyright power, "[t]o promote the Progress of Science and useful Arts," U.S.Const. art. 1, § 8, cl. 8, is best served by allowing all creative works (in a copyrightable format) to be accorded copyright protection regardless of subject matter or content, trusting to the public taste to reward creators of useful works and to deny creators of useless works any reward. It is not surprising that Congress would choose to rely on public acceptability as a measure of a work's worth rather than on the judgment of such public officials as the Register of Copyrights [6] and federal and state judges. As Justice Holmes said, in rejecting the argument that under an earlier version of the Copyright Act the courts had a duty to pass upon the artistic merits of engravings and prints,

> "It would be a dangerous undertaking for persons trained only to the law to constitute themselves final judges of the worth of pictorial illustrations, outside of the narrowest and most obvious limits. At the one extreme, some works of genius would be sure to miss appreciation. Their very novelty would make them repulsive until the public had learned the new language in which their author spoke. It may be more than doubted, for instance, whether the etchings of Goya or the paintings of Manet would have been sure of protection when seen for the first time. At the other end, copyright would be denied to pictures which appealed to a public less educated than the judge. Yet if they command the interest of any public, they have a commercial value,—it would be bold to say that they have not an aesthetic and educational value,—and the taste of any public is not to be treated with contempt."

Bleistein v. Donaldson Lithograph Co., 188 U.S. 239, 251–52 (1903). The Ninth Circuit has recently voiced similar concerns in rejecting the defense of fraudulent content in copyright infringement actions:

> "There is nothing in the Copyright Act to suggest that the courts are to pass upon the truth or falsity, the soundness or unsoundness, of the views embodied in a copyrighted work. The gravity and immensity of the problems, theological, philosophical, economic and scientific, that would confront a court if this view were adopted are staggering to contemplate. It is surely not a task lightly to be assumed, and we decline the invitation to assume it."

Belcher v. Tarbox, 486 F.2d 1087, 1088 (CA9, 1973).

In our view, the absence of content restrictions on copyrightability indicates that Congress has decided that the constitutional goal of encouraging creativity would not be best served if an author had to concern himself not only with the marketability of his work but also with the judgment of government officials regarding the worth of the work.

Further, if Congress were receptive to subject matter restrictions on copyright, there are many reasons why it would be unlikely to choose obscenity as

6. See Schneider, supra note 3, at 703–21; cf. 41 Op.Att'y Gen. 395, 402 (1958) (suggesting that "for policy reasons, it may not be thought appropriate for the Register [of Copyrights] to undertake to be a conservator of public morals").

one of those restrictions. Obscenity law is a concept not adapted for use as a means for ascertaining whether creative works may be copyrighted. Obscenity as a constitutional doctrine has developed as an effort to create a tolerable compromise between First Amendment considerations and police power. It is an awkward, barely acceptable concept that continues to dog our judicial system and society at large. The purpose underlying the constitutional grant of power to Congress to protect writings is the promotion of original writings, an invitation to creativity. This is an expansive purpose with no stated limitations of taste or governmental acceptability. Such restraints, if imposed, would be antithetical to promotion of creativity. The pursuit of creativity requires freedom to explore into the gray areas, to the cutting edge, and even beyond. Obscenity, on the other hand, is a limiting doctrine constricting the scope of acceptability of the written word. . . .

Denying copyright protection to works adjudged obscene by the standards of one era would frequently result in lack of copyright protection (and thus lack of financial incentive to create) [8] for works that later generations might consider to be not only non-obscene but even of great literary merit. See Phillips, Copyright in Obscene Works: Some British and American Problems, 6 Anglo-Am.L.Rev. 138, 168–69 (1977). Many works that are today held in high regard have been adjudged obscene in previous eras. English courts of the nineteenth century found the works of Byron, Southey and Shelley to be immoral. See U.S. v. One Book Entitled Ulysses, 72 F.2d 705, 708 (CA2, 1934). American courts have found these books, among others, obscene: Edmund Wilson, Memories of Hecate County, see People v. Doubleday & Co., 297 N.Y. 687, 77 N.E.2d 6 (1947), aff'd per curiam by an equally divided court, 335 U.S. 848 (1948); Henry Miller, Tropic of Cancer and Tropic of Capricorn, see Besig v. U. S., 208 F.2d 142 (CA9, 1953); Erskine Caldwell, God's Little Acre, see Attorney General v. Book Named "God's Little Acre," 326 Mass. 281, 93 N.E.2d 819 (1950); Lillian Smith, Strange Fruit, see Commonwealth v. Isenstadt, 318 Mass. 543, 62 N.E.2d 840 (1945); D. H. Lawrence, Lady Chatterly's Lover, see Commonwealth v. Delacey, 271 Mass. 327, 171 N.E. 455 (1930); Theodore Dreiser, An American Tragedy, see Commonwealth v. Friede, 271 Mass. 318, 171 N.E. 472 (1930). See generally Lewis, Literature, Obscenity and Law (1976); Alpert, Judicial Censorship of Obscene Material, 52 Harv.L.Rev. 40 (1938).

Further, Congress in not enacting an obscenity exception to copyrightability avoids substantial practical difficulties and delicate First Amendment issues. Since what is obscene in one local community may be non-obscene protected speech in another, see Miller v. California, 413 U.S. 15 (1973), and the copyright statute does not in other respects vary in its applicability from locality to locality, Congress in enacting an obscenity exception would create the dilemma of choosing between using community standards that would (arguably unconstitutionally) [10] fragment the uniform

8. See Comment, The First Amendment Exception to Copyright: A Proposed Test, 1977 Wisc.L.Rev. 1158, 1177–78.

10. Cf. Goldstein v. California, 412 U.S. 546, 555 (1973) ("The objective of the Copyright Clause was clearly to facilitate the granting of rights national in scope.").

national standards of the copyright system and venturing into the uncharted waters of a national obscenity standard. We can only conclude that we must read the facially all-inclusive 1909 copyright statute as containing no explicit or implicit bar to the copyrighting of obscene materials, and as therefore providing for the copyright of all creative works, obscene or non-obscene, that otherwise meet the requirements of the Copyright Act.[12]

II. Constitutionality of the copyright statute

The conclusion that the 1909 Act was all-inclusive and did not provide an exception for obscenity does not end our inquiry, however. We must consider whether the statute, in allowing copyright of obscene material, was constitutional and whether despite congressional intent the courts should take it upon themselves to permit the defense of obscenity in copyright infringement cases. We first turn to the question of constitutionality.

The Copyright and Patent Clause of the Constitution provides that "The Congress shall have Power . . . To promote the Progress of Science and useful Arts, by securing for limited Times to Authors and Inventors the exclusive Right to their respective Writings and Discoveries . . . ." U.S.Const. art. I, § 8, cl. 8. The district court construed this clause to limit the congressional power to grant copyrights solely to works that promote the sciences and useful arts. If one carries the district court's reasoning to its necessary conclusion, Congress acted unconstitutionally in enacting an all-inclusive statute that allows copyrighting of non-useful works (such as, arguably, obscenity) [15] as well as useful works. Several lower courts and commen-

12. Of course, Congress does not approve of obscenity and has enacted several measures armed at reducing the distribution of obscene materials. See, e.g., 18 U.S.C. § 1461 (crime to mail obscene materials); 18 U.S.C. § 1462 (crime to ship obscene materials interstate by common carrier); 18 U.S.C. § 1465 (crime to ship obscene materials interstate for purposes of sale or distribution). However, the existence of such statutes does not indicate that Congress intends obscene material to be uncopyrightable. Rendering obscene materials uncopyrightable would add little to the existing arsenal of weapons against pornography and would have many undesirable consequences, as discussed in the text.

15. The district court apparently was of the view that obscene materials, by definition, could not promote the sciences or useful arts, and at least one commentator agrees. See Rogers, Copyright and Morals, 18 Mich.L.Rev. 390 (1920). Under the *Miller* obscenity test, it would not necessarily be true that an obscene work is completely lacking in utility, for under that standard the work need only be shown to "lack *serious* literary, artistic, political, or scientific value." 413 U.S. at 24 (emphasis added). However, the district court judged the movie in question obscene under both the *Miller* test and the now-obsolete *Memoirs* test. Under the *Memoirs* standard, a work may be found obscene only if "*utterly* without redeeming social value." A Book Named "John Cleland's Memoirs of a Woman of Pleasure" v. Massachusetts, 383 U.S. 413, 419 (1966) (emphasis original). Although a semantical argument can be made that a work that fails the strict *Memoirs* standard cannot possibly promote the useful arts, it is doubtful that a finding of lack of social value for obscenity purposes is equivalent to a finding of lack of utility for purposes of the Copyright and Patent Clause. In fact, if Congress deemed the creation and distribution of sexually explicit works to be beneficial, we do not doubt that this action would be permitted by the Constitution. See, Phillips, Copyright in Obscene Works: Some British and American Problems, 6 Anglo-Am.L.Rev. 138, 166 (1977).

Furthermore, it is doubtful that the question of utility is open to the court in an infringement suit, since the Supreme Court, in construing an earlier copyright statute that contained an arguably content-based restriction, held that a work's worth is sufficiently shown by an infringer's "desire to reproduce [it] without regard to the plaintiffs' rights." Bleistein v. Donaldson Lithograph Co., 188 U.S.

tators have agreed with this construction of the Copyright and Patent Clause.[16] Other commentators disagree, however, and argue that Congress has power to grant copyrights even for individual works that cannot be shown to promote the useful arts so long as Congress in its exercise of its copyright power generally promotes the constitutional goal.[17] In our view the district court's reading of the Copyright and Patent Clause is unduly restrictive of Congress' power and is inconsistent with the Supreme Court's broad view of the congressional powers granted by this Clause. . . .

The all-inclusive nature of the 1909 Act reflects the policy judgment that encouraging the production of wheat also requires the protection of a good deal of chaff. We cannot say this judgment was so unreasonable as to exceed congressional power. We conclude that the protection of all writings, without regard to their content, is a constitutionally permissible means of promoting science and the useful arts.

III. Judicially-created defenses to infringement actions involving immoral or obscene works

Some courts have denied legal redress in infringement suits to holders of copyrights on immoral or obscene works by applying judicially-created doctrines. Two of these doctrines are largely vestiges of a bygone era and need be addressed only briefly. The theory that judges should act as conservators of the public morality was succinctly summarized by the court in Shook v. Daly, 49 How.Prac. 366, 368 (N.Y.Sup.Ct.1895): "The rights of the writer are secondary to the rights of the public to be protected from what is subversive of good morals." Application of this theory by the English courts in the nineteenth century led to the suppression of works because they were inconsistent with Biblical teachings or because they were seditious. . . . Although this theory has been relied on as recently as 1963, see Dane v. M. & H. Co., 136 U.S.P.Q. 426, 429 (N.Y.Sup.Ct.1963) (common law copyright protection denied striptease because it did not "elevate, cultivate, inform, or improve the moral or intellectual natures of the audience"), it is evident to us that it is inappropriate for a court, in the absence of some guidance or authorization from the legislature, to interpose its moral views between an author and his willing audience.

A second judicially-created doctrine, the theory that a person can have no property in obscene works, merely expresses by means of a legal fiction the underlying judicial moral conclusion that the work is not worthy of protec-

239, 252 (1903). In any event, we need not reach issues of utility because of our conclusion that the Constitution does not require that each individual work be shown to promote the useful arts in order to be copyrightable.

16. See Barnes v. Miner, 122 F. 480, 489–90 (C.C.S.D.N.Y.1903); Martinetti v. Maguire, 16 Fed.Cas. p. 920 (No. 9173) (C.C.Cal.1867); Bullard v. Esper, 72 F.Supp. 548 (N.D.Tex.1947); Dane v. M. & H. Co., 136 U.S.P.Q. 426, 429 (N.Y.Sup.Ct.1963); 1 M. Nimmer, On Copyright § 1.03[B] (1978); Rogers, supra note 15; Note, Obscenity and Copyright, 6 S.Dakota L.Rev. at 111–12 (1961); Comment, Copyright Protection of Obscene Material Against Censorship as Correlated with Copyright Protection of Obscene Material Against Infringement, 31 S.Cal.L.Rev. 301, 306 (1958); 6 St. Mary's L.J. 274, 278 (1974); cf. Argos Films, S.A. v. Barry International Properties Inc., 77 Civ. 1062 (S.D.N.Y., July 7, 1977) (constricting Copyright Act to not allow copyright of obscenity apparently adopted to avoid constitutional difficulties).

17. See Phillips, supra note 15, at 165–66; Schneider, supra note 3, at 698 n.36; 74 Colum.L.Rev. 1351, 1353 (1974).

tion. The doctrine has not been adopted in this country, . . . and should not be. Cf. Board of Trade v. Christie Grain & Stock Co., 198 U.S. 236, 251 (1905): "If, then, the plaintiffs' collection of information is otherwise entitled to protection, it does not cease to be so, even if it is information concerning illegal acts. The statistics of crime are property to the same extent as any other statistics, even if collected by a criminal who furnishes some of the data."

The third judicially created doctrine, that of unclean hands, has seldom been relied upon by courts that have denied copyright to obscene or immoral works. For the most part, only English courts have relied on this theory. See generally Chafee, supra note 3, at 1065–70. Of the various American cases allowing obscenity as a defense to a copyright infringement action, few even mention the doctrine of unclean hands. See Bullard v. Esper, 72 F.Supp. 548, 549 (N.D.Tex.1947) (semble); Richardson v. Miller, 20 Fed.Cas. 722 (No. 11,791) (C.C.D.Mass.1877). Nevertheless, since the district court permitted obscenity to be asserted as a defense through the medium of the unclean hands rubric, the concept of unclean hands requires more extended discussion.

Assuming for the moment that the equitable doctrine of unclean hands has any field of application in this case, it should not be used as a conduit for asserting obscenity as a limit upon copyright protection. Creating a defense of obscenity—in the name of unclean hands or through any other vehicle—adds a defense not authorized by Congress that may, as discussed above, actually frustrate the congressional purpose underlying an all-inclusive copyright statute. It will discourage creativity by freighting it with a requirement of judicial approval. Requiring authors of controversial, unpopular, or new material to go through judicial proceedings to validate the content of their writings is antithetical to the aim of copyrights. If the copyright holder cannot obtain financial protection for his work because of actual or possible judicial objections to the subject matter, the pro-creativity purpose of the copyright laws will be undercut.

The Supreme Court and this court have held that equitable doctrines should not be applied where their application will defeat the purpose of a statute. See, e.g., Perma-Life Mufflers, Inc. v. International Parts Corp., 392 U.S. 134, 138 (1968) ("We have often indicated the inappropriateness of invoking broad common-law barriers to relief where a private suit serves important public purposes."); Woolf v. S. D. Cohn & Co., 515 F.2d 591, 601–02 (CA5, 1975), vacated on other grounds, 426 U.S. 944 (1976). . . . Because the private suit of the plaintiff in a copyright infringement action furthers the congressional goal of promoting creativity, the courts should not concern themselves with the moral worth of the plaintiff.[22]

22. Cf. Perma-Life Mufflers, 392 U.S. at 139.

"[T]he purposes of the antitrust laws are best served by insuring that the private action will be an ever-present threat to deter anyone contemplating business behavior in violation of the antitrust laws. The plaintiff who reaps the reward of treble damages may be no less morally reprehensible than the defendant, but the law encourages his suit to further the overriding public policy in favor of competition. A more fastidious regard for the relative moral worth of the parties would only result in seriously undermining the usefulness of the private action as a bulwark of antitrust enforcement."

Furthermore, the need for an additional check on obscenity is not apparent. Most if not all states have statutes regulating the dissemination of obscene materials, and there is an array of federal statutes dealing with this subject, as well. See note 16 supra. As Professor Chafee concluded, the difficulty inherent in formulating a workable obscenity defense to copyright is sufficient reason not to allow such a defense unless the other criminal and civil statutes dealing with the obscenity problem are shown to be plainly ineffective:

"Sometimes the legislature has expressly entrusted questions of obscenity to the courts, as in criminal statutes, and then judges have to do the best they can, but the results have been quite erratic. This should be a warning against rushing into new obscenity jobs which no legislature has told them to undertake.

"The penalties for obscenity are defined by statute. Why should the courts add a new penalty out of their own heads by denying protection to a registered copyright which complies with every provision of the copyright act? . . . I think that the added penalty is justifiable only if there is a serious need for extra pressure to induce obedience to the criminal law. In the obscenity situation, this need is not obvious."

The effectiveness of controlling obscenity by denying copyright protection is open to question. The district court thought that on the whole the long-term discouragement of the creation of obscene works would outweigh the short-term increase in the dissemination of obscene works caused by the refusal of an injunction. This theory, reached without empirical evidence or expert opinion, is at least doubtful. Many commentators disagree and are of the view that denial of injunctions against infringers of obscene materials will only increase the distribution of such works.[23] The existence of this difference of view, which we need not resolve, makes clear that the question of how to deal with the relationship between copyrights and obscenity is not best suited for case-by-case judicial resolution but is instead most appropriately resolved by legislatures. Congress has not chosen to refuse copyrights on obscene materials, and we should be cautious in overriding the legislative judgment on this issue.

Finally, permitting obscenity as a defense would introduce an unmanageable array of issues into routine copyright infringement actions. It was for this reason that the Ninth Circuit rejected the defense of fraudulent content in copyright infringement cases. See Belcher v. Tarbox . . . .

Now, we turn to examine our momentary assumption that the unclean hands doctrine can be invoked at all in this case. For reasons that we have set out, obscenity is not an appropriate defense in an infringement action,

23. See, e.g., Chafee, supra note 3, at 1069; Rogers, supra note 15, at 394; Phillips, supra note 15, at 155–56; Note, supra note 3, 6 S.Dakota L.Rev. at 127. Compare Belcher v. Tarbox, 486 F.2d 1087, 1088 n.3 (CA9, 1973), with id. at 1090 (Wallace, J., concurring and dissenting).

Apart from the question whether denying copyright protection to obscene works will, on balance, produce more or less creation and dissemination of obscenity, there is, of course, a separate issue of the chilling effect upon authors of new or controversial material that is within the bounds of protected speech but, in the eye of some one or more viewers, arguable obscene.

whether piggybacked on the unclean hands rubric or introduced in some other manner. But even if obscenity were not objectionable as a defense, the unclean hands doctrine could not properly be used as the vehicle for that defense.

The maxim of unclean hands is not applied where plaintiff's misconduct is not directly related to the merits of the controversy between the parties, but only where the wrongful acts "in some measure affect the equitable relations between the parties in respect of something brought before the court for adjudication." Keystone Driller Co. v. General Excavator Co., 290 U.S. 240, 245 (1933). The alleged wrongdoing of the plaintiff does not bar relief unless the defendant can show that he has personally been injured by the plaintiff's conduct. Lawler v. Gillam, 569 F.2d 1283, 1294 (CA4, 1978). The doctrine of unclean hands "does not purport to search out or deal with the general moral attributes or standing of a litigant." NLRB v. Fickett-Brown Mfg. Co., 140 F.2d 883, 884 (CA5, 1944). Here it is clear that plaintiffs' alleged wrongful conduct [24] has not changed the equitable relationship between plaintiffs and defendants and has not injured the defendants in any way.

The district court's invocation of unclean hands was based upon an ancient Fifth Circuit case, Stone & McCarrick, Inc. v. Dugan Piano Co., 220 F. 837 (CA5, 1915). *Stone & McCarrick* held that a plaintiff in a copyright infringement action is barred from recovery by the doctrine of unclean hands where the copyrighted material has the effect of fraudulently deceiving or misleading the public. Relying on trademark cases, the court concluded that in copyright cases deceit that causes injury to the public could give rise to unclean hands just as injury to the defendant gives rise to unclean hands in other equitable suits. In the present case, the court coupled this notion of "public injury" assertable as an unclean hands defense with a concept of obscenity as an injury to the public at large.

Stone & McCarrick is inconsistent with subsequent Supreme Court and Fifth Circuit cases holding, as discussed above, that an equitable doctrine should not be applied in a way that will frustrate the purpose of a federal statute. See, e.g., *Perma-Life Mufflers;* Woolf v. S. D. Cohn & Co. *Stone & McCarrick* does not simply apply a traditional equitable doctrine; it goes further and extends the doctrine of unclean hands to a situation not covered by the doctrine at common law and thus subverts a statutory purpose. This is plainly unacceptable under modern precedents.[25]

24. This wrongful conduct presumably is the dissemination of a sexually explicit film in a community where it is obscene. However, there is no evidence in this record that the *plaintiffs* have disseminated "Behind the Green Door" in communities where it is obscene, and we doubt that the mere act of making the movie, if attributable to the plaintiffs, injured the public. Thus, even if we accepted the use of unclean hands based upon asserted injury to the public, discussed infra, a remand for determination of whether the plaintiffs have been responsible for distributing the film where it is obscene would be necessary.

25. Moreover, subsequent Supreme Court cases have made it clear that *Stone & McCarrick* erroneously read prior Supreme Court precedent. *Stone & McCarrick* primarily relied on Manhattan Medicine Co. v. Wood, 108 U.S. 218 (1882), and read this trademark case as though its rationale was that any misuse of a government-granted monopoly (trademark, copyright, or patent) in a way that injures the public permits assertion of an unclean hands defense against the holder of the monopoly right. An independent reading of *Manhattan Medicine* reveals that it was not based on this broad rationale, but rather, it held

It is immediately apparent that limiting copyright protection on a broad public injury rationale would lead to absurd and unacceptable results. Unless the public injury rationale is limited . . . to misuses that frustrate the particular purposes of the copyright (or trademark or patent) statute, an infringer could defend by alleging, for example, that the copyright holder has failed to pay income taxes on revenue derived from the copyright. Arguably an infringer could defend on the ground that the work had been transported into the state in the copyright owner's truck that does not meet federal safety and pollution requirements or by an interstate carrier not certificated as required by the Interstate Commerce Act. The possibilities are well nigh limitless. We have found no copyright, trademark, or patent case subsequent to *Stone & McCarrick* relying on the general principle that the rights of a holder of a government-granted monopoly are limited by an infringer's right to assert as a defense any "injury" to the general public. Whatever vitality, if any, *Stone & McCarrick* presently may have, we decline to extend its holding to this case. Thus, even if we thought obscenity an appropriate defense, *Stone & McCarrick* is an inadequate justification for using unclean hands as the vehicle for allowing the obscenity defense.[26]

In the present case the copyright holders' actions are not inconsistent with any policy of the copyright laws. The infringers' attempt to immunize their illegal acts by wrapping themselves in the mantle of a "public injury" caused by plaintiffs is antithetical to the purpose of these laws. The effort cannot be

that a trademark that deceives the public about the identity of the manufacturer is undeserving of judicial protection because such trademarks undermine the specific purpose of trademark protection—facilitation of public identification of manufacturers. 108 U.S. at 223. This rationale, rather than the broad public injury rationale perceived by *Stone & McCarrick,* is generally accepted in cases involving deceptive trademarks. See Chafee, supra note 3, at 1076. (For a comment pointing out *Stone & McCarrick's* misreading of *Manhattan Medicine,* see 74 Colum.L.Rev. 1351, 1355–56 (1974)). In Morton Salt Co. v. G. S. Suppiger Co., 314 U.S. 488 (1942), the Court held that a patent holder's infringement action is barred by unclean hands where the patent holder is using his invention as part of a tying arrangement. The Court's rationale was much narrower than public injury as a bar. The Court denied relief because the patent holder was using his patent grant to subvert the policy of the patent law itself, extending the patent monopoly to an unpatented item by the tying arrangement. Id. at 493, 494.

In a line of cases following *Morton Salt,* the Court has carefully made clear the limited nature of *Morton Salt* and has stressed that subversion of the policy of the patent is required. See Automatic Radio Mfg. Co. v. Hazeltine Research, 339 U.S. 827, 832 (1950) ("That which is condemned as against public policy by the 'Tie-in' cases is the extension of the monopoly of the patent to create another monopoly or restraint of competition—a restraint not countenanced by the patent grant."); Mercoid Corp. v. Minneapolis-Honeywell Regulator Co., 320 U.S. 680, 684 (1944) (cites *Morton Salt* for proposition that "respondent may not obtain from a court of equity any decree which directly or indirectly helps it to subvert the public policy which underlies the grant of its patent"); U. S. v. Univis Lens Co., 316 U.S. 241, 251 (1942) (states that in *Morton Salt* Court was "construing and applying the patent law so as to give effect to the public policy which limits the granted monopoly strictly to the terms of the statutory grant").

26. We merely note another problem. Plaintiffs seek both legal and equitable relief. The doctrine of unclean hands is equitable in nature and would seemingly not bar recovery of damages for copyright infringement. See 74 Colum.L.Rev. 1351, 1353 (1974). There is authority, however, that in copyright and patent suits the unclean hands doctrine is applicable to both legal and equitable relief. See Chafee, supra note 3, 47 Mich.L.Rev. at 1067, 1070–71; Tempo Music, Inc. v. Myers, 407 F.2d 503, 507 n.8 (CA4, 1969). Since we determine that the defense of unclean hands should not be available to the defendants in this particular case, we need not resolve this issue.

sustained. In an appropriate case a misuse of the copyright statute that in some way subverts the purpose of the statute—the promotion of originality—might constitute a bar to judicial relief.[27] This is not such a case. The unclean hands doctrine was not applicable.

---

1) Throughout his opinion Judge Godbold refers to an article by Zachariah Chafee in the Michigan Law Review. This article was one of Chafee's Cooley lectures at Michigan; these were subsequently reprinted in the first three chapters of a book entitled Some Problems of Equity (1950). He began with these observations:

"The most amusing maxim of equity is 'He who comes into Equity must come with clean hands.' It has given rise to many interesting cases and poor jokes. The maxim has been regarded as an especially significant manifestation of the ethical attitude of equity as contrasted with the common law. Pomeroy, for instance, argues that the principle involved in this maxim is 'merely the expression of one of the elementary and fundamental conceptions of equity jurisprudence.' Pomeroy's theory is that chancery has power to force a defendant to comply with the dictates of conscience as to matters outside the strict rules of law. Correspondingly, it will not interfere on behalf of a plaintiff whose own conduct in this connection has been contrary to conscience. In other words, since equity tries to enforce good faith in defendants, it no less stringently demands the same good faith from plaintiffs.

. . .

"Although it is a pity to take this beautiful statue off its lofty pedestal, I propose to show that the clean hands doctrine does not definitely govern anything, that it is a rather recent growth, that it ought not to be called a maxim of equity because it is by no means confined to equity, that its supposed unity is very tenuous and it is really a bundle of rules relating to quite diverse subjects, that insofar as it is a principle it is not very helpful but is at times capable of causing considerable harm. . . . "

His discussion of the obscenity as unclean hands in a copyright action is at 46–54. Everything Chafee wrote is worth reading. This is especially true here because he wrote articulately and cogently about copyright in addition to equity.

2) Should the *Mitchell Bros.* court generalize from opinions where judges refuse to be aesthetic referees to this lawsuit, where the defendant asks the court to perform a customary judicial task: passing on whether matter is legally obscene? Is the court concerned that the obscenity issue is presented outside the usual, jury-tried criminal action to punish or suppress? Would refusing to enforce the copyright reduce dissemination of "Behind the Green Door?" What effect on dissemination does the decision have? How would either decision affect incentive to create similar motion pictures? Is the court simply hostile to limitations on sexually explicit motion pictures?

3) Something very like the example given in footnote 27 occurred in Russ Berrie & Co., Inc. v. Jerry Elsner Co., Inc., 482 F.Supp. 980 (S.D.N.Y.

27. As, for example, when the copyright is procured by making fraudulent misrepresentations about authorship to the Register of Copyrights. See, e.g., Vogue Ring Creations, Inc. v. Hardman, 410 F.Supp. 609 (D.R.I.1976). . . .

1980). Plaintiff sued charging that defendant had infringed copyrights in toy designs for a Santa Claus, a teddy bear, and a gorilla. The judge concluded that plaintiff "intentionally withheld material information from the Copyright Office in the face of a specific and clear direction to disclose it. . . . The knowing failure to advise the Copyright Office of facts which might have occasioned a rejection of the application constitutes reason for holding the registration invalid and thus incapable of supporting an infringement action, . . . or denying enforcement on the ground of unclean hands." 482 F.Supp. at 988.

If plaintiff lacks any protectable interest, must defendant rely on an affirmative defense like unclean hands to prevail? Isn't unclean hands a makeweight, mentioned after the judge had held that plaintiff lacked a claim? Even so, does the *Russ Berrie* decision spring from copyright law or equity? Should courts grant monopoly power to a copyright obtained by deception? Would the judge dismiss a damage action with equal alacrity?

4) Similarly, where a patentee employs monopoly power to monopolize unpatented matter as well, is the defense to an infringement action equitable unclean hands or something grounded more specifically in patent and antitrust law? See Automatic Radio Manufacturing Co. v. Hazeltine Research, 339 U.S. 827 (1952); and Morton Salt Co. v. G.S. Suppiger Co., 314 U.S. 488 (1942), discussed in *Mitchell Bros.*

IV. Laches

HOSKIN v. RESOR

324 F.Supp. 271 (D.D.C.1971).

GASCH, District Judge.

This matter came on for hearing on cross motions for summary judgment. . . . The Court agrees that there is no issue of material fact and concludes that plaintiffs are entitled to summary judgment as a matter of law. This suit raises the issue of whether the members of the Russian Railway Service Corps were members of the Army of the United States during World War I and whether as such they are entitled to an Honorable Discharge therefrom.

The Court takes judicial notice of the following historical facts: Plaintiffs are a group of railroad men who were recruited, mostly from the Great Northern Railroad, during the course of World War I for service in Siberia as part of a military organization officially designated as the American Expeditionary Force, Siberia. The Czar's government had collapsed. The Kerensky provisional government had been recognized by the Allied Powers. Efforts were being expedited designed to maintain some semblance of pressure on the Central Powers on what was then called the Eastern Front in order to preclude the transfer of some two million German soldiers from that Front to the Western Front. One principal means of supply insofar as the Russian Forces were concerned was via the Trans-Siberian Railway. The Pacific port was Vladivostok. Connections utilizing the Chinese Eastern Railroad through Harbin, China, were also under consideration. Russian railroads, particularly the Trans-Siberian, were in a chaotic state of disrepair. The key to the contemplated operation was repair and maintenance, and if possible, improvement of this vital link.

Mr. Daniel Willard, then President of the Baltimore & Ohio Railroad, was appointed a member of the Advisory Commission of the Council of National Defense by President Wilson. On March 3, 1917, he was elected Chairman of this important Commission. His statement, which is set forth in the affidavit of the plaintiff Hoskin, reflects that following a conference with Sir George Bury, President of the Canadian Pacific, and at the request of the British Prime Minister David Lloyd-George and with the concurrence of President Wilson and Secretary of War Newton D. Baker, Mr. Willard was requested to name a five-man committee to go immediately to Vladivostok for the purpose of evaluating the condition of the Trans-Siberian Railway and reporting thereon to the Allied Powers. Mr. John F. Stevens was named Chairman of this committee. Col. George H. Emerson, formerly general manager of the Great Northern Railroad, became the commanding officer of plaintiffs and those similarly situated.

From the papers filed by the Government in this case, the Court finds the following undisputed material facts: Mr. Daniel Willard's letter dated September 18, 1917, addressed to the Chief of Staff of the United States Army, Gen. Hugh L. Scott, reveals that he was authorized by the Secretary of War to raise and equip a force of approximately two hundred and fifty railroad officers to go to Russia at once for the purpose of acting as instructors of various divisions of the Russian Railroad. Mr. Willard's letter further revealed that the Secretary of War instructed Mr. S.M. Felton (The Director General of Railways, Corps of Engineers, United States Army), working in conjunction with the Chief of Engineers of the United States Army to arrange the details, such as furnishing these men with uniforms. Grades were provided for these railroad men from second lieutenant to colonel. Plaintiffs without exception are in the lower grades. They were given War Department forms on which to apply for commissions in the Officers Reserve Corps. They received direct commissions. . . .

By letter dated October 6, 1917, Brig. Gen. Black, the Army's Chief of Engineers, set forth the authorized ranks of the Russian Railway Service Corps and indicated that they were to be paid by the Russian Government. The Russian Ambassador by letter dated October 10, 1917, addressed to the Assistant Secretary of the Treasury, authorized payment to these men from funds to the credit of the Russian Government. The compensation paid plaintiffs was slightly in excess of compensation paid Army ranks generally. Plaintiffs were issued regulation Army uniforms. United States Army insignia, including that specified for the Corps of Engineers was authorized and was worn. The initials R.R.S. (Russian Railway Service) were also worn. They were armed with regulation Army sidearms. Upon arrival in Siberia, they assisted in the movement of troops and supplies of the Allies and the provisional or Kolchak government. They also assisted in the evacuation of troops and refugees when the Kolchak government was driven back and in the transport of the Czech-Slovak contingent through Siberia. With the collapse of the Kolchak government, these plaintiffs were evacuated from Siberia with other American Troops. The last American transport left Vladivostok April 1, 1920.

On these facts Government counsel contends that these plaintiffs were not members of the United States Army or any branch thereof. The Army has refused to grant these plaintiffs Honorable Discharges, with the rights appertaining thereto, to which they claim they are entitled. The Court finds it difficult under the admitted facts to agree with the Army's conclusion. . . .

Defendant also relies on laches. This is an equitable doctrine based on the principle that equity will not aid a plaintiff whose unexcused delay would be prejudicial to the defendant. Both unreasonable delay and prejudice must be shown for laches to apply. We find the delay here to be neither unreasonable nor prejudicial. Laches is applicable where plaintiffs have elected to sit on their rights and have lacked diligence in pursuing relief. That is not the case here. Though fifty years have passed since the cause of action arose, it should be remembered that mere lapse of time is not the essence of laches. The plaintiffs have been persistent in seeking to obtain legislative relief, although only recently have they instituted judicial action. They have caused [fifteen] bills to be introduced in Congress, drawn for the purpose of achieving the relief now sought in this cause.

The Court finds that the delay has not been unduly prejudicial to the Government in that it has shown by the exhibits filed that it was able to produce extensive and detailed records, letters, and documents which concern the A.E.F. Siberia and the Russian Railway Service Corps and its members. . . .

There is no question here but that these plaintiffs performed the military duties to which they were assigned. There is no issue as to pay. They take the position that having been appointed at the direction of the President of the United States by action of the Adjutant General of the Army they are entitled to an Honorable Discharge as a necessary and proper incident to their military service in the absence of any reason for withholding such an Honorable Discharge. The Court agrees.

---

1) Hoskins's struggle began in 1920. "The Army told me to my face that they'd stall it till we all died off, so they wouldn't have to give us our honorable discharges." When this action was filed, only 33 of the 288 veterans were still alive. "The Army fought for delays," his attorney Selma Samols said. "I kept arguing that I was losing my clients to the Grim Reaper." Judge Gasch held in favor of the veterans in 1971, but the Army delayed sending discharges to the 24 survivors until 1973. Back-pay, insurance, and other military benefits were not settled in 1974. McKeown, Touche, A Few Heartwarming Victories in The People v. The System, The Washington Post/Potomac, April 21, 1974, at 16. Under the G.I. Bill Improvement Act of 1977, if a similar controversy arose today, the Secretary of the Air Force would decide the active military service question. 38 U.S.C. § 106(a)(1) and (2).

2) " 'Laches' is the neglect, for an unreasonable and unexplained length of time under circumstances permitting diligence, to do what in law, should have been done. There is no fixed period within which a person must assert his claim or be barred by laches. The length of time depends upon the cir-

cumstances of the particular case. Mere delay in asserting a right does not of itself constitute laches; the delay involved must work to the disadvantage and prejudice of the defendant. Laches is a question of fact to be determined from all the evidence and circumstances adduced at trial." Lake Development Enterprises, Inc. v. Kojetinsky, 410 S.W.2d 361, 367–68 (Mo.App. 1966).

Laches developed because equity lacked a statute of limitations. It denies relief to plaintiffs who have filed within a general statute of limitations, Los Angeles Heights Independent School District v. Chestnut, 287 S.W. 693 (Tex.Civ.App.1926) (two weeks). It allows plaintiffs who file after a general statute of limitations has run to maintain an action. In addition to *Hoskins,* see Neisius v. Henry, 142 Neb. 29, 5 N.W.2d 291 (1942), where plaintiff recovered thirteen years of illegal salary from defendant.

3) Laches allows the judge to grant or deny relief in a particular action although the statute of limitations appears to dictate a contrary result. It is an extreme example of substituting discretion and individual justice for fixed rules. In a jurisdiction with a catch-all statute of limitations for actions not specifically covered and a general suspension or tolling statute, is laches an anachronism?

4) Laches questions are often litigated in private actions for employment discrimination under Title VII of the 1964 Civil Rights Act. Plaintiff must satisfy two prerequisites before suit: a timely charge with the EEOC and a complaint in the district court within 90 days after receiving notice of the right to sue from the EEOC. In Zipes v. Trans World Airlines, Inc., 455 U.S. 385 (1982), the Supreme Court held "that filing a timely charge of discrimination with the EEOC is not a jurisdictional prerequisite to suit in federal court, but a requirement that, like a statute of limitations, is subject to waiver, estoppel, and equitable tolling." 455 U.S. at 398. The EEOC has jurisdiction over the charge for the first 180 days after filing. The plaintiff may either await EEOC disposition after that, while the agency investigates and conciliates, or she may request the right to sue later after the 180 days expires. In Occidental Life Insurance Co. v. EEOC, 432 U.S. 335 (1977), the Court construed the relevant statute, 42 U.S.C. § 2000e–(5)(f)(1). It held that a complainant who is unhappy with EEOC's progress may seek relief in district court, but not until the EEOC has had the complaint for 180 days. After waiting, the complainant may either 1) file a private action within 90 days after requesting and receiving EEOC notification or 2) leave action on her charge to the EEOC.

The laches issue arises when plaintiff either files her action after waiting for the EEOC process to conclude or waits for years before requesting EEOC notice. State statutes of limitations do not govern. If defendant interposes laches, should any plaintiff who elects the favored method of the EEOC's administrative process be penalized? Does laches, if found, bar either plaintiff's whole claim or just the back pay award? Does it matter whether the EEOC's efforts are active, continual, or dormant? In addition to prejudice from unavailable witnesses and lost records, is the augmented back pay liability from the agency's delay prejudicial to the defendant? See Jones v. Bell Helicopter Co., 614 F.2d 1389 (5th Cir. 1980); Bernard v. Gulf Oil Co., 596 F.2d 1249 (5th Cir. 1979), rehearing granted 604 F.2d 449 (en banc), affirmed 619 F.2d 459 (1980) (en banc); Boone v. Mechanical Specialties Co., 609 F.2d 956 (9th Cir. 1979); Harris v. Ford Motor Co., 487 F.Supp. 429 (W.D.Mo.1980); Richardson v. Delta Drayage Co., 433 F.Supp. 50 (E.D.La.1977); see generally Annot., Laches As a Defense to Action Under Title VII of Civil Rights Act of 1964 (42 U.S.C. § 2000e et seq.) Brought by Private Individual, 52 A.L.R. Fed. 218 (1981).

V. Discretion and Conscience

One theme runs through injunctive litigation, often lending it a certain romance. That theme is discretion. The cases abound with quaint statements: an application for an injunction appeals to the Chancellor's conscience; the injunction is a discretionary remedy; a court of equity has the inherent power to create and fashion a flexible remedy. We suspect that pronouncements such as these provoked Selden's well-known crack: "Equity is according to the conscience of him that is Chancellor, and as that is larger or narrower so is Equity. 'Tis all one as if they should make the standard for the measure we call a foot to be the Chancellor's foot. What an uncertain measure would this be! One Chancellor has a long foot, another a short foot, a third an indifferent foot." The Table-Talk of John Selden (1847).

The Historical Roots: Selden's challenge is no light matter. Too much discretion may not only mean unequal law, but no law at all—for law implies governance through a system of rules that are generally applicable. See K. Davis, Discretionary Justice (1969); Wechsler, Toward Neutral Principles of Constitutional Law, 73 Harv.L.Rev. 1 (1959). But before taking up the challenge or attempting to determine whether there is "too much" discretion in injunctive litigation, we think it is useful to identify the historical roots of this rather distinctive relationship between injunctions and discretion. The history once again indicates the role of accident. In this instance, there are two strands to the accident: (1) preventive relief in the form of the injunction becomes predominantly, if not exclusively, associated with the Court of Chancery even though it may have had its antecedents in the writs of the common law courts; and (2) the delegation to the Chancellor of the task of passing on special petitions to the King led to the rise of a separate court system, Chancery, and this court system in turn adopted the idea of "equity" to justify or rationalize its continued separate existence.

The idea of "equity" stems from Aristotle; but when he spoke of it, he clearly did not have in mind two separate court systems—much less, preventive relief. What Aristotle had in mind when he analyzed the concept of "equity" and its relationship to justice was simply the "rectification of law where it fails through generality." He recognized why law had to be general and why, in some instances, justice could be done only through exception to the general rule. As he said, "All law is couched in general terms, but there are some cases upon which it is impossible to pronounce in general terms." An equitable man is one who will not, in an exceptional situation, insist upon his rights, will not apply the general rule in its full rigor. Equity is a form of dispensation. See generally Nicomachean Ethics bk. 5, ch. 10.

This Aristotelian idea finds its way into English jurisprudence through the work of Christopher St. Germain, Dialogues between a Doctor of Divinity and a Student of the Laws of England, and he in turn derived it from the followers of St. Thomas Aquinas. See P. Vinogradoff, Reason and Conscience in Sixteenth Century Jurisprudence, 24 L.Q.Rev. 373 (1908); reprinted in 2 The Collected Papers of Paul Vinogradoff 190 (1928). Doctor and Student, published in the early sixteenth century, supplied the formal theory of the institutional arrangement that already existed; it was not a summary of the theory that gave rise to the institutional arrangement. Plucknett tells us that during the fourteenth and fifteenth centuries when the Court of Chancery is emerging there is very little talk about "equity." Some of the early petitions appeal to the Chancellor's "conscience," but this concept of "conscience"—unlike the later concept of equity—was not unique to Chancery. "Conscience" was the same as "reason": the way men knew what was the will of God and hence what was just. Both concepts were part of the jurisprudence of the common law. The distinctive concept of Chancery was "equity," and it is only in the sixteenth century—after Chancery has emerged and feels pressure to justify itself—that the idea appears with any frequency. T. F. T. Plucknett, A Concise History of the Common Law 685 (5th ed. 1956).

S.F.C. Milsom, writes:

"The explanation in theory, a commonplace by the late sixteenth century, was that any general rule must work injustice in particular cases, and therefore that the application of positive law must be subject to some dispensing power in the interest of a higher justice. . . .

"The appeal to a higher justice was . . . further explained . . . by St. Germain in his Doctor and Student. St. Germain was a barrister having extensive theological learning; and for him the higher justice was divine in origin, and its human manifestation was a matter of conscience. . . . There was nothing new in the appeal to conscience. The language is found in petitions from the earliest times; but it was not just designed to persuade chancellors who had nearly always been ecclesiastics; still less to persuade them to produce a different result from that reached by 'the law.' Justice was as single as truth, and conscience was man's knowledge of it. Positive law was about the means by which this single justice should be manifested; and the appeal to the chancellor was for the same single justice, in circumstances in which the human machinery was going to fail. . . ."

Historical Foundations of the Common Law 88–89 (1981). For the persistence of this notion of "reason" or "conscience" in the common law, perhaps even up to the time when Selden makes his gibe about the Chancellor's foot, see M. J. Horwitz, The Emergence of an Instrumental Conception of American Law, 1780–1820, in 5 Perspectives in American History 287, 291–298 (Fleming and Bailyn, eds. 1971).

This idea of "equity" fit Chancery naturally because Chancery was viewed as an auxiliary or supplemental legal system to correct the deficiencies of the ordinary court system and the essence of equity was dispensation, relief from the harshness arising from the application of otherwise just rules. There was no reason why "equity" had to become the exclusive property of Chancery; but it did. As the common law rules became increasingly rigid, equity became the Chancery's trademark. Chancery became known as the "court of equity." This identification was so intensive that Maitland could—without embarrassment—begin his famous lectures in 1909 by asking "What is Equity?" and then answering that it is simply the body of rules that had been administered by the Court of Chancery. Equity 1 (1909).

Modern, or merged, procedure incorporates features of formerly equitable procedure like discovery, class actions, and interpleader. Substantive areas formerly associated with equity like trusts, fiduciary relationships, mortgages, wills and estates, and divorce have developed into independent fields. Substantive rules of equity and equitable defenses such as illegality, duress and fraud have been assimilated into unified court systems. Should the idea that equity applied conscience when the legal rules defeated justice survive the merger of the two systems and the end of the inflexible common law writs? Has equity emphasized its moral superiority too much? D. Dobbs, Handbook of the Law of Remedies 56 (1973). Does this emphasis lead the judge to focus on one aspect of a conflict and ignore the total situation? Does the focus on ethics blur policy? Shouldn't all lawsuits be governed by generally applicable rules announced in advance?

Describing equity in terms of a court that is no more cannot be satisfactory. "In an artificial period, say from the middle nineteenth century backwards into the seventeenth, our judges were fond of quoting so called 'maxims of equity.' Some of these made sense, others did not; but they owe their place to 'a bouquet of high-sounding maxims' which the Chancellors obtained from the canon law where Roman law had found a second home. Thus, it was natural for early Chancellors, being churchmen, to draw upon this treasury to point up their deliverances, although they did not intend to 'Romanize the law of England.' One of the 'maxims of equity,' however, has no such definite lineage; and yet, in describing the action of the court, it is, as the late Dean Keener of Columbia used to say, 'the only maxim of equity that is really true.' Such, then, is the rule to which chapters of old treatises used to be devoted, or sections at least, that 'Equity acts against the person.' " Glenn and Redden, Equity: A Visit to the Founding Fathers, 31 Va.L.Rev. 753, 770–771 (1945).

Consider the idea that "Equity acts against the person." Injunctions are the personal orders that this book focuses on. The notion is that the Chancellor ordered people to do things. Common law money judgments, on the other hand, are addressed to the sheriff and not to the defendant; the judgment tells the sheriff to seize defendant's property, sell it, and pay the proceeds to the plaintiff. Defendant owes no personal obedience to a judgment at law; but personal orders like injunctions enforced by contempt may be subject to abuse of power that threatens individuals. Juries are normally excluded from adjudication that leads to injunctions and other personal orders. The maxim that "Equity acts against the person" embodies the enduring uniqueness of equity. Does it also reveal a troublesome concentration of power? Are flexibility and discretion needed to accommodate the institutional necessities of injunctions and other personal relief?

The Variations of Discretion: The classic forms of discretion in injunctive litigation, represented by the doctrines we studied in this chapter, approach the Aristotelian conception of equity. The discretion comes in the form of dispensation—the court is giving or is being asked to give dispensation from its own rules which otherwise dictate the issuance of the injunction.

But discretion takes many other forms in injunctive litigation; and it may be useful to achieve some perspective on the full universe now. This will provide some feel for the magnitude of the theme. A list of seven different ways in which discretion manifests itself in injunctive litigation follows. Discretion means either the decision of the court is 1) not controlled by any rules, or 2) not controlled by reasonably precise rules, or 3) that there is a lax standard for appellate review.

(1) Substantive Doctrine. Some substantive doctrines that define the rights and duties of the parties, telling them what they can and cannot do, employ markedly open-ended concepts. For example, a nuisance may be defined as "unreasonable" use of one's land that "substantially" interferes with the plaintiff's enjoyment of his property.

(2) The General Prerequisites to Injunctive Relief. The prerequisites to injunctive relief transcend all substantive doctrines. They are couched in open-ended terms that defy definition through precise rules; accordingly, they introduce an additional element of discretion. The prerequisites of inadequacy and imminence are good examples.

(3) The General Prerequisites for Interlocutory Injunctions. Thus far the focus has been on permanent injunctions issued after a full evidentiary hearing. Interlocutory injunctions—restraining orders and preliminary injunctions—are issued during the pendency of the litigation, before the evidentiary hearing is complete; and, as we will see later, these injunctions have another set of prerequisites which cut across all substantive areas. Once again, these prerequisites are stated in open-ended terms—for example, a balancing of the harms. They introduce another element of discretion.

(4) How the Plaintiff's Rights Will Be Vindicated. Once the court decides to enjoin it must choose the terms of the injunction. If there are many different ways of vindicating those rights, the choice may be considered a discretionary one. In a school desegregation case, integration can be achieved in a variety of ways, for instance, through the pairing or consolidation of schools. The court has several ways to achieve that goal. In a labor dispute the tribunal may choose whether the employer must post notices proclaiming its intention to obey the law in the future and if so, how many notices and where they need be posted. The details of the remedy and how the rights will be vindicated are often spoken of as discretionary, not prescribed by any sharp rules and subject to slight appellate scrutiny.

(5) When the Plaintiff's Right Will Be Vindicated. Even after the judge decides that the defendant has violated the plaintiff's rights and that relief is due, the question often remains as to when relief must be given or when the injunction will become effective. Courts have given themselves some discretion over this timing issue. That is referred to in the dissent in *Atlantic Cement*; it also occurred in *Reserve Mining*, p. 116. But perhaps the best-known, and most troubling, instance in our injunctive jurisprudence is the "all-deliberate-speed" formula of Brown v. Board of Education, 349 U.S. 294 (1955).

(6) The Equitable Defenses. This is the discretion embodied in the defenses in this chapter—clean hands, balancing the equities, and laches. These equitable defenses seem to cut across all substantive areas and, unlike the other prerequisites, they do not necessarily dispute the need for preventive relief.

(7) Enforcing the Injunction. Even after the injunction is granted, the trial court has some discretion over the sanction to apply to those who violate the injunction. Is civil contempt necessary? Should there be a criminal contempt proceeding? Should punishment be inflicted? What should be the length of the imprisonment or the size of the fine? Once again, appellate courts often say that these decisions lie in the trial judge's "discretion."

This list of the varieties of discretion is not complete. Throughout the course ask yourself whether there are any other manifestations of discretion in injunctive litigation. More importantly, ask whether some types of discretion are more justified than others, whether they should be confined to injunctions, and whether the emphasis on discretion that so marks injunctive litigation can be squared with our notions about equal treatment and the rule of law.

Chapter Three

PERILS OF PREDICTION

I. Imminence

The traditional office of an injunction is to prevent harm, and several rules are tied to this distinctive forward-looking quality. One requires plaintiff to convince the judge that absent relief, harm is imminent—in other words, not premature.

Prematurity as a defense to an injunction raises special problems of prediction. Legislatures and courts formulate general standards abstractly to achieve consensus. The terminology defining the threshold eludes precision; scientific or expert testimony is difficult to relate to legal standards and thresholds. Science's apparent precision fades into the judge's need to consider social and economic factors and to resolve conflicting testimony with concrete judgments about uncertainty and hazards. Carcinogenic effects, in particular, generally do not show up for two decades; to forecast responsibly when the hazard is redoubtable but uncertain is a formidable challenge.

FLETCHER v. BEALEY

28 Ch. 688 (1885).

PEARSON, J.: The Plaintiff complains that the Defendants are placing upon a piece of land on the bank of the River Irwell, higher up the river than his works, a large mass of a substance called "vat waste," the existence of which in that particular spot will, he says, imperil his trade. He has carried on business for many years at the Kearsley Paper Mills, which are situated upon the bank of the River Irwell. The Defendants are alkali manufacturers, their works being on the same river, about six miles higher up the stream. The Plaintiff is a manufacturer of papers of a peculiar description. He says, in one of his affidavits, "I have for many years past especially excelled in trade in the production of the very finest classes of paper which are made in England, such as cigarette paper, the finer kinds of copying papers, and fine and delicate tissues of all kinds. For the purposes of my works I use in the making of paper very high class waste and linen, and in the first processes this has to be bleached, after being boiled and beaten up, to as pure a white as it is possible to get, and this is the secret of my success in trade, that I have, by long experience and care in the use of water and chemicals, succeeded in getting a great purity of white to start the process of paper making. Unless I am able to get this pure white for what is known in the trade as bottom, no amount of washing or use of chemicals in the later processes will enable me to get the delicacy of colour shewn in some of the sample-books now produced, and, if, in order to get rid of deleterious matter, I have to use too much chemicals in the later processes of washing, it quite spoils the paper by rendering the fibre too tender." The Defendants, as I have said, are alkali manufacturers. In the process of manufacturing alkali, a very large quantity is produced of a refuse which is denominated "vat waste." It contains a considerable amount of sulphur, and is hot, and when heaped up it gets, as I conclude, hotter, and unless great care is taken it will ignite, and if a large heap of this "vat waste" should ignite, the result, as one of the witnesses told me, would be to suffocate all the people in the neighbourhood. It is, therefore, a very dangerous material, and the alkali manufacturers are obliged to be exceedingly careful in the handling of it, and, after a large heap of it, the product possibly of many years, has been stored, there flows from it a liquid of a greenish colour, which contains very destructive chemical elements. The Defendants for some years got rid of this refuse by carting it bodily into the River Irwell, but, I think in the year 1881, they were restrained by injunction at the suit of the Salford corporation from continuing that process, and, not having any land in the immediate neighbourhood of their works which is suitable for storing this refuse, they have taken for the purpose, from the Lancashire and Yorkshire Railway Company, a piece of land comprising three and a half acres, adjoining the Bolton, Bury, and Manchester Canal, which belongs to that company, at Nob End Wharf, which is on the bank of the river, and one mile and 740 yards above the Plaintiff's works. The Plaintiff says that if the Defendants proceed to deposit this refuse on this land, depositing, as they do at the present moment, at the rate of 1000 tons a month, the result will be that, sooner or later, there will necessarily come from the heap a large quantity of this green liquid, which will find its way into the River Irwell, and, finding its way into the river, it will be carried down to his works, and when he pumps the water from the river he will take in with it this chemical matter which will be destructive to his paper. There is no dispute between the parties that in process of time a liquid of that character does come from these heaps. There is no dispute that if any reasonably large quantity of that liquid should find its way into the Plaintiff's bleaching works, that is, if it should be pumped by him from the river into his reservoir, it would be very destructive to his manufacture. But the Defendants say: "You need be under no apprehension. We have not the slightest intention of injuring you; we intend to conduct our works in such a way that no appreciable quantity of that liquid shall find its way into the Irwell, and consequently no appreciable quantity will find its way from our heap into your works."

The hearing of this case was commenced in August last; it was continued in December; and neither in August nor in December was there any allegation that the Plaintiff had, in fact, received any injury from the Defendants' operations. It is admitted that the action is brought, not to obtain damages for a past injury, but to prevent that which is feared as a future injury, or, to use the more technical expression, the action is a *quia timet* action.

. . . I do not think, therefore, that I shall be very far wrong if I lay it down that there are at least two necessary ingredients for a *quia timet* action. There must, if no actual damage is proved, be proof of imminent danger, and there must also be proof that the apprehended damage will, if it comes, be very substantial. I should almost say it must be proved that it will be irreparable, because, if the danger is not proved to be so imminent that no one can doubt that, if the remedy is delayed, the damage will be suffered, I think it must be shewn that, if the damage does occur at any time, it will come in such a way and under such circumstances that it will be impossible for the Plaintiff to protect himself against it if relief is denied to him in a *quia timet* action.

Now the circumstances of the present case are these. In the first place, it is said that, do what the Defendants may, if they proceed to cover, as they propose to do, two acres and a half of the land with this refuse, at the rate of 1000 tons a month, necessarily, although not immediately, there will ooze from the heap a large quantity of this pernicious liquid. Moreover, it is said that, inasmuch as the Defendants have taken a lease of the land from the railway company only for the purpose of depositing this refuse on it, and they have the power of giving up the lease when they have made as much use of the land as they can for the purpose, at the end of ten years, at which time it is reasonably concluded they will have deposited on the land as much of the refuse as it will hold, they will give up the lease, and then the heap will be left without any person whose duty it is to take care of it, and the liquid will continue to ooze out of it for a period of forty or fifty years, or even longer, and the Plaintiff will be under a risk, an increasing risk, certainly a much greater risk than he incurs at the present moment, of having the water of the Irwell polluted, and of pumping into his works the water which is so polluted. The quantity of water which the Plaintiff takes from the Irwell is very large indeed, amounting, I think, sometimes to one-third of the water in the river; 1,000,000 gallons in the twenty-four hours.

Now, if that stood alone, would there be a sufficient ground for a *quia timet* action? I think not. There was some conflict in the evidence as to what amount of the liquid would be sufficient to pollute the water so as to injure the Plaintiff. According to the evidence of the Plaintiff, one gallon in 10,000 would be sufficient to produce injury, and it is also in evidence that, if at the end of ten years there were 120,000 tons of the refuse deposited on the land, there would not be less of the liquid oozing from the heap and capable of getting into the Irwell than one gallon in a little more than 5000, and of course, if one gallon in 10,000 would be injurious, one gallon in 5000 would be highly injurious. But the answer of the Defendants is this. They do not intend that any appreciable amount of this liquid should get into the Irwell, and, inasmuch as it is perfectly practicable, according to all that we know, to prevent the liquid which comes from the heap from getting into the Irwell, I cannot think that at the present moment the evidence on this point is sufficient to justify the Court in interfering. In Attorney-General v. Corporation of Kingston [13 W.R. 888], Wood, V. C., spoke of injurious results at the end of 100 years. If an injury does result in the present case it will result in a much shorter time, and, if the heap were left alone without any protection to the river to prevent the liquid from oozing into it, I have no doubt that at the end of ten years the water would be polluted sufficiently to do a great amount of injury to the Plaintiff. But Wood, V. C., pointed out that in 100 years' time chemical processes might be invented which would prevent the sewage from doing any injury to the River Thames, and I think that in ten years' time it is highly probable that science (which is now at work on the subject) may have discovered some means for rendering this green liquid innocuous. But, even if no such discovery should be made in that time, I cannot help seeing that there are contrivances, such as tanks and pumps, and other things of that kind, by which the liquid may, as the Defendants say, be kept out of the river altogether. Therefore, upon that ground alone, I do not think that the action can be supported.

There is another observation to be made on this point of the case. In the first place I think the danger is not imminent, because it must be some years before any such quantity of the liquid will be found issuing from the heap as would pollute the Irwell to the detriment of the Plaintiff. And, in the next place, if any such quantity of the liquid did get into the river so as to injure the Plaintiff, I think it would be discovered immediately, and it would be perfectly possible for him then to apply to the Court for relief, and to obtain an immediate injunction restraining the Defendants from allowing the liquid to get into the river. For both these reasons I think there is not sufficient in this part of the case to sustain a *quia timet* action.

The next point raised on behalf of the Plaintiff was this: It was said, and with force and truth, that the piece of land upon which the Defendants are depositing their refuse is not level, but is on a considerable slope from the wall of the canal down to the River Irwell. The soil is at the surface loamy gravel; under that is clay, and under that rock. There is very conflicting evidence as to how far there have been slips already, and what probability there is of the land continuing to slip. It was stated by some of the witnesses that the land is full of water. In my opinion the only evidence on which I can rely points to there being one spring of water; of that I think there can be no doubt. There is a spring from which water comes close to the bottom of the tip as it at present stands; it is not yet covered by the heap, but it will be in process of time if the heap is extended, as it seems probable that it will be, and if this water, or any portion of it in the neighbourhood, should get between the clay and the rock, the clay will probably slip and bring everything down with it more or less. It is said that there is so much danger of the heap of refuse being brought down by the shifting and slippery nature of the ground on which it is being deposited, and, if it does come down, of its going bodily into the river, that I ought on this ground alone to grant an injunction. There is another piece of evidence in support of the Plaintiff's case which I have not overlooked. A little further to the east, not immediately adjoining the piece of land which the Defendants have leased from the company, but a little beyond it, are some mills called the Cream Paper Mills, and the evidence of one of the witnesses was as distinct as could be that the tanks which have been made there are perpetually crushing in, and, according to his statement, the land has been slipping for years. On the other hand, with regard to this particular piece of land on which the Defendants' refuse is being tipped, I cannot find from the evidence that any change whatever has taken place at the margin of the river. On the contrary, I am satisfied upon the evidence that there has been no slip of this piece of land such as to alter the contour of the river at that particular spot.

I desire to make two observations upon this evidence. The first is, that, whatever may be the condition of the land in the immediate neighbourhood, I am not satisfied that any slip whatever, or, at all events, any slip of any magnitude, has taken place on this particular piece of land. And, in the next place, I can hardly think, looking at all the evidence, that, if any slip should take place, there would be immediately a slip of such magnitude as, according to the fears of the Plaintiff, would bring the whole heap of refuse at once bodily into the river. I think that, if any slip does take place, there will be some premonitory symptoms which will warn the Plaintiff and the Defendants, and give the Defendants time to do whatever may be necessary to prevent the heap from slipping into the river, and at the same time enable the Plaintiff, if he should think it right to do so, to bring an action against the Defendants on the ground of positive and imminent danger at that time. Moreover, the Defendants say that they propose to do that which their own engineer suggested was necessary, viz., to build a retaining wall along the bank of the river to prevent any slip of the ground. The soil along the bank of the river consists of about fourteen feet of clay over rock. At the bottom of the fourteen feet of clay, which is good puddling clay, you come to the rock, and they propose to build a retaining wall along the margin of the river, which the engineer says will be sufficient to prevent any slip. The evidence on this point was most conflicting, the scientific witnesses on the one side declaring that it was perfectly certain that the land would slip, and that the whole heap would before long be brought down bodily into the river, while the scientific witnesses on the other side were equally confident that the land would never slip, and never had slipped. Under these circumstances I cannot say that any case of such imminent danger on this ground has been made out as would entitle me to interfere.

I would also add that, supposing a slip to take place, supposing that to happen which the Plaintiff fears, viz., that the heap is brought down into the river, if it should be a large heap, and it should all come bodily into the river, I imagine the result would be to choke the river and to create a deluge upon the adjoining lands, and in that event the Plaintiff, being one mile and 740 yards lower down, would get ample notice of it long before the water came to him. He would be able to stop pumping, and the damage which would be done to him would be the loss of the power of working for a certain time, a loss which, I need hardly say, would be easily compensated by money.

The third point taken for the Plaintiff is a very curious one, viz., that the wall of the canal is very likely to come down, and, if it falls, it will bring the heap with it, and it will all go bodily into the river. Now the railway company, who are the owners of the canal, seem, so far as I can judge from the evidence, to have had a great deal of trouble with this wall. The wall, as I gather, has fallen at least three times, once a great many years ago, and twice more recently. It fell, I think, in 1876, and it fell again curiously enough confirming the predictions of the Plaintiff's witnesses, between the month of August, when the trial of this action was commenced, and the month of December, when the hearing was resumed. In August the Defendants' witnesses magnified the beauty and excellence of this wall, and said that it had been built with the greatest possible care at an expense of £20,000, and that it would stand as long as the world lasted. But, notwithstanding, in the month of October, another fall occurred. I think, however, that that fall arose from a temporary accident or blunder. Some alterations were being made in the bank of the canal, and the water was carelessly allowed to get on to the newly-made ground, between the canal and a part of the wall, so as to soak all the new earth, and that, pressing with an enormous weight upon a portion of the new wall, broke it, and carried the débris right across the river. This is the same part of the wall which broke on a former occasion, and it is said that the wall immediately behind the heap, and from which the refuse is tipped over, is in a dangerous condition, and is likely, or, as the Plaintiff would say, is certain to break, as the other part of the wall did, and, if it breaks the result will be that the heap must be carried into the river. I do not know how I am to arrive at any conclusion as to the certainty of the wall breaking. It may or it may not break, and, even if it does break, it may break in such a way as not seriously to move the heap, and I think I may fairly take this into account, that the wall belongs, not to the Defendants, but to the railway company, and is put there for the support and maintenance of the canal which the railway company are bound to maintain. It has been built with the greatest care, and they have spent a large sum of money upon it. It is their interest to keep the wall in as good a condition as possible, because, if that should happen which the Plaintiff fears and predicts, the railway company, as I understand, would have no choice, but would be obliged to replace the wall at any expense. They are bound to keep up the canal, and, if they are careless about the wall, they will put themselves to a most serious loss.

Now, under these circumstances, am I to consider that there is an imminent danger to the Plaintiff, or one which will produce irreparable mischief to him, if it should happen? I am unable to say on the evidence before me that the danger is imminent, because it does not follow that the wall, which has broken twice in a different place, will on the next occasion by a freak of fortune break immediately behind the heap. Nor does it follow that, even if it does break there, it will break to such an extent and in such a way as to carry the heap bodily into the river, for, even on the occasion when it broke, not from what I may call natural causes, but from a blunder, or mismanagement of the canal, a large proportion of the wall was left standing for some distance above the ground, and, if the wall should be left standing for a considerable distance above the ground behind the heap, it does not at all follow that all the mischief which the Plaintiff anticipates would occur. I cannot, therefore, in the present state of things say that the danger on this ground is so imminent as to justify me in granting relief in a *quia timet* action.

I think the Plaintiff has been premature in bringing his action, and that, according to the rules which have been laid down (and I cannot go beyond precedent), I must refuse to grant an injunction, and I believe, according to the practice in these cases, I have no choice but to dismiss the action with costs. But I observe that in Attorney-General v. Corporation of Kingston, Wood, V. C., guarded the dismissal of the information by a declaration of the right of the plaintiff to bring another action thereafter if there should be actual damage, or damage whch he could prove to be imminent or likely to be irreparable. The Vice-Chancellor said: "The proper course would be to dismiss the information, such dismissal being prefaced by a declaration that the Court was of opinion that the evidence did not establish the existence of any nuisance in respect of the works executed, or intended to be executed, by the defendants, or any case for the interference of the Court in respect of nuisance to be apprehended, if such works were carried into effect. The order would be without prejudice to any future proceedings on the part of the Attorney-General in case the works should occasion a nuisance." Though I do not think it is necessary, yet if the Plaintiff's counsel desire it, I have no objection to inserting a similar declaration in the order which I am now making.

Cozens-Hardy said that he wished to have the declaration inserted.

---

1) A bill is the equivalent of today's complaint or the early common law writ. It was used to begin a proceeding in a court of equity. The injunction is a remedy that could be awarded in a proceeding commenced by a bill denominated "bill *quia timet*" (which simply means "he fears"). Story points out that these bills were designed "to accomplish the ends of precautionary justice" and that the injunction was one among several remedies that the court of equity could use to prevent the harm. Rather than issuing an injunction, it might appoint a receiver to receive rents or other income or direct that security to be given or money paid over. 2 Commentaries Equity Jurisprudence as Administered in England and America 154–55 (3rd ed. 1843).

2) Does *Fletcher* stand for the idea that judges avoid hypothetical questions and decide only concrete disputes? Does the result prevent anxious litigants from wasting the judge's time and prestige on something that may never happen? Does the test the judge applies allow him to overlook probabilities and long term consequences? Is dynamite all right so long as the fuse is long? What unspoken premises about the social good and the judicial function seem to inform the judge's decision making?

Could the definition of harm transform the issue of imminence? Is the harm that plaintiff seeks to prevent actual injury or exposure to the risk of injury occurring? The court suggests that the imminence and inadequacy requirements are connected: the more the court is able to compensate for injury, if it ever occurs, the more willing the court will be to force the plaintiff to risk future uncertainties. But in applying this test, does the court define the harm correctly? See generally Leubsdorf, Remedies for Uncertainty, 61 B.U.L.Rev. 132 (1981).

If the anticipated harm occurs, can the judge compensate the plaintiff in money? Will the alkali manufacturers be able to pay for all the damage their vat waste may cause? Will compensation be difficult to compute? Considerations like the foregoing led modern legislatures to pass legislation for hazardous substances. The Resource Conservation and Recovery Act, 42 U.S.C. §§ 6901–6986, allows the government to sue to enjoin activities involving hazardous waste. The Comprehensive Environmental Response, Compensation and Liability Act (Superfund) allows the government either to use administrative and judicial orders to force polluters to clean up or to undertake the job itself with money from the fund and recover from responsible parties. 42 U.S.C. §§ 9601–9657. Private plaintiffs may resort to a formidable array of tort theories, and class actions are available for group damage litigation without regard to these statutes.

3) The ripeness issue in large part turns on the specific terms of the injunction sought. Take, for example, the risk of the mud sliding into the river. Could the plaintiff have sought an injunction that would have served his needs—eased his fears—and yet avoided the ripeness problems? Would the court have granted such an injunction?

RESERVE MINING CO. v. ENVIRONMENTAL PROTECTION AGENCY

514 F.2d 492 (8th Cir.1975).

Before LAY, BRIGHT, ROSS, STEPHENSON and WEBSTER, Circuit Judges, En Banc.

BRIGHT, Circuit Judge.

The United States, the States of Michigan, Wisconsin, and Minnesota, and several environmental groups seek an injunction ordering Reserve Mining Company[1] to cease discharging wastes from its iron ore processing plant in Silver Bay, Minnesota, into the ambient air of Silver Bay and the waters of Lake Superior. On April 20, 1974, the district court granted the requested relief and ordered that the discharges immediately cease, thus effectively closing the plant. United States v. Reserve Mining Co., 380 F.Supp. 11 (D.Minn.1974). Reserve Mining Company appealed that order and we stayed the injunction pending resolution of the merits of the appeal. Reserve Mining Co. v. United States, 498 F.2d 1073 (8th Cir. 1974). We affirm the injunction but direct modification of its terms. As to other issues brought before us by appeals during the course of this complex litigation, we affirm in part and reverse in part.

In this lengthy opinion, we undertake a comprehensive analysis of the relevant scientific and medical testimony and evaluate the claims of the plaintiffs that Reserve's conduct violates express provisions of federal law as well as the state laws and regulations and is a public nuisance.

We summarize our key rulings as follows:

1) The United States and the other plaintiffs have established that Reserve's discharges into the air and water give rise to a potential threat to the public health. The risk to public health is of sufficient gravity to be legally cognizable and calls for an abatement order on reasonable terms.

2) The United States and Minnesota have shown that Reserve's discharges violate federal and state laws and state pollution control regulations, also justifying injunctive relief on equitable terms.

3) No harm to the public health has been shown to have occurred to this date and the danger to health is not imminent. The evidence calls for pre-

1. Reserve Mining Company is a jointly owned subsidiary of Armco Steel Corporation and Republic Steel Corporation. The district court joined these parent corporations as parties to this lawsuit at an advanced state of the litigation. . . . Generally we shall make reference only to Reserve, the original defendant.

The following environmental groups intervened as plaintiffs on June 15, 1972, by order of the district court: The Minnesota Environmental Law Institute, the Northern Environmental Council, the Save Lake Superior Association, and the Michigan Student Environmental Confederation. United States v. Reserve Mining Co., 56 F.R.D. 408 (D.Minn.1972). The Environmental Defense Fund intervened pursuant to the court's order of July 31, 1973, and the Sierra Club has filed an amicus curiae brief on behalf of the plaintiffs.

Numerous parties have intervened as defendants. They include the Northeastern Minnesota Development Association, the Duluth Area Chamber of Commerce, the Towns of Silver Bay, Babbitt, and Beaver Bay, and several other civic and governmental units in the area of the Reserve facility. The United Steelworkers of America has submitted an amicus curiae brief on behalf of the defendants.

ventive and precautionary steps. No reason exists which requires that Reserve terminate its operations at once.

4) Reserve, with its parent companies Armco Steel and Republic Steel, is entitled to a reasonable opportunity and a reasonable time period to convert its Minnesota taconite operations to on-land disposal of taconite tailings and to restrict air emissions at its Silver Bay plant, or to close its existing Minnesota taconite-pelletizing operations. The parties are required to expedite consideration and resoluton of these alternatives.

5) The evidence suggests that the threat to public health from the air emissions is more significant than that from the water discharge. Consequently, Reserve must take reasonable immediate steps to reduce its air emissions.

In 1947, Reserve Mining Company (Reserve), then contemplating a venture in which it would mine low-grade iron ore ("taconite") present in Minnesota's Mesabi Iron Range and process the ore into iron-rich pellets at facilities bordering on Lake Superior, received a permit from the State of Minnesota to discharge the wastes (called "tailings") from its processing operations into the lake.

Reserve commenced the processing of taconite ore in Silver Bay, Minnesota, in 1955, and that operation continues today. Taconite mined near Babbitt, Minnesota, is shipped by rail some 47 miles to the Silver Bay "beneficiating" plant where it is concentrated into pellets containing some 65 percent iron ore. The process involves crushing the taconite into fine granules, separating out the metallic iron with huge magnets, and flushing the residual tailings into Lake Superior. The tailings enter the lake as a slurry of approximately 1.5 percent solids. The slurry acts as a heavy density current bearing the bulk of the suspended particles to the lake bottom. In this manner, approximately 67,000 tons of tailings are discharged daily.

The states and the United States commenced efforts to procure abatement of these discharges as early as mid-1969. These efforts, however, produced only an unsuccessful series of administrative conferences and unsuccessful state court proceedings. The instant litigation commenced on February 2, 1972, when the United States—joined eventually by the States of Minnesota, Wisconsin, and Michigan and by various environmental groups—filed a complaint alleging that Reserve's discharge of tailings into Lake Superior violated § 407 of the Rivers and Harbors Act of 1899 [33 U.S.C. § 401 et seq. (1970)], § 1160 of the pre-1972 Federal Water Pollution Control Act (FWPCA) [33 U.S.C. § 1151 et seq. (1970)] and the federal common law of public nuisance.

Until June 8, 1973, the case was essentially a water pollution abatement case, but on that date the focus of the controversy shifted to the public health impact of the tailings discharge and Reserve's emissions into the ambient air. Arguing the health issue in the district court, plaintiffs maintained that the taconite ore mined by Reserve contained an asbestiform variety of the amphibole mineral cummingtonite-grunerite, and that the processing of the ore resulted in the discharge into the air and water of mineral fibers substantially identical and in some instances identical to amosite asbestos. This contention raised an immediate health issue, since inhalation of asbestos at occupational levels of exposure is associated with an increased incidence of various forms of cancer.

Although it is undisputed that Reserve discharges significant amounts of waste tailings into Lake Superior and dust into the Silver Bay air, the parties vigorously contest the precise physical properties of the discharges, their biological effects, and, with respect to the water discharge, the issue of whether a significant proportion of the discharge, instead of flowing to the lake bottom with the density current, disperses throughout the lake. Plaintiffs attempted to show that a substantial amount of the fibers discharged by Reserve could be classified as amosite asbestos, and that these fibers could be traced in the ambient air of Silver Bay and surrounding communities and in the drinking water of Duluth and other communities drawing water from the lake. Reserve countered that its cummingtonite-grunerite does not have a fibrous form and is otherwise distinguishable from amosite asbestos. It further maintained that the discharges do not pose any cognizable hazard to health and that, in any event, with respect to the discharge into water, the tailings largely settle to the bottom of the lake in the "great trough" area as initially planned.

The evidence presented on these points was extensive and complex. Hearings on a motion for a preliminary injunction were consolidated with the trial on the merits and during the nine-month period of 139 days of trial, the trial court heard more than 100 witnesses and received over 1,600 exhibits. The parties introduced testimony comparing the mineralogy of Reserve's cummingtonite-grunerite with amosite asbestos, such testimony based on electron microscope analysis of morphology, x-ray and electron diffraction analysis of crystal structure, laboratory analysis of chemical composition, and other identification techniques. As for the possible dispersion of the tailings throughout Lake Superior, witnesses disputed whether Reserve's discharges provided the sole source of cummingtonite-grunerite in the lake and whether the presence of the mineral could thus be used as a "tracer" for Reserve's discharge. In an effort to assess the health hazard, the parties presented extensive expert scientific and medical testimony, and the court itself appointed certain expert witnesses, who assumed the task of assisting the court in the evaluation of scientific testimony and supervising court-sponsored studies to measure the levels of asbestos fibers in the air near Silver Bay, in Lake Superior water, and in the tissues of deceased Duluth residents.

On April 20, 1974, the district court entered an order closing Reserve's Silver Bay facility. In an abbreviated memorandum opinion, the court held that Reserve's water discharge violated federal water pollution laws and that its air emissions violated state air pollution regulations, and that both the air and water discharges constituted common law nuisances. The court's decision, in part, rested on these core findings:

> The discharge into the air substantially endangers the health of the people of Silver Bay and surrounding communities as far away as the eastern shore in Wisconsin.
>
> The discharge into the water substantially endangers the health of people who procure their drinking water from the western arm of Lake Superior including the communities of Beaver Bay, Two Harbors, Cloquet, Duluth [Minnesota], and Superior, Wisconsin.

The district court issued an extensive supplemental memorandum on May 11, 1974, expanding on its earlier findings of fact and conclusions of law. In proceedings detailed in the following section of this opinion, a panel of this court stayed the injunction and subsequently requested the district court to fully dispose of the litigation and enter final judgment. This court, sitting *en banc*, heard the merits of several consolidated appeals at the December 1974 session. We have also taken under consideration other appeals which have been subsequently submitted to us on briefs, but without oral argument. Our disposition follows.

In its memorandum opinions of April 20, and May 11, ordering Reserve to cease immediately its discharges into the air and water, the district court predicated its determinations on several counts. On the discharge into water, the court found a violation of several sections of the Minnesota water quality standards. . . . Further, the court found that the discharge into Lake Superior endangered the health and welfare of persons in Minnesota, Wisconsin, and Michigan and therefore was subject to abatement pursuant to §§ 1160(c)(5) and (g)(1) of the FWPCA. Finally, the court found that the endangerment to health also constituted both a federal common law nuisance and a nuisance under the applicable laws of Minnesota, Wisconsin, and Michigan.

As for the air emissions, the court also found liability under both federal and state common law nuisance. Additionally, the court cited Reserve for the violation of several Minnesota air pollution control regulations . . . .

The trial court based its closure decision on two independent determinations. First, as noted above, the court had concluded that the discharges "substantially endanger" the exposed populations. Second, the court had concluded that, although a method of abatement providing for an alternate means of disposal of wastes with some turn-around time represented a desirable middle course in this litigation,[14] Reserve had demonstrated such intransigence on the issue of abating its water discharge as to render any such middle course impossible. The court thus believed it had no alternative but to immediately enjoin the discharges:

"Defendants have the economic and engineering capability to carry out an on land disposal system that satisfies the health and environmental considerations raised. For reasons unknown to this Court they have chosen not to implement such a plan. In essence they have decided to continue exposing thousands daily to a substantial health risk in order to maintain the current profitability of the present operation and delay the capital outlay (with its concomitant profit) [sic] needed to institute modifications. The Court has no other alternative but to order an immediate halt to the discharge which threatens the lives of thousands. In that defendants have no plan to make the

14. The court observed that it would like to find a middle ground that would satisfy both considerations. If an alternate method of disposal is available that is economically feasible, could be speedily implemented and took into consideration the health questions involved, the Court might be disposed to fashion a remedy that would permit the implementation of such a system. However, if there is no alternative method available, the Court has no other choice but to immediately curtail the discharge and stop the contamination of the water supply of those downstream from the plant.

necessary modifications, there is no reason to delay any further the issuance of the injunction."

Reserve promptly appealed the injunction order of the district court and we issued a temporary stay of that order on April 22, 1974, and scheduled a hearing on Reserve's application for a stay of injunction pending its appeal. That hearing was held on May 15, 1974, before a panel of this court consisting of Judges Bright, Ross, and Webster, and on June 4, 1974, the court issued an opinion granting Reserve a 70-day stay of the injunction. . . . The court conditioned the stay upon Reserve taking prompt steps to abate its air and water discharges, and provided for further proceedings to review whether Reserve had proceeded with the good faith preparation and implementation of an acceptable plan.

The State of Minnesota applied to the Supreme Court to vacate this stay. The Court denied Minnesota this relief in an order entered July 9, 1974. Minnesota v. Reserve Mining Co., 418 U.S. 911 (1974). Meanwhile, in accordance with the stay order, the district court evaluated compliance with our order that Reserve proceed in good faith to present a plan of abatement. In a memorandum opinion filed August 3, 1974, [380 F.Supp. 11, 71 (D.Minn. 1974)] the district court, taking cognizance of the opposition of the State of Minnesota to Reserve's proffered plan (the so-called Palisades Plan), rejected Reserve's proposal as unreasonable and recommended against any further stay during the pendency of this litigation. Also, pursuant to our earlier request for advice on the status of unresolved claims, the district court indicated that it had "severed for later resolution the issue of the biological effect of Reserve's discharge on the Lake itself" and that several other issues remained under advisement. . . .

Following hearings, this court entered an order continuing the stay. . . .

Minnesota and the United States applied to the Supreme Court for relief from this further stay order. The Court denied the applications, with Mr. Justice Douglas dissenting. Minnesota v. Reserve Mining Co., 419 U.S. 802 (1974).

On October 18, 1974, the district court issued an unpublished memorandum resolving certain other issues in the case and, noting that there was no just reason for delay, directing the entry of final judgment on all claims decided to date. See Fed.R.Civ.P. 54(b). . . .

During oral arguments and by written submissions, Reserve has advised us that it no longer asks Minnesota to accept its plan to dispose taconite tailings at the Palisades location, ... Reserve has now submitted a second proposal to Minnesota for an on-land disposal site in which it proposes to spend approximately $243,000,000 in order to end its discharge of tailings into Lake Superior and curtail its emission of contaminants into the air. This proposed site, which Minnesota has under consideration, is located approximately seven miles inland from the Silver Bay facility, and is referred to as Milepost 7, or Lax Lake site.

The initial, crucial question for our evaluation and resolution focuses upon the alleged hazard to public health attributable to Reserve's discharges into the air and water.

We first considered this issue on Reserve's application for a stay of the district court's injunction pending a determination of the merits of its appeal. We noted the usual formulation of the applicable standards to be met by the party seeking a stay. One of those standards addresses the likelihood of success by the moving party on the merits of the appeal. In applying this standard we made a preliminary assessment of the merits of Reserve's appeal from the trial court's injunction order. We noted that the "rather drastic remedy ordered by the district court . . . was a response to the finding of a substantial danger to the public health," and that our preliminary assessment of whether such a substantial danger was presented "should control our action as to whether to grant or deny a stay." . . .

In this preliminary review, we did not view the evidence as supporting a finding of substantial danger. We noted numerous uncertainties in plaintiffs' theory of harm which controlled our assessment, particularly the uncertainty as to present levels of exposure and the difficulty in attempting to quantify those uncertain levels in terms of a demonstrable health hazard. As we stated then, ". . . it is not known what the level of fiber exposure is, other than that it is relatively low, and it is not known what level of exposure is safe or unsafe." . . . In confirmation of our view, we noted the opinion of Dr. Arnold Brown, the principal court-appointed expert, that no adverse health consequences could be scientifically predicted on the basis of existing medical knowledge. Additionally, we noted the district court's conclusion that there is " '. . . insufficient knowledge upon which to base an opinion as to the magnitude of the risks associated with this exposure.' " . . . We thought one proposition evident:

"[A]lthough Reserve's discharges represent a possible medical danger, they have not in this case been proven to amount to a health hazard. The discharges may or may not result in detrimental health effects, but, for the present, that is simply unknown."

On the basis of the foregoing we forecast that Reserve would likely prevail on the merits of the health issue. We limited this forecast to the single issue before us whether Reserve's plant should be closed immediately because of a "substantial danger" to health:

"While not called upon at this stage to reach any final conclusion, our review suggests that this evidence does not support a finding of *substantial danger* and that, indeed, the testimony indicates that such a finding should not be made. *In this regard*, we conclude that Reserve appears likely to succeed on the merits of its appeal on the health issue. . . . " (Emphasis added).

We reached no preliminary decision on whether the facts justified a less stringent abatement order.

As will be evident from the discussion that follows, we adhere to our preliminary assessment that the evidence is insufficient to support the kind of demonstrable danger to the public health that would justify the immediate closing of Reserve's operations. . . .

As we noted in our stay opinion, much of the scientific knowledge regarding asbestos disease pathology derives from epidemiological studies of asbestos workers occupationally exposed to and inhaling high levels of asbestos dust. Studies of workers naturally exposed to asbestos dust have shown "excess" cancer deaths and a significant incidence of asbestosis. The principal excess cancers are cancer of the lung, the pleura (mesothelioma) and gastrointestinal tract ("gi" cancer). . . .

The comparability of the nature of Reserve's discharge to the nature of the discharge in known disease situations raises two principal questions. The first is whether the discharged fibers are identical or substantially identical to fibers known to cause disease; the second is whether the length of the fibers discharged is a relevant factor in assessing pathogenic effect. The district court found that Reserve's discharge includes known pathogenic fibers and that a lower risk to health could not be assigned to this discharge for reasons of fiber length. . . .

The second major step in the inquiry of the health aspects of Reserve's air emissions is an assessment of the amount of the discharge and the resulting level of exposure. Two principal issues are raised: first, what in fact is the level of exposure; second, does that level present a cognizable risk to health? The district court found the level "significant" and comparable to the levels associated with disease in nonoccupational contexts. . . .

Given the presence of excess fibers, we must now assess the effects of this exposure on the public. We note first, as we did in the stay opinion, that the exposure here cannot be equated with the factory exposures which have been clearly linked to excess cancers and asbestosis. Our inquiry, however, does not end there. Asbestos-related disease, as noted earlier, has been associated with exposure levels considerably less than normal occupational exposure. The studies indicating that mesothelioma is associated with the lower levels of exposure typical of residence near an asbestos mine or mill or in the household of an asbestos worker are of significance. Although these studies do not possess the methodological strengths of the occupational studies, they must be considered in the medical evaluation of Reserve's discharge into the air. . . .

Plaintiffs' hypothesis that Reserve's air emissions represent a significant threat to the public health touches numerous scientific disciplines, and an overall evaluation demands broad scientific understanding. We think it significant that Dr. Brown, an impartial witness whose court-appointed task was to address the health issue in its entirety, joined with plaintiffs' witnesses in viewing as reasonable the hypothesis that Reserve's discharges present a threat to public health. Although, as we noted in our stay opinion, Dr. Brown found the evidence insufficient to make a scientific probability statement as to whether adverse health consequences would in fact ensue, he expressed a public health concern over the continued long-term emission of fibers into the air. We quote his testimony at some length.

"[Dr. Brown]. Based on the scientific evidence, I would be unable to predict that the number of fibers in the air of Silver Bay, as seen on four days in October, that I would be unable to predict that cancer would be found in Silver Bay.

"Now, going beyond that, it seems to me that speaking now in general terms, where it has been shown that a known human carcinogen, sir, and I make that distinction and I shall make it again, I suspect, a human carcinogen is in the air of any community, and if it could be lowered I would say, as a physician that, yes, it should be lowered. And if it could be taken out of the air completely, I would be even more happy.

"But the presence of a known, human carcinogen, sir, is in my view cause for concern, and if there are means of removing that human carcinogen from the environment, that should then be done."

He explained further:

"As a physician, I take the view that I cannot consider, with equanimity, the fact that a known human carcinogen is in the environment. If I knew more about that human carcinogen, if I knew what a safe level was in the air, if I knew what a safe level was in the water, then I could draw some firm conclusions and advise you in precise terms. That information is not available to me and I submit, sir, it's not available to anyone else. And that until that information is developed in a scientific way, using techniques that would be acceptable to the medical community, until that time has arrived, then I take only the view that I have expressed. . . .

"But with asbestos, . . . we're dealing with a different situation, we're dealing with a material which is known to cause cancer not only in animals but in humans. . . ."

Finally, in a post-trial deposition taken December 6, 1974, which the parties have stipulated may be considered by this court, Dr. Brown further testified:

"Q [Mr. Bastow, attorney for the United States]. [I]s there any question in your mind that the people living on the North Shore are being exposed to a human carcinogen in the air and water? . . .

"A [Dr. Brown]. Court studies demonstrated to my satisfaction that similar [asbestiform] fibers are present in the air of Silver Bay and since I am convinced that asbestiform fibers are carcinogenic for humans, my answer to your question would be yes."

He added:

"I took some pains to also say that it was my medical opinion that the presence of a human carcinogen in the air and water was not to be taken lightly . . . . Until I know what the safe level is I therefore could not, as a physician, consider with equanimity the fact that they are being exposed to a human carcinogen."

The claim that Reserve's discharge of tailings into Lake Superior causes a hazard to public health raises many of the same uncertainties present with respect to the discharge into air. . . . In two respects, however, the discharge into water raises added uncertainties: first, whether the ingestion of fibers, as compared with their inhalation, poses any danger whatsoever; and second, should ingestion pose a danger, whether the exposure resulting from Reserve's discharge may be said to present a legally cognizable risk to health. . . .

Recognizing the complete lack of any direct evidence (epidemiological or otherwise) on the issue of whether the ingestion of fibers poses a risk, the trial court directed that a tissue study be conducted to determine whether the tissues of long-time Duluth residents contain any residue of asbestoslike fibers. . . .

The district court decided, and we agree, that the study cannot be deemed conclusive in exonerating the ingestion of fibers in Lake Superior water as a hazard. The negative results must, however, be given some weight in assessing the probabilities of harm from Reserve's discharge into water. The results also weigh heavily in indicating that no emergency or imminent hazard to health exists. Thus, while this study crucially bears on the determination of whether it is necessary to close Reserve down immediately, the negative results do not dispose of the broader issue of whether the ingestion of fibers poses some danger to public health justifying abatement on less immediate terms. . . .

These concepts of potential harm, whether they be assessed as "probabilities and consequences" or "risk and harm," necessarily must apply in a determination of whether any relief should be given in cases of this kind in which proof with certainty is impossible. The district court, although not following a precise probabilities-consequences analysis, did consider the medical and scientific evidence bearing on both the probability of harm and the consequences should the hypothesis advanced by the plaintiffs prove to be valid.

In assessing probabilities in this case, it cannot be said that the probability of harm is more likely than not. Moreover, the level of probability does not readily convert into a prediction of consequences. On this record it cannot be forecast that the rates of cancer will increase from drinking Lake Superior water or breathing Silver Bay air. The best that can be said is that the existence of this asbestos contaminant in air and water gives rise to a reasonable medical concern for the public health. The public's exposure to asbestos fibers in air and water creates some health risk. Such a contaminant should be removed.

As we demonstrate in the following sections of the opinion, the existence of this risk to the public justifies an injunction decree requiring abatement of the health hazard on reasonable terms as a precautionary and preventive measure to protect the public health. . . .

We turn now to Minnesota's claims that its laws are being violated by Reserve's air discharge. In ordering, on April 20, 1974, an immediate cessation of air discharges containing amosite asbestos, the district court relied upon violations by Reserve of APC 5, 6, and 17—regulations published by the Minnesota Pollution Control Agency pursuant to Minn.Stat.Ann. § 116.07—and the state's public nuisance law which is formulated at Minn.Stat.Ann. § 609.74(1). 380 F.Supp. at 17. Subsequently, Minnesota amended its complaint under Fed.R.Civ.P. 15(b) to allege violations of APC 1 and 3, and Minn.Stat.Ann. § 116.081(1) relating to air emission permits. Because the district court held that Reserve's discharge also violates these provisions, . . . we also examine whether these alleged violations provide alternative or additional grounds for injunctive relief.

The district court observed that studies of suspended particulate matter in the air over Silver Bay for the months of July through October 1972 disclosed only isolated instances of violation of the primary and secondary air quality standards of APC 1.

The court noted, however, that

"the data introduced at trial, . . . reveals that since October 1972 there has been a marked increase in the number of days in which the secondary standard was exceeded and several days in which the primary standard was exceeded." [Order of Oct. 18, 1974, at 14–15.]

On the basis of this evidence, the court properly held that Reserve was in violation of APC 1.

APC 5 limits the emission of particulate matter from industrial processes. Generally, it prohibits the operation of an existing emission source unless it has filtration equipment with a collection efficiency of 99 percent by weight. The district court found, and Reserve does not deny, that its present methods of filtration fail to comply with this standard.

APC 3(a)(2)(bb) requires that a person "operating an existing installation which is a source of air contaminants and air pollution shall apply for an operating permit." Minn.Stat.Ann. § 116.081(1) makes unlawful the operation of an "emission facility" without a permit from the Minnesota Pollution Control Agency. The district court properly held that Reserve is in violation of both APC 3 and Minn.Stat.Ann. § 116.081(1) by its failure to obtain a permit for its emissions into the air of Silver Bay. . . .

As we have demonstrated, Reserve's air and water discharges pose a danger to the public health and justify judicial action of a preventive nature.

In fashioning relief in a case such as this involving a possibility of future harm, a court should strike a proper balance between the benefits conferred and the hazards created by Reserve's facility. In its pleadings Reserve directs our attention to the benefits arising from its operations, as found by a Minnesota state district court, as follows:

"In reliance upon the State and Federal permits as contemplated by [Reserve] and the agencies issuing the permits prior to such issuance [Reserve] constructed its plant at Silver Bay, Minnesota. [Reserve] also developed the Villages of Babbitt and Silver Bay and their schools and other necessary facilities where many of [Reserve's] employees live with their families, as do the merchants, doctors, teachers and so forth who serve them. [Reserve's] capital investment exceeds $350,000,000. As of June 30, 1970 [Reserve] had 3,367 employees. During the calendar year 1969, its total payroll was approximately $31,700,000; and it expended the sum of $27,400,000 for the purchase of supplies and paid state and local taxes amounting to $4,250,000. [Reserve's] annual production of 10,000,000 tons of taconite pellets represents approximately two-thirds of the required pellets used by Armco and Republic Steel, the sole owners of Reserve, 15% of the production of the Great Lakes [ore] and about 12% of the total production of the United States. Between four and six people are supported by each job in the mining industry, including those directly involved in the mining industry and those employed in directly and indirectly related fields. . . ."

We understand that plaintiffs do not deny these allegations.

The district court justified its immediate closure of Reserve's facility by characterizing Reserve's discharges as "substantially" endangering the health of persons breathing air and drinking water containing the asbestos-like fibers contained in Reserve's discharges. The term "substantially" in no way measures the danger in terms of either probabilities or consequences. Yet such an assessment seems essential in fashioning a judicial remedy.

Concededly, the trial court considered many appropriate factors in arriving at a remedy, such as a) the nature of the anticipated harm, b) the burden on Reserve and its employees from the issuance of the injunction, c) the financial ability of Reserve to convert to other methods of waste disposal, and d) a margin of safety for the public.[83]

An additional crucial element necessary for a proper assessment of the health hazard rests upon a proper analysis of the probabilities of harm. . . . Gelpe & Tarlock, The Uses of Scientific Information in Environmental Decisionmaking, 48 S.Cal.L.Rev. 371, 412–427 (1974).

With respect to the water, these probabilities must be deemed low for they do not rest on a history of past health harm attributable to ingestion but on a medical theory implicating the ingestion of asbestos fibers as a causative factor in increasing the rates of gastrointestinal cancer among asbestos workers. With respect to air, the assessment of the risk of harm rests on a higher degree of proof, a correlation between inhalation of asbestos dust and subsequent illness. But here, too, the hazard cannot be measured in terms of predictability, but the assessment must be made without direct proof. But, the hazard in both the air and water can be measured in only the most general terms as a concern for the public health resting upon a reasonable medical theory. Serious consequences could result if the hypothesis on which it is based should ultimately prove true.

A court is not powerless to act in these circumstances. But an immediate injunction cannot be justified in striking a balance between unpredictable health effects and the clearly predictable social and economic consequences that would follow the plant closing.

In addition to the health risk posed by Reserve's discharges, the district court premised its immediate termination of the discharges upon Reserve's persistent refusal to implement a reasonable alternative plan for on-land disposal of tailings. . . .

During these appeal proceedings, Reserve has indicated its willingness to deposit its tailings on land and to properly filter its air emissions. At oral argument, Reserve advised us of a willingness to spend 243 million dollars in plant alterations and construction to halt its pollution of air and water. Reserve's offer to continue operations and proceed to construction of land disposal facilities for its tailings, if permitted to do so by the State of Minnesota, when viewed in conjunction with the uncertain quality of the health risk created by Reserve's discharges, weighs heavily against a ruling which closes Reserve's plant immediately.

Indeed, the intervening union argues, with some persuasiveness, that ill health effects resulting from the prolonged unemployment of the head of the family on a closing of the Reserve facility may be more certain than the harm from drinking Lake Superior water or breathing Silver Bay air.

83. See Note, Imminent Irreparable Injury: A Need For Reform, 45 S.Cal.L. Rev. 1025 (1972).

Furthermore, Congress has generally geared its national environmental policy to allowing polluting industries a reasonable period of time to make adjustments in their efforts to conform to federal standards. See, e.g., Federal Water Pollution Control Act, 33 U.S.C. § 1160 (1970); Clean Air Act, 42 U.S.C. §§ 1857c–5 to –8 (1970); National Environmental Policy Act, 42 U.S.C. § 4331 (1970). In the absence of an imminent hazard to health or welfare, any other program for abatement of pollution would be inherently unreasonable and invite great economic and social disruption. Some pollution and ensuing environmental damage are, unfortunately, an inevitable concomitant of a heavily industrialized economy. In the absence of proof of a reasonable risk of imminent or actual harm, a legal standard requiring immediate cessation of industrial operations will cause unnecessary economic loss, including unemployment, and, in a case such as this, jeopardize a continuing domestic source of critical metals without conferring adequate countervailing benefits.

We believe that on this record the district court abused its discretion by immediately closing this major industrial plant. In this case, the risk of harm to the public is potential, not imminent or certain, and Reserve says it earnestly seeks a practical way to abate the pollution. A remedy should be fashioned which will serve the ultimate public weal by insuring clean air, clean water, and continued jobs in an industry vital to the nation's welfare. . . .

Reserve must be given a reasonable opportunity and a reasonable time to construct facilities to accomplish an abatement of its pollution of air and water and the health risk created thereby. In this way, hardship to employees and great economic loss incident to an immediate plant closing may be avoided. *See* Georgia v. Tennessee Copper Co., 206 U.S. 230, 239 (1907). . . .

We cannot ignore, however, the potential for harm in Reserve's discharges. This potential imparts a degree of urgency to this case that would otherwise be absent from an environmental suit in which ecological pollution alone were proved. Thus, any authorization of Reserve to continue operations during conversion of its facilities to abate the pollution must be circumscribed by realistic time limitations. Accordingly, we direct that the injunction order be modified as follows.

Reserve shall be given a reasonable time to stop discharging its wastes into Lake Superior. A reasonable time includes the time necessary for Minnesota to act on Reserve's present application to dispose of its tailings at Milepost 7 (Lax Lake site), or to come to agreement on some other site acceptable to both Reserve and the state. Assuming agreement and designation of an appropriate land disposal site, Reserve is entitled to a reasonable turnaround time to construct the necessary facilities and accomplish a changeover in the means of disposing of its taconite wastes.

We cannot now precisely measure this time. Minnesota must assume the obligation of acting with great expedition in ruling on Reserve's pending application or otherwise determining that it shall, or that it shall not, afford a site acceptable to Reserve. We suggest, but do not determine, that with expedited procedures a final administrative decision should be reached within one year after a final appellate decision in this case. . . .

Pending final action by Minnesota on the present permit application, Reserve must promptly take all steps necessary to comply with Minnesota law applicable to its air emissions, as outlined in this opinion.

Reserve, at a minimum, must comply with [Minnesota law] 5. Furthermore, Reserve must use such available technology as will reduce the asbestos fiber count in the ambient air at Silver Bay below a medically significant level. According to the record in this case, controls may be deemed adequate which will reduce the fiber count to the level ordinarily found in the ambient air of a control city such as St. Paul.[85]

We wish to make it clear that we view the air emission as presenting a hazard of greater significance than the water discharge. Accordingly, pending a determination of whether Reserve will be allowed to construct an on-land disposal site or will close its operations, Reserve must immediately proceed with the planning and implementation of such emission controls as may be reasonably and practically effectuated under the circumstances. We direct that the injunction decree incorporate ¶ B2 of the stipulation between Reserve and Minnesota relating to air emissions, reading as follows:

"However, if following final court or administrative agency action relating to the existing discharge to Lake Superior, Reserve decides to substantially suspend or reduce, or to discontinue, its pelletizing operations at Silver Bay then Reserve, upon giving reasonable notice, shall be relieved from further implementation of the compliance program scheduled in this Stipulation, provided that the Agency may reasonably retain such conditions of this Stipulation, or reasonably impose such other or modified conditions as may be appropriate in connection with such suspension, reduction or discontinuance of operations. . . . "

Assuming that Reserve is granted the necessary permits to build an on-land disposal site, the existing stipulation between Minnesota and Reserve relating to air emissions, subject to modification because of litigation delay to this date, shall serve as a general guideline for time requirements on air controls. If the parties are unable to come to an accord for a time-table for installation of emission controls based upon the stipulation agreement, either Minnesota or Reserve may apply to the district court for an appropriate order to supplement the injunction decree in conformity with the views expressed here. We reserve jurisdiction to review any such supplemental order.

We believe some additional directions will be helpful to the district court in fashioning its decree in conformity with this opinion. The matters of fur-

85. We here order Reserve to meet a court-fashioned standard which may exceed the standards of existing air pollution control regulations, excepting APC 17. The Minnesota Pollution Control Agency may condition issuance of a permit for the emission of air contaminants or the operation of an emission facility, such as the Reserve plant, upon the prevention of air pollution. Minn.Stat.Ann. § 116.07(4a). Minnesota defines air pollution as

". . . the presence in the outdoor atmosphere of any air contaminant or combination thereof in such quantity, of such nature and duration, and under such conditions as *would be injurious to human health or welfare* . . . ." [Minn.Stat. Ann. § 116.06(3) (emphasis added).]

By this injunction we impose upon Reserve the duty not only to comply with APC 1 and 5 but also to take additional steps, if any are necessary, to abate its air pollution within the meaning of Minn. Stat.Ann. § 116.06(3). The broad remedial policy behind Minnesota's pollution control laws authorizes injunctive relief of this scope. See Minn.Stat.Ann. § 115.071(4).

nishing Reserve with an on-land disposal site and issuing necessary permits relevant to the air and water discharges are governed by provisions of Minnesota state law. See Minn.Stat.Ann. §§ 116.07(4a) and 115.05 (Supp.1974). The resolution of the controversy over an on-land disposal site does not fall within the jurisdiction of the federal courts.[87] Moreover, it follows that neither Michigan, Wisconsin, nor the environmental groups have any right of participation in that decision-making process except as may be otherwise provided by Minnesota law.[88]

Although we requested the district court to resolve all issues before it, the court reserved the question of possible fines and penalties against Reserve, stating that

"the Court has some discretion in the matter and it is this Court's view that it is not in a position to evaluate the equities until it is apprised of the course of action defendants must take in order to come into compliance with applicable law. . . ."

Unfortunately, it is possible that some parties may read this statement as a veiled threat that, if Reserve closes its plant rather than acquiesces to Minnesota's proposals for an on-land site for tailings disposal which Reserve deems unsuitable, the district court will levy substantial fines and penalties against it. While we are quite sure the district court intended no such implication and would not use its judicial power for such an improper purpose, we believe it is proper to comment that Reserve is free to close its operation if it cannot practicably meet Minnesota's requirements for an on-land disposal site without the fear of substantial fines and penalties being levied against it because of this election.

Upon remand, we suggest that the district court request Dr. Brown to advise the court concerning new scientific or medical studies which may require a reevaluation of the health hazard (either as more or less serious than as apprehended during this lawsuit) attributable to Reserve's discharges. A similar request should also be posed to Dr. Selikoff and his group of researchers. Either party may apply for a modification of the time requirements specified herein should significant new scientific information justify a reassessment of the hazard to public health.

Additionally, the district court should take proper steps to ensure that filtered water remains available in affected communities to the same extent as is now provided by the Corps of Engineers, although not necessarily at the expense of the Corps.

87. We note that both the district court and this court have sought to encourage a settlement among the parties on an on-land disposal site. While these efforts were judicially proper during the course of the litigation, upon entry of a judgment in this case the federal courts must permit the State of Minnesota and Reserve to resolve the question of an on-land disposal site under the appropriate state procedures.

88. Minnesota, of course, in ruling upon any proposed on-land disposal site must abide by the basic principles of due process of law. Should Minnesota, acting in an arbitrary and capricious manner, deny Reserve a permit for an on-land disposal site, thus forcing Reserve to close, Reserve's claims, if any, against Minnesota resting on provisions of the state or federal constitutions are preserved by reason of our direction that Reserve's counterclaims shall be dismissed without prejudice.

Finally, this court deems it appropriate to suggest that the national interest now calls upon Minnesota and Reserve to exercise a zeal equivalent to that displayed in this litigation to arrive at an appropriate location for an on-land disposal site for Reserve's tailings and thus permit an important segment of the national steel industry, employing several thousand people, to continue in production. As we have already noted, we believe this controversy can be resolved in a manner that will purify the air and water without destroying jobs.

The existing injunction is modified in the respects stated herein. This case is remanded to the district court for the entry of a decree in accordance with our directions and for such further proceedings consistent with this opinion as may be just and equitable.

---

1) Did the court subordinate analysis of the severity of the harm if it occurred to the likelihood that the harm would occur? Did the court ignore "the lesser risk of a greater harm"? Ethyl Corp. v. EPA, 7 Env't Rep. Cas. (BNA) 1353, 1387 (D.C.Cir. 1975) (Wright, J., dissenting), reversed 541 F.2d 1 (D.C.Cir.), certiorari denied 426 U.S. 941 (1976). Does the court impose too much of a threshold burden of proof for an injunction? Should the court grant a remedy that is smaller than plaintiffs' substantive right? Should courts grant delayed, "all deliberate speed," remedies? Did the court hold that the short-term benefits of the discharge outweighed the risk, but that the long run risks outweighed the benefits?

2) Consider the following from Professor Marshall Shapo's book, A Nation of Guinea Pigs 198–99, 205, 208–09 (copyright 1979):

"When issues of causation confront us with uncertainties and wide-ranging statistical estimates like those in Reserve Mining, the practical decision often will turn on this sort of general assessment. In my view, such expressions of concern by dispassionate, qualified scientists present at least a prima facie case for governmental action.

"Responding to such statements, the courts in Reserve Mining seemed at least implicitly to follow a principle of risk–averseness which applies to situations where there is conflicting evidence on the scientific artifacts, where responsible testimony indicates that there is a risk factor, and where what is at issue is a judgment on the quantum of risk. It should be emphasized that this case not only drew into question the effects of what might be called different models of the same product, but involved disagreement about whether what was being measured was one model or another. Certainly when there is controversy relating to the production of scientific knowledge, it seems desirable that regulation should be biased toward avoiding risk in complex situations, and that courts should err on the side of caution in making judgments on the basis of heavily contested expert interpretations.

"Despite the prospect of diminution in productive activity, intervention is justified when the predicted danger is one that would fall fortuitously and severely on groups of persons unable practically to provide protection for themselves. The very dearth of definitive knowledge on the subject, the relative lack of choice in the target population, and the gravity of the potential consequences all argue for legislative regulation, or in its absence, positive judicial response. The possibility that such actions may inflict disproportionate economic hardship on the target population itself presents a special problem that requires further analysis. I shall not explore this problem in detail here. For the moment, we may say that when the judgment is that it is intolerable to permit the hazardous conduct to continue, the solution may lie in direct compensation payments from a combination of sources. A *Reserve* situation would present a classic case for legislative cushioning from the general revenues, at least if one assumes ignorance of the hazard in the population when the process began and while it continued. . . .

"There is common sense as well as legal sense in the decision. By its declaration that there is a risk requiring judicial intervention, the court makes clear that its basic approach favors public protection against even uncertain hazards. At the same time its tailoring of the remedy represents the degree of risk averseness it derives from the relevant statutes, absorbs from general attitudes, and finds responsive to the facts of a difficult case. Taking a somewhat resigned perspective on the previously established existence of the risk, it responds to the tensions created by conflicting interests that rend residents in the same community, at once maintaining the role of the judiciary as legislative interpreter as well as independent preserver of public health and safety. Inculcated in this approach is the idea that all law is a balance. Yet even in its recognition of competing interests, the decision teaches that in a 'day of synthetic living,' the basic line of the balance has shifted toward risk aversion because of the very artificiality of the processes that fuel that life-style. . . .

"The subsequent history of the *Reserve* case emphasized the need for courts and agencies to give fullest implementation to the risk-aversion inherent in the kinds of statutes and regulations at issue in that litigation. These events pointed up in particular the built-in bargaining margin that a prospective injunction involves when it is made subject to negotiation. The initial measure of that margin in the Reserve case was sixteen months: The court of appeals having directed in April 1975 that Reserve and the State of Minnesota should have a 'reasonable time' to agree on an on-land disposal site, it was not until August 1976 that the district court concluded that failure to reach agreement—the parties were 13 miles apart in their proposals—required a halt to the discharges within one year. The court of appeals affirmed this order, and also the imposition of $837,500 in fines.

"Still there was more to come, in the form of a complication of federalism. The court of appeals in its brief opinion left open the possibility of resolving the on-land dumping question 'by agreement or through litigation in state court.' Responding to this invitation, Reserve persuaded a panel of state district judges to require issuance of a permit allowing it to dump the tailings at the point it preferred—Milepost 7—rather than the Milepost 20 contended for by the state's pollution control agency and its department of natural resources. Reserve's advantage in fighting a holding action was evident at that point from the fact that once a site was fixed, it would take two years to construct proper disposal facilities. Thus the combination of a conditional injunction and a state avenue of litigation provided plenty of room for maneuver. The company then capped its defense when the Minnesota Supreme Court unanimously affirmed the state district court's Milepost 7 decision, which included a disposal permit limited to five years and specified the use of the 'best available technology.' The state decided not to appeal to the United States Supreme Court. The judicial process of two systems had thus eventually yielded a result that reduced risk though it did not avoid it entirely. As a generality, this had a satisfactory sound. Its specific outcome would have to abide efforts at compliance—and further measurements."

3) "The discharges into Lake Superior continued under the injunctive compliance schedule until 1980 when the company shifted to on-land disposal at Milepost 7," Minnesota's former Commissioner of Conservation told Professor Plater. Plater, Statutory Violations and Equitable Discretion, 70 Calif. L.Rev. 524, 572 n. 221 (1982).

II. Recurrence

The opinions in this section raise the question: Why does plaintiff seek to enjoin? In addition to injunctions, the courts have a smorgasbord of responses including dismissing the action, retaining jurisdiction, entering a declaratory judgment, or allowing the parties to negotiate a consent decree. Other remedies include criminal prosecutions and actions for money damages, which could be tried by juries. Why the injunction? Examine also the defendants' motives. Why do the defendants object to injunctions that add nothing to the substantive law?

Judges must consider several things in deciding how to respond: the strength and source of plaintiffs' substantive interest; whether, absent an injunction, the defendants will be likely to violate plaintiffs' substantive interest again; and what difference the terms of the injunction seem to make. Many defendants are large organizations. Will an injunction rouse a somnolent sense of bureaucratic urgency? Finally, is it fair to the legislature and the plaintiff to find liability but to deny relief?

HECHT CO. v. BOWLES

321 U.S. 321, 64 S.Ct. 587, 88 L.Ed. 754 (1944).

Justice DOUGLAS delivered the opinion of the Court.

Sec. 205(a) of the Emergency Price Control Act of 1942 . . . provides:

"Whenever in the judgment of the Administrator any person has engaged or is about to engage in any acts or practices which constitute or will constitute a violation of any provision of section 4 of this Act, he may make application to the appropriate court for an order enjoining such acts or practices, or for an order enforcing compliance with such provision, and upon a showing by the Administrator that such person has engaged or is about to engage in any such acts or practices a permanent or temporary injunction, restraining order, or other order shall be granted without bond." The question in this case is whether the Administrator, having established that a defendant has engaged in acts or practices violative of § 4 of the Act is entitled as of right to an injunction restraining the defendant from engaging in such acts or practices or whether the court has some discretion to grant or withhold such relief.

Sec. 4(a) of the Act makes it unlawful for a person to sell or deliver any commodity in violation of specified orders or regulations of the Administrator. A regulation issued under § 2 of the Act and effective in May, 1942 (7 Fed.Reg. 3153) provided that no person should sell or deliver any commodity at a price higher than the authorized maximum price . . . as fixed or determined by the regulation. Since maximum prices were fixed with reference to earlier base periods, the regulation also provided for the preservation and examination of existing records. And provision was likewise made for the keeping of current records reflecting sales made under the regulation and for the filing of maximum prices with the Administrator.

There is no substantial controversy over the facts. Petitioner operates a large department store in Washington, D.C. and did a business of about $20,000,000 in 1942. There are 107 departments in the store and each sells a separate line of merchandise. In the fall of 1942 the Administrator started an investigation to determine whether petitioner was complying with the Act and the regulation. The investigation was a "spot check," confined to seven departments. In each of the seven departments violations were disclosed. As a result this suit was brought. The complaint charged violations of the maximum price provisions of the regulation and violations of the regulations governing the keeping of records and reporting to the Administrator. The Administrator prayed for an injunction enjoining petitioner from selling, delivering or offering for sale or delivery any commodity in violation of the regulation and from failing to keep complete and accurate records as required by the regulation. In its answer petitioner pleaded among other things that any failure or neglect to comply with the regulation was involuntary and was corrected as soon as discovered.

Numerous violations both as respects prices and records were discovered. Thus in six of the seven departments investigated there had occurred between May and October, 1942 some 3,700 sales in excess of the maximum prices with overcharges of some $4,600. The statements filed with the Administrator were deficient, some 400 items of merchandise being omitted. And there were over 300 items with respect to which no records were kept showing how the maximum prices had been determined.

There is no doubt, however, of petitioner's good faith and diligence. The District Court found that the manager of the store had offered it as a laboratory in which the Administrator might experiment with any regulation which might be issued. Prior to the promulgation of the regulation the petitioner had created a new section known as the price control office. That office undertook to bring petitioner into compliance with the requirements of the regulation in advance of its effective date. The head of that office together with seven assistants devoted full time to that endeavor. But the store had about 2,000 employees and over one million two hundred thousand articles of merchandise. In the furniture departments alone there were over fifty-four thousand transactions in the first ten months of 1942. Difficulties were encountered in interpreting the regulation, in determining the exact nature of an article and whether it had been previously sold and at what price, etc. The absence of adequate records made it difficult to ascertain prices during the earlier base-period. Misunderstanding of the regulation, confusion on the part of employees not trained in such problems of interpretation and administration, the complexity of the problem, and the fallibility of humans all combined to produce numerous errors. But the District Court concluded that the "mistakes in pricing and listing were all made in good faith and without intent to violate the regulations."

The District Court also found that the mistakes brought to light "were at once corrected, and vigorous steps were taken by The Hecht Company to prevent recurrence of these mistakes or further mistakes in the future." The company increased its price control office to twenty-eight employees. New methods of internal control were instituted early in November 1942 with the view of avoiding future violations. That new system of control "greatly improved" the situation. Petitioner undertook to make repayment of all overcharges brought to light by the investigation in case of customers who could be identified. It proposed to contribute the remaining amount of such overcharges to some local charity. The District Court concluded that the issuance of an injunction would have "no effect by way of insuring better compliance in the future" and would be "unjust" to petitioner and not "in the public interest." It accordingly dismissed the complaint. 49 F.Supp. 528. On appeal the Court of Appeals for the District of Columbia reversed that judgment, one judge dissenting. 137 F.2d 689. That court held that the findings of the District Court were supported by substantial evidence, except that it did not consider whether the evidence supported the findings that an injunction would not insure better compliance in the future and would be unjust to petitioner. In its view the latter findings were immaterial. For it construed § 205(a) of the Act to require the issuance of an injunction or other order as a matter of course, once violations were found. . . .

Respondent insists that the mandatory character of § 205(a) is clear from its language, history and purpose. He argues that "shall be granted" is not permissive, that since the same section provides that the Administrator "may" apply for an injunction and that, if so, the injunction "shall" be granted, "may" and "shall" are each used in the ordinary sense. It is pointed out that when the bill . . . passed the House, § 205(a) provided that "upon a proper showing" an injunction or other order "shall be granted without bond." The words "upon a proper showing" were stricken in the Senate and were replaced by the words "upon a showing by the Administrator that such person has engaged or is about to engage in any such acts or practices." And the Senate Report in its analysis of § 205(a) stated that "upon a showing by the Administrator that such person has engaged or is about to engage in any such acts or practices, a temporary or permanent injunction, restraining order or other order is to be granted without bond." S.Rep. No. 931, 77th Cong., 2d Sess., p. 25. . . .

We agree that the cessation of violations, whether before or after the institution of a suit by the Administrator, is no bar to the issuance of an injunction under § 205(a). But we do not think that under all circumstances the court must issue the injunction or other order which the Administrator seeks.

It seems apparent on the face of § 205(a) that there is some room for the exercise of discretion on the part of the court. For the requirement is that a "permanent or temporary injunction, restraining order, or other order" be granted. Though the Administrator asks for an injunction, some "other order" might be more appropriate, or at least so appear to the court. Thus in the present case one judge in the Court of Appeals felt that the District Court should not have dismissed the complaint but should have entered an order retaining the case on the docket with the right of the Administrator, on notice, to renew his application for injunctive relief if violations recurred. It is indeed not difficult to imagine that in some situations that might be the fairest course to follow and one which would be as practically effective as the issuance of an injunction. Such an order, moreover, would seem to be a type of "other order" which a faithful reading of § 205(a) would permit a court to issue in a compliance proceeding. However that may be, it would seem clear that the court might deem some "other order" more appropriate for the evil at hand than the one which was sought. We cannot say that it lacks the power to make that choice. Thus it seems that § 205(a) falls short of making mandatory the issuance of an injunction merely because the Administrator asks it.

There is, moveover, support in the legislative history of § 205(a) for the view that "shall be granted" is less mandatory than a literal reading might suggest. We have already referred to a portion of the Senate Report which lends some support to the position of the Administrator. But in another portion of that Report there is the following reference to suits to enjoin violations of the Act: "In common with substantially all regulatory statutes, the bill authorizes the official charged with the duty of administering the act to apply to any appropriate court, State or Federal, for an order enjoining any person who has engaged or is about to engage in any acts or practices which constitute or will constitute a violation of any provision of the bill. Such courts are given jurisdiction to issue whatever order to enforce compliance is proper in the circumstances of each particular case." S.Rep. No. 931, supra, p. 10. A grant of *jurisdiction* to issue compliance orders hardly suggests an absolute duty to do so under any and all circumstances. We cannot but think that if Congress had intended to make such a drastic departure from the traditions of equity practice, an unequivocal statement of its purpose would have been made.

. . . We are dealing here with the requirements of equity practice with a background of several hundred years of history. Only the other day we stated that "An appeal to the equity jurisdiction conferred on federal district courts is an appeal to the sound discretion which guides the determinations of courts of equity." Meredith v. Winter Haven, 320 U.S. 228, 235. The historic injunctive process was designed to deter, not to punish. The essence of equity jurisdiction has been the power of the Chancellor to do equity and to mould each decree to the necessities of the particular case. Flexibility rather than rigidity has distinguished it. The qualities of mercy and practicality have made equity the instrument for nice adjustment and reconciliation between the public interest and private needs as well as between competing private claims. We do not believe that such a major departure from that long tradition as is here proposed should be lightly implied. We do not think the history or language of § 205(a) compel it. It should be noted, moreover, that § 205(a) governs the procedure in both federal and state courts. For § 205(c) gives the state courts concurrent jurisdiction with federal district courts of civil enforcement proceedings. It is therefore even more compelling to conclude that, if Congress desired to make such an abrupt departure from traditional equity practice as is suggested, it would have made its desire plain. Hence we resolve the ambiguities of § 205(a) in favor of that interpretation which affords a full opportunity for equity courts to treat enforcement proceedings under this emergency legislation in accordance with their traditional practices, as conditioned by the necessities of the public interest which Congress has sought to protect. . . .

We do not mean to imply that courts should administer § 205(a) grudgingly. . . . The Administrator does not carry the sole burden of the war against inflation. The courts also have been entrusted with a share of that responsibility. And their discretion under § 205(a) must be exercised in light of the large objectives of the Act. For the standards of the public interest, not the requirements of private litigation, measure the propriety and need for injunctive relief in these cases. That discretion should reflect an acute awareness of the Congressional admonition that "of all the consequences of war, except human slaughter, inflation is the most destructive" (S.Rep. No. 931, supra, p. 2) and that delay or indifference may be fatal. Whether the District Court abused its discretion in dismissing the complaint is a question which we do not reach. The judgment must be reversed and the cause remanded to the Court of Appeals for that determination.

Justice FRANKFURTER agrees that § 205(a) of the Emergency Price Control Act, apart from dispensing with any requirement for a bond, does not change the historic conditions for the exercise by courts of equity of their power to issue injunctions, according to which the Court of Appeals should now dispose of this cause.

Justice ROBERTS is of opinion that the judgment of the Court of Appeals should be reversed and that of the District Court affirmed.

Judge Edgerton's opinion for the Court of Appeals, in Brown v. Hecht Co., 137 F.2d 689, 692 (D.C.Cir.1943) said: "Despite the Company's past and present good intentions, by the express terms of the statute the Company's past violations authorized the District Court to enjoin future violations. In order to justify the granting of an injunction under an express and unrestricted statutory authority, no balancing of equities is necessary and neither threatened irreparable injury nor lack of an adequate remedy at law need be shown. General equitable doctrines 'do not militate against the capacity of a court of equity as a proper forum in which to make a declared policy of Congress effective.'

"The question remains whether the Act merely *authorized* the court to grant an order without regard to equitable considerations, such as the Company's good intentions and the probable effect of granting an order, or whether it *required* the court to do so. Unless it required the court to do so, Congress turned over to the court the important question whether the granting of an order against a violator of the Act should be a matter of course or should depend upon the general principles of equity. But Congress was free to decide that question and there was no apparent reason for leaving it to the court. We think Congress did not leave it to the court. The phrase 'a permanent or temporary injunction, restraining order, or other order shall be granted,' in its context, means in our opinion that an injunction or other order is to be granted as of course when violations of the Act are found. Only the affirmative or negative character of the order, and its other details, are left to the court's discretion.

"To most laymen, the question whether the word 'shall' in a statute is mandatory would doubtless seem to answer itself. The legal proposition that the word is not necessarily mandatory and may be 'merely directory' is a more or less technical one. Sometimes this proposition means only that violation of a statutory mandate may entail no consequences when the statute prescribes none; as when waivers of notice are allowed to validate a corporate meeting held without notice although a statute provides that notice shall be given. Sometimes it means only that the author of a mandate may be privileged to change or break it. Thus it has been held that a court or an administrative body may waive some of its own rules despite the presence in the rules of the word 'shall,' and that a legislature may change the means by which it has itself provided that process 'shall' be served upon a corporation. In some of the State court cases on which the dissenting opinion relies, the proposition is a euphemism which covers judicial refusal to follow a legislative mandate addressed to the court. In some contexts, perhaps, it has been found by way of genuine statutory construction that a particular 'shall' was more or less equivalent to 'may.' It is nonetheless true that the word 'shall' in a statute is normally 'the language of command.' We think the word has its normal meaning in § 205(a). . . .

"Neither the context nor the legislative history of the Emergency Price Control Act suggests any unusual meaning of the word 'shall.' On the contrary, both confirm its common meaning. It is recognized that the use of 'may' and 'shall' in one sentence implies that each word is used in its own ordinary sense and not in the ordinary sense of the other. A single sentence in § 205(a) provides that the Administrator 'may' apply for an order and that an order 'shall' be granted. If Congress had been using 'shall' in the sense of 'may' there would have been no reason for using 'may' instead of 'shall' in regard to the Administrator. . . .

"Inflation is infectious and cumulative. It cannot be prevented in general unless it is prevented in particular. The Emergency Price Control Act is designed to prevent inflation. To that end it provides various means. These include price fixing, subsidy payments, licensing, criminal penalties, damage suits, and the remedy which the Administrator seeks here. There is nothing new or strange in the belief of Congress that an injunction or other order, with the possibility of contempt proceedings, is an effective means of law enforcement. The legislative history of the entire Act, like that of § 205(a), tends to show that Congress meant what it said and why it meant what it said when it provided that an order shall be granted upon a showing that the Act has been violated. The limitation upon the court's discretion is unusual, but the situation which evoked it is extraordinary. The emergency is more acute today than when the Act was passed. 'Any easy attitude of the courts which even remotely suggests that the Act may be violated with impunity strikes at the entire enforcement problem . . . .' "

Judge Eicher concurring said (137 F.2d 689, 695): ". . . It is difficult for me to view an injunction which merely forbids violation of the law as a punishment. Further violations are not only threatened in this case, but are claimed to be unavoidable. If, after injunction, they do occur, and contempt proceedings follow, then for the first time do quasi-criminal sanctions come into play and penalties may be imposed. Before doing so, courts can and will give full weight to a showing that violations have been inadvertent and innocent and not wilful, for in such an inquiry the courts are no longer under statutory mandate, but are exercising their inherent powers."

---

1) Why didn't the government bring a criminal prosecution or an action for damages? Does the court of appeals's position parallel the absolutist-all or nothing nuisance doctrine in New York before *Boomer*? p. 79. If so, does the Supreme Court's decision parallel *Boomer* in freeing the trial judge's discretion?

Professor Plater says "a court has no discretion to allow statutorily proscribed conduct to continue." Plater, Statutory Violations and Equitable Discretion, 70 Cal.L.Rev. 524, 532 (1982). In nonstatutory lawsuits like *Boomer,* however, where they apply court-made rules, judges may find that defendant violated the rule yet not enjoin because "abatement was decided anew in each case." 70 Calif.L.Rev. at 543. Does this illustrate Aristotelian dispensation with rigid legal rules? Should courts analyze the source of the substantive rule without also analyzing the strength of the substantive interest? The Court, Plater writes, decided *Hecht* correctly. 70 Calif.L.Rev. at 546–53. The department store had violated the statute, and its breaches should not have continued. The Court based its narrow holding on the premise that the violation would cease, and it focused on how to choose a remedy to carry out the statutory rule. What is the narrowest way to state the holding? What is the critical language in the statute?

What sort of order should the court of appeals tell the district judge to enter? Do the remedial choices include 1) entering an injunction, 2) reconsidering whether to enjoin, 3) retaining jurisdiction, and 4) affirming dismissal? Does *Hecht* curb overzealous bureaucrats? Would an injunction that restated the statutory standard prevent the inadvertent violations of the complex scheme that were inevitable? Would such an injunction be futile because the judge would exercise another level of discretion in adjudicating charges of contempt? After *Hecht,* the Office of Price Administration concentrated on triple damages to deter. Professor Fleming James, a former OPA attorney, said "that treble damage awards, like criminal penalties in price fixing cases, 'really got the attention of the white collar crowd.'" quoted by Plater, 70 Calif.L.Rev. at 559 n. 142.

2) The *Hecht* dilemma involves both separation of powers and individualization of rules for discrete instances. In a wages and hours case, the judge said: "When an employer has committed a clear violation of the Act without any valid excuse or explanation, an injunction should and will be issued. An injunction subjects the defendant to no penalty or hardship. It merely requires him to do what the Act requires anyhow." Marshall v. Hendersonville Bowling Center, Inc., 483 F.Supp. 510, 518 (M.D.Tenn. 1980). Other decisions under the Fair Labor Standards Act, 29 U.S.C. § 217, (1976) have established that the trial judge should almost always enjoin the defendant. The judge should enjoin even if the employer's violations were inadvertent, the employer otherwise acted in good faith, or the employer is currently com-

plying. The only time a judge might not enjoin is when he is "soundly convinced that there is no reasonable probability of a recurrence of the violations." Marshall v. Chala Enterprises, Inc., 645 F.2d 799 (9th Cir. 1981); Marshall v. Van Matre, 634 F.2d 1115, 1118 (8th Cir. 1980). "When an injunction is explicitly authorized by statute, proper discretion usually requires its issuance if the prerequisites for the remedy have been demonstrated and the injunction would fulfill the legislative purpose." Donovan v. Brown Equipment and Service Tools, Inc., 666 F.2d 148, 157 (5th Cir. 1982). Can you square these decisions with *Hecht?* See also Freedom of Information Act decisions, Long v. IRS, 693 F.2d 907 (9th Cir. 1982); Tennessean Newspapers v. FHA, 464 F.2d 657, 661 (6th Cir. 1972); Soucie v. David, 448 F.2d 1067, 1077 (D.C.Cir. 1971).

Would a court violate the rules of separation of powers if it exempted a defendant from an act of the legislature? Is the court's core function to determine whether the factual circumstances exist to enforce statutes? Plater, 70 Calif.L.Rev. at 591. Does *Hecht* hold that Congress lacks the power to withdraw certain remedies? Plater, 70 Calif.L.Rev. at 553. Lauf v. E.G. Shinner & Co., 303 U.S. 323, 330 (1938), upheld the Norris-LaGuardia Act's prohibition of injunctions in labor disputes. Yakus v. United States, 321 U.S. 414 (1944), like *Hecht,* involved the wartime price control statutes. The 1942 Emergency Price Control Act denied the Emergency Court of Appeals power to grant interlocutory orders enjoining the Administrator's orders and regulations. The *Yakus* Court upheld that denial of power "in the special circumstances of the case." 321 U.S. at 437, 439.

3) In Rondeau v. Mosinee Paper Corp., 422 U.S. 49 (1975), a takeover target company sued the defendant who was acquiring shares. Plaintiff sued under the Williams Act because defendant had failed to disclose properly. As a defense to an injunction, the defendant claimed that he had been unfamiliar with the Act and that no harm had occurred to either plaintiff or its shareholders. The trial judge denied relief for the "technical" violation and entered judgment for defendant. The court of appeals, however, thought that only an injunction would be "appropriate to neutralize [defendant's] violation of the Act and to deny him the benefit of his wrongdoing." Mosinee Paper Corp. v. Rondeau, 500 F.2d 1011, 1017 (7th Cir. 1974). The Supreme Court found no "cognizable danger of recurrent violation" (quoting *W. T. Grant,* the next case). Moreover, the "bare fact" of violation did not justify an injunction against defendant. The Court discussed *Hecht* and held that, even though defendant violated the Act, plaintiff had to "satisfy the traditional prerequisites of equitable relief by establishing irreparable harm," 422 U.S. at 61, and the judge retained the historic discretion to withhold an injunction.

Plater says, discussing *Rondeau,* that "likelihood of future compliance is open to the full scope of equitable discretion." 70 Calif.L.Rev. at 565. What factors should a judge consider to determine whether a defendant who has breached will comply? Do the quality and frequency of the past violations affect the decision to enjoin? If the judge decides not to enjoin, should he 1) dismiss, 2) retain jurisdiction, or 3) issue a declaratory judgment?

4) The Supreme Court enjoined the TVA from completing the Tellico Dam on the Little Tennessee River; Congress's plain words in the Endan-

gered Species Act prohibited the TVA from impounding the river and jeopardizing an endangered fish, the snail darter. TVA v. Hill, 437 U.S. 153 (1978). While some argued that the millions of dollars spent on the dam outweighed the loss of the snail darter, the Court felt that Congress had balanced the interests and concluded that endangered species were more important than dams. 437 U.S. at 187, 188. Justice Rehnquist's dissent cited *Hecht.* He argued that "since the District Court possessed discretion to refuse injunctive relief even though it had found a violation of the Act, the only remaining question is whether this discretion was abused in denying [plaintiff's] prayer for an injunction." He concluded that the district judge had not abused discretion by subordinating the snail darter's habitat to "other equally significant factors" and refusing to enjoin. 437 U.S. at 212, 213. Did Justice Rehnquist read *Hecht* correctly? Plater, 70 Calif.L.Rev. at 554–56. Could the trial judge in *Hecht* decide that price control should not apply to clothes? Plater, Calif.L.Rev. at 556 n. 120.

Congress responded to TVA v. Hill by amending the Act to create an Endangered Species Committee with power to exempt agency action. 16 U.S.C. § 1536(e)–(h). The Committee refused to exempt the Tellico Dam: even though the government had spent $100,000,000, the benefits of completion failed to clearly outweigh the benefits of the alternatives. Congress then told TVA to complete the dam. Energy and Water Development Appropriation Act, 1980, Pub.L. No. 96–69, 93 Stat. 437, 449 (1978). See generally Note, Environmental Law—The Endangered Species Act of 1978: Congress Responds to Tennessee Valley Authority v. Hill, 25 Wayne L.Rev. 1327 (1979). The snail darter has been discovered elsewhere since 1978. In light of these subsequent developments, was TVA v. Hill correctly decided? Did the decision assure that the issue was resolved in the proper forum? Plater, 70 Calif.L.Rev. at 586–88.

5) The Louisiana court dealt with a statute similar to the one in *Hecht* in Gulf States Theatres v. Richardson, 287 So.2d 480, 485–87 (La.1980). Part of a statutory scheme providing for injunctions against obscenity said that the trial judge "shall" grant a temporary injunction if the district attorney alleges "upon information and belief" that obscenity exists. The court held that "shall" meant mandatory interlocutory relief. This invalidated the statute because it allowed the suppression of alleged obscenity without a hearing and a prior judicial determination. The legislature substituted a more flexible system. La.Stat.Ann.—R.S. 13:4711–16.

The Indiana obscenity nuisance statute compels the judge to issue a temporary injunction if plaintiff sustains the allegations in the petition. Ind.Code 35–30–10.5–4. The Ohio statute makes relief mandatory if the judge finds obscenity. The relief takes the form of a perpetual injunction against the nuisance, a $300 tax, and an order that 1) personal property be removed and sold and 2) the theatre be closed for one year. Ohio Rev.Code §§ 3767.01–3767.09. Are these attempts to circumscribe judicial discretion permissible? See State ex rel. Ewing v. "Without a Stitch," 37 Ohio St.2d 95, 103–05, 307 N.E.2d 911, 917–18 (1974), appeal dismissed 421 U.S. 923; Rendleman, Civilizing Pornography: The Case for An Exclusive Obscenity Nuisance Statute, 44 U.Chi.L.Rev. 509, 547–48 (1977).

UNITED STATES v. W. T. GRANT CO.

345 U.S. 629, 73 S.Ct. 894, 97 L.Ed. 1303 (1953).

Justice CLARK delivered the opinion of the Court.

For the first time since the enactment of the Clayton Act in 1914 the Court is called upon to consider § 8's prohibitions against interlocking corporate directorates.[1] The Government appeals from judgments dismissing civil actions brought against Hancock and three pairs of corporations which he served as a director, W. T. Grant Co. and S. H. Kress & Co., Sears Roebuck & Co. and Bond Stores, Inc., and Kroger Co. and Jewel Tea Co., Inc. Alleging that the size and competitive relationship of each set of companies brought the interlocks within the reach of § 8, the complaints asked the court to order the particular interlocks terminated and to enjoin future violations of § 8 by the individual and corporate defendants. Soon after the complaints were filed, Hancock resigned from the boards of Kress, Kroger and Bond. Disclosing the resignations by affidavit, all of the defendants then moved to dismiss the actions as moot. Treated as motions for summary judgment, they were granted by the District Judge. He concluded that there is not "the slightest threat that the defendants will attempt any future activity in violation of Section 8 [if they have violated it already] . . . ." 112 F.Supp. 336, 338. The Government brought this direct appeal, . . . contending that the cases were not rendered moot by Hancock's resignations and that it was an abuse of discretion for the trial court to refuse any injunctive relief. . . .

Both sides agree to the abstract proposition that voluntary cessation of allegedly illegal conduct does not deprive the tribunal of power to hear and determine the case, i.e., does not make the case moot. . . . A controversy may remain to be settled in such circumstances, . . . e.g., a dispute over the legality of the challenged practices. . . . The defendant is free to return to his old ways. This, together with a public interest in having the legality of the practices settled, militates against a mootness conclusion. . . . For to say that the case has become moot means that the defendant is entitled to a dismissal as a matter of right . . . . The courts have rightly refused to grant defendants such a powerful weapon against public law enforcement.[5]

The case may nevertheless be moot if the defendant can demonstrate that "there is no reasonable expectation that the wrong will be repeated." [Unit-

1. "Sec. 8. . . .

"No person at the same time shall be a director in any two or more corporations, any one of which has capital, surplus, and undivided profits aggregating more than $1,000,000, engaged in whole or in part in commerce, . . . if such corporations are or shall have been theretofore, by virtue of their business and location of operation, competitors, so that the elimination of competition by agreement between them would constitute a violation of any of the provisions of any of the antitrust laws. . . . " 38 Stat. 730, 15 U.S.C. § 19.

5. "When defendants are shown to have settled into a continuing practice or entered into a conspiracy violative of antitrust laws, courts will not assume that it has been abandoned without clear proof. . . . It is the duty of the courts to beware of efforts to defeat injunctive relief by protestations of repentance and reform, especially when abandonment seems timed to anticipate suit, and there is probability of resumption." United States v. Oregon State Medical Society, 343 U.S. 326, 333 (1952).

ed States v. Aluminum Co. of America, 148 F.2d 416, 448 (1945)] The burden is a heavy . . . one. Here the defendants told the court that the interlocks no longer existed and disclaimed any intention to revive them. Such a profession does not suffice to make a case moot although it is one of the factors to be considered in determining the appropriateness of granting an injunction against the now-discontinued acts.

Along with its power to hear the case, the court's power to grant injunctive relief survives discontinuance of the illegal conduct. . . . The purpose of an injunction is to prevent future violations, . . . and, of course, it can be utilized even without a showing of past wrongs. But the moving party must satisfy the court that relief is needed. The necessary determination is that there exists some cognizable danger of recurrent violation, something more than the mere possibility which serves to keep the case alive. The chancellor's decision is based on all the circumstances; his discretion is necessarily broad and a strong showing of abuse must be made to reverse it. To be considered are the bona fides of the expressed intent to comply, the effectiveness of the discontinuance and, in some cases, the character of the past violations.

The facts relied on by the Government to show an abuse of discretion in this case are these: Hancock's three interlocking directorates viewed as three distinct violations, his failure to terminate them until after suit was filed despite five years of administrative attempts to persuade him of their illegality, his express refusal to concede that the interlocks in question were illegal under the statute and his failure to promise not to commit similar violations in the future.

Were we sitting as a trial court, this showing might be persuasive. But the Government must demonstrate that there was no reasonable basis for the District Judge's decision. In this we think it fails. An individual proclivity to violate the statute need not be inferred from the fact that three violations were charged, particularly since it is only recently that the Government has attempted systematic enforcement of § 8. The District Court was not dealing with a defendant who follows one adjudicated violation with others. The only material before the District Judge on the supposed five years of administrative persuasion could easily support an inference that during that time the defendant and the Department of Justice were each trying to determine the legality of his directorships. The Government's remedy under the statute was plain. Postponement of suit indicates doubt on the prosecutor's part as much as intransigence on the defendant's. How much contrition should be expected of a defendant is hard for us to say. This surely is a question better addressed to the discretion of the trial court. The same can be said of the limited disclaimer of future intent.

Assuming with the Government that the corporations were properly joined as defendants,[9] the conclusion that there was no abuse of discretion in refusing injunctive relief against Hancock applies *a fortiori* in their case. None of the corporations appeared to have engaged in more than one alleged violation. And affidavits filed with the motions to dismiss indicated that these defendants were ignorant of the Government's interest in the inter-

9. We should not be understood as deciding whether corporations can violate § 8 or, for other reasons, be enjoined under the statute.

locks until the suits were filed. Indeed the emphasis on this branch of the case is placed on the refusal of relief against Hancock. The failure to point to circumstances compelling further relief against the corporations speaks for itself.

Essentially, the Government's claim is that it was deprived of a trial on the relief issue. But at no time was objection raised to the procedure by which the case was handled. Of course summary judgment procedure could not have been employed were there a "genuine issue as to any material fact." Fed.Rules Civ.Proc. 56. However, after the defendants had moved to dismiss, the Government elected not to file any countervailing affidavits or amend its complaint and stated on oral argument that the truth of the defendants' affidavits was not questioned. To frame a factual dispute, that left the complaint, the only relevant paragraph of which reads: "16. The defendants have threatened to continue and will continue *the aforesaid violation* of Section 8 of the Clayton Act unless the relief prayed for herein is granted." (Emphasis added.) "The aforesaid violation[s]," the specific interlocks, had been voluntarily terminated and intention to resume them had been negatived under oath. As to the prayer that the defendants be enjoined from any future violations of § 8, the complaint alleged no threatened violations other than those specifically charged. In these circumstances, the District Judge could decide that there was no significant threat of future violation and that there was no factual dispute about the existence of such a threat.

We conclude that, although the actions were not moot, no abuse of discretion has been demonstrated in the trial court's refusal to award injunctive relief. Moreover, the court stated its dismissals "would not be a bar to a new suit in case possible violations arise in the future." The judgments are

Affirmed.

Justice DOUGLAS, with whom Justice BLACK concurs, dissenting.

Monopoly and restraints of trade are sometimes the products of practices and devices as ingenious as the minds of men. Sometimes they follow a blunt and direct course as is involved in the acquisition of the assets of a competitor—a way of growth of monopoly power to which the decisions of the Court have given a powerful impetus and encouragement. . . . More subtle are interlocking arrangements between directorates. This can accomplish disastrous consequences, as Mr. Justice Brandeis pointed out forty years ago. Interlocking directorates between companies which compete stifle the competition. Or to use the words of Mr. Justice Brandeis, the practice substitutes "the pull of privilege for the push of manhood." [1] Moreover, those entwined relations are the stuff out of which concentration of financial power over American industry was built and is maintained. Mr. Justice Brandeis gave one example: [2]

"They, the bankers, control the railroads, and controlling the railroads, they were able to control the issue and sale of securities. Being bankers,

1. See Brandeis, The Endless Chain, Harper's Weekly, Dec. 6, 1913, p. 13, quoted in Lief, The Brandeis Guide to the Modern World, p. 111.

2. See his testimony in Hearings, H.R. Committee on the Judiciary, 63d Cong., 2d Sess., on Trust Legislation, vol. 2, p. 922, quoted in Lief, op. cit., supra, note 1, p. 113.

they bought those securities at a price which they had a part in fixing or could have a part in fixing. They sold those securities, as bankers, to insurance companies in which they were able to exercise some control as directors. They got the money with which to buy those securities from railroads through their control of the great banking institutions, and then, in their capacity of having control of the railroads, they utilized that money to purchase from great corporations, like the Steel Corporation, what the railroads needed, and in their capacity as controlling other corporations they bought from the Steel Corporation again, and so on until we had the endless chain."

The web that is woven may tie many industries, insurance companies, and financial houses together into a vast and friendly alliance that takes the edge off competition.

That condition is aggravated here. The interlocking control in the present case is not indirect. Mr. Hancock served as a director for each of three sets of companies which, on the state of the pleadings before us, we must assume to have been competitive. The fact that he resigned under the pressure of these proceedings should not dispose of the case. We are dealing here with professionals whose technique for controlling enterprises and building empires was fully developed and well known long before Mr. Justice Brandeis was crying out against the evils of "the money trust." Mr. Hancock is and has been for some years a partner in the investment banking firm of Lehman Bros. In 1940 he testified that when Lehman Bros. did financing for a company it was their "traditional practice" to ask for representation on the board of directors.

It therefore seems to me that a District Judge, faced with violations such as were involved here, would want to know *first,* how investment bankers built their empires; *second,* how this particular firm built its own empire; *third,* the effect of these banker empires on competition between the companies which are tied to them.

The fact that the Lehman partner resigned to avoid a decision on the merits has little, if any, relevancy to the issue in the case, for we are here concerned with the *proclivity* of the house to indulge in the practice.

The relevant issues have never been weighed in this case. The District Court's ruling would be entitled to a presumption of validity if those various factors had been considered. But the District Court made no such considered judgment. It disposed of the case on the basis of mootness, a ruling now conceded to be erroneous. The case should go back for a consideration of the nature and extent of the web which this investment banking house has woven over industry and its effect on the "elimination of competition" within the meaning of § 8 of the Clayton Act.[4] Unless we know that much, we are in no position to judge the service an injunction against future violations may do. Unless we know that much, we are in no position to carry out Woodrow Wilson's policy expressed in § 8 of the Clayton Act that those interlocking directorates should be prevented which make "those who affect to compete

4. In United States v. Sears, Roebuck & Co., 111 F.Supp. 614, 616, decided April 28, 1953, the court ruled that Congress intended by § 8 "to nip in the bud incipient violations of the antitrust laws by removing the opportunity or temptation to such violations through interlocking directorates."

in fact partners and masters of some whole field of business." Message, Joint Session of the Houses of Congress, Jan. 20, 1914.

---

1) Would a criminal prosecution or an action for damages be a better remedy? How would a fact-finder measure money damages under Section 8? Why did the government pursue its application for an injunction after Hancock resigned? Why didn't the government seek a consent decree or a declaratory judgment that "it was illegal for Hancock to serve on the boards of A–B, C–D, and E–F?" Would this declaratory judgment be superior to an injunction forbidding Hancock from conduct forbidden by Section 8? Did the government fear that Hancock would become a director in X and Y corporations? What remedy would best prevent that? Was there more at stake? Did the government "win" 1) when Hancock resigned? 2) when the Supreme Court held the lawsuit not moot? Would the government have preferred an order telling the district judge to retain jurisdiction?

2) Why do defendants who intend to obey the law resist preventive injunctions which merely personalize the existing substantive standards? Professor Andre examines the collateral consequences of Securities Act injunctions, civil or criminal contempt, loss of business and business benefits, and loss of reputation in the The Collateral Consequences of SEC Injunctive Relief: Mild Prophylactic or Perpetual Hazard?, 1981 U.Ill.L.F. 625. He discusses whether the effects of violating an injunction are worse than the effects of violating the law in the absence of an injunction and concludes that they may be. Do these collateral consequences apply outside the securities area? Should a judge consider these factors in deciding whether to enjoin? In particular, should judges enjoin when defendant did not breach intentionally but inadvertently?

3) Reconsider *Reserve Mining* p. 116 in light of *Hecht* and *W. T. Grant.* The court of appeals let the defendant continue to violate the substantive standard after considering the effect and expense of an injunction as well as the health hazards of not enjoining. Was this appropriate where defendant violated not a court-made rule, but a statute? Did the *Reserve Mining* court use reasonable delays to resurrect "all deliberate speed?" Plater asserts "each of the [substantive] grounds implicitly or explicitly permitted the court to balance the question of abatement." 70 Calif.L.Rev. at 572. Does equity have a "residual power to grant defendants a reasonable transition time to move from noncompliance to compliance?" Plater, 70 Calif.L.Rev. at 579–80. Does it matter whether the substantive standard is judge-made, statutory, or constitutional?

Hecht and *W. T. Grant,* involve an easier problem than *Romero-Barcelo:* whether the judge will enjoin if the wrongdoer abandons the illegal conduct before the decree is issued. In *Romero-Barcelo,* the defendant has not ceased the violation and does not appear to intend to cease.

WEINBERGER v. ROMERO-BARCELO

456 U.S. 305, 102 S.Ct. 1798, 72 L.Ed.2d 91 (1982).

Justice WHITE delivered the opinion of the Court.

The issue in this case is whether the Federal Water Pollution Control Act (FWPCA or the Act), 86 Stat. 816, 33 U.S.C. § 1251 et seq. (1976 ed. and Supp. III), requires a district court to enjoin immediately all discharges of pollutants that do not comply with the Act's permit requirements or whether the district court retains discretion to order other relief to achieve compliance. The Court of Appeals for the First Circuit held that the Act withdrew the courts' equitable discretion. 643 F.2d 835 (1981). We reverse.

For many years, the Navy has used Vieques Island, a small island off the Puerto Rico coast, for weapons training. Currently all Atlantic Fleet vessels assigned to the Mediterranean and the Indian Ocean are required to complete their training at Vieques because it permits a full range of exercises under conditions similar to combat. During air-to-ground training, however, pilots sometimes miss land-based targets, and ordnance falls into the sea. That is, accidental bombings of the navigable waters and, occasionally, intentional bombings of water targets occur. The District Court found that these discharges have not harmed the quality of the water.

In 1978, respondents, who include the Governor of Puerto Rico and residents of the island, sued to enjoin the Navy's operations on the island. Their complaint alleged violations of numerous federal environmental statutes and various other acts. After an extensive hearing, the District Court found that under the explicit terms of the Act, the Navy had violated the Act by discharging ordnance into the waters surrounding the island without first obtaining a permit from the Environmental Protection Agency (EPA).

Under the FWPCA, the "discharge of any pollutant" requires a National Pollutant Discharge Elimination System (NPDES) permit. 33 U.S.C. § 1311(a), § 1323(a) (1976 ed. and Supp. III). The term "discharge of any pollutant" is defined as

". . . any addition of any *pollutant* to the waters of the contiguous zone or the ocean from any *point source* other than a vessel or other floating craft." 33 U.S.C. § 1362(12) (emphasis added).

Pollutant, in turn, means,

". . . dredged spoil, solid wastes, incinerator residue, sewage, garbage, sewage sludge, *munitions,* chemical wastes, biological materials, radioactive materials, heat, wrecked or discarded equipment, rock, sand, cellar dirt and industrial, municipal and agricultural waste discharged into water . . . ." 33 U.S.C. § 1362(6) (emphasis added).

And, under the Act, a "point source" is

"any discernible, confined and discrete *conveyance,* including but not limited to any pipe, ditch, channel, tunnel, conduit, well, discrete fissure, container rolling stock, concentrated animal feeding operation, or *vessel* or other *floating craft from which pollutants are or may be discharged . . . .*" 33 U.S.C. § 1362(14) (emphasis added).

Under the FWPCA, the EPA may not issue a NPDES [permit] without state certification that the permit conforms to state water quality standards. A state has the authority to deny certification of the permit application or attach conditions to the final permit. 33 U.S.C. § 1341.

As the District Court construed the FWPCA, the release of ordnance from aircraft or from ships into navigable waters is a discharge of pollutants, even though the Environmental Protection Agency, which administers the Act, had not promulgated any regulations setting effluent levels or providing for the issuance of a NPDES permit for this category of pollutants. Recognizing that violations of the Act "must be cured," 478 F.Supp. at 707, the District Court ordered the Navy to apply for a NPDES permit. It refused, however, to enjoin Navy operations pending consideration of the permit application. It explained that the Navy's "technical violations" were not causing any "appreciable harm" to the environment.[4] "Moreover, because of the importance of the island as a training center, the granting of the injunctive relief sought would cause grievous, and perhaps irreparable harm, not only to Defendant Navy, but to the general welfare of this Nation."[5] The District Court concluded that an injunction was not necessary to ensure suitably prompt compliance by the Navy. To support this conclusion, it emphasized an equity court's traditionally broad discretion in deciding appropriate relief and quoted from the classic description of injunctive relief in Hecht v. Bowles: "The historic injunctive process was designed to deter, not to punish."

The Court of Appeals for the First Circuit vacated the District Court's order and remanded with instructions that the court order the Navy to cease the violation until it obtained a permit. 643 F.2d 835 (1981). Relying on TVA v. Hill, 437 U.S. 153 (1978), in which this Court held that an imminent violation of the Endangered Species Act required injunctive relief, the Court of Appeals concluded that the District Court erred in undertaking a traditional balancing of the parties' competing interests. "Whether or not the Navy's activities in fact harm the coastal waters, it has an absolute statutory obligation to stop any discharges of pollutant until the permit procedure has been followed and the Administrator of the Environmental Protection Agency, upon review of the evidence, has granted a permit." 643 F.2d, at 861. The court suggested that if the order would interfere significantly with military preparedness, the Navy should request that the President grant it an

4. The District Court wrote:

"In fact, if anything, these waters are as aesthetically acceptable as any to be found anywhere, and Plaintiff's witnesses unanimously testified as to their being the best fishing grounds in Vieques. . . . [I]f truth be said, the control of large areas of Vieques [by the Navy] probably constitutes a positive factor in its over all ecology. The very fact that there are in the Navy zones modest numbers of various marine species which are practically nonexistent in the civilian sector of Vieques or in the main island of Puerto Rico, is an eloquent example of *res ipsa loquitur.*" 478 F.Supp., at 667, 682.

5. The District Court also took into consideration the delay by plaintiffs in asserting their claims. It concluded that although laches should not totally bar the claims, it did strongly militate against the granting of injunctive relief. 478 F.Supp., at 707.

exemption from the requirements in the interest of national security." [6]

. . .

It goes without saying that an injunction is an equitable remedy. It "is not a remedy which issues as of course," Harrisonville v. U. S. Dickey Clay Mfg. Co., 289 U.S. 334 (1933), or "to restrain an act the injurious consequences of which are merely trifling." Consolidated Canal Co. v. Mesa Canal Co., 177 U.S. 296 (1900). An injunction should issue only where the intervention of a court of equity "is essential in order effectually to protect property rights against injuries otherwise irremediable." Cavanaugh v. Looney, 248 U.S. 453, 456 (1919). The Court has repeatedly held that the basis for injunctive relief in the federal courts has always been irreparable injury and the inadequacy of legal remedies. Rondeau v. Mosinee Paper Corp., 422 U.S. 49, 61 (1975); Sampson v. Murray, 415 U.S. 61, 88 (1974); Beacon Theaters, Inc. v. Westover, 359 U.S. 500, 506–507 (1959); Hecht Co. v. Bowles.

Where plaintiff and defendant present competing claims of injury, the traditional function of equity has been to arrive at a "nice adjustment and reconciliation" between the competing claims, Hecht Co. v. Bowles. In such cases, the court "balances the conveniences of the parties and possible injuries to them according as they may be affected by the granting or withholding of the injunction." Yakus v. United States, 321 U.S. 414, 440 (1944). "The essence of equity has been the power of the chancellor to do equity and to mold each decree to the necessities of the particular case. Flexibility rather than rigidity has distinguished it." Hecht Co. v. Bowles.

In exercising their sound discretion, courts of equity should pay particular regard for the public consequences in employing the extraordinary remedy of injunction. Railroad Comm'n. v. Pullman Co., 312 U.S. 496, 500 (1941). Thus, the Court has noted that "the award of an interlocutory injunction by courts of equity has never been regarded as strictly a matter of right, even though irreparable injury may otherwise result to the plaintiff," and that "where an injunction is asked which will adversely affect a public interest for whose impairment, even temporarily, an injunction bond cannot compensate, the court may in the public interest withhold relief until a final determination of the rights of the parties, though postponement may be burdensome to the plaintiff." Yakus v. United States, supra, 321 U.S., at 440 (footnote omitted). The grant of jurisdiction to insure compliance with a statute hardly suggests an absolute duty to do so under any and all circumstances, and a federal judge sitting as chancellor is not mechanically obligated to grant an injunction for every violation of law. TVA v. Hill, 437 U.S. 153, 193 (1978); Hecht Co. v. Bowles.

These commonplace considerations applicable to cases in which injunctions are sought in the federal courts reflect a "practice with a background of several hundred years of history," Hecht Co. v Bowles, a practice of which

6. 33 U.S.C. § 1323(a) (Supp. III 1976) provides, in relevant part:

"The President may exempt any effluent source of any department, agency, or instrumentality in the executive branch from compliance with any such a requirement if he determines it to be in the paramount interest of the United States to do so. . . . The President shall report each January to the Congress all exemptions from the requirements of this section granted during the preceding calendar year, together with his reason for granting such exemption."

Congress is assuredly well aware. Of course, Congress may intervene and guide or control the exercise of the courts' discretion, but we do not lightly assume that Congress has intended to depart from established principles. Hecht Co. v. Bowles. As the Court said in Porter v. Warner Holding Co., 328 U.S. 395, 398 (1946):

"Moreover, the comprehensiveness of this equitable jurisdiction is not to be denied or limited in the absence of a clear and valid legislative command. Unless a statute in so many words, or by a necessary and inescapable inference, restricts the court's jurisdiction in equity, the full scope of that jurisdiction is to be recognized and applied. 'The great principles of equity, securing complete justice, should not be yielded to light inferences, or doubtful construction.' Brown v. Swann . . . "

In TVA v. Hill, we held that Congress had foreclosed the exercise of the usual discretion possessed by a court of equity. There, we thought that "one would be hard pressed to find a statutory provision whose terms were any plainer" than that before us. 437 U.S., at 173. The statute involved, the Endangered Species Act, 87 Stat. 884, 16 U.S.C. § 1531 et seq., required the district court to enjoin completion of the Tellico Dam in order to preserve the snail darter, a species of perch. The purpose and language of the statute under consideration in *Hill,* not the bare fact of a statutory violation, compelled that conclusion. Section 1536 of the Act requires federal agencies to "insure that actions authorized, funded, or carried out by them do not jeopardize the continued existence of [any] endangered species . . . or result in the destruction or habitat of such species which is determined . . . to be critical." The statute thus contains a flat ban on the destruction of critical habitats.

It was conceded in *Hill* that completion of the dam would eliminate an endangered species by destroying its critical habitat. Refusal to enjoin the action would have ignored the "explicit provisions of the Endangered Species Act." 437 U.S., at 173. Congress, it appeared to us, had chosen the snail darter over the dam. The purpose and language of the statute limited the remedies available to the district court; only an injunction could vindicate the objectives of the Act.

That is not the case here. An injunction is not the only means of ensuring compliance. The FWPCA itself, for example, provides for fines and criminal penalties. 33 U.S.C. § 1319(c) and (d). Respondents suggest that failure to enjoin the Navy will undermine the integrity of the permit process by allowing the statutory violation to continue. The integrity of the nation's waters, however, not the permit process, is the purpose of the FWPCA.[7] As Congress explained, the objective of the FWPCA is to "restore and maintain the chemical, physical and biological integrity of the Nation's waters." 33 U.S.C. § 1251(a).

This purpose is to be achieved by compliance with the Act, including compliance with the permit requirements. Here, however, the discharge of ordnance had not polluted the waters, and, although the District Court de-

7. The objective of this statute is in some respects similar to that sought in nuisance suits, where courts have fully exercised their equitable discretion and ingenuity in ordering remedies. E.g., Spur Ind. Inc. v. Del E. Webb Development Co., 108 Ariz. 178, 494 P.2d 700 (1972); Boomer v. Atlantic Cement Co.

clined to enjoin the discharges, it neither ignored the statutory violation nor undercut the purpose and function of the permit system. The court ordered the Navy to apply for a permit.[9] It temporarily, not permanently, allowed the Navy to continue its activities without a permit.

In *Hill,* we also noted that none of the limited "hardship exemptions" of the Endangered Species Act would "even remotely apply to the Tellico Project." 437 U.S., at 188. The prohibition of the FWPCA against discharge of pollutants, in contrast, can be overcome by the very permit the Navy was ordered to seek. The Senate Report to the 1972 Amendments explains that it was enacting the permit program because "the Committee recognizes the impracticality of any effort to halt all pollution immediately." S.Rep. 92–414, 92d Cong., 1st Sess. 43 (1971), U.S.Code Cong. & Admin.News 1972, p. 3709. That the scheme as a whole contemplates the exercise of discretion and balancing of equities militates against the conclusion that Congress intended to deny courts their traditional equitable discretion in enforcing the statute.

Other aspects of the statutory scheme also suggest that Congress did not intend to deny courts the discretion to rely on remedies other than an immediate prohibitory injunction. Although the ultimate objective of the FWPCA is to eliminate all discharges of pollutants into the navigable waters by 1985, the statute sets forth a scheme of phased compliance. As enacted, it called for the achievement of the "best practicable control technology currently available" by July 1, 1977 and the "best available technology economically achievable" by July 1, 1983. 33 U.S.C. § 1311(b) (Supp. IV 1970). This scheme of phased compliance further suggests that this is a statute in which Congress envisioned, rather than curtailed, the exercise of discretion.[11]

The FWPCA directs the Administrator of the EPA to seek an injunction to restrain immediately discharges of pollutants he finds to be presenting "an imminent and substantial endangerment of the health of persons or to the

9. The Navy applied for a NPDES permit in December, 1979. In May, 1981, the EPA issued a draft NPDES permit and a notice of intent to issue that permit. The FWPCA requires a certification of compliance with state water quality standards before the EPA may issue a NPDES permit. 33 U.S.C. § 1341(a). The Environmental Quality Board of the Commonwealth of Puerto Rico denied the Navy a water quality certificate in connection with this application for a NPDES [permit] in June, 1981. In February, 1982, the Environmental Quality Board denied the Navy's reconsideration request and announced it was adhering to its original ruling. In a letter dated April 9, 1982, the Solicitor General informed the Clerk of the Court that the Navy has filed an action challenging the denial of the water quality certificate. United States of America v. Commonwealth of Puerto Rico, No. 82–0726 (D.P.R.).

11. We have, however, held some standards related to phased compliance to be absolute. See EPA v. National Crushed Stone Association, 449 U.S. 64 (1980). In Middlesex County Sewerage Authority v. National Sea Clammers Ass'n., 453 U.S. 1 (1981), we concluded that the federal common law of nuisance was preempted by the FWPCA and other similar acts: "In the absence of strong indicia of a contrary congressional intent, we are compelled to conclude that Congress provided precisely the remedies it considered appropriate." 453 U.S., at 15; see Milwaukee v. Illinois, 451 U.S. 304 (1981). But, as we have also observed in construing this Act, "The question . . . is not what a court thinks is generally appropriate to the regulatory process, it is what Congress intended . . . ." E.I. Du Pont de Nemours & Co. v. Train, 430 U.S. 112, 138 (1977). Here we do not read the FWPCA as intending to abolish the courts' equitable discretion in ordering remedies.

welfare of persons." 33 U.S.C. § 1364(a). This rule of immediate cessation, however, is limited to the indicated class of violations. For other kinds of violations, the FWPCA authorizes the Administrator of the EPA "to commence a civil action for appropriate relief, including a permanent or temporary injunction, for any violation for which he is authorized to issue a compliance order . . . ." 33 U.S.C. 1319(b).[12] The provision makes clear that Congress did not anticipate that all discharges would be immediately enjoined. Consistent with this view, the administrative practice has not been to request immediate cessation orders. "Rather, enforcement actions typically result, by consent or otherwise, in a remedial order setting out a detailed schedule of compliance designed to cure the identified violation of the Act." Brief for United States 17. See Milwaukee v. Illinois, 451 U.S. 304, 320–322 (1981). Here, again, the statutory scheme contemplates equitable consideration.

Both the Court of Appeals and respondents attach particular weight to the provision of the FWPCA permitting the President to exempt Federal facilities from compliance with the permit requirements. 33 U.S.C. § 1323. They suggest that this provision indicates Congressional intent to limit the court's discretion. According to respondents, the exemption provision evidences Congress' determination that only paramount national interests justify failure to comply and that only the President should make this judgment.

We do not construe the provision so broadly. We read the FWPCA as permitting the exercise of a court's equitable discretion, whether the source of pollution is a private party or a federal agency, to order relief that will achieve *compliance* with the Act. The exemption serves a different and complementary purpose, that of permitting *noncompliance* by federal agencies in extraordinary circumstances. Exec. Order No. 12088, 43 Fed.Reg. 47707, 47709 (1978), which implements the exemption authority, requires the federal agency requesting such an exemption to certify that it cannot meet the applicable pollution standards. "Exemptions are granted by the President only if the conflict between pollution control standards and crucial federal activities cannot be resolved through the development of a practicable remedial program." Brief for United States.

Should the Navy receive a permit here, there would be no need to invoke the machinery of the Presidential exemption. If not, this course remains open. The exemption provision would enable the President, believing para-

12. The statute at issue in Hecht v. Bowles, contained language very similar to that in § 1319(b). It directed the Administrator to seek "a permanent or temporary injunction, restraining order, or other order" to halt violations. The Court determined that such statutory language did not require the court to issue an injunction even when the Administrator had sued for injunctive relief. In *Hecht*, the court's equitable discretion overrode that of the Administrator. If a court can properly refuse an injunction in the circumstances of *Hecht*, the exercise of its discretion seems clearly appropriate in a case such as this, where the EPA Administrator was not a party and had not yet expressed his judgment. The action of the district court permitted it to obtain the benefit of the EPA's recommendation before deciding to enjoin the discharge.

In *Hecht Co.*, unlike here, the violations had ceased by the time the injunction was sought. The Court, however, explained that "the cessation of violations, whether before or after the institution of a suit by the administrator, is no bar to the issuance of an injunction." 321 U.S., at 327. Thus, contrary to the dissent's characterization, the Court did not base its decision on the fact that violations had ceased.

mount national interests so require, to authorize discharges which the district court has enjoined. Reading the statute to permit the exercise of a court's equitable discretion in no way eliminates the role of the exemption provision in the statutory scheme.

Like the language and structure of the Act, the legislative history does not suggest that Congress intended to deny courts their traditional equitable discretion. Congress passed the 1972 Amendments because it recognized that "the national effort to abate and control water pollution has been inadequate in every vital aspect." S.Rep.No. 92–414, 92d Cong., 1st Sess. 7, U.S.Code Cong. & Admin. News p. 3674. The past failings included enforcement efforts under the Rivers and Harbors Appropriation Act of 1899 (Refuse Act), 33 U.S.C. § 401 et seq. The "major purpose" of the 1972 Act was "to establish a comprehensive long-range policy for the elimination of water pollution." S.Rep. 92–414, at 95, U.S.Code Cong. & Admin. News at 3758. The permit system was key to that policy. "The Amendments established a new system of regulation under which it is illegal for anyone to discharge pollutants into the Nation's waters except pursuant to a permit." Milwaukee v. Illinois, 451 U.S., at 310–311; see generally EPA v. State Water Resources Control Board, 426 U.S. 200 (1976). Nonetheless, "in writing the enforcement procedures involving the Federal Government the Committee drew extensively . . . upon the existing enforcement provisions of the Refuse Act of 1899." S.Rep.No. 92–414, at 63, U.S.Code Cong. & Admin. News p. 3730. Violations of the Refuse Act have not automatically led courts to issue injunctions. See Reserve Mining Co. v. EPA, 514 F.2d 492, 535–538 (CA8 1975); United States v. Rohm & Haas Co., 500 F.2d 167, 175 (CA5 1974), cert. denied, 420 U.S. 962 (1975); United States v. Kennebec Log Driving Co., 491 F.2d 562, 571 (CA1 1973), on remand, 399 F.Supp. 754, 759–760 (D.Me.1975).

This Court explained in Hecht v. Bowles that a major departure from the long tradition of equity practice should not be lightly implied. As we did there, we construe the statute at issue "in favor of that interpretation which affords a full opportunity for equity courts to treat enforcement proceedings . . . in accordance with their traditional practices, as conditioned by the necessities of the public interest which Congress has sought to protect." We do not read the FWPCA as foreclosing completely the exercise of the court's discretion. Rather than requiring a District Court to issue an injunction for any and all statutory violations, the FWPCA permits the District Court to order that relief it considers necessary to secure prompt compliance with the Act. That relief can include, but is not limited to, an order of immediate cessation.

The exercise of equitable discretion, which must include the ability to deny as well as grant injunctive relief, can fully protect the range of public interests at issue at this stage in the proceedings. The District Court did not face a situation in which a permit would very likely not issue and the requirements and objective of the statute could therefore not be vindicated if discharges were permitted to continue. Should it become clear that no permit will be issued and that compliance with the FWPCA will not be forthcoming, the statutory scheme and purpose would require the court to reconsider the balance it has struck.

Because Congress, in enacting the FWPCA, has not foreclosed the exercise of equitable discretion, the proper standard for appellate review is whether the district court abused its discretion in denying an immediate cessation order while the Navy applied for a permit. We reverse and remand to Court of Appeals for proceedings consistent with this opinion.

STEVENS, Justice, dissenting.

The appropriate remedy for the violation of a federal statute depends primarily on the terms of the statute and the character of the violation. Unless Congress specifically commands a particular form of relief, the question of remedy remains subject to a court's equitable discretion. Because the Federal Water Pollution Control Act does not specifically command the federal courts to issue an injunction every time an unpermitted discharge of a pollutant occurs, the Court today is obviously correct in asserting that such injunctions should not issue "automatically" or "mechanically" in every case. It is nevertheless equally clear that by enacting the 1972 amendments to the FWPCA Congress channeled the discretion of the federal judiciary much more narrowly than the Court's rather glib opinion suggests. Indeed, although there may well be situations in which the failure to obtain a NPDES permit would not require immediate cessation of all discharges, I am convinced that Congress has circumscribed the district courts' discretion on the question of remedy so narrowly that a general rule of immediate cessation must be applied in all but a narrow category of cases. The Court of Appeals was quite correct in holding that this case does not present the kind of exceptional situation that justifies a departure from the general rule.

The Court's mischaracterization of the Court of Appeals' holding is the premise for its essay on equitable discretion. This essay is analytically flawed because it overlooks the limitations on equitable discretion that apply in cases in which public interests are implicated and the defendant's violation of the law is ongoing. Of greater importance, the Court's opinion grants an open-ended license to federal judges to carve gaping holes in a reticulated statutory scheme designed by Congress to protect a precious natural resource from the consequences of ad hoc judgments about specific discharges of pollutants.

Contrary to the impression created by the Court's opinion, the Court of Appeals did not hold that the District Court was under an absolute duty to require compliance with the FWPCA "under any and all circumstances," or that it was "mechanically obligated to grant an injunction for every violation of law." The only "absolute duty" that the Court of Appeals mentioned was the Navy's duty to obtain a permit before discharging pollutants into the waters off Vieques Island.[2] In light of the Court's opinion the point is worth repeating—the Navy, like anyone else,[3] must obey the law.

2. "Whether or not the Navy's activities in fact harm the coastal waters, it has an absolute statutory obligation to stop any discharges of pollutants until the permit procedure has been followed and the Administrator of the Environmental Protection Agency, upon review of the evidence, has granted a permit." Romero-Barcelo v. Brown, 643 F.2d 835, 861 (CA1 1981).

This statement by the Court of Appeals is entirely consistent with the comments in the Senate Report on the legislation that "[e]nforcement of violations . . . should be based on relatively narrow fact situations requiring a minimum of discretionary decision making or delay," and that "the issue before the

3. See note 3 on page 154.

The Court of Appeals did not hold that the District Court had no discretion in formulating remedies for statutory violations. It merely "conclude[d] that the district court erred in undertaking a traditional balancing of the parties' competing interests." . . . The District Court was not free to disregard the "congressional ordering of priorities" and "the judiciary's 'responsibility to protect the integrity of the . . . process mandated by Congress.'" . . . The Court of Appeals distinguished a statutory violation that could be deemed merely "technical" from the Navy's "[utter disregard of] the statutory mandate." Id., at 861–862. It then pointed out that an order prohibiting any discharge of ordnance into the coastal waters off Vieques until an NPDES permit was obtained would not significantly affect the Navy's training operations because most, if not all, of the Navy's targets were land based. Finally, it noted that the statute authorized the Navy to obtain an exemption from the President if an injunction would have a significant effect on national security. Id., at 862; see 33 U.S.C. § 1323(a).

Under these circumstances—the statutory violation is blatant and not merely technical, and the Navy's predicament was foreseen and accommodated by Congress—the Court of Appeals essentially held that the District Court retained no discretion to deny an injunction. The discretion exercised by the District Court in this case was wholly at odds with the intent of Congress in enacting the FWPCA. In essence, the District Court's remedy was a judicial permit exempting the Navy's operations in Vieques from the statute until such time as it could obtain a permit from the Environmental Protection Agency or a statutory exemption from the President. The two principal bases for the temporary judicial permit were matters that Congress did not commit to judicial discretion. First, the District Court was persuaded that the pollution was not harming the quality of the coastal waters . . . ; and second, the court was concerned that compliance with the Act might adversely affect national security. The Court of Appeals correctly noted that the first consideration is the business of the EPA [4] and the second is the business of the President.[5]

courts would be a factual one of whether there had been compliance." S.Rep.No. 92–414, 92d Cong., 1st Sess., 64, 80 (1971), U.S. Code Cong. & Admin. News 1972, pp. 3730, 3746.

3. The statute expressly subjects federal agencies to all laws "respecting the control and abatement of water pollution in the same manner, and to the same extent as any nongovernmental entity." 33 U.S.C. § 1323(a). . . .

4. "Not only are the technical problems difficult—doubtless the reason Congress vested authority to administer the Act in administrative agencies possessing the necessary expertise—but the general area is particularly unsuited to the approach inevitable under a regime of federal common law. Congress criticized past approaches to water pollution control as being 'sporadic' and 'ad hoc,' S.Rep.No. 92–414, p. 95 (1971), 2 Leg. Hist. 1511, apt characterizations of any judicial approach applying federal common law, see Wilburn Boat Co. v. Fireman's Fund Ins. Co., 348 U.S. 310 (1955)." Milwaukee v. Illinois, 431 U.S. 304.

5. In my opinion the national security considerations that were persuasive to the District Court are not matters that are suitable for judicial evaluation. Congress has wisely given the President virtually unlimited authority to exempt the military from the statute on national defense grounds. If those grounds justify an exemption in this case, the Navy clearly should have obtained it from its Commander-in-Chief, not from a judge unlearned in such matters. This Court, however, makes the curious argument that the presidential exemption was intended to permit *noncompliance* with the statute and therefore merely complements the equitable discretion of a dis-

The Court unfairly uses the Court of Appeals' opinion in this case as a springboard for a lecture on the principles of equitable remedies. The Court of Appeals' reasoning was correct in all respects. It recognized that the statute categorically prohibits discharges of pollutants without a permit. Unlike the Court, it recognized that the requested injunction was the only remedy that would bring the Navy into compliance with the statute on Congress' timetable.[6] It then demonstrated that none of the reasons offered by the District Court for refusing injunctive relief was consistent with the statute or was compelling under the circumstances. The position of the Court of Appeals in effect was that the federal courts' equitable discretion is constrained by a strong presumption in favor of enforcing the law as Congress has written it. By reversing, the Court casts doubt on the validity of that position. This doubt is especially dangerous in the environmental area, where the temptations to delay compliance are already substantial.[7]

Our cases concerning equitable remedies have repeatedly identified two critical distinctions that the Court simply ignores today. The first is the distinction between cases in which only private interests are involved and those in which a requested injunction will implicate a public interest. Second, within the category of public interest cases, those cases in which there is no danger that a past violation of law will recur have always been treated differently from those in which an existing violation is certain to continue.

Yakus v. United States, 321 U.S. 414, 441, illustrates the first distinction. The Court there held that Congress constitutionally could preclude a private party from obtaining an injunction against enforcement of federal price control regulations pending an adjudication of their validity. In any balancing process, the Court explained, special deference must be given to the public interest:

"Even in suits in which only private interests are involved the award is a matter of sound judicial discretion, in the exercise of which the court balances the conveniences of the parties and possible injuries to them according as they may be affected by the granting or withholding of the injunction. . . .

"But where an injunction is asked which will adversely affect a public interest for whose impairment, even temporarily, an injunction bond cannot compensate, the court may in the public interest withhold relief until a final determination of the rights of the parties, though the postponement may be burdensome to the plaintiff."

In that case, the public interest, reflected in an act of Congress, was in opposition to the availability of injunctive relief. The Court stated, however, that

trict court also to authorize noncompliance.

6. The District Court ordered the Navy to file for a NPDES permit " 'with all deliberate speed.' " . . .

7. It is ironic that the Court comes to the aid of the Navy even though Congress authorized an executive exemption for federal (particularly military) operations but no analogous exemption for important private activities, and even though Congress intended federal agencies to assume a leadership role in the water pollution control effort. To paraphrase the Senate Report, the Federal Government cannot expect private industry to obey the law by ceasing discharges of pollutants until a permit is obtained if the Federal Government is not willing to obey the same law or at least invoke a statutory exemption. See S.Rep.No. 92–414, 92d Cong., 1st Sess., 67 (1971).

the public interest factor would have the same special weight if it favored the granting of an injunction:

"This is but another application of the principle, declared in Virginia Ry. Co. v. System Federation, 300 U.S. 515, 552, that 'Courts of equity may, and frequently do, go much farther both to give and withhold relief in furtherance of the public interest than they are accustomed to go when only private interests are involved.' "

Hecht Co. v. Bowles which the Court repeatedly cites, did involve an attempt to obtain an injunction against future violations of a federal statute. That case fell into the category of cases in which a past violation of law had been found and the question was whether an injunction should issue to prevent future violations. Cf. United States v. W. T. Grant Co.; United States v. Oregon Medical Society, 343 U.S. 326, 332–334. Because the record established that the past violations were inadvertent, that they had been promptly terminated, and that the defendant had taken vigorous and adequate steps to prevent any recurrence, the Court held that the District Court had discretion to deny injunctive relief. But in reaching that conclusion, the Court made it clear that judicial discretion "must be exercised in light of the large objectives of the Act. For the standards of the public interest, not the requirements of private litigation, measure the propriety and need for injunctive relief in these cases." Indeed, the Court emphasized that any exercise of discretion "should reflect an acute awareness of the congressional admonition" in the statute at issue.

In contrast to the decision in *Hecht,* today the Court pays mere lip service to the statutory mandate and attaches no weight to the fact that the Navy's violation of law has not been corrected.[8] The Court cites no precedent for its holding that an ongoing deliberate violation of a federal statute should be treated like any garden-variety private nuisance action in which the chancellor has the widest discretion in fashioning relief.[9] . . .

The Court's discussion of the FWPCA creates the impression that Congress did not intend any significant change in the enforcement provisions of the Rivers and Harbors Appropriation Act of 1899. The Court goes so far as to suggest that the FWPCA is little more than a codification of the common law of nuisance. The contrast between this casual attitude toward the FWPCA and the Court's writing in Milwaukee v. Illinois, 451 U.S. 304, is stark. In that case the Court refused to allow federal judges to supplement the statutory enforcement scheme by enjoining a nuisance, whereas in this case the question is whether a federal judge may create a loophole in the scheme by refusing to enjoin a violation. Why a different standard should be used to define the scope of judicial discretion in these two situations is not explained.

In Milwaukee v. Illinois the Court described the FWPCA in these terms:

"The statutory scheme established by Congress provides a forum for the pursuit of such claims before expert agencies by means of the permit-granting process. It would be quite inconsistent with this scheme if federal courts were in effect to 'write their own ticket' under the guise of federal common

8. The Navy has been in continuous violation of the statute during the entire decade since its enactment.

9. Indeed, I am unaware of any case in which the Court has permitted a statutory violation to continue.

law after permits have already been issued and permittees have been planning and operating in reliance on them." Id., at 326.

Ironically, today the Court holds that federal district courts may in effect "write their own ticket" under the guise of federal common law *before* permits have been issued.

The Court distinguishes TVA v. Hill, 437 U.S. 153, on the ground that the Endangered Species Act contained a "flat ban" on the destruction of critical habitats. But the statute involved in this case also contains a flat ban against discharges of pollutants into coastal waters without a permit. Surely the congressional directive to protect the Nation's waters from gradual but possibly irreversible contamination is no less clear than the command to protect the snail darter. To assume that Congress has placed a greater value on the protection of vanishing forms of animal life than on the protection of our water resources is to ignore the text, the legislative history,[15] and the previously consistent interpretation of this statute.[16]

It is true that in TVA v. Hill there was no room for compromise between the federal project and the statutory objective to preserve an endangered species; either the snail darter or the completion of the Tellico Dam had to be sacrificed. In the FWPCA, the Court tells us, the congressional objective is to protect the integrity of the Nation's waters, not to protect the integrity of the permit process. Therefore, the Court continues, a federal court may compromise the process chosen by Congress to protect our waters as long as the court is content that the waters are not actually being harmed by the particular discharge of pollutants.

On analysis, however, this reasoning does not distinguish the two cases. Courts are in no better position to decide whether the permit process is necessary to achieve the objectives of the FWPCA than they are to decide whether the destruction of the snail darter is an acceptable cost of completing the Tellico Dam. Congress has made both decisions, and there is nothing in the respective statutes or legislative histories to suggest that Congress invited the federal courts to secondguess the former decision any more than the latter.

A disregard of the respective roles of the three branches of government also tarnishes the Court's other principal argument in favor of expansive equitable discretion in this area. The Court points out that Congress intended to halt water pollution gradually, not immediately, and that "the scheme as a whole contemplates the exercise of discretion and balancing of equities." In the Court's words, Congress enacted a "scheme of phased compliance." Eq-

15. The Senate Report emphasized that "if the timetables established throughout the Act are to be met, the threat of sanction must be real, and enforcement provisions must be swift and direct." S.Rep.No. 92-414, 92d Cong., 1st Sess., 65 (1971), U.S.Code Cong. & Admin.News 1972, p. 3731.

16. "The establishment of such a self-consciously comprehensive program by Congress, which certainly did not exist when Illinois v. Milwaukee was decided, strongly suggests that there is no room for courts to attempt to improve on that program with federal common law." Milwaukee v. Illinois, 451 U.S. 304, 319.

Today's holding that a federal court has inherent power to grant exemptions from the statutory permit requirement presents a dramatic contrast with the holding in Milwaukee v. Illinois:

"Federal courts lack authority to impose more stringent effluent limitations under federal common law than those imposed by the agency charged by Congress with administering this comprehensive scheme." Id., at 320.

uitable discretion in enforcing the statute, the Court states, is therefore consistent with the statutory scheme.

The Court's sophistry is premised on a gross misunderstanding of the statutory scheme. Naturally, in 1972 Congress did not expect discharges to end pollution immediately. Rather, it entrusted to expert administrative agencies the task of establishing timetables by which dischargers could reach that ultimate goal. These timetables are determined by the agencies and included in the NPDES permits; the conditions in the permits constitute the terms by which compliance with the statute is measured. Quite obviously, then, the requirement that each discharger subject itself to the permit process is crucial to the operation of the "scheme of phased compliance." By requiring each discharger to obtain a permit *before* continuing its discharges of pollutants, Congress demonstrated an intolerance for delay in compliance with the statute. It is also obvious that the "exercise of discretion and balancing of equities" were tasks delegated by Congress to expert agencies, not to federal courts, yet the Court simply ignores the difference.

The decision in TVA v. Hill did not depend on any peculiar or unique statutory language. Nor did it rest on any special interest in snail darters. The decision reflected a profound respect for the law and the proper allocation of lawmaking responsibilities in our government.[20] There we refused to sit as a committee of review. Today the Court authorizes free thinking federal judges to do just that. Instead of requiring adherence to carefully integrated statutory procedures that assign to nonjudicial decisionmakers the responsibilities for evaluating potential harm to our water supply as well as potential harm to our national security, the Court unnecessarily and casually substitutes the chancellor's clumsy foot for the rule of law.

I respectfully dissent.

---

1) Does *Romero-Barcelo* write a new chapter of government by injunction: government by noninjunction when judges disagree with the legislature? Does the majority a) merely read common law discretion back into the stat-

20. "Our individual appraisal of the wisdom or unwisdom of a particular course consciously selected by the Congress is to be put aside in the process of interpreting a statute. Once the meaning of an enactment is discerned and its constitutionality determined, the judicial process comes to an end. We do not sit as a committee of review, nor are we vested with the power of veto. The lines ascribed to Sir Thomas More by Robert Bolt are not without relevance here:

'The law, Roper, the law. I know what's legal, not what's right. And I'll stick to what's legal. . . . I'm *not* God. The currents and eddies of right and wrong, which you find such plainsailing, I can't navigate, I'm no voyager. But in the thickets of the law, oh there I'm a forester. . . . What would you do? Cut a great road through the law to get after the Devil? . . . And when the last law was down, and the Devil turned round on you—where would you hide, Roper, the laws all being flat? . . . This country's planted thick with laws from coast to coast—Man's laws, not God's—and if you cut them down . . . d'you really think you could stand upright in the winds that would blow then? . . . Yes, I'd give the Devil benefit of law, for my own safety's sake.' R. Bolt, A Man for All Seasons, Act I, p. 147 (Three Plays, Heinemann ed. 1967).

"We agree with the Court of Appeals that in our constitutional system the commitment to the separation of powers is too fundamental for us to pre-empt congressional action by judicially decreeing what accords with 'common sense and the public weal.' Our Constitution vests such responsibilities in the political branches." TVA v. Hill, 437 U.S. 153, 194–195.

ute? b) construe the statute to tell Congress that a statute must override equitable discretion specifically? c) hold the remedy "at law" adequate because the statute is essentially procedural and the purpose of the procedure has been accomplished? d) follow *Brown II-Reserve Mining* phased compliance with an implied "all deliberate speed" to allow defendants to comply? e) find that an injunction was too severe a remedy for technical or *de minimus* violations?

Does the Court fail to distinguish between judge-made and statutory standards? Did the *Romero-Barcelo* Court read *Hecht*'s language and ignore its holding? Professor Plater charges that the majority failed to appreciate that the prior decisions "involved only threshold questions . . . and the choice of remedy." Thus, the majority was "able to presume that equity had always balanced everything." Plater, 70 Calif.L.Rev. at 593 n. 324. Did Congress intend the executive or the judiciary to exercise the statute's flexibility? Plater thinks that *Romero-Barcelo* is the first statutory equity decision where judges have overridden "the specific prohibitions of a statute." 70 Calif.L.Rev. at 594. Is that interpretation correct?

2) On the other hand, reconsider *Romero-Barcelo* in light of *Boomer,* p. 79. Is *Romero-Barcelo* so astounding after all? Don't both courts resort to discretion to deny plaintiffs an injunction that would forbid an activity the court concedes is unlawful? Which decision is easier to justify? Remember that Plater distinguishes nonstatutory from statutory substantive standards on the ground that "abatement was decided anew in each case." 70 Calif.L.Rev. at 543.

3) Afterword: The Commonwealth of Puerto Rico has denied the Navy's application for a discharge permit. The Navy has sued to reverse that decision. The Court's majority said that such a denial might require different considerations on remand. Formulate an order for the court of appeals to enter on remand. Remember the district judge's initial response. See Plater, 70 Calif.L.Rev. at 594.

4) On September 20, 1982 EPA's Administrator sent to Regional Administrators a "Memorandum Outlining Enforcement Policy on Industrial Sources Not in Compliance with Clean Air Act By Dec. 31, 1982 Deadline." Based on *Romero-Barcelo*, the Memorandum dealt with the problem "that some sources will not be able to achieve timely compliance . . ." by the statutory deadline. "[B]oth the Justice Department and EPA's Office of Legal and Enforcement Counsel have concluded that a district court has equity power to fashion relief that allows a source to continue in operation beyond 1982 while taking steps to come into compliance. As a matter of policy, shutdown by 1982 may be the appropriate relief in some cases, but an expeditious compliance schedule going beyond 1982 may be appropriate in others. Proceeding from that conclusion, this policy sets forth criteria to determine the specific equitable relief the Agency should seek in each case. . . . As a general rule, the goal of any EPA enforcement action against a source in a primary non-attainment area is to bring the source into compliance as expeditiously as possible, but no later than the end of 1982. However, when EPA seeks enforcement in Court, we can stipulate to facts that would warrant relief which allows the source to remain in operation and out of compliance beyond 1982 if, at a minimum, all of the following threshold

criteria are met: 1) the source must be unable to comply by December 31, 1982, other than by shutdown, 2) the source must demonstrate that there is a public interest in continued operation of the source which outweighs the environmental cost of an additional period of noncompliance, and 3) if there is any doubt about the source's financial condition, the source must demonstrate that it will have sufficient funds to be able to comply expeditiously."

Before the EPA agrees to stipulate, the three criteria must be met and a complaint must be filed seeking an injunction. The order "should insure" that the defendant commits to comply "as expeditiously as possible," and agrees to a compliance schedule that "contains enforceable increments of progress." The order should require "interim emission limitations and controls to the extent practicable," agree not to increase emissions, include monitoring and reporting requirements, provide for stipulated penalties for failure to meet timetables, compel "payment of a significant cash civil penalty" reflecting "the economic benefit of delayed compliance," and reserve the right to seek further equitable relief including shutdown for noncompliance.

LANKFORD v. GELSTON

364 F.2d 197 (4th Cir. 1966).

Before HAYNSWORTH, Chief Judge, and SOBELOFF, BOREMAN, BRYAN and J. SPENCER BELL, Circuit Judges, sitting en banc.

SOBELOFF, Circuit Judge: Negro families of Baltimore City, four in number but acting in behalf of others similarly situated, as well as in their own behalf, instituted an action in the United States District Court for the District of Maryland, seeking injunctive relief against the Police Commissioner of Baltimore City to prevent further invasions of their right to privacy guaranteed by the Fourth and Fourteenth Amendments to the Constitution. Jurisdiction is grounded on 28 U.S.C.A. § 1343, as authorized by 42 U.S.C.A. § 1983.[1]

The District Court heard the testimony of forty-two witnesses and received a summary of the police records from a team of special masters chosen from the membership of the Junior Bar Association of Baltimore City. This case, which has attained considerable notoriety, stems from the efforts of the Baltimore Police Department to capture Samuel and Earl Veney, two brothers who shot and killed one policeman and seriously wounded another. During a nineteen-day period in December, 1964, and January, 1965, the police conducted searches of more than 300 houses, most of them private dwellings. The searches were based in almost every instance on unverified anonymous tips. In none did the police have a search warrant. Although the court found that the police, in conducting these searches at all hours of the day and night, upon telephone tips from unknown persons, had deprived plaintiffs and others of their constitutional rights, it refused to issue an injunction and denied plaintiffs relief. The court, however, retained jurisdiction of the case

1. Baltimore City is a municipal corporation of the State of Maryland, but its Police Commissioner is an appointee of the Governor. . . . Both at trial and on appeal the Police Commissioner was represented by the Attorney General of Maryland. . . .

in order to process expeditiously any future claim of invasion of the plaintiffs' rights.

There is no dispute over the facts. On the evening of December 24, 1964, several persons committed an armed robbery of a liquor store in Baltimore City, in the course of which Police Lieutenant James Maskell was shot and seriously wounded. A suspect was soon apprehended near the scene of the crime and after questioning him, several police officers visited homes in the area in search of other suspects. At about 4:50 a.m., on December 25, Police Sergeant Jack Cooper, a uniformed officer in a cruising car and a member of the search party, was found fatally shot near his cruiser.

Early in the morning of December 25, warrants were issued for the arrest of Samuel Veney and his brother Earl, charging them with the robbery of the liquor store and with assaulting and shooting Lieutenant Maskell.[2] The Veney brothers were justifiably believed by the police to be armed and extremely dangerous. Later that day, the then Police Commissioner, Bernard Schmidt, authorized a special squad to be formed under the command of Captain Joseph Mahrer to search for the Veneys. About 50 or 60 police officers were members of the squad at one time or another.

Between December 25 and January 12, the Baltimore police made more than 300 "turn-ups" in an unsuccessful effort to locate and arrest the Veneys. In police parlance a turn-up is an investigation of a location and usually includes a search of the premises. Most of the searches here were of private residences. The Veneys are Negroes, and most of the dwellings searched were occupied by Negroes.[3]

The court found that:

"The police records with respect to many of the searches are sketchy and incomplete. Frequently all that is shown is that a particular address was turned-up on a particular day.

"The police did not apply for or obtain search warrants for the search of any of the more than 300 premises they entered." 240 F.Supp. at 553–554.

A policy emergency vehicle carrying shotguns, submachine guns, tear gas apparatus, and bulletproof vests accompanied the men on every search. Before each turn-up a surveillance team of plainclothesmen would drive past the building to locate exits, alleyways, etc., but there were no inquiries in the neighborhoods about the houses to be searched nor was there any other investigation of the tips, except to observe the character of the neighborhood.

2. The police believed that the Veneys had also killed Sergeant Cooper.

3. The special masters' summary of the police records listed 300 searches by dates:

Date	Searches
12/24	0
12/25	4
12/26	39
12/27	16
12/28	16
12/29	28
12/30	35
12/31	54
1/1	26
1/2	23
1/3	7
1/4	18
1/5	5
1/6	10
1/7	4
1/8	7
1/9	4
1/10	2
1/11	1
1/12	1

Four officers carrying shotguns or submachine guns and wearing bulletproof vests would go to the front door and knock. They would be accompanied or followed by supervising officers, a sergeant or lieutenant. Other men would surround the house, training their weapons on windows and doors. "As soon as an occupant opened the door, the first man would enter the house to look for any immediate danger, and the supervising officer would then talk to the person who had answered the door. Few stated any objection to the entry; some were quite willing to have the premises searched for the Veneys, while others acquiesced because of the show of force."

"The officers involved worked exceptionally long hours. Some were polite and considerate of the occupants. Others were abrupt, and without adequate explanation of their purpose, flashed lights on beds where children were sleeping and otherwise upset the occupants of the home being searched."

Few specific instances need be detailed to illustrate the consequences of police reliance on anonymous tips and the terrifying experiences to which occupants of the searched homes were subjected.

Samuel Lankford and his wife, who have six children, have resided at 2707 Parkwood Avenue since 1949. Mr. Lankford has worked at the U.S. Post Office in Baltimore for over ten years. At about 1:15 a.m. on January 2, 1965, Lieutenant Robert Hewes was told by a communications center officer that he had received a call that the Veney brothers were at this address with a family named Garrett. A few minutes before 2:00 a.m. Lieutenant Hewes and his search party converged upon Parkwood Avenue. Upon their arrival in the neighborhood they met on the street a Negro man, described by the lieutenant as "respectable looking," who identified himself as the person that had called the communications center. He told Lieutenant Hewes that he had been told by a newspaper boy that two men resembling the Veneys had entered a house on Parkwood Avenue. At 2:00 a.m. a search party led by the lieutenant knocked on the door, and Mrs. Lankford, awakened by the knock, opened the door. The officers entered the house and began their search while the lieutenant talked with the woman. She told him that her name was not Garrett. At the trial she denied that the officers asked for or were given permission to search, and Lieutenant Hewes acknowledged that his men had already gone to the second floor while he was talking with her. The husband was awakened in his second floor bedroom by two flashlights shining in his face and found four men with shotguns in his room. They questioned him, while other officers searched the remaining rooms including the children's bedrooms, and left.

Mr. and Mrs. Wallace have made their home at 2408 Huron Street for 21 years. They live with a three-year old son, three daughters, Lucinda (a Baltimore public school teacher), Harrietta (a college student), and Sharon (a high school student), and two other relatives. At 8:30 p.m. on December 30, 1964, Lieutenant Coll of the Southwest District was told by a clerk at another police station that she had received an anonymous call from a man who said that the Veneys were being sheltered at this address. Lieutenant Coll testified that since this was the first time that the Veneys had been placed in this neighborhood, he felt that an investigation was in order. A little after

9:00 p.m. Lieutenant Coll led about 14 officers to the house. When the police arrived, Lucinda Wallace was showing slides to a group of her family and guests. Mr. and Mrs. Wallace were both out, Mrs. Wallace at a beauty shop she operated four doors away. Six officers armed with shotguns and rifles entered and searched the home; others who were stationed outside would not allow Mrs. Wallace to enter and refused to explain what was happening. Reduced to tears, she was finally admitted to her home, where she was joined by her children, all crying hysterically. As the policemen were departing, they told Lucinda and her mother that they had received an anonymous call that the Veneys were in the house.

At the trial several police officers, each with long experience on the Baltimore police force, testified that in serious cases it was routine practice to make searches of homes on the basis of anonymous calls. They recognized the difficulty in authenticating such tips, and testified that they attempted to do so by evaluating the tone of voice used by the caller. The officers further stated that not infrequently they would also conduct searches based on tips received from the outside and transmitted to them by police telephone clerks.

On January 8, 1966, plaintiffs' attorneys brought the complaint to the chambers of the District Judge and asked for a temporary restraining order. At a hearing held that afternoon, the Deputy Attorney General represented to the court that the Police Commissioner would promptly issue a general order dealing with the problems raised in the complaint. Based on that representation, the District Court denied the request for a temporary restraining order, and set the case for trial on January 14.

On January 11 the Police Commissioner did issue General Order No. 10388.[4] In the essence the Order forbids police officers from searching "any premises for the purpose of arresting a person for whom an arrest warrant has

4. "*General Order:* January 11, 1965. No. 10388

"*Subject: Service of Arrest Warrants* "The question has recently arisen as to the precise scope of the authority conferred upon police officers by arrest warrants, and specifically whether such warrants authorize entry upon private property for the purpose of locating and arresting the defendant named in the warrant.

"A police officer may make a peaceable or a forcible entry to search any premises for the purpose of arresting a person for whom an arrest warrant has been issued, if, but only if, the officer has probable cause to believe the accused person to be on the premises to be searched.

"In this context, 'probable cause' is said to exist where the facts and circumstances within the officer's knowledge and of which he has reasonably trustworthy information are sufficient in themselves to warrant a man of reasonable caution to believe that the accused person is on the premises to be searched.

"The officer should, where practicable, seek admission to the suspected premises by announcing his identity, the existence of the arrest warrant, and his desire to search for and arrest the accused person. If the officer has any doubt as to the existence of 'probable cause,' he should immediately either seek the issuance of a search warrant, or consult with the office of the State's Attorney for Baltimore City or of the Attorney General of the State of Maryland before attempting entry upon private premises in search of the accused person.

"In all instances, consideration should be given to the convenience of the persons whose premises are to be searched and the other residents of the neighborhood. In this connection, it may at times be necessary, and in the public interest, to make such searches in the nighttime when most of the residents would not be on the street, when the possibility of warning and escape would be less, and when greater safety would be afforded the arresting officer.

"Copies: Inspectors, All Districts, Divisions, Units."

been issued" unless "the officer has probable cause to believe the accused person to be on the premises to be searched." The determination of what constitutes probable cause is still left to the policeman, and there is nothing in the Order which specifically prohibits officers from conducting searches grounded only on anonymous tips, which is precisely the evil to which the Complaint was addressed. We therefore find nothing in General Order No. 10388 which would make the issuance of an injunction unnecessary.

In refusing injunctive relief, the District Court emphasized the reluctance of the federal judiciary to employ its equity power to control police practices and noted that

"this Court has now stated the basic principles which must be observed by the police in determining whether there are reasonable grounds for a contemplated entry. The Court is satisfied that the Police Commissioner and other police officers will make a bona fide effort to observe those rules. They did observe them during the remainder of the search for the Veneys after the Commissioner issued General Order No. 10388 on January 11." 240 F.Supp. at 561.

We conclude, however, that in striking the balance between the role of the federal court in the preservation of the constitutional rights of the appellants and the independence of state officials, the District Court erred when it refused to issue an injunction prohibiting the police from conducting searches based only on uncorroborated anonymous tips and hence without probable cause.

This case reveals a series of the most flagrant invasions of privacy ever to come under the scrutiny of a federal court. The undisputed testimony indicates that the police in conducting the wholesale Veney raids were engaging in a practice which on a smaller scale has routinely attended efforts to apprehend persons accused of serious crime. If denying relief in these circumstances should be held a proper exercise of judicial restraint, it would be difficult to envision any case justifying judicial intervention. The parties seeking redress have committed no acts warranting violation of the privacy of their homes; there has never been any suspicion concerning them or their associations. It was not contended by the Attorney General, nor could it have been contended, that information from an anonymous and unverifiable source is probable cause for the search of a home.

Instances have often come to the attention of courts in which persons accused of crime have sought to prevent the use against them of illegally seized incriminating evidence. But it is only in the rare instance that a person not accused or even suspected of any crime petitions the court for redress of police invasion of his home. The reason is not that such invasions do not occur but, as Mr. Justice Jackson eloquently put it:

"Only occasional and more flagrant abuses come to the attention of the courts, and then only those where the search and seizure yields incriminating evidence and the defendant is at least sufficiently compromised to be indicted. If the officers raid a home, an office, or stop and search an automobile but find nothing incriminating, this invasion of the personal liberty of the innocent too often finds no practical redress. There may be, and I am convinced that there are, many unlawful searches of homes and automobiles of innocent people which turn up nothing incriminating, in which no arrest is made, about which courts do nothing, and about which we never hear.

" . . . There is no opportunity for injunction or appeal to disinterested intervention. The citizen's choice is quietly to submit to whatever the officers undertake or to resist at risk of arrest or immediate violence." Brinegar v. United States, 338 U.S. 160, 181–182 (1949) (Mr. Justice Jackson dissenting).

There can be little doubt that actions for money damages would not suffice to repair the injury suffered by the victims of the police searches. Neither the personal assets of policemen nor the nominal bonds they furnish afford genuine hope of redress. Nor is there any provision for compensation from public funds. In any event the wrongs inflicted are not readily measurable in terms of dollars and cents. Indeed, the Supreme Court itself has already declared that the prospect of pecuniary redress for the harm suffered is "worthless and futile." Moreover, the lesson of experience is that the remote possibility of money damages serves as no deterrent to future police invasions. Mapp v. State of Ohio, 367 U.S. 643, 651–652 (1961), and concurring opinion of Mr. Justice Douglas at 666, 670 . . . .

The appellants' position has been lucidly articulated by their attorneys:

"Unless equity courts find means to protect the innocent homeowners, who are the principal beneficiaries of the Fourth Amendment, their rights will not be protected. It would be a grotesque irony if our courts protect only against the unlawful search which actually uncovers contraband (by the exclusionary rule), while offering no relief against an admittedly unlawful pattern and practice affecting hundreds of innocent homeowners." Brief of Appellants, p. 38.

We are persuaded that the injunction should issue even though the Veney raids have ceased and notwithstanding the Police Commissioner's General Order No. 10388. These raids were not isolated instances undertaken by individual police officers. They were rather the effectuation of a plan conceived by high ranking officials. All members of the Police Department, from the Commissioner down to the raw recruit, are expected to be familiar with the principle that if the police intend to conduct a search of a man's home for a suspect, they must at least have probable cause to believe that he is on the premises. The doctrine is not subtle; it touches the very heart of law enforcement practices, and has found expression in numerous judicial opinions.[6] Its force could not have escaped the Commissioner and other members of the police hierarchy, yet the raids were carried on relentlessly for 19 days. The grave character of the department's conduct places a strong obligation on the court to make sure that similar conduct will not recur. Police protestations of repentance and reform timed to anticipate or to blunt the

6. . . . Even a cursory reading of the Fourth Amendment will not fail to convey the idea that an essential requirement before police may enter a private home is the existence of probable cause:

"The right of the people to be secure in their persons, houses, papers, and effects against unreasonable searches and seizures, shall not be violated, and no Warrants shall issue, but upon probable cause, supported by Oath or affirmation, and particularly describing the place to be searched, and the persons or things to be seized."

force of a lawsuit offer insufficient assurance that similar raids will not ensue when another aggravated crime occurs. See United States v. W. T. Grant Co.; Bailey v. Patterson, 323 F.2d 201, 205–206 (5th Cir. 1963); Anderson v. City of Albany, Georgia, 321 F.2d 649, 656–657 (5th Cir. 1963); Developments in the Law—Injunctions, 78 Harv.L.Rev. 994, 1076 (1965). In fact, it is perhaps more reasonable to view the cessation of the raids and the promulgation of General Order No. 10388 not as belated acts of repentance but as the recognition of the futility of continuing the searches when it had become manifest that the Veneys had made their escape. They were later apprehended in New York State.

The General Order, in reciting no more than that probable cause is required to conduct a search, is in no sense a recognition that the conduct complained of fell short of established legal standards; it adds nothing to the general rule with which the rank-and-file policeman should already have been familiar. It is too vague to provide even a faint warning that searches based only on anonymous tips do not constitute proper police tactics. It would not have been too much to expect in these circumstances a forthright statement that officers conducting such illegal searches in the future will subject themselves to disciplinary action.

The plaintiffs, in their argument in the District Court maintained that the police behavior was racially discriminatory since most of the homes searched were occupied by Negroes. This contention the District Court rejected, reasoning that the police concentrated on Negro residences because the Veneys are Negroes and most of the information received related to their supposed presence in Negro neighborhoods. While this ruling of the District Court is not contested on appeal, we think that it has a substantial bearing on the question of whether injunctive relief is appropriate. The District Judge himself noted that "[t]he evidence does show what has become common knowledge in Baltimore—that the relations between the Negro community and the police have deteriorated seriously."

Baltimore City has escaped thus far the agony and brutality of the riots experienced in New York City, Los Angeles, Chicago, and other urban centers. Courts cannot shut their eyes to events that have been widely publicized throughout the nation and the world. Lack of respect for the police is conceded to be one of the factors generating violent outbursts in Negro communities. The invasions so graphically depicted in this case "could" happen in prosperous suburban neighborhoods, but the innocent victims know only that wholesale raids do not happen elsewhere and did happen to them. Understandably they feel that such illegal treatment is reserved for those elements who the police believe cannot or will not challenge them. It is of the highest importance to community morale that the courts shall give firm and effective reassurance, especially to those who feel that they have been harassed by reason of their color or their poverty.

After so vast a demonstration of disregard of private rights, the complainants are entitled to a clear response. While the immediate pressure of wholesale raids has been withdrawn, the practice of indiscriminate searches of homes has been renounced only obliquely, if at all, and the danger of repetition has not been removed. The sense of impeding crisis in police-community relations persists, and nothing would so directly ameliorate it as a judicial decree forbidding the practices complained of.[7]

In ordering the issuance of an injunction we have not blotted from our consideration the serious problems faced by the law enforcement officer in his daily work. His training stresses the techniques of the prevention of crime and the apprehension of criminals, and what seems to him to be the logical and practical means to solve a crime or to arrest a suspect may turn out to be a deprivation of another's constitutional rights. And where one policeman is killed and another wounded, the police, and the public, too, are understandably outraged and impatient with any obstacle in the search for the murderer. While fully appreciating the exceedingly difficult task of the policeman, a court must not be deterred from protecting rights secured to all by the Constitution.

The police department is society's instrumentality to maintain law and order, and to be fully effective it must have public confidence and cooperation. Confidence can exist only if it is generally recognized that the department uses its enforcement procedures with integrity and zeal, according to law and without resort to oppressive measures. Law observance by the police cannot be divorced from law enforcement. When official conduct feeds a sense of injustice, raises barriers between the department and segments of the community, and breeds disrespect for the law, the difficulties of law enforcement are multiplied.[8]

Baltimore now has a new Interim Police Commissioner whose enlightened efforts to foster better relations between the Negro community and the Police Department have been widely applauded by all elements of the community. The clear assurance which the injunction is designed to give is nevertheless still necessary in the interest of public tranquility. The issuance of the injunction will not prove harmful, but helpful, to the Interim Commissioner temporarily in office and to his successors in the lawful and effective exercise of their authority and in the administration of the department.[9]

7. In the debate over the tentative draft of the American Law Institute's Model Code of Pre-Arraignment Procedure, Judge George C. Edwards, now a member of the United States Court of Appeals for the Sixth Circuit and formerly Commissioner of Police in Detroit, made the same point, that police excesses bear the seed of untoward counter reactions of violence. See 34 U.S.L.Week. 2641, 2642 (May 24, 1966).

8. The classic words of Mr. Justice Brandeis, dissenting in Olmstead v. United States, 277 U.S. 438, 485 (1928), apply with full force in the present context:

"Decency, security and liberty alike demand that government officials shall be subjected to the same rules of conduct that are commands to the citizen. In a government of laws, existence of the government will be imperilled if it fails to observe the law scrupulously. Our Government is the potent, the omnipresent teacher. For good or for ill, it teaches the whole people by its example. Crime is contagious. If the Government becomes a lawbreaker, it breeds contempt for law; it invites every man to become a law unto himself; it invites anarchy. To declare that in the administration of the criminal law the end justifies the means—to declare that the government may commit crimes in order to secure the conviction of a private criminal—would bring terrible retribution. Against that pernicious doctrine this court should resolutely set its face."

9. Though not stressed, the fact was mentioned in oral argument that since the preparation of the briefs the defendant named in the District Court proceeding has retired from office and has been succeeded by General George M. Gelston, as Interim Police Commissioner, whose successor is to be appointed in the near future. This presents no difficulty. Our concern is not with the person who happens to hold the office at a particular

The appellants, however, would have us go further. They urge this court to order an injunction much broader in scope than one limited to prohibiting searches based only on anonymous tips and without probable cause. They contend that the determination of the existence of probable cause should not be left to policemen but should be vested in a judicial officer, and that absent exceptional circumstances the police should be required to obtain a search warrant from a magistrate before entering the private home of a stranger in search of an offender, even when the police have in their possession a warrant for the arrest of the person they are seeking. Appellants point out that the existence of an arrest warrant establishes only that there is probable cause for the arrest of the person named therein, but that it reflects no judgment at all as to where the suspect may be found.

It is settled law, of course, that subject to established exceptions, a search warrant is constitutionally required to enable the police to conduct a search for "things." Agnello v. United States, 269 U.S. 20 (1925). Appellants' contention is that there is no reason to think that police are better judges of probable cause when their quarry is a person rather than a thing. Moreover, appellants' counsel forcefully argue that from the standpoint of the victim the invasion of the privacy of his home is unaffected by the object of the policeman's search. The gravity of the invasion is precisely the same whether the policeman's objective is to search for a person or for an inanimate object, and the resulting injury is not mitigated by the fact that the officer may have a warrant to arrest some person but has not bothered to obtain a warrant from a judicial officer to search specified premises—not the premises of the person named in the arrest warrant. The contention is that the determination of probable cause for searching a particular home for a suspect who does not live there is the function of the magistrate, not the policeman.

Appellants frankly concede that no case explicitly upholds their contention, but they refer us to a few cases which may be construed as supporting their reasoning. See Morrison v. United States, 104 U.S.App.D.C. 352, 262 F.2d 449 (1958); District of Columbia v. Little, 85 U.S.App.D.C. 242, 178 F.2d 13, 17 (1949), aff'd. 339 U.S. 1 (1950). They criticize as inadequately and incorrectly reasoned the contrary statements in Love v. United States, 170 F.2d 32 (4th Cir. 1948), cert. denied, 336 U.S. 912 (1949).

We have no occasion now to accept or reject the legal theory thus advanced by the appellants or to canvass countervailing arguments. The injunction which we order fully protects them and all similarly circumstanced from future violations of the character described in this record, and we find it unnecessary to consider the advisability of a broader decree.

time, but with the office. The named defendant is only a nominal party, and the real aim of the proceeding is not to reach the Commissioner individually but to forbid an evil practice that has long and notoriously persisted in the Police Department. The ancient common law rule of abatement as a result of death or resignation of a public officer was relaxed and generally abandoned even before the 1961 amendment to Rule 25(d) of the Federal Rules of Civil Procedure. Seven Oaks, Inc. v. Federal Housing Administration, 171 F.2d 947, 950 (4th Cir. 1948). . . . The injunctive order may be issued against "The Police Commissioner of Baltimore City," or the name of the present incumbent may, on application and in the discretion of the District Court, be substituted. In either case the order will be binding in the future regardless of the identity of the office holder. . . .

The case will be remanded for the entry of a decree enjoining the Police Department from conducting a search of any private house to effect the arrest of any person not known to reside therein, whether with or without an arrest warrant, where the belief that the person is on the premises is based only on an anonymous tip and hence without probable cause.

The District Judge in Lankford v. Schmidt, 240 F.Supp. 550, 561–62 (D.Md., 1965) said: "We come finally to the question whether under all the circumstances a preliminary injunction should issue.

"Such an injunction would be difficult to frame, in view of the discretion which must be allowed to the police under the Supreme Court decisions quoted above. It would also be difficult to enforce, and its enforcement would place severe burdens on the police and on this Court. Those difficulties, however, should not bar the issuance of an injunction, if an injunction is necessary to protect the important rights of all citizens and residents of Baltimore which are involved in this case.

"The Court said on the opening day of the hearing that everyone in the courtroom was on both sides of this case. Every resident of the City should be interested in protecting the privacy of his home granted by the Fourth and Fourteenth Amendments. On the other hand, every resident of the City should be interested in seeing that the police are not unduly hampered in their efforts to arrest persons who have been charged with crime or whom the police reasonably believe to have been guilty of felonies. Striking a proper balance between those important interests is not always easy.

"One or two of the officers who testified in this case indicated that they would probably act in the future on anonymous tips if they felt the circumstances required it. But this Court has now stated the basic principles which must be observed by the police in determining whether there are reasonable grounds for a contemplated entry. The Court is satisfied that the Police Commissioner and other police officers will make a bona fide effort to observe those rules. They did observe them during the remainder of the search for the Veneys after the Commissioner issued General Order No. 10388 on January 11.

"Where constitutional rights have been violated as the result of discriminatory action by state officials, and it is likely that such discriminatory action will be continued in the future, a court has little or no discretion to refuse an injunction. Henry v. Greenville Airport Commission, 4 Cir., 284 F.2d 631 (1960). In this case, however, there has been no proof of discriminatory action. The rights and interests of all residents of Baltimore are involved in this case. The constitutional rights of some of the plaintiffs of other witnesses and of other citizens have been violated by the police on separate though related occasions. The Court has found that the violations are not likely to be resumed, although some officers will no doubt make mistakes in individual instances in the future.

"Under these circumstances, standards of the public interest measure the propriety and need for injunctive relief. Hecht Co. v. Bowles. 'Courts of equity may and frequently do, go much farther both to give and withhold relief in furtherance of the public interest than they are accustomed to go when only private interests are involved.' Virginian Ry. Co. v. System Federation No. 40, 300 U.S. 515, 552 (1937). . . . And as Mr. Justice Cardozo said in Hawks v. Hamill, 288 U.S. 52, at p. 60 (1933): 'Caution and reluctance there must be in special measure where relief, if granted, is an interference by the process of injunction with the activities of state officers discharging in good faith their supposed official duties.'

"The Veneys have now been arrested. Other frustrating cases will, however, arise in the future, and will tempt the police to engage in searches, raids or other activities which pass the line of reasonableness. The police must remember that although the killing of a police officer in the course of his duty is a most serious crime, which shocks the whole community, it is not an excuse for violating anyone's constitutional rights. Any policemen who have in the past been contemptuous of the rights and feelings of Negroes must recognize that all persons have equal constitutional rights and are equally entitled to courtesy and consideration, whatever their race or station in life. And any members of the Negro community who have considered all policemen their enemies must recognize the responsibilities borne by the police in the difficult and dangerous duty of protecting the public, and must realize their own responsibility to support rather than hinder the officers.

"Since the Court believes that the police will make an honest effort to observe their constitutional responsibilities, no preliminary injunction will be issued. The case will not be dismissed, but may be called for trial if it appears necessary."

---

1) Why didn't plaintiffs in *Lankford* ask for money damages? If you were on a jury, how much would you award the Wallaces? the Lankfords? What torts are analogous? Even though there was no "impact" and the victims suffered no "physical" damages, could they recover for fright? Could plaintiffs have added a claim for money damages to the federal class action? What would an injunction add to a money judgment? Your answer to the preceding questions may depend on the way you answer the following questions. When the Veney brothers were apprehended, wasn't *Lankford* as effectively over as *W.T. Grant* was when Hancock resigned? Are there other reasons to distinguish *W.T. Grant* from *Lankford?* Read 18 U.S.C. § 242 in the Appendix. Why didn't the federal government prosecute under that statute?

2) *Hecht, W.T. Grant,* and *Lankford* involve the relation between trial and appellate courts. Appellate courts supply perspective, detachment, and collegial judgment. If appellate courts seek to preserve the integrity of the substantive law, why is the standard of review whether the trial judge abused discretion? In Albemarle Paper Co. v. Moody, 422 U.S. 405 (1975), the Court discussed whether a trial judge in a Title VII suit for employment discrimination possessed discretion to deny back pay. It said, "The power to award back pay was bestowed by Congress, as part of a complex legislative design directed at a historic evil of national proportions. A court must exercise this power 'in light of the large objectives of the Act,' Hecht Co. v. Bowles. That the court's discretion is equitable in nature . . . hardly means that it is unfettered by meaningful standards or shielded from thorough appellate review." 422 U.S. at 416. What does "abuse of discretion" mean? Does it apply to all decisions granting or denying injunctive relief?

Does the appellate court look more carefully at a final than an interlocutory injunction?

The district judge's opinion in *Lankford* reflects sensitivity to the factors that moved the court of appeals. He recognized, however, that only an application for a preliminary injunction was before him. Did the court of appeals's standard of appellate review ignore the lawsuit's interlocutory status? The trial judge denied plaintiffs' application but threatened to call the case "for trial if it appears necessary." Could we describe that remedy as a declaratory judgment and retained jurisdiction? Was his response as appropriate or effective as the court of appeals's?

The answer to this question depends on whether an effective decree can be framed. Try to draft the order. In what areas of the city would it operate? What would be the conduct prohibited? Can the conduct be defined with sufficient specificity to enable the "wilfullness" requirement of criminal contempt to be satisfied? Could the contempt power be used against individual officers? Could you devise some mechanism for insuring effective policing of the decree? You might begin by criticizing the decree that was actually entered by the district judge on September 21, 1966, on remand in Lankford v. Gelston. It reads in full:

"This cause having been remanded from the United States Court of Appeals for the Fourth Circuit for the entry of a decree in conformity with its opinion and judgment of June 23, 1966, it is hereby ORDERED:

"1. That this Court's order of May 7, 1965, denying plaintiffs injunctive relief, is hereby vacated.

"2. That until further order of this Court, the Police Department of Baltimore City shall be, and hereby is, enjoined from conducting any search of any private house to effect the arrest of any person not known to reside therein, whether with or without an arrest warrant, where the belief that the person is on the premises is based only on anonymous tip and hence without probable cause;

"3. That jurisdiction of this cause shall be retained for the issuance of any and all future orders which may become necessary for the protection of plaintiffs' constitutional rights; and,

"4. That costs shall be awarded to the plaintiffs."

Is this what the court of appeals expected on remand? If so, was there anything of substance that separated the two courts? Does the reversal serve any purpose other than to rebuke the district judge and to give the plaintiffs' lawyers a sense of victory? Is it this sense of victory that is supposed to improve "community morale," whatever that means? Could you improve on the decree? How? Examples of decrees in similar contexts may be found in Wallace v. King, 650 F.2d 529, 531 n. 1 (4th Cir. 1981); and Hairston v. Hutzler, 334 F.Supp. 251, 254–55 (W.D.Pa.1971).

3) Judge Sobeloff was faced with the voluntary cessation issue once again in United States v. Hunter, 459 F.2d 205 (4th Cir. 1972). That was a suit brought by the United States under Title VIII of the Civil Rights Act of 1968, prohibiting racial discrimination in housing. The defendant was the editor and publisher of a Maryland newspaper, The Courier. On two occasions the paper carried an advertisement tendering for rent a furnished apart-

ment in what was denominated as a "white home." The statute has a provision [(§ 804(c) of the Civil Rights Act of 1968, 42 U.S.C.A. § 3604(c)] that prohibits discriminatory advertisements. The defendant argued that the section was not violated by simply specifying that that furnished apartment was located in a white home; that, in any event, the statute was not intended to authorize relief against the newspaper; and that, if it did, the statute was unconstitutional. The district judge—the same one as in Lankford v. Gelston—rejected the defendant's position and issued a declaratory judgment to the effect that the statute had been violated by the defendant and that it could be constitutionally applied to the newspaper. But the district judge refused to issue the injunction. As Judge Sobeloff put it, "[T]he district judge believed a declaration of the law would be as effective a remedy as the issuance of an injunction because he was firmly convinced that the defendant, although opposing the Government's interpretation of § 3604(c), would obey the law as declared by the court." This time Judge Sobeloff affirmed. Can this be reconciled with *Lankford?*

4) A judge has a spectrum of preventive remedies; several ways exist to put substantive law expressed in a statute, judicial precedent, or constitution into practice in a particular lawsuit. First, the judge may retain jurisdiction. Holding the case on the docket implies "I am keeping my eye on you." This is what the trial judge did in *Lankford,* but the court of appeals rejected that approach in favor of an injunction. Second, the judge may enter a declaratory judgment that tells the parties how the substantive law affects a controversy. "A declaratory judgment is a final judicial determination clarifying and settling legal relations by telling the parties to a controversy what their rights and obligations are." Rendleman, Prospective Remedies in Constitutional Adjudication, 78 W.Va.L.Rev. 155, 161–62 (1976). A declaration may be a foundation for later damages and an injunction, or it may be a freestanding separate remedy. Declarations differ from precedents or statutes by relating the "law" to the discrete controversy. The district judge in *Lankford* entered an informal declaratory judgment. Declarations have precedential value, and we normally think of them as entitled to res judicata effect. "The adjudication, not the command, is the essence of judicial power, and in our civilized communities, it is the adjudication, and not the command, which evokes respect and official sanction, because it is a determination by the societal agent appointed to perform that function, and thus irrevocably fixes legal relations." E. Borchard, Declaratory Judgments 10 (1934). Are declaratory judgments a milder, more civilized remedy than injunctions?

The declaratory judgment has failed to achieve its potential. Professor Plater says: "The courts' inclination toward issuing injunctions may also be attributable to judicial recognition of a certain American contumaciousness. In other societies it may be feasible and prudent to rely on voluntary obedience to judicial decisions. But to presume, for example, that American steelworkers will respond forthwith to mere judicial declarations that their strike is illegal betrays a lack of awareness of cultural reality. Given the litigiousness of the Yankee race, it is little wonder that injunctions have become a normal remedy of choice and that the question of whether the conduct is illegal often becomes, in effect, the same question as whether an injunction shall issue." Plater, 70 Calif.L.Rev. at 567. But doesn't *Hecht* tell judges to declare rather than enjoin when defendant will comply after the judge declares rights?

5) How do we tell injunctions from declarations and other orders? See Federal Rule 65(d). Many decisions on this issue occur under statutes defining appellate jurisdiction. In Lessard v. Schmidt, 349 F.Supp. 1078 (E.D. Wis.1972), the three-judge district court's comprehensive opinion concluded: "Alberta Lessard and the other members of her class are entitled to declaratory and injunctive relief against further enforcement of the present Wisconsin scheme against them. . . . [Miss Lessard] is also entitled to an injunction against any further extensions of the invalid order which continues to make her subject to the jurisdiction of the hospital authorities." 349 F.Supp. at 1103. The district court's later judgment stated: "It is Ordered and Adjudged that judgment be and hereby is entered in accordance with the Opinion heretofore entered . . . ." The Supreme Court discussed whether there was an injunction for the purpose of invoking its appellate jurisdiction over "an order granting or denying . . . an . . . injunction" under 28 U.S.C. § 1253. The Court held that the judgment invoked appellate jurisdiction, but that it was an "inadequate foundation" for plenary review because it flunked Federal Rule 65(d)'s precision test. Schmidt v. Lessard, 414 U.S. 473 (1974). The Court reasoned: "Since an injunctive order prohibits conduct under threat of judicial punishment, basic fairness requires that those enjoined receive explicit notice of precisely what conduct is outlawed. . . . In the absence of specific injunctive relief, informed and intelligent appellate review is greatly complicated, if not made impossible." 414 U.S. at 476, 477. Are Rule 65(d)'s policies stronger than Rule 51(a)'s requirement that the trial court "find the facts specially and state separately its conclusions of law thereon?"

Steffel v. Thompson, 415 U.S. 452 (1974), distinguishes declaratory from injunctive relief. The Court dealt with a federal declaration that a state prosecution or statute violates the federal constitution. *Steffel* insists that declarations are less intrusive than injunctions, but it fails to distinguish fully between the two remedies. Whitten, Federal Declaratory and Injunctive Interference with State Court Proceedings: The Supreme Court and the Limits of Judicial Discretion, 53 N.C.L.Rev. 591, 681, 685 (1975). Justice Rehnquist, concurring in *Steffel,* said that federalism prevents a declaration from being the basis for a later injunction; indeed, he said, a declaration is neither res judicata nor binding precedent. 415 U.S. at 479. Justice White disagreed, in a separate concurrence. 415 U.S. at 477–78.

The *Steffel* majority said that if it affirms a declaration that a prosecution is unconstitutional, it will reverse a later criminal conviction. Does this merely accord precedential effect to the declaration? Justice White seems to suggest that a declaration is a nascent injunction? Does Justice Rehnquist mean that a declaration is an advisory opinion? Fiss, Dombrowski, 86 Yale L.J. 1103, 1131–32, 1144–48 (1977); Laycock, Federal Interference with State Prosecutions: The Cases Dombrowski Forgot, 46 U.Chi.L.Rev. 636 (1979); Laycock, Federal Interference with State Prosecutions: The Need for Prospective Relief, 1977 Sup.Ct.Rev. 193; Rendleman, Prospective Remedies in Constitutional Adjudication, 78 W.Va.L.Rev. 155, 167–68 (1976); Comment, Federal Jurisdiction—Declaratory Judgments—Federal Declaratory Relief Not Precluded When No State Prosecution is Pending and Threat of Prosecution is Demonstrated, 28 Rutgers L.Rev. 720 (1975).

6) Does an injunction add anything to a declaration? The two would be equivalent if everyone obeyed the law expressed in precedent and statute. Injunctions command obedience and may be enforced by contempt; they add contempt's bite to the declaration's bark. Federal judges may, however, employ less meddlesome declarations when federalism policies tell them to be gentle with defendants who are state officials. In Roe v. Wade, 410 U.S. 113 (1973), and Doe v. Bolton, 410 U.S. 179 (1973), for example, the Court approved a declaration without an injunction: "We assume the Texas prosecutorial authorities will give full credence to this decision that the present criminal abortion statutes are unconstitutional." 410 U.S. at 166. What should the district judge and court of appeals in *Lankford* have considered in deciding whether to declare or enjoin? See Prospective Remedies, 78 W.Va.L.Rev. at 165–66.

7) Long ago in a faraway land a young lawyer represented a massage parlor. An ordinance that banned "cross-sex" massages was passed by the governing body. The lawyer filed a federal action seeking a declaratory judgment that the ordinance was unconstitutional on due process and equal protection grounds. Since obedience would have reduced its business almost to nothing, the parlor continued to operate. Which equitable defense did the local officials interpose? Should equitable prerequisites and defenses generally limit declaratory relief? These cases say "No." Steffel v. Thompson, 415 U.S. 452, 471–72 (1974); Aetna Life Insurance Co. v. Haworth, 300 U.S. 227, 241 (1937); Age of Majority Educational Corp. v. Preller, 512 F.2d 1241, 1245 (4th Cir. 1975); Airways Theatre, Inc. v. Canale, 366 F.Supp. 343, 346–47 (W.D.Tenn.1973). But cf. Samuels v. Mackell, 401 U.S. 66, 72–73 (1971).

8) *Lankford* has stood the test of time. In Rizzo v. Goode, 423 U.S. 362 (1976), the Supreme Court disapproved a massive injunction that was intended to correct the Philadelphia police department's allegedly unconstitutional practices, but Justice Rehnquist's majority opinion said in a footnote that *Lankford* "intimated" no power to "supervise the functioning of the police department" and that the facts were "obviously distinguishable." 423 U.S. at 373–74 n. 8. The Court apparently felt that the routine and approved unconstitutional searches brought *Lankford* within the realm of a corrective injunction. For a discussion of *Lankford* actions after *Rizzo,* Note, Rethinking Federal Injunctive Relief Against Police Abuse: Picking Up the Pieces after Rizzo v. Goode, 7 Rut.-Cam.L.Rev. 530 (1976). Professor Fiss takes a somewhat more somber view in Dombrowski, 86 Yale L.J. 1103, 1154–60 (1977). Compare Wong v. Nelson, 549 F.Supp. 895 (D.Colo.1982). After an illegal search Judge Kane granted a temporary restraining order and a preliminary injunction; but he declined to "extend the preliminary order to a permanent injunction" because the search was "an isolated incident."

Justice Marshall dissenting in Los Angeles v. Lyons, 103 S.Ct. 1660 (1983), however, found Lankford v. Gelston "indistinguishable." Id. at 1677 n. 15 Lyons sued for an injunction and damages charging injury from a police "chokehold." The majority held that, because of the lack of a "real and immediate threat" that he would be illegally choked again, Lyons lacked "standing" and an Article III "case or controversy." The Court wrote, "A federal court may not entertain a claim by any or all citizens who no more than assert that certain practices of law enforcement officers are unconstitutional." Id. at 1670. The opinion is limited to federal injunctions. The majority told Lyons to pursue his damage action or to seek a state injunction; it also noted that "those who deliberately deprive a citizen of his constitutional rights risk conviction under the federal criminal laws." Id. at 1671. The dissent rejected a separate standing inquiry with respect to each request for relief. at 1678.

In addition, Steagald v. United States, 451 U.S. 204 (1981), confirmed *Lankford* by holding that absent consent or an emergency, an arrest warrant will not substitute for a search warrant as a basis to search third persons' homes for the subject of the arrest warrant. The Court cited and discussed *Lankford* as an example of the "potential for abuse" of allowing the searches. 451 U.S. at 215. The injunction, moreover, has become the plaintiff's preferred remedy. Defendant police officials who rely on departmental policy will be immune from monetary liability: plaintiff's attorney may recover a fee, Wallace v. King, 650 F.2d 529 (4th Cir. 1981). Plaintiff may be able to recover compensatory damages from the municipality, Owen v. City of Independence, 445 U.S. 622 (1980).

9) Professor Plater's article reflects his experience as an environmental litigator, and he concentrates his admirable analytical power on arguing that a judge cannot refuse to enjoin when defendant has breached a statute. Yet he says twice, in "dicta," that, paradoxically, a judge has discretion to withhold an injunction when defendant has violated plaintiff's constitutional rights. 70 Calif.L.Rev. at 531, 546. He argues that separation of powers forbids a judge from overriding a statute. What allows a judge to override the Constitution?

10) The *Lankford* plaintiffs asked the court to appoint a judicial officer who, "absent exceptional circumstances," would determine whether probable cause exists for officers to enter a third person's home to execute an arrest warrant. The court of appeals thought that the injunction ordered "fully protects" plaintiffs' class. "We find it unnecessary to consider the advisability of a broader decree." 364 F.2d 197, 206. Rizzo v. Goode, 423 U.S. 362 (1976), also rejected this sort of judicial intervention in police procedure on somewhat different grounds.

Courts dealing with state institutions have confronted the problem the *Lankford* and *Rizzo* courts avoid: how to deal with an intractable defendant bureaucracy. What if the judge enters an injunction and nobody does anything? In Landman v. Royster, 333 F.Supp. 621 (E.D.Va.1971), Judge Merhige entered a comprehensive injunction setting minimum standards for the Virginia State Penitentiary System. He also ordered the authorities to disseminate the order "to all members of the custodial staff." At a later contempt hearing, security officers testified that they had not been informed "as to the actual meaning and effect of that order." The authorities, moreover, lacked knowledge of "whether lower custodial personnel understood and were carrying out the terms of the injunction." 354 F.Supp. at 1298. Not much of consequence had changed. Judge Merhige entered a civil contempt order that basically reenjoined the defendants to obey the first injunction.

Two sources dealing with the problems involved in changing a bureaucracy are G. Allison, Essence of Decision: Explaining the Cuban Missile Crises (1971), and M. Z. Crozier, Bureaucratic Phenomenon (1967). We return to the problem below in Government By (Structural) Injunction, Chapter 9.

11) Reread footnote 9 of the *Lankford* majority opinion, dealing with succession in public office. What was the violation? How did the court relate the remedy to it? Does the court's theory of liability, expressed in footnote 9, assume that the violation was a social condition as opposed to the discrete illegal searches? In light of the new police commissioner and the arrest of the accused killers, did the injunction grow out of a desire to fit the remedy to a discrete violation? Will this lead to rigid and uncreative ideas about remedies? Or does the court send a message that seeks to eliminate a general threat to protected values? Will such a broad definition lead to government by injunction? Do any of the officials possess enough power or influence to alter the course of the large bureaucracy? See Fiss, The Supreme Court, 1978 Term—Foreword: The Forms of Justice, 93 Harv.L.Rev. 1, 46–50 (1979). Contrast Spomer v. Littleton, 414 U.S. 514 (1974), to footnote 9. Plaintiffs sued a prosecuting attorney, charging racially discriminatory practices and seeking an injunction. While appeals were pending, a successor was elected. The Court refused to substitute the successor but instead sent the action back to the court of appeals to determine whether the dispute was moot and whether plaintiffs may and might amend to include claims against the successor. The Court was not sure that any controversy concerning future injunctive relief remained. See Fiss, Dombrowski, 86 Yale L.J. 1103, 1150–52 (1977). We return to this issue in the final chapter.

III. Fait Accompli

Fletcher v. Bealey, p. 109 introduced us to the idea that the applicant for preventive relief may be too early. *Bell* asks what happens when plaintiff applies for an injunction too late. We generally think that judges award damages to the victims of consummated wrongs and reserve injunctions for prevention. Ask yourself why the court tells the defendants to "do it over again, and do it right this time."

BELL v. SOUTHWELL

376 F.2d 659 (5th Cir. 1967).

Before BROWN, GOLDBERG and AINSWORTH, Circuit Judges.

JOHN R. BROWN, Circuit Judge: A Georgia election was conducted under procedures involving racial discrimination which was gross, state-imposed, and forcibly state-compelled. Nevertheless the District Court by summary judgment held it could not set aside such election or order a new one even though in parallel cases the unconstitutional discriminatory practices were enjoined and all persons arrested were ordered discharged immediately. We reverse.

The underlying facts out of which the controversy grew may be quickly stated. The Justice of the Peace for the 789th Militia District in Americus,

Sumter County, Georgia, died on June 23, 1965. The Ordinary [1] on June 26, 1965, called a special election to fill the vacancy, which was held on July 20, 1965. Mrs. Mary F. Bell, one of the plaintiffs, a Negro, was a candidate as was the winner, J. W. Southwell, a defendant, and four other white men.[2] Following Georgia procedure, the results of the election were canvassed and the defendant J. W. Southwell declared the winner. Of the 2,781 votes cast, Negroes actually voting numbered 403 out of a total of 1,223 registered and qualified Negro voters in the District. On July 29, 1965, and after the expiration of the time for election contest under Georgia laws, this suit was filed. The District Judge by opinion denied relief for three reasons, two Georgia and one Federal. First, even assuming the admitted racial discrimination intimidated Negroes from voting, if all of the qualified Negroes not voting were added to the combined vote of Southwell's opponents, the result could not have been changed.[3] Second, if the election were voided, the Ordinary would be required to appoint the successor and the appointee would surely be Southwell. Third, Federal Courts simply do not have power to void a state election.

This suit, brought on their own behalf and on behalf of other Negroes and other voters in the District by Mrs. Bell, a qualified elector and candidate, and two other named Negro qualified voters, against the defendants Southwell and Horne, the Ordinary, invoked the Civil Rights Acts, 42 U.S.C.A. §§ 1971, 1981, 1983, 1985, 28 U.S.C.A. § 1343(3), (4). The main charge was that the election officials including the Ordinary had conducted the election in violation of the rights established under the Constitution and laws of the United States. The specific allegations fell in two categories, one relating to the election system and the second to specific acts of intimidation. In the first it was alleged that voting lists for the election were segregated on the basis of race. Likewise, voting booths were segregated according to race, with one booth for "white males," another for "white women," and a third for Negroes. During the course of the election, a number of qualified Negro women voters were denied the right to cast their ballots in the "white women's" booth. In the second group were charges that the officials barred representatives of candidate Bell from viewing the voting, another was physically struck by an election official and police allowed a large crowd of white males to gather near the polls thus intimidating Negroes from voting. In

1. The Ordinary, elected by the people of the county for a term of four years, . . . has broad powers, including original, exclusive and general jurisdiction in matters relating to probate, administration of decedent's estates, guardianships, and "all such matters as may be conferred on them by the Constitution and laws." . . . Involved here is a special election called by the Ordinary to fill a vacancy in the office of justice of the peace pursuant to Ga.Code Ann. § 24–406 (Supp.1966).

2. The vote was:

J.W. Southwell	2,001	
Mary F. Bell	332	
4 others	448	
Total vote	2,781	[Eds.]

3. Qualified Negro

Voters:	1,223	
Voting	403	
Not voting	820	
Mary F. Bell	332	
4 others	448	
Negro voters not voting	820	
Total	1,600	
Southwell	2,001	[Eds.]

addition, the plaintiffs were commanded by a deputy sheriff, acting under directions of the Ordinary, to leave the white women's polling booth and after their respectful refusal to do so on the ground that they had the constitutional right to vote without being subjected to racial discrimination, they were arrested. With precision, through simultaneous motions for temporary restraining order, preliminary injunction, show cause orders, and the immediate release from arrest, the plaintiffs requested that the Court declare the defendant Southwell was not the legally elected Justice of the Peace, that he be enjoined from taking office, and that the Ordinary be ordered to call a new election.

In addition to the answer, which in the main admitted the maintenance of segregated voting lists and polling boths (group 1) and denied the specific acts of misconduct (group 2), the defendants filed a motion to dismiss and subsequently three affidavits which bore primarily on the election statistics (see notes 2 and 3, supra) and a verified denial of the physical violence.[4] The Court properly treated it as a motion for summary judgment under F.R. Civ.P. 12(b).

It rounds out the picture to state that this record affirms without contradiction that two parallel companion cases were before the District Court, one by the United States against various officials of Sumter County, the other an identical suit by these appellants-plaintiffs against the same Georgia officials. Hearing them simultaneously with the application for preliminary relief in the instant case, the District Judge in those two cases entered an injunction enjoining the defendants from maintaining racial segregation at the polls, from maintaining segregated voting lists, from arresting or interfering with Negro voters, and from prosecuting the plaintiffs for their conduct leading to their arrest on July 20, 1965.[6] 10 R.Rel.Law Rept. 1247.

Subsequently the Court on the basis of the pleadings and affidavits granted summary judgment, F.R.Civ.P. 12(b) for the defendants. In the opinion the Judge specified the three grounds previously mentioned—(1) the actions complained could not have affected the outcome of the election, (2) if the election were voided, a new election could not be ordered since §§ 24–406 and 408, Ga.Code Ann. requires the Ordinary to fill such a vacancy by appointment, (3) there is no authority, statutory, constitutional or equitable, for a Federal Court to void a state election.

We think that the Georgia problems are inconsequential and deserve only the later brief discussion. The claim invoked the protection of the Federal Court under statutes which assuredly give it jurisdiction to vindicate constitutional rights. Since it is clear that constitutional rights of the plaintiffs, the Negro voters as a class, indeed all voters, Negro and white, of the District were infringed, the sole question remaining is the sort of relief to be granted.

4. The answer categorically denied the specific allegations that the plaintiffs were arrested . . . for having insisted on using the "white women" polling booths. But the affidavits do not touch this incident. Consequently, for motion to dismiss and summary judgment purposes, these allegations must be taken as true.

6. In view of these sweeping injunctions in the companion cases and the assurances of the defendants in the present case that they would maintain the status quo pending determination of the case on the merits, the District Court thought it unnecessary to enter interim relief. This is not questioned here.

By the decrees in the companion cases . . . which all properly consider to be a part of the matter presented additionally by this case, the trial Court in unmistakable terms and action characterized the practices as flagrant violations of the Constitution. These steps were taken, so the Judge said, "to insure that in the future, elections in Sumter County will be free from discrimination." Despite his determination that for the future these glaring racial discriminations could not go on, the trial Judge concluded that a Federal Court was either powerless—or at least ought not to exercise power—to set aside a State election. The Judge was apparently influenced by two factors. The first is one going to the existence of power or the propriety of its exercise. On the basis of Reynolds v. Sims, 1964, 377 U.S. 533, and other reapportionment cases, the trial Court, recognizing that a prohibitory decree could look to the future, nevertheless held that it could not rectify the past since, as the Judge put it, "only a few minutes' reflection is needed to realize that the implications of such a decision would be staggering." The second slipped over into a Georgia reason that, granting the existence of this crude discrimination, there is no way to tell whether the result would have been different in its absence. Hence, no harm or injury is shown by these complainants. Neither of these factors warrant, in our view, the complete denial of relief.

Drastic, if not staggering, as is the Federal voiding of a State election, and therefore a form of relief to be guardedly exercised, this Court in Hamer v. Campbell, 5 Cir., 1966, 358 F.2d 215, cert. denied, 1966, 385 U.S. 851 expressly recognized the existence of this power. Of course as that opinion emphasizes, not every unconstitutional racial discrimination necessarily permits or requires a retrospective voiding of the election. But the power is present and *Hamer,* announced subsequent to the action of the District Court below, would require reversal without more for re-examination by the District Court of the appropriateness of injunctive relief.

As to the second we do not think the Court could justify denial of effective, present relief because of any assumed inability to demonstrate that the outcome would have been different. The appellants seem to suggest that the existence of such flagrant racial discrimination would raise a presumption that the vote of every actual and potential voter was affected. On that approach, it is not Negroes alone who suffer, it is the body politic as a whole, both Negro and white. And this is certainly true at least to the extent that the trial Court legally could not assume—as it evidently did—that all white voters would vote for white candidates, all Negroes for Negroes, or that no whites would vote for Negroes in a free, untainted election. See Hamer v. Campbell, supra, 358 F.2d 215, 219.

As long as we bear carefully in mind the limitations that *Hamer* imposes on this stringent relief, we think it is a mistake to cast this in terms of presumption. The fact is that there are certain discriminatory practices which, apart from demonstrated injury or the inability to do so, so infect the processes of the law as to be stricken down as invalid. . . . Thus in jury-race exclusion cases, once the evidence, either direct or by inference from statistical percentages, cf. Swain v. State of Alabama, 1965, 380 U.S. 202, 205; Whitus v. State of Georgia, 1967, 385 U.S. 545, 552 & n. 2; establishes the existence of racial discrimination, the law requires that the indictment (or the petit jury verdict of guilty) be set aside even though the accused is unable to demonstrate injury in fact. Labat v. Bennett, 5 Cir., 1966 (en banc), 365 F.2d 698, 723 & n. 43. And at times demonstrated actual discrimination is not even required if the racially conscious system affords a ready opportunity for it in practice. . . . Of course the Court discharging an accused from such indictment or conviction as a legalism finds that the accused was "prejudiced," but it is not in terms of the personal harm suffered or a factual demonstration that things would have turned out better. Rather, it is the law's recognition that in areas of such vital importance, state-imposed racial discrimination cannot be tolerated and to eliminate the practice or the temptation toward it, the law must extinguish the judgment wrought by such a procedure.

Even more directly, in connection with the elective process, the Supreme Court gave full play to this approach in striking down the Louisiana law requiring the designation of the race of each candidate on the ballot.[7] Anderson v. Martin, 1964, 375 U.S. 399. It takes little transposition to substitute for the ballot's written racial candidate label the state-supplied racial marker for places and manner of voting. In each situation it is ". . . placing a racial label . . . at the most crucial stage in the electoral process—the instant before the vote is cast . . . ." By each mechanism "the State furnishes a vehicle by which racial prejudice may be so aroused as to operate against one group because of race and for another." And in both situations this "is true because by directing the citizen's attention to the single consideration of race or color, the State indicates that . . . race or color is an important—perhaps paramount—consideration in the citizen's choice, which may decisively influence the citizen to cast his ballot along racial lines." And as much for one as for the other, the ". . . vice lies not in the resulting injury but in the placing of the power of the State behind a racial classification that induces racial prejudice at the polls."

Once we get this far, no difficulty is encountered from the *Hamer* restrictions on the use of injunctive relief setting aside an election.

Although as earlier pointed out, injunctive relief setting aside the election was granted, we emphasized in *Hamer* that this "action does not mean that we necessarily would set aside every election in which a substantial number of citizens have been denied the right to vote." Going further, we remarked, "This is not a case where an election is challenged for the first time after it is held." This leads the Georgia authorities to insist here that the relief sought was properly denied since the injunction was requested after the election was over.

But we certainly intended no such mechanical rule. In *Hamer* the vice sought to be corrected was the denial of the right to vote to Negroes through operation of the registration procedure. That was known to exist before the election was held. It was also known that the effects could not be eradicated except through equitable court relief. Here, of course, the vice occurred on election day upon the opening of the polls. It might be suggested that the

7. This was, of course, a suit prior to a primary and not one after the fact seeking to void the results of a racially tainted election. This distinction, however, bears upon the appropriateness of the relief and *Hamer* limitations to be placed upon it.

Negro voters should have anticipated that the traditional practice of racially segregated lists and polling places would be maintained. But it was equally permissible for them to think that at this late date and in the atmosphere of that moment and the passage of successive Civil Rights statutes increasing protection against racial discrimination,[8] that these Georgia authorities would measure up to the demands of the Constitution.

There was really no effective relief available before the election. The moment the election process began, there was a protest by these Negro voters and others seeking an eradication of the discrimination and an opportunity for all members of that race, indeed for all voters, to vote without regard to race or color. That this self-help was not successful, indeed resulted in the unwarranted arrest and detention of those who protested, does not fault them for want of diligence. And within but a few days after the result of the election was published, this suit was filed as a part of an attack on many fronts.

Considering the gross, spectacular, completely indefensible nature of this state-imposed, state-enforced racial discrimination and the absence of an effective judicial remedy prior to the holding of the election, this is far removed from a belated effort to set aside retrospectively an election held long before on the ground that re-examination of the circumstances indicates a denial of constitutional rights on the part of candidates or voters, or both. Cf. McGill v. Ryals, M.D.Ala.N.D., 1966, 253 F.Supp. 374, 376, appeal dism'd, 385 U.S. 19. The parties here moved with unusual diligence and as was true in *Hamer,* relief ". . . if it is to be had, must perforce come from the Court or the voters must simply be told to wait four more years." Hamer v. Campbell, supra, 358 F.2d 215, 222.

In the face of gross, unsophisticated, significant, and obvious racial discriminations in the conduct of the election and the now established power of a Federal Court to extinguish its effects even to the point of setting aside the election, the Georgia reasons relied on by the District Judge warrant but a brief comment. The Court's fundamental mistake was in assuming that this was an election contest as such in which the winner is challenged because of ineligibility, fraud or irregularities in the conduct of the election, the receipt or counting of illegal ballots which would change the result and the like, and which, as a separate special statutory proceeding, must be timely filed by specified persons following statutory procedures and in particular tribunals. Mrs. Bell and her co-plaintiffs alone or as members of the class did not challenge the eligibility of Mr. Southwell or the fact that he received an over-

8. By the Civil Rights Act of 1957, Congress empowered the Attorney General of the United States to institute suits to protect the right to vote from deprivation because of race or color or because of threats or intimidation. This was supplemented by the Civil Rights Act of 1960, in which Congress gave the Attorney General full powers of inspection of documents in the custody of local voting registrars, and provided for a more comprehensive procedure of registration of Negroes where a pattern or practice of discrimination was disclosed. These initial steps were considerably broadened and strengthened by the Civil Rights Act of 1964. Particularly pertinent here is the provision relating to voting rights, 42 U.S.C.A. § 1971, especially subparts (a) and (e). Approved August 6, 1965, subsequent to the election and suit here involved, is the most recent link in this chain of legislation, the Voting Rights Act of 1965. . . .

whelming majority. Indeed, Mrs. Bell as a former candidate did not seek to be selected over Southwell or any other opponent. What, and all, she and others sought was an election conducted free of such indefensible, racial distinctions. That being so, it was not the usual simple case of counting votes and denying relief for want of affirmative proof of a different result.

Equally lacking in merit is the Court's conclusion that setting aside the election would be ineffectual since, on his interpretation of the Georgia statute, § 24–408, prescribes that when an election is held and is determined not to have been valid, no re-election is held, but rather the Ordinary appoints a Justice of the Peace for the required term. The Court assumed, with unquestioned basis probably, that the Ordinary would have appointed Southwell. Clearly, the Federal Constitution and the Federal Courts are not so helpless or unresourceful as to condemn in words only to let go by default in such an open breach of constitutional demands.

This leaves only a tag end. There is a suggestion that the District Court enjoining Southwell from taking office pursuant to the election would be powerless to grant affirmative relief requiring that the Ordinary call a special election. In this vital area of vindication of precious constitutional rights, we are unfettered by the negative or affirmative character of the words used or the negative or affirmative form in which the coercive order is cast. If affirmative relief is essential, the Court has the power and should employ it. State of Alabama v. United States, 5 Cir., 1962, 304 F.2d 583, 589, affirmed, 1962, 371 U.S. 37; Hamer v. Campbell, supra, 358 F.2d 215, 221.

The cause must therefore be reversed and remanded for the entry of an appropriate order setting aside the election and requiring the calling of a special election.[13]

---

1) In light of footnote 13, what is the misconduct that rendered the election invalid? Could that have been anticipated before the election?

2) Assume that the court is correct in declaring the election invalid. The question then arises as to the proper remedy. We know the court orders that the election be rerun. But where does the court get the authority to order a new election in light of the otherwise valid state law which provides that when an election is determined to be invalid, the ordinary procedure is to appoint a Justice of the Peace for the required term? The Supreme Court addressed these issues in Washington v. Washington State Commercial Passenger Fishing Vessel Association, 443 U.S. 658, 695–96 (1979). The Court said: "State-law prohibition against compliance with the District Court's decree cannot survive the command of the Supremacy Clause of the United States Constitution. Cooper v. Aaron, 358 U.S. 1; Ableman v. Booth, 21 How. 506. . . . The federal court unquestionably has the power to enter the various orders that state official and private parties have chosen to ignore, and even to displace local enforcement of those orders if necessary to remedy the violations of federal law found by the court. E.g.,

13. The racial discriminations in the first category are for all practical purposes admitted, and these alone are sufficient to require the relief here directed. There is no need for further evidence as the specific acts of violence or other racial discrimination, including the arrest and confinement of the Negro plaintiffs, (see note 4, supra), set forth in the second group are superfluous.

Hutto v. Finney, 437 U.S. 678; Milliken v. Bradley, 433 U.S. 267, 280–281, 290; Swann v. Charlotte-Mecklenburg Board of Education, 402 U.S. 1, 15. . . . [T]he District Court has the power to undertake the necessary remedial steps and to enlist the aid of the appropriate federal law enforcement agents in carrying out those steps."

3) The remedy in Bell v. Southwell was to rerun the election. This is the usual remedy utilized by the National Labor Relations Board in the elections it supervises—those determining whether the union represents a majority of the employees and is the one with whom the employer must bargain. The remedy is used almost as a matter of course whenever an unfair labor practice occurs during an election—with the Board making little or no inquiry as to the actual impact of the unfair labor practices on the outcome of the election. See generally J. Getman, S. Goldberg, and J. Herman, Union Representation Elections: Law or Reality (1976). There may be factors that distinguish the labor-management context from Bell v. Southwell; but before speculating on the difference it may be useful to know that on occasion the Board has moved beyond the rerun remedy. It has—to use Professor Getman's apt phrase—resorted to a "powerhouse remedy" and ordered the employer to bargain with a union that had just lost an election.

This occurred in the General Steel Products case, 157 N.L.R.B. 636 (1966), a decision of the Board that was reversed by the Fourth Circuit, 398 F.2d 339 (4th Cir. 1968), but upheld by the Supreme Court in NLRB v. Gissel Packing Co., 395 U.S. 575 (1969). In *General Steel* the union waged an organizational campaign and received authorization cards from 120 of 201 employees in the unit. Those cards read: "I do hereby designate and authorize the Upholsterers International Union of North America, AFL–CIO, and its representatives to act as my representative for the purpose of collective bargaining in respect to rates of pay, wages, hours of employment and other conditions of employment." The company refused to recognize the union, stating its disbelief in the union's claimed majority status. In the meantime, the union filed a petition with the Board for a representation election. The election was held and, by a vote of 83 to 94, the union lost (13 ballots were held invalid).

What illegal practices invalidated the election? For the Supreme Court (395 U.S., at 582, n. 3), it was that over a six-month period—both before and after the union's demand for recognition—"the Company's foremen and supervisors interrogated employees about their Union involvement; threatened them with discharge for engaging in Union activities or voting for the Union; suggested that unionization might hurt business and make new jobs more difficult to obtain; warned that strikes and other dire economic consequences would result (a supervisor informed a group of employees that if the Union came in, 'a nigger would be the head of it,' and that when the Company put in 10 new machines 'the niggers would be the operators of them'); and asserted that, although it would have to negotiate with the Union, it could negotiate endlessly and would not have to sign anything." How does this compare to the election misconduct in Bell v. Southwell? To use Judge Brown's favorite words, is this unlawful conduct "gross" and "spectacular?"

Assuming that this was sufficient to invalidate the election, what should be the remedy? The court of appeals thought a rerun was appropriate: the violations "were not so pervasive that available remedies were not reasonably calculated to assure a free exercise of the employees' choice by secret ballot rather than by resort to a count of questionable cards." 398 F.2d, at 340 n. 3. Did the court of appeals characterize the reliability of authorization cards as "questionable" because of the circumstances surrounding the signing of the cards? The company conceded that 19 authorization cards might be properly read as indicating the signee's desire to have the union represent him in negotiations. But the company claimed that the bulk of the remaining cards (97) were signed by the employees solely for the purpose of getting an election and should be so understood. They did not commit the signer to support the union in the election and should not be used as a substitute for the vote. The Board rejected this contention: "Although solicitors in many cases may have mentioned *a* use of the cards in order to secure an election, all the cards signed are explicit and unambiguous . . . . At first glance, the distinction between representations that an election is the *sole* purpose of the cards and representations that an election is *a* purpose may seem a fine one, but the distinction goes to the basis for the rule. Thus, by stating that the card may or will be used to secure an election, the solicitor neither contradicts the plain statement on the card nor misstates the union's actual intention." 157 N.L.R.B., at 644–645. Was there a counterpart to the authorization cards in Bell v. Southwell?

The Supreme Court found the analysis of the Board persuasive. It concluded that, rather than trying to resolve the ambiguities through a rerun, the Board could order the company to recognize and bargain with the union despite the union's defeat in the election. The Court then turned to the task of identifying the conditions that make the "powerhouse remedy" appropriate (395 U.S., at 613–15):

". . . While refusing to validate the general use of a bargaining order in reliance on cards, the Fourth Circuit nevertheless left open the possibility of imposing a bargaining order, without need of inquiry into majority status on the basis of cards or otherwise, in 'exceptional' cases marked by 'outrageous' and 'pervasive' unfair labor practices. Such an order would be an appropriate remedy for those practices, the court noted, if they are of 'such a nature that their coercive effects cannot be eliminated by the application of traditional remedies, with the result that a fair and reliable election cannot be had.' NLRB v. Logan Packing Co., 386 F.2d 562, 570 (C.A.4th Cir. 1967); see also NLRB v. Heck's, Inc., 398 F.2d 337, 338. The Board itself, we should add, has long had a similar policy of issuing a bargaining order, in the absence of a § 8(a)(5) violation or even a bargaining demand, when that was the only available, effective remedy for substantial unfair labor practices. . . .

"The only effect of our holding here is to approve the Board's use of the bargaining order in less extraordinary cases marked by less pervasive practices which nonetheless still have the tendency to undermine majority strength and impede the election processes. The Board's authority to issue such an order on a lesser showing of employer misconduct is appropriate, we should reemphasize, where there is also a showing that at one point the union had a majority; in such a case, of course, effectuating ascertainable employee free choice becomes as important a goal as deterring employer misbehavior.

In fashioning a remedy in the exercise of its discretion, then, the Board can properly take into consideration the extensiveness of an employer's unfair practices in terms of their past effect on election conditions and the likelihood of their recurrence in the future. If the Board finds that the possibility of erasing the effects of past practices and of ensuring a fair election (or a fair rerun) by the use of traditional remedies, though present, is slight and that employee sentiment once expressed through cards would, on balance, be better protected by a bargaining order, than such an order should issue. . . .

"We emphasize that under the Board's remedial power there is still a third category of minor or less extensive unfair labor practices, which, because of their minimal impact on the election machinery, will not sustain a bargaining order. There is, the Board says, no *per se* rule that the commission of any unfair practice will automatically result in a § 8(a)(5) violation and the issuance of an order to bargain. . . ."

Is this rule better or worse than the one in Bell v. Southwell?

4) Bell v. Southwell introduces a new kind of injunction. Previously we have studied preventive injunctions, mini-criminal statutes forbidding future conduct. We usually think of money to correct completed violations, but *Bell* takes us beyond preventive injunctions. Professor Fiss identifies the *Bell* injunction as reparative: "it compel[s] the defendant to engage in a course of action that seeks to correct the effects of a past wrong." O. Fiss, The Civil Rights Injunction 7 (1978). If a preventive injunction resembles the substantive standard, does a reparative injunction resemble an in-kind damage award? What is there about the events and interests in *Bell* to lead the court to prefer the reparative injunction to the district judge's preventive injunction? See O. Fiss, The Civil Rights Injunction 7–12. Would a criminal prosecution under 18 U.S.C. § 242 send the message home better than any equitable remedy?

5) Toney v. White, 488 F.2d 310 (5th Cir. 1973), traces the way the rerun election doctrine developed. It also illustrates an important lesson for plaintiff. Time is a perishable commodity. The more time that passes before plaintiffs file suit and before the court decides, the more likely the court is to allow the next regularly scheduled election to be plaintiffs' remedy. The rights the law says citizens should enjoy perish while the process of enforcing them proceeds. How much should the judicial need to deliberate be accommodated to the plaintiffs' need to expedite?

6) For an account of the "squeeze play" between prematurity and accomplished fact when defendant possesses the initiative, see Fiss, Dombrowski, 86 Yale L.J. 1103, 1111, 1118–19, 1135 (1977).

PROBLEMS

Try your understanding of the issues raised in this chapter on the following problems.

1) You are a state trial judge. You found that the local public college violated the state's Sunshine (Open Meetings) Act by closing Curriculum Committee meetings to students. The statute allows you to "grant appropriate relief including an injunction against future violations." Another section provides a $500 penalty for wilful violations of the Act. The college's attor-

ney argues that no injunction is in order. First, the faculty has received the message; and from now on, they promise to open all meetings covered by the Act. Second, the judge would be very unlikely to throw faculty members in jail for violating an injunction; and he should not threaten unnecessarily. "Remember the Gurkha soldiers," she argued. "They resheathed their swords only after the swords were bloodied. They understood the seriousness of battle, and thus they didn't brandish weapons lightly. The judge's injunction resembles a sword. You shouldn't unsheath it unless you are willing to employ it vigorously." You silently assent to the idea that you will hesitate a long time before you hold a faculty member in contempt for excluding a student from a faculty committee meeting. Write an opinion expressing your conclusion on the question of whether to grant an injunction.

If you decided not to enjoin, would you change your mind if the statute read either a) "The court shall have jurisdiction to enjoin any violation of this Chapter and to enter any other orders as may be appropriate."; b) "A single instance of denial of the rights conferred herein shall suffice to invoke the remedies herein granted."; or c) "Upon a proper showing, a permanent or temporary injunction shall be granted without bond?"

Compare Common Cause v. Nuclear Regulatory Commission, 522 F.Supp. 457 (D.D.C.1981). The court of appeals affirmed the trial court's ruling that the meeting should be open, but it reversed contempt because the injunction was too imprecise to satisfy Federal Rule 65(d), 674 F.2d 921 (D.C.Cir.1982). The second is based upon the statute at issue in Nageotte v. King George County, 223 Va. 259, 269–70, 288 S.E.2d 423, 428 (1982), and Marsh v. Richmond Newspapers, Inc., 223 Va. 245, 257–58, 288 S.E.2d 415, 421–22, (1982), the latest chapters in the Sunshine Trialogue between Virginia's legislature, courts, and local governments.

2) Frances Nicholson taught gym and health in a rural junior high. The school board learned that while an undergraduate, Ms. Nicholson had written several editorials for the University Daily advocating sexual freedom and experimentation. The board fired her in violation of the first amendment and due process. She seeks back pay and reinstatement. May the judge refuse to reinstate her and simply award back pay? See Allen v. Autauga County Board of Education, 685 F.2d 1302 (11th Cir. 1982); Cain v. McQueen, 580 F.2d 1001 (9th Cir. 1978); Abbott v. Thetford, 534 F.2d 1101 (5th Cir. 1976); Burton v. Cascade School District, 512 F.2d 850 (9th Cir. 1975).

3) The Civil Liberties Union representing a parent and her children, sued the Braxton schools to challenge morning devotional readings conducted by students over the school's public address system. The school cancelled the readings the day after they received notice of the suit and consulted attorneys. The school authorities agree that the readings violate the establishment clause, say that they do not intend to revive them, and express a desire to enter into a "consent declaratory judgment." You represent a plaintiff intervenor, the B'Nai B'Rith and several Jewish families. What are the arguments for an injunction? What do you expect the judge to do if you refuse to agree? See Lubbock Civil Liberties Union v. Lubbock Independent School District, 669 F.2d 1038 (5th Cir. 1982); Hall v. Board of School

Commissioners of Conecuh County, 656 F.2d 999 (5th Cir. 1981); Meltzer v. Board of Instruction of Orange County Florida, 548 F.2d 559 (5th Cir. 1977).

Chapter Four

PRIOR RESTRAINTS AND THE REMEDIAL HIERARCHY

The prior restraint doctrine imposes limitations on injunctions that are not imposed on criminal statutes and liability rules. It incorporates a legal double standard: a criminal statute or liability rule will be judged by one first amendment standard and an injunction will be judged by a more stringent standard. The justification for the double standard emphasizes the preventive character of the injunction—hence the term *prior* restraint. But we remain puzzled, because the injunction is not the only instrument that has preventive ambitions: criminal statutes and liability rules also seek to prevent future conduct. We wonder why they are not subjected to the same standards as injunctions. The prior restraint doctrine is concerned with injunctions addressed to speech, one of our most precious liberties; but nonetheless it provides a rich opportunity to identify the distinctive character of the injunction as a preventive instrument and once again to compare it to other remedies.

Prior restraint opinions help us examine the remedial hierarchy and test the idea that an injunction is simply one way of either stopping illegal or harmful conduct or correcting its effect. We will compare injunctions to parallel criminal statutes and tort doctrines with several questions in mind. Which remedies solve plaintiff's legitimate problem without interferring with protected rights? Why limit injunctions when we tolerate damage suits or criminal prosecutions? Do injunctions possess peculiar features that restrain illegal and harmful conduct excessively? Do injunctions against illegal and harmful conduct somehow threaten or chill people and deter them from engaging in protected activity? If so, should plaintiff first resort to damage or criminal remedies? Or should courts utilize devices that will curb the excesses of injunctions? Are the doctrines that subordinate injunctions to other remedies illogical or anachronistic? Should courts stop talking about prior restraint and curb injunctive excesses by addressing two questions: Was the procedure fair? Do the terms of the injunction violate the first amendment?

The defendant's interest is one of society's most cherished freedoms: to facilitate the dissemination of ideas by forbidding the government from imposing a sanction on constitutionally protected expression. The courts seem to define a prior restraint as a sanction on speech, either protected or not, imposed before the defendant disseminates that speech to the public. One of your editors, Rendleman, thinks that the courts' definition is far too broad to be applied and administered discerningly. He thinks that a prior restraint is a sanction imposed against a person for activity related to protected expression without adjudicating whether the sanctioned activity is constitutionally protected. Both editors wonder whether an injunction should be a disfavored remedy for illegal activity once a court has adjudicated that activity to be both unprotected and illegal.

Courts use the words "prior restraint" for two distinguishable groups of cases: procedural and remedial. Procedural decisions govern the process of sorting protected expression from unprotected activity. Injunction procedure includes three unique features that we will study later. Procedure may be ex parte or nonadversary; a jury may not be available; and the collateral bar rule may preclude injunction defenses in contempt. The casebook contains at least one procedural decision, Carroll v. President and Commissioners of Princess Anne on p. 328. This chapter tries to focus on the restrictions on the injunction as a distinct remedy, although all the opinions examine procedure as well.

A student of prior restraints may consult quite a bit of secondary literature. Both of the editors have taken a crack at it. See O. Fiss, The Civil Rights Injunction 69–74 (1978); Fiss, Chapter 5, Free Speech and the Prior Restraint Doctrine: The *Pentagon Papers Case,* in The Supreme Court and Human Rights (B. Marshall ed. 1982); Rendleman, Civilizing Pornography: The Case for An Exclusive Obscenity Nuisance Statute, 44 U.Chi.L.Rev. 509, 551–57 (1977); Rendleman, Free Press-Fair Trial: Restrictive Orders After Nebraska Press, 67 Ky.L.J. 867, 895–900 (1979); See also Barnett, The Puzzle of Prior Restraint, 29 Stan.L.Rev. 539 (1977); Edelstein and Mott, Collateral Problems in Obscenity Regulation: A Uniform Approach to Prior Restraints, Community Standards, and Judgment Preclusion, 7 Seton Hall 543 (1976); Emerson, First Amendment Doctrine and the Burger Court, 68 Calif.L.Rev. 422, 454–58 (1980); Freedman and Starwood, Prior Restraints on Freedom of Expression by Defendants and Defense Attorneys: Ratio Decidendi v. Obiter Dictum, 29 Stan.L.Rev. 607 (1977); Goodale, The Press Ungagged: The Practical Effect on Gag Order Litigation of Nebraska Press Association v. Stuart, 29 Stan.L.Rev. 497 (1977); Litwack, The Doctrine of Prior Restraint, 12 Harv.C.R.-C.L.L.Rev. 519 (1977); Schauer, Fear, Risk and the First Amendment: Unraveling the "Chilling Effect," 58 B.U.L.Rev. 685, 725–30 (1978).

Near v. Minnesota, the foundation of modern prior restraint doctrine, is the subject of a considerable literature. Mr. Fred Friendly wrote a readable social history of *Near,* Minnesota Rag (1981), and the Minnesota Law Review published a symposium to celebrate *Near*'s 50th anniversary. The symposium contains several helpful articles. Symposium: Near v. Minnesota, 50th Anniversary, 66 Minn.L.Rev. 1 (1981); Blasi, Toward a Theory of Prior Restraint: The Central Linkage; Knoll, National Security: The Ultimate Threat to the First Amendment; Linde, Courts and Censorship; Murphy, Near v. Minnesota in the Context of Historical Developments.

NEAR v. MINNESOTA

283 U.S. 697, 51 S.Ct. 625, 75 L.Ed. 1357 (1930).

Chief Justice HUGHES delivered the opinion of the Court.

Chapter 285 of the Session Laws of Minnesota for the year 1925 provides for the abatement, as a public nuisance, of a "malicious, scandalous and defamatory newspaper, magazine or other periodical." Section one of the Act is as follows:

"Section 1. Any person who, as an individual, or as a member or employee of a firm, or association or organization, or as an officer, director, member or employee of a corporation, shall be engaged in the business of regularly or customarily producing, publishing or circulating, having in possession, selling or giving away.

(a) an obscene, lewd and lascivious newspaper, magazine, or other periodical, or

(b) a malicious, scandalous and defamatory newspaper, magazine or other periodical,

is guilty of a nuisance, and all persons guilty of such nuisance may be enjoined, as hereinafter provided.

"Participation in such business shall constitute a commission of such nuisance and render the participant liable and subject to the proceedings, orders and judgments provided for in this Act. Ownership, in whole or in part, directly or indirectly, of any such periodical, or of any stock or interest in any corporation or organization which owns the same in whole or in part, or which publishes the same, shall constitute such participation.

"In actions brought under (b) above, there shall be available the defense that the truth was published with good motives and for justifiable ends and in such actions the plaintiff shall not have the right to report (*sic*) to issues or editions of periodicals taking place more than three months before the commencement of the action."

Section two provides that whenever any such nuisance is committed or exists, the County Attorney of any county where any such periodical is published or circulated, or, in case of his failure or refusal to proceed upon written request in good faith of a reputable citizen, the Attorney General, or upon like failure or refusal of the latter, any citizen of the county, may maintain an action in the district court of the county in the name of the State to enjoin perpetually the persons committing or maintaining any such nuisance from further committing or maintaining it. Upon such evidence as the court shall deem sufficient, a temporary injunction may be granted. The defendants have the right to plead by demurrer or answer, and the plaintiff may demur or reply as in other cases.

The action by section three, is to be "governed by the practice and procedure applicable to civil actions for injunctions," and after trial the court may enter judgment permanently enjoining the defendants found guilty of violating the Act from continuing the violation and, "in and by such judgment, such nuisance may be wholly abated." The court is empowered, as in other cases of contempt, to punish disobedience to a temporary or permanent injunction by fine of not more than $1,000 or by imprisonment in the county jail for not more than twelve months.

Under this statute, clause (b), the County Attorney of Hennepin County brought this action to enjoin the publication of what was described as a "malicious, scandalous and defamatory newspaper, magazine and periodical," known as "The Saturday Press," published by the defendants in the city of Minneapolis. The complaint alleged that the defendants, on September 24,

1927, and on eight subsequent dates in October and November, 1927, published and circulated editions of that periodical which were "largely devoted to malicious, scandalous and defamatory articles" concerning Charles G. Davis, Frank W. Brunskill, the Minneapolis Tribune, the Minneapolis Journal, Melvin C. Passolt, George E. Leach, the Jewish Race, and members of the Grand Jury of Hennepin County impaneled in November, 1927, and then holding office, and other persons, as more fully appeared in exhibits annexed to the complaint, consisting of copies of the articles described and constituting 327 pages of the record. While the complaint did not so allege, it appears from the briefs of both parties that Charles G. Davis was a special law enforcement officer employed by a civic organization, that George E. Leach was Mayor of Minneapolis, that Frank W. Brunskill was its Chief of Police, and that Floyd B. Olson (the relator in this action) was County Attorney.

Without attempting to summarize the contents of the voluminous exhibits attached to the complaint, we deem it sufficient to say that the articles charged in substance that a Jewish gangster was in control of gambling, bootlegging and racketeering in Minneapolis, and that law enforcement officers and agencies were not energetically performing their duties. Most of the charges were directed against the Chief of Police; he was charged with gross neglect of duty, illicit relations with gangsters, and with participation in graft. The County Attorney was charged with knowing the existing conditions and with failure to take adequate measures to remedy them. The Mayor was accused of inefficiency and dereliction. One member of the grand jury was stated to be in sympathy with the gangsters. A special grand jury and a special prosecutor were demanded to deal with the situation in general, and, in particular, to investigate an attempt to assassinate one Guilford, one of the original defendants, who, it appears from the articles, was shot by gangsters after the first issue of the periodical had been published. There is no question but that the articles made serious accusations against the public officers named and others in connection with the prevalence of crimes and the failure to expose and punish them.

At the beginning of the action, on November 22, 1927, and upon the verified complaint, an order was made directing the defendants to show cause why a temporary injunction should not issue and meanwhile forbidding the defendants to publish, circulate or have in their possession any editions of the periodical from September 24, 1927, to November 19, 1927, inclusive, and from publishing, circulating, or having in their possession, "any future editions of said The Saturday Press" and "any publication, known by any other name whatsoever containing malicious, scandalous and defamatory matter of the kind alleged in plaintiff's complaint herein or otherwise."

The defendants demurred to the complaint upon the ground that it did not state facts sufficient to constitute a cause of action, and on this demurrer challenged the constitutionality of the statute. The District Court overruled the demurrer and certified the question of constitutionality to the Supreme Court of the State. The Supreme Court sustained the statute (174 Minn. 457, 219 N.W. 770), and it is conceded by the appellee that the Act was thus held to be valid over the objection that it violated not only the state constitution but also the Fourteenth Amendment of the Constitution of the United States.

Thereupon, the defendant Near, the present appellant, answered the complaint. He averred that he was the sole owner and proprietor of the publication in question. He admitted the publication of the articles in the issues described in the complaint but denied that they were malicious, scandalous or defamatory as alleged. He expressly invoked the protection of the due process clause of the Fourteenth Amendment. The case then came on for trial. The plaintiff offered in evidence the verified complaint, together with the issues of the publication in question, which were attached to the complaint as exhibits. The defendant objected to the introduction of the evidence, invoking the constitutional provisions to which his answer referred. The objection was overruled, no further evidence was presented, and the plaintiff rested. The defendant then rested, without offering evidence. The plaintiff moved that the court direct the issue of a permanent injunction, and this was done.

The District Court made findings of fact, which followed the allegations of the complaint and found in general terms that the editions in question were "chiefly devoted to malicious, scandalous and defamatory articles," concerning the individuals named. The court further found that the defendants through these publications "did engage in the business of regularly and customarily producing, publishing and circulating a malicious, scandalous and defamatory newspaper," and that "the said publication" "under said name of The Saturday Press, or any other name, constitutes a public nuisance under the laws of the State." Judgment was thereupon entered adjudging that "the newspaper, magazine and periodical known as The Saturday Press," as a public nuisance, "be and is hereby abated." The judgment perpetually enjoined the defendants "from producing, editing, publishing, circulating, having in their possession, selling or giving away any publication whatsoever which is a malicious, scandalous or defamatory newspaper, as defined by law," and also "from further conducting said nuisance under the name and title of said The Saturday Press or any other name or title."

The defendant Near appealed from this judgment to the Supreme Court of the State, again asserting his right under the Federal Constitution, and the judgment was affirmed upon the authority of the former decision. 179 Minn. 40, 228 N.W. 326. With respect to the contention that the judgment went too far, and prevented the defendants from publishing any kind of a newspaper, the court observed that the assignments of error did not go to the form of the judgment and that the lower court had not been asked to modify it. The court added that it saw no reason "for defendants to construe the judgment as restraining them from operating a newspaper in harmony with the public welfare, to which all must yield," that the allegations of the complaint had been found to be true, and, though this was an equitable action, defendants had not indicated a desire "to conduct their business in the usual and legitimate manner."

From the judgment as thus affirmed, the defendant Near appeals to this Court.

This statute, for the suppression as a public nuisance of a newspaper or periodical, is unusual, if not unique, and raises questions of grave importance transcending the local interests involved in the particular action. It is no longer open to doubt that the liberty of the press, and of speech, is within the liberty safeguarded by the due process clause of the Fourteenth Amendment from invasion by state action. It was found impossible to conclude that this essential personal liberty of the citizen was left unprotected by the general guaranty of fundamental rights of person and property. Gitlow v. New York, 268 U.S. 652, 666; Whitney v. California, 274 U.S. 357, 362, 373; Fiske v. Kansas, 274 U.S. 380, 382; Stromberg v. California, 283 U.S. 359, decided May 18, 1931. In maintaining this guaranty, the authority of the State to enact laws to promote the health, safety, morals and general welfare of its people is necessarily admitted. The limits of this sovereign power must always be determined with appropriate regard to the particular subject of its exercise. . . . Liberty of speech, and of the press, is also not an absolute right, and the State may punish its abuse. Whitney v. California, supra; Stromberg v. California, supra. Liberty, in each of its phases, has its history and connotation and, in the present instance, the inquiry is as to the historic conception of the liberty of the press and whether the statute under review violates the essential attributes of that liberty.

The appellee insists that the questions of the application of the statute to appellant's periodical, and of the construction of the judgment of the trial court, are not presented for review; that appellant's sole attack was upon the constitutionality of the statute, however it might be applied. The appellee contends that no question either of motive in the publication, or whether the decree goes beyond the direction of the statute, is before us. The appellant replies that, in his view, the plain terms of the statute were not departed from in this case and that, even if they were, the statute is nevertheless unconstitutional under any reasonable construction of its terms. The appellant states that he has not argued that the temporary and permanent injunctions were broader than were warranted by the statute; he insists that what was done was properly done if the statute is valid, and that the action taken under the statute is a fair indication of its scope.

With respect to these contentions it is enough to say that in passing upon constitutional questions the court has regard to substance and not to mere matters of form, and that, in accordance with familiar principles, the statute must be tested by its operation and effect. . . . That operation and effect we think is clearly shown by the record in this case. We are not concerned with mere errors of the trial court, if there be such, in going beyond the direction of the statute as construed by the Supreme Court of the State. It is thus important to note precisely the purpose and effect of the statute as the state court has construed it.

First. The statute is not aimed at the redress of individual or private wrongs. Remedies for libel remain available and unaffected. The statute, said the state court, "is not directed at threatened libel but at an existing business which, generally speaking, involves more than libel." It is aimed at the distribution of scandalous matter as "detrimental to public morals and to the general welfare," tending "to disturb the peace of the community" and "to provoke assaults and the commission of crime." In order to obtain an injunction to suppress the future publication of the newspaper or periodical, it is not necessary to prove the falsity of the charges that have been made in the publication condemned. In the present action there was no allegation that the matter published was not true. It is alleged, and the statute requires the allegation, that the publication was "malicious." But, as in prosecutions for libel, there is no requirement of proof by the State of malice in fact as distinguished from malice inferred from the mere publication of the defamatory matter. The judgment in this case proceeded upon the mere proof of publication. The statute permits the defense, not of the truth alone, but only that the truth was published with good motives and for justifiable ends. It is apparent that under the statute the publication is to be regarded as defamatory if it injures reputation, and that it is scandalous if it circulates charges of reprehensible conduct, whether criminal or otherwise, and the publication is thus deemed to invite public reprobation and to constitute a public scandal. The court sharply defined the purpose of the statute, bringing out the precise point, in these words: "There is no constitutional right to publish a fact merely because it is true. It is a matter of common knowledge that prosecutions under the criminal libel statutes do not result in efficient repression or suppression of the evils of scandal. Men who are the victims of such assaults seldom resort to the courts. This is especially true if their sins are exposed and the only question relates to whether it was done with good motives and for justifiable ends. This law is not for the protection of the person attacked nor to punish the wrongdoer. It is for the protection of the public welfare."

Second. The statute is directed not simply at the circulation of scandalous and defamatory statements with regard to private citizens, but at the continued publication by newspapers and periodicals of charges against public officers of corruption, malfeasance in office, or serious neglect of duty. Such charges by their very nature create a public scandal. They are scandalous and defamatory within the meaning of the statute, which has its normal operation in relation to publications dealing prominently and chiefly with the alleged derelictions of public officers.[3]

Third. The object of the statute is not punishment, in the ordinary sense, but suppression of the offending newspaper or periodical. The reason for the enactment, as the state court has said, is that prosecutions to enforce penal statutes for libel do not result in "efficient repression or suppression of the evils of scandal." Describing the business of publication as a public nuisance, does not obscure the substance of the proceeding which the statute authorizes. It is the continued publication of scandalous and defamatory matter that constitutes the business and the declared nuisance. In the case of public officers, it is the reiteration of charges of official misconduct, and the fact that the newspaper or periodical is principally devoted to that purpose, that exposes it to suppression. In the present instance, the proof was that nine editions of the newspaper or periodical in question were published on successive dates, and that they were chiefly devoted to charges against public officers and in relation to the prevalence and protection of crime. In such a case, these officers are not left to their ordinary remedy in a suit for libel, or the authorities to a prosecution for criminal libel. Under this statute, a publisher of a newspaper or periodical, undertaking to conduct a campaign to expose

3. It may also be observed that in a prosecution for libel the applicable Minnesota statute (Mason's Minn.Stats., 1927, §§ 10112, 10113), provides that the publication is justified "whenever the matter charged as libelous is true and was published with good motives and for justifiable ends," and also "is excused when honestly made, in belief of its truth, and upon reasonable grounds for such belief, and consists of fair comments upon the conduct of a person in respect to public affairs." The clause last mentioned is not found in the statute in question.

and to censure official derelictions, and devoting his publication principally to that purpose, must face not simply the possibility of a verdict against him in a suit or prosecution for libel, but a determination that his newspaper or periodical is a public nuisance to be abated, and that this abatement and suppression will follow unless he is prepared with legal evidence to prove the truth of the charges and also to satisfy the court that, in addition to being true, the matter was published with good motives and for justifiable ends.

This suppression is accomplished by enjoining publication and that restraint is the object and effect of the statute.

Fourth. The statute not only operates to suppress the offending newspaper or periodical but to put the publisher under an effective censorship. When a newspaper or periodical is found to be "malicious, scandalous and defamatory," and is suppressed as such, resumption of publication is punishable as a contempt of court by fine or imprisonment. Thus, where a newspaper or periodical has been suppressed because of the circulation of charges against public officers of official misconduct, it would seem to be clear that the renewal of the publication of such charges would constitute a contempt and that the judgment would lay a permanent restraint upon the publisher, to escape which he must satisfy the court as to the character of a new publication. Whether he would be permitted again to publish matter deemed to be derogatory to the same or other public officers would depend upon the court's ruling. In the present instance the judgment restrained the defendants from "publishing, circulating, having in their possession, selling or giving away any publication whatsoever which is a malicious, scandalous or defamatory newspaper, as defined by law." The law gives no definition except that covered by the words "scandalous and defamatory," and publications charging official misconduct are of that class. While the court, answering the objection that the judgment was too broad, saw no reason for construing it as restraining the defendants "from operating a newspaper in harmony with the public welfare to which all must yield," and said that the defendants had not indicated "any desire to conduct their business in the usual and legitimate manner," the manifest inference is that, at least with respect to a new publication directed against official misconduct, the defendant would be held, under penalty of punishment for contempt as provided in the statute, to a manner of publication which the court considered to be "usual and legitimate" and consistent with the public welfare.

If we cut through mere details of procedure, the operation and effect of the statute in substance is that public authorities may bring the owner or publisher of a newspaper or periodical before a judge upon a charge of conducting a business of publishing scandalous and defamatory matter—in particular that the matter consists of charges against public officers of official dereliction—and unless the owner or publisher is able and disposed to bring competent evidence to satisfy the judge that the charges are true and are published with good motives and for justifiable ends, his newspaper or periodical is suppressed and further publication is made punishable as a contempt. This is of the essence of censorship.

The question is whether a statute authorizing such proceedings in restraint of publication is consistent with the conception of the liberty of the press as historically conceived and guaranteed. In determining the extent of the constitutional protection, it has been generally, if not universally, considered that it is the chief purpose of the guaranty to prevent previous restraints upon publication. The struggle in England, directed against the legislative power of the licenser, resulted in renunciation of the censorship of the press. The liberty deemed to be established was thus described by Blackstone: "The liberty of the press is indeed essential to the nature of a free state; but this consists in laying no *previous* restraints upon publications, and not in freedom from censure for criminal matter when published. Every freeman has an undoubted right to lay what sentiments he pleases before the public; to forbid this, is to destroy the freedom of the press; but if he publishes what is improper, mischievous or illegal, he must take the consequence of his own temerity." 4 Bl.Com. 151, 152; see Story on the Constitution, §§ 1884, 1889. The distinction was early pointed out between the extent of the freedom with respect to censorship under our constitutional system and that enjoyed in England. Here, as Madison said, "the great and essential rights of the people are secured against legislative as well as against executive ambition. They are secured, not by laws paramount to prerogative, but by constitutions paramount to laws. This security of the freedom of the press requires that it should be exempt not only from previous restraint by the Executive, as in Great Britain, but from legislative restraint also." Report on the Virginia Resolutions, Madison's Works, vol. IV, p. 543. This Court said, in Patterson v. Colorado, 205 U.S. 454, 462: "In the first place, the main purpose of such constitutional provisions is 'to prevent all such *previous restraints* upon publications as had been practiced by other governments,' and they do not prevent the subsequent punishment of such as may be deemed contrary to the public welfare. Commonwealth v. Blanding, 3 Pick. [Mass.] 304, 313, 314 [15 Am.Dec. 214]; Respublica v. Oswald, 1 Dall. 319, 325, 1 L.Ed. 155, 158. The preliminary freedom extends as well to the false as to the true; the subsequent punishment may extend as well to the true as to the false. This was the law of criminal libel apart from statute in most cases, if not in all. Commonwealth v. Blanding, ubi sup.; 4 Bl.Com. 150."

The criticism upon Blackstone's statement has not been because immunity from previous restraint upon publication has not been regarded as deserving of special emphasis, but chiefly because that immunity cannot be deemed to exhaust the conception of the liberty guaranteed by state and federal constitutions. The point of criticism has been "that the mere exemption from previous restraints cannot be all that is secured by the constitutional provisions;" and that "the liberty of the press might be rendered a mockery and a delusion, and the phrase itself a by-word, if, while every man was at liberty to publish what he pleased, the public authorities might nevertheless punish him for harmless publications." 2 Cooley, Const. Lim., 8th ed., p. 885. But it is recognized that punishment for the abuse of the liberty accorded to the press is essential to the protection of the public, and that the common law rules that subject the libeler to responsibility for the public offense, as well as for the private injury, are not abolished by the protection extended in our constitutions. id. pp. 883, 884. The law of criminal libel rests upon that secure foundation. There is also the conceded authority of courts to punish for contempt when publications directly tend to prevent the proper discharge of judicial functions. Patterson v. Colorado, supra; Toledo Newspaper Company v. United States, 247 U.S. 402, 419. In the present case, we have no occasion to inquire as to the permissible scope of subsequent punishment. For whatever wrong the appellant has committed or may commit, by his publications, the State appropriately affords both public and private redress by its libel laws. As has been noted, the statute in question does not deal with punishments; it provides for no punishment, except in case of contempt for violation of the court's order, but for suppression and injunction, that is, for restraint upon publication.

The objection has also been made that the principle as to immunity from previous restraint is stated too broadly, if every such restraint is deemed to be prohibited. That is undoubtedly true; the protection even as to previous restraint is not absolutely unlimited. But the limitation has been recognized only in exceptional cases: "When a nation is at war many things that might be said in time of peace are such a hinderance to its effort that their utterance will not be endured so long as men fight and that no Court could regard them as protected by any constitutional right." Schenck v. United States, 249 U.S. 47, 52. No one would question but that a government might prevent actual obstruction to its recruiting service or the publication of the sailing dates of transports or the number and location of troops. On similar grounds, the primary requirements of decency may be enforced against obscene publications. The security of the community life may be protected against incitements to acts of violence and the overthrow by force of orderly government. The constitutional guaranty of free speech does not "protect a man from an injunction against uttering words that may have all the effect of force. Gompers v. Buck's Stove & Range Co." Schenck v. United States, supra. These limitations are not applicable here. Nor are we now concerned with questions as to the extent of authority to prevent publications in order to protect private rights according to the principles governing the exercise of the jurisdiction of courts of equity.

The exceptional nature of its limitations places in a strong light the general conception that liberty of the press, historically considered and taken up by the Federal Constitution, has meant, principally although not exclusively, immunity from previous restraints or censorship. The conception of the liberty of the press in this country had broadened with the exigencies of the colonial period and with the efforts to secure freedom from oppressive administration. That liberty was especially cherished for the immunity it afforded from previous restraint of the publication of censure of public officers and charges of official misconduct. . . .

The fact that for approximately one hundred and fifty years there has been almost an entire absence of attempts to impose previous restraints upon publications relating to the malfeasance of public officers is significant of the deep-seated conviction that such restraints would violate constitutional right. Public officers, whose character and conduct remain open to debate and free discussion in the press, find their remedies for false accusations in actions under libel laws providing for redress and punishment, and not in proceedings to restrain the publication of newspapers and periodicals. . . .

The importance of this immunity has not lessened. While reckless assaults upon public men, and efforts to bring obloquy upon those who are endeavoring faithfully to discharge official duties, exert a baleful influence and deserve the severest condemnation in public opinion, it cannot be said that this abuse is greater, and it is believed to be less, than that which characterized the period in which our institutions took shape. Meanwhile, the administration of government has become more complex, the opportunities for malfeasance and corruption have multiplied, crime has grown to most serious proportions, and the danger of its protection by unfaithful officials and of the impairment of the fundamental security of life and property by criminal alliances and official neglect, emphasizes the primary need of a vigilant and courageous press, especially in great cities. The fact that the liberty of the press may be abused by miscreant purveyors of scandal does not make any the less necessary the immunity of the press from previous restraint in dealing with official misconduct. Subsequent punishment for such abuses as may exist is the appropriate remedy, consistent with constitutional privilege. . . .

The statute in question cannot be justified by reason of the fact that the publisher is permitted to show, before injunction issues, that the matter published is true and is published with good motives and for justifiable ends. If such a statute, authorizing suppression and injunction on such a basis, is constitutionally valid, it would be equally permissible for the legislature to provide that at any time the publisher of any newspaper could be brought before a court, or even an administrative officer (as the constitutional protection may not be regarded as resting on mere procedural details) and required to produce proof of the truth of his publication, or of what he intended to publish, and of his motives, or stand enjoined. If this can be done, the legislature may provide machinery for determining in the complete exercise of its discretion what are justifiable ends and restrain publication accordingly. And it would be but a step to a complete system of censorship. The recognition of authority to impose previous restraint upon publication in order to protect the community against the circulation of charges of misconduct, and especially of official misconduct, necessarily would carry with it the admission of the authority of the censor against which the constitutional barrier was erected. The preliminary freedom, by virtue of the very reason for its existence, does not depend, as this Court has said, on proof of truth. Patterson v. Colorado, supra.

Equally unavailing is the insistence that the statute is designed to prevent the circulation of scandal which tends to disturb the public peace and to provoke assaults and the commission of crime. Charges of reprehensible conduct, and in particular of official malfeasance, unquestionably create a public scandal, but the theory of the constitutional guaranty is that even a more serious public evil would be caused by authority to prevent publication. "To prohibit the intent to excite those unfavorable sentiments against those who administer the Government, is equivalent to a prohibition of the actual excitement of them; and to prohibit the actual excitement of them is equivalent to a prohibition of discussions having that tendency and effect; which, again, is equivalent to a protection of those who administer the Government, if they should at any time deserve the contempt or hatred of the people, against being exposed to it by free animadversions on their characters and conduct." There is nothing new in the fact that charges of reprehensible conduct may create resentment and the disposition to resort to violent means of redress, but this well-understood tendency did not alter the determination to protect the press against censorship and restraint upon publication. As was said in New Yorker Staats-Zeitung v. Nolan, 89 N.J.Eq. 387, 388; 105 A. 72: "If the township may prevent the circulation of a newspaper for no reason other than that some of its inhabitants may violently disagree with it, and resent its circulation by resorting to physical violence, there is no limit to what may be prohibited." The danger of violent reactions becomes greater with effective organization of defiant groups resenting exposure, and if this consideration warranted legislative interference with the initial freedom of publication, the constitutional protection would be reduced to a mere form of words.

For these reasons we hold the statute, so far as it authorized the proceedings in this action under clause (b) of section one, to be an infringement of the liberty of the press guaranteed by the Fourteenth Amendment. We should add that this decision rests upon the operation and effect of the statute, without regard to the question of the truth of the charges contained in the particular periodical. The fact that the public officers named in this case, and those associated with the charges of official dereliction, may be deemed to be impeccable, cannot affect the conclusion that the statute imposes an unconstitutional restraint upon publication.

Justice BUTLER, dissenting.

The decision of the Court in this case declares Minnesota and every other State powerless to restrain by injunction the business of publishing and circulating among the people malicious, scandalous and defamatory periodicals that in due course of judicial procedure has been adjudged to be a public nuisance. It gives to freedom of the press a meaning and a scope not heretofore recognized and construes "liberty" in the due process clause of the Fourteenth Amendment to put upon the States a federal restriction that is without precedent. . . .

The record shows, and it is conceded, that defendants' regular business was the publication of malicious, scandalous and defamatory articles concerning the principal public officers, leading newspapers of the city, many private persons and the Jewish race. It also shows that it was their purpose at all hazards to continue to carry on the business. In every edition slanderous and defamatory matter predominates to the practical exclusion of all else. Many of the statements are so highly improbable as to compel a finding that they are false. The articles themselves show malice.[1]

The defendant here has no standing to assert that the statute is invalid because it might be construed so as to violate the Constitution. His right is limited solely to the inquiry whether, having regard to the points properly raised in his case, the effect of applying the statute is to deprive him of his liberty without due process of law. This Court should not reverse the judgment below upon the ground that in some other case the statute may be ap-

1. The following article appears in the last edition published, dated November 19, 1927:

"FACTS NOT THEORIES.

" 'I am a bosom friend of Mr. Olson,' snorted a gentleman of Yiddish blood, 'and I want to protest against your article,' and blah, blah, blah, ad infinitum, ad nauseam.

"I am not taking orders from men of Barnett faith, at least right now. There have been too many men in this city and especially those in official life, who HAVE been taking orders and suggestions from JEW GANGSTERS, therefore we HAVE Jew Gangsters, practically ruling Minneapolis. . . ."

plied in a way that is repugnant to the freedom of the press protected by the Fourteenth Amendment. . . .

This record requires the Court to consider the statute as applied to the business of publishing articles that are in fact malicious, scandalous and defamatory. . . .

Defendant concedes that the editions of the newspaper complained of are "defamatory *per se.*" And he says: "It has been asserted that the constitution was never intended to be a shield for malice, scandal, and defamation when untrue, or published with bad motives, or for unjustifiable ends. . . . The contrary is true; every person *does* have a constitutional right to publish malicious, scandalous, and defamatory matter though untrue, and with bad motives, and for unjustifiable ends, *in the first instance,* though he is subject to responsibility therefor *afterwards.*" The record, when the substance of the articles is regarded, requires that concession here. And this Court is required to pass on the validity of the state law on that basis. . . .

The Act was passed in the exertion of the State's power of police, and this court is by well established rule required to assume, until the contrary is clearly made to appear, that there exists in Minnesota a state of affairs that justifies this measure for the preservation of the peace and good order of the State. . . .

The Court quotes Blackstone in support of its condemnation of the statute as imposing a previous restraint upon publication. But the *previous restraints* referred to by him subjected the press to the arbitrary will of an administrative officer. He describes the practice (Book IV, p. 152): "To subject the press to the restrictive power of a licenser, as was formerly done, both before and since the revolution [of 1688], is to subject all freedom of sentiment to the prejudices of one man, and make him the arbitrary and infallible judge of all controverted points in learning, religion, and government." . . .

It is plain that Blackstone taught that under the common law liberty of the press means simply the absence of restraint upon publication in advance as distinguished from liability, civil or criminal, for libelous or improper matter so published. . . . Story defined freedom of the press guaranteed by the First Amendment to mean that "every man shall be at liberty to publish what is true, with good motives and for justifiable ends." His statement concerned the definite declaration of the First Amendment. It is not suggested that the freedom of press included in the liberty protected by the Fourteenth Amendment, which was adopted after Story's definition, is greater than that protected against congressional action. And see 2 Cooley's Constitutional Limitations, 8th ed., p. 886. 2 Kent's Commentaries (14th ed.) Lect. XXIV, p. 17.

The Minnesota statute does not operate as a *previous* restraint on publication within the proper meaning of that phrase. It does not authorize administrative control in advance such as was formerly exercised by the licensers and censors but prescribes a remedy to be enforced by a suit in equity. In this case there was previous publication made in the course of the business of regularly producing malicious, scandalous and defamatory periodicals. The business and publications unquestionably constitute an abuse of the right of free press. The statute denounces the things done as a nuisance on the ground, as stated by the state supreme court, that they threaten morals, peace and good order. There is no question of the power of the State to denounce such transgressions. The restraint authorized is only in respect of continuing to do what has been duly adjudged to constitute a nuisance. The controlling words are "All persons guilty of such nuisance may be enjoined, as hereinafter provided. . . . Whenever any such nuisance is committed . . . an action in the name of the State" may be brought "to perpetually enjoin the person or persons committing, conducting or maintaining any such nuisance, *from further committing, conducting or maintaining any such nuisance.* . . . The court may make its order and judgment permanently enjoining . . . defendants found guilty . . . from committing or continuing the acts prohibited hereby, and in and by such judgment, such nuisance may be wholly abated. . . . " There is nothing in the statute purporting to prohibit publications that have not been adjudged to constitute a nuisance. It is fanciful to suggest similarity between the granting or enforcement of the decree authorized by this statute to prevent *further* publication of malicious, scandalous and defamatory articles and the *previous restraint* upon the press by licensers as referred to by Blackstone and described in the history of the times to which he alludes.

The opinion seems to concede that under clause (a) of the Minnesota law the business of regularly publishing and circulating an obscene periodical may be enjoined as a nuisance. It is difficult to perceive any distinction, having any relation to constitutionality, between clause (a) and clause (b) under which this action was brought. Both nuisances are offensive to morals, order and good government. As that resulting from lewd publications constitutionally may be enjoined it is hard to understand why the one resulting from a regular business of malicious defamation may not.

It is well known, as found by the state supreme court, that existing libel laws are inadequate effectively to suppress evils resulting from the kind of business and publications that are shown in this case. The doctrine that measures such as the one before us are invalid because they operate as previous restraints to infringe freedom of press exposes the peace and good order of every community and the business and private affairs of every individual to the constant and protracted false and malicious assaults of any insolvent publisher who may have purpose and sufficient capacity to contrive and put into effect a scheme or program for oppression, blackmail or extortion.

The judgment should be affirmed.

Justice VAN DEVANTER, Justice McREYNOLDS, and Justice SUTHERLAND concur in this opinion.

---

1) Legislatures have often used equitable doctrine for social control. Depending on the time and mores, public nuisance actions have been brought against saloons, houses of prostitution, and gambling. See Black, The Expansion of Criminal Equity Under Prohibition, 5 Wis.L.Rev. 412 (1930). Contemporary equitable actions against obscenity are described in Rendleman, Civilizing Pornography: The Case For An Exclusive Obscenity Nuisance Statute, 44 U.Chi.L.Rev. 509 (1977).

2) Some parts of *Near* are obsolete as first amendment doctrine. The *Near* Court approved criminal sanctions and civil tort judgments for defama-

tion and libel. Neither would be available today based on the law and facts of *Near.* Garrison v. Louisiana, 379 U.S. 64 (1964); New York Times v. Sullivan, 376 U.S. 254 (1964). Professor Blasi says that "The restraint in *Near* itself . . . would surely be invalidated under the modern vagueness doctrine even if embodied in a criminal statute." Toward a Theory of Prior Restraint: The Central Linkage, 66 Minn.L.Rev. 11, 12 n. 8 (1981).

3) *Near* might be described as a politically motivated lawsuit, brought by government officials against opponents and critics. The Court argues cogently against all libel, tort and criminal as well as equitable. Could you explain *Near* by saying that the Supreme Court viewed the criminal and tort law of libel as so overreaching and unfair that it refused to countenance injunctions against libel? Was the Court ready to say that libel law imposes sanctions on activity the Constitution protects? Why did the Court wait more than 30 years to circumscribe criminal and tort libel?

4) The Restatement of Torts says: "Prior restraint of certain kinds of communications runs afoul of the restriction of the First Amendment, even though the enjoined conduct would be tortious in nature." Restatement (Second) of Torts § 942 comment e (1977). Does an equitable action possess peculiar features that threaten expression more than criminal or tort actions? Minnesota treated fair comment differently in an equitable action. How protective was the trial court procedure? What burden of proof did plaintiff carry? Was defendant entitled to a jury? Do the procedural differences lead you to doubt the propriety of injunctions to regulate expression related activity, even though you might approve tort or criminal regulation? If so, does assuming that the criminal or damage remedy is preferred mean that the prior restraint rule is a special illustration of the inadequacy prerequisite? But remember that the defendant was not subject to concrete punishment until after he violated the injunction and a contempt proceeding was conducted. An injunction merely restates the substantive law without punishing or sanctioning defendant. Is the free violation before an injunctive warning a sufficient reason for the procedural differences?

Is a civil plaintiff's damage remedy adequate? Can a jury measure injury to plaintiff's reputation accurately? The venerable rule is that "equity will not enjoin a libel." D. Dobbs, Handbook of the Law of Remedies 523–25 (1973); Bose Corp. v. Consumers Union of United States, Inc., 529 F.Supp. 357, 361–62 (D.Mass.1981). Does that notion represent a populistic fear of setting judges up as arbiters of truth and falsity? Perhaps *Near* simply reflects a preference for civil and criminal juries in defamation actions. If you were Jay Near's lawyer, would you rather have a jury or a judge? What control do the authorities have over criminal juries that refuse to apply the law? Might the authorities have proceeded against Near in equity because they feared that a criminal jury would not convict him? Is the chance that a criminal jury will refuse to apply the governing law a valid reason to prefer either equity or the criminal sanction? Does the equitable alternative preserve the integrity of the substantive law?

Do decisions enjoining defamation create a menacing aspect that hinders the defendant and "chills" protected expression? Could an injunction threaten censorship because a defendant would seek informal declaratory judgments from the prosecuting attorney or trial judge? Is that as dangerous as executive censorship where the agency develops an interest in suppression? See Schauer, Fear, Risk and the First Amendment: Unraveling the "Chilling Effect," 58 B.U.L.Rev. 685, 727–30 (1978); Developments in the Law: Injunctions, 78 Harv.L.Rev. 994, 1008–12 (1965). But may an injunction that a judge writes precisely for a discrete problem interfere less with related or protected interests?

5) Tort liability rules and criminal statutes threaten damage judgments and criminal sanctions. Do these threats deter speech? Does an injunction resemble a tort rule or criminal statute and a contempt prosecution resemble a criminal prosecution? Does an injunction halt speech only the way a stop sign halts a car: someone must put on the brakes and obey? In what sense is an injunction either "prior" or a "restraint?" Is "prior restraint" an opprobrius epithet the Court employs to upset restrictions on particular speech without addressing the substantive standard?

6) Professor Blasi's article on *Near* asks whether we should regard the injunction generally as "a particularly repressive method of regulating speech, akin to the historically disfavored administrative licensing system?" 66 Minn.L.Rev. at 14. He concludes that injunctions resemble executive licensing in unacceptable ways: both adjudicate abstractly in advance, contain an internal dynamic that leads them to be used excessively, affect adversely the way audiences receive the messages, and are at odds with our premises about limited government. You will not be able to evaluate Professor Blasi's critique fully until we have studied the collateral bar rule, injunction procedure and criminal contempt. You nevertheless may ask some questions: Do the prematurity rules of Fletcher v. Bealey p. 109 and *Reserve Mining* p. 116 ensure a concrete, nonabstract dispute and obviate Professor Blasi's concern? Does Professor Blasi overlook the issue in contempt, whether contemnor violated the injunction, as a way of reducing the abstract nature of the conflict? Does Professor Blasi give an injunction a life of its own and neglect the idea that an injunction is merely a remedy based on, and judged by, substantive law?

7) In order to focus on remedy, consider section 1(a) of the Minnesota statute, and assume it interdicts "commercial exhibition of obscene motion pictures" as well. We know that a criminal statute defining and punishing obscenity is constitutional. Miller v. California, 413 U.S. 15 (1973). The Kozy Theatre is in Lake Nishnabotna, Minnesota. Peter Peterson the manager has booked a feature called "Kitten Goes to Law School." "Kitten" is legally obscene.

One way the government can distinguish merely sexually explicit from obscene movies is licensing. The state may delegate power to an agency to grant or refuse a license to exhibit, and the statute will make it a crime to exhibit without a license. Executive licensing is a traditional prior restraint condemned by Blackstone. "Bambi" without a license would violate a licensing system. Times Film Corp. v. City of Chicago, 365 U.S. 43 (1961). The nation's last statewide movie licensing agency closed in 1981 when Maryland's system expired under the state's "sunset" law. Md.Code 1957, Art. 66A, § 26A. Executive licensing is demonstrably unfashionable. *Near* contributed to free expression by expanding prior restraint doctrine from executive licensing to injunctions. Justice Butler addressed his dissent to this expansion.

The authorities have several remedial alternatives in an obscenity nuisance action under section 1(a): 1) Judge Hunthausen may hold that the Kozy is a public nuisance because of "Kitten," and she may abate the nuisance by padlocking the Kozy's door. Running "Bambi" would be contempt. One wag called such shutdown injunctions "hardcore prior restraints." Obscenity Nuisance, 44 U.Chi.L.Rev. at 551 (1977). 2) Judge Hunthausen may abate the nuisance with an injunction forbidding "obscene movies." Under Rule 65(d) she must copy the legal definition from the criminal statute into the order. If the Kozy exhibits "Swedish Paradise," and the authorities charge contempt, then Peter may defend contempt by proving that "Swedish Paradise" is nonobscene. 3) Judge Hunthausen may view "Kitten," find it obscene, and abate the nuisance by forbidding the Kozy from exhibiting "Kitten Goes to Law School." If Peter books "Swedish Paradise," the authorities must start over.

In *Kingsley Books,* the Supreme Court said that the Minnesota statute in *Near* allowed courts to enjoin a defendant from publishing "future issues of a publication because its past issues have been found offensive." Kingsley Books, Inc. v. Brown, 354 U.S. 436, 445 (1957). Does that misstate *Near?* Does the Court in *Organization for a Better Austin,* below, misstate *Near?* If, after a full evidentiary hearing, Judge Hunthausen convicted Peter of contempt for exhibiting "Swedish Paradise" under order 2) or "Kitten" under order 3), then would that be a prior restraint? Did the injunction in *Near* resemble a padlocking order or an order against "obscene" picture shows? What did the Minnesota Supreme Court think? The dissent? The majority? See also Avenue Book Store v. City of Tallmadge, Ohio, 103 S.Ct. 356 (1982) (Justice White dissenting from denial of certiorari); Felhaber v. North Carolina, 675 F.2d 1365 (4th Cir. 1982).

Jay Near did in fact cease publishing the "Saturday Press" after the preliminary order. Could he have continued to publish a newspaper and, if charged with contempt, argue that it did not violate the injunction? Would it matter if Near had called the paper the "Hennepin Shopper" and filled it with garage sale ads, birth announcements, and high school football scores? See Obscenity Nuisance, 44 U.Chi.L.Rev. at 551–57.

8) Examine Vance v. Universal Amusement Co., Inc., 445 U.S. 308 (1980), with the foregoing questions in mind. In particular, has the Court's analysis improved since *Near?* It contains a related issue, whether the procedure was sufficient.

VANCE v. UNIVERSAL AMUSEMENT CO., INC.

445 U.S. 308, 100 S.Ct. 1156, 63 L.Ed.2d 413 (1980).

PER CURIAM.

The question presented in this unusual obscenity case is whether the United States Court of Appeals for the Fifth Circuit, correctly held a Texas public nuisance statute unconstitutional. The Court of Appeals read the Texas statute as authorizing a prior restraint of indefinite duration on the exhibition of motion pictures without a final judicial determination of obscenity and without any guarantee of prompt review of a preliminary finding of probable obscenity. Cf. Freedman v. Maryland, 380 U.S. 51 (1965); Southeastern Promotions, Ltd. v. Conrad, 420 U.S. 546 (1975). In this Court, appellants argue that such a restraint is no more serious than that imposed by Texas' criminal statutes and that it is therefore constitutional. We find appellants' argument unpersuasive and affirm the judgment of the Court of Appeals.

In 1973, appellee King Arts Theatre, Inc. (hereafter appellee), operated an indoor, adults-only motion picture theater. In October of that year, appellee's landlord gave notice that the theater's lease would be terminated. The notice stated that the County Attorney had informed the landlord that he intended to obtain an injunction to abate the theater as a public nuisance in order to prevent the future showing of allegedly obscene motion pictures. Appellee responded by filing suit in the United States District Court for the Northern District of Texas seeking an injunction and declaratory relief to forestall any action by the County Attorney under the Texas nuisance statutes.

. . .

Two different Texas statutes were in issue at that point. The first, Tex. Rev.Civ.Stat.Ann., Art. 4666 (Vernon 1952),[1] authorizes injunction suits in the name of the State against alleged nuisances. If successful, "judgment shall be rendered abating said nuisance and enjoining the defendants from maintaining the same, and ordering that said house be closed for one year," unless certain conditions are met. The second nuisance statute, Art. 4667(a), (Vernon Supp.1978), provides that certain habitual uses of premises shall constitute a public nuisance and shall be enjoined at the suit of either the State or any citizen. Among the prohibited uses is "the commercial manufacturing, commercial distribution, or commercial exhibition of obscene material." [2]

1. "Art. 4666. Nuisance; prosecution

"Whenever the Attorney General, or the district or county attorney has reliable information that such a nuisance exists, either of them shall file suit in the name of this State in the county where the nuisance is alleged to exist against whoever maintains such nuisance to abate and enjoin the same. If judgment be in favor of the State, then judgment shall be rendered abating said nuisance and enjoining the defendants from maintaining the same, and ordering that said house be closed for one year from the date of said judgment, unless the defendants in said suit, or the owner, tenant or lessee of said property make bond payable to the State at the county seat of the county where such nuisance is alleged to exist, in the penal sum of not less than one thousand nor more than five thousand dollars, with sufficient sureties to be approved by the judge trying the case, conditioned that the acts prohibited in this law shall not be done or permitted to be done in said house. On violation of any condition of such bond, the whole sum may be recovered as a penalty in the name and for the State in the county where such conditions are violated, all such suits to be brought by the district or county attorney of such county."

In the early stages of the litigation the parties appear to have assumed that this statute applied to the exhibition of obscene motion pictures; at least the District Court so understood the statute. The Court of Appeals, however, read Art. 4666 as applicable only to the types of nuisance specified in Art. 4664 none of which relates to obscenity. See n. 6, infra.

2. "Art. 4667. Injunctions to abate public nuisances

"(a) The habitual use, actual, threatened or contemplated, of any premises, place or building or part thereof, for any of the following uses shall constitute a public nuisance and shall be enjoined at

The three-judge District Court held that both of these statutes authorize state judges, on the basis of a showing that obscene films have been exhibited in the past, to prohibit the future exhibition of motion pictures that have not yet been found to be obscene. 404 F.Supp. 33 (1975). Recognizing that it is not unusual in nuisance litigation to prohibit future conduct on the basis of a finding of undesirable past or present conduct, the District Court read Near v. Minnesota ex rel. Olson, to require a special analysis when the prohibited future conduct may be protected by the First Amendment.[3] The routine abatement procedure, which the District Court characterized as "the heavy hand of the public nuisance statute," was considered constitutionally deficient in the First Amendment context.

Specifically, the District Court noted that a general prohibition would operate as a prior restraint on unnamed motion pictures, and that even orders temporarily restraining the exhibition of specific films could be entered *ex parte.*[4] Moreover, such a temporary restraining order could be extended by a temporary injunction based on a showing of probable success on the merits and without a final determination of obscenity. The District Court concluded that the nuisance statutes, when coupled with the Texas Rules of Civil Procedure governing injunctions, operate as an invalid prior restraint on the exercise of First Amendment rights.

. . . The State appealed to the United States Court of Appeals for the Fifth Circuit. A divided panel of that court reversed. The panel majority acknowledged that if Art. 4666 authorized the closing of a motion picture theater for all uses for a year, it "would pose serious first amendment ques-

the suit of either the State or any citizen thereof:

"(1) For gambling, gambling promotion, or communicating gambling information prohibited by law;

"(2) For the promotion or aggravated promotion of prostitution, or compelling prostitution;

"(3) For the commercial manufacturing, commercial distribution, or commercial exhibition of obscene material;

"(4) For the commercial exhibition of live dances or exhibition which depicts real or simulated sexual intercourse or deviate sexual intercourse;

"(5) For the voluntary engaging in a fight between a man and a bull for money or other thing of value, or for any championship, or upon result of which any money or anything of value is bet or wagered, or to see which any admission fee is charged either directly or indirectly, as prohibited by law."

3. "In its defense the state has tried to distinguish the instant case from Near v. Minnesota, supra, but the attempt is not successful. In both cases the state made the mistake of prohibiting future conduct after a finding of undesirable present conduct. When that future conduct may be protected by the first amendment, the whole system must fail because the dividing line between protected and unprotected speech may be 'dim and uncertain.' Bantam Books v. Sullivan, 372 U.S. [58], at 66 (1963). The separation of these forms of speech calls for 'sensitive tools,' Speiser v. Randall, 357 U.S. 513 (1958), not the heavy hand of the public nuisance statute." 404 F.Supp., at 44.

4. In dissent, Mr. Justice White incorrectly assumes that it is "undisputed that any injunction granted under Art. 4667(a) will be phrased in terms of the Miller v. California, 413 U.S. 15 (1973), definition of obscenity." This is by no means necessarily so. Under the Texas statutes a temporary injunction prohibiting the exhibition of specific named films could be entered on the basis of a showing of probability of success on the merits of the obscenity issue. Even if it were ultimately determined that the film is not obscene, the exhibitor could be punished for contempt of court for showing the film before the obscenity issue was finally resolved.

tions," but held that the District Court had misconstrued Art. 4666 in that it was not intended to apply to obscenity cases.[6]

The panel majority disagreed more fundamentally with the District Court's view of Art. 4667(a). It held that the injunction procedure authorized by that statute was "basically sound" in its application to an establishment such as appellee's:

"The statute authorizes an injunction against the commercial manufacture, distribution or exhibition of *obscene* material only. Because the injunction follows, rather than precedes, a judicial determination that obscene material has been shown or distributed or manufactured on the premises and because its prohibitions can apply only to further dealings with obscene and unprotected material, it does not constitute a prior restraint."

Further, the panel majority found no problem under Freedman v. Maryland, because any temporary restraint entered pending a final adjudication on the issue of obscenity would be imposed by a judge, not an administrative censor. The judgment of the District Court was therefore reversed.

The Court of Appeals granted rehearing en banc, and reversed the panel's holding that Art. 4667(a) is constitutional. 587 F.2d 159 (1978).[8] The 8-to-6 majority found the statute objectionable because it "would allow the issuance of an injunction against the future exhibition of unnamed films that depict particular acts enumerated in the state's obscenity statute," id., at 168, and "lacks the procedural safeguards required under Freedman v. Maryland, 380 U.S. 51 . . . ." The dissenters wrote that a pragmatic assessment of the statute's operation indicated that once the contemplated injunction was in effect, it would impose no greater a prior restraint than a criminal statute forbidding exhibition of materials deemed obscene . . . .

The Texas defendants appealed to this Court . . . . We limit our review to the two arguments advanced in appellants' brief: first, that an "obscenity injunction" under Art. 4667(a)(3) constitutes no greater a prior restraint than any criminal statute and, second, that the Court of Appeals erroneously held that no prior restraint of possible First Amendment materials is permissible. . . .

The Court of Appeals was quite correct in concluding both (a) that the regulation of a communicative activity such as the exhibition of motion pictures must adhere to more narrowly drawn procedures than is necessary for the abatement of an ordinary nuisance, and (b) that the burden of supporting an injunction against a future exhibition is even heavier than the burden of justifying the imposition of a criminal sanction for a past communication.[13]

6. The panel interpreted the "such a nuisance" language in the first sentence of Art. 4666, see n. 1, supra, as referring to the definition of "common nuisance[s]" in Art. 4664 (Vernon Supp. 1978): gambling houses, houses of prostitution, and places where intoxicating liquors are kept.

8. It accepted the panel majority's construction of Art. 4666, i.e., that it was inapplicable in obscenity cases.

13. "Any system of prior restraint, however, 'comes to this Court bearing a heavy presumption against its constitutional validity.' Bantam Books, Inc. v. Sullivan, 372 U.S., at 70; New York Times Co. v. United States; Organization for a Better Austin v. Keefe; Carroll v. Princess Anne; Near v. Minnesota ex rel. Olson. The presumption against prior restraints is heavier—and the degree of protection broader—than that against limits on expression imposed by criminal penalties. Behind the distinction is a theory deeply etched in our law: a free society prefers to punish the few who abuse

As the District Court and the Court of Appeals construed Art. 4667(a), when coupled with the Texas Rules of Civil Procedure, it authorizes prior restraints of indefinite duration on the exhibition of motion pictures that have not been finally adjudicated to be obscene.[14] Presumably, an exhibitor would be required to obey such an order pending review of its merits and would be subject to contempt proceedings even if the film is ultimately found to be nonobscene.[15] Such prior restraints would be more onerous and more objectionable than the threat of criminal sanctions after a film has been exhibited, since nonobscenity would be a defense to any criminal prosecution.

Nor does the fact that the temporary prior restraint is entered by a state trial judge rather than an administrative censor sufficiently distinguish this case from Freedman v. Maryland. "*Any* system of prior restraints of expression comes to this Court bearing a heavy presumption against its constitutional validity." Bantam Books, Inc. v. Sullivan, 372 U.S. 58, 70 (1963) (emphasis added). That a state trial judge might be thought more likely than an administrative censor to determine accurately that a work is obscene does not change the unconstitutional character of the restraint if erroneously entered.

Accordingly, we agree with the Court of Appeals' conclusion that the absence of any special safeguards governing the entry and review of orders restraining the exhibition of named or unnamed motion pictures, without regard to the context in which they are displayed, precludes the enforcement of these nuisance statutes against motion picture exhibitors.

Contrary to appellants' second argument, the Court of Appeals did not hold that there can never be a valid prior restraint on communicative activity. The Court of Appeals simply held that these Texas statutes were procedurally deficient and that they authorize prior restraints that are more onerous than is permissible under Freedman v. Maryland and Southeastern Promotions Ltd. v. Conrad, 420 U.S. 546 (1975).

Because we find no merit in the contentions advanced on behalf of appellants, the judgment is affirmed.

Chief Justice BURGER, with whom Justice POWELL joins, dissenting.

I would dismiss the appeal for failure to present a real and substantial controversy "of the immediacy which is an indispensable condition of constitutional adjudication." Poe v. Ullman, 367 U.S. 497 (1961) (plurality opinion). Alternatively, I would abstain from decision until the Texas courts interpret the challenged statute. I would not reach the merits of this "dispute" at this stage.

This Court's power of constitutional review is "most securely founded when it is exercised under the impact of a lively conflict between antagonistic

rights of speech *after* they break the law than to throttle them and all others beforehand. It is always difficult to know in advance what an individual will say, and the line between legitimate and illegitimate speech is often so finely drawn that the risks of freewheeling censorship are formidable. See Speiser v. Randall, 357 U.S. 513 (1958)." Southeastern Promotions, Ltd. v. Conrad, 420 U.S. 546, 558–559 (1975).

14. Those courts believed that a short-lived temporary restraining order could be issued on the basis of an *ex parte* showing, and that a temporary injunction of indefinite duration could be obtained on the basis of a showing of probable success on the merits. . . .

15. Cf. Walker v. City of Birmingham; United States v. Mine Workers.

demands, actively pressed, which make resolution of the controverted issue a practical necessity." Id., at 503. This case quite plainly fails to satisfy that rigorous standard. Here, Texas has conceded at oral argument that the injunctive remedy of Art. 4667(a) is not likely to be used by any Texas prosecutor.[1] . . .

Moreover, the need for constitutional decision could be obviated in this case by permitting the Texas courts an opportunity to interpret Texas law. The Court today assumes (1) that "a temporary injunction of indefinite duration" could be issued against a named motion picture "on the basis of a showing of probable success on the merits," and (2) that an exhibitor would be subject to criminal contempt proceedings for violating such an injunction even if the motion picture is ultimately adjudged nonobscene. If these assumptions are correct, the statute is obviously flawed. See Freedman v. Maryland, 380 U.S. 51 (1965). But there is ample reason to believe that the Court may be wrong in today's conjectures; indeed, there is a serious question as to whether the Texas statute even authorizes an injunction against a *named* film. . . . If such an injunction is permitted, the decision of the Texas Court of Civil Appeals in Locke v. State, 516 S.W.2d 949 (1974), casts doubt on the assumption that it can be obtained on a showing of probable success. There, the Texas court in reviewing the validity of a temporary injunction entered against a motion picture exhibitor made a *de novo* on-the-merits determination of obscenity. Are we really to believe that the trial court applies a less stringent, probable-success standard? At the very least, *Locke* demonstrates that if an injunction is obtainable on such a slender showing, it is likely to enjoy a short life. It provides stark proof that only by abstaining from decision can we know whether Texas law is as the Court today "forecasts" it to be. See Railroad Comm'n v. Pullman Co., 312 U.S. 496, 499 (1941).[4] "So fragile a record is an unsatisfactory basis on which to entertain this action for declaratory relief." Public Affairs Press v. Rickover, 369 U.S. 111, 114 (1962).

In sum, I am unwilling to join the Court in "umpiring" an empty debate on a question of Texas law on which the Texas courts have not yet had an opportunity to speak. I therefore would dismiss the appeal.

Justice WHITE, with whom Justice REHNQUIST joins, dissenting.

The Court of Appeals invalidated Tex.Rev.Civ.Stat.Ann., Art. 4667(a) (Vernon Supp.1978), for what I understand to be two distinct reasons. Neither is valid, and to the extent that the Court falls into the same error, I respectfully dissent.

1. "QUESTION: Well, what does it—why, then, do you need [this statute], if it is the equivalent of the Texas criminal law?

"MR. ZWEINER: I am not sure that we do, to be frank; but—

"QUESTION: What does it add to the criminal law. It changes the burden of proof, it deprives a person of a jury trial.

"MR. ZWEINER: I don't think it adds anything. As a matter of fact I think it is a cumbersome process and I don't know that the prosecutor after more than two rounds will ever use it again. . . ."

4. Equally dubious is the Court's second assumption that an exhibitor could be punished for disobeying a temporary injunction even if the motion picture shown is ultimately found nonobscene. It is an open question whether Texas in these circumstances would apply a rule analogous to that invoked in Walker v. City of Birmingham, to bar a defendant from raising a First Amendment defense in an action for contempt.

The Court of Appeals first characterized Art. 4667(a) as a prior restraint on expression and invalidated it for this reason. I disagree. In my view, Art. 4667(a), standing alone, intrudes no more on First Amendment values than would a criminal statute barring exhibition of obscene films in terms that would be valid under our cases.

The Court of Appeals' analysis of Art. 4667(a), and that of this Court as well, glosses over what I take to be a crucial feature of that law. Before an exhibitor can be found to have violated an Art. 4667(a) injunction, there must be two quite separate judicial proceedings. First, the plaintiff must obtain temporary or permanent injunctive relief against the habitual use of the subject premises for the commercial exhibition of obscene motion pictures. Second, the exhibitor must be found in criminal or civil contempt for violating the terms of the injunction. When these separate proceedings are carefully distinguished, it becomes apparent that neither individually nor jointly do they impose an impermissible burden on the exercise of First Amendment freedoms.

The initial injunctive proceeding is both substantively and procedurally sound under our precedents. Although the lack of an actual Art. 4667(a) injunction in the present case gives a somewhat abstract and hypothetical tone to the analysis, it seems undisputed that any injunction granted under Art. 4667(a) will be phrased in terms of the Miller v. California, 413 U.S. 15 (1973), definition of obscenity. Hence an Art. 4667(a) injunction would not by its terms forbid the exhibition of any materials protected by the First Amendment and would impose no greater functional burden on First Amendment values than would an equivalent—and concededly valid—criminal statute. It simply declares to the exhibitor that the future showing of obscene motion pictures will be punishable.[2] It is true that an Art. 4667(a) injunction is issued by a court of law while a criminal statute is imposed by a legislature. Yet this distinction seems irrelevant for First Amendment purposes.

Of course, an exhibitor who continues to show arguably obscene motion pictures after an Art. 4667(a) injunction has issued against him does run the risk of being held in contempt. The Court implies that this danger renders Art. 4667(a) unconstitutional because under Walker v. City of Birmingham an exhibitor could be held in contempt even if the film is ultimately found to be nonobscene. This conclusion is plainly wrong. As I have noted, and as the majority does not dispute, an Art. 4667(a) injunction, temporary injunction, or temporary restraining order will be phrased in terms of a constitutionally adequate definition of obscenity. Therefore, contrary to the Court's inference, the motion picture's nonobscenity would clearly defeat any contempt proceeding brought under Art. 4667(a), since if the film were not obscene, there would be no violation of the injunction.

There remains the question of whether the procedures employed at a contempt proceeding satisfy First Amendment requirements. I believe that they do. An exhibitor who shows a film arguably violative of the injunction would likely be tried for criminal contempt. At such a proceeding the exhib-

2. Indeed, the Art. 4667(a) procedure provides greater protection to speech than would an equivalent criminal statute, since no one is punishable for violating an Art. 4667(a) injunction unless a plaintiff has already gone to the considerable trouble of first obtaining a public nuisance injunction against the defendant.

itor would have the constitutional rights of any criminal defendant. In particular, the State would bear the burden of proving beyond a reasonable doubt that the film which allegedly violated the injunction was obscene.[3] Such procedures seem more than adequate to satisfy any procedural requirements that may exist with respect to criminal contempt proceedings in the First Amendment context.

The defendant might also be held in civil contempt if he refused to cease showing a specific motion picture proved to be obscene and contrary to the terms of the injunction. A civil contempt proceeding, unlike the original Art. 4667(a) injunction, could result in jailing or fining the exhibitor until he ceased showing a film that had been publicly determined to be obscene. But such procedures would fully satisfy the requirements of our cases. Under Texas law, no one may be held in civil contempt unless he has received notice, in the form of an order to show cause, and a hearing on the charge against him. . . . The burden of bringing civil contempt charges is on the party seeking to suppress the exhibition; presumably, that party as plaintiff also bears the burden of showing noncompliance with the injunction, and in particular of proving that the exhibitor has shown obscene films. Since contempt proceedings are held before a court, a civil contempt order will not issue until there has been a final judicial determination that the defendant has exhibited and continues to exhibit obscene films. And even then the exhibitor could purge his contempt by ceasing to exhibit such films.

The Court of Appeals and the Court, therefore, too easily equate an injunction against the exhibition of unnamed, obscene films with a typical "prior restraint." The Art. 4667(a) injunction does, in a sense, "restrain" future speech by declaring punishable future exhibitions of obscene motion pictures. But in this weak sense of the term criminal obscenity statutes would also be considered "prior restraints." Prior restraints are distinct from, and more dangerous to free speech than, criminal statutes because, through caprice, mistake, or purpose, the censor may forbid speech which is constitutionally protected, and because the speaker may be punished for disobeying the censor even though his speech was protected. Those dangers are entirely absent here. An injunction against the showing of unnamed obscene motion pictures does not and cannot bar the exhibitor from showing protected material, nor can the exhibitor be punished, through contempt proceedings, for showing such material. The Art. 4667(a) injunction, in short, does not impose a traditional prior restraint. On the contrary, it seems to me functionally indistinguishable from a criminal obscenity statute. Since an appropriately worded criminal statute is constitutionally valid, I believe that Art. 4667(a) is valid also.

The second reason given by the Court of Appeals for invalidating Art. 4667(a) and apparently adopted by this Court, was the "failure to provide the safeguards mandated by" Freedman v. Maryland, 380 U.S. 51 (1965), and Southeastern Promotions, Ltd. v. Conrad, 420 U.S. 546 (1975). Those

3. The Fifth Circuit majority expressed some doubt as to whether the State will have the burden of proof of showing that the film is obscene. To the contrary, obscenity is one element of the injunction, and if the State has the burden of showing violation of the injunction beyond a reasonable doubt, it follows that the State as a matter of due process has the burden of showing that the particular film shown was obscene.

cases held that injunctions against showing allegedly obscene films are invalid unless (1) the burdens of instituting proceedings and of proving the material is obscene are on the censor; (2) the restraint prior to judicial review continues only for a limited time and only to preserve the status quo; and, (3) there is an assurance of prompt final judicial determination of the films' obscenity.

I fail to see, however, how the *Freedman* restraints are relevant to the injunction contemplated by Art. 4667(a). The *Freedman* restraints are wholly appropriate with respect to injunctions against specific, named films but the injunction contemplated by Art. 4667(a) is one directed against the future showing of *unnamed* obscene motion pictures. Because the films enjoined are unnamed, a final judicial determination of obscenity is logically impossible prior to or at the time the injunction issues. As I have said, an Art. 4667(a) injunction no more restrains the showing of *particular* films than would a similarly worded criminal statute.

The Court of Appeals referred to the Texas Rules of Civil Procedure and declared that injunctions under those Rules could be issued without compliance with *Freedman* requirements. I would agree that the Texas procedures for enjoining the showing of named films must comply with the First Amendment requirements set out in our cases, but I fail to perceive why the inadequacy of the Texas procedures in this respect invalidates Art. 4667(a), a separate statutory provision, contemplating only injunctions against unnamed films.

In this light, striking down Art. 4667(a) is wholly gratuitous, and I respectfully dissent.

---

1) Does footnote 13 of the majority opinion resolve the enigma of the prior restraint doctrine? Is it "always difficult to know what an individual will say?" What if a book or movie is involved? Does the Court explain why "the risks of freewheeling censorship" are especially pronounced in an injunction proceeding?

2) Justice White, in his dissent, seeks to narrow the scope of the prior restraint doctrine, so that prior restraints are no longer coextensive with injunctions. He speaks of "a traditional prior restraint" and excludes the Texas injunction from that category. Is this consistent with Near v. Minnesota? Justice White assesses the special dangers of prior restraints: the censor may prohibit speech that is protected or the speaker may be punished for disobeying the censor even though his speech is protected. Are these dangers tied to the injunction? The Chief Justice points out in footnote 4 that the collateral bar rule might under special circumstances prevent a criminal contemnor from challenging the constitutional validity of the order he disobeys. We turn to that rule in the next chapter.

3) Does *Vance* emphasize specialized injunction procedure or the nature of an injunction as a remedy? Reread Note 7 after *Near*. Did the *Vance* majority fear a "padlocking" injunction? Did the statute only allow "obscenity" injunctions? Did the dissent analyze the procedural and remedial aspects separately? Properly?

4) In Obscenity Nuisance, 44 U.Chi.L.Rev. 509 (1977), one of the editors asserts that legislatures should repeal criminal obscenity statutes and rely exclusively on civil injunctions under a suggested statute he concocted. The idea has failed to catch on. Why? Was it a good idea anyway?

ORGANIZATION FOR A BETTER AUSTIN v. KEEFE

402 U.S. 415, 91 S.Ct. 1575, 29 L.Ed.2d 1 (1971).

Chief Justice BURGER delivered the opinion of the Court.

We granted the writ in this case to consider the claim that an order of the Circuit Court of Cook County, Illinois, enjoining petitioners from distributing leaflets anywhere in the town of Westchester, Illinois, violates petitioners' rights under the Federal Constitution.

Petitioner Organization for a Better Austin (OBA) is a racially integrated community organization in the Austin neighborhood of Chicago. Respondent is a real estate broker whose office and business activities are in the Austin neighborhood. He resides in Westchester, Illinois, a suburb of Chicago some seven miles from the Austin area.

OBA is an organization whose stated purpose is to "stabilize" the racial ratio in the Austin area. For a number of years the boundary of the Negro segregated area of Chicago has moved progressively west to Austin. OBA, in its efforts to "stabilize" the area—so it describes its program—has opposed and protested various real estate tactics and activities generally known as "blockbusting" or "panic peddling."

It was the contention of OBA that respondent had been one of those who engaged in such tactics, specifically that he aroused the fears of the local white residents that Negroes were coming into the area and then, exploiting the reactions and emotions so aroused, was able to secure listings and sell homes to Negroes. OBA alleged that since 1961 respondent had from time to time actively promoted sales in this manner by means of flyers, phone calls, and personal visits to residents of the area in which his office is located, without regard to whether the persons solicited had expressed any desire to sell their homes. As the "boundary" marking the furthest westward advance of Negroes moved into the Austin area, respondent is alleged to have moved his office along with it.

Community meetings were arranged with respondent to try to persuade him to change his real estate practices. Several other real estate agents were prevailed on to sign an agreement whereby they would not solicit property, by phone, flyer, or visit, in the Austin community. Respondent who has consistently denied that he is engaging in "panic peddling" or "blockbusting" refused to sign, contending that it was his right under Illinois law to solicit real estate business as he saw fit.

Thereafter, during September and October of 1967, members of petitioner organization distributed leaflets in Westchester describing respondent's activities. There was no evidence of picketing in Westchester. The challenged publications, now enjoined, were critical of respondent's real estate practices in the Austin neighborhood; one of the leaflets set out the business card respondent used to solicit listings, quoted him as saying "I only sell to Negroes," cited a Chicago Daily News article describing his real estate activities and accused him of being a "panic peddler." Another leaflet, of the same general order, stated that: "When he signs the agreement, we stop coming to Westchester." Two of the leaflets requested recipients to call respondent at his home phone number and urge him to sign the "no solicitation" agreement. On several days leaflets were given to persons in a Westchester shopping center. On two other occasions leaflets were passed out to some parishioners on their way to or from respondent's church in Westchester. Leaflets were also left at the doors of his neighbors. The trial court found that petitioners' "distribution of leaflets was on all occasions conducted in a peaceful and orderly manner, did not cause any disruption of pedestrian or vehicular traffic, and did not precipitate any fights, disturbances or other breaches of the peace." One of the officers of OBA testified at trial that he hoped that respondent would be induced to sign the no-solicitation agreement by letting "his neighbors know what he was doing to us."

Respondent sought an injunction in the Circuit Court of Cook County, Illinois, on December 20, 1967. After an adversary hearing the trial court entered a temporary injunction enjoining petitioners "from passing out pamphlets, leaflets or literature of any kind, and from picketing, anywhere in the City of Westchester, Illinois."

On appeal to the Appellate Court of Illinois, First District, that court affirmed. It sustained the finding of fact that petitioners' activities in Westchester had invaded respondent's right of privacy, had caused irreparable harm, and were without adequate remedy at law. The Appellate Court appears to have viewed the alleged activities as coercive and intimidating, rather than informative and therefore as not entitled to First Amendment protection. The Appellate Court rested its holding on its belief that the public policy of the State of Illinois strongly favored protection of the privacy of home and family from encroachment of the nature of petitioners' activities.

It is elementary, of course, that in a case of this kind the courts do not concern themselves with the truth or validity of the publication. Under Near v. Minnesota, the injunction, so far as it imposes prior restraint on speech and publication, constitutes an impermissible restraint on First Amendment rights. Here, as in that case, the injunction operates, not to redress alleged private wrongs, but to suppress, on the basis of previous publications, distribution of literature "of any kind" in a city of 18,000.

This Court has often recognized that the activity of peaceful pamphleteering is a form of communication protected by the First Amendment. E.g., Martin v. City of Struthers, 319 U.S. 141 (1943); Schneider v. State, 308 U.S. 147 (1939); Lovell v. Griffin, 303 U.S. 444 (1938). In sustaining the injunction, however, the Appellate Court was apparently of the view that petitioners' purpose in distributing their literature was not to inform the public, but to "force" respondent to sign a no-solicitation agreement. The claim that the expressions were intended to exercise a coercive impact on respondent does not remove them from the reach of the First Amendment. Petitioners plainly intended to influence respondent's conduct by their activities; this is not fundamentally different from the function of a newspaper. See Schneider v. State, supra; Thornhill v. Alabama, 310 U.S. 88 (1940). Petitioners were engaged openly and vigorously in making the public aware of respondent's real estate practices. Those practices were offensive to them, as the views and practices of petitioners are no doubt offensive to others. But so long as the means are peaceful, the communication need not meet standards of acceptability.

Any prior restraint on expression comes to this Court with a "heavy presumption" against its constitutional validity. Carroll v. Princess Anne; Bantam Books, Inc. v. Sullivan, 372 U.S. 58, 70 (1963). Respondent thus carries a heavy burden of showing justification for the imposition of such a restraint. He has not met that burden. No prior decisions support the claim that the interest of an individual in being free from public criticism of his business practices in pamphlets or leaflets warrants use of the injunctive power of a court. Designating the conduct as an invasion of privacy, the apparent basis for the injunction here, is not sufficient to support an injunction against peaceful distribution of informational literature of the nature revealed by this record. Rowan v. United States Post Office Dept., 397 U.S. 728 (1970), relied on by respondent, is not in point; the right of privacy involved in that case is not shown here. Among other important distinctions, respondent is not attempting to stop the flow of information into his own household, but to the public. Accordingly, the injunction issued by the Illinois court must be vacated.

[Justice Harlan's dissent, which relates to appealability, is below p. 445.]

---

1) Did the trial judge's injunction forbid the defendants from handing out the Chicago Tribune in Westchester? Does the Court deny Keefe a remedy because a) the first amendment doctrines of vagueness and overbreadth invalidated his tort cause of action, b) the defendants had a first amendment defense to the tort action, or c) even though money damages were constitutionally permissible, the court could not enjoin the defendant's activity? If the court based *Keefe* on a) or b), then did it treat the damage and equitable remedies the same way? If so, is there any reason to discuss the prior restraint doctrine? Why not say that the first amendment forbids states from making defendants' activity the basis for either a damage judgment or an injunction? Would the injunction's prohibitions have passed the constitutional test if they were embodied in a criminal statute or ordinance?

Is the *OBA* injunction objectionable for the same reason the Court struck down the injunction in *Near*: it generalized from past unlawful conduct to proscribe future expressive activity regardless of content? Is the injunction in *Keefe* more objectionable than the one in *Near*? Would you say that even if OBA's conduct were tortious, the trial judge should refuse to grant an injunction that generalizes from defendants' past torts to forbid their future expressive activity without adjudicating whether the latter activity is protected by the first amendment or violates any legal standard?

Is a prior restraint something different and more effective than the substantive law expressed in the tort, statutory, or criminal law? Does an injunction, which may be called a prior restraint, simply restate the substantive law and threaten contempt? Does an injunction say, in effect, "You have violated the law; go and sin no more?" Felhaber v. North Carolina, 675 F.2d

1365, 1370 (4th Cir. 1982). Defendant goes home unscathed after the judge enjoins. Defendant may not go home after a criminal conviction, and a damage action may result in a judgment that defendant must pay. An injunction entered after fair procedure may be carefully drafted to reduce the risk of uncertainty and self-censorship.

2) The court in Galella v. Onassis, 353 F.Supp. 196 (S.D.N.Y.1972), enjoined intrusive invasions of Jacqueline Onassis's right to privacy by Ron Galella, a self-proclaimed prince of paparazzi. The court of appeals affirmed the injunction after modifying it. 487 F.2d 986 (2d Cir. 1973). Galella argued that an injunction would be an illegal prior restraint, but Judge Cooper subordinated what he felt to be Galella's marginal press interest to Onassis's right to be free from objectionable tortious invasions. Both courts accommodated Galella's interest in pursuing his occupation with Onassis's privacy by forbidding him from coming close to her: he had to stay thirty feet from her children and twenty five from her, and he could not touch her.

Other branches of the privacy tort lead to even murkier consequences. Consider Estate of Presley v. Russen, 513 F.Supp. 1339 (D.C.N.J.1981). Russen simulated stage performances of the late Elvis Presley under the trade name THE BIG EL SHOW. Presley's estate sued under several theories including infringement of the right to publicity, a branch of privacy. The judge measured the plaintiff's right to restrict or sell publicity against the defendant's right to express creative talent and enrich society; he found that Russen used the Elvis mystique primarily to exploit it commercially without any valuable contribution to society. The judge refused, however, to enjoin the name "THE BIG EL SHOW" or the show itself; but he did issue a preliminary injunction forbidding defendant from using the initials TCB, a lightning bolt, and Elvis Presley's likeness or the "Elvis Pose" to identify his service.

3) May we distinguish *Onassis* and *Presley* from *Keefe* on the grounds of commercial motive and marginal social value? Would you expect a judge to enjoin a) a magazine from using Associate Dean Sullivan's name and picture without his permission to advertise conservative three-piece suits? b) defendant's publication of plaintiff's letter that defendant had intercepted? c) a creditor from calling a debtor on the telephone every five minutes to ask when she was going to pay up? d) a disaffected purchaser from displaying a large lemon on his car with the caption "Just another ripped-off buyer from Landerstein's Nash dealership"? e) two people who were picketing a tavern owner's home in a quiet residential neighborhood with signs that read "Save Kelly's, Please Don't Move to the Shopping Center Kelly"?

4) Problem: Johann French is a successful professional tennis player whose income from endorsing "masculine" products exceeds his tournament winnings. Johann's former college roommate writes Mrs. French threatening to call a press conference to reveal that Johann is a "homosexual queer and pervert" and to read selected passages from Johann's secret college diary. Johann says that the whole thing is a lie and that the roommate is a habitual liar and blackmailer who was expelled from college for cheating on a test. Should Johann seek to enjoin the press conference and any repetition of the defamation? Will he prevail?

Which injunction in Note 7 after *Near* would Johann French's resemble: the one against future "obscene movies?" the one against "Kitten Goes to Law School?" May a specific injunction against repeating discrete defamation comport with the first amendment? Does your answer depend on whether you prefer a judge or a jury to pass on truth or falsity? Could an injunction protect Johann against defamation yet be phrased to prevent it from suppressing the truth as well? Do your prefer 1) to let the roommate broadcast the defamation and to impose liability for damage or 2) to enjoin and risk burying the truth? See Z. Chafee, Government and Mass Communications 91–92 (1947). Does "burying the truth" overstate an injunction's effect? Will the legal process leading to an injunction harm Johann more than an injunction will help? May the roommate disseminate information about Johann despite an injunction and defend contempt by arguing that he did not violate the injunction?

NEW YORK TIMES CO. v. UNITED STATES

403 U.S. 713, 91 S.Ct. 2140, 29 L.Ed.2d 822 (1971).

PER CURIAM. We granted certiorari in these cases in which the United States seeks to enjoin the New York Times and the Washington Post from publishing the contents of a classified study entitled "History of U.S. Decision-Making Process on Viet Nam Policy." . . .

"Any system of prior restraints of expression comes to this Court bearing a heavy presumption against its constitutional validity." Bantam Books, Inc. v. Sullivan, 372 U.S. 58, 70 (1963); see also Near v. Minnesota. The Government "thus carries a heavy burden of showing justification for the imposition of such a restraint." Organization for a Better Austin v. Keefe. The District Court for the Southern District of New York in the *New York Times* case and the District Court for the District of Columbia and the Court of Appeals for the District of Columbia Circuit in the *Washington Post* case held that the government had not met that burden. We agree.

The judgment of the Court of Appeals for the District of Columbia Circuit is therefore affirmed. The order of the Court of Appeals for the Second Circuit is reversed and the case is remanded with directions to enter a judgment affirming the judgment of the District Court for the Southern District of New York. The stays entered June 25, 1971, by the Court are vacated. The judgments shall issue forthwith.

Justice BLACK, with whom Justice DOUGLAS joins, concurring.

I adhere to the view that the Government's case against the Washington Post should have been dismissed and that the injunction against the New York Times should have been vacated without oral argument when the cases were first presented to this Court. I believe that every moment's continuance of the injunctions against these newspapers amounts to a flagrant, indefensible, and continuing violation of the First Amendment. Furthermore, after oral argument, I agree completely that we must affirm the judgment of the Court of Appeals for the District of Columbia Circuit and reverse the judgment of the Court of Appeals for the Second Circuit for the reasons stated by my Brothers Douglas and Brennan. In my view it is unfortunate that some of my Brethren are apparently willing to hold that the publication of news may sometimes be enjoined. Such a holding would make a shambles of the First Amendment.

Our Government was launched in 1789 with the adoption of the Constitution. The Bill of Rights, including the First Amendment, followed in 1791. Now, for the first time in the 182 years since the founding of the Republic, the federal courts are asked to hold that the First Amendment does not mean what it says, but rather means that the Government can halt the publication of current news of vital importance to the people of this country.

In seeking injunctions against these newspapers and in its presentation to the Court, the Executive Branch seems to have forgotten the essential purpose and history of the First Amendment. When the Constitution was adopted, many people strongly opposed it because the document contained no Bill of Rights to safeguard certain basic freedoms. They especially feared that the new powers granted to a central government might be interpreted to permit the government to curtail freedom of religion, press, assembly, and speech. In response to an overwhelming public clamor, James Madison offered a series of amendments to satisfy citizens that these great liberties would remain safe and beyond the power of government to abridge. Madison proposed what later became the First Amendment in three parts, two of which are set out below, and one of which proclaimed: "The people shall not be deprived or abridged of their right to speak, to write, or to publish their sentiments; *and the freedom of the press, as one of the great bulwarks of liberty, shall be inviolable.*" (Emphasis added.) The amendments were offered to *curtail* and *restrict* the general powers granted to the Executive, Legislative, and Judicial Branches two years before in the original Constitution. The Bill of Rights changed the original Constitution into a new charter under which no branch of government could abridge the people's freedoms of press, speech, religion, and assembly. Yet the Solicitor General argues and some members of the Court appear to agree that the general powers of the Government adopted in the original Constitution should be interpreted to limit and restrict the specific and emphatic guarantees of the Bill of Rights adopted later. I can imagine no greater perversion of history. Madison and the other Framers of the First Amendment, able men that they were, wrote in language they earnestly believed could never be misunderstood: "Congress shall make no law . . . abridging the freedom . . . of the press . . . ." Both the history and language of the First Amendment support the view that the press must be left free to publish news, whatever the source, without censorship, injunctions, or prior restraints.

In the First Amendment the Founding Fathers gave the free press the protection it must have to fulfill its essential role in our democracy. The press was to serve the governed, not the governors. The Government's power to censor the press was abolished so that the press would remain forever free to censure the Government. The press was protected so that it could bare the secrets of government and inform the people. Only a free and unrestrained press can effectively expose deception in government. And paramount among the responsibilities of a free press is the duty to prevent any part of the government from deceiving the people and sending them off to distant lands to die of foreign fevers and foreign shot and shell. In my view, far from deserving condemnation for their courageous reporting, the New York Times, the Washington Post, and other newspapers should be commended for serving the purpose that the Founding Fathers saw so clearly. In revealing the workings of government that led to the Vietnam war, the newspapers nobly did precisely that which the Founders hoped and trusted they would do.

The Government's case here is based on premises entirely different from those that guided the Framers of the First Amendment. The Solicitor General has carefully and emphatically stated:

"Now, Mr. Justice [Black], your construction of . . . [the First Amendment] is well known, and I certainly respect it. You say that no law means no law, and that should be obvious. I can only say, Mr. Justice, that to me it is equally obvious that 'no law' does not mean 'no law,' and I would seek to persuade the court that that is true. . . . [T]here are other parts of the Constitution that grant powers and responsibilities to the Executive, and . . . the First Amendment was not intended to make it impossible for the Executive to function or to protect the security of the United States."

And the Government argues in its brief that in spite of the First Amendment, "[t]he authority of the Executive Department to protect the nation against publication of information whose disclosure would endanger the national security stems from two interrelated sources: the constitutional power of the President over the conduct of foreign affairs and his authority as Commander-in-Chief."

In other words, we are asked to hold that despite the First Amendment's emphatic command, the Executive Branch, the Congress, and the Judiciary can make laws enjoining publication of current news and abridging freedom of the press in the name of "national security." The Government does not even attempt to rely on any act of Congress. Instead it makes the bold and dangerously far-reaching contention that the courts should take it upon themselves to "make" a law abridging freedom of the press in the name of equity, presidential power and national security, even when the representatives of the people in Congress have adhered to the command of the First Amendment and refused to make such a law. See concurring opinion of Mr. Justice Douglas . . . . To find that the President has "inherent power" to halt the publication of news by resort to the courts would wipe out the First Amendment and destroy the fundamental liberty and security of the very people the Government hopes to make "secure." No one can read the history of the adoption of the First Amendment without being convinced beyond any doubt that it was injunctions like those sought here that Madison and his collaborators intended to outlaw in this Nation for all time.

The word "security" is a broad, vague generality whose contours should not be invoked to abrogate the fundamental law embodied in the First Amendment. The guarding of military and diplomatic secrets at the expense of informed representative government provides no real security for our Republic. The Framers of the First Amendment, fully aware of both the need to defend a new nation and the abuses of the English and Colonial governments, sought to give this new society strength and security by providing that freedom of speech, press, religion, and assembly should not be abridged. . . .

Justice DOUGLAS with whom Justice BLACK joins, concurring.

While I join the opinion of the Court I believe it necessary to express my views more fully.

It should be noted at the outset that the First Amendment provides that "Congress shall make no law . . . abridging the freedom of speech, or of the press." That leaves, in my view, no room for governmental restraint on the press.

There is, moreover, no statute barring the publication by the press of the material which the Times and the Post seek to use. 18 U.S.C. § 793(e) provides that "[w]hoever having unauthorized possession of, access to, or control over any document, writing . . . or information relating to the national defense which information the possessor has reason to believe could be used to the injury of the United States or to the advantage of any foreign nation, willfully communicates . . . the same to any person not entitled to receive it . . . [s]hall be fined not more than $10,000 or imprisoned not more than ten years, or both."

The Government suggests that the word "communicates" is broad enough to encompass publication.

There are eight sections in the chapter on espionage and censorship, §§ 792–799. In three of those eight "publish" is specifically mentioned: § 794(b) applies to "Whoever, in time of war, with intent that the same shall be communicated to the enemy, collects, records, *publishes*, or communicates . . . [the disposition of armed forces]."

Section 797 applies to whoever "reproduces, *publishes,* sells, or gives away" photos of defense installations.

Section 798 relating to cryptography applies to whoever: "communicates, furnishes, transmits, or otherwise makes available . . . *or publishes*" the described material.[2] (Emphasis added.)

Thus it is apparent that Congress was capable of and did distinguish between publishing and communication in the various sections of the Espionage Act.

The other evidence that § 793 does not apply to the press is a rejected version of § 793. That version read: "During any national emergency resulting from a war to which the United States is a party, or from threat of such a war, the President may, by proclamation, declare the existence of such emergency and, by proclamation, prohibit the publishing or communicating of, or the attempting to publish or communicate any information relating to the national defense which, in his judgment, is of such character that it is or might be useful to the enemy." 55 Cong.Rec. 1763. During the debates in the Senate the First Amendment was specifically cited and that provision was defeated. 55 Cong.Rec. 2167.

2. These documents contain data concerning the communications system of the United States, the publication of which is made a crime. But the criminal sanction is not urged by the United States as the basis of equity power.

Judge Gurfein's holding in the *Times* case that this Act does not apply to this case was therefore preeminently sound. Moreover, the Act of September 23, 1950, in amending 18 U.S.C. § 793 states in § 1(b) that:

"Nothing in this Act shall be construed to authorize, require, or establish military or civilian censorship or in any way to limit or infringe upon freedom of the press or of speech as guaranteed by the Constitution of the United States and no regulation shall be promulgated hereunder having that effect." 64 Stat. 987.

Thus Congress has been faithful to the command of the First Amendment in this area.

So any power that the Government possesses must come from its "inherent power."

The power to wage war is "the power to wage war successfully." See Hirabayashi v. United States, 320 U.S. 81, 93. But the war power stems from a declaration of war. The Constitution by Art. I, § 8, gives Congress, not the President, power "[t]o declare War." Nowhere are presidential wars authorized. We need not decide therefore what leveling effect the war power of Congress might have.

These disclosures [3] may have a serious impact. But that is no basis for sanctioning a previous restraint on the press. As stated by Chief Justice Hughes in Near v. Minnesota:

"While reckless assaults upon public men, and efforts to bring obloquy upon those who are endeavoring faithfully to discharge official duties, exert a baleful influence and deserve the severest condemnation in public opinion, it cannot be said that this abuse is greater, and it is believed to be less, than that which characterized the period in which our institutions took shape. Meanwhile, the administration of government has become more complex, the opportunities for malfeasance and corruption have multiplied, crime has grown to most serious proportions, and the danger of its protection by unfaithful officials and of the impairment of the fundamental security of life and property by criminal alliances and official neglect, emphasizes the primary need of a vigilant and courageous press, especially in great cities. The fact that the liberty of the press may be abused by miscreant purveyors of scandal does not make any the less necessary the immunity of the press from previous restraint in dealing with official misconduct." . . .

The Government says that it has inherent powers to go into court and obtain an injunction to protect the national interest, which in this case is alleged to be national security.

Near v. Minnesota, repudiated that expansive doctrine in no uncertain terms.

The dominant purpose of the First Amendment was to prohibit the widespread practice of governmental suppression of embarrassing information. It is common knowledge that the First Amendment was adopted against the

3. There are numerous sets of this material in existence and they apparently are not under any controlled custody. Moreover, the President has sent a set to the Congress. We start then with a case where there already is rather wide distribution of the material that is destined for publicity, not secrecy. I have gone over the material listed in the *in camera* brief of the United States. It is all history, not future events. None of it is more recent than 1968.

widespread use of the common law of seditious libel to punish the dissemination of material that is embarrassing to the powers-that-be. See T. Emerson, The System of Freedom of Expression, c. V (1970); Z. Chafee, Free Speech in the United States, c. XIII (1941). The present cases will, I think, go down in history as the most dramatic illustration of that principle. A debate of large proportions goes on in the Nation over our posture in Vietnam. That debate antedated the disclosure of the contents of the present documents. The latter are highly relevant to the debate in progress.

Secrecy in government is fundamentally anti-democratic, perpetuating bureaucratic errors. Open debate and discussion of public issues are vital to our national health. On public questions there should be "uninhibited, robust, and wide-open" debate. New York Times Co. v. Sullivan, 376 U.S. 254, 269–270.

I would affirm the judgment of the Court of Appeals in the *Post* case, vacate the stay of the Court of Appeals in the *Times* case and direct that it affirm the District Court.

The stays in these cases that have been in effect for more than a week constitute a flouting of the principles of the First Amendment as interpreted in Near v. Minnesota.

Justice BRENNAN, concurring.

I write separately in these cases only to emphasize what should be apparent: that our judgments in the present cases may not be taken to indicate the propriety, in the future, of issuing temporary stays and restraining orders to block the publication of materials sought to be suppressed by the Government. So far as I can determine, never before has the United States sought to enjoin a newspaper from publishing information in its possession. The relative novelty of the questions presented, the necessary haste with which decisions were reached, the magnitude of the interests asserted, and the fact that all the parties have concentrated their arguments upon the question whether permanent restraints were proper may have justified at least some of the restraints heretofore imposed in these cases. Certainly it is difficult to fault the several courts below for seeking to assure that the issues here involved were preserved for ultimate review by this Court. But even if it be assumed that some of the interim restraints were proper in the two cases before us, that assumption has no bearing upon the propriety of similar judicial action in the future. To begin with, there has now been ample time for reflection and judgment; whatever values there may be in the preservation of novel questions for appellate review may not support any restraints in the future. More important, the First Amendment stands as an absolute bar to the imposition of judicial restraints in circumstances of the kind presented by these cases.

The error which has pervaded these cases from the outset was the granting of any injunctive relief whatsoever, interim or otherwise. The entire thrust of the Government's claim throughout these cases has been that publication of the material sought to be enjoined "could," or "might," or "may" prejudice the national interest in various ways. But the First Amendment tolerates absolutely no prior judicial restraints of the press predicated upon surmise or conjecture that untoward consequences may result.* Our cases, it is true, have indicated that there is a single, extremely narrow class of cases in which the First Amendment's ban on prior judicial restraint may be overridden. Our cases have thus far indicated that such cases may arise only when the Nation "is at war," Schenck v. United States, 249 U.S. 47, 52 (1919), during which times "[n]o one would question but that a government might prevent actual obstruction to its recruiting service or the publication of the sailing dates of transports or the number and location of troops." Near v. Minnesota. Even if the present world situation were assumed to be tantamount to a time of war, or if the power of presently available armaments would justify even in peacetime the suppression of information that would set in motion a nuclear holocaust, in neither of these actions has the Government presented or even alleged that publication of items from or based upon the material at issue would cause the happening of an event of that nature. "[T]he chief purpose of [the First Amendment's] guaranty [is] to prevent previous restraints upon publication." Near v. Minnesota. Thus, only governmental allegation and proof that publication must inevitably, directly, and immediately cause the occurrence of an event kindred to imperiling the safety of a transport already at sea can support even the issuance of an interim restraining order. In no event may mere conclusions be sufficient: for if the Executive Branch seeks judicial aid in preventing publication, it must inevitably submit the basis upon which that aid is sought to scrutiny by the judiciary. And therefore, every restraint issued in this case, whatever its form, has violated the First Amendment—and not less so because that restraint was justified as necessary to afford the courts an opportunity to examine the claim more thoroughly. Unless and until the Government has clearly made out its case, the First Amendment commands that no injunction may issue.

Justice STEWART, with whom Justice WHITE joins, concurring.

In the governmental structure created by our Constitution, the Executive is endowed with enormous power in the two related areas of national defense and international relations. This power, largely unchecked by the Legislative and Judicial branches, has been pressed to the very hilt since the advent of the nuclear missile age. For better or for worse, the simple fact is that a President of the United States possesses vastly greater constitutional independence in these two vital areas of power than does, say, a prime minister of a country with a parliamentary form of government.

In the absence of the governmental checks and balances present in other areas of our national life, the only effective restraint upon executive policy and power in the areas of national defense and international affairs may lie in

* Freedman v. Maryland, 380 U.S. 51 (1965), and similar cases regarding temporary restraints of allegedly obscene materials are not in point. For those cases rest upon the proposition that "obscenity is not protected by the freedoms of speech and press." Roth v. United States, 354 U.S. 476, 481 (1957). Here there is no question but that the material sought to be suppressed is within the protection of the First Amendment; the only question is whether, notwithstanding that fact, its publication may be enjoined for a time because of the presence of an overwhelming national interest. Similarly, copyright cases have no pertinence here: the Government is not asserting an interest in the particular form of words chosen in the documents, but is seeking to suppress the ideas expressed therein. And the copyright laws, of course, protect only the form of expression and not the ideas expressed.

an enlightened citizenry—in an informed and critical public opinion which alone can here protect the values of democratic government. For this reason, it is perhaps here that a press that is alert, aware, and free most vitally serves the basic purpose of the First Amendment. For without an informed and free press there cannot be an enlightened people.

Yet it is elementary that the successful conduct of international diplomacy and the maintenance of an effective national defense require both confidentiality and secrecy. Other nations can hardly deal with this Nation in an atmosphere of mutual trust unless they can be assured that their confidences will be kept. And within our own executive departments, the development of considered and intelligent international policies would be impossible if those charged with their formulation could not communicate with each other freely, frankly, and in confidence. In the area of basic national defense the frequent need for absolute secrecy is, of course, self-evident.

I think there can be but one answer to this dilemma, if dilemma it be. The responsibility must be where the power is. If the Constitution gives the Executive a large degree of unshared power in the conduct of foreign affairs and the maintenance of our national defense, then under the Constitution the Executive must have the largely unshared duty to determine and preserve the degree of internal security necessary to exercise that power successfully. It is an awesome responsibility, requiring judgment and wisdom of a high order. I should suppose that moral, political, and practical considerations would dictate that a very first principle of that wisdom would be an insistence upon avoiding secrecy for its own sake. For when everything is classified, then nothing is classified, and the system becomes one to be disregarded by the cynical or the careless, and to be manipulated by those intent on self-protection or self-promotion. I should suppose, in short, that the hallmark of a truly effective internal security system would be the maximum possible disclosure, recognizing that secrecy can best be preserved only when credibility is truly maintained. But be that as it may, it is clear to me that it is the constitutional duty of the Executive—as a matter of sovereign prerogative and not as a matter of law as the courts know law—through the promulgation and enforcement of executive regulations, to protect the confidentiality necessary to carry out its responsibilities in the fields of international relations and national defense.

This is not to say that Congress and the courts have no role to play. Undoubtedly Congress has the power to enact specific and appropriate criminal laws to protect government property and preserve government secrets. Congress has passed such laws, and several of them are of very colorable relevance to the apparent circumstances of these cases. And if a criminal prosecution is instituted, it will be the responsibility of the courts to decide the applicability of the criminal law under which the charge is brought. Moreover, if Congress should pass a specific law authorizing civil proceedings in this field, the courts would likewise have the duty to decide the constitutionality of such a law as well as its applicability to the facts proved.

But in the cases before us we are asked neither to construe specific regulations nor to apply specific laws. We are asked, instead, to perform a function that the Constitution gave to the Executive, not the Judiciary. We are asked, quite simply, to prevent the publication by two newspapers of material that the Executive Branch insists should not, in the national interest, be published. I am convinced that the Executive is correct with respect to some of the documents involved. But I cannot say that disclosure of any of them will surely result in direct, immediate, and irreparable damage to our Nation or its people. That being so, there can under the First Amendment be but one judicial resolution of the issues before us. I join the judgments of the Court.

Justice WHITE, with whom Justice STEWART joins, concurring.

I concur in today's judgments, but only because of the concededly extraordinary protection against prior restraints enjoyed by the press under our constitutional system. I do not say that in no circumstances would the First Amendment permit an injunction against publishing information about government plans or operations.[1] Nor, after examining the materials the Government characterizes as the most sensitive and destructive, can I deny that revelation of these documents will do substantial damage to public interests. Indeed, I am confident that their disclosure will have that result. But I nevertheless agree that the United States has not satisfied the very heavy burden that it must meet to warrant an injunction against publication in these cases, at least in the absence of express and appropriately limited congressional authorization for prior restraints in circumstances such as these.

The Government's position is simply stated: The responsibility of the Executive for the conduct of the foreign affairs and for the security of the Nation is so basic that the President is entitled to an injunction against publication of a newspaper story whenever he can convince a court that the information to be revealed threatens "grave and irreparable" injury to the public interest;[2] and the injunction should issue whether or not the material to be published is classified, whether or not publication would be lawful under relevant criminal statutes enacted by Congress and regardless of the circumstances by which the newspaper came into possession of the information.

1. The Congress has authorized a strain of prior restraints against private parties in certain instances. The National Labor Relations Board routinely issues cease-and-desist orders against employers who it finds have threatened or coerced employees in the exercise of protected rights. See 29 U.S.C. § 160(c). Similarly, the Federal Trade Commission is empowered to impose cease-and-desist orders against unfair methods of competition. 15 U.S.C. § 45(b). Such orders can, and quite often do, restrict what may be spoken or written under certain circumstances. See, e.g., NLRB v. Gissel Packing Co., 395 U.S. 575, 616–620 (1969). Article I, § 8, of the Constitution authorizes Congress to secure the "exclusive right" of authors to their writings, and no one denies that a newspaper can properly be enjoined from publishing the copyrighted works of another. See Westermann Co. v. Dispatch Co., 249 U.S. 100 (1919). Newspapers do themselves rely from time to time on the copyright as a means of protecting their accounts of important events. However, those enjoined under the statutes relating to the National Labor Relations Board and the Federal Trade Commission are private parties, not the press; and when the press is enjoined under the copyright laws the complainant is a private copyright holder enforcing a private right. These situations are quite distinct from the Government's request for an injunction against publishing information about the affairs of government, a request admittedly not based on any statute.

2. The "grave and irreparable danger" standard is that asserted by the Government in this Court. In remanding to Judge Gurfein for further hearings in the *Times* litigation, five members of the Court of Appeals for the Second Circuit directed him to determine whether disclosure of certain items specified with particularity by the Government would "pose such grave and immediate danger to the security of the United States as to warrant their publication being enjoined."

At least in the absence of legislation by Congress, based on its own investigations and findings, I am quite unable to agree that the inherent powers of the Executive and the courts reach so far as to authorize remedies having such sweeping potential for inhibiting publications by the press. Much of the difficulty inheres in the "grave and irreparable danger" standard suggested by the United States. If the United States were to have judgment under such a standard in these cases, our decision would be of little guidance to other courts in other cases, for the material at issue here would not be available from the Court's opinion or from public records, nor would it be published by the press. Indeed, even today where we hold that the United States has not met its burden, the material remains sealed in court records and it is properly not discussed in today's opinions. Moreover, because the material poses substantial dangers to national interests and because of the hazards of criminal sanctions, a responsible press may choose never to publish the more sensitive materials. To sustain the Government in these cases would start the courts down a long and hazardous road that I am not willing to travel, at least without congressional guidance and direction.

It is not easy to reject the proposition urged by the United States and to deny relief on its good-faith claims in these cases that publication will work serious damage to the country. But that discomfiture is considerably dispelled by the infrequency of prior-restraint cases. Normally, publication will occur and the damage be done before the Government has either opportunity or grounds for suppression. So here, publication has already begun and a substantial part of the threatened damage has already occurred. The fact of a massive breakdown in security is known, access to the documents by many unauthorized people is undeniable, and the efficacy of equitable relief against these or other newspapers to avert anticipated damage is doubtful at best.

What is more, terminating the ban on publication of the relatively few sensitive documents the Government now seeks to suppress does not mean that the law either requires or invites newspapers or others to publish them or that they will be immune from criminal action if they do. Prior restraints require an unusually heavy justification under the First Amendment; but failure by the Government to justify prior restraints does not measure its constitutional entitlement to a conviction for criminal publication. That the Government mistakenly chose to proceed by injunction does not mean that it could not successfully proceed in another way.

When the Espionage Act was under consideration in 1917, Congress eliminated from the bill a provision that would have given the President broad powers in time of war to proscribe, under threat of criminal penalty, the publication of various categories of information related to the national defense.[3] Congress at that time was unwilling to clothe the President with such far-

3. "Whoever, in time of war, in violation of reasonable regulations to be prescribed by the President, which he is hereby authorized to make and promulgate, shall publish any information with respect to the movement, numbers, description, condition, or disposition of any of the armed forces, ships, aircraft, or war materials of the United States, or with respect to the plans or conduct of any naval or military operations, or with respect to any works or measures undertaken for or connected with, or intended for the fortification or defense of any place, or any other information relating to the public defense calculated to be useful to the enemy, shall be punished by a fine . . . or by imprisonment . . . ." 55 Cong.Rec. 2100.

reaching powers to monitor the press, and those opposed to this part of the legislation assumed that a necessary concomitant of such power was the power to "filter out the news to the people through some man." 55 Cong.Rec. 2008 (remarks of Sen. Ashurst). However, these same members of Congress appeared to have little doubt that newspapers would be subject to criminal prosecution if they insisted on publishing information of the type Congress had itself determined should not be revealed. Senator Ashurst, for example, was quite sure that the editor of such a newspaper "should be punished if he did publish information as to the movements of the fleet, the troops, the aircraft, the location of powder factories, the location of defense works, and all that sort of thing." Id., at 2009.[4] . . .

The Criminal Code contains numerous provisions potentially relevant to these cases. Section 797 makes it a crime to publish certain photographs or drawings of military installations. Section 798, also in precise language, proscribes knowing and willful publication of any classified information concerning the cryptographic systems or communication intelligence activities of the United States as well as any information obtained from communication intelligence operations. If any of the material here at issue is of this nature, the newspapers are presumably now on full notice of the position of the United States and must face the consequences if they publish. I would have no difficulty in sustaining convictions under these sections on facts that would not justify the intervention of equity and the imposition of a prior restraint.

The same would be true under those sections of the Criminal Code casting a wider net to protect the national defense. Section 793(e)[8] makes it a criminal act for any unauthorized possessor of a document "relating to the national defense" either (1) willfully to communicate or cause to be communicated that document to any person not entitled to receive it or (2) willfully to retain the document and fail to deliver it to an officer of the United States entitled to receive it. The subsection was added in 1950 because pre-existing law provided no penalty for the unauthorized possessor unless demand for

4. Senator Ashurst also urged that " 'freedom of the press' means freedom from the restraints of a censor, means the absolute liberty and right to publish whatever you wish; but you take your chances of punishment in the courts of your country for the violation of the laws of libel, slander, and treason." 55 Cong. Rec. 2005.

8. Section 793(e) of 18 U.S.C. provides that:

"(e) Whoever having unauthorized possession of, access to, or control over any document, writing, code book, signal book, sketch, photograph, photographic negative, blueprint, plan, map, model, instrument, appliance, or note relating to the national defense, or information relating to the national defense which information the possessor has reason to believe could be used to the injury of the United States or to the advantage of any foreign nation, willfully communicates, delivers, transmits or causes to be communicated, delivered, or transmitted, or attempts to communicate, deliver, transmit or cause to be communicated, delivered, or transmitted the same to any person not entitled to receive it, or willfully retains the same and fails to deliver it to the officer or employee of the United States entitled to receive it"; is guilty of an offense punishable by 10 years in prison, a $10,000 fine, or both. It should also be noted that 18 U.S.C. § 793(g), added in 1950, see 64 Stat. 1004; S.Rep.No. 2369, Pt. 1, 81st Cong., 2d Sess., 9 (1950), provides that "[i]f two or more persons conspire to violate any of the foregoing provisions of this section, and one or more of such persons do any act to effect the object of the conspiracy, each of the parties to such conspiracy shall be subject to the punishment provided for the offense which is the object of such conspiracy."

the documents was made.[9] "The dangers surrounding the unauthorized possession of such items are self-evident, and it is deemed advisable to require their surrender in such a case, regardless of demand, especially since their unauthorized possession may be unknown to the authorities who would otherwise make the demand." S.Rep.No. 2369, Pt. 1, 81st Cong., 2d Sess., 9 (1950). Of course, in the cases before us, the unpublished documents have been demanded by the United States and their import has been made known at least to counsel for the newspapers involved. In Gorin v. United States, 312 U.S. 19, 28 (1941), the words "national defense" as used in a predecessor of § 793 were held by a unanimous court to have "a well understood connotation"—a "generic concept of broad connotations, referring to the military and naval establishments and the related activities of national preparedness"—and to be "sufficiently definite to apprise the public of prohibited activities" and to be consonant with due process. 312 U.S., at 28. Also, as construed by the Court in *Gorin*, information "connected with the national defense" is obviously not limited to that threatening "grave and irreparable" injury to the United States.[10]

It is thus clear that Congress has addressed itself to the problems of protecting the security of the country and the national defense from unauthorized disclosure of potentially damaging information. Cf. Youngstown Sheet & Tube Co. v. Sawyer, 343 U.S. 579, 585–586 (1952); see also id., at 593–628 (Frankfurter, J., concurring). It has not, however, authorized the injunctive remedy against threatened publication. It has apparently been satisfied to rely on criminal sanctions and their deterrent effect on the responsible as well as the irresponsible press. I am not, of course, saying that either of these newspapers has yet committed a crime or that either would commit a crime if it published all the material now in its possession. That matter must await resolution in the context of a criminal proceeding if one is instituted by the United States. In that event, the issue of guilt or innocence would be determined by procedures and standards quite different from those that have purported to govern these injunctive proceedings.

9. . . . It seems clear . . ., contrary to the intimations of the District Court for the Southern District of New York in this case, that in prosecuting for communicating or withholding a "document" as contrasted with similar action with respect to "information" the Government need not prove an intent to injure the United States or to benefit a foreign nation but only willful and knowing conduct. The District Court relied on Gorin v. United States, 312 U.S. 19 (1941). But that case arose under other parts of the predecessor to § 793, see 312 U.S., at 21–22—parts that imposed different intent standards not repeated in § 793(d) or § 793(e). Cf. 18 U.S.C. §§ 793(a), (b), and (c). Also, from the face of subsection (e) and from the context of the act of which it was a part, it seems undeniable that a newspaper, as well as others unconnected with the Government, are vulnerable to prosecution under § 793(e) if they communicate or withhold the materials covered by that section. The District Court ruled that "communication" did not reach publication by a newspaper of documents relating to the national defense. I intimate no views on the correctness of that conclusion. But neither communication nor publication is necessary to violate the subsection.

10. Also relevant is 18 U.S.C. § 794. Subsection (b) thereof forbids in time of war the collection or publication, with intent that it shall be communicated to the enemy, any information with respect to the movements of military forces "or with respect to the plans or conduct . . . of any naval or military operations . . . or any other information relating to the public defense, which might be useful to the enemy . . . ."

Justice MARSHALL, concurring.

The Government contends that the only issue in these cases is whether in a suit by the United States, "the First Amendment bars a court from prohibiting a newspaper from publishing material whose disclosure would pose a 'grave and immediate danger to the security of the United States.' " With all due respect, I believe the ultimate issue in these cases is even more basic than the one posed by the Solicitor General. The issue is whether this Court or the Congress has the power to make law.

In these cases there is no problem concerning the President's power to classify information as "secret" or "top secret." Congress has specifically recognized Presidential authority, which has been formally exercised in Executive Order 10501 (1953), to classify documents and information. See, e.g., 18 U.S.C. § 798; 50 U.S.C. § 783. Nor is there any issue here regarding the President's power as Chief Executive and Commander in Chief to protect national security by disciplining employees who disclose information and by taking precautions to prevent leaks.

The problem here is whether in these particular cases the Executive Branch has authority to invoke the equity jurisdiction of the courts to protect what it believes to be the national interest. See In re Debs. The Government argues that in addition to the inherent power of any government to protect itself, the President's power to conduct foreign affairs and his position as Commander in Chief give him authority to impose censorship on the press to protect his ability to deal effectively with foreign nations and to conduct the military affairs of the country. Of course, it is beyond cavil that the President has broad powers by virtue of his primary responsibility for the conduct of our foreign affairs and his position as Commander in Chief. . . . And in some situations it may be that under whatever inherent powers the Government may have, as well as the implicit authority derived from the President's mandate to conduct foreign affairs and to act as Commander in Chief there is a basis for the invocation of the equity jurisdiction of this court as an aid to prevent the publication of material damaging to "national security," however that term may be defined.

It would, however, be utterly inconsistent with the concept of separation of powers for this Court to use its power of contempt to prevent behavior that Congress has specifically declined to prohibit. There would be a similar damage to the basic concept of these co-equal branches of Government if when the Executive Branch has adequate authority granted by Congress to protect "national security" it can choose instead to invoke the contempt power of a court to enjoin the threatened conduct. The Constitution provides that Congress shall make laws, the President execute laws, and courts interpret laws. Youngstown Sheet & Tube Co. v. Sawyer, 343 U.S. 579 (1952). It did not provide for government by injunction in which the courts and the Executive Branch can "make law" without regard to the action of Congress. It may be more convenient for the Executive Branch if it need only convince a judge to prohibit conduct rather than to ask the Congress to pass a law and it may be more convenient to enforce a contempt order than seek a criminal conviction in a jury trial. Moreover, it may be considered politically wise to get a court to share the responsibility for arresting those who the Executive Branch has probable cause to believe are violating the law. But convenience and political considerations of the moment do not justify a basic departure from the principles of our system of government.

In these cases we are not faced with a situation where Congress has failed to provide the Executive with broad power to protect the Nation from disclosure of damaging state secrets. Congress has on several occasions given extensive consideration to the problem of protecting the military and strategic secrets of the United States. This consideration has resulted in the enactment of statutes making it a crime to receive, disclose, communicate, withhold, and publish certain documents, photographs, instruments, appliances, and information. The bulk of these statutes is found in chapter 37 of U.S.C., Title 18, entitled Espionage and Censorship. In that chapter, Congress has provided penalties ranging from a $10,000 fine to death for violating the various statutes.

Thus it would seem that in order for this court to issue an injunction it would require a showing that such an injunction would enhance the already existing power of the Government to act. See Bennett v. Laman, 277 N.Y. 368, 14 N.E.2d 439 (1938). It is a traditional axiom of equity that a court of equity will not do a useless thing just as it is a traditional axiom that equity will not enjoin the commission of a crime. See Z. Chafee & E. Re, Equity 935–954 (5th ed. 1967); 1 H. Joyce, Injunctions §§ 58–60a (1909). Here there has been no attempt to make such a showing. The Solicitor General does not even mention in his brief whether the Government considers that there is probable cause to believe a crime has been committed or whether there is a conspiracy to commit future crimes.

If the Government had attempted to show that there was no effective remedy under traditional criminal law, it would have had to show that there is no arguably applicable statute. Of course, at this stage this Court could not and cannot determine whether there has been a violation of a particular statute or decide the constitutionality of any statute. Whether a good-faith prosecution could have been instituted under any statute could, however, be determined.

At least one of the many statutes in this area seems relevant to these cases. [Justice Marshall then quoted 18 U.S.C. § 793(e).]

It is true that Judge Gurfein found that Congress had not made it a crime to publish the items and material specified in § 793(e): He found that the words "communicates, delivers, transmits . . . " did not refer to publication of newspaper stories. And that view has some support in the legislative history and conforms with the past practice of using the statute only to prosecute those charged with ordinary espionage. But see 103 Cong.Rec. 10449 (remarks of Sen. Humphrey). Judge Gurfein's view of the statute is not, however, the only plausible construction that could be given. See my Brother White's concurring opinion.

Even if it is determined that the Government could not in good faith bring criminal prosecutions against the New York Times and the Washington Post, it is clear that Congress has specifically rejected passing legislation that would have clearly given the President the power he seeks here and made the current activity of the newspapers unlawful. When Congress specifically declines to make conduct unlawful it is not for this Court to redecide those issues—to overrule Congress. See Youngstown Sheet & Tube Co. v. Sawyer, 343 U.S. 579 (1952).

On at least two occasions Congress has refused to enact legislation that would have made the conduct engaged in here unlawful and given the President the power that he seeks in this case. In 1917 during the debate over the original Espionage Act, still the basic provisions of § 793, Congress rejected a proposal to give the President in time of war or threat of war authority to directly prohibit by proclamation the publication of information relating to national defense that might be useful to the enemy. The proposal provided that:

"During any national emergency resulting from a war to which the United States is a party, or from threat of such a war, the President may, by proclamation, declare the existence of such emergency and, by proclamation, prohibit the publishing or communicating of, or the attempting to publish or communicate any information relating to the national defense which, in his judgment, is of such character that it is or might be useful to the enemy. Whoever violates any such prohibition shall be punished by a fine of not more than $10,000 or by imprisonment for not more than 10 years, or both: *Provided*, That nothing in this section shall be construed to limit or restrict any discussion, comment, or criticism of the acts or policies of the Government or its representatives or the publication of the same." 55 Cong.Rec. 1763.

Congress rejected this proposal after war against Germany had been declared even though many believed that there was a grave national emergency and that the threat of security leaks and espionage was serious. The Executive Branch has not gone to Congress and requested that the decision to provide such power be reconsidered. Instead, the Executive Branch comes to this Court and asks that it be granted the power Congress refused to give.

In 1957 the United States Commission on Government Security found that "[a]irplane journals, scientific periodicals, and even the daily newspaper have featured articles containing information and other data which should have been deleted in whole or in part for security reasons." In response to this problem the Commission proposed that "Congress enact legislation making it a crime for any person willfully to disclose without proper authorization, for any purpose whatever, information classified 'secret' or 'top secret,' knowing, or having reasonable grounds to believe, such information to have been so classified." Report of Commission on Government Security 619–620 (1957). After substantial floor discussion on the proposal, it was rejected. See 103 Cong.Rec. 10447–10450. If the proposal that Sen. Cotton championed on the floor had been enacted, the publication of the documents involved here would certainly have been a crime. Congress refused, however, to make it a crime. The Government is here asking this Court to remake that decision. This Court has no such power.

Either the Government has the power under statutory grant to use traditional criminal law to protect the country or, if there is no basis for arguing that Congress has made the activity a crime, it is plain that Congress has specifically refused to grant the authority the Government seeks from this Court. In either case this Court does not have authority to grant the requested relief. It is not for this Court to fling itself into every breach perceived by some

Government official nor is it for this Court to take on itself the burden of enacting law, especially a law that Congress has refused to pass. . . . .

Chief Justice BURGER, dissenting.

So clear are the constitutional limitations on prior restraint against expression, that from the time of Near v. Minnesota, until recently in Organization for a Better Austin v. Keefe, we have had little occasion to be concerned with cases involving prior restraints against news reporting on matters of public interest. There is, therefore, little variation among the members of the Court in terms of resistance to prior restraints against publication. Adherence to this basic constitutional principle, however, does not make these cases simple. In these cases, the imperative of a free and unfettered press comes into collision with another imperative, the effective functioning of a complex modern government and specifically the effective exercise of certain constitutional powers of the Executive. Only those who view the First Amendment as an absolute in all circumstances—a view I respect, but reject—can find such cases as these to be simple or easy.

These cases are not simple for another and more immediate reason. We do not know the facts of the cases. No District Judge knew all the facts. No Court of Appeals judge knew all the facts. No member of this Court knows all the facts.

Why are we in this posture, in which only those judges to whom the First Amendment is absolute and permits of no restraint in any circumstances or for any reason, are really in a position to act?

I suggest we are in this posture because these cases have been conducted in unseemly haste. . . . The prompt setting of these cases reflects our universal abhorrence of prior restraint. But prompt judicial action does not mean unjudicial haste.

Here, moreover, the frenetic haste is due in large part to the manner in which the Times proceeded from the date it obtained the purloined documents. It seems reasonably clear now that the haste precluded reasonable and deliberate judicial treatment of these cases and was not warranted. The precipitate action of this Court aborting trials not yet completed is not the kind of judicial conduct that ought to attend the disposition of a great issue.

The newspapers make a derivative claim under the First Amendment; they denominate this right as the public right-to-know; by implication, the Times asserts a sole trusteeship of that right by virtue of its journalistic "scoop." The right is asserted as an absolute. Of course, the First Amendment right itself is not an absolute, as Justice Holmes so long ago pointed out in his aphorism concerning the right to shout fire in a crowded theater. There are other exceptions, some of which Chief Justice Hughes mentioned by way of example in Near v. Minnesota. There are no doubt other exceptions no one has had occasion to describe or discuss. Conceivably such exceptions may be lurking in these cases and would have been flushed had they been properly considered in the trial courts, free from unwarranted deadlines and frenetic pressures. A great issue of this kind should be tried in a judicial atmosphere conducive to thoughtful, reflective deliberation, especially when haste, in terms of hours, is unwarranted in light of the long period the Times, by its own choice, deferred publication.

It is not disputed that the Times has had unauthorized possession of the documents for three to four months, during which it has had its expert analysts studying them, presumably digesting them and preparing the material for publication. During all of this time, the Times, presumably in its capacity as trustee of the public's "right to know," has held up publication for purposes it considered proper and thus public knowledge was delayed. No doubt this was for a good reason; the analysis of 7,000 pages of complex material drawn from a vastly greater volume of material would inevitably take time and the writing of good news stories takes time. But why should the United States Government, from whom this information was illegally acquired by someone, along with all the counsel, trial judges, and appellate judges be placed under needless pressure? After these months of deferral, the alleged right-to-know has somehow and suddenly become a right that must be vindicated instanter.

Would it have been unreasonable, since the newspaper could anticipate the Government's objections to release of secret material, to give the Government an opportunity to review the entire collection and determine whether agreement could be reached on publication? Stolen or not, if security was not in fact jeopardized, much of the material could no doubt have been declassified, since it spans a period ending in 1968. With such an approach—one that great newspapers have in the past practiced and stated editorially to be the duty of an honorable press—the newspapers and Government might well have narrowed the area of disagreement as to what was and was not publishable, leaving the remainder to be resolved in orderly litigation, if necessary. To me it is hardly believable that a newspaper long regarded as a great institution in American life would fail to perform one of the basic and simple duties of every citizen with respect to the discovery or possession of stolen property or secret government documents. That duty, I had thought—perhaps naively—was to report forthwith, to responsible public officers. This duty rests on taxi drivers, Justices, and the New York Times. The course followed by the Times, whether so calculated or not, removed any possibility of orderly litigation of the issues. If the action of the judges up to now has been correct, that result is sheer happenstance.[1] . . .

The consequence of all this melancholy series of events is that we literally do not know what we are acting on. As I see it, we have been forced to deal with litigation concerning rights of great magnitude without an adequate record, and surely without time for adequate treatment either in the prior proceedings or in this Court. It is interesting to note that counsel in oral argument before this Court were frequently unable to respond to questions on factual points. Not surprisingly they pointed out that they had been working literally "around the clock" and simply were unable to review the documents that give rise to these cases and were not familiar with them. This Court is in no better posture. I agree with Mr. Justice Harlan and Mr. Justice Blackmun but I am not prepared to reach the merits.

1. Interestingly the Times explained its refusal to allow the Government to examine its own purloined documents by saying in substance this might compromise *its* sources and informants! The Times thus asserts a right to guard the secrecy of its sources while denying that the Government of the United States has that power.

I would affirm the Court of Appeals for the Second Circuit and allow the District Court to complete the trial aborted by our grant of certiorari, meanwhile preserving the status quo in the *Post* case. I would direct that the District Court on remand give priority to the *Times* case to the exclusion of all other business of that court but I would not set arbitrary deadlines.

I should add that I am in general agreement with much of what Mr. Justice White has expressed with respect to penal sanctions concerning communication or retention of documents or information relating to the national defense.

We all crave speedier judicial processes but when judges are pressured as in these cases the result is a parody of the judicial process.

Justice HARLAN, with whom THE CHIEF JUSTICE and Justice BLACKMUN join, dissenting.

These cases forcefully call to mind the wise admonition of Mr. Justice Holmes, dissenting in Northern Securities Co. v. United States, 193 U.S. 197, 400–401 (1904):

"Great cases like hard cases make bad law. For great cases are called great, not by reason of their real importance in shaping the law of the future, but because of some accident of immediate overwhelming interest which appeals to the feelings and distorts the judgment. These immediate interests exercise a kind of hydraulic pressure which makes what previously was clear seem doubtful, and before which even well settled principles of law will bend."

With all respect, I consider that the Court has been almost irresponsibly feverish in dealing with these cases.

Both the Court of Appeals for the Second Circuit and the Court of Appeals for the District of Columbia Circuit rendered judgment on June 23. The New York Times' petition for certiorari, its motion for accelerated consideration thereof, and its application for interim relief were filed in this Court on June 24 at about 11 a.m. The application of the United States for interim relief in the *Post* case was also filed here on June 24 at about 7:15 p.m. This Court's order setting a hearing before us on June 26 at 11 a.m., a course which I joined only to avoid the possibility of even more peremptory action by the Court, was issued less than 24 hours before. The record in the *Post* case was filed with the Clerk shortly before 1 p.m. on June 25; the record in the *Times* case did not arrive until 7 or 8 o'clock that same night. The briefs of the parties were received less than two hours before argument on June 26.

This frenzied train of events took place in the name of the presumption against prior restraints created by the First Amendment. Due regard for the extraordinarily important and difficult questions involved in these litigations should have led the Court to shun such a precipitate timetable. In order to decide the merits of these cases properly, some or all of the following questions should have been faced:

1. Whether the Attorney General is authorized to bring these suits in the name of the United States. Compare In re Debs with Youngstown Sheet & Tube Co. v. Sawyer, 343 U.S. 579 (1952). This question involves as well

the construction and validity of a singularly opaque statute—the Espionage Act, 18 U.S.C. § 793(e).

2. Whether the First Amendment permits the federal courts to enjoin publication of stories which would present a serious threat to national security. See Near v. Minnesota (dictum).

3. Whether the threat to publish highly secret documents is of itself a sufficient implication of national security to justify an injunction on the theory that regardless of the contents of the documents harm enough results simply from the demonstration of such a breach of secrecy.

4. Whether the unauthorized disclosure of any of these particular documents would seriously impair the national security.

5. What weight should be given to the opinion of high officers in the Executive Branch of the Government with respect to questions 3 and 4.

6. Whether the newspapers are entitled to retain and use the documents notwithstanding the seemingly uncontested facts that the documents, or the originals of which they are duplicates, were purloined from the Government's possession and that the newspapers received them with knowledge that they had been feloniously acquired. Cf. Liberty Lobby, Inc. v. Pearson, 129 U.S.App.D.C. 74, 390 F.2d 489 (1967, amended 1968).

7. Whether the threatened harm to the national security or the Government's possessory interest in the documents justifies the issuance of an injunction against publication in light of—

a. The strong First Amendment policy against prior restraints on publication;

b. The doctrine against enjoining conduct in violation of criminal statutes; and

c. The extent to which the materials at issue have apparently already been otherwise disseminated.

These are difficult questions of fact, of law, and of judgment; the potential consequences of erroneous decision are enormous. The time which has been available to us, to the lower courts,* and to the parties has been wholly inadequate for giving these cases the kind of consideration they deserve. It is a reflection on the stability of the judicial process that these great issues—as important as any that have arisen during my time on the Court—should have been decided under the pressures engendered by the torrent of publicity that has attended these litigations from their inception.

Forced as I am to reach the merits of these cases, I dissent from the opinion and judgments of the Court. Within the severe limitations imposed by the time constraints under which I have been required to operate, I can only state my reasons in telescoped form, even though in different circumstances I

* The hearing in the *Post* case before Judge Gesell began at 8 a.m. on June 21, and his decision was rendered, under the hammer of a deadline imposed by the Court of Appeals, shortly before 5 p.m. on the same day. The hearing in the *Times* case before Judge Gurfein was held on June 18 and his decision was rendered on June 19. The Government's appeals in the two cases were heard by the Courts of Appeals for the District of Columbia and Second Circuits, each court sitting *en banc*, on June 22. Each court rendered its decision on the following afternoon.

would have felt constrained to deal with the cases in the fuller sweep indicated above.

It is a sufficient basis for affirming the Court of Appeals for the Second Circuit in the *Times* litigation to observe that its order must rest on the conclusion that because of the time elements the Government had not been given an adequate opportunity to present its case to the District Court. At the least this conclusion was not an abuse of discretion.

In the *Post* litigation the Government had more time to prepare; this was apparently the basis for the refusal of the Court of Appeals for the District of Columbia Circuit on rehearing to conform its judgment to that of the Second Circuit. But I think there is another and more fundamental reason why this judgment cannot stand—a reason which also furnishes an additional ground for not reinstating the judgment of the District Court in the *Times* litigation, set aside by the Court of Appeals. It is plain to me that the scope of the judicial function in passing upon the activities of the Executive Branch of the Government in the field of foreign affairs is very narrowly restricted. This view is, I think, dictated by the concept of separation of powers upon which our constitutional system rests. . . .

The power to evaluate the "pernicious influence" of premature disclosure is not, however, lodged in the Executive alone. I agree that, in performance of its duty to protect the values of the First Amendment against political pressures, the judiciary must review the initial Executive determination to the point of satisfying itself that the subject matter of the dispute does lie within the proper compass of the President's foreign relations power. Constitutional considerations forbid "a complete abandonment of judicial control." Cf. United States v. Reynolds, 345 U.S. 1, 8 (1953). Moreover, the judiciary may properly insist that the determination that disclosure of the subject matter would irreparably impair the national security be made by the head of the Executive Department concerned—here the Secretary of State or the Secretary of Defense—after actual personal consideration by that officer. This safeguard is required in the analogous area of executive claims of privilege for secrets of state. . . .

But in my judgment the judiciary may not properly go beyond these two inquiries and redetermine for itself the probable impact of disclosure on the national security.

"[T]he very nature of executive decisions as to foreign policy is political, not judicial. Such decisions are wholly confided by our Constitution to the political departments of the government, Executive and Legislative. They are delicate, complex, and involve large elements of prophecy. They are and should be undertaken only by those directly responsible to the people whose welfare they advance or imperil. They are decisions of a kind for which the Judiciary has neither aptitude, facilities nor responsibility and which has long been held to belong in the domain of political power not subject to judicial intrusion or inquiry." Chicago & Southern Air Lines v. Waterman Steamship Corp., 333 U.S. 103, 111 (1948) (Jackson, J.).

Even if there is some room for the judiciary to override the executive determination, it is plain that the scope of review must be exceedingly narrow. I can see no indication in the opinions of either the District Court or the Court of Appeals in the *Post* litigation that the conclusions of the Executive were given even the deference owing to an administrative agency, much less that owing to a co-equal branch of the Government operating within the field of its constitutional prerogative.

Accordingly, I would vacate the judgment of the Court of Appeals for the District of Columbia Circuit on this ground and remand the case for further proceedings in the District Court. Before the commencement of such further proceedings, due opportunity should be afforded the Government for procuring from the Secretary of State or the Secretary of Defense or both an expression of their views on the issue of national security. . . . And for the reasons stated above I would affirm the judgment of the Court of Appeals for the Second Circuit.

Pending further hearings in each case conducted under the appropriate ground rules, I would continue the restraints on publication. I cannot believe that the doctrine prohibiting prior restraints reaches to the point of preventing courts from maintaining the *status quo* long enough to act responsibly in matters of such national importance as those involved here.

Justice BLACKMUN, dissenting.

I join Mr. Justice HARLAN in his dissent. I also am in substantial accord with much that Mr. Justice WHITE says, by way of admonition, in the latter part of his opinion. . . .

Two federal district courts, two United States courts of appeals, and this Court—within a period of less than three weeks from inception until today—have been pressed into hurried decision of profound constitutional issues on inadequately developed and largely assumed facts without the careful deliberation that, one would hope, should characterize the American judicial process. There has been much writing about the law and little knowledge and less digestion of the facts. In the New York case the judges, both trial and appellate, had not yet examined the basic material when the case was brought here. In the District of Columbia case, little more was done, and what was accomplished in this respect was only on required remand, with the Washington Post, on the excuse that it was trying to protect its source of information, initially refusing to reveal what material it actually possessed, and with the District Court forced to make assumptions as to that possession.

With such respect as may be due to the contrary view, this, in my opinion, is not the way to try a lawsuit of this magnitude and asserted importance. It is not the way for federal courts to adjudicate, and to be required to adjudicate, issues that allegedly concern the Nation's vital welfare. The country would be none the worse off were the cases tried quickly, to be sure, but in the customary and properly deliberative manner. The most recent of the material, it is said, dates no later than 1968, already about three years ago, and the Times itself took three months to formulate its plan of procedure and, thus, deprived its public for that period.

The First Amendment, after all, is only one part of an entire Constitution. Article II of the great document vests in the Executive Branch primary power over the conduct of foreign affairs and places in that branch the responsibility for the Nation's safety. Each provision of the Constitution is important, and I cannot subscribe to a doctrine of unlimited absolutism for the First Amendment at the cost of downgrading other provisions. First Amendment absolutism has never commanded a majority of this Court. See, for example, Near v. Minnesota and Schenck v. United States, 249 U.S. 47, 52 (1919). What is needed here is a weighing, upon properly developed standards, of the broad right of the press to print and of the very narrow right of the Government to prevent. Such standards are not yet developed. The parties here are in disagreement as to what those standards should be. But even the newspapers concede that there are situations where restraint is in order and is constitutional. Mr. Justice Holmes gave us a suggestion when he said in *Schenck,*

"It is a question of proximity and degree. When a nation is at war many things that might be said in time of peace are such a hindrance to its effort that their utterance will not be endured so long as men fight and that no Court could regard them as protected by any constitutional right."

I therefore would remand these cases to be developed expeditiously, of course, but on a schedule permitting the orderly presentation of evidence from both sides, with the use of discovery, if necessary, as authorized by the rules, and with the preparation of briefs, oral argument, and court opinions of a quality better than has been seen to this point. In making this last statement, I criticize no lawyer or judge. I know from past personal experience the agony of time pressure in the preparation of litigation. But these cases and the issues involved and the courts, including this one, deserve better than has been produced thus far. . . .

The Court, however, decides the cases today the other way. I therefore add one final comment.

I strongly urge, and sincerely hope, that these two newspapers will be fully aware of their ultimate reponsibilities to the United States of America. Judge Wilkey, dissenting in the District of Columbia case, after a review of only the affidavits before his court (the basic papers had not then been made available by either party), concluded that there were a number of examples of documents that, if in the possession of the Post, and if published, "could clearly result in great harm to the nation," and he defined "harm" to mean "the death of soldiers, the destruction of alliances, the greatly increased difficulty of negotiation with our enemies, the inability of our diplomats to negotiate . . . ." I, for one, have now been able to give at least some cursory study not only to the affidavits, but to the material itself. I regret to say that from this examination I fear that Judge Wilkey's statements have possible foundation. I therefore share his concern. I hope that damage has not already been done. If, however, damage has been done, and if, with the Court's action today, these newspapers proceed to publish the critical documents and there results therefrom "the death of soldiers, the destruction of alliances, the greatly increased difficulty of negotiation with our enemies, the inability of our diplomats to negotiate," to which list I might add the factors of prolongation of the war and of further delay in the freeing of United States prisoners, then the Nation's people will know where the responsibility for these sad consequences rests.

---

1) On June 14, 1971, the Attorney General sent the following telegram to the Times:

"Arthur Ochs Sulzberger
"President and Publisher
"The New York Times
"New York, New York

"I have been advised by the Secretary of Defense that the material published in The New York Times on June 13, 14, 1971 captioned 'Key Texts From Pentagon's Vietnam Study' contains information relating to the national defense of the United States and bears a top secret classification.

"As such, publication of this information is directly prohibited by the provisions of the Espionage Law, Title 18, United States Code, Section 793.

"Moreover, further publication of information of this character will cause irreparable injury to the defense interests of the United States.

"Accordingly, I respectfully request that you publish no further information of this character and advise me that you have made arrangements for the return of these documents to the Department of Defense.

John N. Mitchell
Attorney General"

The Times then issued the following statement:

"We have received the telegram from the Attorney General asking The Times to cease further publication of the Pentagon's Vietnam study.

"The Times must respectfully decline the request of the Attorney General, believing that it is in the interest of the people of this country to be informed of the material contained in this series of articles.

"We have also been informed of the Attorney General's intention to seek an injunction against further publication. We believe that it is properly a matter for the courts to decide. The Times will oppose any request for an injunction for the same reason that led us to publish the articles in the first place. We will of course abide by the final decision of the court."

Consider the New York Times's commitment to "abide by the final decision of the court" : Why was the New York Times prepared to risk violating the Espionage Act, a criminal statute, but quite eager to announce that it would not continue to publish in the face of an injunction? Why defer more to the injunction than the criminal statute?

2) Professor Harry Kalven viewed the action of Daniel Ellsberg and the New York Times as a form of civil disobedience but found it "puzzling why sanctions for violating an injunction might have inhibited a party who intended disobedience as a political gesture more than criminal sanctions." The Supreme Court, 1970 Term—Foreword: Even When a Nation Is at War, 85 Harv. L. Rev. 3, 34 n.156 (1971). "Perhaps," Kalven continued, "it depended on the quality of direct, personal command of the injunction; perhaps on the different procedural risks involved, as, for example, the loss of a chance to appeal to a jury; and perhaps on the fact that, in this case, the existence of an applicable criminal statute was in doubt." But, regardless of the reasons, it was fair to presume that "the papers were not ready to frontally defy an injunction," and, if so, the Supreme Court action in forbidding the

prior restraint was seen by Professor Kalven "as protecting the chance for civil disobedience"—that is, the only kind of civil disobedience the Times was prepared to undertake. This led him to conclude that "in this context prior and subsequent restraints are not coterminous" (supra at 34).

On November 5, 1971, the General Counsel of the New York Times, James C. Goodale, spoke about the case at the University of Chicago Law School. He made two statements that bear on these issues: (1) the June 14th commitment of the Times to abide by an injunction was a mistake and ill-conceived; and (2) in the three months prior to publication, no one at the Times thought there was any risk of criminal prosecution under the Espionage Act.

3) *New York Times*, sometimes called *Pentagon Papers*, helps us to understand the injunction as a form of preventive relief. Justice White's perspective assumes, indeed invites, a criminal prosecution. Why restrict the injunction as a prior restraint when the threat of a criminal prosecution will deter? Professor Bickel's metaphor was "A criminal statute chills, prior restraint freezes." Morality of Consent 61 (1975). Professor Wright's metaphor differed: "The injunction is not a set of handcuffs. In itself it cannot prevent the defendant from doing the criminal act." Wright, The Law of Remedies as a Social Institution, 18 U.Det.L.J. 376, 391 n.65 (1955).

Does the idea that prior restraints are the most serious and least tolerable infringement on first amendment rights assume that a prior restraint forbids activity protected by the first amendment? If so, is the prior restraint doctrine meaningless? Kalven felt that prior restraint doctrine protected the chance for civil disobedience because "everything, or virtually everything, is entitled to be published at least once." Kalven, The Supreme Court, 1970 Term—Foreword: Even When a Nation is at War—, 85 Harv.L.Rev. 1, 34 (1971). Does this assume a high absolute standard for prior restraints and overstate the effect of an injunction? Is it true only if the defendant incorrectly views the injunction as a "set of handcuffs?" Why not compare an injunction to the criminal statute? The defendant may violate an injunction and defend contempt just as a person may violate a criminal statute and defend the prosecution.

Professor Fiss says that "a distinction must be drawn between two distinct phases of the injunctive process, issuance and enforcement. In its issuance phase, the injunction resembles a criminal statute; it establishes a standard of conduct and threatens to punish those who disobey. It controls through deterrence. An injunction is often classified as a prior restraint because it can be issued before publication. That only means that the injunction controls—deters—before the event to be avoided—here publication—actually occurs. But that is equally true of the criminal statute. It restrains before publication; it deters future conduct. The criminal prosecution takes place after the event, after publication, but that phase of the criminal process should be compared to the enforcement phase of the injunctive process (the contempt proceeding): sanctions are imposed on those who violate the standard of conduct. Contempt and criminal prosecution are retrospective; an injunction and a criminal statute are both preventive." Fiss, Chapter 5, Free Speech and the Prior Restraint Doctrine: The *Pentagon Papers Case*, in The Supreme Court and Human Rights 59 (B. Marshall ed. 1982).

4) If a criminal statute possesses a draconian sanction, say forty years, and if the defendant is certain that the government will prosecute, then does the criminal statute "chill" or "freeze?" Schauer, Fear, Risk and the First Amendment: Unraveling the "Chilling Effect," 58 B.U.L.Rev. 685, 728 (1978). Did Mitchell's June 14 message to the Times threaten a criminal prosecution as clearly as an injunction threatens contempt? See Bantam Books v. Sullivan, 372 U.S. 58 (1963) ("informal" warnings unconstitutional). Is a person who violates a legislative order morally more pure than one who violates a judicial order? Blasi, Toward a Theory of Prior Restraint: The Central Linkage, 66 Minn.L.Rev. 11, 41–43 (1981). Is the question in both whether the order comports with the Constitution?

5) Perhaps the definition of prior restraints encompasses too much or potentially too much activity. What values are advanced by refusing to allow a judge to enjoin unprotected and illegal activity? In *Pentagon Papers*, unlike *Near* and *Keefe*, all the material was then in existence; *Pentagon Papers* presented no question of enjoining unidentified later material or of establishing the judge as an informal censor of future material. "If the Pentagon Papers should have been published, it was the general principles of freedom of speech and freedom of the press not the prior restraint doctrine that commanded the result." Schauer, 58 B.U.L.Rev. at 728 n.213. Did a majority of the Court reject equitable national security because the Times did not breach any constitutional statute? Or does Justice White speak for a majority with his view that condones a criminal prosecution but precludes an injunction?

6) The Times's right to disseminate material it possesses seems to be broader than its right to compel disclosure. Landmark Communications Inc. v. Virginia, 435 U.S. 829 (1978). The government asserts an inherent or nonstatutory power to prevent the press from disseminating the material without regard to its content. Had the government "lost" when Ellsberg handed the Pentagon Papers to the Times? Did the Supreme Court leave intact the executive's structure of authority to classify and protect? Did the court create an anomaly by calling criminal statutes subsequent restraints and judging them by different standards?

7) Could the government have sued Ellsberg and the newspapers for damages? The *Snepp* litigation also involved the integrity of the secrecy system. While a CIA employee, Snepp had signed a contract agreeing to refrain from publishing without prepublication clearance. He published a book about CIA activities in Viet Nam without even submitting his manuscript. The government sued Snepp for damages, not, however, claiming that anything in the book was classified. The court of appeals approved punitive damages but rejected a constructive trust on Snepp's royalties. (See also United States v. Marchetti, 466 F.2d 1309 (4th Cir. 1972), cert. denied, 409 U.S. 1063, enjoining publication of a CIA employee's book not approved pursuant to contract.) The Supreme Court reversed summarily in *Snepp* without oral argument; the Court impressed Snepp's royalties with a constructive trust but denied punitive damages. Snepp v. United States, 444 U.S. 507 (1980). The majority thought the contract a "reasonable means" to protect the executive's interest in secrecy and "the appearance of confidentiality."

Justice Stevens's dissent attacked the contract and remedy as a "drastic new remedy [to] enforce a species of prior restraint on a citizen's right to criticize his government." 444 U.S. at 526. The contract is intended to assure prior to publication that a person will not disseminate material that, except for the contract, he would not have known. Is that a prior restraint? To obtain a preventive injunction or a retrospective, subsequent constructive trust should the CIA have to prove both the contract and a breach of security? If the CIA dawdles in its review or attempts to suppress unclassified but embarrassing material may the employee publish despite a contract or an injunction? See Alfred A. Knopf, Inc. v. Colby, 509 F.2d 1362 (4th Cir. 1975) certiorari denied 421 U.S. 992.

8) Are "prior restraints" good buzz words to caricature an opponent's argument? Did the doctrine of prior restraint allow courts from *Near* to *Pentagon Papers* to strike down particular interdictions of expression related activity without confronting the background of common law, statutory law, and criminal statutes? If so, is prior restraint an evasive device or a salutary safety valve? What would be the consequences of different results in *Near* and *Pentagon Papers*? Should courts define prior restraints more narrowly and precisely but forbid all prior restraints? Would that allow them to spend less time worrying about prior restraints and more time analyzing whether procedures assure fair and intelligent decisions and whether orders ban activity the constitution protects.

9) Reconsider United States v. Philadelphia, p. 36 in light of *Pentagon Papers*, particularly Justice Marshall's opinion. Is *Pentagon Papers* easier than *Near* in that "Congress had not directed courts to enjoin errant newspapers, as Minnesota had."? Junger, Down Memory Lane: The Case of the Pentagon Papers, 23 Case.W.Res. 3 (1971).

10) During the *Pentagon Papers* litigation, a Second Circuit judge asked the Times's attorney Alexander Bickel for an example that justified a prior restraint. Bickel answered "When the hydrogen bomb turns up."

UNITED STATES v. THE PROGRESSIVE, INC.

467 F.Supp. 990 (W.D.Wis. 1979).

March 26, 1979.

Findings of Fact and Conclusions of Law March 28, 1979.

WARREN, District Judge.

On March 9, 1979, this Court, at the request of the government, but after hearing from both parties, issued a temporary restraining order enjoining defendants, their employees, and agents from publishing or otherwise communicating or disclosing in any manner any restricted data contained in the article: "The H-Bomb Secret: How We Got It, Why We're Telling It."

In keeping with the Court's order that the temporary restraining order should be in effect for the shortest time possible, a preliminary injunction hearing was scheduled for one week later, on March 16, 1979. At the request of the parties and with the Court's acquiescence, the preliminary injunction hearing was rescheduled for 10:00 A.M. today in order that both sides might have additional time to file affidavits and arguments. The Court continued the temporary restraining order until 5:00 P.M. today.

In order to grant a preliminary injunction, the Court must find that plaintiff has a reasonable likelihood of success on the merits, and that the plaintiff will suffer irreparable harm if the injunction does not issue. In addition, the Court must consider the interest of the public and the balance of the potential harm to plaintiff and defendants.

Jurisdiction in this action is grounded on 42 U.S.C. § 2280, the Atomic Energy Act and 28 U.S.C. § 1345.

Under the facts here alleged, the question before this Court involves a clash between allegedly vital security interests of the United States and the competing constitutional doctrine against prior restraint in publication.

In its argument and briefs, plaintiff relies on national security, as enunciated by Congress in The Atomic Energy Act of 1954, as the basis for classification of certain documents. Plaintiff contends that, in certain areas, national preservation and self-interest permit the retention and classification of government secrets. The government argues that its national security interest also permits it to impress classification and censorship upon information originating in the public domain, if when drawn together, synthesized and collated, such information acquires the character of presenting immediate, direct and irreparable harm to the interests of the United States.

Defendants argue that freedom of expression as embodied in the First Amendment is so central to the heart of liberty that prior restraint in any form becomes anathema. They contend that this is particularly true when a nation is not at war and where the prior restraint is based on surmise or conjecture. While acknowledging that freedom of the press is not absolute, they maintain that the publication of the projected article does not rise to the level of immediate, direct and irreparable harm which could justify incursion into First Amendment freedoms.

Hence, although embodying deep and fundamental principles of democratic philosophy, the issue also requires a factual determination by a federal court sitting in equity. At the level of a temporary restraining order, or a preliminary injunction, such matters are customarily dealt with through affidavits.

Thus far the affidavits filed are numerous and complex. They come from individuals of learning and renown. They deal with how the information at issue was assembled, what it means, and how injurious the affiant believes it to be.

The Court notes the *amici curiae* briefs filed by the American Civil Liberties Union, the Wisconsin Civil Liberties Union, the Federation of American Scientists and the Fund for Open Information and Accountability, Inc., and expresses thanks for them. The Court gave consideration to the suggestion that a panel of experts be appointed to serve as witnesses for the Court to assist it in determining whether the dangers of publication are as great as the government asserts or as inconsequential as *The Progressive* states. However, the Court concluded that such a procedure really would merely proliferate the opinions of experts arrayed on both sides of the issue.

Both parties have already marshalled impressive opinions covering all aspects of the case. The Court has read all this material and has now heard extensive argument. It is time for decision.

From the founding days of this nation, the rights to freedom of speech and of the press have held an honored place in our constitutional scheme. The establishment and nurturing of these rights is one of the true achievements of our form of government.

Because of the importance of these rights, any prior restraint on publication comes into court under a heavy presumption against its constitutional validity. New York Times v. United States.

However, First Amendment rights are not absolute. They are not boundless. . . .

In Near v. Minnesota, the Supreme Court specifically recognized an extremely narrow area, involving national security, in which interference with First Amendment rights might be tolerated and a prior restraint on publication might be appropriate. The Court stated:

" 'When a nation is at war many things that might be said in time of peace are such a hindrance to its effort that their utterance will not be endured so long as men fight and that no Court could regard them as protected by any constitutional right.' No one would question but that a government might prevent actual obstruction to its recruiting service or the publication of the sailing dates of transports or the number and location of troops."

Thus, it is clear that few things, save grave national security concerns, are sufficient to override First Amendment interests. A court is well admonished to approach any requested prior restraint with a great deal of skepticism.

Juxtaposed against the right to freedom of expression is the government's contention that the national security of this country could be jeopardized by publication of the article.

The Court is convinced that the government has a right to classify certain sensitive documents to protect its national security. The problem is with the scope of the classification system.

Defendants contend that the projected article merely contains data already in the public domain and readily available to any diligent seeker. They say other nations already have the same information or the opportunity to obtain it. How then, they argue, can they be in violation of 42 U.S.C. §§ 2274(b) and 2280 which purport to authorize injunctive relief against one who would disclose restricted data "with reason to believe such data will be utilized to injure the United States or to secure an advantage to any foreign nation . . . ?"

Although the government states that some of the information is in the public domain, it contends that much of the data is not, and that the Morland article contains a core of information that has never before been published.

Furthermore, the government's position is that whether or not specific information is "in the public domain" or has been "declassified" at some point is not determinative. The government states that a court must look at the nature and context of prior disclosures and analyze what the practical impact of the prior disclosures are as contrasted to that of the present revelation.

The government feels that the mere fact that the author, Howard Morland, could prepare an article explaining the technical processes of thermonuclear weapons does not mean that those processes are available to everyone. They lay heavy emphasis on the argument that the danger lies in the exposition of certain concepts never heretofore disclosed in conjunction with one another.

In an impressive affidavit, Dr. Hans A. Bethe, whose affidavit was introduced by the government and whose article, *The Hydrogen Bomb: II*, was a source document for Theodore Postol's affidavit I filed by the defendants states that sizeable portions of the Morland text should be classified as restricted data because the processes outlined in the manuscript describe the essential design and operation of thermonuclear weapons. He later concludes "that the design and operational concepts described in the manuscript are not expressed or revealed in the public literature nor do I believe they are known to scientists not associated with the government weapons programs."

The Court has grappled with this difficult problem and has read and studied the affidavits and other documents on file. After all this, the Court finds concepts within the article that it does not find in the public realm—concepts that are vital to the operation of the hydrogen bomb.

Even if some of the information is in the public domain, due recognition must be given to the human skills and expertise involved in writing this article. The author needed sufficient expertise to recognize relevant, as opposed to irrelevant, information and to assimilate the information obtained. The right questions had to be asked or the correct educated guesses had to be made.

The ability of G. I. Taylor to calculate the yield of the first nuclear explosion from a *Life* magazine photo demonstrates that certain individuals with some knowledge, ability to reason and extraordinary perseverance may acquire additional knowledge without access to classified information, even though the information thus acquired may not be obvious to others not so equipped or motivated. All of this must be considered in resolving the issues before the Court.

Does the article provide a "do-it yourself" guide for the hydrogen bomb? Probably not. A number of affidavits make quite clear that a *sine qua non* to thermonuclear capability is a large, sophisticated industrial capability coupled with a coterie of imaginative, resourceful scientists and technicians. One does not build a hydrogen bomb in the basement. However, the article could possibly provide sufficient information to allow a medium size nation to move faster in developing a hydrogen weapon. It could provide a ticket to by-pass blind alleys.

The Morland piece could accelerate the membership of a candidate nation in the thermonuclear club. Pursuit of blind alleys or failure to grasp seemingly basic concepts have been the cause of many inventive failures. . . .

Although the defendants state that the information contained in the article is relatively easy to obtain, only five countries now have a hydrogen bomb. Yet the United States first successfully exploded the hydrogen bomb some twenty-six years ago.

The point has also been made that it is only a question of time before other countries will have the hydrogen bomb. That may be true. However, there are times in the course of human history when time itself may be very important. This time factor becomes critical when considering mass annihilation weaponry—witness the failure of Hitler to get his V–1 and V–2 bombs operational quickly enough to materially affect the outcome of World War II.

Defendants have stated that publication of the article will alert the people of this country to the false illusion of security created by the government's futile efforts at secrecy. They believe publication will provide the people with needed information to make informed decisions on an urgent issue of public concern.

However, this Court can find no plausible reason why the public needs to know the technical details about hydrogen bomb construction to carry on an informed debate on this issue. Furthermore, the Court believes that the defendants' position in favor of nuclear non-proliferation would be harmed, not aided, by the publication of this article.

The defendants have also relied on the decision in the *New York Times* case. In that case, the Supreme Court refused to enjoin the *New York Times* and the *Washington Post* from publishing the contents of a classified historical study of United States decision-making in Viet Nam, the so-called "Pentagon Papers."

This case is different in several important respects. In the first place, the study involved in the *New York Times* case contained historical data relating to events that occurred some three to twenty years previously. Secondly, the Supreme Court agreed with the lower court that no cogent reasons were advanced by the government as to why the article affected national security except that publication might cause some embarrassment to the United States.

A final and most vital difference between these two cases is the fact that a specific statute is involved here. Section 2274 of The Atomic Energy Act prohibits anyone from communicating, transmitting or disclosing any restricted data to any person "with reason to believe such data will be utilized to injure the United States or to secure an advantage to any foreign nation."

Section 2014 of the Act defines restricted data. " 'Restricted Data' means all data concerning 1) design, manufacture, or utilization of atomic weapons; 2) the production of special nuclear material; or 3) the use of special nuclear material in the production of energy, but shall not include data declassified or removed from the Restricted Data category pursuant to section 2162 of this title."

As applied to this case, the Court finds that the statute in question is not vague or overbroad. The Court is convinced that the terms used in the statute—"communicates, transmits or discloses"—include publishing in a magazine.

The Court is of the opinion that the government has shown that the defendants had reason to believe that the data in the article, if published, would injure the United States or give an advantage to a foreign nation. Extensive reading and studying of the documents on file lead to the conclusion that not all the data is available in the public realm in the same fashion, if it is available at all.

What is involved here is information dealing with the most destructive weapon in the history of mankind, information of sufficient destructive potential to nullify the right to free speech and to endanger the right to life itself.

Stripped to its essence then, the question before the Court is a basic confrontation between the First Amendment right to freedom of the press and national security.

Our Founding Fathers believed, as we do, that one is born with certain inalienable rights which, as the Declaration of Independence intones, include the right to life, liberty and the pursuit of happiness. The Constitution, including the Bill of Rights, was enacted to make those rights operable in everyday life.

The Court believes that each of us is born seized of a panoply of basic rights, that we institute governments to secure these rights and that there is a hierarchy of values attached to these rights which is helpful in deciding the clash now before us.

Certain of these rights have an aspect of imperativeness or centrality that make them transcend other rights. Somehow it does not seem that the right to life and the right to not have soldiers quartered in your home can be of equal import in the grand scheme of things. While it may be true in the long-run, as Patrick Henry instructs us, that one would prefer death to life without liberty, nonetheless, in the short-run, one cannot enjoy freedom of speech, freedom to worship or freedom of the press unless one first enjoys the freedom to live.

Faced with a stark choice between upholding the right to continued life and the right to freedom of the press, most jurists would have no difficulty in opting for the chance to continue to breathe and function as they work to achieve perfect freedom of expression.

Is the choice here so stark? Only time can give us a definitive answer. But considering another aspect of this panoply of rights we all have is helpful in answering the question now before us. This aspect is the disparity of the risk involved.

The destruction of various human rights can come about in differing ways and at varying speeds. Freedom of the press can be obliterated overnight by some dictator's imposition of censorship or by the slow nibbling away at a free press through successive bits of repressive legislation enacted by a nation's lawmakers. Yet, even in the most drastic of such situations, it is always possible for a dictator to be overthrown, for a bad law to be repealed or for a judge's error to be subsequently rectified. Only when human life is at stake are such corrections impossible.

The case at bar is so difficult precisely because the consequences of error involve human life itself and on such an awesome scale.

The Secretary of State states that publication will increase thermonuclear proliferation and that this would "irreparably impair the national security of the United States." The Secretary of Defense says that dissemination of the Morland paper will mean a substantial increase in the risk of thermonuclear proliferation and lead to use or threats that would "adversely affect the national security of the United States."

Howard Morland asserts that "if the information in my article were not in the public domain, it should be put there . . . so that ordinary citizens may have informed opinions about nuclear weapons."

Erwin Knoll, the editor of *The Progressive,* states he is "totally convinced that publication of the article will be of substantial benefit to the United States because it will demonstrate that this country's security does not lie in an oppressive and ineffective system of secrecy and classification but in open, honest, and informed public debate about issues which the people must decide."

The Court is faced with the difficult task of weighing and resolving these divergent views.

A mistake in ruling against *The Progressive* will seriously infringe cherished First Amendment rights. If a preliminary injunction is issued, it will constitute the first instance of prior restraint against a publication in this fashion in the history of this country, to this Court's knowledge. Such notoriety is not to be sought. It will curtail defendants' First Amendment rights in a drastic and substantial fashion. It will infringe upon our right to know and to be informed as well.

A mistake in ruling against the United States could pave the way for thermonuclear annihilation for us all. In that event, our right to life is extinguished and the right to publish becomes moot.

In the *Near* case, the Supreme Court recognized that publication of troop movements in time of war would threaten national security and could therefore be restrained. Times have changed significantly since 1931 when *Near* was decided. Now war by foot soldiers has been replaced in large part by war by machines and bombs. No longer need there be any advance warning or any preparation time before a nuclear war could be commenced.

In light of these factors, this Court concludes that publication of the technical information on the hydrogen bomb contained in the article is analagous to publication of troop movements or locations in time of war and falls within the extremely narrow exception to the rule against prior restraint.

Because of this "disparity of risk," because the government has met its heavy burden of showing justification for the imposition of a prior restraint on publication of the objected-to technical portions of the Morland article, and because the Court is unconvinced that suppression of the objected-to technical portions of the Morland article would in any plausible fashion impede the defendants in their laudable crusade to stimulate public knowledge of nuclear armament and bring about enlightened debate on national policy questions, the Court finds that the objected-to portions of the article fall within the narrow area recognized by the Court in Near v. Minnesota in which a prior restraint on publication is appropriate.

The government has met its burden under section 2274 of The Atomic Energy Act. In the Court's opinion, it has also met the test enunciated by two Justices in the *New York Times* case, namely grave, direct, immediate and irreparable harm to the United States.

The Court has just determined that if necessary it will at this time assume the awesome responsibility of issuing a preliminary injunction against *The Progressive's* use of the Morland article in its current form.

However, the Court is acutely aware of the old legal adage that "bad cases make bad law." This case in its present posture will undoubtedly go to the Supreme Court because it does present so starkly the clash between freedom of press and national security. Does it go there with the blessing of the entire press? The Court thinks not. Many elements of the press see grave risk of permanent damage to First Amendment freedoms if this case goes forward. They feel appellate courts will find, as this Court has, that the risk is simply too great to permit publication.

Furthermore, if there is any one inescapable conclusion that one arrives at after wading through all these experts' affidavits, it is that many wise, intelligent, patriotic individuals can hold diametrically opposite opinions on the issues before us.

Recognizing that both sides at the moment may seem adamant, the Court nonetheless was greatly impressed by the arguments in the *amicus* brief submitted by the Federation of American Scientists through its director, Dr. Jeremy J. Stone.

This group, with half of America's Nobel laureates in its ranks, urged *The Progressive* to recognize the damage the article could do to both nuclear nonproliferation policies and First Amendment rights. It sees the dangers of the present confrontation and suggests that similar cases can arise in the future involving this or other technologies. The group notes that it is possible for example, that a technology such as recombinant DNA could someday surface means of destruction that ought not be published while, at the same time, provoking crucial issues of public policy that badly need to be publicly discussed.

The group suggests that the accommodating of such conflicting interests is not best done in the glare of a judicial spotlight, but that the parties, seemingly at odds can, with effort, satisfy both their interests with a non-legal resolution.

The government seeks only the deletion of certain technical material and, in the Court's opinion, would have an interest in settling this case out of court. On the other hand, the Court believes that *The Progressive* has an obligation to its colleagues in the press and does not really require the objected-to material in order to ventilate its views on government secrecy and the hydrogen bomb.

In this context, the Federation urges that the Court give the parties every last chance to try to resolve the matter out-of-court, so as to simultaneously moot the case and set a desirable precedent for the future.

NOW THEREFORE, acting on this suggestion, the Court herewith poses to the parties a final choice:

We will now adjourn until 2:00 P.M. At that time the case will be recalled. In the interim, each party is to consider whether it would be willing to meet with a panel of five mediators appointed by the Court to attempt to resolve the parties' differences.

The Court recognizes that today is the deadline for the May issue of *The Progressive* and that the temporary restraining order expires at 5:00 P.M. this afternoon. If everyone is willing to attempt mediation, the temporary restraining order would have to be extended by mutual agreement.

If the parties agree to mediation, each side will be asked to submit to the Court the names of two senior weapons scientists and two representatives of the media. From these names the Court will select two people from each category and will then itself approach a respected lawyer or retired jurist and ask that person to chair the group. The given individuals would compose a mediating panel. This panel would have to receive appropriate clearance.

The panel would meet with the parties and report back to the Court in 10 days on its progress or lack of it, in dealing with the specific deletions at issue.

At the time of the report, the Court will then either dismiss the case by stipulation of the parties, or in the event of inability to agree, issue a preliminary injunction.

If, at 2:00 P.M. either or both sides are unable to agree to this proposal, the Court will regretfully issue the preliminary injunction.

SO ORDERED this 26th day of March, 1979, at Milwaukee, Wisconsin.

FINDINGS OF FACT AND CONCLUSIONS OF LAW

The Court, having this day entered a preliminary injunction restraining defendants, *pendente lite,* from publishing or otherwise disseminating restricted data contained in the manuscript which is the subject of this action, hereby makes the following findings of fact and conclusions of law pursuant to Rule 52(a) of the Federal Rules of Civil Procedure:

FINDINGS OF FACT

1. The defendant Howard Morland is a free-lance writer specializing in energy and nuclear weapons issues. His article, "Tritium; the New Genie" appeared in the February, 1979, issue of *The Progressive* magazine. . . .

5. While on assignment for *The Progressive* magazine, defendant Morland completed, at the end of February, an article describing the operation of a hydrogen bomb. The article was entitled, "The H-Bomb Secret—How We Got It, Why We're Telling It."

6. On February 27, 1979, a copy of the Morland article was delivered to the Department of Energy (DOE) offices in Germantown, Maryland. Defendant Day stated in a letter to the Department of Energy accompanying the article that the article contained technical information pertaining to hydrogen weapon design and manufacture. In this letter, Mr. Day stated that he would appreciate the Department verifying the technical accuracy of the enclosures. Copies of this article were forwarded for review to John A. Griffin, Director of Classification of the Department of Energy and to Duane C. Sewell, Assistant Secretary of Energy for Defense Programs.

7. Based on their review of the article, Mr. Griffin and Mr. Sewell determined that a significant portion of the article contained information that the Atomic Energy Act, 42 U.S.C. § 2014(y), requires to be classified as Restricted Data. The Restricted Data contained in the article has not been declassified and remains classified as Secret Restricted Data.

8. On March 1, 1979, Lynn R. Coleman, General Counsel of the Department of Energy, telephoned *The Progressive* magazine and spoke with de-

fendant Day and defendant Knoll. Mr. Coleman informed Mr. Day and Mr. Knoll that he was in possession of a copy of the Morland article, and that, in the opinion of the Department, the article contained Restricted Data, as defined in the Atomic Energy Act of 1954, as amended. He further informed Mr. Day and Mr. Knoll that, in the view of the Department of Energy, the Department of State and the Arms Control and Disarmament Agency, publication of the Restricted Data contained in this article would injure the United States and would give an advantage to other nations. He stated that the release of this information would be contrary to the United States' effort to prevent the proliferation of nuclear weapons and requested that *The Progressive* refrain from publishing the article.

9. On March 2, 1979, Duane Sewell met with representatives of *The Progressive,* including Mr. Day, Mr. Knoll, and Ronald Carbon, publisher. He advised them that the Department of Energy had reviewed the Morland manuscript and, based upon that review, had determined that it contains material which is Secret Restricted Data. He further told the magazine's representatives that publication of the article would constitute a violation of the Atomic Energy Act and would give an advantage to foreign nations in the development of thermonuclear technology. Mr. Sewell assured the magazine's representatives that the Department of Energy did not want to stop the publication of the entire manuscript but only those portions which contained Secret Restricted Data. He suggested to *The Progressive* that they permit the Government to work with them to recast the Secret Restricted Data portions of the manuscript so that they would no longer be classified and publication could go forward.

10. On March 7, 1979, Mr. Gordon Sinykin, counsel for *The Progressive,* advised Mr. Coleman of the Department of Energy that, after careful review of the matter, *The Progressive* intended to publish the article. He stated that publication would proceed unless the United States promptly obtained a temporary restraining order. . . .

13. On March 9, 1979, this Court held a hearing on the Government's request for a temporary restraining order to enjoin the defendants, their employees, and agents from publishing or otherwise disclosing in any manner any of the Restricted Data contained in the Morland article. After hearing from both parties, the Court issued a temporary restraining order to be in effect for the shortest time possible consistent with the opportunity for the Government to substantiate its claim at a hearing on the request for a preliminary injunction. A preliminary injunction hearing was scheduled for one week later, on March 16, 1979.

14. At the request of the parties, and with the Court's acquiescence, the preliminary injunction hearing was rescheduled from March 16, 1979, to March 26, 1979, in order that both sides might have additional time to file affidavits and briefs. The Court continued the temporary restraining order until 5:00 P.M. on Monday, March 26, 1979.

15. The Court has carefully read and studied the affidavits and other documents on file in this action and concludes that the article in question contains concepts that are not found in the public realm, concepts that are vital to the operation of the bomb. Although the Restricted Data portions of the article also contain some information that has been previously disclosed in

scattered public sources, the article provides a more comprehensive, accurate, and detailed analysis of the overall construction and operation of a thermonuclear weapon than any publication to date in the public literature. Although various information in the public realm suggests a number of possible designs for a thermonuclear weapon, nowhere in the public domain is there a correct description of the type of design used in United States thermonuclear weapons.

16. Publication of the Restricted Data contained in the Morland article would be extremely important to a nation seeking a thermonuclear capability, for it would provide vital information on key concepts involved in the construction of a practical thermonuclear weapon. Once basic concepts are learned, the remainder of the process may easily follow. The article could provide sufficient information to allow a medium-size nation to move faster in developing a hydrogen weapon.

17. Publication of the Restricted Data contained in the article could materially reduce the time required by certain countries to achieve a thermonuclear weapon capability.

18. Defendants have reason to believe that publication, or any other disclosure of the Secret Restricted Data, would injure the United States or secure an advantage to a foreign nation, within the meaning of § 2274(b) of the Atomic Energy Act.

19. After careful review of the Morland article and other documents filed in this case, the Court finds that publication or other disclosure of the Secret Restricted Data contained in the Morland article would irreparably harm the national security of the United States.

20. The United States and its citizens will suffer irreparable harm and the public interest will be disserved if a preliminary injunction, *pendente lite,* is not issued. On balance, the defendants will not be substantially harmed by the issuance of such a preliminary injunction.

21. Publication of the Restricted Data in the Morland article will result in direct, immediate and irreparable damage to the United States by accelerating the capacity of certain non-thermonuclear nations to manufacture thermonuclear weapons.

CONCLUSIONS OF LAW

1. This Court has jurisdiction over the subject matter of this action pursuant to 42 U.S.C. § 2280 and 28 U.S.C. § 1345.

2. Publication or other disclosure or communication of the Restricted Data contained in the Morland article would likely constitute a violation of the Atomic Energy Act, 42 U.S.C. § 2274(b).

3. The pertinent provisions of the Atomic Energy Act, 42 U.S.C. § 2274(b) and § 2280, apply to the defendants and are not constitutionally vague or over broad.

4. Because defendants intend imminently to publish the Restricted Data contained in the Morland article, unless restrained by order of the court, plaintiff, United States of America, is entitled to a preliminary injunction,

pendente lite, prohibiting publication or disclosure of the article pursuant to 42 U.S.C. § 2280.

5. In view of the showing of harm made by the United States, a preliminary injunction would be warranted even in the absence of statutory authorization because of the existence of the likelihood of direct, immediate and irreparable injury to our nation and its people. New York Times Co. v. United States (Justice Stewart concurring); see also, Near v. Minnesota.

6. The facts and circumstances as presented here fall within the extremely narrow recognized area, involving national security, in which a prior restraint on publication is appropriate. Issuance of a preliminary injunction does not, under the circumstances presented to the Court, violate defendants' First Amendment rights.

7. Plaintiff has proven all necessary prerequisites for issuance of a preliminary injunction restraining defendants from publishing or disclosing any Restricted Data contained in the Morland article until a final determination in this action has been made by the Court.

SO ORDERED this 28th day of March, 1979, at Milwaukee, Wisconsin.

UNITED STATES v. THE PROGRESSIVE, INC.

486 F. Supp. 5 (W.D.Wis., 1979)

WARREN, District Judge.

On June 12, 1979, the Court heard oral argument *in camera* on defendants' motion to reconsider and to vacate the preliminary injunction issued by this Court on March 26, 1979.

On March 26, 1979, the Court found that the facts and circumstances in this case fall within the extremely narrow recognized area involving national security, in which a prior restraint on publication was appropriate. The Court granted the preliminary injunction pursuant to the Atomic Energy Act, 42 U.S.C. § 2280, and also found that an injunction would be warranted even in the absence of statutory authorization because of the existence of the likelihood of direct, immediate, and irreparable injury to this nation.

Defendants have filed their motion to reconsider, alleging that recent developments and publication of certain articles since the March 26, 1979 hearing have rendered the preliminary injunction moot and ineffectual.

Basically, the defendants argue that they cannot be enjoined from publishing the Morland article under either the Atomic Energy Act of 1954 or the United States Constitution because the information it contains on the three key concepts—separate stages, compression and radiation coupling—is already in the public domain. Therefore, they state that the injunction against *The Progressive* is ineffective in preventing other countries from learning the three essential concepts involved in hydrogen bomb design and construction.

The contention that "the secret is out" and that therefore the injunction must be lifted advances on two fronts. One contention made by the defendants is that the government itself was responsible for the declassification of portions of UCRL 4725 and UCRL 5280 with the inadvertent result that the entire documents were available to the public in the open archives of the Los Alamos Scientific Library for a period of several years. Thus, they argue that the government is now estopped from seeking to enjoin the publication of the very same information which the government itself made available.

A second contention deals with a series of non-governmental publications. Defendants cite several articles, including articles in the *Milwaukee Sentinel*, *Fusion* magazine and *Encyclopedia Americana*, which allegedly reveal one or all of these three key concepts. The defendants emphasize that the *Milwaukee Sentinel* articles, in particular, contain these concepts and were written and published in the context of this case. In light of this, defendants argue that they are authoritative documents.

The government strenuously contends that only two articles contain authoritative information on hydrogen bomb construction: UCRL 4725 and UCRL 5280. Plaintiff states these two documents were erroneously declassified and placed in the public section at the Los Alamos Scientific Library. However, when this error was discovered, these documents were immediately removed from the public shelves at the Los Alamos Scientific Library.

Plaintiff argues that all of the other articles and documents cited by defendants constitute "literature of speculation" and contain isolated bits of information which are so speculative and disjointed as to be meaningless. The government states that these articles fail to contain the accurate and uniquely detailed information on all three concepts found in the Morland article.

Plaintiff counters defendants' argument about the effectiveness of continuing the injunction against *The Progressive* and the other defendants by arguing that the case has not changed since the injunction was first issued. The government states that, unlike the situation in the Pentagon Papers case, no other publications have published the same or similarly accurate, comprehensive and detailed articles on the construction of hydrogen weapons. Thus, the preliminary injunction against the defendants would still be effective and is warranted under the provisions of 42 U.S.C. § 2280. The government argues that, even in the absence of this statutory authority, the injunction would still be warranted because of the existence of the likelihood of direct, immediate and irreparable injury to this country.

The Court is now faced with resolving these conflicting contentions.

Certain basic issues must be addressed by the Court. Admittedly, UCRL 5280 "reveals in a thermonuclear weapons context the three concepts which the government has described as the essential secret of the H-Bomb." (Stipulation of the parties, June 11, 1979). Therefore, the Court must first determine whether documents, such as UCRL 5280 and UCRL 4725 are "in the public domain."

In Alfred A. Knopf, Inc. v. Colby, 509 F.2d 1362, 1370 (4th Cir. 1975), cert. denied, 421 U.S. 992 (1975), reh. denied, 422 U.S. 1049 (1975), the court held that classified information "was not in the public domain unless there has been official disclosure of it." The court continued:

"Rumor and speculations circulate and sometimes get into print. It is one thing for a reporter or author to speculate or guess that a thing may be so or even, quoting undisclosed sources, to say that it is so; it is quite another thing for one in a position to know of it officially to say that it is so. The reading public is accustomed to treating reports from uncertain sources as being of uncertain reliability, but it would not be inclined to discredit reports of sensitive information revealed by an official of the United States in a position to know of what he spoke."

In this case, UCRL 4725 and UCRL 5280 were inadvertently declassified in toto. (Cucchiara Affidavit, ¶¶ 7, 8). They were available to the public at the Los Alamos Scientific Library. (Freed Affidavit, ¶ 4; Sewell Affidavit, ¶ 4). However, as soon as the declassification error was discovered, the documents were removed from the public shelves. (Freed Affidavit, ¶ 7; Sewell Affidavit, ¶ 4).

Whether or not the secret was compromised by this error can only be a matter of conjecture. The Court has reviewed the affidavits regarding access and is unable to conclude one way or another whether the vital data was obtained by scientists or intelligence agents from other nations.

Prior release of classified information should not be binding on the government if, at a later time, it is determined that further release would jeopardize national security. Aspin v. Department of Defense, 453 F.Supp. 520 (E.D.Wis.1978); Halperin v. Central Intelligence Agency, 446 F.Supp. 661 (D.D.C.1978).

The Court is compelled to the conclusion that, from a legal point of view, the government's error in inadvertently declassifying UCRL 4725 and UCRL 5280 did not move these documents into "the public domain" and further, that there is no showing that the injunction became ineffectual.

The Court must now determine whether any published materials admittedly in the public domain contain information on the three key concepts.

At the time of the issuance of the preliminary injunction, the Court found that information was available on possibly two of the key concepts. However, the Court found that the concept of radiation coupling had not previously been revealed in the public literature and that the maintenance of the secrecy of this concept was so vital to the security of this nation that a preliminary injunction against the defendants was justified.

In support of their motion, the defendants have filed copies of several recently published articles with the Court. The Court has conducted a detailed examination of these articles, especially the *Milwaukee Sentinel* articles of April 30 and May 1, 1979 by Joe Manning and recent *Fusion* magazine articles.

The *Milwaukee Sentinel* article of May 1, 1979 is pertinent on this concept of radiation coupling because, as defendants argue, there is one statement that bears on the utilization of soft x-ray pressure. The relevant paragraph states:

"Recent information published in Fusion magazine suggests that Teller and Ulam may have come up with some kind of arrangement that would compress the fuel through the use of soft x-rays from the atomic bomb blast reflected off the bomb casing wall. Soft x-rays are low energy rays like those given off by a color television set."

The Court notes that this statement is couched in terms of speculation and conjecture. It utilizes such generalized terms and touches the key concept so obliquely that it can hardly be considered a definitive affirmation of one crucial step in the construction of a thermonuclear weapon.

Similar problems exist with the *Fusion* magazine articles cited by defendants. Any information on the key concepts in these articles is stated in a highly speculative and generalized framework.

In the Court's opinion, there is a distinct and marked difference between specifying with particularity the three key concepts necessary to construct a hydrogen weapon and merely mentioning numerous concepts that may or may not be important and relevant in the construction of a thermonuclear device.

In this regard, the Court finds that the *Milwaukee Sentinel* articles, the *Fusion* magazine articles and other publications cited by the defendants are clearly dissimilar from the Morland article which provides an accurate, detailed and comprehensive description and analysis of hydrogen weapon construction.

Therefore, after detailed study of the documents filed by the parties and due consideration of the oral arguments of counsel, the Court concludes that the article, "The H-Bomb Secret—How We Got It, Why We're Telling It," contains a comprehensive description of radiation coupling, along with the other two key concepts, that is not found in the public realm. Some articles in the public domain contain information on one or another of the other two concepts. However, only the Morland article contains a comprehensive, accurate and detailed analysis of all three concepts utilized in the construction of a thermonuclear weapon.

Therefore, the Court finds that publication or other disclosure of the restricted data contained in the Morland article would likely constitute a violation of the Atomic Energy Act, 42 U.S.C. § 2274(b) and would likely cause a direct, immediate and irreparable injury to this nation.

Accordingly, the Court hereby denies defendants' motion for reconsideration and vacation of the preliminary injunction issued by the Court on March 26, 1979. This memorandum and order constitutes the Court's findings of fact and conclusions of law pursuant to Rule 52(a) of the Federal Rules of Civil Procedure.

---

1) Charles R. Hanson wrote an 18-page letter concerning the availability of information about weapons design. That letter contained much of the same material as Morland's article. Hanson sent the letter to eight newspapers. The Madison Press Connection published the information on September 16, 1979. Two days later the Chicago Tribune reprinted Hanson's letter. On motion of the government, the court dismissed the Progressive's appeal and the lawsuit. 610 F.2d 819 (7th Cir. 1979). Morland's article appeared in the November, 1979 issue of the Progressive. Most of the sealed court record was made public in September 1980 after the Justice Department announced that it would not prosecute. The Progressive asked Judge Warren to repudiate the opinions above. He declined.

The Progressive won in the law reviews. See Cheh, The *Progressive* Case and the Atomic Energy Act: Waking to the Dangers of Government Information Controls, 48 Geo.Wash.L.Rev. 163 (1980); Note, United States v.

Progressive, Inc.: The Faustian Bargain and the First Amendment, 75 Nw. U.L.Rev. 538 (1978); Note, A Journalist's View of the *Progressive* Case: A Look at the Press, Prior Restraint, and the First Amendment From the Pentagon Papers to the Future, 41 Ohio St.L.J. 1165 (1980); Comment, United States v. Progressive, Inc.: The National Security and Free Special Conflict, 22 Wm. & Mary L. Rev. 141 (1980).

2) Do both *Pentagon Papers* and *Progressive* contain internal evidence of the time pressure under which the judges worked? Does the time pressure mean that judges subordinate articulating guiding precedent to drafting prompt decisions for discrete controversies? If time is a perishable commodity, both decisions may reveal that rights may be lost while a court adjudicates whether they exist. Are interlocutory orders to preserve a controversy to adjudicate necessary to the judicial function even though, in retrospect, some interlocutory orders deprive defendants of their constitutional rights to speak?

Problem: Questionable material is scheduled for the December issue of the Restitution Review. It will be mailed to subscribers on November 10. On November 1, Judge Kucan grants Professor Dobbs's motion for an order barring publication for ten days. During the ten days Judge Kucan will determine whether the issue defames Professor Dobbs sufficiently to be enjoined. Is the order forbidding dissemination, before the periodical intended to publish in any event, a prior restraint?

3) In *Progressive,* if the statute allowed the injunction and if the judge held the statute to govern and be constitutional, then was the injunction a prior restraint? Would an incorrect decision that the statute was constitutional and that the statute barred the activity, combined with the issuance of an injunction based on that decision, be a prior restraint?

4) The prior restraint test, *Progressive* reminds us, fails to define the level of protection against prior restraints. Courts apply a "presumption" against prior restraints, but "evidence" may overcome the presumption. Justices Black and Douglas rejected injunctions under any circumstances, and even the dissenters in *Pentagon Papers* opposed prior restraint. *Progressive* applies the Stewart-White test from *Pentagon Papers.* Did Judge Warren apply that test correctly? Does that test merely restate the "clear and present danger" test? Comment, 22 Wm. & Mary L. Rev. at 147. How does Justice Brennan's test differ?

The prior restraint presumption is said to be especially formidable. Brandenburg v. Ohio, 395 U.S. 444 (1969), struck down a syndicalism conviction on the ground that it punished mere advocacy not directed "to inciting or producing imminent lawless action and is likely to incite or produce such action." 395 U.S. at 447. Did Morland incite? Was the harm imminent? Was action probable? Did the *Progressive* court approve an injunctive restriction that would be unconstitutional as a criminal statute? Schauer, Categories and the First Amendment: A Play in Three Acts, 34 Vand.L.Rev. 265, 297–98 (1981). Did the magnitude of the threatened harm compel the judge to enjoin? Cheh, 48 Geo.Wash.L.Rev. at 199. Compare Reserve Mining, p. 116. Does Judge Warren also calculate risk and harm but hold that if the harm is great, the risk need not be probable to enjoin?

5) The test for overcoming the presumption against prior restraints was stated differently in Nebraska Press Association v. Stuart, 427 U.S. 539

(1976). The trial judge forbade publication of specified information about a locally notorious criminal suspect. The judge intended to protect the defendant's right to an untainted jury. Striking the order down, Chief Justice Burger's opinion determined whether a prior restraint is valid by asking whether "the gravity of the 'evil,' discounted by its improbability, justifies such invasion of free speech as is necessary to avoid the danger." 427 U.S. at 562. Among other things, Professor Benno Schmidt says that *Nebraska Press* took "its standard for judging the legality of prior restraints from a precedent [United States v. Dennis, 183 F.2d 201 (2d Cir.1950), affirmed, 341 U.S. 494 (1951)] widely thought to represent the nadir of first amendment protection in modern subsequent punishment cases." Schmidt, *Nebraska Press Association:* An Expansion of Freedom and Contraction of Theory, 29 Stan.L. Rev. 431, 458–66 (1977). Justice Brennan, concurring in *Nebraska Press,* rejected injunctions to protect criminal trials and repeated his view that military security, the troop movement example not the clear and present danger test, is the exclusive basis for prior restraints. 427 U.S. at 588, 592–93. Chief Justive Burger might not speak for a majority in *Nebraska Press.* O. Fiss, The Civil Rights Injunction 103 n.2 (1978). Whatever the standard, *Nebraska Press* was easy. Professor Blasi, after citing cases, says "the prohibition against publication at issue in *Nebraska Press* would have been invalidated even if it had been imposed by criminal statute rather than judicial order." Toward a Theory of Prior Restraint: The Central Linkage, 66 Minn.L.Rev. 11, 13 n.10 (1981).

Should the courts stop talking about a presumption against prior restraints and ask whether the challenged order prohibits expression that the constitution protects? At a minimum, is a "heavy presumption" against prior restraints "the kind of judicial formula by which courts reserve to themselves the power of future judgments?" Linde, Courts and Censorship, 66 Minn.L. Rev. 171, 207 (1981). Have we learned that the prior restraint "test" is loose and illusory?

6) In the final analysis, do *Pentagon Papers* and *Progressive* teach that national security injunctions are unworkable? Why can Coca-Cola and Kentucky Fried Chicken keep their formulae secret but the United States government cannot? Judicial orders to enforce government secrecy seem to become ineffective at the approximate time the government asks the judge to stop dissemination. Ellsberg gave the Pentagon Papers to about a score of newspapers, and Judge Robb of the court of appeals asked the government if it was "asking us to ride herd on a swarm of bees." Justice White's opinion mentions this phenomenon. See 403 U.S. at 733. Could the district judges have enjoined "all newspapers in the United States" and assumed that the Times and Post represented their interest?

The Court in *Nebraska Press* discusses "the reality of the problems of managing and enforcing" silence orders: "The territorial jurisdiction of the issuing court is limited by concepts of sovereignty." 427 U.S. at 565. See also Hanson v. Denckla, 357 U.S. 235 (1958); Pennoyer v. Neff, 95 U.S. 714 (1877). The need for *in personam* jurisdiction also presents an obstacle to a restraining order that applies to publication at large as distinguished from restraining publication within a given jurisdiction. Assuming the court has jurisdiction, "even a cursory examination suggests how awkwardly broad prior restraints on publication, directed not at named parties but at large, would fit into our jurisprudence." 427 U.S. at 566 n.10. Moreover, "rumors would travel swiftly, . . . [P]lainly a whole community cannot be restrained from discussing a subject intimately affecting life within it." 427 U.S. at 567.

Is the only way for the government to keep secrets to keep them? Do *Pentagon Papers* and *Progressive* show that it is impossible to keep information a secret once it is out of the government's control? Are the equity actions last-ditch efforts to reduce embarrassment? Should judges, to keep the secrecy system on its toes, allow the press to publish anything it learns? May judges assume that if security is permeable enough for a reporter to penetrate, the enemy is inside it too? If you answered affirmatively, is the dicta in *Near* about the location of troops and the sailing date of ships ill-considered? Remember that "a prohibition against publicly describing what the government is doing is a prohibition against effectively urging that it change course." The troops may already be in another nation. The ships may be about to shell an ally. And neither Congress nor the public may know. Linde, 66 Minn.L.Rev. at 197. Is the fact that an alert person learns something a reason to tell the inert also?

7) Should the courts apply secrecy controls to privately developed information? Must a scientist who creates this data comply with the restrictions on espionage? Will the scientist be subject to security controls? Cheh, 48 Geo.Wash.L.Rev. at 176, 188.

8) "Erwin Knoll, editor of *The Progressive,* said that his decision to obey the injunction, which delayed publication of an article on the 'making' of a hydrogen bomb for more than six months, was 'the most serious moral error I've made in my whole life.' Knoll, however, would grant that the government has a responsibility for keeping short term secrets in time of war.

"Knoll said that *Near* was invoked as a pretext for gagging his publication (a temporary restraining order and a preliminary injunction). The national security exception assures an emotionally charged climate in which no one will think rationally or constitutionally. 'There was a reason', Knoll added, 'for the first amendment to be written without exceptions of any kind—even those no one would question.'

"Professor Blasi, nevertheless, was concerned that the ethic of disobeying injunctions may cause government to escalate its efforts toward social control and to use more extreme forms of incapacitating speakers." Gillmor, Prologue, 66 Minn.L.Rev. 1, 6 (1981).

Floyd Abrams is a "distinguished first amendment advocate." With the late Professor Bickel, he argued *Pentagon Papers* before the Supreme Court. He moderated the symposium that celebrated *Near*'s 50th birthday. Abrams rejects what he calls Erwin Knoll's "promiscuous" defiance of court orders: "One ought to pause a few seconds more before one says no to the rule of law." Gillmor, 66 Minn.L.Rev. at 9. Compare Mr. Goodall's statements at the University of Chicago Law School, p. 240.

Why did the Times publish the Pentagon Papers in installments instead of all at once? Why did the Progressive's staff submit Morland's article to verify accuracy? Why did both publications obey the interlocutory orders? Do your answers teach us anything about the rule of law or the mystique of injunctions?

9) Appellate courts have operated secretly. Except for formal written opinions, the public knows almost nothing about the way the courts function. Obviously the veil of secrecy hides debates, discussions, tentative votes, drafts, compromises, and confrontations. Some of the inside information could be employed to take advantage of opportunities for profit. Unwritten traditions and civilities preserve internal secrecy. In a footnote in his *Pentagon Papers* dissent, Chief Justice Burger said:

"With respect to the question of inherent power of the Executive to classify papers, records, and documents as secret, or otherwise unavailable for public exposure, and to secure aid of the courts for enforcement, there may be an analogy with respect to this Court. No statute gives this Court express power to establish and enforce the utmost security measures for the secrecy of our deliberations and records. Yet I have little doubt as to the inherent power of the Court to protect the confidentiality of its internal operations by whatever judicial measures may be required." 403 U.S. at 752 n. 3.

The Brethren's authors pierced this secrecy. The authors claim to have based their chronicle of the internal workings of the Supreme Court during Chief Justice Burger's tenure on interviews with several Justices, 170 former law clerks, internal memoranda, conference notes, assignment sheets, diaries, and unpublished drafts. B. Woodward and S. Armstrong, The Brethren 1–4 (1979).

Problem: A judicial administrator proposes a statute. It defines sensitive judicial information as all written or spoken matter about lawsuits submitted to courts that is created by judges or clerks, except for final published opinions. It makes it an offense for a court employee to divulge sensitive judicial information to any person not employed by the court. It also requires that each employee sign a contract agreeing not to disseminate or participate in the dissemination of sensitive judicial information to any person not employed by the court. Violation of this contract shall be the basis for an action for damages and for an injunction. Damages will be measured by profits acquired. Finally, courts have jurisdiction to enjoin any other person from disseminating or repeating sensitive judicial information. See Landmark Communications, Inc. v. Virginia, 435 U.S. 829 (1978). Evaluate this proposal.

Chapter Five

ENHANCED DUTIES TO OBEY INJUNCTIONS

This chapter deals with facilitating preventive injunctive relief for plaintiff by imposing enhanced duties to obey on defendant. Defendant must obey a decree obtained ex parte and informally communicated; this departs from our usual ideas of notice and personal jurisdiction. Defendant may even be charged with disobedience of an inchoate decree; this alters the normal way we understand court orders. Finally, defendant must comply with an incorrect, even unconstitutional injunction even though he lacked an opportunity to challenge its validity. Judges achieve legitimacy by bringing people affected into court and allowing them to participate in the decisions. Ask whether the enhanced duties exact a toll on procedural fairness and whether they can be reconciled with the overarching principles that govern our legal system. Why are injunctions special?

I. The Informally Communicated Order

CAPE MAY AND SCHELLINGER'S RAILROAD CO. v. JOHNSON

35 N.J.Eq. 422 (1882).

VAN FLEET, V.C. . . . On the 20th day of June, 1881, an order was made directing the city council of the city of Cape May to desist and refrain from passing a certain ordinance, and also to show cause, at a subsequent day, why an injunction should not issue restraining the same act. The order was granted at Newark about midday on the day of its date. The council, it was understood, were to meet on the evening of the same day for the purpose of doing the act which the order was intended to restrain. The distance between the point where the order was made and the point where the defendants were to meet, rendered an actual service of the order impossible before the next day. Notice of the fact that an order had been made prohibiting the passage of the ordinance was sent to the president of the council by telegraph, which he received before the council convened on the evening of the 20th, and afterwards read to the council in open meeting. A special messenger, sent by the complainants, gave the council the same notice while they were in session on the evening of the 20th. The council the next day (June 21st) passed the ordinance.

The facts just stated are undisputed. They show that the defendants are guilty. The regularity, validity or correctness of the order contemned cannot be examined on this proceeding. While an order of a court remains in force it must be obeyed. Even if it was improvidently granted or irregularly obtained, it must nevertheless be respected until it is annulled by the proper authority. . . .

The notice that the defendants had of the order, at the time they violated the command, was, according to the authorities, entirely sufficient. Where the charge is that the defendant has willfully contemned the authority of the court, all that need be shown is that he knew of the existence of the order at the time he violated it. Haring v. Kauffman, 2 Beas. 397. Lord Eldon held that if a defendant is in court when an injunction is granted, he has sufficient notice of it to make it his duty to respect it. He also held that if the defendant is not in court when an order for an injunction is made, but is informed that such an order has been made, by a person who was in court when the order was made, he has sufficient notice of the injunction to render him liable to punishment for its breach. Vansandau v. Rose, 2 Jac. & Walk. 264. . . .

Notice, to be sufficient, need possess but two requisites—first, it must proceed from a source entitled to credit; and second, it must inform the defendant clearly and plainly from what act he must abstain. The notice in the case under consideration possessed both requisites. It was sent by the counsel who obtained the order, and it not only informed the defendants what act the order prohibited, but warned them, if they disregarded the order, their disobedience would be a contempt of the authority of the court. There is nothing in the conduct of the defendants indicating that they had the least doubt concerning the authenticity of the notice or the truth of its contents. They made no inquiry respecting its authenticity or its truth, but say that they consulted counsel whether or not they could safely disregard it, and were advised that they could. This advice, to say the least of it, was both injudicious and dangerous. It affords the defendants neither justification nor palliation. They must be adjudged guilty of contempt.

The complainants, since the proceeding for contempt was instituted, have voluntarily brought the order to show cause why an injunction should not issue to hearing, and it has been decided against them. While the fact that the order contemned was improvidently or erroneously made, neither justifies nor excuses the defendants, it is a matter which it is proper the court should consider in awarding punishment. . . .

Each of the six defendants must pay to the clerk, for the use of the state, a fine of $10, and they must also jointly pay the taxed costs of this proceeding.

---

1) Ten contemnors were convicted of breaching an injunction while protesting the construction of the Seabrook nuclear plant. The district judge held that notice of the injunction was not proved. The court of appeals found "three sources from which it could be fairly inferred that all petitioners had notice: general group discussion prior to entry, at least one posted sign, and two loud speaker broadcasts, one prior to entry, and one after entry to the effect that the protestors could be purged of contempt if they left immediately, (met by a chorus of "no's")." Adams v. Sampson, 588 F.2d 317, 318 (1st Cir. 1978).

2) "[K]nowledge, like any other fact, may be established by circumstantial evidence; and we think there were enough circumstances shown by the

evidence to justify the court in making a finding that Karns and Hill did have knowledge of the injunction, particularly in view of the absence of any sworn denial on their part. The evidence establishes the relationship of these parties; indicates concert of action in the maintenance of the unlawful business; shows the smallness of the community, the notoriety of the 'Tommie Hill Roadhouse,' and the obvious interest of the defendants in evading any interference with their unlawful business as long as possible. These and other circumstances indicated to the trial judge, and indicate to us, that it was so highly improbable that these defendants did not know of this injunction as to make a finding that they did know proper. It would seem just as probable that one could successfully drop a stone into a bird's nest without disturbing the birds as that a temporary injunction of this kind could, under the circumstances proven, be thrust into a nest of bootleggers without all of them knowing of it, even though all were not served." Hill v. United States, 33 F.2d 489, 491 (8th Cir. 1929), certiorari denied 280 U.S. 592. See also Consolidation Coal Co. v. Disabled Miners, 442 F.2d 1261, 1267–8 (4th Cir. 1971); Backo v. Local 281, United Brotherhood of Carpenters & Joiners, 438 F.2d 176, 180 (2d Cir. 1970); Garrigan v. United States, 163 F. 16, 21 (7th Cir. 1908); United States ex rel. Carter v. Jennings, 333 F.Supp. 1392, 1396 (E.D.Pa.1971); In re Herndon, 325 F.Supp. 779 (M.D.Ala.1971); United States v. Puerto Rico Independence Party, 324 F.Supp. 1333 (D.C.Puerto Rico 1971); Walker v. City of Birmingham, 279 Ala. 53, 63–64, 181 So.2d 493, 503–04 (1965), affirmed 388 U.S. 307 (1967); Reihe v. District Court, 184 N.W.2d 701, 705 (Iowa 1971); United Packing House Workers of America v. Boynton, 240 Iowa 212, 222–23, 35 N.W.2d 881, 888 (1949).

3) Are these equity doctrines consistent with accepted standards of personal jurisdiction? Normally, either plaintiff must serve defendant or defendant must appear voluntarily. "[T]he validity of every judgment depends on the jurisdiction of the court before it is rendered, not upon what may occur subsequently." Pennoyer v. Neff, 95 U.S. 714, 728 (1877). A judgment without notice is void, and it will be vulnerable to collateral attack. Mullane v. Central Hanover Bank & Trust Co., 339 U.S. 306, 320 (1950). A court will deny a void judgment res judicata and full faith and credit. McDonald v. Mabee, 243 U.S. 90 (1917). Generally after the judge approves a judgment or decree, the clerk enters it and mails a copy to all parties not in default.

Notice serves two functions: the symbolic function of signifying that the government is exercising sovereignty and power over the defendant, and the pragmatic function of providing the defendant a chance to appear and defend. When did personal jurisdiction over defendants begin in *Cape May?* Did the *Cape May* procedure satisfy the reasons for notice? Did defendants have a chance to argue the law and facts? Are defendants who are enjoined after attenuated procedure more likely to feel overreached? Does the *Cape May* rule frustrate the adversary system's premise? Is the *Cape May* rule necessary to protect plaintiff's right to preventive relief?

4) In More on Void Orders, 7 Ga.L.Rev. 246 (1973), one of the editors argued that when an injunction affects defendant's present conduct, plaintiff must give notice before enjoining. Notice may be informal. If defendant

receives no notice, however, the court fails to attain personal jurisdiction over defendant and the injunction is void. Defendant may ignore a void injunction and assert lack of jurisdiction to prevent contempt. We will deal in more depth with the collateral bar rule later in this chapter, and we will learn why the injunction must be void rather than simply erroneous.

5) In both *Cape May* and *Griffin,* the following decision, an attorney advises the defendant to go ahead with conduct later held to be contempt. Should that advice negate the wilfullness element of criminal contempt? Should it affect the choice and severity of the contempt sanction? If the policy is to punish disrespect for the court, should the fact that the attorney's advice turned out to be substantively correct affect the judge's decisions about contempt?

Attorneys have a duty to represent their clients zealously within the bounds of the law. Should an attorney advise clients to obey all injunctions? Does it suffice to outline the possible consequences of disobedience including the application of the collateral bar rule? Should an attorney reduce this advice to writing? If an attorney advises the client to obey and he violates, how does she handle the client's request to defend a contempt citation?

II. The Inchoate Decree

GRIFFIN v. COUNTY SCHOOL BOARD OF PRINCE EDWARD CO.

363 F.2d 206 (4th Cir.), certiorari denied 385 U.S. 960 (1966).

Before HAYNSWORTH, Chief Judge, and SOBELOFF, BOREMAN, BRYAN and BELL, sitting en banc.

ALBERT V. BRYAN, Circuit Judge: A judgment of civil contempt upon the Board of Supervisors of Prince Edward County and its members is moved for by the appellants-plaintiffs. The ground of the motion is that the Board disbursed public funds to private segregated schools while the right to do so was under consideration by this court. A remedial order requiring the Board to restore these moneys to the County Treasurer is also asked. We grant the motion.

The episode developed in the enforcement of decrees of the District Court reopening the Prince Edward County public schools. The history of the litigation is laid out, ab ovo usque ad mala, in Griffin v. County School Board, 377 U.S. 218, 224 (1964). There the facts of the present controversy are related, commencing with the District Court's injunction dated November 16, 1961. This injunction was issued on the supplemental complaint of the Negro children and parents who were plaintiffs in the District Court and are the appellants here.

Specifically, the injunction commanded the Board and the State not to pay out further funds in tuition grants while the public schools of Prince Edward County remained closed. Allen v. County School Board, 198 F.Supp. 497, 503–504 (E.D.Va. August 25, 1961). The grants had been used for the support of Prince Edward County Educational Foundation, a privately organized corporation conducting a school for white children only. The Court refrained at the time from passing on the County's right to refuse to operate its public schools until the question could be ruled on by the State courts.

With no ruling in the State courts by the summer of 1962, the District Court resumed consideration of the issue, ordered the schools reopened and continued the injunction of tuition grants until the schools were reopened. Allen v. County School Board, 207 F.Supp. 349 (E.D.Va. July 25, 1962). On appeal this decree was stayed by the Court of Appeals awaiting decision in a case then pending in the Supreme Court of Appeals of Virginia. Griffin v. Board of Supervisors, 322 F.2d 332 (4 Cir. 1963). The abstention order was reversed in Griffin v. County School Board, supra, 377 U.S. 218, and the injunction and reopening orders of the District Court approved. Upon receipt of the mandate, the District Court set a hearing for June 17, 1964 to formulate a decree thereon.

This hearing resulted in an order to Prince Edward's Board of Supervisors to appropriate, by June 25, 1964, such moneys as were reasonably necessary to open and maintain the public schools on a nondiscriminatory basis, beginning with the 1964 fall term. In obedience the Board arranged to open the public schools, voted appropriations for them and voted also a larger sum for 1964–65 session tuition grants. On June 29, 1964 the plaintiffs moved the District Court to enjoin permanently the processing of tuition grants and to require the Board to augment the sums available for public schools.

With the schools now open, on July 1, 1964 the State Board of Education authorized the reimbursement of parents, to the extent of the tuition grants enjoined for the 1963–64 session, for the amounts they had paid for their children's school attendance in private schools during that session. Thereupon, plaintiffs obtained a temporary injunction barring the payment retroactively of any tuition grants until the hearing on the motion for the permanent injunction, then set for July 9, 1964. The Board agreed to a permanent injunction of the proposed reimbursement of 1963–64 grants. However, the Court declined to enjoin *future* grants and an appeal was noted on July 17, 1964 to this refusal. On July 28, 1964 the appellants moved this court to accelerate the appeal.

As we were then not in session, the Chief Judge requested the Clerk to ask the Board of Supervisors to stipulate that no tuition grants would be paid pending the appeal. On August 4, 1964 the Clerk transmitted this message to the office of the Attorney General of Virginia. In reply the Clerk was told "during the late evening of August 4," that the Board would not make the stipulation. The next morning the Clerk explained that a satisfactory stipulation would be an agreement that the grants would not be paid before the normal time for processing and paying grants, that is not until after the private schools opened in September 1964.

Meanwhile, during the night of August 4 and early morning of August 5, 1964 the Board met and decided to enlarge substantially the tuition grants for the session 1964–65, and ordered that payment of one-half of the total grants be made before September 1, 1964. That night white parents were notified of the Board's action. Checks totalling about $180,000 were distributed before 9 o'clock A.M. and most of them cashed at that hour, August 5, 1964.

On August 13, 1964 in their appeal, the appellants moved to cite the Board for contempt of this court and for an order restoring the moneys distributed during the night and morning of August 4–5, 1964. After argument of the appeal in regular course, the District Court was directed to enjoin the Board from paying any tuition grants to send children to private schools so long as these schools remained segregated. Griffin v. Board of Supervisors, 339 F.2d 486, 493 (4 Cir. December 2, 1964).

Our decision did not pass upon the contempt motion, but remanded it to the District Court for "further inquiries into the facts surrounding the payments." The District Judge was authorized to consider also the charge of the appellants that the defendants had in effect paid 1963–64 grants retrospectively, by authorizing and paying increased amounts for 1964–65, and thus were in contempt of the District Judge's order of July 9, 1964.

Pursuant to the remittitur, the District Court on February 8, 1965 cited the individual members of the Board of Supervisors to show cause, if any, why they should not be held in contempt of the District Court for failure to comply with its injunction of July 9, 1964 against the retroactive payment of the 1963–64 grants. The rule came on for hearing April 23, 1965, at which time all of the parties in interest were present in person and represented by counsel. In addition to the facts heretofore recited, the District Judge made the following undisputed findings in regard to the questioned events of July and August 1964:

"The Board of Supervisors of Prince Edward County held a meeting on the morning of August 4, 1964 at which time Warren Scott and four of the Negro citizens appeared and filed an unsigned petition bearing ten hundred four typewritten names requesting that the Board of Supervisors allocate additional funds to be used for the purpose of public education. No action was then taken.

"Shortly after adjournment of the Board meeting, Supervisor Jenkins and Supervisor Steck met with a Mr. Taylor and other interested citizens for the purpose of finding a way to pay the '64–'65 tuition grants prior to the time the Court of Appeals could enter an order staying these payments. (It was then known to Mr. Jenkins and to the other members of the group that there had been discussions between Mr. Gray [counsel for the State Superintendent of Public Instruction] and Mr. Dean [Clerk of the Court of Appeals] in re the possibility of the County agreeing not to make any tuition grant payments during the pendency of the appeal.)

"The Commonwealth Attorney and two other members of the Board of Supervisors were then called. Those assembled agreed that if the Board of Supervisors would increase the tuition grants to $310.00 for high school and $290.00 for elementary school and authorize the immediate payment thereof, this could be done before the Court of Appeals could do anything about it.

"The four Board members and the Commonwealth Attorney then went to the home of the chairman of the Board of Supervisors to advise him of what they had in mind and to determine whether or not a special meeting of the Board of Supervisors could be called the next morning for the purpose of expediting the payment of the '64–'65 tuition grants. The chairman, after being advised by the Board's special counsel* and the Commonwealth Attorney that such a resolution on the part of the Board of Supervisors would be legal, called a special meeting of the Board for 8:00 a.m. August 5th. At that meeting the Board passed the resolution which provided that the grants should be paid half on or before September 1, 1964 and half on or before January 1, 1965.

"In the interim, that is, between the meeting at Chairman Vaughan's house and eight o'clock the next morning, Board Member Jenkins and other members of the citizens' committee made arrangements to telephone the parents of the children then attending the Prince Edward School Foundation schools advising them if they came down that night and made application they could get half the tuition money that morning.

"Some twenty or thirty volunteers assisted the secretary of the Board in processing the applications and making out the necessary checks. County bonds were sold in Richmond the next morning to raise the money necessary for the payment of these checks.

"Twelve hundred seventeen tuition grant applications were filed during the night of August 4–5. All of these applications were for the '64–'65 school year. Each applicant was paid one-half of the amount applied for. Most, if not all, of the applicants were children enrolled in the Prince Edward School Foundation schools for the year '64–'65.

"There being no evidence that the money thus paid covered school years prior to '64–'65, the Court concludes that the payments made August 4–5, 1964 were not violative of the order entered herein July 9, 1964. The show cause order issued against the members of the Board of Supervisors February 8, 1965 will be dismissed, and it is SO ORDERED."

That these acts of the Board of Supervisors constituted a contempt of this court is beyond cavil. The Board undertook to put the money then available for tuition grants—and then wholly subject to its orders—beyond its control as well as that of the court. In doing so the Board took upon itself to decide its right to exercise, in favor of the private school, the Board's general power to appropriate public funds. This use of power was, as the Board was acutely aware, an arrogation of this court's responsibility. Obviously, the aim was to thwart the impact of any adverse decree which might ultimately be forthcoming on the appeal. In effect it was a "resistance to its [this court's] lawful writ, process, order, rule, decree, or command." 18 U.S.C. § 401(3). The authorities are quite clear on the point.

The Board would escape the judgment of contempt on the argument that the statute limits the power of the court to violations of orders or decrees then extant. But precedent does not so contract the statute or constrict its intent. Although this court had not issued an injunction against the appropriation of the moneys to tuition grants, the Board knew that if the plaintiffs succeeded this would be its ultimate decree, as in fact it became. That potential decree was thus then within the statute. Furthermore, the appeal was itself a "process" which was alive at the time of the disbursement and was resisted by the disbursement.

* The appellants note in their brief that Mr. Gravatt, the Special Counsel for the Board, in fact requested the Board not to pay the grants.

In Merrimack River Savings Bank v. Clay Center, 219 U.S. 527 (1911), a temporary injunction had been issued by a Federal District Court to prevent the destruction by a municipality of a public utility's poles and wires, located in the city streets under an authorized franchise. The suit was dismissed on jurisdictional grounds. However, for and during an appeal to the Supreme Court, the injunction was continued in force. On this review the dismissal was upheld. But before the mandate of dismissal had been issued or could issue, and in the period allowed for presenting an application for a rehearing, the city cut down the poles, destroyed a large section of the wires and thus put the utility out of business. This conduct was declared to be contempt of the Supreme Court, Justice Lurton saying at 535–536:

"It does not necessarily follow that disobedience of such an injunction, intended only to preserve the status quo pending an appeal, may not be regarded as a contempt of the appellate jurisdiction of this court, which might be rendered nugatory by conduct calculated to remove the subject-matter of the appeal beyond its control, or by its destruction. This we need not decide, since *irrespective of any such injunction actually issued the wilful removal beyond the reach of the court of the subject-matter of the litigation* . . . [on] *appeal* . . . *is, in and of itself, a contempt of the appellate jurisdiction of this court.* . . . Unless this be so, a reversal of the decree would be but a barren victory, since the very result would have been brought about by the lawless act of the defendants which it was the object of the suit to prevent." (Accent added.)

The contempt power declared in the *Merrimack* case was not suggested to be rooted in the inherent power of the Supreme Court rather than in the statute now embodied in 18 U.S.C. § 401(3). Incidentally, the Court has never excluded itself from the statute. Cf. Ex parte Robinson, 19 Wall. 505, 86 U.S. 505, 509 (1873). But *Merrimack* is not now cited to power. It is cited as warranting our finding that the putting of the subject-matter of this litigation beyond our reach was a defiance of this court, an anticipatory resistance to its ultimate orders or process.

That inferior courts have the same contempt power as the Supreme Court exerted in *Merrimack,* and that similar conduct is contempt of the lower courts, were unequivocally enunciated in Lamb v. Cramer, 285 U.S. 217, 219 (1932). There, as in the case now on review, no injunction or order had been issued restraining disposition of the property in suit. Nevertheless, receipt and possession of a part of the res, pendente lite, by a transferee of the defendant-owner was adjudged a contempt of the trial court. The Court had no difficulty in concluding that there was contempt despite the absence of a current restraining order.

While Lamb v. Cramer, supra, did not specifically mention the statute, the Court obviously did not think it barred prosecution of the transferee for contempt. Essentially, the Court followed the statutory terms—"resistance to its [the court's] lawful writ, process, order, rule, decree, or command"—by not limiting its application to an immediately outstanding precept. The anticipated final judgment was not considered to be presently beyond the contemplation of the statute. Indeed, the contrary is implicit in the opinion. The diversion of the res was held to be contumacious because it "tended to defeat any *decree* which the court *might ultimately* make in the cause." (Accent added.)

Civil and not criminal contempt was the gravamen of Lamb v. Cramer and is here too. This was a predominant consideration of the Supreme Court and probably accounts for no advertence to the contempt statute, which seems worded more appropriately for criminal contempt. The omission means nothing, for the primary reasoning of the Court was that the res was in gremio legis and the conveyance of it in part was a disturbance of the constructive possession of the trial court. Whether the decision in Lamb v. Cramer was founded on this conception of judicial custody or on the statute, of which the Court was hardly unaware, is immaterial. Either ground supports our holding that the Board of Supervisors was in contempt. . . .

In our case the disbursement of the moneys seriously impaired the appeal. The suit and the appeal were directed to a specific subject, the Board's right to apply to a certain purpose moneys within its power. The Board assumed the right in utter and wilful disregard of this court's views. As was said in Merrimack River Savings Bank v. Clay Center, and again in Lamb v. Cramer, such conduct constituted contempt although not formally and explicitly under injunction.

We find the Board of Supervisors and its members guilty of civil contempt. Accordingly, the Board and its constituent individuals, namely, W.W. Vaughan, C.W. Gates, H.M. Jenkins, Charles B. Pickett, John C. Steck and H.E. Carwile, Jr., personally and in their own right, will be ordered jointly and severally to restore to the County Treasurer of Prince Edward County, through recapture or otherwise, an amount equal to the disbursements authorized and made by their resolutions of August 4–5, 1964. This cause will be continued for a period of 90 days from this date for report by the Board and its members of what has been done towards compliance with this order, as well as for the passage of such further orders as may appear proper. . . .

HAYNSWORTH, Chief Judge, with whom BOREMAN, Circuit Judge, joins (dissenting):

. . . I am not in disagreement that the conduct of the Supervisors was unconscionable. However, I must disagree with the majority in their interpretation of the power of this Court to adjudge parties in contempt.

It is clear that this Court has an inherent power to punish contempts. It was originally defined by the seventeenth section of the Judiciary Act of 1789 as the power to punish by fine or imprisonment all contempts of authority in any cause or hearing before the Court. But the power has since been limited and redefined by the Act of Congress of March 2, 1831, now 18 U.S.C. § 401. The statute prescribes:

"A court of the United States shall have power to punish by fine or imprisonment, at its discretion, such contempt of its authority, and none other, as—

"(1) Misbehavior of any person in its presence or so near thereto as to obstruct the administration of justice;

"(2) Misbehavior of any of its officers in their official transactions;

"(3) Disobedience or resistance to its lawful writ, process, order, rule, decree, or command."

Considerable doubt was expressed in Ex parte Robinson, 19 Wall. 505, 86 U.S. 505, as to whether this statute could limit the contempt power of the Supreme Court, which derives its existence and powers from the Constitution, and it is obvious from *Merrimack* that the Court has since gone beyond the statute. But *Robinson* [86 U.S. 505] made it clear that there can be no question about the limiting effect the statute has upon the courts of appeals and the district courts. As courts created, not by the Constitution, but, through the power that document vested in Congress, exercise of their inherent contempt powers must be confined to the bounds that Congress has fixed.

Measuring the facts in the present case by the word of Congress, I am unable to find a basis in the statute for a contempt citation here. Phrases (1) and (2) of the statute are not applicable here. The majority finds, under phrase (3), that there was disobedience or resistance to a lawful writ, process, order, rule, decree, or command of this Court. Yet none in fact existed to be disobeyed or resisted. The plaintiffs sought no temporary restraining order or injunction, and none was issued preventing the action taken by the Supervisors. The stipulation requested of the defendants by this court cannot be expanded to fit into any of the things specified in § 401(3).

The word "process," as used in the statute in its context of writs, orders and decrees, obviously means more than the pendency of an appeal or of some other relevant judicial proceeding. It has been traditionally used to encompass such things as a summons, a subpoena, an attachment, a warrant, a mandate, a levy and, generically, other writs and orders. In the context of other orders and writs, "process" can reasonably be understood to mean no more than the sum of more explicit terms, such as "original process," "summary process," "mesne process" and "final process," all of which clearly refer to papers issuing from the court and embodying its commands or judgments, or notice of them. Construed so expansively as the majority's suggestion of equivalence with the pendency of any relevant judicial proceeding, it would entirely contravene the clearly limiting purpose of the congressional act.

Since the suggested construction of the word "process," as used in the statute, is original with the majority, it has never been treated in any reported opinion. The suggestion is inconsistent with the substantially uniform course of decision, however, while the primary theory of the majority is explictly at odds with the precedents in this and other courts.

This court declared itself in Ex parte Buskirk, 4 Cir., 72 F. 14. There it was held not only that an anticipatory, partial avoidance of a potential decree was not a punishable contempt within the confines of the limiting statute; violation of a stipulation made in open court, without which mesne process might, and probably would, have issued, was held not to be. Implicit in the decision is a narrow, literal reading of the word "process."

Buskirk was a party in a judicial proceeding in a district court for a determination of the ownership of a tract of timber. In open court, he entered into a stipulation that none of the timber would be cut until the court had decided the question of ownership. Nevertheless, pending the court's decision, he began cutting the timber and intentionally removed it beyond the reach of the court. This court held because of the statute, "[h]owever reprehensible such conduct . . . may have been . . . it nevertheless did not constitute a contempt to the court or its orders."

My brothers now overrule *Buskirk* without deigning to mention it.

Our own decision in *Buskirk* is not an aberration. It is the exemplar of uniform decision. Four of our sister circuits have embraced the same construction of the statute, and have done so in no uncertain terms. No court of appeals, until now, has toyed with any other reading. . . .

The holding in Lamb v. Cramer, 285 U.S. 217, is of some comfort to the majority, but I find myself unable to accept it as an authoritative interpretation of a statute which the Supreme Court and the lower courts did not even mention.

Lamb was a lawyer, who, assertedly in payment of accrued legal fees, accepted a transfer of some of the property in litigation, upon which the adverse parties had specific liens. Concurrently, a supplemental bill in equity to require his restoration of the property to the custody of the court was filed and a rule issued against Lamb to show cause why he should not return the property to the custody of the court or be held in contempt. Lamb claimed immunity from service, and the district court upheld him in both cases. In both cases, the Court of Appeals for the Fifth Circuit reversed, holding that service upon Lamb was good, and that the supplemental bill in equity and the citation were each appropriate means to require restoration of the property to the control of the court, and that each means might be pursued concurrently. Lamb appealed both cases to the Supreme Court, which affirmed the Fifth Circuit in each.

Clearly, the only purpose of the citation in *Lamb* was the procurement of the return of property in the actual possession and under the control of the attorney, an officer of the court. It was not to punish him or to compel him to replace out of his own funds dissipated assets or money. The most significant thing about the *Lamb* cases, however, is that attention in both the Court of Appeals for the Fifth Circuit and the Supreme Court was focused upon a very different problem. In neither court was there a citation of the statute with which we are concerned or of the cases which had established a uniform interpretation of it. The Supreme Court wrote in Lamb v. Cramer as if the affront had been to itself. One can only suppose that it did so because the statute had not been called to its attention,[6] for the Supreme Court had made it perfectly clear in *Robinson* that the subordinate, statutory federal courts are subject to the statute, and that their powers to punish contempts are effectively limited by it.

If the holding in *Lamb* may be regarded as an interpretation of the unmentioned statute, one may more reasonably conclude that it was an application of § 401(2) rather than § 401(3) with which, alone, we are concerned.[8]

6. It was of little moment in any event, for clearly the court had the power to compel the attorney to restore the property which he had taken with notice not only of the pendency of the proceeding, but with notice as well of the specific liens held by the adverse parties.

8. . . . Twenty-four years after Lamb's case was decided, the Supreme Court held that an enrolled attorney was not an officer of the court within the meaning of § 401(2), Cammer v. United States, 350 U.S. 399, but that was not the prevailing notion when Lamb sought to

The large issue in this case was the constitutionality of a continuing program of disbursement of tuition grants allegedly for the purpose of continued maintenance of segregated school systems. The payment of such tuition grants for one-half year did not abort the appeal or frustrate adjudication of the large issue. It was an unwarranted disbursement of public funds, but the Supervisors, themselves, are not now in possession of any part of those moneys. They are not officers of this court punishable under § 401(2) for official transgressions. What is attempted here is far from what was accomplished in Lamb v. Cramer, and, to me, is inconsistent with an appropriate deference to an explicit congressional command of unquestioned constitutionality which limits our jurisdiction and authority.

I would not quibble with the majority's finding of fact that the conduct of the Supervisors was contemptible, but I do dissent from their conclusion that it was contemptuous and punishable as such, when the conclusion is dependent upon a reading of the statute which relegates it to meaninglessness. Such an unsympathetic construction is particularly inappropriate when the statute was clearly intended to inhibit our authority, has been declared by the Supreme Court to have that effect and has been uniformly construed by the courts of appeals in accordance with that evident intention. Such a statute limiting the jurisdiction of the federal courts is largely enforceable only by the limited courts, themselves. Above all other statutory commands, courts should be scrupulous to conform themselves to jurisdictional statutes, so that they do not appropriate to themselves powers which have been constitutionally withdrawn from them. If we exceed our authority, if we exercise powers we do not possess, the Supreme Court may correct us, but with the swelling volume of demand upon that court, the congressional scheme can be effectively and promptly implemented only if the lower courts take great care to move only within the lawful boundaries of their authority.

Respectfully, I dissent from the conclusion that the Supervisors be held in contempt.

---

1) Berry v. Midtown Service Corp., 104 F.2d 107 (2d Cir. 1939), certiorari granted 308 U.S. 536, dismissed per stipulation of counsel, 308 U.S. 629, grew out of a judgment for plaintiff in a wrongful death action. Defendant was granted a twenty day stay of execution to decide whether to appeal. During the stay, defendant "denuded itself of substantially all its assets by transferring them to various affiliated corporations." 104 F.2d at 109. The court of appeals held that the conduct of the debtor and the transferees was not contempt: under the federal contempt statute a judgment debtor who succeeds in staying execution without posting bond and then, during the period of the stay, transfers all assets does not commit contempt that would lead to a compensatory award for the damages that plaintiff sustained. There was no injunction, the judgment debtor did not stipulate anything, and the stay that restrained the creditor did not implicitly order the debtor to keep

retain the fruits of his malfeasance. See e.g. Ex parte Bradley, 74 U.S. 364, 374; Tanner v. United States, 10 Cir., 62 F. 601; Ex parte Davis, C.C.Fla., 112 F. 139. If the explanation of Lamb's failure, and that of the courts which decided his case, to deal with the statute does not lie in an absence of awareness of it, speculation about the reason for ignoring it must be against a background of the law as it was understood at the time.

enoungh assets to satisfy the judgment. The court construed the federal contempt statute strictly to mean that unless specific property was dissipated "a party must have violated an express court order before he can be punished for contempt. . . . " 104 F.2d at 110. The creditor has two other remedies: she could have demanded a supersedeas bond, and she may yet pursue the assets as fraudulent conveyances.

2) Contrasting *Berry* with *Griffin* helps to focus on questions of judicial power as well as the difference between legal and equitable remedies. Consider several creditors' remedies: a) Could the *Griffin* plaintiffs have used the Virginia Fraudulent Conveyances Act to recover the money? The act protected creditors and "other persons" against conveyances intended to defraud. Prejudgment transfers by defendants are fraudulent if the defendant is left unable to pay a judgment. 1 G. Glen, Fraudulent Conveyances and Preferences § 339 (rev.ed. 1940). b) Could the *Griffin* plaintiffs have sued the people who received the money, charging that they held it as constructive trustees for the proper beneficiaries? Restatement of Restitution § 168(1) (1937). c) Was money had and received plaintiffs' proper remedy? d) One who interferes with property *in custodia legis* may be held in contempt. Converse v. Highway Construction Co., 107 F.2d 127, 132 (6th Cir. 1939). Does the court of appeals's theory in *Griffin* resemble *in custodia legis?* Does compensatory contempt frustrate substantive and procedural limits on creditor process developed to protect debtors and third parties? Does reviewing traditional creditors' theories reveal that only injunctions and contempt are flexible enough to protect constitutional and "new property" entitlements? Does procedural advantage to plaintiffs lurk in state v. federal forum or jury v. judge trial?

3) Did the defendants' disbursements "impair" the appeal? In any event, Rule 62 and Appellate Rule 8 allow losing plaintiffs to seek stays and injunctions pending appeal. Should the court rescue plaintiffs' attorney from failure to seek a stay or an appellate injunction? Was Chief Judge Haynsworth's request to stipulate a "process"? If *Buskirk* had held that breach of a stipulation was not contempt, why did Judge Haynsworth ask the Board to stipulate? How would the court have enforced the stipulation?

4) Judge Wyzanski held that breach of a settlement agreement incorporated by reference into a judgment could not be contempt. "Before either the compensatory or the coercive aspects of a court's civil contempt power can be brought into play first, there must have been disobedience of 'an operative command capable of enforcement' . . . and second, that command, if it is in substance an injunction, must comply with Rule 65(d). . . . Rule 65(d) is no mere extract from a manual of procedural practice. It is a page from the book of liberty . . . . The failure of the equity court to spell out in a decree's text the specific obligations resting upon the defeated litigant is fatal to any contempt proceeding unless we are to disregard the teachings of the masters of our law . . . and the political struggles to limit the powers of the federal judiciary." H.K. Porter Co. v. National Friction Products Corp., 568 F.2d 24 (7th Cir. 1977).

5) Is criminal contempt even more clearly interdicted? How would you feel if the *Griffin* court had sentenced each board member to six months in jail? The court ordered the *Griffin* contemnors to pay money. Was the or-

der preventive? Does *Griffin*'s rule enhance the courts' ability to effect preventive relief? To protect rights not susceptible to compensation with money? The court called its order contempt. Could it just as well be called an injunction? Would characterization as an injunction have avoided some of the difficulty? If so, why did the court choose contempt?

6) J.B. Wall, editor of the Farmville paper, wrote that "restitution was made by the parents and friends of the county." What if, however, the board members had dug in their heels and refused to pay? Could the district judge have imprisoned them to coerce them to pay money? Would it be significant that they did not have the money? Would this coercion imprison them for a civil debt? Would a board member be likely to sell exempt property to buy his way out? Would friends and relatives be likely to pay plaintiffs to bail them out? Generally judges cannot imprison to coerce defendants to do impossible things such as pay money they no longer have. Potter v. Wilson, 609 P.2d 1278 (Okl.1980); Knaus v. Knaus, 387 Pa. 370, 127 A.2d 669 (1956).

7) *Griffin* raises a basic question about injunctions and contempt. Is contempt power inherent? Do judges possess a roving commission to correct injustice? Do statutes, rules, and the idea of limited government constrain judges' ability to use equitable power?

8) One of your editors wrote an article about these problems. Rendleman, Compensatory Contempt to Collect Money, 41 Ohio St.L.J. 625 (1980). Bob Smith's They Closed Their Schools (1965), deals with the Prince Edward County school desegregation between 1951–64 from a journalist's perspective.

III. The Invalid Order: The Collateral Bar Rule

UNITED STATES v. UNITED MINE WORKERS

330 U.S. 258, 67 S.Ct. 677, 91 L.Ed. 884 (1946).

[This case, involves a strike by the United Mine Workers at a time when the United States was in possession of the coal mines. Here are some excerpts from the opinion of Chief Justice Vinson dealing with the duty to obey a void order and which—along with Cox's article—should be read as the backdrop to Walker v. City of Birmingham. These excerpts are from 330 U.S. at 289–95. Parts of the Norris-LaGuardia Act are in the Appendix.]

Although we have held that the Norris-LaGuardia Act did not render injunctive relief beyond the jurisdiction of the District Court, there are alternative grounds which support the power of the District Court to punish violations of its orders as criminal contempt.

Attention must be directed to the situation obtaining on November 18. The Government's complaint sought a declaratory judgment in respect to the right of the defendants to terminate the contract by unilateral action. What amounted to a strike call, effective at midnight on November 20, had been issued by the defendant Lewis as an "official notice." Pending a determination of defendants' right to take this action, the Government requested a temporary restraining order and injunctive relief. The memorandum in support of the restraining order seriously urged the inapplicability of the Norris-La-Guardia Act to the facts of this case, and the power of the District Court to grant the ancillary relief depended in great part upon the resolution of this jurisdictional question. In these circumstances, the District Court unquestionably had the power to issue a restraining order for the purpose of preserving existing conditions pending a decision upon its own jurisdiction.

The temporary restraining order was served on November 18. This was roughly two and one-half days before the strike was to begin. The defendants filed no motion to vacate the order. Rather, they ignored it, and allowed a nationwide coal strike to become an accomplished fact. This Court has used unequivocal language in condemning such conduct, and has in United States v. Shipp, 203 U.S. 563 (1906), provided protection for judicial authority in situations of this kind. In that case this Court had allowed an appeal from a denial of a writ of *habeas corpus* by the Circuit Court of Tennessee. The petition had been filed by Johnson, then confined under a sentence of death imposed by a state court. Pending the appeal, this Court issued an order staying all proceedings against Johnson. However, the prisoner was taken from jail and lynched. Shipp, the sheriff having custody of Johnson, was charged with conspiring with others for the purpose of lynching Johnson, with intent to show contempt for the order of this Court. Shipp denied the jurisdiction of this Court to punish for contempt on the ground that the stay order was issued pending an appeal over which this Court had no jurisdiction because the constitutional questions alleged were frivolous and only a pretense. The Court, through Mr. Justice Holmes, rejected the contention as to want of jurisdiction, and in ordering the contempt to be tried, stated:

"We regard this argument as unsound. It has been held, it is true, that orders made by a court having no jurisdiction to make them may be disregarded without liability to process for contempt. In re Sawyer, 124 U.S. 200; Ex parte Fisk, 113 U.S. 713; Ex parte Rowland, 104 U.S. 604. But even if the Circuit Court had no jurisdiction to entertain Johnson's petition, and if this court had no jurisdiction of the appeal, this court, and this court alone, could decide that such was the law. It and it alone necessarily had jurisdiction to decide whether the case was properly before it. On that question, at least, it was its duty to permit argument and to take the time required for such consideration as it might need. See Mansfield, Coldwater & Lake Michigan Ry. Co. v. Swan, 111 U.S. 379, 387. Until its judgment declining jurisdiction should be announced, it had authority from the necessity of the case to make orders to preserve the existing conditions and the subject of the petition, just as the state court was bound to refrain from further proceedings until the same time. Rev.Stat. § 766; act of March 3, 1893, c. 226, 27 Stat. 751. The fact that the petitioner was entitled to argue his case shows what needs no proof, that the law contemplates the possibility of a decision either way, and therefore must provide for it." 203 U.S. 573.

If this Court did not have jurisdiction to hear the appeal in the *Shipp* case, its order would have had to be vacated. But it was ruled that only the Court itself could determine that question of law. Until it was found that the Court had no jurisdiction, " . . . it had authority from the necessity of the case to make orders to preserve the existing conditions and the subject of the petition . . . ." . . .

In the case before us, the District Court had the power to preserve existing conditions while it was determining its own authority to grant injunctive relief. The defendants, in making their private determination of the law, acted at their peril. Their disobedience is punishable as criminal contempt.

Although a different result would follow were the question of jurisdiction frivolous and not substantial, such contention would be idle here. The applicability of the Norris-LaGuardia Act to the United States in a case such as this had not previously received judicial consideration, and both the language of the Act and its legislative history indicated the substantial nature of the problem with which the District Court was faced.

Proceeding further, we find impressive authority for the proposition that an order issued by a court with jurisdiction over the subject matter and person must be obeyed by the parties until it is reversed by orderly and proper proceedings. This is true without regard even for the constitutionality of the Act under which the order is issued. . . . Violations of an order are punishable as criminal contempt even though the order is set aside on appeal . . . or though the basic action has become moot . . . .

We insist upon the same duty of obedience where, as here, the subject matter of the suit, as well as the parties, was properly before the court; where the elements of federal jurisdiction were clearly shown; and where the authority of the court of first instance to issue an order ancillary to the main suit depended upon a statute, the scope and applicability of which were subject to substantial doubt. The District Court on November 29 affirmatively decided that the Norris-LaGuardia Act was of no force in this case and that injunctive relief was therefore authorized. Orders outstanding or issued after that date were to be obeyed until they expired or were set aside by appropriate proceedings, appellate or otherwise. Convictions for criminal contempt intervening before that time may stand.

It does not follow, of course, that simply because a defendant may be punished for criminal contempt for disobedience of an order later set aside on appeal, the plaintiff in the action may profit by way of a fine imposed in a simultaneous proceeding for civil contempt based upon a violation of the same order. The right to remedial relief falls with an injunction which events prove was erroneously issued . . . and *a fortiori* when the injunction or restraining order was beyond the jurisdiction of the court. Nor does the reason underlying United States v. Shipp, supra, compel a different result. If the Norris-LaGuardia Act were applicable in this case, the conviction for civil contempt would be reversed in its entirety.

Assuming, then, that the Norris-LaGuardia Act applied to this case and prohibited injunctive relief at the request of the United States, we would set aside the preliminary injunction of December 4 and the judgment for civil contempt; but we would, subject to any infirmities in the contempt proceedings or in the fines imposed, affirm the judgments for criminal contempt as validly punishing violations of an order then outstanding and unreversed.

H. B. Cox, THE VOID ORDER AND THE DUTY TO OBEY

16 U.Chi.L.Rev. 86 (1948) (Copyright 1948 University of Chicago Law Review).

It is familiar law that the duty of a litigant to obey a temporary restraining order or a temporary injunction does not always depend upon the validity of the court's command. Even though the order or injunction may ultimately be held erroneous by the courts, the order or injunction may be entitled to obedience until it is reversed or set aside on appeal, and disobedience of its provisions in the interim may be punished in a proceeding for criminal contempt.

In what circumstances does an invalid order or temporary injunction issued by a federal court possess this kind of vitality pendente lite? Discussion of this question may well begin by reference to the general principle that courts and commentators have sometimes said is applicable. This principle distinguishes between restraining orders and injunctions that are void because made without jurisdiction, on the one hand, and orders and injunctions that are merely improvident, irregular, or erroneous, on the other. If the court issuing the restraining order or injunction does not have jurisdiction, the order or injunction is said to be void, and to be a nullity; it may be disregarded with impunity. But if the court has jurisdiction over the persons of the litigants and of the subject matter of the litigation, the restraining order or injunction, no matter how improvident or erroneous it may be, must be obeyed until reversed on appeal, and the litigant who disobeys the order may be punished for contempt. The federal courts that have stated this principle have done so without reference to the language of Section [401] of the Judicial Code, the statutory source of the power of the federal courts to punish for contempt. Since 1831 that statute has provided that the authority of the federal courts to punish those who disobey or resist orders of the courts shall extend only to disobedience or resistance "to any lawful writ, process, order, rule, decree or command." To reconcile the principle with the statute, it is necessary to conclude that a restraining order or an injunction, even though ultimately held invalid, is nevertheless "lawful" within the meaning of the statutory language until reversed, provided that the order or the injunction has been issued by a court that has jurisdiction of the person and of the subject matter.

[Mr. Cox then discussed the case law leading up to *Mine Workers,* emphasizing how the concept of jurisdiction is often manipulated.]

The tendency of the Supreme Court in the past to expand the concept of jurisdiction when necessary to excuse litigants from the duty of obeying an erroneous order was also apparent in In re Sawyer. In that case the Supreme Court held that a lower federal court lacked jurisdiction to entertain a bill in equity to restrain the mayor and certain members of the city council of Lincoln, Nebraska from removing a police judge of the city on charges of malfeasance. The Supreme Court concluded that this absence of jurisdiction rendered the lower court's temporary restraining order void. Consequently, the defendants, who had been convicted of contempt for having violated the restraining order, were discharged upon a writ of habeas corpus.

The jurisdiction of the lower federal court had been invoked on the ground that the defendants' activities violated rights of the plaintiff secured to him by the Constitution of the United States. But the Supreme Court did not hold that the lower court lacked jurisdiction because no substantial constitutional question was involved. Instead, the Court based its conclusion as to the lower court's absence of authority to entertain the litigation primarily on the premise that a court of equity has no jurisdiction over the appointment or removal of public officers, the power to determine title to a public office resting exclusively in the courts of law. In other words, the Supreme Court decided that the cause of action asserted in the lower court was not the type of suit of which the courts of equity historically took cognizance; that is to say, that there was a lack of "equity jurisdiction."

The question raised by the decision in In re Sawyer is whether "equity jurisdiction" should be regarded as the kind of jurisdiction whose absence makes an order void. Originally the term "equity jurisdiction" doubtless referred to the category of controversies that a court of equity was authorized to decide. So long as the principles of equity were administered by separate courts, questions of equity jurisdiction were jurisdictional questions in the strict sense; if the cause of action was not of a kind that fell within the province of the chancellor, a court of equity had no power to decide the cause. But the abolition of the distinction between courts of law and courts of equity and the establishment of a single system of courts authorized to administer both the principles of law and the principles of equity tended to give the term "equity jurisdiction" a somewhat different meaning. In the case of a single court authorized to apply the principles of both law and equity, the statement that there is lack of "equity jurisdiction" does not necessarily mean that the court lacks power to adjudicate the controversy. The statement is usually intended to mean merely that under the historic principles of equity the plaintiff is not entitled to the relief he seeks. Thus, today the concept of equity jurisdiction is one that relates rather to the question of the merits of a controversy than to the basic power of the court to decide the case. . . .

It may be useful to pause at this point to inquire whether there is any explanation for the Supreme Court's willingness in such cases as . . . In re Sawyer to regard infirmities as jurisdictional when the better view would seem to have been that although the orders involved were erroneous, they were not void. It has been suggested that the Court's decisions in these cases were influenced by the fact that when the cases were decided a person convicted of criminal contempt could obtain appellate review only by the writ of habeas corpus. It was well settled at the time of these decisions that the writ of habeas corpus would not be used as a writ of error to review the decisions of lower courts on the merits, but that it would be used only to reach those exercises of authority which were void because in excess of jurisdiction. Consequently, if the Court wished to give the petitioner, in such cases as . . . In re Sawyer, any relief whatever, the Court was forced to take the position that the invalidity of the order that had been disobeyed was jurisdictional in character. . . .

The decision in the *Shipp* case can hardly be regarded as an unqualified application of the doctrine of jurisdiction to determine jurisdiction. To the extent that it embodies or applies that notion at all, it deals with a special kind of jurisdiction. In that case the order that was vindicated was not an order made by the lower federal court but an order made by the Supreme Court in aid of its own appellate jurisdiction. The Supreme Court held, in effect, that it had appellate jurisdiction regardless of the question of the jurisdiction of the lower court, and that, therefore, the order that it had made in aid of its own jurisdiction was not void. The conclusion that the Supreme Court had appellate jurisdiction regardless of the jurisdiction of the lower court was consistent with decisions of the Supreme Court both before and after In re Shipp.

One other aspect of In re Shipp deserves comment. Doubtless the petitioners in the *Shipp* case had violated that part of the order of the Supreme Court that directed "that . . . custody of said appellant be retained pending this appeal." But the gravamen of the charge against Shipp and the other petitioners was not merely that Shipp had failed to retain custody of the prisoner, but that Shipp and the others had conspired to destroy Johnson so that the appellate power of the Supreme Court was rendered wholly nugatory. It seems quite possible that even in the absence of the order petitioners could have been punished for contempt of court. [Mr. Cox cited Merrimack River Savings Bank v. Clay Center, 219 U.S. 527, 535–36 (1911).] The destruction of the subject matter of litigation is a direct, violent and irrevocable interference with the judicial process. It would not be unreasonable to say that the criminality of that kind of contempt does not depend upon the existence of a court order forbidding the destruction. . . .

One of the fundamental issues in . . . [*United Mine Workers*] was whether the restraining order and the temporary injunction, which the union and its president were charged with disobeying, had been issued in violation of the provisions of the Norris-LaGuardia Act. It seems appropriate to begin the discussion of the case by considering whether the limitations imposed upon the courts by the Norris-LaGuardia Act are truly jurisdictional in the sense that an order issued in disregard of the limitations should be regarded as void.

The Norris-LaGuardia Act does not deprive the federal courts of jurisdiction over cases involving labor disputes. It does not deprive the federal courts of power to issue injunctions in cases involving labor disputes. Speaking generally, the effect of the statute may be described in the following terms: In any case in which the statute applies, two consequences follow: 1) The federal courts are forbidden to grant injunctions that restrain the commission of certain specified acts. 2) The courts are forbidden to grant injunctions except in compliance with certain procedural requirements with respect to the taking of evidence in open court, notice and the making of appropriate findings of fact, etc.

In a number of cases arising before the *Mine Workers* case, the Supreme Court referred to the Norris-LaGuardia Act as a statute intended to limit and to restrict the exercise of the equitable powers of the federal courts. . . .

It has already been pointed out that the decisions of the Supreme Court dealing with the concept of equity jurisdiction support the conclusion that questions about the existence of equity jurisdiction are not the kind of jurisdictional questions that, if erroneously decided, make a judicial order void. If this is true of the existence of equity jurisdiction, why should it not be equally true of questions that arise with respect to limitations on the exercise of equitable jurisdiction once it is found to exist? These considerations suggest that had the Supreme Court chosen to do so, it might properly have rested its decision in the *Mine Workers* case on the ground that the Norris-LaGuardia Act is not an act affecting the basic jurisdiction of the courts; that, at most, it merely limits the exercise of equitable jurisdiction, and that the questions that arise with respect to its application are not the kind of jurisdictional questions that, if erroneously decided, make an order void.

At least two objections might be made to this suggestion. In the first place, it might be said that the statute itself speaks in terms of jurisdiction—that the important prohibitory sections of the statute begin: "No Court of the United States shall have jurisdiction . . . ." Because of this explicit command, it could be argued that the Court was bound to decide that infirmities caused by disregard of the statute were truly jurisdictional in character.

But the use of the word "jurisdiction" in the statute hardly seems conclusive. . . . Justice Holmes pointed out that words of a statute that "might seem to affect the power of the court" may merely "fix the law by which the court should decide." In any event, the word "jurisdiction" is used in the Norris-LaGuardia Act in a context that shows that the word refers to "equity jurisdiction." Accordingly, even if the word is given full weight, its use does not require the conclusion that a restraining order or preliminary injunction issued in regard of the Act's requirements is void, because the better view would seem to be, as pointed out above, that even total absence of equity jurisdiction does not make a judicial order void.

In the second place, it may be argued that, apart from the use of the word "jurisdiction" in the statute, the prohibitions of the Norris-LaGuardia Act are so explicit and unqualified that it is obvious that Congress intended any restraining order or preliminary injunction issued in disregard of those prohibitions to be void. But the fact that the command of the statute is explicit and unqualified is not in itself conclusive of the point now under consideration. . . .

Whatever merit may exist in the view of the statute just suggested, it is fairly clear that the view was not adopted by the Supreme Court in the *Mine Workers* case. True enough, there are passages in the opinion of Chief Justice Vinson that suggest the district court had jurisdiction even if the Norris-LaGuardia Act applied. For example, the Chief Justice said: "[W]e find impressive authority for the proposition that an order issued by a court with jurisdiction over the subject matter and person must be obeyed by the parties until it is reversed by orderly and proper proceedings." In addition, he continued, "We insist upon the same duty of obedience where, as here, the subject matter of the suit, as well as the parties, was properly before the court; where the elements of federal jurisdiction were clearly shown; and where the authority of the court of first instance to issue an order ancillary to the main suit depended upon a statute, the scope and applicability of which were subject to substantial doubt."

But other passages in the Chief Justice's opinion are inconsistent with the view that no truly jurisdictional question was involved. Thus, Chief Justice Vinson qualified the scope of his decision by this assertion: "Although a different result would follow were the question of jurisdiction frivolous and not substantial such contention would be idle here." This statement seems to imply that the true issue in the case was one of jurisdiction and not merely whether the court below had improperly issued an order ancillary to the main suit. In another passage of his opinion, the Chief Justice, after describing the circumstances in which the district court issued the restraining order, declared: "In these circumstances, the District Court unquestionably had the power to issue a restraining order for the purpose of preserving existing conditions pending a decision upon its own jurisdiction." In this sentence the Chief Justice appears to be applying the doctrine of jurisdiction to determine jurisdiction.

If, in fact, the application of the Norris-LaGuardia Act did not raise a truly jurisdictional question, that is to say, if the district court had jurisdiction of the subject matter notwithstanding any error it may have made in construing the Norris-LaGuardia Act, then both the non-frivolous character of the issue involved and the notion of jurisdiction to determine jurisdiction would be beside the point. The references to both of these matters in the opinion of the Chief Justice make it difficult to determine whether he believed that the issue in the case related to the jurisdiction of the district court, in the strict sense of the word "jurisdiction," or that the issue related only to the authority of that court to issue an ancillary order in a case in which it had jurisdiction.

The opinion of Justice Frankfurter, whose concurrence was necessary to establish a majority of the Court, raises less doubt. It seems clear that Justice Frankfurter was prepared to hold that in some situations an injunction issued in violation of the provisions of the Norris-LaGuardia Act would be void and need not be obeyed pendente lite.[74] Justice Frankfurter appears to have reached the conclusion that the defendants were bound to obey the temporary restraining order and the preliminary injunction by the following reasoning: The question whether the Norris-LaGuardia Act applied to the dispute between the defendants and the United States raised a "complicated and novel" issue; the district court had power to decide whether the case was properly before it, and therefore it could make appropriate orders "to afford the necessary time for fair consideration and decision while existing conditions were preserved. . . . To say that the authority of the Court may be flouted during the time necessary to decide is to reject the requirements of the judicial process." In his opinion Justice Frankfurter discussed at greater length than did the Chief Justice the non-frivolous character of the issue which had been raised with respect to the authority of the district court.

This is an appropriate point to comment briefly on the importance attached by the majority of the Court in the *Mine Workers* case to the conclusion that the assertion of authority by the district court was not frivolous. Little in the older decisions of the Supreme Court suggests that the question of the duty to obey pendente lite an invalid restraining order turns on whether the assertion of jurisdiction is frivolous. . . .

74. For example, Justice Frankfurter said, "Thus, the explicit withdrawal from federal district courts of the power to issue injunctions in an ordinary labor dispute between a private employer and his employees cannot be defeated, and an existing right to strike thereby impaired, by pretending to entertain a suit for such an injunction in order to decide whether the court has jurisdiction. In such a case, a judge would not be acting as a court. He would be a pretender to, not a wielder of, judicial power."

Whatever may be said about the historical basis of the doctrine of the non-frivolous order, the decision in the *Mine Workers* case has given that doctrine a stature that it has not heretofore possessed. Henceforth, a litigant who wishes to disregard a temporary restraining order must be sure not only that the order was made without jurisdiction but also that the assertion of jurisdiction is frivolous. It is difficult to say what degree of frivolity will be required before the order made without jurisdiction may safely be disregarded. . . .

The decision in the *Mine Workers* case, read against the background of the earlier decisions, raises the question whether the time has come, at least so far as concerns jurisdiction of subject matter, to discard the distinction between orders void because made without jurisdiction and merely erroneous orders, and to adopt instead a different test to determine whether an erroneous order should be obeyed pendente lite. This suggestion is restricted to jurisdiction of the subject matter for two reasons (although there may be others of equal weight):

1. Although the existence of jurisdiction over the person is sometimes a difficult question, in general the concept of jurisdiction of the person is more certain in its outline and content and easier of application to particular situations than is the concept of jurisdiction of subject matter.

2. The relationship between jurisdiction and the duty to obey seems more direct in the case of an order made without jurisdiction of the person than it is in the case of an order made without jurisdiction of the subject matter. The remark of Justice Holmes that "the foundation of jurisdiction is physical power" applies to jurisdiction over the person in a sense in which it does not apply to jurisdiction of the subject matter. It appears not unreasonable to say that an order made by a court that has no physical power over the litigant is an order that need not be obeyed. Certain practical considerations may apply when a court lacks jurisdiction of the person that may not be present if the court lacks jurisdiction of the subject matter: An order made without jurisdiction of the person may be an order made without notice to the litigant or issued in circumstances in which it is difficult, or impossible, for the litigant to contest the order. Attempts to contest the validity of orders made without jurisdiction of the person sometimes raise questions of consent and waiver that are not raised by attempts to contest jurisdiction over the subject matter.

The suggestion that the existence of jurisdiction of the subject matter should be discarded as a test of the duty of the litigant to obey an invalid order is not intended to lead to the conclusion that the litigant should obey, pendente lite, every invalid restraining order, no matter what its character or effect may be, made by a court having jurisdiction of the litigant's person. There will be cases in which the litigant should be free to disregard an invalid restraining order. But the circumstances that should be regarded as justifying that disobedience have no necessary relevance to the distinction between orders void because made without jurisdiction of the subject matter and orders that are merely erroneous.

In determining whether a litigant should be required to obey, pendente lite, a restraining order or temporary injunction that the litigant believes is invalid because the court issuing it did not have jurisdiction of the subject matter, two points are of substantial importance:

1. As long as the litigant has an adequate opportunity to seek appellate review of the order's validity in the normal way, there seems to be no reason to permit him to resort to disobedience as a means of testing the order's validity.[86] It seems reasonable, therefore, to say that unless the litigant has exhausted his opportunities (by the prompt filing of an appeal and by the application for stays, pending appeal) to have the order reviewed in the usual way, he has no standing to insist upon testing the order's validity by disobedience. Situations may arise, however, in which there is no right of appeal. For example, there is serious doubt whether the provisions of the Judicial Code permit an appeal to a circuit court of appeals from an order of a district court granting a temporary restraining order as distinguished from a preliminary injunction.

It may well be, therefore, that circumstances may exist in which a litigant, either because he has no right of appeal or because he has not been able to obtain a stay pending appeal, is faced with a choice between immediate obedience to a restraining order that he believes to be invalid or defiance of the order. In those situations, the second consideration comes into play.

2. The second consideration deals with the effect that obedience will have upon the litigant's position and rights. If the temporary restraining order or the preliminary injunction in effect decides the only question involved in litigation and thus really disposes of the merits of the case, it is the kind of order that a litigant should not be compelled to obey pending its review.

On the other hand, if the order injures or affects the litigant only in an abstract or theoretical sense, then no matter how erroneous or improper it may be, there is no good reason for the litigant not to obey the order while the order is being reviewed in the usual way. Thus, if an order prohibits the commission of certain acts by the litigant and the postponement of the commission of those acts pending review will not, in fact, seriously prejudice the litigant, the rule suggested would require the litigant to obey even though his rights, considered in the abstract, may be infringed by the order and even though he may be to some extent inconvenienced.

In instances in which the order requires the litigant to take affirmative action, the question to be decided is whether the affirmative action will, in fact, irrevocably injure or prejudice the litigant's rights. The possibility of making this showing will always presumably be greater in the case of an affirmative order than it will be in the case of an order that is merely prohibitory. But even in the case of the affirmative order, there may well be instances in which the action required can be recalled or undone after the invalidity of the order has been established, without real prejudice to the litigant.[91]

86. In the *Mine Workers* case the defendants made no attempt to obtain appellate review of the temporary restraining order. They did not move to vacate that order. The first motion which the defendants made in the case was a motion made on November 26, 1946 to discharge and to vacate the rule which had previously issued requiring them to show cause why they should not be punished for contempt. Apparently, however, their counsel had appeared on the previous day, pursuant to the order to show cause, and denied the jurisdiction of the court.

91. I venture to think that this was the situation in the *Mine Workers* case. In all probability the union would not have been seriously prejudiced if the no-

Thus, if the injury that will be inflicted upon the litigant's interest by compliance with the order believed to be invalid will be substantial and irreparable, then and only then should disobedience of the order be immune from punishment in the event that the litigant ultimately establishes the invalidity of the order.

In short, I suggest that the general rule should be that it is the duty of the litigant to obey all orders made by a court having jurisdiction of his person, pendente lite, regardless of the decision that is made with respect to the ultimate validity of those orders, with this exception: If the litigant has exhausted all the normal methods of appellate review and if obedience to the order will substantially and irrevocably injure legal interests of the litigant that are not remote and abstract in character, then the litigant should be entitled to take his chance on the invalidity of the order. If he prevails in his attack upon its validity, he should be immune from punishment for contempt. This rule should be applied in those cases in which the temporary order is merely erroneous as well as those cases in which it is asserted to have been made without jurisdiction. The fact that under the traditional rule a litigant, who is prohibited from taking action or required to take action by an order that is merely erroneous and not void because without jurisdiction, has no remedy even though he has no opportunity for appellate review, is an anomaly that should be removed from the law. As indicated earlier in this article, the unfairness of this result may well have induced the Supreme Court in some cases in the past to treat infirmities as jurisdictional when strictly they should not have been so regarded.

In conclusion, it will be helpful to refer briefly to arguments that may be made for and against the proposal advanced:

In support of the proposal, it can be said that, in general, public policy looks with favor upon the principle that litigants should comply with orders issued by the courts until those orders are reversed or set aside by normal appellate procedures. If there are to be exceptions to that public policy, the exceptions should be stated in terms that are, as far as possible, free from ambiguity and that have some relevance to the practical considerations that may justify disobedience in particular situations. The concept of jurisdiction of the subject matter is so elusive and has been treated with so much inconsistency by the courts that it is both unsatisfactory and difficult of application to particular situations if used as a test of the duty to obey. It is not a test having any necessary relevance to the reasons that may justify disobedience in particular situations.

It may be objected, however, that the two considerations that have been suggested as tests of the right to disobey an invalid order are just as vague and unsatisfactory as absence of jurisdiction of the subject matter. But the question of whether the litigant has exhausted his normal appellate remedies is one that can usually be determined without difficulty. A judgment about the effect which obedience to the order will have upon the litigant's rights may be difficult in particular situations. But surely it is less difficult to make this decision than it is to decide (1) whether the court issuing the order had

tice of termination of the contract had been suspended pending determination of the right to terminate the contract, assuming, of course, as I think it is proper to assume, that speedy review of that question would have been possible.

jurisdiction of the subject matter and (2) whether the assertion of jurisdiction is so irrational that it may be disregarded as frivolous.

The procedural and substantive peculiarities of a proceeding for criminal contempt and the confusion between civil and criminal contempt that to some extent still exists make the contempt proceeding an inappropriate device for reviewing the validity of judicial orders. This is an additional reason for restricting any exception to the general principle that a litigant must seek review of any erroneous orders by the normal appellate procedure within the narrowest compass consistent with the public interest.

It may be said that to do away with the distinction between orders void because made without jurisdiction and those that are merely erroneous will remove an important restraint on the usurpation of power by the courts. There is weight in this objection. But if the commands of Congress and the lessons of the earlier decisions are clear, it may be assumed that the courts will stay within the limits of their authority. In doubtful cases, the courts may exceed their authority. If they do so, under the rule suggested, their orders may have to be obeyed until reversed. But that seems to be the law under the *Mine Workers* case. Certainly it would be a rash litigant today who would conclude that he could safely disregard an order made in disregard of some statutory limitation on the powers of a federal court so long as there was any possible ground for argument that the assertion of the authority was not frivolous. As matters now stand, the doctrine of the order that is void because made without jurisdiction is rather an enigma for the litigant than a limitation on the courts.

---

1) One aspect of the *Mine Workers* problem was felicitously named the bootstrap principle in Note, Res Judicata and Jurisdiction: The Bootstrap Doctrine, 53 Harv.L.Rev. 652 (1940). The bootstrap doctrine allows a judge to raise himself to jurisdiction as if by tugging on his bootstraps. His decision that the court possesses jurisdiction is res judicata. A judge without jurisdiction may decide jurisdiction incorrectly and confer jurisdiction on the court: the judge validates a void judgment by deciding jurisdiction incorrectly. The conflict between fairness and finality has generated an extensive and thoughtful literature. See, in addition to Mr. Cox's article, Z. Chafee, Some Problems of Equity 296–380 (1950); Currie, Full Faith and Credit, Chiefly to Judgments: A Role for Congress, 1964 Sup.Ct.Rev. 89; Dobbs, Beyond Bootstrap: Foreclosing the Issue of Subject-Matter Jurisdiction Before Final Judgment, 51 Minn.L.Rev. 491 (1967); Dobbs, The Decline of Jurisdiction by Consent, 40 N.C.L.Rev. 49 (1961); Dobbs, Trial Court Error as an Excess of Jurisdiction, 43 Tex.L.Rev. 854 (1965); Dobbs, The Validation of Void Judgments: The Bootstrap Principle (pts. 1 & 2), 53 Va.L.Rev. 1003, 1020–24; 1241 (1967); Hazard, Revisiting the Second Restatement of Judgments: Issue Preclusion and Related Problems, 66 Cornell L.Rev. 564, 586–91 (1981); Moore, Collateral Attack on Subject Matter Jurisdiction: A Critique of the Restatement (Second) of Judgments, 66 Cornell L.Rev. 534 (1981); Rendleman, More on Void Orders, 7 Ga.L.Rev. 246, 251–55 (1973); Watt, The Divine Right of Government by Judiciary, 14 U.Chi.L. Rev. 409 (1947); Note, Filling the Void: Judicial Power and Jurisdictional Attacks on Judgments, 87 Yale L.J. 164, 202–05 (1977). Most bootstrap

decisions give the first suit res judicata effect, but the reader should be aware that *Mine Workers* refines the defendant's calculus with more than merely litigative constraints.

2) Contemporary labor injunctions are of three general types: (a) Injunctions against "illegal" strikes by government employees, see United States v. Professional Air Traffic Controllers, 653 F.2d 1134 (7th Cir. 1981), certiorari denied 454 U.S. 1083; Peters v. South Chicago Community Hospital, 44 Ill.2d 22, 253 N.E.2d 375 (1969); Board of Education v. Redding, 32 Ill.2d 567, 207 N.E.2d 427 (1965); School Committee v. Westerly Teachers Association, 111 R.I. 96, 299 A.2d 441 (1973). (b) Injunctions against mass picketing and violence. See Youngdahl v. Rainfair, 355 U.S. 131 (1957); Eads Coal Co. v. United Mine Workers of America District No. 12, 131 Ill. App.2d 1082, 269 N.E.2d 359 (1971); United Steelworkers of America, Local 8417 v. Newport News Shipbuilding and Dry Dock Co., 220 Va. 547, 260 S.E.2d 222 (1979). (c) Injunctions against strikes that violate agreements to arbitrate disputes. See Boys Markets, Inc. v. Retail Clerks Union, 398 U.S. 235 (1970); Bituminous Coal Operators' Association, Inc. v. International Union, United Mine Workers of America, 585 F.2d 586 (3d Cir. 1978); Latrobe Steel Co. v. United Steelworkers of America, 545 F.2d 1336 (3d Cir. 1976).

F. Frankfurter & N. Green, The Labor Injunction (1930), was a brief for the Norris-LaGuardia Act, which Congress passed in 1932. The book is nevertheless still worth reading. The Act is codified at 29 U.S.C. § 101–115. Shatz, Picketing Injunctions in California: A Study of the Role of the Courts in Farm Labor Disputes, 28 Hastings L.J. 801 (1977), is a contemporary chronicle.

WALKER v. CITY OF BIRMINGHAM

388 U.S. 307, 87 S.Ct. 1824, 18 L.Ed.2d 1210 (1967).

Justice STEWART delivered the opinion of the Court.

On Wednesday, April 10, 1963, officials of Birmingham, Alabama, filed a bill of complaint in a state circuit court asking for injunctive relief against 139 individuals and two organizations. The bill and accompanying affidavits stated that during the preceding seven days:

"[R]espondents [had] sponsored and/or participated in and/or conspired to commit and/or to encourage and/or to participate in certain movements, plans or projects commonly called 'sit-in' demonstrations, 'kneel-in' demonstrations, mass street parades, trespasses on private property after being warned to leave the premises by the owners of said property, congregating in mobs upon the public streets and other public places, unlawfully picketing private places of business in the City of Birmingham, Alabama; violation of numerous ordinances and statutes of the City of Birmingham and State of Alabama . . . ."

It was alleged that this conduct was "calculated to provoke breaches of the peace," "threaten[ed] the safety, peace and tranquility of the City," and placed "an undue burden and strain upon the manpower of the Police Department."

The bill stated that these infractions of the law were expected to continue and would "lead to further imminent danger to the lives, safety, peace, tranquility and general welfare of the people of the City of Brimingham," and that the "remedy by law [was] inadequate." The circuit judge granted a temporary injunction as prayed in the bill, enjoining the petitioners from, among other things, participating in or encouraging mass street parades or mass processions without a permit as required by a Birmingham ordinance.[1]

Five of the eight petitioners were served with copies of the writ early the next morning. Several hours later four of them held a press conference. There a statement was distributed, declaring their intention to disobey the injunction because it was "raw tyranny under the guise of maintaining law and order."[2] At this press conference one of the petitioners stated: "That they had respect for the Federal Courts, or Federal Injunctions, but in the past the State Courts had favored local law enforcement, and if the police couldn't handle it, the mob would."

That night a meeting took place at which one of the petitioners announced that "[i]njunction or no injunction we are going to march tomorrow." The next afternoon, Good Friday, a large crowd gathered in the vicinity of Sixteenth Street and Sixth Avenue North in Birmingham. A group of about 50 or 60 proceeded to parade along the sidewalk while a crowd of 1,000 to 1,500 onlookers stood by, "clapping, and hollering, and [w]hooping." Some of the crowd followed the marchers and spilled out into the street. At least three of the petitioners participated in this March.

Meetings sponsored by some of the petitioners were held that night and the following night, where calls for volunteers to "walk" and go to jail were made. On Easter Sunday, April 14, a crowd of between 1,500 and 2,000 people congregated in the midafternoon in the vicinity of Seventh Avenue and Eleventh Street North in Birmingham. One of the petitioners was seen organizing members of the crowd in formation. A group of about 50, headed by three other petitioners, started down the sidewalk two abreast. At least one other petitioner was among the marchers. Some 300 or 400 people

1. The text of the injunction is reproduced as Appendix A to this opinion.

The Birmingham parade ordinance, § 1159 of the Birmingham City Code, provides that:

"It shall be unlawful to organize or hold, or to assist in organizing or holding, or to take part or participate in, any parade or procession or other public demonstration on the streets or other public ways of the city, unless a permit therefor has been secured from the commission.

"To secure such permit, written application shall be made to the commission, setting forth the probable number of persons, vehicles and animals which will be engaged in such parade, procession or other public demonstration, the purpose for which it is to be held or had, and the streets or other public ways over, along or in which it is desired to have or hold such parade, procession or other public demonstration. The commission shall grant a written permit for such parade, procession or other public demonstration, prescribing the streets or other public ways which may be used therefor, unless in its judgment the public welfare, peace, safety, health, decency, good order, morals or convenience require that it be refused. It shall be unlawful to use for such purposes any other streets or public ways than those set out in said permit.

"The two preceding paragraphs, however, shall not apply to funeral processions."

2. The full [text of Dr. King's speech] is reproduced as Appendix B to this opinion.

from among the onlookers followed in a crowd that occupied the entire width of the street and overflowed onto the sidewalks. Violence occurred. Members of the crowd threw rocks that injured a newspaperman and damaged a police motorcyle.

The next day the city officials who had requested the injunction applied to the state circuit court for an order to show cause why the petitioners should not be held in contempt for violating it. At the ensuing hearing the petitioners sought to attack the constitutionality of the injunction on the ground that it was vague and overbroad, and restrained free speech. They also sought to attack the Birmingham parade ordinance upon similar grounds, and upon the further ground that the ordinance had previously been administered in an arbitrary and discriminatory manner.

The circuit judge refused to consider any of these contentions, pointing out that there had been neither a motion to dissolve the injunction, nor an effort to comply with it by applying for a permit from the city commission before engaging in the Good Friday and Easter Sunday parades. Consequently, the court held that the only issues before it were whether it had jurisdiction to issue the temporary injunction, and whether thereafter the petitioners had knowingly violated it. Upon these issues the court found against the petitioners, and imposed upon each of them a sentence of five days in jail and a $50 fine, in accord with an Alabama statute.[3]

The Supreme Court of Alabama affirmed.[4] That court, too, declined to consider the petitioners' constitutional attacks upon the injunction and the underlying Birmingham parade ordinance:

"It is to be remembered that petitioners are charged with violating a temporary injunction. We are not reviewing a denial of a motion to dissolve or discharge a temporary injunction. Petitioners did not file any motion to vacate the temporary injunction until after the Friday and Sunday parades. In-

3. "The circuit court, or judges thereof when exercising equity jurisdiction and powers may punish for contempt by fine not exceeding fifty dollars, and by imprisonment, not exceeding five days, one or both." Ala.Code, Tit. 13, § 143. See also id., §§ 4–5, 126.

The circuit court dismissed the contempt proceedings against several individuals on grounds of insufficient evidence.

Those petitioners who participated in April 11 press conference contend that the circuit court improperly relied on this incident in finding them guilty of contempt, claiming that they were engaged in constitutionally protected free speech. We find no indication that the court considered the incident for any purpose other than the legitimate one of establishing that the participating petitioners' subsequent violation of the injunction by parading without a permit was willful and deliberate.

4. The Alabama Supreme Court quashed the conviction of one defendant because of insufficient proof that he knew of the injunction before violating it, and the convictions of two others because there was no showing that they had disobeyed the order. 279 Ala. 53, 64, 181 So.2d 493, 504.

Two of the petitioners here claim that there was a complete dearth of evidence to establish that they had knowledge of the injunction before violating it, and that their convictions are therefore constitutionally defective under the principle of Thompson v. Louisville, 362 U.S. 199. The Alabama Supreme Court's recitation of the evidence on this issue, which is supported by the record, plainly shows this claim is without foundation. It is, of course, a familiar doctrine that proof of the elements of criminal contempt may be established by circumstantial evidence. Bullock v. United States, 265 F.2d 683, cert. denied sub nom. Kasper v. United States, 360 U.S. 932.

stead, petitioners deliberately defied the order of the court and did engage in and incite others to engage in mass street parades without a permit. . . .

"We hold that the circuit court had the duty and authority, in the first instance, to determine the validity of the ordinance, and, until the decision of the circuit court is reversed for error by orderly review, either by the circuit court or a higher court, the orders of the circuit court based on its decision are to be respected and disobedience of them is contempt of its lawful authority, to be punished. Howat v. State of Kansas, 258 U.S. 181." 279 Ala. 53, 60, 62–63, 181 So.2d 493, 500, 502.

Howat v. Kansas, 258 U.S. 181, was decided by this Court almost 50 years ago. That was a case in which people had been punished by a Kansas trial court for refusing to obey an antistrike injunction issued under the state industrial relations act. They had claimed a right to disobey the court's order upon the ground that the state statute and the injunction based upon it were invalid under the Federal Constitution. The Supreme Court of Kansas had affirmed the judgment, holding that the trial court "had general power to issue injunctions in equity and that, even if its exercise of the power was erroneous, the injunction was not void, and the defendants were precluded from attacking it in this collateral proceeding . . . that, if the injunction was erroneous, jurisdiction was not thereby forfeited, that the error was subject to correction only by the ordinary method of appeal, and disobedience to the order constituted contempt."

This Court, in dismissing the writ of error, not only unanimously accepted but fully approved the validity of the rule of state law upon which the judgment of the Kansas court was grounded:

"An injunction duly issuing out of a court of general jurisdiction with equity powers upon pleadings properly invoking its action, and served upon persons made parties therein and within the jurisdiction, must be obeyed by them however erroneous the action of the court may be, even if the error be in the assumption of the validity of a seeming [valid] but void law going to the merits of the case. It is for the court of first instance to determine the question of the validity of the law, and until its decision is reversed for error by orderly review, either by itself or by a higher court, its orders based on its decision are to be respected, and disobedience of them is contempt of its lawful authority, to be punished."

The rule of state law accepted and approved in Howat v. Kansas is consistent with the rule of law followed by the federal courts.

In the present case, however, we are asked to hold that this rule of law, upon which the Alabama courts relied, was constitutionally impermissible. We are asked to say that the Constitution compelled Alabama to allow the petitioners to violate this injunction, to organize and engage in these mass street parades and demonstrations, without any previous effort on their part to have the injunction dissolved or modified, or any attempt to secure a parade permit in accordance with its terms. Whatever the limits of Howat v. Kansas,[6] we cannot accept the petitioners' contentions in the circumstances of this case.

6. In In re Green, 369 U.S. 689, the petitioner was convicted of criminal contempt for violating a labor injunction issued by an Ohio court. Relying on the pre-emptive command of the federal labor law, the Court held that the state

Without question the state court that issued the injunction had, as a court of equity, jurisdiction over the petitioners and over the subject matter of the controversy. And this is not a case where the injunction was transparently invalid or had only a frivolous pretense to validity. We have consistently recognized the strong interest of state and local governments in regulating the use of their streets and other public places. . . . When protest takes the form of mass demonstrations, parades, or picketing on public streets and sidewalks, the free passage of traffic and the prevention of public disorder and violence become important objects of legitimate state concern. As the Court stated, in Cox v. Louisiana, "We emphatically reject the notion . . . that the First and Fourteenth Amendments afford the same kind of freedom to those who would communicate ideas by conduct such as patrolling, marching, and picketing on streets and highways, as these amendments afford to those who communicate ideas by pure speech." 379 U.S. 536, 555. . . .

The generality of the language contained in the Birmingham parade ordinance upon which the injunction was based would unquestionably raise substantial constitutional issues concerning some of its provisions. Schneider v. State, 308 U.S. 147; Saia v. New York, 334 U.S. 558; Kunz v. New York, 340 U.S. 290. The petitioners, however, did not even attempt to apply to the Alabama courts for an authoritative construction of the ordinance. Had they done so, those courts might have given the licensing authority granted in the ordinance a narrow and precise scope . . . . Here . . . it could not be assumed that this ordinance was void on its face.

The breadth and vagueness of the injunction itself would also unquestionably be subject to substantial constitutional question. But the way to raise that question was to apply to the Alabama courts to have the injunction modified or dissolved. The injunction in all events clearly prohibited mass parading without a permit, and the evidence shows that the petitioners fully understood that prohibition when they violated it.

The petitioners also claim that they were free to disobey the injunction because the parade ordinance on which it was based had been administered in the past in an arbitrary and discriminatory fashion. In support of this claim they sought to introduce evidence that, a few days before the injunction issued, requests for permits to picket had been made to a member of the city commission. One request had been rudely rebuffed,[9] and this same official

courts were required to hear Green's claim that the state court was *without jurisdiction* to issue the injunction. The petitioner in *Green,* unlike the petitioners here, had attempted to challenge the validity of the injunction *before* violating it by promptly applying to the issuing court for an order vacating the injunction. The petitioner in *Green* had further offered to prove that the court issuing the injunction had agreed to its violation as an appropriate means of testing its validity.

9. Mrs. Lola Hendricks, *not* a petitioner in this case, testified that on April 3:

"I went to Mr. Connor's office, the Commissioner's office at the City Hall Building. We went up and Commissioner Connor met us at the door. He asked, 'May I help you?' I told him, 'Yes, sir, we came up to apply or see about getting a permit for picketing, parading, demonstrating.' . . .

"I asked Commissioner Connor for the permit, and asked if he could issue the permit, or other persons who would refer me to, persons who would issue a permit. He said, 'No, you will not get a permit in Birmingham, Alabama to picket. I will picket you over to the City Jail,' and he repeated that twice."

had later made clear that he was without power to grant the permit alone, since the issuance of such permits was the responsibility of the entire city commission.[10] Assuming the truth of this proffered evidence, it does not follow that the parade ordinance was void on its face. The petitioners, moreover, did not apply for a permit either to the commission itself or to any commissioner after the injunction issued. Had they done so, and had the permit been refused, it is clear that their claim of arbitrary or discriminatory administration of the ordinance would have been considered by the state circuit court upon a motion to dissolve the injunction.[11]

This case would arise in quite a different constitutional posture if the petitioners, before disobeying the injunction, had challenged it in the Alabama courts, and had been met with delay or frustration of their constitutional claims. But there is no showing that such would have been the fate of a timely motion to modify or dissolve the injunction. There was an interim of two days between the issuance of the injunction and the Good Friday march. The petitioners give absolutely no explanation of why they did not make some application to the state court during that period. The injunction had issued *ex parte;* if the court had been presented with the petitioners' contentions, it might well have dissolved or at least modified its order in some respects. If it had not done so, Alabama procedure would have provided for an expedited process of appellate review.[12] It cannot be presumed that the Alabama courts would have ignored the petitioners' constitutional claims. Indeed, these contentions were accepted in another case by an Alabama appellate court that struck down on direct review the conviction under this very ordinance of one of these same petitioners.[13]

The rule of law upon which the Alabama courts relied in this case was one firmly established by previous precedents. We do not deal here, therefore, with a situation where a state court has followed a regular past practice of entertaining claims in a given procedural mode, and without notice has abandoned that practice to the detriment of a litigant who finds his claim foreclosed by a novel procedural bar. . . . This is not a case where a procedural requirement has been sprung upon an unwary litigant when prior practice did not give him fair notice of its existence. Wright v. Georgia, 373 U.S. 284, 291.

10. Commissioner Connor sent the following telegram to one of the petitioners on April 5:

"Under the provisions of the city code of the City of Birmingham, a permit to picket as requested by you cannot be granted by me individually but is the responsiboity [*sic*] of the entire commission. I insist that you and your people do not start any picketing on the streets in Birmingham, Alabama.

"Eugene 'Bull' Connor, Commissioner of Public Safety."

11. In its opinion, that court stated: "The legal and orderly processes of the Court would require the defendants to attack the unreasonable denial of such permit by the Commission of the City of Birmingham through means of a motion to dissolve the injunction at which time this Court would have the opportunity to pass upon the question of whether or not a compliance with the ordinance was attempted and whether or not an arbitrary and capricious denial of such request was made by the Commission of the City of Birmingham. Since this course of conduct was not sought by the defendants, the Court is of the opinion that the validity of its injunction order stands upon its prima facie authority to execute the same."

12. Ala.Code, Tit. 7, App., Sup.Ct. Rule 47.

13. Shuttlesworth v. City of Birmingham, 43 Ala.App. 68, 180 So.2d 114. The case is presently pending on certiorari review in the Alabama Supreme Court.

The Alabama Supreme Court has apparently never in any criminal contempt case entertained a claim of nonjurisdictional error. . . .

These precedents clearly put the petitioners on notice that they could not bypass orderly judicial review of the injunction before disobeying it. Any claim that they were entrapped or misled is wholly unfounded, a conclusion confirmed by evidence in the record showing that when the petitioners deliberately violated the injunction they expected to go to jail.

The rule of law that Alabama followed in this case reflects a belief that in the fair administration of justice no man can be judge in his own case, however exalted his station, however righteous his motives, and irrespective of his race, color, politics, or religion.[16] This Court cannot hold that the petitioners were constitutionally free to ignore all the procedures of the law and carry their battle to the streets. One may sympathize with the petitioners' impatient commitment to their cause. But respect for judicial process is a small price to pay for the civilizing hand of law, which alone can give abiding meaning to constitutional freedom.

Affirmed.

APPENDIX A TO OPINION OF THE COURT

"TEMPORARY INJUNCTION—April 10, 1963.

"A verified Bill of Complaint in the above styled cause having been presented to me on this the 10th of April 1963 at 9:00 O'Clock P.M. in the City of Birmingham, Alabama.

"Upon consideration of said verified Bill of Complaint and the affidavits of Captain G.V. Evans and Captain George Wall, and the public welfare, peace and safety requiring it, it is hereby considered, ordered, adjudged and decreed that a peremptory or a temporary writ of injunction be and the same is hereby issued in accordance with the prayer of said petition.

"It is therefore ordered, adjudged and decreed by the Court that upon the complainant entering into a good and sufficient bond conditioned as provided by law, in the sum of Twenty-five Hundred Dollars ($2500.00), same to be approved by the Register of this Court that the Register issue a peremptory or temporary writ of injunction that the respondents and the others identified in said Bill of Complaint, their agents, members, employees, servants, followers, attorneys, successors and all other persons in active concert or participation with the respondents and all persons having notice of said order from continuing any act hereinabove designated particularly: engaging in, sponsoring, inciting or encouraging mass street parades or mass processions or like demonstrations without a permit, trespass on private property after

16. The same rule of law was followed in Kasper v. Brittain, 245 F.2d 92. There, a federal court had ordered the public high school in Clinton, Tennessee, to desegregate. Kasper "arrived from somewhere in the East," and organized a campaign "to run the Negroes out of the school." The federal court issued an *ex parte* restraining order enjoining Kasper from interfering with desegregation. Relying upon the First Amendment, Kasper harangued a crowd "to the effect that although he had been served with the restraining order, it did not mean anything . . . ." His conviction for criminal contempt was affirmed by the Court of Appeals for the Sixth Circuit. That court concluded that "an injunctional order issued by a court must be obeyed," whatever its seeming invalidity, citing Howat v. Kansas, 258 U.S. 181. This Court denied certiorari, 355 U.S. 834.

being warned to leave the premises by the owner or person in possession of said private property, congregating on the street or public places into mobs, and unlawfully picketing business establishments or public buildings in the City of Birmingham, Jefferson County, State of Alabama or performing acts calculated to cause breaches of the peace in the City of Birmingham, Jefferson County, in the State of Alabama or from conspiring to engage in unlawful street parades, unlawful processions, unlawful demonstrations, unlawful boycotts, unlawful trespasses, and unlawful picketing or other like unlawful conduct or from violating the ordinances of the City of Birmingham and the Statutes of the State of Alabama or from doing any acts designed to consummate conspiracies to engage in said unlawful acts of parading, demonstrating, boycotting, trespassing and picketing or other unlawful acts, or from engaging in acts and conduct customarily known as 'kneel-ins' in churches in violation of the wishes and desires of said churches.

"W.A. Jenkins, Jr., As Circuit Judge of the Tenth Judicial Circuit of Alabama, In Equity Sitting."

APPENDIX B TO OPINION OF THE COURT

"In our struggle for freedom we have anchored our faith and hope in the rightness of the Constitution and the moral laws of the universe.

"Again and again the Federal judiciary has made it clear that the privileges guaranteed under the First and the Fourteenth Amendments are too sacred to be trampled upon by the machinery of state government and police power. In the past we have abided by Federal injunctions out of respect for the forthright and consistent leadership that the Federal judiciary has given in establishing the principle of integration as the law of the land.

"However we are now confronted with recalcitrant forces in the Deep South that will use the courts to perpetuate the unjust and illegal system of racial separation.

"Alabama has made clear its determination to defy the law of the land. Most of its public officials, its legislative body and many of its law enforcement agents have openly defied the desegregation decision of the Supreme Court. We would feel morally and legally responsible to obey the injunction if the courts of Alabama applied equal justice to all of its citizens. This would be sameness made legal. However the issuance of this injunction is blatant of *difference* made *legal.*

"Southern law enforcement agencies have demonstrated now and again that they will utilize the force of law to misuse the judicial process.

"This is raw tyranny under the guise of maintaining law and order. We cannot in all good conscience obey such an injunction which is an unjust, undemocratic and unconstitutional misuse of the legal process.

"We do this not out of any disrespect for the law but out of the highest respect for *the* law. This is not an attempt to evade or defy the law or engage in chaotic anarchy. Just as in all good conscience we cannot obey unjust laws, neither can we respect the unjust use of the courts.

"We believe in a system of law based on justice and morality. Out of our great love for the Constitution of the U.S. and our desire to purify the judicial system of the state of Alabama, we risk this critical move with an awareness of the possible consequences involved."

Chief Justice WARREN, whom Justice BRENNAN and Justice FORTAS join, dissenting.

Petitioners in this case contend that they were convicted under an ordinance that is unconstitutional on its face because it submits their First and Fourteenth Amendment rights to free speech and peaceful assembly to the unfettered discretion of local officials. They further contend that the ordinance was unconstitutionally applied to them because the local officials used their discretion to prohibit peaceful demonstrations by a group whose political viewpoint the officials opposed. The Court does not dispute these contentions, but holds that petitioners may nonetheless be convicted and sent to jail because the patently unconstitutional ordinance was copied into an injunction—issued *ex parte* without prior notice or hearing on the request of the Commissioner of Public Safety—forbidding all persons having notice of the injunction to violate the ordinance without any limitation of time. I dissent because I do not believe that the fundamental protections of the Constitution were meant to be so easily evaded, or that "the civilizing hand of law" would be hampered in the slightest by enforcing the First Amendment in this case.

The salient facts can be stated very briefly. Petitioners are Negro ministers who sought to express their concern about racial discrimination in Birmingham, Alabama, by holding peaceful protest demonstrations in that city on Good Friday and Easter Sunday 1963. For obvious reasons, it was important for the significance of the demonstrations that they be held on those particular dates. A representative of petitioners' organization went to the City Hall and asked "to see the person or persons in charge to issue permits, permits for parading, picketing, and demonstrating." She was directed to Public Safety Commissioner Connor, who denied her request for a permit in terms that left no doubt that petitioners were not going to be issued a permit under any circumstances. "He said, 'No, you will not get a permit in Birmingham, Alabama to picket. I will picket you over to the City Jail,' and he repeated that twice." A second, telegraphic request was also summarily denied, in a telegram signed by "Eugene 'Bull' Connor," with the added information that permits could be issued only by the full City Commission, a three-man body consisting of Commissioner Connor and two others.[1] Ac-

1. The uncontradicted testimony relating to the rebuffs of petitioners' attempts to obtain a permit is set out in footnotes 9 and 10 of the majority opinion. Petitioners were prevented by a ruling of the trial court from introducing further proof of the intransigence of Commissioner Connor and the other city officials toward any effort by Negroes to protest segregation and racial injustice. The attitude of the city administration in general and of its Public Safety Commissioner in particular are a matter of public record, of course, and are familiar to this Court from previous litigation. See Shuttlesworth v. City of Birmingham, 382 U.S. 87 (1965); Shuttlesworth v. City of Birmingham, 376 U.S. 339 (1964); Shuttlesworth v. City of Birmingham, 373 U.S. 262 (1963); Gober v. City of Birmingham, 373 U.S. 374 (1963); In re Shuttlesworth, 369 U.S. 35 (1962). The United States Commission on Civil Rights found continuing abuse of civil rights protesters by the Birmingham police, including use of dogs, clubs, and firehoses. 1963 Report of the United States Commission on Civil Rights 114 (Government Printing Office, 1963). Commissioner Eugene "Bull" Connor, a self-proclaimed white supremacist (see Congress and the Nation 1945–1964: A Review of Government and Politics in the Post-war Years 1604 (Congressional Quarterly Service, 1965)), made no secret of his personal attitude toward the rights

cording to petitioners' offer of proof, the truth of which is assumed for purposes of this case, parade permits had uniformly been issued for all other groups by the city clerk on the request of the traffic bureau of the police department, which was under Commissioner Connor's direction. The requirement that the approval of the full Commission be obtained was applied only to this one group.

Understandably convinced that the City of Birmingham was not going to authorize their demonstrations under any circumstances, petitioners proceeded with their plans despite Commissioner Connor's orders. On Wednesday, April 10, at 9 in the evening, the city filed in a state circuit court a bill of complaint seeking an *ex parte* injunction. The complaint recited that petitioners were engaging in a series of demonstrations as "part of a massive effort . . . to forcibly integrate all business establishments, churches, and other institutions" in the city, with the result that the police department was strained in its resources and the safety, peace, and tranquility were threatened. It was alleged as particularly menacing that petitioners were planning to conduct "kneel-in" demonstrations at churches where their presence was not wanted. The city's police dogs were said to be in danger of their lives. Faced with these recitals, the Circuit Court issued the injunction in the form requested, and in effect ordered petitioners and all other persons having notice of the order to refrain for an unlimited time from carrying on any demonstrations without a permit. A permit, of course, was clearly unobtainable; the city would not have sought this injunction if it had any intention of issuing one.

Petitioners were served with copies of the injunction at various times on Thursday and on Good Friday. Unable to believe that such a blatant and broadly drawn prior restraint on their First Amendment rights could be valid, they announced their intention to defy it and went ahead with the planned peaceful demonstrations on Easter weekend. On the following Monday, when they promptly filed a motion to dissolve the injunction, the court found them in contempt, holding that they had waived all their First Amendment rights by disobeying the court order.

These facts lend no support to the court's charges that petitioners were presuming to act as judges in their own case, or that they had a disregard for the judicial process. They did not flee the jurisdiction or refuse to appear in the Alabama courts. Having violated the injunction, they promptly submitted themselves to the courts to test the constitutionality of the injunction and the ordinance it parroted. They were in essentially the same position as persons who challenge the constitutionality of a statute by violating it, and then defend the ensuing criminal prosecution on constitutional grounds. It has never been thought that violation of a statute indicated such a disrespect for the legislature that the violator always must be punished even if the statute was unconstitutional. On the contrary, some cases have required that persons seeking to challenge the constitutionality of a statute first violate it to establish their standing to sue. Indeed, it shows no disrespect for law to

of Negroes and the decisions of this Court. He vowed that racial integration would never come to Birmingham, and wore a button inscribed "Never" to advertise that vow. Yet the Court indulges in speculation that these civil rights protesters might have obtained a permit from this city and this man had they made enough repeated applications.

violate a statute on the ground that it is uconstitutional and then to submit one's case to the courts with the willingness to accept the penalty if the statute is held to be valid.

The Court concedes that "[t]he generality of the language contained in the Birmingham parade ordinance upon which the injunction was based would unquestionably raise substantial constitutional issues concerning some of its provisions." That concession is well-founded but minimal. I believe it is patently unconstitutional on its face. Our decisions have consistently held that picketing and parading are means of expression protected by the First Amendment, and that the right to picket or parade may not be subjected to the unfettered discretion of local officials. Cox v. Louisiana, 379 U.S. 536 (1965); Edwards v. South Carolina, 372 U.S. 229 (1963); Thornhill v. Alabama, 310 U.S. 88 (1940). Although a city may regulate the manner of use of its streets and sidewalks in the interest of keeping them open for the movement of traffic, it may not allow local officials unbridled discretion to decide who shall be allowed to parade or picket and who shall not. "Wherever the title of streets and parks may rest, they have immemorially been held in trust for the use of the public and, time out of mind, have been used for purposes of assembly, communicating thoughts between citizens, and discussing public questions. Such use of the streets and public places has, from ancient times, been a part of the privileges, immunities, rights, and liberties of citizens. The privilege of a citizen of the United States to use the streets and parks for communication of views on national questions may be regulated in the interest of all; it is not absolute, but relative, and must be exercised in subordination to the general comfort and convenience, and in consonance with peace and good order; but it must not, in the guise of regulation, be abridged or denied." Hague v. C.I.O., 307 U.S. 496, 515–516 (1939) (opinion of Mr. Justice Roberts). When local officials are given totally unfettered discretion to decide whether a proposed demonstration is consistent with "public welfare, peace, safety, health, decency, good order, morals or convenience," as they were in this case, they are invited to act as censors over the views that may be presented to the public. The unconstitutionality of the ordinance is compounded, of course, when there is convincing evidence that the officials have in fact used their power to deny permits to organizations whose views they dislike. The record in this case hardly suggests that Commissioner Connor and the other city officials were motivated in prohibiting civil rights picketing only by their overwhelming concern for particular traffic problems. Petitioners were given to understand that under no circumstances would they be permitted to demonstrate in Birmingham, not that a demonstration would be approved if a time and place were selected that would minimize the traffic difficulties. The only circumstance that the court can find to justify anything other than a *per curiam* reversal is that Commissioner Connor had the foresight to have the unconstitutional ordinance included in an *ex parte* injunction, issued without notice or hearing or any showing that it was impossible to have notice or a hearing, forbidding the world at large (insofar as it knew of the order) to conduct demonstrations in Birmingham without the consent of the city officials. This injunction was such potent magic that it transformed the command of an unconstitutional statute into an impregnable barrier, challengeable only in what likely would have been protracted legal proceedings and entirely superior in the meantime even to the United States Constitution.

I do not believe that giving this Court's seal of approval to such a gross misuse of the judicial process is likely to lead to greater respect for the law any more than it is likely to lead to greater protection for First Amendment freedoms. The *ex parte* temporary injunction has a long and odious history in this country, and its susceptibility to misuse is all too apparent from the facts of the case. As a weapon against strikes, it proved so effective in the hands of judges friendly to employers that Congress was forced to take the drastic step of removing from federal district courts the jurisdiction to issue injunctions in labor disputes. The labor injunction fell into disrepute largely because it was abused in precisely the same way that the injunctive power was abused in this case. Judges who were not sympathetic to the union cause commonly issued, without notice or hearing, broad restraining orders addressed to large numbers of persons and forbidding them to engage in acts that were either legally permissible or, if illegal, that could better have been left to the regular course of criminal prosecution. The injunctions might later be dissolved, but in the meantime strikes would be crippled because the occasion on which concerted activity might have been effective had passed. Such injunctions, so long discredited as weapons against concerted labor activities, have now been given new life by this Court as weapons against the exercise of First Amendment freedoms. Respect for the courts and for judicial process was not increased by the history of the labor injunction.

Nothing in our prior decisions, or in the doctrine that a party subject to a temporary injunction issued by a court of competent jurisdiction with power to decide a dispute properly before it must normally challenge the injunction in the courts rather than by violating it, requires that we affirm the convictions in this case. The majority opinion in this case rests essentially on a single precedent, and that a case the authority of which has clearly been undermined by subsequent decisions. Howat v. Kansas, 258 U.S. 181 (1922), was decided in the days when the labor injunction was in fashion. Kansas had adopted an Industrial Relations Act, the purpose of which in effect was to provide for compulsory arbitration of labor disputes by a neutral administrative tribunal, the "Court of Industrial Relations." Pursuant to its jurisdiction to investigate and perhaps improve labor conditions in the coal mining industry, the "Court" subpoenaed union leaders to appear and testify. In addition, the State obtained an injunction to prevent a strike while the matter was before the "Court." The union leaders disobeyed both the subpoena and the injunction, and sought to challenge the constitutionality of the Industrial Relations Act in the ensuing contempt proceeding. The Kansas Supreme Court held that the constitutionality of the Act could not be challenged in a contempt proceeding, and this Court upheld that determination.

Insofar as Howat v. Kansas might be interpreted to approve an absolute rule that any violation of a void court order is punishable as contempt, it has been greatly modified by later decisions. In In re Green, 369 U.S. 689 (1962), we reversed a conviction for contempt of a state injunction forbidding labor picketing because the petitioner was not allowed to present evidence that the labor dispute was arguably subject to the jurisdiction of the National Labor Relations Board and hence not subject to state regulation. If an injunction can be challenged on the ground that it deals with a matter arguably subject to the jurisdiction of the National Labor Relations Board, then *a fortiori* it can be challenged on First Amendment grounds.[9]

It is not necessary to question the continuing validity of the holding in Howat v. Kansas, however, to demonstrate that neither it nor the *Mine Workers* case supports the holding of the majority in this case. In *Howat* the subpoena and injunction were issued to enable the Kansas Court of Industrial Relations to determine an underlying labor dispute. In the *Mine Workers* case, the District Court issued a temporary antistrike injunction to preserve existing conditions during the time it took to decide whether it had authority to grant the Government relief in a complex and difficult action of enormous importance to the national economy. In both cases the orders were of questionable legality, but in both cases they were reasonably necessary to enable the court or administrative tribunal to decide an underlying controversy of considerable importance before it at the time. This case involves an entirely different situation. The Alabama Circuit Court did not issue this temporary injunction to preserve existing conditions while it proceeded to decide some underlying dispute. There was no underlying dispute before it, and the court in practical effect merely added a judicial signature to a preexisting criminal ordinance. Just as the court had no need to issue the injunction to preserve its ability to decide some underlying dispute, the city had no need of an injunction to impose a criminal penalty for demonstrating on the streets without a permit. The ordinance already accomplished that. In point of fact, there is only one apparent reason why the city sought this injunction and why the court issued it: to make it possible to punish petitioners for contempt rather than for violating the ordinance, and thus to immunize the unconstitutional statute and its unconstitutional application from any attack. I regret that this strategy has been so successful.

It is not necessary in this case to decide precisely what limits should be set to the *Mine Workers* doctrine in cases involving violations of the First Amendment. Whatever the scope of that doctrine, it plainly was not intended to give a State the power to nullify the United States Constitution by the simple process of incorporating its unconstitutional criminal statutes into judicial decrees. I respectfully dissent.

Justice DOUGLAS, with whom THE CHIEF JUSTICE, Justice BRENNAN, and Justice FORTAS concur, dissenting. . . .

The record shows that petitioners did not deliberately attempt to circumvent the permit requirement. Rather they diligently attempted to obtain a permit and were rudely rebuffed and then reasonably concluded that any further attempts would be fruitless.

9. The attempt in footnote 6 of the majority opinion to distinguish In re Green is nothing but an attempt to alter the holding of that case. The opinion of the Court states flatly that "a state court is without power to hold one in contempt for violating an injunction that the state court had no power to enter by reason of federal preemption." 369 U.S., at 692 (footnote omitted). The alleged circumstance that the court issuing the injunction had agreed to its violation as an appropriate means of testing its validity was considered only in a concurring opinion. Although the petitioner in *Green* had attempted to challenge the order in court before violating it, we did not rely on that fact in holding that the order was void. Nor is it clear to me why the Court regards this fact as important, unless it means to imply that the petitioners in this case would have been free to violate the court order if they had first made a motion to dissolve in the trial court.

The right to defy an unconstitutional statute is basic in our scheme. Even when an ordinance requires a permit to make a speech, to deliver a sermon, to picket, to parade, or to assemble, it need not be honored when it is invalid on its face. . . .

By like reason, where a permit has been arbitrarily denied, one need not pursue the long and expensive route to this Court to obtain a remedy. The reason is the same in both cases. For if a person must pursue his judicial remedy before he may speak, parade, or assemble, the occasion when protest is desired or needed will have become history and any later speech, parade, or assembly will be futile or pointless.

Howat v. Kansas, 258 U.S. 181, states the general rule that court injunctions are to be obeyed until error is found by normal and orderly review procedures. See United States v. Mine Workers. But there is an exception where "the question of jurisdiction" is "frivolous and not substantial." Id., at 293. Moreover, a state court injunction is not *per se* sacred where federal constitutional questions are involved. In re Green, 369 U.S. 689, held that contempt could not be imposed without a hearing where the state decree bordered the federal domain in labor relations and only a hearing could determine whether there was federal pre-emption. In the present case the collision between this state court decree and the First Amendment is so obvious that no hearing is needed to determine the issue.

As already related, petitioners made two applications to Commissioner "Bull" Connor for a permit and were turned down. At the trial, counsel for petitioners offered to prove through the city clerk that the Commission never has granted a permit, the issuing authority being the city clerk who acts at the request of the traffic division. But he was not allowed to answer the question. And when asked to describe the practice for granting permits an objection was raised and sustained.

It is clear that there are no published rules or regulations governing the manner of applying for permits, and it is clear from the record that some permits are issued. One who reads this record will have, I think, the abiding conviction that these people were denied a permit solely because their skin was not of the right color and their cause was not popular.

A court does not have *jurisdiction* to do what a city or other agency of a State lacks *jurisdiction* to do. The command of the Fourteenth Amendment, through which the First Amendment is made applicable to the States, is that no "State" shall deprive any person of "liberty" without due process of law. The decree of a state court is "state" action in the constitutional sense (Shelley v. Kraemer, 334 U.S. 1, 14–18), as much as the action of the state police, the state prosecutor, the state legislature, or the Governor himself. An ordinance—unconstitutional on its face or patently unconstitutional as applied—is not made sacred by an unconstitutional injunction that enforces it. It can and should be flouted in the manner of the ordinance itself. Courts as well as citizens are not free "to ignore all the procedures of the law," to use the Court's language. The "constitutional freedom" of which the Court speaks can be won only if judges honor the Constitution.

Justice BRENNAN, with whom THE CHIEF JUSTICE, Justice DOUGLAS, and Justice FORTAS join, dissenting.

Under cover of exhortation that the Negro exercise "respect for judicial process," the Court empties the Supremacy Clause of its primacy by elevating a state rule of judicial administration above the right of free expression guaranteed by the Federal Constitution. And the Court does so by letting loose a devastatingly destructive weapon for suppression of cherished freedoms heretofore believed indispensable to maintenance of our free society. I cannot believe that this distortion in the hierarchy of values upon which our society has been and must be ordered can have any significance beyond its function as a vehicle to affirm these contempt convictions. . . .

The holding of the Alabama Supreme Court, and the affirmance of its decision by this Court, rest on the assumption that petitioners may be criminally punished although the parade ordinance and the injuction be unconstitutional on their faces as in violation of the First Amendment, and even if the parade ordinance was discriminatorily applied. It must therefore be assumed, for purposes of review of the Alabama Supreme Court's decision, and in assessing the Court's affirmance, that petitioners could successfully sustain the contentions (into which the Alabama courts refused to inquire) that the ordinance and injunction are in fact facially unconstitutional as excessively vague prior restraints on First Amendment rights and that the ordinance had been discriminatorily applied. It should be noted, without elaboration, that there is clearly sound basis in fact for this assumption: the Alabama Court of Appeals, in a case involving one of these petitioners, has held that the ordinance is "void for vagueness because of overbroad, and consequently meaningless, standards for the issuance of permits for processions," and that the ordinance has been enforced discriminatorily. Shuttlesworth v. City of Birmingham, 43 Ala.App. 68, 180 So.2d 114 (1965). However, it is not the merits of such claims, but the refusal of the Alabama courts to consider them, that is here involved.

Like the Court, I start with the premise that States are free to adopt rules of judicial administration designed to require respect for their courts' orders. See Howat v. Kansas. But this does not mean that this valid state interest does not admit of collision with other and more vital interests. Surely the proposition requires no citation that a valid state interest must give way when it infringes on rights guaranteed by the Federal Constitution. The plain meaning of the Supremacy Clause requires no less.

In the present case we are confronted with a collision between Alabama's interest in requiring adherence to orders of its courts and the constitutional prohibition against abridgment of freedom of speech, more particularly "the right of the people peaceably to assemble," and the right "to petition the Government for a redress of grievances." . . . Special considerations have time and again been deemed by us to attend protection of these freedoms in the face of state interests the vindication of which results in prior restraints upon their exercise, or their regulation in a vague or overbroad manner, or in a way which gives unbridled discretion to limit their exercise to an individual or group of individuals. To give these freedoms the necessary "breathing space to survive," NAACP v. Button, 371 U.S. 415, 433, the Court has modified traditional rules of standing and prematurity. See Dombrowski v. Pfister, 380 U.S. 479. We have molded both substantive rights and procedural remedies in the face of varied conflicting interests to conform to our overriding duty to insulate all individuals from the "chilling effect" upon exercise of First Amendment freedoms generated by vagueness, overbreadth and unbridled discretion to limit their exercise.

The vitality of First Amendment protections has, as a result, been deemed to rest in large measure upon the ability of the individual to take his chances and express himself in the face of such restraints, armed with the ability to challenge those restraints if the State seeks to penalize that expression. The most striking examples of the right to speak first and challenge later, and of peculiar moment for the present case, are the cases concerning the ability of an individual to challenge a permit or licensing statute giving broad discretion to an individual or group, such as the Birmingham permit ordinance, despite the fact that he did not attempt to obtain a permit or license. In Staub v. City of Baxley, 355 U.S. 313, the accused, prosecuted for soliciting members for an organization without a permit, contended that the ordinance was invalid on its face because it made exercise of freedom of speech contingent upon the will of the issuing authority and therefore was an invalid prior restraint—the same contention made by petitioners with regard to the Birmingham ordinance. The Georgia Court of Appeals held that "[h]aving made no effort to secure a license, the defendant is in no position to claim that any section of the ordinance is invalid or unconstitutional . . . ." Staub v. City of Baxley, supra, at 318. We refused to regard this holding as an adequate nonfederal ground for decision, stating:

> "The decisions of this Court have uniformly held that the failure to apply for a license under an ordinance which on its face violates the Constitution does not preclude review in this Court of a judgment of conviction under such an ordinance. Smith v. Cahoon, 283 U.S. 553, 562; Lovell v. Griffin, 303 U.S. 444, 452. 'The Constitution can hardly be thought to deny to one subjected to the restraints of such an ordinance the right to attack its constitutionality, because he has not yielded to its demands.' Jones v. Opelika, 316 U.S. 584, 602, dissenting opinion, adopted *per curiam* on rehearing, 319 U.S. 103, 104."

See also Cox v. Louisiana, 379 U.S. 536, 556–557.

Yet by some inscrutable legerdemain these constitutionally secured rights to challenge prior restraints invalid on their face are lost if the State takes the precaution to have some judge append his signature to an *ex parte* order which recites the words of the invalid statute. The State neatly insulates its legislation from challenge by mere incorporation of the identical stifling, overbroad, and vague restraints on exercise of the First Amendment freedoms into an even more vague and pervasive injunction obtained invisibly and upon a stage darkened lest it be open to scrutiny by those affected. The *ex parte* order of the judicial officer exercising broad equitable powers is glorified above the presumably carefully considered, even if hopelessly invalid, mandates of the legislative branch. I would expect this tribunal, charged as it is with the ultimate responsibility to safeguard our constitutional freedoms, to regard the *ex parte* injunctive tool to be far more dangerous than statutes to First Amendment freedoms. One would expect this Court particularly to remember the stern lesson history taught courts, in the context of the labor injunction, that the *ex parte* injunction represents the most devastating of restraints on constitutionally protected activities. Today, however, the weapon is given complete invulnerability in the one context in which the danger from broad prior restraints has been thought to be the most acute. Were it not for the *ex parte* injunction, petitioners could have paraded first and challenged the permit ordinance later. But because of the *ex parte* stamp of a judicial officer on a copy of the invalid ordinance they are barred not only from challenging the permit ordinance, but also the potentially more stifling yet unconsidered restraints embodied in the injunction itself.

The Court's religious deference to the state court's application of the *Mine Workers'* rule in the present case is in stark contrast to the Court's approach in In re Green, 369 U.S. 689. The state court issued an *ex parte* injunction against certain labor picketing. Green, counsel for the union, advised the union that the order was invalid and that it should continue to picket so that the order could be tested in a contempt hearing. The court held Green in contempt without allowing any challenge to the order. This Court stated that the issue was "whether the state court was trenching on the federal domain." In re Green. It remanded for a hearing to determine whether the activity enjoined was "arguably" subject to Labor Board jurisdiction. In *Green,* therefore, we rejected blind effectuation of the State's interest in requiring compliance with its court's *ex parte* injunctions because of the "arguable" collision with federal labor policy. Yet in the present case the Court affirms the determination of a state court which was willing to assume that its *ex parte* order and the underlying statute were repugnant on their face to the First Amendment of the Federal Constitution. One must wonder what an odd inversion of values it is to afford greater respect to an "arguable" collision with federal labor policy than an assumedly patent interference with constitutional rights so high in the scale of constitutional values that this Court has described them as being "delicate and vulnerable, as well as supremely precious in our society." NAACP v. Button, 371 U.S. 415, 453.

It is said that petitioners should have sought to dissolve the injunction before conducting their processions. That argument is plainly repugnant to the principle that First Amendment freedoms may be exercised in the face of legislative prior restraints, and *a fortiori* of *ex parte* restraints broader than such legislative restraints, which may be challenged in any subsequent proceeding for their violation. But at all events, prior resort to a motion to dissolve this injunction could not be required because of the complete absence of any time limits on the duration of the *ex parte* order. See Freedman v. Maryland, 380 U.S. 51. Even the Alabama Supreme Court's Rule 47 leaves the timing of full judicial consideration of the validity of the restraint to that court's untrammeled discretion.

The shifting of the burden to petitioners to show the lawfulness of their conduct prior to engaging in enjoined activity also is contrary to the principle, settled by Speiser v. Randall, 357 U.S. 513, 526, that

"The man who knows that he must bring forth proof and persuade another of the lawfulness of his conduct necessarily must steer far wider of the unlawful zone than if the State must bear these burdens. . . . In practical operation, therefore, this procedural device must necessarily produce a result which the State could not command directly. It can only result in a deterrence of speech which the Constitution makes free."

The suggestion that petitioners be muffled pending outcome of dissolution proceedings without any measurable time limits is particularly inappropriate in the setting of this case. Critical to the plain exercise of the right of protest was the timing of that exercise. First, the marches were part of a program to arouse community support for petitioners' assault on segregation there. A cessation of these activities, even for a short period, might deal a crippling blow to petitioners' efforts. Second, in dramatization of their cause, petitioners, all ministers, chose April 12, Good Friday, and April 14, Easter Sunday, for their protests hoping to gain the attention to their cause which such timing might attract. Petitioners received notice of the order April 11. The ability to exercise protected protest at a time when such exercise would be effective must be as protected as the beliefs themselves. . . . It is a flagrant denial of constitutional guarantees to balance away this principle in the name of "respect for judicial process." To preach "respect" in this context is to deny the right to speak at all.

The Court today lets loose a devastatingly destructive weapon for infringement of freedoms jealously safeguarded not so much for the benefit of any given group of any given persuasion as for the benefit of all of us. We cannot permit fears of "riots" and "civil disobedience" generated by slogans like "Black Power" to divert our attention from what is here at stake—not violence or the right of the State to control its streets and sidewalks, but the insulation from attack of *ex parte* orders and legislation upon which they are based even when patently impermissible prior restraints on the exercise of First Amendment rights, thus arming the state courts with the power to punish as a "contempt" what they otherwise could not punish at all. Constitutional restrictions against abridgments of First Amendment freedoms limit judicial equally with legislative and executive power. Convictions for contempt of court orders which invalidly abridge First Amendment freedoms must be condemned equally with convictions for violation of statutes which do the same thing. I respectfully dissent.

---

1) In considering the validity of the Birmingham decree, two subsequent decisions of the Supreme Court during the 1968 Term of the Supreme Court should be noted. The first is the decision in Carroll v. Princess Anne, p. 328. It required adversary procedure before an injunction that forbade a rally. The second is the decision of the Supreme Court in reviewing the conviction of the Reverend Shuttlesworth for violating the Birmingham parade ordinance in the course of the Easter marches led by Dr. King. Shuttlesworth v. City of Birmingham, 394 U.S. 147 (1969). In that case the Court held, first, that the Birmingham parade-permit ordinance was invalid on its face because of the unfettered discretion that it vested in the city officials and, second, that the Reverend Shuttlesworth was able to void his conviction for parading without a permit even though he did not refrain from parading until he had sought judicial review of the decision by the city officials denying him a permit. Why should Shuttlesworth be allowed to challenge the parading statute but not the injunction granted to enforce it?

2) What may be said in behalf of the collateral bar rule? In Iolanthe, Gilbert and Sullivan had the Lord Chancellor intone:

The law is the true embodiment
Of everything that's excellent.
It has no kind of fault or flaw
And I, m'lords embody the law.

The Mississippi court said that "[r]espect for courts is that voluntary esteem the public has for judicial rectitude. Punishment for contempt will not ensure or preserve respect, for it cannot be compelled." Boydstun v. State, 259 So.2d 707, 709 (Miss.1972). Did the contemnors disrespect the legal process? On the other hand, did Dr. King sufficiently justify disobeying an injunction by saying that the Alabama government had ignored judicial precedent?

The California courts reject the collateral bar rule. In re Berry, 68 Cal. 2d 137, 65 Cal.Rptr. 273, 436 P.2d 273 (1968), allowed a contemnor to disobey an injunction and challenge it in contempt. The court felt that the injunction was sufficiently incorrect to be void. See also Justice Douglas's dissent in *Walker.* Does this approach comport with usual ideas about direct and collateral attack? More on Void Orders, 7 Ga.L.Rev. at 273–74, 282–85 (1973). "In [California] a person affected by an injunctive order may conclude that the exigencies of the situation or the magnitude of the rights involved render immediate action worth the cost of peril." 436 P.2d at 281. Did the California court reach a fair result for unstated reasons while justifying the result on unsatisfactory technical grounds? Z. Chafee, Some Problems of Equity 334–36 (1950). Does California's rejection of the collateral bar rule frustrate plaintiffs' effective preventive relief? "Who can trust himself or be trusted, to be 'judge in his own case—however righteous his motives . . .'?" Bickel, Civil Disobedience and the Duty to Obey, 8 Gonz.L.Rev. 199, 213 (1973).

3) The Supreme Court created exceptions to Alabama's collateral bar rule on both procedural and substantive grounds. Consider whether either exception applies to the facts in the case. Was the injunction effective final relief? Would a motion to dissolve have tested the order's validity? Remember the social and political environment in Birmingham in 1963. Assume the defendants moved to dissolve on Friday morning and the judge set the motion for hearing on Monday morning. Should defendants have paraded on Friday and Sunday? How likely was it that the judge would have dissolved the injunction either on Friday or on Monday? Perhaps the motion to dissolve possessed a ritualistic but not a functional significance. Did the obligation to file merge into symbolism like the obligation to touch Mezuzah on the doorpost of a Jewish home? Is the motion a ritualistic prerequisite to a later hearing on the injunction's constitutional validity? Is forcing the defendant to utilize the opportunity for a timely challenge a substitute for personal jurisdiction? Is the exception for "transparently invalid" injunctions "merely a makeweight argument?" Blasi, Prior Restraints on Demonstrations, 68 Mich.L.Rev. 1482, 1561–62 (1970). Does the collateral bar rule as qualified satisfactorily accommodate the tension between full exercise of constitutional rights and the need to channel controversies into the formal system of adjudication?

4) Why forbid a contemnor from attacking the constitutional validity of an injunction while allowing a defendant to challenge the validity of a criminal statute in a criminal prosecution? Professor Bickel distinguished betwen the duty to obey legislative and judicial commands. People could disobey statutes as acts of "law formation" and take their chances on having them declared unconstitutional. But after an injunction, "disobedience of a court's judgment does not question the judgment, for it is in theory and in practice irreversible. Here disobedience questions the very legal order itself, which must in the end rest on something more than its power to coerce." Bickel, 8 Gonz.L.Rev. at 200, 212–13. Is this convincing? Did the city, by proceeding ex parte, destroy any unique moral duty defendant owed to obey an injunction? Is there a principle that every exercise of governmental power must be tested against constitutional norms? Must directly affected citizens be assured an opportunity to test the constitutional validity of government power?

5) *Walker* elevates the collateral bar rule to a constitutional context. It has been the subject of extensive comment. One of your editors contributed two lengthy articles: Rendleman, More on Void Orders, 7 Ga.L.Rev. 246 (1973); Toward Due Process in Injunction Procedure, 1973 U.Ill.L.F. 221. See also the following discussions: Blasi, Prior Restraints on Demonstrations, 68 Mich.L.Rev. 1482 (1970); Rogers, The Elusive Search for the Void Injunction: Res Judicata Principles in Criminal Contempt Proceedings, 49 B.U.L.Rev. 251 (1969); Selig, Regulation of Street Demonstrations by Injunction: Constitutional Limitations on the Collateral Bar Rule in Prosecutions for Contempt, 4 Harv.C.R.-C.L.L.Rev. 135 (1968); Tefft, Neither Above the Law nor Below It: A Note on Walker v. Birmingham, 1967 Sup. Ct.Rev. 181; Note, Constitutional Law: The First Amendment and the Right to Violate an Injunction: 56 Calif.L.Rev. 517 (1968); Note, Defiance of Unlawful Authority, 83 Harv.L.Rev. 626 (1970); Note, Collateral Attack of Injunctions Restraining First Amendment Activity, 45 S.Cal.L.Rev. 1083 (1972); Note, Injuria Non Excusat Injuriam: Unconstitutional Injunctions and the Duty to Obey, 1970 Wash.U.L.Q. 51. Alan Westin and Barry Mahoney's The Trial of Martin Luther King (1974) is a readable account of *Walker's* social, political, and legal environment written for nonlawyers.

6) Finally, in what sense did the dissenters think that Judge Jenkins's injunction was a prior restraint? Four possible answers emerge. The statute granted the authorities too much discretion. The procedure that led to the order was insufficient. The injunction was too vague and broad, and it forbade or arguably forbade activity the first amendment protected. Would a court have to declare a similar injunction a prior restraint to find that it violated the defendant's first amendment rights on any of these suggested grounds? Does it make sense for the Court to approve the collateral bar rule for an injunction against first amendment activity and disapprove prior restraints?

UNITED STATES v. DICKINSON

465 F.2d 496 (5th Cir. 1972).

Before JOHN R. BROWN, Chief Judge, and BELL and SIMPSON, Circuit Judges.

JOHN R. BROWN, Chief Judge:

The civil libertarians' nightmare with which we here are haunted presents a classic confrontation between "two of the most cherished policies of our civilization"—freedom of the press, encased in the armor of the First Amendment, pitted against the right of the accused to a fair and impartial trial, shielded by the Sixth Amendment and reinforced in this case by a protective order of the District Court which is the real cause of the battle. In the skirmish that ensues, both sides glimpse victory and both sides taste defeat. But the Day of Armageddon has not yet dawned on this great conflict, and accordingly at our hands there is a forced withdrawal to the District Court.

A Prohibited Publication

Cast against a backdrop of assassination and political intrigue, the case began when Frank Stewart, a VISTA worker active in civil rights endeavors on behalf of the black community of Baton Rouge, Louisiana, was indicted in Louisiana State Court on a charge of conspiring to murder the Mayor of Baton Rouge. Alleging that the State Court prosecution was completely groundless and intended solely and exclusively to harass the accused in order to suppress his exercise of First Amendment rights, Stewart, calling on the full arsenal of Federal Civil Rights Statutes, sought to foreclose the pending State criminal prosecution by requesting injunctive relief from the United States District Court for the Eastern District of Louisiana. The District Court declined to restrain the State Court (Stewart v. Dameron, D.C.La., 1971, 321 F.Supp. 886), but this Court vacated that order and remanded the case for a new evidentiary hearing, since "Stewart had not been allowed to put on any evidence concerning his allegations of bad faith prosecution and harassment" at the original proceeding. Stewart v. Dameron, 5 Cir., 1971, 448 F.2d 396.

In accordance with the mandate of this Court, the District Court held a Younger v. Harris hearing on November 1, 1971, limited solely to the question of whether the State prosecutorial motive was legitimate or contrived. This hearing likewise resulted in a holding for the State, but again the District Court's order was reversed on appeal and the case remanded for another evidentiary hearing. Stewart v. Dameron, 5 Cir., 1972, 460 F.2d 278.

Meanwhile, during the second hearing, the opening shot of the present battle had been fired. Dickinson and Adams, appellants, were newspaper reporters, employed by the City Press and assigned to cover that hearing for the *Morning Advocate* and the *State Times.* During the course of the morning's proceedings the Judge pronounced this order from the bench:

"And, at this time, I do want to enter an order in the case, and that is in accordance with this Court's Rule in connection with Fair Trial—Free Press provisions, the Rules of this Court,

"It is ordered that no, no report of the testimony taken in this case today shall be made in any newspaper or by radio or television, or by any other news media. This case will, in all probability, be the subject of further prosecution; at least, there is the possibility that it may. In order to avoid undue publicity which could in any way interfere with the rights of the litigants in connection with any further proceedings that might be had in this or other courts, there shall be no reporting of the details of any evidence taken during the course of this hearing today.

"This order is made subject to the sanctions provided by law in the event of any violation of this order.

"Now, gentlemen, by that I do not mean that the press cannot report the fact that a hearing has been held or that a hearing is being held, but it's obvious that the testimony here today could impede another court in its progress toward selecting a jury in this case if such became necessary. Consequently, I do not want—and this order means that there shall be no reporting of the details of the evidence taken in this court today or in any continuation of this trial—of this hearing."

Notwithstanding that order, and with admitted knowledge that their actions violated its terms, Dickinson and Adams wrote articles for their newspapers summarizing the day's testimony in detail. Accordingly, a show cause order was issued and following a hearing thereon, the District Court found the appellants guilty of criminal contempt for knowingly having violated the November 1 order. Each defendant was sentenced to pay a fine of $300.00. This appeal resulted.

Free Press vs. Fair Trial—Constitutionality Of The Court's Order

The initial question with which we are confronted concerns the constitutionality of the District Court's order. Sympathetic as we are to the legitimate objective earnestly pursued by the conscientious Trial Judge (preservation of an impartial venire within the local community whenever the state criminal prosecution should reach trial), we must conclude that a blanket ban on publication of Court proceedings so far transgresses First Amendment freedoms that any such absolute proscription "cannot withstand the mildest breeze emanating from the Constitution." Southeastern Promotions Ltd. v. City of West Palm Beach, 5 Cir., 1972, 457 F.2d 1016, p. 1017.

We start, of course, with the proposition repeatedly reaffirmed by the Supreme Court that "a trial is a public event. What transpires in the courtroom is public property. . . . Those who see and hear what transpired may report it with impunity. There is no special perquisite of the judiciary which enables it, as distinguished from other institutions of democratic government, to suppress, edit, or censor events which transpire in proceedings before it." Craig v. Harney, 1947, 331 U.S. 367, 374; Stroble v. California, 1952, 343 U.S. 181, 193; Estes v. Texas, 1965, 381 U.S. 532, 541; Sheppard v. Maxwell, 1966, 384 U.S. 333, 350. Moreover, "reporters of all media . . . are plainly free to report whatever occurs in open court through their respective media." *Estes,* supra, 381 U.S. at 541–542.

Particularly is maximum freedom of the press required where the trial is intended to "determine whether a charge is founded upon reason or was dictated by an intimidating power or by malice and personal ill will." Wood v. Georgia, 1962, 370 U.S. 375, 390 . . . .

The Younger v. Harris hearing generating the present case, involving as it did allegations of bad faith, harassment, political machinations, and racial motivation on the part of the State prosecutorial officials, was peculiarly one of public concern. In fact, it was precisely the *widespread* interest in the case which led the Court to issue the controversial order. Accordingly, in the circumstances of this case, the prior restraint of the press imposed by the questioned order "comes to this Court bearing a heavy presumption against its constitutional validity." Bantam Books, Inc. v. Sullivan, 1963, 372 U.S. 58, 70, 83; Organization for a Better Austin v. Keefe; New York Times Co. v. United States; Near v. Minnesota.

Of course, the accused has constitutional rights, too, and particularly important among these are rights to a speedy trial before a fair and impartial tribunal in the venue where the alleged offense occurred. Clearly, pervasive and irresponsible news coverage of a pending criminal proceeding can so inflame and prejudice a community that it becomes virtually impossible to select an impartial jury therefrom. And without a doubt it is the Trial Court's responsibility to protect the defendant from such inherently prejudicial influences which threaten the fairness of his trial and an abrogation of his constitutional rights. *Sheppard,* supra; *Estes,* supra . . . .

Thus does Alexander again confront the Gordian Knot. For our history demands that breaches of the unqualified commands of the First Amendment cannot be tolerated and freedom of the press must be given the broadest scope that a liberty-loving people can allow. . . . On the other hand, our fundamental concepts of absolute fairness in trials dictate that the environment within which justice is administered must be maintained unpolluted by the potential infamous notoriety and biased predilections which a completely unfettered but omnipresent press can irrevocably engender in an age of the mass media. . . . The balance is delicate with so much at stake, and the equipollence of the interests defies a simple resolution by mere judicial tug-of-war, with the "lesser" bantam liberty giving way to a weightier, more Herculean one. . . .

The Clash An Ancient One

But the clash between the First and the Sixth Amendments is by no means endemic only to a modern age of electronic technology and instantaneous dissemination of information. Rather it is a conflict dramatically traced by our history. The District Court, in promulgating his order, relied on the Free Press—Fair Trial Rules for the Eastern District of Louisiana. To perceive why his order overreached those Rules to constitutionally unsupportable extents, it is necessary to understand the historical context in which the Rules came into being.

Our tale begins in 1830 when United States District Judge James H. Peck was tried on Articles of Impeachment for having imprisoned and disbarred one Lawless for publishing a criticism of one of Judge Peck's opinions in a case which was then pending on appeal. Although Judge Peck was eventually acquitted (despite an impassioned prosecution by James Buchanan), Congress acted the very next day to limit severely the Federal Court's power to punish summarily contempt by publication. . . .

The years that followed were marked by a feeling of jealous solicitude for freedom of the press in areas touching upon the administration of justice. A temporary departure from the previous consistent holdings favoring publication of commentary on court proceedings occurred in 1918 when the Supreme Court in Toledo Newspaper Co. v. United States, 1918, 247 U.S. 402, greatly enlarged the District Court's power to punish contemptuous publications by adopting a "reasonable tendency to obstruct the administration of justice" standard for determining whether or not a particular publication was contemptuous. The *Toledo Newspaper* rule proved aberrational, however, and was shortlived. In Nye v. United States, [313 U.S. 33 (1941)], it was specifically overruled.

During the very next term after *Nye* the Supreme Court reaffirmed and, in fact, strengthened the *Nye* holding in Bridges v. California, [314 U.S. 252 (1941)]. In that case, Mr. Justice Black, writing for the majority, engrafted the "clear and present danger" test of *Gitlow* to the contemptuous publication of court proceeding situation, declaring that even (or perhaps especially) within the courtroom context "minor matters of public inconvenience or annoyance [cannot be transformed] into substantive evils of sufficient weight to warrant the curtailment of liberty or expression. . . . [T]he substantive evil must be extremely serious and the degree of imminence extremely high before utterances can be punished."

Problems Of A New Era

At about this time, however, modern technology catapulted the news industry into the electronic age, endowing the press with theretofore unimagined powers of instantaneous dissemination of information, literally to the entire world. With the advent of this capacity for mass communications, the potential of the news media to influence the outcome of court proceedings, long recognized as a likelihood, was finally seen really to be more than theoretical.

Mr. Justice Frankfurter had early warned that press exploitation of court proceedings could so inflame potential jurors that a conviction could not be obtained in the local community consistent with due process. . . . That position did not achieve authoritative judicial acceptance, however, until 1959, when, apparently for the first time, the Supreme Court reversed a criminal conviction solely because of prejudicial news articles read by the jurors. Marshall v. United States, 1959, 360 U.S. 310.

Though that case was decided on supervisory rather than constitutional grounds, the Court two years later invoked the Due Process Clause to invalidate a State murder conviction where continued adverse publicity had created an atmosphere of "sustained excitement," "strong prejudice" and "public passion." Irvin v. Dowd, 1961, 366 U.S. 717. Shortly thereafter, the Court recognized the inherent impossibility of obtaining an impartial jury in a community where a video tape replay of the defendant's confession had been televised to an estimated 100,000 home viewers. Rideau v. Louisiana, supra.

The next few years saw the courts flooded with a torrent of complaints that prejudicial publicity had prevented the convicted defendant from obtaining a fair trial. Over 100 such cases are reported for the brief two-year span from January, 1963 to March, 1965. See R. Ainsworth, Fair Trial—Free Press, 45 F.R.D. 417, 419 (1968). As a result of this flurry of litigation, several federal and local law enforcement agencies, bar associations, national, state and local press groups and judicial conferences convened committees to study the problem and to propose solutions.[8] Despite this intense

8. Some of the better known commissions included the Reardon Committee of the American Bar Association's Advisory Committee on Fair Trial and Free Press, the Medina Committee of the Association of the Bar of the City of New York, and the Special Committee of the Board of Directors of the American Newspaper Publishers Association. . . .

activity, however, effective measures to curb prejudicial publicity while protecting freedom of the press were virtually non-existent. Report of the Committee on the Operation of the Jury System on the "Free Press—Fair Trial" Issue, 45 F.R.D. 391, 399 (1968).

Sheppard v. Maxwell

Such was the situation when, in 1966, the Supreme Court announced its landmark decision in the case of Sheppard v. Maxwell, 1966, 384 U.S. 333. Sam Sheppard's trial for the murder of his wife had been carnivalized by relentless, irresponsibly over-anxious reporters who displayed a remarkable insensitivity to accuracy, fairness or justice. Before the trial pervasive news coverage had branded Sheppard "a bare-faced liar," a "Jekyll-Hyde" and a "perjuror." A picture of Mrs. Sheppard's bloodstained pillow was "doctored" and then published on the front page of a local newspaper. Much attention was devoted to the extrajudicial claims of a woman convict that Sheppard was the father of her illegitimate child. During the trial, bedlam reigned at the courthouse as hundreds of reporters and photographers jammed the entire courtroom, causing constant confusion, disruption and commotion. A radio broadcast booth was established adjacent to the jury room. Jurymen, witnesses, attorneys and even the Judge were "forced to run the gauntlet of reporters and photographers each time they entered or left the courtroom." 384 U.S. at 355. The newsmen exploited the "free reign" which had been allowed them and turned the trial into a "Roman holiday."

Finding that the "state trial judge did not fulfill his duty to protect Sheppard from the inherently prejudicial publicity which saturated the community and to control disruptive influences in the courtroom," 384 U.S. at 363, the Supreme Court ordered a writ of habeas corpus releasing Sheppard from custody. In so holding the Supreme Court laid to rest the notion that the trial court was impotent to protect the defendant from prejudicial influences of an omnipresent press. Indeed the Court suggested a number of ways in which the Courts could "protect their processes from prejudicial outside interferences." 384 U.S. at 363. More importantly, the Court in *Sheppard* not only sanctioned efforts to effect this insulation but *demanded* that trial courts adopt "strong measures to insure that the balance is never weighed against the accused." 384 U.S. at 362. "If publicity during the proceedings threatens the fairness of the trial, a new trial should be ordered. But we must remember that reversals are but palliatives; the cure lies in those remedial measures that will prevent the prejudice at its inception."

Free Press—Fair Trial Rules

In response to the mandate of *Sheppard,* the Judicial Conference of the United States took action. Its standing Committee on the Operation of the Jury System [was] headed by Judge Irving Kaufman . . . .

The Kaufman Committee Report was subsequently adopted by the Judicial Conference of the United States and implemented by Local "Free-Press—Fair-Trial" Rules promulgated by each District Court. The Report and the

Local Rules embodying it, however, must be viewed in light of the historically delicate balance the recommendations sought so zealously to preserve. Painstakingly harmonizing history with contemporary realities, freedom of the press with fundamental fairness of trials, the Kaufman Committee explored every aspect of the problem and its Report synthesizes all relevant considerations. The result is a catalogue of explicit proposals, most taken directly from the *Sheppard* opinion, inventorying the tools available to the trial Judge in discharging his affirmative duty to protect the accused from prejudicial publicity and disruptive influences at trial, but carefully avoiding any but the most limited, tangential and indispensable controls on the press.

Indeed, the *Sheppard* opinion had specifically declined to "place any direct limitations on the freedom traditionally exercised by the news media" and had expressly asserted that "of course, there is nothing that proscribes the press from reporting events that transpire in the courtroom." In recognition of those dictates the Kaufman Committee's recommendations deliberately eschew any suggestions for direct control of newsmen except in two very carefully delineated situations—(i) the seating of news media representatives so as to minimize disruptive influences during trial and (ii) the televising, photographing or broadcasting from the courtroom. Other than those exceptions, the Kaufman Committee's recommendations are directed exclusively to parties, witnesses, attorneys, jurors, and courthouse personnel. Of course, the provision for special orders in widely publicized and sensational cases,[11] on which the District Court here relied so heavily, provides great elasticity and room for judicial inventiveness. However, the Report makes clear that this provision was intended to apply only "where necessary to preserve decorum in and around the courtroom and to maintain the integrity of the trial." More importantly, in an effort to insure that the Rule would be invoked only within the framework of constitutionally permissible limits, the Committee went on to identify certain specific subjects to which orders might be addressed. . . . Significantly, none of these permissive special provisions includes a suggestion that the content of news reports might be judicially supervised or otherwise controlled, and the local Rule does not undertake to do so. Without so holding—since no such Rule exists—we have grave reservations whether such a limitation could be promulgated without making impermissibly serious inroads into the purview of the First Amendment. Censorship in any form—judicial censorship included—is simply incompatible with the dictates of the constitution and the concept of a free press.

Now To The Case At Hand

Translating that rich history to the case before us, one significant circumstance is readily apparent—no decision, opinion, report or other authoritative proposal has ever sanctioned by holding, hint, dictum, recommendation or otherwise any judicial prohibition of the right of the press to publish accurate-

11. "RULE 9. SPECIAL ORDERS

In a widely publicized or sensational case, the Court on motion of either party or on its own motion, may issue a special order governing such matters as extrajudicial statements by parties and witnesses likely to interfere with the rights of the accused to a fair trial by an impartial jury, the seating and conduct in the courtroom of spectators and news media representatives, the management and the sequestration of jurors and witnesses, and any other matters which the Court may deem appropriate for inclusion in such an order. . . .

ly reports of proceedings which transpire in open court.[14] Indeed, the *Sheppard* opinion, amid a host of suggestions which inevitably limit the press to some extent, specifically and plainly repudiates the notion that the Trial Judge may also bar news reports of public proceedings. "Of course, there is nothing that proscribes the press from reporting events that transpire in the courtroom." 384 U.S. at 362–363. The Kaufman Committee Report likewise rejects direct influence over the newsmen's domain. "The Committee does not presently recommend any direct curb or restraint on publication by the press of potentially prejudicial material. Such a curb, it feels, is both unwise as a matter of policy and poses serious constitutional problems." [15]

Even if special exigencies might justify curtailment of the right to publish court proceedings in some extraordinary circumstance—and that *if* is a very big one indeed—the present case is peculiarly ill-suited for abandonment of the traditional reluctance of courts to supervise the content of news accounts of public proceedings. In the first place, since the cases make clear that before First Amendment freedoms can be abridged "the substantive evil must be extremely serious and the degree of imminence extremely high," *Bridges,* supra, 314 U.S. at 263, and that "the fires which [the expression] kindles must constitute an immediate, not merely a likely, threat to the administration of justice. The danger must not be remote or even probable; it must immediately imperil," *Craig,* 331 U.S. at 376, "the specific freedom of public comment should weigh heavily against a possible tendency to influence pending cases [particularly in borderline instances]." *Pennekamp,* supra, 328 U.S. at 347. With these guides in mind, it is significant that the hearing here in issue was not before a jury, and trial on the merits was by no means immediate. Nor was there any certainty as to the place of the State Court trial. It is the nature of news that it is so readily forgotten—time can erase impressions, even sensational ones. Thus, while prejudicial news coverage may poison the minds of jurors or immediate prospective jurors for the present, the contamination may be only temporary and while allowing the press possibly to generate an inflamed temper in the community is regrettable, this was no indication that change of venue would not likely suffice. Therefore, the District Court's cure was worse than the disease.

14. One possible exception to this broad statement may be found by way of dictum in Mr. Justice White's very recent opinion for the Court in Branzburg v. Hayes, 1972, 408 U.S. 665, that newsmen "may be prohibited from attending or publishing information about trials if such restrictions are necessary to assure a defendant a fair trial before an impartial tribunal." 408 U.S. at 685. It seems unlikely that he meant for this dictum to be read too literally, since he immediately cites *Sheppard, Estes* and *Rideau* as support for this proposition. Of course, as we have already pointed out, each of these three cases expressly and explicitly disavows any suggestion that newsmen can be prohibited from publishing reports of what transpires in open court.

15. Footnote 17 of the Report explained, "Both the Reardon and Medina Committees reject an expanded use of the contempt power to control the news media. Because of 'the constitutional problems that would be raised' and 'the inhibitory effect on speech that ought not to be prohibited,' the Reardon Committee proposes the use of the contempt power only, 'when a serious threat to the fairness of an ongoing trial by jury is created by an extrajudicial public statement calculated to affect the outcome of that trial.' Reardon Report, Recommendation 4.1, Proposed Final Draft, p. 27. The Medina Committee is of the view that 'as a matter of both constitutional law and policy, . . . extension of the contempt power is neither feasible nor wise. . . . " (Medina Report, p. 11)."

Second, the situation which the trial court faced in the present case was in no way the "Roman holiday"—"carnival atmosphere" created by hundreds of reporters at the Sheppard trial, or the "cause celebre"-show-must-go-on environment of the Estes trial, or the total "bombardment of the community with the sights and sounds of a two-day hearing" at the Rideau trial, for example. The order here covered only two reporters whose in-court conduct was unobtrusive and whose articles appeared deeply buried within the oft-overlooked interiors of the daily paper. Of course this was not the object of the Judge's concern relating to possible prejudice in a future trial at another time and place, but the factor of disruption did not warrant the restrictive measures employed.

Third, the public's right to know the facts brought out in this specific hearing was particularly compelling here, since the issue being litigated was a charge that elected state officials had trumped up charges against an individual solely because of his race and political civil rights activities. "Particularly in matters of local political corruption and investigation is it important that freedom of communications be kept open and that the real issues not become obscured . . . ." *Wood,* supra, 370 U.S. 390.

Fourth, while the Court's power over particular conduct committed in his presence within the courtroom is unquestioned, the injunction challenged in this case was not directed at any named party or court official involved in the underlying litigation, but rather it sought to control activities of non-parties to the lawsuit—namely, two reporters—in matters not going to the merits of the substantive issues of the ongoing trial or the court's ability to effectuate any ultimate judgment on them.

Fifth, a Federal Court's responsibility to protect a State Court defendant from anticipated unconstitutional influences is generally limited to situations where there is an antecedent showing of bad faith harassment or other special circumstances. Younger v. Harris, companion cases and progeny. Since the State Courts are presumed to be no less capable of protecting the defendants' constitutional rights in the context of a pending criminal prosecution than is a Federal Court, Becker v. Thompson, 5 Cir., 1972, 459 F.2d 919, it is generally inappropriate for a Federal Court to attempt by way of anticipation to protect the potential defendant from some possible denial of constitutional right by the State Court. See especially, Perez v. Ledesma, 1971, 401 U.S. 82. Although this sensitivity to the accused's rights was laudable both in the sense of protection to the accused and in eliminating the possible generation of deplorable community-wide prejudice, the restrictive measures adopted practically put the Federal Judge in the role of policing the climate of the community to insure a sterile trial in the State Court.

Finally, there are available alternative cures for prejudicial publicity far less disruptive of constitutional freedoms than an absolute ban on publication. Thus, if as the Judge apprehended, the expected pretrial publicity generated a prejudicial atmosphere which had not abated by time for the State trial, the traditional remedies of continuance or change of venue would be readily available to insure a fair trial. The inconvenience or expense to State or defendant in such a course was not enough to justify the extreme ban on publication.

Of course with mass dissemination of news being what it is today there is no way of being positive that change of venue or postponement by continuance eradicates all prejudice, but with competing values at stake this possibly is not enough. For if allowing the press to publish reports of the proceedings in the present case carried the prospect of poisoning the minds of potential jurors, it likewise offered the promise of administering an antidote against the societal diseases of corruption, oppression and abuse of power by government officials. Enforced silence in the name of preserving the sterility of a future trial can suffocate the First Amendment, particularly when the very issue then on trial is the serious charge of flagrant, wilfull abuse of power. Tabulating this rich history, these factors add up to our compelled conclusion that the District Court's order banning publication of matters transpiring in open court was constitutionally unacceptable, and hence illegal.

It Doesn't End Here

The conclusion that the District Court's order was constitutionally invalid does not necessarily end the matter of the validity of the contempt convictions. There remains the very formidable question of whether a person may with impunity knowingly violate an order which turns out to be invalid. We hold that in the circumstances of this case he may not.

We begin with the well-established principle in proceedings for criminal contempt that an injunction duly issuing out of a court having subject matter and personal jurisdiction *must be obeyed,* irrespective of the ultimate validity of the order. Invalidity is no defense to criminal contempt. United States v. United Mine Workers; Howat v. State of Kansas; Gompers v. Buck's Stove and Range Co; Walker v. City of Birmingham.

It is clear that this principle applies even where the invalidity of the order is of constitutional proportions, as Walker v. Birmingham plainly holds. In *Walker* the contemnors, including Dr. Martin Luther King, had violated an Alabama circuit court ex parte injunction prohibiting participation in street demonstrations planned for the forth coming Easter weekend. Forsaking numerous appellate routes left open for contesting the circuit court's order, the demonstrators marched anyway in knowing disobedience to the injunction and without having taken any judicial steps to dissolve or overturn it. The Supreme Court affirmed the resulting contempt convictions. Admittedly the injunction in *Walker* was merely a judicial paraphrase of an existing municipal ordinance which prohibited street demonstrations without authority of a permit secured from the Commissioner of Public Safety (Eugene "Bull" Conner), which ordinance was shortly declared unconstitutional by a unanimous court in Shuttlesworth v. City of Birmingham, 1968, 394 U.S. 147. Nevertheless, the Court, emphasizing that "respect for judicial process is a small price to pay for the civilizing hand of law," 388 U.S. at 321, emphatically rejected the suggestion that an individual may disregard a court order simply because the injunction interfered with—albeit impermissibly—his exercise of First Amendment rights. Absent a showing of "transparent invalidity" or patent frivolity surrounding the order, *it must be obeyed* until reversed by orderly review or disrobed of authority by delay or frustration in the appellate process, regardless of the ultimate determination of constitutionality, or lack thereof.

Uniqueness Of The Judiciary

Admittedly, the inviolability of court orders, typified by the *Walker* rule, is unique among governmental commands. When legislators or executive agencies—State or Federal—have transgressed constitutional or statutory bounds, their mandates need not be obeyed. Violators, of course, risk criminal sanctions if their prediction of illegality should fail, but if the directive is invalid, it may be disregarded with impunity. Shuttlesworth v. City of Birmingham. In fact, in certain situations, intentional disobedience to the statute may be the only means of obtaining a judicial determination of its constitutionality. See, e.g., Becker v. Thompson, 5 Cir., 1972, 459 F.2d 919; Boyle v. Landry, 1971, 401 U.S. 77. Similarly, "one cannot be punished for failing to obey the command of a [police] officer if that command is violative of the Constitution." Wright v. Georgia, 1963, 373 U.S. 284, 291–292.

Likewise, disobedience to a Congressional demand for information cannot be punished as contempt of Congress if the demand was constitutionally infirm. Watkins v. United States, 1957, 354 U.S. 178. And obviously, refusal to submit to an order of induction into the armed forces is not punishable where the order issued in violation of the inductee's constitutional or statutory rights. United States v. Wingerter, 5 Cir., 1970, 423 F.2d 1015.

Significantly, it is only the orders of judicial authorities which must be tested in the courts before deliberate transgression can be excused on an eventual determination that the order was invalid.

The criminal contempt exception requiring compliance with court orders, while invalid non-judicial directives may be disregarded, is not the product of self-protection or arrogance of Judges. Rather it is born of an experience-proved recognition that this rule is essential for the system to work. Judges, after all, are charged with the final responsibility to adjudicate legal disputes. It is the judiciary which is vested with the duty and the power to interpret and apply statutory and constitutional law. Determinations take the form of orders. The problem is unique to the judiciary because of its particular role. Disobedience to a legislative pronouncement in no way interferes with the legislature's ability to discharge its responsibilities (passing laws). The dispute is simply pursued in the judiciary and the legislature is ordinarily free to continue its function unencumbered by any burdens resulting from the disregard of its directives. Similarly, law enforcement is not prevented by failure to convict those who disregard the unconstitutional commands of a policeman.

On the other hand, the deliberate refusal to obey an order of the court without testing its validity through established processes requires further action by the judiciary, and therefore directly affects the judiciary's ability to discharge its duties and responsibilities. Therefore, "while it is sparingly to be used, yet the power of courts to punish for contempts is a necessary and integral part of the independence of the judiciary, and is absolutely essential to the performance of the duties imposed on them by law. Without it they are mere boards of arbitration whose judgments and decrees would be only advisory." Gompers v. Buck's Stove & Range Co.

No Distinction Between Press and Speech

Appellants do not challenge the *Walker* case or its predecessors. Rather they argue that these cases simply do not apply to injunctions or other judicial orders infringing freedom of the press. No rationale has been offered to justify different treatment where free press instead of free speech issues are at stake, and we perceive no basis for such a distinction. On the contrary, particular language in the recent Supreme Court decision of New York Times Co. v. United States suggests that that Court would not sanction disobedience of a court order, even where the injunction unconstitutionally restrains publication of news. In the *Times* case, the lower courts had issued temporary restraining orders prohibiting further publication of the Pentagon Papers pending judicial determination of the merits of the Government's objections. Six of the Justices agreed that these injunctions were violative of the First Amendment. Nevertheless, no one suggested that the injunctions could have been ignored with impunity. On the contrary, Mr. Justice Black, with whom Mr. Justice Douglas concurred, vehemently asserted that "every moment's continuance of the injunctions against these newspapers amounts to a flagrant, indefensible, and continuing violation of the First Amendment." 403 U.S. at 715. Obviously, if the *Times* were free to disregard the unreversed injunctions because of their incompatibility with the First Amendment, the mere presence of impotent and unenforceable restraining orders could not be deemed an ominous immediate denial of First Amendment rights. Mr. Justice Brennan announced an equivalent position. Accordingly, an assumption that courts may punish as contempt violations of even its constitutionally defective orders infringing freedom of the press underlies the *Times* decision.

A Few Inapplicable Qualifications

Of course, the rule that unconstitutional court orders must nevertheless be obeyed until set aside presupposes the existence of at least three conditions: (i) the court issuing the injunction must enjoy subject matter and personal jurisdiction over the controversy; (ii) adequate and effective remedies must be available for orderly review of the challenged ruling, and (iii) the order must not require an irretrievable surrender of constitutional guarantees. Regarding (i), there is no problem in this case at all.

Regarding (ii), the Supreme Court made quite clear in *Walker* that its decision was influenced by the fact that there was a two-day interim between the issuance of the injunction and the planned Good Friday march, during which time some effort to secure judicial relief could and should have been made. However, Mr. Justice Stewart emphasized that "this case would arise in quite a different constitutional posture if the petitioners, before disobeying the injunction, had challenged it in the Alabama courts, and had been met with delay or frustration of their constitutional claims." 382 U.S. at 318. If there had been no real opportunity to contest the unconstitutional order, as, for example, if it had been issued at the very moment the march was scheduled to commence, then the premise that effective judicial remedies were available would be undermined and the result would likely have been different.

The "News Is Today's News" Argument–Newsmen Are Citizens, Too

Where the thing enjoined is publication and the communication is "news," this condition presents some thorny problems. Timeliness of publication is the hallmark of "news" and the difference between "news and history" is merely a matter of hours. Thus, where the publishing of news is sought to be restrained, the incontestable inviolability of the order may depend on the immediate accessibility of orderly review. But in the absence of strong indications that the appellate process was being deliberately stalled—certainly not so in this record—violation with impunity does not occur simply because immediate decision is not forthcoming, even though the communication enjoined is "news." Of course the nature of the expression sought to be exercised is a factor to be considered in determining whether First Amendment rights can be effectively protected by orderly review so as to render disobedience to otherwise unconstitutional mandates nevertheless contemptuous. But newsmen are citizens, too. See Branzburg v. Hayes. They too may sometimes have to wait. They are not yet wrapped in an immunity or given the absolute right to decide with impunity whether a Judge's order is to be obeyed or whether an appellate court is acting promptly enough.

Regarding (iii) it is obvious that if the order requires an *irrevocable* and permanent surrender of a constitutional right, it cannot be enforced by the contempt power. For example, a witness cannot be punished for contempt of court for refusing a court order to testify if the underlying order violates Fifth, Fourth or perhaps First Amendment rights. Malloy v. Hogan, 1964, 378 U.S. 1; Silverthorne Lumber Co. v. United States, 1920, 251 U.S. 385; Gelbard v. United States, 1972, 408 U.S. 41. In each of these cases the unconstitutionality of the court's order served as a valid defense to a charge of contempt. The rationale of these cases is that once the witness has complied with an order to testify he cannot thereafter retrieve the information involuntarily revealed, even if it subsequently develops that compelling the testimony violated constitutional rights. In such a predicament, the damage is irreparable. No remedies are available which can effectively cure the constitutional deprivation after the order has been unwillingly obeyed.

But none of these exculpating factors was present in the case before us. As a matter of jurisdiction (i), the District Court certainly has power to formulate Free Press-Fair Trial orders in cases pending before the court and to enforce those orders against all who have actual and admitted knowledge of its prohibitions. Secondly, as the District Court's findings of fact establish, both the District Court and the Court of Appeals were available and could have been contacted that very day,[18] thereby affording speedy and effective

18. The court order was issued on November 1. It was violated on November 2. On November 15 the defendants were convicted of contempt of court. Until this time defendants had made no effort whatsoever to have the injunction set aside. They had not sought reconsideration by the District Court, appeal, mandamus or any other judicial review of the order. *Thereafter,* on December 1 the defendants filed an application for writ of mandamus in this Court seeking to have this Court order the District Court to vacate the injunction. The response filed by the District Court explained that the order had been dissolved and that the mandamus action was therefore moot. On December 7 a panel of this Court (Judges Wisdom, Coleman and Simpson) denied the petition for writ of mandamus

but *orderly* review of the injunction in question swiftly enough to protect the right to publish news while it was still "news." Finally, unlike the compelled testimony situations the District Court's order required that information be withheld—not forcibly surrendered—and accordingly, compliance with the Court's order would not require an irrevocable, irretrievable or irreparable abandonment of constitutional privileges.

Under the circumstances, reporters took a chance. As civil disobedients have done before they ran a risk, the risk being magnified in this case by the law's policy which forecloses their right to assert invalidity of the order as a complete defense to a charge of criminal contempt. Having disobeyed the Court's decree, they must, as civil disobeyers, suffer the consequences [19] for having rebelled at what they deem injustice, but in a manner not authorized by law. They may take comfort in the fact that they, as their many forerunners, have thus established an important constitutional principle—which may be all that was really at stake—but they may not now escape the inescapable legal consequence for their flagrant, intentional disregard of the mandates of a Court.

Retrospective Invalidity Taints Guilty Finding

The fact that the District Court in the circumstances of this case could validly have punished the defendants for contempt of court despite the unconstitutionality of the underlying order still does not dispose of the case. There remains the question whether the conviction should stand in view of the fact that the District Court's action rested on the good faith but mistaken belief that the order was perfectly valid.

Contempt, of course, is a *sui generis* proceeding, and "there is no doubt that a contempt proceeding has play in the joints." United States v. Barnett, 5 Cir. (en banc), 1965, 346 F.2d 99, 107 (Wisdom, J., dissenting). Indeed, contempt may well be the last vestige of the so-called "common law crimes," insofar as a determination that particular conduct should be punished as contempt depends not so much on specific prohibited acts having occurred as on the Judge's subjective determination that the conduct was culpable, blameworthy and deserving of punishment. It may well be that particular conduct is in direct and flagrant disobedience to a court order but the issuing court whose order is violated may nevertheless decide, for whatever reasons, that no sanctions ought to be imposed. See United States v. Barnett.

Given that flexibility in contempt cases, an erroneous view regarding the lawfulness of the underlying order may well taint the judgment of contempt. The case of Donovan v. City of Dallas, 1964, 377 U.S. 408, is illustrative. In *Donovan* the Texas Court of Civil Appeals had issued a Writ of Prohibition barring certain Federal Court plaintiffs from prosecuting their claims in the United States Court of Appeals for the Fifth Circuit because the issues had already been litigated in the State Courts. The Federal plaintiffs violated this order and were adjudged to be in contempt. When the case ultimately reached the United States Supreme Court, that Court held that the Texas Writ of Prohibition constituted an unlawful deprivation of a Federal Court

"without prejudice to petitioners' appeal from the criminal contempt convictions." . . .

19. In this case the consequences came relatively painlessly. The defendants were merely fined $300.00 each.

litigant's rights to pursue Federal appellant remedies. The invalidity of the Texas order, however, did not in and of itself vitiate the contempt convictions. Rather, the Supreme Court remanded the case for a determination by the Texas Court as to whether or not it still would consider the conduct contemptuous, in view of the subsequent pronouncement that the restraining order was unconstitutional. . . .

On remand the Texas Court of Civil Appeals determined that the judgments of contempt were inappropriate in view of the Supreme Court pronouncement that the restraining orders were unlawful. Accordingly, the contempt convictions were vacated.

. . . Undeniably, there is no absolute prohibition to such a result ensuing but where the premise (*lawful* order disobeyed) is erroneous, the conclusion (conduct contemptuous) is tainted.

In the case before us the conclusion of contempt was bottomed irrevocably on a mistake of law—"It was the opinion of this Court then and it is its opinion now that the order issued was authorized by [paragraph 9 of the Court's Free Press-Fair Trial] Rule." It was not. Since the determination that the conduct of the respondents was contemptuous was premised on this erroneous view, it is appropriate to remand the case to the District Court for a determination of whether the judgment of contempt or the punishment therefor would still be deemed appropriate in light of the fact that the order disobeyed was constitutionally infirm.

Upon the "forced withdrawal to the District Court," Judge WEST wrote [349 F.Supp. 227, 228 (M.D.La.1972)]:

[A]fter making this positive finding, the Court of Appeals remanded the case to this Court for reconsideration and for a determination of "whether the judgment of contempt or the punishment therefor would still be deemed appropriate in light of the fact that the order disobeyed was constitutionally infirm." In view of the positive findings of the Court of Appeals, with which views I wholeheartedly agree, it would be too great a contradiction for me, on the one hand, to recognize the principle approved by the Court of Appeals that "Having disobeyed the Court's decree, they must, as civil disobeyers, suffer the consequences for having rebelled at what they deem injustice, but in a manner not authorized by law," and at the same time hold that because the order, issued in utter good faith by this Court, was subsequently held by another Court to be constitutionally infirm, the defendants should *not* suffer the consequences for "having rebelled at what they deem injustice, but in a manner not authorized by law." I deem it inappropriate in this case for me to try to imitate the proverbial catfish who could talk out of both sides of his mouth and whistle all at the same time.

Furthermore, the Court of Appeals mistakenly concludes that "the conclusion of contempt was bottomed irrevocably on a mistake of law." On the contrary, the conclusion of contempt was bottomed on the very law recognized, approved, and reiterated by the Court of Appeals in this very case, i.e., that the defendants may not assert invalidity of the order as a defense to the charge of criminal contempt in this case; that having disobeyed the Court's decree they must, as civil disobeyers, suffer the consequences, and that they may not now "escape the inescapable legal consequence for their flagrant, intentional disregard of the mandates of a Court."

"It was not the fact that this Court then and now believes that its order was a valid one that alone gave rise to the contempt citation. It was the fact that these defendants, rather than seek an available judicial review of the Court's order, decided instead to announce to court personnel that they were going to violate the order and then, after violating the order, contemptuously announced to the public, at the end of their published articles, that they had published this story despite an order of Court ordering them not to do so. It was primarily this public display of utter contempt for this Court's order that prompted the contempt citation. The defendants, as noted by the Court of Appeals, may "not now escape the inescapable legal consequence for their flagrant, intentional disregard of the mandates of a Court." Of course this Court was of the opinion that its order was a valid one. It would be difficult to conceive of a court issuing an order, knowing it to be invalid, and then having the audacity to cite a person for contempt for disobeying it. The very purpose of the law which has been cited with approval by the Court of Appeals, and under which a person must suffer the consequences for willfully and intentionally disregarding a court order, is to protect the integrity of court orders, issued in good faith, unless and until they are judicially determined to be invalid. At the time of the contempt citation, it was not the validity vel non of the Court's order that was primarily at issue. It was the intentional, willful, flagrant and contemptuous disregard of the Court's order before in any way attempting to have the order, which was obviously issued in good faith, judicially reviewed. It was upon this action, rather than a mistake of law, that the contempt citation was bottomed.

"For these reasons, the conviction of the defendants for criminal contempt of Court, and the fines heretofore imposed, must remain unchanged."

---

1) Dickinson and Adams appealed again. A different panel of the court of appeals disposed of the appeal without reaching the merits. "We do not have on this appeal any issue of free press-fair trial. The determination which we make is that the prior opinion and decision of this Court established the law of the case from which we do not depart. Orderly judicial procedure requires that there be an adherence to a decision upon an earlier appeal of the same case. . . . Although the Court has power to adopt a position different from that of the earlier appeal, we are not persuaded that such action is required in this cause. It is to be noted that the appellants did not seek a rehearing or make application for certiorari of the decision on the prior appeal. The judgment of the district court is affirmed." 476 F.2d 373, 374 (5th Cir. 1973). The Supreme Court denied certiorari 414 U.S. 979 (1973).

2) Rendleman reacted to *Dickinson* with two articles: Free Press—Fair Trial: Restrictive Orders After Nebraska Press, 67 Ky.L.J. 867 (1979); Free Press—Fair Trial: Review of Silence Orders, 52 N.C.L.Rev. 127 (1973). Two problems pervade analysis. The reporters were not parties to the underlying action; if it had been a criminal prosecution, they would not be parties to it. Yet they were constrained to obey the order. How did they become "parties"? Second, can the reporters proceed promptly enough for

the November 2 edition of the paper? Was timing as important for Dickinson as it was for the *Walker* defendants?

Did Judge West's order exercise legislative power to declare conduct unlawful instead of judicial power to decide discrete lawsuits? Would you find it easier to say that Dickinson and Adams were parties if Judge West had extended the usual procedural amenities of notice and an opportunity to be heard to them? Was there a legal proceeding in which they could become parties? Would formal procedure complicate and delay the Stewart trial?

Was Judge Brown correct in saying that because Judge West "required that information be withheld" it did "not require an irrevocable, irretrievable, or irreparable abandonment of constitutional privileges"? Was Judge West's order effective final relief against the reporter's right to expression on November 2? The *Pentagon Papers* Court divided on the question of whether the time it took the courts to decide the lawsuit interfered with the newspaper's first amendment right, p. 217. Which view does Judge Brown appear to adopt, Justice Brennan's or Justice Harlan's?

If one of the reporters had left Judge West's courtroom right after the judge announced the order and consulted you, what could you have done for him? A short review of procedural options follows: a) Ask Judge West to modify or dissolve the order. b) Seek a permissive interlocutory appeal, 28 U.S.C. § 1292(b). c) File a final order appeal, 28 U.S.C. § 1291. d) Appeal the order as a preliminary injunction, 28 U.S.C. § 1292(a)(1). e) File mandamus in the court of appeals, Fed.R.App.P. 21, 28 U.S.C. § 1651(a). If any of b)–e) is used, seek a stay from Judge West or the court of appeals. Fed.R.Civ.P. 62(d), Fed.R.App.P. 8(a). f) Publish the story and take your chances.

3) Judge West's order lacked the usual amenities of notice and an opportunity to be heard. It affected expressive activity and bound nonparties to the underlying action. The reporters had little time to appeal. Was this an appropriate time to apply the collateral bar rule? Did Judge Brown test the order against all the limitations of the *Walker* rule? Is jurisdiction as easy as he thinks? Why not apply *Walker's* "transparently invalid" exception? Is Judge Brown's rationale for the *Walker* rule adequate? Does one contempt hearing interfere with the performance of the judicial function? Did Judge Brown, instead of reversing the order, give Judge West a chance to correct his error? Did Judge West get the message? Why didn't the court of appeals reverse on the reporters' second appeal? Research revealed no other reported opinion that imposed contempt on a reporter who disseminated judicial material despite an unconstitutional order. Free Press-Fair Trial, 67 Ky.L.J. at 891; Free Press-Fair Trial, 52 N.C.L.Rev. at 153–63.

4) Problem: Heather Wilson asks Judge Bryson to seal one client's civil settlement agreement pending a jury decision in a related trial arising from the same accident. The judge sends notice to the Register, holds a hearing, and orders the settlement sealed citing Federal Rule 26(c). The Register neglects to send anyone to the hearing. A reporter named Dudley Warner takes a member of the clerk's staff to lunch two weeks later, learns that *Heather's* client settled the related case for 5% of what she had asked, and publishes a story the night before the jury begins to deliberate. The jury finds against *Heather's* client. May *Heather* charge contempt? Will Judge Bryson employ

the collateral bar rule to prevent the Register and Dudley Warner from arguing that the sealing order misapplied Rule 26(c)? Free Press-Fair Trial, 67 Ky.L.J. at 893.

5) The term prior restraint is one way of expressing skepticism about using injunctions to govern expression-related activity. Is *Dickinson* really a prior restraint decision? Would a criminal statute against a truthful report of a public trial abridge protected expression? Reconsider note 4) after *Walker.* Does the collateral bar rule justify the presumption against prior restraints? Is an injunction more likely than a criminal statute to prevent or deter protected expression because the collateral bar rule increases the chance that someone will be punished for engaging in protected expression? Is Judge West's order a prior restraint only because the court of appeals finds that it is an injunction and that the collateral bar rule insulates it from scrutiny? If we reject the collateral bar rule, should we reject prior restraint analysis with it? See generally Barnett, The Puzzle of Prior Restraint, 29 Stan.L.Rev. 539, 557–58 (1977). Professor Blasi argues that the presumption against prior restraints remains viable for injunctions even without the collateral bar because the injunctive process still assumes that speech is a threatening force, contributes to premature and abstract constitutional decisions, and will be employed more and more promptly than subsequent measures would be. Blasi, Toward a Theory of Prior Restraint: The Central Linkage, 66 Minn.L.Rev. 11, 85–92 (1981).

Is rejection of the collateral bar rule more consistent with the first amendment because a reporter may, like breaching a criminal statute and defending a prosecution, violate an order and take his chances in contempt? Sanford and Mortimer Kadish treat the collateral bar rule as part of "civil disobedience." They observe that "the law-and-order arguments used in the case of disobedience to court orders are just as appropriate in the case of disobedience to statutes." Discretion to Disobey 114 (1973). Does Judge Brown distinguish injunctions from statutes satisfactorily?

6) Four of the newspapers enjoined in the *Pentagon Papers* litigation filed affidavits in the *Dickinson* appeal. The affidavit filed by Evarts Graham, managing editor of the St. Louis Post-Dispatch is typical. "The decision of this newspaper not to publish these documents [the Pentagon Papers] in defiance of the order was based on the knowledge that the Supreme Court was going to decide the controversy. The government was asserting novel questions allegedly involving the national security. While we did not agree with the government's contention, we refrained from publishing while those important issues were being decided. In so doing, we in no way conceded that we had no right to print, and we in no way conceded that a prior restraint clearly unconstitutional on its face must be obeyed. On the contrary, in the normal case of a prior restraint, we are strongly of the view that the public has an immediate right to the news and that the media have a responsibility to the public under the constitution to publish news promptly, even in the face of a court order so long as that court order is patently unconstitutional, as in the *Dickinson* case." The New York Times filed a similar affidavit. Compare Mr. Goodale's statements at the University of Chicago Law School, p. 240 and Mr. Abrams's later comment, p. 259.

Chapter Six

INTERLOCUTORY INJUNCTIONS

Interlocutory injunctions prevent harm that plaintiff asserts will occur before the judge can adjudicate plaintiff's claims for final relief fully. The court must adjust its normal procedures to accommodate plaintiff's request for immediate, or at least prompt, action. Temporary restraining orders and preliminary injunctions come after attenuated procedure. Temporary restraining orders dispense with adversary procedure, and judges grant preliminary injunctions after assessing the facts incompletely at a short hearing. How do trial judges reduce the risk of error and ameliorate damage to defendant? This chapter is concerned with the procedural accommodations occasioned by interlocutory injunctions and the devices that guard against the dangers they present to defendants and the integrity of the legal system. Ask yourself whether plaintiff's expedited relief is purchased by compromising the adversary system's basic premises. Nussbaum, Temporary Restraining Orders and Preliminary Injunctions—The Federal Practice, 26 Sw.L.J. 265 (1972), is a readable general introduction to the subject.

I. Temporary Restraining Orders

CARROLL v. PRESIDENT AND COMMISSIONERS OF PRINCESS ANNE

393 U.S. 175, 89 S.Ct. 347, 21 L.Ed.2d 325 (1968).

Justice FORTAS delivered the opinion of the Court.

Petitioners are identified with a "white supremacist" organization called the National States Rights Party. They held a public assembly or rally near the courthouse steps in the town of Princess Anne, the county seat of Somerset County, Maryland, in the evening of August 6, 1966. The authorities did not attempt to interfere with the rally. Because of the tense atmosphere which developed as the meeting progressed, about 60 state policemen were brought in, including some from a nearby county. They were held in readiness, but for tactical reasons only a few were in evidence at the scene of the rally.

Petitioners' speeches, amplified by a public address system so that they could be heard for several blocks, were aggressively and militantly racist. Their target was primarily Negroes and, secondarily, Jews. It is sufficient to observe with the court below, that the speakers engaged in deliberately derogatory, insulting, and threatening language, scarcely disguised by protestations of peaceful purposes; and that listeners might well have construed their words as both a provocation to the Negroes in the crowd and an incitement to the whites. The rally continued for something more than an hour, concluding at about 8:25 p.m. The crowd listening to the speeches increased from about 50 at the beginning to about 150 of whom 25% were Negroes.

In the course of the proceedings it was announced that the rally would be resumed the following night, August 7.[1]

On that day, the respondents, officials of Princess Anne and of Somerset County, applied for and obtained a restraining order from the Circuit Court for Somerset County. The proceedings were *ex parte,* no notice being given to petitioners and, so far as appears no effort being made informally to communicate with them, although this is expressly contemplated under Maryland procedures.[2] The order restrained petitioners for 10 days from holding rallies or meetings in the county "which will tend to disturb and endanger the citizens of the County." [3] As a result, the rally scheduled for August 7 was not held. After the trial which took place 10 days later, an injunction was issued by the Circuit Court on August 30, in effect extending the restraint for 10 additional months. The court had before it, in addition to the testimony of witnesses, tape recordings made by the police of the August 6 rally.

On appeal, the Maryland Court of Appeals affirmed the 10-day order, but reversed the 10-month order on the ground that "the period of time was unreasonable and that it was arbitrary to assume that a clear and present danger of civil disturbance and riot would persist for ten months."

Petitioners sought review by this Court asserting that the case is not moot and that the decision of the Maryland Court of Appeals continues to have an adverse effect upon petitioners' rights. We granted certiorari.

We agree with petitioners that the case is not moot. Since 1966, petitioners have sought to continue their activities, including the holding of rallies in Princess Anne and Somerset County, and it appears that the decision of the Maryland Court of Appeals continues to play a substantial role in the response of officials to their activities.[4] In these circumstances, our jurisdiction is not at an end. . . .

1. Petitioner Norton said, "I want you to . . . be back here at the same place tomorrow night, bring every friend you have . . . . We're going to take it easy tonight . . . " and "You white folks bring your friends, come back tomorrow night. . . . Come on back tomorrow night let's raise a little bit of hell for the white race."

2. Maryland Rule of Procedure BB72 [reproduced after the opinion].

3. The text of the Writ of Injunction is as follows:

"We command and strictly enjoin and prohibit you the said Joseph Carroll, Richard Norton, J. B. Stoner, Connie Lynch, Robert Lyons, William Brailsford and National States Rights Party from holding rallies or meetings in Somerset County which will tend to disturb and endanger the citizens of the County and to enjoin you, the said defendants, from using and operating or causing to be operated within the County any devices or apparatus for the application [*sic*] of the human voice or records from any radio, phonograph or other sound making or producing device thereby disturbing the tranquility of the populace of the County, until the matter can be heard and determined in equity, or for a period of ten days from the date hereof.

"Hereof, fail not, as you will act to the contrary at your peril."

4. Petitioners recite that they were denied the right to hold a rally in Princess Anne on July 17, 1967, and that the letter of rejection relied upon the Court of Appeals' decision. They acknowledge that on July 25, they were authorized to hold rallies in Princess Anne on July 28, 29, and 30, 1967; but they appear to complain that the permit stipulated that the sound should not be amplified for more than 250 feet, and that "you will not be permitted to use racial epithets or to make slanderous remarks about the members of any race or ethnic group."

. . . The underlying question persists and is agitated by the continuing activities and program of petitioners: whether, by what processes, and to what extent the authorities of the local governments may restrict petitioners in their rallies and public meetings.

This conclusion—that the question is not moot and ought to be adjudicated by this Court—is particularly appropriate in view of this Court's decision in Walker v. Birmingham. In that case, the Court held that demonstrators who had proceeded with their protest march in face of the prohibition of an injunctive order against such a march, could not defend contempt charges by asserting the unconstitutionality of the injunction. The proper procedure, it was held, was to seek judicial review of the injunction and not to disobey it, no matter how well-founded their doubts might be as to its validity. Petitioners have here pursued the course indicated by *Walker;* and in view of the continuing vitality of petitioners' grievance, we cannot say that their case is moot.

Since the Maryland Court of Appeals reversed the 10-month injunction of August 30, 1966, we do not consider that order. We turn to the constitutional problems raised by the 10-day injunctive order.

The petitioners urge that the injunction constituted a prior restraint on speech and that it therefore violated the principles of the First Amendment which are applicable to the States by virtue of the Fourteenth Amendment. In any event, they assert, it was not constitutionally permissible to restrain petitioners' meetings because no "clear and present danger" existed.

Respondents, however, argue that the injunctive order in this case should not be considered as a "prior restraint" because it was based upon the events of the preceding evening and was directed to preventing a continuation of those events, and that, even if considered a "prior restraint," issuance of the order was justified by the clear and present danger of riot and disorder deliberately generated by petitioners.

We need not decide the thorny problem of whether, on the facts of this case, an injunction against the announced rally could be justified. The 10-day order here must be set aside because of a basic infirmity in the procedure by which it was obtained. It was issued *ex parte,* without notice to petitioners and without any effort, however informal, to invite or permit their participation in the proceedings. There is a place in our jurisprudence for *ex parte* issuance, without notice, of temporary restraining orders of short duration; but there is no place within the area of basic freedoms guaranteed by the First Amendment for such orders where no showing is made that it is impossible to serve or to notify the opposing parties and to give them an opportunity to participate.

We do not here challenge the principle that there are special, limited circumstances in which speech is so interlaced with burgeoning violence that it is not protected by the broad guaranty of the First Amendment. In Cantwell v. Connecticut, 310 U.S. 296, at 308 (1940), this Court said that "[n]o one would have the hardihood to suggest that the principle of freedom of speech sanctions incitement to riot." . . . Ordinarily, the State's constitutionally permissible interests are adequately served by criminal penalties imposed after freedom to speak has been so grossly abused that its immunity is breached. The impact and consequences of subsequent punishment for such abuse are materially different from those of prior restraint. Prior restraint upon speech suppresses the precise freedom which the First Amendment sought to protect against abridgment.

The Court has emphasized that "[a] system of prior restraints of expression comes to this Court bearing a heavy presumption against its constitutional validity." Bantam Books v. Sullivan, 372 U.S. 58, 70 (1963); Freedman v. Maryland, 380 U.S. 51, 57 (1965). And even where this presumption might otherwise be overcome, the Court has insisted upon careful procedural provisions, designed to assure the fullest presentation and consideration of the matter which the circumstances permit. As the Court said in Freedman v. Maryland, supra, at 58, a noncriminal process of prior restraints upon expression "avoids constitutional infirmity only if it takes place under procedural safeguards designed to obviate the dangers of a censorship system."

Measured against these standards, it is clear that the 10-day restraining order in the present case, issued *ex parte,* without formal or informal notice to the petitioners or any effort to advise them of the proceeding, cannot be sustained. Cf. Marcus v. Search Warrant, 367 U.S. 717, 731 (1961);[6] A Quantity of Books v. Kansas, 378 U.S. 205 (1964).[7] In the latter case, this Court disapproved a seizure of books under a Kansas statute on the basis of *ex parte* scrutiny by a judge. The Court held that the statute was unconstitutional. Mr. Justice Brennan, speaking for a plurality of the Court, condemned the statute for "not first affording [the seller of the books] an adversary hearing." In the present case, the reasons for insisting upon an opportunity for hearing and notice, at least in the absence of a showing that reasonable efforts to notify the adverse parties were unsuccessful, are even more compelling than in cases involving allegedly obscene books. The present case involves a rally and "political" speech in which the element of timeliness may be important. As Mr. Justice Harlan, dissenting in A Quantity of Books v. Kansas, pointed out, speaking of "political and social expression":

"It is vital to the operation of democratic government that the citizens have facts and ideas on important issues before them. A delay of even a day or two may be of crucial importance in some instances. On the other hand, the subject of sex is of constant but rarely particularly topical interest."

In the present case, the record discloses no reason why petitioners were not notified of the application for injunction. They were apparently present in Princess Anne. They had held a rally there on the night preceding the application for and issuance of the injunction. They were scheduled to have another rally on the very evening of the day when the injunction was issued.[8]

6. Marcus rejected the contention that Kingsley Books, Inc. v. Brown, 354 U.S. 436 (1957), supported "the proposition that the State may impose the extensive restraints imposed here on the distribution of these publications prior to an adversary proceeding on the issue of obscenity." 367 U.S., at 736. In Kingsley, a New York statute authorizing an injunction *pendente lite* against the distributon of obscene books was upheld. By statute, the person enjoined could get a hearing "within one day after joinder of issue." The New York courts have subsequently held that no *ex parte* injunction may be issued under the statute. Tenney v. Liberty News Distribs., Inc., 13 App.Div.2d 770, 215 N.Y.S.2d 663 (1961).

7. Compare the considerations leading to the Norris-LaGuardia Act, 47 Stat. 70, 29 U.S.C. §§ 101–115. See F. Frankfurter & N. Greene, The Labor Injunction 200–205 (1930).

8. The petition for the temporary injunction recited that Carroll and the others against whom the injunction was

And some of them were actually served with the writ of injunction at 6:10 that evening. In these circumstances, there is no justification for the *ex parte* character of the proceedings in the sensitive area of First Amendment rights.

The value of a judicial proceeding, as against self-help by the police, is substantially diluted where the process is *ex parte,* because the Court does not have available the fundamental instrument for judicial judgment: an adversary proceeding in which both parties may participate. The facts in any case involving a public demonstration are difficult to ascertain and even more difficult to evaluate. Judgment as to whether the facts justify the use of the drastic power of injunction necessarily turns on subtle and controversial considerations and upon a delicate assessment of the particular situation in light of legal standards which are inescapably imprecise. In the absence of evidence and argument offered by both sides and of their participation in the formulation of value judgments, there is insufficient assurance of the balanced analysis and careful conclusions which are essential in the area of First Amendment adjudication.[10]

The same is true of the fashioning of the order. An order issued in the area of First Amendment rights must be couched in the narrowest terms that will accomplish the pin-pointed objective permitted by constitutional mandate and the essential needs of the public order. In this sensitive field, the State may not employ "means that broadly stifle fundamental personal liberties when the end can be more narrowly achieved." Shelton v. Tucker, 364 U.S. 479, 488 (1960). In other words, the order must be tailored as precisely as possible to the exact needs of the case. The participation of both sides is necessary for this purpose.[11] Certainly, the failure to invite participation of the party seeking to exercise First Amendment rights reduces the possibility of a narrowly drawn order, and substantially imperils the protection which the Amendment seeks to assure.

Finally, respondents urge that the failure to give notice and an opportunity for hearing should not be considered to invalidate the order because, under Maryland procedure, petitioners might have obtained a hearing on not more than two days' notice. Maryland Rule of Procedure BB72. But this procedural right does not overcome the infirmity in the absence of a showing of justification for the *ex parte* nature of the proceedings. The issuance of an injunction which aborts a scheduled rally or public meeting, even if the restraint is of short duration, is a matter of importance and consequence in view of the First Amendment's imperative. The denial of a basic procedural right in these circumstances is not excused by the availability of post-issuance procedure which could not possibly serve to rescue the August 7 meeting, but, at best, could have shortened the period in which petitioners were prevented from holding a rally.

sought "are presently in Somerset or Wicomico Counties of the State of Maryland."

10. There is a danger in relying exclusively on the version of events and dangers presented by prosecuting officials, because of their special interest. Freedman v. Maryland.

11. Cf. Williams v. Wallace, 240 F.Supp. 100 (D.C.M.D.Ala.1965). There District Judge Johnson initially refused to issue an injunction *ex parte* against the absent state officials. Then, after a hearing at which the plaintiffs submitted a detailed plan for their proposed Selma-Montgomery march, he enjoined the State from interfering with the march as proposed in the plan.

We need not here decide that it is impossible for circumstances to arise in which the issuance of an *ex parte* restraining order for a minimum period could be justified because of the unavailability of the adverse parties or their counsel, or perhaps other reasons. In the present case, it is clear that the failure to give notice, formal or informal, and to provide an opportunity for an adversary proceeding before the holding of the rally was restrained, is incompatible with the First Amendment. Because we reverse the judgment below on this basis, we need not and do not decide whether the facts in this case provided a constitutionally permissible basis for temporarily enjoining the holding of the August 7 rally.

Reversed.

---

1) The significance of the *Carroll* rule might be assessed by determining what it adds to the requirements imposed by the Maryland rule of civil procedure that was in existence at the time of the case. The pertinent rule (Md. Ann.Code, Rules of Procedure, BB72 Ex Parte Injunctions, (1957)) provides:

"a. *When May Be Granted.*

"Any ex parte injunction shall not be granted unless it appears from specific facts shown by affidavit, or a verified pleading with or without supporting affidavit or sworn testimony, that immediate, substantial and irreparable injury will result to the applicant before an adversary hearing can be had. The judge to whom application is made for an ex parte injunction may, in his discretion, communicate informally with the person against whom the injunction is sought, or his attorney, prior to taking action upon the application.

"b. *Service—Contents—Expiration—Extension.*

"An ex parte injunction shall be served forthwith on the adverse party by the quickest possible means; it shall give the adverse party leave to move for a hearing on not more than two days' notice; and it shall expire by its terms within such time after entry as the court may fix. Such time shall not exceed ten days, in case of a resident, and shall not exceed thirty-five days, in case of a nonresident. The court may within the time so fixed, for good cause shown, extend such time for a like period or for a longer period if the party against whom the injunction is directed consents.

"c. *Motion for Relief—Early Hearing.*

"A motion for relief against an ex parte injunction shall be set down for hearing at the earliest possible time.

"d. *Hearing—Burden on Applicant—Dissolution.*

"At the hearing, the applicant who obtained the ex parte injunction shall have the burden of showing the necessity or propriety of continuing the injunction, and if he does not, the court shall dissolve the injunction."

The federal counterpart, Federal Rule of Civil Procedure 65(b), is in the Appendix. Compare both to 29 U.S.C. § 107, also in the Appendix.

2) United Farm Workers of America v. Superior Court, 14 Cal.2d 902, 122 Cal.Rptr. 877, 537 P.2d 1237 (1975), mandated procedural safeguards before enjoining picketing. The California court forbade ex parte restraining orders against activity "within the area" of expression unless plaintiff first

made good faith efforts to notify defendants. What sort of notice is required? How much notice must plaintiff extend? What type of hearing should the judge hold? Does defendant have a right to insist on sworn testimony, subject to cross examination?

3) Interlocutory injunctions preserve the status quo. What exactly is the status quo? When plaintiff appeared before the judge? When plaintiff began the lawsuit? The last noncontested status that preceded the lawsuit? Is the term status quo too unstable to be used to reach intelligent decisions? The Harvard Developments Note argues that when granting interlocutory orders, the judge should consider how to preserve or create a situation in which he can award effective relief to either party at the end of the trial. Note, Developments in the Law—Injunctions, 78 Harv.L.Rev. 994, 1056 (1965). If combined with the collateral bar rule and ex parte procedure, does that definition of status quo lead to hair triggered injunctions? More on Void Orders, 7 Ga.L.Rev. 246, 286 n. 200 (1973). The judge seeks to preserve a controversy to decide and allow the victor to profit from the victory. Remember that the lower court in *Pentagon Papers*, p. 217 preserved a controversy for the Supreme Court to decide but that Justice Black said that the interlocutory orders were final for every day they blocked publication. Did the temporary relief in *Carroll* grant effectively final relief against the August 7th rally? Did it preserve plaintiffs' status quo but alter defendants'?

4) Did plaintiffs' lawyer violate any professional duty by not notifying the apparently available defendants? In 1966, J.B. Stoner, one of the defendants, was a licensed attorney. Would Stoner's presence at the hearing have assisted the judge in deciding the plaintiffs' application? (In May 1980, Stoner was convicted of setting dynamite dangerously near or in an inhabited building for events stemming from the bombing of a black church in Birmingham in 1958, and his license to practice was suspended. In re Stoner, 246 Ga. 581, 272 S.E.2d 313 (1980).)

Canon 16 of the 1924 Canons of Judicial Ethics reads:

"A judge should discourage ex parte hearings of applications for injunctions and receiverships where the order may work detriment to absent parties; he should act upon such *ex parte* applications only where the necessity for quick action is clearly shown; if this be demonstrated, then he should endeavor to counteract the effect of the absence of opposing counsel by a scrupulous cross-examination and investigation as to the facts and the principles of law on which the application is based, granting relief only when fully satisfied that the law permits it and the emergency demands it. He should remember that an injunction is a limitation upon the freedom of action of defendants and should not be granted lightly or inadvisedly. One applying for such relief must sustain the burden of showing clearly its necessity and this burden is increased in the absence of the party whose freedom of action is sought to be restrained even though only temporarily."

Should the trial judge have insisted that someone notify the defendants or refused to enjoin until notice?

5) Assume the NSRP plans to conduct a rally in the town square of Grove, a largely black community. The authorities seek and receive an ex parte injunction from Judge Nagle. The NSRP defies the injunction and rallies. A criminal contempt trial follows. The NSRP argues that procedure

leading to the injunction violated *Carroll.* Plaintiff interposes *Walker,* p. 286. If defendant disobeys, does *Walker* insulate *Carroll* issues from scrutiny in contempt? Does a *Carroll* defense fit an exception to the *Walker* rule? Should the Court have based *Carroll* on due process rather than on the first amendment? When does it become "impossible" to notify defendants? Does *Carroll* go far enough? Should the rule be limited to first amendment interests? Will plaintiffs strive to avoid the *Carroll* rule by alleging a theory unrelated to free expression? Won't plaintiff argue that the rally creates a clear and present danger, the movie is obscene, or the picketing will be violent? Doesn't the answer to the question of what interests are affected by the injunction turn on the result of the hearing that was not held? What options does the defendant have? Could defendant move to dissolve, citing *Carroll*? Does service of the order retroactively cure lack of prior notice?

One of your editors has argued that plaintiffs should notify defendants formally or informally before any interlocutory order that prohibits conduct in progress or soon to begin. Failure to notify defendant will deprive the court of jurisdiction. The injunction will be void and vulnerable to collateral attack in contempt. This will encourage plaintiffs to notify defendants, yet it will allow the judge to apply the collateral bar rule when defendants were notified and the adversary system functioned. Rendleman, More on Void Orders, 7 Ga.L.Rev. 246 (1973); Toward Due Process in Injunction Procedure, 1973 U.Ill.L.F. 221. Does this apparent blanket ban include any exception for emergencies? The New Due Process: Rights and Remedies, 63 Ky.L.J. 532, 582–89 (1975). See also Krohn-Hite Corp. v. Berube, 372 F.Supp. 1262 (D.Mass.1974).

6) *Carroll* may be understood as a procedural prior restraint opinion. The government legitimately regulates activity on the borderline of expression like obscenity, defamation, and traffic. The Maryland procedure failed, however, to extend a sufficiently protective process to sort unprotected from protected activity. Because the Court found the procedure defective, it did not reach the substantive validity of the injunction. Assume that the judge had granted the injunction in note 3 after notice to the NSRP and a sufficient hearing. Could the NSRP have held an unamplified rally that didn't "tend to disturb and endanger the citizens of the County?" Would that injunction have been unconstitutional as a criminal statute? Brandenburg v. Ohio, 395 U.S. 444 (1969). How would the collateral bar rule affect the NSRP's defense in contempt?

Would an injunction that forbade the NSRP from inciting white members of the audience to immediate violence against black spectators be a prior restraint? Do the courts that follow prior restraint analysis prefer criminal prosecutions to injunctions because of the hazards of predicting from one rally that the next rally will become a riot? Is an individualized injunction more likely than a criminal statute to prevent a planned rally? Does the collateral bar rule affect your answer? If instead of enjoining, the prosecuting attorney had called on the NSRP before the second rally and told them that he planned to prosecute if the rally got out of hand, would that have been a prior restraint?

7) Problem: Billy Bob and his band travel about the country giving concerts. An unnamed and unknown "merchant" follows them surreptitiously

from town to town; on concert evenings about twenty people appear to sell "bootleg" records and merchandise bearing Billy Bob's name and picture to the throngs of people. The sales personnel differ from town to town. Billy Bob thinks that gross bootleg sales average over $10,000 at each concert. Unauthorized use of Billy Bob's name and picture violates his right to publicity and section 43(a) of the Lanham Act. Billy Bob arrives for a concert and files a federal action against "various unnamed individuals" to enjoin unauthorized marketing that evening. He seeks a temporary restraining order, needless to say, without notice. Is the order barred by *Carroll*?

8) Rendleman, Legal Anatomy of an Air Pollution Emergency, 2 Envrtl. Aff. 90 (1972), explores the dilemmas of an ex parte restraining order against stable-source particulate pollution in an apparent health emergency.

II. Preliminary Injunction Procedure

The rules governing the issuance of preliminary injunctions govern temporary restraining orders as well. Both are generally thought of as devices to preserve the status quo or to prevent irreparable harm during the pendency of a lawsuit. Both are interlocutory injunctions. Indeed, a preliminary injunction is sometimes called a "temporary injunction," heightening the confusion. The critical difference is, however, that preliminary injunctions are not issued ex parte. There is some adversary hearing. But, since the essence of the applicant's claim is that he needs the injunctive relief during the suit, before the full trial can be completed and sometimes even before it can be started, one of the most difficult problems for the trial judge is deciding how much of an adversary hearing to hold: Are the parties entitled to the normal privileges of pretrial discovery? Can the number of witnesses be limited? How extensive is the defendant's right of cross-examination?

SIMS v. GREENE

160 F.2d 512 (3d Cir. 1947).

Before BIGGS, GOODRICH and KALODNER, Circuit Judges.

BIGGS, Circuit Judge. On December 2, 1946, the plaintiff, David H. Sims, filed a complaint against the defendant, Sherman L. Greene, alleging that he, Sims, is a citizen of Pennsylvania and a Bishop of the African Methodist Episcopal Church and that he was assigned by a General Conference of the AME Church held in 1944 to the First Episcopal District to serve as the presiding bishop of that district until the next General Conference to be held in 1948; that the defendant, another bishop of the same church, has appeared in the First Episcopal District and within the jurisdiction of the court below and has proclaimed that he is the presiding bishop of the First District and is attempting to function as such; that by reason of the foregoing the plaintiff's office and functions as presiding bishop and his salary and emoluments are threatened as is the administration of the church and its conferences in the district; and that irreparable injury will result to the church, to its property and to the plaintiff unless the defendant is enjoined from pursuing the course complained of. An affidavit supporting the allegations of the complaint was filed with it.

On December 2, 1946, the court below, ex parte, issued an order restraining the defendant from interfering with the plaintiff as the presiding bishop of the district. The restraint originally imposed was continued by order for an additional ten days, to expire on December 22, 1946. . . . On December 20 the defendant consented to the restraint being extended until January 14, 1947 and the court made an order to such effect on December 20, 1946. See note 7 infra.

On December 24, 1946 the defendant filed his answer and with it a counterclaim containing prayers for affirmative relief. He admitted the allegations of the amended complaint in respect to diversity of citizenship and jurisdictional amount, but asserted that the plaintiff was no longer a bishop of the AME Church because he had been unfrocked by an extra session of the General Conference and by the Episcopal Committee meeting in Little Rock, Arkansas, about November 20, 1946; that he, the defendant, had been assigned by the extra session of the General Conference and by the Bishops' Council to the First Episcopal District as its presiding bishop; that by virtue of the foregoing he is the lawful presiding bishop of the district and his right to that office and its emoluments and his administration of the church and its property within the district are imperilled by the plaintiff's actions. The counterclaim ends with a prayer that the plaintiff be enjoined from interfering with the defendant.

On January 13, 1947 the court below extended the restraining order until January 24 [7] and proceeded to a hearing on the question of whether or not a preliminary injunction should be granted.[8] This hearing continued from January 13 to January 17, inclusive, and twelve hundred pages of argument, colloquy and testimony were taken down and have been transcribed. On January 17, at the close of the day the defendant's counsel made a motion to dissolve the restraint. . . .

On January 23, 1947 the defendant appealed to this court from the restraining order and moved for a stay of all proceedings in the District Court.[9]

7. The dates of the orders granting or continuing the restraint are as follows:

December 2, 1946, restraining order issued, to expire on December 12, 1946.

December 9, 1946, order entered extending the restraining order for a period of ten days from December 12, 1946, viz., December 22, 1946.

On December 20, 1946, the restraining order was continued by consent until January 14, 1947.

On January 13, 1947, the restraining order was continued until January 24, 1947.

On January 23, 1947, the restraining order was continued until February 3, 1947.

8. On December 19, 1946 the trial court suggested that it might be desirable to "consolidate" the hearing "into a preliminary and final proceeding," i.e., to proceed to final hearing. It does not appear, however, that this suggestion was acted upon.

9. At the same time the defendant filed a petition for a writ of prohibition or for a writ of peremptory mandamus to prohibit or restrain the trial judge from proceeding with the case on the ground that he had demonstrated bias and prejudice. At or about the same time the defendant filed an affidavit of bias and prejudice in the court below pursuant to Section 21 of the Judicial Code, 28 U.S.C.A. § 25. A rule issued, was made returnable on February 10, 1947, and was set down to be heard on February 13. Our disposition of that case (In re Petition of Greene, 3 Cir., 160 F.2d 517) is dealt with in an opinion filed concurrently with this.

We stayed the proceedings in the District Court and restrained the defendant from acting as the presiding bishop of the First Episcopal District pending the disposition of the appeal, setting February 13 as the day for argument. . . .

In our opinion the restraining order now in effect in the District Court must be treated as a temporary injunction, issued without the consent of the defendant, in the face of his motion to dissolve it, and contrary to the provisions of Rule 52(a). It is clear that an appeal lies from a temporary injunction. Deckert v. Independence Shares Corporation, 311 U.S. 282. The appeal at bar therefore may not be dismissed and the order restraining the defendant must be reversed. Our conclusions in this regard, however, are not intended to indicate that the court below may not enter a temporary injunction in accordance with the provisions of Section 381 of 28 U.S.C.A. and Rules 52 and 65, if the facts and the law warrant such a course. . . .

In view of the fact that the defendant has filed an answer and a counterclaim we can perceive no reason why the court below should not, as it itself suggested, proceed to final hearing. A prompt disposition of the cause is necessary in the public interest. The witnesses should not be permitted to give extended irrelevant testimony. Counsel should be restricted to relevant examination and cross-examination. The proceedings in the court below, as the record shows, were repeatedly interrupted by demonstrations by the spectators and the learned trial judge took no strong step to prevent such demonstrations. The dignity and decorum of a court of the United States must be maintained at all times.

The court below should sit from day to day and without unnecessary interruptions until the hearing is concluded.

The motion to dismiss the appeal will be denied. The order appealed from will be reversed. The stay order entered by this court on January 31, 1947 will be vacated. The court below will be directed to sit from day to day until the hearing is concluded.

SIMS v. GREENE

161 F.2d 87 (3d Cir. 1947).

Before BIGGS, GOODRICH, and KALODNER, Circuit Judges.

BIGGS, Circuit Judge. Many of the facts pertinent to the present appeal are stated in our opinion in Sims v. Greene, 3 Cir., 160 F.2d 512, and need not be repeated here. It is sufficient to state that following our reversal of the temporary restraining order or injunction originally issued by the court below on December 2, 1946, and after the remand of the case the learned trial judge on March 12, 1947, entered a preliminary injunction in form and effect substantially identical with the temporary restraining order or injunction disposed of by this court on the prior appeal. At or about the same time the court below filed findings of fact and conclusions of law. See Rule 52(a) of the Federal Rules of Civil Procedure . . . . Greene appealed from the order of March 12. We granted supersedeas and set the appeal down for argument on April 7, specifically directing the District Court to proceed to hear the case pending the disposition of the appeal.

We conclude that the preliminary injunction must be set aside. There are several reasons for our conclusion. The preliminary injunction was issued on the identical record which was before this court on the prior appeal. The allegations of the pleadings and affidavits filed in the cause are conflicting. Such conflicts must be resolved by oral testimony since only by hearing the witnesses and observing their demeanor on the stand can the trier of fact determine the veracity of the allegations made by the respective parties. If witnesses are not heard the trial court will be left in the position of preferring one piece of paper to another. Greene was given no opportunity to present oral testimony on his behalf except for one witness whose testimony was immaterial to any issue presented by the pleading. Sims insists that Greene was permitted to offer in evidence certain documents material to the issue but an examination of the record indicates that these documents, at least the most important of them, were read into the record by Greene's counsel in his protracted cross-examination of Sims. Questions asked by counsel are not evidence. The truth of the matter is that Greene was given no fair opportunity to present testimony prior to the issuance of the preliminary injunction.

The issuance of a preliminary injunction under such circumstances is contrary not only to the Rules of Civil Procedure but also to the spirit which imbues our judicial tribunals prohibiting decision without hearing. Rule 65(a) provides that no preliminary injunction shall be issued without notice to the adverse party. Notice implies an opportunity to be heard. Hearing [3] requires trial of an issue or issues of fact. Trial of an issue of fact necessitates opportunity to present evidence and not by only one side to the controversy. It should be pointed out also that subsection (b) of Rule 65 provides that a motion for a preliminary injunction "shall be set down for *hearing* . . . " and speaks of the motion coming on for "hearing."

It is also pertinent to observe that the predecessor to Rule 65 was Equity Rule 73, and that this rule was copied in haec verba from Section 17 of the Clayton Act. It has never been supposed that a temporary injunction could issue under the Clayton Act without giving the party against whom the injunction was sought an opportunity to present evidence on his behalf. The theory of Rule 65, of Equity Rule 73, and of Section 17 of the Clayton Act, is that the trial judge may issue a temporary restraining order if he thinks it necessary to preserve the status quo; that the order may endure for twenty days but for no longer without the consent of the party against whom it issued; that within the twenty day period, which affords the opportunity for hearing, such facts must be presented to the court as will justify the tribunal, in the exercise of its sound legal discretion, to issue a preliminary injunction.

If anything more was required to indicate with certainty that a preliminary injunction may not issue without giving the party sought to be enjoined an opportunity to present evidence on his behalf, it is furnished by the provisions of Rule 52(a) which requires the court, in all actions "tried upon the facts without a jury" to state separately its conclusions of law and "in granting or refusing interlocutory injunctions" "similarly [to] set forth the findings of fact and conclusions of law which constitute the grounds of its action." The conclusion is inescapable that since a district court is required by the rule to

3. At common law, the word "Hearing" meant the trial of a chancery suit. See 1 Bouv.Law Dict., Rawle's Third Revision, p. 1429.

make findings of fact, the findings must be based on something more than a one-sided presentation of the evidence. Finding facts requires the exercise by an impartial tribunal of its function of weighing and appraising evidence offered, not by one party to the controversy alone, but by both. . . . It is appropriate to point out also that after evidence has been presented by both sides an opportunity must also be afforded to both sides to argue the effect of that evidence to the court. . . . Since Greene was not given the opportunity to present evidence on his behalf (and of course was not afforded the opportunity to argue it), the preliminary injunction should be set aside even if there were no other ground for doing so.

The court erred in another respect, however. The findings of fact are insufficient. Finding 17 [5] will not sustain the preliminary injunction and Sims can point to no stronger finding. To justify the granting of a preliminary injunction there must be a showing of irreparable injury during the pendency of the action and, of course, a finding of fact to such effect. . . . In the case at bar the learned judge made no finding that irreparable injury would be wrought to Sims if a preliminary injunction was not granted.

The order of the court below granting the preliminary injunction will be reversed.

MARSHALL DURBIN FARMS, INC. v. NATIONAL FARMERS ORGANIZATION, INC.

446 F.2d 353 (5th Cir. 1971).

Before THORNBERRY and GODBOLD, Circuit Judges, and BOOTLE, District Judge.

GODBOLD, Circuit Judge:

National Farmers Organization (NFO) and several of its members appeal from the District Court's order granting a preliminary injunction against them in an action alleging violations of §§ 1 and 2 of the Sherman Act, 15 U.S.C. §§ 1–2. We reverse.

The fourteen plaintiffs are processors of broiler chickens and operators of feed mills. They have large numbers of plants and facilities located in numerous different towns in many counties of North Alabama. Generally speaking, the growing of broilers is contracted out to farmers, each of whom feeds and cares for chickens owned by a processor, using feed and supplies the processor sells him, until the chickens are ready for processing. NFO is active in North Alabama, and many of its members in the area are farmers who grow broilers under such contracts with processors.

In April, 1970 NFO began in the North Alabama area what it terms a "holding action" pursuant to which, NFO says, its members refused to grow broilers for plaintiffs until such time as the processors entered into new con-

5. As follows:

"By virtue of the circumstances recited in the foregoing findings, the salary and emoluments due the plaintiff have been discontinued by the A. M. E. Church, confusion exists as to the authority and power to supervise the affairs of the Church in the District, and the general management and direction of the affairs and property of the A. M. E. Churches within the First Episcopal District have been adversely affected."

tractual arrangements sought by NFO. Pickets were set up at some of plaintiffs' plants. On June 8 picketing began on a round-the-clock basis.

On June 18, 1970 the plaintiffs filed suit, charging NFO and some of its Alabama officers and members with conspiring to restrain trade, conspiring to monopolize, and attempting to monopolize. Plaintiffs charged that the defendants had effectuated the alleged offenses in three general ways: conspiring with and inducing producers not members of NFO to refrain from growing broilers under contracts with plaintiffs; interfering with plaintiffs' businesses, plant operations, and sales; and picketing at plaintiffs' plants to induce employees and Department of Agriculture inspectors to refrain from entering.

The lengthy complaint alleges more than 50 specific incidents or activities in which it was charged that NFO had engaged in threats, intimidation, harassment, acts of violence and destruction of property, to effectuate the alleged antitrust offenses. The locations of most of the incidents were not alleged. More than 50 persons were named as victims of the incidents charged. The largest number were broiler producers who did not belong to NFO, and members of their families. Their places, or even counties, of residence were not specified. A substantial number of the alleged victims were said to be employees of plaintiffs, but, as to most of them, the complaint does not reveal of which plaintiff.

The complaint was verified by the affidavit of an officer or managerial employee of each plaintiff. Each verification was the same, stating only that the averments of the complaint were true and correct according to affiant's knowledge, information and belief.

Simultaneously with the filing of the complaint plaintiffs filed a motion for a preliminary injunction, relying upon the verified complaint and nine attached affidavits. Several of the affidavits described specific threats of violence and of destruction of property, and such occurrences as the burning of two chicken houses with evidence of arson, unexplained rifle shots fired in the vicinity of an affiant, and the unexplained death of a cow. Two affidavits concerned suggestions to persons by NFO members not to accept chicks for growing. One affidavit related the unexplained presence of unidentified persons near the butane gas tanks of a processing plant. Some of the affidavits concerned incidents not alleged in the complaint.

On the date of filing, June 18, the court set the motion for hearing at Birmingham, Alabama, on June 25, stating in its order that the parties could present evidence at the hearing by affidavit and oral testimony if they desired. The complaint, motion for injunction (with the nine affidavits), and order were served on the defendants at various times from Friday, June 19 to Tuesday, June 24. NFO's agent for service of process was served on the 19th. On June 23, defense counsel moved for a continuance of the hearing, and it was denied.

At the commencement of the hearing on the morning of June 25, defense counsel renewed the motion for a continuance on the grounds, inter alia, that the issues were complex and that counsel had not had an opportunity to confer with the witnesses. Counsel requested time to prepare adequately. The court denied the motion, stating:

"Of course that request is not unreasonable in the light of the facts. On the other hand today is the only day before the first of October that I have open and for that reason I just can't continue the case. I do not consider the request unreasonable."

Defense counsel renewed the request for a postponement pointing out the substantial impact of the proceedings on what counsel described as "thousands of Alabama farmers," and asked that the matter be set prior to October 1 before whatever district judge might be available. The court declined.

Plaintiffs opened their case by introducing, over objection by the defendants, approximately 77 affidavits, including the nine attached to the motion. Of the approximately 68 affidavits theretofore unrevealed, defendants were handed copies of approximately 47. Plaintiffs did not have copies of 21 affidavits to furnish to defendants.

The defense then introduced 14 affidavits, all but one of them executed prior to June 25. The court recessed for slightly less than an hour to afford it and counsel an opportunity to examine the affidavits. When court reconvened the trial judge announced that he had read all of the defendants' affidavits and, of those submitted by plaintiffs, more than half selected at random from each category (i.e., those describing threats, violence, etc., to non-member producers, those describing interference with plaintiffs' business operations, and those relating to picket line activities.) Plaintiffs then put on the live testimony of the Alabama manager for plaintiff Pillsbury, who described the facilities of the plaintiffs in North Alabama and the general operation of the broiler business. At the conclusion of his testimony (the most lengthy of the day), the court announced that it would only have until 4:30 of that afternoon to receive live testimony, and at 4:30 it would take the case under submission on the affidavits and the live testimony. The court gave each side half of the time remaining. Plaintiffs put on nine more witnesses, and in the remaining one hour and 45 minutes available to them defendants put on eight.

At the conclusion of the testimony, the court announced that it would grant the injunction. The following day it entered findings of fact, which stated that they were based upon all the evidence presented—affidavits, written exhibits and oral testimony—and conclusions of law. It issued an injunction enjoining defendants from acting in concert to interfere with plaintiffs' business activities; from picketing or assembling at or near plaintiffs' plants and mills; from threatening, intimidating (etc.) employees of plaintiffs and persons contracting with plaintiffs; from interfering with plaintiffs' vehicles; and from interfering with ingress and egress of goods at plaintiffs' plants and mills. A $2,500 bond was required. A motion of defendants to increase the bond to $1,000,000 was denied. On motion of defendants this court modified the injunction pending appeal to eliminate restraints on peaceful picketing. [This decision is dated July 9.]

In reversing, we emphasize that we understand the deep concern of the experienced trial judge arising from the picture presented to him of threats, intimidation and disorder that might reach beyond the interests of the immediate parties, and we give full regard to his discretion in granting or denying injunctive relief. Reversal is, in large part, laid at the doors of the plaintiffs themselves.

Two interrelated rights of the defendants are critical to the case: fair notice and an effective opportunity to controvert the facts adduced in support of plaintiffs' motion. Rule 65(a) requires notice. It does not define what "notice" must be. But we know that it implies a hearing. Hawkins v. Board of Control, 253 F.2d 752 (5th Cir. 1958); Sims v. Greene. "Hearing requires a trial of [issues] of fact. Trial of [issues] of fact necessitates an opportunity to present evidence," *Hawkins,* and not by only one side to the controversy, *Sims.*

The right of defendants to present controverting factual data is illusory unless there is adequate notice of plaintiffs' claims. "It goes without saying that the requirements of a fair hearing include notice of the claims of the opposing party and an opportunity to meet them." [4]

Plaintiffs thrust the defendants into an impossible position insofar as both preparing and presenting an effective response to the motion for preliminary injunction. Prior to the hearing the defendants were obliged, within a few days, to undertake a task which was at least difficult and at most almost insurmountable. They were under the necessity of retaining counsel, locating the numerous persons and investigating the multitude of occurrences alleged in the complaint and separate affidavits, determining if there was evidence to controvert what was said to have occurred, and either procuring affidavits or arranging for live testimony from witnesses. This task was none the easier for the dearth of identifying information in the complaint, which we have pointed out.

At the hearing what had been difficult but perhaps possible became impossible. There was hardly time for defense counsel to read the flood of additional affidavits, which occupy approximately 175 pages of the appendix (even the court had no opportunity to read them all). When one has the opportunity to read them against the incidents and persons specified in the complaint and the original affidavits, it is seen that they have a kaleidoscopic effect, opening numerous new areas of factual inquiry—including, inter alia, additional specific instances of threats, fires at chicken houses, vehicles struck

4. The extent to which the court is required to take oral testimony in a hearing on a motion for a preliminary injunction, and the extent to which it may rely upon affidavits, a choice only tangential to this case, "reflect a tension between the need for speedy action and the desire for certainty and complete fairness." SEC v. Frank, 388 F.2d 486, 490 (2d Cir. 1968). There is a diversity of views in this regard. E.g., compare, Sims v. Greene . . . (suggesting that evidentiary conflicts in such cases may never be resolved on the basis of affidavits alone but only by oral testimony), with, Warner Bros. Pictures v. Gittone, 110 F.2d 292 (3d Cir. 1940) (suggesting the trial judge ought to resolve such conflicts through oral testimony), with 7 Moore's Federal Practice, ¶ 65.04 [3] at pp. 1639, 1641 (suggesting that the court should be more reluctant to decide controverted factual issues in favor of the movant on affidavits alone since they are at best not too trustworthy), with Ross-Whitney Corp. v. Smith, Kline & French Lab., 207 F.2d 190 (9th Cir. 1953) (which indicates the grant of a preliminary injunction may be proper on affidavits alone).

We observe that the instant controversy is at that end of the spectrum where so very much turns upon an accurate presentation of numerous facts that the propriety of proceeding upon affidavits becomes the most questionable. SEC v. Frank.

by rifle fire, items thrown at trucks, activities on NFO picket lines at processing plants, activities among government-employed inspectors at processing plants, demands by the Teamsters' union to protect its members from violence if they crossed NFO picket lines, and the transcript of a speech allegedly made by NFO's president. Some were more or less connected to NFO activities, some not at all, some did not rise above the level of suspicion and innuendo. More than 50 of the new affidavits were from persons not named in the complaint as victims of, or having knowledge of, the incidents originally charged.

There was no way in which the defendants, in a hearing required to be held and completed that day, could controvert with opposing affidavits or live testimony the details of the dozens of newly revealed occurrences said to have taken place at numerous different locations over a substantial area of North Alabama, over a time span of more than two weeks, and involving many persons not previously identified. Indeed, defendants had no opportunity even to determine if evidence existed that might contradict the new affidavits.

In addition, to only a limited extent, if at all, were the corporate officers and managers who verified the complaint shown to have had first hand knowledge of any of the specific incidents charged in the complaint. None filed a separate affidavit, and the one who testified described only background matters. Insofar as the record before us deals in specifics, the complaint is not shown to have been any more than a massive compilation of hearsay.[6] While we do not rule out the possibility that hearsay may form the basis for, or contribute to, the issuance of a preliminary injunction, the district courts have shown appropriate reluctance to issue such orders where the moving party substantiates his side of a factual dispute on information and belief. See, e.g., Humble Oil & Refining Co. v. Harang, 262 F.Supp. 39 (E.D.La.1966). Under the circumstances of this case, in the context of plaintiffs' overall presentation, the extensive use of what appears to be hearsay with respect to disputed factual issues contributes to the error requiring reversal.

Finally, the majority of those incidents described in the complaint were never verified in any manner, affidavit or oral testimony, by any person purporting to have actual knowledge, and, of those which were, several were the subject of affidavits executed prior to the filing of the complaint and motion for injunction (some as early as June 9, a number on June 15) but, for reasons never explained, not served upon or furnished to defendants until the hearing was in progress. Of the nine whose affidavits were attached to plaintiffs' motion, only one gave oral testimony and was thereby subjected to cross-examination.

Rule 6(d), F.R.Civ.P., which we think applicable to motions for preliminary injunctions, requires not only five days notice to the non-moving party of a hearing on the motion, but also that, when a motion is supported by affidavit, the affidavit must be served with the motion and notice of hearing. In another context we have held that the five-day provision of 6(d) is not a

6. This is not to say that the corporate officers and managers who verified the complaint had no knowledge, but only that, if they did, the specific content thereof was not revealed to any significant degree.

hard and fast rule, and that technical compliance may be dispensed with if "it is shown that a party had actual notice and time to prepare to meet the questions raised by the motion of an adversary . . . ." Herron v. Herron, 5 Cir., 255 F.2d 589, 593. In this case, we need not reach the question whether, in considering an application for a preliminary injunction, the court is barred from considering any affidavit that has not been served in compliance with Rule 6(d). The procedure followed by plaintiffs in this case cannot be sustained under any standard. And the defendants were not extricated, as they might have been, by a recess of a few days or by entry of a temporary restraining order during the pendency of which they could have had an opportunity to ascertain precisely what the claims were against them and adequately prepare to meet them.

Whatever ultimate efficacy is given to affidavits as opposed to oral testimony, the opportunity *vel non* of a defendant to contradict a plaintiff's factual showing may have a determinative effect on the outcome, since, understandably, the courts are more cautious about invoking the extraordinary remedy of the preliminary injunction where critical facts are in dispute. . . . Had the defendants been given adequate opportunity to prepare and present a factual showing controverting that of the plaintiffs, they might have tipped the scales against the grant.

We pretermit comment on other grounds asserted to be reversible error.

The order of the District Court granting the preliminary injunction is reversed and the cause remanded.

---

1) Excerpts from 1 Wigmore, On Evidence § 4, at 15, 19–21 (3rd ed. 1940): "The orthodox and broad proposition, then, always was and has continued to be that the rules of Evidence at common law trials obtained also in chancery. . . .

"Evidence is constantly being offered to a judge in establishing the grounds of a motion made and heard 'ex parte' only. In such cases the usual system of rules of Evidence is not applied, partly because there is no opponent to invoke them, partly because the judge's determination is usually discretionary, partly because it is seldom final, but mainly because the system of Evidence rules was devised for the special control of trials by jury. . . .

"The most notable deviation, in 'ex parte' proceedings, from the ordinary rules of Evidence is seen in the use of *affidavits,* the cross-examination being dispensed with . . . .

"So, too, in all interlocutory proceedings, even when responsory and not 'ex parte'—for example, a motion . . . for an *injunction*—the usual system of rules is ignored, again partly because of the subsidiary and provisional nature of the inquiry, but chiefly because there is no jury, and the rules of Evidence are, as rules, traditionally associated with a trial by jury."

2) Hearings for preliminary injunctions may rely on affidavits, and the rules clearly make them admissible. One question that has frequently arisen concerns the admissibility of pretrial depositions. In United States v. Fox, 211 F.Supp. 25 (E.D.La.1962), depositions that would not be admissible in the trial on the merits (because the witnesses lived less than 100 miles from

the courthouse) were held admissible on the motion for preliminary injunction. Judge Ainsworth reasoned (at 30):

". . . We reject this contention because in a proceeding for preliminary injunction oral testimony, although permissible, is not absolutely required. The court may receive and consider both affidavits and other documents which are the equivalent of affidavits. The depositions were taken under oath and we hold that they are at least as good as affidavits on the hearing for a motion for preliminary injunction."

In Medeco Security Locks Inc. v. Swiderek, 680 F.2d 37 (7th Cir. 1981), the court reversed a preliminary injunction on procedural grounds. Medeco charged that defendant had infringed its copyright in a book of lock and key code numbers; defendant argued that he personally measured and examined "tens of thousands of Medeco's publicly available keys." Medeco established its theory "solely from the direct examination of [defendant] by Medeco during [defendant's] deposition, and the consequent 'cross' examination of [defendant] by his own counsel, . . . without briefing or holding any type of prior hearing." 680 F.2d at 38. The court quoted *Sims* for the idea that "Normally, an evidentiary hearing is required to decide credibility issues." It continued: "Practitioners rarely engage in extensive interrogation of their clients at depositions called by an opponent. At oral argument, counsel for Medeco conceded the correctness of this statement. Discovery deposition testimony, in fact, will often, if not usually, present even less of a complete picture of a party's position than affidavits presented by that party. The trial court's reading of such a deposition is an inadequate substitute for the hearing of oral testimony and the observing of a witness' demeanor in these highly contested cases where the proper characterization of the factual occurrences is crucial and where credibility is a major determinative factor. . . . This is especially true in the trademark and patent area where a plaintiff can totally prevent the conduct of a defendant's business through the use of these injunctions." 680 F.2d at 38–39.

3) Another question concerns the quality of the affidavits: Need they measure up to the strict standards that govern affidavits with the motion for summary judgment under Federal Rule of Civil Procedure 56(e)? Rule 56(e) provides that the affidavits supporting or opposing a motion for summary judgment "shall be made on personal knowledge, shall set forth facts as would be admissible in evidence, and shall show affirmatively that the affiant is competent to testify to the matters stated therein." Professor Moore argues that this stringent standard should not govern affidavits filed with a motion for a preliminary injunction. 7 Moore's Federal Practice ¶ 65.04 [3] (2d ed. 1982). The strict standard of Rule 56(e) is attributable to: (a) the function of a motion for summary judgment, to dispense with the trial when no genuine issue of triable fact exists; (b) a judgment on the merits will be entered if the motion is granted; and (c) speed is not an important factor in motions for summary judgment. Professor Moore addresses motions for preliminary injunctions:

". . . The function of a preliminary injunction is, on the other hand, quite different. It is, in general, to preserve the status quo pending a trial on the merits. And while a decision at the preliminary injunction stage may be conclusive, in general the decision of either the trial or appellate court in granting or denying a temporary injunction does not conclude the parties or the court as to the merits of the case. Also a grant of the injunction can usually be conditioned as to terms and security so that the party against whom it runs is not unduly prejudiced, although this is not invariably true as labor injunctions eloquently testify; and, of course, a preliminary injunction can be dissolved prior to trial on the merits. Furthermore, speed is often extremely important both in relation to restraining orders and preliminary injunctions, and both the movant and the opposing party may often be unable to obtain and marshal their evidence in a manner that would be proper for a summary judgment hearing or for an actual trial. Affidavits at best are not too trustworthy either for a summary judgment or injunction hearing; and undoubtedly in relation to the latter hearing affidavits that measure up to the standard for summary judgment are preferable to those of a more general character, and oral testimony is even better. But we conclude that a court may properly consider affidavits at the preliminary injunction hearing, which do not measure up to the standards of the summary judgment affidavit, bearing in mind that the party moving for a preliminary injunction has the burden of showing that he is entitled thereto, and that such an injunction should not be granted unless the movant has established a fairly reliable factual basis therefor."

4) How does the judge's decision to grant or deny interlocutory relief relate to other stages of the lawsuit? a) Graduating high-school seniors sought to enjoin a religious invocation and benediction in the graduation ceremony. Three days before the ceremony, Judge Merhige denied plaintiffs' request for a preliminary injunction. Then, after the plaintiffs had graduated, he held that the case was not moot and denied defendant's motion to dismiss for failure to state a claim. He refused to "transpose what was explicitly a preliminary hearing into a final adjudication on the merits," which would "cut against the spirit of Rule 65(a)(2)" where "resolution involves a delicate factual balance and the Court's initial ruling was deliberately tentative." Grossberg v. Deusebio, 380 F.Supp. 285, 293 (E.D.Va.1974). Was that an indirect way of saying that he had changed his mind? Wasn't the lawsuit really moot after an effectively final decision denying the preliminary injunction?

b) After a three day hearing on plaintiff's motion for a preliminary injunction, the trial judge consolidated that hearing with trial on the merits under Rule 65(a)(2), converted defendant's "intimated" oral motion to dismiss for failure to state a claim into a summary judgment motion, and granted summary judgment for defendant. The court of appeals, reversing the summary judgment, looked askance at consolidation without "clear and unambiguous notice" because it ended discovery and could prejudice full presentation. The court affirmed the denial of the preliminary injunction. Gellman v. Maryland, 538 F.2d 603 (4th Cir. 1976). Why are three days not enough?

c) In Miller Brewing Co. v. G. Heileman Brewing Co., 561 F.2d 75, 77 (7th Cir. 1977), certiorari denied 434 U.S. 1025 (1978), the court of appeals reversed a preliminary injunction and held that "light" is a generic or common descriptive word and that neither Lite nor Light could support a trademark for beer. Two years later, Miller sued the Schlitz Company to enforce the same trademark. Both the trial judge and the appellate court accorded the *Heileman* decision preclusive effect to bar Miller from enforcing the trademark against Schlitz, a nonparty to the *Heileman* action. That the "judgment in *Heileman* was rendered in an appeal from a preliminary injunction order does not preclude application of collateral estoppel." Miller Brewing Co. v. Jos. Schlitz Brewing Co., 605 F.2d 990, 995 (7th Cir. 1979).

Does the term "preliminary injunction" describe a fixed category of orders, or is it a variable concept depending on the nature of the issues involved and the amount of energy previously devoted to resolving them? Might an order be a preliminary injunction for one purpose, for example, appeal, but not for another purpose, for example, res judicata?

III. Preliminary Injunction Standard

The issuance of a preliminary injunction usually turns on the judge's estimation of: (1) the probability that the plaintiff will ultimately succeed on the merits; (2) the irreparability and extent of the harm to the plaintiff during the litigation if the preliminary injunction is not granted; (3) the balance of hardship—how the plaintiff's harm compares to the harm to the defendant (that cannot be avoided even by the requirement of a bond) if the preliminary injunction is granted; (4) the impact that granting or denying the preliminary injunction will have on other, more general societal interests.

The open-ended nature of these inquiries leads courts to speak of the issuance of a preliminary injunction as "discretionary," and not a matter of "right." The classic statement of that view occurs in Yakus v. United States, 321 U.S. 414 (1944). In the Emergency Price Control Act of January 30, 1942, Congress established an exclusive statutory procedure for judicial review of the price control regulations in the Emergency Court of Appeals and prohibited interlocutory relief until there was a final determination that the regulation was invalid. In evaluating that statutory provision the Court, by Chief Justice Stone, said (at 439–42):

"In any event, we are unable to say that the denial of interlocutory relief pending a judicial determination of the validity of the regulation would, in the special circumstances of this case, involve a denial of constitutional right. If the alternatives, as Congress could have concluded, were wartime inflation or the imposition on individuals of the burden of complying with a price regulation while its validity is being determined, Congress could constitutionally make the choice in favor of the protection of the public interest from the dangers of inflation. Compare Miller v. Schoene, 276 U.S. 272, in which we held that the Fourteenth Amendment did not preclude a state from compelling the uncompensated destruction of private property in order to preserve important public interests from destruction.

"The award of an interlocutory injunction by courts of equity has never been regarded as strictly a matter of right, even though irreparable injury may otherwise result to the plaintiff. . . . Even in suits in which only private interests are involved the award is a matter of sound judicial discretion, in the exercise of which the court balances the conveniences of the parties and possible injuries to them according as they may be affected by the granting or withholding of the injunction. . . . And it will avoid such inconvenience and injury so far as may be, by attaching conditions to the award, such as the requirement of an injunction bond conditioned upon payment of any damage caused by the injunction if the plaintiff's contentions are not sustained. . . .

"But where an injunction is asked which will adversely affect a public interest for whose impairment, even temporarily, an injunction bond cannot compensate, the court may in the public interest withhold relief until a final determination of the rights of the parties, though the postponement may be burdensome to the plaintiff. . . . This is but another application of the principle, declared in Virginian Ry. Co. v. System Federation, 300 U.S. 515, 552, that 'courts of equity may, and frequently do, go much farther both to give and withhold relief in furtherance of the public interest than they are accustomed to go when only private interests are involved.'

"Here, in the exercise of the power to protect the national economy from the disruptive influences of inflation in time of war Congress has seen fit to postpone injunctions restraining the operations of price regulations until their lawfulness could be ascertained by an appropriate and expeditious procedure. In so doing it has done only what a court of equity could have done, in the exercise of its discretion to protect the public interest. What the courts could do Congress can do as the guardian of the public interest of the nation in time of war. The legislative formulation of what would otherwise be a rule of judicial discretion is not a denial of due process or a usurpation of judicial functions. . . . "

Professor Hammond observes that "A discretionary formula, though fashionable, raises the dangers of potential judicial arbitrariness with respect to a remedy which is often dispositive of litigation and the difficulties of mounting an appeal from a discretion. These difficulties are not really solved by assuming that there will always be a succession of level-headed men called judges on the Clapham omnibus who will exercise considered judgment." Interlocutory Injunctions: Time for a New Model?, 30 U. Toronto L.J. 240, 272 (1980). While reading the decisions that follow, ask yourself how each court applies each of the four inquiries in the standard formulation. Does the test constrain discretion enough to avoid risking arbitrariness?

UNITED STATES v. HAYES INTERNATIONAL CORP.

415 F.2d 1038 (5th Cir. 1969).

Before TUTTLE and SIMPSON, Circuit Judges, and CASSIBRY, District Judge.

TUTTLE, Circuit Judge: On March 25, 1968, the Attorney General filed a complaint in the district court pursuant to Title VII of the Civil Rights Act of 1964, 42 U.S.C.A. § 2000e–6(a). The complaint alleged that the company maintained racially segregated divisions and lines of progression; discriminated in its hiring practices; and assigned whites to jobs offering higher pay, better advancement and security than similarly qualified black employees. The complaint requested that the company be permanently enjoined from continuing such violations and from failing to take reasonable steps to correct the effects of past discriminatory practices.

The company repairs and rebuilds airplanes and airplane parts largely pursuant to government contracts. As of March 11, 1968 eight percent or 145 of the company's 1781 production and maintenance employees were black. The jobs in the unit were arranged in ten seniority divisions. Each division contained from one to seven lines of progression. Each line contained jobs requiring similar job skills in which the employee could normally expect to advance as he gained experience and vacancies occurred. Because some seniority divisions contained a number of lines of progression which involved similar job skills, in some cases it was possible to move laterally or upward between lines. Further, in case of layoff some employees could "bump" less senior men in their present line as well as in related lines within the seniority division.

One hundred twenty-two of the 145 blacks were employed in two seniority divisions. Many held "Cleaner" jobs (washing the outside of airplanes) in seniority division 7. There was but one line of progression in this division. The remainder were employed in maintenance and janitorial jobs in division 8. From a practical standpoint, there was virtually no chance to move from the lines of progression containing the predominantly black jobs into the white lines in this division.

The remaining blacks were scattered in seven of the other divisions. What their jobs were did not appear in the record. However, the company did concede that 138 of the black employees were in "predominantly Negro" jobs.

There were 13 pay grades. Ninety-six percent of the white employees were in the seven highest grades while 77 percent of the blacks were in the three lowest grades. The company's board chairman testified that the average annual pay of "selected" white employees was $7865 and of blacks $7117. . . .

The company apparently had no formal policy of filling job vacancies from among its present black employees even if they were qualified. At least once in the past it provided black employees with limited transfer opportunities but at the cost of loss of seniority and a drop in pay. The company could and did, however, transfer white employees into vacancies ahead of more senior employees. The distribution of black and white employees demonstrates that the company chose not to transfer black employees into white jobs and vice versa even though qualified blacks may have been available or could have been trained. Whatever in-service training programs were offered obviously did not provide black employees with a chance to gain the skills necessary to fill the jobs held by whites.

In short, black employees performed the lowest paid, unskilled jobs. Although the plant was operative since 1951, the company apparently was unable to recruit or train black employees to perform skilled jobs except in the most token manner. This condition remained substantially unchanged even after the effective date of Title VII of the Civil Rights Act of 1964. The black employees were segregated in their jobs in a manner which deprived them of the opportunity for advancement that white employees enjoyed.

The case in this posture never reached the court. One month after the filing of the original complaint [i.e., on April 28], the Attorney General filed a motion for a preliminary injunction. This was occasioned by three significant changes at the plant. First, on March 28 the government awarded the company a contract for the repair of KC–135 jet tankers. This contract would create 740 jobs, of which 294 would not be filled by employees with transfer, promotion or recall rights. Second, on April 8, the company and union signed a new collective bargaining agreement which made some changes in the prior seniority divisions and in seniority provisions which would effect transfer, promotion, recall and layoff rights. Third, on April 12, the company instituted a transfer program which gave black employees an opportunity to transfer to some formerly white jobs.

The government contract provided a unique opportunity to provide black employees with equal employment opportunities. The collective bargaining agreement largely merged the black lines of progression with white lines * . . . .

After some initial confusion, the company adequately explained the transfer program to the black employees. Each was told to fill out an application blank and designate which five from among the 57 available job titles he was interested in transferring to. They were given a week to return the forms. After the company made an offer, the employee had three days to accept. Failure to comply with either rule was a waiver of rights under the program although in practice these limitations were not strictly adhered to. Any employee who accepted a transfer had no further rights under the program.

The program made available 57 largely entry-level job titles previously closed to blacks. The remainder of the company's 140 job titles were not affected.[5]

Because of the unique opportunities thus present to rectify past discriminatory practice, the Attorney General moved for a preliminary injunction. [The hearing was held on June 3, 4 and 5. The District Court opinion was rendered on June 21, 1968.] The denial of this request is the subject of this appeal. [The Court of Appeals decision is dated August 19, 1969.]

The district court's decision largely turned on the conclusion that the transfer program did not violate Title VII.[6] The court found that the trans-

* [Specifically, the line of progression consisting of the cleaner jobs was transferred and merged into a seniority division containing five other lines of progression which had been manned predominantly by white employees. Similarly, the maintenance jobs were consolidated into a single job and placed in a previously predominantly white line of progression containing other jobs involving the operation of plant vehicles, 295 F.Supp. 803, 805 (N.D.Ala.1968).]

5. Ninety-three black employees submitted transfer requests and 47 had transferred at the time of the hearing below. Seventeen refused offers and 23 were awaiting openings. Six were medically disqualified. Of these who transferred, 18 went to General Mechanic Beginner jobs, 12 to Sheet Metal Beginner, 11 Material Handler-Stampers and the rest were scattered in various other entry-level positions.

6. The court also noted that the collective bargaining agreement merged the predominantly black lines of progression into white lines. It also upgraded the wage rates of the Cleaner line of progression and broadened the recall rights of laid-off employees.

The Court also relied in a general manner on Whitfield v. United Steelworkers Local 2708, 263 F.2d 546 (5th Cir.), cert. den., 360 U.S. 902 (1959), wherein it was held that a union which in the past had negotiated discriminatory contracts was presently only required to cease such practices and had no obligation to remove the continuing effects of past discrimination. Whitfield was not a Title VII case and therefore is not controlling. Furthermore, to the extent that it can be read as limiting the power of courts to order "such affirmative action as may be appropriate," 42 U.S.C.A. § 2000e–5(g), to simply barring any further application

fer program did not violate the Act because: (1) The black employees who transferred to Beginner positions in the Sheet Metal and General Mechanic lines would be promoted to permanent "B" level jobs during the life of the KC-135 contract. They would then be protected against layoff in accordance with their plant-wide seniority. (2) Remanning provisions would allow white employees to be promoted to higher level positions in the Sheet Metal and General Mechanic lines in preference to more senior black employees then at the "B" level in those lines only in remote cases.[7] (3) Those black employees who chose not to transfer did so for personal reasons. (4) The program was fairly administered.

The United States argues that the district court's view of the case was erroneous. We agree.

The question was not whether the transfer program itself violated Title VII. The question, rather, was: In view of the prima facie case established by the government that the company was intentionally engaged in a pattern or practice of resistance to the full enjoyment of Title VII rights, did the fact that the new collective bargaining agreement and the transfer program partially corrected the violations negate the need for the preliminary injunction? That issue was not decided by the district court.

We are met initially by the company contention that the United States is now arguing an entirely new theory of the case and it should be limited to the theory that the transfer program violated Title VII.

However, we do not view the matter that way. Of course, if the United States were now setting forth new arguments on facts never presented to the trial court, the company would be correct. But its position is bottomed on the fact that after all the evidence was in and the court requested counsel for both sides to summarize their positions, government counsel concentrated on the transfer program. There is no doubt about that. But he also argued the relevance to his case of the KC-135 contract and the collective bargaining agreement. Furthermore, he was responding to a request by the trial judge to discuss but one aspect of the case: the irreparable harm requirement for issuance of a preliminary injunction.

It seems unlikely that the court was misled by the oral argument. The motion for preliminary injunction clearly set forth the government's theory as to what established the pattern or practice of resistance and the impact on that of the changed events. Furthermore, the United States sought to develop details of when the company knew about the new contract and what its job requirements would be. While it is true that the focus of the United States here is broader than adopted at oral argument, its basic position as shown by the pleadings and the conduct of the hearing is the same, albeit better defined. The district court had the whole theory before it.

of discriminatory practices, Whitfield is inconsistent with the words of the statute, its purposes and the thrust of recent cases in this circuit. See, e.g., Local 53, Asbestos Workers, 407 F.2d 1047, 5 Cir., Jan. 15, 1969; United States v. Local 189, United Papermakers, 282 F.Supp. 39 (E.D.La.1968).

7. The court apparently referred to Art. IV, § 10(a) of the collective agreement which gives first claim to a vacancy to an employee who, without regard to seniority, had been laid off or downgraded due to a work force reduction if the employees previously performed the job satisfactorily.

The company also argues that in any case the transfer program and new collective bargaining agreement negated the need for preliminary relief because they provided the black employees with all they were entitled to under Title VII. That, of course, is the nub of the matter.

Because the case is before us in a preliminary posture, it is unwise to discuss the merits except in a limited fashion. It will be sufficient to briefly note some of the ways in which the black employees still may have been denied the "full enjoyment" of their rights as provided by the law.

We are not persuaded by the argument that the Company, four years after the enactment of the 1964 Civil Rights Act and three years after the effective date of Title VII of the Act, acted on its own initiative and instituted this transfer program for the *sole purpose* of extending to its Negro employees "special opportunities" for transfer, training and advancement. Moreover, this Court will not be misled by the "equal pay" or "substantial pay" test as indicating the absence of a violation of Title VII, for Title VII of the 1964 Civil Rights Act is not an equal pay provision but an equal opportunity to the *full* enjoyment of employment rights.

First, the transfer program was limited in a number of ways. It covered but 57 of the 140 job classifications in the production and maintenance unit. Yet among the black employees some may have possessed the qualifications to perform jobs not on the program. Also the employees were given but one chance to transfer—if they did not accept they were barred from further rights under the program. The company does not argue that it was administratively impossible to extend its duration. There may be nontransferring employees who now see that the company was correct when it assured them that no dire consequences would follow a transfer and who now would like to be considered.

Second, the employment statistics discussed . . . amply demonstrated a preliminary showing that the company hiring practices violated Title VII. Yet the hiring practices were not affected by the transfer program or the collective bargaining agreement.

Third, the collective bargaining agreement still gives the company unlimited power to transfer employees from one permanent position to another subject only to the limitation that there are no employees laid off or downgraded from the job in which the vacancy exists.

It is most difficult to understand why a company such as Hayes whose collective bargaining agreement gives the unlimited right to the employer to transfer its employees [8] would find a need for a "special transfer program" for its Negro employees where the prerequisites, vacancy and qualification, under both provisions are the same. Absent any justifiable reason, which does not appear in either the appellees' brief or in the Record, the logical reason in light of all the facts presented would be race.

Fourth, although the district court found that remanning provisions would provide only the remote possibility of filling a job with a less senior white employee in preference to an equally qualified black, the finding was limited

8. The Company may transfer an employee permanently or temporarily from one job group seniority division to another, provided only that if the transfer is permanent, there are no employees laid off or downgraded from the job group to which he is being transferred. (Art. IV § 17(a)).

to the situation created by the transfer program. However, in other circumstances the possibility still exists that a qualified black employee would be denied a chance to fill a job because a less senior white employee had superior (remanning) rights denied the black because of race. For example, if a white employee had held a position at or near the top of a line of progression and because of race blacks had been excluded from that position (such may be the case even under the transfer program) and through remanning the white employee is in a lower rated job within the seniority division, he will fill a vacancy in the higher rated job in preference to black employees equally qualified and with more seniority even though both employees are presently performing the same job. The present preference for the white can only be explained on the basis of Hayes's long established practices of racial discrimination in employment and hence would violate Title VII.

Finally, the present application of layoff rights gained by whites but denied to blacks in the past could also result in a Title VII violation in a manner similar to that discussed above relative to the remanning problem.

Under the transfer program, a Negro employee would only be allowed to transfer if he qualified and there existed a vacancy. A vacancy would exist only after all employees with remanning rights or recall rights under the layoff pool arrangement had exercised the right or waived the right.[9]

As a practical matter, in most cases this would mean that a white employee with less seniority than a Negro employee participating in the transfer program would get first preference to jobs which neither had formerly held and for which both were equally qualified.

Thus it is clear that the transfer program and collective bargaining agreement did not provide the full vindication of the Title VII rights to which the employees were entitled.

This amply demonstrates the requisite showing that the United States would prevail on the merits. A pervasive pattern of discriminatory employment practices was demonstrated. Against this background, the transfer program and collective bargaining agreement provided only a partial correction of past illegal actions. The remaining pattern and practices remained.

The appellee chooses to believe that the "single ultimate issue" on this appeal is whether the district court abused its discretion in not granting the appellant's motion for preliminary injunction. This contention should also be placed to rest. The trial judge should have granted the appellant's motion for preliminary injunction. It is true that this court has followed the view that an injunction does not follow as a matter of course upon either a finding or stipulation of violation of some Act of Congress. . . . However, it is equally true that this court has consistently held that the decision of the lower court is subject to review and where it is clear that its discretion has not been

9. All employees who were on March 29, 1968 in Seniority Division VII or held jobs of Janitor, Boiler Tender, Facility Maintenance Man, Automotive Maintenance Man or Cement Finisher and Plasterer in Seniority Division VIII, as defined in the Hayes-UAW Agreement dated April 1, 1965, shall be given, before *new* employees are hired, a *single* opportunity to transfer in accordance with their seniority to any beginning or entry level job in any Seniority Division for which *they are qualified to fill vacancies in such job existing after all employees have exercised their seniority and other rights under the collective bargaining agreement.*

exercised with an eye to the purpose of the Act, . . . or exercised in light of the objective of the Act, . . . we have nevertheless not hesitated to reverse an order of the trial court denying an injunction without the need of a discussion of abuse and discretion.

Where, as here, the statutory rights of employees are involved and an injunction is authorized by statute [10] and the statutory conditions are satisfied as in the facts presented here, the usual prerequisite of irreparable injury need not be established and the agency to whom the enforcement of the right has been entrusted is not required to show irreparable injury before obtaining an injunction. . . . We take the position that in such a case, irreparable injury should be presumed from the very fact that the statute has been violated. Whenever a qualified Negro employee is discriminatorily denied a chance to fill a position for which he is qualified and has the seniority to obtain, he suffers irreparable injury and so does the labor force of the country as a whole.

Moreover, we hold as did the court in Vogler v. McCarty, Inc., 294 F.Supp. 368, 372 (E.D.La.1967) affirmed 407 F.2d 1047 (5th Cir., 1969) that where an employer has engaged in a pattern and practice of discrimination on account of race, etc., in order to insure the *full* enjoyment of the rights protected by Title VII of the 1964 Civil Rights Act, affirmative and mandatory preliminary relief is required.

As the court in Quarles v. Philip Morris, Inc., 279 F.Supp. 505, 516 (E.D.Va.1968) concluded, "Congress did not intend to freeze an entire generation of Negro employees into discriminatory patterns that existed before the Act" we add that neither did Congress intend for an entire generation of Negro employees to be given a one chance limited opportunity under the guise of "special opportunities" to break the discriminatory pattern which might exist at a company.

It was error to refuse to issue the preliminary injunction. The case is reversed and remanded for further proceedings not inconsistent with this opinion.

Excerpts from the District Court opinion by Judge Lynne in United States v. Hayes International Corporation, 295 F.Supp. 803 (N.D.Ala.1968):

"For some time prior to the institution of this action, the Company had been considering, and had discussed with the Union, procedures for the transfer of Negro employees in the cleaner jobs and maintenance jobs to other seniority divisions.

"The Company, acting on its own initiative, instituted this transfer program on April 12, 1968, some four days after the collective bargaining agreement became effective. The sole purpose of the program was to extend to its Negro employees special opportunities for transfer, training and advancement in other areas of work. Similar privileges have not been extended to white employees.

10. § 707(a) Civil Rights Act of 1964, 42 U.S.C.A. 2000e–6(a)—The Attorney General is authorized to bring a civil action "requesting such relief, including an application for a permanent or temporary injunction, restraining order or other order against the person or persons responsible for such pattern or practice, as he deems necessary to insure the full enjoyment of the rights described herein."

"It is not disputed that this transfer program provides for the Negro employees in the cleaner line of progression and maintenance jobs, rights of transfer which have never before been available to any employee of the Company. In broad outline, the program provides that the Negro employees in the cleaner line of progression and maintenance jobs may transfer to any of fifty-seven entry level jobs in every line of progression in each seniority division. The program further provides that these transfers are to be effective without reduction in the transferring employees' wage rate and that they will take their seniority with them. The sole conditions of transfer are that a vacancy exist in the job to which transfer is sought and that the employee seeking transfer be qualified to perform the job sought.

"Pursuant to the transfer program, forty-seven out of ninety-three employees in the cleaner and maintenance jobs who submitted transfer request forms have been moved to jobs in other seniority divisions. All of such employees have retained their rate of pay, with the result that all but one of them is earning an hourly wage in excess of that they would have earned but for the special rights provided by the transfer program. All of such employees will be promoted and downgraded in the future on the basis of a comparison of their plant-wide seniority with other employees, white and Negro, similarly situated.

"Of the remaining forty-six employees who submitted transfer request forms, seventeen have subsequently rejected transfer to jobs selected for transfer, and twenty-three have selected jobs which have not become vacant since the inception of the program and which will be offered to such employees when they become vacant.[3]

"Attacking the transfer program, the plaintiff alleges that it is operating in violation of Title VII and will irreparably injure those employees who are the intended beneficiaries of it.

"The court will consider separately the plaintiff's basic contentions of irreparable injury and the evidence relating to each such allegation.

"(1) The plaintiff's first contention is that some twenty-five Negro employees who have transferred to the Beginner jobs in the General Mechanic line of progression and the Sheet Metal line of progression are subject to a risk of layoff to which other employees with comparable seniority in the higher rated jobs in these lines of progression are not subject.

"The court will assume, for the purpose of the motion for preliminary injunction, that in cases of a reduction in the work force, employees in Beginner jobs are subject to layoff before employees in the higher rated jobs.[4] But so assuming, the court cannot accept the thesis that the employees who have transferred pursuant to the transfer program are in the position argued by the plaintiff. On the contrary, with the KC–135 contract in the process of active build-up, there is no credible evidence from which to infer or even speculate that there is a likelihood of a layoff in the General Mechanic or the Sheet

3. "Six employees have been disqualified for jobs they selected for transfer either for medical reasons or lack of qualifications. There is no evidence in the record that any of these disqualifications was without justification."

4. "Since there was testimony regarding layoffs in some higher rated jobs while employees in Beginner jobs are retained, this is an assumption for purposes of the present motion only."

Metal lines of progression within the period of time that the Negro employees in question will remain in the Beginner jobs.

"The Negro employees who have transferred to these Beginner jobs will, as a matter of right, be automatically promoted at the end of twenty-four weeks of service in the Beginner jobs to the higher rated jobs in their lines of progression, and this is so without regard to the need or lack of need for employees in the higher rated jobs.

"The result of the automatic promotion rule, together with the present and anticipated strength of the work force, is that the Negro employees who have transferred to the Beginner jobs in the General Mechanic and Sheet Metal lines of progression will, no later than the end of twenty-four weeks of service in such jobs, be promoted and protected against layoff in accordance with their length of continuous service with the Company.

"The plaintiff's contention that these employees have been subjected to a discriminatory risk in employment security is for these reasons without foundation.

"(2) The plaintiff's second contention is based on the 'remanning' provision of the collective bargaining agreement, under which an employee who has been laid off or downgraded due to a reduction in the work force is entitled to return to a higher rated job which he has previously performed satisfactorily before other employees are promoted to such job. Plaintiff insists that because of this provision, employees working in the higher rated jobs in the lines of progression to which the Negro employees were transferred will be entitled to jobs in the line in preference to such Negro employees.

"This contention is supportable only by considerable speculation with regard to the alignment of a host of variables in the future. The court has carefully considered manpower projections, current and past seniority rosters, and the employment history of employees in the production and maintenance unit in light of the plaintiff's argument. On the basis of this evidence, the court finds that employees who could conceivably have remanning rights over the Negro employees transferred to the Beginner jobs before they are eligible for promotion to higher rated jobs will have such rights only as a result of long years of experience in their lines of progression. Without detailing the evidence on this point, the sum total is that employees with some fifteen years' experience in jobs in the General Mechanic and Sheet Metal lines of progression might be benefited by the remanning provision by being entitled to return to jobs they have held before employees with fifteen years less relevant experience are promoted to such jobs. That this remote possibility exists is not a basis on which the court should properly issue an injunction negating the operation of the remanning provision.

"(3) The plaintiff's third contention is that the transfer program is irreparably injuring those Negro employees who did not exercise their privilege to transfer.

"However the evidence before the court compels the conclusion that the employees who elected not to take advantage of the transfer privileges offered to them have done so either because they preferred the work of their jobs or because they believed that their seniority would better protect them from layoffs in their present seniority division.[5]

"(4) The plaintiff's final contention is that the administration of the transfer program was beset with confusion and that the employees misunderstood their opportunities thereunder.

"That simply isn't so. The testimony of the witnesses, both for the plaintiff and the Company, showed the fact to be that the most meticulous attention was devoted to administering the transfer program and to explaining to the Negro beneficiaries their rights thereunder, both in group meetings and in conferences with individual employees.

"The court is further of the opinion that it would require a departure from the applicable law on the subject to treat the transfer program as a violation of the rights of the Negro employees of the Company.

"The leading authority is the decision of our court of appeals in Whitfield v. United Steelworkers of America, 263 F.2d 546 (5th Cir. 1959), cert. denied, 360 U.S. 902 (1959), which concerned a procedure by which Negro employees could transfer from previously segregated lines of progressions to entry level jobs in lines of progression which had previously been restricted to white employees. Rejecting the claim that the requirement of transferring to entry level jobs perpetuated racial discrimination, the court spoke through Judges Hutcheson, Rives, and Wisdom as follows:

" 'An employee without the proper training and with no proof of potential ability to rise higher, cannot expect to start in the middle of the ladder, regardless of plant seniority. It would be unfair to the skilled, experienced, and deserving employee to give a top or middle job to an unqualified employee. It would also destroy the whole system of lines of progression, to the detriment of efficient management and to the disadvantage of Negro as well as white employees having a stake in orderly promotion.'

"The subject of transfer rights was similarly at issue in Quarles v. Philip Morris, Inc., 279 F.Supp. 505 (E.D.Va.1968). There, the court expressed the opinion that the *Whitfield* case was applicable under Title VII with respect to transfers to jobs which required skill and training.[6] From the evidence before the court on the present record, such is the case with respect to the higher rated jobs under consideration here.

"The provisions of Title VII, as any student of the legislative history will discover, are the product of an extended and careful consideration of the rights not only of Negroes but of other employees in the light of the complex realities of industrial life. The statute was not intended to accord privileges to Negro employees in blind disregard of the seniority rights of others, and it was not intended to be administered in disregard of the interest of employers in efficiency and ability. . . .

5. "The record shows that employees in the cleaner and maintenance jobs have substantial seniority against layoffs as compared with other employees in the plant."

6. "While the rationale of *Whitfield* may be substantially eroded by future cases arising under Title VII, its caveat that 'fairness is not achieved by treating the white incumbents unfairly,' 263 F.2d at 550, should remain a polestar to guide the courts through yet uncharted seas."

"The fact that Title VII contemplates and requires a triangular adjustment of the rights of minority group employees, the rights of other employees, and the interest of management and labor is abundantly clear and indisputable. Here, as in the *Whitfield* case, the transfer program at issue has, in the considered opinion of the court, resolved this triangular adjustment in an entirely fair and nondiscriminatory manner.[7]

"In sum total, then, the court finds that the employees with respect to whom the plaintiff alleges irreparable injury have in fact been accorded by the transfer program the opportunity to take advantage of special and unequal advantages which have never been accorded any other employee. The court is accordingly firmly of the opinion, and so holds, that the plaintiff's motion for preliminary injunction is to be denied.[8] "

---

1) Judge Lynne apparently concluded that the transfer program disturbed the status quo. The government moved for a preliminary injunction to bar the defendant from effecting that program. The court of appeals rejected Judge Lynne's view. What does the court of appeals think the government sought to prevent by moving for a preliminary injunction? Does the court of appeals try to preserve the status quo or to alter it substantially?

The traditional rule, rooted in the conception of the preliminary injunction to preserve the status quo, disfavored preliminary injunctions that required an affirmative act. As then Circuit Judge Taft wrote, even under that view of interlocutory relief, a preliminary injunction compelling affirmative conduct may be in order. "The office of a preliminary injunction is to preserve the status quo until, upon final hearing, the court may grant full relief. Generally this can be accomplished by an injunction prohibitory in form, but it sometimes happens that the status quo is a condition not of rest, but of action, and the condition of rest is exactly what will inflict the irreparable injury upon complainant, which he appeals to a court of equity to protect him from. In such a case courts of equity issue mandatory writs before the case is heard on its merits." Toledo, Ann Arbor & North Michigan Railway v. Pennsylvania Co., 54 F. 730, 741 (C.C.N.D. Ohio 1893). Does this endorsement include orders, such as in *Hayes,* that seek to restructure a large institution?

2) Does the preliminary injunction the court of appeals thinks the district judge should enter on remand differ from the permanent injunction the United States sought as final relief? Did the United States move for a preliminary injunction to accelerate final consideration? Did the court of appeals grant the plaintiffs almost complete relief because it thought that plaintiffs were certain to prevail at the trial?

7. "Thus, this case is clearly distinguishable from United States v. Local 189, United Papermakers & Paperworkers, 282 F.Supp. 39 (E.D.La.1968) where the holdings of the court emanated from the finding that the company and the union there had 'actively engaged, prior to January, 1966, in a pervasive pattern of discrimination.' "

8. "In ruling on this motion the court has carefully refrained from discussing, or expressing an opinion on, the merits of all the issues tendered by the pleadings, which await determination on a full record after final hearing. For this reason the court has pretermitted a critical analysis of the several remedies proposed by the plaintiff."

3) The court of appeals says that if the defendant has violated a statute, the court will relieve the plaintiff from demonstrating irreparable harm. Many courts have indicated that defendant's breach of a statute or the constitution obviates irreparability. Elrod v. Burns, 427 U.S. 347, 373 (1976); Sampson v. Murray, 415 U.S. 61, 88–90 (1974); Wolff v. Selective Service, 372 F.2d 817, 824 (2d Cir. 1967); Henry v. Greenville Airport Commission, 284 F.2d 631, 633 (4th Cir. 1960); Sierra Club v. Coleman, 405 F.Supp. 53, 54 (D.D.C.1975). Compare *Weinberger*, p. 146.

Is this another way of saying that plaintiff is entitled to an injunction when success on the merits is assured? Does it evade the judge's duty of searching for and comparing irreparable harm? Is the court deferring excessively to an executive agency that lacks power to grant injunctions? Leubsdorf, The Standard for Preliminary Injunctions, 91 Harv.L.Rev. 525, 561–5 (1978).

AMERICAN CYANAMID CO. v. ETHICON LTD.

[1975] 1 All E.R. 504.

[LORD DIPLOCK stated the facts and continued:] My Lords, the question whether [Ethicon's] use of XLG as an absorbable surgical suture is an infringement of Cyanamid's patent depends upon the meaning to be given to the three words "a polyhydroxyacetic ester" in the principal claim. Cyanamid's contention is that at the date of publication of the patent those words were used as a term of art in the chemistry of polymerisation not only in the narrower meaning of a homopolymer of which the units in the chain, apart from the end stabilisers, consisted solely of glycolide radicals but also in the broader meaning of a copolymer of which up to 15 per cent. of the units in the chain would be lactide radicals; and that what was said in the body of the patent made it clear that in the claim the words were used in this wider meaning.

Ethicon's first contention is that the words "a polyhydroxyacetic ester" in the principal claim bear the narrower meaning only, viz. that they are restricted to a homopolymer of which all the units in the chain except the end stabilisers consist of glycolide radicals. In the alternative, as commonly happens where the contest is between a narrower and a wider meaning in a patent specification, they attack the validity of the patent, if it bears the wider meaning, on the grounds of inutility, insufficiency, unfair basis and false suggestion. These objections are really the obverse of their argument in favour of the narrower construction. They are all different ways of saying that if the claim is construed widely it includes copolymers which will not have as surgical sutures the characteristics described in the body of the patent. Ethicon also attacks the validity of the patent on the ground of obviousness.

Both Graham J. and the Court of Appeal felt constrained by authority to deal with Cyanamid's claim to an interlocutory injunction by considering first whether, upon the whole of the affidavit evidence before them, a prima facie case of infringement had been made out. As Russell L.J. put it in the concluding paragraph of his reasons for judgment with which the other members of the court agreed [1974] F.S.R. 312, 333:

". . . if there be no prima facie case on the point essential to entitle the plaintiffs to complain of the defendants' proposed activities, that is the end of the claim to interlocutory relief."

"Prima facie case" may in some contexts be an elusive concept, but the sense in which it was being used by Russell L.J. is apparent from an earlier passage in his judgment. After a detailed analysis of the conflicting expert testimony he said, at p. 330:

"I am not satisfied on the present evidence that on the proper construction of this specification, addressed as it is to persons skilled in the relevant art or science, the claim extends to sterile surgical sutures produced not only from a homopolymer of glycolide but also from a copolymer of glycolide and up to 15 per cent. of lactide. That is to say that I do not consider that a prima facie case of infringement is established."

In effect what the Court of Appeal was doing was trying the issue of infringement upon the conflicting affidavit evidence as it stood, without the benefit of oral testimony or cross-examination. They were saying:

"If we had to give judgment in the action now without any further evidence we should hold that Cyanamid had not satisfied the onus of proving that their patent would be infringed by Ethicon's selling sutures made of XLG."

The Court of Appeal accordingly did not find it necessary to go into the questions raised by Ethicon as to the validity of the patent or to consider where the balance of convenience lay.

Graham J. had adopted the same approach as the Court of Appeal; but, upon the same evidence he had come to the contrary conclusion on the issue of infringement. He considered (at p. 321) that on the evidence as it stood Cyanamid had made out a "strong prima facie case" that their patent would be infringed by Ethicon's selling sutures made of XLG. He then went on to deal briefly with the attack upon the validity of the patent and came to the conclusion that upon the evidence before him none of the grounds of invalidity advanced by Ethicon was likely to succeed. He therefore felt entitled to consider the balance of convenience. In his opinion it lay in favour of maintaining the status quo until the trial of the action. So he granted Cyanamid an interlocutory injunction restraining Ethicon from infringing the patent until the trial or further order.

The grant of an interlocutory injunction is a remedy that is both temporary and discretionary. It would be most exceptional for your Lordships to give leave to appeal to this House in a case which turned upon where the balance of convenience lay. In the instant appeal, however, the question of the balance of convenience, although it had been considered by Graham J. and decided in Cyanamid's favour, was never reached by the Court of Appeal. They considered that there was a rule of practice so well established as to constitute a rule of law that precluded them from granting any interim injunction unless upon the evidence adduced by both the parties on the hearing of the application the applicant had satisfied the court that on the balance of probabilities the acts of the other party sought to be enjoined would, if committed, violate the applicant's legal rights. In the view of the Court of

Appeal the case which the applicant had to prove before any question of balance of convenience arose was "prima facie" only in the sense that the conclusion of law reached by the court upon that evidence might need to be modified at some later date in the light of further evidence either detracting from the probative value of the evidence on which the court had acted or proving additional facts. It was in order to enable the existence of any such rule of law to be considered by your Lordships' House that leave to appeal was granted.

The instant appeal arises in a patent case. Historically there was undoubtedly a time when in an action for infringement of a patent that was not already "well established," whatever that may have meant, an interlocutory injunction to restrain infringement would not be granted if counsel for the defendant stated that it was intended to attack the validity of the patent. . . .

My Lords, when an application for an interlocutory injunction to restrain a defendant from doing acts alleged to be in violation of the plaintiff's legal right is made upon contested facts, the decision whether or not to grant an interlocutory injunction has to be taken at a time when ex hypothesi the existence of the right or the violation of it, or both, is uncertain and will remain uncertain until final judgment is given in the action. It was to mitigate the risk of injustice to the plaintiff during the period before that uncertainty could be resolved that the practice arose of granting him relief by way of interlocutory injunction; but since the middle of the 19th century this has been made subject to his undertaking to pay damages to the defendant for any loss sustained by reason of the injunction if it should be held at the trial that the plaintiff had not been entitled to restrain the defendant from doing what he was threatening to do. The object of the interlocutory injunction is to protect the plaintiff against injury by violation of his right for which he could not be adequately compensated in damages recoverable in the action if the uncertainty were resolved in his favour at the trial; but the plaintiff's need for such protection must be weighed against the corresponding need of the defendant to be protected against injury resulting from his having been prevented from exercising his own legal rights for which he could not be adequately compensated under the plaintiff's undertaking in damages if the uncertainty were resolved in the defendant's favour at the trial. The court must weigh one need against another and determine where "the balance of convenience" lies.

In those cases where the legal rights of the parties depend upon facts that are in dispute between them, the evidence available to the court at the hearing of the application for an interlocutory injunction is incomplete. It is given on affidavit and has not been tested by oral cross-examination. The purpose sought to be achieved by giving to the court discretion to grant such injunctions would be stultified if the discretion were clogged by a technical rule forbidding its exercise if upon that incomplete untested evidence the court evaluated the chances of the plaintiff's ultimate success in the action at 50 per cent. or less, but permitting its exercise if the court evaluated his chances at more than 50 per cent. . . .

[A]uthority was treated by Graham J. and the Court of Appeal in the instant appeal as leaving intact the supposed rule that the court is not entitled to take any account of the balance of convenience unless it has first been satisfied that if the case went to trial upon no other evidence than is before the court at the hearing of the application the plaintiff would be entitled to judgment for a permanent injunction in the same terms as the interlocutory injunction sought.

Your Lordships should in my view take this opportunity of declaring that there is no such rule. The use of such expressions as "a probability," "a prima facie case," or "a strong prima facie case" in the context of the exercise of a discretionary power to grant an interlocutory injunction leads to confusion as to the object sought to be achieved by this form of temporary relief. The court no doubt must be satisfied that the claim is not frivolous or vexatious; in other words, that there is a serious question to be tried.

It is no part of the court's function at this stage of the litigation to try to resolve conflicts of evidence on affidavit as to facts on which the claims of either party may ultimately depend nor to decide difficult questions of law which call for detailed argument and mature considerations. These are matters to be dealt with at the trial. One of the reasons for the introduction of the practice of requiring an undertaking as to damages upon the grant of an interlocutory injunction was that "it aided the court in doing that which was its great object, viz. abstaining from expressing any opinion upon the merits of the case until the hearing": Wakefield v. Duke of Buccleugh (1865) 12 L.T. 628, 629. So unless the material available to the court at the hearing of the application for an interlocutory injunction fails to disclose that the plaintiff has any real prospect of succeeding in his claim for a permanent injunction at the trial, the court should go on to consider whether the balance of convenience lies in favour of granting or refusing the interlocutory relief that is sought.

As to that, the governing principle is that the court should first considered whether, if the plaintiff were to succeed at the trial in establishing his right to a permanent injunction, he would be adequately compensated by an award of damages for the loss he would have sustained as a result of the defendant's continuing to do what was sought to be enjoined between the time of the application and the time of the trial. If damages in the measure recoverable at common law would be adequate remedy and the defendant would be in a financial position to pay them, no interlocutory injunction should normally be granted, however strong the plaintiff's claim appeared to be at that stage. If, on the other hand, damages would not provide an adequate remedy for the plaintiff in the event of his succeeding at the trial, the court should then consider whether, on the contrary hypothesis that the defendant were to succeed at the trial in establishing his right to do that which was sought to be enjoined, he would be adequately compensated under the plaintiff's undertaking as to damages for the loss he would have sustained by being prevented from doing so between the time of the application and the time of the trial. If damages in the measure recoverable under such an undertaking would be an adequate remedy and the plaintiff would be in a financial position to pay them, there would be no reason upon this ground to refuse an interlocutory injunction.

It is where there is doubt as to the adequacy of the respective remedies in damages available to either party or to both, that the question of balance of convenience arises. It would be unwise to attempt even to list all the various matters which may need to be taken into consideration in deciding where the balance lies, let alone to suggest the relative weight to be attached to them. These will vary from case to case.

Where other factors appear to be evenly balanced it is a counsel of prudence to take such measures as are calculated to preserve the status quo. If the defendant is enjoined temporarily from doing something that he has not done before, the only effect of the interlocutory injunction in the event of his succeeding at the trial is to postpone the date at which he is able to embark upon a course of action which he has not previously found it necessary to undertake; whereas to interrupt him in the conduct of an established enterprise would cause much greater inconvenience to him since he would have to start again to establish it in the event of his succeeding at the trial.

Save in the simplest cases, the decision to grant or to refuse an interlocutory injunction will cause to whichever party is unsuccessful on the application some disadvantages which his ultimate success at the trial may show he ought to have been spared and the disadvantages may be such that the recovery of damages to which he would then be entitled either in the action or under the plaintiff's undertaking would not be sufficient to compensate him fully for all of them. The extent to which the disadvantages to each party would be incapable of being compensated in damages in the event of his succeeding at the trial is always a significant factor in assessing where the balance of convenience lies; and if the extent of the uncompensatable disadvantage to each party would not differ widely, it may not be improper to take into account in tipping the balance the relative strength of each party's case as revealed by the affidavit evidence adduced on the hearing of the application. This, however, should be done only where it is apparent upon the facts disclosed by evidence as to which there is no credible dispute that the strength of one party's case is disproportionate to that of the other party. The court is not justified in embarking upon anything resembling a trial of the action upon conflicting affidavits in order to evaluate the strength of either party's case.

I would reiterate that, in addition to those to which I have referred, there may be many other special factors to be taken into consideration in the particular circumstances of individual cases. The instant appeal affords one example of this.

Returning, therefore, to the instant appeal, it cannot be doubted that the affidavit evidence shows that there are serious questions to be tried. Graham J. and the Court of Appeal have already tried the question of infringement on such affidavit evidence as was available and have come to contrary conclusions. Graham J. has already also tried the question of invalidity on these affidavits and has come to the conclusion that the defendant's grounds of objection to the patent are unlikely to succeed, so it was clearly incumbent upon him and on the Court of Appeal to consider the balance of convenience.

Graham J. did so and came to the conclusion that the balance of convenience lay in favour of his exercising his discretion by granting an interlocutory injunction. As patent judge he has unrivalled experience of pharmaceutical patents and the way in which the pharmaceutical industry is carried on. Lacking in this experience, an appellate court should be hesitant to overrule his exercise of his discretion, unless they are satisfied that he has gone wrong in law.

The factors which he took into consideration, and in my view properly, were that Ethicon's sutures XLG were not yet on the market; so they had no business which would be brought to a stop by the injunction; no factories would be closed and no work-people would be thrown out of work. They held a dominant position in the United Kingdom market for absorbent surgical sutures and adopted an aggressive sales policy. Cyanamid on the other hand were in the course of establishing a growing market in PHAE surgical sutures which competed with the natural catgut sutures marketed by Ethicon. If Ethicon were entitled also to establish themselves in the market for PHAE absorbable surgical sutures until the action is tried, which may not be for two or three years yet, and possibly thereafter until the case is finally disposed of on appeal, Cyanamid, even though ultimately successful in proving infringement, would have lost its chance of continuing to increase its share in the total market in absorbent surgical sutures which the continuation of an uninterrupted monopoly of PHAE sutures would have gained for it by the time of the expiry of the patent in 1980. It is notorious that new pharmaceutical products used exclusively by doctors or available only on prescription take a long time to become established in the market, that much of the benefit of the monopoly granted by the patent derives from the fact that the patented product is given the opportunity of becoming established and this benefit continues to be reaped after the patent has expired.

In addition there was a special factor to which Graham J. attached importance. This was that, once doctors and patients had got used to Ethicon's product XLG in the period prior to the trial, it might well be commercially impracticable for Cyanamid to deprive the public of it by insisting on a permanent injunction at the trial, owing to the damaging effect which this would have upon its goodwill in this specialised market and thus upon the sale of its other pharmaceutical products.

I can see no ground for interfering in the learned judge's assessment of the balance of convenience or for interfering with the discretion that he exercised by granting the injunction. In view of the fact that there are serious questions to be tried upon which the available evidence is incomplete, conflicting and untested, to express an opinion now as to the prospects of success of either party would only be embarrassing to the judge who will have eventually to try the case. The likelihood of such embarrassment provides an additional reason for not adopting the course that both Graham J. and the Court of Appeal thought they were bound to follow, of dealing with the existing evidence in detail and giving reasoned assessments of their views as to the relative strengths of each party's cases.

I would allow the appeal and restore the order of Graham J.

VISCOUNT DILHORNE. My Lords, I have had the advantage of reading the speech of my noble and learned friend, Lord Diplock. I agree with it and that this appeal should be allowed and the order of Graham J. restored.

LORD CROSS OF CHELSEA. My Lords, for the reasons given by my noble and learned friend, Lord Diplock, in his speech, which I have had the advantage of reading in draft, I would allow this appeal.

LORD SALMON. My Lords, I agree with the opinion of my noble and learned friend, Lord Diplock, and for the reasons he gives I would allow the appeal and restore the order of Graham J.

LORD EDMUND-DAVIES. My Lords, for the reasons given by my noble and learned friend, Lord Diplock, I would also allow this appeal.

---

1) Litigants often use preliminary injunctions for quick, inexpensive trials. For example, a high school student sues the school to be reinstated after suspension or to be placed on a sports team. After the interlocutory decision, neither the student nor the school presses for a final decision. The parties may be able to afford only one stage. Moreover, interlocutory relief for plaintiff may be effective final relief because the school year or season will end before a final hearing. The same sequence also unfolds in commercial disputes. Plaintiffs' tactic is to select a court with a hair trigger for interlocutory relief but a clogged trial calendar.

Does the *American Cyanamid* approach eliminate the practice of using the motion for a preliminary injunction to jump the courthouse queue? Has the House of Lords "simply shifted the strength of the party's case to another rubric (the balance of convenience)" ? Hammond, Interlocutory Injunction: Time for a New Model?, 30 U. Toronto L.J. 240, 258 (1980). If you interpreted the court of appeals decision in *Hayes* as hinging on the court's view that plaintiff would prevail in the end, would *American Cyanamid's* analysis militate against a preliminary injunction? Does *American Cyanamid* preserve the injunction as a preventive remedy without creating an excessive chance of judicial error?

2) Subsequent English decisions dealing with interlocutory, or as the British have it, interim injunctions include: BBC v. Hearn, [1978] 1 All E.R. 111 (C.A.—Lord Denning), NWL v. Woods, [1979] 3 All E.R. 614 (H.L.); Express Newspapers Ltd. v. McShane, [1979] 2 All E.R. 360 (C.A.—Lord Denning); [1980] 1 All E.R. 65 (H.L.); Dupont Steele Ltd. v. Sirs, [1980] 1 All E.R. 529 (Q.B.) 534 (C.A.—Lord Denning), 540 (H.L.); Fellowes v. Fisher, [1975] 21 All E.R. 829 (C.A.—Lord Denning); and Hubbard v. Pitt, [1975] 3 All E.R. 1 (C.A.—Lord Denning).

SONESTA INTERNATIONAL HOTELS CORP. v. WELLINGTON ASSOCIATES

483 F.2d 247 (2d Cir. 1973).

Before HAYS, MANSFIELD and MULLIGAN, Circuit Judges.

MANSFIELD, Circuit Judge:

Sonesta International Hotels Corp. ("Sonesta") appeals from the denial of a preliminary injunction sought against Wellington Associates . . . to enjoin Wellington, during the pendency of this action, from (a) acquiring or attempting to acquire in any manner any shares of stock of Sonesta, (b) voting any shares of Sonesta stock held or acquired after the initiation of the plan, combination or conspiracy of the defendants alleged by Sonesta in its complaint, (c) exercising, directly or indirectly, any influence upon the management of Sonesta, and (d) otherwise utilizing any such stock or shares of Sonesta stock previously acquired as a means of controlling or affecting the management of Sonesta. Sonesta also sought an order directing Wellington to vote its shares of Sonesta stock in favor of Proposals Nos. 3 and 4 set forth in Sonesta's Notice of Annual Meeting, dated April 16, 1973, which relate to shareholder authorization for the sale of Sonesta's interests in two hotels and the distribution of the net proceeds of the sales to common shareholders, expected to amount to about $2 per share, subject to a favorable tax ruling and the adoption of a plan of partial liquidation by Sonesta's Board of Directors.

The gravamen of Sonesta's complaint, brought on by order to show cause before Judge Ryan, is that Wellington failed to disclose, in connection with its cash tender offer announced in the Wall Street Journal on May 9, 1973, for 1,000,000 shares of Sonesta common at $7 per share, several material facts which were necessary to make the cash offer, as published, and the Schedule 13D filed with the SEC on May 8 concerning the cash offer, not misleading, in violation of §§ 10(b), 13(d), 14(d), and 14(e) of the Securities Exchange Act of 1934, 15 U.S.C. §§ 78j(b), 78m(d), 78n(d), and 78n(e) (1971). These laws are founded on the principle that full and fair disclosure of all material facts must be made to investors so that they may have the benefit of the facts in making their investment decisions. . . .

Sonesta filed its complaint on May 14, 1973. Judge Ryan heard argument on May 17, and on May 22 he rendered a written decision denying Sonesta's request for a preliminary injunction, finding no showing of irreparable injury on the part of Sonesta or likelihood of success on the merits, and specifically finding no false or misleading statements or omissions in the 13D statement or in the tender offer. The offer expired on May 21, according to its terms, with 419,623 shares having been tendered to Wellington. On May 23 Judge Ryan entered an order in accordance with his decision of the previous day. Sonesta thereupon sought and obtained a stay from another panel of this court, which also expedited the appeal. Sonesta's Annual Meeting, scheduled for May 24, went forward as planned, and the necessary two-thirds shareholder approval was obtained for Sonesta's Proposals 3 and 4, described above.

For reasons hereinafter stated we hold that Wellington failed to disclose material facts in its Schedule 13D filed with the SEC and in its Tender Offer announced to the public. We therefore reverse with directions to enter a preliminary injunction preventing consummation of the offer subject to the conditions of supplemental disclosure and rescission noted below.

Sonesta claims that in four respects Wellington omitted to state information material to an informed choice by Sonesta shareholders as to whether they should accept Wellington's cash offer of $7 per share. More specifically, it is claimed that the Schedule 13D and the published offer failed to disclose (1) that Wellington owed Sonesta approximately $2.4 million, which amount might be compromised on terms adverse to Sonesta's stockholders if Wellington should acquire control, (2) that Wellington's plan to abstain from voting on Proposals 3 and 4 at the Annual Meeting could result in the defeat of these Proposals for failure to obtain the required approval of two-thirds of

Sonesta's issued outstanding shares, thereby causing Sonesta shareholders to be deprived of a partially tax-free cash distribution of about $2 a share, (3) that Sonesta might lose its listing on the New York Stock Exchange if Wellington should receive the number of tenders it sought, and (4) that a number of buildings owned by Wellington had received adverse notoriety in certain publications which had described the buildings as havens of prostitution, illicit massage parlors, pornographic film theaters, and peep shows, and that this negative publicity could harm the business reputation and credit standing of Sonesta if Wellington should acquire control.

Before turning to consideration of the alleged omissions in greater detail, it is important to restate the standard to be applied in determining whether, at the instance of a target corporation, a preliminary injunction should be issued against the continuation of a proposed tender offer when it is claimed that the offer and supporting materials, such as a Schedule 13D required by 17 C.F.R. § 240.14d–1 (1972), fail to adequately disclose material information necessary to make the statements contained in the offer not misleading. The settled rule is that a preliminary injunction should issue only upon a clear showing of either (1) probable success on the merits *and* possible irreparable injury, *or* (2) sufficiently serious questions going to the merits to make them a fair ground for litigation *and* a balance of hardships tipping decidedly toward the party requesting the preliminary relief. . . . Assuming that such a showing is made prior to consummation of the tender offer, a preliminary injunction will normally afford prompt relief against a violation of § 14(e), which makes it unlawful to make any untrue statement of a material fact in connection with any tender or to omit to state any material fact necessary in order to make the statements made, in the light of the circumstances under which they are made, not misleading. . . .

Where the foregoing standard has been met preliminary injunctive relief is a particularly useful remedy for prevention of probable violations of the disclosure requirements of the Act, for the reason that prior to consummation of the offer the court still has a variety of methods available to it for correction of the misstatements or omissions. . . . But once the tender offer has been consummated it becomes difficult, and sometimes virtually impossible, for a court to "unscramble the eggs." . . . On the other hand, preliminary relief does not, in assuring that the offer will be lawfully made, sacrifice the legitimate desires of shareholders to accept the offer. If the offeror is subsequently vindicated after a trial on the merits, the offer may be renewed. Thus, in the normal situation, when it appears likely that the offer may contain materially misleading statements or omissions as made, the interest of the shareholders and of the public in full disclosure of relevant circumstances renders preliminary injunctive relief an appropriate method of remedying the deficiencies in disclosure before the offer is consummated.

The probability of success on the merits in any application for injunctive relief turns greatly upon whether the plaintiff has shown that the tender offer under attack has misstated or omitted *material* facts. The materiality of facts allegedly misstated or omitted depends, in turn, upon whether a reasonable investor might have considered them to be important in deciding whether to accept the tender offer. . . .

To be material a statement in a tender offer need not necessarily relate to a past or existing condition or event. It may refer to a prospective event, even though the event may not occur, provided there appears to be a reasonable likelihood of its future occurrence. . . . A reasonable stockholder, once informed of the contingency, can then determine whether to assume the risk of its occurrence or non-occurrence in accepting or rejecting the tender offer. Where the event, if it should occur, could influence the stockholder's decision to tender, the chance that it might well occur is a factor that should be disclosed to the investor for consideration in making his or her decision.

Applying these principles here, we are satisfied that Sonesta has made a clear showing, upon undisputed facts, that Wellington failed in violation of § 14(e) to disclose certain material facts in its tender offer. After making due allowance for the wide discretion normally permitted the district court in deciding whether to issue a preliminary injunction, . . . it appears that in this case the district judge plainly erred in applying an incorrect standard as to materiality and in concluding that certain of the omissions charged by Sonesta did not entitle it to preliminary relief.

The most persuasive claim by Sonesta is that Wellington did not sufficiently disclose that it owed more than $2.4 million to Sonesta and that this debt might be compromised on terms adverse to Sonesta shareholders if Wellington should succeed in acquiring control of Sonesta. Wellington's offer neglected to mention that Sonesta had obtained a judgment in New York State Supreme Court against Wellington in the sum of $1,896,584.32 arising out of a property dispute concerning the land underlying the Plaza Hotel, which is owned 50% by each of the parties, and that Sonesta had asserted against Wellington a claim for over $500,000 in back real estate taxes which has not been disputed. Wellington's tender offer limited itself to informing Sonesta's stockholders of the existence of a dispute between it and Sonesta over the valuation of the land underlying the Plaza Hotel, which had resulted in a decision fixing the value of that land (upon which the rental formula was dependent) at $18,500,000, from which Wellington had appealed, claiming that the value should be materially greater.

Judge Ryan concluded that "while it might have been better to have stated the actual dollar figure [of the judgment] . . . this is not a major or deceptive omission" and that the disclosure of the dispute "was more than adequate." We disagree. Disclosure of the dispute over the valuation of the land, while a step in the right direction, hardly put Sonesta's stockholders on notice that Sonesta had obtained an $1,896,584 judgment against Wellington which, when supplemented by a separate claim for over $500,000, brought Wellington's total indebtedness to Sonesta up to more than $2.4 million, an amount equal to nearly 10% of Sonesta's equity and nearly $1 per Sonesta share. By describing the dispute in more general terms, Wellington deprived Sonesta's shareholders of the knowledge of just how much was actually at stake in litigation which admittedly might be resolved on terms less favorable to Sonesta shareholders if Wellington should succeed in its takeover bid. As Judge Friendly observed in Gerstle v. Gamble-Skogmo, Inc. [478 F.2d 1281, 1298 (2d Cir. 1973)], "the English language has sufficient resources that the draftsman could have done better than he did." Here a simple reference in relevant Arabic numerals to the money judgment in favor of Sonesta and to its claim for back taxes (which the tender offer did not even mention) would have alerted Sonesta stockholders to the potential significance of the possible compromise of the judgment and of the tax claim. The standard of materiality was not whether the non-disclosure was "major," as Judge Ryan indicated, but whether a reasonable stockholder might have attached importance to the omitted facts. If these simple facts had been disclosed in the present case, we have no hesitancy in concluding that a reasonable shareholder, contemplating a sale of all or part of his shares, might well have considered the information to be of considerable importance in making his decision.

We turn next to Sonesta's claim that Wellington failed to disclose certain material facts with respect to the possible effect of its decision to abstain from voting on Propositions 3 and 4 at Sonesta's Annual Meeting scheduled for May 24, 1973. These resolutions, if affirmatively approved by two-thirds of Sonesta's issued and outstanding shares, called for liquidation of its leasehold interest in two hotels for approximately $5,150,000. Subject to a favorable income tax ruling from the Internal Revenue Service and adoption of a plan of partial liquidation and approval by Sonesta's Board of Directors, the net proceeds of the sale were to be distributed to Sonesta stockholders, who would receive nearly $2 per share (or approximately 28.5% of the $7 tender offer price), partially free of income tax. Although Wellington's tender offer stated that it would abstain from voting on the two proposals, it failed to disclose that if its offer to purchase 1,000,000 shares (out of Sonesta's 2,393,817 outstanding common shares) should be reasonably successful and result in its acquiring more than 767,440 shares,[5] the defeat of the proposals would be certain, since the remaining shares outstanding, even if voted in favor of the proposals, would be less than the two-thirds required for approval.

Judge Ryan concluded that it was unnecessary for Wellington to have pointed out that a successful completion of its tender offer could defeat the liquidation proposals because it was "purely hypothetical and an 'if' situation" since it was unknown at the time of the offer how many shares would be tendered and whether other shareholders would vote for the proposals. We disagree. The test of materiality is not whether a possible consequence of the offer was contingent or hypothetical, Gerstle v. Gamble-Skogmo, Inc., supra, but whether it was a factor that might be considered of some importance by a Sonesta stockholder in making his decision. We believe that it was. It is true that Wellington's offer has not been as successful as it had hoped (undoubtedly due in part to Sonesta's opposition) and that the two proposals have since been approved by a small margin at Sonesta's Annual Meeting. But this post-offer occurrence does not render the offer any the less misleading. Section 14(e) prohibits omissions which are misleading "in the light of the circumstances under which they are made." . . . No sound reason appears why the full circumstances of the possible defeat of the proposals (which might have yielded the shareholders an amount equal to approximately 28.5% of Wellington's $7 offering price) should not have been set forth in the offer in the first instance.

5. Wellington had previously acquired 30,500 shares of Sonesta which, if added to 767,440 or more shares received pursuant to the tender offer, would amount to more than one-third of the 2,393,817 total outstanding shares.

Nor do we have any difficulty in concluding that Wellington should have disclosed the prospect that if its offer should be fully successful Sonesta common stock could have lost its listing privileges on the New York Stock Exchange. Judge Ryan concluded that the possibility of delisting was too speculative to make this omission material. We disagree. Section A–16 of the Exchange Rules permits but does not require removal or suspension of a listed security if the publicly held shares number less than 600,000 and their aggregate market value is less than $5 million. Of Sonesta's 2,393,817 outstanding shares, 1,572,839 were publicly held according to the Exchange's definition, the balance of 820,978 being owned by officers and directors of Sonesta and their immediate families. If Wellington had achieved its goal of acquiring 1,000,000 shares, the publicly held stock would have been reduced below the Exchange standards in both number and aggregate value. Wellington again suggests that it could not know in advance how many Sonesta shareholders would accept its offer. Sonesta counters, by affidavit of its general counsel, that the Exchange had advised Sonesta that it could lose its listing privileges if Wellington's offer was successful. Under these circumstances the risk of delisting was sufficiently appreciable to require disclosure. . . . Loss of listing on the Exchange would deprive Sonesta shareholders of a ready market for their shares and of the protection of certain Exchange requirements, including its disclosure rules. The possibility of losing these advantages could certainly have been of importance to a Sonesta shareholder in deciding whether to retain some Sonesta shares or to tender all. Although Wellington has not received as many tenders as it sought and there does not now appear to be a prospect of immediate delisting as a result of the immediate offer, the consequences of Wellington's nondisclosure cannot on that account be dismissed as moot since there remains the possibility of further offers which could have the cumulative result of subjecting Sonesta common to the possibility of delisting.

Finally, Sonesta complains that Wellington should have disclosed that it has been the subject of adverse comment in the New York Post and other publications for allegedly owning properties which have been used by prostitutes, illicit massage parlors, pornographic film theaters, and peep shows. Sonesta notes that Wellington has instituted an action for libel against the Post and others for alleged damage to its reputation and suggests that Wellington was under an obligation to state that, should it acquire control of Sonesta, Sonesta's reputation might be similarly impaired. On this issue, we agree with Judge Ryan's conclusion that Sonesta's claim lacks an adequate basis. . . .

On the basis of what is before us, we see no reason why Wellington should have described the allegations of unsavory conduct which it had not only denied but has claimed to be libelous in a suit instituted by it against the New York Post. Sonesta does not assert that the allegations are true but only that they have given Wellington notoriety. But Wellington owes no duty to repeat what it considers to be false statements about itself, thereby giving currency to the allegedly libelous matter and increasing the risk that it might unjustly incur notoriety.

Wellington attempts to excuse its failure to disclose the facts we have found material on the grounds (1) that although Sonesta published a message to its shareholders on May 14 (five days after the offer was first made) it did not refer to the money judgment, to the effect of abstention or to the possibility of delisting, from which we are asked to infer that Sonesta did not consider these facts material, and (2) that any deficiencies have been overcome by the generosity of Wellington's $7 offer, which exceeded the prices at which Sonesta common had been trading in previous weeks. While the failure of a target company to seize an opportunity to rectify claimed omissions may have some bearing on their materiality, . . . and while it would have been in the interests of disclosure for Sonesta itself to have drawn its stockholders' attention to the possible consequences of their tendering Sonesta shares, which Wellington had omitted, it would emasculate the purposes of the Williams Act to allow the offeror to look to the target company to remedy the offeror's own material deficiencies in disclosure. The obligation is placed squarely on those making the offer in the first instance to disclose all material factors necessary to make *their offer* not misleading. That duty cannot be shifted to the shoulders of others. As for the suggestion that the generosity of the offer should reduce Wellington's obligation to inform the shareholders of all relevant circumstances, we must reject any such nullification of the disclosure requirements of the Act, as did the Supreme Court in a similar situation with respect to proxy violations in Mills v. Electric Auto-Lite, supra, 396 U.S. at 381–385.

As the tender offer has not yet been consummated and the interests of all parties may be protected in allowing only a lawful offer to be completed, we reverse and remand with directions to enter a preliminary injunction enjoining the consummation of the offer unless Wellington makes a supplemental disclosure to Sonesta stockholders setting forth (1) the facts concerning the money judgment Sonesta presently has against it and Sonesta's claim against it for back real estate taxes, and (2) the possibility of delisting of Sonesta's common stock by the New York Stock Exchange if Wellington should receive a greater number of shares on any future offer, and unless Wellington offers to those tendering shareholders who responded to its current offer an opportunity within a reasonable period of time to rescind their tenders. . . .

---

1) Do business takeover suits illustrate litigants using a preliminary injunction to speed a decision and obtain a final resolution before events outrun the litigation process? Should the standard preliminary injunction test apply? John Leubsdorf argued that, "Rather than try to predict how a fictional final hearing would apply a hypothetical final standard, courts should develop a standard for the single hearing that does occur. . . . The dilemma of interlocutory inaccuracy is missing . . . ." Leubsdorf, The Standard for Preliminary Injunctions, 91 Harv.L.Rev. 525, 557 (1978). See Easterbrook and Fischel, Takeover Bids, Defensive Tactics, and Shareholders' Welfare, 36 Bus.Law. 1733 (1981); Note, Preliminary Injunctive Relief and Tender Offers: An Analysis Under the Williams Act, 49 Geo.Wash.L.Rev. 563 (1981).

What if the target company's management uses an interlocutory injunction to stop the clock on a tender offer while it organizes a defense? Can defendant be compensated for these losses from plaintiff's bond? What about losses to the investing public? Can a preliminary injunction maintain any kind of status quo? Will the offeror have to pay interest on borrowed money while a preliminary injunction is in effect? Will a preliminary injunction destroy many tender offers as a practical matter?

2) Does the second branch of the "bicephalous" *Sonesta* inquiry eliminate from consideration the threat of irreparable harm to plaintiff if the judge denies a preliminary injunction? Or is the threat of irreparable harm part of the balance of hardships? In Doran v. Salem Inn, 422 U.S. 922, 931 (1975), the Supreme Court said, "The traditional standard for granting a preliminary injunction requires the plaintiff to show that in the absence of its issuance he will suffer irreparable injury and also that he is likely to prevail on the merits. It is recognized, however, that a district court must weigh carefully the interests on both sides." Similar statements appear in Rondeau v. Mosinee Paper Corp., 422 U.S. 49, 57 (1975), and Sampson v. Murray, 415 U.S. 61, 88 (1974), both quoting Beacon Theatres, Inc. v. Westover, 359 U.S. 500, 506–507 (1959).

Judge Mulligan of the Second Circuit concluded that *Sonesta* is "based on a cumulative misreading of the traditional standards for a preliminary injunction," and he unequivocally called on his court to repudiate *Sonesta* "to the extent that it would indicate that irreparable harm is not necessary for every preliminary injunction." Mulligan, Foreword: Preliminary Injunction in the Second Circuit, 43 Brooklyn L.Rev. 831, 836, 839 (1977).

3) Should it suffice for plaintiff to show only a reasonable chance of ultimate success if nothing short of a preliminary injunction will prevent defendant from destroying any chance of final relief and rendering the judicial process futile? For example, Professor Hammond suggests that a low threshold of success is appropriate to ground an airplane thought to be potentially unsafe. Interlocutory Injunctions: Time for a New Model?, 30 U. Toronto L.J. 240, 279 (1980). Compare the calculations in the court employed in *Reserve Mining* to determine whether the request for an injunction was premature, p. 116. Did the court develop the *Sonesta* approach because the requirement of showing a likelihood of success on the merits is too restrictive? The Courts of Appeals for the Third and Fourth Circuits balance four factors, emphasizing that no single factor controls: 1) the plaintiff's likelihood of success on the merits, 2) the threat of irreparable harm to the plaintiff, 3) the possibility of harm to the defendant, and 4) the public interest. Constructors Association v. Kreps, 573 F.2d 811, 815 (3d Cir. 1978); Blackwelder Furniture Co. v. Seilig Manufacturing Co., 550 F.2d 189, 196 (4th Cir. 1977).

Examine the following excerpts from Dataphase Systems, Inc. v. CL Systems, Inc., 640 F.2d 109, 112–113 (8th Cir. 1981). Did the court clarify the standard?

"The court has considered this case *en banc* in an effort to clarify the standard to be applied by the district courts of this circuit in considering requests for preliminary injunctive relief. We apprehend that in recent years some misunderstanding of the standard has developed. We recognize that language in some of our recent opinions may have contributed to uncertainty as to the appropriate test or tests. Thus, we take this opportunity to reaffirm that there is a single "test" or list of considerations to be used in every case and to suggest its proper application.

"In Minnesota Bearing Co. v. White Motor Corp., 470 F.2d 1323 (8th Cir. 1973), we enumerated four factors to be weighed by the district court in deciding whether to grant or deny preliminary injunctive relief: (1) whether there is a substantial probability movant will succeed at trial; (2) whether the moving party will suffer irreparable injury absent the injunction; (3) the harm to other interested parties if the relief is granted; and (4) the effect on the public interest. . . . This statement of the standard, in particular the requirements of 'substantial probability' and 'irreparable injury,' has become known as the 'traditional test.' . . .

"Perhaps due to dissatisfaction with restrictive practical application of the language of the traditional test, this court offered a restated version in Fennell v. Butler, 570 F.2d 263. In that case we suggested that a preliminary injunction should issue: upon a clear showing of either (1) probable success on the merits *and* possible irreparable injury, *or* (2) sufficiently serious questions going to the merits to make them a fair ground for litigation *and* a balance of hardships tipping decidedly toward the party requesting preliminary relief. . . .

"Some confusion apparently has been spawned by our characterization of the *Fennell* standard as an 'alternative test.' Despite this label, we find no contradiction between *Fennell* and *Minnesota Bearing.* Whatever the verbal formulation, the relevant factors remain the same. Whether a preliminary injunction should issue involves consideration of (1) the threat of irreparable harm to the movant; (2) the state of the balance between this harm and the injury that granting the injunction will inflict on other parties litigant; (3) the probability that movant will succeed on the merits; and (4) the public interest.

"The major difficulty with application of the traditional test has arisen from the phrase 'probability of success on the merits.' Some have read this element of the test to require in every case that the party seeking preliminary relief prove a greater than fifty per cent likelihood that he will prevail on the merits. Under this view, even if the balance of the other three factors strongly favored the moving party, preliminary relief would be denied if the movant could not prove a mathematical probability of success at trial. Although this construction of the 'probability of success' requirement is technically possible, we reject it.

"The very nature of the inquiry on petition for preliminary relief militates against a wooden application of the probability test. At base, the question is whether the balance of equities so favors the movant that justice requires the court to intervene to preserve the status quo until the merits are determined. The equitable nature of the proceeding mandates that the court's approach be flexible enough to encompass the particular circumstances of each case. Thus, an effort to apply the probability language to all cases with mathematical precision is misplaced.

"In balancing the equities no single factor is determinative. The likelihood that plaintiff ultimately will prevail is meaningless in isolation. In every case, it must be examined in the context of the relative injuries to the parties and the public. If the chance of irreparable injury to the movant should relief be denied is outweighed by the likely injury to other parties litigant should the injunction be granted, the moving party faces a heavy burden of demonstrating that he is likely to prevail on the merits. Conversely, where the movant has raised a substantial question and the equities are otherwise strongly in his favor, the showing of success on the merits can be less.

"It follows that the court ordinarily is not required at an early stage to draw the fine line between a mathematical probability and a substantial possibility of success. This endeavor may, of course, be necessary in some circumstances when the balance of equities may come to require a more careful evaluation of the merits. But where the balance of other factors tips decidedly toward movant a preliminary injunction may issue if movant has raised questions so serious and difficult as to call for more deliberate investigation."

4) Professor Leubsdorf addresses the confusion you are now experiencing in The Standard for Preliminary Injunctions, 91 Harv.L.Rev. 525 (1978). He observes that the "standard" preliminary injunction formula is less a test than a list of factors to consider and that courts state the test differently, even inconsistently. Courts lack a theory of interlocutory relief. The early decision may differ from the final judgment because of the incomplete procedure. If the judge denies a preliminary injunction, plaintiff may lose irreplaceable interests; but if the judge grants it, defendant may similarly lose rights. Accordingly the standard should aim to reduce irreparable loss caused by errors that flow from a hasty decision.

The judge, according to Leubsdorf, should investigate harm from an incorrect interlocutory decision and seek to minimize harm final relief cannot redress. The judge should ask two questions: 1) Who will be more likely to win in the end? 2) What irreparable interlocutory loss will each party suffer if the preliminary injunction decision is erroneous? The judge should compare impairments: which will lose less if the other incorrectly prevails.

More precisely, the judge should adopt the solution with the smaller probable loss from the following calculations. If the judge grants an incorrect preliminary injunction, the probability the defendant will win is multiplied by the defendant's irreparable interlocutory loss. If the judge incorrectly denies a preliminary injunction, the probability plaintiff will win is multiplied by plaintiff's irreparable interlocutory loss.

Professor Leubsdorf posits this example: "Suppose the plaintiff is an indigent who claims additional welfare payments of $20 per month. With these payments, he could buy food in bulk at reduced rates, increasing his purchasing power by $32 per month. If five months will elapse before final judgment, the defendant agency has $100 at stake and the plaintiff $160. Although calculable, these potential losses are irreparable because the plaintiff is judgment-proof and the defendant has sovereign immunity from a judgment for payments due in previous months. The judge also estimates that the plaintiff's claim has a 40% chance of success at trial. On these assumptions, the judge can calculate the probable irreparable loss of rights resulting from the grant or denial of preliminary relief. If the defendant must pay the plaintiff's claim during the litigation, it will spend $100 with a 60% chance that the payments will be found legally unnecessary. Therefore, the defendant's probable irreparable loss of rights from the grant of relief is $60. The plaintiff's probable irreparable loss from the denial of relief, based on a similar calculation, is 40% of $160, or $64. Since the estimated $64 loss from denying relief exceeds the estimated $60 loss from granting it, the judge should grant a preliminary injunction." 91 Harv.L.Rev. at 542.

Professor Leubsdorf's example used hard figures, but he admits that precision may not always be possible for the factors are not susceptible to quantitative estimate. For example, change the probability of success ratio above to 38/62. In theory, moreover, money damages are inadequate for the rights at issue because they are difficult or impossible to value. Finally, evidence may be scarce at the preliminary stage. Try applying Leubsdorf's test to United States v. Progressive, p. 242 and Lankford v. Gelston, p. 160.

Professor Hammond puts Leubsdorf in the same basket with the courts Leubsdorf bemoans. "[T]he solution really suggested by the contemporary formulations—the ubiquitous balancing exercise within a broad judicial discretion—is both a blunt vehicle and largely unreviewable. Moreover, the philosophies of pragmatic instrumentalism and procedural fairness which have enjoyed such contemporary fashionability cannot lead, ultimately, to anything but impotent legal relativism. This typically expresses itself in a meaningless Burkean formula—add, subtract, multiply, and divide—and its modern analogue, the balancing exercise." Interlocutory Injunctions: Time for a New Model?, 30 U. Toronto L.J. 240, 278 (1980).

Professor Hammond's test is to "require a judge to ask three preliminary questions: 1) is there a real dispute (in the sense of the claim being nonfrivolous)? 2) what is the nature of that dispute? 3) Assuming that question 1 is answered affirmatively and after the analysis required in question 2 is undertaken, what threshold test is appropriate for that kind of dispute?" Hammond, 30 U. Toronto L.J. at 278. Examples of the variable threshold model that require the plaintiff to show a strong probability of success are patent and free speech cases. Hammond, 30 U. Toronto L.J. at 280.

5) Are the recent formulations too hair-triggered? Have all the courts and scholars ignored the procedural foundations of judicial legitimacy? The judge's inaction in refusing to grant a preliminary injunction differs from action in granting an order because judicial action must be preceded by adversary procedure. The courts' legitimacy depends on whether they observe the procedural norms of the adversary system. Should the rules be changed to put pressure on plaintiffs to ask for hearings and to mount more thorough presentations? Does the *Jack Kahn* decision below administer an antidote to promiscuous preliminary injunctions?

JACK KAHN MUSIC CO., INC. v. BALDWIN PIANO & ORGAN

604 F.2d 755 (2d Cir. 1979).

Before MEDINA and TIMBERS, Circuit Judges, and SAND, District Judge.

MEDINA, Circuit Judge:

Having failed in its opposition before District Judge Charles S. Haight, Jr., in the Southern District of New York, to the granting of a preliminary mandatory injunction in a private antitrust action, defendant Baldwin Piano & Organ Company appeals. The controversy between plaintiff, Jack Kahn Music Co., Inc., a seller at retail of pianos, organs and other musical instruments at various locations in Eastern Long Island, New York, and Baldwin arises out of the cancellation of a dealership contract by Baldwin. The preliminary mandatory injunction enjoins Baldwin from terminating Kahn's dealership until the final hearing of the antitrust suit.

In recent years there has been developing a substantial body of decisional law affecting a small but important segment of the law relating to the cancellation of retail dealerships by manufacturers. The procedural device employed in this group of cases is the service of a complaint in a private triple-damage antitrust action in which the retailer charges the manufacturer with various violations of the Sherman and Clayton antitrust laws and the simultaneous service of motion papers seeking a preliminary mandatory injunction preventing the manufacturer from cancelling the dealership agreement between the parties until the disposition of the antitrust suit. As the conclusion of the trial on the merits of the antitrust suit will in the normal course of events in all likelihood not take place for some years, if at all, the granting of such a preliminary mandatory injunction amounts as a practical matter, as here, to freezing plaintiff's revocable and hence temporary dealership into a dealership non-revocable for a substantial period. Thus here Baldwin thought it had entered into a two-year dealership, renewable from year to year and revocable on six months' notice. By the decision below it winds up with a non-revocable dealership of considerable duration, which is the very thing Baldwin thought the terms of the contract made impossible. The dealership contract was made on August 7, 1976. The notice of termination was given, one year, five months, and twenty-three days later, on January 30, 1978, to take effect on August 7, 1978. The complaint and the motion papers were served on July 20, 1978.

In this narrow field there are numerous opinions reporting decisions by many federal Courts of Appeals, including several in this, the Second Circuit. As is to be expected there is to be found in these opinions a certain amount of digressions and glosses, perhaps due to the circumstance that with overcrowded dockets and overworked judges there is always a feeling of urgency promptly to dispose of appeals involving injunctions.

As we are convinced that the decision below is wrong and that the result is not a just one and that we should reverse and vacate the injunction, we have given the appeal our most careful consideration and, in deference to the similar careful consideration below, by an able and conscientious judge, we shall try to explain in some detail our reasons for the view we take of the case. We start with an analysis of the fundamental principles involved.

I.

As a general rule, an appellate court will reverse the grant or denial of a preliminary injunction only upon a clear showing that the District Judge abused his discretion, Doran v. Salem Inn, Inc., 422 U.S. 922 (1975), or erred in his application of the relevant law, Triebwasser & Katz v. American Telephone & Telegraph Co., 535 F.2d 1356 (2d Cir. 1976). But as there was no evidentiary hearing in the District Court and the injunction was granted on a paper record containing only the affidavits, the pleadings and the briefs, we are, as stated by Chief Judge Kaufman, "in as good a position as the district judge to read and interpret the pleadings, affidavits and depositions." Dopp v. Franklin National Bank, 461 F.2d 873, 879 (2d Cir. 1972). . . . And this is particularly true where, as here, the affidavits are replete with flat contradictions, discrepancies, and unsupported conclusory statements. The trial judge saw and listened to no witnesses and he had no demeanor impressions to affect his judgment. We think that there can be no reasonable doubt that in this Circuit we have appellate power of "full review" over the grant of this preliminary injunction. Judge Friendly has been hammering away at this point for years. . . .

This Circuit has long provided two alternative tests for the grant of a preliminary injunction. The tests both require a finding of irreparable injury and differ regarding the potential for success on the merits which the plaintiff is able to demonstrate at this early stage of the litigation. A recent statement of these tests is found in Seaboard World Airlines, Inc. v. Tiger International, Inc., 600 F.2d 355, 359–360 (2d Cir. 1979), quoting Jackson Dairy, Inc. v. H.P. Hood & Sons, Inc., 596 F.2d 70, 72 (2d Cir. 1979) (per curiam):

"Preliminary injunctive relief in this Circuit calls for a showing of '(a) irreparable harm and (b) either (1) likelihood of success on the merits or (2) sufficiently serious questions going to the merits to make them a fair ground for litigation and a balance of hardships tipping decidedly toward the party requesting the preliminary relief.' "

Accord, Caulfield v. Board of Education of the City of New York, 583 F.2d 605, 610 (2d Cir. 1978); Triebwasser & Katz v. American Telephone & Telegraph Co., supra, 535 F.2d at 1358–59; Foreword Sonesta International Hotels Corp. v. Wellington Associates; Mulligan, Preliminary Injunctions in the Second Circuit, 43 Brooklyn L.Rev. 831 (1977). In the present case Judge Haight granted the preliminary injunction on the basis of his findings of irreparable injury, a substantial question amounting to a fair ground for litigation, and a balance of hardships tipping decidedly in Kahn's favor.

This Court recognized in Jackson Dairy, Inc. v. H.P. Hood & Sons, Inc. that "[a]s to the kind of irreparable harm that the party must show, the language of some past cases has suggested to some a spectrum ranging from possible to probable, which is defined as 'not remote or speculative but . . . actual and imminent.' " Judge Haight relied on the formulation of the test stated in Caulfield v. Board of Education of the City of New York in which appears the phrase "possible irreparable injury." The great Voltaire once wrote in *Candide,* his most entertaining and perhaps most influential philosophical novel, that anything is possible in this best of all possible worlds.

The basic statute we are construing here is Section 16 of the Clayton Act, 15 U.S.C. § 26, which requires "a showing that the danger of irreparable loss or damage is immediate," and the principles of "courts of equity, under the rules governing such proceedings" are made applicable. Ever since the establishment of the English Court of Chancery, hundreds of years ago, the basic rule has always been that there must be a showing that there is "no adequate remedy at law." We do not think that this fundamental rule has been changed so as to regard as sufficient proof of a lack of any remedy at law a mere speculation that there is a possibility that the party seeking the injunction may in some unproved way suffer loss or damage. In any event, Judge Mulligan's ruling in Triebwasser & Katz v. American Telephone &

Telegraph Co. disposes of this point, especially where, as here, the District Judge granted the preliminary injunction only on a showing of a fair ground for litigation. He wrote:

"If the element of irreparable harm is prerequisite for relief where the plaintiff must show probable success on the merits, then *a fortiori* where the plaintiff establishes something less than probable success on the merits, need for proof of the threat of irreparable damage is even more pronounced."

As we shall demonstrate in a later section of the opinion, we believe that Kahn has wholly failed to meet its burden of proving the requisite probability of irreparable injury upon termination of its Baldwin dealership. The injuries which Kahn alleges that it will incur on termination of its Baldwin dealership are in every sense ordinary and are compensable in light of the liberal rule for proving damages in antitrust cases. SCM Corp. v. Xerox Corp., 507 F.2d 358 (2d Cir. 1974).

II.

Kahn has engaged in the retail sale of pianos, organs and other musical instruments at discount prices since 1930. At the time this action was commenced Kahn stores were located in Freeport, Huntington, and Centereach, Long Island, and in Manhattan. Kahn sells numerous makes and models of pianos and organs at these stores other than those manufactured by Baldwin.

Baldwin is a leading manufacturer of premier pianos and organs in the United States. Baldwin grand pianos are considered a standard of excellence. Baldwin studio pianos are also considered among the finest of their kind and are a favorite of institutional purchasers such as schools, churches, and the like. Baldwin markets its instruments through approximately nine hundred independent dealers and through some twenty-three company-owned stores. Baldwin has operated a company store in Manhattan for approximately forty years.

In August 1976 the former Baldwin dealer in Huntington, Freeport and Jamaica, Long Island, went out of business. Kahn then approached Baldwin about possibly obtaining a Baldwin dealership. On August 7, 1976, Baldwin and Kahn executed a written agreement whereby Kahn was appointed a dealer for the sale and service of Baldwin pianos and organs. The initial term of the Agreement was for only two years and for successive one-year terms unless either party terminated the Agreement on six months' written notice.

The Agreement contained the following "location clause":

"2. *Sale of Instruments.* Baldwin shall sell to Dealer and Dealer shall purchase from Baldwin Instruments, the quantity and kind of said Instruments to be determined from time to time by mutual agreement of the parties. All Instruments shall be held for sale in the ordinary course of Dealer's retail business but only at the addresses set forth in Schedule 1, attached hereto, or such additional locations as shall have the prior written consent of Baldwin."

Though the parties did not attach a Schedule 1 to the Agreement, there is no dispute that at the time the Agreement was made Kahn was permitted to sell Baldwin instruments only at its Freeport and Huntington stores. Approximately one year later Baldwin extended its authorization to Kahn's store in

Centereach. There is no dispute that on at least one occasion Baldwin enforced this location clause against Kahn.

Baldwin has never authorized Kahn to sell Baldwin instruments at the Kahn Manhattan store. Nor did the Agreement give Kahn exclusive rights to market Baldwin pianos and organs on Long Island. As the trial judge . . . states that the White Plains situation "is not material to these motions," we shall not make any further reference to that peripheral phase of the case.

There is an irreconcilable conflict in the affidavits relating to conversations and various other matters that in our judgment have a very considerable bearing upon the ultimate decision we must make on the subject of whether or not the decision below brings about a miscarriage of justice, as we think it does. Despite a sprinkling of talismanic phrases and cliches, such as the reluctance of courts to issue mandatory injunctions, and the requirement that plaintiff make a "clear showing" to satisfy its undoubted burden of proof of irreparable damage and the other necessary requirements, it is not possible to discern any clear view by the trial judge concerning these conflicting and disputed issues. In our full review of the case, in order to reach a just result, we think we must give our reasoned views on the subject . . . .

During the negotiations prior to the execution of the Agreement, Kahn and Baldwin officials discussed sales goals for the balance of 1976, 1977 and 1978 which Kahn was expected to meet. These goals were:

Balance of 1976:			Balance of 1977:		
	Pianos —	200		Pianos —	500
	Organs —	100		Organs —	300
		300			800

Balance of 1978:		
	Pianos —	600
	Organs —	350
		950

These original goals were memorialized in a letter from Baldwin to Kahn dated July 20, 1976. It is significant, we think, that there was no reply by Kahn to this letter of transmittal and no prompt denial of the statement that these goals had been agreed upon. In any event, the very terms of the Agreement itself demonstrate, in our view of the record, that Kahn was only to start with a two-year dealership, with single-year extensions, unless on six months' written notice the dealership was revoked and cancelled. Bearing in mind the explosive increase in population in Eastern Long Island in the past decade and the very large potential market consisting of colleges, public and private schools, churches, theatres, hotels, and private homes, we think it highly improbable, contrary to Kahn's allegation, that any of the Baldwin officials referred to these original goals as "ridiculous."

The fact is that the purchases made by Kahn in 1976 and 1977, despite Kahn's unsupported assertions that the Baldwin line was "the cornerstone of its marketing effort" and that it had "expended large sums promoting and advertising Baldwin products," were:

Balance of 1976:			Balance of 1977:		
	Pianos —	97		Pianos —	291
	Organs —	38		Organs —	116
		135			407

On January 30, 1978, Baldwin notified Kahn in writing of its intention to terminate the Agreement effective August 7, 1978. In its letter of termination Baldwin assured Kahn that in the event Kahn was awarded contracts after the effective date on bids submitted before that date, Baldwin would supply the instruments necessary to meet these commitments.

Just prior to the time the cancellation notice became effective, and on July 20, 1978, Kahn caused to be simultaneously served its antitrust complaint against Baldwin and its motion papers on the application for the temporary preliminary injunction. It was agreed that the dealership should continue pending the determination of the motion.

III.

We do not believe that Judge Haight placed any special reliance on the word "possible" in the test for the grant of a preliminary injunction enunciated in Caulfield v. Board of Education of the City of New York. Rather, the gist of his position on the subject of irreparable damage is in the following sentence . . . :

"Under these circumstances it is the finding of this Court that, although a substantial portion of Kahn's threatened injury would be ascertainable in money damages, there is another component of the injury which is also substantial and which cannot be calculated—the public's reaction and its influence on Kahn's goodwill."

This finding does not derive any support whatsoever from the record in this case. The Second Circuit cases as well as other cases relied upon by the District Court and Kahn are distinguishable since in each of them there was clear proof of an imminent threat of irreparable injury and not mere unsupported speculation as here.

One of the Second Circuit cases strongly relied upon is Semmes Motors, Inc. v. Ford Motor Co., 429 F.2d 1197 (2d Cir. 1970). The most significant feature of this case is that the dealership had continued over twenty years during which Semmes had built up a very considerable goodwill in Scarsdale and the dealer's son had recently entered the business, doubtless with hopes of succeeding to it when his father became too old.

In Jacobson & Co., Inc. v. Armstrong Cork Co., 548 F.2d 438 (2d Cir. 1977), we have the sort of thing referred to in the early part of this opinion. From some of the phraseology of Judge Hays' opinion one might almost suppose that the requirement of irreparable damage had been eliminated and that all the law required was "a fair ground for litigation" of the antitrust issues and a showing that the balance of hardships was in plaintiff's favor. But a close study of the opinion shows that Judge Hays is applying the same old rule. And this must always be true because of the basic requirement in all cases in equity that there must be proof that there is no adequate remedy at law. And so it was with the seminal case of Hamilton Watch Co. v. Benrus Watch Co., 206 F.2d 738 (2d Cir. 1953), in which Judge Jerome Frank wrote his famous opinion that originated the doctrine we are now applying, and Judge Hincks, then a District Judge in Connecticut, held the prolonged hearings resulting in his characteristically complete and detailed findings.

And so we would expect to find ample proof of a threat of irreparable damage in *Jacobson* and that is precisely what we do find.

Jacobson had been a dealer of Armstrong products in New York City, Long Island, Westchester and Rockland Counties in New York State, Fairfield County in Connecticut, and in northern New Jersey for eight years. The Armstrong products were so varied and so widely used, especially in flooring and in acoustical walls and ceilings, and they were specified in the contracts of so many architects and builders, that the loss of the dealership was likely to put Jacobson at a decided competitive disadvantage as virtually all of Jacobson's competitors carried Armstrong products.

Interphoto Corp. v. Minolta Corp., 417 F.2d 621 (2d Cir. 1969), is a case similar to *Jacobson*. Minolta products amounted to forty per cent of Interphoto's sales of Japanese cameras and lenses. Another phase of both *Jacobson* and *Interphoto* was that each was a full line dealer with a full range of products in its particular field. The loss of either of these dealerships would cause a loss of customers to other dealers who could provide a full range of services and products. . . .

Curiously enough, the principal reliance by Judge Haight was on a Fourth Circuit case that first appeared in Kahn's reply brief in the District Court. The case is Blackwelder Furniture Co. of Statesville, Inc. v. Selig Manufacturing Co., Inc., 550 F.2d 189 (4th Cir. 1977), and the quotation relied on refers to potential irreparable injury to the dealer's goodwill due to "grumbling customers" who complained because of Blackwelder's inability to honor Selig orders. It was said this might give the dealer "a reputation for unreliability." There was no such claim in the Kahn affidavits and there is no proof whatever in this case of any grumbling customers. The facts of the two cases differ so radically that we think reliance on this case is completely misplaced.

Blackwelder was a discount distributor of many types of furniture and had been a successful Selig dealer for over ten years. Blackwelder made thirty-five per cent of its purchases of "contemporary upholstered furniture" from Selig, which manufactured one of the top three lines of this type of furniture. While Blackwelder was based outside the Washington, D.C. area, part of its sales were to mail-order customers in that area. Often these customers would go to the showrooms of local retailers, select the models they desired, and then place their orders with Blackwelder at discount prices. This practice brought on the ill will of the Washington dealers, who allegedly pressured Selig to remove Blackwelder as a factor in the Washington market. Cancellation of its Selig dealership left Blackwelder unable to fill outstanding and accumulating orders for Selig furniture in excess of $15,000. On this record the Fourth Circuit determined that "[w]ord-of-mouth grumbling of customers can convert Blackwelder's inability to honor Selig orders into a reputation for general unreliability as a merchant. Losing Selig can set back Blackwelder's efforts to become known as a 'full line' furniture discounter." The Court concluded that this injury to goodwill was incalculable. It is highly significant that in its letter terminating Kahn's dealership, Baldwin assured Kahn that in the event Kahn was awarded contracts on bids submitted before the effective date of termination, Baldwin would supply the instruments necessary to meet these commitments.

Thus the record in this appeal provides absolutely no evidence suggesting that the loss of the Baldwin line will result either in various customers abandoning Kahn for other dealers who can provide a full range of services or with Kahn unable to fill outstanding orders for Baldwin instruments. Cutting through the morass of unsupported allegations of irreparable damage, the essence of Kahn's claim is for the loss of the alleged profitable business of selling Baldwin pianos, organs and other musical instruments. There is no doubt that any such loss is provable. So also, even if we take at face value Kahn's statement that it had "expended large sums promoting and advertising Baldwin's products," all these are clearly also provable as part of Kahn's damages, if the cancellation was wrongful.

One of the reasons given for highly praising the private triple-damage antitrust case for the efficient way it is used to enforce the antitrust laws is that there is applicable to this type of case a very liberal rule for the proving of damages. It is critical to this case to keep in mind the fact that the tentative and exploratory dealership lasted only one and one-half years from the date of signing the agreement to the date of sending the written cancellation notice. This short period of time and the performance record of Kahn above referred to make it doubtful that there was sufficient time to build up much reputation and goodwill. We do not think the record supports Kahn's expansive claim that Kahn "made Baldwin instruments a cornerstone of its marketing effort."

As noted above, Judge Haight ruled that while Kahn had failed to demonstrate a probability of success on the merits, it had made out a "fair ground for litigation," satisfying the alternative test for the grant of a preliminary injunction. The trial judge's analysis of this feature of the case is clear, precise and correct. As we agree with Judge Haight's treatment of this phase of the case, we shall do no more than briefly restate his position. Our disagreement with the decision below relates to the requirements of irreparable harm and a balance of hardships decidedly in Kahn's favor.

Considering the short period of time, one and one-half years, that the dealership was in operation before Baldwin served the notice of cancellation, it seems surprising that Kahn had discovered so many and such comprehensive violations by Baldwin of the Sherman and Clayton Acts. The complaint reads as though everything in the books was included. But the support in the affidavits is sketchy and on all but a single phase of the claim Baldwin has submitted affidavits denying what was stated in the Kahn affidavits. For this and for other reasons it was clear that Kahn had not shown any "probable success on the merits."

On the other hand, the dealership agreement on its face showed that Kahn's right to sell the Baldwin pianos and organs was limited to certain physical locations in certain designated places, and Baldwin asserted its right to insist upon Kahn's compliance. This is what is called a "vertical" restraint. And the reason this phase of the case presented "a fair ground for litigation" is that the Supreme Court had fairly recently overruled an earlier case on this very subject and had held that such vertical restraints were not *per se* violations but rather that they were governed by the rule of reason. This necessarily meant a long drawn out trial, as a decision with respect to the reasonable nature of the location clause in Kahn's dealership contract could only be decided after full and complete proof of the nature and extent of Baldwin's operations, and its system of dealerships. This is what made this phase of the antitrust claim "a fair ground for litigation."

Having already held that Kahn has failed to prove a probability of irreparable damage resulting from termination of its Baldwin dealership, there is little to add on the subject of the balance of hardships.

Even if Kahn's profits of operation of its discount business diminish because it is less competitive after the loss of the Baldwin line, it should have foreseen this result if it failed to live up to its overly optimistic representations during the preliminary negotiations leading to the original sales goals memorialized in Baldwin's letter to Kahn dated July 20, 1976.

And it seems significant that, although the trial judge denied all Kahn's applications for preliminary injunctive relief relative to its multiple antitrust claims, the order disposing of the motion contains not a single word of protective relief for the benefit of Baldwin during the pretrial and trial of the antitrust case. We think it not unlikely that Kahn might and probably would proceed to act in this interval as though the location clause in the dealership agreement had already been found by some court to be illegal.

Despite the fact that the notice of termination was given in strict conformity with the terms of the Agreement, and six months before the expiration of the short two-year initial period of the dealership, if the preliminary mandatory injunction is sustained Baldwin will be frozen into an intimate and continuous relationship with a dealer it no longer wishes to be associated with. It seems inevitable that a firm of Kahn's aggressive character will cause continual friction over the delivery and servicing of the pianos and organs, and other matters. One of the reasons the contract was of so short duration and subject to such short cancellation notice may be assumed to be that one of the undoubted rights a manufacturer still has is to use its own judgment with respect to those whom it wishes to appoint as its dealers. To bear this burden for an indefinite number of years is a great hardship.

Under the above circumstances we do not see how we can do otherwise than to hold and decide, as we do, that Kahn has not sustained its burden of proving that the balance of hardships tips decidedly in Kahn's favor.

The order is reversed and the injunction is vacated, with costs.

---

1) Does *Jack Kahn* repudiate earlier approaches? Or does it, like *American Cyanamid*, simply restore to a central place in the analysis the question of whether plaintiff will suffer irreparable injury while the suit is pending, in short the inadequacy prerequisite? Does the court apply the inadequacy prerequisite properly? In particular, should the court have limited the harms that cannot be compensated in money? Can a court measure the damages from losing a) a well-established dealership? b) customers to competitors with a fuller line of brands? c) goodwill? Note, The Irreparable Harm Requirement for Preliminary Injunctive Relief in Antitrust Distributor Termination Cases: Jack Kahn Music Co. v. Baldwin Piano & Organ Co. and the Wholesaler-Retailer Distinction, 61 B.U.L. Rev. 507, 519–21 (1981); Note, Granting Preliminary Injunctions Against Dealership Terminations in Antitrust Actions, 67 Va.L.Rev. 1395, 1414–18 (1981).

2) May *Jack Kahn* be explained by amorphous substantive standards in antitrust law which always allow plaintiff to show a "fair ground for litigation"? Does the court seek to prevent plaintiffs with weak claims from using preliminary injunctions and crowded dockets to coerce generous settlements? Antitrust remedies include liberal ways to prove damages and treble damages once damage is proved. Does that limit *Jack Kahn*? Money might be inadequate for some claims without these features, but liberal provision for money may obviate the need for equity.

3) The Virginia Note concludes that, with the public interest also considered, *Jack Kahn* states "the best test for preliminary relief yet articulated." 67 Va.L.Rev. at 1411. The Boston University Note concludes that *Jack Kahn* was incorrectly decided. 61 B.U.L. Rev. at 508, 510.

MARINO v. JOSEPHSON BAR REVIEW CENTER OF AMERICA., INC.

517 F.Supp. 674 (S.D.N.Y.1981).

EDWARD WEINFELD, District Judge.

The rule in this Circuit requires one seeking a preliminary injunction to establish irreparable injury and either (1) a likelihood of success on the merits or (2) sufficiently serious questions going to the merits to make them fair ground for litigation and a balance of hardships tipping decidedly in favor of the party requesting the preliminary relief.[1]

The hearings on the plaintiff's application for preliminary injunctive relief extended over three days. Clearly the case bristles with disputed issues of fact and presents substantial questions of law as to which the parties are in disagreement. A primary issue, the nature of the contractual relationship between the plaintiff and the defendants, is sharply disputed and on its resolution depends in large measure the right to certain videotapes made by plaintiff and used by the defendants after their relationship had been terminated by plaintiff.

Plaintiff, among other matters, contends that his agreement with defendants was oral, which in no respect granted to defendants either a copyright or other property right in his recordings or lectures and excluded any restrictive covenant. The defendants, on the other hand, contend that plaintiff failed to send in as promised a written "independent service agreement," a form of agreement executed by all their lecturers, and that in any event, every arrangement between plaintiff and defendants incorporated by reference the provisions of the "independent service agreement" and is confirmed by plaintiff's conduct and actions. The serious factual dispute on the issue of the parties' contractual relationship, which must await resolution upon a trial, precludes a finding at this time that plaintiff has established a likelihood of success on the merits.[2] Moreover, while the case clearly presents sufficiently

1. Union Carbide Agricultural Products Co. v. Costle, 632 F.2d 1014, 1017 (2d Cir. 1981); Jack Kahn Music Co. v. Baldwin Piano & Organ Co.

2. The parties declined the Court's suggestion to consolidate the preliminary injunction hearing with a trial on the merits pursuant to Rule 65(a)(2) of the Federal Rules of Civil Procedure.

serious questions going to the merits of the controversy to make them fair ground for litigation, plaintiff, to prevail on his application for preliminary relief, must also establish that the balance of hardship tips decidedly in his favor.

Plaintiff, under his arrangement with the defendants, whatever its true nature, had lectured in the past in defendants' bar examination review courses. He last lectured in person in the January-February 1981 course in New York City and videotape recordings of that lecture were played in other areas of the state (also Boston, Washington, D.C. and elsewhere) to those enrolled in the course and who were unable to attend in New York City. He terminated his relationship on about April 1981. The defendants are using, in the current course, videotapes of plaintiff's prior lectures in preparation for the July 1981 New York State bar examination. Plaintiff contends that the presentation of his earlier videotapes in the present review sessions has somehow injured and tarnished his reputation because they have not been brought up to date; that they were shown out of turn and without coordination with the substantive law lectures; and further, that defendants have failed to distribute certain supplemental written material referred to by plaintiff in his lecture with the result that there has been confusion among the students, thereby causing him irreparable injury.

The defendants deny plaintiff's charges and assert that under their contractual relationship with plaintiff, they are entitled to the use of the videotapes and lectures; further that the videotapes are accurate and current as to subject matter and entirely adequate for instruction to those taking the bar review course. It is questionable upon the present state of the record, with its sharply conflicting testimony as to the adequacy of the tape recordings and lectures for instruction to the current students, that plaintiff has established irreparable injury. In any event, while there are sufficiently serious questions going to the merits to make them fair ground for litigation, plaintiff has failed to establish that the balance of hardship tips decidedly in his favor. Some 1,200 students are taking the preparatory bar examination offered by the defendants. Thus the issue of the balance of hardship is really not limited to the respective interests of plaintiff and defendants. An injunction would have an adverse impact upon 1,200 individuals now taking the review course and who plan to take the bar examination at the end of this month. With the examination scheduled less than three weeks from this date, they will be deprived of the benefit of whatever value may inhere in the materials that are the subject of the parties' controversy. These students are caught in the crossfire of the conflicting claims of plaintiff and defendants. They are innocent persons who should not be deprived of the benefits of the videotapes and other items which are the subject of the plaintiff's claims and for which no adequate replacement can be found at this late date. The motion for a preliminary injunction is denied.

Does Judge Weinfeld, in fact, apply the *Jack Kahn* test? If the judge resolves legal and factual doubt against the plaintiff, does that allow the defendant to inflict irreparable interlocutory harm? Should the judge consider nonparties? Does the judge's commiseration for the cramcourse zombies illustrate *Yakus*'s desire to consider the public interest? p. 343. Shouldn't consideration of nonparties' interests depend on the contract and substantive law? "Those whom the law excludes from protection at the final hearing have no greater claim to be taken into account earlier. This is implicit in the basic perception that preliminary relief guards against irreparable loss of rights, not against *damnum abseque injuria.*" Leubsdorf, The Standard for Preliminary Injunctions, 91 Harv.L.Rev. 525, 549 (1978). Has Judge Weinfeld accepted the defendants' version anyway?

IV. Interlocutory Injunction Bonds

MONROE DIVISION, LITTON BUSINESS SYSTEMS v. DE BARI

562 F.2d 30 (10th Cir. 1977).

Before SETH, BREITENSTEIN and McWILLIAMS, Circuit Judges.

BREITENSTEIN, Circuit Judge.

This is a proceeding to recover damages allegedly resulting from an overly broad preliminary injunction. The district court, after entering a narrower permanent injunction, denied damages. We reverse.

Defendant-appellant De Bari was employed by plaintiff-appellee, Monroe Division, Litton Business Systems, Inc., as assistant branch manager of its Santa Fe, New Mexico, office. His employment was terminated on June 27, 1975. Monroe sued to enforce a provision of the employment contract which prohibited the employee from competing against the employer for one year after contract termination, and sought injunctive relief.

Monroe is a division of Litton Industries, Inc., a conglomerate. It is concerned with the production and marketing of adding machines, calculators and similar devices. Other Litton divisions are engaged in a variety of fields involving business systems and equipment, defense and marine systems, industrial systems and equipment, and professional services and equipment.

After an evidentiary hearing, the court on July 22 issued a preliminary injunction barring defendant from competing with "the Company or its parent or any affiliate or subsidiary of the Company or its parent." The injunctive order did not require, and the plaintiff did not post, the security required by Rule 65(c), F.R.Civ.P. The case was set for trial on October 6 and was continued on the motion of defendant. On October 14, defendant moved for the posting of security. Monroe opposed the motion. It relied on Continental Oil Co. v. Frontier Refining Co., 10 Cir., 338 F.2d 780, 782–783, and argued that security need not be posted by a corporation which has sufficient assets to assure its ability to pay damages. On October 22, the court denied the motion for security, saying that it would be inequitable to require security on a preliminary injunction "which, but for defendant's motion for continuance, would have reached a final decision on the merits." On December 23, after trial on the merits, the court found that defendant had had no contact with Litton subsidiaries other than Monroe, permanently enjoined defendant from competing with Monroe, and deleted the broader restriction of competition with any Litton enterprise.

Defendant then moved "to enforce liability on the wrongful preliminary injunction," and filed a supporting memorandum of points and authorities. The memorandum referred to an affidavit of plaintiff, previously filed, in which he stated loss of income. It also asserts the right to recover on the theory of restitution and unjust enrichment arising from business opportunities made possible by the wrongful restraint on defendant's activities. The motion for enforcement contained a request for a hearing. The court denied the motion without a hearing. This appeal is from the denial of the motion.

Monroe argues that, absent a security bond, there is no liability for damages or restitution because of a wrongful injunction unless the circumstances give rise to a claim for malicious prosecution. Rule 65(c), F.R.Civ.P., provides that no "preliminary injunction shall issue except upon the giving of security by the applicant" for the payment of damages that may be suffered by a party wrongfully enjoined. Rule 65.1 provides that liability may be enforced on motion without an independent action. Monroe's reliance on cases such as Meyers v. Block, 120 U.S. 206, 211 and Russell v. Farley, 105 U.S. 433, which antedated the Federal Rules of Civil Procedure, is misplaced. We questioned the continued viability of Russell v. Farley in Atomic Oil Co. of Oklahoma, Inc. v. Bardahl Oil Company, 10 Cir., 419 F.2d 1097, 1100–1101, cert. denied 397 U.S. 1063. We pointed out that Rule 65(c) creates a cause of action for costs and damages incurred by an enjoined party by reason of a wrongful injunction. The rule controls and negates the concept that recovery may only be based on malicious prosecution.

In Continental Oil Company v. Frontier Refining Company, 10 Cir., 338 F.2d 780, 782–783, we held that the security requirement of Rule 65 gave the trial judge a discretion to dispense with a security bond when the applicant for the injunction had "considerable assets" and was "able to respond in damages." Monroe argues that without the posting of security, there may be no recovery of damages or restitution from the applicant for the injunction even though the preliminary injunction was modified to make it less restrictive. Implicit in our decision in *Atomic Oil* is recognition that Rule 65 mandates security for the protection of the person enjoined. That protection is not eliminated when the court relies on the financial strength of the party seeking the injunction in place of the security of a bond. To hold otherwise would make a farce of the rule and of our *Continental Oil* decision.

When the court granted the preliminary injunction, it did not comply with the security requirement of Rule 65. The court's violation of this rule does not destroy the defendant's right to recover for a wrongful preliminary injunction. The security bond both protects the enjoined party and limits the liability of the applicant for the injunction. Where, as here, the applicant opposes a motion for posting of security on the basis of its financial responsibility and does not seek to limit its liability, it may not avoid liability on the ground that a bond was not required.

The court's denial of defendant's motion to require security was based not on *Continental Oil* but on the supposed inequity of requiring the applicant to post bond at a time when, if not for the defendant's motion for a continuance, the case would already have been tried on the merits. The case was tried on November 11, and the wrongful preliminary injunction remained in effect until December 23.

The request for continuance did not waive the security requirement of Rule 65. The grant of the continuance was not conditioned in any way. Whatever effect the requested continuance may have had, it did not preclude defendant from seeking to recover damages for a wrongful injunction. *Atomic Oil* recognized the right to seek recovery. Equity comes into play in determining whether there may be recovery and the amount thereof.

The parties presented evidence at both the hearing on the preliminary injunction and that on the permanent injunction. In denying defendant's motion for damages because of the wrongful preliminary injunction, the court said that there was sufficient evidence in the record to decide the matter. The court then recited defendant's noncompliance with the preliminary injunction, his failure to mitigate damages by seeking other employment, and insufficiency of the evidence to sustain the claim of damage. Defendant asserts that he would have produced evidence on these points if given the requested opportunity to do so at a hearing on his motion. The two evidentiary hearings held by the court were concerned with Monroe's right to injunctive relief. At those hearings the claim for damages because of a wrongful preliminary injunction was neither presented nor considered; indeed, the claim for damages had not yet arisen. The principles of collateral estoppel were therefore inapplicable. . . . Evidence adduced at hearings on other matters might be relevant to, but in this case not conclusive on, the question of damages.

Defendant requested, and was entitled to, a hearing on his claim of damages arising from the wrongful injunction. The presentations of the parties in the trial court and on this appeal show genuine disputes as to material facts relating to the damage to the defendant. "The fundamental requisite of due process of law is the opportunity to be heard." Grannis v. Ordean, 234 U.S. 385; see also Goss v. Lopez, 419 U.S. 565. Defendant was unconstitutionally denied that right.

We express no opinion on any matter relating to defendant's right to damages or restitution. Those matters are for determination, in the first instance, by the trial court after an evidentiary hearing followed by appropriate findings of fact and conclusions of law.

Reversed and remanded for further proceedings in the light of this opinion.

ROCKY MOUNTAIN TIMBER CORP. v. FEDERAL INSURANCE CO.

502 F.Supp. 433 (D.Or.1980).

REDDEN, Judge:

Plaintiffs, Rocky Mountain Timber Corporation (RMT) and Montana Lumber Sales, Inc. (MLS), brought this [diversity] action for wrongful injunction against defendant, Federal Insurance Company (FIC). Plaintiffs seek damages of $35,935.72.

The case is before the court on plaintiffs' motion for partial summary judgment on the issue of liability.

On February 12, 1980, an Oregon State circuit court awarded judgments to RMT and MLS against Georgia-Pacific Corporation (GP) in excess of $2 million. At the same time, GP was awarded a judgment on its counterclaim against RMT and MLS for more than $700,000. These judgments were final non-appealable orders.

On the same date, GP filed a complaint in state court alleging that RMT and others owed GP more than $7 million. The complaint also requested an injunction preventing the parties from enforcing the judgments entered on that date. GP filed a motion for a temporary restraining order on February 12, 1980, accompanied by an undertaking executed by its surety, FIC, promising to pay the costs and damages incurred by plaintiffs if the injunction were subsequently determined to have been wrongfully obtained.

The temporary restraining order was issued on February 12. On February 28, 1980, FIC filed a second, identical undertaking which superseded the first one and continued the temporary restraining order until further order of the court. On March 24, 1980, the court dissolved the temporary restraining order on the ground that there was insufficient proof to warrant injunctive relief.

It is well-settled that plaintiffs are entitled to damages caused by a wrongfully obtained temporary injunction. . . . The action is against the surety on the undertaking filed in order to obtain the injunction. The requirement of the undertaking is designed to protect the person enjoined from injustices caused by hasty orders of injunction. . . .

In Oregon, the bond requirements are set forth in O.R.S. 32.020, which provides:

"An injunction may be allowed by the court, or judge thereof, at any time after the commencement of the suit and before decree. Before allowing the injunction, the court shall require of the plaintiff, an undertaking, with one or more sureties, to the effect that he will pay all costs and disbursements that may be decreed to the defendant, and such damages, not exceeding an amount therein specified, as he may sustain by reason of the injunction if the same be wrongful or without sufficient cause."

It is not necessary for the court to find that the injunction was obtained maliciously or without probable cause before liability on the bond attaches. . . . Nor is it a defense that the injunction was sought in good faith and with sufficient cause if it is ultimately determined that the party who obtained the preliminary injunction was not entitled to a permanent injunction. . . .

Here, the state court judge dissolved the temporary restraining order and denied a preliminary injunction on the ground that GP failed to prove by clear and convincing evidence that injunctive relief was appropriate. Plaintiffs therefore contend that, by virtue of the dissolution of the restraining order, GP is liable for wrongful injunction as a matter of law.

GP raised two defenses: (1) Partial summary judgment is premature because the merits of the case in which the injunction was sought have yet to be decided; and (2) defendant is not obligated on the undertaking because no preliminary injunction was issued.

GP sought and obtained the temporary restraining order in connection with the underlying $7 million action against plaintiffs. That action has not been resolved. Generally, there can be no recovery of damages caused by a preliminary injunction, even if set aside, unless final judgment after trial is in favor of the party who has been enjoined. . . . The purpose of this requirement is to insure that a final decision is rendered on the merits of the issues relating to injunctive relief. See generally, 11 Wright and Miller, Federal Practice and Procedure, § 2972. But as pointed out by Wright and Miller, "[a] final determination may take the form of a decree dismissing the suit, total or partial dissolution of the injunction, *or the failure to carry the burden of proof at the hearing on the preliminary injunction.*" (Emphasis added). Here, the temporary restraining order was dissolved because GP failed to carry its burden at the preliminary injunction hearing.

The remainder of the lawsuit now pending is unrelated to the issue of injunctive relief. Nothing will be gained by waiting until that case is resolved before allowing the wrongful injunction action to proceed. I consider the state court's decision on the preliminary injunction to be a final decision on the merits *for the purposes of this action.* Therefore, I conclude that this action is not premature.

The undertaking provided:

"WHEREAS plaintiffs have applied to the court in this case for a preliminary injunction against defendants, restraining them from doing certain acts set forth in the motion for preliminary injunction. NOW THEREFORE, in consideration of the issuance of that preliminary injunction, [GP and FIC] . . . do jointly and severally undertake and promise that they will pay all costs and disbursements that may be decreed to defendants, and such damages, not exceeding $3,600,000, as defendants may sustain by reason of said injunction if the same be wrongful or without sufficient cause."

This undertaking was filed in order to obtain the ex parte temporary restraining order, and a second identical undertaking was filed to continue the temporary restraining order. Yet, defendant now contends that the undertaking applied only if a preliminary injunction was issued. This contention is belied by GP's own memorandum in support of the motion for preliminary injunction:

"Plaintiffs have obtained a temporary restraining order pending this motion, upon filing an undertaking herein in the sum of $3,600,000."

The undertakings filed by defendant were intended to help secure the temporary restraining order as well as a preliminary injunction. Plaintiffs are entitled to protection from the surety as to both types of restraints.

Finally, defendant argues that it is not obligated on the undertakings because undertakings are not required under Oregon law for the issuance of a temporary restraining order. I disagree. O.R.S. 32.020 requires the filing of an undertaking by the party seeking an injunction. O.R.S. 32.010 defines an injunction as "an order requiring a defendant in a suit to refrain from a particular act. . . . " These statutes do not differentiate between temporary restraining orders and preliminary injunctions. Defendant argues that

O.R.S. 32.050 does differentiate, however, by setting forth terms for obtaining a temporary restraining order without referring to the need for an undertaking. This argument is without merit. O.R.S. 32.050 provides a mechanism for the issuance of a show cause order before the issuance of an injunction. That section does not, in my opinion, delete the requirement of an undertaking in order to obtain a temporary restraining order. O.R.S. 29.060 bolsters that conclusion. It provides that, where a hearing on a show cause order is pending, the court may issue a temporary restraining order preventing the disposal, destruction, transfer or removal of property "if an undertaking has been filed by the plaintiff in accordance with O.R.S. chapter 32. . . . " I conclude that an undertaking was necessary before a temporary restraining order could issue in this case. It is apparent from the record that all parties involved here thought that was the case also.

I therefore find that defendant FIC is liable on the undertakings because the temporary restraining order entered and continued by the state court was wrongfully issued.

Plaintiffs' motion for partial summary judgment is granted.

---

1) Federal Rule 65(c) governs interlocutory injunction bonds, and Rule 65.1 deals with recovery on injunction bonds. Requiring plaintiff to post a bond departs from the usual American approach of keeping the costs of litigation down to encourage people to resort to courts. The bond grows out of the idea that because of attenuated procedure, an interlocutory order has a higher than usual chance of being wrong. Bonds are common for prejudgment remedies like attachment, garnishment, and replevin. The bond deters rash applications for interlocutory orders; the bond premium and the chance of liability on it causes plaintiffs to think carefully beforehand. An incorrect interlocutory order may harm defendant, and a bond provides a fund to use to compensate incorrectly enjoined defendants. A bond facilitates the interlocutory relief that prevents plaintiff from losing irreparably before final judgments.

Discussions of injunction bonds are found in Dobbs, Should Security Be Required as a Pre-Condition to Provisional Injunctive Relief?, 52 N.C.L.Rev. 1091 (1974); Note, Interlocutory Injunctions and the Injunction Bond, 73 Harv.L.Rev. 333 (1959); Comment, The Triggering of Liability on Injunction Bonds, 52 N.C.L.Rev. 1252 (1974). Henson and Gray, Injunction Bonding in Environmental Litigation, 19 Santa Clara L.Rev. 541 (1979), and Comment, Injunction Bond Amounts in Federal NEPA Litigation, 61 Iowa L.Rev. 580 (1975), deal with bonds in the environmental area.

2) Is a bond mandatory under Rule 65(c)? See Dobbs, 52 N.C.L.Rev. 1091 (1974); Crowley v. Local No. 82, 679 F.2d 978, 999–1001 (1st Cir. 1982). Was the Monroe company, in the first case, too clever by half to argue at different stages: 1) we are rich and don't need to post a bond, and yet 2) if no bond is posted, no money for defendant? If the bond is mandatory, does the judge have discretion to set a low or nominal bond? The bond should cover defendant's interlocutory costs and damages. What if defendant neither proves nor argues any? See Northern Pennsylvania Legal Services v. County of Lackawanna, 513 F.Supp. 678, 685–686 (M.D.Pa.

1981) ($100). If there is no likelihood of harm to defendant, may the judge dispense with security? In Brookins v. Bonnell, 362 F.Supp. 379, (E.D.Pa. 1973), a student who had been expelled from school argued that the expulsion violated due process and the first amendment. The judge reinstated the student pending plenary trial with an unbonded injunction on the ground that no harm would occur to defendant if the injunction were wrong.

3) The bond premium is a price on justice that may restrict plaintiffs' access to the courts and prevent them from litigating their just claims. Denying an interlocutory injunction for failure to post a bond leaves plaintiff to her damage remedy in the teeth of the decisions that she would suffer irreparable interlocutory harm and that her damage remedy is inadequate. Dispensing with the bond may inflict uncompensated damage on defendant. In Boddie v. Connecticut, 401 U.S. 371 (1971), the Court forbade the state from interposing filing fees that prevented an indigent plaintiff from suing for divorce. In United States v. Kras, 409 U.S. 434 (1973), the Court refused to waive a bankruptcy filing fee and left Kras too poor to go bankrupt. In Little v. Streater, 452 U.S. 1 (1981), the Supreme Court held that a non-waivable fee for paternity tests deprived an indigent paternity defendant of access to courts because without corroborating evidence, his defenses were insufficient as a matter of law. May a court require an injunction bond of an indigent plaintiff asserting a constitutional right? What about a class action brought by welfare recipients to enjoin a reduction in medical benefits? Should the judge weigh the preliminary injunction factors carefully, schedule an early hearing on the final injunction, and grant an unbonded preliminary injunction? See Orantes-Hernandez v. Smith, 541 F.Supp. 351, 385–386 n. 42 (C.D.Cal.1982); Bass v. Richardson, 338 F.Supp. 478 (S.D.N.Y.1971); Tenants and Owners in Opposition to Redevelopment v. United States Department of Housing and Urban Development, 406 F.Supp. 1024, 1041 (N.D.Cal.1970).

In environmental litigation, plaintiffs seek to enjoin huge construction projects. Requiring a bond premium may prevent the suit. See Henson and Gray, 19 Santa Clara L.Rev. 541 (1979); Comment, 61 Iowa L.Rev. 580 (1975). In Natural Resources Defense Council, Inc. v. Morton, 337 F.Supp. 167, 168–169 (D.D.C.1971), the judge used his discretion to reduce a government request of up to $2,500,000 per month to $100 total. In Environmental Defense Fund, Inc. v. Corps of Engineers, 331 F.Supp. 925, 927 (D.D.C.1971), a $387,000,000 project was bonded for $1. Are these bonds jokes? Do you distinguish injunction bonds from filing fees on the ground that the bond protects the defendant instead of the government? If the judge dispenses with the bond, should he impose personal liability? Should plaintiffs suing the government be excused from bonds on the ground that they are private attorneys general? Dobbs, 52 N.C.L.Rev. at 1112–21, 1159–63.

In Crowley v. Local No. 82, 679 F.2d 978, (1st Cir. 1982), the trial judge found and exercised discretion to dispense with bond after being guided by four factors: "the possible harm to the enjoined party if the order is unlawful, the likelihood of applicant's success on the merits, applicant's ability to post a substantial bond or surety, and the possible adverse impact that requiring substantial security might have on the enforcement of rights created by remedial legislation." The court of appeals affirmed the discretion and decision but shortened the list of factors: "First, at least in noncommercial cases, the court should consider the possible loss to the enjoined party together with the hardship that a bond requirement would impose on the applicant. Applicants in commercial cases—merchants, manufacturers, and others—can be assumed capable of bearing most bond requirements, so hardship to them is less of a factor. Second, in order not to restrict a federal right unduly, the impact that a bond requirement would have on enforcement of the right should also be considered. One measure of the impact lies in a comparison of the positions of the applicant and the enjoined party. A bond requirement would have a greater adverse effect where the applicant is an individual and the enjoined party an institution that otherwise has some control over the applicant than where both parties are individuals or institutions." The court thought that the likelihood of success factor "is already accounted for in the decision whether to grant preliminary relief at all and generally seems to be irrelevant to the issue of a bond requirement." 679 F.2d at 1000. It answered your shades of *Sonesta* question in a footnote: "[W]here the likelihood of success is extraordinarily high, this factor may be an additional reason not to require a bond." 679 F.2d at 1000 n. 25.

4) Assume that the bond is mandatory. In Gompers v. United States, 233 U.S. 604 (1914), on December 18, 1907 the judge restrained AFL President Samuel Gompers from listing the Bucks Stove and Range Company in the "We Don't Patronize" list of the Federationist. The injunction provided that Bucks should "first execute and file a bond"; but Bucks waited until December 23 to file. Between the 18th and the 23rd, the AFL rushed the Federationist to press. It named Bucks on the forbidden list. Bucks charged Gompers with contempt. Gompers argued that he could not be in contempt of an order before it was effective. Compare *Griffin*, p. 264. The appeal was decided on other grounds, but it raises an important issue: Is the mandatory bond jurisdictional? Is an unbonded injunction simple error, correctible on appeal? Or is it the same type of fundamental procedural blunder as lack of personal or subject matter jurisdiction?

The Alabama Supreme Court dealt with that state's version of Rule 65(c). It said that a bond is "mandatory, unless the trial court makes a specific finding based upon competent evidence that one or more of the exceptions, stating them, do exist." The defendant had disobeyed the injunction and been held in contempt. The court quoted another decision: "there can be no injunction, and consequently no contempt for its violation, until the bond has been given." It exonerated the contemnor. This result, the court noted, did not impinge upon Alabama's tenacious adherence to the collateral bar rule. Lightsey v. Kensington Mortgage and Finance Corp., 294 Ala. 281, 315 So. 2d 431 (1975).

The Harvard Note says that an unbonded injunction "deprives the defendant of a fair opportunity to present an argument and might be better held to be a jurisdictional error." Note, 73 Harv.L.Rev. at 339 n. 42. Dobbs says: "the practicalities of the voidness rule do not recommend it very highly as a means of either protecting the defendant or forcing the plaintiff to claim such relief in extreme cases." Dobbs, 52 N.C.L.Rev. at 1155.

5) Does a bond lessen the chance that a court will hold that an ex parte TRO forbidding conduct in progress violates due process? Rendleman, More on Void Orders, 7 Ga.L.Rev. 246 (1973). In Fuentes v. Shevin, the Court said:

"If the right to notice and a hearing is to serve its full purpose, then, it is clear that it must be granted at a time when the deprivation can still be prevented. At a later hearing, an individual's possessions can be returned to him if they were unfairly or mistakenly taken in the first place. Damages may even be awarded to him for the wrongful deprivation. But no later hearing and no damage award can undo the fact that the arbitrary taking that was subject to the right of procedural due process has already occurred. . . .

"The minimal deterrent effect of a bond requirement is, in a practical sense, no substitute for an informed evaluation by a neutral official. More specifically, as a matter of constitutional principle, it is no replacement for the right to a prior hearing that is the only truly effective safeguard against arbitrary deprivation of property. While the existence of these other, less effective, safeguards may be among the considerations that affect the form of hearing demanded by due process, they are far from enough by themselves to obviate the right to a prior hearing of some kind." 407 U.S. 67, 81–84 (1971).

In Mitchell v. W. T. Grant, 416 U.S. 600 (1974), the Court approved repossession of personal property without notice or a hearing. The plaintiff had an economic interest in the items because the defendant had not paid for them. The Court stressed several features of the procedure that it felt obviated the need for notice. A judge, not a clerical official, decided. The existence of a sale, a debt, and a default could be proved with documents. Plaintiff verified the petition and posted bond double the value of the property. If property were wrongfully taken, defendant could recover damages and attorney fees.

6) The question of when the defendant is liable has several dimensions. Despite *Rocky Mountain,* should courts forbid separate actions for wrongful injunction and limit the defendant to a Rule 65.1 procedure? Should a federal court in a diversity action follow state practice or Rules 65(c) and 65.1? See Walker v. Armco Steel Co., 446 U.S. 740 (1980). Would a separate malicious prosecution action be available if plaintiff proceeded in bad faith? Annot., 70 A.L.R.3d 536 (1976). Is plaintiff's blameworthiness relevant? Absent malicious prosecution, should defendant's recovery be limited to the amount of the bond? Or should the judge impose personal liability apart from the bond? Do your answers depend on whether the judge set the bond ex parte or hastily, without considering how much the order might harm defendant?

Should other courts follow *Rocky Mountain*? Does defendant's recovery on the bond depend on the ultimate merits? Must defendant wait until after final judgment even when the judge denies a permanent injunction before final judgment? Comment, 52 N.C.L.Rev. at 1260. By Professor Leubsdorf's standard, Judge Goebel correctly grants a preliminary injunction, but he finds on final hearing that a permanent injunction is unwarranted. Is plaintiff liable for defendant's loss on the ground that the bond is to compensate people injured by attenuated procedure? Note, 73 Harv.L.Rev. at 340–41. Should plaintiff be liable when the permanent injunction is merely narrower than the preliminary injunction? Comment, 52 N.C.L.Rev. at 1270.

7) What should the amount of liability be? Dobbs, 52 N.C.L.Rev. at 1121–46. Except for malicious prosecution, plaintiff's liability is limited to the bond. No one quarrels with the idea that defendant must prove actual loss. A rule prevents defendants from recovering losses not measurable in money. Assume that the defendants in *Walker,* p. 286 cancelled the parades on Friday and Sunday, moved successfully to dissolve the injunction as unconstitutional, and proceeded against plaintiffs' $2,500 bond. What were their actual losses? The judge will not enjoin unless money is an inadequate remedy for plaintiff; but if an incorrect interlocutory injunction causes damages irreparable by money, defendant must bear that loss. Would liability on bonds deter rash applications for injunctions? Should judges bond these injunctions with a liquidated figure like $10,000? Note, 73 Harv.L.Rev. at 340–41.

Defendant recovers special and general damages usually including attorney fees. De Bari's argument in the *Monroe* case for restitution is somewhat far fetched. Assume a preliminary injunction allows Bill Vance to possess Red Acres. Vance sells all the timber for firewood. Because of the woodstove craze he takes in three times more than the injunction bond. The judge refuses to grant Vance a final injunction and holds that defendant Walt Dabney owned the property. If Vance gained something valuable from the incorrect preliminary injunction, should Dabney be entitled to restitution? Could Dabney recover for conversion in a separate action? How would damage be measured? Dobbs, 52 N.C.L.Rev. at 1136. May restitution exceed the bond when necessary to take all of plaintiff's ill-gotten gains?

8) Suppose that in the prior note Dabney had leased Red Acres to Roosevelt Washington's boy scout troop, but that after the preliminary injunction, Vance revokes permission. What may Washington's scouts recover? From whom? Should courts allow nonparties to sue plaintiffs for damages caused by incorrect preliminary injunctions? Comment, 52 N.C.L. Rev. at 1255.

9) Is it fair for Rule 65(c) to exempt government plaintiffs from posting interlocutory injunction bonds? Dobbs, 52 N.C.L.Rev. at 1165; Rendleman, Civilizing Pornography: The Case for an Exclusive Obscenity Nuisance Statute, 44 U.Chi.L.Rev. 509, 540–542 (1977).

Chapter Seven

APPELLATE PERSPECTIVES ON INTERLOCUTORY RELIEF

This chapter deals with litigation that strains the technical rules and statutes that govern appellate jurisdiction and procedure. We use the federal appellate system as the subject of study. We start with the basic norm of that system: the function of the Court of Appeals is to review the final decisions of district courts. One exception is embodied in 28 U.S.C. § 1292(a); it allows appeals from interlocutory orders granting or denying injunctions. The first two sections of the chapter are concerned with the final judgment rule, as well as the injunction exception and its underlying theory. In the final two sections we consider an even more striking departure from the basic norm. If the need for preventive relief is great and the claim of justice moving, appellate tribunals issue injunctions, sometimes in aid of their appellate jurisdiction, but sometimes to fill a void left by the trial courts. These decisions test our commitment to procedural rules that are independent of substance.

I. Appeals of Preliminary Injunctions

SWITZERLAND CHEESE ASSOCIATION v. HORNE'S MARKET

385 U.S. 23, 87 S.Ct. 193, 17 L.Ed.2d 23 (1966).

Justice DOUGLAS delivered the opinion of the Court.

Petitioners brought this suit for trademark infringement and unfair competition under the trademark laws. . . . They sought a preliminary injunction during the pendency of the action, a permanent injunction, and damages. After issue was joined, petitioners moved for a summary judgment granting a permanent injunction and awarding damages against respondent. The District Court could not say that there was "no genuine issue as to any material fact" within the meaning of Rule 56 of the Federal Rules of Civil Procedure which governs summary judgments and accordingly denied the motion. Petitioners appealed, claiming that order to be an "interlocutory" one "refusing" an injunction within the meaning of . . . 28 U.S.C. § 1292(a)(1).

Unlike some state procedures, federal law expresses the policy against piecemeal appeals. . . . Hence we approach this statute somewhat gingerly lest a floodgate be opened that brings into the exception many pretrial orders. It is earnestly argued, however, that, although this order denied a permanent injunction, it was nonetheless "interlocutory" within the meaning of § 1292(a)(1) because the motion for summary judgment did service for a motion for a preliminary injunction . . . and that therefore "interlocutory" must also include a denial of a permanent injunction.

We take the other view not because "interlocutory" or preliminary may not at times embrace denials of permanent injunctions, but for the reason that the denial of a motion for a summary judgment because of unresolved issues of fact does not settle or even tentatively decide anything about the merits of the claim. It is strictly a pretrial order that decides only one thing—that the case should go to trial. Orders that in no way touch on the merits of the claim but only relate to pretrial procedures are not in our view "interlocutory" within the meaning of § 1292(a)(1). We see no other way to protect the integrity of the congressional policy against piecemeal appeals.

Justice HARLAN would affirm the judgment below on the basis of the reasoning set forth in Judge Waterman's opinion for the Second Circuit in Chappell & Co., Inc. v. Frankel.

Justice STEWART concurs in the result.

CHAPPELL & CO. v. FRANKEL

367 F.2d 197 (2d Cir. 1966).

Before LUMBARD, Chief Judge, and WATERMAN, MOORE, FRIENDLY, SMITH, KAUFMAN, HAYS, ANDERSON and FEINBERG, Circuit Judges.

WATERMAN, Circuit Judge: Appellants commenced this action in the United States District Court for the Southern District of New York on June 10, 1964, alleging that the manufacture and sale of certain phonograph records by two corporations, which appellee controlled,[1] infringed copyrights owned by appellants, in violation of federal copyright law. . . . The complaint sought a temporary and a permanent injunction, . . . a royalty, . . . an order directing the appellee to deliver up for destruction all infringing phonograph records and all means for producing them, . . . and for other relief. In his answer, appellee alleged as his defense that the corporations he controlled had been licensed to manufacture and sell the phonograph records containing the compositions subject to appellants' copyrights which are alleged to have been infringed. Appellants took the position that it was incontrovertible that the defendant's corporations had not been so licensed. Therefore, prior to trial, pursuant to federal rule 56, Fed.R.Civ.P. 56, appellants moved on affidavits and counter affidavits for "an interlocutory summary judgment . . . on the issue of liability," and for the appointment of a special master to compute the royalties and damages due them, ". . . reserving for the Court upon the conclusion of such hearings the question of such other relief to which each of plaintiffs shall be entitled . . . ." The court below denied the motion for summary judgment on the ground that there was a genuine issue whether the appellee had been issued licenses for the musical compositions in question or whether, in any event, the appellants were at least estopped to deny appellee's right to sell and dis-

1. Both of the corporations controlled by appellee have been in bankruptcy proceedings since late 1962 and are no longer producing phonograph records.

tribute phonograph records containing musical compositions copyrighted by appellants. . . .

At the outset it is completely clear that an order refusing to grant a motion for summary judgment is not a "final decision" within 28 U.S.C. § 1291, and we thus have no appellate jurisdiction to review the lower court's order under that section. . . . What is more, the lower court's denial of appellants' motion for summary judgment was directly concerned with the merits of appellants' substantive claim for relief and thus cannot be brought within the judicially created exception to the final decision rule, which permits appeal from "collateral" orders where irreparable harm is threatened in the absence of immediate review. See, e.g., United States v. Wood (1962). See generally, Note, Appealability in the Federal Courts, 75 Harv.L.Rev. 351, 364–67 (1961). It is almost equally clear that we ought not review a lower court's denial of a summary judgment motion by means of a prerogative writ, which we can on occasion issue pursuant to the All Writs Statute, 28 U.S.C. § 1651(a). We have only recently received a scholarly reminder that the prerogative writs are of "limited scope." A. Olinick & Sons v. Dempster Bros., Inc., 365 F.2d 439 (2 Cir. August 8, 1966) (Friendly, J., concurring). Traditionally, the prerogative writs have been reserved for extraordinary circumstances. In re Josephson, 218 F.2d 174 (1 Cir. 1954). And a garden variety denial of a summary judgment motion on the ground that there is a genuine issue as to a material fact can hardly satisfy this "extraordinary circumstances" test. . . . Of course, in some cases we can review interlocutory denials of summary judgment motions under the Interlocutory Appeals Act of 1958 which grants the courts of appeals discretion to review any interlocutory order in a civil case if the trial judge decides that the issue he ruled upon involves a controlling question of law as to which there is a substantial ground for difference of opinion and that an immediate appeal from the interlocutory order may materially advance the ultimate termination of the litigation. 28 U.S.C. § 1292(b). Here, however, the Interlocutory Appeals Act is inapplicable because the trial judge has not certified that he is of the opinion that his order should be reviewed immediately under the provisions of that Act.[4] Thus, it would appear we have jurisdiction to review the trial court's denial of appellants' motion for summary judgment if, but only if, this jurisdiction is granted by 28 U.S.C. § 1292(a)(1), which grants the courts of appeals jurisdiction to hear appeals from interlocutory orders "granting, continuing, modifying, refusing or dissolving injunctions, or refusing to dissolve or modify injunctions . . . ."

. . . We hold that the denial of appellants' motion for summary judgment is not appealable under Section 1292(a)(1), and as our result here is inconsistent with the result reached in the above cases we are reversing the rule set forth therein which until now has settled the matter in this circuit in favor of appealability. Peter Pan Fabrics, Inc. v. Dixon Textile Corp., 280 F.2d 800 at 802.

. . . First the rule of our circuit has commanded no following in other federal courts of appeals and has been much criticized by the commentators.

4. It is doubtful whether the denial of summary judgment when the applicable law is clear but there is a genuine issue as to a material fact can properly be certified under Section 1292(b), for that section is limited only to certifying an order involving a "controlling question of law."

This unfavorable reaction to our earlier decisions has led us to the ". . . strong . . . view that the challenged precedent is probably wrong . . . ." Mississippi River Fuel Corp. v. United States, 314 F.2d 953, 958, 161 Ct.Cl. 237 (1963) (Davis, J., concurring). Second, the present case is proof enough that our earlier decisions tend to encourage interlocutory appeals, thereby both delaying an ultimate resolution of the case and unnecessarily consuming judicial resources at the trial and appellate levels. Third, and most important, the enactment of the Interlocutory Appeals Act of 1958 would seem to be the sort of "intervening development in the law, . . . " ibid., that frequently justifies a court's reconsideration of its prior rulings, for that Act, which allows interlocutory appeals in those cases in which the argument for interlocutory appeal is most persuasive removes much of the initial justification for our earlier decisions. . . .

. . . In light of past differences of opinion on this issue in this circuit, and the disturbing fact that most other federal courts have reached a result precisely opposite to the result we reached in our earlier decisions, it would be truly extraordinary if it were argued today that the result reached in those decisions was compelled by reliance on the literal language of Section 1292(a)(1) standing alone. This court is not sympathetic to arguments that seek to have statutes interpreted on the basis of literalness, irrespective of purpose. . . . It is instead with reference to the policy underlying Section 1292(a)(1) that this issue must be resolved.

As a general rule, ever since the Judiciary Act of 1789, appeals within the federal court system have been allowed from final judgments only. . . . Since 1891, however, Congress has excepted from this general rule a group of interlocutory orders, and the most significant of these is the exception now embodied in Section 1292(a)(1). In a considered elaboration of the purpose underlying Section 1292 the Supreme Court held that the genesis of that section was ". . . a developing need to permit litigants to effectually challenge interlocutory orders of serious, perhaps irreparable consequence." Baltimore Contractors v. Bodinger, 348 U.S. 176, 181 (1955). This statement of the purpose of that section makes it clear that Section 1292(a)(1) gives us jurisdiction to review an interlocutory district court order refusing to grant a preliminary injunction. Indeed, we think this statement and an examination of the differences between preliminary and permanent injunctions establish that only district court orders refusing to grant the former are appealable as a class under Section 1292(a)(1).

A motion for a preliminary injunction invariably raises an issue as to ". . . how best to create or preserve a state of affairs such that [the court] will be able, upon conclusion of the full trial, to render a meaningful decision for either party." Developments in the Law—Injunctions, 78 Harv.L.Rev. 994, 1056 (1965). Its grant or denial depends on the trial court's equitable balancing of several factors: the severity of plaintiff's injury if preliminary relief is denied, the severity of defendant's injury if preliminary relief is granted, and the likelihood that one party or the other will prevail at trial. . . . If the grant or denial of a preliminary injunction was reviewable only after a "final decision" had been entered below it would frequently be too late for the courts of appeals to undo the harm caused by an erroneous ruling below and recreate a state of affairs in which meaningful relief could be granted to the party entitled to prevail. There thus is a good reason to hold Section 1292(a)(1) empowers the courts of appeals to review, as a class, without delay, all orders granting or denying preliminary injunctions.

At the same time, the Court's explication in Baltimore Contractors v. Bodinger of the purpose of Section 1292 casts considerable doubt on the proposition that Section 1292(a)(1) similarly was intended to empower the courts of appeals to review as a class orders denying plaintiffs' motions for summary judgment and permanent injunctive relief. A permanent injunction [12] is ordinarily issued only "after a full trial on the merits." Developments in the Law—Injunctions, supra, at 1055. To be sure, the summary judgment procedure makes it possible for a party to argue, prior to final judgment, that, as a matter of law, upon admitted or established facts he is entitled to relief—here a permanent injunction. . . . But summary judgment motions will be denied whenever there is a genuine issue as to a material fact or it is unclear that the moving party is entitled to judgment as a matter of law. Fed.R.Civ.P. 56. And in most cases the denial of a summary judgment motion to which a request for a permanent injunction has been attached will not be of "serious, perhaps irreparable consequence." Baltimore Contractors v. Bodinger. A denial of a plaintiff's motion for summary judgment does not finally deny the relief sought but only indicates that the district court has been uncertain enough of the complaint's merits to grant it at that time: the relief frequently will be granted at a later date when "final judgment" is entered. If in a particular case a motion for summary judgment is, on the facts, denied, but there remains a need for relief during the pendency of the litigation, a preliminary injunction may nevertheless be obtained. See Holt Howard Associates, Inc. v. Goldman, 177 F.Supp. 611 (SDNY 1959).[13] And if the relief requested is not granted when "final judgment" is entered, an appeal can, of course, be immediately taken under Section 1291. . . . We hardly deny that in some cases the denial of a plaintiff's motion for summary judgment conjoined to a request for a permanent injunction may present an especially convincing case for immediate interlocutory review. . . . But resolution of the issue before us should not depend on the persuasive facts of a particular case. And when denials of plaintiffs' motions for summary judgment conjoined with requests for permanent injunctions are viewed as a class we think the foregoing makes it reasonably clear that they cannot with reason be classed as likely to cause serious and irreparable harm if not corrected without delay. Thus we doubt they should, as a class, be appealable under Section 1292(a)(1).

It has been argued, nevertheless, that to permit interlocutory appeals from orders denying plaintiffs' motions for preliminary injunctions but to forbid interlocutory appeals from orders denying plaintiffs' motions for summary judgment conjoined with requests for permanent injunctive relief, would be "sheer ritualism." Federal Glass Co. v. Loshin . . . 217 F.2d at 938 (Frank, J., concurring). This view seems wrong for several reasons. First, as

12. Also sometimes termed a perpetual or final injunction. The duration of a permanent injunction in theory is unlimited. See generally, Note, Are All Permanent Injunctions Temporary?, 23 Mich.L. Rev. 382 (1924).

13. Both motions can be made simultaneously, but in the alternative. . . . It is hard to agree with Judge Frank's view . . . that this process is more time-consuming than the process of interlocutory appeal.

we have just explained, it is only the grant or denial of a preliminary injunction that as a class can be said to pose a threat of irreparable harm unless reviewed without delay. Second, as Chief Judge Lumbard has acutely noted, the issues raised on a motion for a preliminary injunction are distinct from those raised when permanent injunctive relief is sought. American Visuals Corp. v. Holland, 261 F.2d 652, 654 (2 Cir. 1958). There thus is no inconsistency in treating each differently for purposes of Section 1292(a)(1). Finally, there is the very practical point that it is much more likely that interlocutory review can resolve the issues raised by an order granting or denying a preliminary injunction than that such review can resolve the issues raised by the denial of summary judgment. Motions for preliminary injunctive relief invariably raise the issue of the propriety of injunctive relief to preserve or create a state of affairs, in which relief can be awarded to either party at the conclusion of the trial. An appellate court can review the lower court's resolution of this issue without delving deeply into the merits of the case, which are not directly relevant, and, by hypothesis have not yet been fully developed. . . . On the other hand, to permit an interlocutory appeal from an order refusing summary judgment and permanent injunctive relief would bring before the appellate court in every case not merely the propriety of injunctive relief but also the merits of the case. . . . But the merits of the case will frequently be uncertain during its early stages, foreclosing the possibility of meaningful appellate review. And this would almost always seem to be so when, as is usually the case, . . . the district court denies summary judgment on the ground that there exists a genuine issue as to a material fact.[14]

It has also and more persuasively been argued in favor of our prior rulings that an order denying a plaintiff's motion for summary judgment and permanent injunctive relief is an important order, and that, especially when the denial is based on the trial court's decision that a plaintiff is not entitled to a judgment as a matter of law, it frequently will "finally settle a great deal." Federal Glass Co. v. Loshin . . . 217 F.2d at 937 . . . . We admit that when summary judgment and injunctive relief is denied as a matter of law the argument for interlocutory review is most appealing. And when our former rule was first announced, there was merit to the view that, in order to assure review in the important case that might require review, all interlocutory denials of motions for summary judgment and permanent injunctive relief should be immediately reviewable under Section 1292(a)(1), even though in many cases no threat of irreparable harm in the absence of immediate review was apparent. But this view has considerably less merit since passage of the Interlocutory Appeals Act of 1958 . . . . That Act explicitly grants to the courts of appeals discretion to review any interlocutory order if the trial judge determines that the order involves a controlling question of law as to which there is substantial ground for difference of opinion and that an immediate appeal from the order may materially advance the ultimate termination of the litigation. 28 U.S.C. § 1292(b). This new avenue of interlocutory review, with its carefully devised limitations, seems well suit-

14. The present case well illustrates this point. Were we to reaffirm our earlier decisions and permit appeal, our only course, once we reached the merits of the district court's order, would be to affirm on the ground it did not err in finding genuine issues as to material fact.

ed to permit appeal from a lower court order denying summary judgment and permanent injunctive relief in those cases in which appeal should be available immediately. There thus no longer is need to interpret Section 1292(a)(1) in a way that seems plainly inconsistent with its purpose, as that purpose is explicated by the court in Baltimore Contractors v. Bodinger. To be sure, Section 1292(b) assumes that the district courts will employ discretion prudently in deciding which of their orders should receive immediate review, whereas under our former rule the courts of appeals always had the opportunity to pass upon the interlocutory denials of summary judgment and permanent injunctive relief. But this would clearly seem to be a virtue rather than a fault of the new Section 1292(b) procedure, for the district courts are best able to discern the presence of dilatory motives in applications for interlocutory appeals, and thus can best protect the courts of appeals from a deluge of applications.

Appeal dismissed for want of appellate jurisdiction.

ABERCROMBIE & FITCH CO. v. HUNTING WORLD, INC.

461 F.2d 1040 (2d Cir. 1972).

Before FEINBERG and TIMBERS, Circuit Judges, and THOMSEN, District Judge.

THOMSEN, District Judge: Abercrombie & Fitch Co. (plaintiff) sued Hunting World, Inc. (defendant) in the district court, seeking an injunction against defendant's uses of the word "Safari," which plaintiff had registered as a trademark for various classes of goods. Defendant moved for summary judgment under Rule 56(b), F.R.Civ.P., on the ground that it had not infringed plaintiff's trademark rights in the word "Safari." After considering the pleadings, several affidavits and many exhibits filed by the respective parties, and after hearing argument, the district judge filed an opinion, 327 F.Supp. 657 (S.D.N.Y.1971), and entered an order which included the following provisions: (1) "that the defendant's motion for summary judgment is granted to the extent of holding that defendant's use of the word 'Safari' to describe its safari hat, 'Minisafari' to describe its smaller safari hat, and the further use by the defendant of the coined word 'Safariland' to describe a part of its shop, as a corporate name, and as the name of a newsletter, do not infringe such rights as plaintiff may have in the use of the word 'Safari,' and to the further extent of holding that defendant is entitled to use the word 'Safari' to describe those of its products which relate to the practice or cult of safari"; (2) "that summary judgment be awarded to each of the parties against the other in relation to the respective claims of misrepresentation made by each of them"; and (3) "that in all other respects" defendant's motion for summary judgment be denied.

Plaintiff sought and was denied a certification by the district court under 28 U.S.C. § 1292(b) and Rule 54(b), F.R.Civ.P. It then appealed to this court, relying on § 1292(a)(1) . . . .

In granting in part defendant's motion for summary judgment, the district court's order in effect constituted a final denial on the merits of the injunctive relief prayed for by plaintiff as to those uses by defendant of the word "safari" which the district court found not to violate any trademark rights plaintiff may have in the word "safari." In these respects the order is appealable as an interlocutory order refusing an injunction under § 1292(a)(1).

Defendant argues that the order is not appealable, relying on Switzerland Cheese Association, Inc. v. E. Horne's Market, Inc. . . . and Western Geophysical Co. of America v. Bolt Associates, Inc., 440 F.2d 765 (2 Cir. 1971). Those cases, however, are distinguishable.

In *Switzerland Cheese* the Court held that the *denial* of a *plaintiff's* motion for summary judgment seeking injunctive relief was not a denial or refusal of an injunction within § 1292(a)(1) because it did not "settle or even tentatively decide anything about the merits of the claim. It is strictly a pretrial order that decides only one thing—that the case should go to trial." 383 U.S. at 25. The present appeal deals with a *grant* in part of *defendant's* motion for summary judgment, which was, in effect, a final denial on the merits of plaintiff's request for an injunction as to certain uses of the word "safari" by defendant.

In *Western Geophysical* this court declined to take appellate jurisdiction under § 1292(a)(1) where the district court had granted in part motions by a plaintiff and a third-party defendant for summary judgment with respect to portions of several defenses and counterclaims raised by the defendant, which portions sought injunctive relief against the movants. The rationale of the decision was that no single counterclaim had been dismissed in its entirety and that the full extent of injunctive relief prayed for by the defendant could still be secured in each of its counterclaims. 440 F.2d at 771. In the present case, however, there are no remaining claims for injunctive relief which would encompass those uses of the word "safari" as to which the district court granted summary judgment in favor of defendant. Even if plaintiff should prevail on the remaining issues, the summary judgment in favor of defendant with respect to certain uses of the word "safari" by defendant would remain in effect.

Although a part of the district court's order is therefore appealable under § 1292(a)(1), the scope of appellate review is limited to that part of the order which resulted in a final denial of a major portion of plaintiff's requested injunction. . . .

The judge . . . discussed several of defendant's uses of the word "Safari," alone or in compound words. He found that in certain instances defendant uses the word descriptively rather than as a trademark, despite evidence to the contrary, e.g., the letters "TM" after the words "Minisafari" and "Safariland." He concluded that some of the uses of the word were not infringements, but that a genuine issue of fact exists as to whether plaintiff may be entitled to an injunction with respect to other items, specifically shoes, and granted defendant's motion for summary judgment only in part.

We intimate no opinion as to the ultimate merits of the case. But viewing the inferences to be drawn from the underlying facts in the light most favorable to the party opposing the motion for summary judgment, we conclude that genuine issues of fact exist which made it improper to enter a summary judgment finally denying even in part the injunctive relief sought by plaintiff.

TIMBERS, Circuit Judge (concurring): . . . If the relief sought below by plaintiff had been cast in the form of a claim for preliminary injunction, rather than for summary judgment, then I take it that the court's interlocutory order refusing such injunction quite clearly would be appealable under § 1292(a)(1). That being so, it seems to me that the order here under review which finally dismissed certain of plaintiff's claims for injunctive relief with respect to the alleged infringement of plaintiff's trademark rights *a fortiori* is appealable under § 1292(a)(1). Although other claims for injunctive relief are still pending, the dismissed claims sought relief on a legal theory distinct from the retained claims. . . .

FEINBERG, Circuit Judge (dissenting): I dissent from the majority opinion because the district court's order is not appealable. In my view, there is no compelling reason in cases like this to justify abandoning the historic federal policy against piecemeal appeals. Nor can justification be found in the purpose of 28 U.S.C. § 1292(a)(1), which must be our guide rather than the statute's literal language. See Chappell & Co. v. Frankel . . . . The clear purpose of section 1292(a)(1) is to "permit litigants to effectually challenge interlocutory orders of serious, perhaps irreparable, consequence." Baltimore Contractors v. Bodinger, 348 U.S. 176, 181 (1955). Moreover, when Congress amended the original exception to the final judgment rule for the grant or continuance of injunctive relief, to add the refusal of such relief, "it seems rather plain that Congress was thinking primarily of the case where erroneous denial of a *temporary* injunction may cause injury quite as irreparable as an erroneous grant of one." See Stewart-Warner Corp. v. Westinghouse Elec. Corp., 325 F.2d 822, 830 (2d Cir. 1963) (dissent), cert. denied, 376 U.S. 944 (1964). But plaintiff does not, and indeed cannot, claim that it will suffer special or irreparable temporary harm unless allowed to appeal the trial court's order immediately. Any such assertion would be belied by plaintiff's failure to seek preliminary injunctive relief in the district court in the period since the complaint was filed in January 1970.

Plaintiff's suit asks for a permanent injunction against the use by defendant of plaintiff's mark "Safari" on various classes of goods and an accounting from defendant. That suit still remains untried, except that the district judge has limited plaintiff's case as follows: Plaintiff cannot stop defendant from using "Safari" on a safari hat, "Minisafari" on a smaller hat, "Safariland" in the name of its shop and newsletter, or "Safari" on products relating to "the practice or cult of safari." What the latter are we do not know. But we do know that plaintiff still has a case to prove regarding defendant's use of "Safari" on other products, such as shoes. In that sense, and in the absence of any threat of imminent irreparable injury, the situation resembles a pre-trial order limiting the type of damages plaintiff may prove, e.g., in a contract suit, eliminating lost profits. Cf. Clark v. Kraftco Corp., 447 F.2d 933, 936 (2d Cir. 1971). In such a case, a plaintiff should not be able to appeal the adverse determination until the entire case has been tried, unless there is ground for an immediate appeal under Fed.R.Civ.P. 54(b) or 28 U.S.C. § 1292(b), . . . The permanent injunction plaintiff seeks has not yet been fully and finally granted or denied. Until it is, and in the absence of a motion in the trial court for a preliminary injunction, . . . we should not allow the appeal.

Admittedly, this position perhaps conflicts with the reasoning of our decision in Glenmore v. Ahern, 276 F.2d 525 (2d Cir.), cert. denied, 362 U.S. 964 (1960). There we allowed, over strong dissents, an appeal under section 1292(a)(1) from a district court order which dismissed one count of a multi-count complaint. The dismissed count requested the same injunctive relief as did other counts in the complaint but was based on a "distinct legal theory." But one of the principal cases on which the court in *Glenmore* relied in reaching its decision, Federal Glass Co. v. Loshin, 217 F.2d 936 (2d Cir. 1954), was subsequently overruled by this court in Chappell & Co. v. Frankel, . . . and disapproved by the Supreme Court in Switzerland Cheese Ass'n, Inc. v. E. Horne's Market, Inc., ... Moreover, the writer of the majority opinion in *Glenmore*, now Chief Judge Friendly, has suggested that "it may be appropriate for us to give further consideration to . . . [the appealability question] should it again arise." Western Geophysical Co. of America v. Bolt Associates, Inc., 440 F.2d 765, 770–71 n. 4 (2d Cir. 1971). In holding that an order granting partial summary judgment against defendant was not appealable under section 1292(a)(1), the court in *Western Geophysical* distinguished *Glenmore* on the ground that in the case then before it "no single counterclaim . . . had been dismissed in its entirety." 440 F.2d at 770–71.

Thus, the question of appealability in cases such as this is far from closed. Arguably, since the district court's order here did not dismiss a separate "count" of plaintiff's complaint, there is no right to an interlocutory appeal under our cases. That argument, of course, is complicated by the fact that the effect of the trial court's order was to narrow the scope of injunctive relief sought by plaintiff. . . . But aside from such technical arguments, both the policy behind section 1292(a)(1) and considerations of judicial administration, . . . support the conclusion that the order here is not now appealable. The remainder of this case should be tried promptly and concluded, rather than have it surface in this court in bits and pieces.

---

1) Judge Feinberg relies on Judge Friendly's dissent in *Stewart-Warner.* There Judge Friendly urged that the § 1292(a)(1) exception to the final judgment rule be confined to "cases of true hardship," and that it not be expanded "to include mere practice orders simply because a pleading contains the talismanic word 'injunction.'" To support this view he reviewed the history of the statute (325 F.2d 822, 829–30 (2d Cir. 1963)):

". . . In the Evarts Act, the sole exception to the final judgment rule was 'where, upon a hearing in equity . . . an injunction shall be granted or continued by an interlocutory order or decree . . . ,' 26 Stat. 828 (1891). In such cases the court had brought its force to bear, and the need for immediate appeal was obvious. Four years later the exception was broadened to include cases 'where, upon a hearing in equity . . . , an injunction shall be granted, continued, refused, or dissolved by an interlocutory order or decree or an application to dissolve an injunction shall be refused . . . ,' 28 Stat. 666–667 (1895). This was because the implications of 'the lack of all review over the action of a single judge in denying interlocutory injunctions' 'had not been adequately considered,' Frankfurter and Landis, The Business of the Supreme Court, 108–09 (1928); although the language is broader, as the *General Electric* case was later to hold, it seems rather plain that Congress was thinking primarily of the case where erroneous denial of a *temporary* injunction may cause injury quite as irreparable as an erroneous grant of one. After a retreat to the original wording in 1900, 31 Stat. 660, the 1895 version was restored in § 129 of the Judicial Code of 1911, 36 Stat. 1134. The reference to 'a hearing in equity'—strongly suggesting the pressing of a demand for interlocutory relief—has suffered drafting erosion that has tended to obscure the original aim. The words 'in equity' were dropped in 1925 when the section was broadened to include orders modifying or refusing to modify injunctions. 43 Stat. 937, but the omission 'was not intended to remove that limitation.' Schoenamsgruber v. Hamburg American Line, 294 U.S. 454, 457 fn. 3 (1935); Baltimore Contractors, Inc. v. Bodinger, 348 U.S. 176, 180 fn. 6 (1955). Then the words 'upon a hearing' fell by one of those unexplained changes in the 1948 revision of the Judicial Code, 62 Stat. 929, which we have been wisely instructed to disregard. Fourco Glass Co. v. Transmirra Prod. Corp., 353 U.S. 222, 227–228 (1957).

"The Supreme Court has characterized this history of the injunction exception to the final judgment rule as reflecting 'a developing need to permit litigants to effectually challenge interlocutory orders of serious, perhaps irreparable, consequence.' Baltimore Contractors, Inc. v. Bodinger, supra, 348 U.S. at 181. An order granting or denying a request for a temporary injunction fits that description. So does an order striking a claim for injunctive relief on the merits or on grounds of jurisdiction or venue since, as said in a case cited in *General Electric*, 287 U.S. at 433, 'the greater includes the less.' . . . "

2) Is *Abercrombie & Fitch* consistent with *Switzerland Cheese* and *Chappell*? Is there a distinction between an order denying plaintiff's motion for summary judgment and one granting defendant's motion? Does appellate jurisdiction in *Abercrombie & Fitch* frustrate the limited purpose of the statute because plaintiff failed to seek a preliminary injunction and did not claim irreparable interlocutory injury? When reading *Build of Buffalo*, below, ask whether it approaches appealability more like *Switzerland Cheese-Chappell* or *Abercrombie & Fitch.*

BUILD OF BUFFALO, INC. v. SEDITA

441 F.2d 284 (2d Cir. 1971).

Before LUMBARD, Chief Judge, KAUFMAN and ANDERSON, Circuit Judges.

IRVING R. KAUFMAN, Circuit Judge. . . . On March 13, 1970, Judge Henderson dismissed plaintiffs' omnibus civil rights action (brought under 42 U.S.C. §§ 1981–1983, 1986, 1988–1990) as to three of many defendants for failure to state an actionable claim, F.R.Civ.P. 12(b)(6). The initial question is whether the order is appealable because it is undoubtedly not a final order, 28 U.S.C. § 1291, or whether it is maintainable nonetheless pursuant to 28 U.S.C. § 1292(a)(1) as an interlocutory order "refusing" an injunction. Since we are of the view that the latter statute applies we reach the merits of the appeal and hold that the partial dismissal was improper.

. . . Plaintiffs include numerous individuals who claim that defendants have violated rights guaranteed to them by the Constitution, as well as nine civic and other private organizations.[1] Suing individually and as representatives of a rather amorphous class of "others similarly situated," [2] they seek monetary damages and a variety of equitable relief, including some quite drastic remedies, as will appear. The three defendants as to whom the complaint has been dismissed are Frank A. Sedita, the Mayor and Chief Executive of the City of Buffalo, New York; the Commissioner of the Buffalo Police Department, Frank Felicetta; and the Department of Human Relations of Buffalo. Plaintiffs here appeal from the dismissal as to Mayor Sedita and Commissioner Felicetta. In addition, the complaint joins as defendants various members of the Buffalo Police Department, some named and others anonymous, who have allegedly engaged in "a systematic pattern of conduct resulting in numerous, separate and distinct violations of the rights, privileges, and immunities" of plaintiffs and the class they seek to represent. Appellees Sedita and Felicetta are said by plaintiffs to "have condoned or encouraged," or to have "directed" or "permitted" such conduct. Also (and alternatively) the Mayor and Police Commissioner are charged with having so "lost control" over some of the Buffalo police "as to make effective law enforcement impossible" and also with having failed to respond in any manner to "numerous specific complaints" by plaintiffs and others of police conduct in violation of the federal Constitution, New York law, and Police Department Regulations.

The dismissal as to appellees of course did not affect the continuing vitality of the action against the other defendants, the individual police officers. Because the district court did not direct the entry of a final judgment against appellees or determine that there was "no just reason for delay" prior to entering a final order, his order granting defendants' Rule 12(b)(6) motion is not appealable under 28 U.S.C. § 1291 or Rule 54(b). Nor did the district court accompany its order with a statement as to the desirability of an interlocutory appeal required if plaintiffs were to attempt to proceed under 28 U.S.C. § 1292(b).

Plaintiffs' complaint, however, included several prayers for permanent injunctive relief against all defendants. Moreover, on March 3, 1970, plaintiffs added a motion for a preliminary injunction to restrain defendants *pendente lite* from committing a formidable list of specific kinds of abusive police practices. By granting the motion of the Mayor, the Police Commissioner and the Department of Human Relations, to dismiss,[3] the district court effectively denied at the same time plaintiffs' motion for a preliminary injunction as against

1. The class is described in the fifth paragraph of the complaint as "all of those persons who reside in, are employed in, or are entitled to enjoy the benefits, services and facilities of the City of Buffalo."

2. The complaint alleges that these organizations "are concerned and effected" by the alleged police abuses and that their membership includes "members of the class which plaintiffs seek to represent."

3. On February 24, appellees moved to dismiss the class action, strike certain matter from the complaint, and to sever the causes of action, as well as to dismiss under Rule 12(b), both for failure to state a claim and for lack of jurisdiction over the subject matter.

those defendants.[4] The resultant denial of an injunction is appealable under 28 U.S.C. § 1292(a)(1). The reasoning and decision in General Electric Co. v. Marvel Rare Metals Co., 287 U.S. 430 (1932)[5] is persuasive and, in this context, is also authority that would be difficult to ignore:

"But by their motion to dismiss, plaintiffs themselves brought on for hearing the very question that, among others, would have been presented to the court upon formal application for an interlocutory injunction. That is, whether the allegations of the answer are sufficient to constitute a cause of action for an injunction. And the court necessarily decided that upon the facts alleged in the counterclaim defendants were not entitled to an injunction. It cannot be said . . . that the dismissal did not deny to defendants the protection of the injunction prayed in their answer. Id. at 433."

Judge Henderson's dismissal for failure to state a claim was not a mere practice order "controlling the sequence in which portions of the case would be tried," Spangler v. United States, 415 F.2d 1242, 1248 (9th Cir. 1969),[6] or simply consigning plaintiffs' claim against appellees to a separate action as an exercise of the court's control over the scope of the litigation. See Stewart-Warner Corp. v. Westinghouse Electric Corp., 325 F.2d 822, 829 (2d Cir. 1963) (Friendly, J., dissenting), cert. denied, 376 U.S. 944 (1964). Rather, the district court's determination that plaintiffs were entitled to no relief under federal law, including preliminary relief, was as decisive to plaintiffs as would have been a refusal to grant a preliminary injunction on the grounds that plaintiffs failed to demonstrate either likelihood of ultimate success or irreparable injury.

Judge Anderson dissents from this portion of our holding on the premise that the dismissal of the action against the Mayor, the Chief of Police, and the Department of Human Relations did not "affect . . . the quality of the relief prayed for by the plaintiffs." Our response to this is that we need not decide that most dismissals as against some defendants in suits seeking injunctive relief are appealable. It is sufficient to say that our jurisdiction here is clearly established under the second of Judge Anderson's own proposed tests. The dismissal did not merely limit the number of defendants against which any injunctive relief might ultimately run. In Judge Anderson's words, it resulted in "contracting the scope of the injunctive relief originally sought." It is apparent that the gist of plaintiffs' claim was the systematic and knowledgeable failure of responsible authorities to take any measures to correct a pattern of abusive police practices. In order to establish that there was in fact a *pattern* of police misbehavior, plaintiffs seek to prove a number of separate

4. Both appellants' and appellees' motions were returnable March 9. On that date, during argument before Judge Henderson, plaintiffs volunteered to postpone the argument on the motion for a preliminary injunction but the offer was mooted when the court from the bench granted appellees' motion to dismiss.

5. *In Marvel*, a patent infringement action, the district court had dismissed, for lack of jurisdiction, a counterclaim asserted by defendant which included a prayer for an injunction and accounting. The Court held that the dismissal was appealable under old 28 U.S.C. § 227, predecessor of the present Section 1292(a)(1).

6. *Spangler* [p. 499], was a class action by individual students seeking to desegregate three Pasadena, California, public high schools. The motion of the United States to intervene was granted and the Government enlarged the action by requesting an injunction to desegregate the entire Pasadena public school system. The district court granted defendants' motion to strike the claims of the complaint with respect to all but the three high schools originally in the suit.

instances of misconduct. So far as the relief sought against the appellees before us, the claims against the individual officers are only exemplary. Thus, even if injunctive relief were eventually awarded against each of the named individual police defendants, it would not at all satisfy plaintiffs' claim for relief from systematic misbehavior at levels of authority higher than that of the patrolman on the beat. Indeed, for an injunction only against individual policemen to substitute adequately for the relief plaintiffs seek against the present appellees, it would have to run against every officer in the Buffalo Police Department. Thus, the dismissal against the Mayor, Chief of Police, and Department of Human Relations, operated as a refusal of a distinct and separate claim for an injunction, for which any other relief that might emerge from the case could never adequately substitute.

Finally, Judge Anderson is concerned that disposition of the present appeal may affect the rights of the other defendants in the case, without affording them an opportunity to be heard. But the disposition of this appeal will have no greater impact on the rights of the individual police defendants than if plaintiffs had adopted a different strategy of litigation and chosen not to join their claims against the individual policemen with their separate claim against the present appellees. Courts inevitably announce legal principles that affect people unrepresented in the adjudications from which the principles emerge. And specifically, the other defendants in this action will not be affected in the least by our disposition of the question whether plaintiffs' complaint stated a cause of action against the present appellees.

Hence we reach the merits of the dismissal, and we find ourselves in partial disagreement with Judge Henderson. The venerable standard for judging the propriety of a dismissal on the pleadings under the Federal Rules is not contested here. Accepting the allegations in the complaint as true, as we must on a Rule 12(b)(6) motion . . . the complaint may not be dismissed "unless it appears 'to a certainty that the plaintiff would be entitled to no relief under any state of facts which could be proved in support of his claim.'" Holmes v. New York City Housing Authority, 398 F.2d 262, 265 (2d Cir. 1968). Such elementary formulas show their worth in the unusual case and this particular standard is especially useful here, where plaintiffs have combined traditional pleas for injunctive relief with a more exotic plea that may tend to distort one's perception of the complaint.

As indicated above, the essence of the plaintiffs' theory as it is developed in the complaint is that certain members of the Buffalo Police Department have engaged in "a systematic pattern of conduct" over a period of many years which has resulted in plaintiffs being subjected under color of state law to the deprivation of constitutional rights. Plaintiffs by no means confine themselves to such generalities, however. After alleging broadly that defendants have engaged in illegal "acts of violence, intimidation, humiliation, and other . . . misconduct," plaintiffs enumerate fourteen separate varieties of police abuses to which they have allegedly been subjected.[7] There

7. The sprawling nature of this part of the complaint is conveyed by plaintiffs' motion for a preliminary injunction, which requested that defendants be restrained "from beating, intimidating, and humiliating members of plaintiffs' class in the course of affecting arrest or while in custody, from denying members of plaintiffs' class the right to make telephone calls to counsel or families upon being arrested, from indiscriminately arresting members of plaintiffs' class with-

follows what might be described as a bill of particulars reciting in seventeen lettered paragraphs specific instances of the kinds of abuses complained of.

It is in this context of specific allegations that the more expansive and diffuse allegations directed against appellees Sedita and Felicetta occur.

Although we need not now decide the question we have little doubt that upon these allegations plaintiffs will not succeed in establishing a right to the most drastic remedy they request, namely that appellees be required to adopt a complaint mechanism approved by the district court for processing and remedying police misconduct. If that mechanism should fail, plaintiffs propose a still more extraordinary measure: that the district court appoint a special master as receiver for the Police Department to establish "a fair and equitable complaint machinery to investigate and provide redress for complaints of police misconduct or police violence."

The question of the propriety of remedies prayed for by plaintiffs, however, is not the issue on this appeal. The question here is whether plaintiffs might conceivably have some remedy, whether or not suggested by them, and on the face of this complaint we cannot say "to a certainty" that they will not be able to make out a case against Felicetta and Sedita calling for at least part of the equitable relief they request, or some other appropriate relief. Of course, that is based on the assumption that the plaintiffs are proper representatives of the "class" and that this extraordinary and diffuse "class" is appropriate, questions we are not called upon to decide on this appeal.[8] . . .

Despite the diffuseness and broadside nature of their claims, we believe that plaintiffs' allegations in the complaint are sufficient to satisfy the generous pleading requirements of the Federal Rules. Deliberate, purposeful activity resulting in widespread police abuses and perhaps rising to the level of *de facto* policy were held to be an appropriate occasion for injunctive relief in such cases as *Lankford* . . . . Whether plaintiffs can establish this pattern of police abuse, and, if so, what relief is justified, must be left initially to the district court. Moreover, as we have indicated the propriety of the class suit remains to be determined. But we believe Judge Henderson should not have dismissed the suit as against appellees Sedita and Felicetta simply because some of the relief sought seemed far-fetched.

LUMBARD, Chief Judge (concurring): I agree that Judge Henderson's order dismissing the complaint as against the Mayor and the Commissioner of

out reason or probable cause to believe that a crime has been committed, from making false charges or 'cover charges' against members of plaintiffs' class, from arresting members of plaintiffs' class when attempting to exercise their rights under the Constitution of the United States, from referring to members of plaintiffs' class by derogatory, obscene, or racial epithets, from refusing to give members of plaintiffs' class proper protection from criminal acts perpetrated against them by various persons, including members of the Buffalo Police Department. . . . "

8. The parties to this appeal have directed our attention to a subsequent order by Judge Henderson entered January 22, 1970, apparently dismissing the complaint on the ground that it is not maintainable as a class action. During oral argument, this panel requested counsel for all parties to submit supplementary briefs discussing the question whether this interlocutory appeal was properly before us, an issue we have resolved in part I of this opinion. In response to the panel's request, counsel for plaintiffs-appellants have informed the court that they do not intend to appeal Judge Henderson's dismissal of January 22. We intimate no view on the question whether the action against these appellees is maintainable as a class action. . . .

Police is reviewable as an interlocutory order "refusing" an injunction under 28 U.S.C. § 1292(a)(1), but I feel it would be unwise at this time to attempt to establish broad propositions of law to govern all situations where an appeal is sought under that section. First, the confusion generated by this case may unduly color our judgment as to the general desirability of appeals at this stage of litigation when, in practical effect, all injunctive relief against the appellees has been denied. Second, although we requested and received supplementary briefs on the appealability of Judge Henderson's order, the parties did not consider the possibility that review could be had under § 1292(a)(1), and we all agree that this is the only relevant statute. Thus, we are without the customary benefit of assistance from the parties in resolving a difficult question of law. For these reasons, I would avoid statements more general than are necessary to resolve the instant case.

Judge Anderson's dissent recognizes that we have jurisdiction where the dismissal for all practical purposes effectively terminates the litigation, or where the scope of injunctive relief originally sought is necessarily contracted. I agree that in such cases immediate review is justified. Since I also agree with Judge Kaufman that the instant litigation does meet these standards proposed by the dissent, I find it unnecessary to decide whether some or most other cases dismissing an action against some parties where injunctive relief is sought should be appealable.

In my view, Judge Henderson's dismissal of the Mayor and the Commissioner of Police as defendants effectively terminated this litigation, and certainly nullified the injunctive relief that was requested. The complaint plainly sought to restrain the Buffalo police from committing alleged massive and systematic violations of the constitutional rights of the named plaintiffs and other citizens of Buffalo who are similarly situated. After Judge Henderson's dismissal, plaintiffs were placed in a logically untenable position: a "class" action against several named and anonymous police officers seeking injunctive and declaratory relief against systematic violations of constitutional rights, and institution of an adequate grievance machinery. Without the Mayor and the Police Commissioner as parties, Judge Henderson had no choice but to dissolve the class action, dismiss the suit entirely, and consign the individual plaintiffs to separate actions for the specific deprivations they allegedly suffered. Judge Henderson so acted on January 22, 1971, and plaintiffs inform us by letter dated March 12, 1971, that they do not intend to appeal this determination.

The above letter also claims that the allegations against the individual police officers were included in the complaint "primarily as illustrations of the abuse which the defendants-appellees herein, encouraged and condoned." This contention obviously is well-founded, for the plaintiffs would accomplish virtually nothing by obtaining equitable relief against a handful of police officers. The detailed and specific nature of this complaint may well have been a response to the holding of at least one circuit that conclusory allegations of police misconduct failed to state a cause of action under the Civil Rights Act. Peek v. Mitchell, 419 F.2d 575, 579 (6th Cir. 1970).

For these reasons, I conclude that the order appealed from meets both of Judge Anderson's proposed tests, and is reviewable under § 1292(a)(1). On the merits, I join in Judge Kaufman's opinion.

ANDERSON, Circuit Judge (dissenting):

I dissent from the majority's determination that the order from which Build of Buffalo Inc. has appealed is an interlocutory order refusing an injunction, appealable under 28 U.S.C. § 1292(a)(1). This holding . . . involves a needless extension of appellate jurisdiction over an order that exhibits none of the potential harm to the litigants which § 1292(a)(1) was designed to alleviate.

. . . Rule 54(b) of the Federal Rules of Civil Procedure cannot be the source of jurisdiction over this appeal, as its requirements have not been met, and an order dismissing an action as to some but not all the defendants, at least where the defendants are jointly liable, is not a final order appealable under 28 U.S.C. § 1291 in the absence of compliance with Rule 54(b). . . . Thus, the sole question of appealability is the one identified by the majority, whether the district court's dismissal as to the Mayor, Chief of Police and Department of Human Relations of the City of Buffalo constitutes an interlocutory order denying an injunction within the meaning of the interlocutory appeals statute, 28 U.S.C. § 1292(a)(1).

The majority asserts that the appealability of the present order is settled by General Electric Co. v. Marvel Rare Metals Co., 287 U.S. 430, where the Supreme Court held that an order dismissing a counterclaim for injunctive relief against a single plaintiff, was appealable as an interlocutory order denying an injunction. . . . The reliance on *Marvel,* however, overlooks the important fact that the present appeal is not from an order completely disposing of *a claim for injunctive relief* but is merely an appeal from an order dismissing a *single cause of action as to some of the defendants.* . . .

The liability of the Mayor, the Chief of Police and the Department of Human Relations of Buffalo is derivative of the liability of the individual police officers. Dismissing the action as to these three defendants did not affect the action as to the remaining defendants, and no argument has been presented that the dismissal affected the quality of the relief prayed for by the plaintiffs. As such, the present appeal is distinguishable from those cases, like *Marvel,* sustaining jurisdiction over the dismissal of a separate action for injunctive relief in a multiple claim case, because there the district court's determination operated as a complete adjudication of the claim. The order was properly characterized, therefore, as a denial of injunctive relief, because the court's action completely foreclosed that avenue of relief. Here, however, the order merely held that if any injunctive relief is ultimately obtained, it may not run against the appellees herein.

Moreover, an important policy consideration points up the difference between the multiple-claim and multiple-defendant case, because, in the latter, where the liability of the defendants is derivative and joint, the adjudication of piecemeal appeals involving some but not all the defendants may operate to determine issues common to all the defendants without a corresponding opportunity for all the defendants to participate in that determination. . . . Under these circumstances it is unwise to stretch the meaning of § 1292(a)(1) to include as the denial of an injunction an order which merely holds that the requested injunctive relief may not run against some of the defendants.[9] Rather, jurisdiction should be denied unless it can be shown that for all practical purposes the dismissal of these defendants effectively terminates the litigation or that it fully nullifies any potential injunctive relief by contracting the scope of the injunctive relief originally sought. Spangler v. United States, 415 F.2d 1242 (9th Cir. 1969). Both approaches are familiar analytical concepts; the former has been utilized in this Circuit to determine whether the dismissal of the class action aspect of a complaint is appealable under the collateral order doctrine, . . . and the latter has been utilized by the Fourth Circuit to determine whether the same question is appealable under § 1292(a)(1) as a denial of injunctive relief. . . . Such an approach to the question of the appealability of orders like the one before us would provide the needed flexibility to deny jurisdiction where the order, as in this case, will not cause serious injury to the plaintiffs by effectively terminating the action but would, on the other hand, deprive the remaining defendants of the opportunity to be heard on issues that may work a collateral estoppel effect against them. . . .

It is clear, however, that the district court's dismissal as to the appellees herein did not sound the "death knell" of the action. The action remained pending as to the individual police officers, and complete relief could have been had against them.

In their supplemental papers, appellants argue that the district court's subsequent action as to the individual officers disposes of the uncertainty surrounding our jurisdiction over the appeal and makes it clear that jurisdiction may be based on Rule 54(b). As stated earlier, however, the district court made no attempt to enter the order in accordance with Rule 54(b), and the subsequent action is of no moment in determining whether § 1292(a)(1) provides jurisdiction. In its latest order, the district court severed the organizational plaintiffs as not properly representative and dismissed the class action aspect of the complaint, letting stand the actions by individual plaintiffs against the individual officers for violations of their civil rights.[11] This order itself presents serious questions of appealability, . . . and no coherent argument has been presented that explains how this subsequent order can affect the appealability of the order now before us.

I would dismiss the appeal for lack of statutory jurisdiction.

---

1) The plaintiffs' theory is questionable today in light of Rizzo v. Goode, 423 U.S. 362 (1976). How does the injunction plaintiffs sought differ from

9. Because § 1292(a)(1) provides a limited exception to the general policy against piecemeal appeals as expressed by the rule that only final orders of the district courts are subject to review, 28 U.S.C. § 1291, it should be construed with some strictness. Switzerland Cheese Association, Inc. v. E. Horne's Market, Inc. . . . .

11. Judge Henderson's second order, entered on January 22, 1971, does, however, point up the undesirability of reviewing, at this stage, the earlier order, because in the last paragraph of the order he indicates that the individual plaintiffs are now free to prosecute individual actions against the individual officers *and their responsible superiors.* As there was no opinion written as to the first order, this latter determination suggests that the motion to dismiss as against the Mayor, Chief of Police and Department of Human Relations was granted as to the class action aspect of the complaint alone, not for failure to state a claim as the order purports to do. The unraveling of such confusion as exists would better await a time when the posture of the case before this court permits a treatment of the entire case.

the injunction ultimately entered in Lankford v. Gelston, p. 160? Should *Build of Buffalo* have cited note 9, p. 167 from *Lankford*?

2) In Kershner v. Mazurkiewicz, 670 F.2d 440 (3d Cir. 1982), the trial judge denied plaintiff both a preliminary injunction and certification of a plaintiff class. An order denying class certification is neither a final decision nor a denial of injunctive relief. Plaintiffs asked the court of appeals to adopt "pendant appellate jurisdiction": jurisdiction to review the decision to deny the preliminary injunction carries discretion to review otherwise nonappealable matters such as class certification. The court of appeals rejected a broad view of § 1292(a)(1) in light of the basic policy against piecemeal appeals. It denied pendant jurisdiction over the certification issue "unless the preliminary injunction issue cannot properly be decided without reference to the class certification question." 670 F.2d at 449. Judge Higginbotham thought the rule too narrow; he favored review of the certification issue because it was "intertwined with the court's denial of injunctive relief." 670 F.2d at 452.

II. Review of Temporary Restraining Orders

Two of the decisions that follow, United States v. Wood, the next opinion, and United States v. Lynd, in the following section are classic Fifth Circuit civil rights decisions. Both grew out of efforts in the early 1960s to ensure fairness in voter registration. These efforts were greatly enhanced by the 1965 Voting Rights Act which suspended literacy tests and provided for federal examiners to register voters. Judge Harold Cox was the federal district judge in both *Wood* and *Lynd.* "Although Cox wasn't alone as an obstructionist judge in voting cases, his blatantly outrageous conduct and publicized antics probably contributed to passage of the Voting Rights Act by helping make Congress conclude that nothing less would solve the problem." J. Bass, Unlikely Heroes 270 (1981). Chapman, Expediting Equitable Relief in the Courts of Appeals, 53 Cornell L.Rev. 12 (1967), and Note, Judicial Performance in the Fifth Circuit, 73 Yale L.J. 90 (1963), are helpful legal accounts of this evolution. Important background material on *Wood* and *Lynd* is found in J. Bass, Unlikely Heroes 216–20 (1981), and F. Read and L. McGough, Let Them Be Judged: The Judicial Integration of the Deep South 293–303, 411–12 (1978). Chapter 1 of D. Garrow, Protest at Selma: Martin Luther King, Jr. and the Voting Rights Act of 1965 (1978), reviews voting rights enforcement prior to 1964, including enforcement of the 1957 and 1960 acts; that is a preface to the story of the Voting Rights Act of 1965 which comprises the balance of the book.

These decisions strain the legal process in a special way. Time is a perishable commodity; delay equals denial. On the other hand, the goal of judicial independence led to life-tenured judges. Their superiors cannot fire them or reduce their pay. They cannot assign them to teach undesirable courses, in undesirable classrooms, at undesirable hours. How can an appellate court respond when the trial judge exploits every opportunity in an apparent effort to frustrate the substantive law? What happens to the features of the appellate process that are intended to ensure a balanced, deliberative, and collegial decision?

UNITED STATES v. WOOD

295 F.2d 772 (5th Cir. 1961).

Before RIVES, CAMERON and BROWN, Circuit Judges.

RIVES, Circuit Judge. The United States appeals from the denial of a temporary restraining order pending a hearing for a preliminary injunction.[1] The Government seeks to restrain the defendants from prosecuting one John Hardy, a Negro, before a Justice of the Peace in Walthall County, Mississippi. The case was filed in the Southern District of Mississippi under the Civil Rights Act of 1957, 42 U.S.C.A. § 1971, on the theory that the continued prosecution of John Hardy was designed to, and would, intimidate the qualified Negroes of Walthall County from attempting to register to vote.[2] The defendants are John Q. Wood, Registrar of Walthall County; Edd Craft, Sheriff of Walthall County; Breed O. Mounger, City Attorney of Tylertown, county seat of Walthall; and Michael Carr, District Attorney of that judicial district of Mississippi. The suit was filed on September 20, 1961, just two days before the scheduled date of Hardy's trial, which was set for 9:00 a.m., September 22; service was made on the evening of September 20; the hearing on the temporary restraining order was set for September 21, when the Government submitted its case on affidavits. These affidavits were not disputed, the defendants claiming insufficient notice or time for obtaining counter-affidavits. At 5:00 p.m. on the 21st, the district court entered its decision denying the order. The district judge refused to sign a certificate under 28 U.S.C.A. § 1292(b) allowing the Government to seek appeal of an interlocutory order. On the evening of the 21st, an attorney for the Government, accompanied by a Mississippi Assistant Attorney General representing the defendants, flew to Montgomery, Alabama, to submit to Judge Rives a petition for stay of the state prosecution pending appeal of the district court's decision. There, decision on whether the stay should issue became unnecessary when the Mississippi Assistant Attorney General commendably agreed to continue the prosecution of Hardy pending disposition of the Government's appeal. Judge Rives then entered an order expediting the appeal and setting argument for 9:00 a.m., October 3, 1961. Over the Government's objection, Judge Rives further ordered that the defendants, because of the minimum of time allowed them before the hearing in the district court, would be permitted to obtain counter-affidavits, provided they served them on the

1. In the alternative, if the order is not appealable, the Government insists that this Court has jurisdiction of its petition for injunction under the all writs statute, 28 U.S.C.A. § 1651.

2. The district court, in announcing the reasons for its decision, said: "We are not concerned in this hearing with anything outside the very sharp question as to whether or not that criminal proceeding should be enjoined." The complaint was framed in two counts, called "First Claim" and "Second Claim." The "First Claim" was limited to an attempt to enjoin the continued prosecution of John Hardy. The "Second Claim" charged a conspiracy to deprive Negro citizens of Walthall County, Mississippi, of the right secured by 42 U.S.C.A. § 1971(b), of which the prosecution of John Hardy was alleged to form a part, and prayed for very broad relief.

Government by September 29, and that the Government could then obtain rebuttal affidavits up until the argument on October 3. He stated that any such affidavits would be considered by this Court if that proved legally permissible.[3] [This opinion is dated Oct. 27].

The facts as stated in the complaint and affidavits of the Government are as follows:

There are at the present time some 2,490 Negroes of voting age in Walthall County, Mississippi, none of whom are registered to vote. There are some 4,530 white persons of voting age in Walthall County, a substantial majority of whom are registered. In July 1961, John Hardy, a Negro citizen, resident of Nashville, Tennessee, having completed two years at the Tennessee Agricultural and Industrial State College, came to Mississippi as a member of the "Student Non-Violent Coordinating Committee" for the purpose of encouraging Negroes to register and vote. This organization is currently sponsoring a voter registration project in Walthall, Amite, and Pike Counties, Mississippi. In early August, John Hardy and several other Negro students came to Walthall County to set up a voting registration school to teach the qualified local Negroes how to register and to encourage them to make application to the Voting Registrar. From August 18 to September 9, they conducted classes for several hours a day. In these classes, Hardy and his helpers would issue facsimiles of the necessary registration forms and a copy of the Constitution of Mississippi. Those attending the classes would practice filling out the forms, copying sections of the Mississippi Constitution, and explaining their meaning. Attendance varied from 25 to 50 each evening.

The first attempt of participants in the school to register took place on August 30, when Hardy accompanied five Negroes to the Registrar's office, where at least two completed the registration forms. Outside the Registrar's office, Hardy encountered the Sheriff of Walthall County, Edd Craft (a defendant), in the company of the editor of the Tylertown Times. The Sheriff asked Hardy a number of questions about the registration school and whether he had a driver's license. The Sheriff soon left, but the editor of the Tylertown Times interviewed Hardy more extensively for an article which appeared on the front page of the Tylertown Times the next day. On September 5, 1961, three more Negroes went to register; on September 6, one Negro; on September 7, two Negroes. The incident giving rise to this action took place on September 7, and since then no Negroes have attempted to apply for registration in Walthall County.

On September 4, Mrs. Edith Simmons Peters, a negro, aged 63, owner of an 80-acre farm in Walthall County, having had an eighth-grade education, attended her first registration class. On about the same day, Lucius Wilson, a Negro, aged 62, owner of a 70-acre farm in Walthall County, also started attendance. By September 6, they thought they were ready to apply and agreed to accompany Hardy to the Registrar's office the next morning. They arrived in Tylertown in Mrs. Peters' pickup truck at about 9:30 on the

3. Counter-affidavits have been attached to the brief for appellees. Those affidavits might properly be considered in connection with the alternative relief sought in this Court under the all-writs statute (see n. 1, supra). We are not, however, permitted to consider them if the appeal is allowed. . . .

morning of September 7 and went to the Registrar's office in the courthouse. The Registrar, John Q. Wood, a defendant, was in an inner office; Mrs. Peters and Wilson went in and Hardy remained just outside the door. When Registrar Wood looked up, Mrs. Peters told him that they desired to register. Wood then replied that, "I am not registering anyone now. You all have got me in court and I refuse to register anyone else until this court is cleared up." John Hardy heard this from his position outside the door of the office some 5 or 6 feet away and came in. According to the affidavits of the Government, Hardy had given Wood only his name when Wood got up and said, "I want to see you John." He then brushed past Hardy into the main room and from the drawer of a desk took out a revolver. Holding the gun down by his right side he pointed to the door going outside and said, "Do you see that door, John?" Hardy replied, "Yes." Wood told him, "You get out of it." Hardy said OK, and turned to go. Wood followed him, and just as Hardy got to the door, Wood struck him on the back of the head, saying, "Get out of here you damn son-of-a-bitch and don't come back in here." Mrs. Peters and Wilson rushed on out, held Hardy up, and helped him out of the building. Hardy went first to the newspaper office, where he told the editor what had happened. The editor instructed him to get medical attention. Meanwhile, Wilson went to get the pickup truck, and Mrs. Peters helped Hardy eventually to a little cafe. Wilson returned and they headed out to the street. When asked what he was going to do, Hardy then told several people that he had better find the sheriff. Going up the street, they met the sheriff and, according to the affidavit of Mrs. Peters,

"They met right where I was standing and the sheriff asked, 'What happened to you, boy.' John told the sheriff what had happened. The sheriff told him he didn't have no business in that courthouse. Wilson walked up at this time. The sheriff then said to John, 'If that boy (pointing to Wilson) wants to register he know how to go down to that courthouse and he don't need you to escort him. You didn't have a bit of business in the world down there. You is from Tennessee, you was in Tennessee and you ought to have stayed there.' The sheriff told him to 'Come on.' John asked him, 'Are you arresting me?' The sheriff said 'Yes.' John asked 'On what charges' and the sheriff said for disturbing the peace and bringing an uprising among the people. John said, 'Will you allow me to tell my side of the story.' The sheriff said, 'Don't give me none of your head boy, or I will beat you within an inch of your life.' After the sheriff took John, I went home."

At the Tylertown jail, Hardy ws interviewed twice during the day of the 7th—first, by the defendants Sheriff Edd Craft and City Attorney Breed Mounger, and later by the same two plus defendant Michael Carr, the local District Attorney for the State of Mississippi. That evening, because the feeling about the incident was evidently running high in the community, Hardy was transferred by the defendants to the jail in Magnolia, Mississippi. Hardy was released on bond the next morning and his trial for disturbing the peace was set for the 22nd of September.

Hardy claims in his affidavit that, about the time the formal charge was entered, the District Attorney took him into a room "and several white people whom I can't identify told me that I was in a lot of trouble and that I was asking for a lot of trouble to come down there; that they had good Negroes here and that they treated their darkies good but that I was causing a lot of trouble. The Justice of the Peace was present but the sheriff was out." There are no allegations that Hardy was otherwise mistreated in any way during his confinement.

The appellees move this Court to dismiss the appeal, and, at the very outset, this Court is faced with the question of its jurisdiction. The appeal is from the denial of a temporary restraining order. The Government admits that ordinarily the denial of a temporary restraining order is not an interlocutory order refusing an injunction within the meaning of 28 U.S.C.A. § 1292(a), and is not otherwise appealable. The Government claims that, under the special circumstances of this case, the denial of the temporary restraining order is in the nature of a final decision from which an appeal may be taken under 28 U.S.C.A. § 1291.

The substance of the Government's case under the "First Claim" of its complaint is that the prosecution of Hardy, regardless of outcome, will effectively intimidate Negroes in the exercise of their right to vote in violation of 42 U.S.C.A. § 1971. This, it insists, is a claim entitling it to injunctive relief. As a practical matter, the time between the arrest and prosecution of a person for breach of the peace is usually very short—in this case, 15 days. If the Government states a claim entitling it to injunctive relief, then the effect of denying the temporary restraining order is to moot its case. The denial of the restraining order is thus equivalent to the dismissal of the First Claim of the complaint on the ground that it does not state a claim upon which the requested injunctive relief can be granted. To then call this de facto dismissal a nonappealable interlocutory order is to preclude review altogether. As a practical matter, then, it is clear that the denial of the restraining order is a final disposition of the Government's claimed right to prevent the prosecution of Hardy.[5] The question is whether such a practical construction may be put on the meaning of a final decision as used in § 1291.

It does not appear that the Supreme Court or any of the Circuits has directly considered whether the denial of a temporary restraining order may under certain circumstances be considered a final decision within the meaning of 28 U.S.C.A. § 1291. However, the Supreme Court has given a number of guides to be used for the construction of section 1291 and the meaning of "final" in cases concerning the appealability of orders deciding collateral issues, separable from the main claim. In Cohen v. Beneficial Indus. Loan Corp., 1949, 337 U.S. 541, it was said that the purpose of § 1291 is to "disallow appeal from any decision which is tentative, informal or incomplete," or from a consummated decision which is a mere step towards a final judgment with which it will merge. The Court found, however, that the collateral issue involved in that case was not of such a nature. "When that

5. One of the questions posed by the appellees is how the denial of an order can be final when, admittedly, granting it would only be interlocutory and nonappealable. A very similar issue was presented in Swift & Co. Packers v. Compania Colombiana Del Caribe, 1950, 339 U.S. 684. There, the collateral order involved was the vacating of an attachment on a ship under an admiralty libel. The Court pointed out that only the vacating of the attachment would have the practical effect of finally and irreparably determining the rights of the appellant to the ship, and the denial of the motion to vacate would have been only interlocutory since the rights of all the parties could have been protected pending the final determination of the primary claim. 339 U.S. at page 689.

time comes [to appeal the final disposition of the case], it will be too late effectively to review the present order and the rights conferred by the statute, if it is applicable, will have been lost, probably irreparably." The Court then held the order to be appealable within the meaning of section 1291, and concluded, "This Court has long given this provision of the statute this practical rather than a technical construction." . . . On the basis of these cases, we feel that the Supreme Court has approved a practical construction of section 1291 and that an order, otherwise nonappealable, determining substantial rights of the parties which will be irreparably lost if review is delayed until final judgment may be appealed immediately under section 1291. We, therefore, determine the denial of the temporary restraining order to be a final decision, appealable under 28 U.S.C.A. § 1291.[6]

Turning to the merits of the appeal, the Government asks the court to enjoin a state criminal court proceeding. We are immediately met with the strictures of 28 U.S.C.A. § 2283 . . . . It is the contention of the Government that this statute does not apply where the suit is brought by the United States.[7] This question was before the Supreme Court in the case of Leiter Minerals, Inc. v. United States, 1957, 352 U.S. 220, where the United States brought suit in the federal court to protect its title to certain public lands. The issue of title was already before a state court for determination. The United States asked the Court to enjoin the state proceedings, which request was upheld on appeal. Mr. Justice Frankfurter . . . wrote for the Court, stating:

"There is, however, a persuasive reason why the federal court's power to stay state court proceedings might have been restricted when a private party was seeking the stay but not when the United States was seeking similar relief. The statute is designed to prevent conflict between federal and state courts. This policy is much more compelling when it is the litigation of private parties which threatens to draw the two judicial systems into conflict than when it is the United States which seeks a stay to prevent threatened irreparable injury to a national interest. The frustration of superior federal interests that would ensue from precluding the Federal Government from obtaining a stay of state court proceedings except under the severe restrictions of 28 U.S.C. § 2283, would be so great that we cannot reasonably impute such a purpose to Congress from the general language of 28 U.S.C. § 2283 . . . ."

The Court then expressly construed section 2283 as inapplicable to a suit brought by the United States.

The appellees attempt to distinguish the *Leiter Minerals* case on the ground that the Court there dealt with the protection of federal property rights and the enjoining of state civil proceedings, and here the United States sues on

6. It is significant to note that Courts of Appeals have considered the merits of denials of temporary restraining orders in deportation cases, evidently on the theory that unless review is had the entire controversy would be mooted by the deportation of the appellant. . . .

7. The Government contends also that the Civil Rights Act of 1957, in effect, expressly authorized the stay of the proceedings in the State court, and further that such stay was necessary in aid of the jurisdiction of the federal court. We find it unnecessary to decide those questions.

behalf of a class of private citizens and seeks to enjoin state criminal proceedings. As far as the type of proceeding is concerned, the statute must be read as applicable to all state proceedings. Admittedly, the policy against interference with state criminal proceedings is stronger than that with respect to state civil proceedings, but this policy is not one of statutory derivation. It applies even where section 2283 does not. Thus, the type of state court proceeding may not be used as a ground for distinguishing the *Leiter Minerals* construction of section 2283. It is also difficult to see how the nature of the interests the United States asserts can make a difference so long as the United States asserts them. The method of construction used in *Leiter Minerals* is that the statute will not be imputed to apply to the United States in the absence of some congressional indication to the contrary. We are unaware that Congress even considered the applicability of section 2283 to the United States, much less that it distinguished between the type of rights the United States may happen to assert.

Following further, however, the appellees' contention, they claim that the rights the United States asserts here are private rights such that applying section 2283 could not lead to the "frustration of superior federal interest" within the meaning of *Leiter Minerals.* In fact, they further contend that the lack of a federal interest precludes the Attorney General from bringing the suit under any circumstances. We are unable to agree. In United States v. Raines, 1960, 362 U.S. 17, the Supreme Court said with respect to a claim based on the same Civil Rights Act as this case, 42 U.S.C.A. § 1971:

"It is urged that it is beyond the power of Congress to authorize the United States to bring this action in support of private constitutional rights. But there is the highest public interest in the due observance of all the constitutional guarantees, including those that bear the most directly on private rights, and we think it perfectly competent for Congress to authorize the United States to be the guardian of that public interest in a suit for injunctive relief."

Thus, whatever doubt there may have been as to the right of the United States to bring the suit or as to the extent of the federal interest involved has been put to rest.

The determination that section 2283 is inapplicable to the present suit does not, however, dispose of this appeal. For, as the Court went on to say in the *Leiter Minerals* case, "The question still remains whether the granting of an injunction was proper in the circumstances of this case."

The district court in this case did not deny the restraining order on the ground that it had no jurisdiction or could not in a proper case enjoin a state criminal proceeding. Rather, it denied the motion on the ground that it was within its discretion to refuse to extend its equitable powers to interfere with a state criminal proceeding. It pointed out that, as to Hardy himself, the Government does not even contend that the state proceeding will result in irreparable injury to Hardy's constitutional rights. As for the Government's contention that the prosecution will intimidate other Negroes in Walthall County and lead to the irreparable injury of their constitutional right to vote, which injury the United States may assert under section 1971 of the Civil Rights Act, Judge Cox states:

"In the argument it is asserted that the trial of that case tomorrow will irreparably damage the United States in deterring colored people in Walthall

County from registering. That statement is without any substantial support in the record before the Court and appears as a non sequitur. . . .

"It is difficult to find any satisfactory definition of irreparable, but it is equally difficult to conceive how the United States can possibly be irreparably damaged by this criminal case down in Walthall County, Mississippi, regardless of its outcome."

He then goes on to base his decision on the holding of the Supreme Court in Douglas v. City of Jeannette, 1943, 319 U.S. 157, 163, where it said:

"It is a familiar rule that courts of equity do not ordinarily restrain criminal prosecutions. No person is immune from prosecution in good faith for his alleged criminal acts. Its imminence, even though alleged to be in violation of constitutional guaranties, is not a ground for equity relief since the lawfulness or constitutionality of the statute or ordinance on which the prosecution is based may be determined as readily in the criminal case as in a suit for an injunction."

This same rationale is the substance of the appellees' case on appeal.

It is necessary at this point to clearly state what right the Government claims, and the facts it believes sufficient to entitle it to injunctive relief.

The Civil Rights Act of 1957, 42 U.S.C.A. § 1971(b), provides: "No person, whether acting under color of law or otherwise, shall intimidate, threaten, coerce . . . any other person for the purpose of interfering with the right of such other person to vote or to vote as he may choose . . . ." Section 1971(c) provides: "Whenever any person has engaged or there are reasonable grounds to believe that any person is about to engage in any act or practice which would deprive any other person of any right or privilege secured by subsection . . . (b), the Attorney General may institute for the United States . . . a civil action . . . for preventive relief, including an application for a permanent or temporary injunction . . . ." The Government states that under Mississippi law registration is prerequisite for voting in any election, such that intimidation to prevent registration is a primary means for preventing the Negro citizens of Mississippi from exercising their right to vote. The complaint sets out the acts of the defendants calculated to intimidate, which include: the Registrar striking Hardy with gun; Hardy's subsequent arrest for breach of the peace; the numerous comments indicating that the purpose of acts of the Registrar, the Sheriff and the other defendants are in part to punish Hardy for his registration activities; the interviews in jail with respect to these activities; the placing of charges known to be unjustified; and finally the scheduled prosecution for September 22. The crux of the action is then stated in paragraph XV of the complaint:

"The continued prosecution of and participation in the criminal proceedings by the defendants is without justification and was and is being continued solely to attempt to intimidate, threaten and coerce Negro citizens of Walthall County for the purpose of interfering with the right of such Negro citizens to register and vote . . . ."

In the affidavit supporting the request for an order restraining Hardy's prosecution, the Government alleges the belief of its counsel "that, unless restrained by this Court, the act of John Q. Wood in physically striking a Negro citizen in the presence of other Negroes who were attempting to register, the act of Edd Craft in arresting and molesting a Negro citizen and the acts of all the defendants in continuing and participating in the prosecution of a Negro citizen who encouraged registration, have caused, and will continue to cause, irreparable injury, loss and damage to plaintiff, the United States of America, in that the inevitable effect of such acts on the part of defendants is to deter Negro citizens in Walthall County, Mississippi, who are eligible, from exercising their right to become registered voters and to vote for federal candidates." In the argument here, and in the court below, the Government makes very clear that the rights the Government asserts are not the rights of Hardy; it assumes that Hardy will obtain a fair trial and that the existence of adequate state remedies will protect all of Hardy's constitutional rights. Hardy is not qualified to register or vote in Walthall County and the Government does not seek to assert Hardy's rights under section 1971. Rather, the Government here asserts the rights of all those Negro citizens in Walthall County who are qualified to register and vote. The rights of these citizens are not at issue in Hardy's prosecution, and remedies available to Hardy in his trial are in no way available to them. Thus, if the prosecution of Hardy does injure them, they have no adequate relief in his trial.

The question then arises how the arrest and prosecution of Hardy can irreparably injure these other citizens, especially if we must assume that Hardy will receive a fair trial and that his acquittal is a possible result. It is the contention of the Government that, under the circumstances of this case, the alleged acts of unlawfully striking Hardy, arresting him without cause, and proceeding with his prosecution constitute sufficient facts to establish an equitable claim under the Civil Rights Act, even if Hardy were acquitted at the trial.[9] . . .

9. The Government's brief sets out at length why these acts alone will cause such injury as to warrant injunctive relief:

"In spite of the fact that Negroes constitute a large percentage of the county's population, there are presently no Negro voters in Walthall County. John Hardy and others, members of the Student Non-Violent Coordinating Committee, came to Walthall County this summer to sponsor a voter registration drive. After the registration school was set up, eleven Negroes went to the registrar's office to seek to register for voting, on four different occasions, in spite of the fact that the registrar, under one pretext or another, simply refused to take any action. Since the incident of September 7, 1961, however, when John Hardy was struck by the registrar and then arrested, no Negroes have made any attempt to be registered. On the basis of the record in this Court and in view of the conditions and circumstances prevailing in Mississippi, it is most unlikely that, if the appellees are allowed to proceed with Mr. Hardy's trial, further Negro registration will take place. The blunt truth is that it can really not be expected that Negroes who have lived all their lives under the white supremacy conditions which exist in that area of Mississippi will continue their efforts to register and otherwise to exercise their rights and privileges of citizenship if in addition to being threatened and beaten, they will also be prosecuted in state court with all that such a prosecution entails. Such prosecutions, experience has shown, not only are expensive, but it is becoming increasingly difficult for Negroes accused of offenses in the civil rights context even to secure competent legal assistance. There are no Negro attorneys in Walthall County and scarcely a half-dozen Negro attorneys in the entire State of Mississippi. Because of the tremendous political and economic pressures brought to bear by the State of Mississippi, it is difficult, if not impossible, to secure competent white counsel for Negroes in cases such as this. Certainly this will be so if, upon success in this case, some officials of the State of Mississippi will be further emboldened to use harassment by prosecution to an even greater extent than heretofore."

. . . Based on the allegations of the complaint, the supporting affidavits, the statutory language of section 1971(b–c) and its legislative history, we are convinced that the Government states a claim for which relief is warranted.

This brings us to the district court's reliance upon Douglas v. City of Jeannette for the points that injunctive relief was not available against a state court criminal action, and that the denial of the temporary restraining order was within the court's discretion.

For a number of reasons we cannot agree with the district court's conclusion or its reliance on Douglas v. City of Jeannette. First, this suit is brought by the United States under an obligation charged to it by the Civil Rights Act for the protection of constitutional rights in which, according to the Supreme Court in United States v. Raines there is the "highest public interest." As was also pointed out by the Supreme Court in the *Leiter Minerals* case, where the United States does seek to stay irreparable injury to a national interest, the normal equitable doctrines of comity between the court systems, doctrines which are the basis of the Douglas v. City of Jeannette rationale, have little or no bearing. Further, where the United States has instituted the suit, we must assume that the considered judgment of the Attorney General has concluded that a violation of a national interest has taken place, a judgment unbiased by the subjective opinion of the private individuals who have in fact been injured. This judgment should not be lightly put aside by the courts on a preliminary motion as in this case. Thus, the presence of the United States seriously tests the strictures of Douglas v. City of Jeannette.

Second, the court in this action is not operating under common-law equitable and discretionary doctrines, but under a mandatory jurisdictional statute. As already pointed out, the district court considered that it had jurisdiction over this action but that such jurisdiction should not be exercised to the extent of issuing the temporary restraining order. Under the applicable jurisdictional section, we do not believe the court had that choice. Section 1971(d) states:

"The district courts of the United States shall have jurisdiction of proceedings instituted pursuant to this section and shall exercise the same without regard to whether the party aggrieved shall have exhausted any administrative or other remedies that may be provided by law."

Since the United States has, in our opinion, stated a valid claim under the section, we read this section as directing the district court to exercise its jurisdiction. It might be argued that this is not a direction to exercise "equitable" jurisdiction, but both the rationale of the section and the legislative history refute this interpretation. For having established a claim, the only "preventive relief" available to the United States is injunctive relief through the federal courts. If the United States may not act until after the process of intimidation is complete, the United States no longer has available a worthwhile civil remedy for preventive relief. And, as was pointed out by the Supreme Court in the *Leiter Minerals* case, the fact that the United States has no available remedy other than action through the federal courts weighs heavily towards the conclusion that the court must grant the relief to which it is entitled. . . .

The mandatory duty of the district courts to exercise jurisdiction of proceedings under section 1971 does not, of course, indicate in any way whether such exercises shall culminate in granting or in denying the relief prayed, or in any relief. It does, however, include some opportunity for the hearing of the merits of a properly asserted claim, and precludes the district court from, in effect, dismissing the claim upon the hearing of a motion for a temporary restraining order.

Finally, there is in Douglas v. City of Jeannette considerable emphasis on the nature of the injury. The allegation in that case was that members of Jehovah's Witnesses were being arrested and prosecuted under an unconstitutional ordinance because of the method of proselytizing they were using in private homes. . . . They also claimed that the city officials threatened to continue the arrests. The nature of the injury was that, in the absence of injunctive relief, the threatened arrests and prosecutions would deter Jehovah's Witnesses in the exercise of their constitutional rights. This is precisely the nature of the injury in this case, although the activity to be enjoined is different. Here, the Government claims that if Hardy's trial continues other Negroes in Walthall County will be afraid to apply for registration for fear they will be subjected to unjustified official acts, including arrest and prosecution. At this point, it should be noticed what the Supreme Court did in Douglas v. City of Jeannette. The import of the decision is not to deny as a question of fact that Jehovah's Witnesses were deterred in the exercise of their constitutional rights. Rather, it stated that, "No person is immune from prosecution in good faith for his alleged criminal acts. Its imminence, even though alleged to be in violation of constitutional guaranties, is not a ground for equity relief . . . ," except in the rare instance where it can be shown that the irreparable injury is "both great and immediate." The effect of this is to say that even where an actual deterrent is found to exist by the trier of fact, it will not be judicially recognized to fulfill the equitable element of "irreparable injury." The primary reason given by the Court being one of comity—that interference with the state criminal system is not warranted when adequate safeguards exist in the state proceedings. For several reasons, we hold that this theory is not applicable to the present case.

First, section 1971 creates a cause of action in the United States for "preventive relief" where a person has intimidated or has attempted to intimidate another in the exercise of his right to vote. Where a federal statute has specifically created a cause of action for preventive relief for intimidation, it may no longer be said that this intimidation will not be judically recognized for the purpose of establishing an equitable cause of action.

Second, we believe that the affirmative defense of adequate state remedies has been specifically removed by statute, for subsection (d) expressly states that the district court is to exercise jurisdiction without regard to whether the aggrieved party shall have exhausted other remedies provided by law. With this defense removed, there are no longer any grounds for judicially ignoring that intimidation may exist in fact or that irreparable injury is not present. . . .

The foundation of our form of government is the consent of the governed. Whenever any person interferes with the right of any other person to vote or to vote as he may choose, he acts like a political termite to destroy a part of that foundation. A single termite or many termites may pass unnoticed, but each damages the foundation, and if that process is allowed to continue the whole structure may crumble and fall even before the occupants become aware of their peril. Eradication of political termites, or at least checking their activities, is necessary to prevent irreparable damage to our Government. On the other hand, the temporary postponement of trial of a misdemeanor case before a justice of the peace causes either no injury or very slight injury. The public interest demanded the granting of temporary relief by the district court.

Nothing said in this opinion is intended to pass upon, or intimate any views as to the merits of the claim asserted by the United States. The importance of the case is such as to require a full hearing, either upon the motion for a preliminary injunction or upon a final hearing, including an opportunity to examine and cross-examine the witnesses. The claim should not be allowed to become moot before some such hearing can be had. To that end, unless there is a further agreement to continue the prosecution of Hardy at least until determination of the motion for preliminary injunction, the district court should grant the Government's request for a temporary restraining order.

CAMERON, Circuit Judge (dissenting).

I respectfully dissent from the majority opinion in this case. The exigencies of time [1] arising from the desirability of returning to State hands the enforcement of its laws make it impossible for me to set down, point by point, the reasons for my dissent. This opinion will, therefore, be confined to a detailed discussion of one or two points whose decision seem to me so glaringly wrong in the majority opinion and so distressingly destructive of the cooperative relationship which should exist between state and federal sovereignties.

I do not think that the order by the district court denying the motion for a temporary restraining order was appealable, and I do not, therefore, think that the case decided by the majority was properly before us. The majority admits that the question has never been decided by the Supreme Court or any Court of Appeals, but accepts the government's argument that the denial of the temporary restraining order was a final decision because of the special circumstances existing in this case. . . .

In the public press (The Tylertown Times of September 7, 1961) the editor of a newspaper stated:

"In our interview, Hardy expressed skepticism to me about the existence of God. He said 'Why should I believe in a God that I can't see?' He told

1. An urgency springing from the self-imposed delay of the government in beginning this action. The prosecution was instituted against Hardy in the state courts of Walthall County, Mississippi on September 7, 1961. The United States chose not to file its complaint in the present action until September 20, 1961, when it prayed for an immediate restraining order. The court below required notice to the defendants and heard and denied the motion at 5:00 P.M. September 21, 1961. As stated in the majority opinion, its author was importuned in his home at 10:30 P.M. on September 21st, 1961, for a stay of the proceedings before us. The clerk of the District Court was required to rush the filing of the record and appellee was called upon to file, a brief, all in the course of twelve days. The whole procedure was in keeping with the government's practice of demanding, and most often receiving, special treatment.

me he did not believe in service in the armed forces. 'Why should I go to defend a lie?' he said."

The same statement appears in a number of affidavits the originals of which are attached to the brief of appellees. Appellee's brief states: "It was agreed at this time [that is, when the application of appellant for injunction pending appeal was presented to Judge Rives] that the appellees may file and make parts of their briefs as part of the record any affidavits which they so desired."

Appellee's brief further showed that all of the original affidavits filed had been served on the appellant within the time fixed by Judge Rives at that hearing. As far as I am advised, the appellant has never moved to strike the affidavits, or taken any other step to take them out of the record. Such an attitude would appear to be requisite in view of the fact that the government had not given the county and state officers an opportunity to file affidavits prior to the hearing before the court below.

---

1) Can you state the rule in *Wood?* Whose rights are threatened by the state prosecution? How does the court answer that question in considering the § 2283 bar to the injunctive suit? If review were delayed, would the United States's rights be irreparably lost?

2) Since *Wood,* the standards for granting federal injunctions to prevent state criminal prosecutions have evolved and, Professor Fiss thinks, regressed. Fiss, Dombrowski, 86 Yale L.J. 1103 (1977). Perhaps the standards today are about the same as they were under Douglas v. City of Jeannette when the court decided *Wood;* perhaps, however, the court would refuse to enjoin the prosecution against Hardy. O. Fiss, The Civil Rights Injunction 61–68 (1978). The government sued in *Wood,* and it asserted the rights of people who are not criminal defendants. Is *Wood* distinguishable from criminal defendants seeking federal injunctions against arguably unconstitutional state criminal prosecutions? *Wood* accepts the idea of civil rights litigants' access to federal courts, "the primary guardians of constitutional rights." Fiss, 86 Yale L.J. at 1116. Is this access necessary in the changed climate of the 1980s?

WIRTZ v. POWELL KNITTING MILLS CO.

360 F.2d 730 (2d Cir. 1966).

Before SMITH, KAUFMAN and FEINBERG, Circuit Judges.

J. JOSEPH SMITH, Circuit Judge [paragraphs of the original opinion have been rearranged]:

The Secretary of Labor appeals from an order of the United States District Court for the Eastern District of New York, Joseph C. Zavatt, Chief Judge, vacating a temporary restraining order issued against Powell Knitting Mills, Inc. and against Meinhard Commercial Corp. Powell has not appeared. . . .

The vacated order prohibited the sale in interstate commerce of certain sweaters, produced by Powell, and acquired by Meinhard, a factor, when it foreclosed its lien. The prohibition was grounded on an asserted violation of

§ 6 and § 7 of the Fair Labor Standards Act, 29 U.S.C. §§ 201, 206, 207, in that 86 employees of Powell were not paid wages for the weeks ending February 18, February 25, and March 5, 1966, so that the sale of the sweaters would be a violation of § 15(a) of the Act, 29 U.S.C. § 215, if applicable, and enjoinable under § 17, 29 U.S.C. § 217. Powell had made an assignment for the benefit of creditors and was said to be insolvent. The unpaid wages totalled $8425. Section 15 makes it unlawful for "any person . . . to . . . sell in commerce . . . any goods in the production of which any employee was employed in violation of section 206 or section 207 of this title . . . "

Meinhard commenced financing Powell on September 2, 1965; cash advances said to have been around $700,000 were made, secured by inventory and equipment liens. Financing statements were filed. The liens covered inventory to be produced. Powell's financial condition worsened, and on about March 8, 1966, it ceased operations, and made an assignment for the benefit of creditors to the New York Creditmen's Adjustment Bureau, Inc. Meinhard foreclosed on its security, and the Secretary brought this action to prevent sale of the sweaters, some of which evidently were produced during the time when wages were not paid. Without deciding on the application for a preliminary injunction, Judge Zavatt vacated the restraining order he had previously signed ex parte. The Secretary applied for a stay pending appeal, which Judge Lumbard granted. . . .

As a general rule, it is true, the denying or vacating of a temporary restraining order is not appealable. . . . But this is not always so. In the first place, the appellate court is not bound by what the parties or the District Court may call the order appealed from. That is not this case, for there is no doubt that the original ex parte order was a temporary restraining order. The order vacating it, therefore, though after a hearing, and contested, is an order vacating a temporary restraining order. . . . But there is another reason in some cases for appealability of the granting, denial, or vacating of a temporary restraining order. Where dismissing the appeal may moot the underlying case for an injunction, the appeal should be heard. . . . The rationale of these cases in that the matter is appealable not under 28 U.S.C. § 1292, dealing with injunctions, but rather under § 1291, under the collateral order doctrine . . . .

Here dismissing the appeal, together with refusing to continue the stay ordered by Judge Lumbard, could very well moot the whole case for Meinhard could dispose of the sweaters before Judge Zavatt acted on the request for a preliminary injunction. Hence the matter is appealable quite apart from the fact that both parties were heard on the motion, and that a hearing occurred. . . .

On the merits, we find no error, and affirm the order vacating the temporary restraining order. . . .

[I]t is sufficient for this and similar cases to adopt a rule that frees from § 15 only a creditor foreclosing like Meinhard, for nonpayment of funds previously advanced. One purpose of making the sale illegal was to prevent adverse competitive effects on those who comply with the Act. Here there can be no connection between the asserted violation and any effects on competition. Another purpose of § 15 is to assure that the wage earners would be paid. With Powell insolvent and having made the assignment for the benefit of creditors, it is hardly possible that Powell may be forced to pay them. Hence the only way this purpose of the Act could be served would be to force Meinhard to pay them. But without some reasonably clear reference to the problem in the Act or in its history we find it hard to believe that Congress contemplated that the foreclosing creditor would have to pay the wage earners to avoid § 15. An exception should be read into § 15 for these particular facts. . . .

FEINBERG, Circuit Judge (concurring in the result):

I concur in the result. However, I believe the order under attack is not appealable. The majority's [position] would swallow up the rule denying appealability from denial or vacation of a temporary restraining order. Under Fed.R.Civ.P. 65(b), a party is entitled to a temporary restraining order only upon proof of the threat of "immediate and irreparable injury," and such an order can last no longer than twenty days, unless the party restrained consents. Erroneous denial of a temporary restraining order, by hypothesis, leaves a plaintiff unprotected from immediate and irreparable injury; hence, mootness will ordinarily follow unless immediate corrective appellate action is sought or a motion for a preliminary injunction is pressed in the trial court. The latter course can be taken as quickly as circumstances require and allows the trial court to consider the matter on a fuller record with a clear right of appeal to the parties thereafter. I believe this is the procedure envisaged by the Federal Rules of Civil Procedure and 28 U.S.C. § 1292(a)(1). . . .

---

1) Judge Feinberg asserts that the majority opinion's exception would "swallow up the rule." Is he correct?

2) If the employees, as creditors, filed to put Powell Knitting in involuntary bankruptcy, the automatic stay would stop Meinhard; and the issue would be adjudicated on Meinhard's motion to abandon the collateral and to dissolve the automatic stay. 11 U.S.C. §§ 362(a)(5), 554. The employees would be entitled to a wage priority in bankruptcy, 11 U.S.C. § 507(a)(3); but whether Meinhard's lien on the sweaters would defeat the employees remains to be seen.

3) A line of decisions related to *Wood* and *Wirtz* holds that an order denying a TRO may be appealed because it effectively denies a preliminary injunction. Coalition for Basic Human Needs v. King, 654 F.2d 838 (1st Cir. 1981); Belo Broadcasting Corp. v. Clark, 654 F.2d 423 (5th Cir. 1981). Is that the basis of the following decision? Or has Judge Friendly formulated a new rule?

BELKNAP v. LEARY

427 F.2d 496 (2d Cir. 1970).

Before LUMBARD, Chief Judge, and FRIENDLY and HAYS, Circuit Judges.

FRIENDLY, Circuit Judge: On May 27, 1970, plaintiffs asked Judge Motley in the District Court for the Southern District of New York, to issue, without notice to defendants, an order in an action instituted by plaintiffs under the Civil Rights Act, 42 U.S.C. § 1983, to restrain the Police Commissioner of New York City and his subordinates from failing to accord protection against physical harm at any legally constituted public demonstration over the Memorial Day weekend. The judge directed the plaintiffs to notify the defendants to appear at 3:00 P.M. that day. On May 28 she issued an order restraining the Police Commissioner, a named inspector, and all the other inspectors, captains, lieutenants, sergeants, and police officers of the City from:

"1) failing to protect plaintiffs and members of their class, while engaged in the peaceful and orderly exercise of their constitutional right to protest present Government war policies, from physical assaults and threats of physical assaults on May 29, 30, 31, 1970;

"2) failing to guarantee to these plaintiffs and members of the class they represent proper and adequate police protection while said plaintiffs and members of their class are engaged in exercising their constitutional right to meet and assemble in a peaceful and orderly manner and protest against the Government's war policies on May 29, 30, and 31, 1970;

"3) refusing or failing to take all reasonable precaution and means to protect plaintiffs and others similarly situated from acts of violence or other interference with the exercise of their right to peacefully assemble and protest present Government war policies on May 29, 30, and 31, 1970."

The order was to apply only to demonstrations of which the Police Department had prior notice. The court further directed that the order "be read or otherwise conveyed by the Police Commissioner, or his designated deputy, to every member of the Police Department who will be on duty on May 29, 30, 31, 1970." In view of the urgency as to time we heard the defendants' appeal on an expedited basis. [The appeal was argued and decided on May 29.]

We are met at the outset by a question of our appellate jurisdiction. The order is not a final decision under 28 U.S.C. § 1291, and the grant or denial of a temporary restraining order is generally not appealable as the grant or denial of an injunction under 28 U.S.C. § 1292(a)(1). . . . However, "in applying this distinction the label put on the order by the trial court is not decisive." Wright, Federal Courts 459 (2d ed. 1970). Unlike most temporary restraining orders, the one here under appeal is essentially affirmative. We regard it as a mandatory injunction, appealable under 28 U.S.C. § 1292(a)(1), even though it is of short duration.

Responsibility for protecting the people of the City of New York in the exercise of their First Amendment right "peaceably to assemble and petition the Government for the redress of grievances" rests in the first instance on their elected Mayor and his designee, the Commissioner of Police. Proper discharge of that duty is not likely to be enhanced by a necessarily vague order from a federal judge, which the Commissioner is commanded to read or otherwise convey to the men and women on his force, with the attendant threat of contempt proceedings if their conduct falls short of what the judge thinks proper. Responsibility, as Mr. Justice Brandeis once said, "is the great developer of men." St. Joseph Stock Yards Co. v. United States, 298 U.S. 38, 92 (1936) (concurring opinion).

Plaintiffs' argument for a departure from these principles hangs almost entirely on alleged gross neglect by a number of police officers during the deplorable events of May 8, 1970, when a group of construction workers assaulted anti-war demonstrators in downtown New York. They say this created an atmosphere of intimidation which nothing but a federal injunction can cure.

If there had been a continuation of police failure to protect anti-war demonstrators, such as the judge was justified in thinking had occurred on May 8, or even if City officials had done nothing about the incident, plaintiffs' case might have merit. But the facts are to the contrary. On May 9 Mayor Lindsay issued a statement characterizing the previous day's violence as "appalling" and saying that what was "most appalling" was "that the people of this city witnessed a breakdown of the police as the barrier between them and wanton violence." He added that the Police Commissioner and the Department's high command were equally disturbed "by failures of police performance," that an investigation had been started, and that other corrective procedures were being initiated. Even before that the Commissioner had issued a statement emphasizing the policy of the Department "to provide protection of the safety of those exercising their rights of free speech." The Department has had guidelines on the handling of mass demonstrations since September, 1969; a revised version of these which emphasizes the duty of the police to protect the peaceful exercise of the rights of free speech and assembly is about to be promulgated.

Indeed, at the argument before us plaintiffs' counsel affirmed confidence in the Mayor and the Police Commissioner but expressed doubt whether these high officials could get their views through to the force without assistance from a federal injunction. We perceive no basis for this fear.

. . . The injunction in Lankford v. Gelston was directed against an instance of large scale police violation of the Fourth Amendment which, as the court found, "on a smaller scale has routinely attended efforts to apprehend persons accused of serious crime." The very statement of these cases shows their inapplicability to a situation involving a single although grave failure by the police to discharge their responsibilities, followed by speedy criticism and the taking of corrective measures by the Mayor and the Police Commissioner. The apparent effectiveness of their action seems to have been shown by the handling of two major demonstrations, one pro-war and one anti-war, since May 8. There is thus no basis at present for any reasonable citizen to assume that these measures will be ineffective so that he must refrain from exercising his First Amendment rights to protest peaceably against the war—or anything else.

We therefore vacate the order as an abuse of discretion. The mandate shall issue forthwith.

---

1) Why does the "essentially affirmative" property of the TRO make it appealable? Why cite § 1292(a)(1)?

2) Fernandez-Roque v. Smith, 671 F.2d 426 (11th Cir. 1982), concerned Cubans who had come to the United States as part of the 1981 Freedom Flotilla. The trial judge entered a TRO to prevent their deportation. About eight weeks later, the government appealed on the theory that the TRO had ripened into an appealable preliminary injunction. The court of appeals disagreed: the TRO preserved the status quo instead of granting relief, and the government had consented to the extension. The court of appeals found a way to keep the trial judge on a short rein. It treated the government's appeal as a petition for a writ of mandamus, directed the trial judge to resolve crucial subject matter jurisdictional issues promptly, and certified a permissive interlocutory appeal from that decision under § 1292(b).

3) The final scorecard on appealability looks something like this:

	Denial	Grant
Motion for Summary Judgment	No Switzerland Cheese, Chappell	Yes Abercrombie & Fitch
Motion to Dismiss	No	Yes Build of Buffalo
Motion for Preliminary Injunction	Yes	Yes
Application for TRO	No? Wood, Wirtz	No? Belknap v. Leary

III. Appellate Orders to Fill a Trial Court Void

UNITED STATES v. LYND

1) Decision of April 10, 1962—301 F.2d 818 (5th Cir.).

Before TUTTLE, Chief Judge, and HUTCHESON and WISDOM, Circuit Judges.

TUTTLE, Chief Judge. This is a motion for an injunction pending an appeal which the United States seeks to have this Court issue following a refusal by the District Court for the Southern District of Mississippi to grant a temporary injunction, which the government sought under the provisions of 42 U.S.C.A. § 1971(a) . . . , it being charged in the government's complaint that Negro applicants for registration in Forrest County, Mississippi, were not being treated "without distinction of race [or] color." The government has filed a notice of appeal from the denial of the temporary injunction. Pending the disposition of this appeal on the merits, the government has filed this motion by which this Court is asked to enjoin the alleged violations of the voting rights of the Negro residents of Forrest County in certain particulars as to which the government claims that it offered undisputed proof. Such a motion for an injunction pending an appeal is to be found in the All-Writs Statute, 28 U.S.C.A. § 1651, which provides that:

"The Supreme Court and all courts established by Act of Congress may issue all writs necessary or appropriate in aid of their respective jurisdictions and agreeable to the usages and principles of law."

Rule 62(g) of the Federal Rules of Civil Procedure, 28 U.S.C.A. also provides that the authority granted to the District Court to grant relief pending an appeal does "not limit any power of an appellate court or of a judge or justice thereof . . . to suspend, modify, restore, or grant an injunction during the pendency of an appeal or to make any order appropriate to preserve the status quo or the effectiveness of the judgment subsequently to be entered." *

The basis of the government's appeal and its subsequent motion for injunction pending appeal is its contention that it has been completely frustrated in an effort to obtain an order of the trial court putting an end to alleged racially discriminatory acts and practices which the government contended in its complaint have deprived Negro citizens of Forrest County of their right to register and to vote without distinction of race or color. The government's efforts to redress the wrongs which it alleges exist in Forrest County commenced on August 11, 1960, ten months prior to the filing of this suit. At that time the United States formally requested that the defendant Lynd, the Registrar of Forrest County, make his registration records available for inspection and copying under Title III of the Civil Rights Act of 1960, 42 U.S.C.A. § 1974 et seq. These efforts proving fruitless, the government, on January 19, 1961, filed an enforcement proceeding in the District Court to require production of such records. This action also proved fruitless for, although as this Court said in the recent case of Kennedy, Attorney General v. Bruce, 5 Cir., 298 F.2d 860, an order granting the government the right to make such an inspection should have been issued "as a matter of course," the trial court failed for nearly six months to grant such order. Thereupon, on July 6, 1961, this present suit was filed. Thereafter, on February 15, 1962, the court dismissed the enforcement proceeding as "abandoned." This action was taken, so the trial court said, because after the government filed its suit for injunction on July 6, 1961, and moved for discovery of the official registration records of Forrest County under Rule 34 of Federal Rules of Civil Procedure, the trial court considered that this effort, which it also blocked, superseded the enforcement proceeding.

In the meantime, the instant litigation was delayed from time to time by dilatory motions, including motions to quash the Rule 34 motion, and including motions to make more definite statement, none of which, of course, should stand in the way of a prompt disposition of a motion for temporary injunction.

Briefly stated, the net effect of the several procedural steps taken by the parties is that the trial court finally set down for hearing the motion for temporary injunction on March 1, 1962, eight months after the suit for injunction was filed, and the posture of the parties was that defendants had objected to, and the trial court had sustained their objections to, giving any access to the records of the Registrar, although at the same time defendants had insisted, and the court had sustained their insistence, on the government's amending its complaint to allege in great detail the name of each applicant who had sought and been denied the right to register, the date of each such applica-

[* Federal Rules of Appellate Procedure, Rule 8, adopted subsequently, is in the Appendix.]

tion, the name of each Negro who had been refused the right to register, the dates involving any discriminatory mishandling of any Negro registration applications, the names of white people allowed to register who possessed no better qualifications than such Negroes denied the same privilege, and other facts and circumstances showing such discrimination in each of said instances. Moreover, the court had sustained objections by the defendants to the inclusion among the alleged complaining Negro applicants of any who had been denied the right to register or who claimed a discriminatory practice which had occurred prior to February 26, 1959, the beginning of defendant Lynd's term of office. Out of the 63 Negroes whose names the government had supplied by an amendment to the complaint, the trial court required that all but 40 of these be eliminated because the incidents as to which they were identified occurred prior to this date.

The injunction hearing finally came on for trial on March 5th and continued through March 7th. At this time sixteen of the Negroes whose names had been furnished by an amendment to the complaint testified as to experiences with which they were familiar. The government also undertook to prove discriminatory practices by sixteen white witnesses who had been found to be willing to testify in spite of the refusal of the Registrar, with approval of the Court, to make any records of white voters available to the complainant. During the trial it appeared that the defendants actually had in court certain voting records of the Negro witnesses, and the court required that these be turned over to the United States. The court also required that the records touching on the registration experiences of the white witnesses be turned over to the United States, but that they should not be turned over until after the government completed its case in chief. They were actually turned over as to six white witnesses only after the government closed.

Notwithstanding the well-nigh impossible task of showing the true facts, the witnesses produced by the government proved without question that certain serious discriminations had taken place during the term of office of the defendant Lynd. At the conclusion of the presentation by the government of its evidence, the State and the defendant Lynd both reserved the right of cross examination and deferred such cross examination. The defendants then declined to put on any evidence but stated that it would take thirty days to be prepared to file answers to the amended complaint and to prepare for introducing defense witnesses. Thereupon the government moved the Court to issue a temporary injunction. Without doing so, and declining either to grant or refuse a temporary injunction, in terms, the court failed to comply with the motion and granted a recess of thirty days to permit the defendants to file their answer and to prepare for proving their defensive case.

At the time the government made its motion for temporary injunction it is plain that the following facts relevant to the complaint that Negro applicants had been denied equal rights to register and vote in Forrest County had occurred:

(1) No Negro had been registered in Forrest County during defendant Lynd's term of office. There were forty Negroes who were named in the amended complaint who attempted to register during this period; sixteen of them testified that they attempted to register on one or more occasions since February 26, 1959, one of them four times. None was registered.

(2) No Negro was permitted even to apply for registration prior to January 31, 1961. Those who attempted to do so were told by one of the deputies that they had to see Mr. Lynd personally, and if they saw Mr. Lynd they were told by him that he couldn't register them, but he gave no reason and gave no time when he would undertake to do so.

(3) Prior to January 31, 1961, most, if not all, of the white applicants were permitted to register without filling out an application form. It is undisputed that many persons were registered without these formalities.

(4) From January 31, 1961, to the present, obviously qualified Negroes were rejected for registration unless the Registrar has some basis for denying the right to register which has not been communicated to them. Among these are five school teachers in the public schools of Hattiesburg or Forrest County, Mississippi; six of them hold baccalaureate degrees from colleges, and three of them have degrees of Master of Arts.

(5) In spite of the government's contention that no named white person during the defendant's entire tenure in office had been rejected for registration, none of the defendants nor their deputies were able to testify to any individual white person who had been rejected.

(6) From the date when the defendant started to use the application forms for white applicants, the defendant's deputies received applications from white applicants, but refused to receive them from Negro applicants. It was conceded that the Registrar himself was engaged in court as the Circuit Court Clerk two and one-half weeks each month, and was thus frequently unavailable.

(7) The defendant Lynd and his deputies assisted white applicants in filling out their application forms, but refused assistance to Negro applicants. Among the few white registered voters who were found to testify for the government, most of them testified either that they had not been required to fill out forms at all, that they filled them out incorrectly and received aid from the defendant, or were otherwise assisted in completing their registration.

(8) The defendant Lynd refused to give reasons to Negro applicants as to the reason or cause for their rejection, and he required that such applicants wait six months before reapplying for registration, although there is no provision in the statute authorizing such conduct.

(9) All of the sixteen Negro witnesses who testified at the trial were required to write and interpret different provisions of the Mississippi constitution from those provisions of the Mississippi constitution that were submitted to white applicants who testified.

We are not now considering the appeal from the refusal of the trial court to grant the temporary injunction on the merits. We are considering only the motion of the government that we grant a temporary injunction pending the hearing of the appeal. We, therefore, do not have for decision the numerous rulings of the trial court, either in relation to the original enforcement suit seeking access to the records or in the present suit for injunction. However, we cannot fail to comment briefly on the course of the litigation because of its direct bearing on the contention of the government that the refusal of the trial court to grant the temporary injunction justifies our granting this relief pending the appeal. We, therefore, point to the fact that this Court has . . . clearly laid down the rule that the government is entitled to have an order of the trial court authorizing it to inspect the voting records such as are here involved upon the simple assertion by the Attorney General of the United States that there are reasonable grounds for belief that certain voters are being discriminatorily denied their voting rights in a given county. See 42 U.S.C.A. § 1971(c). We have thus held that such allegation need not be enlarged or expanded by supplying detailed information such as was required by the Court in the case on appeal. Likewise, it is clear that there was no justification for the Court's requiring the government to amend its complaint in this civil rights action to allege specific details of voter discrimination as if this were an action for fraud or mistake under Rule 9, Federal Rules of Civil Procedure. These matters are commented on not as a final adjudication of the legal points involved, since they have not been briefed and are not now before us on appeal, but because they are relevant in our considering the need at this time, after nearly nine months following the filing of the suit, to enjoin such discriminatory practices as now appear to be fully proved.

The first objection of the defendants to our granting this relief is that the trial judge did not enter a formal order "refusing" a temporary injunction. He simply failed to do so, although the government made a formal motion during and at the end of its presentation of evidence for the issuance of such an injunction. The movant, under such circumstances, was clearly entitled to have a ruling from the trial judge, and since he did not grant the order his action in declining to do so was in all respects a "refusal," so as to satisfy the requirements of Section 1292, 28 U.S.C.A. We hold, therefore, that the failure of the trial judge to grant the temporary injunction constituted an "interlocutory order of the district court . . . refusing . . . an injunction." Such order is appealable.

The defendants' next contention is that it would be entirely inappropriate for the court at this time, as they claim it would have been for the trial court at the end of plaintiff's testimony, to grant a temporary injunction, because the State has not filed its answer and has not put on its proof. This contention entirely overlooks the nature of a temporary injunction, which is a writ of the trial court, or, in this instance, of an appellate court, issued to protect the rights of any person moving for it upon his making a showing that he is entitled to it. The grant of a temporary injunction need not await any procedural steps perfecting the pleadings or any other formality attendant upon a full-blown trial of this case. The defendant may, of course, make such counter showing as it deems wise or necessary to meet such proof as is produced by the moving party. Where, however, as is here the case, the plaintiff made a clear showing that rights which it sought to vindicate were being violated, and that no response or counterproof would be available for some considerable period after these rights should have been, but had not been, taken under consideration by the trial court, the plaintiff has satisfied every requirement for the granting of temporary relief pending a final adjudication of the appeal.

We conclude that the likelihood that the court's refusal to grant the temporary injunction will be reversed as an abuse of discretion is sufficiently great that we are warranted in protecting the rights of the Negro registrants pending a decision on this issue by this Court.

Therefore, pending a final determination of the appeal now pending in this Court, the defendants, their agents, employees, successors, and all persons in concert with them are hereby enjoined from engaging in discriminatory acts and practices based on race in the registration for voting in Forrest County, Mississippi, and they are expressly enjoined from:

(1) Denying Negro applicants the right to make application for registration on the same basis as white applicants;

(2) Failing to process applications for registrations submitted by Negro applicants on the same basis as applications submitted by white applicants;

(3) Failing to register and to issue registration cards to Negro applicants on the same basis as white applicants;

(4) Denying Negro applicants the right to be registered by the same office personnel and with the same expedition and convenience as are being permitted to white applicants, and from failing or refusing to give to Negro applicants the same privileges as to reviewing their application forms at the time they are filled out and advising Negro applicants of such omissions as appear on their forms as they are now or heretofore have given to white applicants under similar circumstances;

(5) From administering the constitutional interpretation test to Negro applicants by including as sections to be read and interpreted any sections other than those which at the time of the trial had been used for submission to white applicants;

(6) From requiring rejected Negro applicants to wait any different period before reapplying for registration than may be authorized under the laws of Mississippi and other than is required of white applicants.

In view of the immediate pendency of termination of registration proceedings prior to an early election, it is ordered that this injunction shall be effective immediately, and that the judgment and order of this Court be transmitted forthwith to the Clerk of the District Court for the Southern District of Mississippi, and that the Clerk of this Court send a certified copy hereof to each party defendant, said service to be made upon counsel of record.

---

2) Decision of July 15, 1963—321 F.2d 26 (5th Cir.).

Before BROWN, WISDOM and BELL, Circuit Judges.

PER CURIAM.

When this case was first appealed, the Government sought and this Court granted a preliminary injunction pending appeal. United States v. Lynd, 5 Cir., 1962, 301 F.2d 818.

Since that time the full record has been filed together with extensive briefs of all parties. For all practical purposes, the issues on the merits of the appeal are the same as those with which we had to deal earlier. These are set out with sufficient fullness in our prior opinion. Reconsideration of them in the light of the full briefs and record leads us to reaffirm our former conclusions. We therefore hold that there was an appealable order. Likewise, on the merits, we hold that, under appropriate standards of appellate review, the facts were such that it was error for the District Court in effect to deny the application for preliminary injunction.

Since a further trial is required it is necessary that we rule on those procedural points which may have a bearing on the proceedings on remand. As to the problem of pleading, we adhere to our former ruling . . . .

The District Court also imposed unjustified restrictions on the scope of the evidence. The evidence to establish a pattern and practice is not confined to the incumbency of Registrar Lynd. Neither is it limited as to the State by the effective date of the 1960 amendments to the Civil Rights Act. 42 U.S.C.A. § 1971. A broad latitude is to be allowed. . . . So far as the Government's complaint on production of voter records is concerned we doubt that it will any longer be a problem in light of Kennedy v. Lynd, 5 Cir., 1962, 306 F.2d 222, cert. denied, 371 U.S. 952, and the District Court's own subsequent decision in In re Coleman, S.D.Miss., 1962, 208 F.Supp. 199, which we affirmed, Coleman v. Kennedy, 5 Cir., 1963, 313 F.2d 867.

Consequently, the case must be reversed and remanded for further and not inconsistent proceedings, including the full trial on the merits. As our procedural rulings bear closely on the showing of a right to injunctive relief, all parties, the Government and Defendants alike, are entitled to offer further evidence in the proceedings on remand. The mandate to be issued hereon will provide that the preliminary injunction previously entered by us is continued in full force and effect until such time as the District Court finally disposes of the case. However, as issuance of an injunction by this Court is most unusual, it is more than ordinarily important that the further proceedings in the District Court move with dispatch.[1] The objective is to terminate the preliminary injunction of this Court at the earliest possible time so that all further or other orders will be those of the District Court. This is in keeping with the general proposition that an appeal from the denial or granting of a preliminary injunction should not ordinarily delay the final trial of the case on its merits. . . .

GRIFFIN B. BELL, Circuit Judge (concurring specially). . . . This court had the power under the All Writs Statute, 28 U.S.C.A. § 1651, to take the action it took on the former appeal. . . . However, in my judgment it was more properly a matter for mandamus. The issue did not go to a denial of temporary relief as such, but to a delay in granting or denying the relief and this court should have spoken to the District Court through a Writ of Mandamus.

This would have afforded the District Court a chance to be heard. It might have avoided the necessity of this court taking the case over prior to a decision in the District Court. It would have avoided the multitudinous handling, by way of contempt hearings and otherwise, since the grant of the original relief by this Court, with no further action having been taken in the interim on the main case in the District Court. This case serves as a classic example of the pitfalls to be encountered, with the attendant disruption and

1. The pendency of the proceedings for civil and criminal contempt against Appellee Lynd as respondent affords no basis for delay in the proceedings on remand since the record of the evidence in the contempt cases is fully closed and those matters have been taken under submission.

delays in the orderly administration of justice when courts depart from the time-tested processes of law.

Judge Bell apparently favored using mandamus to tell Judge Cox to enter and enforce a particular order. As you read on, ask if it made a big difference whether the court of appeals or Judge Cox enforced the order and conducted the contempt proceedings.

---

3) Decision of June 16, 1965—Injunctive Proceeding—349 F.2d 785 (5th Cir.).

GRIFFIN B. BELL, Circuit Judge: . . . Suit was filed on July 6, 1961 against Mr. Lynd and the State. The United States moved for an injunction in this court pending appeal upon the refusal of the District Court to grant a preliminary injunction after a three day hearing in March, 1962. The matter was heard in this court on April 6, 1962 with the result that an injunction pending appeal prohibited discrimination against Negroes in the registration process was entered on April 10, 1962. . . .

Thereafter and in the same month, the United States alleged that Mr. Lynd had violated the terms of the injunction. A rule nisi was issued by this court on May 1, 1962 requiring Mr. Lynd to show cause why he should not be held in civil and criminal contempt. He was tried on the rule in Hattiesburg, Mississippi by the present panel of this court in September, 1962, and an order adjudicating him in civil contempt was entered on July 15, 1963. No action has been taken to date relative to disposition of the criminal contempt charge. The civil contempt order required Mr. Lynd to meet certain conditions in the registration procedures which were designed to prevent discrimination against Negroes, and also to register certain applicants previously denied registration. He took all action required of him at the time, and agreed in writing to abide the terms of the order.

Meanwhile, no further proceedings had been had in the District Court on the case and this court, also under date of July 15, 1963, ordered a prompt trial on the merits with the injunction of April 10, 1962 to remain in full force and effect until such time as the District Court finally disposed of the case. United States v. Lynd, 5 Cir., 1963, 321 F.2d 26. The case was tried on the merits in the District Court during April, 1964 and the final decision of that court was entered on January 20, 1965. It forms the subject matter of this appeal.

During this period of delay in the District Court after July 15, 1963, the United States alleged in this court that Mr. Lynd was violating the terms of the injunction of April 10, 1962 and the civil contempt order in the registration process by using a double standard in the administration and grading of the tests which form a part of the application for registration as between white and Negro applicants, and by failing to comply with the terms of the order respecting assistance to applicants. The rule nisi issued on that complaint was heard in conjunction with the argument of this appeal and a separate order is being simultaneously entered thereon. . . .

This brings us to the subject matter of relief by way of freezing. As is now settled in the decisions of this court, such relief is in order where discrimination has resulted from a pattern or practice. . . . We hold that such relief is demanded in this case. It is the duty of the court to render a decree which will insofar as possible eliminate the discriminatory effects of the past as well as bar like discrimination in the future. . . .

The relief to be granted by way of freezing has had the careful consideration of this court. The registration accommodations available, the number of Negroes who may seek registration, and the past discriminatory record in Forrest County have all been weighed. The District Court is directed upon remand to enter forthwith the following judgment in this matter:

"In accordance with and pursuant to the opinion of the United States Court of Appeals for the Fifth Circuit in the within matter, this court finds that the successive registrars of voters of Forrest County, Mississippi have engaged in acts and practices which have deprived Negroes citizens of Forrest County of their right to register to vote without distinction by reason of race, and that such deprivation has been pursuant to a pattern or practice of discrimination against Negro citizens in the registration processes in Forrest County, Mississippi.

"By virtue of and pursuant to the mandate of the United States Court of Appeals for the Fifth Circuit in this cause, it is ordered, adjudged, and decreed by the Court that Defendant Theron C. Lynd, his agents, officers, employees and successors in office be and each is hereby permanently enjoined from

"1. Engaging in any act or practice which involves or results in distinctions based on race or color between Negro citizens and other citizens in the registration for voting process in Forrest County, Mississippi.

"2. Determining the qualifications of citizens in Forrest County, Mississippi in any manner or by any procedure different from or more stringent than the following which have heretofore been used by registrars of Forrest County and their agents in determining the qualifications of white applicants:

"(a) He is a citizen and is or will be 21 years of age or older at the time of the next election;

"(b) He, at the time of the next election, has or will have resided in the State two years and in the election district in which he intends to vote one year;

"(c) He embraces the duties and obligations of citizenship as demonstrated by his willingness to take and sign the oath to bear allegiance to the Constitution of the United States and the State of Mississippi; provided, however, that any errors or omissions in filling out or signing the oath on the application form shall not be a basis for rejection, except that an applicant may be rejected if he refuses to sign the oath (or affirmation) after being shown by the registrar or his agent where to sign;

"(d) He is not disqualified by reason of conviction of a disqualifying crime, insanity or idiocy;

"(e) He is able to demonstrate a reasonable ability to read and write by completion of Questions 1–18 of the application form with informational assistance by the registrar or his agents, as needed; provided, however, the section of the Mississippi Constitution to be copied under question 18 shall in no event exceed two lines as printed in the Mississippi Constitution, Mississippi Code of 1942. The registrar is ordered to judge the literacy of applicants on the basis of responses to these questions, but in judging literacy, the registrar is further ordered not to take into account bad handwriting and spelling so long as the answers to the questions are legible and responsive, provided that no applicant shall be rejected for an error or omission in his application which is not material in determining whether the applicant meets the substantive requirements set out in paragraph 2(a), (b), (c), and (d); nor shall any applicant be rejected for any other error or omission relating to his substantive qualifications as set forth in paragraph 2(a), (b), (c), and (d) in his application unless such error or omission has been specifically pointed out and explained to him by the registrar or his agent and the applicant refuses to supply the requested information. The provisions of this paragraph 2 shall remain in full force and effect until such time as: (a) the proper local officials of Forrest County, Mississippi, order an entirely new registration of all voters in Forrest County . . . ; [or (b)] . . . it has been shown to the satisfaction of this Court that the effect of the pattern or practice of discrimination against Negroes seeking to register to vote in Forrest County have been overcome, and provided further, no such showing may be made to this Court until after two years from the entry of this Judgment. . . .

"3. It is further Ordered that defendant, Theron C. Lynd, shall review in light of the requirements in this Order the application forms of those rejected Negro applicants who applied during his tenure in office and who are not now registered, and whose names and applications in a number not to exceed 350 are submitted to him by the United States, and register all such citizens who meet the requirements of this Order. . . .

"4. It is further ordered that defendant Theron C. Lynd, his agents, employees, and successors in conducting registration of voters in Forrest County, Mississippi, are enjoined and ordered to:

"(a) Afford each applicant for registration an opportunity to apply and complete the application form whether either the registrar or a deputy registrar is present;

"(b) Advise each applicant, when he or she applies, whether the applicant is accepted or rejected; if accepted, the applicant must be registered at that time; if rejected the applicant must be informed of the reason or reasons for his rejection and must be advised of his right to apply directly to this Court to be registered as provided in paragraph 5 hereof.

"(c) Receive and process each applicant as expeditiously as possible to the extent that the physical facilities of the registration office permit but in no case less than six applicants at one time and in no case refuse to process fewer than six applicants at one time. The office of the registrar shall be open during the office hours observed by defendant Lynd in his capacity as the clerk of the courts of Forrest County for registration from Monday through Friday of each week except on holidays during the twenty four month period following the entry of this order.

"5. Any applicant for registration hereafter rejected or not given the opportunity to apply by the defendant Lynd, his agents, employees, or successors, may in accordance with 42 U.S.C. 1971(e) apply to this court, or to a voting referee to be appointed by and in the discretion of this court no more than 20 days after receipt by the court of the first application, to have his qualifications determined. The court or such referee shall register all such applicants who meet the standards established in this order.

"6. It is further ordered that the defendant Lynd, his agents, employees, and successors in office shall file a written report with the clerk of this Court and shall mail a copy thereof to the Plaintiff's attorneys on or before the tenth day of each month. Said reports shall contain the name and race of each applicant for registration from the previous monthly period, the date of the application, the action taken on the application, and if the applicant is rejected, the specific reason or reasons for rejecting the application. . . .

"7. The defendant Lynd, his deputies, agents, and successors in office shall, until further order of this Court, make the registration records of Forrest County, Mississippi available to attorneys or agents of the United States at any and all reasonable times in the circuit clerk's office in Hattiesburg for the purpose of inspection, copying, and photographing.

"8. Jurisdiction is retained of this cause for all purposes and especially for the purpose of issuing any and all additional orders as may become necessary or appropriate for the purposes of modifying and/or enforcing this order.

"9. Costs in this Court are awarded to plaintiff."

. . . With respect to the last assignment of error, the District Court erred in ordering applicants for registration and all persons representing and acting in concert with them to cooperate with the registrar and his office, and to desist from any acts on the courthouse premises calculated to interfere with the registration process. No applicant for registration was a party to the suit. It was brought by and in the name of the United States. Thus there was no jurisdictional basis for the order. . . .

Reversed and remanded for further proceedings not inconsistent herewith, and the mandate is to issue forthwith.

The court of appeals writes the decree to be entered by the District Judge. Is this a wiser strategy than the one previously employed, the appellate court issuing its own injunction? What happened to all that easy talk about the terms of an injunction being within the discretion of the trial judge?

---

4) Decision of June 16, 1965—Contempt Proceeding—349 F.2d 790 (5th Cir.).

Before BROWN, WISDOM, and BELL, Circuit Judges.

JOHN R. BROWN, Circuit Judge: This proceeding for civil contempt for disobedience of the orders of this Court is an outgrowth of the Government's suit for injunction forbidding racial discrimination by Respondent Theron C. Lynd, Registrar of Forrest County, in the Registration of Negro citizens, the appeal therein being this day decided. . . .

The history traced briefly in that opinion reflects the tortuous path of this effort to vindicate this clear constitutional right. . . . Simultaneously with the latter opinion remanding the case for an early trial on the merits, we entered the order of July 15, 1963, adjudging Lynd guilty of contempt. Besides compelling compliance with our 1962 orders prohibiting racial discrimination, the sanctions imposed forbad rejection of applications for errors or omissions if the applicant satisfied seven specified qualifications, required nondiscriminatory selection from a list of 14 sections of the Mississippi Constitution, and prescribed that Lynd and his deputies notify any rejected applicant "of the specific deficiency or deficiencies and afford such applicant the opportunity to correct the error or omission and supply the needed information with respect to the" specified qualifications. We also provided that our orders of April 1962 and July 15, 1963, were effective until final disposition of the case by the District Court. About the time of the further trial on remand the Government on April 15, 1964, filed a petition requesting additional contempt orders because of continued violations subsequent to our July 15, 1963 order. This was supplemented by a similar petition of August 28, 1964. We purposely withheld action in the hope that the decision of the District Court would effectually dispose of such matters occurring up to date of trial. Subsequent to the District Court's judgment of January 20, 1965, a third supplement was filed March 5, 1965. Upon a show cause order of March 15, 1965, a hearing [1] has now been held on charges of violations occurring between August 11, 1962 through January 19, 1965.[2]

. . . [W]e have concluded that Registrar Lynd has violated our orders in several major and significant respects. The unfortunate fact is that despite our orders of April 1962 and July 15, 1963—the latter of which we hoped would be an inducement to eliminate any vestige of discriminatory practices—Negroes have been denied this precious Constitutional right because they are Negroes. There has been improvement, but both on the appeal and contempt, mandatory orders are required to erase discrimination altogether for all time.

We need mention only briefly the more glaring types of discrimination.

In the grading of answers to Questions 19 and 20,[3] the use of a double standard was frequent, glaring and often flagrant.[4] This case graphically

1. By previous order the appeal . . . and the contempt citations, Docket No. 19576, were consolidated for hearing and argument at New Orleans June 14, 15, 1965.

2. The record on the contempt case comprises oral testimony and documentary exhibits offered June 14, 15, 1965; the full transcript (with exhibits) of the 1961–62 and April 1964 trial in the District Court; and the transcript of our five-day contempt hearing at Hattiesburg, September 1962. This record exceeds 1000 pages of testimony and several thousand exhibits. Over 50 witnesses have testified in person before us.

3. Q. 18 requires the applicant to "write and copy" a section of the Mississippi Constitution selected by the Registrar.

Q. 19 states: "Write . . . a reasonable interpretation (the meaning) of the section" copied in Q. 18.

Q. 20 requires "Write . . . a statement setting forth your understanding of the duties and obligations of citizenship under a constitutional form of government."

4. See, e.g., A–4 Demonstrative Notebook filed in this record. A white voter's application October 17, 1964, was accepted with Q. 20 answered: "It is the duty of every citizen to be law abiding and vote." A Negro application October 6, 1964, was rejected on this answer: "The duties and obligation of a Citizen under a constitution form of government, that you should be able to vote in all election, pay your poll taxes, respect private property and obey all laws." According to Lynd's June 1965 testimony, he now says the white answer was not adequate and should have been rejected. See B–4, as to Sec. 16 of the Constitution:

"Ex post facto laws, or laws impairing the obligation of contracts, shall not be passed."

demonstrates how such tests are the engine of discrimination. . . . Likewise in the selection from the 14 permitted sections of the Mississippi Constitution, there was continued racial discrimination. There was, to be sure, improvement, but significant traces still remained.[5] There was like disparity in grading other answers, such as place of residence and statutory voter residence requirements.

And in the face of our contempt order of July 15, 1963, requiring that he give assistance to applicants by pointing out errors, omissions, or other deficiencies in the application, Lynd handed to applicants for a substantial time a printed card [6] and posted a large printed sign [7] which plainly stated the contrary. Equally important, this message discouraged these persons from even asking for this court-ordered assistance. Moreover, with or without signs or cards, Lynd's practice was to afford no assistance although this was plainly required.[8]

Obviously the denial of these rights—at one and the same time a violation of the Constitution and the orders of this Court—demands correction. At the snail's pace to date, it will take decades to eradicate the evil.[9] The Judici-

According to Lynd, not a lawyer, the important thing was impairment of contracts. He rejected many Negroes who gave answers worthy of a law review editor on ex post facto laws. He accepted a white answer, "that all laws such as ex post facto laws impairing obligations of contracts cannot be passed" while rejecting this perfect Negro answer: "If a person has committed a crime he cannot be convicted of a crime if no such law exist. No law can be passed right then for that person. No law shall be passed to impair contract's obligation."

5. The figures themselves are startling as to some long "hard" sections opposed to some short "easy" sections, and when figures talk, Courts listen. . . .

6. "You have just filled out an application for registration. THIS DOES NOT REGISTER YOU. You must check back with us in 30 days to see if your application has been accepted or rejected. If accepted you must then sign the registration book personally. If rejected you can then fill out another application. We cannot point out errors to you on rejected applications. You may fill out as many applications as you desire until registered."

This was used from early fall 1963 through January 1964 at which time it was discontinued upon advice of his counsel after protest by the United States.

7. "NOTICE

"STATE LAW REQUIRES

"Application for Registration must be completely filled out without any assistance or suggestions of any person or memorandum.

"After 10 days applicant's names and addresses are published for two consecutive weeks in the newspaper. They cannot be ruled on until 14 days after the second publication. Therefore it can take as long as 33 days before we can give you an answer as to your application being accepted or rejected.

"Your indulgence is appreciated."

8. From July 23, 1963, through December 1964 numerous rejected Negro applications show pencilled arrows to errors. The obvious sense of our July 15, 1963 order was to require that such deficiencies be then and there pointed out for immediate correction.

9. Of 29,926 persons of voting age in Forrest County (1960 census), 75% (22,431) are white and 25% (7,595) are Negroes. As of March 1964 the registration was:

	White	Negro
Number	17,738	196
Percent	74.62%	2.58%

From November 1960 through March 1964 acceptance-rejection was:

	Applied	Accepted Number	Percent	Rejected
White	2,055	1,446	70.4%	608
Negro	1,066	135	12.7%	924

(Discrepancies in figures due to some applicants not being positively identified as to race.)

From August 1962 through January 20, 1965 it was:

	Applied	Accepted
White	1,620	914
Negro	1,835	281

ary has the power and the duty to fashion appropriate relief. We have done so in the appeal by directing the entry of a mandatory order. . . . And sanctions are permissible and called for to coerce compliance. . . .

By our order in this case, we are requiring the registration of approximately 280 applicants, subject to deletion of those shown to be disqualified under a procedure similar to that approved in State of Alabama v. United States, supra, 304 F.2d at 594. As to this group, we have not taken into account the answers to Questions 19 and 20 (note 3, supra). Of course, our order of July 15, 1963, permitted their non-discriminatory use. But in view of the discrimination in the five categories discussed, we think it appropriate that the sanctions imposed require registration of these applicants. As immediate and clearly identifiable subjects of discriminatory practices, this will put them on a parity with those who will apply in the future and as to whom the injunctive order . . . [in the companion case] forbids use of Questions 19 and 20.

For like reasons, we think it appropriate that as a sanction we require the conspicuous posting of the District Court's order when entered pursuant to our mandate in No. 22477. All—and this includes voter applicants, Registrar Lynd and his staff, and interested citizens—will know precisely what is expected.

Only a tag end remains. A question is raised as to our considering both the contempt and the appeal case. The answer to that is simple and twofold. First, the contempt concerns violation of our orders up to January 19, 1965, the day before the District Court's judgment, since our orders were expressly viable to that time. Second, the District Court's judgment had a built-in suspension clause.[11] Obviously, it would have been intolerable that through a judgment having no worthwhile effect, the power of orders would simultaneously evaporate.

The order and mandate of the Court shall issue forthwith.

APPENDIX

This matter having come on for a hearing on June 14 and 15, 1965, on the Order requiring Theron C. Lynd to show cause why he should not be held in civil contempt of this Court, and all parties having been represented by counsel in open court, and the Court having filed its findings of fact which are incorporated by reference, it is:

1. Adjudged that Theron C. Lynd, Respondent, is guilty of civil contempt of this Court for violation, after notice and service thereof of the orders of this Court of April 10 and 16, 1962, and the Judgment and Order of Civil Contempt of July 15, 1963.

11. The judgment of January 20, 1965, provided:

"This judgment shall be and become effective only after the United States Court of Appeals for the Fifth Circuit completes its handling of all matters in this case presently pending before said Court."

2. It is further ordered and adjudged that Theron C. Lynd, Respondent, in order to purge himself of civil contempt of this Court as herein declared and as prescribed in the judgment of July 15, 1963, shall:

a. Register forthwith and place upon the current voter registration rolls of Forrest County, Mississippi, and do all other acts necessary to complete the registration for voting in Forrest County, the Negro citizens listed in Attachment A to this judgment and order and herein incorporated, all of whom applied for and were improperly denied registration in Forrest County, Mississippi, in violation of this Court's orders. Such registration shall be effective in all respects and for all purposes as of the date of the most recent application forms of these respective citizens.

b. Notify each of said citizens listed in Attachment A by United States Mail, postage prepaid, that they are now registered voters and identify to them the effective date of their registration. Respondent Lynd shall not require any of these applicants to return to his office to complete their registration.

c. Remove forthwith the sign in his office suggesting that applicants may not receive assistance.

d. Post in his office in a conspicuous place where it may be read by applicants a copy of the Order entered by the United States District Court for the Southern District of Mississippi pursuant to the mandate of this Court . . . .

e. Within twenty (20) days of the date of this Order and Judgment, file with the Clerk of this Court a written signed report showing that he has complied with Paragraph 2a, b, and c of this Judgment, and that he will hereafter faithfully abide by and comply with this Order. Filing of this statement and compliance therewith shall not restrict or abridge the right of Theron C. Lynd to appeal from the Judgments or Orders therein enumerated or to contest the validity thereof in a Court of appropriate jurisdiction.

3. As to any applicant who, since the date of his last application, has subsequently become disqualified by reason of conviction of a disqualifying crime, insanity, or idiocy, change of residence, or upon death of such applicant, or who is not entitled to register because of lack of citizenship, age, residence or conviction of a disqualifying crime, the Respondent, Theron C. Lynd, need not take the action prescribed in Par. 2a and b above. But he shall in writing and under oath submit to this Court within 20 days hereof the detailed facts respecting such claimed disqualification for approval or disapproval by the Court. Upon the disapproval of any such claimed disqualification by the Court he shall within 10 days of the date of such order comply with Par. 2a and b, and file a report of compliance within 5 days thereafter.

4. It is further ordered and adjudged that all costs of this proceeding taxable as Court costs are taxed against Theron C. Lynd and shall be paid within 60 days after assessment by the Clerk of this Court.

---

1) Why did the court of appeals issue its own injunction in 1962 and continue it in 1963 rather than to remand to the District Court for entry of an injunction? One possible answer is that the court of appeals wanted to control enforcement—it believed that it would be "tough" with Theron Lynd

in a way that the District Judge would not. Can that theory be reconciled with the enforcement measures the court of appeals actually employed? The failure to use the criminal contempt power is most striking. On two occasions—July 15, 1963, and June 16, 1965—the court of appeals enters orders denominated "civil contempt." Are these contempt orders at all, or simply appellate injunctions in a new guise.

2) Two possible reasons to avoid criminal contempt should be mentioned here. First, when dealing with a known heel dragger like Lynd, does 2.a in the civil contempt order, p. 441, place the court at the mercy of a litigant who may use that order to become a martyr? Is it possible that Lynd sought to be the victim of the federal court's stern response? Perhaps the court of appeals tried to avoid allowing Lynd to force it to resort to the punitive measures that would make a martyr of him and ensure his political future. Second, Lynd's recalcitrance went a long way toward creating the national political climate that made the 1965 Voting Rights Act possible. When the court of appeals adjudicated Lynd's contempt in 1965, was anything more necessary? One thousand blacks were registered to vote in Forrest County in the summer of 1965 "with the threat of federal registrars hanging in the air." D. Garrow, Protest at Selma 256 (1978).

The court of appeals's problem is endemic to *in personam* enforcement. Huston tells us that orders to defendants to convey specific property enforced by imprisonment in the Fleet were "frequently quite unsuccessful as a means of procuring the performance of the commands of the court, which was after all the thing to be aimed at." C. Huston, The Enforcement of Decrees in Equity 15–16 (1915). The response to "dogged contumacy" was to allow a court official to execute a deed. See Rule 70 in the Appendix. Could the court of appeals invoke Rule 70 as an analogy and order a federal officer to register the voters?

3) The judiciary contributed "freezing" injunctions to the development of voting rights. Judges ordered boards to apply the same standard to blacks that they had applied to whites during the period of discrimination. These orders departed from orders to stop discrimination in the future. See United States v. Penton, 212 F.Supp. 193, 199 (M.D.Ala.1962). This created a precedent for Congress to suspend literacy requirements in the Voting Rights Act. See Fiss, Gaston County v. United States: Fruition of the Freezing Principle, 1969 Sup.Ct.Rev. 379. In a later essay, Professor Fiss has also called similar orders reparative injunctions because they eliminate the effects of a past wrong. O. Fiss, The Civil Rights Injunction 10 (1978). Compare Bell v. Southwell p. 176.

4) Reconsider the plight of Dickinson and Adams in United States v. Dickinson, p. 305. The judge tells them to publish nothing about the proceedings. The trial will continue. Assume that the order happens today and that one of the reporters consults you. What could you tell him? *Nebraska Press* held that these orders are presumptively incorrect. Would you seek a permissive interlocutory appeal under § 1292(b)? Mandamus? An appeal of a final decision by right under § 1291? Review as an interlocutory injunction under § 1292(a)(1)? Rendleman, Free Press-Fair Trial: Restrictive Orders after Nebraska Press, 67 Ky.L.J. 867, 879–88 (1979). What makes the order final? Why is mandamus appropriate? Would you seek a stay?

Should trial court orders in the first amendment area be automatically stayed? Would granting a stay end the controversy? Does relief by a stay subordinate the appellate goal of considered, collegial, and reasoned decisions? What if the appellate court grants a stay, the newspaper publishes, and it turns out on full consideration that the trial judge was right? Should the appellate court allow the trial judge's order to remain in effect and decide the reporters' appeal after the trial ends? If the appellate court allowed the trial judge's order to remain in effect, would you reconsider your advice not to disobey the order?

5) Single judges may grant stays. United States Servicemen's Fund v. Shands, 440 F.2d 44 (4th Cir. 1971). Injunctions pending an appeal are the functional equivalents of stays, although the court stays a situation rather than a lower court order. The appellate courts apply roughly the same standards as trial judges apply for preliminary injunctions. Washington Metropolitan Area Transit Commission v. Holiday Tours, Inc., 559 F.2d 841 (D.C.Cir. 1977). Some may stress the likelihood that the stay will coincide with the ultimate relief. Rainey v. Jackson State College, 481 F.2d 347, 351 (5th Cir. 1973). A judge may couple a stay with an accelerated briefing schedule. In re Bradley, 456 F.2d 6 (4th Cir. 1972).

Inescapably, some stays are dispositive. In Application of the President and Directors of Georgetown College, 331 F.2d 1010 (D.C.Cir. 1964), certiorari denied 377 U.S. 978, a single circuit judge ordered a blood transfusion for a dying woman who was prevented by religious scruples from consenting. When the matter came before the full court for "rehearing," it was moot. The court denied rehearing over dissents that registered doubt about deciding lawsuits with stays instead of preserving the status quo.

6) The need for appellate courts to control trial judges continues. Southeastern Promotions v. City of Mobile, 457 F.2d 340 (5th Cir. 1972), grew out of the problems of scheduling the musical production "Hair" in the Mobile, Alabama auditorium. The trial judge denied the promotor's request for a preliminary injunction; the court of appeals vacated and remanded for immediate reconsideration; the trial judge set the hearing for after the scheduled opening; and the court of appeals said "We cannot countenance this prior restraint on freedom of speech . . . " The February 29, Supplemental Opinion said that plaintiff "is entitled to have an injunction pending appeal which will direct the use of the Mobile Municipal Auditorium on the dates of February 29, March 1 and 2, 1972. Therefore, this Court's order of February 28, 1972 is herewith amended, so as to provide that the District Court shall immediately and forthwith, today, upon receipt of the text of this order by telephone communication from the Clerk of this Court to the Clerk of the District Court, grant a preliminary injunction in the manner and form sought by plaintiff in order that the production of 'Hair' may be presented in the Mobile Municipal Auditorium on the dates above referred to, beginning today."

7) We saved the last page of *Reserve Mining*, p. 116 for here because it shows the continuing struggle between trial and appellate courts. The court of appeals issued this order on remand:

"For reasons stated below, we find it necessary to issue this special order on remand to protect the integrity of the processes of this court.

"We filed our detailed and carefully drawn, unanimous *en banc* opinion in these cases on March 14, 1975. Although these cases remained exclusively in our jurisdiction subject to any request for reconsideration by any of the parties, *see* Fed.R.App.P. 40, and before issuance of any mandate, the district court called the parties and other persons together for a hearing the very next day, March 15, 1975. After learning of this hearing through news dispatches published in the daily press, we requested that the clerk of the district court furnish each member of the *en banc* court with a transcript of the hearing.

"We have reviewed this transcript. We can only characterize the district court proceedings of March 15 as irregular. Indeed, since no mandate had yet been issued from this court to the district court, the various orders, directions to parties, suggestions to the Governor of Minnesota, members of Congress, and the Minnesota State Legislature, and all other actions taken by the trial judge at these proceedings are a complete nullity. Until we issue our mandate, the district court lacks jurisdiction over these cases. . . .

"We have an additional concern over the actions of the district court judge at that hearing. The judge initiated steps which appear to be in conflict with the express language of this court's opinion of March 14, 1975. Moreover, the district court judge and counsel for certain of the plaintiffs suggested in that hearing that Reserve Mining Company will be able to continue its present discharges for seven to ten years as a consequence of our modification of the district court's injunction. We made no such prediction nor authorized any unnecessary delay in abatement of air and water discharges.[1]

"We recognize that by March 15 insufficient time had elapsed from the issuance of our opinion for the district court judge and counsel to study and reflect on all matters covered in it. This lack of time may explain but it does not excuse conduct, statements, or requests for and the issuance of orders contrary to this court's opinion.

"Because of the nature of the March 15 proceedings, we deem it necessary to advise the trial judge and counsel for all parties, including intervenors, that they must respect the letter and spirit of our opinion as incorporated in the mandate of this court. . . . Neither the district court nor any party is free to ignore our determinations, including the determination that "[t]he resolution of the controversy over an on land disposal site does not fall within the jurisdiction of the federal courts[,]" . . . . We think it inappropriate to characterize such a determination as "advisory" or dictum. Until modified by us or reversed or modified by the Supreme Court, our opinion governs the rights and obligations of the parties and all intervenors.

1. "See our opinion of March 14, 1975. In light of the comments which surfaced at this March 15 hearing, we think it appropriate to note that during oral argument before us on December 9, 1974, Reserve stated that following approval by the State of the tailings disposal site now proposed, it could complete construction of new facilities in three years or less. We also understand that partial abatement of discharges into Lake Superior would take place in advance of such construction completion date. Reserve also represented during this oral argument that it could begin installing air pollution control equipment on existing facilities immediately. The initiation of this timetable in part now depends upon action yet to be taken by the State of Minnesota on Reserve's application for a disposal site."

"We expect and insist that our mandate be carried out promptly, fairly, efficiently, and without deviation from its letter and spirit. See Cascade Natural Gas Corp. v. El Paso Natural Gas Co., 386 U.S. 129, 136 (1967). Furthermore, the district court judge should not interfere in matters concerning the parties which lie outside his jurisdiction in these cases.

"Finally, we believe it is appropriate to caution counsel that although each may be an adversary with regard to opposing parties, all serve as officers of the court and all are bound to respect and follow the law as laid down by a final appellate judgment in this case.

"We direct that a copy of this order be incorporated into and made a part of the judgment on remand."

IV. The Supreme Court and Interlocutory Relief

The Supreme Court's role in deciding particular lawsuits is minute. That Court exists to refine our jurisprudence and to guide lower courts, lawyers, and the public. Moreover, fast-paced injunctive litigation will usually have spent its force before it reaches the Court. Nonetheless, the Court and the Justices must grapple with issues of interlocutory relief similar to those confronted by the courts of appeals. First, its jurisdiction over the decisions of state courts is confined to "final judgments or decree." Organization for a Better Austin v. Keefe asks whether it can review interlocutory injunctions issued by a state court. Second, like any appellate tribunal, the Court will be asked to stay or enjoin pending appeal. These orders may allow the Court to preserve the opportunity to discharge its appellate functions, whether that be to declare constitutional doctrine, to protect especially perishable constitutional rights, or to supervise those lower courts adjudicating federal rights. Third, as in *Pentagon Papers,* Carroll v. Princess Anne, and the free speech cases that follow, the Court must consider whether interlocutory relief is consistent with certain, especially time-bound constitutional rights.

For general overviews of the Supreme Court practice on interlocutory relief, we especially recommend C. Wright, Federal Courts, chap. 12 (4th ed. 1983); and R. L. Stern & E. Gressman, Supreme Court Practice, chap. 2 (5th ed. 1978). Several of the Court's rules are in our Appendix.

ORGANIZATION FOR A BETTER AUSTIN v. KEEFE

402 U.S. 415, 91 S.Ct. 1575, 29 L.Ed.2d 1 (1971).

[The majority opinion, at p. 213 struck down a state court injunction against picketing and distributing pamphlets. There was, however, an issue about the jurisdiction of the Supreme Court, since the injunction was termed a "temporary injunction" and 28 U.S.C. § 1257 limits the Supreme Court review to "final judgments or decrees rendered by the highest court of a state in which a decision could be had." The majority opinion, written by Chief Justice Burger, dealt with the issue in a footnote in these terms: "The injunction is termed a 'temporary' injunction by the Illinois courts. We have therefore considered whether we may properly decide this case. 28 U.S.C. § 1257. We see nothing in the record that would indicate that the Illinois courts applied a less rigorous standard in issuing and sustaining this injunction than they would with any permanent injunction in the case. Nor is there any indication that the injunction rests on a disputed question of fact that might be resolved differently upon further hearing. Indeed, our reading of the record leads to the conclusion that the issuance of a permanent injunction upon termination of these proceedings will be little more than a formality. Moreover, the temporary injunction here, which has been in effect for over three years, has already had marked impact on petitioners' First Amendment rights. Although the record in this case is not such as to leave the matter entirely free from doubt we conclude we are not without power to decide this case."]

Justice HARLAN, dissented.

In deciding this case on the merits, the Court, in my opinion, disregards the express limitation of our appellate jurisdiction to "[f]inal judgments or decrees," 28 U.S.C. § 1257, and does so in a way which undermines the policies behind limiting our review to judgments "rendered by the highest court of a State in which a decision could be had," ibid., and interferes with Illinois' arrangements for the expeditious processing of litigation in its own state courts.

It is plain, and admitted by all, that the "temporary" or "preliminary" injunction entered by the Circuit Court of Cook County and affirmed by the Appellate Court, First District, is not a final judgment. Review of preliminary injunctions is a classic form of interlocutory appeal, which Congress has authorized in limited instances not including review by this Court of state decrees. See 28 U.S.C. §§ 1252, 1253; cf. 28 U.S.C. § 1292(a)(1). Despite the seemingly absolute provision of the statute, the Court holds that this case is within the judicially created exception for instances in which the affirmance of the interlocutory order by the highest state court decides the merits of the dispute for all practical purposes, leaving the remaining proceedings in the lower courts as nothing more than a formality. See Pope v. Atlantic Coast Line R. Co., 345 U.S. 379, 382 (1953); Construction Laborers' Local 438 v. Curry, 371 U.S. 542, 550–551 (1963); Mills v. Alabama, 384 U.S. 214, 217–218 (1966). The apparent, though unstated, justification for this is the petitioners' representation in this Court that they have no defense to offer other than their First Amendment contentions, which they assert the Illinois courts have decided against them on the merits. Pet. for Cert. 6.

Even assuming that the latter position is correct,* this case does not fit into the mold of the cases in which this Court has reviewed orders of state supreme courts affirming the grant of preliminary relief, for here the Illinois Supreme Court has never passed on the merits of petitioners' constitutional contentions. If this case were permitted to return to the trial court for con-

* . . . In argument before the Illinois chancellor, petitioners' attorney stated:

"We don't wish to go into lengthy argument on constitutional provisions at this time. We feel that it is only fair that both sides prepare briefs in preparation for a full hearing on the permanent injunction. And, to that end, we just want to point out that these are constitutional questions, on which we feel the law is abundantly clear, and that is a further reason why Your Honor in his discretion, should not see fit to issue a temporary injunction." R. 56.

sideration of the merits of petitioners' contentions and the entry of final judgment, petitioners would have an appeal as of right directly to the Illinois Supreme Court if that judgment were adverse to them. Ill.Const., Art. 6, § 5; Ill.Sup.Ct.Rules 301, 302(a). That court would then have an opportunity to correct the errors, if any, in the lower court judgment; or if it failed to do so we would have the benefit of that court's views on the issues here presented. Such review by "the highest court of a State in which a decision could be had" is particularly important in the context of Illinois procedure, which places primary responsibility for review of constitutional contentions in the State Supreme Court. All appeals from final judgments in cases involving a constitutional question must be taken directly to that court, see Ill.Sup.Ct. Rule 302(a)(2); consequently the intermediate Appellate Court rarely has occasion to engage in constitutional adjudication.

To be sure, the Illinois Supreme Court, by denying petitioners' motion for leave to appeal from the order of the Appellate Court, had an opportunity to rule on the issue presented by this case and declined to do so. However, Illinois has a strong policy against Supreme Court review of interlocutory orders. Until recently the Supreme Court had no direct appellate jurisdiction over judgments of the Appellate Court on interlocutory appeals, but simply reviewed the issues presented by the subsequent final judgment. 6 C. Nichols, Illinois Civil Practice § 5998 (1962 rev. vol. H. Williams & M. Wingersky). Although interlocutory review is now available in the discretion of the Supreme Court, it is "not favored." Ill.Sup.Ct.Rule 318(b); see also Ill.Sup. Ct.Rule 315(a). We have ourselves often made a similar resolution of the competing interests in prompt correction of lower courts' errors on the one hand and in expeditious processing of litigation to final judgment on the other. See R. Stern & E. Gressman, Supreme Court Practice § 4.19 (4th ed. 1969). Under today's decision, Illinois will have to surrender its judgment in these matters if it desires to interpose the State Supreme Court between the subordinate state courts and review by this Court, as the highest-state-court requirement permits it to do. If this Court would respect the final-judgment limitation on our jurisdiction, Illinois would not be put to this choice.

It is, of course, tempting to ignore the proper limitations on our power when the alternative is to delay correction of what the Court today holds was a flagrant error by lower courts. This is particularly true where, as here, a "temporary" injunction has been outstanding for a lengthy period. But the question is not whether we think our intervention in the dispute at this stage would be desirable—although with our overall docket running at about 4,000 cases a Term there is surely much to be said for giving each litigant only one bite at the apple. The policy judgment involved was expressly committed to Congress by Art. III, § 2, of the Constitution, and Congress has spoken in § 1257.

I would respect that congressional judgment and dismiss the writ for lack of jurisdiction.

MORELAND v. SPRECHER

443 U.S. 709, 99 S.Ct. 3086, 61 L.Ed.2d 860 (1979).

PER CURIAM.

On March 29, 1979, the District Court for the Western District of Wisconsin entered a preliminary injunction restraining petitioners from publishing or otherwise disseminating an article entitled "The H-Bomb Secret: How We Got It, Why We're Telling It." On June 21, 1979, one judge of the Court of Appeals for the Seventh Circuit denied in part petitioners' motion for an expedited hearing of their appeal. That hearing is currently set for September 10, 1979.

Petitioners seek a writ of mandamus to the Court of Appeals ordering it to expedite their appeal. They claim that parties who have been enjoined from engaging in constitutionally protected speech have a right to prompt appellate review of that injunction. See National Socialist Party v. Skokie . . . . In view of their conduct in prosecuting their appeal before the Court of Appeals, however, we conclude that petitioners have effectively relinquished whatever right they might otherwise have had to expedited consideration.

The District Court's preliminary injunction was entered on March 26, 1979, yet, petitioners waited until June 15, 1979, to file a meaningful motion for expedited review before the Court of Appeals. Prior to that time, petitioners (1) waited two weeks after the District Court entered its injunction before filing a notice of appeal, and then waited another week before proposing that the appeal be accorded special scheduling treatment; (2) in that proposal, suggested an 89-day briefing schedule that—as they knew—provided for oral argument in the case, at the earliest, 10 days after the Court of Appeals' summer recess was to begin; (3) at a subsequent prehearing conference held by the Senior Staff Attorney of the Court of Appeals, asked that the briefing and argument schedule they had originally proposed be extended by an additional three weeks, i.e., into the latter half of July; (4) participated in a second prehearing conference in which a panel of the Court of Appeals discussed scheduling with the parties, and did not object either to the briefing schedule ordered by the Court or to the September 10 hearing date; and (5) pursuant to the schedule discussed at the conference, took 81 days to file their opening brief on the merits. It was only upon the filing of that brief on June 15, 1979 (just four days before the Seventh Circuit's scheduled recess was to begin), that they sought expedition. Accordingly, as proposed by petitioners, the onus of expedition would have fallen entirely on the Government, which would have had a severely limited opportunity to respond to petitioners' opening brief, and on the Court of Appeals, whose conscientious attempts during the preceding two months—by way of two prehearing conferences and numerous additional discussions with the parties—to manage its docket in an orderly fashion, would have been frustrated.

It is true that between May 8, 1979, and June 15, 1979, petitioners were unsuccessfully seeking reconsideration by the District Court based on newly discovered information. But that information did not affect the essentials of petitioners' legal argument in favor of expedited review of the District

Court's March 26 order—i.e., that ever since the order was issued, petitioners had been operating under an allegedly unconstitutional and irreparably injurious prior restraint against the publication of information subject to First Amendment protection. Because they chose not to make that argument to the Court of Appeals until long after it had ripened, and until they had taken close to three months to prepare their own brief on the merits, petitioners forbore any right to expedition that the Constitution might otherwise have afforded them.

The motion for leave to file a petition for writ of mandamus is denied.

Justice WHITE, with whom Justice BRENNAN joins, dissenting.

It is my view that the Court of Appeals, by declining to hear arguments until the conclusion of its summer recess, has unduly delayed plenary consideration of this case. And I do not agree with my Brothers that the petitioners have forfeited whatever rights to an early hearing they might otherwise have had. Our cases indicate that the proffered justification for an injunction against publication should be considered and verified or rejected by appellate courts without unnecessary delay. See New York Times Co. v. United States . . . ; Freedman v. Maryland, 380 U.S. 51 (1965); cf. National Socialist Party of America v. Village of Skokie . . . . As I see it, the Court of Appeals should schedule a hearing herein at the earliest date that is both practicable and consistent with mature consideration of the questions involved. I would have preferred the Court to have reached and stated this conclusion and then, on the assumption that the Court of Appeals would follow this Court's suggestion, to have withheld the issuance of the writ of mandamus. See Connor v. Coleman, 440 U.S. 612 (1979); Connor v. Coleman, 425 U.S. 675, 679 (1976); Bucolo v. Adkins, 424 U.S. 641, 644 (1976); Deen v. Hickman, 358 U.S. 57, 58 (1958); cf. National Socialist Party of America v. Village of Skokie; . . . Nebraska Press Association v. Stuart, 423 U.S., at 1325–1326. Of course, with or without advancement of the hearing schedule in the Court of Appeals, the petitioners, pursuant to 28 U.S.C. § 1254(1), may request this Court to grant certiorari prior to judgment in the Court of Appeals.

TIMES–PICAYUNE PUBLISHING CORP. v. SCHULINGKAMP

419 U.S. 1301, 95 S.Ct. 1, 42 L.Ed.2d 17 (1974).

Justice POWELL, Circuit Justice.

This is an application for stay of an order of the Louisiana Criminal District Court for the Parish of Orleans restricting media coverage of the trials of two defendants accused of committing a highly publicized rape and murder in the city of New Orleans. The applicant, a Louisiana corporation that owns and publishes two of the city's daily newspapers, has asked that I stay that order pending filing and disposition of a petition for a writ of certiorari in this Court. Respondent, the Honorable Oliver P. Schulingkamp, has at my request filed a memorandum in opposition to the application. The record before me indicates a substantial possibility that the state court's order is inconsistent with this Court's decisions governing prior restraint of the news media and that continuance of the order pending consideration of a petition for a writ of certiorari would inflict irreparable harm. I therefore have granted the requested stay.

In April 1973, a young white nursing student was raped and murdered following her visit to an elderly patient living in one of the city's public housing projects. Shortly thereafter, two Negro suspects were arrested and charged with the crime. The case immediately became the focal point in the media for a number of more generalized concerns. The state university program that prompted the student's unescorted visit to the housing project was called into sharp question, as was the sufficiency of law enforcement efforts in high-crime areas of New Orleans. The case also occasioned criticism of the criminal and juvenile justice systems.

Much of the initial publicity was directed toward one defendant, a 17-year-old with an apparently extensive history of juvenile offenses. Newspaper stories recounted in some detail the circumstances leading to his arrest and his subsequent alleged disclosure of the location where the victim's body was recovered. Additionally, stories dwelt on his prior juvenile offenses. Almost all of the many newspaper references characterized him as a youth with a history of 43 juvenile arrests, the accuracy of which has since been disputed. Some newspaper accounts referred to his previous arrest on charges of murder and armed robbery without simultaneously revealing that those charges had been dropped for insufficient evidence. Others reported a psychiatric diagnosis of this defendant made several years earlier and apparently contained in the records of the juvenile probation officer.

Within a few days reports concerning the crime, the accused, and other related concerns ceased to be of banner importance. Stories became shorter and began to move from the first page to less prominent positions in the papers. Newspaper coverage appears to have ceased within some 10 days of the arrest and the papers apparently published no stories about the defendants from the latter part of April until late January of the following year, when one subdued story announced the anticipated initiation of pretrial motions in the case.

Some of the newspaper reporting that occurred in April can hardly be characterized as responsible journalism. Like many States, Louisiana maintains the confidentiality of the records of juvenile offenders. La.Rev.Stat. Ann. § 13:1586.3 (Supp.1974). The record does not indicate how reporters came into possession of some of their information. Additionally, there appear to be inaccuracies or partial truths in matters that are of obvious importance.

In March 1974, some 11 months after the crime and attendant extensive publicity, counsel for the defendant who had received the most journalistic attention moved that the Criminal District Court for the Parish of Orleans impose restrictions on reporting of the case. The court granted the motion on June 17, 1974. The court's order imposes a total ban on reporting of testimony given in hearings on pretrial motions until after the selection of the jury and also places other selective restrictions on reporting before and during trial.

At the time the order was issued, the court apparently contemplated only one trial. By its terms the order was to remain in effect until termination of the trial. The court later severed the defendants' cases and ordered separate trials of the rape and murder charges against each. It made no modification of its media coverage order to reflect this changed circumstance. The applicant has represented that the court stated that the order would remain in effect until the termination of the last trial. Respondent has not contradicted this representation, and I assume it to be correct.

The applicant sought relief from both the lower federal courts and the state court system prior to addressing this application to me. After failing to obtain immediate injunctive relief from the federal courts,[2] the applicant asked the state court to vacate its order. That request was denied, as was a request that the court stay its order pending submission of application for supervisory and remedial writs in the Louisiana Supreme Court. On July 9, 1974, the applicant sought writs of certiorari, review, prohibition, and mandamus, and a stay of the state trial court's order in the Louisiana Supreme Court. That same day the Louisiana Supreme Court denied relief by a vote of four to three, stating that the "[s]howing made does not justify the relief demanded." Following one more unsuccessful attempt to obtain an injunction in the United States District Court, the applicant has requested that I, as Circuit Justice for the Fifth Circuit, stay the state court's order pending this Court's consideration of a petition for a writ of certiorari.

I have previously expressed my reluctance, in considering in-chambers stay applications, to substitute my view for that of other courts that are closer to the relevant factual considerations that so often are critical to the proper resolution of these questions. Graves v. Barnes, 405 U.S. 1201, 1203 (1972). In my in-chambers opinion in that case, I articulated the general standards governing the grant of a stay application: there must be a reasonable probability that four members of the Court would consider the underlying issue sufficiently meritorious for the grant of certiorari or the notation of probable jurisdiction; there must be a significant possibility of reversal of the lower court's decision; and there must be a likelihood that irreparable harm will result if that decision is not stayed.

The question of the possibility of irreparable harm is particularly troublesome in this case. It presents a fundamental confrontation between the competing values of free press and fair trial, with significant public and private interests balanced on both sides. If the order is not stayed, the press is subjected to substantial prior restraint with respect to a case of widespread concern in the community. If, on the other hand, the order is stayed and the press fails to act with scrupulous responsibility, the defendants' constitutional right to a fair trial may be seriously endangered.

The challenged portions of the order of the Criminal District Court for the Parish of Orleans impose a total prohibition on publication of testimony adduced in pretrial hearings until after selection of a jury. Noting that extensive testimony would be required in considering the many pretrial motions, including motions to suppress an alleged confession and other evi-

2. The United States District Court conducted a hearing at which it heard argument of counsel and the testimony of the respondent herein. Thereafter, the court determined that it should abstain from interfering with the state proceedings at that stage. The applicant noted an appeal from that decision and requested that the United States Court of Appeals for the Fifth Circuit stay the state court order pending appeal. A panel of the Fifth Circuit denied the request for a stay. Neither of these decisions is before me today.

dence, the court specifically ordered "that the reporting of such testimony be deferred until after the jury has been selected in order to preclude the possibility of such testimony influencing, in any way, prospective jurors yet to be selected, and rendering more difficult the task of selecting said jurors." In addition, the state court order imposes other selective restrictions on what may be published both before and during trial. These restrictions are aimed at the content of news reporting. The order requires that the media avoid publication of interviews with subpoenaed witnesses. It also prohibits publication of any of the defendants' criminal records or discreditable acts or of any possible confessions or inculpatory statements unless made part of the evidence in the court record. The order forbids publication of any testimony stricken by the court unless identified as having been stricken and bars publication of any leaks, statements, or conclusions of guilt or innocence that might be expressed or implied by statements of the police, prosecuting attorneys, or defense counsel. Finally, the order prohibits any editiorial comment preceding or during trial "which tends to influence the Court, jury, or witnesses." By its terms, the order remains in effect "until the conclusion of the trial." The court's decision to continue the order during pendency of all of the trials ensures that it will extend over an indefinite and possibly lengthy period of time.

The court's order imposes significant prior restraints on media publication. As such, it would come to this Court " 'bearing a heavy presumption against its constitutional validity.' " New York Times Co. v. United States; Organization for a Better Austin v. Keefe; Bantam Books, Inc. v. Sullivan, 372 U.S. 58, 70 (1963); Near v. Minnesota ex rel. Olson. Decisions of this Court repeatedly have recognized that trials are public events. See, e.g., Sheppard v. Maxwell, 384 U.S. 333, 349–350 (1966); Estes v. Texas, 381 U.S. 532, 541 (1965); Craig v. Harney, 331 U.S. 367, 374 (1947). And "reporters . . . are plainly free to report whatever occurs in open court through their respective media." Estes v. Texas, 381 U.S. at 541–542.

This Court also has shown a special solicitude for preserving fairness in a criminal trial. "Legal trials are not like elections, to be won through the use of the meeting hall, the radio, and the newspaper." Bridges v. California, 314 U.S. 252, 271 (1941). The task of reconciling First Amendment rights with the defendant's right to a fair trial before an impartial jury is not an easy one. This Court has observed in dictum that newsmen might be prohibited from publishing information about trials if such restrictions were necessary to assure a defendant a fair trial. Branzburg v. Hayes, 408 U.S. 665, 685 (1972). There was no indication in that opinion, however, that the standards for determining the propriety of resort to such action would materially differ from those applied in other decisions involving prior restraints of speech and publication.

I need only consider this question in the limited context of an application for a stay. On the record before me, and certainly in the absence of any showing of an imminent threat to fair trial, I cannot say that the order of the state court would withstand the limitations that this Court has applied in determining the propriety of prior restraints on publication. Cf. United States v. Dickinson. The state court was properly concerned that the type of news coverage described above might be resumed and might threaten the defendants' rights to a fair trial. But the restraints it has imposed are both pervasive and of uncertain duration. They include limitations on the timing as well as the content of media publication, cf. Miami Herald Publishing Co. v. Tornillo, 418 U.S. 241 (1974). Moreover, the court has available alternative means for protecting the defendants' rights to a fair trial.[3]

The issues underlying this case are important and difficult. Without anticipating my views on the merits, I have concluded that this application satisfies the standards for the grant of a stay. Accordingly, I have decided to stay that portion of the order of the Louisiana Criminal District Court that imposes direct limitations on media reporting pending the timely filing and disposition of a petition for a writ of certiorari in this Court.[4]

---

1) Subsequent decisions vindicate the view Justice Powell took in *Times-Picayune.* Oklahoma Publishing Co. v. District Court, 430 U.S. 308 (1977) (per curiam); Nebraska Press Association v. Stuart, 427 U.S. 539 (1976). A Justice's stay may be as effective to end the controversy as a court of appeals stay. Should the Supreme Court let the trial judge's order remain in effect if that means deciding the newspaper's appeal after the trial? Would the end of the trial moot the newspaper's appeal? The Court in *Nebraska Press* said no. Did the Court write an opinion without deciding the lawsuit? What if a Justice "stays" the effectiveness of a trial judge's order not to publish, the newspaper publishes, and when the full Court considers the order it decides that the trial judge was right? Should the chagrined Court decide this lawsuit without writing an opinion? Rendleman, Free Press—Fair Trial: Restrictive Orders After *Nebraska Press,* 67 Ky.L.J. 867, 885–88 (1979).

3. The court has already invoked several of these procedures. For example, portions of the court's order prohibit members of the bar and other persons under the court's supervision and control from making extrajudicial statements prior to the termination of trial. These prohibitions are not challenged here. Additionally, respondent has indicated his intention to sequester the juries. This will protect against many of the hazards that the selective restrictions on reporting during trial are designed to prevent.

Some other options may yet be used to protect the defendants' rights. The defendant who sought the order apparently did not request that the pretrial hearings be closed to the public and press, and the court does not seem to have contemplated that possibility. As an initial matter, the court's power to take such action is a question governed by state law. Unlike some States, Louisiana does not appear to have a specific provision authorizing such action. Cf. Cal.Penal Code § 868 (1970); Iowa Code § 761.13 (1973); Mont. Rev.Codes Ann. § 95–1202(c) (1969). This Court has not been called upon to determine whether these provisions are constitutional, and I express no view on that question. Of course, the court must conduct *voir dire* of the prospective jurors in these cases with particular care. Finally, the court retains the power to hold persons, including members of the media, in contempt in particular limited circumstances. See Craig v. Harney, 331 U.S. 337 (1947); Pennekamp v. Florida, 328 U.S. 331 (1946); Bridges v. California, 314 U.S. 252 (1941).

4. The applicant has not questioned the portions of the court's order that relate to the conduct of other persons, and this stay order does not affect them. My order is limited to the portion of the respondent's order directed specifically to the news media. It does not, however, stay the portion of the court's order prohibiting the use of electronic or mechanical equipment within the court during the trial or related proceedings.

The Reporters Committee for Freedom of the Press and the Vieux Carre Courier Publishing Co., as *amici curiae,* have requested additionally that I enjoin any court proceeding about which the press is prohibited from reporting pending final disposition of this case on the merits. I find that action to be unwarranted and unwise.

2) Remember that the stays in *Pentagon Papers*, p. 217, prevented publication pending a final decision. Was the stay each day in retrospect a final, incorrect decision? How did Justices Black and Harlan react to the stay?

NATIONAL SOCIALIST PARTY OF AMERICA ET AL. v. VILLAGE OF SKOKIE

432 U.S. 43, 97 S.Ct. 2205, 53 L.Ed.2d 96 (1977).

June 14, 1977

PER CURIAM.

On April 29, 1977, the Circuit Court of Cook County entered an injunction against petitioners. The injunction prohibited them from performing any of the following actions within the village of Skokie, Ill.: "[m]arching, walking or parading in the uniform of the National Socialist Party of America; [m]arching, walking or parading or otherwise displaying the swastika on or off their person; [d]istributing pamphlets or displaying any materials which incite or promote hatred against persons of Jewish faith or ancestry or hatred against persons of any faith or ancestry, race or religion." The Illinois Appellate Court denied an application for stay pending appeal. Applicants then filed a petition for a stay in the Illinois Supreme Court, together with a request for a direct expedited appeal to that court. The Illinois Supreme Court denied both the stay and leave for an expedited appeal. Applicants then filed an application for a stay with Mr. Justice Stevens, as Circuit Justice, who referred the matter to the Court.

Treating the application as a petition for certiorari from the order of the Illinois Supreme Court, we grant certiorari and reverse the Illinois Supreme Court's denial of a stay. That order is a final judgment for purposes of our jurisdiction, since it involved a right "separable from, and collateral to" the merits, Cohen v. Beneficial Loan Corp., 337 U.S. 541, 546 (1949). See Abney v. United States, 431 U.S. 651 (1977); cf. Cox Broadcasting Corp. v. Cohn, 420 U.S. 469, 476–487 (1975). It finally determined the merits of petitioners' claim that the outstanding injunction will deprive them of rights protected by the First Amendment during the period of appellate review which, in the normal course, may take a year or more to complete. If a State seeks to impose a restraint of this kind, it must provide strict procedural safeguards, Freedman v. Maryland, 380 U.S. 51 (1965), including immediate appellate review, see Nebraska Press Assn. v. Stuart, 423 U.S. 1319, 1327 (1975) (Blackmun, J., in chambers). Absent such review, the State must instead allow a stay. The order of the Illinois Supreme Court constituted a denial of that right.

Reversed and remanded for further proceedings not inconsistent with this opinion.

Justice REHNQUIST, with whom THE CHIEF JUSTICE and Justice STEWART join, dissenting.

The Court treats an application filed here to stay a judgment of the Circuit Court of Cook County as a petition for certiorari to review the refusal of the Supreme Court of Illinois to stay the injunction. It summarily reverses this refusal of a stay. I simply do not see how the refusal of the Supreme Court of Illinois to stay an injunction granted by an inferior court within the state system can be described as a "[f]inal judgmen[t] or decre[e] rendered by the highest court of a State in which a decision could be had," which is the limitation that Congress has imposed on our jurisdiction to review state-court judgments under 28 U.S.C. § 1257. Cox Broadcasting Corp. v. Cohn, 420 U.S. 469, 476–487 (1975), relied upon by the Court, which surely took as liberal a view of this jurisdictional grant as can reasonably be taken, does not support the result reached by the Court here. In *Cox* there had been a final decision on the federal claim by the Supreme Court of Georgia, which was the highest court of that State in which such a decision could be had. Here all the Supreme Court of Illinois has done is, in the exercise of the discretion possessed by every appellate court, to deny a stay of a lower court ruling pending appeal. No Illinois appellate court has heard or decided the merits of applicants' federal claim.

I do not disagree with the Court that the provisions of the injunction issued by the Circuit Court of Cook County are extremely broad, and I would expect that if the Illinois appellate courts follow cases such as Freedman v. Maryland, 380 U.S. 51 (1965), and Nebraska Press Assn. v. Stuart, 423 U.S. 1319 (1975), relied upon by the Court, the injunction will be at least substantially modified by them. But I do not believe that in the long run respect for the Constitution or for the law is encouraged by actions of this Court which disregard the limitations placed on us by Congress in order to assure that an erroneous injunction issued by a state trial court does not wrongly interfere with the constitutional rights of those enjoined.

NATIONAL SOCIALIST PARTY OF AMERICA v. VILLAGE OF SKOKIE

434 U.S. 1327, 98 S.Ct. 14, 54 L.Ed.2d 38 (1977).

Aug. 26, 1977.

Justice STEVENS, Circuit Justice.

Following the entry of this Court's order of June 14, 1977, the Illinois Appellate Court reviewed and substantially modified the injunction entered against applicants by the Circuit Court of Cook County, upholding only that portion of the injunction that prevented applicants from displaying the swastika "in the course of a demonstration, march or parade." Thereafter, the Illinois Supreme Court scheduled an expedited review of the Appellate Court's decision, but it denied an application for a stay of the injunction pending that review. On August 18, 1977, a similar application was submitted to me as Circuit Justice. I requested a response from the village of Skokie and have now decided to deny the application.

Applicants have not demonstrated that a stay is necessary to protect this Court's appellate jurisdiction. There appears to be no danger that the controversy will become moot while the appeal is pending in the Illinois Supreme Court. Nor have applicants demonstrated that the Illinois courts have failed to comply with the "immediate appellate review" requirement of this Court's order of June 14, 1977. After the entry of that order, both the Illinois Appellate Court and the Illinois Supreme Court expedited their consideration of the case, and I am confident that the Illinois Supreme Court will make its decision without any unnecessary delay. Even "immediate" appellate review of an important and difficult issue necessitates appropriate deliberation. Considering these facts, the fact that the injunction has been substantially modified, and the fact that the entry of the stay would be tantamount to a decision on the merits in favor of the applicants, it seems clear that a stay should not be granted.

The application submitted to me as Circuit Justice is denied.

---

1) David Goldberger, the Illinois Civil Liberties Union attorney who represented the Nazis in *Skokie*, describes the lawsuits in Skokie: The First Amendment Under Attack by its Friends, 29 Mercer L.Rev. 761 (1978).

2) Does the *Skokie* opinion grow out of the unstated premise that the injunction is unconstitutionally broad? Does the prompt appellate review *Skokie* mandates cut across the grain of our appellate process? Has the Court subordinated correctness to promptness? Does *Skokie* favor deciding particular controversies over creating a body of precedent? Free Press—Fair Trial, 67 Ky.L.J. at 883–85.

3) The Court has accelerated other decisions. In Oklahoma Publishing Co. v. District Court, 430 U.S. 308 (1977), after an order banning publication took ten weeks to reach decision in the state supreme court, the Court stayed, pending a timely certiorari petition, before simultaneously granting certiorari and reversing per curiam.

Snepp v. United States, 444 U.S. 507 (1980), was more controversial. We discussed the prior restraint issue above p. 241, and we return to the jury trial question below. Both Snepp and the United States asked the Supreme Court to review the court of appeals decision. That decision allowed the government to recover punitive damages from Snepp for publishing despite his contract with the CIA. The Court granted both petitions for certiorari and, without briefs and arguments, held that a constructive trust was the government's proper remedy. Three Justices dissented. Why expedite review in *Snepp?*

SCHLESINGER v. HOLTZMAN

414 U.S. 1321, 94 S.Ct. 11, 38 L.Ed.2d 33 (1973).

Justice MARSHALL, Circuit Justice.

On August 1, 1973, I, as Circuit Justice for the Second Circuit, denied an application to vacate a stay, 414 U.S. 1304, entered by the United States Court of Appeals for the Second Circuit on July 27, 1973, staying the order of the District Court for the Eastern District of New York dated July 25, 1973.

On August 2, Elizabeth Holtzman and others, plaintiffs in the original action, presented an application to Mr. Justice Douglas. A hearing was then set in Yakima, Washington, on Friday, August 3. On August 3, an order was issued by Mr. Justice Douglas, vacating the stay entered by the Court of Appeals on July 27, 1973, and thereby reinstating the order of the United States District Court for the Eastern District of New York.

On August 4, the Solicitor General presented an application for a stay of the order of the United States District Court for the Eastern District of New York. [This opinion is dated August 4.]

Since the action of the Court of Appeals in granting a stay is set aside, the only order extant in this case is the order of the District Court dated July 25, 1973. The instant application calls on me to deal directly with that order of the District Court.

In the ordinary course, a Justice acting as a Circuit Justice would defer acting with respect to a District Court order until the Court of Appeals had acted, but in the present circumstances the Court of Appeals has already acted and the consequence of the order of Mr. Justice Douglas is to set aside the Court of Appeals order.

The consequence of the Court of Appeals' stay order of August 1, 1973, was to preserve the status quo until it could act on the merits. The Court of Appeals, having originally expedited a hearing on the merits to August 13, 1973, has since further expedited the hearing on the merits to August 8, 1973.

Now therefore, the order of the District Court dated July 25, 1973, is hereby stayed pending further order by this Court.

I have been in communication with the other Members of the Court, and The Chief Justice, Mr. Justice Brennan, Mr. Justice Stewart, Mr. Justice White, Mr. Justice Blackmun, Mr. Justice Powell, and Mr. Justice Rehnquist agree with this action.

Mr. Justice DOUGLAS (dissenting). . . . My order of August 3, 1973, reads as follows:

"ORDER

"On application of petitioners and after oral argument it is ordered:

"(1) that the stay of the District Court's order entered by the Court of Appeals on July 27, 1973 is vacated and

"(2) that the order of the District Court of July 25, 1973 enjoining Defendants from participating in any way in military activities in or over Cambodia or releasing any bombs which may fall on Cambodia is hereby restored.

"W. O. Douglas

"August 3, 1973."

My Brother Marshall in his opinion of August 4, 1973, misstates the facts when he says that "the only order extant in this case is the order of the District Court." A correct statement would be that the most recent order in this case was my order of August 3, 1973, reinstating the order of the District Court, which would thus leave the Court of Appeals free to act on the merits and give full relief or, alternatively, permit this Court to reverse me. Under my Brother Marshall's order of August 4, 1973, only this Court can act to give injunctive relief.[1]

1. The Court takes a bite out of the merits, for the order of August 4, 1973, bars the Court of Appeals from reinstating the judgment of the District Court until and unless this Court acts, as the order states that the order of the District Court "is hereby stayed pending further order by this Court."

The Court has unquestioned power to reverse me; and although I disagree with the Court's action on the merits, that is not the point of this dissent. If we who impose law and order are ourselves to be bound by law and order, we can act as a Court only when at least six of us are present. That is the requirement of the Act of Congress; [2] and heretofore it has been the practice to summon the Court to Special Term. Seriatim telephone calls cannot, with all respect, be a lawful substitute. A Conference brings us all together; views are exchanged; briefs are studied; oral argument by counsel for each side is customarily required. But even without participation the Court always acts in Conference and therefore responsibly.

Those of the Brethren out of Washington, D.C., on August 4, 1973, could not possibly have studied my opinion in this case. For, although I wrote it late on August 3, it was not released until 9:30 a.m. on August 4; and before 3 p.m., August 4, I was advised by telephone that eight Members of the Court disagreed with me. The issue tendered in the case was not frivolous; the Government on oral argument conceded as much. It involved a new point of law never yet resolved by the Court. I have participated for enough years in Conferences to realize that profound changes are made among the Brethren once their minds are allowed to explore a problem in depth. Yet there were only a few of the Brethren who saw my opinion before they took contrary action.

Whatever may be said on the merits, I am firmly convinced that the telephonic disposition of this grave and crucial constitutional issue is not permissible. I do not speak of social propriety. It is a matter of law and order involving high principles. The principles are that the Court is a deliberative body that acts only on reasoned bases after full consideration, and that it is as much bound by the law of the land as is he who lives in the ghetto or in the big white house on the hill. With all respect, I think the Court has slighted that law. The shortcut it has taken today surely flouts an Act of Congress providing for a necessary quorum. A Gallup Poll type of inquiry of widely scattered Justices is, I think, a subversion of the regime under which I thought we lived.

One Justice, who grants bail, issues a stay of a mandate, or issues a certificate of probable cause cannot under the statutory regime designed by Congress vacate, modify, or reverse what another Justice does.[3] The Court, of course, can do so—and only the Court [4]—but when the Court acts it must have six Members present.

2. "The Supreme Court of the United States shall consist of a Chief Justice of the United States and eight associate justices, any six of whom shall constitute a quorum." 28 U.S.C. § 1.

3. The statutes authorizing individual Justices of this Court to affirmatively grant applications for such actions do not authorize them to rescind affirmative action taken by another Justice. See, e.g., 28 U.S.C. § 2101(f) (stays of mandate); 28 U.S.C. § 2241(a) (writs of habeas corpus); 18 U.S.C. § 3141 and Fed.Rule Crim.Proc. 46(a)(2) (granting of bail).

4. This requirement of collegial action is confirmed by the Rules of this Court and by this Court's prior decisions and practices.

Rules 50 and 51 govern the in-chambers practices of the Court. Rule 50(5) provides that, when one Justice denies an application made to him, the party who has made the unsuccessful application may renew it to any other Justice. It was pursuant to this Rule that application for the stay in this case was made to me. But neither Rule 50 nor Rule 51 authorizes a party, once a stay has been

Under the law as it is written, the order of Mr. Justice Marshall of August 4, 1973, will in time be reversed by that Higher Court which invariably sits in judgment on the decisions of this Court. . . . Therefore, I respectfully dissent.

---

1) After Justice Marshall denied the stay on August 1, Justice Douglas granted it. Was Justice Douglas acting properly? Should the plaintiffs be allowed to shop for a stay?

2) Did Justice Marshall outfox Justice Douglas? Did Justice Marshall "vacate, modify, or reverse" Justice Douglas's order? Or did Justice Marshall stay the district court order? Could Justice Douglas have prevented Justice Marshall's last move?

3) This lawsuit was part of the movement to stop the Viet Nam war. In the early summer of 1973, Congress forbade the expenditure of funds for combat activities in Cambodia after August 15. President Nixon signed the bill but escalated combat in Cambodia asserting that Congress had approved combat before August 15. Congresswoman Holtzman sued to stop combat activity in Cambodia.

Does this background shed any light on the propriety of Justice Marshall's actions? Justice Douglas's? Is procedure independent of substance? Has Justice Douglas's "Higher Court" spoken? Did the proceedings to impeach Nixon and his resignation vindicate Justice Douglas?

4) On August 8, the parties argued the appeal from the district judge's injunction before the court of appeals. The court of appeals reversed and ordered the complaint dismissed on the ground that the issue was not justiciable. The court announced its opinion late in the afternoon of the 8th; a published opinion followed later. Holtzman v. Schlesinger, 484 F.2d 1307 (2d Cir. 1973). Judge Oakes dissented.

granted, to contest that action before another individual Justice.

The Court has previously deemed it necessary and proper to meet together in Special Term before stays granted by an individual Justice out of Term could be overturned. In Rosenberg v. United States, 346 U.S. 273, the full Court felt constrained to consider its power to vacate a stay issued by an individual Justice, finally resting that power on the Court's position—as a body—as final interpreter of the law. . . .

Finally, it is our procedure during a Term of Court to take an application that has already been denied or acted upon by one of the Justices to the entire Court upon an application made by the opposing side, so that the entire Court can act and thus prevent "shopping around." That course is not possible during recess when the Justices are scattered around the country and throughout the world. Therefore it has been my practice if I grant a stay during recess to make that stay effective only until the Court convenes in October. This course could not be followed in the instant case because after August 15, 1973, the case will be moot.

Chapter Eight

PROCEDURES FOR GRANTING AND MODIFYING PERMANENT INJUNCTIONS

This chapter is concerned with two distinguishing features of the injunctive process. One is the absence of the jury in the issuance of injunctions. The other is requests to modify or dissolve an injunction already issued, either to make the injunction more effective or to relieve the defendant of various obligations because of changed circumstances.

I. Juryless Equity

The civil jury remains central to any discussion of legal and equitable remedies. The seventh amendment states that in "suits at common law where the value in controversy shall exceed twenty dollars, the right of trial by jury shall be preserved." Judges decide equitable issues without juries because equitable issues are not deemed "suits at common law."

Opponents of particular exercises of equitable power have focused on the absence of a jury. Colonial Americans associated Chancery with foreign and authoritarian institutions, the King and the Council. Many of the states in the new United States did without equity; others tinkered with equity juries. Van Hecke, Trial By Jury in Equity Cases, 31 N.C.L.Rev. 157 (1953). Critics of the labor injunction attacked the absence of a jury for both the injunction and contempt. F. Frankfurter & N. Greene, The Labor Injunction 189–97 (1930).

The dialogue about the civil jury will be with us for some time. One of the editors summarized the basic positions:

"An ideological debate about the lay jury rings through Anglo-American legal history. Defenders of the jury view it as expressing a Rousseauian 'collective earthy wisdom,' a natural sense of fairness based on shared morality. Staunch believers in the jury emphasize the people, political freedom, citizen participation in government, and the need to adjust the law's harsh strictures to human realities. . . .

"Detractors of the jury stress judicial expertise and intellectual consistency. 'To overrate the function of the jury (or other trier of the facts),' Professer Griswold wrote, 'is to shirk the function of the court, and to fail to administer justice rationally, consistently, and soundly.' Detractors perceive the argument for the jury to be ephemeral and illusory rhetoric, a cloak for mean-spirited prejudice. They agree, however, that the jury represents the community. A premise opposed to decisions based on majority sentiment appears. What a jury approves or disapproves, a community approves or disapproves; and the 'town meeting' may become a plebicite or, at worst, a lynch mob. Racial issues have proved particularly intractable, perhaps because 'the concept of an impartial trial by one's peers did not originate in a country containing visually distinct racial and national groups one of which had not been the peers but the slaves of the other.' . . .

"Practical questions about the jury's role cut to the core of the type of society we desire to create and maintain. In a pluralistic society, tension, change, and conflict are inevitable. The adjudicatory process simply reflects society. Contemporary jury issues grow out of present controversies. In a complex, pluralistic, and law-laden society, a civil jury as a miniature legislature may soften the substantive law's impact, but we purport to be governed by a democratically elected legislature and to live under a judicially construed constitution. Serious questions arise when a jury, or even one juror, creates regional or individual variations in substantive law developed by courts and legislatures. To ensure that litigants receive their just desserts, must the process appear capricious, arbitrary, and irresponsible?"

Rendleman, Chapters of the Civil Jury, 65 Ky.L.J. 769, 794, 796, 797 (1977).

To compound matters, your editors do not agree completely about the jury's role; their disagreement emerges in their analysis of the inadequacy prerequisite, which, it is said, protects the jury's domain from equitable encroachment. Professor Fiss argues that neither the prerequisite nor juryless equity are inevitable:

"The relationship between the injunction and the right to trial by jury is the product of a threefold historical accident: (a) Two independent legal systems developed in England, the common law courts and Chancery, and one of them, Chancery, did not recognize a jury trial right. It could be expected that Chancery would not utilize the jury, but there is no functional explanation of why there had to be two legal systems, why the dispensation (equity) function of Chancery could not be integrated into the existing legal system. (b) The injunction was used only by the Chancery, the legal system in which there was no jury trial right. The injunction could (also) have been an instrument of the common law courts, the ones that did recognize a jury trial right. (c) The American Constitution did not aspire to create a jury trial right afresh or to expand it beyond the English bounds, but rather sought to codify the English practice as it then existed, thereby freezing into the American jury trial right the late eighteenth-century English distinction between law and equity.

"I emphasize the accidental character of this relationship not to deny its reality, but rather to deny its inevitability. The relationship between the jury trial right and the injunction could be altered. The jury could be integrated into the injunctive process. This is relevant for our purposes for it means that the absence of the jury trial cannot be the defect that justifies the subordination of the injunction. If the absence of the jury were really perceived as a defect, we could integrate it into the injunctive process, and the failure to do so should not count as a reason for subordinating the injunction, but rather should be read as a sign, along with others, of an ambivalence toward the jury right. . . .

"The jury can be easily integrated with the reparative injunction since it is like an in-kind damage judgment. But additional problems arise with the preventive injunction, and even more with the structural one. The jury would have to design the decree, and, in the structural context, continuously modify that design in light of the defendant's performance and changed conditions.

"This objection to integration might be muted if a bifurcated procedure were employed—letting the jury decide whether the substantive right was violated, and letting the judge design the decree. But such a scheme would be subject to an objection that I consider to be sound, namely that it incorrectly presupposes too clear a distinction between violation and remedy. The remedy and violation are interdependent. A judgment about violation should reflect, and in fact does reflect, a judgment about remedy. Accordingly, we must confront the possibility that the jury will decide not just whether an injunction should issue, but also what its terms should be.

"Such a scheme would of course put a new strain on the jury, and yet I do not regard the tasks as unmanageable. The lay status of the jury could be compensated for by fuller evidentiary presentations on the remedy; such presentations might include testimony of experts, and they could be structured and interpreted by judicial instructions. The group nature of the jury would not preclude its use in designing the decree: most statutes are drafted by committee. Admittedly, the structural decree would require a single jury to remain in existence for a long period of time—that would be an onerous burden but not an impossible one, as reference to grand jury practice reveals.

"The truth of the matter is, once again, that this integration of the jury into the injunctive process will not occur . . . . The constitutional preference for the jury is at its weakest in the issuance phase. This is in part due to the fact that at issue is a second right: assuming the jury trial right is honored in the enforcement phase, as it surely is with criminal contempt, then the demand for the jury in the issuance phase is in essence a demand for a second jury. The constitutional preference for the jury is not that strong.

"The weakness of the preference for the jury in the issuance phase also stems from the fact that it entails the promulgation of future standards of conduct, and in those matters there seems little demand for a jury. This is not true for reparative injunctions since the command is roughly analogous to the command to pay money damages but is true for the structural injunction, which does not have a ready comparison in traditional legal domains, where the jury is found. Its closest analog may be found in administrative law. And as for preventive injunctions, I have argued that the proper analog is not the damage action or the criminal prosecution, proceedings where the jury is traditionally found, but rather those processes—some judicial and others legislative—that precede the promulgation of liability rules and criminal prohibitions. No one suggests that these tasks be turned over to the jury.

"True, injunctions are capable of greater individuation than, say, liability rules or criminal prohibitions, but I fail to see why that quality of an injunction, even if realized, provides the foundation for a jury trial claim. The claim for a jury trial does not, in my judgment, get stronger as one moves from a nonindividuated injunction (do not discriminate on the basis of race) to a highly individuated one (admit James Meredith to the University of Mississippi).

"Similarly, I do not believe that a preference for the jury in the issuance phase of the injunctive process can be predicated on the unique nature of the decisional agency. For the moment, I am willing to assume that the judge is a nonrepresentative decisional agency and that this nonrepresentativeness is a special source of concern with the issuance phase of the injunctive process, a source of concern not present with the criminal statute that is promulgated by a legislature. It still remains to be seen whether the jury is the proper antidote: we may not want the kind of representatives that comes from the jury. The jury is not a representative body in the same sense that a legislature is.

"The properly constituted (i.e., randomly chosen) jury panel is a representative body in the same sense that a scepter might be said to represent the sovereign—it *stands for* the public (the pictorial or ornamental sense of representation). But there is no sense in which the jury . . . can be said to *speak for* the public (the agency sense of representation) as a legislature might. This is due not just to the unanimity requirement, which could be modified, but also to the absence of any mechanism of accountability between the public and the jury, and the conceptual impossibility of developing such an accountability mechanism. The secrecy of the jury's deliberations (the fact that it need not discuss the case in public), the fact that the jury need not explain or justify decisions, and its one-shot quality (i.e., the fact that a new jury is convened for each case) preclude the development of a proper mechanism of accountability. And these are core features of the jury. If we tried to eliminate those features, and also abrogated the unanimity requirement, we would cease to have a jury and instead would have created a six-to-twelve person legislature. We may prefer the legislature to the judge, and for that reason subordinate the injunction, an argument still to be considered, but we should not let a demand for a jury be a proxy for the preference for the legislature."

O. Fiss, The Civil Rights Injunction 50–51, 55–58 (1978).

Professor Rendleman reflects a more sympathetic perspective and allows a more active role for the inadequacy prerequisite and thus for the jury. He asks whether practical and institutional reasons support juryless equity:

"Judges consider some important substantive interests too basic to be compensable with money. They perceive the same interests to be too important to be frustrated by jurors. Perverse jury verdicts damage substantive interests and nullify substantive law. Preventing distorted factfinding preserves the substantive law's integrity. Thus, as the potential for social harm from an incorrect jury verdict increases, the likelihood that the judge will defer to the jury decreases. The decision that the remedy at law is inadequate in a category of lawsuits may reflect the moral determination that the jury should not be permitted to frustrate the underlying substantive law.

"Three other features of the jury system may influence the inadequacy decision. New jurors are picked for each trial, jury members lack expertise, and juries deliberate secretly until they achieve unanimity. These characteristics become pivotal when it is realized that many equity actions last for years. Federal judges have undertaken to reform schools, mental hospitals, and prisons with what Professor Fiss calls structural injunctions. These judges have learned that reorganizing a social institution is no easy task. Deciding where substantive rights exist, formulating satisfactory remedial standards for future conduct, and enforcing the remedy become coextensive tasks. In asking whether the remedy at law is adequate, the judge compares the jury's amateurism with judicial professionalism, accountability, and continuity. Thus, the characteristics of juries determine, in part, whether a remedy at law is inadequate. As juryless equity is somewhat a contradiction in terms, some jurisdictions established binding equity juries. But the candid observer must ask whether the federal judiciary could perform many of the tasks it presently undertakes, particularly structural injunctions, with an equity jury."

Rendleman, The Inadequate Remedy at Law Prerequisite for an Injunction, 33 U.Fla.L.Rev. 346, 355 (1981).

This debate continues in the context of resolving the most pointed of questions: how to distinguish "suits at common law" from "equitable issues." The difficult contemporary decisions are those where plaintiff seeks an injunction and something else.

VAN ERMEN v. SCHMIDT

374 F.Supp. 1070 (W.D.Wis.1974).

JAMES E. DOYLE, District Judge.

This is a civil action under 42 U.S.C. § 1983 for injunctive and monetary relief. . . . Defendants have made a timely demand for trial by jury. Rule 38(b), Fed.R.Civ.P. Plaintiff has moved to strike the demand for jury trial.

. . . [P]laintiff alleges that from 1968 until March, 1972, he was confined at the Wisconsin State Prison, Waupun, and that since March, 1972, he has been confined at the Winnebago State Farm. The . . . complaint challenges the constitutionality of several prison regulations that were applied to plaintiff while he was at the Wisconsin State Prison. Acting pursuant to these regulations, the defendant corrections officials allegedly refused to deliver to plaintiff law books purchased by him and brought to the prison by his relatives, prohibited plaintiff from keeping law books from the prison library in his cell overnight and on weekends, and limited plaintiff's use of law books in the prison library to two hours per week. Plaintiff alleges that the application to him of these regulations denied him the opportunity to pursue post-conviction remedies while at the Wisconsin State Prison and violated his constitutional right of access to the courts. He seeks damages for himself and injunctive relief on his own behalf and on behalf of all inmates confined at institutions under the jurisdiction of the Wisconsin Division of Corrections.

. . . For the reasons stated herein, I conclude that defendants are entitled to a jury trial on the damage claim. . . . For purposes of this opinion only, I will assume that the proposed class action can be maintained, and that the claim for injunctive relief is not moot.

Defendants argue that the Seventh Amendment preserves their right to a jury trial on the damage claim and that this right was expressly recognized by Congress in the original Civil Rights Act of 1871. They also maintain that "legal" issues, issues cognizable at law prior to the merger of law and equity, are triable to a jury regardless of the presence of equitable issues in the same case. Beacon Theatres v. Westover, 359 U.S. 500 (1959); Dairy Queen, Inc. v. Wood, 369 U.S. 469 (1962); Ross v. Bernhard, 396 U.S. 531 (1970). Noting that the Supreme Court has viewed § 1983 actions against a background of tort liability,[2] they contend that plaintiff's damage claim sounds in tort, that tort claims are traditional legal issues, and that defendants are entitled to a jury trial of those issues. . . .

Plaintiff contends that the legislative history of the Civil Rights Act of 1871 discloses the intent of Congress to bar jury trials in non-criminal suits under the Act; that § 1983 actions are "statutory" proceedings unknown to the common law and thus beyond the scope of the Seventh Amendment, N.L.R.B. v. Jones & Laughlin Steel Corp., 301 U.S. 1 (1937); that plaintiff's action is predominantly equitable and that the incidental damage claim would have been cognizable at equity; that juries reflect general public prejudices and are, therefore, ill-suited for deciding § 1983 actions seeking to vindicate unpopular claims.

Statutory Right to Jury Trial

42 U.S.C. § 1983 and its predecessors contain no specific provision for jury trial. Plaintiff urges that I read a denial of jury trial into the statute from debates in the Forty-Second Congress which preceded enactment of the Civil Rights Act of 1871. I find it unnecessary to delve into the legislative background since I conclude that the Act recognized that some civil actions arising under it would be tried to a jury and implied that the courts were to follow customary practice on the right to jury trial. . . .

Constitutional Right to Jury Trial

The Seventh Amendment provides:

"In Suits at common law, where the value in controversy shall exceed twenty dollars, the right of trial by jury shall be preserved, and no fact tried by a jury, shall be otherwise reexamined in any Court of the United States, than according to the rules of the common law."

The right to a jury trial has been extended not only to those actions known to the common law at the time of passage of the Amendment in 1791 but also to all:

". . . suits in which *legal* rights were to be ascertained and determined, in contradistinction to those where equitable rights alone were recognized, and equitable remedies were administered. . . . In a just sense, the amendment then may well be construed to embrace all suits which are not of equity and admiralty jurisdiction, whatever may be the peculiar form which they may assume to settle legal rights." Parsons v. Bedford, 3 Pet. 433, 447 (1830) (emphasis in original), quoted in Ross v. Bernhard, 396 U.S. 531 (1970).

No distinction is made for purposes of jury trial between legal claims arising under the common law and legal claims arising under statutory law.[6] Curtis v. Loether, 415 U.S. 189, 193–196 (1974).

2. Monroe v. Pape, 365 U.S. 167 (1961).

6. Plaintiff cites N.L.R.B. v. Jones & Laughlin Steel Corp., 301 U.S. 1 (1937), in support of his argument that no jury trial is required of a claim arising under statute since such a claim would have been unknown to the common law in 1791. *Jones & Laughlin* held that the Seventh Amendment did not apply to a hearing on an unfair labor practice charge before the Labor Board: "The instant case is not a suit at common law or in the nature of such a suit. The pro-

Where equitable and legal claims are joined in the same action and a jury trial is demanded, only the most extraordinary circumstances can justify a denial of a jury trial on the legal claims. [Citing Beacon Theatres v. Westover]. Characterization of the legal claims as incidental to the equitable claims cannot justify striking the jury demand. Dairy Queen v. Wood, 369 U.S. 469, 470 (1962). The right to a jury "depends on the nature of the issue to be tried rather than the character of the overall action [footnote omitted]." Ross v. Bernhard, 396 U.S. 531, 538 (1962).

Plaintiff here seeks injunctive and monetary relief. Clearly, the injunctive claim is equitable and a jury is not required. There is no simple answer to the question of whether the damage claim requires a jury. Not every claim for monetary relief is triable to a jury as a matter of right.[8] Traditionally, where a new cause of action was created by Congress, and nothing was said about the mode of trial, the courts looked to the "nearest historical analogy" at common law to decide whether there was a right to a jury. 9 Wright and Miller, Federal Practice and Procedure, Civil § 2302; cited with approval in Rogers v. Loether, 467 F.2d 1110, 1116 n. 20 (7th Cir. 1972). Two additional guides to the right to jury trial were suggested in *Ross* (396 U.S. at 538 n. 10):

"As our cases indicate, the 'legal' nature of an issue is determined by considering, first, the pre-merger custom with reference to such questions; second, the remedy sought; and, third, the practical abilities and limitations of juries. Of these factors, the first, requiring extensive and possibly abstruse historical inquiry, is obviously the most difficult to apply."

Curtis provides some clarification of the *Ross* footnote. While acknowledging the continued vitality of the historical approach, it makes clear that the nature

ceeding is one unknown to the common law. It is a statutory proceeding."

The Seventh Amendment was held inapplicable to the Labor Board hearing not because the substantive rights were created by statute but because the forum was administrative rather than judicial. Administrative proceedings are not in the nature of a suit at common law. *Curtis,* supra, at 4261; Hart and Wechsler, The Federal Courts and the Federal System 338 (2d ed. 1973).

8. Jury trials on claims for monetary relief have been denied in the following circumstances: (1) In an action for refund of excess rent under the Emergency Price Control Act of 1942 on the alternative grounds that the refund was restitution or was mandatory injunctive relief to restore the status quo from changes that took place during the pendency of the action. Porter v. Warner Co., 328 U.S. 395 (1946). (2) In an action by the Secretary of Labor under the Fair Labor Standards Act for payment of overtime compensation withheld and minimum wage on grounds that public rights were being enforced and, implicitly, on restitution theory, Wirtz v. Jones, 340 F.2d 901 (5th Cir. 1965). (3) In actions for back pay and reinstatement under § 1983 and Title VII of the 1964 Civil Rights Act on the ground that back pay was not a separable legal claim. McFerren v. County Board of Education, 455 F.2d 199 (6th Cir. 1972), cert. denied, 407 U.S. 934 (1972); Harkless v. Sweeny Independent School District, 427 F.2d 319 (5th Cir. 1970), cert. denied, 400 U.S. 991 (1971); Smith v. Hampton Training School for Nurses, 360 F.2d 577 (4th Cir. 1966); Hayes v. Seaboard Coast Line R.R. Co., 46 F.R.D. 49 (S.D.Ga.1968). (4) On claims for exemplary damages and attorney fees in an action for patent infringement on the ground that such awards are available only at law but that historically there is no right to jury trial on these matters. Swofford v. B & W, Incorporated, 336 F.2d 406 (5th Cir. 1964). (5) In an action for damages under § 1983 on grounds that the Seventh Amendment does not apply to statutory actions and that the unpopularity of plaintiff's claim makes impossible empanelling an impartial jury. Lawton v. Nightingale, 345 F.Supp. 683 (N.D.Ohio 1972).

Only the *Lawton* case deals with the issues raised in the present action and, for reasons stated herein, I cannot agree with its conclusion.

of the relief sought is a more important test. 415 U.S. at 193–196. It is silent on the limitations of a jury as a guide to the legal nature of an issue.

In the present action, both the relief sought and historical analogy indicate a right to jury trial. Plaintiff seeks money damages for an injury suffered. Such relief has customarily been awarded by a jury at law. The nearest historical analogy I have found to a damage claim for denial of access to the courts is a damage claim for denial of the right to vote.[10] . . .

It is clear that a damage action for denial of voting rights was a suit at common law and could be tried as a matter of right to a jury.

The right of access to the courts, like the right to vote, is fundamental to our constitutional system. The existence of an action at law for deprivation of voting rights argues strongly for recognition of plaintiff's damage claim as a legal issue within the protection of the Seventh Amendment.[12]

The remaining consideration, the practical abilities and limitations of juries, has been subject to varying interpretations. Plaintiff argues that it is directed to potential jury prejudice and notes one recent commentary which reads the three *Ross* criteria as an abandonment of the historical analogy approach in favor of a functional approach to the right to jury trial.[13] Defendants respond that this factor is directed only to the jury's ability to comprehend complex issues and that the factual issues present here are readily understandable and appropriate for jury determination.

The cases have not considered possible jury prejudice as one of the guides to whether an issue is legal in nature. *Ross* gives no hint that it contemplates prejudice as a limitation on juries. *Curtis* treats prejudice only in relation to statutory intent. Lawton v. Nightingale, 345 F.Supp. 683 (N.D.Ohio, 1972), holds that denial of a jury trial because of the risk of prejudice accords with the purposes of § 1983. Since it views the Seventh Amendment as not applicable to § 1983 actions, *Lawton* does not consider the *Ross* standards.

I view the third *Ross* standard as simply a reaffirmation of the traditional common law practice of equity taking jurisdiction where transactions between parties were too complicated for jury determination. . . . Without much more specific direction from the Supreme Court, I will not elevate risk of jury prejudice to a determinant of Seventh Amendment protection. Other means are readily available to counter the danger of prejudice.[15] The issues

10. The analogy is employed in another context in Basista v. Weir, 340 F.2d 74, 88 (3rd Cir. 1965), and suggested for this context in a thoughtful note, Jury Trial in 1983 Actions, 24 Case Western Reserve Law Review 406, 412, 413 (1973).

12. There is no indication in the amended complaint that the $100,000 damages sought are other than compensatory damages. The line between compensatory and punitive damages in civil rights actions can easily become blurred. See e.g., Basista v. Weir, 340 F.2d 74, 85 (3rd Cir. 1965). If punitive damages were to be sought, they also would be tried to the jury.

13. Note, Congressional Provision for Nonjury Trial, 83 Yale L.J. 401 (1973).

15. Protection of the right to be tried before a jury without prejudice is afforded by the Jury Selection and Service Act of 1968 (28 U.S.C. §§ 1861–1874); by recognition of independent actions challenging juror selection practices, e.g., Carter v. Jury Comm'n, 396 U.S. 320 (1970); and by procedural devices such as change of venue, challenge of jurors for cause, and peremptory dismissals. Further protection from a verdict reached on improper consideration is afforded by the court's authority under Rule 50, Fed.R. Civ.P., for directing a verdict or granting judgment notwithstanding the verdict.

presented here are no different in nature from those common to tort actions typically tried to a jury. . . .

In summary, the relief sought and historical analogy strongly indicate a right to jury trial on plaintiff's damage claim. Since I do not view possible jury prejudice as one of the limitations contemplated by *Ross.* I find that the damage claim is appropriate for a jury in light of that institution's abilities and limitations. I conclude that the Seventh Amendment guarantees defendants the right to a jury trial.

---

1) If a jury hears and decides factual issues pertaining to both legal and equitable relief, the judge may grant equitable relief commensurate with the jury's fact-finding. Beacon Theatres v. Westover, 359 U.S. 500, 509 (1959). In a later damage action against an equitable defendant, a nonparty to the equitable action may preclude the losing defendant from relitigating decided issues, although defendant would otherwise be entitled to summon a jury. Parkland Hosiery Co. v. Shore, 439 U.S. 322 (1979).

2) The question of whether hideously complex damage trials may be kept from juries remains unsettled. See Annot., 54 A.L.R.Fed. 733 (1981). The Ninth Circuit denied that there is a complexity exception, In re United States Financial Securities Litigation, 609 F.2d 411 (9th Cir. 1979); the Supreme Court declined to hear the case, Gant v. Union Bank, 446 U.S. 929 (1980). The Third Circuit compared judicial and lay abilities and found that the fifth amendment right to due process justifies a complexity exception. In re Japanese Electronic Products Antitrust Litigation, 631 F.2d 1069 (3d Cir. 1980).

The debate between proponents of legitimacy and those of efficiency bears on much equitable litigation. Judge Gibbons dissented in *Japanese Electronic Products;* he framed the issues in the broadest manner. "It is often said that the judicial process involves the search for objective truth. We have no real assurance, however, of objective truth whether the trial is to the court or to a jury. The judicial process can do no more than legitimize the imposition of sanctions by requiring that some minimum standards of fair play, which we call due process, are adhered to. In this legitimizing process, the seventh amendment is not a useless appendage to the Bill of Rights, but an important resource in maintaining the authority of the rule of law. In the process of gaining public acceptance for the imposition of sanctions, the role of the jury is highly significant. The jury is a sort of ad hoc parliament convened from the citizenry at large to lend respectability and authority to the process. Judges are often prone to believe that they, alone, can bear the full weight of this legitimizing function. I doubt that they can. Any erosion of citizen participation in the sanctioning system is in the long run likely, in my view, to result in a reduction in the moral authority that supports the process." 631 F.2d at 1093.

3) What did the Supreme Court mean by saying that "the practical abilities and limitations of juries" may help determine the legal or equitable nature of an issue? Ross v. Bernhard, 396 U.S. 531, 538 n. 10 (1970). That local prejudice and community resentment would frustrate legislation intended to counteract that prejudice and resentment? Kane, Civil Jury Trial: The Case for Reasoned Iconoclasm, 28 Hastings L.J. 1, 34–35 (1976).

Are constitutional litigants entitled to avoid juries? Professor Monaghan considers jurors to be insensitive to first amendment interests. Monaghan, First Amendment "Due Process," 83 Harv.L.Rev. 518, 527 (1970). The Missouri court set up a complex system to submit obscenity issues to juries and provide a judicial check. See McNary v. Carlton, 527 S.W.2d 343, 348 (Mo.1975). One of your editors concluded that "it helps to be a constitutional litigant." Chapters of the Civil Jury, 65 Ky.L.J. at 797. In what way?

4) In Edelman v. Jordan, 415 U.S. 651 (1974), we learned that an injunction may be deemed to be money for eleventh amendment purposes if it imposes "a liability which must be paid from public funds." The Court also said that, for the purposes of seventh amendment "we need not, and do not, go so far as to say that any award of monetary relief must necessarily be 'legal' relief." Curtis v. Loether, 415 U.S. 189, 196 (1974). What is the test?

5) In some ways, the right to a jury trial has expanded. Pernell v. Southall Realty, 416 U.S. 363 (1974) (landlord tenant dispute); Curtis v. Loether, 415 U.S. 189 (1974) (fair housing); Ross v. Bernhard, 396 U.S. 531 (1970) (stockholder derivative action); Dairy Queen, Inc. v. Wood, 369 U.S. 469 (1962) (complex actions and masters); Beacon Theatres, Inc. v. Westover, 359 U.S. 500 (1959) (equitable cleanup). Merger, moreover, "could have the effect of permitting a litigant to demand a jury trial on legal issues which previously would have been tried without a jury because of the equitable cleanup doctrine." Kirst, Administrative Penalties and the Civil Jury: The Supreme Court's Assault on the Seventh Amendment, 126 U.Pa.L. Rev. 1281, 1290 (1978).

GNOSSOS MUSIC v. MITKEN, INC.

653 F.2d 117 (4th Cir. 1981).

Before WINTER, RUSSELL and SPROUSE, Circuit Judges.

SPROUSE, Circuit Judge:

This is an appeal by a defendant, Mitken, Inc., from a March 5, 1980, district court order granting plaintiffs' motion to strike defendants' request for a jury trial in two consolidated copyright infringement cases.

Mitken, Inc., is the owner and operator of a nightclub in Asheville, North Carolina, the Cosmic Ball Room, that regularly presented live music for dancing in 1979. . . . The plaintiffs/appellees (hereinafter "copyright owners") are eight owners of copyrights in original musical compositions and are members of the American Society of Composers, Authors and Publishers ("ASCAP"). Their works are registered, printed, and published in accordance with the copyright laws, thus entitling them to the exclusive right to publicly perform, or permit performance of, their music. 17 U.S.C. § 106(4).

Six of the copyright owners brought suit in the district court against Mitken and Mitchell in April 1979, alleging five instances of copyright infringement by public performance for profit of protected works. Three copyright owners filed another suit against Mitken in October 1979, alleging two additional infringements. The suits sought permanent injunctions, damages, and costs.

The defendants denied any infringements and requested a jury trial in both cases. The copyright owners waived any recovery in excess of the $250.00 minimum statutory damages and costs, stipulating that they would not offer proof of actual damages. Plaintiffs then moved the district court to strike the defendants' demands for a jury trial.

The district court consolidated the cases for trial, granted the copyright owners' motion to strike the demand for a jury trial, and entered judgment for them on five of the seven counts of infringement. Defendants were permanently enjoined from infringing specifically named compositions and ordered to pay $250.00 statutory damages for each of the five infringements and costs (including $1,250.00 attorney fees).

The sole issue on appeal concerns the denial of trial by jury to alleged copyright infringers when the copyright owners seek only an injunction and minimum statutory damages.

The 1976 Copyright Act provides, in part:

"(a) In General.—Except as otherwise provided by this title, an infringer of copyright is liable for either—

"(1) the copyright owner's actual damages and any additional profits of the infringer, as provided by subsection (b); or

"(2) statutory damages, as provided by subsection (c). . . .

"(c) Statutory Damages.—

"(1) . . . the copyright owner may elect, at any time before final judgment is rendered, to recover, instead of actual damages and profits, an award of statutory damages for all infringements involved in the action, with respect to any one work, . . . in a sum of not less than $250 or more than $10,000 as the court considers just."

17 U.S.C. §§ 504(a), (c)(1). The owners of the infringed copyrights are thus entitled to an injunction, actual damages, and profits *or,* in the alternative, an injunction plus statutory damages—the latter requiring no proof beyond the infringement. A plaintiff in an infringement suit who seeks only the alternative statutory damages is, of course, relieved of the often difficult burden of proving actual damages or infringer's profits. Douglas v. Cunningham, 294 U.S. 207, 209 (1935).

Appellant contends it is entitled to jury trial both by the terms of section 504(c) of the Act and by the seventh amendment to the United States Constitution. We observe initially that the question of the right to a jury in litigating a statutorily-created right should be decided as a matter of statutory construction rather than of constitutional interpretation wherever possible.

Appellees first argue that the language of section 504(c) is ambiguous but, properly read, indicates a congressional intent that the amount of statutory damages be determined by the court without a jury. We agree that the language is ambiguous, but cannot interpret it as the copyright owners contend. As the courts concluded in Curtis v. Loether, 415 U.S. 189 (1974), and Barber v. Kimbrell's, Inc., 577 F.2d 216 (4th Cir.), cert. denied, 439 U.S. 934 (1978), "court" could mean either "judge" singularly or "judge and jury" in tandem. The language of the fair housing statute interpreted in *Curtis* read "[t]he court may grant as relief, as it deems appropriate." 415

U.S. at 189. The language of the Truth in Lending statute interpreted in *Barber* states that damages can be awarded in "such amount as the court may allow" and "as determined by the court," and sets out factors that "the court shall consider." 577 F.2d at 219 n. 3 (quoting 15 U.S.C. § 1640(a) (1975)). In each case the courts held that Congress meant a determination by a jury. If anything, the language of section 504(c) enforces rather than detracts from an interpretation requiring a jury trial, but it is not sufficiently clear to mandate either a bench trial or a jury trial. *Barber*, supra. But see Sid & Marty Krofft Television Productions, Inc. v. McDonald's Corp., 562 F.2d 1157 (9th Cir. 1977); Chappell & Co. v. Palermo Cafe Co., 249 F.2d 77 (1st Cir. 1957).

Since neither a reading of section 504(c) nor a review of its congressional history reveals whether it creates the right of trial by jury for statutory damages, we must decide whether the seventh amendment requires a jury trial in litigation involving minimum statutory damages.

The language of the seventh amendment is concise: "In Suits at common law, where the value in controversy shall exceed twenty dollars, the right of trial by jury shall be preserved . . . ." U.S. Const. amend.VII. In *Curtis* the Supreme Court quoted Justice Story in summarizing the accumulated understanding of "suits at common law" as that term was used by the drafters of the Bill of Rights in framing the seventh amendment:

"The phrase 'common law,' found in this clause, is used in contradistinction to equity, and admiralty, and maritime jurisprudence . . . . By *common law,* [the framers of the amendment] meant . . . not merely suits, which the *common* law recognized among its old and settled proceedings, but suits in which *legal* rights were to be ascertained and determined, in contradistinction to those where equitable rights alone were recognized, and equitable remedies were administered . . . . In a just sense, the amendment, then, may well be construed to embrace all suits which are not of equity and admiralty jurisdiction, whatever may be the peculiar form which they may assume to settle legal rights."

415 U.S. at 193 (quoting Parsons v. Bedford, 28 U.S. (3 Pet.) 433, 446–47 (1830)).

In Beacon Theatres, Inc. v. Westover, 359 U.S. 500 (1959), the Supreme Court held that the seventh amendment afforded a right to jury trial of legal issues even when equitable issues are involved in the same case: "Only under the most imperative circumstances . . . can the right to a jury trial of legal issues be lost through prior determination of equitable claims." That principle was reaffirmed in Dairy Queen, Inc. v. Wood, 369 U.S. 469 (1962), which found that jury trials must be provided even where the trial judge characterizes the legal issues as "incidental" to equitable issues. Neither language in the pleadings nor the nature of the defenses could render a matter "purely equitable" so as to preclude a jury trial where there were legal issues.

There had been some uncertainty as to whether a suit to enforce rights created by congressional action should be characterized under the legal/equitable analytical framework as a "suit at common law." The Supreme Court in *Curtis,* supra, dissipated that confusion. The Court there said:

"Whatever doubt may have existed should now be dispelled. The Seventh Amendment does apply to actions enforcing statutory rights, and requires a jury trial upon demand, if the statute creates legal rights and remedies, enforceable in an action for damages in the ordinary courts of law [and] . . .

". . . when Congress provides for enforcement of statutory rights in an ordinary civil action in the district courts, where there is obviously no functional justification for denying the jury trial right, a jury trial must be available if the action involves rights and remedies of the sort typically enforced in an action at law." 415 U.S. at 194–95.

The decision as to a jury trial right in the case *sub judice* is thus reduced to determining whether the right to statutory damages provided by section 504(c) is a remedy that has been typically enforced in an action at law. We think both *Curtis* and *Barber* require an affirmative answer.

As we indicated in *Barber,* this pivotal analysis requires a two-part test. "*First,* are the rights and duties created by the statute analogous to rights and duties historically comprehended by the common law? *Second,* are the remedies sought legal rather than equitable in nature?" 577 F.2d at 225.

First, the underlying question is whether a legal or equitable base supports that part of the statutory scheme allowing a plaintiff to recover damages. The copyright statute, when first enacted, defined a new legal duty, but recovery for breach of that duty is analogous to recovery for a number of tort actions traditionally recognized at common law. See Screen Gems-Columbia Music, Inc. v. Metlis & Lebow Corp., 453 F.2d 552, 554 (2d Cir. 1972); Ted Browne Music Co. v. Fowler, 290 F.2d 751, 754 (2d Cir. 1923). So viewed, copyright infringement is a tortious interference with a property right for which Congress created the remedy for damages. See *Screen Gems,* supra; *Ted Browne Music,* supra. The fact that it was created by statute makes it no less sounding in tort. See *Curtis,* supra, 415 U.S. at 195. We conclude that, as was the case regarding the statutes interpreted in *Curtis* and *Barber,* a civil action seeking damages for copyright infringement under 504(c) is basically an action for the enforcement of a legal right.

Second, section 504(c), the copyright infringement statute we now consider, provides a remedy of a type which traditionally would have been enforced at law. The copyright owners, in addition to the injunction, sought the minimum statutory damages of $250.00 for each infringement. As the trial court held in Chappell & Co. v. Pumpernickle Pub Inc., 79 F.R.D. 528 (D.Conn. 1977), this is analogous to the ancient civil action for debt. The analysis does not stop there, however. Even had the owners requested statutory damages in the allowable range above $250 (i.e., not a specific amount), such would yet have been a remedy recoverable in an action at common law. The statute creates a concomitant right to injunctions but this says no more than that the total new package contains both equitable and legal remedies.

It is true that the fact-finder's discretion is limited by section 504(c) to fixing damages within a specified range. This, however, is not a recent innovation. Statutory rights created by state legislatures have circumscribed damage-fixing by juries in wrongful death actions, tortious interference with mineral rights, usury actions, and many others. Congress has given the fact-finder discretion in assessing damages in a number of statutes, including the Truth in Lending Act, *Barber,* supra; the fair housing provisions of the Civil Rights Act, *Curtis,* supra; and the antitrust laws, Bigelow v. RKO Radio Pictures, Inc., 327 U.S. 251, 264 (1946).

In our view, the application of the seventh amendment to the facts of this case mandates a trial by jury. This result is required by our holding in *Barber* and by the Supreme Court's holding in *Curtis.* The judgment of the district court denying the defendant's motion for a jury trial is therefore reversed and the case remanded for further proceedings consistent with the views expressed in this opinion.

---

1) Broadcast Music Inc. v. Papa John's Inc., 201 U.S.P.Q. (BNA) 302 (N.D.Ind.1979), turned on comparable parts of the repealed copyright act. The judge said: "The remedy sought in this case is statutory damages, a form of monetary relief which is to be awarded 'in the discretion of the court' in lieu of actual damages and profits. 17 U.S.C. § 101(b). While the court recognizes that money damages are normally accepted as a form of legal relief, entitling the parties to trial by jury, not all forms of monetary damages are 'legal' in nature. See Curtis v. Loether . . . . It is the opinion of this court that the statutory damages provided by Congress for the violation of a copyright are not legal in nature, but are solely equitable, and do not entitle either party in the suit to a trial by jury. Accord, Chappell & Co. v. Palermo Cafe Co., 249 F.2d 77 (1st Cir. 1957) (alternative holding); Cayman Music, Ltd. v. Reichenberger, 403 F.Supp. 794 (W.D.Wis.1975). Contra, Chappell & Co. v. Cavalier Cafe, Inc., 13 F.R.D. 321 (D.Mass.1952).

"In finding that the money relief demanded here is not of a legal nature, the court has relied on a variety of factors. First, the relief is to be awarded only in lieu of actual damages and profits and then only at the discretion of the court, within certain guidelines. It is not contested that either party would be entitled to a jury trial if the plaintiff were seeking actual damages and profits. See, e.g., Arnstein v. Porter, 154 F.2d 464 (2nd Cir. 1946). But these statutory damages were provided by Congress to create a remedy where actual damages are not provable at law, but yet where it is proven that a violation of the copyright has occurred. In this sense at least, Congress has simply authorized by statute what equity courts have long done as a matter of course, i.e., not to suffer a wrong to be without a remedy. In codifying this remedy, Congress did not remove it from the equitable jurisdiction of the courts, instead they simply provided guidelines to be used by the courts in the exercise of their discretion.

"A second factor relied upon by this court in making its determination is the similarity between the copyright statutory damage provision and the back pay provisions of Title VII. Compare 17 U.S.C. § 101(b) with 42 U.S.C. § 2000e–5(g). The majority of courts passing on the question have found back pay awards to be solely in the discretion of the trial courts, not entitling the parties to a jury. See, e.g., Slack v. Havens, 522 F.2d 1091 (9th Cir. 1975); EEOC v. Laucke & Joys Co., 375 F.Supp. 852 (E.D.Wis.1974). This approach seems to be founded upon both the statutory language authorizing such awards and the very nature of the awards. Back pay awards, like statutory damages in copyright infringement actions, are very similar in nature to the equitable relief of restitution. See 5 Moore's Federal Practice ¶ 38.24[2]. Like restitution, these statutory damages are used to force a party to disgorge profits or money unlawfully gained by the infringement of another's copyrighted work. This analogy also persuades the court that the statutory damages are committed to the equitable discretion and jurisdiction of the court.

"A final factor persuasive to this court is the language of the statute. The statute provides that the infringer shall be liable, 'in lieu of actual damages and profits, [to pay] such damages as to the court shall appear to be just, and in assessing such damages the court may, in its discretion, allow the amounts as hereinafter stated . . . .' 17 U.S.C. § 101(b). The statute then lists certain guidelines for the assessment of such damages, leaving the final determination of the amount solely in the discretion of the court. For the instant case the statute provides that the minimum damages to be allowed on each showing of infringement is $250 and a maximum of $5,000. Within this range, the court has full discretion.

"Two items in this language are worthy of particular note. The fact that Congress specifically speaks in terms of the court and the fact that the Congress leaves the court a broad discretion in awarding the final amount. Certainly the Congress may have used the term 'court' to include both judge and jury; however, juries are not normally thought of as exercising discretion. Their function is to find facts and to apply the law, as it is explained to them, to those facts. Its seems unlikely that Congress would have meant to commit such a great deal of discretion to juries in circumstances where proof of actual damages would not be given. Moreover, the very nature of equity is the power which evolves from the discretion a court possesses to do that which is just, and the greater the discretion involved, the less likely it is that Congress meant to deprive the court of that power. See Albemarle Paper Co. v. Moody, 422 U.S. 405 (1975) (Rehnquist, J., concurring); Comment, The Right to Jury Trial Under the Age Discrimination in Employment and Fair Labor Standards Acts, 44 U.Chi.L.Rev. 365 (1977). See also Campbell v. Wireback, 269 F. 372 (4th Cir. 1920), where the court states:

" '[W]here the damages are indirect and not capable of ascertainment, the compensation which the copyright proprietor shall receive for the injuries caused by the infringer is committed to the *discretion of the trial judge.'* (emphasis added).

"For the reasons set forth above, this court [finds] that because of the traditionally equitable character of suits such as this, the explicit statutory commitment to the court of discretion in the assessment and awarding of just damages, and the integral relation of the damages to the injunctive relief requested, there is no right to trial by jury in cases such as the one now at bar." 201 U.S.P.Q. (BNA) at 305–06.

2) The Fifth Circuit rejected a jury trial under § 504(c) of the Copyright Act. Twentieth Century Music Corp. v. Frith, 645 F.2d 6 (5th Cir. 1981). Other decisions that reject a jury under the repealed act are Chappell & Co. v. Palermo Cafe Co., 249 F.2d 77, 81–82 (1st Cir. 1957); Cayman Music,

Ltd. v. Reichenberger, 403 F.Supp. 794, 796 (W.D.Wis.1975) (per Judge Doyle of Van Ermen v. Schmidt, p. 464). Judge Doyle based the *Cayman Music* decision on *Chappell's* three-step argument: 1) statutory damages are a minimum recovery where actual damages are hard to prove; 2) "the court is required to award at least the minimum statutory damages once it has made the determination that there is a basis for injunctive relief," and 3) "just damages are an integral part of the injunctive remedy and not a separate basis for recovery." 403 F.Supp. at 796–797. Is that argument more faithful than that of the *Gnossos* court to the idea of granting an injunction because money is inadequate? If money is "an integral part" of the injunction, isn't *Gnossos* wrong?

3) Why do copyright infringement defendants seek jury trials? Are they home town businesses who conclude that local jurors will serve some home cooking to out-of-state copyright proprietors? Are the jury demands dilatory tactics based on long delays before trial? Is either reason legitimate? Why do the plaintiffs ask for minimum damages? Why not spurn the gold and seek a preliminary injunction plus attorney fees?

"[S]tatutory damages arose from an inability to prove actual damages . . . . It is clear that all actions to collect statutory damages prior to the 1909 [Copyright] Act were at law. . . . Regardless of the statutory right, there is a seventh amendment right to a jury when statutory damages are sought. . . . Statutory damages were and are legal in nature . . . the right to a jury is one of our most cherished rights. It cannot be denied on the grounds of expediency, or on the ground that judges are allegedly more flexible or just than juries. The reasons our forefathers fought for the right to a jury are as valid today as they ever were." Patry, The Right to a Jury in Copyright Cases, 29 J.Bull. Copyright Soc'y USA 139, 193–94 (1981).

HILDEBRAND v. BOARD OF TRUSTEES OF MICHIGAN STATE UNIVERSITY

607 F.2d 705 (6th Cir. 1979).

Before WEICK and KEITH, Circuit Judges, and CECIL, Senior Circuit Judge.

KEITH, Circuit Judge.

In recent years, the genteel academic world has been rocked with controversies which have required adjudication by federal judges. This case presents an increasingly common dispute—a non-tenured professor whose employment is terminated, claims that his first amendment and due process rights were abridged. The issues presented in this appeal, however, do not directly implicate the merits of how and why the plaintiff was fired. Instead, plaintiff complains of . . . the district court's denial of his right to trial by jury. We find merit in his contentions and reverse and remand for a new trial.

For a number of years prior to 1967, the plaintiff, Dr. John R. Hildebrand, was a full professor at Texas Technological University. He applied for a position on the faculty of Michigan State University and was accepted in

April of 1967. Hildebrand began teaching courses in the Department of Social Science at Michigan State in September of 1967.

At the time, Michigan State's social science program followed a standard format to which all professors were expected to conform. The plaintiff became dissatisfied with this mechanical approach since it left no room for variation by individual instructors. He voiced these and other concerns to his colleagues, some of those criticisms were contained in a report entitled *Improving Undergraduate Education.* He also successfully sought election to a position on the Departmental Advisory Committee. In early June of 1968, shortly after his successful election, the plaintiff met with Douglas Dunham, Chairman of the Department of Social Sciences. The two discussed Dr. Hildebrand's future in what appeared to be a frank and cordial fashion.

Approximately one month later, during the summer recess, Dr. Dunham met with a number of the department's full professors. They discussed Dr. Hildebrand's upcoming reappointment and voted unanimously not to recommend him for reappointment. On September 12, 1968, Dr. Dunham informed the plaintiff by letter that he would not be reappointed. By this time, the plaintiff had returned from the summer recess. Dr. Hildebrand commenced a series of intra-University appeals, but to no avail. He then filed two unsuccessful unfair labor practice charges with the Michigan Employment Relations Commission. The Michigan State courts denied leave to appeal and the plaintiff turned to federal court. Dr. Hildebrand's employment with Michigan State terminated on August 31, 1969.

Suit was filed on October 12, 1971, against the defendants—The Board of Trustees of Michigan State and various University employees. Plaintiff alleged that his termination was in retaliation for the exercise of his first amendment rights and that the University procedures which were followed contravened the due process clause of the 14th Amendment. The cause of action was based on 42 U.S.C. §§ 1983 and 1985. Plaintiff prayed for reinstatement, back pay and compensatory and punitive damages.

Both plaintiff and defendant made timely requests for a jury trial. The jury trial issue was not raised at all throughout pre-trial proceedings, including a motion to dismiss, motion for a preliminary injunction and motion for summary judgment. At the final pre-trial conference on August 16, 1974, everyone assumed that the case would be tried by a jury and the pre-trial statements so indicated. The case went to trial before a jury for approximately five days. Both sides presented their evidence; neither side moved for a directed verdict at any point. After both sides rested but before the jury was instructed, the district court, on its own motion, questioned whether a jury was appropriate.

After considering the issue, the court concluded that the case sounded in equity and that the case would not be submitted for a jury verdict after all. Instead, the court decided that it would treat the jury as advisory under F.R. Civ.Pro. 39(c) and have it answer certain interrogatories to help out with the final decision. And so it happened: The jury answered four interrogatories; both sides submitted proposed findings of fact and conclusions of law; and the case was submitted to the district court for decision. Over two years later, on March 18, 1977, the court issued an extensive opinion finding in favor of the defendants on all counts and dismissing the complaint. The plaintiff appeals.

The plaintiff contends that the district judge erred in taking the case over from the jury and deciding it himself. We agree. The Seventh Amendment guarantees that a trial by jury be had in all federal cases presenting "legal" claims over $20.00. Before 1938, this presented little problem since cases at law were separate from cases in equity. In 1938, everything changed; law and equity were merged. The merger of law and equity is universally acknowledged to be a good thing, but it has created problems in the jury trial area since one is entitled to a jury trial on legal claims, but not equitable ones. Some clarity was brought to this area by Dairy Queen v. Wood, 369 U.S. 469 (1962), and Beacon Theatres Inc. v. Westover, 359 U.S. 500 (1959), which command that where a case presents both legal and equitable issues, jury trial rights must be preserved.

The question remains, what is a "legal" issue? Guidance is provided by Ross v. Bernhard, 396 U.S. 531, 538 n. 10 (1970), where the Court stated:

"As our cases indicate, the 'legal' nature of an issue is determined by considering, first, the pre-merger custom with reference to such question; second, the remedy sought; and third, the practical abilities and limitations of juries."

The first part of the test created confusion. Some courts took the view that no jury trial right attached to purely statutory causes of action which had no direct common-law counterpart. Whatever merit there might have been to this expansive notion, it was quickly deflated by Curtis v. Loether, 415 U.S. 189 (1974). There, the Court ruled that a jury trial was available in a housing discrimination suit under Title VIII of the Civil Rights Act where the plaintiff sought actual and punitive damages. Curtis v. Loether shifts the focus to the second issue: the nature of the relief sought.

A key dividing line between law and equity has historically been that the former deals with money damages and the latter with injunctive relief. This distinction has been blurred by court decisions indicating that not all money damages claims will be deemed "legal." See Curtis v. Loether; McFerren v. County Board of Ed. of Fayette Co., Tenn., 455 F.2d 199, 202–04 (6th Cir. 1972); Local No. 92, Int'l Ass'n of Bridge, S. & O. Workers v. Norris, 383 F.2d 735, 740–42 (5th Cir. 1967). See also Georgia Power Co. v. 138.30 Acres of Land, 596 F.2d 644 (5th Cir. 1979). A common example is an employment discrimination claim brought under Title VII of the Civil Rights Act of 1964, 42 U.S.C. § 2000e et seq. which seeks injunctive relief (i.e. reinstatement) and back pay. Although the Supreme Court has never directly addressed this question,[2] the courts of appeals have uniformly held that no jury trial right exists. See Slack v. Havens, 522 F.2d 1091, 1094 (9th Cir. 1975); EEOC v. Detroit Edison Co., 515 F.2d 301, 308 (6th Cir. 1975), vacated and remanded on other grounds, 431 U.S. 951 (1977); Robinson v. Lorillard Corp., 444 F.2d 791, 802 (4th Cir.), cert. dismissed, 404 U.S. 1006 (1971); King v. Laborers Int. Union, 443 F.2d 273, 279 (6th Cir. 1971) (dicta); Johnson v. Georgia Highway Express, Inc., 417 F.2d 1122, 1125 (5th Cir. 1969).

2. The Court has continued to leave the issue open. See Lorillard v. Pons, 434 U.S. 575 (1978); Curtis v. Loether, 415 U.S. 189 (1974).

The rationale for this view is that a back pay award is a discretionary, "make whole" remedy which is incidental to injunctive relief. See Lorillard v. Pons, 434 U.S. 575 (1978); Albemarle Paper Co. v. Moody, 422 U.S. 405 (Rehnquist, J., concurring); Slack v. Havens; EEOC v. Detroit Edison Co.; Johnson v. Georgia Highway Express, Inc. In contrast a claim for actual and/or punitive damages is viewed as purely "legal." See Curtis v. Loether; EEOC v. Detroit Edison. See also United States v. Snepp, 595 F.2d 926, 935–38 (4th Cir. 1979), petition for cert. filed June 18, 1979, 47 U.S.L.W. 3826. . . .

The above-cited authorities mandate that the chief focus to be made when determining whether a jury trial right exists is the nature of the relief sought. If the remedy sought is injunctive relief and/or back pay, no jury trial right attaches. In the ordinary case, if the relief sought includes compensatory and/or punitive damages, then there does exist a right to trial by jury. . . .

In this case, the plaintiff sought actual and punitive damages in addition to reinstatement and back pay. There is direct authority that such claims entitle one to a jury trial in a first-amendment retaliatory discharge case. Burt v. Board of Trustees of Edgefield City School District, 521 F.2d 1201 (4th Cir. 1975); Amburgery v. Cassady, 507 F.2d 728 (6th Cir. 1974). Subsequent suits similar to this one have been tried to a jury. See Cooper v. Johnson, 590 F.2d 559 (4th Cir. 1979) (J.N.O.V. entered) (2–1 decision); Goss v. San Jacinto Junior College, 588 F.2d 96 (5th Cir. 1979); Wagle v. Murray, 546 F.2d 1329 (9th Cir. 1976), vacated and remanded, 431 U.S. 935 (1977), on remand, 560 F.2d 401 (9th Cir. 1977), cert. denied, 434 U.S. 1014 (1978); Norbeck v. Davenport Community School District, 545 F.2d 63 (8th Cir. 1976); Bertot v. School District No. 1, 522 F.2d 1171 (10th Cir. 1975) (J.N.O.V. entered on appeal). These authorities mandate a jury trial in cases such as this.

At the time it removed the case from the jury, the district court did not have the benefit of *Burt,* supra, or our decision in *Amburgery,* supra. In its subsequent opinion the district court attempted to distinguish these decisions. We are unable to do so.

The court stated that in order to be entitled to a jury trial, a party must sustain its burden of coming forward with the evidence as to the legal issues in the case. The court went on to analyze the plaintiff's claim for compensatory damages for mental anguish and for punitive damages and found them insubstantial. The court pointed to Lynch v. Pan American World Airways, 475 F.2d 764, 765 (5th Cir. 1973), where the Fifth Circuit stated that "unsupported allegations for compensatory and punitive damages" under 42 U.S.C. § 1981 could not "unilaterally alter the genre" of an essentially equitable employment discrimination proceeding.

We will assume that the district court correctly determined that the damages counts were insubstantial.[5] Plaintiff urges that this makes no difference and that *Lynch* cannot survive Curtis v. Loether. We disagree. A plaintiff already has considerable power to determine whether there will be a jury

5. Defendants argue that actual and punitive damages as well as backpay were unavailable because of sovereign immunity. Edelman v. Jordan, 415 U.S. 651 (1974) . . . . It is unnecessary for us to address this issue now.

trial since he can decide whether to add actual or punitive damages counts to his complaint. This right should not extend to a case where the actual or punitive damages counts are frivolous or clearly not meritorious. The question then becomes, at what point must this determination be made?

There is surprisingly little authority on when a jury trial determination need be made. The Supreme Court expressly left the question open in Curtis v. Loether. Judge Stevens' opinion in Rogers v. Loether, 467 F.2d 1110, 1118–19 (7th Cir. 1972), aff'd sub nom. Curtis v. Loether, 415 U.S. 189 (1974) stated that a jury demand should be decided on the allegations and relief sought in the plaintiff's complaint.

We think that this view is too strict. Under the liberal pleading allowances of the Federal Rules of Civil Procedure, allegations made in pleadings must be broadly construed. A complaint cannot be dismissed unless a plaintiff could advance no set of facts which would entitle him to relief. See Conley v. Gibson, 335 U.S. 41, 45–46 (1957). When examining a complaint, one must look solely at the allegations made and assume that they are true. . . . If a trial judge could look only at the pleadings, then too many meritless damages claims could be made on which to base jury demands.

We think that the pre-trial standard contained in F.R.Civ.Pro. 56 is preferable. If it becomes clear prior to trial that no genuine issue exists as to any material facts, a district court can grant summary judgment as to some or all issues. This standard can operate to eliminate meritless damages requests and thus moot a jury demand.[6] Under this standard, the district court is free to examine all of the record and not just the pleadings. If a demand for damages is so insubstantial that it cannot meet the standard contained in Rule 56, then it should not be allowed to convert equitable issues into legal ones.

. . .

In this case, however, the district court let the case be tried before a jury and then withdrew it from them. His conclusion that the damages claims were frivolous was based on the testimony at trial. In effect, the district court held that if damages claims cannot survive a motion for directed verdict, then it is proper to abort a jury trial and convert the proceedings into a bench trial.

We think that considerations of fundamental fairness and judicial economy militate against this view. Any good trial lawyer will testify that there are significant tactical differences in presenting and arguing a case to a jury as opposed to a judge. To convert a trial from a jury trial to a bench trial (or vice-versa) in the middle of the proceedings is to interfere with counsel's presentation of their case and, quite possibly, to prejudice one side or the other. Further, it is a waste of the additional time and money which is inherent to a jury trial.

Even if we were to adopt the district court's view, we would have to reverse. In this case *both* sides requested a jury trial. Neither side ever moved to strike the jury demands. Indeed, neither side ever moved for a directed verdict. Since both parties apparently wanted the jury to decide this case and

6. We do not formalistically require that actual summary judgment be entered as to damages counts before trial so long as the district judge makes it clear to the parties that no jury trial will be had because the money damages claims were not meritorious when tested against F.R.Civ.Pro. 56 standards.

since the jury had heard both sides' presentation, the district judge's conduct in *sua sponte* taking the case away from the jury is particularly difficult to understand.

Even if the court was correct that no jury trial right existed in this case, F.R.Civ.Pro.Rule 39(c) [7] permits both sides to stipulate to a jury trial. To be sure, a district court does not have to go along with the stipulation, but once that occurs, it does not have unbridled discretion to change its mind. . . . Assuming that the district court in this case had the authority to abort the jury's decision-making role, we would find an abuse of discretion in the exercise of that authority.

One final issue requires examination—the effect of the use of the jury in an advisory role. We do not have a situation here where the entire case was submitted to the jury for an advisory verdict. Despite counsel's requests that the whole case be submitted, the district court submitted only four interrogatories for the jury to answer. These interrogatories . . . indicate that the jury concluded that no due process violation took place, but that the plaintiff should have been reinstated to his position at Michigan State. Presumably, the basis for the jury's conclusion was that the plaintiff's firing was done in retaliation for the exercise of his first amendment rights. Plaintiff urges that we enter judgment on this verdict and remand solely for a determination of damages.

Defendants, on the other hand, suggested at oral argument that we treat the jury trial matter as harmless error and that we affirm the district court's findings of fact and conclusions of law. They point to dicta in the district court's opinion where it states that the proof was such that it would have granted a directed verdict in any event.[9]

This case presents a procedural nightmare worthy of inclusion in a first year of law school civil procedure [or injunctions, Eds.] examination authored by the most cunning of professors. The district court erroneously withdrew the case from the jury, but allowed it to answer certain interrogatories in an advisory capacity. The court then entered findings of fact and conclusions of law, but stated that a directed verdict would have been granted in any event.

We do not think that we can enter judgment on the interrogatories. After deciding to take the case away from the jury, the district judge told both the jury and counsel that the jury's role would be solely advisory.[10] The

7. F.R.Civ.Pro. 39(c) provides:

"In all actions not triable of right by a jury the court upon motion or of its own initiative may try any issue with an advisory jury or, except in actions against the United States when a statute of the United States provides for trial without a jury, *the court with the consent of both parties may order a trial with a jury whose verdict has the same effect as if trial by jury had been a matter of right.*" (emphasis added)

9. The district court stated, in relevant part: ". . . this Court's examination of the evidence leads to the rather inescapable conclusion that a directed verdict would have been justified here at the close of the evidence. . . . Considering the strong evidence already surveyed at some length, this [directed verdict standard] certainly appears to have been met. Indeed, a successful directed verdict at the close of plaintiff's case also seems a distinct possibility."

10. The issue of whether an advisory jury verdict could ever be treated as a "regular" jury verdict is unsettled. Dicta in Parklane Hosiery Co., Inc. v. Shore, 439 U.S. 322 (1979), indicates that it could not be. (". . . an advisory jury . . . would not in any event have been a Seventh Amendment jury.")

entire case was not submitted to the jury for a general verdict. Nor can we ignore the district judge's statement that the evidence was such that a directed verdict would have been in order. At the very least it appears that the district court would have granted a Motion for New Trial had the case been in that procedural posture. In addition, the jury was not—could not have been—instructed in accord with the standards which the Supreme Court subsequently set forth in Mt. Healthy School District v. Doyle, 429 U.S. 274 (1977).

At the same time, we cannot sustain the district court's findings of fact and conclusions of law as a directed verdict. Neither side briefed or argued this issue in this court or in the court below and the district court's opinion was not written as a directed verdict. Neither side ever moved for a directed verdict and the district court never suggested prior to issuing its opinion that such a verdict was being considered. A motion for directed verdict is ordinarily a prerequisite to the filing of a motion for judgment notwithstanding the verdict. In this case, both sides were apparently willing to let the jury decide the outcome since neither moved for a directed verdict, thus waiving their right to request [Judgment] N.O.V. Although some cases have indicated that a district judge has independent authority to direct a verdict, the judge in this case never purported to do so. Under these circumstances, we would have difficulty treating the district court's opinion as one granting a directed verdict.

Moreover, the district court, in finding against plaintiff's claim that he was denied tenure because he exercised his first amendment rights, relied heavily upon the fact that the plaintiff spoke in private to his co-workers and not in public. The distinction which the district court drew between private and public speech cannot survive Givhan v. Western Line Consolidated School District, 439 U.S. 410 (1979). Especially given this intervening clarification in the law, we cannot affirm the district court under directed verdict standards.

The only fair solution to this tangled and protracted case is to reverse and remand for a prompt jury trial on all issues. We are aware of the Western District of Michigan's glutted docket, but we see no other solution here. On these facts especially with both sides requesting a jury trial, Dr. Hildebrand was entitled to have a jury decide the issues.

Reversed and remanded for a prompt trial by jury.[16]

WEICK, Circuit Judge, concurring:

I concur in the result.

This case involves legal as well as equitable claims. The legal claim is for compensatory and punitive damages charging a conspiracy and violations of the constitutional rights of plaintiff, an untenured teacher at Michigan State University, arising out of the failure of the University to reappoint plaintiff at the expiration of his term of employment so that he could obtain tenure.

16. Nothing in this opinion should be construed as precluding the entry of a directed verdict or [Judgment] N.O.V. as to some or all issues on retrial. Given the length of time that this case has been pending, however, we recommend that any motion for directed verdict be held in abeyance until after the jury renders its verdict. Similarly, we recommend that trial of this case, be expedited, although we impose no time requirements.

The equitable claim is for reinstatement with back pay under 42 U.S.C. § 1983.

Under federal law, the legal claim must be tried first before a jury and the equitable claim resolved subsequently in the light of the determination of the legal claim by the jury. Dairy Queen v. Wood, 369 U.S. 469 (1962).

Whether or not the issues in the legal claim are to be submitted to the jury for determination will necessarily depend on the sufficiency of the evidence which must be determined by the court applying the applicable rules if a motion is made for a directed verdict. I express no views on the sufficiency of the evidence as it is not properly before us. No motion for a directed verdict was made at the trial of this case and the court did not direct a verdict.

---

1) When plaintiff sues to be reinstated and seeks back pay, why is back pay equitable? "The prayer for back pay is not a claim for damages, but is an integral part of the equitable remedy of injunctive reinstatement. Reinstatement involves a return of the plaintiffs to the positions they held before the alleged unconstitutional failure to renew their contracts. An inextricable part of the restoration to prior status is the payment of back wages properly owing to the plaintiffs, diminished by their earnings, if any, in the interim. Back pay is merely an element of the equitable remedy of reinstatement." Harkless v. Sweeny Independent School District, 427 F.2d 319, 324 (5th Cir. 1970). See also Wirtz v. Jones, 340 F.2d 901 (5th Cir. 1965) (injunction to pay wages due "not to collect a debt . . . but to correct a continuing offense against the public interest.") See Chapters of the Civil Jury, 65 Ky. L.J. at 772–78.

2) Is back pay restitution in the sense that plaintiff's deprivation unjustly enriched defendant? Or is back pay simply a damage claim for wrongful discharge? Is it important that both Hildebrand and Harkless asserted that defendants had deprived them of constitutional rights? That Harkless was a black teacher asserting that she had been unconstitutionally discharged by a Southern school board? If back pay were "legal," would future plaintiffs ask only to be reinstated? Would reinstatement alone be a satisfactory remedy?

Judge Lumbard wrote: "If community resentment was a legitimate factor to consider, few Southern school districts would have been integrated. One of the major purposes of the Constitution is to protect individuals from the tyranny of the majority. That purpose would be completely subverted if we allowed the feelings of the majority to determine the remedies available to a member of a minority group who has been the victim of unconstitutional actions." Burton v. Cascade School District, 512 F.2d 850, 855–856 (9th Cir. 1975), certiorari denied 423 U.S. 839 (dissent).

3) In Albemarle Paper Co. v. Moody, 422 U.S. 405, 443 (1975), Justice Rehnquist, concurring, said: "To the extent, then, that the District Court retains substantial discretion as to whether or not to award back pay notwithstanding a finding of unlawful discrimination, the nature of the jurisdiction which the court exercises is equitable, and under our cases neither party may demand a jury trial. To the extent that discretion is replaced by awards which follow as a matter of course from a finding of wrongdoing, the action

of the court in making such awards could not be fairly characterized as equitable in character, and would quite arguably be subject to the provisions of the Seventh Amendment." May the legislature or an appellate court change issues from equitable to legal by altering the standards for awarding money? Does the grant and amount of "legal" awards follow "as a matter of course" from the finding of liability? Chapters of the Civil Jury, 65 Ky.L.J. at 775–76.

4) Carey v. Piphus, 435 U.S. 247 (1978), holds that violations of due process are constitutional torts and actionable without proof of damage, but that to recover damages plaintiff must prove compensable harm such as emotional distress caused by the denial of due process. Generally, plaintiffs who suffer only procedural deprivations will recover only nominal damages. Is an action for denial of due process alleging no actual damages legal or equitable? Are nominal damages legal but less than the seventh amendment's twenty dollar threshold? Burt v. Abel, 585 F.2d 613, 616–617 n. 7 (4th Cir. 1978). Does the parsimonious damage measure for deprivations of due process mean that judges should grant injunctions freely because the legally cognizable injury to plaintiff's constitutionally protected interest consists of uncompensable, unmeasurable, and intangible impairments? Inadequacy Prerequisite, 33 U.Fla.L.Rev. at 348–52.

5) Jared Sparks taught American Government in a conservative suburban high school. He took a strong stand against what he called Israel's "fascist racism and bloodthirsty aggression." After Jared made an intemperate speech at an open meeting to protest the invasion of Lebanon in 1982, numerous parents confronted the school authorities and demanded that he be fired. Mr. Sparrow, the principal, went to Jared's class the next day and said: "Mr. Sparks has suffered a severe mental breakdown. He will not be teaching you anymore." Jared refused to leave the classroom; but Mr. Sparrow and two teachers removed him forcibly, dislocating Jared's shoulder in the process. That evening, the school board held a closed, secret meeting and fired Jared for "incompetence." Jared Sparks sued Mr. Sparrow and the school officials in federal district court. He charged that they had denied him due process, retaliated against him for exercising a constitutional right, defamed him, and battered him. He asked to be reinstated, paid lost salary, and compensated for defamation and battery. The defendants answered. They denied liability, asserted that Jared was incompetent, and demanded a jury trial. Draft the argument in support of Jared's motion to strike defendant's jury demand.

6) A principal issue in the contractual prior restraint case, United States v. Snepp, was remedy. After Frank Snepp published "Decent Interval," the government sued him to enforce a contract that called for prepublication review and approval. The book, the government conceded, contained no nonpublic, classified matter. The lower courts agreed almost without discussion that Snepp should be enjoined from future publishing before submission to and review by the CIA. United States v. Snepp, 456 F.Supp. 176, 182 (E.D. Va.1978), affirmed in part, reversed in part and remanded 595 F.2d 926 (4th Cir. 1979), reversed and remanded 444 U.S. 507 (1980). District Judge Lewis, Judge Hoffman dissenting in the court of appeals, and the Su-

preme Court majority agreed that Snepp held all receipts from "Decent Interval" as constructive trustee.

The court of appeals majority felt that, because the government proved no fiduciary breach, the government could recover compensatory and punitive contractual damages measured roughly by injury, punishment, and deterrence. The government's damage, however, was not quantifiable. The Supreme Court found a fiduciary breach and reinstated a constructive trust measured by Snepp's gains and intended to remove the incentive to breach the contract. The Supreme Court majority said: "Nominal damages are a hollow alternative, certain to deter no one. The punitive damages recoverable after a jury trial are speculative and unusual. Even if recovered, they may bear no relation to either the Government's irreparable loss or Snepp's unjust gain." 444 U.S. at 514. Snepp had demanded a jury trial, and he argued vigorously for a jury. Damages for breach of the contract would be tried to a jury, but a constructive trust action is equitable, and it would be tried to the judge alone. United States v. Snepp, 595 F.2d at 938 n. 3 (Hoffman, J., dissenting). See also Robair v. Dahl, 80 Mich.App. 458, 264 N.W.2d 27 (1978).

Since the government could not prove any quantifiable loss, was its remedy at law inadequate, entitling it to equitable relief? In these circumstances, are punitive damages an adequate remedy at law? Nominal damages? Did the government choose equity to avoid a criminal jury? Comment, Enforcing the CIA's Secrecy Agreement Through Postpublication Civil Action, 32 Stan.L.Rev. 409, 419–20 (1980). Why did Snepp seek a jury? Did punitive damages threaten Snepp because they are "an invitation to the jury to engage in prejudice and irrationality"? Comment, 32 Stan.L.Rev. at 427. Since the book revealed nothing classified, did the constructive trust unjustly enrich the government? 444 U.S. at 521 (Stevens, J., dissenting).

The courts assumed, but omitted to discuss, that Snepp would not be entitled to a jury in a constructive trust action. Why have a jury for one money remedy, compensatory and punitive damages, but not for another money remedy, constructive trust? A constructive trust assures specie recovery. Plaintiff must show that the res exists before the judge will grant a personal order to convey it. The judge orders the constructive trustee to execute the trust by conveying the res or corpus to the beneficiary. This personal order is enforced with coercive contempt if defendant balks. Restatement of Restitution § 160, Comments e, i (1936). The administrative difficulties of coercive enforcement are reasons to ration equitable remedies only to plaintiffs who show that prompt, impersonal legal remedies are inadequate. Inadequacy Prerequisite, 33 U.Fla.L.Rev. at 355–57. To prevent imprisonment for a civil debt and coercion to perform the impossible, plaintiff must show that the trust res exists before being awarded a constructive trust. Rendleman, Compensatory Contempt to Collect Money, 41 Ohio St.L.J. 625, 629 n. 24 (1980).

Did these considerations enter into the Court's decision to deny Snepp a jury trial? What unstated premises led the Court to the constructive trust? Is there a compelling reason to deny a jury trial to defendants who breach a fiduciary duty? Unless a plaintiff shows that it needs and should have the peculiarly equitable features of a constructive trust like coercive enforcement, should plaintiff be limited to a legal remedy for unjust enrichment, tried to a jury, but measured by defendant's gain? See D. Dobbs, Handbook on the Law of Remedies 248 (1973).

7) The authorities sue the Kozy Theatre in Lake Nishnabotna, Minnesota to enjoin further exhibition of "Sex Kitten Goes to Law School" on the ground that "Sex Kitten" is obscene. Miller v. California anticipates that the material will be evaluated according to the values of "the average person, applying contemporary community standards." 413 U.S. 15, 24 (1973). May Peter Peterson, the Kozy's proprietor, demand a jury? Rendleman, Civilizing Pornography: The Case for an Exclusive Obscenity Nuisance Statute, 44 U.Chi.L.Rev. 509, 542–46 (1977).

In Alexander v. Virginia, 413 U.S. 836 (1973), defendant challenged juryless civil obscenity, but the Court held laconically that "a trial by jury is not constitutionally required in this state civil proceeding." This holding reflects the long tradition that the seventh amendment does not apply to the states. Is the community-based nature of the substantive standard more important in determining the right to a jury than the relief plaintiff asks? If you were drafting a civil obscenity statute would you provide for jury trials?

What standard of proof does the Constitution call for in civil obscenity: beyond a reasonable doubt, clear and convincing, or a preponderance? In Cooper v. Mitchell Brothers' Santa Ana Theatre, 454 U.S. 90 (1981), a nuisance action tried to a jury, the Court said that the state could require proof beyond a reasonable doubt but that the Constitution did not compel it. What standard should a legislature provide? Civilizing Pornography, 44 U.Chi.L. Rev. at 546.

II. Motions to Modify and Dissolve

UNITED STATES v. SWIFT & CO.

286 U.S. 106, 52 S.Ct. 460, 76 L.Ed. 999 (1932).

Justice CARDOZO delivered the opinion of the Court.

A decree of the Supreme Court of the District of Columbia has modified an earlier decree of the same court which enjoined the continuance of a combination in restraint of trade and commerce.

Separate appeals, one by the United States of America, and the others by associations of wholesale grocers intervening by leave of court, have brought the case here, . . .

In February, 1920, a bill was filed by the Government under § 4 of the Act of July 2, 1890 . . . , known as the Sherman Antitrust Act, against the five leading meat-packers in the United States to dissolve a monopoly. The packers joined as defendants were Swift & Company, Armour & Company, Wilson & Company, the Morris Packing Company, and the Cudahy Packing Company, together with their subsidiaries and also their chief officers. The charge was that by concert of action the defendants had succeeded in suppressing competition both in the purchase of live stock and in the sale of dressed meats, and were even spreading their monopoly into other fields of trade. They had attained this evil eminence through agreements apportioning the percentages of live stock to which the members of the combinations were severally entitled; through the acquisition and control of stockyards and stockyard terminal railroads; through the purchase of trade papers and journals whereby cattle raisers were deprived of accurate and unbiased reports of the demand for live stock; and through other devices directed to unified control. "Having eliminated competition in the meat products, the defendants next took cognizance of the competition which might be expected" from what was characterized as "substitute foods." To that end, so it was charged, they had set about controlling the supply of "fish, vegetables, either fresh or canned, fruits, cereals, milk, poultry, butter, eggs, cheese and other substitute foods ordinarily handled by wholesale grocers or produce dealers." Through their ownership of refrigerator cars and branch houses as well as other facilities, they were in a position to distribute "substitute foods and other unrelated commodities" with substantially no increase of overhead. Whenever these advantages were inadequate, they had recourse to the expedient of fixing prices so low over temporary periods of time as to eliminate competition by rivals less favorably situated. Through these and other devices there came about in the view of the Government an unlawful monopoly of a large part of the food supply of the nation. The prayer was for an injunction appropriate to the case exhibited by the bill.

The defendants consented to dismemberment, though answering the bill and traversing its charges. With their answer there was filed a stipulation which provided for the entry of a decree upon the terms therein set forth and provided also that the decree "shall not constitute or be considered as an adjudication that the defendants, or any of them, have in fact violated any law of the United States." The decree entered on February 27, 1920, enjoined the defendants from maintaining a monopoly and from entering into or continuing any combination in restraint of trade and commerce. In addition they were enjoined both severally and jointly from (1) holding any interest in public stockyard companies, stockyard terminal railroads or market newspapers, (2) engaging in, or holding any interest in, the business of manufacturing, selling or transporting any of 114 enumerated food products, (principally fish, vegetables, fruit and groceries), and thirty other articles unrelated to the meat packing industry; (3) using or permitting others to use their distributive facilities for the handling of any of these enumerated articles, (4) selling meat at retail, (5) holding any interest in any public cold storage plant, and (6) selling fresh milk or cream. No injunction was granted in respect of the sale or distribution of poultry, butter, cheese and eggs, though these had been included in the bill among the substituted foods with the defendants were seeking to engross. The decree closed with a provision whereby jurisdiction of the cause was retained for the purpose of taking such other action or adding at the foot such other relief "as may become necessary or appropriate for the carrying out and enforcement" thereof, "and for the purpose of entertaining at any time hereafter any application which the parties may make" with reference thereto.

The expectation would have been reasonable that a decree entered upon consent would be accepted by the defendants and by those allied with them as a definitive adjudication setting controversy at rest. The events that were to follow recount a different tale. In April, 1922, the California Co-operative Canneries Corporation filed an intervening petition alleging that the effect of the injunction was to interfere with the performance by Armour & Company of a contract by which Armour had agreed to buy large quantities of California canned fruit, and praying that the decree be vacated for lack of jurisdiction. Leave to intervene was granted by the Court of Appeals of the District, which ordered "that such further proceedings thereupon be had as are necessary to determine the issue raised." In November, 1924, motions for like relief were made by Swift and by Armour, their subsidiaries and officers. The motions were denied by the Supreme Court of the District, and thereafter were considered by this court, which upheld the consent decree in the face of a vigorous assault. Swift & Co. v. United States, 276 U.S. 311. In the meantime, however, an order had been made on May 1, 1925, by the Supreme Court of the District at the instance of the California Canneries whereby the operation of the decree as a whole was suspended "until further order of the court to be made, if at all, after a full hearing on the merits according to the usual course of chancery proceedings" (see United States v. California Canneries, 279 U.S. 553, 555). This order of suspension remained in force till May, 1929, when a decision of this court swept the obstacle aside. United States v. California Canneries, supra.

The defendants and their allies had thus been thwarted in the attempt to invalidate the decree as of the date of its entry, and again the expectation would have been reasonable that there would be acquiescence in its restraints. Once more the expectation was belied by the event. The defendants, or some of them, discovered as they thought that during the years that had intervened between the entry of the decree and its final confirmation, conditions in the packing industry and in the sale of groceries and other foods had been transformed so completely that the restraints of the injunction, however appropriate and just in February, 1920, were now useless and oppressive. The discovery or supposed discovery had its fruit in the proceeding now before us. On April 12, 1930, the defendants Swift & Company and Armour & Company and their subsidiaries, being no longer under the shelter of an order suspending the injunction, filed a petition to modify the consent decree and to adapt its restraints to the needs of a new day. The prayer was that the petitioners be permitted (1) to own and operate retail meat markets; (2) to own stock in stockyard companies and terminal railroads; (3) to manufacture, sell and deal in the 144 articles specified in paragraph fourth of the decree, which for convenience will be spoken of as "groceries," (4) to use or permit others to use their distributive facilities in handling such commodities; and one of the defendants, Swift & Company, asked in addition that the defendants be permitted to hold interests in public cold-storage warehouses and to sell fresh milk and cream. Of the five defendants named in the original suit, one, Morris & Company, sold out to Armour & Company in 1923, and discontinued business. The two other defendants, Wilson and Cudahy, did not join in the petition to modify the decree, but stated in open court that they would consent to such modification as the court might order provided it be made applicable to the defendants equally. All the requests for modification were denied except numbers 3 and 4, of which 4 is merely ancillary to 3, and calls for no separate consideration. The modification in respect of number 3 gave permission to deal at wholesale in groceries and other enumerated commodities, but maintained the injunction against dealing in them at retail.

In every other respect, the decree of February 27, 1920, was continued in force as originally entered. The modifying decree, which was entered January 31, 1931, is the subject of this appeal.

We are not doubtful of the power of a court of equity to modify an injunction in adaptation to changed conditions though it was entered by consent. The power is conceded by the Government, and is challenged by the interveners only. We do not go into the question whether the intervention was so limited in scope and purpose as to withdraw this ground of challenge, if otherwise available. Standing to make the objection may be assumed, and the result will not be changed. Power to modify the decree was reserved by its very terms, and so from the beginning went hand in hand with its restraints. If the reservation had been omitted, power there still would be by force of principles inherent in the jurisdiction of the chancery. A continuing decree of injunction directed to events to come is subject always to adaptation as events may shape the need. . . . The distinction is between restraints that give protection to rights fully accrued upon facts so nearly permanent as to be substantially impervious to change, and those that involve the supervision of changing conduct or conditions and are thus provisional and tentative. . . . The result is all one whether the decree has been entered after litigation or by consent. . . . In either event, a court does not abdicate its power to revoke or modify its mandate if satisfied that what it has been doing has been turned through changing circumstances into an instrument of wrong. We reject the argument for the interveners that a decree entered upon consent is to be treated as a contract and not as a judicial act. A different view would not help them, for they were not parties to the contract, if any there was. All the parties to the consent decree concede the jurisdiction of the court to change it. The interveners gain nothing from the fact that the decree was a contract as to others, if it was not one as to them. But in truth what was then adjudged was not a contract as to any one. The consent is to be read as directed toward events as they then were. It was not an abandonment of the right to exact revision in the future, if revision should become necessary in adaptation to events to be.

Power to modify existing, we are brought to the question whether enough has been shown to justify its exercise.

The defendants, controlled by experienced business men, renounced the privilege of trading in groceries, whether in concert or independently, and did this with their eyes open. Two reasons, and only two, for exacting the surrender of this adjunct of the business were stated in the bill of complaint. Whatever persuasiveness the reasons then had, is theirs with undiminished force today.

The first was that through the ownership of refrigerator cars and branch houses as well as other facilities, the defendants were in a position to distribute substitute foods and other unrelated commodities with substantially no increase of overhead. There is no doubt that they are equally in that position now. Their capacity to make such distribution cheaply by reason of their existing facilities is one of the chief reasons why the sale of groceries has been permitted by the modified decree, and this in the face of the fact that it is also one of the chief reasons why the decree as originally entered took the privilege away.

The second reason stated in the bill of complaint is the practice followed by the defendants of fixing prices for groceries so low over temporary periods of time as to eliminate competition by rivals less favorably situated.

Whether the defendants would resume that practice if they were to deal in groceries again, we do not know. They would certainly have the temptation to resume it. Their low overhead and their gigantic size, even when they are viewed as separate units, would still put them in a position to starve out weaker rivals. Mere size, according to the holding of this court, is not an offense against the Sherman Act unless magnified to the point at which it amounts to a monopoly (United States v. United States Steel Corp., 251 U.S. 417 . . .), but size carries with it an opportunity for abuse that is not to be ignored when the opportunity is proved to have been utilized in the past. The original decree at all events was framed upon that theory. It was framed upon the theory that even after the combination among the packers had been broken up and the monopoly dissolved, the individual units would be so huge that the capacity to engage in other forms of business as adjuncts to the sale of meats should be taken from them altogether. It did not say that the privilege to deal in groceries should be withdrawn for a limited time, or until the combination in respect of meats had been effectually broken up. It said that the privilege should be renounced forever, and this whether the units within the combination were acting collectively or singly. The combination was to be disintegrated, but relief was not to stop with that. To curb the aggressions of the huge units that would remain, there was to be a check upon their power, even though acting independently, to wage a war of extermination against dealers weaker than themselves. We do not turn aside to inquire whether some of these restraints upon separate as distinguished from joint action could have been opposed with success if the defendants had offered opposition. Instead, they chose to consent, and the injunction, right or wrong, became the judgment of the court. Groceries and other enumerated articles they were not to sell at all, either by wholesale or by retail. Even the things that they were free to sell, meats and meat products, they were not to sell by retail. The court below annulled the restraint upon sales of groceries by wholesale, but retained the prohibition in respect of sale by retail both for groceries and for meats. The one prohibition equally with the other was directed against abuse of power by the individual units after the monopoly was over; and the death of the monopoly, the breaking up of the combination, if an adequate reason for terminating one of them, is an adequate reason for terminating both.

We have said that the defendants are still in a position, even when acting separately, to starve out weaker rivals, or at least that the fear of such abuses, if rational in 1920, is still rational today. The meat monopoly has been broken, for the members now compete with one another. The size of the component units is substantially unchanged. In 1929, the latest year for which any figures are furnished by the record, the sales made by Swift and Armour, each, amounted to over a billion dollars; those made by all the defendants together to over $2,500,000,000; and those made by their thirteen chief competitors to only $407,000,000. Size and past aggressions induced the fear in 1920 that the defendants, if permitted to deal in groceries, would drive their rivals to the wall. Size and past aggressions leave the fear unmoved today. Changes there have been that reduce the likelihood of a monopoly in the business of the sale of meats, but none that bear significantly upon the old-time abuses in the sale of other foods. The question is not whether a modification as to groceries can be made without prejudice to the interests of producers of cattle on the hoof. The question is whether it can be made without prejudice to the interests of the classes whom this particular restraint was intended to protect. Much is made in the defendants' argument of the rise of the chain stores to affluence and power, and especially of chains for the sale of groceries and other foods. Nothing in that development eradicates the ancient peril. Few of the chain stores produce the foods they have for sale, and then chiefly in special lines. Much, indeed most, of what they offer, they are constrained to buy from others. They look to the defendants for their meats, and if the ban of this decree is lifted, they will look to the defendants for other things as well. Meats and groceries today are retailed at the same shops, departments of a single business. The defendants, the largest packers in the country, will thus hold a post of vantage, as compared with other wholesale grocers, in their dealings with the chains. They will hold a post of vantage in their dealings with others outside the chains. When they add groceries to meats, they will do so, they assure us, with substantially no increase of the existing overhead. Thus in the race of competition they will be able by their own admission to lay a handicap on rivals overweighted at the start. The opportunity will be theirs to renew the war of extermination that they waged in years gone by.

Sporadic instances of unfair practices even in the meat business are stated in the findings to have occurred since the monopoly was broken, practices as to which the defendants' officers disclaim responsibility or knowledge. It is easy to make such excuses with plausibility when a business is so huge. They become less plausible when the size of the business is moderate. Responsibility is then centered in a few. If the grocery business is added to the meat business, there may be many instances of unfair pressure upon retailers and others with the design of forcing them to buy from the defendants and not from rival grocers. Such at any rate was the rationale of the decree of 1920. Its restraints, whether just or excessive, were born of that fear. The difficulty of ferreting out these evils and repressing them when discovered supplies an additional reason why we should leave the defendants where we find them, especially since the place where we find them is the one where they agreed to be.

There is need to keep in mind steadily the limits of inquiry proper to the case before us. We are not framing a decree. We are asking ourselves whether anything has happened that will justify us now in changing a decree. The injunction, whether right or wrong, is not subject to impeachment in its application to the conditions that existed at its making. We are not at liberty to reverse under the guise of readjusting. Life is never static, and the passing of a decade has brought changes to the grocery business as it has to every other. The inquiry for us is whether the changes are so important that dangers, once substantial, have become attenuated to a shadow. No doubt the defendants will be better off if the injunction is relaxed, but they are not suffering hardship so extreme and unexpected as to justify us in saying that they are the victims of oppression. Nothing less than a clear showing of grievous wrong evoked by new and unforeseen conditions should lead us to change what was decreed after years of litigation with the consent of all concerned.

The case comes down to this: the defendants had abused their powers so grossly and persistently as to lead to the belief that even when they were acting separately, their conduct should be subjected to extrordinary restraints. There was the fear that even when so acting they would still be ready and able to crush their feebler rivals in the sale of groceries and kindred products by forms of competition too ruthless and oppressive to be accepted as fair and just. Wisely or unwisely, they submitted to these restraints upon the exercise of powers that would normally be theirs. They chose to renounce what they might otherwise have claimed, and the decree of a court confirmed the renunciation and placed it beyond recall.

What was then solemnly adjudged as a final composition of an historic litigation will not lightly be undone at the suit of the offenders, and the composition held for nothing.

The decree should be reversed and the petitions dismissed.

Justice BUTLER, dissenting.

. . . Conditions affecting competition in the lines of business carried on by defendants have changed since 1920. Indeed, the Government, after the introduction of evidence by appellees, formally stipulated that they "are in active competition with each other" etc.[1] The facts negative any suggestion that danger of monopolistic control now exists. Each of the principal packers has suffered discouraging operating losses. One of them, retiring from business, sold its plants to another. The purchaser, in order to avoid failure, was compelled to refinance and has not earned reasonable profits in any year. Another, being embarrassed, passed into the hands of a receiver, was subsequently adjudged bankrupt and later reorganized. Only two have continued able to sustain themselves. It is shown without dispute that defendants' earnings, whether considered in relation to sales or to the worth of property invested, are low and substantially less than those of others carrying on the same lines of business.[2]

1. Census figures in respect of slaughtering and meat packing establishments in 1921 and 1927 are as follows:

Value of production per year:	1921	1927
\$5,000 to \$20,000	142	64
\$20,000 to \$100,000	304	267
\$100,000 to \$500,000	360	429
\$500,000 to \$1,000,000	112	163
\$1,000,000 and over	266	327
Total	1,184	1,250

The relations between each of the defendant packers' production of meat and lard and total production of these articles in the United States during the years 1920 and 1929 are as follows:

	1920	1929
Swift	13.2%	15.2%
Armour (including Morris)	15.8%	14.1%
Wilson	5.2%	4.3%
Cudahy	4.0%	4.7%

2. The following table groups the defendants' earnings and compares them with the combined earnings of 15 competitors from 1920 to 1929:

Year	Percentage of defendants' earnings on sales	Percentage of competitiors' earnings on sales	Percentage of defendants' earnings on net worth	Percentage of competitors' earnings on net worth
1920	0.18	0.76	0.88	2.48
1921	[a]3.05	[a].17	[a]10.27	[a]5.80
1922	.10	2.72	.35	10.87
1923	1.58	3.40	5.65	12.00
1924	1.77	3.39	6.46	13.28
1925	1.44	2.03	5.82	9.11
1926	1.35	2.65	5.03	12.24
1927	.63	2.07	2.49	9.83
1928	1.24	3.17	5.13	14.10
1929	1.06	2.68	4.55	14.02

[a] Loss.

Since 1920 the manufacture and distribution of food have grown greatly and to a large extent have come to be carried on by integrated concerns in strong hands, which have taken over and are handling many products from the sources of production to consumers. More and more, meat—formerly distributed through shops selling little if anything else—is sold in stores carrying groceries and other articles of food. The diversification of the business of defendants permitted by the modification of the injunction is in harmony with present legitimate tendencies in the business of producing and selling meat, groceries and other articles of food. In all branches of such activities there is strong and active competition. The use by defendants of their employees and facilities for the sale and distribution of groceries as well as meat would not give them any undue advantage over their competitors. Under present conditions the relief granted below would not enable them to inflict the evils of monopoly upon any part of the food industry. The denial of that relief makes against competition intended to be preserved by the Sherman Act. Defendants should be permitted more efficiently to use their help and equipment to lessen their operating expenses. That makes for lower prices and so is in the public interest.

The wholesale grocers, represented here by objecting interveners, are not entitled to the court's protection against the competition of non-members or of defendants carrying on separately and competing actively. They may not avoid the burden of sustaining themselves in a free and open market by protestation of fear that, if allowed to engage in the grocery business at all, defendants will unfairly compete in violation of the federal antitrust laws. If and whenever shown necessary for the protection of the commerce safeguarded by the original decree, the Government may have the modified provisions restored or new ones added.

There is nothing in the original complaint that makes for reversal here. The Government's allegations were denied by answer. The decree was entered without evidence or findings pursuant to a written stipulation between the Government and the defendants expressly providing that "this stipulation shall not constitute or be considered as an admission, and the rendition or entry of the decree, or the decree itself, shall not constitute or be considered as an adjudication that the defendants, or any of them, have in fact violated any law of the United States." And that provision was in exact words incorporated in and made a part of the decree. Thus the Government consented to, and the court adopted, this provision quite as much as the defendants consented to the other parts of the decree.

The fact that defendants thereafter applied to have the decree vacated upon grounds directed only to the power of the court to enter it ought not to be regarded as militating against them or their good faith—particularly when it is recalled that this court, when reviewing that proceeding, deemed the questions presented of sufficient importance to call for their argument a second time. 276 U.S. 311.

I am of opinion that the facts found, taken with those conceded or established by uncontradicted evidence, justly entitle appellees to the measure of relief given below. and that the modifying decree should be affirmed.

1) If there had been no consent decree, a suit by the Department of Justice in the early 1930's to prevent Armour, Swift, and other large packers from entering the retail grocery business almost certainly would have failed. No contemporary precedent existed to prohibit, on the ground of size, a firm in one market, meat packing, from expanding or acquiring to enter another market, retail groceries. Even in the absence of a theory, the packers' position in the meat industry had declined during the 1920's, and the chains would have competed vigorously. How should this conclusion affect the Court's decision on the motion to modify?

2) Requests for modification continued. United States v. Swift & Co., 189 F.Supp. 885 (N.D.Ill.1960), affirmed per curiam 367 U.S. 909 (1961); United States v. Swift & Co., No. 58/c/613 (N.D.Ill.1969); United States v. Armour & Co., 398 U.S. 268 (1970); United States v. Armour & Co., 402 U.S. 673 (1971). See Note, Flexibility and Finality in Antitrust Consent Decrees, 80 Harv.L.Rev. 1303 (1967).

UNITED STATES v. UNITED SHOE MACHINERY CORP.

391 U.S. 244, 88 S.Ct. 1496, 20 L.Ed.2d 562 (1968).

Justice FORTAS delivered the opinion of the Court.

In 1953, in a civil suit brought by the United States, the District Court for the District of Massachusetts held that appellee had violated § 2 of the Sherman Antitrust Act by monopolizing the manufacture of shoe machinery. The court found that "(1) defendant has, and exercises, such overwhelming strength in the shoe machinery market that it controls that market, (2) this strength excludes some potential, and limits some actual, competition, and (3) this strength is not attributable solely to defendant's ability, economies of scale, research, natural advantages, and adaptation to inevitable economic laws." United States v. United Shoe Machinery Corp., 110 F.Supp. 295, 343 (1953). The court did not order the relief requested by the Government—that appellee be dissolved into three separate shoe machinery manufacturing companies. Rather, the court imposed a variety of restrictions and conditions designed "to recreate a competitive market." [1] Appellee appealed to this Court, which affirmed the decision of the District Court. United Shoe Machinery Corp. v. United States, 347 U.S. 521 (1954).

1. Some of the major provisions of the decree were as follows: United was enjoined from further monopolization; it was ordered to offer for sale all types of machines (previously only leased) at "such terms . . . as do not make it substantially more advantageous for a shoe factory to lease rather than to buy a machine"; if United continued leasing it was required to lease for no more than five-year terms under certain specified conditions; it was not to refuse a prospective customer's request to lease or buy a machine "except for good cause"; it was to submit a plan for disposing of certain sectors of its business; it was to grant to any applicant, except a deliberate infringer, a nonexclusive license under any or all patents held by it on reasonable nondiscriminatory royalty terms; it was not to acquire any patents or patent applications except those acquired by reason of bona fide employment of the inventor, nor was it to acquire patents or patent applications under exclusive license; it was not to acquire any secondhand shoe machinery or any shoe machinery manufacturer or a manufacturer or distributor of supplies for shoe factories.

The decree of the District Court, entered on February 18, 1953, and subsequently modified on July 12, and September 17, 1954, provided in paragraph 18 that:

> "On [January 1, 1965] both parties shall report to this Court the effect of this decree, and may then petition for its modification, in view of its effect in establishing workable competition. If either party takes advantage of this paragraph by filing a petition, each such petition shall be accompanied by affidavits setting forth the then structure of the shoe machinery market and defendant's power within that market." 110 F.Supp., at 354.

Pursuant to this provision, the Government reported to the District Court on January 1, 1965, that appellee continued to dominate the shoe machinery market, that workable competition had not been established in that market, and that additional relief was accordingly necessary. The Government asked that appellee be required to submit to the Court a plan, pursuant to which United's business would be reconstituted so as to form two fully competing companies in the shoe machinery market. It also requested "such other and further relief as may be necessary to establish workable competition in the shoe machinery market."

The District Court, after a hearing, denied the Government's petition.[2] It held that under United States v. Swift & Co., its power to modify the original decree was limited to cases involving "(1) a clear showing of (2) grievous wrong (3) evoked by new and unforeseen conditions." United States v. United Shoe Machinery Corp., 266 F.Supp. 328, 330 (1967). Analyzing its 1953 decree, as amended, the court said that the object of the decree was "not to restore so-called workable competition but to move toward establishing it," and that "the 1953 decree has operated in the manner and with the effect intended. It has put in motion forces which, aided by new technology, have eroded United's power and already dissipated much of the effect of United's monopolization." 266 F.Supp., at 330, 334. Accordingly, in view of the stringent requirements of *Swift* as the court construed that decision, the District Court denied the Government's petition. . . .

The District Court misconceived the thrust of this Court's decision in *Swift.* That case in no way restricts the District Court's power to grant the relief requested by the Government in the present case. In *Swift,* a consent decree had been entered in 1920 ordering a measure of divestiture by and imposing a variety of restraints upon the defendant meat packers. In 1930, after various unsuccessful attempts to secure modification or vacation of the decree, the packers filed a petition "to modify the consent decree and to adapt its restraints to the needs of a new day," as Justice Cardozo phrased it. 286 U.S., at 113. The lower court granted a measure of relief and the United States appealed. This Court reversed. It emphasized the power of a court of equity "to modify an injunction in adaptation to changed conditions though it was entered by consent." Id., at 114. The question, it held, is "whether enough has been shown to justify its exercise." Id., at 115. After reviewing the evidence, the Court concluded that the danger of monopoly and of the elimination of competition which led to the initial government

2. A petition by appellee, seeking to be relieved of certain restrictions contained in the original decree, was similarly denied. The judgment in this regard is not before us, since appellee has not appealed to this Court.

complaint and the decree had not been removed and that, although in some respects the decree had been effectuated, there was still a danger of unlawful restraints of trade. The Court's language, quoted and relied on by the trial court here, to the effect that "nothing less than a clear showing of grievous wrong evoked by new and unforeseen conditions should lead us to change," id., at 119, the decree, must, of course, be read in light of this context. *Swift* teaches that a decree may be changed upon an appropriate showing, and it holds that it may *not* be changed in the interests of the defendants if the purposes of the litigation as incorporated in the decree (the elimination of monopoly and restrictive practices) have not been fully achieved.

The present case is the obverse of the situation in *Swift* if the Government's allegations are proved. Here, the Government claims that the provisions of the decree were specifically designed to achieve the establishment of "workable competition" by various means and that the decree has failed to accomplish this result. Because time and experience have demonstrated this fact, according to the Government, it seeks modification of the decree. Nothing in *Swift* precludes this. In *Swift,* the defendants sought relief not to achieve the purposes of the provisions of the decree, but to escape their impact. Accordingly, we conclude that the District Court erred in denying the Government's petition "on the authority of United States v. Swift & Co.," 266 F.Supp., at 334.

Decision as to the Government's petition to modify the decree in the present case must be based upon the specific facts and circumstances that are presented. In urging affirmance of the 1953 decision, the Government advised this Court that, in framing the decree, the District Court had "proceeded on the premise that relatively mild remedies should be tried as a first resort, and that the possibility of more drastic measures should be held in abeyance." Paragraph 18 of the decree appeared to be in confirmation of this statement since it expressly required a report after 10 years of experience under the decree and contemplated that petitions for modification might be filed "in view of [the decree's] effect in establishing workable competition." Paragraph 18 then specifically provided that any such petition would have to be accompanied by "affidavits setting forth the then structure of the shoe machinery market and defendant's power within that market." [3]

These specifications were peculiarly apt because this is a monopoly case under § 2 of the Sherman Act and because the decree was shaped in response to findings of monopolization of the shoe machinery market. That the purpose of the 1953 decree was to eliminate this unlawful market domination was made clear beyond question by the District Court's statement at the beginning of the section of its opinion dealing with relief. This read as follows:

"Where a defendant has monopolized commerce in violation of § 2, the principal objects of the decrees are to extirpate practices that have caused or

3. In paragraph 23 of the original decree jurisdiction was expressly retained "for the purpose of enabling either of the parties to apply to this Court at any time for such further orders and directions as may be appropriate for the correction, construction, or carrying out of this Decree, and to set aside the Decree and take further proceedings if future developments justify that course in the appropriate enforcement of the Anti-Trust Act."

may hereafter cause monopolization, and to restore workable competition in the market." 110 F.Supp., at 346–347.

It is of course established that, in a § 2 case, upon appropriate findings of violation, it is the duty of the court to prescribe relief which will terminate the illegal monopoly, deny to the defendant the fruits of its statutory violation, and ensure that there remain no practices likely to result in monopolization in the future. . . . The trial court is charged with inescapable responsibility to achieve this objective, although it may, if circumstances warrant, accept a formula for achieving the result by means less drastic than immediate dissolution or divestiture. The decree in the present case was carefully devised within the limits of this principle. Measures short of divestiture were prescribed with provisions for review and possible revision after 10 years.[4]

The District Court has now denied the Government's petition for modification of the decree on the ground that the decree is "still working at its long-range task of freeing the market from all consequences of United's monopolization and keeping the door wide open for the arrival of an adequately provided challenger." According to the court, this was the intended effect of the decree.

If the decree had not contained paragraph 18—if it had been silent as to the time for submitting reports and, if necessary, petitions for modification—and if after 10 years it were shown that the decree had not achieved the adequate relief to which the Government is entitled in a § 2 case, it would have been the duty of the court to modify the decree so as to assure the complete extirpation of the illegal monopoly. The court's power to do this is clear. See, e.g., United States v. Swift & Co.; Chrysler Corp. v. United States, 316 U.S. 556 (1942). Its duty is implicit in the findings of violation of § 2 and in the decisions of this Court as to the type of remedy which must be prescribed.

We find nothing in the 1953 decree, as amended, or in the District Court's opinion relating thereto which presents an obstacle or embarrassment to the application of this principle in the present case. If the decree has not, after 10 years, achieved its "principal objects," namely, "to extirpate practices that have caused or may hereafter cause monopolization, and to restore workable competition in the market"—the time has come to prescribe other, and if necessary more definitive, means to achieve the result. A decade is enough.[5] Even if we should assume that paragraph 18, as the District Court now states, had only the limited purpose of calling for a 10-year report as to whether the decree was "gradually eroding United's 1953 power to monopolize the market," 266 F.Supp., at 330, its specific provisions did not exhaust the District Court's power. Relief in a Sherman Act case "should put an end

4. In rejecting the suggestion that United be forbidden to lease on any terms, the District Court stated specifically that it "agrees that it would be undesirable, at least until milder remedies have been tried, to direct United to abolish leasing forthwith." 110 F.Supp., at 349.

5. We emphasize that there is no issue here regarding the timing of the Government's petition for modification. No claim is made that the Government has petitioned for modification before the running of a reasonable period during which the effects of the original decree have become clear. Moreover, the Government may claim, persuasively, that paragraph 18 of the original decree specifically contemplated that the Government would petition when it did.

to the combination and deprive the defendants of any of the benefits of the illegal conduct, and break up or render impotent the monopoly power found to be in violation of the Act." United States v. Grinnell Corp., 384 U.S. 563, 577 (1966). . . . The District Court should proceed to determine whether the relief in this case has met the standards which this Court has prescribed. If not, the District Court should modify the decree so as to achieve the required result with all appropriate expedition.

Justice MARSHALL took no part in the consideration or decision of this case.

---

1) Does *United Shoe* modify *Swift*'s standard for modification? Can you reconcile the decisions on the grounds that (a) the *United Shoe* plaintiff sought to modify? (b) the *United Shoe* decree followed trial rather than consent? (c) the motion to modify in *United Shoe* sought to strengthen the injunction and to make it more effective rather than to relax it?

2) Courts attempt, with post-injunction procedure, to keep personal orders in tune with the world about them. Like all post-judgment procedure, motions to modify and dissolve strive to reconcile the competing policies of finality and correctness. Finality is important. Disputes must end sometime to keep the public peace, to prevent harassment, and to allow stability to plan the future. Yet most of us find it incongruous to have conduct controlled by an order out of tune with present law and circumstances.

Res judicata perpetuates error. For example, when the Wilsons divorced in 1970, the Texas trial judge apportioned a military pension to grant the wife $225.25 per month. Even after the Supreme Court held in McCarty v. McCarty, 453 U.S. 210 (1981), that such pensions were not divisible, the Texas decision received res judicata-full faith and credit, and the wife received a judgment for arrearages *plus* future payments. Wilson v. Wilson, 667 F.2d 497 (5th Cir. 1982). It took an Act of Congress to avoid *McCarty* for those spouses who lacked a Texas judgment. Uniformed Services Former Spouse's Protection Act, Pub.L. No. 97–252, §§ 1001–1006, 96 Stat. 718 (1982) codified 10 U.S.C.A. § 1408.

3) When prior judicial decisions guide future conduct, however, courts hate to perpetuate "bad" law. In Commissioner of Internal Revenue v. Sunnen, 333 U.S. 591 (1948), a court had adjudicated the tax impact of a contract favorably to the taxpayer; but when the decisional law changed in unrelated litigation, the authorities successfully sought to tax later income under that contract on the theory that the unrelated decisions controlled and that the earlier adjudication should be denied res judicata effect for tax years after those decisions. The Supreme Court held that each tax year is a separate claim or cause of action to advance the policy of treating all taxpayers the same and to avoid "inequalities in the administration of the revenue laws."

4) Res judicata doctrines are inappropriate for injunctions that continue in effect. Even so, conflict between approaches resembling *Wilson* and *Sunnen* is apparent. United States v. Swift & Co. embodies the *Wilson* approach. Lubben v. Selective Service System Local Board No. 27, 453 F.2d 645 (1st Cir. 1972), reveals the *Swift-Wilson* approach. The issue was the manner and time in which a Viet Nam war draftee could interpose a conscientious objec-

tion that crystalized after he received notice of induction. The trial judge relied on a similar decision by another trial judge, Lane v. Local Board No. 17, 315 F.Supp. 1355 (D.Mass.1970), to enjoin the government from inducting Lubben into the armed services. The government appealed both decisions. The other inductee, Lane, cross-appealed but Lubben did not. The government stipulated to dismiss both appeals. The court of appeals held in *Lane,* the cross appealed decision, that, in light of a Supreme Court decision, the trial judge lacked jurisdiction. The government then moved under Rule 60(b) to vacate Lubben's injunction:

"In United States v. Swift & Co. the Court held that it was the inherent right of a court of equity to modify an injunction in adaptation to changed circumstances which rendered the injunction an instrument of wrong. The clause of Rule 60(b)(5) allowing for relief from the inequitable prospective application of a judgment was designed primarily to incorporate that inherent power, and the clause should be used in light of the *Swift* decision.

" 'There is need to keep in mind steadily the limits of inquiry proper to the case before us. We are not framing a decree. We are asking ourselves whether anything has happened that will justify us now in changing a decree. The injunction, *whether right or wrong,* is not subject to impeachment in its application to the conditions that existed at its making . . . . *Nothing less than a clear showing of grievous wrong evoked by new and unforseen conditions* should lead us to change what was decreed after years of litigation with the consent of all concerned.' [Emphasis by *Lubben* court]

"The government has not met its burden of demonstrating that inequity results from continued enforcement of the injunction against appellant's Local Board. Indeed, the conditions of the injunction could have been easily complied with in the year since the dismissal of the *Lubben* appeal, and compliance at this time would not prejudice the Selective Service System. The *Ehlert* and *Lane* decisions were not such subsequent events as to render continued application of the injunction inequitable." 453 F.2d at 651.

5) The last decade reveals the decline of the *Swift-Lubben* approach. We may identify several reasons. Protracted structural injunctive litigation about schools, prisons, hospitals, and other institutions became prominent. Rules 25(d) and 65(d) give injunctions against government officials long lives, and Rule 23(b)(2) makes a "plaintiff" almost perpetual. A realistic approach to changing the law, and an alacrity to interpret, expand, and contract the governing substantive law became the more prominent if not the pervasive view. Finally, remedial pragmatism and experimentation achieved favor. Fiss, The Forms of Justice, 93 Harv.L.Rev. 1, 45–57 (1979). The process of determining and defining rights in injunctions blends imperceptibly into the process of enforcing those rights through motions to modify; post-injunction enforcement blends into the contempt process.

PASADENA CITY BOARD OF EDUCATION v. SPANGLER

427 U.S. 424, 96 S.Ct. 2697, 49 L.Ed.2d 599 (1976).

Justice REHNQUIST delivered the opinion of the Court.

In 1968, several students in the public schools of Pasadena, Cal., joined by their parents, instituted an action in the United States District Court for the Central District of California seeking injunctive relief from allegedly unconstitutional segregation of the high schools of the Pasadena Unified School District (PUSD). This action named as defendants the Pasadena City Board of Education, which operates the PUSD, and several of its officials. Before the defendants had filed an answer, the United States moved to intervene in the case pursuant to . . . 42 U.S.C. § 2000h–2. . . .

[T]he District Court held a trial on the allegations that the Pasadena school system was unconstitutionally segregated. On January 23, 1970, the court entered a judgment in which it concluded that the defendants' educational policies and procedures were violative of the Fourteenth Amendment. The court ordered the defendants "enjoined from failing to prepare and adopt a plan to correct racial imbalance at all levels in the Pasadena Unified School District." The defendants were further ordered to submit to the District Court a plan for desegregating the Pasadena schools. In addition to requiring provisions for the assignment of staff and the construction and location of facilities, the District Court ordered that

"[t]he plan shall provide for student assignments in such a manner that, by or before the beginning of the school year that commences in September of 1970 there shall be no school in the District, elementary or junior high or senior high school, with a majority of any minority students."

The court went on to retain

"jurisdiction of this cause in order to continue to observe and evaluate the plans and the execution of the plans of the Pasadena Unified School District in regard to the hiring, promotion, and assignment of teachers and professional staff members, the construction and location of facilities, and the assignment of students." Ibid.

The defendant school officials voted to comply with the District Court's decree and not to appeal. They thereupon set out to devise and submit the plan demanded by the District Court. In February the defendants submitted their proposed plan, the "Pasadena Plan," and on March 10, 1970, the District Court approved the plan, finding it "to be in conformance with the Judgment entered herein January 23, 1970." The "Pasadena Plan" was implemented the following September, and the Pasadena schools have been under its terms ever since.

In January 1974, petitioners, successors to the original defendants in this action, filed a motion with the District Court seeking relief from the court's 1970 order. Petitioners sought four changes: to have the judgment modified so as to eliminate the requirement that there be "no school in the District, elementary or junior high or senior high school, with a majority of any minority students"; to have the District Court's injunction dissolved; to have the District Court terminate its "retained jurisdiction" over the actions of the

Board; or, as an alternative, to obtain approval of petitioners' proposed modifications of the "Pasadena Plan."

The District Court held hearings on these motions and, on March 1, 1974, denied them in their entirety. In an opinion filed May 3, the court discussed its reasons for refusing the relief requested by petitioners. 375 F.Supp. 1304 (1974). Petitioners appealed to the Court of Appeals for the Ninth Circuit. A divided panel of that court affirmed the District Court, 519 F.2d 430 (1975), but all three members of the panel expressed substantial reservations about some of the District Court's actions and the implications of some portions of its orders as they bore on the future operations of the Pasadena schools. Judges Ely and Chambers were apparently satisfied that the District Judge would heed the reservations expressed in their separate opinions, however, and they were content to affirm the District Court's order and remand the case. Judge Wallace dissented from the affirmance. Because the case seemed to present issues of importance regarding the extent of a district court's authority in imposing a plan designed to achieve a unitary school system, we granted certiorari. . . . We vacate the judgment of the Court of Appeals and remand the case to that court for further proceedings.

We must first deal with petitioners' contention that there no longer exists any case or controversy sufficient to support our jurisdiction. Petitioners assert that all the original student plaintiffs have graduated from the Pasadena school system, and that since the District Court never certified this suit as a class action pursuant to Fed.Rule Civ.Proc. 23, the case is moot. Respondents advance several theories why it is not moot.

Counsel for the individual named respondents, the original student plaintiffs and their parents, argue that this litigation was filed as a class action, that all the parties have until now treated it as a class action, and that the failure to obtain the class certification required under Rule 23 is merely the absence of a meaningless "verbal recital" which counsel insists should have no effect on the facts of this case. But these arguments overlook the fact that the named parties whom counsel originally undertook to represent in this litigation no longer have any stake in its outcome. As to them the case is clearly moot. And while counsel may wish to represent a class of unnamed individuals still attending the Pasadena public schools who do have some substantial interest in the outcome of this litigation, there has been no certification of any such class which is or was represented by a named party to this litigation. Except for the intervention of the United States, we think this case would clearly be moot.

The case did not remain an individual private action seeking to desegregate the Pasadena schools, however. The United States intervened in this case pursuant to 42 U.S.C. § 2000h–2. That section provides that "the United States shall be entitled to the same relief as if it had instituted the action." The meaning of this provision is somewhat ambiguous, and there is little legislative history to shed any light upon the intention of Congress. But we think the statute is properly read to authorize the United States to continue as a party plaintiff in this action, despite the disappearance of the original plaintiffs and the absence of any class certification, so long as such participation serves the statutory purpose, and that the presence of the United States as a party ensures that this case is not moot.

Petitioners requested the District Court to dissolve its injunctive order requiring that there be no school in the PUSD with a majority of any minority students enrolled. The District Court refused this request, and ordered the injunction continued. The court apparently based this decision in large part upon its view that petitioners had failed properly to comply with its original order. This conclusion was in turn premised upon the fact that although the School Board had reorganized PUSD attendance patterns in conformity with the court-approved Pasadena Plan, literal compliance with the terms of the court's order had been obtained in only the initial year of the plan's operation. Following the 1970–1971 school year, black student enrollment at one Pasadena school exceeded 50% of that school's total enrollment. The next year, four Pasadena schools exceeded this 50% black enrollment figure; and at the time of the hearing on petitioners' motion some five schools, in a system of 32 regular schools, were ostensibly in violation of the District Court's "no majority of any minority" requirement. It was apparently the view of the majority of the Court of Appeals' panel that this failure to maintain literal compliance with the 1970 injunction indicated that the District Court had not abused its discretion in refusing to grant so much of petitioner's motion for modification as pertained to this aspect of the order.[1] We think this view was wrong.

We do not have before us any issue as to the validity of the District Court's original judgment, since petitioners' predecessors did not appeal from it. The District Court's conclusion that unconstitutional segregation existed in the PUSD; its decision to order a systemwide school reorganization plan based upon the guidelines which it submitted to the defendants; and the inclusion in those guidelines of the requirement that the plan contain provisions insuring that there be no majority of any minority in any Pasadena school, all became embodied in the 1970 decree. All that is now before us are the questions of whether the District Court was correct in denying relief when petitioners in 1974 sought to modify the "no majority" requirement as then interpreted by the District Court.

The meaning of this requirement, as originally established by the District Court, was apparently unclear even to the parties. In opposing the petitioners' request for relief in 1974, counsel for the original individual plaintiffs and counsel for the Government jointly stipulated that they were aware "of no violations of the Pasadena Plan up to and including the present." These parties were, of course, aware that some of the Pasadena schools had "slipped out of compliance" with the literal terms of the order. The stipulation was based upon the fact that the plaintiffs never understood the District Court's order to require annual reassignment of pupils in order to accommodate

1. In addition to several other factors, Judge Ely cited the fact that the defendants had been found in violation of the District Court's 1970 order as supplying evidence that the court "could rightly determine that the 'dangers' which induced the original determination of constitutional infringements in Pasadena have not diminished sufficiently to require modification or dissolution of the original Order." 519 F.2d 430, 434 (1975). Judge Chambers, concurring in the result, relied only upon the fact that petitioners had apparently not yet complied with what he viewed as the "continuing duty to homogenize" imposed upon them by the District Court's 1970 order. Judge Chambers thought that as soon as the PUSD was brought in compliance with that order, the mandatory injunction should be terminated.

changing demographic residential patterns in Pasadena from year to year, as the Government candidly admits in its brief here.

Petitioners have argued that they never understood the injunction, or the provisions of the plan which they drafted to implement that order, to contain such a requirement either.[3] But at the hearing on petitioners' motion for relief the District Court made it clear that *its* understanding of the decree was quite different from that of the parties. In response to the arguments of petitioners' counsel, the judge stated that his 1970 order "meant to me that at least during my lifetime there would be no majority of any minority in any school in Pasadena."

When the District Court's order in this case, as interpreted and applied by that court, is measured against what this Court said in its intervening decision in Swann v. Board of Education, 402 U.S. 1 (1971), regarding the scope of the judicially created relief which might be available to remedy violations of the Fourteenth Amendment, we think the inconsistency between the two is clear. The District Court's interpretation of the order appears to contemplate the "substantive constitutional right [to a] particular degree of racial balance or mixing" which the Court in *Swann* expressly disapproved. It became apparent, at least by the time of the 1974 hearing, that the District Court viewed this portion of its order not merely as a "starting point in the process of shaping a remedy," which *Swann* indicated would be appropriate, but instead as an "inflexible requirement," ibid., to be applied anew each year to the school population within the attendance zone of each school.

The District Court apparently believed it had authority to impose this requirement even though subsequent changes in the racial mix in the Pasadena schools might be caused by factors for which the defendants could not be considered responsible. Whatever may have been the basis for such a belief in 1970, in *Swann* the Court cautioned that "it must be recognized that there are limits" beyond which a court may not go in seeking to dismantle a dual school system. These limits are in part tied to the necessity of establishing that school authorities have in some manner caused unconstitutional segregation, for "[a]bsent a constitutional violation there would be no basis for judicially ordering assignment of students on a racial basis." While the District Court found such a violation in 1970, and while this unappealed finding afforded a basis for its initial requirement that the defendants prepare a plan to remedy such racial segregation, its adoption of the Pasadena Plan in 1970 established a racially neutral system of student assignment in the PUSD. Having done that, we think that in enforcing its order so as to require annual readjustment of attendance zones so that there would not be a majority of any minority in any Pasadena public school, the District Court exceeded its authority.

3. There is some disagreement whether petitioners, or their predecessors at least, understood the District Court's order in the same manner as it was interpreted in 1974. There are some suggestions in the record that petitioners may have made some attempts to stay in compliance with the "no majority of any minority" guideline as demographic patterns in Pasadena changed. But there are no factual assessments in the record as to the understanding of the petitioners, and they have argued before us that their reading of the 1970 order was the same as that of the plaintiffs. However this factual issue might be resolved, we think petitioners were not foreclosed from challenging the District Court's decree as interpreted and applied in 1974.

In so concluding, we think it important to note what this case does not involve. The "no majority of any minority" requirement with respect to attendance zones did not call for defendants to submit "step at a time" plans by definition incomplete at inception. See, e.g., United States v. Montgomery Board of Education, 395 U.S. 225 (1969). Nor did it call for a plan embodying specific revisions of the attendance zones for particular schools, as well as provisions for later appraisal of whether such discrete individual modifications had achieved the "unitary system" required by Brown v. Board of Education, 349 U.S. 294, 300 (1955). The plan approved in this case applied in general terms to all Pasadena schools, and no one contests that its implementation did "achieve a system of determining admission to the public schools on a nonracial basis."

There was also no showing in this case that those post-1971 changes in the racial mix of some Pasadena schools which were focused upon by the lower courts were in any manner caused by segregative actions chargeable to the defendants. The District Court rejected petitioners' assertion that the movement was caused by so-called "white flight" traceable to the decree itself. It stated that the "trends evidenced in Pasadena closely approximate the state-wide trends in California schools, both segregated and desegregated." 375 F.Supp., at 1306. The fact that black student enrollment at 5 out of 32 of the regular Pasadena schools came to exceed 50% during the 4-year period from 1970 to 1974 apparently resulted from people randomly moving into, out of, and around the PUSD area. This quite normal pattern of human migration resulted in some changes in the demographics of Pasadena's residential patterns, with resultant shifts in the racial makeup of some of the schools. But as these shifts were not attributed to any segregative actions on the part of the petitioners, we think this case comes squarely within the sort of situation foreseen in *Swann:*

"It does not follow that the communities served by [unitary] systems will remain demographically stable, for in a growing, mobile society, few will do so. Neither school authorities nor district courts are constitutionally required to make year-by-year adjustments of the racial composition of student bodies once the affirmative duty to desegregate has been accomplished and racial discrimination through official action is eliminated from the system."

It may well be that petitioners have not yet totally achieved the unitary system contemplated by this quotation from *Swann.* There has been, for example, dispute as to the petitioners' compliance with those portions of the plan specifying procedures for hiring and promoting teachers and administrators. . . . But that does not undercut the force of the principle underlying the quoted language from *Swann.* In this case the District Court approved a plan designed to obtain racial neutrality in the attendance of students at Pasadena's public schools. No one disputes that the initial implementation of this plan accomplished *that* objective. That being the case, the District Court was not entitled to require the PUSD to rearrange its attendance zones each year so as to ensure that the racial mix desired by the court was maintained in perpetuity. For having once implemented a racially neutral attendance pattern in order to remedy the perceived constitutional violations on the part of the defendants, the District Court had fully performed its function of providing the appropriate remedy for previous racially discriminatory attendance patterns.

At least one of the judges of the Court of Appeals expressed the view that while all of the petitioners' contentions which we have discussed might be sound, they were barred from asserting them by their predecessors' failure to appeal from the 1970 decree of the District Court. But this observation overlooks well-established rules governing modification of even a final decree entered by a court of equity. See Pennsylvania v. Wheeling & Belmont Bridge Co., 18 How. 421 (1856); United States v. Swift & Co.; System Federation v. Wright, 364 U.S. 642 (1961). In the latter case this Court said:

"There is also no dispute but that a sound judicial discretion may call for the modification of the terms of an injunctive decree if the circumstances, whether of law or fact, obtaining at the time of its issuance have changed, or new ones have since arisen. The source of the power to modify is of course the fact that an injunction often requires continuing supervision by the issuing court and always a continuing willingness to apply its powers and processes on behalf of the party who obtained that equitable relief."

Even had the District Court's decree been unambiguous and clearly understood by the parties to mean what that court declared it to mean in 1974, the "no majority of any minority" provision would, as we have indicated previously, be contrary to the intervening decision of this Court in *Swann,* supra. The ambiguity of the provision itself, and the fact that the parties to the decree interpreted it in a manner contrary to the interpretation ultimately placed upon it by the District Court, is an added factor in support of modification. The two factors taken together make a sufficiently compelling case so that such modification should have been ordered by the District Court.

. . .

There is little real dispute among the parties with our observations thus far.[5] Indeed, as the Government points out, each of the judges of the Court of Appeals disapproved both the District Court's statement regarding its lifetime commitment to the "no majority of any minority" rule and the substance of that rule itself, to the extent that either indicated a continuing, rigid insistence upon some particular degree of racial balance. The Government adds that these disapprovals were, in its view, quite proper, and it concludes they were sufficient to remove the "no majority of any minority" requirement from this case.

It is here that we disagree with the Government. Violation of an injunctive decree such as that issued by the District Court in this case can result in punishment for contempt in the form of either a fine or imprisonment. Federal Rule Civ. Proc. 65(d) concomitantly provides that "[e]very order granting an injunction and every restraining order shall . . . be specific in terms; shall describe in reasonable detail, and not by reference to the complaint or other document, the act or acts sought to be restrained . . . ." Because of the rightly serious view courts have traditionally taken of violations of injunctive orders, and because of the severity of punishment which

5. Counsel for the original plaintiffs has urged, in the courts below and before us, that the District Court's perpetual "no majority of any minority" requirement was valid and consistent with *Swann,* at least until the school system achieved "unitary" status in all other respects such as the hiring and promoting of teachers and administrators. Since we have concluded that the case is moot with regard to these plaintiffs, these arguments are not properly before us. It should be clear from what we have said that they have little substance.

may be imposed for such violation, such orders must in compliance with Rule 65 be specific and reasonably detailed.

Because of related concern that outstanding injunctive orders of courts be obeyed until modified or reversed by a court having the authority to do so, this Court has held that even though the constitutionality of the Act under which the injunction issued is challenged, disobedience of such an outstanding order of a federal court subjects the violator to contempt even though his constitutional claim might be later upheld. United States v. Mine Workers. The Court has likewise held that a State is constitutionally free to adopt a similar rule respecting punishment as contempt of violation of injunctive orders issued by its courts. Walker v. City of Birmingham.

There is necessarily a counterpart to this well-established insistence that those who are subject to the commands of an injunctive order must obey those commands, notwithstanding eminently reasonable and proper objections to the order, until it is modified or reversed. That counterpart is that when such persons heed this well-established rule and prosecute their remedy first by a motion to modify in the issuing court and then, failing there, by appeal of that court's denial of their motion, they are entitled in a proper case to obtain a definitive disposition of their objections. Here a majority of the Court of Appeals for the Ninth Circuit in separate opinions strongly intimated that the District Court erred in refusing to amend the "no majority of any minority" provision of its order, but the Court nonetheless affirmed the order of the District Court denying *in toto* the motion to modify that order.

Petitioners have plainly established that they were entitled to relief from the District Court's injunction insofar as it required them to alter school attendance zones in response to shifts in demographics within the PUSD. The order of the District Court which was affirmed by the Court of Appeals equally plainly envisioned the continuation of such a requirement. We do not think petitioners must be satisfied with what may have been the implicit assumption of the Court of Appeals that the District Court would heed the "disapproval" expressed by each member of the panel of that court in his opinion. Instead, we think petitioners were entitled on this phase of the case to a judgment of the Court of Appeals reversing the District Court with respect to its treatment of that portion of the order.

Because the case is to be returned to the Court of Appeals, that court will have an opportunity to reconsider its decision in light of our observations regarding the appropriate scope of equitable relief in this case. We thus think it unnecessary for us to consider petitioners' other contentions: that the District Court's 1970 injunction should in all respects be dissolved; that the District Court's jurisdiction over the PUSD should be terminated; or that petitioners' suggested modifications of the Pasadena Plan should be accepted as an alternative to the present plan. The record in this case reflects the situation in Pasadena as it was in 1974. At oral argument the Solicitor General discussed the Government's belief that if, as petitioners have represented, they have complied with the District Court's order during the intervening two years, they will probably be entitled to a lifting of the District Court's order in its entirety. And while any determination of compliance or noncompliance must, of course, comport with our holding today, it must also depend on factual determinations which the Court of Appeals and the District Court are in a far better position than we are to make in the first instance.

Accordingly the judgment of the Court of Appeals is vacated, and the case is remanded to that court for further proceedings not inconsistent with this opinion.

Justice STEVENS took no part in the consideration or decision of this case.

Justice MARSHALL, with whom Justice BRENNAN joins, dissenting.

I cannot agree with the Court that the District Court's refusal to modify the "no majority of any minority" provision of its order was erroneous. Because at the time of the refusal "racial discrimination through official action," Swann v. Board of Education, 402 U.S. 1, 32 (1971), had apparently not yet been eliminated from the Pasadena school system, it is my view that the District Court did not abuse its discretion in refusing to dissolve a major part of its order.

In denying petitioners' motion for modification of the 1970 desegregation order, the District Court described a 3-year pattern of opposition by a number of the members of the Board of Education to both the spirit and letter of the Pasadena Plan. It found that "the Pasadena Plan has not had the cooperation from the Board that permits a realistic measurement of its educational success or failure." 375 F.Supp. 1304, 1308 (CD Cal. 1974) (footnote omitted). Moreover, the 1974 Board of Education submitted to the District Court an alternative to the Pasadena Plan, which, at least in the mind of one member of the Court of Appeals, "would very likely result in rapid resegregation." 519 F.2d 430, 435 (CA9 1975). I agree with Judge Ely that there is "abundant evidence upon which the district judge, in the reasonable exercise of his discretion, could rightly determine that the 'dangers' which induced the original determination of constitutional infringements in Pasadena have not diminished sufficiently to require modification or dissolution of the original Order."

The Court's conclusion that modification of the District Court's order is mandated is apparently largely founded on the fact that during the Pasadena Plan's first year, its implementation did result in no school's having a majority of minority students. According to the Court, it follows from our decision in *Swann,* that as soon as the school attendance zone scheme had been successful, even for a very short period, in fulfilling its objectives, the District Court should have relaxed its supervision over that aspect of the desegregation plan. It is irrelevant to the Court that the system may not have achieved " 'unitary' status in all other respects such as the hiring and promoting of teachers and administrators."

In my view, the Court, in so ruling, has unwarrantedly extended our statement in *Swann* that "[n]either school authorities nor district courts are constitutionally required to make year-by-year adjustments of the racial composition of student bodies *once the affirmative duty to desegregate has been accomplished and racial discrimination through offical action is eliminated from the system."* (emphasis added). That statement recognizes on the one hand that a fully desegregated school system may not be compelled to adjust its attendance zones to conform to changing demographic patterns. But on the other hand, it also appears to recognize that *until* such a unitary system is established, a district court may act with broad discretion—discretion which includes the adjustment of attendance zones—so that the goal of a wholly unitary system might be sooner achieved.

In insisting that the District Court largely abandon its scrutiny of attendance patterns, the Court might well be insuring that a unitary school system in which segregation has been eliminated "root and branch," Green v. County School Board, 391 U.S. 430, 438 (1968), will never be achieved in Pasadena. For at the point that the Pasadena system is in compliance with the aspects of the plan specifying procedures for hiring and promoting teachers and administrators, it may be that the attendance patterns within the system will be such as to once again manifest substantial aspects of a segregated system. It seems to me singularly unwise for the Court to risk such a result.

We have held that "[o]nce a right and a violation have been shown, the scope of a district court's equitable powers to remedy past wrongs is broad, for breadth and flexibility are inherent in equitable remedies." Swann v. Board of Education. As the Court recognizes, there is no issue before us as to the validity of the District Court's original judgment that unconstitutional segregation existed in the Pasadena school system. Thus, there is no question as to there being both a "right and a violation." Moreover, at least as of the time that the District Court acted on the request for modification, the violation had not yet been entirely remedied. Particularly, given the breadth of discretion normally accorded a district court in fashioning equitable remedies, I see no reason to require the District Court in a case such as this to modify its order prior to the time that it is clear that the entire violation has been remedied and a unitary system has been achieved.[1] We should not compel the District Court to modify its order unless conditions have changed so much that "dangers, once substantial, have become attenuated to a shadow." United States v. Swift & Co. I, for one, cannot say that the District Court was in error in determining that such attenuation had not yet taken place and that modification of the order would "surely be to sign the death warrant of the Pasadena Plan and its objectives." Accordingly, I dissent.[2]

---

1) Which standard did Justice Rehnquist use: *Swift* or *United Shoe?* Or a special school desegregation standard?

2) A lighted cross was located in a state park. Judge Ward found that it breached the establishment clause; the court of appeals affirmed. American Civil Liberties Union of Georgia v. Rabun County Chamber of Commerce, 678 F.2d 1379 (11th Cir. 1982). How should he draft the injunction? Judge Ward "ordered the cross to be removed." 678 F.2d at 1382. Should

1. In the course of final argument, the District Judge did make the spontaneous statement that the 1970 order "meant to me that at least during my lifetime there would be no majority of any minority in any school in Pasadena." As did the Court of Appeals, I disapprove the statement to the extent that it suggests that continuous redistricting can be required "even *after* the court has determined that its plan has been effectively implemented and *racial discrimination [has been] eliminated from the system.*" 519 F.2d, at 438 (emphasis added).

2. While I dissent from the Court's opinion, I do acknowledge the narrowness of its holding. For instance, the Court intimates that it would view this case differently if the demographic changes were themselves a product of a desegregation order. Moreover, as the Court observes, this case does not involve an attendance-zone requirement calling "for defendants to submit 'step at a time' plans by definition incomplete at inception." Ibid.

he have simply told the defendants to "cease violating the establishment clause"? Which order would Justice Rehnquist favor? See also Newman v. Alabama, 683 F.2d 1312, 1318 (11th Cir. 1982). How would the terms of the order bear on the modification problem? Compare the *Spangler* injunction with Judge Frank Johnson's in Wyatt v. Stickney, 344 F.Supp. 387 (M.D. Ala.1972); Wyatt v. Aderholt, 503 F.2d 1305 (5th Cir. 1974). It contained more than 75 specific requirements for two state institutions including dishwashing, washroom, and shower water temperature. Was the *Spangler* injunction too vague to administer or was it, in fact, quite specific?

A judge who views remedy passively will decide whether the challenged situation violates the substantive law. He will neither choose nor implement the remedy. Instead the remedial burden falls on defendant. The judge may, however, resort to contempt if necessary. We question whether this approach can be the basis for effective structural relief. Will the game of "guess what's on my mind" be a sterile and wasteful way to implement constitutional reforms against obstreperous bureaucracies? Should judges announce positive instead of negative directives? Should they participate in the shaping of remedies?

Many judges seek to tailor positive injunctions to fit the violations they find. This often emerges from the idea that the object of a remedy is to prevent discrete incidents. In Newman v. Alabama, 683 F.2d at 1319, the court said that injunctive relief "must be no broader than necessary to remedy the constitutional violation." Does the *Spangler* majority represent that idea? In The Forms of Justice, 93 Harv.L.Rev. 1 (1979), Professor Fiss criticized what he calls the "tailoring principle." He thinks it impoverishes remedy because it a) "suggests that the relationship between remedy and violation is deductive or formal," b) views the violation as the exclusive source of the remedy, c) refers each provision of the remedy to the violation, d) assumes that each violation has a unique remedy, and e) suggests that the remedy follows certainty from the violation. 93 Harv.L.Rev. at 47.

Fiss thinks that remedy is less formalistic and he stresses two sets of intermediate factors. The judge should shape the remedy after considering normative countervalues; federalism, fairness and evenhandedness. He should also assess efficacy pragmatically. Thus a structural order may be both positive and specific. Precise orders define the bureaucratic task and decrease the risk of evasion. Moreover, the judge should be instrumental and willing to revise a burdensome or ineffective remedy.

The judge who considers fairness and strategy will vary the remedial pattern based on discrete circumstances. This exposes the dilemma of instrumentalism. 93 Harv.L.Rev. at 53. The judge desires to be efficacious. He may exaggerate the hazards of interdependent decisionmaking and distort both right and remedy to accomplish the possible. The tailoring principle's intellectual bonds may emerge in a new guise.

3) Two views of remedy compete for attention in desegregation lawsuits. First, jurisdiction "should extend only so far as is necessary to remedy racial imbalance caused by school officials' unconstitutional acts." Second, "a desegregation remedy must [also] eliminate racial prejudice from school board decisionmaking." Note, Retention of Jurisdiction in Desegregation Cases: A Causal and Attitudinal Analysis, 52 S.Cal.L.Rev. 195, 200 (1978). Did

the *Spangler* injunction order the school to revise the desegregation plan annually to accommodate to changing demography? Did the Supreme Court majority think that the district judge could adjust the remedy to changing demographic patterns not caused by PUSD's constitutional violations?

Does a judge's attitude toward remedy determine his approach to modification? Does the majority's decision in *Spangler* turn on the vague or ambiguous order? the parties' interpretation? the change in decisional law? Why didn't plaintiff adjudicate the issues with a motion to hold PUSD in contempt? Would a motion for contempt be simply bad form under the circumstances? The specificity requirement is based in part on the idea that injunctions that are the basis for contempt must warn defendants of the conduct they forbid. If neither the parties nor the judge anticipate basing contempt on an injunction, should courts be allowed to enjoin defendants generally to "go forth and sin no more"?

Are general injunctions a more realistic way to respond to complex structural enforcement? If defendant drags its feet or displays recalcitrance, should the judge then modify a general order to make it more specific? Would the specific order then be a basis for contempt? In Newman v. Alabama, 683 F.2d 1312 (11th Cir. 1982), the court insisted that plaintiffs should have enforced a prison consent decree with contempt instead of entering an order telling defendants to release 352 named inmates.

4) Judge Friendly's opinion on motion to modify the Willowbrook consent judgment allows us to examine how the courts adopt that procedural device to the unique features of administering structural decrees. New York State Association for Retarded Children v. Carey, 706 F.2d 956, 967–71 (2d Cir. 1983). The New York defendants argued that the consent judgment which limited community placements to 15-bed facilities should be modified to allow placements in 50-bed facilities. Judge Friendly wrote:

"An injunction, as a final judgment with prospective application, may be modified by the court upon motion by a party and a showing that continuation of the injunction would be inequitable. F.R.Civ.P. 60(b)(5) expressly authorizes a district court to relieve a party from a final judgment if 'it is no longer equitable that the judgment should have prospective application.' The power of a court of equity to modify a decree of injunctive relief is long-established, broad, and flexible. 'A continuing decree of injunction directed to events to come is subject always to adaptation as events may shape the need. . . . The distinction is between restraints that give protection to rights fully accrued upon facts so nearly permanent as to be substantially impervious to change, and those that involve the supervision of changing conduct or conditions and are thus provisional and tentative.' United States v. Swift & Co. . . .

"In denying defendants' motion for modification of the limitation on the size of community placement facilities, Judge Bartels relied on other language of Justice Cardozo in United States v. Swift & Co., supra, quoted here *in extenso:*

" 'There is need to keep in mind steadily the limits of inquiry proper to the case before us. We are not framing a decree. We are asking ourselves whether anything has happened that will justify us now in changing a decree. The injunction, whether right or wrong, is not subject to impeachment in its application to the conditions that existed at its making. We are not at liberty to reverse under its application to the conditions that existed at its making. We are not at liberty to reverse under the guise of readjusting. Life is never static, and the passing of a decade has brought changes to the grocery business [the subject of the decree] as it has to every other. The inquiry for us is whether the changes are so important that the dangers, once substantial, have become attenuated to a shadow. No doubt the defendants will be better off if the injunction is relaxed, but they are not suffering hardship so extreme and unexpected as to justify us in saying that they are the victims of oppression. Nothing less than a clear showing of grievous wrong evoked by new and unforeseen conditions should lead us to change what was decreed after years of litigation with the consent of all concerned.'

"This apparent hardening of the usual standard for modifying decrees of injunctive relief did not stem from the fact that in *Swift* the Court was dealing with a consent decree. Justice Cardozo explicitly ruled that '[t]he result is all one whether the decree has been entered after litigation or by consent' and rejected the argument that for purposes of modification by the court, 'a decree entered upon consent is to be treated as a contract and not as a judicial act. . . . The consent is to be read as directed toward events as they then were. It was not an abandonment of the right to exact revision in the future, if revision should become necessary in adaptation to events to be.'[15] Rather, the considerations underlying the language just quoted from *Swift* were based on the specific facts then before the Court.

"The consent decree at issue in *Swift* had been entered into by the United States and five major meatpackers in February, 1920, enjoining the meatpackers from violating the antitrust laws and from holding any interest in several lines of business, including the wholesale and retail provision of other foodstuffs such as fish, vegetables, fruit and groceries, as to which the market power arising from defendants' domination of the meatpacking business was thought to give them unfair competitive advantages and to encourage practices violative of the antitrust laws. The ink had hardly become dry on the decree when the meatpackers began to assail it, see Swift & Co. v. United States, 276 U.S. 311 (1928); United States v. California Cooperative Canneries, 279 U.S. 553, 555 (1929), the latter of which attempts led to a suspension of the decree for several years. Not daunted by the adverse results in these cases, several of the meatpackers within a year sought major modification in the decree, which the lower court granted to the extent of eliminating the prohibitions mentioned above. The modification on which the Supreme Court passed in *Swift* would have robbed the 1920 consent decree of so much of its force that the Court considered it 'revers[al] under the guise of readjusting.'

"The *Swift* decision was analyzed by the Supreme Court in Chrysler Corp. v. United States, 316 U.S. 556, 562 (1942) and, more particularly, in United States v. United Shoe Machinery Corp. (1968). There the United States, rather than the defendant, sought modification of an antitrust decree. The

"**15.** This position was reaffirmed in System-Federation v. Wright, 364 U.S. 642, 650–52 (1961). Resort to a contractual analogy would be particularly inappropriate in the present case. This court has noted in a previous decision with respect to Willowbrook that even for purposes of interpretation, the 'Consent Judgment is no mere contract,' "

district court read *Swift* as limiting its power to modify to cases involving '(1) a clear showing of (2) grievous wrong (3) evoked by new and unforeseen conditions,' 266 F.Supp. 328, 330 (D. Mass. 1967). The Supreme Court held the district court had read *Swift* too rigidly. The language we have quoted in extenso must, the Court said, be read in the light of context. '*Swift* teaches that a decree may be changed upon an appropriate showing, and it holds that it may *not* be changed in the interest of the defendants if the purposes of the litigation as incorporated in the decree (the elimination of monopoly and restrictive practices) have not been fully achieved.' (emphasis in original).

"Our case differs from both *Swift* and *United Shoe Machinery.* Here, as in *Swift*, the modification is proposed by the defendants. But it is not, as in *Swift,* in derogation of the primary objective of the decree, namely, to empty such a mammoth institution as Willowbrook; indeed defendants offered substantial evidence that, again in contrast to *Swift,* the modification was essential to attaining that goal at any reasonably early date. To be sure, the change does run counter to another objective of the decree, namely, to place the occupants of Willowbrook in small facilities bearing some resemblance to a normal home, but any modification will perforce alter some aspect of the decree. An analogy closer than either *Swift* or *United Shoe* is King-Seeley Thermos Co. v. Aladin Industries, Inc., 418 F.2d 31 (2d Cir. 1969). We there considered a district court's refusal to modify a 1962 consent decree between two manufacturers regarding use by one, Aladdin Industries, of the generic term "thermos" in labels and advertising. Aladdin had sought modification of the decree insofar as it applied to advertising. We noted that the heavy burden applied in *Swift* must be read in the context of that case, in which, for reasons previously outlined, the meatpackers were obliged 'to stake their claim on drastic changes in conditions.' When a case involves drawing the line between legitimate interests on each side, modification will be allowed on a lesser showing:

" 'While changes in fact or in law afford the clearest bases for altering an injunction, the power of equity has repeatedly been recognized as extending also to cases where a better appreciation of the facts in light of experience indicates that the decree is not properly adapted to accomplishing its purposes.'

"We therefore remanded in *King-Seeley* for consideration whether, 'in the light of experience, the detailed provisions of the decree seriously and needlessly impeded [Aladdin's] exploitation of the generic term and that modification was necessary to achieve the results intended, even though this would take the form of reducing the restrictions imposed upon it,' See also Sec. v. Warren, 583 F.2d 115, 119–20 (3d Cir. 1978) (commentary on *Swift* and *King-Seeley*).[16]

"**16.** Some cases have steadfastly hewed to the *Swift* line. See, e.g., Humble Oil and Refining Co. v. American Oil Co., 405 F.2d 803, 813 (8th Cir.) (Blackmun, J.), cert. denied, 395 U.S. 905 (1969); United States v. Work Wear Corp., 602 F.2d 110, 112 n. 6 (6th Cir. 1979); Holiday Inns, Inc. v. Holiday Inn; Roberts v. St. Regis Paper Co., 653 F.2d 166, 174 (5th Cir. 1981).

"Other circuits have distinguished the *Swift* standard in different ways. See Tobin v. Alma Mills, 192 F.2d 133, 136–37 (4th Cir. 1951); United States v. City of Chicago, 663 F.2d 1354, 1359–60 (7th Cir. 1981) (en banc)."

"Two other considerations reinforce our conclusion that the district court imposed far too drastic a standard upon defendants' request for modification. It is well recognized that in institutional reform litigation such as this, judicially-imposed remedies must be open to adaptation when unforeseen obstacles present themselves, to improvement when a better understanding of the problem emerges, and to accommodation of a wider constellation of interests than is represented in the adversarial setting of the courtroom. In one of the earliest scholarly explications of institutional reform litigation, Professor Abram Chayes recognized as its most important characteristic that 'the trial judge has increasingly become the creator and manager of complex forms of ongoing relief, which have widespread effect on persons not before the court and require the judge's continuing involvement in administration and implementation,' Chayes, The Role of the Judge in Public Law Litigation, 89 Harv. L.Rev. 1281, 1284 (1976).[17] A principal advantage of the use of injunctive relief in such cases, Chayes added, is that '[o]ver time, the parties may resort to the court for enforcement or modification of the original order in light of changing circumstances.'

"As experience with this type of litigation increases, a consensus is emerging among commentators in favor of modification with a rather free hand. . . . The best statement we have found with respect to the appropriate legal standard for evaluating a defendant's motion for modification of a consent judgment in institutional reform litigation is that of Professor Owen Fiss:

" 'The judge must search for the 'best' remedy, but since his judgment must incorporate such open-ended considerations as effectiveness and fairness, and since the threat and constitutional value that occasions the intervention can never be defined with great precision, the intervention can never be defended with any certitude. It must always be open to revision, even without the strong showing traditionally required for modification of a decree, namely, that the first choice is causing grievous hardship. A revision is justified if the remedy is not working effectively or is unnecessarily burdensome.' [Citation omitted.]

Fiss, The Supreme Court, 1978 Term, Foreword: The Forms of Justice, 93 Harv.L.Rev. 1, 49 (1979). . . . Applications to modify a decree such as that in this case should thus be viewed with generosity. . . .

"In System Federation No. 91 v. Wright, 364 U.S. 642 (1961), the Supreme Court held that a consent decree prohibiting certain acts must be modified when the statutory requirement on which the decree was based was amended so as to permit them. Justice Harlan noted that 'the District Court's authority to adopt a consent decree comes only from the statute which the decree is intended to enforce'; hence the court must 'be free to modify the terms of a consent decree when a change in law brings those terms in conflict with statutory objectives,' 364 U.S. at 651. Justice Harlan took as undisputed the proposition that 'a sound judicial discretion may call for the modification of the terms of an injunctive decree if the circumstances,

"17. Professor Chayes has recently reaffirmed his view that injunctions in institutional reform cases "are not so much peremptory commands to be obeyed in terms, as they are future-oriented plans designed to achieve broad public policy objectives in a complex, ongoing fact situation," Chayes, The Supreme Court—1981 Term—Foreword: Public Law Litigation and the Burger Court, 96 Harv.L. Rev. 4, 56 (1982)."

whether of law or fact, obtaining at the time of its issuance have changed, or new ones have arisen.' We can see no reason for a different view when the requirement is constitutional and a subsequent decision of the Court has made clear that the court entering the decree interpreted the requirement too broadly. Theriault v. Smith, 523 F.2d 601 (1st Cir. 1975).

". . . [T]he district judge felt free to choose between the different views of plaintiffs' and defendants' experts with respect to the value of the limitations on the size of the units to which the residents of Willowbrook were to be transferred. We now know, . . . that this was not the appropriate inquiry. Once the defendants had established, as they unquestionably did, that abandoning the $^{15}/_{10}$ and $^{6}/_{3}$ bed limitations in favor of a 50 bed limitation would facilitate the emptying of Willowbrook and like institutions, the question was whether, in Chief Judge Seitz's phrase, 'professional judgment in fact was exercised' or, in Justice Powell's formulation, 'the decision by the professional is such a substantial departure from accepted professional judgment, practice or standards as to demonstrate that the person responsible actually did not base the decision on such a judgment.' We see no merit in the argument of the United States as *amicus curiae* that defendants irrevocably exercised their professional judgment when they agreed to the consent here; defendants' agreement was premised on their belief, now shown to have been untenable, that they could find enough small facilities to empty Willowbrook within a reasonable time. As said in *Swift*, '[t]he consent is to be read as directed to things as they were.' Since there is no suggestion that defendants' experts testified in bad faith, we very likely could simply reverse the denial of the defendants' request for modification and direct that it be granted. However, since *Youngberg* was not available to the parties at the time of the hearing or to the district judge at the time of his decision, fairness seems to make preferable a remand on the narrow issue whether the views expressed by defendants' experts as to the propriety of the 50 bed limitation constituted 'professionally acceptable choices' or were 'such a substantial departure from accepted, professional judgment, practice or standards as to demonstrate that the person responsible actually did not base the decision on such a judgment.'[19]"

5) The modification problems in other complex lawsuits are similar to *Spangler* although the opinions are heavy with substantive lore. See, e.g., a) Title VII, United States v. City of Chicago, 663 F.2d 1354 (7th Cir. 1981) (quotas); United States v. Georgia Power, 634 F.2d 929 (5th Cir. 1981) (seniority system); Patterson v. American Tobacco Co., 634 F.2d 744 (4th Cir. 1980) (seniority system); b) Prisons, Nelson v. Collins, 659 F.2d 420 (4th Cir. 1981).

"**19.** In this connection we note that defendants are by no means alone in contending that placement in small community facilities is not appropriate for all mentally retarded persons. Recent decisions in Kentucky Ass'n for Retarded Citizens v. Conn, 510 F.Supp. 1233, 1250 (W.D.Ky. 1980), aff'd, 674 F.2d 582, 585 (6th Cir. 1982), and Garrity v. Gallen, 522 F.Supp. 171, 195 (D.N.H. 1981), recognize the growing perception among professionals in this field that placement in small group homes in the community may prove neither the "least restrictive" nor the safest alternative for some severely and profoundly retarded persons. . . ."

HOLIDAY INNS, INC. v. HOLIDAY INN

645 F.2d 239 (4th Cir. 1981).

Before BRYAN, Senior Circuit Judge, PHILLIPS, Circuit Judge and HOFFMAN, District Judge.

ALBERT V. BRYAN, Senior Circuit Judge:

This appeal is from the Federal District Court of South Carolina's denial of the motion by defendant Holiday Inn (the Local), a motel-restaurant in Myrtle Beach, South Carolina, for relaxation of an injunction the Court had granted in 1973 to Holiday Inns, Inc. (the Chain), a national and international operation in the same business with its name duly registered under 15 U.S.C. § 1111.[1] The injunction prohibited the Local from indicating that its name HOLIDAY INN was registered by the U.S. Patent Office. Specifically it proscribed the Local's usage of the symbol ® in connection with its insignia. The order on appeal reaffirmed the injunction and declared that the subsequent acquisition by the Local of a limited registration from the Court of Customs and Patent Appeals in 1976, did not warrant the modification. Maintaining the continued efficacy of the injunction, we refuse to overrule the trial judge's order denying the motion.

For decision upon the District Court's refusal to relax its injunction, our course is charted by Mr. Justice Cardozo's cautions in United States v. Swift & Co.

"There is need to keep in mind steadily the limits of inquiry proper to the case before us. We are not framing a decree. We are asking ourselves whether anything has happened that will justify us now in changing a decree. *The injunction, whether right or wrong, is not subject to impeachment* in its application to the conditions that existed at its making. . . . The inquiry for us is whether the changes are *so important that dangers, once substantial, have become attenuated to a shadow.* No doubt the defendants will be better off if the injunction is relaxed, but they are not suffering hardship so extreme and unexpected as to justify us in saying that they are the victims of oppression."

The words are an immediate reminder that we are not to question the right or wrong of the issuance of the injunction decreeing that:

"Defendant [Holiday Inn], its officers, agents, servants, employees and attorneys and all those persons in active concert or participation therewith, who receive actual notice hereof, are hereby perpetually enjoined and restrained from . . . :

"(e) Using directly or indirectly any indication that the defendant's name is registered in the United States Patent Office."[4]

To begin with, incontrovertibly the injunction was violated whenever the Local used the symbol ® in connection with its name in advertisements, publications or elsewhere. Of course, this litigation is not confined to the use of

1. 15 U.S.C. § 1111:

"[A] registrant of a mark registered in the Patent Office, may give notice that his mark is registered by displaying with the mark as used the words 'Registered in U.S. Patent Office' or 'Reg. U.S. Pat. Off.' or the letter R enclosed with a circle, thus ®; . . . ."

4. The right of the Local to continue in the use of the name Holiday Inn within the town of Myrtle Beach was not questioned.

the ® just in itself but, rather, embraces also the significance accorded the symbol by statute, i.e., it is the equivalent of the words "Registered in U.S. Patent and Trademark Office" or "Reg. U.S. Pat. & Tm. Off.," 15 U.S.C. § 1111. Nor is there any question of the *power* of this court to continue the exclusivity preserved by the District Court. The single inquiry is whether the change now sought is warranted by the evidence. There is no basis for assuming that the Court of Customs and Patent Appeals' award of concurrent registration of the Local's trademark lends any force of law tempering or modulating the injunction; that award does not *ex proprio vigore* override in any degree the District Court's injunction.

Returning to the question of this court's abatement or modification of the injunction, our first ground for refutation of appellant's motion rests on the premise of Justice Cardozo: the decree is "not subject to impeachment in its application to the *conditions that existed at its making* . . . " . . . Justification for the injunction was laid, in the appeal of it to this court, "upon the District Court's findings of fact." . . . No longer open to "impeachment" or to vacation when, as here, they are not assertedly erroneous, Rule 52, Fed.R.Civ.P., the following findings accurately reflect the "conditions" before, and as of, March 14, 1973 when the injunction issued.

1. Holiday Inns, Inc. (the Chain) was founded in 1952 in Memphis, Tennessee and since that time has become the largest factor in the restaurant and lodging business in the United States. Permanent displays were developed and placed on each facility, including the one at Myrtle Beach. One was the "great sign," having a green background with HOLIDAY INN in distinctive script lettering, a large star at the top, and an orange arrow running from the top to the bottom pointing to the location of the restaurant. In addition, the name is printed in large lettering in script on the side or face of the building. Its slogan was "your host from coast to coast."

2. The United States Patent Office registered the Chain's service marks beginning in 1954. They have been well known to the American traveling public. Numerous advertisements, appearing in magazines and newspapers as well as on radio, television and billboards, embody the symbol ® or the words, "Reg. U.S. Pat. Office."

3. The Local was incorporated in 1960, having prior thereto operated as a partnership or proprietorship. In 1948 it began business under the name of Ocean Front Lodge, consisting of eight frame structures. In August 1955, a new sign was erected bearing the words HOLIDAY INN. The lettering was in script and materially identical to that of the Chain's, which had been adopted in 1952 and, as mentioned, registered in 1954. In recent years the Local has placed stars near the words HOLIDAY INN. It has also distributed towels, parking lot identification stickers and notices to guests bearing the insignia "HOLIDAY INN ®."

4. In 1968 the Local erected a sign in its parking lot across the street from its facility. The manager of the Local requested the sign maker to provide a sign which would resemble, but not exactly duplicate, the plaintiff's "great sign." He was given one of the Chain's brochures to copy. The production so resembled the "great sign" of the Chain that the manager in

his testimony could not describe any differences between the Local's sign and the Chain's without first seeing photographs of them.

"When comparing the two photographs the Court can distinguish one from the other, but the signs are so similar that the traveling public would be easily confused and upon seeing defendant's sign would conclude that it was a franchise of plaintiff or affiliated with it. The colors of the two signs are almost identical. The use of stars, the big arrow, the attraction panel and the script of Holiday Inn are so similar that the Court *can only conclude that defendant erected this sign with the intent and purpose of infringing the rights of the plaintiff and unfairly competing* with it." . . .

In the past confusion has been deliberately and systematically nurtured by the *defendant* [the Local] in an *effort to profit from the national recognition and good will* of the plaintiff [the Chain]. . . .

[Again,] [in] the present case, the [Chain's] wrong, if any, is delay, while the [Local's] wrong is intentional deception and use of the [Chain's] marks to the detriment of the [Chain] and the confusion of the public. . . .

The foregoing numbered sections are the unassailable findings of the District Court (repeated in direct quotation or, for brevity, in substance) upon which it issued the injunction. The findings are essential to the pending issue for *they foretell why the injunction should not be modified.*

The Local's behavior in the past predicts what its conduct may, with reason, be expected in the future if the Chain's trademarks are stripped of their potency by the duplication. Clearly, it will allow the Local to "identify with and trade upon the [Chain's] good will," to quote the language of the trial judge.

To repeat, appellant's motion does not meet Justice Cardozo's measure of justification for "changing" the injunction. Truth is the Local's misconduct evinces no hint of cessation or dilution. On the contrary, it has never lessened in its constancy. Amazing, indeed is the failure of the Local to give evidence of any diminution in its imitating of the Chain's presentations.

In his findings precedent to refusal of the modification, the District Judge squarely refutes the contention that the injunction, unmodified, deprived the Local of economic benefits to the point of "oppression" as enunciated by Justice Cardozo. The pertinent parts of the trial court's findings are these:

"After careful review of defendant's memorandum and supplemental memorandum in support of its present motion, the Court can see little, if any practical benefit to be derived by the defendant by use of ® in the restricted area of Myrtle Beach, South Carolina. In the original Order this Court found that most of the confusion in Myrtle Beach was caused by efforts of the defendant Holiday Inn (a South Carolina corporation with one motel at Myrtle Beach) to identify itself with the plaintiff Holiday Inns, Inc. (the national chain). In that Order it was found that the defendant's summer season is always full and it enjoys approximately 80% repeat business, which had not suffered because of the construction and operation of motels in the Myrtle Beach area affiliated with the plaintiff."

The closely reasoned conclusions of the District Court will be

Affirmed.

JAMES DICKSON PHILLIPS, Circuit Judge, dissenting:

Mindful that we review a ruling committed to trial court discretion, and that the discretion was here exercised by an able judge carefully informed in the matter, I would nevertheless reverse. In my view the unique change in legal circumstances upon which the motion to modify the injunction was based could not properly be ignored in the exercise of a sound judicial discretion. I think it compelled granting the narrow relief from the comprehensive injunction that the Local Inn sought.

The unique quality of the change in circumstance can only be appreciated by putting the motion to modify in full procedural and historical context. The critical facts are these. From the late 1960's to the time of the ruling under review these parties had been embroiled in controversy spawned by the use of identical Holiday Inn service names. The Local Inn—and this is a fact not to be forgotten—was the first user, having operated a local motel and restaurant in Myrtle Beach, South Carolina, under the style Holiday Inn since 1949. The Chain was only founded in 1952 but has since expanded to its present status as a major national and international operator of motels, restaurants and related facilities under the same service name. In 1954, 1960 and 1962 the Chain registered with the United States Patent Office a number of service marks and slogans for use in promoting its operation. As will later be developed, the Local Inn did not seek registration of any mark until 1970, and only obtained a concurrent use registration in 1976.

Direct conflict between the parties began around 1956 when the Chain first franchised a facility in Myrtle Beach. Since then the controversy has proceeded in and out of court. From the outset the Local Inn boldly and, as it developed, illegally sought to capitalize on the Chain's mounting reputation by near duplications of its service mark signs and slogans. In the meantime, the Chain expanded its operations in the Myrtle Beach area while seeking in various ways to fend off the Local Inn's damaging competitive maneuvers. Eventually, inevitably, litigation ensued.

In 1970 the Local Inn, which had not until then registered any service mark, began a concurrent use proceeding in the Patent and Trademark Office, seeking registration of its distinctive Holiday Inn service mark for concurrent use in the Myrtle Beach area. While this proceeding was pending, the Chain commenced the instant action against the Local Inn in United States District Court, alleging unfair competition and service mark infringement. The concurrent use proceeding in the Patent Office was suspended during the pendency of the unfair competition and infringement action which then proceeded to final judgment in 1973. This 1973 judgment granted the permanent injunction whose modification is here in issue, based upon findings and conclusions that the Local Inn had engaged in specific acts of unfair competition and service mark infringement. The injunctive decree tracked in its specific prohibitions the specific acts of unfair competition and infringement alleged by the Chain and determined by the court to have been established by the evidence: using the registered script Holiday Inn mark; using the Chain's registered "great sign"; using any slogans or symbols suggestive by their similarity to the Chain's registered ones of a connection with the Chain. Also specifically prohibited was the use here in issue of "any indication that the [Local Inn's] name is registered in the United States Patent Office." Finally, and most importantly, the decree authorized the Local Inn to continue use of a distinctive, noninfringing Holiday Inn service mark within the Town of Myrtle Beach.

Following affirmance of the district court's judgment by this court, . . . the concurrent use proceeding in the Patent and Trademark Office was resumed, with the Chain there actively contesting the restricted registration now sought by the Local Inn. In 1976, following appeal from an administrative denial of the registration, the Court of Customs and Patent Appeals reversed. Holiday Inn v. Holiday Inns, Inc., 534 F.2d 312 (C.C.P.A.1976). The Local Inn was awarded a registration for its service mark, restricted in style to plain block letters and in location to Myrtle Beach, in conformity with the restriction on style and location embodied in the 1973 decree.

The restricted registration was granted under section 2(d), of the Lanham Act, 15 U.S.C. § 1052(d), which allows concurrent registration "when a court of competent jurisdiction has finally determined that more than one person is entitled to use the same or similar marks in commerce." The Court of Customs and Patent Appeals held that concurrent registration was proper under section 2(d) provided that the registration contained conditions and limitations corresponding to those contained in the district court judgment. This applied the rule that where a court has previously allowed more than one person to use a mark in commerce, concurrent registration is proper without an additional determination that there is no likelihood of confusion, mistake or deception, but that the registration must contain whatever conditions and limitations were imposed by the prior judgment and may not be unrestricted.

It was with this restricted registration of its service mark that the Local Inn returned to the district court seeking a modification of only that part of the broad 1973 injunction that prohibited any direct or indirect indication that its name was registered. Arguing that as an incident to registration, the owner of a trademark or service mark is entitled by section 29 of the Lanham Act, 15 U.S.C. § 1111,[1] to give appropriate notice of registration, the Local Inn sought permission to use the circled R, ®, with its now duly registered service name HOLIDAY INN. In denying the motion the district court explicitly relied upon its conclusions that there would be little damage resulting from an inability to use the ®, that few practical benefits would result, and that confusion would increase rather than decrease were the local establishment allowed to use the ® with its name.

Without questioning the validity of these general conclusions of the district court about the likely practical consequences of granting or withholding the relief sought, I would nevertheless find reversible error in the denial of the motion to modify. In my view, the critical factor that should have controlled decision here did not lie in any practical consequences attending the grant or denial of relief that could fairly be predicted for either of the parties or the public. With the district court, I would assess those consequences—

1. 15 U.S.C. § 1111 provides:

"Notwithstanding the provisions of section 1072 of this title, a registrant of a mark registered in the Patent and Trademark Office, may give notice that his mark is registered by displaying with the mark as used the words 'Registered in U.S. Patent and Trademark Office' or 'Reg. U.S. Pat. & Tm. Off.' or the letter R enclosed within a circle, thus ®; . . ."

for all interested parties—as essentially insignificant or merely speculative. With those consequences therefore discounted, the critical factor that remained was the Local Inn's intervening acquisition in a valid, contested proceeding against the Chain of a legal right to use the registration symbol in conjunction with its noninfringing service mark—a right that it did not have when the 1973 injunction was entered. Both the district court and the majority have erred in my judgment in applying an overly rigid standard for relief that has obscured this factor's controlling significance. To show why requires an analysis of the power whose exercise is at issue.

Analysis must start with the specific authority invoked by the Local Inn in seeking relief from the 1973 injunction. The basic authority is clear enough. Under Fed.R.Civ.P. 60(b)(5) a district court may grant partial or total relief from a permanent injunction if "it is no longer equitable that the judgment should have prospective application." Though codified by rule, this simply expresses the inherent power, not dependent upon rule, possessed by courts of equity to modify or vacate their decrees "as events may shape the need." United States v. Swift & Co. In the traditional formulation, if the circumstances of law or of fact existing at the time an injunction is issued have changed, then "a sound judicial discretion *may* call for the modification of [its] terms . . . ." System Federation No. 91 v. Wright, 364 U.S. 642, 647 (1961). The rub of course has come in determining whether a particular change *does* call for modification. This determination is necessarily committed in the first instance to trial court discretion—preferably that of the injunction court—and the discretion thus committed is necessarily "wide" though "never without limits." The precise nub of the rub has been in devising a standard by which the discretion—wide but not unlimited—may be guided in the trial court and reviewed on appeal.

Justice Cardozo's famous formulation in United States v. Swift—quoted and extensively relied upon by the majority here as supplying the appropriate standard—has inevitably come to be the starting point in subsequent judicial analysis. Inevitably also—given the authorship—courts have sometimes been tempted to ascribe to its several felicities of phrase—"dangers . . . attenuated to a shadow," "hardship so extreme and unexpected," "victims of oppression," "instrument of wrong"—a talismanic significance that, with all deference, I suggest the author of *The Nature of the Judicial Process* would never have claimed for them. If the *Swift & Co.* formulation is given that general significance and treated as embodying cumulative specific tests, it would allow modification only if a party seeking relief from an injunction could demonstrate *both* a lack of any further need for it to achieve the purposes of the litigation *and* hardship resulting from the denial of relief so "extreme" as to constitute "oppression." Admittedly, some courts have seemed so to read *Swift & Co.* See SEC v. Thermodynamics, Inc., 464 F.2d 457 (10th Cir. 1972); Humble Oil & Refining Co. v. American Oil Co., 405 F.2d 803 (8th Cir. 1969). With all respect for those courts, I do not think that the equity powers whose exercise we review should be considered so generally circumscribed and rigidly ordered.

The *Swift & Co.* formulation must, I think, be read simply as a description of the proper exercise of those powers in the particular context of the case before that Court rather than as a general prescription for their exercise in all cases. In *Swift & Co.* general relief was being sought from the historic antitrust consent decree involving the big five meat packers. The public stakes in maintenance of the decree were great; the complexity of the economic harm being sustained was equally great and difficult to assess. The case was in consequence a very special one for application of the modification power, and the application made was correspondingly a quite special one. The Supreme Court has since cautioned against overly rigid, general applications of the *Swift & Co.* formulation. See United States v. United Shoe Machine Co. Judge Friendly has sounded a similar caution, noting that the usual case "involves no such sharp conflict between wrong-doing and right-doing as did *Swift.*" King-Seeley Thermos Co. v. Aladdin Industries, Inc., 418 F.2d 31, 35 (2d Cir. 1969). In this circuit we have, I submit, been properly selective and flexible in our application of the *Swift & Co.* standard, depending upon the nature of the litigation, the injunction at issue and the scope of relief sought. Compare Tobin v. Alma Mills, 192 F.2d 133 (4th Cir. 1951) (FLSA injunction dissolved) with Brooks v. County School Board of Arlington County, Virginia, 324 F.2d 303 (4th Cir. 1963) (school desegregation decree not dissolved).

Remembering that we are dealing with the exercise of discretionary equity powers, I suggest that *Swift & Co.*'s general teaching—as opposed to its specific application—is merely that harm and continuing need must always be weighed in the balance in deciding whether continued enforcement of any injunctive decree is equitable in the light of specific changed circumstances. See United States v. Swift & Co., 189 F.Supp. 885, 905 (N.D.Ill. 1960). The proper test is therefore necessarily a flexible one, greatly dependent upon the particular facts of the case. In another *Swift & Co.* setting fraught with massive public interest in preventing a resumption of massive wrong-doing, the Cardozo formulation might properly be treated as having narrow precedential force. But not every case is a *Swift & Co.,* and this one most assuredly is not.

Stripped to its essentials, the situation presented to the district court here was a much simpler one. The court's comprehensive 1973 injunction had recognized the Local Inn's right—acquired by prior use—to continue a concurrent use, restricted in location and to a noninfringing style, of the shared service name, Holiday Inn. The specific style and locality restrictions on the Local Inn's use of its mark were complemented in the decree by a variety of specific prohibitions against continued acts of adjudicated infringement of the Chain's various registered marks. Also included as a specific prohibition was the Local Inn's indicating that any service mark used by it was registered in the Patent Office. The 1973 judgment had found as fact that the Local Inn had been giving such indications and that this tended to add to the confusion of marks; but this had neither been charged nor was it determined in the litigation to have been a specific act of infringement. It was simply an unauthorized act at the time because the Local Inn then had no registered mark. So far as the record shows, at the time the Local Inn applied in 1979 for modification of the decree it had scrupulously complied for the six years since its entry in 1973 with all its restrictions on the authorized concurrent use of its service mark and with all of the decree's prohibitions, including that against indicating that its mark was registered.[2]

2. In this connection, I do not understand the majority's statement, that "the injunction was violated whenever the Local used the symbol ® . . . "; nor its

In the interval since the 1973 decree the Local Inn had been awarded the registration of its mark which it had not possessed but was already seeking when the 1973 decree was entered. This award was by a valid judgment of a court with competence to grant it. The judgment had been entered following a contested proceeding in which the Chain was an adversary party and in which the district court infringement action was fully taken into account. The registration awarded was expressly conformed in its restrictions to the restrictions on style and locality embodied in the 1973 decree. The judgment awarding it was subject to appellate review.

In this setting, the district court addressed itself essentially to an assessment of the extent to which denial of the relief sought—lifting of the prohibition against indicating service mark registration—would create actual economic or practical harm to the Local Inn, and of the extent to which granting the relief would practically add to any existing confusion of service marks. With the burden properly imposed upon it, the Local Inn sought to demonstrate both that it would suffer practical harm if it were not given relief and that granting the relief would in fact tend to reduce any existing confusion.

On the harm aspect, the Local Inn pointed to certain procedural benefits flowing from registration that would improve its position in respect of infringers. Specifically, a trade mark registrant has the right to invoke federal jurisdiction, the benefit of certain evidentiary presumptions in trademark litigation, and most importantly, the benefit of constructive notice which deprives infringers of the innocent appropriation defense. These, the Local Inn urged, demonstrated a clear economic value incident to use of its registration, hence clear economic harm to it if the injunction against its use were continued. The district court dismissed this contention on the basis that, in view of the extreme unlikelihood that anyone would now risk infringement of the two Holiday Inn marks in the Town of Myrtle Beach, the potential harm was more theoretical than real.

On the confusion aspect—essentially the question whether the need for continuation of the injunction had been removed—the Local Inn argued that enabling it to use its registration symbol would actually reduce any public confusion resulting from the appearance of both registered and apparently unregistered Holiday Inn marks in the locality. The district court dismissed this as too speculative and ephemeral for acceptance. It concluded instead that the inevitable effect of allowing the Local Inn now to affix an ® to its service mark would be to increase any existing public confusion created by

implication, that the Local Inn could be expected to repeat its specifically prohibited acts of infringement if it were given the narrow relief that it seeks; nor the basis of its statements, that " . . . [T]he Local's misconduct evinces no hint of cessation or dilution. On the contrary, it has never lessened in its constancy."

I do not find any suggestion in the record that the Local Inn has failed in any way since the injunction was entered in 1973 to obey its specific prohibitions and to observe its specific restrictions on concurrent service mark use, including the prohibition against indicating that its service mark was registered. So far as the record shows, that latter prohibition has been observed as well after registration as before.

Obedience to an injunction is not in itself reason for granting relief from its terms, see Goldberg v. Ross, 300 F.2d 151 (1st Cir. 1962), but neither is pre-injunction misconduct that ceases with issuance of the injunction a reason for denying relief. It is also true, as the majority emphasizes, that an injunction cannot be impeached under the guise of seeking modification of its terms. United States v. Swift & Co. But the Local Inn is not here seeking in any way to impeach the injunction in its relation to adjudicated pre-injunction misconduct.

the two marks since by this means they would be made at least that much more similar.

These factual findings as to likely consequences—of practical harm if the relief were denied and of the effect on confusion if it were granted—are not clearly erroneous. For the district court and the majority, they are dispositive as they stand against the Local Inn's request for injunctive relief.

For me they merely reduce the final balancing problem to two simple conflicting considerations that, properly weighed, conclusively demonstrate the inequity of continuing the prohibition. Discounting any significant practical harm from denying the relief or any significant reduction in confusion of service marks from granting it, we are left with the following two considerations. On the one hand there is the fact that granting the relief would increase—by the addition of an ® mark to the Local Inn's authorized, noninfringing service mark—any confusion already existing in the public's mind between the two service marks that had now long been in concurrent use. On the other hand is the fact that the right to use that registration symbol in conjunction with the Local Inn's service mark is one generally authorized by federal statute and now specifically established by an intervening, unchallenged federal judicial decision.[3]

When one contemplates that since 1973 the noninfringing service marks had been in constant legally authorized concurrent use in the limited area of the Town of Myrtle Beach, it is inconceivable to me that now merely adding to the Local Inn's distinctive block letter service mark the small symbol ® would increase above a de minimus level any already existing public confusion resulting from the six years of legally approved concurrent use. That was the only reason addressed to the continuing need factor that was presented to the district court. Sufficient to overpower that tenuous threat of added confusion is the simple matter of newly acquired legal right, whether or not accompanied by any objective economic or practical value.[4] . . .

To deny the relief sought was in effect to nullify this legal right fairly acquired in the interval for no reason but to avoid a highly speculative, obviously minimal, increase in confusion of service marks already long in concurrent use. In my judgment, under the flexible test of harm and continuing

3. Even if the *Swift & Co.* "attenuated to a shadow" language were rigidly applied as a general test for granting relief from injunctions, I would find it met here. Admittedly, it all depends upon how one defines the "danger" whose attenuation is being assessed. That can only be done by looking to the context and evident purposes of the injunction litigation. Here, looking to that source, the danger was that the Local Inn would continue its *unauthorized* use of the ® as an added element of confusion. By the intervening authorization of its use that danger has been not merely attenuated to a shadow but utterly removed.

4. Even if any objective economic value be discounted—a position to which I concede we are bound by the clearly erroneous standard of review—there remains an intrinsic, subjective value in having the public know of the existence of any legal right that has been in public dispute. This is a value that has not, and could not properly, be discounted by the district court in assessing harm. Ultimately at stake was the right publicly to signal by the registration symbol a fact long since established, but not generally signalled, by the injunction decree itself—that the Local Inn's concurrent use of its service mark was legally authorized. In view of the high likelihood—clearly a matter for judicial notice—that public doubt about the legality of the use might continue, the significant intangible (if no other) value of this right is manifest. So, necessarily, is the significance of the harm resulting from its denial.

need properly applied to the Local Inn's motion, its request for limited relief could not be denied in the exercise of a sound legal discretion. . . .

I would reverse and direct a grant of the relief sought.

---

1) The injunction decision teaches us that in 1956 when the chain began the first franchise in Myrtle Beach, the local objected to the franchise's projected name. The Myrtle Beach Holiday Inn franchise began to operate as the Holiday Lodge. After a vigorous campaign on behalf of its own rights, the local capitalized on the Holiday Inn reputation and good will with Holiday Inn ® towels and supplies, its name in Holiday Inn script, a sign nearly identical to the "great sign," and a slogan, "Your Host on the Coast," that resembled the registered "Your Host from Coast to Coast" more than slightly. Holiday Inns, Inc. v. Holiday Inn, 364 F.Supp. 775 (D.S.C.1973), affirmed mem. 498 F.2d 1397 (4th Cir. 1974).

The Court of Customs and Patent Appeals granted the local's request for concurrent registration specifically and sua sponte said that the injunction should be modified to allow the local to display the ® to evidence the newly registered mark. The injunction that barred the local from displaying the ® was appropriate only so long as the local lacked valid registration; but the statute says that valid registration confers the right to display the symbol, and no reason existed to deny that right to the local.

Consider the way substantive law interacts with the courts' remedial power. Does the Fourth Circuit decision pay proper deference to the concurrent use proceeding in the Patent and Trademark Office and the Court of Customs and Patent Appeals? Does the Fourth Circuit ignore the executive's prerogative under statute to grant concurrent use? Was the Court of Customs and Patent Appeals's decision res judicata to preclude the district judge and the court of appeals from reexamining the question of whether the local could display the ®? If the South Carolina infringement litigation had been initiated after the C.C.P.A. decision on concurrent use, would it have been proper to bar the local from displaying the ®? Is the majority resolving disputes under substantive law or punishing sinners?

2) Note, Injunction Modification Standards: Uniformity v. Flexibility, 39 Wash. & Lee L.Rev. 490, 500 (1982), suggests that the court of appeals in *Holiday Inn* refused to modify because it would "foster confusion": the court "may have believed that by granting concurrent registration, the patent appeals court had adhered to the language of the Lanham Act but failed to recognize that the intended purpose of the Act's concurrent registration provision was to avoid the possibility of confusion."

Did the Fourth Circuit decision harm the local? Myrtle Beach supported three franchised Holiday Inns plus the local. Is it likely that a fifth but unfranchised Holiday Inn would establish itself there and that the local would be denied the right to recover damages in an infringement action because it had failed to display the ®? Does the dissent respond to this argument satisfactorily?

3) Two decisions concern modifications of trademark injunctions when the trademark becomes generic, that is, passes into common usage to describe the type of goods. King-Seeley Thermos Co. v. Aladdin Industries, Inc., 418

F.2d 31 (2d Cir. 1969), dealt with "thermos." King-Seeley registered "thermos" as part of a trademark, and a court enjoined Aladdin from using the term "thermos." The term became generic, Aladdin asked the court to modify, and the court granted modification. Coca-Cola Co. v. Standard Bottling Co., 138 F.2d 788 (10th Cir. 1943), is similar concerning "cola." Do these decisions present more compelling arguments for modification than *Holiday Inn* because only the enjoined competitors were barred from using the terms?

4) In Tobin v. Alma Mills, 192 F.2d 133 (4th Cir. 1950), certiorari denied 343 U.S. 933 (1952), the Fourth Circuit dissolved a nine-year-old Fair Labor Standards Act injunction on the ground that good faith evidenced by compliance constituted a sufficient change. Did *Holiday Inn* reverse *Tobin?*

5) Should the modification question differ depending on whether legal change comes from statute or decisions? Courts traditionally modify injunctions when statutory law changes. System Federation No. 91 v. Wright, 364 U.S. 642, 648 (1961); Pennsylvania v. The Wheeling and Belmont Bridge Co., 59 U.S. (18 How.) 421 (1855). Do courts hesitate to treat changes in decisional law the same because they find it hard to tell when decisional law changes?

An "all-fours" Supreme Court decision is clear. But consider an injunction that prohibits the Marine Corps from enforcing a regulation against long hair at summer camp. The Supreme Court upheld police requirements of short hair. The court refused to modify the summer camp injunction: neither exceptional circumstances nor grievous wrong evoked by unforeseen circumstances were shown. De Fillipis v. United States, 567 F.2d 341 (7th Cir. 1977).

Do contrary decisions in lower courts signal modification? Courts say no. Berryhill v. United States, 199 F.2d 217 (6th Cir. 1952); Loney v. Scurr, 474 F.Supp. 1186 (S.D. Iowa 1979). When the decisions were overwhelming, one court recognized their effect. Coca-Cola Co. v. Standard Bottling Co., 138 F.2d 788 (10th Cir. 1943) ("cola" generic).

Should the judge simply ask whether he would enjoin again under the state of the law the decisions currently reveal?

6) Mr. Steinberg has identified five standards: "First, *Swift* itself requires a clear showing that the dangers that gave rise to the decree have ceased and that the movants have suffered grievous wrong from unforeseen changed conditions. Second, the decisions in *United Shoe* and *System Federation* have encouraged courts to recognize a change in law or fact as sufficient equitable basis for modification or dissolution. Third, Judge Friendly's opinion in *King-Seeley* held that although a change of fact or law provides the clearest basis for relief, 'a better appreciation of the facts in light of experience' may indicate that 'the decree is not properly adapted to accomplishing its purposes,' and therefore should be altered. Fourth, the trial court in *Warren* balanced the 'alleged danger the injunction was designed to eliminate against the continuing necessity for an injunction and the hardship brought by its prospective application.' [SEC v. Warren, 76 F.R.D. 405, 408 (W.D.Pa. 1977), affirmed on other grounds, 583 F.2d 115 (3d Cir. 1978)]. Finally, the district court's order in *Blazon* implies that dissolution after a fixed period of time is appropriate if the enjoined party complies with the decree's terms unless the applicable government entity satisfies the court that the public in-

terest requires the continued protection of the injunction. [SEC v. Blazon Corp., 609 F.2d 960, 966–968 (9th Cir. 1979)]." Steinberg, SEC and Other Permanent Injunctions—Standards for Their Imposition, Modification, and Dissolution, 66 Cornell L.Rev. 27, 59 (1980).

If defendant intends to obey the substantive law, why does it seek to modify an "obey the law" injunction? Should the standard for modification differ for a burdensome injunction like a busing decree that imposes additional costs on defendant? Mr. Steinberg points out that an SEC injunction has collateral consequences: a basis to suspend or revoke defendant's registration, a ground to prohibit persons from associating with a defendant, a reason to disqualify defendant from service with a registered company, or a bar to prevent a professional from practice before the SEC. Should these collateral consequences make an SEC injunction harder to grant and easier to modify?

Mr. Steinberg suggests that "courts should engage in an *ad hoc* balancing test, considering such factors as (1) subsequent change of fact or law, (2) the extent of adverse, unforeseen collateral consequences, (3) whether the injunction has fulfilled its objectives, (4) whether the individual deterrent effect of the injunction has ceased, (5) the decree's effect on societal deterrence, (6) whether a government entity is a party to the litigation and the adverse effect that granting of the motion would have on the entity's resources and (7) the extent and nature of the public or other countervailing interest involved. This list of considerations is not exhaustive, but should serve as a fairly comprehensive benchmark for assessing motions for modification or dissolution. Although the formulation may resemble a balancing test, such a characterization may be misleading. The importance of each factor may change from case to case, depending on the totality of the circumstances. Further, if the factors are to be weighed, they should not be weighed equally. For example, when a party seeks modification or dissolution of an injunction that was obtained by a government entity, the public interest criteria should be of paramount importance. In such a case, dissolution or modification may still be granted—but only if the public interest is relatively minute or, in the alternative, if the other variables clearly are predominant.

"This standard would undoubtedly vest wide discretion in the trial court. Such discretion, however, is wholly consistent with equity jurisdiction. The proposal's greatest deficiency is its lack of a uniform standard, which invites *ad hoc* variations and disparate rationales among the courts. The proposal does have a common thread, however, that would link all such cases involving modification or dissolution: the above factors would be relevant in each court's determination and some factors, such as the public interest, would be more important than others." Steinberg, 66 Cornell L.Rev. at 71–73.

Does Mr. Steinberg help you understand *Holiday Inns?* Why not simply ask whether the original injunction would be granted again under present legal and factual conditions?

7) Problem: Inventor Walter S. Cyrenius secured a patent on an improved bicycle seat. Litigation against Moncure Manufacturer Inc. ensued. The lawsuit was settled with a negotiated consent decree. The consent decree agreed that Cyrenius's patent was valid, and Moncure admitted that it had infringed the patent. As part of the settlement, Cyrenius and Moncure entered into a license providing that Moncure would pay royalties to Cyreni-

us. After five years, Moncure ceased paying royalties. Cyrenius sought a contempt order. Moncure moved to modify or set the consent decree aside. Moncure interposed a judgment against Cyrenius in unrelated litigation with another alleged infringer; the judgment declared Cyrenius's patent void; Moncure argued that Cyrenius was barred from enforcing the invalid patent. Cyrenius replies that the consent judgment is res judicata and that, in any event, Moncure cannot argue in contempt that the injunction is incorrect. Schlegel Manufacturing Co. v. USM Corp., 525 F.2d 775 (1975) certiorari denied 425 U.S. 912 (1976); Langsam, Res Judicata Effects of Consent Judgments in Patent Infringement Litigation, 36 Fed.B.J. 171 (1977); McCarthy, "Unmuzzling" the Patent Licensee: Chaos in the Wake of Lear v. Adkins, 45 Geo.Wash.L.Rev. 429 (1977); Comment, Res Judicata Effect of Consent Judgments in Patent Litigation, 18 B.C.Indus. & Com.L.Rev. 66 (1976).

8) When does it all end? Are permanent injunctions perpetual? If the defendant is complying, when should the court cease to retain jurisdiction and dissolve the injunction? The *Spangler* litigation ended in 1979. Spangler v. Pasadena City Board of Education, 611 F.2d 1239 (9th Cir. 1979). The Board showed present compliance and "pledged continued good faith efforts to comply with the letter and spirit of the law." The court considered three factors: "The first factor is the nature and scope of the constitutional violation. The second is the remedial objective: to restore, as nearly as possible, the victim of discrimination to the position they would have occupied in the absence of illegal conduct. The third factor is the interests of state and local authorities in managing their own affairs, consistent with the Constitution."

Judge Kennedy said: "Retention of jurisdiction when there is no longer a demonstrated need to monitor compliance may defeat important governmental and personal interests. Legitimate changes in educational policy are more difficult to implement. Where the court retains jurisdiction, a board may feel obliged to take racial factors into account in each of its decisions so that it can justify its actions to the supervising court. This may make it more, rather than less, difficult to determine whether race impermissibly influences board decisions, for the subject is injected artificially into the decision process, and the weight that racial considerations might otherwise have had is more difficult to determine."

The courts in the Deep South take a different view as revealed in the following short opinion, Youngblood v. Board of Public Instruction of Bay County, 448 F.2d 770 (5th Cir. 1971):

"PER CURIAM:

"The District Court, sua sponte, dismissed this school integration case after making a finding that the school system was desegregated and unitary in nature. Plaintiffs-appellants urge on this appeal that the cause should not have been dismissed, but rather should be maintained on the inactive docket for the next three school years, during which time the school district would be required to file status reports on the state of desegregation in the school system. Appellants further ask that the District Court be directed to dismiss the suit at the termination of the three year period only after notice and hearing at which appellants would be permitted an opportunity to show why dismissal of the cause should be further delayed.

"It is ordered by the Court:

"1. The order of the District Court dismissing this action is vacated, and the cause is remanded to the District Court with directions to reinstate the action, and to retain jurisdiction over the action for a period not less than three school years. During the next three school years the school district shall be required by the court below to file semi-annual reports with the District Court similar to those required in United States v. Hinds County School Board, 5 Cir., 1970, 433 F.2d 611, 618–619.

"2. At the conclusion of three school years the District Court should again consider whether the cause should be dismissed. In no event, however, shall the District Court dismiss the action without notice to the plaintiffs below and a hearing providing opportunity to plaintiffs-appellants to show cause why dismissal of the cause should be further delayed. See Wright v. Board of Public Instruction of Alachua County, Florida, 5 Cir., 1971, 445 F.2d 1397."

In Singleton v. Jackson Municipal Separate School District, 541 F.Supp. 904 (S.D. Miss. 1981), Judge Russell dismissed the Jackson, Mississippi school case. The opinion concluded that the district had achieved unitary status with integrated faculty, staff, transportation, extracurricular activities, facilities, and composition of student body.

Note, 52 S.Cal.L.Rev. at 228–31, suggests that, instead of dismissing, the judge should substitute a general injunction not to discriminate for the detailed order and retain jurisdiction on the inactive docket. The Board, the Note argues, will be free to govern the school without the judge peering over its shoulders; but the judge is keeping his eye on them from a distance. Intervenors and plaintiffs would not need to file a new action; but they might move for supplemental relief, modification, or contempt. This approach compromises the view that the remedy should address only the harm caused by past illegal acts with the view that the remedy should extirpate prejudiced decisionmaking and advance constitutional values. The Note quotes Judge McMillan's "Swann song" from Swann v. Charlotte-Mecklenburg Board of Education, 67 F.R.D. 648 (W.D.N.C. 1975).

Chapter Nine

GOVERNMENT BY (STRUCTURAL) INJUNCTION

The injunction is a judicial command that prohibits or compels some discrete act of the defendant. Disobedience is punished by contempt. For the most part we have treated the injunction in this classic form; but now we consider a legal instrument, the structural injunction, that bears only a formal resemblance to the classic preventive injunction. The structural injunction achieved its greatest prominence in the civil rights era. Federal courts used structural injunctions to desegregate the schools of the nation. In the late 1960s and 1970s that experience was transferred to prisons, mental institutions, and police departments. During the 1970s the structural injunction emerged as one of the most prominent and controversial exercises of modern equity.

The structural injunction recognizes the bureaucratic nature of the modern state. It seeks to safeguard constitutional values from the threats posed by bureaucratic organizations. It is premised on the view that these threats will not be eliminated by some specific command or prohibition, but only through restructuring of the bureaucratic organization. The injunction is the medium the judge uses to direct or manage the reconstruction of the bureaucratic organization. Given the magnitude of the task and the limitations of our knowledge, this usually creates a long-term relationship between the judge and the organization. See generally O. Fiss, The Civil Rights Injunction (1978). An example of a structural decree is found below on p. 774.

We believe that the structural injunction is best understood by studying a single case over a significant period of time. The first edition of this book examined the structural injunction through Judge Johnson's efforts to desegregate the schools of Montgomery, Alabama over a ten-year period. Judge Johnson was the chancellor of the 1960s. The choice reflected the primacy of the school litigation in shaping this new form of injunction in addition to Judge Johnson's creative use of the equity power. Now we turn to the Arkansas prison litigation. Other studies of these prisons are the movie "Brubaker" and Bruce Jackson's photographic essay "Killing Time" (1977). We examine the way Judge Henley used the injunctive power to reform Arkansas's prisons. This case study builds on the civil rights experience, and poses the issues of efficacy and legitimacy in a particularly compelling way. Can a court reorganize a bureaucratic organization in a way that effectively protects constitutional values and respects the limitations on the judicial power?

I. Case Study: The Arkansas Prisons

CHRONOLOGY

1965	Media coverage and public awareness of conditions in state prison system begin to escalate.
Oct. 13	Talley v. Stephens. Trial begins, evidence on prisoners' claims reveals conditions inside prisons.
Nov. 1	Talley v. Stephens. Evidentiary hearing on consolidated claims previously set for this date is cancelled when respondent agrees to consent decrees as to these claims.
Nov. 2	Arkansas A & M teacher ousted for circulating petition among students criticizing whippings in state prisons.
Nov. 6	State legislature's resolution "hails" College action.
Nov. 15	Talley v. Stephens decision and order. Chief Judge Henley of the Eastern District of Arkansas renders decree in Talley restraining the use of corporal punishment by state prison authorities until such time as adequate safeguards should be established, enjoins authorities from interfering with prisoners' access to courts, and requires improvement in medical services and care for ill inmates.
1966	
March 22	Gov. Faubus declares he will not seek a 7th term. He cites personal and administrative difficulties.
Aug. 19	Gov. Faubus orders state police into Tucker Reformatory for Men to investigate incidents that came to public attention, including inmate drunkenness, extortion, and conversion of state property for personal use. Police report back to Faubus.
Aug. 30	Faubus orders state police back into Tucker Reformatory for Men.
Aug. 31	Superintendent O.E. Bishop fires all free world employees at Tucker.
Sept. 5	Severe riot in Cummins Prison Farm.
Sept. 14	State Police use tear gas to end attempted strike by 144 Cummins inmates. Eleven punished by whipping.
Sept. 15	Accusations appear in press that only blacks were punished.
Sept.–Nov.	Bitter campaign for Governor between Winthrop Rockefeller and segregationist J.D. "Justice" Johnson.

Nov. 8	Rockefeller wins election. The black vote is believed to be pivotal in electing the 1st Republican Governor since reconstruction.
1967	
Jan. 16	Gov. Rockefeller releases report of the State Police revealing beatings and corruption. At a press conference he calls for intensive study of the prison system.
Feb.	Bob Scott, Rockefeller aide, gains publicity by posing as inmate to obtain first hand knowledge of prison conditions.
Feb. 3–4	Rockefeller fires supervisor Booker and his 3 wardens at Tucker; Governor denies this action is related to the recent death of an inmate.
Feb. 15	Governor appoints T.O. Murton, criminologist, as assistant farm superintendent, with directive to reform prisons. Murton takes charge at Tucker.
March 18	First meeting of the Arkansas Penitentiary Study Commission. Study lasts nine months and publishes a report.
May 28	Courtney v. Bishop. Petition filed in District Court seeking relief from cruel and unusual punishment in solitary confinement at Cummins. Case before Judge Oren Harris.
June 3	Jackson v. Bishop. Decision and Order by Judges Harris and Young enjoins corporal punishment pending the implementation of "proper and adequate" safeguards for its use.
Oct. 6	E.H. Clardy dismissed as Cummins Prison Farm warden for attending church while drunk.
1968	
Jan.	C. Clark, ex-convict and right-wing political organizer, testifies before Arkansas Senate. He lauds prisons as having finest atmosphere in the world, rejects murder charges, gets standing ovation.
Jan. 1	Arkansas Penitentiary Study Commission Report Released.
Jan. 8	C. Smith, Cummins Farm manager, resigns in protest over Murton appointment to Cummins.
Jan. 15–28	Murton reveals his findings about conditions to national media, and expresses fear that many inmates have been shot or beaten to death and secretly buried on prison grounds.
Jan. 26	Courtney v. Bishop. Judge Harris finds that inmate not subjected to cruel and unusual punishment and dismisses the case.

Jan. 29	Human skeletons found by Murton crew on Cummins grounds. Search set for more bodies.
Jan. 30–31	State police probe deaths. Gov. Rockefeller "shocked." Press runs account of one inmate's testimony about 12 slayings during his term in prison.
Feb. 1–2	Governor's office first indicates police probe of burials will be halted to allow "speculation on political problems involved"; then in face of charges of political whitewash, Governor indicates the investigation will continue. Press continues to run prisoners' reports of killings, eyewitness accounts.
Feb. 2–7	Investigation continues. Inmate witnesses report most of slayings have occurred since 1960. Prisoners tell newsmen they have been threatened for giving information. Rockefeller reports he will ask Legislature to create a Corrections Department to facilitate overhaul of system. Press publishes prison records showing that at least 70 of the 254 deaths reported at State Penitentiary since 1936 were caused by violence and brutality. Records reveal no prior outside investigation of deaths. Murton indicates belief that records "disguise some criminal activity." Prison board approves search for nine bodies and directs Murton to relocate discovered bodies.
Feb. 7–9	Murton asks for independent state investigator to be present at exhumations. Reports he will resign, then withdraws his intention to resign. Rockefeller bars further digging pending decision on legality of moving human remains under state law. He says Murton acts independently and creates problems for him.
Feb. 9–12	Press reports growing political opposition to Murton and investigation. State law making removal of a body from a grave a felony effectively diffuses further investigation. State Judge Henry W. Smith impanels Grand Jury instructing it to determine if any laws have been violated in digging up the bodies.
Feb. 12	Governor releases state medical examiner's report. Findings about the skeletons inconclusive.
Feb. 15	A.H. McCormick, Chief Consultant to Penitentiary Study Commissions, testifies before state senate that Arkansas has the "worst prison system in the country."
Feb. 21	After special sessions the legislature passes two bills to reform prisons. Governor indicates he is satisfied. Influential legislators criticize Murton.
March 5	Governor Rockefeller sends letter to state Correction Board indicating he wants Murton relieved, claiming Murton created a completely untenable situation.

March 7	Murton fired, replaced by V. Urban.
March 8	Murton accused by Lincoln County Grand Jury of a publicity stunt in opening 3 unmarked graves, indicates remains were found in an established prison cemetery and recommends prisons revert to whipping, which was abolished by Murton. Four Murton appointees resign.
March 15	Eight inmates reported to have escaped from Cummins.
March 27	State Police complete new report on mistreatment in prisons, incidents of slayings and brutality described. Rockefeller says he is not "terribly excited" by findings, and that he will release report with names deleted.
May 11	Governor Rockefeller releases "condensed" version of state police report on study of the Cummins prison begun in January. He dismisses report as a "mish-mash" that contains nothing on which he could officially act and nothing that contributes to reform.
May 13	State Circuit Court dismisses criminal brutality charges against 3 former aides at state prison. J. Bruton, former state representative and former Tucker Superintendent among those acquitted. (See July 12, 1969).
May 19	State prosecutor says he does not intend to follow up on report.
June 9	Murton charges that there is a "total conspiracy in the state to suppress the truth" about prison conditions. Calls the police report a fraud.
Oct. 14	Guards and trustys at Cummins wound 24 convicts by firing shotgun blasts into crowd of penned-up prisoners to force them to work in the fields. Prisoners were staging a sit-down strike insisting on improved conditions.
Nov. 15	Robert Sarver appointed as Commissioner of Corrections.
Dec. 9	Jackson v. Bishop. 8th Cir. orders the state to abolish whipping to discipline prisoners.
1969	
March 4	Murton testifies before U.S. Senate subcommittee about torture, discrimination, and other aspects of Arkansas prisons. Claims that Rockefeller ordered him to stop digging up bodies and that his removal was political whitewash.
March 25	C. Poze, former inmate, sues state on charge that his eye was put out by guard's beating.
April 12	Holt v. Sarver (Holt I). Eight pro se class action petitions challenging overall prison system under 42

	U.S.C. § 1983 are consolidated and set for trial by Judge Henley.
April 21	Courtney v. Bishop. 8th Cir. affirms decision below not to give relief as to petitioners complaint about solitary confinement.
June 20	Holt I. Judge Henley finds several aspects of prison system to be unconstitutional. The court issues guidelines and orders administrators to report back in one month about remedial steps taken.
June–July	Justice Department asks Eastern District of Arkansas to convene Grand Jury; Grand Jury convened.
July 12	U.S. Grand Jury indicts 15 former prison officials and guards under 18 U.S.C. § 242 on charges of performing brutal acts against inmates at Tucker and Cummins and at county penal farms. J.L. Bruton and 2 others indicted have previous state informations quashed when the State Supreme Court declares the statute under which they had been charged unconstitutional. (See May 13, 1968).
Nov.	A number of jury trials end in verdicts of not guilty for all defendants. Jury acquits Bruton on 8 of 9 charges of cruel and unusual treatment. A mistrial declared on the count that Bruton ordered electric shock treatment as torture, jury unable to return a verdict.
1970	
Jan. 18	Bruton pleads no contest to remaining brutality count and sentenced by Judge Henley to 1 year suspended sentence and fine. Henley "deplores" light sentence but fears that Bruton would be murdered by inmates if sent to prison. Bruton to face still another trial on cruelty charges stemming from 1964 incidents.
Feb. 18	Holt II. Decision and Order. Judge Henley, after considerable inmate testimony, rules that still more aspects of the prison system are unconstitutional, warns that he would close the farms if conditions do not improve, and orders State Correction Board to present a plan for compliance by April 11, and rejects prisoners attack on uncompensated labor. Commissioner Farber and Correction Board Chairman Haley back Henley's views.
April 15	Holt II. Defendants ordered to file progress reports that provide information on isolation units, and other aspects of Cummins confinement procedures.
Nov. 2	Group of armed inmates seize 4 hostages and threaten to kill them in attempt to gain freedom from Cummins. Hostages released and inmates surrender after talks with State Commissioner Sarver and prison Su-

	perintendent Steed, who placed themselves in the hands of the prisoners for release of 2 of the hostages.
Nov. 22	Fifty-five armed state troopers remain at Cummins following 2 days of fighting stemming from demand for separate living quarters for blacks and whites.
1971	
March 5	T.O. Murton testifies before U.S. Senate Subcommittee on Juvenile Delinquency and calls for taking prisons out of control of state officials in Arkansas.
May	Terrell Don Hutto appointed by Gov. Dale Bumpers to replace Robert Sarver as Commissioner of Corrections. District Court continues to receive numerous complaints from prisoners.
May 5	Holt II. Judge Henley's decision affirmed by the 8th Circuit.
June 16	Holt II. Memorandum and Order. Judge Henley requires defendants to file more specific and detailed progress reports by July 20.
Dec. 11	State officials end policy of sending youthful first time offenders for one-day shock treatment at state prisons following death of 17-year-old black W.E. Stewart at Cummins. Stewart's death, attributed to disease akin to sickle cell anemia, came one day after he was hazed by prison guards and after a hard day's work in the cotton fields.
Dec. 20	Holt II. Supplemental Decree. Judge Henley enjoins defendants from inflicting cruel and unusual punishment on inmates and interfering with prisoners' access to court.
1972	
Sept. 8	Holt III. Begins with Memorandum and Order by Judge Henley consolidating 34 individual and class actions by prisoners and ordering a hearing under the heading of Holt v. Hutto.
Nov.–Dec.	Holt III. Evidentiary hearings held on the merits.
1973	
Aug. 13	Holt III. Decision and Second Supplemental Decree. Judge Henley issues further orders to correct what he finds to be continued deficiencies in prisons (e.g. treatment of Black Muslims, racial segregation and discrimination, and improper disciplinary procedures.) Henley finds several other inmate complaints without merit; finding substantial improvements in operation of the prisons, he holds that it is no longer necessary to retain jurisdiction over the case. He recommends an alternative administrative grievance machinery to take over the role the court filled in preceding years.

Aug.	Holt III. Several petitioners appeal. Appeals consolidated in Finney v. Arkansas Board of Correction.
1974	
Oct. 10	Finney v. Arkansas Board of Correction (Holt III on appeal). 8th circuit reverses District Court in part and remands, requiring Judge Henley to retain jurisdiction citing the continuing shortcomings of Arkansas's correctional system. The Court of Appeals further instructs Judge Henley to hold hearings, and to grant additional appropriate relief as warranted.
Oct. 28	Two prison inmates, trying to escape, run into Cummins guard force lying in wait outside the prison. Both wounded; the informant who had gone over the wall with them in the escape attempt unharmed.
Nov. 4	Finney v. Arkansas Board of Correction. Rehearing and rehearing en banc denied by 8th Circuit.
1975	
Jan.–July	Finney v. Hutto (Holt III on remand). Judge Henley conducts extensive evidentiary hearings as required by the remand order.
March 24	Henley becomes circuit judge of the 8th circuit. Continues to sit by designation.
1976	
March 19	Finney v. Hutto (Holt III on remand). Judge Henley sets forth findings and opinion derived from remand hearings, offers a comprehensive evaluation of the existing state of Arkansas prisons, concludes that several intolerable practices are still prevalent and issues orders accordingly.
July 15	Commissioner files report on compliance as required by March 19 order in Finney v. Hutto.
Oct. 19	Civil Rights Attorney's Fees Award Act of 1976, Pub. L. 94–559, signed into law.
1977	
Jan. 6	Finney v. Hutto. 8th circuit affirms the District Court.
Feb. 3	Finney v. Hutto. Rehearing denied by the 8th circuit.
1978	
June 23	Hutto v. Finney. Supreme Court affirms award of attorney's fees to prisoners' attorneys.
Oct. 5	Consent Decree entered.

1978–1981	
	Arkansas prisons operate under the Oct. 5, 1978 Consent Decree.
1981	
March	Cooperation of parties necessary for continued progress within the Consent Decree no longer forthcoming. Plaintiff class requests a hearing.
Aug.–Sept.	Five week hearing on extent of compliance before Judge Eisele, who replaces Judge Henley. The hearings end with oral arguments on September 28 and October 5, 1981.
Oct. 6	Court requests parties to brief issues relating to policy of administrative segregation in prisons.
Dec. 15	Finney v. Mabry. Opinion by Judge Eisele concerning due process in administrative segregation contains specific directives about compliance.
1982	
Feb. 19	Finney v. Mabry. Memorandum opinion by Judge Eisele concerning compliance.
March 2	Finney v. Mabry. Order entered.
March 25	Department of Corrections presents a new plan for integration, taking into account safety, to the court and petitioner class attorney in conference.
May 7	Final report on compliance filed by respondents.
Aug. 9	Hearing before Judge Eisele. At the conclusion, Judge Eisele finds that respondents are in compliance with Consent Decree.
Aug. 20	Finney v. Mabry. Case dismissed.

Excerpts from M. Harris and D. Spiller, After Decision: Implementation of Judicial Decrees in Correctional Settings: A Case Study of Holt v. Sarver, National Institute of Law Enforcement and Criminal Justice, Law Enforcement Assistance Administration, U.S. Department of Justice (1976) (hereafter: **Harris & Spiller Report**).

During the mid–1960's, because of widely-reported abuses in all phases of prison life, the Arkansas penitentiary system became perhaps the most notorious prison system in the United States. Revelations of corruption, neglect and abuse led to national publicity, official investigations and a series of lawsuits that attacked conditions existing in the system. The most prominent of the lawsuits was a civil rights action litigated in the United States District Court for the Eastern District of Arkansas as Holt v. Sarver. The *Holt* case ". . . amount[ed] to an attack on the [penitentiary] [s]ystem itself." It was, in the words of the court, " . . . the first time that convicts have attacked an entire penitentiary system in any court, either State or Federal."

Analysis of the extent of compliance with court orders, the factors that affected compliance, and the impact of the Holt v. Sarver litigation, depends upon understanding at the outset the philosophy that governed the prison system, conditions that existed in the system, early litigation that affected the system, and investigations and reports that focused attention upon the need for prison reform in Arkansas.

Throughout its history, the Arkansas penal system emphasized punishment and hard work for convicts and profits for the state. The penitentiary system was optimally expected to utilize inmate labor to produce revenue for the state. It was minimally expected to be self-sufficient. This philosophy had significant programmatic repercussions that adversely affected inmates. It led sequentially to a convict-leasing system, the hiring out of inmates to work on roads and private farms, and creation of the inmate trusty system—the most infamous feature of the prison system's recent past.

The convict-leasing system flourished during the early years of the penitentiary system. Under the leasing system, private individuals paid the state for the use of inmates. The inmates were under the care and custody of private individuals with little actual supervision and control exercised by the state. The system was intended to save state money but was the cause of gross mistreatment and neglect of prisoners. It was estimated that, during the period from 1873 until 1893, one fourth of all prisoners in the Arkansas penitentiary system died each year. Although the convict-leasing system was discontinued during the 1920s, abuse and neglect continued as convicts were "hired out" by the state to work on roads and private farms. In 1933 the prison system converted to the present "penal plantation" model composed of three units located in sparsely populated, rural areas of southeast Arkansas. The units were: Tucker Reformatory for Men, located on 4,500 acres of farmland approximately 35 miles from Little Rock, Arkansas; Cummins Prison Farm, located on 16,227 acres of land approximately 75 miles from Little Rock; and the Reformatory for Women, which was located on the Cummins Prison Farm. [In 1967 the population of Cummins was approximately 1600 inmates, of Tucker, approximately 275 inmates, most of them young first offenders.]

The transition to a penal plantation model signalled the official end of the convict-leasing system in its various forms. Nevertheless, the penitentiary system remained true to its heritage. Inmates worked on the prison farms to produce crops for sale and consumption and a new system developed whereby inmate trusties performed tasks normally performed by free world personnel. The penal plantation system and the inmate trusty system embodied the dominant historical theme of the Arkansas prison system—hard work and punishment for the inmates and profits for the state.

1. *Report of the Arkansas State Police*

[Starting in 1965 a series of events called attention to the corruption and brutality within the state prison system. By late 1966 and early 1967, in the face of growing controversy, both outgoing Governor Faubus and newly elected Governor Rockefeller repeatedly ordered the state police into the prisons. The findings of the state police, based on their observations and investigations while in control of the prisons, were eventually compiled in a report which was first made available to the public by Governor Rockefeller in 1967.] . . .

Perhaps the most shocking practice revealed by the report was the torture of inmates at the direction of prison personnel. Especially infamous among the various torture instrumentalities described in the report was the "Tucker telephone," an instrument that ". . . consisted of an electric generator taken from a ring-type telephone, placed in sequence with two dry cell batteries, and attached to an undressed inmate strapped to the treatment table at the Tucker hospital by means of one electrode to a big toe and a second electrode to the penis, at which time a crank was turned sending an electric charge into the body of the inmate . . . [S]everal charges were introduced into the inmate of a duration designed to stop just short of the inmate 'passing out.'" According to the report, the Tucker telephone was used both to punish inmates and to extract information from them. In addition to the Tucker telephone, other devices and practices were reportedly used to torture inmates. One such practice involved the application of wire pliers to pinch, pull, and squeeze inmates' fingers, toes, ears, noses and genitals. Other practices were jabbing needles under inmates' fingernails, extinguishing cigarettes on inmates' bodies and beating inmates' fingers with wire pliers.

According to the report, inmates were viciously beaten by other inmates, and by or at the direction of free world personnel. A large percentage of such beatings were either directly or implicitly sanctioned by prison officials. The most frequently mentioned reasons for beatings were inmate escapes, improper work performance, or talking to other inmates. The report alleged that beatings were performed with leather straps (often administered to the bare buttocks of inmates), chains, automotive fan belts, knotted ropes, shovels, clubs, blackjacks and brass knuckles. A prison search conducted during the course of the investigation resulted in the discovery of 61 knives, five pair of "fighting knuckles," two "palm weights" for fighting, five blackjacks, three straight razors, a hatchet, illegal drugs, gambling equipment, and whiskey bottles.

The report told of the existence within Tucker of an informal but thriving entrepreneurial system, based upon the sale of goods and services. Those involved in the system included inmates, employees of the prison, local businessmen and even members of the Penitentiary Board which had responsibility for overseeing the operations of the penitentiary system. One inmate reported that " . . . almost anything could be had at Tucker Farm if you could get the money." Inmate entrepreneurs were usually trustees who, with staff complicity, sold goods and services that ranged from items routinely provided inmates by prison management to items that were contraband. There was abundant evidence of the ingenuity of the inmate entrepreneurs. Inmates charged other inmates a fee for a good bed. The sale of prison jobs was commonplace. The going price for jobs was as much as the traffic would bear—as low as $30 and as high as $1,000. Inmates reportedly paid up to $10,000 for early release. They paid trusties who worked in the laundry room to have their clothes cleaned. It was necessary for inmates to pay an inmate "doctor" to receive medical treatment or to remain in the prison hospital (often to recover from injuries the inmate had suffered because of beatings administered by other trusties). Money paid to certain trusties could result in an inmate receiving better food than was generally available. There was a money-lending operation in which money was loaned to inmates on a $2 for $1 basis. Because of the pervasive brutality and lack of security, an extortion business thrived in Tucker. Inmates paid trusties for protection against being whipped, beaten or brutalized. Narcotic drugs and alcoholic beverages were always available for a price. Inmates were allowed to have sexual contact with their wives and girlfriends in cells and rooms on the prison grounds by paying money for use of the cell or room.

Sexual abuse of inmates by other inmates was commonplace. Sometimes such abuse was physically forced (particularly in the case of younger inmates), while in other cases sexual favors were exchanged for food. Sexual misconduct reportedly extended to prison employees, who offered preferential treatment or early release to inmates in exchange for sexual favors from the inmates' wives or female friends.

The report stated that widescale private use was made by prison employees of prison equipment, supplies and manpower. Employees took large quantities of food from the prison kitchen for their own use and the use of their families. Prison employees had their families' clothes cleaned in the prison laundry. Vehicles and farm equipment belonging to prison employees and their families were maintained at no charge in the prison garage. Employees' livestock and horses were kept on prison property, fed state-owned grain and cared for by inmates. It was reported that the superintendent used inmate labor to train on prison property horses which he then sold at a substantial profit. Inmates reportedly performed free labor on property belonging to private individuals. The report also alleged that employees stole state property from the prison, including cattle and feed.

Included within the report were allegations that certain unidentified members of the Penitentiary Board participated in the corruption at Tucker. Board members allegedly took large amounts of meat from the prison. It was alleged in addition that one member of the parole board granted release on parole to certain inmates with the understanding that those inmates would work on his private farm. It was reported that, if they did not agree to the arrangement in advance, they would not be paroled. Regular beatings were a normal part of the purported operations of this farm and, if the inmates protested, their parole was revoked and they were sent back to prison.

The practices described in the state police report were exacerbated by the environmental conditions under which the inmates lived. The report contained a partial description of the condition of the facilities and appearance of the inmates. The field workers' physical appearance was described as dreadful. It was estimated that each of them was between 40 and 60 pounds underweight. Their clothing was filthy and torn. Their shoes were worn out and too large. They were issued no underwear. The kitchen was filthy. Flies were thick on food and meat that had been left exposed. Used tin cans served as drinking utensils. Meals contained very little protein. Meat was served only once each month and milk and eggs were used only in cooking or were given to trusties. Otherwise, each inmate received one egg a year, usually at Christmas time. Mattresses were filthy, rotten and discolored. The sheets were dirty and no pillows were provided. Water leaked from the showers and the commodes and urinals were stopped up. The floors were littered with debris and were filthy. A foul odor permeated the entire area where inmates were housed. . . .

2: *Early Federal Lawsuits Affecting the Prison System*

Beginning in 1965, three lawsuits were filed in the Federal District Court for the Eastern District of Arkansas, under the authority of the Civil Rights Act, concerning conditions and practices in the Tucker and Cummins prisons. These suits were Talley v. Stephens, Jackson v. Bishop, and Courtney v. Bishop. Talley v. Stephens involved lack of access by inmates to court for the redress of grievances, inadequate provision of medical services, unduly harsh working conditions, and the use of corporal punishment. Jackson v. Bishop was limited to considering the constitutionality of administering beatings with "the strap" as a punishment. Courtney v. Bishop involved a generalized attack upon the procedures leading to disciplinary sanctions and the conditions existing in the solitary confinement areas of Cummins. Though unsuccessful at both the district and appellate court levels, *Courtney* foreshadowed the Holt v. Sarver decisions that would soon follow. . . .

TALLEY v. STEPHENS

247 F.Supp. 683 (E.D.Ark.1965).

HENLEY, Chief Judge.

This is a suit in equity brought by three inmates of the Arkansas State Penitentiary, namely Winston Talley, William Warren Hash, and Vernon Sloan, against Dan D. Stephens, Superintendent of that institution, for the purpose of restraining respondent from continuing certain prison practices which petitioners claim are violative of rights secured to them by the 14th Amendment to the Constitution of the United States. Federal subject matter jurisdiction is to be found in 42 U.S.C.A. § 1983.

Petitioners contend, in essence, that they have been unconstitutionally subjected to cruel and unusual punishments, and that they have been denied unconstitutionally access to the Courts to secure redress of their alleged grievances. They do not question the legality of their confinements or claim that they are entitled to release from custody at this time.

Petitioners have been represented most capably by Bruce T. Bullion of Little Rock and Louis L. Ramsay, Jr. of Pine Bluff, appointed by the Court to represent petitioners without charge. The Court is grateful to Messrs. Bullion and Ramsay for their services.

All petitioners assert that they have been denied access to the Courts; Talley and Hash, and Sloan to some extent, contend that they have been subjected to severe corporal punishment which, in the case of Talley, includes alleged unlawful assaults by a fellow inmate, James Pike. Hash and Sloan contend that they have been forced to perform heavy manual labor on the Penitentiary farm which they were not and are not capable of performing. All petitioners complain also that they have been refused needed medical attention.

Respondent denies that Talley is entitled to any relief. Respondent originally took the same position with respect to Hash and Sloan, but now concedes, as will more fully appear, that the Court should enter a decree awarding them some relief.

Following a pre-trial conference held in September of the current year, the case was set for trial to the Court on Monday, October 13. On that date testimony was taken with respect to the Talley petition. The Court heard the testimony of Talley and that of a considerable number of inmate witnesses called by Talley and respondent, respectively. Assistant Warden Mose Harmon, Jr., who has had Talley in charge during much of his incarceration at the Penitentiary, was also heard.[2] Respondent did not testify, but he has made a number of statements in the course of the proceedings which the Court has taken into consideration.

At the conclusion of the hearing on the Talley petition, the Court adjourned the proceedings until November 1, at which time it was planned to take testimony in connection with the applications of Hash and Sloan. However, a few days before November 1 respondent filed two documents consenting to the entry of judgments in favor of those two petitioners; and no further evidentiary hearing was held.

Both sides have filed memorandum briefs and both sides have requested or suggested certain specific findings of fact and conclusions of law. All of those requests and suggestions are denied, except to the extent that they are included in this memorandum which incorporates the Court's findings of fact and conclusions of law. . . .

Although persons convicted of crimes lose many of the rights and privileges of law abiding citizens, it is established by now that they do not lose all of their civil rights, and that the Due Process and Equal Protection Clauses of the 14th Amendment follow them into the prison and protect them there from unconstitutional administrative action on the part of prison authorities carried out under color of State law, custom, or usage. More specifically, prison authorities are not permitted to inflict upon convicts cruel and unusual punishments for violations of prison rules; they may not discriminate invidiously against a prisoner or class of prisoners; and they may not deny to a prisoner reasonable access to the courts to test the validity of his confinement or to secure judicial protection of his constitutional rights. . . .

On the other hand, convicts must be disciplined, and prison authorities must be given wide latitude and discretion in the management and operation of their institutions, including the disciplining of inmates. The Courts cannot take over the management of prisons, and they cannot undertake to review every complaint made by a convict about his treatment while in the prison. . . . It must be recognized also that the administration of prison discipline must in many instances be summary, and that the punishment administered to a convict for a violation of prison rules may differ quantitatively and qualitatively from the punishment prescribed by a criminal statute and imposed initially by a court following an individual's conviction of a crime. See State v. Revis, 193 N.C. 192, 136 S.E. 346, 50 A.L.R. 98.

Taking up first the claims of Hash and Sloan that they have been required to do field work in excess of their physical capabilities, it is conceded, and the Court finds, that both of those men are laboring under serious physical handi-

2. The Court has been caused some difficulty by the fact that none of the inmate witnesses, including Talley, is particularly worthy of belief, and because of the patent interest of Mr. Harmon whose conduct as Assistant Warden has been called into serious question in the course of the proceedings.

caps, that their physical condition has been classified as "poor" by the prison physician; that despite their condition and classification thereof they have been required to engage in work which they are not physically able to perform. They have now been assigned to light work. Respondent has consented that injunctive relief should be granted to Hash and Sloan in this area, and such relief will be granted.

In this connection the Court has no difficulty with the proposition that for prison officials knowingly to compel convicts to perform physical labor which is beyond their strength, or which constitutes a danger to their lives or health, or which is unduly painful constitutes an infliction of cruel and unusual punishment prohibited by the Eighth Amendment to the Constitution of the United States as included in the 14th Amendment. See Robinson v. State of California, 370 U.S. 660.

Not entirely unrelated to the claim of Hash and Sloan just discussed is the claim of all three petitioners that needed medical assistance has been withheld and that attendance at "sick calls" has been unreasonably restricted.

Proposed Conclusion of Law No. (14)A(b) submitted by petitioners is that respondent should be required to "furnish reasonable medical attention for injuries and disabilities, at all reasonable times, and to permit attendance at sick call at reasonable times . . . ." Respondent does not object to the Court drawing that conclusion, and it will be incorporated in the decree to be entered.

The Court next turns to the most serious complaint of petitioners, namely, the infliction of corporal punishment. As administered at the Penitentiary, that punishment consists of blows with a leather strap five feet in length, four inches wide, and about one-fourth inch thick, attached to a wooden handle or shaft about six inches long. Ordinarily, the punishment is inflicted by the Assistant Warden having in his charge the inmate to be punished. A prisoner who is to be whipped is required to lie down on the ground fully clothed, and the blows are inflicted on his buttocks.

Under governing provisions of Arkansas law control of the Penitentiary is vested in the State Penitentiary Board, which is an honorary board consisting of five members appointed by the Governor of Arkansas. In practice the Board has largely left the administration of the Penitentiary to the discretion of the Superintendent.

Act 76 of 1893, § 62, p. 121, Ark.Stats., 1947, § 46–158, makes it the duty of the Board to prescribe the mode and extent of punishments to be inflicted on convicts for the violation of prison rules, and it is a felony for any Superintendent, subordinate officer or guard having convicts in charge to inflict or cause to be inflicted on any convict any greater or more severe punishment than is prescribed by the Board, and if death results from the infliction of excessive punishment, the person responsible is deemed to be guilty of murder or manslaughter "as the case may be."

It is probably true that corporal punishment has been used at the Penitentiary for many years. However, its use was not formally authorized by the Board, at least as far as the record here reflects, until March 1962. At that time, which was before the commencement of respondent's tenure as Superintendent, the Board adopted a brief resolution authorizing the infliction of corporal punishment whenever in the judgment of the Superintendent it appears that such punishment is necessary to maintain prison discipline or to enforce respect for Penitentiary policies. The resolution did not prescribe the form of such punishment, or the extent to which it may be employed. Its administration in practice has been described.

There are no written rules or regulations prescribing what conduct or misconduct will bring on a whipping or prescribing how many blows will be inflicted for a given act of misconduct. The punishment is administered summarily, and whether an inmate is to be whipped and how much he is to be whipped are matters resting within the sole discretion of the prison employee administering the punishment, subject to the present informal requirement of respondent that the blows administered for a single offense shall not exceed ten.

Adult male inmates of the Penitentiary are confined at either Cummins Farm Unit, where petitioners are incarcerated, or at the smaller Tucker Farm Unit. As their names imply, the primary activity carried on at those farms is agriculture. Large quantities of food are produced for consumption by inmates of the Penitentiary and of other State institutions. In addition, field crops are produced for marketing.

The actual physical labor incident to the farming operations is performed by convicts, known as "rankers," who work ordinarily ten hours a day, six days a week without pay. The rankers, including petitioners, are guarded by other convicts known as "trusty guards," armed with shotguns, pistols, and high powered rifles. Those guards are frequently hardened criminals themselves.

The rankers are assigned to work squads known as "long lines"; each long line is under the supervision of an Assistant Warden who is a paid employee of the State. In addition, each line has assigned to it a trusty guard known as a "line rider." He performs not only a security function but also has some supervisory authority over the rankers, at least in the absence of the Assistant Warden.

The number of paid employees of the Penitentiary, in addition to the Superintendent, is very few. Since the Penitentiary farms have very little direct labor expense, they are entirely self-supporting and ordinarily show annual profits, if the value of the convict labor employed be disregarded.

Certain of the crops produced at the Penitentiary, including cotton and cucumbers, are harvested by hand. The amount of such a crop which an inmate will harvest during a given work period depends not only upon his physical condition, skill, and dexterity, but also upon his diligence and willingness to work. Those same factors influence both the quantity and quality of work performed.

No individual convict has set for him in advance a quota of work which he is expected to perform within a given time. A convict is expected to do "the best he can," and if his performance is not satisfactory to his Assistant Warden, he may be whipped. Here again the infliction of punishment is determined upon and administered summarily.

Petitioner Talley has been whipped on a number of occasions by Assistant Warden Harmon both for infractions of discipline and for insufficient work. Hash has been whipped at least once by Assistant Warden Chadick.

The evidence is sharply conflicting as to how many times Talley has been whipped since he came to the Penitentiary about 1961. He says that he has been whipped about 70 times. Harmon says that Talley has been whipped only six or seven times. Talley probably exaggerates; Harmon probably minimizes. In the Court's eyes that conflict in the testimony is not material.

The evidence also discloses that on two occasions Talley has been assaulted and beaten by James Pike, the line rider assigned to Talley's long line. Pike, an illiterate, is a convicted murderer serving a sentence for beating to death a warden at the Mississippi County Penal Farm where Pike was formerly confined on a misdemeanor charge.

The evidence is conflicting as to the reasons for the assaults of Pike on Talley and as to the extent of the injuries inflicted upon the latter. Again the Court finds it unnecessary to resolve those conflicts. Regardless of why or how severely Pike beat Talley, the Court finds that the assaults were committed by Pike in his capacity as line rider and were for the purpose of disciplining Talley. In connection with the first beating Talley unquestionably received injuries to his teeth which necessitated the furnishing to him of a partial denture.

Still further disclosed by the evidence is the fact that on occasions Talley has been whipped by Harmon on the report of Pike that Talley had done insufficient work. Pike's reports seem to have been acted upon by Harmon automatically and without investigation.

It is contended by petitioners that the infliction of corporal punishment in any degree and in any circumstances upon an adult human being, either as an initial punishment for crime or as punishment for an infraction of prison discipline by a convict, is abhorrent to the modern mind, and that whatever view of it may have been taken in times past it is today a cruel and inhuman punishment prohibited by the Constitution.

In evaluating that contention it should be said first that in present context it is beside the point whether the use of such punishment is good or bad penology, or whether its infliction is necessary to control Arkansas convicts or to run the Penitentiary efficiently, or whether the Judge of the Court, as an individual, approves of such punishment. The question is whether the use of the strap at the Arkansas Penitentiary is a cruel and unusual punishment in the constitutional sense.

The criminal code of Arkansas does not prescribe whipping as a punishment for any crime, and as early as 1884 the Supreme Court of Arkansas deprecated the whipping of convicts and refused to presume that the then Penitentiary Board had authorized it. Werner v. State, 44 Ark. 122. And the infliction of such punishment has been banned in many jurisdictions. It must be recognized, however, that corporal punishment has not been viewed historically as a constitutionally forbidden cruel and unusual punishment, and this Court is not prepared to say that such punishment is per se unconstitutional. See 18 C.J.S. Convicts § 11; State v. Revis, supra; Balser v. State

(Del.), 195 A.2d 757; State v. Cannon (Del.), 190 A.2d 514; United States v. Jones, S.D.Fla., 108 F.Supp. 266, 270.

But, the Court's unwillingness to say that the Constitution forbids the imposition of any and all corporal punishment on convicts presupposes that its infliction is surrounded by appropriate safeguards. It must not be excessive; it must be inflicted as dispassionately as possible and by responsible people; and it must be applied in reference to recognizable standards whereby a convict may know what conduct on his part will cause him to be whipped and how much punishment given conduct may produce.

The Court finds that those safeguards do not exist at the Arkansas Penitentiary today, and until they are established the further corporal punishment of petitioners must and will be enjoined. It is not the function of the Court to undertake to prescribe appropriate safeguards; that is the function of the Board or of respondent subject to the Board's approval. For the guidance of those in charge of the Penitentiary the Court will say, in a general way, that it has particular trouble with the fact that there is no established schedule of punishments, that punishments are inflicted summarily and by Assistant Wardens who may or may not be men of judgment and temperate nature, and that Talley as an individual has been subjected to physical beatings at the hands of Pike. The Court is also troubled by the fact that the question of whether a convict has produced "sufficient work" during a particular period is left to the subjective judgment of the Assistant Warden, who may, at times, act uncritically upon the recommendation or report of the line rider.

There remains for consideration the complaint of petitioners that they have been denied access to the Courts. The record indicates that prior to the tenure of respondent at the Penitentiary, the authorities of that institution certainly discouraged and perhaps prevented inmates from addressing petitions to the Courts either for the purpose of testing the legality of their confinements or for the redress of grievances within the prison. However, the policy of respondent has been to permit access to the Courts, both State and federal, and at the present time such access is theoretically both adequate and reasonable.[4]

It must be recognized, however, that a theoretical right of access to the Courts is hardly actual and adequate if its exercise is likely to produce reprisals, physical or otherwise, from Penitentiary personnel. And it must be recognized also that a complaint to a Court about physical mistreatment inside the Penitentiary is more apt to produce such reprisals than is a petition whereby a convict simply seeks release from the institution.

4. In the course of the proceedings respondent stated that it was the policy of the Penitentiary to screen petitions to the Courts for the purpose of preventing inmates from sending out petitions containing obscene, abusive, or otherwise objectionable allegations or statements. The Court pointed out at the hearing on October 13, and repeats now, that while respondent's motive in so screening petitions is understandable and laudable, the wiser course for him to pursue is to permit all petitions for relief to be sent out, regardless of their language or tone, and to leave it to the Courts to protect themselves from improper matter, which they can do. Respondent and his subordinates have the right, of course, and indeed the duty to make sure before sending out a petition that the addressee is in fact a judge or court official, and that the communication is related to a request for judicial relief. But, beyond that the Penitentiary authorities probably should not go.

The Court regrets to say that the record discloses that reprisals have been visited upon Talley on account of his recourse to this Court and on account of his testimony in support of his claims.

Process in this case was served on respondent on August 6 of the current year. On the evening of that day after work in the fields had been concluded and after the rankers had been confined in their barracks, Pike, who has been mentioned, and two other inmates, apparently trusties or quasi-trusties, entered the barracks where Talley was confined and assaulted him and certain other prisoners who had been complaining about conditions in the Penitentiary and who refer to themselves as "writ writers."

The evidence also shows that for some days after August 6 the writ writers, including Talley, were put into special squads and were worked under the immediate supervision of a shotgun guard; on one occasion that guard discharged his weapon deliberately into the ground behind one of the working men and in such close proximity to him that a buckshot pellet penetrated the man's cotton sack.

While there is no evidence that respondent personally authorized or knew of the August 6 assaults on Talley and his associates, or that he ordered the formation of the special squads, and while it appears that respondent abolished the squads as soon as he learned of their existence, it does not appear that respondent has ever undertaken to discipline or reprimand the convicts concerned, or that Assistant Warden Harmon was disciplined or reprimanded, at least at the time, although he certainly knew about the special squads.

More serious in the Court's eyes is the treatment which Talley received on the day following his testimony in this case. It is admitted that on the morning of October 14 Talley and the other members of his squad were put to work picking cotton, and that after the work proceeded about 30 minutes Warden Harmon called Talley out of the long line and administered to him nine blows with the strap.

When that occurrence was reported to the Court, respondent was called upon to make an investigation and submit a report to the Court. In due course respondent submitted sworn statements of Talley and Harmon and of certain other convicts who witnessed the whipping.

According to Talley, Harmon administered the nine blows as a punishment to Talley for "lying in court." Talley says that Harmon stated that he considered that he still "owed" Talley about 25 strokes and that he had just as well "get started right now."

According to Harmon, Talley was whipped for "agitating work-stoppage and insolence." The Harmon version is that he was advised by inmates that Talley was urging his fellows to slow down or refuse to work and was telling them that "the 'people in Little Rock' were on his side and none of them would be punished because the Institution Officials were afraid to do anything." Harmon proceeds to state that on the morning of the 14th the men under his charge "all but quit work and a general rebellion appeared in the making or worse if something was not done to correct it. Talley's attitude was both openly defiant and insolent and, knowing that he was the ring-leader, I called him out of the Line and punished him for the above charges."

Harmon says that the punishment was not inflicted because Talley filed his petition or on account of his testimony. He concedes, however, that in the course of the punishment he remarked that "perhaps it would teach him not to lie in Court."

The affidavits of the inmate witnesses of the whipping to some extent corroborate Talley's version and to some extent corroborate that of Harmon. The truth is hard to determine. The Court thinks it probable that Talley was agitating to some extent, perhaps to an extent sufficient to justify punishment of some sort. On the other hand, he could not have done very much agitating prior to his whipping, and Harmon concedes that he at least took into consideration Talley's alleged "lying in court."

It was not the function of Harmon to pass upon the question of whether the testimony given by Talley was truthful or otherwise, and it was certainly not the function of Harmon to punish Talley for perjury, if any was committed. Moreover, at the time of the punishment now being discussed it was contemplated that a further hearing would be held in connection with the complaints of Hash and Sloan, and it might well have been expected that Talley would be called upon to give further testimony.

From its observation of the individuals involved the Court thinks that it was foreseeable to a penitentiary superintendent of ordinary prudence and foresight that following the October 13th hearing Talley might engage in some boasting or agitation and, on the other hand, that Harmon or Pike, or both, would visit some reprisal on Talley on account of his testimony. Although both risks were foreseeable, respondent apparently took no steps to prevent the occurrence of either.

In view of the events which have been described in this section of this opinion the Court finds itself unable to say that injunctive relief is unnecessary to protect petitioners in their access to the Courts. The granting of such access will be ordered and all reprisals against petitioners should they seek further access to the Courts or on account of their present proceeding will be enjoined.

The Court does not think that it should bring this opinion to a close without stating that nothing said herein should be construed as a claim that respondent personally is an evil, brutal, or cruel man or that he personally approves of all long standing practices of the penitentiary system. On the contrary, the record in this case reflects that respondent has undertaken with some success to ameliorate the condition of Penitentiary inmates in a number of areas of prison life. For his efforts in that connection respondent is entitled to a full measure of credit.

It is also true that the record does not disclose that respondent authorized or had personal advance knowledge of some of the events mentioned herein. However, it must not be overlooked that respondent is in charge of the Penitentiary and is responsible for the acts of his subordinates, including trusty guards. He is not relieved of that responsibility by personal ignorance of abuses practiced in fields and barracks.

A decree in accordance with the foregoing will be entered.

---

1) Did Judge Henley treat corporal punishment correctly? Should the opinion specify acceptable procedural safeguards?

2) How can Judge Henley effectively enjoin to assure "access" to the courts? Can he protect prisoners from retaliation?

3) Does the closing portion of Judge Henley's opinion belong in a judicial decision?

JACKSON v. BISHOP

268 F.Supp. 804 (E.D.Ark.1967).

OREN HARRIS and GORDON E. YOUNG, District Judges.

These are suits in equity brought under 42 U.S.C.A. § 1983 by three inmates of the Arkansas State Penitentiary against O.E. Bishop, Superintendent of the Penitentiary. The cases first became known to the court through handwritten petitions filed by each of the prisoners seeking various forms of relief. The court allowed the petitions to be filed in forma pauperis and treated each one as a complaint for equitable relief under 42 U.S.C.A. § 1983. Counsel was appointed for the prisoners, and after investigation an amended complaint was filed seeking an injunctive relief and making the cases class actions. Although one of the cases was assigned to Judge Harris and the other two to Judge Young, they were consolidated for trial due to the similarity of the issues presented, and both judges sat as a panel of two for the trial.

The plaintiffs make several alternative claims or contentions for themselves and other prison inmates:

First, they contend that the infliction of corporal punishment in any form constitutes cruel and unusual punishment contrary to the prohibitions of the Eighth Amendment to the United States Constitition as made applicable by the Fourteenth Amendment to the States.

Secondly and alternatively, they contend that the use of the strap or "hide" as a means of punishing inmates in the Penitentiary under any circumstances is cruel and unusual so as to be unconstitutional.

Thirdly, they contend that the imposition of administrative rules or regulations concerning the use of the strap does not make it a constitutionally permissible method of prison discipline.

Plaintiffs' fourth contention is actually twofold: (1) they claim that the rules concerning corporal punishment adopted by the Arkansas State Penitentiary Board do not adequately protect the prisoners from unconstitutional treatment nor do they conform to the requirements that this court set out in the *Talley* decision; and (2) the rules which have been promulgated by the Prison Board have been violated in the administration of corporal punishment upon the inmates.

Finally, each of the plaintiffs contends that although he has some physical impairment which would prevent him from doing the work of an average man, he nevertheless is classified as "average" for prison work purposes, is required to perform difficult physical labor, and is whipped when he fails to perform. Each claims that this is contrary to his constitutional right to due process and equal protection of the law and that it is also unconstitutionally cruel and unusual punishment.

The defendant denies that corporal punishment *per se* or use of the strap as carried out by prison officials is cruel and unusual in the constitutional sense. He relies primarily upon this court's earlier decision in the *Talley* case and upon the rules and regulations adopted by the Penitentiary Board pursuant to that decision. He admits that certain rule violations and other unlawful acts occurred at the Penitentiary but claims that these matters have been remedied by administrative action. Defendant denies that any injunctive relief for these plaintiffs or anyone in their class is necessary or justified.

The court appointed Edward L. Wright of Little Rock and William S. Arnold of Crossett, both highly respected and experienced members of the Arkansas Bar, to represent the plaintiffs without charge. They have done so most capably, and the court thanks them for their services.

. . . [A]t the outset we want to point out that the court is especially conscious of the limitations of its function in cases of this kind.

It is well settled that the administration of state prison discipline is the primary responsibility of state officials, and federal courts have an extremely limited area in which they may act pertaining to the treatment of prisoners confined to state penal institutions. State officials must of necessity have wide discretion and control over disciplinary measures in order to properly maintain the prison system as well as to protect the public. . . . Therefore this court cannot and will not become appellate in nature and review each prison administration decision to punish a prisoner.

However, it is equally well settled that there are exceptions to these rules when special circumstances exist and constitutional rights are involved. . . .

As was said in *Talley,* "Although persons convicted of crimes lose many of the rights and privileges of law abiding citizens, it is established by now that they do not lose all of their civil rights, and that the Due Process and Equal Protection Clauses of the 14th Amendment follow them into the prison . . . ."

We feel that the complaints in these cases raise several constitutional questions which merit the court's attention.

In order to understand the issues in their proper perspective, it is necessary to set out some of the facts about, and the recent history of the Arkansas State Penitentiary. . . .

In the fall of 1965 certain irregularities at the Penitentiary were brought to the court's attention by three inmates who filed suits similar to the ones now before the court. This court, with Judge Henley presiding, heard those cases and rendered its decision in November 1965. Talley v. Stephens. The chief contention of the plaintiffs in those cases was that the use of corporal punishment at the Arkansas State Penitentiary for disciplinary purposes was cruel and unusual and violative of the constitutional rights of the plaintiffs.

The court found that it could not say that corporal punishment *per se* was unconstitutional. It went on to say:

"But, the Court's unwillingness to say that the Constitution forbids the imposition of any and all corporal punishment on convicts presupposes that its infliction is surrounded by appropriate safeguards. It must not be excessive; it must be inflicted as dispassionately as possible and by responsible people; and it must be applied in reference to recognizable standards whereby a convict may know what conduct on his part will cause him to be whipped and how much punishment given conduct may produce."

Shortly after this decision, the Superintendent of the Penitentiary resigned; and on January 1, 1966, Mr. O.E. Bishop, the present Superintendent, was appointed. On January 10, 1966, the Penitentiary Board through Mr. Bishop promulgated a set of rules and regulations for the Penitentiary which include, *inter alia,* the following rules setting forth the offenses which merit corporal punishment as well as the procedures to be followed in administering such punishment.

"OFFENSES AND PUNISHMENT:

"A great part of your time here will be spent in the barracks you are assigned to. Barracks rules and procedure will be posted in the barracks. Your conduct, personal cleanliness and attitude while in the barracks is an important part of your prison record.

"These major offenses will warrant corporal punishment:

(1) Homosexuality.

(2) Agitation (defined as one who creates turmoil and disturbances).

(3) Insubordination (resisting authority or refusing to obey orders).

(4) Making or concealing of weapons.

(5) Refusal to work when medically certified able to work.

(6) Participating in or inciting a riot.

(7) No inmate shall ever be authorized to inflict any corporal punishment under color of prison authority on another inmate.

"Punishment shall not, in any case, exceed Ten lashes with the strap, the number of lashes to be administered shall be determined by a Board of Inquiry, consisting of at least two officials of the Arkansas State Penitentiary, The Superintendent or Assistant Superintendent, and the head Warden or an associate Warden. The Board of Inquiry will request that the accused inmate appear before the Board and speak in his own behalf. No Punishment will be administered in the field."

(Although these rules were adopted as a result of the *Talley* case, they were never approved by the court.) Each inmate, as well as the employees of the Penitentiary, was given a copy of the rules and was instructed to become familiar with and understand each of them. New prisoners were similarly instructed.

In August of 1966 Superintendent Bishop became aware of irregularities at the Tucker Prison Farm and requested that the Criminal Investigation Division of the Arkansas State Police conduct an investigation. The investigation disclosed rank violations of the rules by certain of the Prison officials.

Shortly thereafter all of the wardens at Tucker Farm were discharged or allowed to resign. Since that time there have been three new assistant superintendents in charge of Tucker Farm in quick succession, as well as other personnel changes.

Subsequently the Arkansas Legislature through a special commission, as well as the Penitentiary Board, conducted various investigations of the penal system. As a result, many desirable changes have been brought about in the administration of the two farms.

These cases were filed in the fall of 1966 and it was during their preparation for trial that the aforementioned investigations were taking place. Therefore, by the time of the trial many of the activities complained of had ceased and many of the individuals involved no longer were employed by the Penitentiary.

The trial of these cases lasted some three days, in which the court heard testimony from fifteen prisoners, several members and ex-members of the Prison personnel, one doctor, and two expert penologists. Some of the testimony pertained to strappings and other whippings which took place prior to the *Talley* decision in 1965. The court ruled that this testimony would be admitted only for the purpose of showing the background or history and would not be relevant to the type of punishment used in the Prison system since the changes brought about by the *Talley* decision, or more particularly since the rules were promulgated in January of 1966.

The strap which is referred to throughout this opinion is made of leather and is between four and five feet long and four inches wide. This leather is bradded to a wooden handle approximately six inches in length. The strap is about one-fourth inch thick at the end attached to the wooden handle and is gradually tapered toward the end which comes in contact with the person being whipped. The evidence showed that there is more than one strap used at the Penitentiary but all are of approximately the same construction. . . .

The evidence showed that the plaintiff Jackson, age 28, entered the prison in 1963 to serve a five year sentence for burglary. Jackson testified to having been subjected to physical beatings three times since he has been in prison. First, in 1965, James Pike, a trusty and long line rider, (an escapee at the time of this trial) hit him several times with his fist, as well as kicking him two or three times. The testimony was unclear as to what the purpose of this whipping was. In November of 1965 Jackson was whipped with the strap by Captain Harmon, a field warden at the Penitentiary, for not picking enough cotton. He has been whipped only once since the rules were promulgated in January 1966.

On July 29, 1966, Jackson and seven other inmates received eight lashes with the strap for leaving okra in the field. Jackson testified that he was charged by the long line rider with overlooking okra and was taken by Captain Harmon to the office of Clay Smith, Head Warden at Cummins Farm. In the process of conducting a hearing on the matter, Captain Smith informed the inmates of the charges against them and asked if each was familiar with the rules of the Penitentiary. He then asked if anyone would like to make a statement, and Jackson told Captain Smith that he had picked all the okra he could see and that he was having eye problems and needed glasses. Captain

Smith called for Jackson's medical record to determine the condition of Jackson's eyes. After checking these records and finding that Jackson had been certified as physically able for normal work, he then sentenced each prisoner to receive eight lashes with the strap. These lashes were administered by Captain Dean, another warden at the Prison. Prisoners were required to lie face down on a concrete floor while Captain Dean administered the licks to the buttocks. Jackson testified that the whipping caused much pain and left his buttocks bruised and sore for a number of days. The prisoners were returned to the field, where they continued to pick okra for the rest of the day without incident.

Further evidence shows that at the time of the whipping Jackson had, and still has, a visual defect of the left eye. There is also a slight variance from normal vision in the right eye but this is within the normal vision for reading. Shortly after the whipping he was taken to the nearby city of Pine Bluff for an eye examination and the examining doctor did not recommend glasses for him.

Plaintiff Ernst is 24 years old and has been in the penitentiary (Tucker Farm) since January 19, 1963. He has received seven whippings during his entire stay. The first three of these were administered before the rules were promulgated. They involve charges of scuffling in the barracks, not working hard enough in the fields, and cursing a trusty guard.

In January of 1966, shortly after the rules were promulgated, Ernst received ten lashes upon a charge of talking back to an overseer known as a yardman. He was called to Assistant Superintendent Bruton's office on the morning following the alleged offense and was told that he was charged with talking back to the yardman, was required to lie face down on the floor, and receive ten licks with the strap. No other wardens or other prison officials were present during the charge or the whipping.

Sometime later in 1966 he received ten licks from Captain Mayes for throwing his hat across the Prison yard. The prisoners are told that they must wear their hats in the field and also that they must care for and not misuse the clothing issued to them. Ernst testified that on this evening as he returned to the barracks from the field he took off his hat and threw it across the Prison yard onto the ground. Upon seeing this, Captain Mayes called him over, took him into the barracks, made him lie down and gave him ten lashes with the strap. There were no other wardens or other prison personnel present at this whipping.

On July 20, 1966, plaintiff Ernst was picking cucumbers in the field and was charged by the long line rider with not working and leaving cucumbers on the vines. Ernst responded by saying that he was working the best he could on the food that was fed him and that he was feeling ill. The rider reported Ernst to Captain Mayes, who took him from the fields to the barracks and gave him ten lashes with the strap. This time Ernst was required to lower his pants and was whipped on the bare buttocks, which he testified cut and bruised him and caused a great deal of pain. There was no hearing or formal charge and there were no other wardens present. Ernst was then returned to the field to continue his work. Some forty-five minutes or an hour later, the long line rider approached Ernst and started picking cucumbers back down the row upon which Ernst had just been working. He picked approximately a half bushel of cucumbers from the area in which Ernst had been working since returning from the first whipping. The rider again reported Ernst to Captain Mayes. Ernst was returned to the barracks and taken to Captain Bruton, who was shown the cucumbers and told what had happened. Captain Bruton instructed Captain Mayes to give Ernst ten lashes. He was again required to lower his pants and lie face down on the concrete floor to receive the licks. Ernst testified that this whipping left large bruises and caused him to bleed. Captain Bruton was present during this whipping and when it was over he ordered Ernst to stand on the "teeter board"[7] inside the barracks until he was told to get off. Ernst testified that he was required to remain on the teeter board for the rest of the day or about three or four hours. According to Ernst this treatment caused his legs and ankles to swell and ache. He has not been whipped since that day.

Plaintiff Mask is twenty years old and has been in prison since November 12, 1965. He spent his first four and a half months at the Cummins Farm and was then sent to Tucker and has been there since that time. He has received five whippings with the strap since coming to Tucker. The first such whipping was in June of 1966, when he was charged by a long line rider with being the last in the field or working too slow and was taken to Captain Fletcher. Captain Fletcher administered ten licks. One week later he was reported leaving cucumbers in the field. He was taken to Captain Bruton, who told him to get his pants down and lie on the floor. Captain Fletcher gave him ten licks. Plaintiff testified that two months later he was caught putting rotten tomatoes in the box they were using to carry tomatoes from the field where they were being picked. Captain Bruton gave him nine licks for this offense. In September of 1966 he was charged with not picking enough cotton. He testified that he had picked ninety pounds that day. He was taken to Captain Goodwin, the Assistant Superintendent at that time, who sentenced him to six lashes which were administered by Captain Heston. On December 7, 1966, he and several other inmates were charged with sitting down and smoking when they should have been picking cotton. He received eight lashes for this offense and was put in an isolation cell for eight days. While plaintiff was in this cell, he received regular meals, although he was denied his mail privileges and could not purchase anything from the commissary.

Plaintiff Mask also testified concerning an altercation between him and Captain Goodwin sometime in the last of November 1966. Mask said that Captain Goodwin hit him on the chin and then had him brought into the office where he was hit four or five times in the stomach and kicked once. Captain Goodwin testified that he had not hit Mask but merely grabbed him and shook him and pushed him in a corner. The testimony is not clear just why this altercation arose; however, it appears it had something to do with Mask's attitude toward work and his work performance.

7. The teeter board is a device formed by two 2-inch by 4-inch boards, one approximately three and one-half feet in length and the other about eighteen inches long. The two boards are nailed together so that the longer board is on top and also so that nails will protrude from beneath the bottom board. The prisoner is required to stand on the top or longer board and balance himself rocking on the nails and the smaller board.

Plaintiff Mask also complained that his knee bothers him when he works for long periods of time. This causes him not to be able to do as much work as is required of him. His knee was injured in a tractor accident in 1960 to such an extent that it required surgery to repair. There is some evidence that it might have been re-injured in 1964. However, medical evidence was introduced to show that there were no significant residual effects of the earlier injury and also that there had been no recent re-injury.

The court also heard testimony from twelve other inmates of the Arkansas State Penitentiary, most of which was cumulative to that given by the three named plaintiffs as well as corroborating some of their testimony set out above. These prisoners related the facts surrounding whippings which the various prisoners had received for offenses such as insufficient work, insubordination, and scuffling among prisoners. According to these witnesses, some of the whippings were administered without a formal hearing, also some hearings were conducted with only one warden present. The general pattern of these whippings as related by the prisoners is that a prisoner is charged by a trusty or other inmate in the capacity of an overseer such as a long line rider or yardman with some infraction of the Penitentiary rules. He is taken to a warden. The warden then takes him before another Penitentiary official and there charges him with a rule infraction. In most cases the prisoner is given a chance to explain his actions; then sentence is handed down. If the prisoner is found guilty and sentenced to a whipping, he is required to lie face down on the floor and receive the lashes on his buttocks. The prisoners claim that the word of the trusty or accusing warden is usually summarily accepted without further investigation or questioning.

The prisoners also testified to certain beatings which inmates had received at the hands of trusties or other inmates in positions of authority. These beatings seem to have no connection with the disciplining of the beaten prisoners; however, testimony showed that yardmen, floorwalkers, and occasionally a night warden have seen these beatings and have not reported the inmates for fighting nor have they tried to interfere with the beatings. Most of this type activity takes place at night in the barracks; however, there were a few instances in which one or two blows were struck in the field.

Investigator H.H. Atkinson of the Criminal Investigation Division of the Arkansas State Police testified as to the facts and circumstances of his investigation of the Tucker Prison Farm in August of 1966. Atkinson's investigation arose out of some alleged violations of the rules involving possession of liquor by some of the inmates. He testified that as his investigation progressed he and his men uncovered various acts of brutality and cruel treatment of the inmates by certain officials and trusties at Tucker Farm. Immediately upon report of his findings to Superintendent Goodwin, all the wardens at Tucker Farm were discharged. Although new personnel was appointed, Atkinson's investigation continued for some twenty-two days. He revealed that he had uncovered such torturous devices as a crank telephone device which was used to electrically shock prisoners, as well as use of the teeter board and strapping upon the bare buttocks. He testified that in the first part of his investigation he witnessed such a strapping of an inmate by Captain Mayes. He further testified that all persons responsible for such treatment have been discharged.

He was later placed in charge of Tucker Farm as Acting Assistant Superintendent during the administrative changes in December of 1966 and January of 1967. He said that he found it necessary to use the strap while he was in charge. He strapped four of twelve prisoners who had been sentenced by a three-man board of inquiry to six lashes because they had picked an insufficient amount of cotton. He was told later by the inmates that they were "trying him to see if he would use the whip." He also said that he got better work from the prisoners after they found out he would use the strap.

Superintendent O.E. Bishop has been Superintendent for the Prison system since January 1, 1966. He testified that when the rules were promulgated he made every effort to make sure that each prisoner had a copy of the rules and understood them. His efforts included reading the rules to the prisoners over a loud speaker system and answering any questions they might have. He instructed all the personnel of the Prison that anyone who was found not following the rules would be fired immediately. He also told the trusties that they would be "ranked" (lose their privileges as trusties) at the first violation of the rules. The evidence showed in fact that some trusties have been ranked and several wardens have been fired because of violations.

He testified that he was not aware of the activities that had taken place at Tucker Farm prior to August of 1966 because his duties required him to spend the largest part of his time at Cummins Farm. He also said that the two farms were fifty miles apart and that he could not leave Cummins to go to Tucker without the wardens at Tucker knowing of his visit beforehand.

Superintendent Bishop said that disciplinary methods other than the use of the strap are also used in the Penitentiary system. These include loss of the few privileges which exist for the prisoners, administrative isolation or solitary confinement, and removal from the plasma program, which is a means by which the prisoners earn money. He said that often prisoners charged with violations of the rules were found not guilty and were not punished. The evidence showed that substantial improvements have been made in the facilities and in the administrative procedure of the Penitentiary system since Mr. Bishop has taken over.

The court heard the testimony of five of the wardens who were discharged or permitted to resign from the staff at Tucker Farm. Captain Clay Smith, Head Warden, and two other wardens at Cummins Farm also testified. These witnesses related the facts and circumstances surrounding each of the whippings complained of in this case. They said that in each case involving a whipping there had been a violation of the rules by the prisoners and except in a few instances (which have been admitted by the defendant) the procedure for the administration of corporal punishment as set out in the rules was followed. They maintained that at all hearings at least two wardens were present. They also said that they treated the whipping of prisoners as just another part of their jobs and had no personal feelings against the prisoners while the whipping was being administered.

Captain Clay Smith testified that he usually sits on the board of inquiry at Cummins Farm and that he always asked the prisoner being charged if he knew of and understood the rules and regulations. He then would ask if the prisoner had anything to say before he decided the case or gave any punishment. Captain Smith said that he could not set a work quota for each inmate because of the many variables involved in the day-to-day work at the Prison. He stated that all the Prison administration asked of the inmates was an honest day's work. Upon being questioned by the court, Captain Smith said that of the 1,600 inmates at Cummins, in 1966 approximately 200 were whipped. He said the great majority of prisoners adjusted satisfactorily to Prison conditions and are never punished. There are some whose conduct is such that discipline in some form becomes necessary. There is a smaller group who are rebellious and, because of their recalcitrance, require repeated disciplinary measures.

The court reconvened some two and a half weeks after the close of the first two days of this hearing to hear the testimony of two expert penologists presented by counsel for the plaintiffs.

Dr. James V. Bennett, who was Director of the Federal Prisons from 1937 to 1964, and whose qualifications as an eminent penologist are far too numerous to mention here, gave his views on the use of the whip for disciplinary purposes in a penitentiary. He said that in all the many years in which he was connected with the federal prisons he never used strapping or corporal punishment for disciplinary purposes. He felt that it was brutal and medieval and did no real good. He also testified that to his knowledge only one other state used the whip officially in its penitentiary system. He said that it was possible, however, that other states used it unofficially. He said that he had never visited the Arkansas Penitentiary System and that he was familiar with it only through discussions with prisoners who had been incarcerated there.

He had read and was familiar with the rules of the Penitentiary. Even if corporal punishment were permitted, it was his opinion that these rules were too indefinite and could be easily circumvented so as to make them ineffective. He said that an inmate should be entitled to a completely objective hearing by a qualified employee whose decision should be approved by a high ranking official in the system before corporal punishment is administered to that prisoner. He also suggested that a cooling-off period should be allowed between the charge and the decision or sentence. He advocated the use of incentives for good behavior rather than punishment.

Mr. Fred Wilkinson, Director of Corrections for the State of Missouri, who is also an eminently qualified penologist with many years of experience in the federal prisons, also testified for plaintiffs. It is his opinion that all forms of corporal punishment should be abolished. He said that he also knew of only one other state that uses the whip officially in disciplining prison inmates. In his experience the most commonly used punishment was forfeiture of good time credits, deprivation of privileges, and administrative separation. He said that if the strap were used, there should be a commission or board to rule on the appropriate discipline rather than just one person. Both he and Mr. Bennett testified at some length as to the type of facilities and the forms of punishment used in the prisons with which they had been connected.

According to Mr. Wilkinson, in the Missouri Prison System there is one paid employee for each four or five prisoners; nationally the average is one paid employee to about seven or eight prisoners. It appears that in Arkansas the ratio is one paid employee to approximately 58 prisoners.

The Eighth Amendment to the Constitution of the United States provides " . . . excessive bail shall not be required, nor excessive fines imposed, *nor cruel and unusual punishments inflicted.*" (Emphasis supplied.) Although the prohibitions of this Amendment originally applied only to the federal government, it is now well settled that they apply equally to the States through the due process clause of the Fourteenth Amendment. Robinson v. State of California, 370 U.S. 660; United States ex rel. Bryant v. Fay, 211 F.Supp. 812 (D.C.N.Y.1962).

The courts have never arrived at a satisfactory definition of "cruel and unusual punishment." As was said recently by the Eighth Circuit, "It is settled doctrine that except in extreme cases the courts may not interfere with the conduct of a prison, with its regulations and their enforcement, or with its discipline. (Citation of authorities.)" However, in the same case the court went on to say, "Unlawful administration can exist where there are aspects of institutional treatment of such character or consequences as to shock general conscience or to be intolerable in fundamental fairness. Such treatment is entitled to be held to be within the ban of the Eighth Amendment as representing cruel and unusual punishment and so constituting unlawful administration of prison sentence." Lee v. Tahash, 352 F.2d 970, 971, 972 (1965). See also Carey v. Settle, 351 F.2d 483 (8 Cir. 1965).

The court has weighed the evidence in these cases, along with the arguments and authorities set forth in the excellent briefs of both parties. We think it is fair to say, however, as this court said in *Talley,* " . . . corporal punishment has not been viewed historically as a constitutionally forbidden cruel and unusual punishment." Neither are we willing to say that the use of the strap in and of itself is contrary to the Eighth Amendment's prohibitions.

. . .

. . . A punishment, like a law, may be constitutional in its bare form and yet be unconstitutionally administered. Certainly proper safeguards against capricious administration are necessary to keep such punishment from violating constitutional standards.

There can be no doubt that the brutal and sadistic atrocities which were uncovered by the investigation of the State Police in August and September of 1966 cannot be tolerated. The court has reference to the use of a telephone shocking apparatus, the teeter board, strapping on the bare buttocks, and other torturous acts of this nature. The defendant admits that these acts were committed but claims that they were carried on without the knowledge or approval of the Superintendent, that they are contrary to the Prison rules as well as the State law, that all personnel responsible for such acts have been discharged, that the offending objects of torture have been disposed of, and that administrative steps have been taken to assure that such acts will not recur.

The court commends the actions of the Superintendent, under the supervision of the Prison Board, which have produced more efficient administration and improved standards of discipline, as well as other improvements; however, we feel that the inmates' right to be free of such treatment as disclosed in the testimony cannot depend upon the competence of the administrative personnel which changes from time to time; therefore, these and other actions of this character will be permanently enjoined.

As we have indicated, the court is aware that there has been much improvement in the disciplining of prisoners since the rules were promulgated in January 1966. However, the court finds that the "Rules and Regulations" adopted by the Penitentiary Board January 10, 1966 do not provide the adequate safeguards required by this court in *Talley.*

As an example, they are unnecessarily ambiguous in prescribing the composition of the "board of inquiry" described in the rules. We agree with Mr. Bennett's observation that this portion of the rules is so indefinite as to be easily circumvented. It is obvious from the testimony that experience under these rules has proven this to be true.

The court refers particularly to the convening of hearings in connection with the administration of corporal punishment without a proper "board of inquiry."

The court will enjoin the use of the strap as punishment at the penitentiary until proper and adequate safeguards surrounding its use are provided by those in charge of prison administration.

It is neither this court's duty nor its inclination to tell the defendant or the Penitentiary Board what rules should be promulgated in order to comply with the Constitution. However, the court will make these general observations.

First, more than one person's judgment should be required for a decision to administer corporal punishment. This is implicit in the existing rules which require such a decision to be made by a board of inquiry. In this procedure, the accuser should not be counted among those who sit in judgment.

Secondly, that circumvention of the rules and regulations by an official in time of anger is intolerable. Certainly a prisoner charged with a rule violation is entitled to and should be provided with an objectively reasoned, dispassionate decision as to whether or not he should be punished.

Third, that summary acceptance of one inmate's report on another without further investigation in determining whether punishment should be administered voids the effectiveness of any rules and regulations.

And, finally, it is suggested that the Superintendent or an Assistant Superintendent of the Prison participate in or review any decision to inflict corporal punishment.

The court finds that the evidence is insufficient to sustain the contention of each plaintiff concerning his physical impairment. Each claims that he has been unconstitutionally punished because of failure to do work which he is physically unable to do.

There can be no doubt that as we stated in the *Talley* decision:

" . . . for prison officials knowingly to compel convicts to perform physical labor which is beyond their strength, or which constitutes a danger to their lives or health, or which is unduly painful constitutes an infliction of cruel and unusual punishment prohibited by the 8th Amendment to the Constitution of the United States as included in the 14th Amendment."

However, such a situation does not exist in this case. Upon request of plaintiffs' counsel the court appointed Dr. Dale Alford (an ophthalmologist) to examine plaintiff Jackson's eyes, and Dr. John Hundley and Dr. Charles McKenzie (orthopedic surgeons) to examine plaintiff Mask's knee. Relying upon these doctors' reports, as well as the prison medical records of each plaintiff and the testimony surrounding the incidents concerning the alleged physical impairments, the court can find no merit in these contentions.

An injunction will be issued permanently restraining the defendant and any personnel of the Prison System from:

"The use of any such devices as the crank telephone or teeter board; or

The application of any whipping to the bare skin of prisoners."

Such officials are further restrained from the "use of the strap" on any prisoner until additional rules and regulations are promulgated with appropriate safeguards in accordance with this opinion and filed with the Clerk of this court.

An order will be issued in accordance with this opinion.

DECREE

In accordance with the Memorandum Opinion of the court filed this date, the defendant, O.E. Bishop, Superintendent of the Arkansas State Penitentiary, and any personnel of the Prison System are permanently restrained from:

"The use of any such devices as the crank telephone or teeter board; or

The application of any whipping to the bare skin of prisoners."

Such officials are further restrained from the "use of the strap" on any prisoner until additional rules and regulations are promulgated with appropriate safeguards in accordance with said opinion and filed with the Clerk of this court.

---

1) How does *Talley* differ from Jackson v. Bishop? What explains those differences?

2) What legal theory forbids the crank telephone or teeter board? How do you distinguish the whippings?

3) Is Jackson v. Bishop a class action? The court examines the testimony of the individual plaintiffs to demonstrate the need for general procedural requirements or safeguards concerning the strap. How does the court move from the particular to the general? What legal theory requires the safeguards? Why doesn't the court describe those safeguards, rather than merely making some "general observations"?

4) How will the decree be enforced? The court bases the need for injunctive relief on the conclusion that the Superintendent lacks full control of his staff. Should it place the obligation to ensure compliance on his shoulders? How might the decree be written to ensure greater compliance? Should the court require reports? appoint auxiliary personnel to police performance?

5) The court denies relief on the claim that prison officials are compelling convicts to work beyond their capacities. It bases this on a physical examination of two of the plaintiffs and the testimony surrounding certain "incidents." Is this a sufficient basis to deny relief on this claim? Would it make

a difference if this proceeding were a class action? Does this retreat from *Talley?*

6) Judges Young and Harris consolidated these cases and issued a single opinion and decree. Was that correct under Rule 42(a)?

JACKSON v. BISHOP

404 F.2d 571 (8th Cir. 1968).

Before VAN OOSTERHOUT, Chief Judge, BLACKMUN, Circuit Judge, and VAN PELT, District Judge.

BLACKMUN, Circuit Judge.

The three plaintiffs-appellants, inmates of the Arkansas penitentiary, in separate actions call upon us to direct the entry of an injunction barring the use of the strap as a disciplinary measure in Arkansas' penal institutions. The claim is that the district court

"erred in refusing to hold that corporal punishment of prisoners is cruel and unusual punishment within the meaning of the Eighth Amendment to the United States Constitution, and in holding that the whipping of prisoners was not unconstitutional per se."

The plaintiffs' cases are not dissimilar, in tone and complaint, to an earlier non-class action by another trio of Arkansas prisoners. Talley v. Stephens. Chief Judge Henley in *Talley* granted, in part by consent, a substantial measure of relief, including restraint against forcing prisoners to work beyond their physical capabilities, against the withholding of reasonable medical attention, against the infliction of corporal punishment until "appropriate safeguards" were established, and against reprisals for seeking access to the courts. Neither side appealed.

The present cases were filed in the Eastern District of Arkansas and were assigned respectively to Judge Young and Judge Harris. Upon agreement, the judges consolidated the three actions and, as a panel of two, jointly heard and decided them. After a full hearing, the court granted relief against "[t]he use of any such devices as the crank telephone or teeter board" and against "[t]he application of any whipping to the bare skin of prisoners." It also restrained the use of the strap "until additional rules and regulations are promulgated with appropriate safeguards. . . . " Jackson v. Bishop.

The use of the strap, therefore, as in the *Talley* case, was not totally restrained. Because it was not, the plaintiffs appeal and seek here to remove that vestige. The defendant Superintendent has taken no cross appeal. Thus, the relief granted in the district court remains effective and is not in issue before us.

We conclude that the plaintiffs are correct in their position and that Arkansas' use of the strap, irrespective of safeguards, is to be enjoined. . . .

[S]o far as the Supreme Court cases are concerned, we have a flat recognition that the limits of the Eighth Amendment's proscription are not easily or exactly defined, and we also have clear indications that the applicable standards are flexible, that disproportion, both among punishments and between punishment and crime, is a factor to be considered, and that broad and idealistic concepts of dignity, civilized standards, humanity, and decency are useful and usable. We recognize that some of these utterances by the Court were made in concurrence or dissent or in the approach, evidently now superseded, through the Fourteenth Amendment's due process clause rather than jointly through the Fourteenth and Eighth Amendments. All this, however, strikes us as of no import because we read and ascertain in the totality of the language used the basic attitude of the entire Court to the Eighth Amendment.

With these principles and guidelines before us, we have no difficulty in reaching the conclusion that the use of the strap in the penitentiaries of Arkansas is punishment which, in this last third of the 20th century, runs afoul of the Eighth Amendment; that the strap's use, irrespective of any precautionary conditions which may be imposed, offends contemporary concepts of decency and human dignity and precepts of civilization which we profess to possess; and that it also violates those standards of good conscience and fundamental fairness enunciated by this court in the *Carey* and *Lee* cases.

Our reasons for this conclusion include the following: (1) We are not convinced that any rule or regulation as to the use of the strap, however seriously or sincerely conceived and drawn, will successfully prevent abuse. The present record discloses misinterpretation and obvious overnarrow interpretation even of the newly adopted January 1966 rules. (2) Rules in this area seem often to go unobserved. Despite the January 1966 requirement that no inmate was to inflict punishment on another, the record is replete with instances where this very thing took place. (3) Regulations are easily circumvented. Although it was a long-standing requirement that a whipping was to be administered only when the prisoner was fully clothed, this record discloses instances of whippings upon the bare buttocks, and with consequent injury. (4) Corporal punishment is easily subject to abuse in the hands of the sadistic and the unscrupulous. (5) Where power to punish is granted to persons in lower levels of administrative authority, there is an inherent and natural difficulty in enforcing the limitations of that power. (6) There can be no argument that excessive whipping or an inappropriate manner of whipping or too great frequency of whipping or the use of studded or overlong straps all constitute cruel and unusual punishment. But if whipping were to be authorized, how does one, or any court, ascertain the point which would distinguish the permissible from that which is cruel and unusual? (7) Corporal punishment generates hate toward the keepers who punish and toward the system which permits it. It is degrading to the punisher and to the punished alike. It frustrates correctional and rehabilitative goals. This record cries out with testimony to this effect from the expert penologists, from the inmates and from their keepers. (8) Whipping creates other penological problems and makes adjustment to society more difficult. (9) Public opinion is obviously adverse. Counsel concede that only two states still permit the use of the strap. Thus almost uniformly has it been abolished. It has been expressly outlawed by statute in a number of states. See for example, N.D.Cent.Code § 12–47–26 (1960); S.D.Code § 13.4715 (1939). And 48 states, including Arkansas, have constitutional provisions against cruel or unusual punishment. Ark.Const. art. 2, § 9.

We are not convinced contrarily by any suggestion that the State needs this tool for disciplinary purposes and is too poor to provide other accepted means of prisoner regulation. Humane considerations and constitutional requirements are not, in this day, to be measured or limited by dollar considerations or by the thickness of the prisoner's clothing. . . .

We choose to draw no significant distinction between the word "cruel" and the word "unusual" in the Eighth Amendment. See Trop v. Dulles, 356 U.S. 86, 100 n. 32 (1958). We would not wish to place ourselves in the position of condoning punishment which is shown to be only "cruel" but not "unusual" or vice versa. In any event, the testimony of the two expert penologists clearly demonstrates that the use of the strap in this day is unusual and we encounter no difficulty in holding that its use is cruel.

Neither do we wish to draw, in this context, any meaningful distinction between punishment by way of sentence statutorily prescribed and punishment imposed for prison disciplinary purposes. It seems to us that the Eighth Amendment's proscription has application to both.

The district court's decree is vacated and the case is remanded with directions to enter a new decree embracing the injunctive relief heretofore granted but, in addition, restraining the Superintendent of the Arkansas State Penitentiary and all personnel of the penitentiary system from inflicting corporal punishment, including the use of the strap, as a disciplinary measure.

---

1) Does the court's ban on corporal punishment apply only to named plaintiffs? extend to present prisoners?

2) Is Judge Blackmun's reasoning convincing? Why were Judges Harris, Young, and Henley unwilling to endorse it? Did they have different information? Or just different sensibilities?

3) Why didn't the superintendent appeal from the portions of the decree that banned the crank phone and the teeter board? Can you answer that question consistently with the contention that an injunction was necessary in the first place?

Further Excerpts from **Harris & Spiller Report.**

The Arkansas Penitentiary Study Commission was created by Act No. 22 of the Arkansas legislature for 1967 as a response to adverse publicity regarding the penal system. The act authorized appointment of 13 members to the commission, all of whom were recognized community leaders. The last section of the act explained the reason for the commission's existence and its general purpose.

"It is hereby found and determined by the General Assembly that there has recently been much publicity regarding the penal system in Arkansas; that such publicity has raised serious questions in the minds of the public officials and the general public regarding the facilities, practices and disciplinary procedures at the State Penitentiary; and that it is necessary that a thorough study and evaluation of the penal system be made as soon as possible. . . ."

The commission's first meeting was held in Little Rock, Arkansas on March 18, 1967. Thereafter, for the next nine months, it studied, evaluated and ultimately reported on the Arkansas penitentiary system. The report covered nine specific areas and authorized a broad, general inquiry:

"1. A study and review of the existing facilities and holdings of the State Penitentiary and the adequacy thereof.

2. The feasibility of establishing a first offenders unit at the State Penitentiary.

3. The feasibility of providing separate facilities at the Penitentiary for the separation of persons by age, especially in regard to young inmates.

4. The need for, and suggested standards and regulations for the use of, rehabilitation facilities and services at the Penitentiary, including educational and vocational-technical training facilities.

5. Evaluation of the disciplinary facilities and procedures at the Penitentiary.

6. A study and evaluation of the facilities and programs of the Women's Reformatory at the State Penitentiary.

7. A study and evaluation of the State's parole system and a need for revisions or improvements thereof.

8. A study of the trusty system at the Penitentiary.

9. A study of the financial operations of the Penitentiary, including the source of income, and purposes for which expenditures are made.

10. A study of such other aspects of the State Penal System that the Commission may deem advisable and necessary, including a study and review of the penal systems of other states."

The Study Commission submitted its report to the governor and the Arkansas General Assembly on January 1, 1968. The report characterized rehabilitation of the offender as a legal and moral obligation of the state and affirmed that rehabilitation should be the primary mission of the Arkansas penal system. In the report the commission called for financial and moral support for all of the rehabilitative programs in the system. Included in the report was a description of the composition and methodology of the Commission, the history of the Arkansas penitentiary system, an assessment of its status, and specific recommendations for improvement. The recommendations touched management of the system, improving existing facilities, upgrading prison personnel, utilizing inmate labor, and provisions regarding the custody, discipline and rehabilitation of prisoners.

Prominent in the report were recommendations designed to restructure the financing and management of the prison system. In a radical departure from the existing notion that the prison system should pay for itself, the commission proposed that revenue generated by the prison system through "prison industries" should be placed in a general revenue fund and that the amount of the prison system's expenditures should not be limited to the previous year's net income from the prison industries. This recommendation envisioned that, rather than making money for the state, the system would cost the state large sums of money. Proposals concerning management of the prison system bore implications of similar magnitude.

The commission recommended that a separate state department of correction administered by a director of correction be legislatively established and given responsibilities for administration of the prison system. It proposed that Tucker, Cummins, and the Women's Reformatory be designated separate institutions and each placed under the direction of a superintendent responsible to the director of correction. Specific recommendations were proposed concerning each institution. According to the report, Tucker should be designated an institution for youthful male offenders and should continue farming operations for production of its own food and for training inmates. Cummins should become an institution for prisoners above youthful offender level, with major emphasis on the production of agriculture for profit, for consumption by inmates and for training inmates. The report proposed that the Reformatory for Women be made into a separate institution and moved to a new location near Little Rock. It was recommended that each facility provide "treatment," education, vocational training and other rehabilitative programs. In addition to the changes to the existing facilities, the report recommended the construction of several new facilities at a site near Little Rock. The proposed facilities were a small maximum security facility for men, a reception center for all newly admitted prisoners, and a pre-release center.

Acknowledgment was made in the report that the "improvement of personnel, diversified utilization of prison labor, methods of custody and discipline, and rehabilitative programs . . . [should] be considered of prime importance and the improvement of buildings of secondary importance . . . ." The commission thus established priorities for improving the system that were illustrated by specific recommendations.

The report recommended that personnel be increased in number and improved in quality with the goal of replacing armed inmate trusty guards and of increasing the supervision of inmates by free world personnel. It proposed higher qualifications, better training and higher salaries for prison personnel. "The positive rehabilitative value of a varied work program . . . " was emphasized, and several recommendations were advanced concerning the use of inmate labor in various work situations. The commission recommended that major emphasis continue to be placed on agricultural operations. However, it recommended that the farm operations be modernized and better coordinated, and that working conditions for inmates be upgraded. Although agricultural operations were emphasized, the report recommended that inmate labor be utilized in a number of other programs. It recommended that " . . . a few relatively small productive industries . . . " be developed; that a ". . . limited number of carefully selected prisoners be employed . . . " on public works projects; that a work furlough program be developed, under which prisoners would be allowed to work at free world jobs during the day and return to institutions at night; and, that the maintenance work of the institution be performed by inmates as part of a vocational training program.

Several recommendations were advanced concerning the custody and discipline of inmates. It was recommended that use of the strap be discontinued and that only disciplinary sanctions that were ". . . accepted as defensible and effective by the American Correctional Association . . . ," such as reprimands, loss of privileges, loss of good time, solitary confinement, loss of trusty status, reduced rations, and the imposition of new sentences for serious disciplinary offenses, should be imposed upon inmates. The report did not recommend completely dismantling the prisoner trusty system but it advocated substantial change in the way the trusty system operated in Arkansas. According to the report, trusties should ". . . no longer be given duties, responsibilities, or authority that should be given only to civilian employees . . . ." It was suggested that, because many inmates in medium security custody actually presented maximum security problems, the medium security buildings be made more secure, and a maximum security facility be constructed.

Despite the fact that improvements in structures were assigned a relatively low priority by the commission, the report nevertheless made several proposals that were intended to upgrade existing physical structures. According to the report, construction defects in the existing buildings should be corrected as fast as funds for building materials became available; living quarters should be expanded or modified to provide single occupancy residences for prisoners who should not be housed in open dormitories; farm buildings should be modified or replaced; new kitchen equipment should be provided at Cummins; new laundry equipment should be provided at both Cummins and Tucker; new sewing machines should be provided at the Reformatory for Women; the hospital building at Cummins should be modified and expanded; and a gymnasium should be constructed at Tucker. . . .

COURTNEY v. BISHOP

409 F.2d 1185 (8th Cir. 1969).

Before VAN OOSTERHOUT, Chief Judge, MATTHES and BRIGHT, Circuit Judges.

MATTHES, Circuit Judge.

Robert Courtney has appealed from the order of the United States district court dismissing his petition for relief under 42 U.S.C. § 1983.

On May 28, 1967, appellant acting pro se filed a petition in the United States district court seeking relief from alleged cruel and unusual treatment inflicted upon him during solitary confinement in Cummins Farm, a penal institution in the state of Arkansas. Philip K. Lyon and Robert L. Robinson, Jr., lawyers of Little Rock, Arkansas, were appointed to represent petitioner. At the time of the filing of the original petition appellant had been released from solitary confinement. Subsequently, however, he was again placed in isolation. This precipitated a second complaint. The allegations in the second complaint were incorporated along with the first one in a final amended complaint filed by counsel on December 18, 1967. Essentially appellant alleged that he had been arbitrarily placed in solitary confinement, and that while there he was deprived of adequate and sanitary food, medical and psychiatric treatment, and was subjected to beatings by prison officials. These circumstances and conditions, he claimed, constituted cruel and unusual punishment as applied to him.

After a hearing before Honorable Oren Harris on January 26, 1968, at which appellant was afforded a full opportunity to offer evidence in support of his charges, the court found that appellant had not been subjected to cruel and unusual punishment and dismissed his claim for relief. At that time appellant had been released from solitary confinement and had been transferred to Tucker Farm, another penal institution in Arkansas.

The sole issue here is whether the court below was wrong in dismissing the claim for relief.

The law to be applied is well settled. Lawful incarceration necessarily operates to deprive a prisoner of certain rights and privileges he would otherwise enjoy in the free society, a retraction justified by considerations underlying our penal system. Price v. Johnston, 334 U.S. 266, 285 (1948); Jackson v. Bishop. A convict, however, does not lose all of his civil rights—for those that are fundamental follow him, with appropriate limitations, through the prison gate, and the walls do not foreclose his access to the courts to protect those rights. Sharp v. Sigler, 408 F.2d 966 (8th Cir., 1969); Jackson v. Bishop. On the other hand, prison officials are vested with wide discretion in controlling prisoners committed to their custody, Douglas v. Sigler, 386 F.2d 684 (8th Cir. 1967); Stroud v. Swope, 187 F.2d 850, 851 (9th Cir. 1951), and it is elementary that unless an infringement upon constitutional or fundamental rights is involved, federal courts are naturally reluctant to interfere with a prison's internal discipline, whether the institution is federal or state. . . . Jackson v. Bishop.

In *Jackson,* applying the above principles, this court found that strapping a prisoner violated his fundamental right to be free from cruel and unusual punishment as guaranteed by the Eighth Amendment, and we did not hesitate to intervene to restore that right. But in *Sharp,* we sustained the district court's finding that confinement of four inmates of the Maximum Security Unit did not constitute a denial of the free exercise of their religion guaranteed by the First Amendment, and refrained from interfering with prison administration there.

Appellant frankly concedes that solitary confinement is not unconstitutional pro se. The authorities so hold. Graham v. Willingham, 384 F.2d 367 (10th Cir. 1967); Kostal v. Tinsley, 337 F.2d 845 (10th Cir. 1964). He argues, however, that the particular conditions of his confinement do constitute cruel and unusual punishment. Thus it follows that appellant's contention presented an issue of fact for determination by the district court.

The following events, gleaned from the hearing, are pertinent:

Appellant had been placed in solitary confinement on or about April 23, 1967, and remained there for seven days. This resulted from his being intoxicated and "scratching" another inmate with a knife.

On July 17, 1967, after his first complaint had been filed, appellant assaulted another inmate, Ronnie Elser, who on January 5, 1967, had attacked appellant with a knife. It is evident that as a result of this attack there was bad blood between appellant and Elser. In explanation of his assault on Elser, appellant stated that he had been warned that Elser intended again to assault him. On the day in question, July 17, appellant was in the barracks on Cummins Farm. He observed Elser approaching and also saw a knife partly protruding from Elser's pocket. At the opportune time appellant stabbed Elser twice in his back. Appellant was immediately placed in solitary confinement and remained there until January 4, 1968. The evidence at the hearing in large measure related to the conditions attending appellant's confinement and the alleged inhuman treatment inflicted upon him during that period.

Judge Harris found that appellant was not arbitrarily subjected to solitary confinement: "It was his own conduct that made it necessary for the officials of the penitentiary, by his own admission, that required his being placed in solitary confinement." The other circumstances relied upon, such as inadequate food, improper medical attention, lack of sanitation in the cell and an assault upon appellant in November, 1967, by two guards, were also carefully considered by Judge Harris. He found that appellant had failed to prove the existence of the claimed cruel and unusual punishment.

". . . particularly with reference to medical treatment, with reference to the allegation of being placed in cells with active TB patients, with reference to unsanitary food being prepared, and matters of that kind. The petitioner's own witnesses failed to sustain that contention, and therefore there is no merit to such contentions whatsoever.

"With reference to the physical abuse, which seems to have surrounded the incident of November 7th and 8th, the Petitioner Courtney admitted the incidents that he himself brought on with reference to disciplinary action in not only tearing up the cell but destroying the property and defying the officers or the officials of the penitentiary when they themselves came in to try to do something about it. By his own admission he resisted and by the description of his own witnesses he had to be restrained."

Our examination of the record convinces us that the district court's findings are supported by appellant's own evidence and that such findings are in no sense clearly erroneous.

Appellant also complains of the district court's holding that he was not entitled to a hearing before an appropriate prison board of inquiry prior to being placed in solitary confinement or shortly thereafter. Judge Harris' interpretation of the prison rules designed to regulate the treatment of inmates persuaded him to conclude that appellant's misconduct did not necessitate a hearing. This phase of the case obviously relates to the internal affairs of the penal institution. Where, as here, the lack of an inquiry did not deprive the prisoner of a fundamental constitutional right, the courts will not interfere.

We have considered the contentions of appellant relating to procedural matters in the district court and find them lacking in substance.

The judgment is affirmed.

---

1) Judge Harris insisted on procedural safeguards for corporal punishment. Why not require the same for solitary confinement?

2) Plaintiffs claimed that solitary confinement was improper because of inadequate food, improper medical attention, and lack of sanitation. Are you convinced that this claim failed because of inadequate proof?

HOLT v. SARVER [HOLT I]

300 F.Supp. 825 (E.D.Ark. 1969).

HENLEY, Chief Judge.

The several petitioners in subject cases are inmates of the Cummins Farm Unit of the Arkansas State Penitentiary . . . . Petitioners complain that those in charge of the Farm are depriving them of rights protected by the Fourteenth Amendment to the Constitution of the United States. Federal jurisdiction under 28 U.S.C.A. § 1343(3) and 42 U.S.C.A. § 1933, is not questioned and is established. Under those sections the Court is authorized to grant both declaratory and injunctive relief to the extent that petitioners may have shown that they are entitled to relief.

The principal complaints of petitioners are that confinement in cells in the isolation unit of the Farm amounts to cruel and unusual punishment prohibited by the Eighth Amendment as carried forward into the Fourteenth, Robinson v. California, 370 U.S. 660; Jackson v. Bishop; Talley v. Stephens; that they are denied adequate medical attention, Talley v. Stephens; and that the Penitentiary authorities have failed to take adequate steps to protect inmates from assaults by other inmates, Cf. Johnson v. United States Government, E.D.Va., 258 F.Supp. 372, and Cohen v. United States, N.D.Ga., 252 F.Supp. 679. . . .

At this juncture it may be noted that the Court's inquiry here is limited to whether Arkansas convicts as a class, or individual convicts, have been and are being deprived of federal constitutional rights. The Court is not concerned in general with prison policies, administration, or discipline. However, if the State, acting through its penal authorities, is depriving convicts of rights which the Constitution protects, including the right to be free from cruel and unusual punishment, the Court may and should intervene to protect those rights and to put an end to unconstitutional practices. Courtney v. Bishop; Jackson v. Bishop; Talley v. Stephens.

The opinion of the Court of Appeals in Jackson v. Bishop makes clear that the concept of "cruel and unusual punishment" is a flexible and expanding one, and that a punishment or system of punishment is unconstitutional if it offends concepts of decency and human dignity and precepts of civilization which Americans profess to possess, or if it is disproportionate to the offense, or if it violates fundamental standards of good conscience and fairness.

Solitary confinement or close confinement in an isolation unit of a prison is not unconstitutional per se, but depending on the circumstances it may be. Courtney v. Bishop; Graham v. Willingham, 10 Cir., 384 F.2d 367; Kostal v. Tinsley, 10 Cir., 337 F.2d 845; Jordan v. Fitzharris, N.D.Cal., 257 F.Supp. 674.

In *Jordan* the Court held that solitary confinement in "slit cells" in a California correctional institution was in the circumstances shown by the evidence unconstitutional. It was said, 257 F.Supp. at 680, that the prison authorities had "abandoned elemental concepts of decency by permitting conditions to prevail of a shocking and debased nature" to the extent that the Court was required promptly to intervene "to restore the primal rules of a civilized community in accord with the mandate of the Constitution of the United States."

It is plain, then, that the State must refrain from imposing cruel and unusual punishments on its convicts. And the Court is convinced that the State owes to those whom it has deprived of their liberty an even more fundamental constitutional duty to use ordinary care to protect their lives and safety while in prison. The Government owes that duty to federal prisoners, . . . and the Court thinks that a State prisoner is entitled to the same measure of care from the State, although the State, of course, is not an insurer of the safety of its convicts.

Where an unconstitutional situation is found to exist in a given prison, the prison authorities cannot escape responsibility for it by merely pointing to the existence of the same situation in other prisons, or by establishing that conditions in their prison are "better" or "no worse than" conditions prevailing elsewhere.

The record in this case is voluminous and covers a number of areas of prison life. The burden is upon the petitioners to show by a preponderance of the evidence that their constitutional rights and those of other inmates similarly situated have been violated, and that they are entitled to equitable relief with respect to the alleged violations.

The Court has considered the entire record in the light of the principles heretofore mentioned. The Court thinks it desirable to state at this point its ultimate findings and conclusions and to discuss some of them in detail at later points in the opinion.

Plaintiffs have failed to sustain their burden of proof with respect to the medical and dental facilities. While those facilities leave a good deal to be desired, the Court does not consider that the deficiencies are such as to raise a constitutional problem.

Plaintiffs have also failed to sustain their complaint about food served to prisoners while in isolation. As will be seen, the food is not appetizing; it is not intended to be, and the Constitution does not require that prisoners in isolation be served tasty or attractive dishes.

The Court heard some evidence as to alleged assaults on certain prisoners by prison employees and trusty guards. The Court does not think that evidence sufficient to justify relief in this case. Respondent and his subordinates are already forbidden by the injunction issued in the Jackson case from inflicting corporal punishment on convicts, and the Court is not persuaded that that injunction has been violated.

The Court does find from a preponderance of the evidence that the State has failed and is failing to discharge its constitutional duty with respect to the safety of certain convicts, and that the conditions existing in the isolation cells, including overcrowding, render confinement in those cells under those conditions unconstitutional.

With respect to the areas in which unconstitutionalities are found to exist, there is persuasive evidence that when a new maximum security unit is completed and put into operation in the next year or so the Farm's problems of inmate safety and confinement in isolation will be much ameliorated if not eliminated entirely. However, the Court is persuaded that present inmates are entitled to some injunctive relief in those areas at this time. . . .

. . . The Superintendent at Cummins is Ralph Roberts, and the Associate Superintendent is J.R. Price, both of whom appear to be competent men. The Chief Security Officer is Ed Walker, and he has 17 free world armed guards working under him. In addition, a member of the Arkansas State Police is regularly stationed at Cummins. The total number of paid employees at the Farm is 56.

Prisoners who are not confined in the isolation unit sleep in open barracks. There are two barracks for trusties and two for "do pops" * and rankers. Those barracks amount to enclosed dormitories in which the inmates sleep on cots arranged in rows. At night there are one or more free world guards on duty outside the barracks proper, but they are not actually inside the sleeping area. Those areas are supposedly patrolled by inmate "floorwalkers" whose duty it is to report disturbances to the guards.

Since the inmates sleep together in the barracks, an inmate has ready access to any other inmate sleeping in the same barracks. Many of the inmates have weapons of one sort or another, and the evidence indicates that in spite of efforts to do so it is impossible from a practical standpoint to prevent inmates from having small weapons such as knives or scissors in their possession.

At times deadly feuds arise between particular inmates, and if one of them can catch his enemy asleep it is easy to crawl over and stab him. Inmates who commit such assaults are known as "crawlers" and "creepers," and other inmates live in fear of them. The Court finds that the "floorwalkers" are ineffective in preventing such assaults; they are either afraid to call the guards or, in instances, may be in league with the assailants.

The undisputed evidence is to the effect that within the last 18 months there have been 17 stabbings at Cummins, all but one of them taking place in the barracks, and four of them producing fatal results. At least two of the petitioners now in isolation have been assailants in stabbing incidents and others have been the victims of such incidents.

Respondent and his subordinates deplore the situation just described but insist that until the maximum security unit can be put into use there is nothing that they can do about it. Respondent testified that when he was the head of a penitentiary in another State convicts there slept in individual cells and there were 170 paid guards; he also testified that the incidence of stabbings at Cummins was no higher than that at the other institution he had headed. He conceded, however, that more free world guards at Cummins might ameliorate the situation somewhat.

The Court recognizes, of course, that assaults, fights, stabbings, and killings may and do occur in penal institutions that are unquestionably well equipped, well staffed, and well managed. It occurs to the Court, however, that such incidents in such institutions take place in spite of all reasonable precautions taken by prison authorities. At Cummins there are no precau-

[* T.O. Murton, Prison Superintendent February 1967 To March 1968, explains that these prisoners were so named because they were required to "pop" open doors for trusties. T.O. Murton and J. Hyams, Accomplices to the Crime 23 (1969).]

tions worthy of the name, and the "creepers" and "crawlers" take deadly advantage of that fact.

The Court is of the view that if the State of Arkansas chooses to confine penitentiary inmates in barracks with other inmates, they ought at least to be able to fall asleep at night without fear of having their throats cut before morning, and that the State has failed to discharge a constitutional duty in failing to take steps to enable them to do so.

The isolation unit at Cummins consists of a one-story concrete block building surrounded by a tall metal fence. Inside that building are 12 cells arranged in a single row on one side of the building. Eleven of those cells are used to confine inmates; the other has been fitted up as a shower room. The building is heated by gas, and there are blowers to provide ventilation. In hot weather the exterior door or doors of the building are left open to provide circulation.

The building has no windows; however, electric lights are burned so that the inmates are not confined in darkness during daylight hours. The fronts of the individual cells are closed in part by concrete walls and for the rest by solid metal doors. At the bottom of each door is a small movable grating through which food trays are pushed and later recovered.

The individual cells are ten feet long by approximately eight feet wide; the record does not reflect how high they are, but photographs indicate that the distance from floor to ceiling substantially exceeds the height of a man. The cells are completely bare of furniture, probably due to the tendency of inmates to tear up pieces of furniture that might be put in the cells. Each cell contains a drinking fountain, and each is equipped with a concrete toilet. An examination of the photographs makes it rather clear that while the toilets will flush, they cannot be flushed by a person inside the cell. It is not clear whether the toilets can be covered firmly so as to hold down odors; the photographs suggest that some of them are covered with pieces of tarpaulin or other material.

There seem to be three classes of inmates in the isolation cells: (1) Prisoners confined in isolation for rule infractions; (2) Prisoners held in the cells as a measure of "protective custody," the purpose of which is to protect them from other inmates; (3) Prisoners who are general escape or security risks or who are awaiting trial on additional criminal charges.

Theoretically, a prisoner is not committed to isolation for a rule infraction until he has been found guilty by the administrative court described in the evidence. In practice, however, a prisoner may be put in the unit before hearing and may stay there for several days prior to hearing. An infraction of rules usually produces a sentence of a definite number of days, and some of the sentences are for rather long periods. Common rule infractions resulting in confinement in the unit are insubordination, fighting, and refusing to work, and it appears that some prisoners deliberately refuse to work or temporarily disable themselves to avoid work.

An inmate of the Farm may be put into the unit for protective custody if he requests that action provided that the Penitentiary authorities think that he needs protection. Protective custody confinements are usually of indefinite duration.

Inmates in protective custody usually are sent to their regular work each day and are served regular prison food. Inmates who are kept in the unit 24 hours a day are served a food mixture known as "grue." "Grue" consists of meat, potatoes, vegetables, eggs, oleo, syrup, and seasoning baked all together in a pan and served in four inch squares. The Court finds that while "grue" is not appetizing and is not served attractively, it is a wholesome and sufficient diet for men in close confinement day after day. The Court observed all of the petitioners, and none of them appeared to be suffering from malnutrition.

The "grue" is delivered at the isolation unit on plates or trays and is pushed to the inmates through the gratings at the bottoms of the doors. At times portions of the food are knocked off the plates as they are pushed through the gratings. There is some evidence that at times trays of food are left on the ground outside the unit, and that in instances the food has been tainted by dogs or birds. However, the Court is convinced that such instances have been rare if they have occurred at all.

The Court finds that the isolation cells are dirty and unsanitary, that they are pervaded by bad odors from the toilets, and that the plain cotton mattresses on which the inmates sleep are uncovered and dirty. Those conditions are due at least in part to the fact that the inmates take little or no interest in keeping their cells clean and in part to the overcrowded conditions of the cells presently to be described.

Confinement in the isolation cells is not "solitary confinement" in the conventional sense of that term. On the contrary, the cells are substantially overcrowded. As of the time of the hearing only two of the cells were occupied by one man only, and they were so occupied only because of the fact that the two individuals confined therein are too dangerous to be put with other prisoners. The average number of men confined in a single cell seems to be four, but at times the number has been much higher. In extreme circumstances as many as ten or eleven men have been in the same cell at the same time.

As stated, inmates of the isolation unit sleep on mattresses which are spread on the cell floors. During daylight hours the mattresses are removed from the cells of the men who are required to remain in the cells 24 hours a day. The mattresses of the "protective custody" inmates who work remain in the cells all day. The mattresses that are removed from the cells are piled indiscriminately in the corridor of the unit and are indiscriminately returned to the inmates at night. Thus an inmate has no assurance that the mattress allotted to him on any night is the same one that he had the night before or the same one that he will have the next night. That problem is aggravated by the fact that some of the inmates of the cells suffer from infectious diseases. In that connection the evidence discloses that one inmate died recently in the infirmary of infectious hepatitis after having been confined in isolation for a number of days. And one of the petitioners who is in the same cell as other men testified that he is suffering from venereal disease. It should be said, however, that there is no evidence that any inmate has as yet contracted a serious contagious disease from another inmate.

Theoretically, inmates are permitted to take showers twice a week. In practice, that schedule is not adhered to consistently, and it is possible that individual inmates may not avail themselves of an opportunity to shower.

Inmates of the cells who are there for purposes of discipline are not permitted to exercise outside their cells. Prior to May 28 the same rule applied to inmates in protective custody who did not work; the Court understands, however, that since that date such inmates have been allowed reasonable exercise. The inmates who work get exercise, of course, while they are at their daily tasks.

Without undertaking to state with specificity the exact point at which one of the isolation cells becomes "overcrowded" rather than simply "crowded," and two men are a crowd in an 8 × 10 cell when they have to stay there 24 hours a day for days or weeks on end, the Court finds that the cells have been chronically overcrowded, and that overcrowding to a greater or lesser extent will unavoidably continue until such time as more isolation cells are available.

In evaluating from a constitutional standpoint confinement in isolation as practiced at Cummins, the Court will observe that it does not find that any of the present inmates of the isolation were put there unnecessarily, unjustly, arbitrarily, or discriminatorily. The inmates of the unit who are there for discipline have deserved their punishment. Those who are there for the protection of themselves and other inmates should be kept away from the general prison population.

Confinement in isolation is now the only stringent disciplinary measure available at Cummins since the Court of Appeals has enjoined the use of the strap. If confinement of that type is to serve any useful purpose, it must be rigorous, uncomfortable, and unpleasant.

However, there are limits to the rigor and discomfort of close confinement which a State may not constitutionally exceed, and the Court finds that those limits have been exceeded here. The Court finds that the prolonged confinement of numbers of men in the same cell under the conditions that have been described is mentally and emotionally traumatic as well as physically uncomfortable. It is hazardous to health. It is degrading and debasing; it offends modern sensibilities, and, in the Court's estimation, amounts to cruel and unusual punishment.

The task of the Court in devising a remedy in this case is both difficult and delicate.

Subject to constitutional limitations, Arkansas is a sovereign State. It has a right to make and enforce criminal laws, to imprison persons convicted of serious crimes, and to maintain order and discipline in its prisons. This Court has no intention of entering a decree herein that will disrupt the Penitentiary or leave Respondent and his subordinates helpless to deal with dangerous and unruly convicts.

The Court has recognized heretofore the financial handicaps under which the Penitentiary system is laboring, and the Court knows that Respondent cannot make bricks without straw.

However, the Court is convinced that given the will, Respondent, with the means now available to him and that will become available to him at the commencement of the new fiscal year that begins on July 1 [this opinion is dated June 20], can make a substantial start toward alleviating the conditions that the Court has found to be unconstitutional. He will be ordered to do so.

The Court will not undertake at this time to prescribe any specific immediate steps to be taken by Respondent. The Court would like to know first what Respondent thinks that he can do, and what he is willing to undertake to do. There are some suggestions that the Court is prepared to make.

First, in allocating funds and assigning free world personnel to duties, Respondent should give the highest priority to the safety of inmates of the barracks and to alleviating existing conditions in the isolation unit. If that is done, Respondent may find that he can put free world guards into the barracks proper and dispense with the "floorwalkers." Although the Court recognizes that it might be unwise to spend a large amount of money on temporary facilities in view of the contemplated construction of the new maximum security unit, Respondent may also find that he will be able to build some additional isolation cells.

Second, there is evidence to the effect that some inmates are more of a problem at one farm than they are at the other. Consideration might be given to transferring certain individual inmates from Cummins to Tucker.

Third, every effort should be made to hold the number of persons confined in a single isolation cell at one time to a minimum. That may involve more selectivity in imposing isolation as a punishment, or shorter sentences, or more flexible sentences. In the field of criminology it has been observed that long terms of imprisonment imposed on persons convicted of crime are not necessarily more efficacious as crime deterrents than shorter sentences, and the same thing may hold good within the walls of penal institutions.

Fourth, in ordinary cases inmates should not be long confined in isolation in advance of hearing, and consideration might be given to an automatic review of the actions of all sentencing panels.

Finally, Respondent ought to be able at minimum expense to do something about the sanitary conditions of the cells and he might give consideration to doing so without much regard to the attitudes of the inmates. Certainly, something can be done about the condition of the mattresses and it can be assured at least that an inmate will sleep on the same mattress every night. Most important, seriously ill men should not be confined in close contact with other prisoners.

The foregoing suggestions happen to be those that occur to the Court at the moment; the Court does not suggest that they are necessarily all of the steps that can and should be taken.

In the decree to be entered Respondent will be directed to report to the Court within 30 days as to what steps he in fact plans to take, and jurisdiction of the case will be retained for all appropriate purposes.

---

1) Do Courtney v. Bishop and *Holt I* conflict on the issue of the isolation cell? What might have produced the divergent responses of Judges Harris and Henley? Could it have been simply a difference in the factual presentation? Which decision must the prison authorities follow?

2) Why didn't Courtney v. Bishop settle the matter? What prompted the *Holt* litigation in the first place? In an interview in August 1982, Sarver, the new Commissioner of Corrections, said that he drew up some of the papers against himself: "I wrote out the writs on a yellow pad and gave them to the inmates, who typed them up and signed them." Wells, Dark and Evil World is Banished, Changed By Inmate Complaints, Arkansas Gazette, Aug. 15, 1982 at Al, col. 8. Do you think Judge Henley knew about this? Should he have dismissed the suit under Article III for lack of sufficient adversity?

3) The Constitution prohibits the state from inflicting cruel and unusual punishment. Is Arkansas responsible for the "creepers" and "crawlers"? What legal theory makes threats posed by other prisoners violate the ban on cruel and unusual punishments?

4) Should the relief in *Holt* be confined to the named plaintiffs? Can it be? Does it make any difference whether *Holt* was a class action? Does the scope of relief depend on the nature of the wrong or on the identity of the plaintiff?

5) The reform of the barracks contemplated by Judge Henley will command public revenues. The taxpayers, legislators, and the governor are responsible for generating and allocating those funds. Do they have a right to participate in the litigation? How can that right be exercised? Is their right merely one to be represented? Who represents them?

6) Judge Henley concluded that the prison system was operated unconstitutionally. He ordered the Commissioner to "make a substantial start toward alleviating the conditions that the Court has found to be unconstitutional." Why only a "substantial start"? Why allow any illegal conditions to persist?

7) Judge Henley declines "to prescribe any specific immediate steps to be taken by" the Commissioner. Does he have the authority to prescribe steps? If so, why decline to use it? He does, however, make "some suggestions" about what might be done. Does he have authority to make "suggestions"? Is this conception of the judicial power consistent with Article III? If you were representing the Commissioner, how would you state the binding force of such "suggestions"?

Winthrop Rockefeller was governor of Arkansas from 1966 to 1970. Dale Bumpers was governor from 1971 until 1974.

HOLT v. SARVER [HOLT II]

309 F.Supp. 362 (E.D.Ark.1970).

HENLEY, Chief Judge. . . .

Petitioners' complaints are well summarized in Paragraph 20 of the Consolidated Amended and Substituted Complaint which is as follows:

"20. The action of defendants have deprived members of the plaintiff class of rights, privileges and immunities secured to them by the due process and equal protection clauses of the Fourteenth Amendment to the Constitution of the United States, including (a) the right not to be imprisoned without meaningful rehabilitative opportunities, (b) the right to be free from cruel and unusual punishment, (c) the right to be free from arbitrary and capricious denial of rehabilitation opportunities, (d) the right to minimal due process safeguards in decisions determining fundamental liberties, (e) the right to be fed, housed, and clothed so as not to be subjected to loss of health or life, (f) the right to unhampered access to counsel and the courts, (g) the right to be free from the abuses of fellow prisoners in all aspects of daily life, (h) the right to be free from racial segregation, (i) the right to be free from forced labor, and (j) the right to be free from the brutality of being guarded by fellow inmates."

The prayer is for a declaratory judgment to the effect that Respondents' acts, policies, and practices violate Thirteenth and Fourteenth Amendment rights and for appropriate permanent injunctive relief.

Shortly before the cases, hereinafter called collectively at times simply "the case" or "this case," were tried, Respondents, represented by Messrs. Don Langston and Mike Wilson of the Office of the Arkansas Attorney General, moved to dismiss the petitions on the ground that the case was nothing more than an effort to coerce the Arkansas Legislature into appropriating more money for the System, and that the Court was without jurisdiction to entertain such an action. The Court did not and does not so characterize the case, and the motion was denied. The Court is satisfied that it has jurisdiction under the federal statutes heretofore cited, and so finds.

On the merits, Respondents do not contend that they are operating a "good" prison or a "modern" prison. With commendable candor they concede that many of the conditions existing at the Penitentiary are bad. However, they deny that they are operating an unconstitutional prison or are engaging in unconstitutional practices. They say that they are doing the best they can with extremely limited funds and personnel. They point, justly, to the fact that over the past several years a number of significant improvements have been made within the System and they say that more are in the offing.

This case, unlike earlier cases to be mentioned which have involved specific practices and abuses alleged to have been practiced upon Arkansas convicts, amounts to an attack on the System itself. As far as the Court is aware, this is the first time that convicts have attacked an entire penitentiary system in any court, either State or federal.

The cases were consolidated for purposes of trial and were tried to the Court without a jury for almost an entire week. Much testimony was taken and a substantial body of documentary evidence was introduced. The Court had the benefit of the expert testimony of a recognized authority on prisons and their administration, Mr. James V. Bennett who for many years was Director of the Federal Bureau of Prisons. The Court had indirectly the benefit of the views of Mr. Austin McCormick of New York City, another recognized penologist, who is Executive Director of the Osborne Association, Inc., and who served as Chief Consultant to the Penitentiary Study Commission created by the Arkansas Legislature in 1967. (Act 22 of 1967, approved January 31, 1967.) The views of Mr. McCormick are set forth in the formal report of the Commission submitted on January 1, 1968, a copy of which report was introduced in evidence. There has also been made available to the Court a copy of a report in letter form from Dr. Charles M. Friel, Director of Research, Institute of Contemporary Corrections and the Behavioral Sciences, Sam Houston State University, Huntsville, Texas, to the Arkansas Commission on Crime and Law Enforcement. That report is dated January 29, 1970, which date was the third day of the trial of this case. While the report was not formally introduced in evidence, it will be made part of the record, and the Court feels at liberty to consider it.

Apart from the foregoing, the Court heard the testimony of inmates and free world employees of the Penitentiary System; the Court also saw a motion picture film depicting certain prison conditions and has examined a number of photographs and other documentary material.

This Memorandum incorporates the Court's findings of fact and conclusions of law. In view of the serious nature of the case, in view of the fact that in a sense the real Respondents are not limited to those formally before the Court but include the Governor of Arkansas, the Arkansas Legislature, and ultimately the people of the State as a whole, the issues presented have been given the most careful consideration of which the Court has felt itself capable. The questions presented are grave and will be discussed fully. The Court deems it well, however, to state in advance of discussion its ultimate findings and conclusions on the constitutional issues presented.

1. The Court rejects the contention of the Petitioners that the forced, uncompensated labor of Arkansas convicts violates the Thirteenth Amendment.

2. The Court sustains the claim that conditions and practices in the Penitentiary System are such that confinement of persons therein amounts to a cruel and unusual punishment prohibited by the Eighth and Fourteenth Amendments.

3. The Court sustains the claim that to the extent that unconstitutional racial discrimination is being practiced in the System it must be eliminated.

Having so stated its findings and conclusions, the Court will proceed to discuss them and thereafter will pass to a consideration of the relief to be awarded. . . .

The inmate population at Cummins now consists of somewhat less than 1,000 persons; about 325 persons most of whom are under 21 years of age are confined at Tucker. Prior to the passage of Act 377 of 1969 the Tucker Intermediate Reformatory was known simply as the Tucker Farm Unit of the Arkansas State Penitentiary. It is a much smaller institution than Cummins and its problems and those of its inmates are not nearly as severe as those existing at Cummins. For that reason discussion will be directed chiefly at Cummins, and references to the "Penitentiary" will in general be references to Cummins. Specific mention of Tucker will be made where such mention appears necessary or desirable. . . .

Tucker was designed primarily for the confinement of young white convicts and for the confinement of both whites and Negroes awaiting execution. Negro convicts, other than those condemned to die, were confined at Cummins, and Cummins was also used as a place of confinement for more hardened white convicts.

Prior to the Civil War Arkansas convicts were leased to private employers and were frequently mistreated seriously by the lessees. There was strong public opposition to the system for both humanitarian and economic reasons and it was abolished in 1913. Since that time Arkansas convicts have been required to work for the State, and their work has consisted largely of agricultural and other manual labor for which they are paid nothing either actually or constructively.

At both Cummins and Tucker the inmate population is divided into three categories. At the bottom of the list are ordinary laboring convicts known as "rankers." At the top of the list are privileged inmates known as "trusties." Between those two categories is a third class of convicts known as "do pops." . . .

As indicated, most of the inmates at Tucker are young men who are not, in general, a particularly vicious lot, although there are exceptions. The Cummins population is extremely varied. Some are run-of-the-mill non-violent criminals; others are extremely violent and dangerous; many are incorrigibles; some are properly classified as either sociopathic or psychopathic, if not psychotic. A few of them have to be kept in isolation cells for 24 hours a day to protect them from other inmates or to protect other inmates from them.

Certain characteristics of the Arkansas prison system serve to distinguish it from most other penal institutions in this country. First, it has very few paid employees; armed trusties guard rank and file inmates and trusties perform other tasks usually and more properly performed by civilian or "free world" personnel. Second, convicts not in isolation are confined when not working, and are required to sleep at night in open dormitory type barracks in which rows of beds are arranged side by side; there are large numbers of men in each barracks. Third, there is no meaningful program of rehabilitation whatever at Cummins; while there is a promising and helpful program at Tucker, it is still minimal.

Prior to about 1965 the people of Arkansas as a whole knew little or nothing about their penal system although there were sporadic and sensational "exposes" from time to time about alleged conditions at the farms.

Those "exposes" created little, if any, lasting impressions on the Arkansas public. As of that time it is probably fair to say that many otherwise well informed Arkansas people viewed the Penitentiary as a self-sustaining even profit-making institution, operated by a few strong willed men who were able to make the convicts behave themselves and work; while it was recognized that the life of the convicts was probably hard, that was as it should be; they had been sent to the Penitentiary to be punished and were not entitled to lead a "country club" existence. Reports of whippings might cause passing concern which was easily allayed by the thought that the convicts who were whipped deserved to be whipped, and that a man who went down to the Penitentiary and behaved himself and did his work would be treated fairly and would get along fairly well.

That popular impression of the Penitentiary was not accurate in former years, and to the extent that it is still present it is not accurate today, as will be seen presently. However, the myth tends to be preserved by glowing reports of members of conducted tours of the farms who are shown in daylight hours what their conductors want them to see, who talk to selected convicts, and who are fed a good meal accompanied by the assurance that they are eating "just what the inmates eat." . . .

By 1965 Arkansas convicts were becoming more articulate about the conditions under which they lived than in years past and were having more success in bringing their complaints to the attention of free world authorities, including the federal courts sitting in this State. . . .

In all of those cases, except *Courtney,* it was found that unconstitutional practices were being carried on at the Penitentiary, and injunctive relief was granted. The final result of the Talley and Jackson cases was that corporal punishment of inmates, practiced for years at the farms, was outlawed along with the use of such devices of torture as the "Tucker Telephone" and the "teeter board." In *Holt I* this Court held that the State owed a constitutional duty to inmates at Cummins to use ordinary care for their safety, and that the State had failed and was failing to discharge that duty; the Court also found that due to overcrowding confinement in the Cummins isolation cells was unconstitutional.

The decree entered in *Holt I* in the summer of 1969 brought about some improvements in conditions at Cummins, notably what appears to be an elimination of gross overcrowding in the isolation cells. However, continuing complaints from inmates of both Cummins and Tucker and disturbing information that financial difficulties might have caused a retrogression to former conditions to set in prompted the Court not to approve the report of the Commissioner filed in *Holt I* and to give further consideration to overall conditions at both institutions.

Aside from the litigation just outlined, there have been significant recent developments at the farms. In the late summer of 1966 serious trouble with inmates broke out that led to a full investigation of conditions at both farms by the Arkansas State Police and by the Federal Bureau of Investigation. That investigation plus an additional investigation brought about by another violent episode at Cummins in October 1968 produced certain prosecutions in the Circuit Court of Jefferson County, Arkansas, and in this Court.[4]

4. Following the 1966 investigation certain former employees at the Tucker Farm were charged in the Circuit Court of Jefferson County, Arkansas, with having violated Ark.Stats. § 46–158 which made it a felony for any Penitentiary employee to inflict a punishment on a convict in excess of the punishment prescribed by the then Penitentiary Board. The Circuit Court held that the Arkansas statute was violative of the Arkansas Constitution in that it involved an invalid delegation of legislative power to the Board. The informations were dismissed by the Circuit Court, and the Supreme Court of Arkansas affirmed. State v. Bruton, 246 Ark. 288, 437 S.W.2d 795.

In 1968 a number of prisoners at Cummins went on a sit down strike and refused to disperse. They were fired upon with shotguns loaded with birdshot by a number of free world people and trusty guards. Some inmates were wounded, one seriously. Fortunately, no one was killed.

The abortion of the State court prosecutions and the 1968 episode just described caused the United States Department of Justice to ask the Court to call the federal Grand Jury for the Eastern District of Arkansas into special session in the summer of 1969. That was done, and a number of indictments were returned against Penitentiary employees and former employees and against a number of former inmates charging violations of 18 U.S.C.A. § 242. The Court conducted a number of jury trials which with one exception resulted in verdicts of not guilty, although the evidence in all of the cases was ample to convict. In one case the jury was not able to agree. As to that case the defendant ultimately pleaded nolo contendere, and another plea of nolo contendere was entered by another defendant.

When the Legislature convened in January 1967 it promptly created the Penitentiary Study Commission. The Emergency Clause included in Act 22 of 1967 creating the Commission and directing it to make a detailed study of the farms recited that widespread publicity about the Penitentiary had "raised serious questions in the minds of public officials and the general public regarding the facilities, practices, and disciplinary procedures at the State Penitentiary and that it is necessary that a thorough study and evaluation of the penal system in Arkansas be made as soon as possible."

The Commission's study was detailed, and its report was sharply critical of many aspects of the prison system; numerous reforms were recommended. Responding to the report, the Legislature in special session in early 1968 adopted Act 50 of that year, a sweeping statute dealing with the prison system and which recognized that training and rehabilitation should be essential objectives of the farms. That Act, among other things, created the Department of Corrections which took the place of the old Penitentiary Board.

The legislation adopted in 1967 and 1968 and Act 377 of 1969 establishing the Tucker Intermediate Reformatory are forward looking; but at least as yet they have not had any significant impact on the distinctive characteristics of the Arkansas penal system mentioned heretofore.

Returning now to this case, the testimony of Director Bennett, the report of the Study Commission, and the 1969 report of Dr. Friel to the Commission on Crime and Law Enforcement, are all to the effect that the Arkansas Penitentiary System is substandard and outmoded when measured by accepted penological standards, and that improvements are needed in many areas. Commissioner Sarver himself has come forward with sweeping recommendations for radical improvements to be made over a period of about ten years.

The Court, however, is limited in its inquiry to the question of whether or not the constitutional rights of inmates are being invaded and with whether the Penitentiary itself is unconstitutional. The Court is not judicially concerned with questions which in the last analysis are addressed to legislative and administrative judgment. A practice that may be bad from the standpoint of penology may not necessarily be forbidden by the Constitution. And a prison system that would be excellent from the point of view of a modern prison administrator may not be required by the provisions of the Constitution with which the Court is concerned. . . .

The Thirteenth Amendment, adopted immediately after the Civil War, provides explicitly that:

"Neither slavery nor involuntary servitude, except as a punishment for crime whereof the party shall have been duly convicted, shall exist within the United States, or any place subject to their jurisdiction."

The purpose of the Amendment was, of course, to abolish African slavery and practices related or analogous thereto. It will be observed that the Thirteenth Amendment, unlike the Fourteenth and certain other Amendments, is more than a prohibition upon the States. The Thirteenth Amendment abolishes slavery and involuntary servitude, except as punishment for crime, everywhere in the United States, its Territories, and possessions.

The Thirteenth Amendment claim with which the Court is concerned relates primarily to the requirement that Arkansas convicts work for long hours without pay in the fields on the farms for the financial benefit of the State. Not all rank and file Arkansas convicts are required to perform labor of that type, but substantial numbers of them are. As in other contexts, the principal problem is at Cummins. That is true because the farming operation now being conducted at Tucker is limited to the production of food for inmate consumption. Tucker farmlands not used for that purpose have been leased to private operators.

Cummins Farm is located on fertile land well adapted to producing just about any kind of crop that can be grown in Arkansas. The principal crops produced on the farm are cotton, soybeans, rice, vegetables, fruits, and berries. Other substantial farm operations include livestock, dairying, and poultry production.

According to the report of the Study Commission, there were 9,070 acres of land in cultivation at Cummins as of December 15, 1967. As of the same date the Farm had 2,070 cattle, 800 hogs, 40 horses, 160 mules, and 1,600 poultry.

Again according to the Commission, during 1967 60 percent of the cultivated acreage at Cummins was devoted to crops raised for sale on the market; 30 percent to crops that supported the livestock and poultry; and 10 percent to garden vegetables and other crops for the feeding of civilian personnel and inmates.

The Commission's report reflects that with respect to the fiscal year ending June 30, 1966, the Penitentiary, both farms apparently, derived an income of $1,415,419.43 from the sale of crops, including field crops, vegetables, fruit, and pecans; the corresponding figure for the year ending June 30, 1967, was $1,242,191.38. Sales of farm products other than crops amounted to $213,561.22 for fiscal '66 and to $131,806.13 for fiscal '67.

Total receipts of the Penitentiary from all sources for fiscal '66 was $1,763,487.09 and total expenditures came to $1,473,497.70. Corresponding figures for fiscal '67 were $1,566,712.76 and $1,785,570.33.

The December 15, 1967, inventory of equipment at Cummins indicates that there has been substantial mechanization of the Farm's operation. However, the evidence reflects that much of the work is still done by hand, and the fact that in 1967 the Farm owned 160 mules indicates that a good deal of power utilized at the Farm is "mule power."

In 1967 the Farm had a cotton allotment of 962 acres worked largely by hand, and the production of fruits and vegetables involves a great deal of what is commonly called "stooped labor."

Men assigned to the fields are required to work long hours six days a week, except for a few holidays, if weather permits. They are worked regardless of heat, and summers can be very hot at Cummins; in the winter they are not required to work when the temperature is below freezing, but they are required to work in merely bad or wet weather regardless of the season of the year. The men are not supplied by the State with particularly warm clothing for winter work, nor are they furnished any bad weather gear. There is evidence that at times men have been sent to the fields without shoes or with inadequate shoes. The field work is arduous and is particularly onerous in the case of men who have had no previous experience in chopping and picking cotton or in harvesting vegetables, fruits, and berries. What skills they may require in connection with their field work are of very little, if any, value to them when they return to the free world.

Naturally, the inmates do not like to work in the fields. Prior to the decision of the Court of Appeals in *Jackson,* most of them could be forced to do so by applications of the strap. Now there is no sanction, except confinement in isolation, to compel the men to work, and many of them are willing to undergo solitary confinement in order to avoid field work.

Rankers assigned to work in the fields do so in groups known as "long lines." The numbers of men in long lines may vary considerably. Theoretically, each long line is under the supervision of a free world employee known as a field warden. Actually, the rankers are under the immediate and direct supervision of trusties known as "long line riders" and inmate "pushers." As his name implies, the long line rider is a mounted man who rides back and forth among the working men. Since he is in very close proximity to the rankers and is somewhat vulnerable to attack from them, he ordinarily does not carry a firearm, although he may do so on occasions. The real guarding of the rankers in the field is done by other trusties armed either with high powered rifles and known as "high powers," or with shotguns and known, logically, as "shotguns."

According to the Study Commission's report, a long line at Cummins on a typical date might be made up of, say, 56 rankers, nine trusty guards, and a long line rider. The perimeter of the plot in which the rankers are working is occupied by guards armed with rifles; guards armed with shotguns work in closer proximity to the rankers.

If a ranker tries to escape, the trusties are instructed to fire one warning shot into the air; if the ranker persists in his effort to get away, the trusties fire at him to "stop" him; it makes no difference whether he is killed or not. Whether a ranker is trying to escape is at times subject to question, and the question is answered summarily by the guards. Thus, a ranker who unwittingly strays across an imaginary deadline may be fired upon. In addition to running the risk of being shot by an overzealous guard or by one with merely poor judgment there is always the possibility that a guard will deliberately murder an inmate on the pretense that he was trying to escape.

As stated, the men are paid nothing for their work. If an inmate wants to earn money legitimately in his spare time while in the Penitentiary, there are only two ways in which he can do it. The inmates as a class are permitted to have an Inmate Welfare Fund which operates a commissary type store and which also operates a blood bank. Profits from the store and the blood bank inure to the Fund which, parenthetically, appears as of this moment to have more money available to it than Respondents have available to them to run the Penitentiary. A very limited number of inmates are employed in the store and are paid small monthly salaries. Other inmates can sell their blood once a week at the blood bank and receive $5 per visit. The inmates refer to selling their blood as "bleeding at the blood bank." However, not all inmates are permitted to "bleed" and, hence, cannot earn the $5; for example, the bank will not accept blood from an inmate with a morbid condition of the liver.

What small comforts and luxuries the inmates have legitimately are not furnished by the State but by the Welfare Fund, and it is the Fund, not the State, that gives a departing inmate the nominal sum of $25 to see him on his way.

Director Bennett testified that inmates of federal prisons and of many State prisons can earn legitimate although usually very low wages while confined. He thinks that such wage payments are desirable for several reasons: they give a man an incentive to work; they improve his morale; they enable him to be of some assistance to his dependents; and they perhaps enable him to build up a small stake for himself against the day on which he is to be released from prison. Mr. Bennett conceded, however, that there are still some States, like Arkansas, that pay their convicts nothing.

The picture of working conditions at Cummins that has been painted is not attractive, and the system would not be called humane by modern standards. But, the question for decision at this moment is whether the system is prohibited by the Thirteenth Amendment.

The Arkansas system of working convicts is not "slavery" in the constitutional sense of the term. The State does not claim to own the bodies of its prisoners. The situation does involve "servitude," and there is no doubt whatever that the "servitude" is "involuntary."

But, it is equally clear that this servitude has been imposed as punishment for crimes whereof the inmates have been duly convicted. Conceding that the work required is hard and tedious, that it is performed under harsh conditions, that the State requires it to produce income for the State, and that the system serves little other purpose, if any, the Court is not persuaded that the system violates the Thirteenth Amendment.

According to Director Bennett, the idea that prisons and prisoners ought to support themselves is as old as American penology. He referred to the fact that the convict-leasing system came into existence at a very early stage as the States found that it was more profitable to lease their convicts than to work them themselves. And he pointed out that one of the best descriptions of the leasing system is to be found in Margaret Mitchell's Civil War novel, "Gone With The Wind."

When Congress submitted the Thirteenth Amendment to the States, it must have been aware of generally accepted convict labor policies and practices, and the Court is persuaded that the Amendment's exception manifested a Congressional intent not to reach such policies and practices.

Heflin v. Sanford, 5 Cir., 142 F.2d 798, is instructive on this phase of the case although it did not involve convict labor. Heflin, a conscientious objector, was ordered to report for work of national importance during World War II; his compensation would have been but nominal. He refused to report and was sent to the penitentiary for violating the Selective Service Act. On habeas corpus he contended that to require him to do work of national importance with little or no pay amounted to prohibited slavery and involuntary servitude. His contention was rejected. The Court pointed out that there is a difference between "involuntary servitude" and "uncompensated service," and that the Thirteenth Amendment prohibits the one, except as punishment for crime, but does not prohibit the other.

The Eighth Amendment to the Constitution of the United States prohibits the infliction of "cruel and unusual punishments." Originally a restriction on the federal government, it has been held that the Eighth Amendment has been carried forward into the Fourteenth Amendment . . . and it was on the basis of the Eighth Amendment that relief was granted in *Talley, Jackson,* and *Holt I.*

An individual convict may, of course, be subjected to a cruel and unusual punishment actually inflicted on him personally, as by his being beaten with the Penitentiary strap, or by being shocked electrically by the Tucker Telephone, or by being compelled to stand upon the "teeter board" for long periods of time, or by other means of punishment or torture.

It appears to the Court, however, that the concept of "cruel and unusual punishment" is not limited to instances in which a particular inmate is subjected to a punishment directed at him as an individual. In the Court's estimation confinement itself within a given institution may amount to a cruel and unusual punishment prohibited by the Constitution where the confinement is characterized by conditions and practices so bad as to be shocking to the conscience of reasonably civilized people even though a particular inmate may never personally be subject to any disciplinary action. To put it another way, while confinement, even at hard labor and without compensation, is not considered to be necessarily a cruel and unusual punishment it may be so in certain circumstances and by reason of the conditions of the confinement. That is certainly the law in the case of prisoners confined in isolation, Courtney v. Bishop, *Holt I,* and cases there cited; and the Court sees no reason why it is not the law in cases of prisoners confined "in population," as it is called.

In the instant case Petitioners contend that overall conditions in the Arkansas penal system, including but not limited to those relating to inmate safety, may be so bad that it amounts to an unconstitutional cruel and unusual punishment to expose men to those conditions, regardless of how those conditions may operate fortuitously on particular individuals. Is that contention sustained by the evidence?

The distinguishing aspects of Arkansas penitentiary life must be considered together. One cannot consider separately a trusty system, a system in which men are confined together in large numbers in open barracks, bad conditions in the isolation cells, or an absence of a meaningful program of rehabilitation. All of those things exist in combination; each affects the other; and taken together they have a cumulative impact on the inmates regardless of their status. That should be borne in mind as one reads the following descriptions of the trusty system, the barracks system, the isolation cells, and other aspects of prison life.

Again, these descriptions are based primarily on conditions at Cummins. They are based on a large volume of testimony much of which was really a repetition of what the Court heard when it tried *Holt I.*

No one questions the propriety or desirability of according trusty status to deserving convicts, and perhaps all prisons do. But the trusty system as it exists in Arkansas is *sui generis.* The trusties run the prison. They not only guard other inmates; they also perform many administrative tasks normally performed by free world people, and their authority over other convicts of lesser rank is great. Commissioner Sarver testified without contradiction that more than 90 percent of prison functions relating to inmates are performed by trusties. The few free world people are only nominally in command of the situation at Cummins, and the trusties could take it over in a moment. Perhaps the reason they do not do so is that they do not want to spoil a good thing.

The extent of Arkansas' reliance on trusties is apparent when it is realized that there are only 35 free world employees at Cummins in ostensible charge of slightly less than 1,000 men. Of those 35 only eight are available for guard duty, and only two of them are on duty at night.

The use of trusty guards is universally condemned by penologists, and the system is now in use only in Arkansas, Louisiana, and Mississippi. According to Director Bennett, the reliance that Louisiana places upon trusty guards is much less than that which exists in Arkansas. He did not testify with respect to Mississippi. The reasons for penological disapproval of the use of trusty guards are that it creates an unhealthy prison climate and atmosphere; it breeds fear and hatred between the guards, on the one hand, and those guarded, on the other hand; it tends to be brutal and to endanger the lives of inmates who live and work "under the guns" of other convicts; and it leads to other abuses.

In this connection it may be observed that some inmates of the Penitentiary have refused to accept trusty guard status due to their feeling that it is "wrong" for one convict to guard another and to their fear of what might happen to them should they ever be demoted to the ranks. And Mr. Bennett testified that when he was head of the Bureau of Prisons, it was frequently necessary to take strong protective measures with respect to inmates of federal prisons who had formerly been trusty guards in Arkansas.

Apart from the use of trusties as guards, they can be given too much authority in other areas of prison life. When that is done, various abuses come into existence. When all is said and done, the fact remains that a trusty is a convict, and many trusties will on occasions act like felons and thieves. They will take bribes, they will engage in extortion, they will smuggle contraband, and they will connive at violations of prison rules. Opportunity for abuse is particularly present where, as in Arkansas, trusties have access to prison records pertaining to themselves and to other inmates. A trusty with such access can remove damaging material, such as a detainer, from an inmate's file; he can insert improper material; or he can impart to other inmates confidential information that ought not to be imparted. The undesirability of having prison telephone communications with the outside world in the control of trusties, as it is in Arkansas, is too obvious to require description.

This does not mean that trusties should never be given responsible jobs. One of the chief functions of rehabilitation is to teach convicts to assume and discharge responsibilities. But, it does mean that the areas of trusty responsibility should be limited, and that the trusties, both individually and as a body, should be under the full control and adequate supervision of free world people.

The danger of excessive reliance on trusties was discussed fully in the report of the Study Commission, and one of the recommendations of the Commission was that the system be retained "insofar as it conforms to the type found in the better American state and federal prisons," but that "trusties no longer be given duties, responsibilities or authority that should be given only to civilian employees who can be held legally responsible."

As the Court's description of the trusty system in Arkansas proceeds, it will be seen, to the extent that it has not become apparent already, that just about every abuse which the system is capable of producing has been produced and is being practiced in this State.

An inmate gets to be a trusty in Arkansas by promotion from the ranks or from "do pop" status. While promotions and demotions are formally made by committees of free world personnel, as a practical matter such actions are usually based uncritically on initial recommendations of trusties. In the case of a field worker, the recommendation is usually made by a long line rider.

Actually, few, if any, objective criteria are used in selecting trusties; that a man is a bad man, or a dangerous man, or that he has a bad criminal record is by no means a disqualification; on the contrary, it may be a recommendation. In the case of a trusty guard probably the principal criterion of promotion is his willingness to prevent escapes and support the free world people vis a vis the general inmate population, shooting to kill if necessary to achieve those objectives. A trusty is not expected to take any steps to protect an inmate from violence at the hands of another inmate, and the trusties do not do so.

In a very real sense trusty guards have the power of life and death over other inmates. Some guards are doubtless men of some judgment and humanity; others are not. It is within the power of a trusty guard to murder another inmate with practical impunity, and the danger that such will be done is always clear and present. Very recently a gate guard killed another inmate "carelessly." One wonders. And there is evidence that recently a guard on night duty fired a shotgun into a crowded barracks because the inmates would not turn off their television set. In any event, the rankers live in deadly fear of the guards and entertain deadly hatred for them, and their feelings are reciprocated fully.

The Study Commission recommended that the guard system be phased out as soon as possible, starting with the trusties guarding field workers. The Court thinks that that is a good recommendation, but the trusty guard system itself, bad as it is, does not give the Court as much trouble as do other facets of the overall trusty system.

By virtue of their positions of authority and the functions they perform trusties can make or break rankers and "do pops." They can make prison life tolerable or they can make it unbearably hard. They can and do sell favors, easy jobs, and coveted positions; they can and do extort money from inmates on any and all pretexts. They operate rackets within the prison, involving among other things the forcing of inmates to buy from them things like coffee at exorbitant prices. They lend money to rankers and then use force or threats of force to collect the debts.

Controlling the slaughter house, the kitchen, and the prison stores, trusties steal food and other commodities from the institution and then sell them to other inmates. An inmate can eat well at the Penitentiary if he can pay for what he gets; if he cannot pay, he eats as regular issue what the trusties have seen fit to leave.

Trusties have rather broad privileges about leaving the farms. Coming back they bring with them weapons, liquor, and drugs which they sell to less privileged inmates. As might be expected liquor is much in demand, and its price is high. A pint of taxpaid whiskey sells for $10, much more than twice its free world price.

When a new inmate arrives at the Penitentiary, about the first person to interview him is a trusty who frequently starts out to relieve him by threats or promises of what money and property he may possess.

An enterprising trusty who makes the most of his opportunities can do quite well for himself. Some do so well that they do not want to leave the institution. While it can hardly be said that the trusty system in Arkansas is a "free" enterprise system, it is certainly a capitalistic system with some of the worst features commonly attributed to "Mafia" techniques in organized crime.

One of the worst features of the system is that the trusties form a living barrier between ordinary inmates and institutional facilities and services that are available and to which an inmate ought to be able to have access as a matter of course. If a ranker can pay or is on good terms with the trusties, he can get what he needs when he needs it; he can get to the infirmary when the doctor is there; he can get prescribed medications. If he cannot pay or does not get along with the trusties, the case is far otherwise.

Additionally, inmate access to free world personnel too often depends on trusty good will, whim, or caprice. This Court has long been convinced that many of the complaints that it receives from inmates stem from a simple lack of communication between the complainants and civilian personnel, the lack being due to trusty interference or indifference.

Not only can the trusties prevent a ranker from getting into contact with a civilian employee; they can and frequently do bring unmerited discipline down on the head of a ranker by "writing him up" for unsatisfactory work or for refusal to work; their reports are frequently, if not usually, taken at face value by the employees to whom they are made.

In fairness to the trusties it should perhaps be said that their roses are not without thorns. Just as a trusty can make or break a ranker, so can he be broken or demoted by a superior trusty or by free world personnel. And if he is demoted to the ranks, he is at the tender mercy of those whom he may have persecuted or exploited, and it may become necessary to put him in isolation for his own protection.

Before leaving its description of the trusty system, the Court will say that it has not overlooked the fact that many of the abuses practiced by trusties could also be practiced by free world personnel, but the Court thinks that free world people, carefully selected and properly paid, would be far less likely to commit such abuses than are the felons now holding positions of authority.

The report of the Study Commission reflects that there are eight barracks at Cummins and three at Tucker. Only five of the barracks at Cummins appear to be in use at the present time perhaps due to the fact that the population of Cummins is lower now than it has been in years past. White trusties occupy one barracks; Negro trusties occupy another barracks; white rankers have a barracks of their own; and Negro rankers have a barracks of their own. At the present time "do pops" at Cummins have their own barracks; the record does not disclose whether there are any Negro "do pops." The Commission's report indicates that when "do pops" are not sleeping in their own barracks, they are housed with rankers.

A barracks is nothing more than a large dormitory surrounded by bars; the barracks are separated from each other by wide hallways, and the complex of hallways is referred to as the "yard." At the present time the barracks house more than 100 men each assigned without regard to anything but rank and race. The inhabitants of a given barracks have free access to each other at all times. Only two free world people are on duty in the yard at night. Inmate "floor walkers" are stationed inside the barracks proper for the purpose of keeping order and reporting disturbances. In their barracks the trusties are not armed except with their own knives which they continually keep at hand; however, there are probably one or more armed trusties in picket posts within the barracks building.

In *Holt I* the Court discussed life in the Cummins barracks in some detail.

. . .

Conditions in [the Cummings] barracks have not changed significantly since *Holt I* was decided, except that there has been a decline in the rate of stabbings. There is, however, something more to be said about the barracks in the light of the evidence produced in this case.

The Court heard much testimony about homosexuality in the barracks and elsewhere at Cummins. Homosexuality probably is practiced in all prisons in the United States, and there is a great deal of it practiced at Cummins, some consensual, a great deal nonconsensual. An inmate who is physically attractive to other men may be, and frequently is, raped in the barracks by other inmates. No one comes to his assistance; the floor walkers do not interfere; the trusties look on with indifference or satisfaction; the two free world people on duty appear to be helpless.

Inmates who are passively homosexual are called "punks." There are varieties of "punks," including the "pressure punks" who will engage in homosexual acts if more or less pressure is put upon them to induce or compel them to do so.

In an effort to protect young men from sexual assaults, they are generally assigned to the two rows of cots nearest the front bars of the barracks, which portion of the barracks is called "punk row." It appears, however, that if would-be assailants really want a young man, his being assigned to the "row" is no real protection to him.

To the extent that consensual homosexual acts take place in the barracks, they are not carried out in any kind of privacy but in the full sight and hearing of all of the other inmates.

Sexual assaults, fights, and stabbings in the barracks put some inmates in such fear that it is not unusual for them to come to the front of the barracks and cling to the bars all night. That practice, which is of doubtful value is called "coming to the bars" or "grabbing the bars." Clearly, a man who has clung to the bars all night is in poor condition to work the next day.

Conditions in the barracks are worsened by the prevalent consumption of liquor and beer and by the use of drugs. It is not uncommon for many, if not all, of the inmates of a particular barracks to become intoxicated by drugs and alcohol all at the same time. The resulting commotion, violence, and confusion are quite imaginable. The free world people cannot control the situation; the trusties will not and are not supposed to; and the floor walkers frequently participate in the orgies.

All of this is not to say that a barracks system of confinement properly regulated and limited may not have a place in a well run penal institution. If barracks assignments are confined to small groups of men, properly classified and selected and subject to adequate control, the barracks system is not objectionable and in certain respects may be preferable to confinement in individual cells. It is obvious, however, that the Cummins barracks do not satisfy those conditions.

The isolation cells at Cummins, located in a building set apart to itself and surrounded by a fence, were considered by the Court in *Holt I.* They were found to be overcrowded, filthy, and unsanitary. Pursuant to the Court's order in that case, the overcrowding seems to have been ameliorated; the other conditions still exist.

The Study Commission's report refers to the existence of 12 isolation cells and the construction of 28 more. After the Commission's report was filed, the Legislature authorized the construction of a maximum security unit at Cummins which will be in operation, hopefully, in 1971. After that authorization was given, construction of the additional isolation cells was halted. While there are 12 cells in the isolation unit, one of them has been fitted up as a shower room so that actually there are only 11 cells for the confinement of prisoners.

The isolation unit is guarded by trusties, and free world people seldom come around it. That situation is a source of constant trouble. The trusties threaten and harass the prisoners, and the prisoners probably reciprocate in kind. The isolation diet is carelessly served to the inmates of the cells and at times is permitted to become cold and wet.

The cells are occupied by prisoners who have been confined there for disciplinary reasons or for "protective custody." The isolation inmates who are in "protective custody" are some of the most incorrigible and dangerous prisoners in the Penitentiary. They are sociopathics with no constructive motivation whatever. They damage and destroy fixtures in the cells to the extent of their ability to do so; they set fire to their bedding and to their clothing. They take no interest in the conditions of the cells except to complain about them. They refuse to obey at times the lawful orders of free world people, and obedience has to be compelled by force exerted by free world people and trusty guards; the inmates resist violently and then complain about their "ill treatment."

As the Court understands it, the isolation cells at Tucker are located in the main building of the institution. Some of them are, or at least have been from time to time, occupied by Cummins inmates sent to Tucker for protective custody. The condition of the Tucker isolation cells is about the same as that of the Cummins cells, except that the Tucker cells are inexcusably infested by rats, a problem that does not seem to be particularly troublesome at Cummins.

In view of the fact that the isolation cells are no longer grossly overcrowded, and in view of the fact that most of the conditions existing therein are due to the conduct of the inmates themselves, the cells do not give the Court as serious a constitutional problem as do other aspects of Penitentiary life.

In Act 50 of 1968 the Legislature recognized the important place of training and rehabilitation in the Arkansas penal program and directed the Department of Corrections to initiate and prosecute such a program. A program has been initiated at Tucker and is doing much good. Nothing has been done at Cummins.

While inmates newly arriving at the Penitentiary are given intelligence and aptitude tests disseminated by the Vocational Rehabilitation Service, the results of the tests are of little official interest. No regard is paid to the tests and their results in assigning prisoners to barracks or to work. As far as the inmates are concerned, the tests are of no benefit whatever.

A large proportion, perhaps a majority, of the inmates of the Penitentiary are ignorant and unskilled. Many are illiterate. The contribution of ignorance and lack of skills and specialization to crime today is well known. If a man who is ignorant and unskilled when he goes into prison can come out with some education and some usable skill, he has an improved chance of staying out of prison in the future. If he comes out as ignorant and unskilled as he goes in, recidivism on his part is almost inevitable.

Since it costs money to confine convicts, more than many taxpayers realize, it would seem to be in the enlightened self-interest of all States to try to rehabilitate their convicts, as the Arkansas Legislature and Respondents have recognized. But, does the Constitution require a program of rehabilitation, or forbid the operation of a prison without such a program?

Many penologists hold today that the primary purpose of prisons is rehabilitation of convicts and their restoration to society as useful citizens; those penologists hold that other aims of penal confinement, while perhaps legitimate, are of secondary importance. That has not always been the prevailing view of what penitentiaries are for, if, indeed, it is today. In years past many people have felt, and many still feel, that a criminal is sent to the penitentiary to be punished for his crimes and to protect the public from his further depredations. Under that view, while there is no objection to rehabilitation, it is not given any priority.

This Court knows that a sociological theory or idea may ripen into constitutional law; many such theories and ideas have done so. But, this Court is not prepared to say that such a ripening has occurred as yet as far as rehabilitation of convicts is concerned. Given an otherwise unexceptional penal institution, the Court is not willing to hold that confinement in it is unconstitutional simply because the institution does not operate a school, or provide vocational training, or other rehabilitative facilities and services which many institutions now offer.

That, however, is not quite the end of the matter. The absence of an affirmative program of training and rehabilitation may have constitutional significance where in the absence of such a program conditions and practices exist which actually militate against reform and rehabilitation. That is the situation that exists in Arkansas today, completely at Cummins and to a lesser degree at Tucker.

It can be said safely that except in a very, very few and unusual cases confinement in the Arkansas State Penitentiary today is the opposite of beneficial. As a generality, it may be stated that few individuals come out of it better men for their experience; most come out as bad as they went in, or worse.

Living as he must under the conditions that have been described, with no legitimate rewards or incentives, in fear and apprehension, in degrading surroundings, and with no help from the State, an Arkansas convict will hardly be able to reform himself, and his experience in the Penitentiary is apt to do nothing but instill in him a deep or deeper hatred for and alienation from the society that put him there. And the failure of the State to help him become a good citizen will be compounded by the ever present willingness of his fellow inmates to train him to be a worse criminal.

Thus, the absence of rehabilitation services and facilities of which Petitioners complain remains a factor in the overall constitutional equation before the Court.

Like the absence of a meaningful rehabilitation program, there are other aspects of prison life which in and of themselves do not rise to constitutional dignity but which aggravate the more serious prison defects and deficiencies. The Court will mention some of those aspects briefly.

Medical and dental facilities leave much to be desired. It is not so much that the facilities and services themselves are particularly inadequate for institutions like Cummins and Tucker; rather, it is their unavailability to an inmate when needed that creates the problem. That is largely the fault of the trusty system. If an inmate needs to see the doctor or the dentist, that need is not filled if he is not permitted to go to the infirmary; and it does him no good to go to the infirmary if the doctor is not there when he arrives. Nor does prescribed medication do him any good if it is withheld by a trusty. Making due allowance for malingering, and the Court is sure that there is much of it, there is a great deal of room for improvement in this area of prison life.

Sanitary conditions in the kitchen at Cummins are deplorable according to the testimony of Respondents' own medical witness. Again, that is due largely to the fact that trusties are in charge of the kitchen and do not care whether it is kept clean or not.

The evidence is to the effect that the State supplies its convicts with nothing but the bare necessities of life; no niceties are supplied. Granted, that the State may not be required constitutionally to make it possible for a convict to live comfortably, its failure to do so certainly operates to lower inmate morale. A man who gets only one toothbrush and one tube of toothpaste, who is supplied with no towels, and with insufficient socks and underclothing, and who is required to sleep night after night on filthy bedding is certainly not stimulated to take any pride in himself or to try to be a good inmate of the Penitentiary to say nothing of being a good citizen in the free world when he is released.

It now becomes necessary for the Court to consider in combination the aspects of the Penitentiary System which it has endeavored to describe separately, and to determine whether the situation as a whole is such that confinement in the Arkansas Penitentiary constitutes a cruel and unusual punishment within the prohibition of the Constitution.

In Jackson v. Bishop the Court discussed the concept of "cruel and unusual punishment" in some detail; and in the recent criminal cases that have been mentioned this Court undertook to define the term to trial juries.

The term cannot be defined with specificity. It is flexible and tends to broaden as society tends to pay more regard to human decency and dignity and becomes, or likes to think that it becomes, more humane. Generally speaking, a punishment that amounts to torture, or that is grossly excessive in proportion to the offense for which it is imposed, or that is inherently unfair, or that is unnecessarily degrading, or that is shocking or disgusting to people of reasonable sensitivity is a "cruel and unusual" punishment. And a punishment that is not inherently cruel and unusual may become so by reason of the manner in which it is inflicted. . . .

For the ordinary convict a sentence to the Arkansas Penitentiary today amounts to a banishment from civilized society to a dark and evil world completely alien to the free world, a world that is administered by criminals under unwritten rules and customs completely foreign to free world culture.

After long and careful consideration the Court has come to the conclusion that the Fourteenth Amendment prohibits confinement under the conditions that have been described and that the Arkansas Penitentiary System as it exists today, particularly at Cummins, is unconstitutional.

Such confinement is inherently dangerous. A convict, however cooperative and inoffensive he may be, has no assurance whatever that he will not be killed, seriously injured, or sexually abused. Under the present system the State cannot protect him.

Apart from physical danger, confinement in the Penitentiary involves living under degrading and disgusting conditions. This Court has no patience with those who still say, even when they ought to know better, that to change those conditions will convert the prison into a country club; the Court has not heard any of those people volunteer to spend a few days and nights at either Tucker or Cummins incognito.

The peril and the degradation to which Arkansas convicts are subjected daily are aggravated by the fact that the treatment which a convict may expect to receive depends not at all upon the gravity of his offense or the length of his term. In point of fact, a man sentenced to life imprisonment for first degree murder and who has a long criminal record may expect to fare better than a country boy with no serious record who is sentenced to a term of two years for stealing a pig.

It is one thing for the State to send a man to the Penitentiary as a punishment for crime. It is another thing for the State to delegate the governance of him to other convicts, and to do nothing meaningful for his safety, well being, and possible rehabilitation. It is one thing for the State not to pay a convict for his labor; it is something else to subject him to a situation in which he has to sell his blood to obtain money to pay for his own safety, or for adequate food, or for access to needed medical attention.

However constitutionally tolerable the Arkansas system may have been in former years, it simply will not do today as the Twentieth Century goes into its eighth decade.

The Fourteenth Amendment prohibits racial discrimination within prisons, and the prohibition extends to the racial segregation of inmates. . . .

As to Tucker the Court finds that that facility is essentially integrated, and that no substantial desegregation problem exists there. With respect to Cummins, certain aspects of prison life have been integrated, and Respondents recognize their duty to eliminate all vestiges of racial segregation, including separate barracks for white and Negro inmates, both rankers and trusties.

Respondents contend, however, and the Court agrees, that to order immediate desegregation of the barracks would create disciplinary problems that Respondents are not able to solve at the moment and would tend to make the already bad situation at the Penitentiary substantially worse than it is.

It must be remembered that we are not dealing here with school children. We are not dealing with free world housing; we are not dealing with theatres, restaurants, or hotels. We are dealing with criminals, many of whom are violent, and we are dealing with a situation in which the civilian personnel at the Penitentiary are not in control of the institution.

In such circumstances, while the inmates at Cummins are going to have to be integrated, the Court thinks that the process should be part of the overall transition of the Penitentiary from an unconstitutional to a constitutional institution, which transition will be discussed in the following and final section of this opinion.

As has been seen, Petitioners seek both declaratory and injunctive relief. They also seek relief for themselves as individuals and for other convicts similarly situated. Two aspects of those prayers give the Court little or no trouble.

As far as the individual claims of the individual Petitioners are concerned, including the individual complaints of inmates now in isolation, the Court does not consider that any of the Petitioners has made a case for specific individual relief.[5] However, all of the Petitioners are subject to the overall situation which renders the Penitentiary unconstitutional and all are entitled to class relief with respect to that situation.

As to the claim for declaratory relief, the Court will declare that to the extent indicated heretofore confinement in the Arkansas Penitentiary System under existing conditions amounts to a cruel and unusual punishment consti-

5. One of the Petitioners, James E. Jackson, a Negro inmate of the isolation unit at Cummins wrote the Court in advance of trial expressing the view that the Court was biased, prejudiced and corrupt, and that the Court is a racist. Jackson repeated his statements when called to the witness stand. While the Court is not sensible of any feelings of bias or prejudice in the case and is not aware of anything that would justify a charge of racism or corruption, the Court nevertheless disqualified itself in open court as far as Jackson's individual claim is concerned. He is free to litigate that claim further before some other Judge if he cares to do so.

tutionally prohibited. While the situation at Tucker is much better than that which exists at Cummins, the fact remains that Tucker inmates, like those at Cummins, are subject to the trusty system, including the trusty guard system, and are also confined in large numbers in open barracks. That the situation at Tucker is less severe than that at Cummins seems to the Court to be more significant from the standpoint of the injunctive relief to be ordered than from the standpoint of declaratory relief.

The Court will also declare that racial discrimination in the Penitentiary System, including racial segregation of inmates, is a violation of the Equal Protection Clause of the Fourteenth Amendment and must be eliminated. . . .

Respondents will be ordered to make a prompt and reasonable start toward eliminating the conditions that have caused the Court to condemn the System and to prosecute their efforts with all reasonable diligence to completion as soon as possible. The lives, safety, and health of human beings, to say nothing of their dignity, are at stake. The start must be prompt, and the prosecution must be vigorous. The handwriting is on the wall, and it ought not to require a Daniel to read it. Unless conditions at the Penitentiary farms are brought up to a level of constitutional tolerability, the farms can no longer be used for the confinement of convicts.

The questions that trouble the Court at this juncture are: What must be done within the immediate future, and how long should Respondents be allowed to achieve their ultimate objective? In approaching those questions certain things should be kept in mind.

First, over the past several years conditions at the Penitentiary have ameliorated somewhat, due in part, but by no means entirely, to the decrees of this Court in the earlier stages of the overall litigation. The alleviation began in the mid-sixties when Dan D. Stephens became Superintendent of the Penitentiary, and it has continued under his successors. While the Penitentiary is still a bad place, an unconstitutional place in the Court's eyes, it is in some respects a better place than it was several years ago.

Second, the legislation adopted in 1967, 1968, and 1969, the report of the Study Commission, and the report to the Commission on Crime and Law Enforcement, indicate that the Arkansas State government is more interested than ever before in the prison system and is aware of the fact that the system is deficient. That increasing awareness of the problem is evidenced not only by the items just mentioned but also by increased appropriations for the Penitentiary over the past several years.

Third, notice may be taken of the fact that the Governor of Arkansas has issued his call for the Legislature to meet in special session on March 2 of the current year. Legislation for the benefit of the Penitentiary is included among the numerous items on the agenda, although the specific nature of the legislation to be sought has not yet been spelled out, and the scope of it may depend to some extent on the provisions of the Court's decree in this case.

It is obvious that money will be required to meet the constitutional deficiencies of the institution, and there is no reason to believe that, subject to the overall financial needs and requirements of the State, the Legislature will be unwilling to appropriate necessary funds.

Finally, if Respondents had unlimited funds at their disposal tomorrow, they could not solve their constitutional problem overnight. Obviously, free world people are going to have to be recruited and employed, and that is going to take some time. In this connection it should be emphasized that to replace trusties with venal, corrupt, sadistic, and underpaid civilian employees would be but to substitute another form of tyranny for that which now exists. Thus, Respondents are going to have to be allowed some reasonable period of transition within which to achieve their objective, but that period is going to have to be measured in months, not years.

The Court thinks in this context, as it has thought in other contexts, that Respondents should be given an opportunity to come forward with a plan to eliminate existing unconstitutionalities, to state what they plan to do, and how long they plan to take to do it. The Court also thinks, however, that it should now proceed to lay down some guidelines for Respondents and should mention what it now considers will probably be minimum requirements if persons are going to continue to be confined in the Penitentiary.

This Court rejects out of hand any approach that would phase out the trusty guard system as such while leaving intact other aspects of the overall trusty system even more objectionable than the guard system itself. All of the trusties are going to have to be brought under control; and trusties, whether guards or not, are going to have to be stripped of their authority over the lives and living conditions of other convicts. Responsibilities that ought to be discharged by free world people may no longer be delegated to trusties whether in the office, in the infirmary, the kitchen, or the fields. Trusties must not have it in their power to bring about promotions or demotions of other inmates and must not be allowed to stand as obstacles to reasonable access of ordinary inmates to civilian employees. The right of a man to talk to the Superintendent or the Assistant Superintendent, or to go to the infirmary when necessary, or receive necessary treatment or medication, must not be permitted to depend on the whim of one or more trusties. It should be taken out of the power of trusties to steal prison food for resale, and it should go without saying that trusties ought not to have access to addictive or stimulating drugs in the prison pharmacy.

The Court thinks that when the trusties as a class are deprived of their authority over inmates, they will largely lose the power of extortion and other undesirable powers which they now possess. This does not mean that trusties may not be assigned responsible jobs, but they must be "jobs," not "offices of profit," and they must be performed under adequate supervision.

While the Court is not prepared at this juncture affirmatively to order the elimination of the trusty guard system or a commencement of a general phase out of the system, the system is going to have to be overhauled. The tower guards and picket guards give the Court no particular problem; the gate guards and the field guards do.

As to the gate guards, it seems evident to the Court that without the connivance of such guards the widespread smuggling of contraband into the prison which is now practiced would be impossible or at least would be made much more difficult. Additionally, gate guards have opportunities for extortion and corruption that other guards do not possess. The gate guards should be replaced by free world personnel as soon as possible.

The system of field guards and the system of using trusty long line riders and inmate pushers go hand in hand, and the combination of the two is one of the things that makes the field guard system so dangerous to rankers. Field guards are much less likely to fire on a ranker or on a group of rankers in the immediate presence of a civilian long line supervisor than they are in a situation where the rankers are actually being worked by other inmates. It appears to the Court that the answer, however unpalatable it may be, is to eliminate the positions of long line rider and inmate pusher and to put each long line under the immediate charge of one or more free world people.

The barracks system of confinement has got to be changed, and the change cannot wait on the completion of the maximum security unit that has been mentioned. The barracks are going to have to be made smaller by subdividing existing barracks or otherwise, and more discrimination, other than racial, is going to have to be practiced in assigning men to barracks. It may be necessary to proceed with the construction of more isolation cells at Cummins to take care of men who simply should not be assigned to barracks.

Apart from the foregoing Respondents are going to have to do more than they have done in the past about keeping order in the barracks at night and about protecting inmates from violent assaults of whatever kind.

As to the isolation cells, while the plight of the inmates is largely of their own doing, they are suffering seriously from neglect. Free world people may no longer leave those inmates to the mercies of trusty guards; additionally, the Court thinks that the method of serving them their food must be changed so as to make sure that it gets to them in more sanitary and palatable condition. In that connection the report to the Commission on Crime and Law Enforcement points out, among other things, that the people in isolation have "no decent or Christian" way in which to eat their food. The report suggests that prisoners in isolation be taken from the cells to the main dining hall to eat either before or after other inmates have been served. That recommendation should be within the power of Respondents to follow without substantial expense and without danger to any inmates.

If Respondents will move in good faith and with diligence in the areas of prison life just discussed, namely, the trusty system, the barracks system, inmate safety, and the isolation cells, the Court thinks that subsidiary problems will tend to take care of themselves. It would be a mistake to order too much at this time; but, in the areas just mentioned Respondents will be required to move. And, of course, the remaining vestiges of racial segregation must be eliminated.

The Court will not be dogmatic about time just now. If there are things that Respondents can do now with available funds and personnel, they will be expected to do them now. If necessary steps cost money, and they will, Respondents must move as rapidly as funds become available. The opening of the new maximum security unit in 1971 should be set as at least a tentative target date for the completion of the removal of unconstitutional conditions and practices. The schedule on which Respondents will be required to move may be shortened or lengthened as circumstances and developments may dictate.

At the moment Respondents will be ordered to submit to the Court and to counsel for Petitioners not later than April 1 of this year a report and plan showing what, if anything, they have done up to that time to meet the requirements of the Court, what they plan to do, and when they plan to do it.

If the initial report is approved, the Court may require additional reports from time to time and may require specific information in certain areas. If the initial report is not approved, it will then become necessary for the Court to consider what specific steps it will take to implement its declarations of the unconstitutionality of the existing system.

Let there be no mistake in the matter; the obligation of the Respondents to eliminate existing unconstitutionalities does not depend upon what the Legislature may do, or upon what the Governor may do, or, indeed, upon what Respondents may actually be able to accomplish. If Arkansas is going to operate a Penitentiary System, it is going to have to be a system that is countenanced by the Constitution of the United States.

A decree in accordance with the foregoing will be entered.

---

1) Judge Henley notes that certain officers or institutions, such as the Governor or the Legislature, that will be affected by the litigation and decree are not formally parties to the suit. Should they have been made parties? Could they have been parties in light of the Eleventh Amendment?

2) Judge Henley said: "[T]he Court does not consider that any of the Petitioners has made a case for specific individual relief." What does that mean? What is the difference between "specific individual relief" and the structural relief that Judge Henley orders? Can he give the latter without also giving the former? Reread footnote 5. What do you think about the way Judge Henley treats the charge of bias?

3) Are you convinced by the Judge's treatment of the rehabilitation claim? Should he consider the absence of rehabilitation a "factor in the overall constitutional equation" when it is not itself unconstitutional? He says "[m]edical and dental facilities leave much to be desired." Do statements like that belong in a judicial decision?

4) Judge Henley describes the remedial objective as transforming "the penitentiary from an unconstitutional to a constitutional institution." Later he speaks of the obligation to bring the conditions up to "a level of constitutional tolerability." Should these objectives be achieved immediately? He allows the Commissioner "some reasonable period of transition within which to achieve their objective." Compare the "all-deliberate-speed" formula of *Brown II.* Inquire into the theory in either *Brown II* or *Holt* for delaying the remedy. Does it make the remedy more effective? Vindicate the values underlying the Constitution? Accommodate other goals and interests of the state that are competing for the resources? Does your attitude toward the delay change depending on the reasons for it? Gewirtz, Remedies and Resistance 92 Yale L.J. 585 (1983).

5) The Judge gives the Commissioner "an opportunity to come forward with a plan to eliminate existing unconstitutionalities." (This follows a practice rooted in the school desegregation cases of the late 1950s and early 1960s.) Remember the failure of *Holt I* to remedy the situation. Why is the Commissioner given this opportunity? Does the opportunity to formulate a plan reflect certain strategic or pragmatic considerations? Is it based on in-

trinsic limitations of the court's competence and authority? If the latter, consider whether the court should "lay down some guidelines" or even state "what it now considers will probably be minimum requirements."

HOLT v. SARVER

442 F.2d 304 (8th Cir. 1971).

Before MATTHES, Chief Judge, VAN OOSTERHOUT and LAY, Circuit Judges.

VAN OOSTERHOUT, Circuit Judge.

This is an appeal by respondents Robert Sarver, Commissioner of Corrections, et al., from judgment entered in favor of petitioners in eight consolidated class actions brought by Holt, et al., inmates of the Cummins Farm Unit and the Tucker Intermediate Reformatory, parts of the Arkansas prison system, against Commissioner Sarver and the members of the Board of Corrections. The respondents under Arkansas law administer the State penitentiary system. . . .

The respondents have taken this timely appeal from such judgment and decree. Respondents, as required by the court order, filed the April 1, 1970, report setting out the steps taken and contemplated to meet the constitutional violations. On April 15, 1970, the court approved such report as an interim report, noting that a reasonable start had been made to eliminate the unconstitutional conditions and that "the Court is most pleased with the response of the Governor and of the Legislature to the fiscal needs of the Penitentiary and has no reason to believe that the institution will not be adequately funded in the future, taking into consideration, of course, the overall financial condition of the State."

A report requested by the court giving further information as to disarming prison inmates and measures taken to protect the inmates from attacks by other inmates and the condition of the isolation cells was made on May 8 and was approved and accepted as an interim report by order of May 28, 1970. A required progress report showing prison conditions as of June 30, 1970, was filed by the Commissioners. The record shows no action taken thereon. . . .

It is desirable at this point to observe that some issues decided by the trial court are not before us on this appeal. It appears from the interim reports and the court's action thereon that the racial integration requirement of the court's decree has been fully met. No contrary contention is made in the briefs.

Petitioners on March 18, 1970, filed notice of cross-appeal. No brief in support of the cross-appeal has been filed.

Petitioners in the trial court raised the issue that their Thirteenth Amendment protection against involuntary servitude had been violated by requiring inmates to perform forced labor. The trial court rejected such contention. Petitioners in response to an inquiry in oral argument advised us that they are not here attacking the trial court's determination on the Thirteenth Amendment issue. The cross-appeal was dismissed on motion of appellant on January 8, 1971. . . .

The court overruled respondents' motion to dismiss, based on the ground that the suit is in effect a suit against the State and as such is barred by the Eleventh Amendment. It is quite true that the prison units here in controversy are state agencies and that the funds necessary to operate the institutions must come from State appropriations.

The Eleventh Amendment argument here made is completely answered by Judge Matthes in Board of Trustees of Arkansas A & M College v. Davis, 8 Cir., 396 F.2d 730, 732–733. The college in that case, like the prisons in our present case, is a State agency. As pointed out in *Davis,* the Supreme Court has since the foundation case of Ex parte Young, 209 U.S. 123, repeatedly recognized that an act of a state official which violates a federally guaranteed constitutional right may be enjoined upon the basis that the officer is "stripped of his official or representative character and is subjected in his person to the consequences of his individual conduct. The state has no power to impart to him any immunity from responsibility to the supreme authority of the United States." 396 F.2d 730, 732, quoting from Ex parte Young, 209 U.S. pp. 159–160. Numerous applications of such principle are cited in *Davis.* We adhere to the legal principles there stated.

In Jackson v. Bishop, an action against the superintendent of the two identical prisons here involved, we determined that corporal punishment administered in the prisons constituted cruel and inhuman punishment. We enjoined the administration of corporal punishment. We adhere to the principles stated in *Jackson* including the admonition that a federal court should be reluctant to interfere with the operation and discipline of a state prison and that intervention is warranted only upon a clear showing of a violation of a federally guaranteed constitutional right. See Burns v. Swenson, 8 Cir., 430 F.2d 771, 775; Sostre v. McGinnis, 2 Cir., 442 F.2d 178 (1971); Wilwording v. Swenson, 8 Cir., 439 F.2d 1331 (1971).

Petitioners in their amended complaint did not contest the validity of the imposed sentences which they are serving nor do they ask to be released from custody. No claim for money damages is made. The Commissioner of Corrections and the members of the Board of Corrections are made parties both in their official and individual capacities. Relief sought is to enjoin the respondents from inflicting punishment violative of the Eighth Amendment. Jurisdiction is established under 42 U.S.C.A. § 1983 and 28 U.S.C.A. § 1343(3).

The motion to dismiss was properly denied.

Respondents' contention that the court committed prejudicial error in receiving and refusing to strike expert testimony of James W. Bennett, retired director of federal prisons, and the report of Dr. Friel made to the Arkansas Commission on Crime and Law Enforcement, lacks merit. A proper foundation for expert testimony on the part of Mr. Bennett has clearly been laid. We placed considerable reliance upon Mr. Bennett's testimony in Jackson v. Bishop, supra. The fact that Mr. Bennett had not visited the Arkansas prisons recently does not disqualify him as an expert witness but goes to the weight of his testimony.

Respondents, as required by FRAP Rule 28(e), have not set out in brief or appendix or given record citations to the questions, objections and answers of which they complain. We are not required to search the record for error. Moreover, as is pointed out in the next division, the evidence supporting the court's findings is strong.

Neither the appendix nor the part of the original record certified to us shows the report made by Dr. Friel to the Arkansas Commission on Crime or the circumstances under which such report was made. Apparently Dr. Friel made the report by virtue of his employment by the Arkansas Commission on Crime. Respondents have failed to establish that the report was improperly received over appropriate objection. Respondents have likewise failed to demonstrate that prejudicial error was committed in receiving the report.

In non-jury cases tried to the court it is well settled that we will not reverse for the erroneous reception of evidence unless it appears that the competent evidence is insufficient to support the judgment or that the court was induced by incompetent evidence to make an essential finding which it would not otherwise have made. . . . No such showing has here been made.

Respondents in their brief urge that the evidence is insufficient to support some subsidiary fact findings made by the court. We are convinced from an examination of the voluminous record that Judge Henley's basic findings upon which the judgment and decree are predicated are supported by overwhelming substantial evidence and that such findings afford a firm basis for his determination that imprisonment of inmates at the Cummins and Tucker units constitutes cruel and unusual punishment violative of the Eighth Amendment under conditions shown to have existed at the time of the decree. No useful purpose will be served by a detailed discussion of the events and the retreading of the ground so well covered by Judge Henley in his opinion. Judge Henley had previously determined in Holt I that substantially the same constitutional deficiencies existed at the institutions here involved. No appeal was taken from that determination. . . .

Commissioner Sarver, who also served as superintendent at the Cummins unit, as a witness frankly admitted that the physical facilities at both units were inadequate and in a total state of disrepair that could only be described as deplorable. Additionally, he testified that trusty inmates, some of whom were serving life or long term sentences, constituted 99% of the security force of the prison system. For the approximately 1,000 inmate population only eight free world (non-inmate) guards were employed and these guards were poorly paid and lacked proper training. One hundred and fifty gun carrying trusties, who control all of the weapons at the prison, must be relied upon to guard and protect the prisoners.

The trusties sell desirable jobs to prisoners and also traffic in food, liquor and drugs. Prisoners frequently become intoxicated and unruly. The prisoners sleep in dormitories. Prisoners are frequently attacked and raped in the dormitories and injuries and deaths have resulted. Sleep and rest are seriously disrupted. No adequate means exist to protect the prisoners from assaults. There is no satisfactory means of keeping guns, knives and other weapons away from the prison population.

The reports filed by the Commissioner at the court's direction clearly confirm the findings of Eighth Amendment violations. We deem it unnecessary to go into any greater detail in discussing the substantial evidence supporting the court's findings.

Eighth Amendment violations form the basis for federal court intervention in the administration of a state prison. A factual showing of cruel and unusual punishment violative of the Eighth Amendment is a prerequisite. Jackson v. Bishop; Sostre v. McGinnis. In *Sostre,* Judge Kaufman aptly states:

"For a federal court, however, to place a punishment beyond the power of a state to impose on an inmate is a drastic interference with the state's free political and administrative processes. It is not only that we, trained as judges, lack expertise in prison administration. Even a lifetime of study in prison administration and several advanced degrees in the field would not qualify us *as a federal court* to command state officials to shun a policy that they have decided is suitable because to us the choice may seem unsound or *personally* repugnant. As judges we are obliged to school ourselves in such objective sources as historical usage, see Wilkerson v. Utah, 99 U.S. 130 (1870), practices in other jurisdictions, see Weems v. United States, 217 U.S. 349 (1910), and public opinion, see Robinson v. California, 370 U.S. 660, 666 (1962), before we may responsibly exercise the power of judicial review to declare a punishment unconstitutional under the Eighth Amendment.

"Accordingly, we have in the past declined to find an Eighth Amendment violation unless the punishment can properly be termed 'barbarous' or 'shocking to the conscience.' " 442 F.2d 178, 183–185.

Judge Henley recognized such standards as is reflected by his statement reading:

"The Court, however, is limited in its inquiry to the question of whether or not the constitutional rights of inmates are being invaded, and with whether the Penitentiary itself is unconstitutional. The Court is not judicially concerned with questions which in the last analysis are addressed to legislative and administrative judgment. A practice that may be bad from the standpoint of penology may not necessarily be forbidden by the Constitution. And a prison system that would be excellent from the view point of a modern prison administrator may not be required by the provisions of the Constitution with which the Court is concerned."

No criticism is made by any party of the form of relief granted. Judge Henley in his opinion expressed a realization that conditions at a prison cannot be corrected overnight. Legislative appropriations are required to obtain funds needed for the correction of constitutional deficiencies. Time is needed to recruit and train qualified free world guards. . . .

The reports on file show substantial progress in meeting the constitutional deficiencies. Money has been appropriated for new buildings and needed improvements and for the employment of additional free world guards. The trial court has recognized that the State is making a sincere effort to remedy the deficiencies. The last report before us covers the period to June 30, 1970. The court upon remand should require an up-to-date report on the progress made in meeting the constitutional violations. A hearing thereon should be held to determine whether appropriate steps have been taken to cure the constitutional deficiencies found by the court, after which such further order as may be appropriate should be entered.

Supervision over the state prisons by a federal court should of course not be kept in force for any longer period than necessary to provide reasonable assurance that incarceration therein will not constitute cruel and inhuman punishment violative of the Eighth Amendment.

The judgment is affirmed. The case is remanded to the trial court for further proceedings consistent with the views herein expressed.

LAY, Circuit Judge (concurring).

I fully concur. I sincerely hope it is not wasted rhetoric to express additional judicial condemnation of the conditions and practices carried out by the State of Arkansas in operating its system of "correction." Contemporary conditions in Arkansas do not vary greatly from those condemned in England in the 1700's.[1] The Eighth Amendment prohibiting "cruel and unusual punishment" relates to "evolving standards of decency that mark the progress of a maturing society." See Trop v. Dulles, 356 U.S. 86, 101 (1958). The present record reflects the prison system at Cummins Prison Farm to be not only shocking to "standards of decency," but immoral and criminal as well.

New buildings and additional guards, although essential for compliance with the court's decree, fall far short of remedying the defilement of individuals and the inhumane treatment of prisoners practiced in the name of the state. Imprisonment in buildings of newly laid brick with the most rigid security will not alleviate the depravity and criminality which are fostered by the Arkansas prison system. The district court recognized this when it stated:

"The absence of an affirmative program of training and rehabilitation may have constitutional significance where in the absence of such a program conditions and practices exist which actually militate against reform and rehabilitation."

Until immediate and continued emphasis is given to an affirmative program of rehabilitation the district court should retain jurisdiction.[2]

---

1. Toward the end of the 18th Century John Howard was Sheriff of Bedfordshire. Because of the deplorable conditions in London prisons he resigned to spend the remainder of his life working for prison reform in England. He found that prisons were not sanitary or secure; there was no effective supervision of prisoners; there existed "physical and moral corruption of the common wards and yards"; there were no separate cells for safe sleeping; there was no useful work performed by the prisoners, no educational efforts made on their behalf, and no moral or religious instruction to restore them as useful members of society. C.B. Beccaria, On Crimes & Punishments (1764); J. Howard, The State of the Prisons, etc. (1777), as found in Encyclopedia Britannica, "Prison," Vol. 18, pp. 514–515 (1956).

2. As far back as 1870 the American Prison Association recognized rehabilitation and moral regeneration, rather than vindictive retribution, to be the fundamental aims of correction. See paper given to American Correctional Ass'n by Robert Kutak, Omaha, Nebraska, Oct. 15, 1970. Monograph, Outside Looking In (LEAA 1970).

Several states have recognized the need for implementation of correctional treatment. See e.g. N.Y. Correc.Law § 136 (McKinney's Consol.Laws, c. 43, 1968):

"The objective of prison education in its broadest sense should be the socialization of the inmates through varied impressional and expressional activities, with emphasis on individual inmate needs. The objective of this program shall be the return of these inmates to society with a more wholesome attitude toward living, with a desire to conduct themselves as good citizens and with the skill and knowledge which will give them a reasonable chance to maintain themselves and their dependents through honest labor. To this end each prisoner shall

Does the appellate court discharge its normal duties? Does it try to strengthen Judge Henley's hand in dealing with the state of Arkansas? Does it become part of the remedial enterprise?

HOLT v. HUTTO [HOLT III]

363 F.Supp. 194 (E.D.Ark.1973).

HENLEY, Chief Judge.

These 34 individual and class actions have been brought by Arkansas convicts against the members of the Arkansas State Board of Correction, Terrell Don Hutto, the Arkansas Commissioner of Correction who administers the prisons within the jurisdiction of the Arkansas Department of Correction, and certain lesser prison officials. Petitioners are inmates of the Cummins Unit of the Department which is located in Lincoln County, Arkansas, and of the Tucker Intermediate Reformatory located in Jefferson County.

While different individual inmates naturally complain about different things, petitioners as a class contend that in spite of previous decrees and opinions of this Court conditions in and practices at both of the institutions that have been mentioned are such as to render the confinement of human beings there a cruel and unusual punishment prohibited by the Eighth and Fourteenth Amendments to the Constitution of the United States. They also complain of racial discrimination and make a number of other complaints which will be mentioned in due course. Respondents deny that the complaints have merit.

This litigation today stands in a posture quite different from that in which it stood in 1969 and 1970. In those years the Court was dealing with officially prescribed or sanctioned conditions and practices which were claimed to be unconstitutional, and the controlling facts were essentially undisputed. Today, most of the practices and conditions alleged by petitioners to exist and of which they complain are not officially approved or sanctioned, and a number of them are specifically prohibited by rules and regulations of the Department which appear in the Department's Inmate Handbook and Employee Handbook, copies of which are in the record. Additionally, controlling facts are sharply disputed in many areas.

Inmate complaints extend over practically the entire spectrum of prison life, and in trying to resolve the disputed factual issues the Court has encountered in full measure the credibility problems inherent in litigation of this kind. In resolving the issues of fact before it, the Court has done the best

be given a program of education which, on the basis of available data, seems most likely to further the process of socialization and rehabilitation. The time daily devoted to such education shall be such as is required for meeting the above objectives. The director of education, subject to the direction of the commissioner of correction and after consultation by such commissioner with the state commissioner of education, shall develop the curricula and the education programs that are required to meet the special needs of each prison and reformatory in the department."

Mo.Ann.Stat. § 216.090(1) (1962) reads:

"[I]n the correctional treatment applied to each inmate, reformation of the inmate, his social and moral improvement, and his rehabilitation toward useful, productive and law-abiding citizenship shall be guiding factors and aims."

that it could, employing in that connection its own common sense and its experience with the Department which extends over a period of at least eight years, and which has involved the reading of literally hundreds of inmate complaints or "writs."

From its consideration of the evidence as a whole, the Court finds ultimately that none of the individual petitioners, as individuals, have shown that they are entitled to specific equitable relief. But, the Court further finds that notwithstanding significant progress and improvements that have been made at both Cummins and Tucker, some problem areas of constitutional significance continue to exist, and that the inmates as a class stand in need of some additional injunctive relief, and that respondents need to be admonished about a number of things.

To accentuate the positive, the Court will say first that as a result of changing attitudes and efforts on the part of the Arkansas Legislature, the present Governor of Arkansas and his predecessor, the Board of Correction, incumbent Commissioner of Correction, Terrell Don Hutto, and his predecessor, C. Robert Sarver, and some of Mr. Hutto's subordinates, the Arkansas prison system is simply not the same system that existed in 1969 and 1970 and in prior years.

To start with the iniquitous "trusty system" described in detail in *Holt I* and *Holt II*, has essentially been dismantled. Free world personnel have replaced the trusties in positions of authority throughout both prisons. While there are still a few trusty guards, they do not represent the threat to ordinary inmates that they have done in years past, and the Court is confident that the few that remain will soon be phased out.

Writing in prior years, the Court was gravely concerned with the risk that inmates confined in barracks ran of homosexual or deadly assaults by other inmates. While the barracks are still seriously overcrowded, and while additional housing facilities are still needed, particularly at Cummins, and while inmate assaults on other inmates and fights between inmates still occur, as they do in all prisons, the problem is not what it was in former days.

Since *Holt II* was written, the Department has constructed a maximum security unit at Cummins in which are housed the most dangerous and unstable inmates, and they are thus removed from the general and more tractable prison population. It appears to the Court that somewhat less than 10 percent of the total population of Cummins is confined in the maximum security unit, and a very large portion of the complaints that the Court receives come from the inmates of the unit, a fact which is not without significance.

As its name implies, Tucker is a reformatory type institution, and it has an advancing program of education and training for its comparatively young and unhardened inmates. Tucker is a much smaller institution than Cummins; its population is generally a little over 300 as compared to an average population at Cummins of some 1100 or 1200 inmates. Prior to the 1972–73 hearings the Court received substantial numbers of complaints from the inmates of Tucker; however, during the last few months section 1983 complaints from Tucker inmates have become almost nonexistent.

There is a limited program of vocational and educational training available at Cummins, but inmate participation therein is not as encouraging as that at Tucker. That, however, is explainable by reference to a number of factors, including ages, dispositions, and criminal records of many of the inmates of Cummins.

The Department has recently acquired law libraries for the use of inmates at both institutions, and the Court finds that those libraries are adequate for legitimate inmate purposes, and that rules for the use of the libraries are not unreasonable. The Department has also employed a lawyer who serves full time as Legal Adviser for the inmates at both institutions, and he is of substantial assistance to them in connection with many of their legal problems, although he is not in a position to assist them when they come into conflict or controversy with prison personnel.

A third institution administered by the Department but not directly involved in this particular phase of the overall prison litigation is the Women's State Reformatory presently located on the same tract of State owned lands as is the Cummins Unit where male prisoners are confined. The Women's Reformatory houses a small number of female inmates. It has given some constitutional trouble in the past. However, the Court has had no complaints about it for months. It is capably administered by a Negro matron or Superintendent, and it appears to be a constitutionally tolerable institution. It is to be moved from its present location to a new site near the City of Pine Bluff, and initial phases of construction of the new facility are now under way.

In pointing out significant improvements that have been made at both institutions the Court does not overlook the fact that serious deficiencies, whether constitutional or not, exist at both Cummins and Tucker. Contributing factors to those deficiencies, some of which will be mentioned, are lack of funds and the rural locations of both institutions a substantial distance by road away from each other.

While many inmates have complained that they have been intentionally denied medical and dental services which it was within the power of the Department to provide, the Court does not so find. And it appears to the Court that many of the inmate complaints have stemmed from the fact that they were not treated as quickly or cured as rapidly as they desired or were not given the quantity or quality of medication that they wanted. A great many people in the free world would have the same complaints.

The Court finds that the Department has done the best that it could in the area of medical services with the resources at its command. That is not to say, however, that deficiencies have not existed and do not continue to exist. As of the date upon which the hearings were closed, the Department had never had a full time physician whose services were available to inmates. Inmates were treated by paramedical personnel who generally had to work without the direct supervision of a doctor. Inmates in need of hospitalization were, and still are, carried to Little Rock or Pine Bluff for treatment. Dental services apparently are largely limited to extractions and the supplying of false teeth.

Since the hearings closed, the Department has been able to employ a full time physician, and his services should be quite helpful. However, his services alone will not by any means solve all of the medical problems of the Department.

One serious problem is that a number of inmates are mentally ill or emotionally disturbed and probably should not be in a penal institution at all. Unfortunately, a viable alternative to their confinement in the Department does not exist in Arkansas today since the Arkansas State Hospital for Nervous Diseases in Little Rock will not care for them except when they are violent. Some of these people are extremely dangerous to themselves and to their keepers and other inmates and tend to keep other inmates in states of unrest and excitement.

Apart from mentally ill inmates, there are also some inmates who have serious and chronic physical ailments which render confinement in an ordinary penal institution undesirable, but, again, there is no viable alternative existing today. The problem is complicated by the fact that the Arkansas State Sanitorium at Booneville, an institution for the treatment of tuberculosis, has now been closed. It goes without saying that prison inmates who are active tuberculars or who have other infectious or contagious diseases must be segregated from other inmates, and the Court assumes that respondents can and will work out methods whereby such segregation can be effected.

Kitchen and sanitary facilities at Tucker stand in serious need of improvement, and improvements are contemplated. Improvements are also needed at Cummins. The overcrowding of the barracks should be eliminated or mitigated, and there is a strong need for a minimum security unit at Cummins.

In the course of the hearings the Court heard some testimony involving complaints about clothing issues, and after the hearings were closed a number of inmates of Barracks No. 7 at Cummins submitted a complaint about alleged insufficiencies of issues of underwear and about inadequate laundry facilities. The Court denied that petition summarily but stated that it would take up the matter of clothing in this opinion.

The Court does not find that clothing issues and issues of footwear are seriously deficient. Of course, shortages of particular items occur from time to time, and laundry service may be deficient from time to time. It might also be observed that at times inmates are careless with their clothing, and at times steal items of clothing from other inmates.

The deficiencies that have been mentioned and others like them call for correction, but they are not such, in the Court's opinion, as to render confinement today at either Cummins or Tucker unconstitutional. The main problem at both institutions from a constitutional standpoint lies in prison administration. The quality of the Department's personnel at both institutions is seriously deficient, and the Court is convinced that that deficiency lies at the root of most of the serious problems in the Department.

Commissioner Hutto, A.L. Lockhart, Superintendent at Cummins, R.G. Britton, Superintendent at Tucker, and some of their subordinates came to the Department from the Texas Penal System. Cecil Boren, Associate Superintendent at Cummins, did not come from Texas and, indeed, was an employee of the Department when C. Robert Sarver was Commissioner. Those four men, plus a very few others, make up the top echelon of the administration of the prisons; they are, so to speak, the "management" of the institutions. Lower ranking employees grade down through tables of organization to the lowest grade of ordinary guard.

With some reservations as to particular individuals, the Court finds that Messrs. Hutto, Lockhart, Britton, and Boren are qualified for their jobs, and the Court thinks that up to a point at least they are trying to do good jobs and to run an efficient, reasonably humane, and constitutional prison system.

The Court cannot say as much for lower echelon personnel as a class. Those employees have in general been recruited locally; they are poorly paid by modern standards; they have had little training or experience; many of them are uncultured and poorly educated; some of them are quite young, perhaps too young to be in position of authority over convicts; some of them are quick tempered. If one adjective is to be used to describe them, it would be "unprofessional."

From top to bottom the personnel of the Department are predominantly white notwithstanding the fact that the inmate population of both institutions is approximately 50 percent black. There are very few black employees, and with one or two exceptions there are no blacks in positions of any real authority at either institution. Important as the Classification Committees and Disciplinary Committees at both institutions are, there has been, except for perhaps a few isolated instances, no black representation on those Committees.

A prison staff and the population of the prison naturally react on each other. Ignoring distinctions between Cummins and Tucker, inmates of the Department are not only racially mixed; they also differ greatly in ages, cultural levels, dispositions, criminal records, intelligence, education, training, and experience. Most of them, indeed the great majority of them, had extremely poor work records in the outside world. And, they have carried into the prisons with them the same weaknesses and deficiencies that they had in the outside world and that got them into prison in the first place.

With particular regard to the black inmates as a group, it is probably safe to say that they are drawn from the lower strata of the black population. As a class, they are neither well educated nor industrious; and they appear to be highly suspicious of those in authority over them. Some have difficulty in communicating intelligently, particularly under conditions of stress.

The personnel that have been described and the inmate population that has been described are in day to day contact within the abrasive atmosphere of penal institutions. Given the quality of the personnel and the quality of the inmates, the contacts between them will inevitably produce friction, stress, unrest, and at times violence.

With certain exceptions to be mentioned the Court finds that if the prescribed rules and regulations of the Department were in fact administered conscientiously and with reasonable efficiency and with appropriate supervision by higher echelon prison employees, it would not have any real constitutional problem with either Cummins or Tucker. Unfortunately, the Court is not able to find that the declared policies and prescribed rules and regulations of the Department are in fact being carried out conscientiously and effectively, and, on the contrary, the Court is persuaded that the Department's policies, rules, and regulations are not being carried out properly in some significant areas.

In other words, and subject to certain exceptions, the Court is convinced that today it is dealing not so much with an unconstitutional prison system as with a poorly administered one. However, unconstitutionality can arise from poor administration of valid policies as well as from policies that are constitutionally invalid themselves.

The Court will make no effort here to discuss every problem that has arisen or conceivably may arise in the Department in the future. Rather, the Court will confine itself to certain specific serious problem areas. While institutional problems of constitutional significance fall into well defined categories, it is necessary to keep in mind that the categories are not mutually exclusive; they tend to overlap, particularly where race is involved.

In this section of the opinion the Court will take up claims of racial discrimination against black inmates, and the claim of Black Muslim inmates that they are subjected to additional discrimination and oppression on account of their religion. The Court will take up, first, the peculiar problems of the Black Muslims.

(a) It is now thoroughly established by judicial opinions too numerous to mention that the Black Muslims confined in prisons in this country constitute a religious sect and are entitled, within reasonable limitations dictated by the conditions of prison life, to the protection of the First Amendment as carried over into the Fourteenth and by the Fourteenth Amendment itself. That means that Black Muslims may not be discriminated against on account of their religion, that they are not to be unreasonably restricted in the exercise or practice thereof, and that at least some accommodations must be made by prison authorities to some requirements and taboos of their professed religious belief.

There are a few Muslims in both Cummins and Tucker. Without any particular elaboration the Court finds that the Muslims at both institutions have some problems that are not without constitutional significance. Their problems are mainly dietary in that Muslims are forbidden by their religion to consume pork in any form. While the Muslims are not required to eat pork as such, a good deal of the food served at both institutions is cooked in pork grease or fat, and the Muslims cannot always tell what dishes they can eat on a given day without offending the dietary requirements of their faith. The Court also finds that there are some restrictions on the number and places of Muslim meetings which do not exist with respect to other religious groups who are represented in the prison population. And the Court also finds that Muslims are not permitted to use the Christian chapel at Tucker, and that, at least at Tucker, Muslim meetings must be attended by the prison chaplain who is a black man but who is also a Christian. The Court still further finds that for a time at least lists of inmates who attended Muslim meetings were kept and turned over to the Federal Bureau of Investigation.[4]

The Court does not find that the prison administration has intentionally discriminated against Muslims as such. For example, denial to the Muslims of the use of the chapel at Tucker is attempted to be justified by reference to

4. The Court doubts that such lists are now being kept in view of the fact that according to the media the Washington headquarters of the F.B.I. denied following the Court's November 1972 hearings that it was Bureau policy to require the keeping and delivery of such lists.

the small number of Muslims at Tucker and to security problems in connection with guarding a small number of people meeting in a building that is outside the main prison compound. It appears to the Court that some of the difficulties of the Muslims are due to the fact that the prison authorities are simply not familiar with Muslim problems, and that the administration is prepared to meet reasonable Muslim requests for consideration.

The Court is going to enjoin in general terms discrimination against the undue restrictions upon the Muslims. The Court will say, however, that the Court doubts that as of today the Muslims as a class have any real problems that cannot be disposed of administratively. And the Court will observe in this connection that since the hearings were concluded in January of this year it has received no more than a very few Muslim complaints emanating from either Cummins or Tucker except a number that have come from Negro inmates of the maximum security unit at Cummins who are or claim to be Muslims, and whose complaints about religious discrimination the Court considers to be baseless.

(b) In years prior to 1967 the population of both Cummins and Tucker was strictly segregated from top to bottom on the basis of race. By 1970 when *Holt II* was decided, segregation had been essentially eliminated at Tucker but still existed in large measure at Cummins. The Court discussed the problem in some detail in *Holt II*, and ordered it eliminated to the extent that it still existed in that institution.

The Court finds that as of now the populations of both institutions are fully desegregated, except that inmates of the maximum security unit at Cummins are still assigned to racially segregated cells. Desegregation of the barracks has been accomplished without the creation of any problems in the areas of security and discipline, and the Court cannot accept the argument put forward by respondents that members of both races cannot dwell peaceably together in the cells in the maximum security unit. And it should be pointed out in this connection that not all of the inmates of the unit have been put there for disciplinary reasons.

This is not to say, of course, that there may not be some inmates, whether white or black, who cannot safely be confined in a cell with a member or members of the other race. In such cases the Constitution does not require assignment to integrated cells. Lee v. Washington, 1968, 390 U.S. 333, 334. But the existing general policy of racial segregation in the maximum security cells cannot be approved and must be brought to an end.

Respondents will be directed forthwith to consider the situations of all inmates now in the unit and determine on an individual basis which of those inmates, if any, cannot safely be put in a cell with a member of the other race. The rest of the inmates presently confined in the unit are to be assigned to cells on a nonracial basis.

No present or future inmate of the unit is to be assigned to a cell on the basis of race unless the Superintendent of the institution personally finds in writing and with a statement of supporting reasons that the inmate in question should not be confined in an integrated cell; such finding is to be made a part of the inmate's prison record.

(c) Passing on to the more general problem of racial discrimination in such fields as inmate classifications, job assignments, personal appearance, privileges, and prison discipline, the Court will say first that the prison rules and regulations do not authorize racial discrimination against inmates and, in fact, prohibit it in the field of language used in addressing inmates. On the other hand, the Employee Handbook (Defendants' Exhibit 4031) which is issued to all employees of the Department and which spells out the Department's rules and regulations as to employee conduct, does not in terms prohibit racial discrimination in the areas now being discussed. Perhaps the author or authors of the Handbook did not consider such prohibition to be necessary.

Actually, however, it makes no real difference what the Handbook says or does not say. Racial discrimination between convicts in any form which it may take is unconstitutional and must be eliminated to the extent that it exists.

Racial discrimination can be overt and ingenuous, and that type of discrimination is easy to detect and ought to be easy to eradicate. On the other hand, such discrimination may be covert, subtle, or even unconscious. That kind of discrimination is extremely hard to establish and may be extremely hard to get rid of. The problem is complicated by the fact that the appearance of racial discrimination may be present even if the reality is not, and until such appearance is eliminated to the greatest extent possible, race relations in a prison will not be good.

As has been seen, the proportions of blacks and whites in both institutions are just about equal. It must be recognized, however, that the general educational, vocational, and cultural levels of the black inmates as a class are substantially lower than the corresponding levels of the white inmates. And it is possible that black inmates confined in an integrated institution which is administered by white personnel may create administrative problems disproportionate to their numbers.

The Court does not find from the evidence that any open or gross discrimination against black inmates exists at either Cummins or Tucker, except to the extent that the maximum security cells are still segregated. But the Court is not at all sure that there is not some covert discrimination in the areas of classifications, job assignments, and punishments.

With particular regard to punishments, the Court does not have before it a substantial body of statistical material relating to Tucker, but it does have monthly operating reports from Cummins covering the months of June through November, 1972, and the last of those reports (Defendants' Exhibit 3018) also contains information covering the first eleven months of that year.

A consideration of those reports leads the Court to conclude that a black inmate accused of a disciplinary violation is as likely to be found not guilty or to receive a mild sentence as is a white inmate. But when we come to severe penalties, such as reductions in classification, adverse changes in job assignments, loss of good time, and confinement in punitive isolation, the Court is impelled to the view that a black inmate is more likely than a white inmate to be subjected to such penalties, and if he is sentenced to punitive isolation, he is likely to stay there longer than is a white inmate.

That black inmates may receive more severe sentences than white inmates does not necessarily justify the inference that white members of Disciplinary Committees are intentionally discriminating against blacks in the area of prison discipline. As has been suggested, black inmates in the environment of Cummins and Tucker may as a class present more serious disciplinary problems than do whites as a class and may deserve more severe penalties, although the Court does not so find. Moreover, in view of long held and deep seated racial attitudes, words or acts, if said or done by blacks, may be simply more offensive to some white members of disciplinary panels than are similar words or acts of white convicts. And white prison administrators sitting in judgment on black inmates actually may not consciously be aware that their reactions to rule violations by blacks, as opposed to whites, may constitute a form of discrimination against the former.

Looking at the question of job assignments, there are two things that must be recognized. First, it is probably safe to say that the majority of black inmates at both institutions are not qualified to do anything but work involving more or less arduous physical labor. Second, from an inmate's standpoint a comparatively low status job may be easier than a job of higher status or may have some fringe benefits not attached to a more highly rated job and thus more desirable than some other task which the inmate might be capable of performing.

When those things are borne in mind, the Court cannot find that blacks, as a class, are intentionally assigned to menial or disagreeable jobs while whites are intentionally assigned to "better" jobs. And if one looks at what is probably the lowest prison job, namely, manual agricultural labor as a member of a "hoe squad," the Court concludes that about as many white inmates as blacks are assigned to such jobs.

On the other hand, the Court is not persuaded that the white members of Classification Committees are doing as much as they could and should to classify inmates and to assign them to work on the basis of qualifications. It would appear to the Court that Negroes should occupy some job slots that they are not now occupying, and that certain categories of jobs should have more than their present number of black assignees.

Apparent racial inequities in punishments, job assignments, and other aspects of prison life relate not only to the actual existence of racial discrimination but also to the appearance of such discrimination. And it should be obvious that apart from any question of constitutional law black inmates will make a better adjustment to prison life and will conform better to prison routine and requirements if they believe affirmatively that members of their race are being treated fairly and without discrimination on account of race.

The Court's previous decrees will be supplemented so as to enjoin racial discrimination in any form and in all areas of prison life. However, the Court is not willing to leave this subject without some suggestions to respondents as to what can and should be done to alleviate the racial situation in the Department.

To start with, existing prison rules about employee language should be enforced rigorously and higher echelon personnel should set an example to their subordinates.

Second, positive rules prohibiting racial discrimination should be formulated and published. Employees at all levels must be made familiar with those rules, and must be made to realize that if they want to keep their jobs, they must abide by the rules.

Third, and this is extremely important, more black employees should be recruited, and blacks should be assigned to meaningful positions of authority, including assignments to Classification and Disciplinary Committees.

Not any of those things will be easy to accomplish, and the accomplishment of the third one may be the most difficult of all. The Court realizes that qualified blacks who are willing to fill positions of responsibility and authority in prison administration may be in short supply. Other more appealing positions are open to them in today's society. But, the difficulty of hiring qualified blacks should certainly not deter respondents from trying to do so.

The Court considers next the question of the constitutional acceptability of the disciplinary procedures employed in the Department with respect to inmates who violate prison rules, or who refuse to work, or who loiter at their tasks. . . .

All inmates upon entering the Department are exposed to a period of "orientation," and are furnished with an Inmate Handbook. A copy of that Handbook, revised to November 1, 1972, is in the record as Defendants' Exhibit No. 4023.[6]

The Handbook, among other things, advises the inmate of the types of conduct that may bring on disciplinary proceedings against him, the punishments that may be imposed, and disciplinary procedures that are to be followed if charges are filed. There are 25 listed offenses and 11 possible punishments which may be imposed singly or in combination.

Some of the sentences are relatively mild; others are quite severe. The severe penalties include loss of good time, reduction in classifications, extra duty, job changes, and confinement in punitive isolation. Another severe penalty is a postponement of an inmate's appearance before the Board of Pardons and Paroles for a period of not less than three nor more than six months.

Each of the two units of the Department has a Disciplinary Committee . . . . The Assistant Superintendent of the institution is Chairman of the Committee, and the Chief Security Officer of the institution is the Vice Chairman. A Shift Supervisor, Security, serves as one ordinary member, and a member of the treatment staff of the institution serves as the other ordinary member.

The rules provide that an inmate charged with a violation is to be brought before the Committee and is to be afforded an opportunity to give his version of the episode leading up to the charge. Other witnesses may be called in the discretion of the Committee. The inmate is not entitled to representation at the hearing, and he is not in terms accorded any right of confrontation or any right to call witnesses to testify in his own behalf.

6. Such a handbook may be of little or no value to an illiterate inmate or to one with a limited ability to read.

After the Committee concludes a day's work, it reports its actions to the Superintendent for approval. If the Superintendent notes his approval, the report is forwarded to the Commissioner. While the Superintendent is required to approve the actions of the Committee, it does not appear to the Court that he is required to review specific actions taken by the Committee, although the Court is sure that he does so in some instances.

An inmate who is dissatisfied with a decision of the Committee may appeal in writing to the Superintendent and from him to the Commissioner. It is provided, however, that if the inmate wilfully and knowingly makes false statements in connection with an appeal, or wilfully tries to mislead or deceive the Superintendent or the Commissioner, his action in itself constitutes a major disciplinary offense.

The proceedings of the Committee in a given case are reflected in a document entitled "Disciplinary Report." The Court has seen quite a number of those reports which are made on mimeographed forms. The forms identify the accused inmate, identify the offense and the employee filing the charge. There is a space entitled "Offense in Detail." That space is filled out by the charging employee and signed by him. Next comes a much narrower space entitled "Statement of Inmate to Committee." It is not clear whether the inmate is permitted to fill this space out himself; more probably, the substance of his statement, if any, is written down by a committee member; the inmate may or may not sign the statement. It appears that an inmate is required to plead either "Guilty" or "Not Guilty" to the charge. The report notes the inmate's attitude as being either cooperative, uncooperative, or hostile. The members of the Committee are then identified. The decision of the Committee and the sentence imposed are shown on the report, and the document is signed by the Chairman and by the Superintendent.

As the Court of Appeals for this Circuit has recently pointed out, the law as to what procedural due process requires with respect to a prison inmate charged with a violation of prison rules is in a state of flux. . . . It is clear that such an inmate is not entitled to a full fledged judicial trial or to all of the guarantees and protections afforded by the Fourteenth Amendment to a person charged in court with a criminal offense. On the other hand, he is entitled to be advised of the charge against him, and to be heard, and to have his case considered seriously, dispassionately, and objectively, although he naturally cannot expect an "impartial" fact finding body in the sense that a criminal defendant is entitled to an "impartial" jury.

The Department's procedures themselves are probably not ideal, and the Court is troubled by the fact that the Committees seem to be rather heavily weighted in favor of what may be termed the "prosecution." It should be observed, however, that substantial numbers of inmates are acquitted or receive mild punishments, and that probably the vast majority of inmates accused of disciplinary violations are guilty, just as the majority of persons accused of crime in the outside world are guilty.

The Court thinks that the procedures in question would pass constitutional muster if they were properly administered, and if the Committees were willing to spend some time on individual cases and to make considered, rather than perfunctory, determinations of guilt or innocence, would make clear to the accused what the charges against him are, and what his rights are, and what the consequences of conviction may be, and would adopt an attitude that would encourage an accused inmate to state his side of the case, if he has one.

Unfortunately, the procedures are not so administered. On the contrary, in a given case the Committee tends to act summarily and in a very short space of time, and it may display an attitude of hostility toward the inmate calculated to intimidate him and suppress his version of the incident involved.

The Court is under the impression that disciplinary hearings frequently are held at night, and if the Court is correct in that impression, the night sessions may be part of the trouble with the administration of the procedures. Some or perhaps all of the members of the disciplinary panel probably have been working all day, and they want to go home. That is understandable, but it does not contribute to the proper administration of prison justice.

The Court is going to issue three directives in this area: (1) The rules provide that the Committees are to perform their functions "as quickly as possible." The Court is going to make that requirement more specific by requiring that in cases other than highly exceptional an accused inmate must be given a hearing within 72 hours after the occurrence of the disciplinary episode. In exceptional cases limited extensions of time may be granted by the respective Superintendents. (2) Insofar as possible hearings are to be conducted between the hours of 6 A.M. and 6 P.M. It occurs to the Court that this will not only improve administration of the procedures but may also suggest to respondents that the Committees be restructured so as to include more noncustodial personnel who may be available during ordinary business hours but not at night. (3) All hearings must be reported in such manner that if the occasion arises a reviewing authority, including a court, may determine exactly how much time was taken at the hearing and essentially what was said and done by the individuals involved. This means, of course, that the tapes or transcripts of the hearings must be preserved for at least a reasonable time after the hearings take place.

With regard to the reporting of disciplinary proceedings the Court is advised that as of the present time disciplinary proceedings are being taped, and that tape recordings are also being made of certain types of interviews of prison officials with inmates. Assuming of course that the recordings are complete and accurate, the practice should be of value in dealing with inmate complaints about disciplinary proceedings and certain other types of inmate complaints.

As mentioned, one of the punishments that may be imposed on an inmate is confinement in isolation. At Tucker that confinement is in individual cells that were used for years for the confinement of persons convicted of capital offenses and condemned to die. At Cummins the confinement is in cells in the maximum security unit. The Court finds that the cells are not overcrowded, that they are properly lighted and ventilated, and that confinement in them does not constitute any violation of the Eighth Amendment's prohibition of cruel and unusual punishments. As in years past, convicts confined in isolation have a restricted diet consisting of a food substance known as "grue," which is nourishing but tasteless; however, a convict confined in isolation receives a regular meal every third day. In earlier stages of the litigation the Court concluded that "grue" is not unconstitutional, and it adheres to that view.

Before leaving this phase of the case, the Court desires to comment briefly on conditions of confinement in the maximum security unit in general. An inmate is placed in the unit either as a disciplinary measure, or for his own protection, or for purposes of "administrative segregation." While it appears to the Court that some of the conditions of confinement in the unit are perhaps somewhat more rigorous than may be absolutely necessary, the Court does not find that those conditions are such as to render confinement in the unit unconstitutional.

A word needs to be said about the "quiet" cells in the maximum security unit. Those cells which are soundproof are located in the middle of the building; each one of them has a double door; when the outer door is closed, the inmate is in complete darkness. The cells are essentially devoid of furniture and fixtures; bedding is not supplied. As the Court recalls, there was a somewhat excessive use of the quiet cells soon after the maximum security unit was activated, but the Court finds that as of now the cells are not used excessively or in an inhumane manner. Use of the cells is limited to violent inmates who cannot be controlled in any other manner, and usually an inmate's stay in a quiet cell is quite brief. Further, it is not uncommon for an inmate to be placed in a quiet cell without being placed in darkness; the outer door of the cell is simply left open.

One problem in the field of disciplinary procedures that calls for comment arises out of the fact that at times it is necessary for purposes of discipline and good order to transfer young inmates from Tucker to Cummins, and at times emergency situations arise in which it appears necessary to the authorities at Tucker to move a young inmate or young inmates immediately. The Court has no trouble with such transfers, including emergency transfers, because the Court knows that young convicts can and frequently do present serious disciplinary and other problems and at times are more violent and irresponsible than older convicts. What does trouble the Court is what happens to a young inmate after he goes to Cummins.

Evidence taken in November of last year described an illustrative case. In early 1972 authorities at Tucker had cause to believe that a number of youths confined there were planning to incite a riot or promote a sit down strike. This information was obtained during the late afternoon or night of a particular day, and the riot or sit down strike was supposed to take place the next morning. The young men were summarily moved in the night time from the one institution to the other, and at the time of the November hearing one of them was still there.

There are educational and vocational facilities at Tucker that are not available at Cummins, and many of the inmates of Cummins are hardened criminals with whom a youth of comparatively tender years should not be confined any longer than reasonably necessary. As has been pointed out, there is as yet no minimum security unit at Cummins, and young convicts sent down from Tucker have to be confined either in the maximum security unit or in the barracks among the general prison population. Confinement in neither place is desirable for a young convict, and it is hard to tell which is worse.

The Court finds that prior to the November hearing there was no set policy with respect to getting young transferees back to the milder regime at Tucker, and that nobody seemed to care particularly whether or when a young transferee was retransferred. That situation gave the Court a serious problem, particularly in view of the contention of counsel that a young Arkansas convict has a constitutional right not to be unreasonably deprived of opportunities for improvement that exist at Tucker.

Following the November hearings Commissioner Hutto issued a Policy Memorandum which addressed itself to the problem. The Memorandum provides in substance that in other than emergency situations inmates are not to be transferred from Tucker to Cummins without a hearing before the Tucker Disciplinary Committee or the Tucker Classification Committee, or both, and that after prisoners reach Cummins their cases are to be evaluated every 90 days by the Cummins Classification Committee with the end in view of getting them back to Tucker as soon as possible. If a Tucker inmate is transferred in an emergency situation, he is entitled to a hearing before the Cummins Classification Committee within 72 hours of his arrival at Cummins. All transfer and retransfer decisions may be appealed to the Commissioner by the affected inmates.

Subject to one qualification the Court finds that the Commissioner's Memorandum appears to solve the problem satisfactorily. The Court does not think the Cummins Classification Committee should wait 90 days before reviewing the case of a transferee because it may not take the transferee 90 days to realize the error of his ways and to become ready to behave himself if sent back to Tucker. The Court thinks that the first evaluation should be not later than two weeks after the transferee arrives at Cummins, and that a second evaluation should not be later than 30 days after the first one. If by that time the transferee is not ready to go back to Tucker, the Court thinks that later evaluations at 90 day intervals are adequate.

The Commissioner will be directed to amend his Memorandum accordingly. Of course, it goes without saying that authorities at Cummins will take proper precautions for the safety of young transferees while they are confined at Cummins.

Before discussing claims of abuse of inmates, the Court will take up the question of the validity of institutional rules governing inmate correspondence, a question that actually is of interest to only a small number of inmates who desire to engage in correspondence of which the Department disapproves.

As the Court understands the state of the law in this field today, a prison inmate has a practically unrestricted right to correspond privately with courts and with his attorney. His right to correspond generally with people in the outside world is by no means so unfettered; that right is subject to reasonable regulation and restriction. However, the right of prison authorities to control and regulate inmate correspondence of a general type is not as broad as it was considered to be in prior years. Today, prison restrictions on inmate correspondence must be related to a legitimate institutional interest, and at times the validity of a given restriction must be determined by balancing the interest of the institution in maintaining it against the interest of the inmate in being free from it. . . .

Under the rules of the Department appearing at Pages 42–44 of the Inmate Handbook as supplemented by a later Policy Memorandum, inmate correspondence is divided into three classes, privileged, general, and special purpose. The principal complaints in this area go to the rules relating to general correspondence. No attack is made on the rules relating to special purpose correspondence, and the attack on the privileged correspondence rules is limited.

Taking up, first, the attack on the privileged correspondence rules the Court finds that all outgoing inmate mail to judges, court officials, lawyers, and certain other categories of addressees can be sent out of the institutions sealed; such letters are not opened, inspected, or read. Incoming privileged correspondence, with certain limited exceptions, incuding letters from the federal courts, is subject to being opened and inspected for contraband, principally money that an attorney, unfamiliar with prison rules, might undertake to send to his client.

The specific complaint about privileged correspondence with which the court is concerned is that, as just stated, incoming letters from lawyers may be opened. The Court does not consider that any lawyers of common sense would put anything in a letter to a convict client that the lawyer did not want to be read by prison authorities, but the Court can easily see how a lawyer might mail his client a check, money order, or currency. It has long been prison policy to prohibit inmates from having in their possession what is called "free world" or "green" money. The reasons for the prohibition are obvious. An inmate with currency in his possession may be the subject of attack by other inmates; an inmate with funds is in a better position after escape than an inmate who has no money; the money in the possession of an inmate may be used to bribe guards or other prison employees.

The Court thinks that the rule in question is a reasonable one, and with one modification the Court approves it. The modification is that if prison authorities desire to open and inspect the contents of a letter to an inmate from a lawyer, they should do so in the presence of the inmate so that he will know that the letter has not been read. Compliance with this requirement should not be unduly burdensome.

The Court finds it unnecessary to describe all of the Department's rules dealing with general correspondence. They are doubtless stricter than those that prevail in some jurisdictions and doubtless more liberal than those that prevail in others. In general, they closely track the recommendations of the Association of State Correctional Administrators which appear in a bulletin or handbook entitled "Uniform Correctional Policies & Procedures." The Court observes that Commissioner Hutto is a member of that Association.

Two provisions of the general correspondence rules are attacked here: First, complaint is made that outgoing correspondence may be opened, inspected, and in instances read. Second, complaint is made about general correspondence being limited to persons whose names appear on individual mailing lists which are subject to the approval of the Department.

As to outgoing correspondence, respondents concede that there is no real reason to examine such correspondence for contraband. The Department's trouble with contraband relates to that which comes into the prison rather than to the possibility that inmates will smuggle something out. Thus, the rule cannot be justified on that basis.

However, if an inmate is permitted to send out sealed and unexamined general correspondence, there is always the possibility that he will take advantage of the opportunity to plot an escape or to counsel with the addressee about outside criminal conduct. It is evident that respondents do not claim any right to read all outgoing correspondence, and the Court is sure that the mail room personnel do not do so. The Court doubts that they even examine a great many of the outgoing letters. The Department does reserve the right to read letters in instances where there is reason to believe that a letter may constitute a "clear and present danger" to the security of the institution.

The Court finds that the rule permitting the examination and limited reading of outgoing general correspondence is reasonable and not unconstitutional.

The attack on the mailing list requirement has three aspects. First, it is contended that respondents have no constitutional right to limit the general correspondence of an inmate to persons approved by the Department and whose names appear on the inmate's mailing list. Second, complaint is made that before approving persons for inclusion on a mailing list, the Department sends a questionnaire to the prospective correspondent and also makes certain limited inquiries of local law enforcement officers as to the proposed correspondent's criminal record and connection with drugs. One reason for such inquiries would appear to be that persons on an inmate's mailing list are likely to desire to visit him at the prison from time to time in accordance with prison rules governing visitation. Third, an adult person will not be included on an inmate's list without the consent of the proposed correspondent, and in the case of a proposed correspondent under the age of 18 the consent of a parent or guardian must be given; and it is claimed that this provision is unconstitutional.

As to the first and second claims, the Court notes to begin with that there is no limit to the number of names that an inmate may include on his list, that his list may be changed from time to time, that correspondence between the sexes is permitted, and that the fact that a proposed correspondent has a criminal record does not in and of itself make that person ineligible for inclusion on the list. In general, inmates are permitted to correspond with their close relatives and with anyone else with whom they may have legitimate business.

The Court rejects the claim that respondents may not constitutionally limit the correspondence of an inmate to persons the inclusion of whose names on the inmate's list has been approved by the Department. And the Court thinks that if approval is to be given or withheld intelligently, the Department has a right to find out something about the people with whom the inmate desires to correspond. The Court does not consider that the questionnaires and inquiries addressed to law enforcement officers are designed or calculated to inhibit seriously correspondence with free world people with whom an inmate has a legitimate reason to correspond.

The Court suspects that a good deal of the dissatisfaction in this area stems from the fact that some inmates do not understand the mailing list requirement, and do not understand that adding names to the list or making changes in the list may take some time. Like many people in the free world, inmates tend to want instantaneous gratification of their wants and tend to complain when they do not receive it.

So, the first two attacks on the mailing list requirement are rejected. The third ground of attack is more troublesome, as far as adults who are prospective correspondents are concerned. The Court has no trouble with the requirement that the parent or guardian of a young person give his approval before that person's name is included on the list.

As to adults, the case is somewhat different. The requirement that an adult give his consent to be included on an inmate's mailing list is obviously designed to protect the former from unwanted mail communications. There are many reasons why a person in the outside world may not want to receive letters from a convict, even though he may be a close relative, spouse, or former spouse. Such a person may welcome a prison rule or policy which will insulate him or her from such correspondence. And the willingness of prison administrators to provide such insulation in the interest of public relations or for other reasons is understandable.

The problem of unwanted correspondence, of course, is not limited to situations in which the mailer of the letters is confined in prison. Whether the mailer is inside or outside of a penal institution, a person who does not want to read his letters need not do so. Letters can be thrown away unread or returned unopened.

The Court observes that the publication "Uniform Correctional Policies & Procedures," which has been mentioned, recognizes the propriety of requiring approved mailing lists, and the propriety of limiting an inmate's correspondence with a juvenile to cases in which the consent of the juvenile's parent or guardian is forthcoming. The publication says nothing about any requirement that an adult give his permission before having his name included on an inmate's list.

The Court is of the view that the requirement just discussed is really not necessary and might be dispensed with readily, but the Court does not think that it presents a problem of constitutional dimension and is not prepared to strike it down.

Before leaving this particular aspect of the case the Court would emphasize that prison mail room employees ought to understand the rules thoroughly themselves and faithfully follow them, and that they should realize that many inmates of both Cummins and Tucker are not highly literate or intelligent people, and where necessary the employees should spend a little time with inmates having correspondence problems and explain to them in terms that they can understand just what they can do and what they cannot do, and the procedures to be followed in getting a name on a mailing list or in making changes in a list.

Much of the testimony that the Court heard related to claims of petitioners that they are habitually harassed, retaliated against, and physically and verbally abused by prison personnel. Such claims would be significant if made in connection with any prison, but they are particularly significant here in view of the long history of brutality to inmates of both Cummins and

Tucker that was practiced for so many years and that has been described in detail in earlier opinions of this Court and of the Court of Appeals.

The Court finds, first, that it is not the policy of the Department to abuse inmates in any way or to treat them brutally or abusively. The rules of the Department appropriately limit the use of force on inmates to situations in which the use of force is both legitimate and necessary and specify that the force used must not in any event exceed the reasonable necessities of a particular case. The rules also prohibit the use by employees of vulgar, profane, or insulting language to inmates. And the Court thinks that it is safe to say that if an inmate, whether white or black, of either institution behaves himself and does the work assigned to him to the best of his ability, he will be able to do his time without serious difficulties as far as prison personnel are concerned.

However, the prison staff is required to deal constitutionally not only with tractable inmates but also with inmates who are not so tractable, and there are many inmates who fall within the latter category. Those inmates make a great deal of trouble for themselves. While they are quick to assert what they consider to be their rights, they have little regard for their obligations as inmates. They refuse to obey orders, they loiter at their tasks or positively refuse to work; they fight with each other; and they curse and abuse and sometimes assault or fight with their keepers. Indeed, some inmates appear at times to deliberately engage in conduct which they know will result in the use of force upon them.

In view of such inmate conduct, it is not strange that the relations between prison personnel, on the one hand, and certain inmates, particularly those in the maximum security unit, are bad, to put it conservatively. As indicated, much and perhaps most of the blame for such relations should be laid at the door of the inmates, but at times unprofessional reaction of prison employees to situations of stress is at least a contributing factor. In this overall problem area, as in other areas of prison life, the ultimate answer may lie more in the upgrading of prison personnel than in anything else.

At one time or another inmates of the respective units have charged those in authority over them with every kind of abuse that the inmate mind can imagine. No effort will be made to list, let alone discuss, all of the charges. The Court will confine itself to the principal ones and will start with complaints about working conditions.

While the Court finds that many of the inmates, particularly those assigned to the "hoe squads," are required to work long hours and to work hard, the Court does not find that prison working conditions are so harsh or adverse as to constitute cruel and unusual punishment. Now, the Court does have some trouble with the possibility that at times inmates may be assigned to work that is beyond their strength, or that is medically contraindicated, and that older inmates may be required to try to keep up with younger inmates which they sometimes cannot do. However, the Court does not find that those things are done deliberately or wilfully, and the Court thinks that to the extent that they are done they symptomize simply poor communication and administration. It has been pointed out that the Department has now been able to employ a full time physician who will doubtless evaluate inmates with respect to the types of work that they are able to do, and the Classification Committees and supervisory employees will be expected to pay heed to what the doctor orders or recommends.

With further regard to working conditions, it has been alleged that inmates are forced at times to run to and from work or while at work, or that one crew has been required to race with another crew in the performance of the same type of work. The Court does not find that such practices have ever been employed generally, but the evidence in the overall litigation has reflected that there have been instances in which inmates have been required to run in front of moving vehicles or ridden horses. It is hardly necessary for the Court to say that such practices cannot be tolerated, and it is the responsibility of respondents to prevent them.

The Court takes up next the claim of inmates that prison personnel at all levels employ toward inmates profane, threatening, abusive, and vulgar language which is replete with racial slurs and epithets and sexual and scatological terms. As indicated, prison rules specifically prohibit the use of language of that kind.

The Court is sure that the inmates of both institutions in their own speech use language of the types of which they now complain, and in view of the quality of prison personnel that we have in the Department at this time, the Court knows as a matter of common sense that at least some employees on occasion do use profane or "gutter" language when addressing inmates, and that the objectionable language may include offensive racial and other allusions.

The Court doubts that prison employees use language of the types in question to the extent that such use, standing alone, would present a substantial constitutional problem, but its use, to the extent that it is in fact employed, can contribute to problems that do have constitutional significance. In any event, the use of objectionable language by members of the prison staff, of whatever rank, is completely unnecessary, is unprofessional, and can cause serious trouble. The Court is going to expect higher echelon personnel to set an example for their subordinates in this field, and to enforce the institutional rules that have been mentioned.

Before leaving this subject the Court notes with approval that the prison rules not only prohibit profane and similar language but also admonish employees not to be overly familiar with inmates and that undue familiarity "decreases the effectiveness of an employee as well as sometimes placing the employee in a compromising position." Those admonitions are salutary indeed and should be observed. The Court suspects that many complaints of inmates about language are afterthoughts, and that some of the words involved may have been used, if at all, in jest or flippantly and without realization that they might give offense. Employees of the Department today simply cannot afford to joke or jest coarsely with inmates, particularly black inmates who, whether rightly or wrongly, are obviously "up tight" and prone to take offense.

The Court's Supplemental Decree herein specifically enjoins prison personnel from retaliating against or threatening to retaliate against any inmate for having petitioned for judicial relief or for having testified or for having offered to testify in any judicial proceeding. Despite inmate claims, the Court is not able to find from a preponderance of the evidence that there has been any substantial amount of retaliation or threatened retaliation, and, on the other hand, the Court suspects that some writ writers, witnesses, and potential witnesses have been permitted to take liberties that they otherwise would not have been allowed to take because prison personnel have feared being charged with retaliation. However, in the course of this litigation the Court has seen some indications that in instances some reprisals have been taken against inmates who have testified in this Court. There have been some job changes and disciplinary proceedings that have followed with suspicious closeness the appearances in court of certain inmate witnesses.

The Court's injunction in this area is as specific as it can be made, and further discussion of the subject in this opinion would not be profitable. If a serious question of retaliation arises in the future, it may well be considered in the context of a contempt proceeding.

This brings us at length to inmate claims that they are subjected to unnecessary and unreasonable force. Respondents naturally deny that that claim has any basis, and point out the fact that in instances where employees have been found to have used unnecessary or excessive force they have been discharged or otherwise disciplined.

The Court recognizes at the outset that at times force has to be used by prison personnel on recalcitrant inmates, and that an inmate who has been the subject of force is not likely to concede that its use was necessary or that the amount used was reasonable. The Court also recognizes that an employee charged with improper use of force is not to be judged by hindsight but in the light of facts and circumstances as they reasonably appeared to him to exist at the time.

Force is used from time to time at both Cummins and Tucker, as it is in prisons all over the United States. It is properly employed in self defense, in breaking up fights between inmates, in compelling obedience to lawful orders where milder measures fail, in protecting State property, and in connection with preventing escapes and at times in connection with recapturing escaped convicts.

The force employed by Department personnel is largely simply manual force, but at times striking weapons such as "slappers" must be used. At other times subduing chemicals such as "mace" may be employed. Occasionally, firearms have to be used to break up fights, or to prevent escapes, or in connection with the recapture of escaped inmates. Generally speaking, the use of firearms involves nothing more than the firing of warning shots to induce inmates to stop fighting or to stop trying to run away.

The majority of incidents involving use of force take place in the maximum security unit at Cummins, as might be expected. However, incidents occur in the barracks in both institutions, and in the fields, and in other prison areas. But such incidents do not occur every day or with great frequency. A number of the incidents occurring in the maximum security unit have involved extremely violent and unstable inmates, and some inmates are involved repeatedly in such incidents.

As far as incidents of force in the maximum security unit, the barracks, and the fields are concerned, the Court simply does not find that the problem is as serious as the inmates would make it. While the Court suspects that some of such incidents were unnecessary, and that employees may have over reacted in certain situations, the Court finds that by and large the inmates who have been subjected to force have brought it on themselves, and that in general the degree of force used has been in reasonable proportion to the violence displayed by the inmates involved.

The Court does find that there have been instances in which unnecessary and unreasonable force has been used on escapees after their recapture and after they ceased to be a source of any real danger to their captors. And Superintendent Britton was involved personally in two of such incidents.

The Court realizes that escapes and recaptures can be and frequently are irritating and exasperating to prison administrators and lesser personnel, particularly where as occasionally happens the escape involves a breach of trust reposed in an inmate, as where he does not return to the prison at the expiration of a furlough. And the Court realizes that at times inmates resist recapture and have to be subdued forcibly. But, people who are engaged in custodial work must learn to take such episodes in stride and must learn to control themselves. And there is simply no excuse for hitting, slapping, or kicking an escapee after he has been recaptured and reduced to subjection.

The record reflects that after the November 1972 hearings were concluded, the Commissioner issued a Policy Memorandum dealing with procedures to be followed after an escapee has been recaptured. Those procedures are designed to determine whether the inmate was injured in connection with his recapture and whether improper use of force was made in connection with the recapture. Hopefully, that Memorandum will be of value in solving problems arising out of escapes.

The Court has considered the body of evidence dealing with the use of force, and does not consider that it calls for any drastic action at this moment, although the Court is going to make its injunction somewhat more specific than it is in defining what the Court will consider to amount to a cruel and unusual punishment.

There is one thing that the Court is going to suggest strongly that Mr. Lockhart and Mr. Britton do in connection with incidents of force. If such an incident results in a disciplinary proceeding against the inmate, as many of such incidents do, there is an opportunity in the course of the proceedings to develop the facts of the incident more or less contemporaneously. But all incidents of force do not result in disciplinary proceedings, or at least the Court is of that impression. The Court thinks that it would be highly desirable for such incidents to be investigated at once, and that the investigations should include the development, where possible, of the inmate's version of the event. Many of the complaints that the Court receives about violence practiced upon inmates have been prepared by writ writers and signed by the complaining inmates. What a writ writer puts into his writ may be nothing in the world but the product of his own imagination, and the allegations of the writ may have little or no resemblance to what the complainant actually recalls about the incident or to what he would have said about it if interviewed at the time. The value of the Court's suggestion to prison personnel ought to be apparent to them without further elaboration.

Another supplemental decree in accordance with the foregoing will be entered, and respondents and all Department personnel from the highest in rank to the lowest will be expected to comply with it and with the earlier decrees that have been entered in this litigation.

However, in view of the marked improvements that have been made in the Department and that are continuing to be made the Court does not consider it either necessary or desirable to retain further supervisory jurisdiction with respect to the Department and such jurisdiction will not be retained. Let the Court hasten to add that this release of jurisdiction will not impair the validity and continuing effect of its injunctions, and if those injunctions are violated, those guilty may be faced with contempt proceedings either civil or criminal.

The Court hopes that this will be the last long opinion dealing with the Department that the Court will be called upon to write. But the Court knows that regardless of what has been said here, and regardless of what its decrees may forbid, or command, and regardless of how diligently respondents may seek to obey the orders of the Court or to follow the Court's suggestions, inmate complaints are going to continue to be received by the Court.

Judging from experience, many, if not most, of those complaints will be insubstantial from a constitutional standpoint, and can be ignored or disposed of summarily. Some can be handled administratively, as a number have been over the past year; and the Court will say at this point that it would be most desirable if the Board and the Commissioner could work out a grievance procedure that will be effective and readily available to inmates who have or think they have legitimate grievances. Should such a procedure be evolved, the Court might well be inclined, to the extent legally open to it, to refuse to consider inmate complaints until that procedure has been exhausted.

But, there will be complaints that cannot be brushed aside and that cannot be mediated. Those complaints will require formal judicial determinations. Some, if found meritorious, may call for further injunctive orders; in connection with others the Court may find it necessary or desirable to impose sanctions for violations of existing decrees.

The Court does not now foresee that circumstances will arise which would require the Court to impose the ultimate sanction available to it, that of closing one or both of the prisons or enjoining the further reception of inmates at one or both institutions. Less rigorous, but effective, sanctions are available. The Court can direct the discharge of offending employees; the Court can punish for contempt, and it can award attorney's fees and expenses of litigation. So far, the Court has avoided the imposition of sanctions and hopes that it will not have to impose any in the future; but, the sanctions are at hand, if needed.

Finally, there remain to be considered the question of the allowance of a fee to counsel for respondents and the form of the supplemental decree to be entered pursuant to this opinion.

Messrs. Holt and Kaplan have requested that they be allowed a fee and that they be reimbursed for what they have paid to four law students for assistance in working up these cases. The Court thinks that their request should be granted not by way of punishment or sanction but in recognition of the fact that they have performed valuable services not only to the inmates and to the Court but to the people of the State of Arkansas as well. The Arkansas prison system belongs to the people of this State. They have an interest in their prisons being brought up to constitutional standards and properly administered; and they have an interest in full disclosures about their prisons and conditions and practices therein. Counsel for petitioners have certainly advanced those interests.

Considering the amount of time and effort that counsel have expended in this case, the Court thinks that they are entitled to substantial compensation, and that a fee of $8,000.00 should be awarded to them jointly; they can divide it between themselves in any manner they see fit. The amount paid to the law students totals $502.80, and reimbursement to counsel to that extent will be allowed. The members of the Board will be directed to make those payments out of available Department funds as soon as possible.

The decree to be entered will be entitled "Second Supplemental Decree." It will be self explanatory; in places it will refer to specific sections of this opinion. As in the case of earlier decrees, it will be applicable to all members of the Board of Correction, to the Commissioner, the Superintendents, the Assistant or Associate Superintendents, and to all subordinate employees of the Department.

As has been said, the Court does not find that individual petitioners are entitled to specific individual relief, but all inmates are entitled to the benefits of the decree. Since this is so, the Court is going to dismiss all of the individual cases except the anchor case of Holt v. Hutto, PB–69–C–24.

The decree to be entered will of course be appealable. Respondents may appeal, or the inmates as a class may appeal, or individual inmates may appeal from the decree to the extent that it dismisses their individual cases or fails to award them specific individual relief. The Court thinks it safe to assume that any inmates desiring to appeal will wish to do so in forma pauperis. Notices of appeal should be lodged with the Clerk of this Court not later than 30 days after the decree is filed, and the Court will not be inclined to allow belated appeals.

The Court now requests either Mr. Holt or Mr. Kaplan or both to visit the prisons as soon as possible after the decree is filed and discuss the matter of appeal with individual petitioners. If an individual petitioner wishes to appeal and wants the Court to make specific findings in his case, the Court will do so to the extent that it is able to do so from the record. The Court might point out, however, that not all of the individual petitioners were called as witnesses, and no specific testimony was taken with respect to certain individual cases.

---

1) Judge Henley is careful to define his task to insure that the administration of the prisons is brought up to constitutional standards. Does he observe this limitation on his power? Does he become involved with management? If you believe he exceeded the limits of his office, identify where this occurred and the dynamic that might have led a conscientious judge astray.

2) In *Holt III* Judge Henley issues what he terms a "Second Supplemental Decree." Would he have been entitled to use the contempt power for violations of the previous decrees? If so, why did he not do so? Remember his

discussion of the claim that racial discrimination has continued in the imposition of severe penalties. In his opinion, Judge Henley states that "previous decrees will be supplemented so as to enjoin racial discrimination in any form and in all areas of prison life"; then he goes on to make "some suggestions to respondents as to what can and should be done to alleviate the racial situation." Suppose respondents do not follow these particular "suggestions." Are they subject to contempt? At the end of his opinion, Judge Henley warns that next time sanctions might be imposed. Is this a credible threat? He also says that by way of sanction he can "order the discharge of offending employees." See Lance v. Plummer, p. 1018. Does he have that power? Does he have power to close the prisons? To prohibit the admission of new inmates? See Newman v. Alabama, 683 F.2d 1312 (11th Cir. 1982).

3) The Judge says that at this juncture the "main problem . . . lies in prison administration" and, more particularly, in the low quality of the lower echelon personnel. Assuming Judge Henley's diagnosis is correct, how does he address this problem? Could some provision be included in the decree to deal with this problem effectively? Judge Henley says that the Second Supplemental Decree will be "applicable . . . to all subordinate employees of the Department." Read Rule 65(d) in the Appendix. What is the basis of his power over these employees? Are they parties in the case or adequately represented by some party? Is he likely to use the contempt power against such employees? If not, why specifically make the decree "applicable" to them?

4) Judge Henley considers various rules or policies adopted by the Department pertaining to such matters as correspondence, transfer, and disciplinary hearings. Sometimes he seems to think that his task is to approve or disapprove these rules; for example, he writes: "The Court thinks that the rule in question is a reasonable one, and with one modification the Court approves it." Where does he get the power to "approve" such a rule? Is such a power a necessary concomitant of the power to disapprove the rule? Other times he modifies the rules in some specific detail; for example, while the departmental rule requires disciplinary hearings to be held "as quickly as possible," Judge Henley requires that, except in highly exceptional cases, the hearing must be held within 72 hours. Does Judge Henley have the power to make such a specific modification? Is this an appropriate occasion to exercise the power?

5) After entering a Second Supplemental Decree, Judge Henley seeks to relinquish "further supervisory jurisdiction." Why? Should a judge ever relinquish jurisdiction when an injunction is outstanding? Certainly the court must have jurisdiction to enforce or modify the decree. Did Judge Henley have something else in mind by "supervisory jurisdiction?"

6) Once again, Judge Henley lacks interest in individual prisoners' specific complaints. He denies specific relief, and he even acknowledges that "no specific testimony was taken with respect to certain individual cases." Individual prisoners are protected only insofar as they are members of the group protected by the more general structural relief. Is this lack of interest in individual complaints consistent with his constitutional office? Has this lack of interest grown over time, as the judge became more and more involved with the problems of reforming the system? Is there a risk that he has be-

come over involved with the reform of the prison system and over-protective of the reforms that have been instituted under his prodding? It appears from his opinion that, especially since *Holt III,* he has received an enormous number of individual complaints from prisoners; he acknowledges that the flow will probably continue even if the respondents implement *Holt III* fully. He adds: "Judging from experience, many, if not most, of those complaints will be insubstantial from a constitutional standpoint, and can be ignored or disposed of summarily. . . . [I]t would be most desirable if the Board and the Commissioner could work out a grievance procedure. . . . Should such a procedure be evolved, the Court might well be inclined, to the extent legally open to it, to refuse to consider inmate complaints until that procedure has been exhausted." Evaluate this passage.

FINNEY v. ARKANSAS BOARD OF CORRECTIONS

505 F.2d 194 (8th Cir. 1974).

Before LAY and HEANEY, Circuit Judges and DEVITT, D.J.

LAY, Circuit Judge.

In August 1973, the United States District Court for the Eastern District of Arkansas rendered its decision in this class action brought by Arkansas prisoners against the members of the Arkansas State Board of Correction, Terrell Don Hutto, the Arkansas Commissioner of Correction, and other prison officials. The petitioners are inmates at the Cummins Prison Farm and the Tucker Intermediate Reformatory. The petitions challenge the Arkansas prison system as a constitutional system of correction. Seven of the petitioners have appealed. They assert error in the district court's findings. We reverse in part and remand the case to the district court for further proceedings consistent with this opinion. . . .

We recognize that the district court has received literally hundreds of complaints from Cummins prisoners and that until prison conditions change, the steady stream of prisoner complaints will continue. We are mindful as well of the administrative burden placed upon the Arkansas prison officials who must respond to individual grievances. We further realize that the judicial process often fails to provide needed relief promptly. Surely prisoners are also aware of the slowness of the judicial process, but until conditions change, prisoners have no recourse but to take their constitutional complaints to the courts. By now state correctional authorities should have provided facilities and programs consistent with constitutional standards. As the respondents urge, there is no such thing as a "perfect" prison system, but this does not relieve respondents of their duty to make their system a constitutional one in which the human dignity of each individual inmate is respected.

. . . It has been said many times that the courts possess no expertise in the conduct and management of correctional institutions. This court has long recognized that it is only in the exceptional case where the internal administration of prisons justifies judicial supervision. On the other hand, courts need not be apologetic in requiring state officials to meet constitutional standards in the operation of prisons.

The district court found that significant progress and improvements had been made at both the Cummins and Tucker institutions since *Holt II.* It noted a "changing attitude and effort" on the part of the Arkansas Legislature, the present governor of Arkansas, his predecessor, the Board of Correction, the Commissioner and many employees of the institutions. The court found that those practices complained of in *Holt II* were now not officially approved or sanctioned. The district court did acknowledge that some constitutional deficiencies still existed and on that basis granted the class certain additional injunctive relief. However, the court found no need to retain jurisdiction of the case.

This court recognizes the difficult issues the district court has passed upon since the commencement of this litigation in 1969. We are nevertheless compelled to find on the basis of the overall record that there exists a continuing failure by the correctional authorities to provide a constitutional and, in some respects, even a humane environment within their institutions. As will be discussed, we find major constitutional deficiencies particularly at Cummins in housing, lack of medical care, infliction of physical and mental brutality and torture upon individual prisoners, racial discrimination, abuses of solitary confinement, continuing use of trusty guards, abuse of mail regulations, arbitrary work classifications, arbitrary disciplinary procedures, inadequate distribution of food and clothing, and total lack of rehabilitative programs. We are therefore convinced that present prison conditions, now almost five years after *Holt I,* requ[illegible] the retention of federal jurisdiction and the granting of further relief.

In *Holt II,* the district court set forth a detailed description of "life in the barracks" at the Cummins and Tucker Farms:

"A barracks is nothing more than a large dormitory surrounded by bars; the barracks are separated from each other by wide hallways, and the complex of hallways is referred to as the 'yard.' At the present time the barracks house more than 100 men each assigned without regard to anything but rank and race."

The court also described the total absence of personal safety and security. It observed that if the State of Arkansas chose to confine penitentiary inmates in barracks, some means had to be provided to protect those inmates from assault and physical harm by other inmates. At the trial of that case, then-Commissioner Sarver "frankly admitted that the physical facilities at both units were inadequate and in a total state of disrepair that could only be described as deplorable."

In the report submitted to the court in 1971, Commissioner Hutto expressed a realization of the problem he had inherited when he said: "The Board of Correction and this Administration feel strongly that the greatest problem in the so-called barracks is the problem of overcrowding." Despite this realization, however, and the passage of more than 1½ years, there is continued use of the barracks and continued overcrowding without adequate supervision. Approximately 125 to 135 men are still confined in each of the various barracks despite Mr. Hutto's concession that the barracks cannot be successfully operated with more than 60 to 80 inmates.

Some major improvements have been undertaken. A minimum security unit is under construction at the Cummins facility. It will provide individual rooms for each of 248 inmates. Many of the trusties will be housed there. The new unit will reduce overcrowding in the barracks. In addition a new maximum security unit has been built to house 80 to 90 inmates.

While these improvements were necessary to comply with the decree in *Holt II,* the record indicates that serious overcrowding has not been eliminated and that inmate assaults on other inmates still occur. Moreover, relief will apparently be short-lived, for the testimony reveals that inmate population increases each year.

When a state confines a person by reason of a conviction of a crime, the state must assume an obligation for the safekeeping of that prisoner. One means of protecting inmates from each other is provision of adequate physical facilities. Long-range plans provide no satisfactory solution to those who are assaulted and physically harmed today. The fact that assaults and physical injuries have diminished does not demonstrate compliance with the court's decree of four years ago. The fact that there is *some* compliance is not good enough. As long as barracks are used respondents *must* assure that they are not overcrowded and are safe and sanitary for every inmate. There can be no exceptions. Upon remand, the district court shall meet with counsel and the respondents to devise a program to eliminate immediately the overcrowding of the barracks and to ensure the safety of each inmate. Lack of funds is not an acceptable excuse for unconstitutional conditions of incarceration. An immediate answer, if the state cannot otherwise resolve the problem of overcrowding, will be to transfer or release some inmates. The district court shall also satisfy itself that no additional prisoners will be confined at the Cummins Prison Farm if their confinement will result in continued overcrowding and perpetuation of conditions which fail to provide optimum safety and sanitation for every inmate.

One further problem arises from the overcrowding and inhumane conditions at Cummins. Youthful offenders confined at Tucker, the reformatory have been transferred to Cummins, the adult facility, because they posed disciplinary problems for Tucker personnel. At Cummins the youths are housed either in solitary confinement for their own protection or placed in the general prison population. As Judge Henley observes, one could seriously question which is worse. Apparently, some such transfers have been completed quite summarily. The petitioners state that Tucker offers better conditions of confinement with greater possibilities for rehabilitation. They contend that any transfer to Cummins, since it amounts to a material change in their conditions of confinement, must be accompanied by procedures consistent with due process. The trial court agreed and granted some relief by requiring hearings on retransfer within a shorter period of time and at more frequent intervals. We need not pass on the due process issue for we feel that the transfer of juvenile offenders to Cummins is cruel and unusual punishment while unconstitutional conditions continue to exist there. We therefore direct the district court to enjoin any transfers from Tucker to Cummins until the constitutional infirmities within the latter institution are removed.

The respondents, through the testimony of Mr. Lockhart and Commissioner Hutto, agree that the medical facilities within the Arkansas correctional system are totally inadequate.

At the time of the hearings, no physician, dentist or psychiatrist was employed by Cummins, although Mr. Hutto testified that a full-time doctor was being hired. A number of Cummins inmates are either mentally or emotionally disturbed. These people are, as the district court found, "dangerous to themselves and to their keepers and other inmates and tend to keep other inmates in states of unrest and excitement." . . . In addition the district court found that many inmates have serious physical ailments which render confinement in the ordinary penal institution unbearable for them and, in the case of contagious diseases, dangerous for others. The district court found that deficiencies have existed and continue to exist but that "the Department has done the best that it could in the area of medical services with the resources at its command." We find the problem to be much more complex and serious than this, and assuming the deficiencies are of a constitutional nature, we again cannot agree that lack of funds or facilities justify lack of competent medical care.

Subsequent to the decision in *Holt II,* Dr. T.H. Wortham, a member of the Board of Correction, requested the Arkansas Department of Health to evaluate the medical facilities of the Department of Correction. Its report, which was offered in evidence, is a comprehensive and detailed study encompassing the whole health delivery system, including the future workload, the facility needs and recommended action. The report states:

> "One basic assumption is made upon which this study is built. It is this: the primary purpose of the correction system is to rehabilitate inmates so that they become productive citizens and a basic level of medical care is a necessary part of the rehabilitation process. This assumption includes the notion that a poor state of physical or psychological health will detract from rehabilitation efforts. Also included in this assumption is the concept that medical facilities, acceptable in quality and quantity, are a necessary part of providing this level of medical care."

The report itself illuminates a total deficiency in both manpower and equipment resources. We highlight only some of those deficiencies found to exist at Cummins:

"1. Lack of sufficient personnel to staff the facility on a 24-hour basis with free world help. Along with the added staffing, salary increases are necessary to retain those now employed.

"2. The equipment is completely inadequate to continue present operations at an acceptable level. . . .

"3. There is a tremendous need for more professional assistance. The lack of a physician at more frequent intervals places an unreasonable burden upon the present employees since they are called upon to do work which they are not qualified to perform.

"4. Better transportation is needed if the present operation is maintained. There is an immediate need for an ambulance. The time and effort involved in transfers to Little Rock is very time consuming for the already overworked staff. In addition, it has resulted in 4 escapes during the period studied. . . .

"There is no registered professional nursing supervision at either of these medical facilities. Also, data gathered strongly suggests that in some cases a physician is not responsible for some of the medical care which is rendered. Therefore, even if only temporary medical care was offered at these facilities, the standards for licensure as an infirmary would not be met.

"Some definitive, non-temporary, medical care is provided at Cummins. The length of stay of admitted patients indicates that the medical unit could be better defined as a hospital. If the Cummins unit is, in fact, a hospital and not an infirmary, deficiencies exist in all major areas of the licensure regulations.

"Hospital requirements for physicians' care, nursing, medical records, patient accommodations, diagnostic and treatment service, dietary services, and physical facility are all significantly lacking.

"In fact, some patients appear to not be under the care of a physician, there is no professional nursing, required medical records are only partially maintained, basic laboratory and x-ray services are only partially available, no professional dietary service is provided, and a great many facility and environmental standards are not currently being met."

The Committee summarized:

"Current facilities do not meet state licensure standards.

"Diagnosis and treatment of emergency and acute illness is not adequately provided for due to a lack of facilities, equipment, and only part-time availability of professional medical staff.

"Efforts of the Rehabilitative Services unit are not fully coordinated with efforts of the other medical disciplines.

"Convalescent care and chronic illness treatment is provided in State Health facilities located in Little Rock and Booneville. A security problem is related.

"Construction of adequate medical care facilities is justified on the basis of workload."

The record additionally shows that there are no dentists at Cummins or Tucker. When a dentist does visit, no restorative work is done. Although the evidence indicates that prisoners who need major dental work, such as extractions, are taken into the dentist at Pine Bluff, the record likewise shows that none of the 1200 inmates at Cummins had made such a visit for a period of at least eight months prior to the district court hearing.

The long-range studies conducted by the Board of Correction were made over two years ago. Mr. Hutto testified that a complete medical facility was to be built in the future. There is no question that Commissioner Hutto and the Board of Correction feel that they "*must* have a full service medical and dental program, even to the point of restorative medical and dental problems." Nevertheless, on the present record, we are convinced that they have achieved little more than a study and a *hope* to improve the present inadequate care. This court fully realizes, as did the district court, that this is a difficult problem for the Board of Correction and prison officials. In the meantime, however, 1200 inmates are continuously denied proper medical and dental care, and individuals with contagious diseases, as well as some who are mentally and emotionally ill, are at large in the general prison population. There is not even basic emergency service, much less any assurance of more complete medical treatment when necessary. We think it incumbent upon the court to hold additional hearings and to delineate within specific terms and time limitations not only an overall long-range plan but an immediate plan to update all medical equipment at all facilities, ensuring that every inmate in need of medical attention will be seen by a qualified physician when necessary. We refer the court to the comprehensive decree of Chief Judge Johnson, in Newman v. Alabama, 349 F.Supp. 278, 286–288 (M.D. Ala.1972), as a guide.

Perhaps the most offensive practice in the Arkansas correctional system at the time of *Holt II* was the use of armed trusties as prison guards. As recently as 1969, fully 90 percent of the security force of the Arkansas prison system consisted of such inmate guards. They virtually ran the prison. They sold desirable jobs to other prisoners and trafficked in food, liquor and drugs. There was no way to protect prisoners from assaults if the trusty guards permitted them. Several months after the district court ordered abolition of the trusty system in *Holt II,* Commissioner Hutto reported:

"*The Trusty System of armed guards has not in fact been dismantled at either Cummins or Tucker.* The efforts which have been made have succeeded reasonably well in removing much of the power formerly held by the trusties and placing this power into the hands of civilian personnel. Armed Trusties are being used on the towers at both Tucker and Cummins *and are used to guard outside work forces.* This is done, however, under the direct supervision of a civilian supervisor, who is present at all times with the work forces. Trusties have been removed completely from any responsibility or authority regarding inmate job assignments, promotions and demotions, and all disciplinary matters are handled by free world personnel. Even in institutions where there is a large number of experienced employees there is the constant danger that 'trusted' inmates exercise subtle influences on staff in the area of job assignments and discipline. In a system such as this where there is still some shortage of employed personnel and many of these have little or no experience, this problem is more acute and, realistically, one must admit that this is a daily problem with which we have to deal." (Emphasis added).

The record is deficient in updating this report. However, the inmate complaints make it appear that the Commissioner's 1971 report represents the situation as of January 1973. Apparently some use of trusty guards continues at this time. This court affirmed the district court's opinion in *Holt II,* with emphasis on the admonition that trusty guards were not to perform prison jobs which ordinarily would be performed by free world personnel.

. . .

We feel the time for dismantling the entire system has long passed. The district court shall order that it be completely phased out within a few months.

The district court supplemented its decree of December 30, 1971, by stating:

"(g) Without limiting the generality of the term "cruel and unusual punishment" appearing in Paragraph 4 of the Court's Supplemental Decree of December 30, 1971, that term is now defined as including the infliction upon any inmate of the Department of Correction of any unreasonable or unnecessary force in any form, the assigning of any inmate to tasks inconsistent with his medical classification, the use of any punishment which amounts to torture, the forcing of any inmate to run to or from work, or while at work, or in front of any moving vehicle or animal, and the infliction of any punishment not authorized by the Department's rules and regulations."

In its memorandum order the district court pointed out that Commissioner Hutto, Superintendent Lockhart and the other high-level officers were qualified for their jobs and were attempting to perform well. However, the court expressed concern over the lower echelon of prison personnel. The court's findings and discussion concerning habitual harassment of inmates by prison personnel, through physical and mental abuse, covers several pages of its opinion. . . . Unquestionably the Department of Correction has adopted a policy condemning all forms of abuse of inmates. Commissioner Hutto issued his policy memoranda prohibiting "physical abuse of inmates" in December of 1971. Nevertheless, there is evidence as of January 1973 that excessive force, verbal abuse and various forms of torture and inhumane punishment continue.

The district court demonstrated a keen perception and understanding of how conflicts arise between prison personnel and inmates. The court points out that the overall working conditions and prison environment provide a fertile ground for continued abuses and violations of earlier decrees. Although the district court did not find the prison working conditions so harsh as to constitute cruel and unusual punishment in themselves, it observed that the inmates on the "hoe squads" are required to work long hours under constant prodding; that at times inmates are assigned to work at tasks beyond their strength or medical ability; and that older or weaker inmates are required to keep up with the younger inmates at arduous tasks under threat of disciplinary proceedings. The court found evidence that the inmates are at times still forced to run to and from work or while at work, and that some crews are required to race with another crew in the performance of the same type of work. The record indicates that the inmates have been required to run in front of moving vehicles or ridden horses. Finally, even after *Holt II*, a young boy named Willie Stewart was given a *one-day* sentence. On that day he was put through all forms of mental and physical torture, ending when the guards shot at his feet and inadvertently killed him. This "treatment," according to Mr. Hutto, has stopped. Unfortunately, it took the life of a young prisoner, rather than the court's prior decree, to accomplish it.

In addition to physical abuse the record reveals that the prison personnel at all levels employ profane, threatening, abusive and vulgar language, together with racial slurs, epithets, and sexual and scatalogical terms when addressing inmates. Conduct prohibited by official prison rules is freely engaged in.

We have discussed previously the departmental obligation to protect inmates against both physical and mental abuse by the correctional staff and other inmates. The continued infliction of physical abuse, as well as mental distress, degradation, and humiliation by correctional authorities demonstrates that mere words are no solution. Such unlawful conduct by correctional personnel is of major significance leading to this court's finding that the present correctional system in Arkansas is still unconstitutional. For this reason, as well as those stated elsewhere, the district court shall retain jurisdiction and take, if it deems advisable, additional evidence on those conditions of confinement, hiring policies, working conditions and disciplinary measures which must be changed in order to provide a continuing prophylaxis against such cruel and inhumane treatment.

This court finds that the present working conditions are unconstitutional and must be radically changed. If a man works too slowly or refuses to work he not only loses his entitlement to statutory good time . . . , but faces solitary confinement as well. In effect, lower echelon personnel are given the power to impose additional mental punishment by threatening solitary confinement to those who do not work to their satisfaction. Arbitrary power is thus placed in the hands of persons obviously lacking the discretion to exercise it wisely. Absent evidence of qualified supervisors for the work crews, a possible solution is to deprive the line guards of this power. The district court should review these conditions bearing in mind this court's concern for the lack of rehabilitation and treatment for the prison population and the resultant physical and mental abuse.

One of the principal grievances in both *Holt I* and *Holt II* concerned the intolerable conditions in the old maximum security units at Cummins. Since *Holt II,* a new facility has been constructed alleviating to a great extent problems of sanitation and overcrowding. Some problems remain, however. One such problem is the practice of placing inmates awaiting disciplinary hearings in *punitive* solitary confinement. This court has previously held that solitary confinement is not, per se, cruel and unusual punishment.[8] Burns v. Swenson, 430 F.2d 771, 777–778 (8th Cir. 1970) cert. denied, 404 U.S. 1062 (1972). Under certain circumstances, such confinement can violate the Eighth Amendment. This fact was demonstrated in the original *Holt* decisions.

Complaint is made by prisoners who are placed in isolation for "administrative segregation," pending disciplinary action for rule infraction. Judge Henley limited this segregation to three days' duration. We find such administrative segregation as limited by the trial court to fall within correctional discretion and not to violate due process. We assume, of course, that if disciplinary action is not taken against the inmate for lack of evidence, full privileges will be restored and any good time he would have earned if the opportunity had been available will be credited to him.

In the punitive wing, we note the prisoners are denied the regular prison diet. "Grue" is the term applied to the tasteless, unappetizing paste-like food which is served to prisoners in solitary confinement as a form of further punishment. In *Holt I,* the district court found that grue constituted a nutritionally sufficient diet. The procedure followed by prison authorities when an inmate is placed on "grue", however, makes that conclusion dubious. The

8. At the same time we cannot help but observe that a recent study conducted by the National Advisory Commission on Criminal Justice led to the following observation by that group:

"The Commission recognizes that the field of corrections cannot yet be persuaded to give up the practice of solitary confinement as a disciplinary measure. But the Commission wishes to record its view that the practice is inhumane and in the long run brutalizes those who impose it as it brutalizes those upon whom it is imposed."

Report on Corrections, The National Advisory Committee on Criminal Justice Standards and Goals, p. 32.

prisoner receives one full meal at least every three days and six consecutive full meals every 14 days. At the end of that period, he is given a thorough physical examination. If medical reasons dictate a regular diet then it is ordered. Otherwise the prisoner is continued on this punitive treatment. This, in itself, indicates an awareness of possible dietary insufficiencies. There exists a fundamental difference between depriving a prisoner of privileges he may enjoy and depriving him of the basic necessities of human existence.[9] We think this is the minimal line separating cruel and unusual punishment from conduct that is not. On remand, the district court's decree should be amended to ensure that prisoners placed in punitive solitary confinement are not deprived of basic necessities including light, heat, ventilation, sanitation, clothing and a proper diet.

The district court reviewed the disciplinary procedures employed in the Arkansas prison system and found them lacking in several particulars of due process. It granted a measure of injunctive relief. We agree with the relief granted, but in view of the Supreme Court's subsequent decision in Wolff v. McDonnell, 418 U.S. 539 (1974), we feel more is required. . . .

The petitioners on appeal object to the following aspects of the disciplinary procedure now in force: (1) the possibility that the same person who wrote the disciplinary may sit in judgment, (2) the absence of a right of confrontation, (3) lack of sufficient prior notice of charges, and (4) the lack of any duty upon the "court" to explain the basis for the result reached. In *McDonnell,* the Court held that prison disciplinary proceedings must contain the following safeguards: (A) written notice of charges at least 24 hours prior to the hearing; (B) a qualified right to call witnesses, and (C) a written statement by the committee of the factual basis for its decision. These procedures constitute the minimum assurance of due process.

There is evidence that on occasion the same officer who invokes disciplinary measures sits on the committee to review the matter. This practice has been unanimously condemned by those courts which have considered it. . . . As stated in Morrissey v. Brewer, 408 U.S. 471 (1972), with reference to parole revocations: "The officer directly involved in making recommendations cannot always have complete objectivity in evaluating them." Id. at 486. The district court should bar the charging officer from sitting in judgment on his own complaint in disciplinary proceedings.

In Jackson v. Indiana, 406 U.S. 715, 738 (1972), Mr. Justice Blackmun stated: "At the least, due process requires that the nature and duration of commitment bear some reasonable relation to the purpose for which the individual is committed." Id. at 738. The Supreme Court has recognized rehabilitation as one of the ends of correctional confinement. See, e.g., Procunier v. Martinez, 416 U.S. 396, 412–413 (1974). Arkansas statutes as

9. See, e.g., Landman v. Royster, 333 F.Supp. 621 (E.D.Va.1971), where the court considered a bread and water diet:

"The practice is therefore both generally disapproved and obsolescent even within this penal system. It is not seriously defended as essential to security. It amounts therefore to an unnecessary infliction of pain. Furthermore, as a technique designed to break a man's spirit not just by denial of physical comforts but of necessities, to the end that his powers of resistance diminish, the bread and water diet is inconsistent with current minimum standards of respect for human dignity. The Court has no difficulty in determining that it is a violation of the eighth amendment. Jackson v. Bishop; Wright v. McMann, 321 F.Supp. 127 (N.D.N.Y.1970)." Id. at 647.

well stipulate that efforts should be directed toward the rehabilitation of persons committed to the institutional care of the Department of Correction.[11]

In *Holt II,* the district court said that the lack of rehabilitative programs could, in the face of "other conditions," be violative of the Eighth Amendment. With this we agree. Furthermore, we find that those other conditions persist. Convicts in the Arkansas system are forced to labor long hours under arduous conditions. They are faced with constant threats of physical and mental abuse if their work or conduct falls below often arbitrary standards. They are left almost no time for self-advancing activities or recreation, and the testimony of prison officials indicates that even if time were available, rehabilitative programs are generally not available. The Commissioner has testified concerning the building trades apprenticeship program and the increasing opportunity for basic schooling. However, these programs at Cummins are still very limited, accommodating a relatively small number of inmates. We thus deem it necessary that the respondents be required to submit to the court an overall program for treatment and rehabilitation of the inmates at both Cummins and Tucker.

When *Holt II* was before the district court in 1970, racial discrimination was a serious problem within all the institutions operated by the Arkansas Board of Correction. Living facilities were segregated at that time and there was convincing evidence of racial discrimination in other areas of prison life from job assignments to class status. The court ordered immediate elimination of all racial discrimination. By the time the district court heard this case, there had been a marked improvement in this regard. Living facilities, with the exception of the punitive segregation wing at Cummins, were integrated. Nonetheless, the court found that discrimination still pervaded other facets of prison life. Accordingly, the district court again enjoined racial discrimination in several particulars, including: (1) interference with Black Muslim religious practices; (2) segregation of prisoners in maximum security, and (3) discrimination in such areas as inmate classification, job assignments, privileges, personal appearance, disciplinary proceedings and punishments. With this we agree, but once again we find that the court's decree stops short of its intended goal.

The court specifically found that the more intangible forms of racial discrimination could not be eliminated until the Arkansas Department of Correction was integrated. This is especially true in the areas of job classification and disciplinary proceedings, where preconceived ideas and often unconscious prejudices may seriously affect an inmate's life. The assistant superintendent in charge of the disciplinary court testified that, with the exception of a non-voting black minister, no blacks had ever sat in judgment on the disciplinary court, although at the time of trial fully 48% of the inmate population was black. A compilation of disciplinary proceedings leads to an unmistakable inference of racial discrimination, be it intentional or not. In the area of job classification and admission to the few available rehabilitative programs, the same inference arises, for blacks occupy the menial positions while the more desirable programs are dominated by white inmates. . . .

Very little has been accomplished in the recruitment of black employees. Those who have been hired assume, with slight exception, no position of

11. Ark.Stat.Ann. § 46–116 (1973).

control, influence or even persuasion. Resources, according to Commissioner Hutto, will not permit offering salaries sufficient to attract the qualified individuals he seeks. We need only repeat that inadequate resources cannot justify the imposition of constitutionally prohibited treatment. Even assuming qualified blacks cannot be found, we are not persuaded that an alternative such as establishing a program in which blacks could be trained until qualified is not viable.

On remand the district court should amend its decree to include an affirmative program directed toward the elimination of all forms of racial discrimination. In doing so it should consider the standards now employed in the hiring and promotion of prison personnel. The court must assure itself that those standards are reasonably related to proper correctional goals and not designed to preserve institutional racial discrimination.

The petitioners in the trial court also contested restrictions placed upon the use of the mails. Inmate correspondence is divided by Arkansas prison officials into three classes: privileged, general and special purpose. Privileged correspondence involves mail to or from courts, federal and state officials and inmates' attorneys. General correspondence includes mail between a prisoner and friends or business acquaintances. Special purpose correspondence is described only as mail to or from persons not qualifying under the general or privileged categories.

The petitioners challenge that provision which allows prison officials to open and search privileged mail and to open and read general and special purpose correspondence. They also challenge the "approved mailing list" procedure whereby a prisoner must submit the name of a potential correspondent for approval both by the intended correspondent and prison officials before he may send or receive mail from that person. The district court considered these issues at length but ordered only that privileged correspondence be examined in the presence of the inmate.

In Procunier v. Martinez, 416 U.S. 396 (1974), the Supreme Court considered a challenge to the California prisons' mail censorship policies.[13] Basing its decision on the infringement of "liberties of free citizens . . . implicated in censorship of prisoner mail" rather than on the right of the prisoners themselves to be free from unnecessary interference with their communications, the Court held that censorship of prison mail is justified only if the particular regulations were necessary to further a substantial government interest unrelated to the suppression of expression and the limitations imposed were no greater than necessary to accomplish that objective. If deemed necessary inspection of outgoing or incoming mail in the presence of an inmate is never objectionable. However, any kind of censorship regulations carry a heavy burden. The district court should review the mail regulations under the standards set out in *Martinez.*

The petitioners' second complaint concerns the mailing list requirement, whereby a prisoner may not correspond with any person who has not previously consented. This procedure affects potential correspondents whenever prison officials refuse permission to include a name on the list. However, it more directly places prior restraint on a prisoner's freedom to correspond

13. The district court's opinion was written at a time prior to the Supreme Court's decision in *Martinez* and *McDonnell.*

with whomever he chooses. It is now well settled that a prisoner does not shed his basic constitutional rights at the prison gate. While it has been recognized that these rights and immunities do not always assume the same form in prison that they do in free society, Wolff v. McDonnell, 418 U.S. 539 (1974), they are, nonetheless, present. We need go no further to recognize that a prisoner's First Amendment right should not be restricted by governmental interference unrelated to any legitimate governmental objective. . . .

The district court, while granting injunctive relief to the class, denied singular relief to the individual petitioners. The district judge stated that he would make specific findings as to an individual petitioner only upon individual request. No requests were made, but on appeal petitioners cite as one ground of error the district court's failure to make specific findings.

We find that this was error. Rule 52(a) of the Federal Rules of Civil Procedure requires the district court to make findings of fact in each individual case. The burden should not be upon the petitioner to request specific findings when it is incumbent upon the court to make the findings in each individual case.[15] The district court's error does not deprive this court of jurisdiction to review the record. However, the absence of specific findings does make appellate review more difficult.

We think that Willie Montgomery and Larry Gray stated claims upon which individual relief could possibly be proper. The testimony of Willie Montgomery indicates that he was wrongfully assaulted by prison guards and that, although the correctional employees were discharged, Montgomery was sentenced to the maximum security unit and suffered loss of good time. As for Larry Gray, he alleges that he is unable to work due to a foot ailment. He complains of receiving disciplinaries resulting in loss of good time and class status. In Wilwording v. Swenson, 502 F.2d 844 (8th Cir. 1974), we pointed out that an individual is not entitled to have his record expunged or corrected simply because the full panoply of due process procedures was not granted to him prior to the effective date of *McDonnell.* The Supreme Court made it clear in *McDonnell* that the procedural due process requirements set forth therein were not retroactive. However, where the challenge is made that good time was arbitrarily taken without any supporting evidence whatsoever, the prisoner states a valid claim for relief. This we construe to be the primary thrust of the complaints of Montgomery and Gray and we feel that it was prejudicial error to fail to make specific findings in their individual cases. Denial of individual findings to the other petitioners, however, was harmless error for, as we review their appeals, it appears they did not state a claim upon which relief could be granted.

We have consolidated with the *Finney* case the several pending appeals of James C. Ellingburg, a Cummins prisoner. Most of his petitions relate to

15. This requirement fulfills a threefold purpose: (1) to aid appellate review by affording a clear and concise statement of the basis for the court's decision, Cross v. Pasley, 267 F.2d 824 (8th Cir. 1959); (2) to make the decision of the court definite to aid in future application of the doctrine of *res judicata;* and (3) to cause the trial judge to fully and conscientiously consider the basis for his decision, United States v. Birnbach, 400 F.2d 378 (8th Cir. 1968). None of these purposes is fulfilled when a court dismisses a claim or claims for relief without specified findings.

conditions of confinement at Cummins and therefore present issues of common concern with our discussion in *Finney.* Some of the district court rulings in the Ellingburg cases adopt Judge Henley's decision in *Finney* as the basis for dismissal.

In 74–1369, petitioner Ellingburg asserts, *inter alia,* that Cummins inmates are prohibited from giving legal assistance to one another. It appears that there is one attorney available for inmate consultation at Cummins (the record is silent as to the situation at Tucker) but that he is not permitted to assist the prisoners in civil litigation. The Supreme Court in *McDonnell* said:

"The right of access to the courts, upon which *Avery* was premised, is founded in the Due Process Clause and assures that no person will be denied the opportunity to present to the judiciary allegations concerning violations of fundamental constitutional rights. It is futile to contend that the Civil Rights Act has less importance in our constitutional scheme than does the Great Writ. The recognition by this Court that prisoners have certain constitutional rights which can be protected by civil rights actions would be diluted if inmates, often 'totally or functionally illiterate,' were unable to articulate their complaints to the courts. Although there may be additional burdens on the Complex, if inmates may seek help from other inmates, or from the inmate adviser if he proves adequate, in both habeas and civil rights actions, this should not prove overwhelming. At present only one inmate serves as legal adviser and it may be expected that other qualified inmates could be found for assistance if the Complex insists on naming the inmates from whom help may be sought." 94 S.Ct. at 2986.

Upon remand the district court should re-examine procedures relating to inmate assistance to satisfy the alternative requirements of Johnson v. Avery, 393 U.S. 483 (1969). Cf. McDonnell v. Wolff, 483 F.2d 1059, 1064–1066 (8th Cir. 1973).

In 74–1202, Ellingburg seeks to hold prison officials in contempt for failing to phase out the armed trusty guard system in the towers and for failing to completely segregate diseased prisoners from the general prison population. We have now issued specific directions concerning these conditions. The district court's earlier opinions strongly implied that these measures should be taken, but until today there has been no specific order to that effect. Before contempt may lie the parties must have actual knowledge of the order and the order must be sufficiently specific to be enforceable. United States v. Di Mauro, 441 F.2d 428, 439 (8th Cir. 1971). The appeal is dismissed.

In 74–1205, Ellingburg disputes the type of medical care received for his tuberculosis and other alleged ailments. The district court deferred to the judgment of prison medical personnel. This was the subject of an earlier petition dismissed as failing to state a claim for relief under § 1983. This court affirmed the dismissal. See Ellingburg v. Loyd, 491 F.2d 728 (8th Cir. 1974). This appeal is dismissed.

In 74–1330, Ellingburg attacks the prison mail regulations. For the reasons discussed above we find the district court's dismissal of this claim erroneous. We reverse and remand this claim with directions that it be considered by the district court in accord with our opinion above.

In 74–1406, the petitioner complains about the safety of inmates; he sets forth specific facts on appeal. We dealt with this overall concern above, and since the general relief afforded there is applicable here, the judgment of dismissal should be affirmed as modified by our prior discussion.

In 74–8102, Ellingburg v. Sewell, petitioner seeks damages by reason of an alleged "conspiracy" to murder him. The district court, The Honorable Paul X Williams presiding, refused to file the petition since the complaint was deemed frivolous on its face. We disapprove this procedure of failing to file petitions in the court record. See Jones v. Lockhart, 484 F.2d 1192 (8th Cir. 1973). This was error and the complaint should be filed. If the district court is still satisfied that the complaint is frivolous or fails to state a claim for federal relief, an appropriate judgment should be rendered. The court's refusal to file the complaint is set aside.

In 74–1642, petitioner appeals from the denial of separate injunctive relief on his allegation that a correctional employee, A. A. Lucas, the Food Service Supervisor at Cummins, had an active tubercular condition. On August 14, 1974, the district court denied relief relying on a report from David Crittenden, M.D., Mr. Lucas' physician, which states that although Mr. Lucas has a tubercular condition he is no danger to others and recommends that he be allowed to continue as a prison employee. The district court's dismissal was proper. See Cates v. Ciccone, 422 F.2d 926 (8th Cir. 1970). Ellingburg's petition for a writ of mandamus to provide an immediate hearing in this case is dismissed as moot. . . .

The two Ellingburg appeals that are remanded for reconsideration, 74–1330 and 74–1369, are hereby ordered consolidated with the *Finney* case so that the propriety of the mail regulations and the adequacy of legal assistance may be determined at the same time as the *Finney* challenges are heard on remand.

This case and the individual Ellingburg appeals remanded herein are to be retained by the district court for the holding of additional evidentiary hearings. The district court, if it deems it necessary, should call its own witnesses in order to fully explore the viable alternatives in meeting respondents' immediate responsibility to eliminate the unlawful conditions which now exist in the Arkansas prison system. The district court may consider appointing federal monitors or a committee of lawyers or other responsible citizens to assist in eliminating the present practices of physical abuse and torture. . . . We do not suggest that the district court must do this, we merely recommend it as worthy of consideration in light of the history of these cases. The district court must decide whether continued abuse of its process and of its decree require such measures.

We regret the continued court supervision required by our decision since we are aware of the tremendous docket load under which the district court labors. We realize that the district court's opinions in *Holt I* and *Holt II* viewed unconstitutional conditions in a state prison system in an unprecedented light. Our opinion here is in no sense intended to detract from our recognition of the conscientious and responsible manner in which the district court has undertaken its task. The problems it continues to encounter in these decisions are monumental. Our decision is intended to reinforce its view in a newly developed area of constitutional law. Our continuing confidence and respect for the district court gives us assurance that a suitable end will be quickly attained.

Based on the overall record before us, it is our firm conviction that the Arkansas correctional system is still unconstitutional. We are fully cognizant of the considerable progress which has been made by the Board of Correction with the minimal resources at hand. However, we confront a record and factual history of a sub-human environment in which individuals have been confined under the color of state law. The effort to make *some* amelioration of those conditions will simply not suffice. The fact that an individual has violated the criminal law, is generally uneducated and in poor health is no justification for inhumane treatment and brutality. Segregation from society and loss of one's liberty are the only punishment the law allows.

Affirmed in part and reversed in part; the cause is remanded to the district court with directions contained herein.

On Petition for Rehearing

PER CURIAM.

Respondents have filed a petition for rehearing and alternatively for a rehearing en banc. They allege that this court's opinion is factually and legally erroneous in all respects. The basic thrust of their complaint is that the latest evidentiary hearing preceding this appeal occurred 21 months before this court's opinion was handed down and that the opinion fails to reflect the *facts* as they are now. The respondents list a long line of physical improvements and changes primarily directed toward upgrading the glaring medical deficiencies set out in the prior record. The respondents' brief on rehearing states that since the district court's opinion they have as well invoked a grievance procedure, instituted rehabilitation programs, improved security measures, broadened inmate assistance programs and are in compliance with seven of the major concerns condemned in this court's opinion. At this stage of the proceeding we can only express our sincere hope that this is true.

This court is aware that major improvements have been taking place within the Arkansas Correction System since the evidentiary hearings. However, an appellate court is not a fact-finding court and must necessarily render its decisions on the evidence and record before it. It cannot receive new evidence. One of the fundamental reasons this court ordered a remand of this case to the district court was to allow the district court the opportunity to take additional evidence concerning interim improvements in the prior deficient procedures and practices. The trial court is the only court equipped to test evidentiary compliance and the only forum in which to raise any allegations of continuing deficiencies. Our remand was additionally based on the fact that two decisions of the Supreme Court of the United States, Wolff v. McDonnell, 418 U.S. 539 (1974), and Procunier v. Martinez, 416 U.S. 396 (1974), shed new light on disciplinary procedures and mailing regulations. Both of these decisions were handed down over a year and one-half after the district court's rulings on these areas. It is for the district court to judge on the basis of these decisions whether the disciplinary procedures and mailing regulations are in compliance with the guidelines set forth in those decisions. As was our earlier observation the standards set forth in the district court's earlier decree did not fully contemplate the limits set out later in *Procunier* and *McDonnell.*

We do not consider it too great a burden on the Board of Correction and prison officials to require them to make an evidentiary showing in the district court. If, as urged, there is now constitutional compliance, it should be fairly simple for respondents to demonstrate it to the district court. Once the district court is convinced that constitutional standards, as we defined them, have been met, it may terminate its jurisdiction of the case. We recognize that the sooner the district court may discharge its jurisdiction of the case, the better it is for everyone.

Without minimizing the other areas discussed in this court's opinion, our major concern related to (1) the overcrowding in the barracks and the multi-faceted problems this breeds, (2) the lack of medical supervision and equipment, including proper supervision and treatment of the emotionally ill, and (3) the continuing evidence of physical and mental brutality.

If overcrowding and its subhuman effects have been eliminated, the respondents can easily demonstrate this by affidavit. If changes in the medical treatment and facilities have raised them to conformity with constitutional standards, this, too, can be demonstrated by documentary proof. Notwithstanding some dimunition in the physical and mental brutality, revealed in the first *Hutto* cases, the district court concluded, based on the evidence of 21 months ago, that it was still necessary to further enjoin such abuse. Respondents now say that this has come to an end and that security is such that it is unfair to still appraise the prison system in this light. Yet prisoner complaints continue to be filed alleging verbal abuse, assaults and beatings on inmates by those in authority. Petitioner Ellingburg has filed a motion in response to this motion for rehearing. In his motion he alleges that on October 14, Superintendent Lockhart announced to some 500 or more inmates "that appeals court ruling is nothing but a bunch of shit and don't mean nothing." He alleges that on October 17 an incompetent inmate, one Herschel Spears, was physically assaulted and beaten by an inmate yard security man; that on the same date three inmate floor walkers assaulted another inmate. We do not assume the truth of these allegations; however, if any of the allegations are true it is continuing proof that glaring constitutional deficiencies still exist. The truth of these allegations is for the district court to determine. We found sufficient basis in the previous record to justify further federal jurisdiction to determine what steps must be taken to assure an end to physical and mental abuse.

The respondents' motion for rehearing is overruled.

---

1) What is the proper standard of review for the court of appeals? Is it the lenient standard of review embodied in Rule 52: "Findings of fact shall not be set aside unless clearly erroneous . . . ."? Does the standard change from issue to issue? What factors might account for the divergent views of the court of appeals and the district court? How should these differing perspectives be reflected in the standard of review?

2) At various points the court of appeals proclaims that budgetary considerations are irrelevant in fixing the constitutional obligations of the defend-

ants: "Lack of funds is not an acceptable excuse for unconstitutional conditions of incarceration." Should these proclamations be taken at face value? The court says "an immediate answer" to the problem of overcrowding might be to release some inmates. Would that be "a full answer"? Is it merely a bluff? Are there other ways to deal with the lack-of-funds defense? Does the answer to lack-of-funds depend on whether it is asserted to defend overcrowding, lack of medical services, or lack of rehabilitation?

3) In responding to the petition for rehearing, the court of appeals says that certain issues can be disposed of on the basis of "affidavit" or "documentary proof." This statement is made to minimize the burden on the defendants on remand; but we question whether it is credible. On what theory would any of the contested issues be tried with "affidavits"? What about the plaintiffs' right to cross-examine?

4) Verbal and physical abuse of inmates by correctional staff and other inmates continued to concern the court of appeals. That court orders the district court to retain jurisdiction to establish appropriate protective measures. Consider the dynamics of a prison social system and the potential for violence and abuse from the inmates and the lower echelon correctional officials. Will it ever be appropriate for the jurisdiction of the district court to end?

5) The court of appeals invites the district court to consider the establishment of "federal monitors" or a "committee of lawyers." Why? What is gained by auxiliary institutions? Would such institutions be consistent with the allocation of the judicial power contemplated by Article III?

FINNEY v. HUTTO

410 F.Supp. 251 (E.D.Ark.1976).

HENLEY, Circuit Judge, Sitting by Designation.

These consolidated cases are now before the court pursuant to the mandate of the Court of Appeals in Finney v. Arkansas Board of Correction reversing the decision of this court in Holt v. Hutto and remanding the litigation for further proceedings. The remand requires the court to inquire again into the federal constitutionality of practices and conditions existing and prevailing in the principal penal institutions administered by the Arkansas Department of Correction, an agency of the State of Arkansas. . . .

Pursuant to the remand extensive hearings have been held,[2] and in mid-August, 1975 the court accompanied by court personnel and counsel on both sides visited the principal units of the Department and also visited the new Reformatory for Women which was then nearing completion in the City of Pine Bluff, Arkansas.

2. The hearings extended from January through early July, 1975. Initial hearings were conducted by the court personally. Later hearings were by agreement held before a United States Magistrate, and the testimony heard by him was taken, transcribed, and filed as depositions in the case. In a final hearing conducted by the court personally the testimony of certain expert witnesses was taken in connection with a mental health program recently adopted by the Department.

The cases before the court are in part class actions brought by and on behalf of inmates of the Department generally, and in part individual complaints of particular inmates. In view of the large number of complaints that have been consolidated, this opinion will be confined to the class claims in which petitioners seek for themselves and other inmates similarly situated declaratory and injunctive relief with respect to alleged institutional conditions and practices which they claim deprive inmates of rights protected by the Constitution of the United States. Inmate claims of personal deprivations, including claims for money damages, will be dealt with later. . . .

In approaching the issues before it the court recognizes that it should not embroil itself unreasonably in the affairs of the Department; in areas of prison administration and security, the classification of inmates, prison discipline, and the like, much must be left to the discretion of the prison administrators. The court is concerned ultimately with constitutional deprivations, and if it finds that such deprivations exist or have existed, the court has the power to intervene and devise appropriate relief. . . .

The court first considers whether the principal units of the Department are now overcrowded to a point of unconstitutionality. The matter was discussed in Finney v. Arkansas Board of Correction.

As to the Women's Reformatory, the court found, on the basis of its own observation of that facility in August, 1975, and of the fact that the new Women's Reformatory had still not been completed and put into use as of mid-February, 1976, that the institution was hopelessly overcrowded. And on February 18, 1976 the court entered an order directing that the institution be closed and the inmates transferred or released not later than June 30 of the current year.

Since that order was entered, Commissioner Hutto has indicated compliance with it and has stated publicly that the June 30 deadline will give the Department no trouble. The court hopes that the new Reformatory will be completed and put into use substantially before June 30.

Turning now to Cummins and Tucker, the court recognizes at the outset that the serious overcrowding of a prison operates adversely on inmate safety, morale, and welfare, on the security and good order of the institution, and on the administration of the prison in general. The question of whether a prison is overcrowded to the point of unconstitutionality involves more than determining how many square feet of living space are allocated to individual inmates. Regard must be had to the quality of the living quarters and to the length of time which inmates must spend in their living quarters each day; further some small housing units although cramped may be more comfortable and livable than more spacious quarters.

The question of overcrowding actually involves two questions: First, is the institution as a whole overcrowded? Second, are individual housing units within the institution overcrowded? In other words, the question is not only how many inmates are housed in the prison but also how the prison population is distributed throughout the institution.

Roughly speaking, Cummins houses about three times as many inmates as does Tucker, and, as a class, the Cummins inmates are older men and more hardened criminals than are the inmates of Tucker.

In both *Holt I* and *Holt II* the court found that both of the institutions in question were seriously overcrowded, and that the overcrowding constituted a serious threat to inmate safety, particularly when considered in connection with the trusty guard system which was still in use when *Holt II* was decided in 1970. As of that date the population of Cummins had been declining for some time, and amounted to somewhat less than 1,000 men; at the same time Tucker was housing about 325 inmates.

In those days the basic housing units for inmates at both institutions were large, dormitory type barracks, which are still in use. Each barracks contained, and still contains, about 5,000 square feet of floor space, and each has a maximum capacity of not more than 100 men. Additionally, at Cummins there was a separate building which contained a number of isolation cells. At Tucker there were two rows of small cells reserved for persons who had been condemned to die and who were awaiting execution.

By 1973, when *Holt III* was decided, the Cummins population had grown to about 1200 and that of Tucker had grown to about 349. The basic housing units were still the barracks, and each barracks probably had more than 100 men in it. The old isolation cells at Cummins had been abandoned in favor of a new maximum security facility commonly referred to as the East Building. At Tucker the "death cells" had ceased to be used as such, and were being used to hold prisoners in "administrative segregation" or in "punitive isolation." That was the condition that the Court of Appeals found to be unconstitutional in *Finney.* The holding of that court was based in part on the testimony of Commissioner Hutto that the barracks could not "be successfully operated with more than 60 to 80 inmates," whereas in truth and fact the respective barracks were housing from 125 to 135 men.

When the 1975 hearings were held, the overcrowding at both institutions was worse than it was in either 1973 or 1974. The population at Cummins had grown to 1518 and that at Tucker had grown to 501. According to Mr. Hutto, the population growth was not attributable to any defect or malfunction of the Arkansas parole system, but solely to the fact that inmate intake began to exceed releases about the first of 1974.

The 1975 record reflects a difference between the testimony that Mr. Hutto gave about barracks capacity in 1973 and that which he gave in 1975. In 1973 he had said that there should not be more than 60 to 80 men in a given barracks; in 1975 he raised that figure to 100. He explained the difference by saying that when he was testifying in 1973 he had convenience of administration, rather than overcrowding, in mind, and that as far as overcrowding is concerned, each barracks can properly house 100 men without loss of administrative efficiency. However that may be, the fact remains that as late as the date of the court's August, 1975 inspection of the prisons all of the barracks at both Cummins and Tucker had substantially more than 100 men in them, and inmates who could not be housed in the barracks and who were not in the East Building at Cummins or in the administrative segregation-punitive isolation cells at Tucker, were being housed in facilities that were not designed originally for the housing of inmates.

A report filed with the court and which is a part of the record reflects conditions as they existed on November 12, 1975. That report reveals that since August, 1975 the overcrowded conditions at both Cummins and Tucker had been alleviated substantially as a result of a number of factors.

To start with, in the late summer and early fall of 1975 the rate of inmate discharges began to exceed the rate at which new inmates were being received at the prisons. As a result of this trend, the population of Cummins had declined to 1451, and that of Tucker had gone down to 486.

In the second place a modern minimum security building equipped with cells for single occupancy had been largely completed and put into active use.

And finally the Department had been able to acquire and install a large number of house trailers to provide housing for some 12 inmates per trailer.

However, the report reflects that 27 inmates of Cummins were being housed in a gymnasium area, and that 57 inmates who were not ill were being housed in part of the infirmary facilities. And the report also shows that at Tucker a substantial number of inmates were being housed temporarily in what had been a part of the commissary facility.

The November report reveals that the Department estimates that the capacity of Cummins is 1638 men, and that the capacity of Tucker is 632 men. Those capacity figures are based on 100 men for each of the large barracks and 12 men for each of the house trailers. The Cummins figures show four minimum security "pods" with a capacity of 62 men each, and another minimum security building with a capacity of 62 men. The Cummins figures also show continued use of the gymnasium area with a capacity of 30 men, part of the infirmary building with a capacity of 59 men, the infirmary proper with 25 beds, and the "dog kennel" with a capacity of six men.[4] The Cummins report also reflects that East Building has a capacity of 120 men. The report indicates that at Tucker all of the inmates are housed in the large barracks, the house trailers, and the maximum security unit, which unit has a rated capacity of 28 men, the "dog kennel" with a four man capacity, and the eight bed infirmary. . . .

In *Holt III* the court was not disturbed by the idea that two men were being housed in the same cell in the East Building, but the court now finds that frequently the cells have been used to house three or four men at a time with the men being required to use a single wash basin and toilet. And when one of the cells is used to house more than two people, one or more of them has to sleep on the floor. Regardless of what the theoretical capacities of the cells may be, the court finds that the East Building, or particular units thereof, has been chronically overcrowded and that something must be done about the situation. . . .

The disparities of occupancies among the individual housing units appear to the court to be due in large measure, if not principally, to the policy of the Department to assign men to living quarters on the basis of their job assignments. That policy is understandable from the standpoint of security and convenience of administration, but it can bring about the overcrowding of particular units, and it does not contribute to the efficient use of living space, as such.

4. The dog kennel is the building where the prison bloodhounds are kept. The building has certain living facilities in which inmate dog handlers are housed.

While ordinary inmates do not spend all of their waking hours or even most of them in their living quarters, they do sleep there and spend most of their nonworking time in their quarters where they have essentially no privacy. Living in the barracks at Cummins or Tucker is not nearly as dangerous for an inmate as it was some years ago. However, incidents of violence do occur in the barracks, and two men have been murdered in barracks by other inmates since the court visited the prisons last August. It should be said, however, that the first of those two killings broke the Department's very enviable record of not having had an inmate killed by another inmate since 1971.

The court has given very careful consideration to this aspect of the case. Assuming at least for purposes of argument that Cummins and Tucker were not unconstitutionally overcrowded in November of last year or in February of this year, and assuming that they are not overcrowded today either from the standpoint of the over-all institutions or from the standpoint of individual housing units, the fact remains that they have been seriously overcrowded in the recent past, and unless prevented the overcrowding may recur.

The problem has long-term and short-term solutions. The housing of convicts in parts of gymnasiums or infirmaries or in essentially short-term housing units such as house trailers, is not an acceptable long-term solution. Long-term the problem can be solved only by replacing the existing main buildings at Cummins and Tucker, which contain the old barracks, and which are old and outmoded, by modern and adequate housing facilities, or by reducing prison populations as by dispersing inmates to off-stations or by constructing one or more smaller prisons conveniently located. That Mr. Hutto and the Board of Correction may favor the latter approach is indicated by Mr. Hutto's testimony last summer that no additional construction at Cummins is contemplated, and that it is not felt that Cummins should be a larger institution than it now is.

There is very little, if anything, that the court can do immediately about long-term solutions to the housing problem. As to the short-term solution, the court finds and concludes that the maximum population at Cummins should not exceed 1650 inmates, and that the maximum population at Tucker should not exceed 550, and the decree to be entered will freeze the maximum populations at those numbers. Additionally, respondents will be required generally or in circumstances other than exceptional not to exceed the unit capacities set forth with respect to the various individual housing units, other than the East Building, set forth in the report of November 12, 1975. The court recognizes, of course, that in emergency situations unit capacities may have to be exceeded to some extent for limited periods of time. The court will deal specifically with the East Building in a later section of this opinion.

A state owes to its convicts a constitutional duty to provide them reasonable and necessary medical and surgical care, and this duty extends to the field of mental health and also to other fields of health care. Finney v. Hutto. . . . The existence of this duty was recognized by the Arkansas penal system as early as Talley v. Stephens.

On the other hand, except in cases of emergencies, the need or desire of an inmate for medical service at a particular point in time must be balanced against legitimate institutional interests of the prison administration.

The Arkansas Department of Correction furnishes its inmates both on-station and off-station health care. The on-station care is provided by a full time physician employed by the Department who divides his time between Cummins and Tucker and who also treats female inmates of the Women's Reformatory. The doctor is assisted in his work by paramedical personnel at both Cummins and Tucker, whom the court considers to be adequately qualified to perform the tasks appropriate to their professions. Infirmaries, including pharmacies, are maintained at both Cummins and Tucker. The court finds that the infirmaries are reasonably well equipped and are adequate to provide ordinary types of care reasonably to be expected in a prison infirmary. No one claims that the infirmaries are hospitals or that they are equipped as such.

The Department also provides its inmates with somewhat rudimentary dental care which is administered by two part time dentists. The care appears to be limited to the filling and extraction of teeth and the furnishing of prison made dentures. The equipment at Cummins and Tucker appears to be adequate for the limited uses to which it is put.

When an inmate is admitted to the Department, he is given a physical examination which includes an examination of his eyes. Inmates are advised that if they develop eye complaints while in the institution, they should follow regular sick call procedures. If an inmate needs glasses, they are supplied, and the initial furnishing is gratis. If an inmate loses his glasses through carelessness or neglect, he may be required to pay for a replacement. Since most inmates are indigent and opportunities for an inmate to earn money legitimately while in the Department are quite limited, it may be difficult if not impossible for an inmate to pay for a new set of glasses. The court doubts that the on-station facilities at either Cummins or Tucker are adequate to detect eye diseases or conditions such as cataracts or glaucoma particularly at the early stages of development.

Contagious diseases can create problems for any prison, and the matter of the spread of contagious diseases is closely connected to the sanitary conditions of the institution. A common ailment of prison inmates is infectious hepatitis, and while fortunately there has not been to the court's knowledge a serious epidemic of hepatitis in the Department, there are and have been many cases of it. Likewise, there has been some apprehension about the incidence and possible spread of tuberculosis in the Department. As far as tuberculosis is concerned, the record contains detailed descriptions of the steps that are being taken by the Department in cooperation with the Arkansas Department of Health to detect the disease, to treat it and to render it non-communicable if it appears in an inmate. The court finds that the sanitary conditions that prevail in the Department are reasonably satisfactory on the whole, but there are some improvements that ought to be made, and a particular effort should be made to keep flies out of the prison buildings, including kitchens and dining areas. Naturally, the incidence of flies varies substantially with the seasons; and flies may be able to get inside the buildings to a greater extent during days on which there is an unusual amount of activity in the buildings than on ordinary days.

For many years inmates who required off-station care were transported to Little Rock where they were treated and hospitalized, if need be, at the Arkansas State Hospital which is located in close proximity to the University of Arkansas School of Medicine and to the University Medical Center, including University Hospital.

In August of last year following the closing of the hearings that have been described, the Department for reasons not appearing of record seems to have terminated its arrangement with the State Hospital and to have supplanted it with a contract with the Jefferson County Hospital in Pine Bluff under the terms of which the Hospital, which is publicly owned, will provide compensated in-patient hospital services to inmates of the Department who may be sent there from the prisons. That care is administered by physicians and surgeons engaged in private practice in Pine Bluff and who are willing to participate in the program. The contract is terminable at the will of either party.

Transportation between the units of the Department and the Hospital is now provided by ambulances owned by the Department and stationed at both Cummins and Tucker. Pine Bluff is much closer to Cummins than is Little Rock and is somewhat closer to Tucker. Until last summer, the Department owned no ambulances.

The arrangement between the Department and the Jefferson County Hospital is not intended as a permanent one. The Department now has under construction a hospital of its own in Pine Bluff located near the new Women's Reformatory that has been mentioned. This hospital when completed will be in all respects a modern, up-to-date and fully equipped and staffed hospital facility. It will not only provide medical and surgical care for inmates but will also serve as a reception and evaluation center for all new inmates. The staff will include one or more psychiatrists or clinical psychologists.

The Department hopes to have this new hospital completed and in operation by 1977. However, the court's experience with the construction of the Women's Reformatory causes it to be somewhat skeptical about target dates for the completion of Department construction, particularly in view of the fact that much of the work is done by prison labor.

The court will observe, as it has done in the past, that many of the inmates of the Department suffer from serious mental and emotional illnesses and disturbances. Historically, the Department has done nothing for those people except treat them with drugs, and send violent inmates to the State Hospital to be held temporarily until their periods of violence subside or are brought under control. Until very recently the Department has never had any systematic mental health program for inmates; nor has the Department ever employed a full time psychiatrist or psychologist although it has had from time to time the benefit of part time services of members of those professions who have not had any meaningful opportunity to engage in any extended counselling with or treatment of disturbed inmates.

Last year the Department adopted and put into limited operation a group therapy program designed to aid inmates having correctible character or emotional defects. This program was devised and its practice is taught by the Asklepieion Foundation of Carbondale, Illinois and is sometimes called "AF." Mr. Hutto testified at some length about the program, and the court personally heard a good deal of expert testimony about it on the final day of the 1975 hearings. The program is closely akin although not identical to transactional analysis, and the witnesses expressed great hopes for it as applied to convicts.

The court thinks that the establishment of the program in the Department is certainly a step in the right direction and that it should be extended to the extent feasible if it appears to be getting results. However, the program is probably not suited to all inmates, and it should not be used to the automatic exclusion of other programs of mental health that may show promise. Nor does the court think that the initiation of a program or programs of group therapy takes the place of regular psychiatrists or psychologists to be used in diagnosing, evaluating and endeavoring to treat individual inmates by conventional methods of individual psychotherapy.

Getting back to the subject of on-station care and the adequacy of the facilities and services available at Cummins and Tucker, it appears to the court that the Court of Appeals in reaching its adverse decision on this phase of the case was influenced in substantial measure by the results of a study that was made in 1972 by the Arkansas State Department of Health at the request of the Board of Correction. The report of the results of the study pointed out many serious deficiencies in the health care offered by the Department and was discussed at some length in Finney v. Arkansas Board of Correction. Since that report was made, there have been numerous and substantial improvements at both Cummins and Tucker, but the court thinks that remediable deficiencies probably still exist. It has been some four years since the study was conducted, and the court is going to direct the Department to request that another study be made as soon as practicable. The Department will be expected to follow any reasonable suggestions that the Health Department may make. The study requested should not be limited to the adequacy of personnel and equipment at the prisons, but should also extend to the adequacy of on-station services offered and to such things as sanitary conditions at the prisons and the adequacy of the means being taken to prevent or control the spread of contagious diseases, including tuberculosis.

The existing arrangement between the Department and the Jefferson County Hospital is not ideal. The Hospital was not designed as a prison hospital; it is not under the control of the Department or any other agency of the State itself, and the doctors practicing therein are not state employees. Moreover, the court is not willing to permit the Department entirely to sever its connection with perhaps more advanced facilities and services that may be available at Little Rock. The court thinks it probable that the Department in fact has a contingency arrangement with the State Hospital or the Medical Center whereby inmates can have the benefit of facilities and services that may be available at those institutions and which may not be available at Pine Bluff. If no such contingency arrangement exists, the Department will be expected to undertake to negotiate one as soon as possible.

What has just been said is not to be taken as a disparagement of the Jefferson County Hospital or of the physicians who practice in that hospital or as a disapproval of the existing contract. The court is simply not willing to permit the Department to rely entirely on the Pine Bluff facility to provide off-station care that inmates may need.

As has been said, the court thinks that the Department should now proceed to employ on a full time basis one or more psychiatrists or psychologists for the purposes that have been indicated, and to provide adequate quarters and facilities for the work of the new employees. Those requirements will be made.

With regard to inmate access to available health care services the court finds that the Department has no custom or policy of denying necessary care to any inmate who needs it, and further finds that inmate access to the prison physician and to the infirmaries and their personnel is reasonably adequate. Regular sick calls and "pill" calls are made at both Cummins and Tucker each day. A sick call is made by paramedics at the East Building each day, and the prison physician visits the East Building once a week.

It is true that in some isolated instances inmates may have been denied treatment improperly or may have not been given proper treatment. Such isolated instances, however, would appear to be the result of nothing but administrative or professional error, and they do not result from any departmental policy. Of course, it ought to be unnecessary to point out that it is absolutely impermissible for any Department employee deliberately to refuse to treat an inmate or to deny him prescribed medication for reasons of spite or as a means of retaliation or punishment for misconduct.

To the extent that individual inmates complain that on particular occasions they have been denied treatment or medication, the court thinks that such claims can be dealt with adequately when the court considers the individual claims for relief that are before it.

Before concluding this section of this opinion, the court desires to deal to some extent with the problem of malingering by inmates. Unless they are physically or mentally disabled, inmates of the Department are expected to work, and many of them are required to work hard and for long hours. Some inmates will feign illness to avoid work, and some will go so far as to injure themselves to avoid duty. This tendency of inmates to shirk work by feigning illness creates a real problem for the prison administration, and malingering is quite properly a major disciplinary offense and may be punished severely.

There is one aspect of the problem, however, that gives the court some trouble. Inmates can and do become ill on occasion while at work. If an inmate complains of illness while working in the fields, for example, and expresses a desire to go to the infirmary, his request will ordinarily be granted by his supervisor and he will be transported to the infirmary from his place of work. But, when the inmate asks to be taken to the infirmary in such circumstances he runs the risk of being charged with malingering unless the doctor or the paramedic who examines him finds that he is sick enough to be put to bed or at least to receive an excuse from working for the remainder of the day. If the inmate is so charged and found guilty, he may be confined in punitive isolation, or may lose good time or be reduced in classification, or he may be subjected to a combination of those sanctions.

The court recognizes that an inmate may go to work on a particular day and later pretend to be ill in order to obtain at least a brief respite from labor while being carried to the infirmary, and that this gives a problem to those in charge of inmate work crews. But, an inmate who becomes ill or honestly thinks that he is sick should not be discouraged from seeking medical attention by fear of being exposed to a major disciplinary proceeding should the person who examines him conclude that there is nothing serious the matter with him.

The court thinks that the problem can be solved, at least in part, by providing that before an inmate can be found guilty of malingering by a disciplinary committee or a panel thereof, the committee or panel must consult with the doctor or other person who examined the inmate and determine that in the opinion of the examiner the accused inmate was in fact a malingerer on the occasion in question. The mere fact that the inmate in question was returned to his place of work without being put to bed or given a "lay-in" for the day is not enough automatically to justify a conviction. The decree to be entered will so provide.

Unlike the situation that existed in 1973, the rehabilitation picture within the Department is now quite bright, and the court finds it free of constitutional deficiencies.

With the possible exception of the livestock operation at Booneville, all of the off-stations mentioned in an earlier portion of this opinion were established in 1975, and their rehabilitative value is obvious.

In 1973 the Arkansas Legislature established the Department of Correction School District, and the educational program offered by that district is comparable to the program available in the public schools of the State. If a trustworthy inmate completes his high school education while an inmate of the Department, he can arrange to pursue his education at the college level if he desires to do so. The educational program, which is available to all inmates of the Department, was discussed in some detail by the court in Rutherford v. Hutto, 377 F.Supp. 268 (E.D.Ark.1974), to which opinion reference is now made. . . .

Extensive vocational training is available at both Cummins and Tucker. An inmate at Cummins may be trained in the repair of farm equipment and furniture, in upholstering, welding, building maintenance, and "graphic arts." A Tucker inmate may be trained in the repair of automobile bodies, in the tuning up of automobile engines, welding, woodwork and drafting.

The graphic arts program at Cummins deserves particular mention. It teaches offset printing and perhaps other forms of duplication, and inmates who have completed the course and have been released have been quite fortunate in finding jobs in which their newly developed skill can be employed.

Finally, although the health care provided by the Department has been criticized, it appears to the court that a good many inmates emerge from the Department in better physical condition than they were in when they were received as inmates, and that in itself has rehabilitative value.

The Department's regulations relating to inmate mail which gave the Court of Appeals trouble were promulgated prior to the decision of the Supreme Court in Procunier v. Martinez, 416 U.S. 396 (1974). Since that decision the regulations, which appear as part of Chapter IV of the January, 1975 edition of the Department's Inmate Handbook, have been revised. The court finds that the revised regulations are quite liberal and comply with constitutional requirements.

Regulations dealing with visits between inmates and members of their families and friends also appear in Chapter IV of the Handbook, and they appear to the court to be reasonable and appropriate.

The opinion in *Finney* deals in part with the adequacy of legal assistance available to inmates, and this court was directed to "reexamine procedures relating to inmate assistance to satisfy the alternative requirements of Johnson v. Avery, 393 U.S. 483 (1969)." Finney v. Arkansas Board of Correction.

The court finds that the legal assistance available to inmates, including assistance rendered by fellow inmates, at times called "writ writers," is and has been adequate, and that the Court of Appeals may not have been advised fully in this area.

As to inmate assistance to other inmates, the court knows full well that writ writers have functioned freely and without hindrance in the Department for years, and that the representation to the contrary made to the Court of Appeals by one of the appellants in *Finney* was simply false.[5]

The Court of Appeals was also not fully informed as to the status and function of the Legal Adviser to Inmates. The Legal Adviser is a full time employee of the Department, and is a licensed lawyer. His services are available without charge to inmates of all of the units of the Department. The Adviser is in a position to serve and does serve inmates in numerous fields, and the statement that the Adviser "is not permitted to assist the prisoners in civil litigation," is not an accurate one.

It is true that the Adviser is not in a position to represent inmates who wish to file § 1983 petitions seeking relief against their keepers. But he can and does represent inmates in civil proceedings generally, including proceedings for post-conviction relief either in the Arkansas state courts or in the federal courts. That the efforts of the Adviser have not been unsuccessful in habeas corpus context is demonstrated by the recent decision of this court and of the Court of Appeals in Sanford v. Hutto, 394 F.Supp. 1278 (E.D.Ark.), aff'd, 523 F.2d 1383 (8th Cir. 1975). See also Bumgarner v. Lockhart, 361 F.Supp. 829 (E.D.Ark.1973).

Before leaving this subject the court will point out that apart from the assistance of the Legal Adviser to Inmates and of fellow inmates, Arkansas convicts who can afford to do so are always free to employ counsel of their choice, and that indigent inmates are entitled in proper cases to judicially appointed counsel in connection with either civil or criminal proceedings in the state or federal courts.

5. The representation in question was made in connection with one of the appeals of James G. Ellingburg, which appeals were consolidated with the appeal in *Finney* proper. See 505 F.2d at 213. Ellingburg is himself a notorious prison writ writer and prepared many petitions both for himself and other inmates while confined in Cummins from about 1972 until his release in the summer of 1975. As the court recalls, Ellingburg handled his own appeals, and the representation in question is not to be attributed to counsel for petitioners in *Finney*.

The court recognizes that if the legal assistance to be given by one inmate to another is to be effective, the inmate giving the assistance must have reasonable access to some library facilities. Law libraries have been purchased at both Cummins and Tucker. The court has inspected them and finds them adequate for inmate use and that access to them is reasonably available subject to restrictions which are not inappropriate.

In this section of the opinion the court will discuss the question of whether the Department is exercising ordinary care for the safety of inmates from abuse and violence at the hands of other inmates, and the question of whether living conditions at Cummins or Tucker are so unreasonably dangerous to inmates as to make confinement in either of those institutions unconstitutional.

The questions have been stated as above because it may be doubted that any prison is a "safe" place for an inmate to live. Regardless of how well constructed, organized, and administered a prison may be, incidents of violence of various kinds, including homosexual violence, are going to occur from time to time. And the court has already mentioned the killing of two inmates by other inmates since August of last year.

In the very nature of things a state cannot be held to be an insurer of the safety of the inmates of its penal institutions. But a state does owe to convicts the duty to use ordinary care for their safety, and a state cannot be permitted to maintain a penal institution in which conditions are so dangerous that the inmates must exist in dread of imminent injury or death inflicted by other inmates.

In years past an ordinary inmate of the Department, referred to then as a "ranker," was in almost constant danger from other rankers, and he was also in danger of being killed by armed inmate guards. His danger of attack from other rankers was enhanced by the fact that the trusty guards would do little or nothing to protect him and that the inmate floorwalkers assigned to patrol the barracks at night were of little, if any, value as far as inmate safety was concerned.

In *Holt II* the trusty guard system (and other aspects of the trusty system) was held to be unconstitutional and was ordered to be phased out with the trusties being replaced by civilian personnel.

By the time of *Holt III* the trusty guards had been replaced except for a few armed inmates who were stationed in the towers and the inmate dog handlers who were armed when the prison bloodhounds were being used in pursuit of an escaped convict or a criminal.[6]

The court finds that at the present time the Department uses no armed inmates as guards or in any other capacity, including the handling of dogs. Thus, an inmate today is in no danger of death or injury at the hands of another inmate in whose hands a weapon has been placed by the Department.

6. The court will note at this point that the bloodhounds used by the Department are not "guard" or "attack" dogs. They are not vicious; they are not trained to pursue or attack human beings but simply to follow human scent. When a dog is working, he is under the immediate physical control of the handler. Bloodhounds such as those used by the Department can be, and are, used not only to track fleeing criminals and escapees, but also to track lost or missing persons, including children.

In the course of the hearings counsel for petitioner suggested in their examination and cross-examination of witnesses that the continued use of inmate floorwalkers to patrol the barracks at night was a relic of the old system, and that it should be prohibited. The court does not agree.

The floorwalkers are unarmed and have no authority with respect to the inmates over whom they are supposed to watch. While the court doubts, as it has doubted in the past, that the floorwalkers are of much protection to sleeping inmates, they are not a source of danger to inmates; their presence may have some deterring effect on the "creepers" and "crawlers" mentioned in *Holt II,* and according to Commissioner Hutto and Superintendent Lockhart they serve certain other useful purposes as well.

What has just been said about the floorwalkers who operate in the barracks is generally applicable to the inmate turnkeys who are stationed outside the doors of the respective barracks.

The actual guarding of inmates from other inmates is now done by civilian guards who are always stationed outside the barracks and who can readily come to the assistance of an imperilled inmate. And inmates who are working in the fields are under the guard of free world personnel who are in a position to come to the help of an inmate who is threatened or assaulted by a fellow convict.

Further, regardless of what may be thought about conditions in the East Building at Cummins, a subject that will be reached in due course, the fact remains that the authorities at Cummins have been able to use the building to remove from general population a number of inmates who ordinarily would live in barracks and who would constitute a particular source of danger to other inmates.

The two killings that have taken place in recent months occurred after the record in the case was closed, and the circumstances of the killings have not been developed in the evidence.

While those incidents and other nonfatal incidents that have doubtless occurred are highly regrettable, the court finds that all in all officers and employees of the Department have done a reasonably good job in the field of inmate safety over the past three or four years, and the court does not find that the Department is failing to use ordinary care for inmate safety, or that either Cummins or Tucker is today such a dangerous place for an inmate to live as to raise a constitutional problem as far as inmate safety in itself is concerned.

As is well known, social conditions existing in a given community at a given time are apt to be reflected in its prisons. And if a social problem is of a kind that can arise in a prison, it is almost sure to do so and probably in exacerbated form due to the very nature of prison life. No one questions that race relations constitute a major social problem all over the United States today, and it is not surprising to find that the problem exists in prisons all over the country, and the institutions operated by the Arkansas Department of Correction are no exceptions. Indeed, the problem of race relations at both Cummins and Tucker is perhaps the most vexing one to beset the Department, and it manifests itself in a number of areas of prison life and administration.

In discussing certain prison practices and conditions race relations can be ignored up to a point, and the discussions appearing in the preceding sections of this opinion have not made any particular reference to race. However, when one approaches such areas as prison discipline, alleged brutality practiced upon inmates, inmate classifications, and job assignments, racial consists of inmate populations and prison staffs cannot be overlooked, nor can there be overlooked the effect that racial attitudes and prejudices may have, or be alleged to have, on relationships between inmates and between inmates and prison officers and employees.

Race relations, whether in a prison or somewhere else, depend ultimately on the subjective feelings of the people involved. As long as the subjective feelings involved are no more than feelings, no federal constitutional problem is presented. Where, however, those feelings manifest themselves objectively in words, actions, or policies in prison context, constitutional deprivations can result.

Racial attitudes in this country have developed over a very long period of time, and in many people are so deep seated that the persons holding them are not actively conscious that they exist and influence their objective conduct. Thus, a white prison employee may discriminate against black inmates without being really conscious that he is doing so. The reverse of that proposition is also true. Moreover, a member of a minority racial or ethnic group who believes that he is a member of a class that has been systematically discriminated against by members of a dominant majority may see discrimination where none exists. Further, a member of a minority, including a convict, may seek to excuse his own failings, incapacities, or shortcomings by claiming that he has been the victim of racial discrimination when such is not the case.

It is probably unnecessary to say that when one deals with race relations in the Arkansas Department of Correction, one is dealing with members of the Negro and the Caucasian races. If other racial or ethnic groups are represented in the Department at all, the number of their members is so small as to be insignificant.

Negroes in Arkansas are in a substantial minority when compared with the population of the State as a whole. In the Department of Correction, however, black inmates make up nearly one-half of the total prison population and have done so for as long as this court has been familiar with the Arkansas prison system.

Administration of the Department, on the other hand, is clearly under the control of white people. Although in recent years the Department has employed a substantial number of blacks and is trying to hire more, a large majority of the employees are white, and Negroes occupying positions of any real authority are very few indeed.

Regardless of the fact that at Cummins, and presumably at Tucker as well, one finds a number of black employees bearing titles such as Captain, Lieutenant or Sergeant, it appears to the court that the only black person who occupies a position of any real authority in the administration of the prison system is Ms. Helen Carruthers, the Superintendent of the Women's Reformatory. And the court will say at this point that she has done an excellent job with a racially mixed female population in spite of the difficulties, including overcrowding, under which she has been required to work.

Prior to the Department's voluntary integration of Tucker and prior to the integration of Cummins pursuant to the decision in *Holt II,* the court had no real occasion to consider race relations in the Department apart from the question of segregation itself. However, in *Holt III* the court had urgent occasion to discuss those relations and did so in several contexts. . . .

In *Holt III* the court found that race relations in the Department were bad, to say the least, and the Court of Appeals certainly did not disagree with that finding. Finney v. Arkansas Board of Correction.

Most of what the court had to say in *Holt III* by way of criticism of the Department in the field of race relations is still valid today, and the court sees no occasion to repeat those statements here in any detail. While conditions in the Department have probably improved somewhat over the last two years and several months, the court finds that in spite of Departmental regulations and memoranda designed to improve race relations and to eliminate or mitigate the effects of poor race relations, the relations between whites and blacks are still bad at both Cummins and Tucker, particularly at the former institution. And the court further finds that the poor relations are still due to the factors that the court found causative in *Holt III,* namely a paucity of blacks in positions of real authority that are meaningful to inmates in their day to day prison life, the low caliber of the inmates in general, including black inmates, and the poor quality and lack of professionalism of the lower echelons of prison employees who are in close and abrasive contact with inmates every day.

On the positive side, the court thinks that the members of the Board of Correction, Commissioner Hutto, and Superintendents Lockhart and Britton are conscious of the problem and are working toward at least a partial solution, although in candor the court doubts that race relations, as such, will ever be any better in the Department than they are in the free world; and that observation is as applicable to any prison in the country as it is to the Arkansas prisons.

One hopeful sign is the establishment of the rehabilitative programs that have been described. If they do nothing else, such programs tend to ameliorate the rigors and harshness of prison life, and that amelioration in itself would seem to have a tendency to improve relations between inmates and prison personnel regardless of race. Moreover, providing ignorant or illiterate black inmates with what amounts to a public school education should tend to upgrade them and qualify them for better assignments and a better life inside the prison as well as in the outside world.

Conversely, systematic training of prison employees is calculated to improve their general competency and professionalism, to make them aware of racial attitudes and problems, and to equip them better to deal with inmates of a race other than their own. And it appears from the record that training programs for employees of the Department have been instituted and are being prosecuted.

Respondents' Exhibit No. 687 is a copy of the Department's "Affirmative Action Plan" which was initiated in March, 1974 and which was approved in

February, 1975. The plan indicates that the major concern of the Department has been to promote blacks already hired by the Department, and that since March, 1974, out of 198 promotions, 64 or 32.32% have gone to blacks.

The plan further reflects that since March, 1974 the Department has terminated 260 persons of whom 61 or 23.46% were black, whereas during the same period of time the Department hired 274 people, 78 of whom or 28.47% were black. Thus, the hiring of blacks has been in excess of black terminations percentagewise.

According to the plan, new employees are hired without regard to race and entirely as a result of referrals by the Arkansas Employment Security Division, and the plan recites that prior to the utilization of the ESD as a referring service application forms used by the Department did not refer to race. The plan states that between August 30, 1973 and June 30, 1974 the Department's black work force was increased by 2.4%, and that during the period between March, 1974 and May, 1975 the black work force increased by 5.1%.

While the progress reported in the plan is commendable, and while the plan is doubtless sufficient to serve the purpose for which it was formed, and while it has evidently gained the approval of the governmental agency, the approval of which was required, the court doubts that it really reaches the problem that is involved here.

This is not a fair employment practices case. The question is not whether the Department is discriminating against blacks in matters of hirings, promotions, or discharges, but whether the recruitment and promotional policies of the Department are designed to correct or alleviate the racial imbalance of the Department's staff which has contributed so much to the difficulties that the Department has had in the area now under consideration.

What the Department needs to do is not to hire people without regard to race but to make a conscious effort to hire qualified blacks in additional numbers and to place them in positions in the institutions which will enable them to exercise some real authority and influence in the aspects of prison life with which black inmates are primarily concerned.

The Department needs more blacks who are in positions that will entitle them to sit on classification committees and on disciplinary panels, to counsel with inmates about their problems, and to supervise inmates while at work. This need was recognized by this court in *Holt III,* and it was recognized by the Court of Appeals in *Finney.*

To illustrate that need: Many of the disciplinary problems of the Department arise in the prison fields where large numbers of black inmates work as members of prison "hoe squads" or "garden squads." An examination of Respondents' Exhibit No. 659 reveals as of June 11, 1975 the field security force at Cummins consisted of a Field Major, a Field Captain, three Field Lieutenants, and fifteen "Correctional Officers II." The major, the captain, and the lieutenants were all white, and of the fifteen correctional officers twelve were white. On the other hand, Respondents' Exhibit 658 reflects that on June 10, 1975 282 inmates were assigned to hoe squads; 54.9% of those inmates were black. The same exhibit shows that on the same date 137 inmates were assigned to the garden squads; 52.5% of those inmates were black. In such a situation racial difficulties, including claims of discrimination, are certain to arise, and they do.

There is no constitutional objection, of course, to the Department's using the ESD as a referring service, but the exclusive use of that agency is not apt to produce applicants the hiring of whom will meet the Department's need to correct the existing racial imbalance of the staff.

The court recognizes, as it has recognized in the past, that it is difficult to recruit blacks who are qualified and willing to hold responsible positions in the Department; a number of factors are involved, including the rural location of the prisons. But the court is not satisfied that Commissioner Hutto and others connected with recruiting prison personnel have really exerted themselves to the fullest extent possible or have exhausted their resources as far as hiring responsible blacks is concerned.

There is nothing to indicate that the Department's need in this connection has been made known generally to the black population in Arkansas through advertising or otherwise, or that anyone connected with the Department has sought to enlist the good offices of the University of Arkansas at Pine Bluff, which is a predominantly black institution of higher learning and which used to be an all black college, or that help has been sought from such agencies or organizations as the Urban League or the National Association for the Advancement of Colored People, or from any governmental agencies concerned with the welfare of minorities.

Such approaches to the problem might not turn out to be fruitful, but at least they should be explored. Respondents will be directed to make further efforts in the field of black employment and in that connection to give consideration to the court's suggestions although the court is not going to command that any particular suggestion be followed.

In this section of the opinion the court has undertaken to discuss race relations in the Department in a general way. The court will now proceed to examine other specific prison problems. The problems to be considered will include racial discrimination per se and other problems in which race is involved to a greater or lesser extent.

The racial discrimination now to be considered is alleged discrimination by white prison personnel against black inmates. At this time at least, "reverse discrimination" is not any real problem in the Department.

In a prison which is controlled by white people and in which large numbers of black inmates are confined, opportunities for racial discrimination against the blacks exist in a number of principal fields, namely: inmate classification, including promotions to a higher class or demotions to a lower class, job assignments, disciplinary proceedings, and punishments imposed for infractions of prison rules.

. . . The court has reviewed what it had to say in *Holt III* in the light of the opinion of the Court of Appeals and in the light of the evidence developed in 1975, and finds that it has nothing really substantial to add to what it said in 1973, taking into consideration the fact that there probably has been some improvement in race relations at the prisons since *Holt III* was decided.

As indicated in *Holt III,* racial discrimination is not officially countenanced by the Department and is specifically prohibited by its rules and regulations. As it found in 1973, the court now finds that there is no hard evidence that overt discrimination is being practiced in the Department, although many black inmates think or claim to think that they have been the victims of discrimination. But again as in 1973 the court has the feeling that in instances racial discrimination that is covert and perhaps even unconscious is still going on and that it is going to continue to go on until such time as the Department itself is adequately integrated along the lines laid down in the preceding section of this opinion.

In its Second Supplemental Decree filed in connection with its *Holt III* opinion the court specifically enjoined racial discrimination in any form and in all significant areas of prison life, and the court does not consider that additional injunctive relief in connection with the problem is necessary or would be helpful at this time.[7]

A viable grievance procedure in a prison ought to serve to alleviate a number of prison problems, including claims of racial discrimination. The value of such a program generally has been recognized by the Court of Appeals for this circuit in Willis v. Ciccone, 506 F.2d 1011 (8th Cir. 1974). . . . Where such a procedure exists, it can be used to settle expeditiously many inmate grievances without requiring the inmates involved to resort to time consuming litigation which places extremely heavy burdens on the courts, prison administrators, and attorneys. As the law now appears to stand, a state prisoner is not required to exhaust administrative remedies, including grievance procedures, before seeking judicial relief under § 1983. That is not to say, however, that if a state establishes an adequate grievance procedure and administers it fairly and properly, the federal courts might not be inclined at some future date to require the exhaustion of the procedure before the inmate may have his grievance heard in the courts.

The record in this case reflects that in 1974 the Department initiated a formal grievance procedure which is set out in detail at pages 12–14 of the Inmate Handbook. If an inmate with a grievance is not able to obtain relief from his immediate supervisor, he may carry his grievance to the Administrative Review Officer. If that officer does not solve the problem satisfactorily, the inmate is entitled to review by an "Institutional Review Board," consisting of the Superintendent of the institution and two high ranking staff members. The grievance may be carried still further to the "Department Review Committee" and ultimately to the Board of Correction itself. Provision is made for having the grievance considered by impartial people, and it is expressly provided that unless the inmate makes false statements in the prosecution of his grievance, he is not to be subjected to any sort of retaliation for having invoked the grievance procedure.

Mr. Lockhart testified that some use of the procedure has been made at Cummins, and that some grievances have been adjusted satisfactorily. Of course, if inmates will not use a grievance procedure, it is valueless, and they

7. The court will note at this point that this is not a contempt proceeding in which prison officials are sought to be held liable for violations of previous decrees or orders of the court.

will not use it unless they believe that there is a reasonable possibility of obtaining relief by means of it.

Apart from any formal grievance procedure, the court thinks that the higher echelon officials of the Department should be more available to inmates than perhaps they are, and should keep themselves personally familiar with day to day life in the prisons including the work activities of inmates.

The Department has a number of black inmates who are members of the Black Muslim religious sect. Some of those inmates claim that they are subjected to religious discrimination along with or apart from racial discrimination.

The Muslims in the Department fall broadly into two groups, namely, Muslims who abide generally by prison rules and regulations and who live in general prison population, and Muslims who are more or less consistent rule violators and trouble makers and who spend at least large portions of their time confined under maximum security conditions, principally in the East Building at Cummins. This section of the opinion will deal with the Muslims who live in population, but what is said here will not be irrelevant to the conditions of Muslims in the East Building.

The problem of the Muslims in general population was considered by the court in *Holt III.* The court found that the claims of the Muslims were not without substance, although the court did not find that Department personnel were intentionally discriminating against Muslims as such and that much of the problem arose from the fact that the prison administrations were simply unaware of what the problems of the Muslims were. The court found that the administration was willing to meet reasonable Muslim demands, and that for the most part the problems of the Muslims could be handled administratively. However, in its Second Supplemental Decree the court specifically enjoined the respondents from discriminating against the Muslims on account of their religious beliefs or the teachings of their religion. And the *Finney* court took note of this court's action in that regard.

The court finds that today the Muslims are not unduly restricted in the exercise of their religion. They can hold meetings as can members of other religious sects, the services of Muslim clergymen are not denied to them, and they are free to receive generally circulating Muslim publications.

As it was in 1973, the principal problem of the Department's Muslims today is dietary. As is now generally known, Muslims eschew the consumption of pork in any form; they are not permitted by their religion to eat pork, nor are they permitted to eat any food which has been cooked in pork grease or that has been contaminated otherwise by coming into contact with pork. Unfortunately for the Muslims, pork is frequently served as a food item in the Department, and a good many of the vegetables served to inmates are cooked in pork grease.

The court finds that the Department has made and is making a conscientious effort to supply the Muslims with a pork free diet and to advise Muslim inmates in connection with each meal what dishes they can eat without danger of being contaminated. However, the Muslims are not fully satisfied because in the last analysis they do not trust the Department's cooks and food handlers, including non-Muslim employees and non-Muslim inmates assigned to work in the prison kitchens. And the Muslims fear that they may unwittingly consume food that is taboo to them on religious grounds.

The court does not think that there is much that it can do to remove this distrust by means of further injunction or otherwise. However, the court will enjoin the Department from serving pork to Muslims against their will and from exposing them to food that has been contaminated by contact with pork or pork grease or lard made from pork fat.

Due in part to the small number of Muslims in the Department, the court is not going to order that special kitchens be established for the Muslims or that only Muslims be employed in the preparation of food for the Muslims. Assuming that Muslims will work in a kitchen in which pork is being used as an item of diet or a cooking ingredient, the court thinks that it would be helpful if Muslims were assigned to the kitchens, and the court thinks that in any event non-Muslim kitchen personnel should be properly supervised to prevent the overt or covert, direct or indirect, serving of pork to the Muslim inmates.

While the court does not deem it necessary to order the step to be taken, it might not be amiss for Commissioner Hutto to arrange to have the prisons inspected by free world Muslims and to get their ideas and suggestions about the conditions from the standpoint of religion under which their co-religionists are confined.

The court will now take up the claim of inmates in general population that they are unconstitutionally subjected to brutality, including verbal abuse, cursing, and the like, by prison personnel. This section of the opinion will be limited to class claims of inmates in general population; similar claims of inmates confined under maximum security conditions will be treated in other portions of this opinion, and individual claims of specific instances of brutality will be dealt with within the framework of individual complaints.

The history of brutality in what is now the Department of Correction is a long one and it has been discussed in detail by judges of this court and by the Court of Appeals. . . .

When the *Holt* cases were first filed in 1969, the grosser abuses considered in Courtney v. Bishop, Jackson v. Bishop, and Talley v. Stephens, supra, had been eliminated. However, brutality of various kinds was still prevalent when *Holt II* was decided, and it was still a problem at the time of *Holt III.*

On December 30, 1971, a date between the decisions in *Holt II* and *Holt III,* the court felt constrained to file a supplemental decree enjoining respondents from inflicting any cruel and unusual punishment on any individual inmate and from engaging in any general practices or procedures amounting to the infliction of such punishment and also enjoining respondents from interfering with inmates in their efforts to obtain relief in the courts and from retaliating upon inmates for having sought such relief or for having testified or offered to testify in judicial proceedings.

Contemporaneously with the filing of the opinion in *Holt III,* the court filed another supplemental decree which, among other things, defined "cruel and unusual punishment" in broad terms so as to include: the infliction upon any inmate of any unreasonable or unnecessary force in any form; the assigning of an inmate to tasks inconsistent with his medical classification; the use of any punishment amounting to torture; the practice of forcing any inmate to run to or from work, or while at work, or in front of any moving vehicle or animal; and the infliction of any punishment not authorized by the Department's rules and regulations.

Brutality, whether broadly or narrowly defined, is not countenanced in the Department today. Like racial discrimination, brutality in its various forms is strictly forbidden by the prison rules for employees. And it appears that in instances employees who have been guilty of brutality have been discharged or required to resign.

It should always be kept in mind that the reasonable use of force by prison authorities is not only permissible but positively required on occasions. Hence, every incident of violence involving an inmate and a prison employee is not necessarily an incident of brutality.

In other sections of this opinion the court deemed it well to mention the killing of two inmates by other inmates that took place after the record herein had been closed. And the court now feels it necessary to mention another fatal incident that took place in August of last year. This incident, unlike the killings that have been described, involved prison personnel to some extent. A young inmate was received at Cummins during the early morning hours on the date of the incident and was put to work with other inmates clearing a ditch bank; he was given no breakfast prior to being put to work, although he did eat lunch. In the afternoon he died in circumstances that were at least suspicious. The incident evoked considerable publicity and stirred up the usual inmate rumors, including charges that the young man had been beaten to death by his guards. An autopsy was performed on the body, and after a rather strange period of delay, the State Medical Examiner reported his finding that the inmate had not been physically assaulted and had come to his death as a result of heat exhaustion. There is at least some reason to believe that the young man was subjected to "hazing" by fellow inmates and that one or more prison employees may have participated to some extent in the process.

If the foregoing description of the incident is substantially correct, and the court does not know that it is and is making no finding on the subject, the incident was inexcusable, and points up as much as anything else the fact that some employees of the Department are still sadly lacking not only in professionalism but also in ordinary good sense. The court hopes that Commissioner Hutto and Superintendent Lockhart have investigated the incident properly and have taken such disciplinary action, if any, as might have appeared appropriate.

Getting back to the record, the court does not doubt that incidents of violence still occur in the Department and that some of them may amount to physical brutality. Nor does the court doubt that in spite of Department prohibitions some employees are still using foul language and racial epithets when addressing inmates, and that at times inmates are improperly threatened by their guards and supervisors.

The court has given very careful consideration to the question of whether the inmates are entitled to additional class relief in the matter of brutality. In view of the announced policies of the Department and in view of the relief that has already been granted in this sphere of prison life, the court does not consider that much more relief is called for or that it would do any good. However, the court will in the decree to be entered specifically enjoin all Department personnel from verbally abusing, or cursing, inmates, and from employing racial slurs or epithets when addressing or talking with inmates. That specific prohibition may be of some value to higher echelon employees in their efforts to improve the professionalism and conduct of those who are required to work in close proximity to inmates and who have occasion to deal with inmates.

In *Holt III* the court considered disciplinary procedures that were followed by the Department at that time and that had been devised in 1972 or earlier. The procedures were discussed at some length and were approved subject to the Department's compliance with certain specific directives of the court. On the appeal, the Court of Appeals considered the procedures in question in the light of the then very recent decision of the Supreme Court in Wolff v. McDonnell, 418 U.S. 539 (1974). The appellate court approved of the directives of this court but felt that the procedures in question had to be revamped in the light of the *McDonnell* decision, supra. 505 F.2d at 208.

Wolff v. McDonnell was decided on June 26, 1974. Shortly thereafter the Board of Correction promulgated rules and regulations relating to disciplinary matters which appear in the record as Respondents' Exhibit 688 and most of which appear in the 1975 edition of the Inmate Handbook which has been mentioned. The court finds ultimately that the procedures in question meet the requirements of *McDonnell* and are constitutional.

Each institution has a major disciplinary committee and a minor disciplinary committee. The major disciplinary committee consists of at least four prison officials and must include the Associate Superintendent of the institution or his designee; one member of the security staff of the institution, one member of the treatment staff, and the Chief Security Officer of the institution who is a member of the committee but has no vote. The minor disciplinary committee, which deals with rule infractions deemed to be of a minor or trivial nature, consists of the Shift Supervisor, who serves as Chairman, and any two other department personnel of the Chairman's choosing. While the major disciplinary committee consists of at least four persons, the committee usually sits in panels of three as was the case in 1973 and 1972. A minor disciplinary committee always consists of three members.

A minor disciplinary committee can impose only minor punishments. It cannot sentence an inmate to confinement in punitive isolation, or deprive him of good time, or change his classification or job assignment. The punishments that it can impose are limited to warnings or reprimands, loss of privileges, and limited extra duty. Once a minor disciplinary committee has acted in a given case, its decision cannot be altered by the major disciplinary committee if the inmate accepts the decision of the minor committee. An inmate is not required to accept the decision of the minor disciplinary committee; if he chooses to do so, he may insist upon being proceeded against before the major disciplinary committee in accordance with the procedures applicable to that committee.

It is not entirely clear from the materials before the court what procedures are followed in connection with a minor disciplinary procedure. The rules do provide that a minor disciplinary committee is to function as "expeditiously as possible," and in view of the limitations on the punishments that such a committee can impose and in view of the nature of the violations considered by such a committee, and the fact that an inmate is not required to accept a minor disciplinary decision adverse to him, the court assumes that the minor disciplinary committee acts in a more summary manner than does the major disciplinary committee. The court has no difficulty with that, and thinks that Wolff v. McDonnell recognizes at least by implication that the requirements of procedural due process where only minor rule infractions are involved are less than the requirements that exist where an inmate faces a serious charge that may result in severe punishment.

Turning now to major disciplinary procedures, an inmate facing a major disciplinary charge is required to be served with a written copy of the charge not less than twenty-four hours before the disciplinary hearing that must be held within seventy-two hours after the occurrence of the disciplinary episode, except that in unusual circumstances the Superintendent of the institution may grant limited extensions of time.

The inmate is entitled to appear before the committee, including a panel thereof, and is entitled to present his version of the incident. He may also "call witnesses" in the sense that he may identify potential witnesses to the officer who notifies him of the charge against him. The committee is authorized to call all necessary witnesses. The testimony of a witness may be taken in writing before the hearing or orally before the committee in the course of the hearing.

If in the course of a hearing the panel calls witnesses, the accused is not permitted to be present while the witnesses are testifying; on the other hand, the charging officer is not permitted to be present during the testimony of witnesses. Commissioner Hutto explained this procedure by saying that in view of the conditions of prison life an inmate witness is simply not going to say anything adverse to the accused and is not likely to say anything that may bring him into the bad graces of the charging officer. Consequently, the testimony of inmate witnesses if taken in the presence of either the accused or the charging officer would probably be essentially worthless. The accused is not permitted to cross-examine the employee who prepared the initial disciplinary report and who is frequently the charging officer; in Mr. Hutto's view such cross-examination would be worthless and would be quite likely to cause increased hostility between the inmate and the employee involved and might lead to future confrontations between them. In the court's opinion, Mr. Hutto's views are reasonable, and the court does not consider that the practices just described offend Wolff v. McDonnell or that they violate due process of law.

At the conclusion of the hearing the panel decides the case, and if the accused is found guilty, punishment is assessed. The court presumes that the decision and action of the panel in a given case is determined by the vote of a majority of the members of the panel. If the accused is found guilty, the panel is required to state in writing the reasons for its decision.

An inmate may appeal an adverse disciplinary ruling to the Superintendent of the institution by filing a written notice of appeal within three days after the adverse decision is rendered. However, the Superintendent is not required to review the decision unless he considers that the facts of the case warrant review. If the Superintendent's ruling is adverse to the inmate, the latter may appeal to the Commissioner and finally to the Board of Correction itself. However, the rules provide that if in connection with any appeal an inmate wilfully and knowingly makes a false statement or deliberately tries to deceive the reviewing authority, the inmate's action is in itself a major disciplinary violation.

While Wolf v. McDonnell makes it clear that an inmate is not entitled to counsel in the course of a disciplinary proceeding, the Department's rules provide that if an inmate is illiterate or "is otherwise unable to properly present his case, the Chairman may appoint a member of the staff to assist the inmate in his presentation." And the Superintendent is required to provide the Chairman of the committee with a list of staff members who do not regularly sit on the Disciplinary Committee who are available to assist inmates. The court will pause at this point to commend the Board of Correction for adopting that particular rule because a great many inmates, even if not illiterate, are simply too inarticulate to present their contentions systematically or intelligently. The court hopes that the Disciplinary Committee will make liberal use of the rule in question.

The rules further provide that no disciplinary action is to be taken against any inmate save in accordance with the prescribed procedures, except that a shift supervisor may place an inmate in administrative segregation or barracks arrest pending disciplinary committee action.

The court finds that black employees now sit from time to time as members of disciplinary panels. Assuming that the Department is able to and does employ more blacks and that it pursues its announced policy of promoting blacks where possible, increased black participation in disciplinary proceedings is to be anticipated.

In considering the case the Court of Appeals expressed concern lest a charging officer be a member of the panel hearing the charge, and directed this court to prohibit the charging officer from sitting in judgment on his own complaint. That, of course, will be done.[9]

The rules of the Department specify eight punishments that may be imposed singly or in combination upon an inmate who is found guilty of a disciplinary infraction. Some of the punishments are very light and, as has been seen, may be imposed by a minor disciplinary committee. Other punishments are more severe and can be imposed only by a major disciplinary committee.

The serious punishments take a rather wide range, but there is no question that the punishment that is one of the most dreaded by the inmates and that creates a serious constitutional problem is confinement in punitive isolation.

9. The present rules were issued shortly before the *Finney* decision was handed down. The rules, as written, do not in terms prohibit the practice condemned by the appellate court. It is the court's recollection that when Cecil Boren was Assistant Superintendent at Cummins, he, on one occasion, sat on a disciplinary panel in connection with a matter in which he was the charging officer. Mr. Boren admitted the impropriety of his action, and the court doubts that such a thing would happen again. However, the decree to be entered will specifically prohibit the practice.

This section of the opinion will be devoted principally to a discussion of punitive isolation as it is practiced in the Department, and most of the discussion will be based on conditions at Cummins where the problem is more severe than it is at Tucker. Also discussed herein will be the "administrative segregation" in small cells of inmates who are awaiting trial on disciplinary charges.

The placing of inmates of a prison in punitive isolation or solitary confinement as punishment for violation of prison rules is not necessarily unconstitutional, but it may be, depending upon the duration of the confinement and the conditions thereof. Finney v. Arkansas Board of Correction. . . .

In 1973 the court found in *Holt III* that confinement in punitive isolation in the former "death cells" at Tucker and in the punitive wing of the East Building at Cummins was not unconstitutional, and in that connection specifically found that the cells in use at the two institutions were not overcrowded, and that the diet of "grue," described in *Holt I,* was not unconstitutional. The Court of Appeals took a somewhat dimmer view and expressed particular concern as to whether or not inmates held in punitive isolation were adequately supplied with the necessities of life such as proper and sufficient food, heat, light, ventilation and sanitary facilities. Finney v. Arkansas Board of Correction.

From testimony that the court heard in June, 1974, prior to the rendition of the decision of the Court of Appeals in *Finney,* and from additional testimony taken in 1975, and from the court's own inspection of the facilities in question, including both the punitive cells and the administrative segregation cells at both Cummins and Tucker, the court now finds that either conditions were not as good in 1973 as the court thought that they were or that the conditions have deteriorated since 1973. Whichever may be the case, the court now finds from the evidence that unconstitutionalities now exist with respect to both punitive isolation and administrative segregation, and that substantial changes are going to have to be made within the immediate future if the Department is to be allowed to continue to place inmates charged with offenses in administrative segregation and to punish inmates by what is called without entire accuracy punitive "isolation."

An inmate sentenced to punitive isolation receives a sentence to confinement in an extremely small cell under rigorous conditions for an indeterminate period of time with his status being reviewed at the end of each fourteen day period. While most inmates sentenced to punitive isolation are released to population within less than fourteen days, many remain in the status in question for weeks or months, depending upon their attitudes as appraised by prison personnel. It is rare indeed that a prisoner is confined in a cell by himself. Usually, he must share a cell with at least one other inmate, and at times three or more inmates are kept in the same cell which is equipped with extremely limited facilities. Assuming, and the court is not at all sure that the assumption is valid, that all of the isolation cells are equipped with two bunks, it follows that if three or four men are put in the same cell, and that frequently happens, one or two of them are going to have to sleep on the floor.

Convicts being what they are, that means that the stronger and more aggressive inmates are going to occupy the bunks, and they are also likely to persecute the weaker inmate or inmates. A variant of this is that where three convicts are confined in a single cell, two of them are apt to team up against the third one.

Assuming that an inmate in punitive isolation or in administrative segregation has a bunk to sleep on, he also has a cotton mattress to lie upon during sleeping hours, but the mattress is taken away during each day.

During each basic fourteen day period of confinement, an inmate in a punitive cell is fed on a diet of "grue" unless such a diet is medically contraindicated. He gets no other solid food, except that every third day he receives or is supposed to receive a regular prison meal. And on every third day the inmate is permitted or required to leave his cell for the purpose of taking a shower and probably changing his clothes. While inmates in punitive isolation may now be allowed some limited outdoor exercise, for a long time the only exercise that the inmates in question could take was that involved in going to the shower room, taking the shower, and returning to the cells.

At the end of a basic fourteen day period of punitive confinement, the inmate is weighed to see how much weight he has lost on the "grue" diet; [12] and if it is determined that he should be returned to punitive isolation, he is given regular food for two days and returned to the "grue" diet on the seventeenth day. It is to be observed that the rules specify that during this two day "interim" or "intermission," the inmate need not be moved from the punitive cell to other quarters, and as a matter of practice they are not moved; they simply stay where they are.

An inmate in punitive isolation is not only held in cramped quarters and fed a limited diet, he also loses practically all privileges and opportunities available to inmates in general population. Such an inmate can receive visits from a clergyman, which visits are probably very rare, and he can engage in such correspondence as the Constitution of the United States guarantees or which the prison administration deems to be otherwise "privileged."

As a class, the convicts confined in punitive isolation or in administrative segregation, for that matter, are violent men. They are filled with frustration and hostility, some of them are extremely dangerous, and others are psychopaths. Confined together under rigorous conditions in the same cell or in immediately adjacent cells, the convicts identify with each other and reinforce each other in confrontation with custodial personnel, and those personnel in turn identify with each other and reinforce each other in confrontation with the convicts.

As a result, the punitive wing in the East Building at Cummins is not infrequently a scene of violence. The inmates vandalize their cells to the extent possible, and that extent has been very substantial; they scream and curse; they abuse the guards and at times attempt to assault and injure them. The trouble is made worse by the poor administrative practice of dispatching,

12. While the evidence is to the effect that "grue," a tasteless and unappetizing substance, will not only sustain life but is adequate nutritionally for an inmate who is not leading an active life, the evidence also discloses that some inmates simply will not eat the "grue" or will not eat much of it, and that practically all inmates lose weight while in punitive isolation. The court will note at this point that inmates in administrative segregation are not required to eat "grue." While they are awaiting trial, they receive regular prison food.

say, two correctional officers to quell a disturbance in a cell containing three or four men or to remove one or two convicts from such a cell. Such an approach invites and results in trouble.

From testimony in the record the court is convinced that as a class the inmates of the punitive cells hate those in charge of them, and that they may harbor particular hatreds against prison employees who have been in charge of the same inmates for a substantial period of time. In his hatred of guards in general or of a particular guard, an inmate may deliberately run the risk of injury to himself in order to obtain an opportunity to inflict injury upon prison personnel or upon a particular prison employee.

Inmate violence unavoidably produces a forcible response from prison personnel who may be required to use such things as night sticks and the chemical known as "Mace" to quell disorders. And the court is satisfied that at times the response is excessive, and is further satisfied that many of the episodes of violence that take place in the maximum security facility could be avoided readily if the guards were more professional and used better judgment and common sense in dealing with refractory inmates. This lack of professionalism and good judgment on the part of maximum security personnel in the Department was one of the things that led the court to say in 1973 that the Department's prisons were not so much unconstitutional as they were poorly administered. 363 F.Supp. at 202.

The court agrees with Dr. Arthur Rogers, a clinical psychologist who testified as an expert in the 1974 hearings, that punitive isolation as it exists at Cummins today serves no rehabilitative purpose, and that it is counterproductive. It makes bad men worse. It must be changed.

The court thinks that from the standpoint of orderly and efficient prison administration the Department would be better off if inmates sentenced to punitive isolation were kept alone in individual cells. However, the court is not prepared to go so far as to say that it is unconstitutional to confine as many as two men in the punitive isolation and administrative segregation cells at Cummins and Tucker provided that each man has a bunk to sleep on at night and to sit upon during the day. The court will enjoin the confining of more than two men at any one time in one of the individual cells in question and will require that where two men are placed in the same cell, each must have a bunk.

This does not mean that in cases of serious emergency as for example a riot or other type of disorder involving large numbers of inmates at the same time, the prescribed cell capacity may not be exceeded for limited periods of time. But the court does not accept the proposition that every disciplinary incident in the Department creates an emergency, or that an emergency continuously exists at either Cummins or Tucker.

As to "grue," it may be arguable as to whether what the Court of Appeals had to say about that substance amounted to a holding that its use as food is unconstitutional. But, even if the language in question does not amount to such holding, which would be binding on this court, it is clear to the court that the constitutional handwriting is on the wall as far as "grue" is concerned, and that its use had as well be outlawed now rather than at some later time or by the appellate courts. And that will be done.

The practice of removing mattresses from the cells during daylight hours, like the diet of "grue," is defended on the ground that if living conditions in the cells are made too comfortable inmates will contrive to get themselves consigned to the cells to avoid work. The court does not accept that particular argument either as to "grue" or as to the removal of the mattresses.

However, with respect to the mattresses a more cogent argument is made that the court does accept. The evidence reflects that when a violent inmate of one of the cells is "acting out," as the psychologists call it, he is quite apt to set his mattress on fire, or to tear the mattress up and stuff fragments in the toilet; and it is inferable that this "acting out" is more apt to take place during daylight hours when it is apt to gain more peer approval than if it took place at night when other inmates are trying to sleep or after the violent inmate himself has become fatigued. The court thinks that the respondents' argument is valid, and the practice of removing the mattresses in the daytime, while perhaps questionable, will be permitted to continue.

The court holds that the policy of sentencing inmates to indeterminate periods of confinement in punitive isolation is unreasonable and unconstitutional. The court thinks that determinate sentences of no more than a prescribed number of days must be imposed. In so holding the court does not imply for a moment that there are not some inmates who must be segregated from the general population for any one or more of a number of reasons, and does not condemn that practice. But segregated confinement under maximum security conditions is one thing; segregated confinement under the *punitive* conditions that have been described is quite another thing.

As to the length of the maximum sentences that may be imposed, the court notes that Mr. Hutto is of the view that basically the maximum period of time in which a man should be confined in punitive isolation with a restricted diet, with no mattress in the daytime, and perhaps without a bunk to sleep in at night is fourteen days. In view of the changes in the conditions of confinement in punitive isolation that the court is ordering, the court feels that a maximum sentence of thirty days is permissible. If at the end of that maximum period, it is found that an inmate should not be returned to population, he may be kept segregated but under conditions which are not punitive. Of course, a disciplinary committee may impose a sentence of less than thirty days, and the Superintendent of the institution or the Commissioner may direct that a convict be released from punitive isolation at any time prior to the expiration of his sentence.

Let the court point out in this connection that many acts which constitute serious violations of prison rules also amount to felonies under the laws of the State of Arkansas, and if an inmate commits such an offense he can always be prosecuted in the state courts and may receive a sentence in addition to the one that he was serving when he committed the offense.

The court is well aware of the fact that the changes that are being ordered with respect to punitive isolation and administrative segregation may cause a degree of consternation in the Department and, indeed, outside the Department. But, the court sincerely believes that these changes are not only constitutionally required, but also that they will produce both a more humane prison system and a system that is going to be more peaceful and orderly and easier to administer efficiently in the long run.

In the section of this opinion that dealt with overcrowding the court stated that the population of the East Building at Cummins would have to be reduced. As far as the punitive wing and the administrative segregation wings of the East Building are concerned, the directives of the court in the immediately preceding section hereof ought to take care of the problem of overcrowding. However, there is a third wing of the building that must be dealt with, and there are some other conditions in the East Building that call for attention.

The third wing which may be thought of simply as a "maximum security" wing houses inmates who cannot safely be kept in general population. Some of those inmates require protective custody to prevent them from being killed or injured by other inmates; some are sources of danger to other inmates or to prison personnel; others are high escape risks; and some may be in the wing under consideration for other reasons. While it is not so called in the Department, this wing in some institutions would probably be called the "administrative segregation" wing. Further references to inmates in this section of the opinion will be to persons who are not being held for trial on charges of disciplinary violations and who are not being punished for such violations, but who nevertheless are confined in the wing of the East Building which the court may refer to simply as the "third wing."

Third wing inmates are in certain respects better off than inmates confined in the punitive isolation and administrative segregation wings of the East Building, and are better off than inmates who are held under maximum security conditions in certain other prisons. They receive regular prison food; they have the same correspondence privileges as do inmates in general population; they have certain commissary privileges; and they are permitted to spend part of their time outside their cells in what is known as the "day room." Moreover, they are not kept in the East Building all day. They work in the prison fields and gardens, and "10 Hoe" and "5 Garden" Squads are made up of inmates of the third wing of the building.

Due to the deficiency that has been mentioned in the report of November 12, 1975 and the lack of other figures the court does not know how many men were confined in the third wing on November 12 or how many are confined there today. The court is sure, however, that at times more than two men have been confined to a single cell in the third wing, and the court finds that a single cell in the third wing is overcrowded when it is has more than two men in it just as the cells in the punitive wing and the administrative segregation wing are overcrowded when occupied by more than two men at the same time. The requirements of the preceding section with respect to cell capacity and bunks will also be made applicable to the third wing of the East Building.

While, as indicated, third wing inmates are better off in certain respects than the inmates of the other wings, there is no question that they are not as well off as inmates in general population and suffer deprivations that general population inmates do not suffer.

Such being the case, the Constitution requires that the status of inmates of the third wing be evaluated and reevaluated periodically in order to determine whether or not particular inmates can safely be returned to population or whether they should be transferred to other institutions.

The matter of periodic evaluations of the situations of convicts held in maximum security and segregated from the general population was before the Court of Appeals in Kelly v. Brewer [525 F.2d 394 (8th Cir. 1975).] In that case the court held that such evaluations must take place and that they must be made in the light of relevant, objective criteria, although the court recognized that the proper evaluation of the status of one inmate might require less effort and consideration than the evaluation of the status of another inmate.

In *Brewer* the court also held that there are certain criteria that may not properly be employed in the evaluation process. Specifically, the court held that the evaluating authority may not properly consider adverse staff reaction to a return of an inmate to population, or the deterring effect on other inmates that might result from holding a particular inmate or inmates in segregated confinement. And it was further held that the evaluating authority is not to give undue or artificial weight to the offense of which the inmate in question was convicted originally, although, of course, the nature of that offense is a factor for consideration.

The determination of whether an inmate is to be retained in segregation or returned to population is not so much a question of what he has done in the past but of what he is likely to do or have done to him in the future if he is returned to population. In the last analysis the question is one of behavior prediction, and its answer must be left largely to the discretion of the prison administration. Ordinarily, judicial review of an administrative determination that an inmate should remain in segregated status should be limited to an inquiry as to whether the action in question was arbitrary or capricious or was invidiously discriminatory.

The requirement of evaluation and reevaluation of inmates held under maximum security conditions may seem burdensome to some prison administrators, but it is necessary to protect inmates from being held indefinitely in that status after the original reason for their being placed in it has ceased to be valid or relevant.

The court is going to direct Superintendent Lockhart to review as soon as practicable the status of all convicts now confined in the third wing, and to return to population such inmates, if any, of that wing who can be returned without serious risk to the inmate, to other inmates, to prison personnel or to the security of the prison.

In the future, the cases of all inmates of the third wing are to be re-evaluated by at least the Assistant Superintendent in charge of security at Cummins not less often than once every sixty days, and the cases of all inmates in that wing are to be reviewed at least once a year by the Superintendent personally.

The evaluation process should involve interviews with the inmates out of the presence of other inmates, and should also involve consideration of psychiatric or psychological opinions to the extent that the same may be available. And the court will say that one of the things that it had in mind in directing the employment of one or more full time psychologists or psychiatrists by the Department is the useful function that such specialists can perform in determining whether or not an inmate should continue to be held in segregated status.

It occurs to the court that friction and confrontations between inmates of the East Building and East Building staff may be due in part to the fact that some of the higher ranking personnel of the East Building may have been kept on that station too long and have been dealing with the same inmates too long. Commissioner Hutto and Superintendent Lockhart should give serious consideration to rotating the higher ranking employees assigned to the East Building as well as to rotating ordinary correctional officers.

One problem that arises in the East Building is the failure at times to repair promptly damage to the cells and their furnishings resulting from inmate vandalism. In consequence inmates at times have been removed from badly damaged cells and placed in other cells with other inmates thus overcrowding them or aggravating an already overcrowded condition.

The record reflects that those who designed the East Building assured the Department that the building and its facilities were proof against damage by inmates. Such has been far from the case. It is hard for the court to believe, however, that American technology and engineering is not sufficiently advanced in this day and age to equip prison cells with facilities such as lighting and plumbing facilities and locks that inmates cannot destroy or seriously damage with their bare hands or such simple tools or other means as they may be able to devise. If anything practical can be done in that direction, it should be.

Some of the most dangerous and troublesome of the occupants of the East Building are blacks who are or claim to be Black Muslims. Like Muslims in general population, they claim to be the victims of religious as well as racial discrimination. Their principal complaints relate to diet, a subject with respect to which the court has already undertaken to deal, and about restrictions on religious assemblages and access to the inmates by Muslim ministers.

The Muslim inmates of the East Building are entitled to the same, but no greater, privileges in the area of religious worship, including visits by clergymen, as are accorded to inmates of the building who profess other religious faiths. It must be kept in mind that if an inmate is being held legitimately under maximum security conditions of confinement, his exercise of his religion is necessarily somewhat more circumscribed for legitimate security reasons than is such exercise by an inmate who is not a security risk and who is living in the general prison population. For example, the prison administration may legitimately prevent an inmate in general population from visiting an East Building inmate even though the former may be or claim to be a minister and even though the ostensible reason for his calling on the other inmate is to serve the latter's religious needs. Moreover, free world ministers who desire to pay religious calls on inmates of the East Building are subject to reasonable security measures such as reasonable searches for weapons or other contraband. However, the restrictions imposed on visitations by free world clergymen must not be unreasonable or such as are purposely designed to discourage ministers from the outside world from visiting maximum security inmates or other inmates for that matter.

Returning now to the subject of overcrowding of the administrative segregation and punitive isolation cells at Tucker and the overcrowding of the cells in all three wings of the East Building at Cummins, the court observes from the report of November 12, 1975 that as of that date the punitive isolation cells at Tucker with a capacity of 14 men had only three men in them, and that there were 13 men in the administrative segregation cells with an equal capacity of 14 men. Thus by the court's standards, if there were no more than two men in the same cell and if each man had a bunk, the maximum security facilities at Tucker were not overcrowded on that date. What the situation is today, the court does not know.

It is possible that when this opinion and its accompanying decree are filed, none of the maximum security cells at either institution will be overcrowded. While the court thinks that the existence of such a situation is improbable, if it does exist, well and good. Respondents will simply be required not to let the cells become overcrowded.

Assuming, however, that compliance with the court's decree will require a substantial reduction of the populations of the maximum security cells at either Cummins or Tucker, or both, the court does not think that the respondents should be required to effect the reduction over night or in a haphazard manner. The court feels that respondents should have a reasonable but comparatively short period of time within which to effect necessary reductions, and now sets that period at thirty days from the filing date of the decree. However, the court's prohibition against limited diets will go into effect immediately.

It will be remembered that in the preceding section of this opinion the court fixed thirty days as the maximum period of time during which an inmate may be confined in punitive isolation. Any inmates who have been confined in punitive isolation for thirty days or longer must be returned to population or held in maximum security under conditions that are not punitive. And inmates who at the time of the filing of the decree herein who have been in punitive isolation for less than thirty days are to be deemed as serving sentences of not more than thirty days.

This section of the opinion is the last of what may be called its "substantive" sections. There are, however, some other matters to be considered.

When this litigation was first commenced, the court appointed Messrs. Steele Hays and Jerry T. Jackson, capable members of the Little Rock Bar, to represent petitioners, and their efforts contributed to the *Holt I* decision from which there was no appeal. The court did not award Mr. Hays or Mr. Jackson any fee, and the court does not recall that they requested an award.

After *Holt I* was decided, the attorneys just mentioned were excused from further duty. When the litigation was reactivated, the court appointed Messrs. Jack Holt, Jr. and Philip Kaplan of Little Rock to represent the inmates. Mr. Holt and Mr. Kaplan have been in the case ever since and have rendered yeoman service to their clients. In 1974 when certain inmates of the East Building were permitted to institute a class action of their own, Mr. Phillip H. McMath of Little Rock was appointed to represent them, and he remained actively in the case after the East Building suits were consolidated with the others.

In 1973 in connection with the *Holt III* decision the court allowed Messrs. Holt and Kaplan an $8,000.00 fee and certain expenses. Those items were paid by the Department of Correction. However, Mr. McMath has never received anything for his services, and Mr. Holt and Mr. Kaplan have received nothing attributable to the *Holt III* appeal or to the present phase of this litigation.

The court's 1973 award that has been mentioned was based in part on the theory that counsel had performed valuable services not only to the inmates but also to the people of the State of Arkansas as well. In other words, the award was based in part on the "private attorney general" theory.

After the decision in *Holt III,* the Supreme Court of the United States decided Edelman v. Jordan, 415 U.S. 651 (1974), and Alyeska Pipeline Service Co. v. Wilderness Society, 421 U.S. 240 (1975). While the court is of the opinion that Mr. Holt and Mr. Kaplan deserve an additional award of fee and expenses, and that Mr. McMath ought to receive a fee for his services, it is necessary for the court to consider whether in the light of either or both of the Supreme Court decisions just mentioned it has the power to make the awards in question. In approaching the problem the court recognizes that as far as the class action phase of the litigation is concerned, the real party respondent is the Department of Correction itself which is an agency of the State of Arkansas. And the court recognizes that any valid award made by it will be paid and should be paid out of state funds in the hands of the Department rather than by the individual respondents personally.

In Edelman v. Jordan the Supreme Court held that while a federal court may grant prospective injunctive relief against state agencies and state officials which may impose financial burdens on the treasury of the state, the eleventh amendment to the Constitution prohibits the federal courts from making retroactive pecuniary awards that will have to be paid out of the funds of the state, unless the state has waived its sovereign immunity.

In *Alyeska,* the Supreme Court rejected the "private attorney general" theory as a basis for awards of attorneys' fees to prevailing parties in federal court litigation, and held that such fees are allowable only when authorized by statute or when a case falls within one of the long-established exceptions to the "American Rule" which prescribes that each litigant must pay his own lawyer. The exceptions to the rule are that a court of equity may award an attorney's fee where (1) the losing party has been in violation of a court order; (2) the prevailing party has created a fund for the benefit of himself and others, in which case a fee payable out of the fund may be allowed; and (3) the losing party has acted in bad faith, vexatiously, wantonly or oppressively. . . .

As to whether *Edelman* precludes an award of attorney's fees against state agencies or against state officers sued in their official capacities, the Courts of Appeals appear to be divided, and the question will probably have to be settled ultimately by the Supreme Court. . . .

The cases holding that *Edelman* does not preclude the award of an attorney's fee that must be paid out of state funds characterize the allowance of the fee as being purely ancillary to prospective equitable relief properly granted against a state or a state agency. This court now takes that view. . . .

That the award of an attorney's fee in a civil rights case on the "private attorney general" theory is improper in the absence of a statute allowing such an award was recognized by the Court of Appeals for this circuit in Gilliam v.

City of Omaha, 524 F.2d 1013, 1017 (8th Cir. 1975). But, in the earlier case of Doe v. Poelker, 515 F.2d 541, 546–48 (8th Cir. 1975), the same court held that the case before it fell within one of the *Alyeska* exceptions where the defendant Mayor had obstinately insisted on maintaining an anti-abortion policy in municipally owned hospitals in St. Louis after being on full and ample notice that the policy was unconstitutional or was probably unconstitutional. See also Doe v. Poelker, 527 F.2d 605 (8th Cir. 1976).

As indicated, this court does not feel that the allowance of a fee, costs, and expenses is precluded by *Edelman.* With respect to *Alyeska,* the court thinks that the case before it is markedly different in quality from *Alyeska* and also that it falls within the "bad faith" exception to the American Rule recognized in *Alyeska* and in Doe v. Poelker, supra.

In the first place, *Alyeska* was a private civil suit brought by environmentalists to prevent the construction of a pipeline in Alaska. No constitutional issues were involved. The instant case on the other hand involves the grave constitutional question of whether those in charge of the Arkansas Department of Correction and the prisons of the Department are continuing to deprive indigent convicts of fundamental rights and immunities guaranteed to them by the fourteenth amendment.

In the second place, the attorneys in this case who have labored so diligently on behalf of their inmate clients are not in the litigation on their own motion or by their own volition. They did not voluntarily enroll themselves under the banner of convict rights as the attorneys in the *Alyeska* case enlisted under the banner of environmental protection. Counsel in this case are here because they were appointed by the court and for no other reason.

The very variety of the issues discussed and the length of this opinion and of earlier opinions make it obvious that the claims of the convicts could not have been presented to the court intelligently by petitioners themselves; they had to have counsel. And their attorneys have been of assistance to the court as well as to the inmates.

Assuming arguendo, however, that the considerations just mentioned do not serve adequately to distinguish this case from *Alyeska*, the court thinks that in a legal sense respondents and their predecessors in office and employment have acted in bad faith and oppressively, and that the case falls within the "bad faith" exception to the *Alyeska* rule.

If one looks at the history of the Arkansas prison system from 1965 or 1966 down to the present day, one may note a continuous albeit erratic course of improvement. Some of that improvement would no doubt have taken place even in the absence of this litigation; and the court will observe that in recent years Arkansas governors and legislators, and members of what is now the Board of Correction, have shown marked sympathy with and affirmative response to prison needs, an attitude that was not always characteristic of former years. On the other hand, it is only fair to say that this litigation has served to impress upon Arkansas policy makers that if the prisons are to be operated at all, they must be operated in a constitutional manner, and has served as a spur to improvement. Moreover, the ligitation, including the efforts of petitioners' counsel herein, has served to bring to light certain problem areas that might have been overlooked otherwise.

In earlier stages of the case, when the grossest constitutional violations were brought to light, the prison administration tended to be cooperative in moving against the conditions and practices in question and indeed appeared to welcome the action of the court in requiring them to do what they wanted to do anyway but felt unable to do voluntarily.

It would be unfair to say that the attitude of the respondents is uncooperative today, but the court thinks that it has noted that with the passage of time and with improvements in prison conditions being made, there has been some hardening of Departmental attitudes and an unwillingness on the part of the prison administrators to go much if any farther than they have gone, and as has been seen the progress that has been made to this date is still insufficient.

Another observation that may be made is that at practically every stage of the litigation evidence has brought to light practices of which those in higher prison authority were ignorant, and which they eliminated when the facts were disclosed. It seems to the court that the prison authorities should have discovered at least some of those conditions and practices for themselves and corrected them without waiting for them to be developed in the course of evidentiary hearings in this lawsuit.

Since 1968 the Department of Correction has been in what may be called a period of transition from a patently unconstitutional penal system and in the direction of a constitutional system. But, each major transitional step has followed the mandate of this court or of the Court of Appeals. And significantly at each stage of the litigation, remaining constitutional deficiencies have been discovered. In 1973 the court thought that the Department had moved far enough down the transitional road to permit this court to release its supervisory jurisdiction over the Arkansas prisons, but, as all concerned know, the Court of Appeals sharply disagreed.

Enough on this subject has been said. The court is going to allow petitioners' attorneys a fee and certain expenses of litigation.

In fixing the amount of the fee, which counsel may divide among themselves as they see fit, the court will make no effort to adequately compensate counsel for the work that they have done or for the time that they have spent on the case. Adequate compensation would run into many thousands of dollars. On the other hand, the court is not willing to allow merely a nominal fee or one that has no relation to the work that counsel have done. The court is going to allow a substantial fee for the work done by counsel since the remand. Not only are the attorneys entitled to such a fee, but also the allowance thereof may incline the Department to act in such a manner that further protracted litigation about the prisons will not be necessary.

From its consideration of the matter the court now awards a fee of $20,000.00 to be paid out of Department of Correction funds.

As to costs, the principal item of costs has been the fees paid to the court reporter for transcripts of depositions and testimony. As the litigation has proceeded, the court has entered certain orders under the terms of which a portion of those fees has been paid by the Department. The court now confirms those orders. This action, however, is without prejudice to the right of the Department at some later date or dates to seek reimbursement or recoupment from certain individual inmates whose individual claims now pending when considered may turn out to be frivolous or patently insubstantial. The court is not saying that there are such claims, but there may be.

It is now necessary to wrap up procedurally the class action phase of this litigation so that it may be on its way to the Court of Appeals if either side cares to appeal, and the court assumes that one side or the other will so desire. It is also necessary to give some directions to the Clerk as to how this opinion and its accompanying decree should be handled.

Pursuant to this opinion the court will enter its Third Supplemental Decree. In order that the decree amount to an appealable order, the court, pursuant to Fed.R.Civ.P. 54(b), now determines that there is no just reason for delaying entry of the decree until disposition of the individual claims and directs that the decree be entered forthwith.

The Clerk is now directed to file the original of this opinion and of the decree in the anchor case before the court, namely, Holt, et al. v. Hutto, Commissioner of Correction, et al. Copies of the opinion and of the decree will be considered as having been filed in all of the cases consolidated with *Holt,* and a copy of the opinion and decree will be filed physically in any particular one of the consolidated cases upon the request of either side. Since the court may well have to consider individual inmate claims in all of the individual cases, the Clerk should not close for statistical purposes any of the cases at this time.

Just as the court sees no just reason for delay in entering a decree dealing with the class action aspect of the case, the court likewise sees no reason to delay disposition of the individual claims until an appeal, if there is one, from the class action decree is decided. That is true because decision of an individual claim either in favor of or against a particular inmate is not likely to run counter to the class action decision or to any probable holding of the Court of Appeals with respect to that decision. For example, a claim of Inmate X, that he was denied needed medication on a particular occasion can be decided one way or the other without particular regard to the over-all sufficiency of the health care provided by the Department for inmates in general. The court, therefore, will proceed to adjudicate the individual claims with all convenient speed. The court is probably going to need the help of counsel in connection with the individual claims, and, as a matter of fact, counsel for respondents have requested leave to brief the issues raised by certain individual claims separately from the general issues raised by the class claims. That leave will be granted; it occurs to the court that counsel for petitioners may likewise want to brief some individual claims separately, and the court will shortly be in touch with counsel on both sides in connection with the individual claims.

While the court would like to relieve counsel for petitioners of their duties in the case at this time and while the court is sure that counsel would like to be relieved, the court does not think it practicable to release them until after the appeal, if any, from the class action decision has been disposed of and until after the court rules on the individual claims.

Since jurisdiction of the case is being retained, the Commissioner will be directed to file not later than July 15, 1976 a report showing what has been done toward complying with the directives and requirements of this opinion and its accompanying decree. The report must include data on the prison population in all institutions administered by the Department as of June 30 or July 1. Those data should be reported in a form conforming generally to the report filed on November 12, 1975, but there must be a breakdown among wings and a cell by cell statement of population in the East Building at Cummins. Further reports may be required in the discretion of the court.

---

1) By the time of Finney v. Hutto, Judge Henley was a member of the court of appeals. Should he continue to sit as a trial judge? What are the risks of such a procedure? What would have been the costs of trying to avoid it?

2) Were the earlier decrees defective? Would it have been appropriate to consider a contempt citation on the overcrowding issue? on the continued use of the barracks? on the persistence of racial discrimination? If so, why did the attorneys omit that option and instead ask the court to enter a third supplemental decree?

3) Has Judge Henley's attitude or posture changed? He mentions his personal visits to the prisons; he stresses his personal inspections in dealing with the law library, the facilities used for punitive isolation, and administrative segregation. Are personal inspections an appropriate fact-finding technique? What are the special strengths and weaknesses of such a technique? Judge Henley also notes that some of his trial responsibility was delegated to a magistrate by "agreement" and transmitted to the judge in documentary form as depositions. What are the strengths and weaknesses of this trial technique?

4) Review those portions of the opinion that justify the award of attorney fees as an application of the bad faith exception to the so-called American rule. Has Judge Henley shown that the defendants demonstrated bad faith within the meaning of the traditional exception to the American rule?

FINNEY v. HUTTO

548 F.2d 740 (8th Cir. 1977).

Before HEANEY and ROSS, Circuit Judges, and VAN PELT, Senior District Judge.

ROSS, Circuit Judge.

This appeal is the latest chapter in the seemingly endless litigation involving the constitutionality of the Arkansas state prisons. The respondent-appellants are officials of the Arkansas Department of Correction. The petitioner-appellees are prisoners confined in Arkansas state prisons. In Finney v. Hutto, the district court, pursuant to remand of this court, Finney v. Arkansas Board of Corrections, held that the Arkansas prison system is still unconstitutional in certain respects. The court held, *inter alia*, that the Department's policy of sentencing inmates to indeterminate periods of confinement in punitive isolation is unconstitutional under the eighth and fourteenth amendments. Finney v. Hutto, supra. The court awarded an attorneys' fee to petitioners' court appointed counsel in the amount of $20,000 to be paid out of funds allocated to the Department of Correction. The court also ordered the Department to pay the costs of litigation. The appellants contest these aspects of the judgment entered below. We affirm.

Judge Henley described the conditions of punitive isolation in the following terms:

"An inmate sentenced to punitive isolation receives a sentence to confinement in an extremely small cell under rigorous conditions for an indeterminate period of time with his status being reviewed at the end of each fourteen day period. While most inmates sentenced to punitive isolation are released to population within less than fourteen days, many remain in the status in question for weeks or months, depending upon their attitudes as appraised by prison personnel. It is rare indeed that a prisoner is confined in a cell by himself. Usually, he must share a cell with at least one other inmate, and at times three or more inmates are kept in the same cell which is equipped with extremely limited facilities. Assuming, and the court is not at all sure that the assumption is valid, that all of the isolation cells are equipped with two bunks, it follows that if three or four men are put in the same cell, and that frequently happens, one or two of them are going to have to sleep on the floor. . . .

"As a class, the convicts confined in punitive isolation or in administrative segregation, for that matter, are violent men. They are filled with frustration and hostility, some of them are extremely dangerous, and others are psychopaths. Confined together under rigorous conditions in the same cell or in immediately adjacent cells, the convicts identify with each other and reinforce each other in confrontation with custodial personnel, and those personnel in turn identify with each other and reinforce each other in confrontation with the convicts. . . .

"Inmate violence unavoidably produces a forcible response from prison personnel who may be required to use such things as night sticks and the chemical known as 'Mace' to quell disorders. And the court is satisfied that at times the response is excessive, and is further satisfied that many of the episodes of violence that take place in the maximum security facility could be avoided readily if the guards were more professional and used better judgment and common sense in dealing with refractory inmates."

The court concluded that " . . . punitive isolation as it exists at Cummins today serves no rehabilitative purpose, and that it is counterproductive. It makes bad men worse. It must be changed." Accordingly, the court held, *inter alia,* that confinement in punitive isolation for more than thirty days is cruel and unusual punishment and thus impermissible.[3]

We affirm this holding on the basis of Judge Henley's well-reasoned opinion.

The appellants vigorously contest the attorneys' fee award of $20,000 to be paid out of the funds allocated to the Department of Correction. We affirm the award.

3. The court carefully noted that the thirty day maximum applies only to punitive isolation, not segregated confinement under maximum security conditions.

On October 19, 1976, at a time when this case was pending resolution on appeal, the Civil Rights Attorney's Fees Awards Act of 1976, Pub.L. No. 94–559 (Oct. 19, 1976), 90 Stat. 2641, was signed into law. This Act permits an award of a reasonable attorneys' fee to the prevailing party in an action such as this brought under 42 U.S.C. § 1983. It is clear that Congress intended the Act to apply to cases such as this pending resolution on appeal. Since the Act was passed by Congress under, *inter alia,* the enabling clause of the fourteenth amendment, S.Rep. No. 94–1011, 94th Cong., 2d Sess. 5, U.S.Code Cong. & Admin.News, 1976, p. 5908, the award of attorneys' fees is not barred by the eleventh amendment. Fitzpatrick v. Bitzer, 427 U.S. 445, 457 (1976).

The appellants complain that the district court erroneously forced the Department to pay the fee in view of the fact that the Department is not a named party. We disagree. The Act permits an order, as was entered in this case, requiring the award to be paid directly from the funds of a state agency, such as the Department of Correction, whether or not the agency is a named party.

The petitioners, as private attorneys general, have vindicated the constitutional rights of Arkansas state prisoners. The award is thus justified under Public Law No. 94–559.[6] Furthermore, in view of the protracted nature of this litigation, the results obtained by the petitioners, and other factors enumerated in Johnson v. Georgia Highway Express, Inc., 488 F.2d 714, 717–719 (5th Cir. 1974), the $20,000 award is reasonable.

The appellants also attack the award of costs which is to be paid by the Department of Correction. This award is both permissible under the eleventh amendment, Fairmont Creamery Co. v. Minnesota, 275 U.S. 70, 73–74 (1927), and reasonable.

---

1) Why did the defendants limit their appeal to the time limit on punitive isolation and the award of attorney's fees? What other issues might they have attacked on appeal?

2) Do you detect a change in the Eighth Circuit's attitude between *Holt III* and Finney v. Hutto? Does the *Finney* court seem determined to support, indeed applaud, Judge Henley's action? What might account for the change?

HUTTO v. FINNEY

437 U.S. 678 (1978).

Justice STEVENS delivered the opinion of the Court.

After finding that conditions in the Arkansas penal system constituted cruel and unusual punishment, the District Court entered a series of detailed remedial orders. On appeal to the United States Court of Appeals for the

6. Although, in view of the statute, we are not required to pass on the issue of bad faith, the record fully supports the finding of the district court that the conduct of the state officials justified the award under the bad faith exception enumerated in Alyeska Pipeline Service Co. v. Wilderness Society, 421 U.S. 240, 258–259 (1975).

Eighth Circuit, petitioners challenged two aspects of that relief: (1) an order placing a maximum limit of 30 days on confinement in punitive isolation; and (2) an award of attorney's fees to be paid out of Department of Correction funds. The Court of Appeals affirmed and assessed an additional attorney's fee to cover services on appeal. We granted certiorari . . . and now affirm.

This litigation began in 1969; it is a sequel to two earlier cases holding that conditions in the Arkansas prison system violated the Eighth and Fourteenth Amendments. Only a brief summary of the facts is necessary to explain the basis for the remedial orders.

The routine conditions that the ordinary Arkansas convict had to endure were characterized by the District Court as "a dark and evil world completely alien to the free world." Holt v. Sarver (*Holt II*). That characterization was amply supported by the evidence.[3] The punishments for misconduct not serious enough to result in punitive isolation were cruel,[4] unusual,[5] and unpredictable.[6] It is the discipline known as "punitive isolation" that is most relevant for present purposes.

Confinement in punitive isolation was for an indeterminate period of time. An average of 4, and sometimes as many as 10 or 11, prisoners were crowded into windowless 8′ × 10′ cells containing no furniture other than a source of water and a toilet that could only be flushed from outside the cell. . . . (*Holt I*). At night the prisoners were given mattresses to spread on the floor. Although some prisoners suffered from infectious diseases such as

3. The administrators of Arkansas' prison system evidently tried to operate their prisons at a profit. Cummins Farm, the institution at the center of this litigation, required its 1,000 inmates to work in the fields 10 hours a day, six days a week, using mule-drawn tools and tending crops by hand. The inmates were sometimes required to run to and from the fields, with a guard in an automobile or on horseback driving them on. Holt v. Hutto (*Holt III*). They worked in all sorts of weather, so long as the temperature was above freezing, sometimes in unsuitably light clothing or without shoes. *Holt II.*

The inmates slept together in large, 100-man barracks, and some convicts, known as "creepers," would slip from their beds to crawl along the floor, stalking their sleeping enemies. In one 18-month period, there were 17 stabbings, all but 1 occurring in the barracks. *Holt I.* Homosexual rape was so common and uncontrolled that some potential victims dared not sleep; instead they would leave their beds and spend the night clinging to the bars nearest the guards' station.

4. Inmates were lashed with a wooden-handled leather strap five feet long and four inches wide. Talley v. Stephens. Although it was not official policy to do so, some inmates were apparently whipped for minor offenses until their skin was bloody and bruised. Jackson v. Bishop.

5. The "Tucker telephone," a hand-cranked device, was used to administer electrical shocks to various sensitive parts of an inmate's body. Jackson v. Bishop.

6. Most of the guards were simply inmates who had been issued guns. *Holt II.* Although it had 1,000 prisoners, Cummins employed only eight guards who were not themselves convicts. Only two nonconvict guards kept watch over the 1,000 men at night. While the "trusties" maintained an appearance of order, they took a high toll from the other prisoners. Inmates could obtain access to medical treatment only if they bribed the trusty in charge of sick call. As the District Court found, it was "within the power of a trusty guard to murder another inmate with practical impunity," because trusties with weapons were authorized to use deadly force against escapees. "Accidental shootings" also occurred; and one trusty fired his shotgun into a crowded barracks because the inmates would not turn off their TV. Another trusty beat an inmate so badly the victim required partial dentures. Talley v. Stephens.

hepatitis and venereal disease, mattresses were removed and jumbled together each morning, then returned to the cells at random in the evening. Prisoners in isolation received fewer than 1,000 calories a day;[7] their meals consisted primarily of 4-inch squares of "grue," a substance created by mashing meat, potatoes, oleo, syrup, vegetables, eggs, and seasoning into a paste and baking the mixture in a pan.

After finding the conditions of confinement unconstitutional, the District Court did not immediately impose a detailed remedy of its own. Instead, it directed the Department of Correction to "make a substantial start" on improving conditions and to file reports on its progress. *Holt I.* When the Department's progress proved unsatisfactory, a second hearing was held. The District Court found some improvements, but concluded that prison conditions remained unconstitutional. *Holt II.* Again the court offered prison administrators an opportunity to devise a plan of their own for remedying the constitutional violations, but this time the court issued guidelines, identifying four areas of change that would cure the worst evils; improving conditions in the isolation cells, increasing inmate safety, eliminating the barracks sleeping arrangements, and putting an end to the trusty system. The Department was ordered to move as rapidly as funds became available.

After this order was affirmed on appeal, . . . more hearings were held in 1972 and 1973 to review the Department's progress. Finding substantial improvements, the District Court concluded that continuing supervision was no longer necessary. The court held, however, that its prior decrees would remain in effect and noted that sanctions, as well as an award of costs and attorney's fees, would be imposed if violations occurred. (*Holt III*).

The Court of Appeals reversed the District Court's decision to withdraw its supervisory jurisdiction, Finney v. Arkansas Board of Correction, and the District Court held a fourth set of hearings. It found that, in some respects, conditions had seriously deteriorated since 1973, when the court had withdrawn its supervisory jurisdiction. Cummins Farm, which the court had condemned as overcrowded in 1970 because it housed 1,000 inmates, now had a population of about 1,500. The situation in the punitive isolation cells was particularly disturbing. The court concluded that either it had misjudged conditions in these cells in 1973 or conditions had become much worse since then. There were twice as many prisoners as beds in some cells. And because inmates in punitive isolation are often violently antisocial, overcrowding led to persecution of the weaker prisoners. The "grue" diet was still in use, and practically all inmates were losing weight on it. The cells had been vandalized to a "very substantial" extent. Because of their inadequate numbers, guards assigned to the punitive isolation cells frequently resorted to physical violence, using nightsticks and Mace in their efforts to maintain order. Prisoners were sometimes left in isolation for months, their release depending on "their attitudes as appraised by prison personnel."

7. A daily allowance of 2,700 calories is recommended for the average male between 23 and 50. National Academy of Sciences, Recommended Dietary Allowances, Appendix (8th rev. ed. 1974). Prisoners in punitive isolation are less active than the average person; but a mature man who spends 12 hours a day lying down and 12 hours a day simply sitting or standing consumes approximately 2,000 calories a day.

The court concluded that the constitutional violations identified earlier had not been cured. It entered an order that placed limits on the number of men that could be confined in one cell, required that each have a bunk, discontinued the "grue" diet, and set 30 days as the maximum isolation sentence. The District Court gave detailed consideration to the matter of fees and expenses, made an express finding that petitioners had acted in bad faith, and awarded counsel "a fee of $20,000.00 to be paid out of Department of Correction funds." The Court of Appeals affirmed and assessed an additional $2,500 to cover fees and expenses on appeal.

The Eighth Amendment's ban on inflicting cruel and unusual punishments, made applicable to the States by the Fourteenth Amendment, "proscribe[s] more than physically barbarous punishments." Estelle v. Gamble, 429 U.S. 97, 102. It prohibits penalties that are grossly disproportionate to the offense, Weems v. United States, 217 U.S. 349, 367, as well as those that transgress today's " 'broad and idealistic concepts of dignity, civilized standards, humanity, and decency.' " Estelle v. Gamble, supra, at 102, quoting Jackson v. Bishop. Confinement in a prison or in an isolation cell is a form of punishment subject to scrutiny under Eighth Amendment standards. Petitioners do not challenge this proposition; nor do they disagree with the District Court's original conclusion that Arkansas' prisons, including its punitive isolation cells, constituted cruel and unusual punishment. Rather, petitioners single out that portion of the District Court's most recent order that forbids the Department to sentence inmates to more than 30 days in punitive isolation. Petitioners assume that the District Court held that indeterminate sentences to punitive isolation always constitute cruel and unusual punishment. This assumption misreads the District Court's holding.

Read in its entirety, the District Court's opinion makes it abundantly clear that the length of isolation sentences was not considered in a vacuum. In the court's words, punitive isolation "is not necessarily unconstitutional, but it may be, depending on the duration of the confinement and the conditions thereof." [8] It is perfectly obvious that every decision to remove a particular inmate from the general prison population for an indeterminate period could

8. The Department reads the following sentence in the District Court's 76-page opinion as an unqualified holding that any indeterminate sentence to solitary confinement is unconstitutional: "The court holds that the policy of sentencing inmates to indeterminate periods of confinement in punitive isolation is unreasonable and unconstitutional." But in the context of its full opinion, we think it quite clear that the court was describing the specific conditions found in the Arkansas penal system. Indeed, in the same paragraph it noted that "segregated confinement under maximum security conditions is one thing; segregated confinement under the *punitive* conditions that have been described is quite another thing." (emphasis in original).

The Department also suggests that the District Court made rehabilitation a constitutional requirement. The court did note its agreement with an expert witness who testified "that punitive isolation as it exists at Cummins today serves no rehabilitative purpose, and that it is counterproductive." The court went on to say that punitive isolation "makes bad men worse. It must be changed." We agree with the Department's contention that the Constitution does not require that every aspect of prison discipline serve a rehabilitative purpose. Novak v. Beto, 453 F.2d 661, 670–671 (CA5 1971); Nadeau v. Helgemoe, 561 F.2d 411, 415–416 (CA1 1977). But the District Court did not impose a new legal test. Its remarks form the transition from a detailed description of conditions in the isolation cells to a traditional legal analysis of those conditions. The quoted passage simply summarized the facts and presaged the legal conclusion to come.

not be characterized as cruel and unusual. If new conditions of confinement are not materially different from those affecting other prisoners, a transfer for the duration of a prisoner's sentence might be completely unobjectionable and well within the authority of the prison administrator. Cf. Meachum v. Fano, 427 U.S. 215. It is equally plain, however, that the length of confinement cannot be ignored in deciding whether the confinement meets constitutional standards. A filthy, overcrowded cell and a diet of "grue" might be tolerable for a few days and intolerably cruel for weeks or months.

The question before the trial court was whether past constitutional violations had been remedied. The court was entitled to consider the severity of those violations in assessing the constitutionality of conditions in the isolation cells. The court took note of the inmates' diet, the continued overcrowding, the rampant violence, the vandalized cells, and the "lack of professionalism and good judgment on the part of maximum security personnel." The length of time each inmate spent in isolation was simply one consideration among many. We find no error in the court's conclusion that, taken as a whole, conditions in the isolation cells continued to violate the prohibition against cruel and unusual punishment.

In fashioning a remedy, the District Court had ample authority to go beyond earlier orders and to address each element contributing to the violation. The District Court had given the Department repeated opportunities to remedy the cruel and unusual conditions in the isolation cells. If petitioners had fully complied with the court's earlier orders, the present time limit might well have been unnecessary. But taking the long and unhappy history of the litigation into account, the court was justified in entering a comprehensive order to insure against the risk of inadequate compliance.[9]

The order is supported by the interdependence of the conditions producing the violation. The vandalized cells and the atmosphere of violence were attributable, in part, to overcrowding and to deep-seated enmities growing out of months of constant daily friction. The 30-day limit will help to correct these conditions.[11] Moreover, the limit presents little danger of interference with prison administration, for the Commissioner of Correction himself stated that prisoners should not ordinarily be held in punitive isolation for more than 14 days. Finally, the exercise of discretion in this case is entitled to special deference because of the trial judge's years of experience with the problem at hand and his recognition of the limits on a federal court's authori-

9. As we explained in Milliken v. Bradley, 433 U.S. 267, 281, state and local authorities have primary responsibility for curing constitutional violations. "If, however '[those] authorities fail in their affirmative obligations . . . judicial authority may be invoked.' Swann [v. Charlotte-Mecklenburg Board of Education, 402 U.S. 1] 15. Once invoked, 'the scope of a district court's equitable powers to remedy past wrongs is broad, for breadth and flexibility are inherent in equitable remedies.' " Ibid. In this case, the District Court was not remedying the present effects of a violation in the past. It was seeking to bring an ongoing violation to an immediate halt. Cooperation on the part of Department officials and compliance with other aspects of the decree may justify elimination of this added safeguard in the future, but it is entirely appropriate for the District Court to postpone any such determination until the Department's progress can be evaluated.

11. As early as 1969, the District Court had identified shorter sentences as a possible remedy for overcrowding in the isolation cells. *Holt I.* The limit imposed in 1976 was a mechanical—and therefore an easily enforced—method of minimizing overcrowding, with its attendant vandalism and unsanitary conditions.

ty in a case of this kind. Like the Court of Appeals, we find no error in the inclusion of a 30-day limitation on sentences to punitive isolation as a part of the District Court's comprehensive remedy.

The Attorney General of Arkansas, whose office has represented petitioners throughout this litigation, contends that any award of fees is prohibited by the Eleventh Amendment. He also argues that the Court of Appeals incorrectly held that fees were authorized by the Civil Rights Attorney's Fees Awards Act of 1976. We hold that the District Court's award is adequately supported by its finding of bad faith and that the Act supports the additional award by the Court of Appeals.

Although the Attorney General argues that the finding of bad faith does not overcome the State's Eleventh Amendment protection, he does not question the accuracy of the finding made by the District Court and approved by the Court of Appeals. Nor does he question the settled rule that a losing litigant's bad faith may justify an allowance of fees to the prevailing party.[14] He merely argues that the order requiring that the fees be paid from public funds violates the Eleventh Amendment.

In the landmark decision in Ex parte Young, 209 U.S. 123, the Court held that, although prohibited from giving orders directly to a State, federal courts could enjoin state officials in their official capacities. And in Edelman v. Jordan, 415 U.S. 651, when the Court held that the Amendment grants the States an immunity from retroactive monetary relief, it reaffirmed the principle that state officers are not immune from prospective injunctive relief. Aware that the difference between retroactive and prospective relief "will not in many instances be that between day and night," id., at 667, the Court emphasized in *Edelman* that the distinction did not immunize the States from their obligation to obey costly federal-court orders. The cost of compliance is "ancillary" to the prospective order enforcing federal law.[15] The line between retroactive and prospective relief cannot be so rigid that it defeats the effective enforcement of prospective relief.

The present case requires application of that principle. In exercising their prospective powers under Ex parte Young and Edelman v. Jordan, federal courts are not reduced to issuing injunctions against state officers and hoping for compliance. Once issued, an injunction may be enforced. Many of the court's most effective enforcement weapons involve financial penalties. A

14. An equity court has the unquestioned power to award attorney's fees against a party who shows bad faith by delaying or disrupting the litigation or by hampering enforcement of a court order. Alyeska Pipeline Co. v. Wilderness Soc., 421 U.S. 240, 258–259; . . . cf. Fed. Rule Civ.Proc. 56(g) (attorney's fees to be awarded against party filing summary judgment affidavits "in bad faith or solely for the purpose of delay"); Fed.Rule Civ.Proc. 37(a)(4) (motions to compel discovery; prevailing party may recover attorney's fees). The award vindicates judicial authority without resort to the more drastic sanctions available for contempt of court and makes the prevailing party whole for expenses caused by his opponent's obstinacy. Cf. First Nat. Bank v. Dunham, 471 F.2d 712 (CA8 1973). Of course, fees can also be awarded as part of a civil contempt penalty. See, e.g., Toledo Scale Co. v. Computing Scale Co., 261 U.S. 399; Signal Delivery Service, Inc. v. Highway Truck Drivers, 68 F.R.D. 318 (ED Pa.1975).

15. "Ancillary" costs may be very large indeed. Last Term, for example, this Court rejected an Eleventh Amendment defense and approved an injunction ordering a State to pay almost $6 million to help defray the costs of desegregating the Detroit school system. Milliken v. Bradley, 433 U.S., at 293 (Powell, J., concurring in judgment).

criminal contempt prosecution for "resistance to [the court's] lawful . . . order" may result in a jail term or a fine. 18 U.S.C. § 401 (1976 ed.). Civil contempt proceedings may yield a conditional jail term or fine. United States v. Mine Workers. Civil contempt may also be punished by a remedial fine, which compensates the party who won the injunction for the effects of his opponent's noncompliance. Gompers v. Bucks Stove & Range Co. If a state agency refuses to adhere to a court order, a financial penalty may be the most effective means of insuring compliance. The principles of federalism that inform Eleventh Amendment doctrine surely do not require federal courts to enforce their decrees only by sending high state officials to jail. The less intrusive power to impose a fine is properly treated as ancillary to the federal court's power to impose injunctive relief.

In this case, the award of attorney's fees for bad faith served the same purpose as a remedial fine imposed for civil contempt. It vindicated the District Court's authority over a recalcitrant litigant. Compensation was not the sole motive for the award; in setting the amount of the fee, the court said that it would "make no effort to adequately compensate counsel for the work that they have done or for the time that they have spent on the case." The court did allow a "substantial" fee, however, because "the allowance thereof may incline the Department to act in such a manner that further protracted litigation about the prisons will not be necessary." [17] We see no reason to distinguish this award from any other penalty imposed to enforce a prospective injunction. Hence the substantive protections of the Eleventh Amendment do not prevent an award of attorney's fees against the Department's officers in their official capacities.

Instead of assessing the award against the defendants in their official capacities, the District Court directed that the fees are "to be paid out of Department of Correction funds." Although the Attorney General objects to the form of the order,[19] no useful purpose would be served by requiring that it be recast in different language. We have previously approved directives that were comparable in their actual impact on the State without pausing to attach significance to the language used by the District Court.[20] Even if it

17. That the award had a compensatory effect does not in any event distinguish it from a fine for civil contempt, which also compensates a private party for the consequences of a contemnor's disobedience. Gompers v. Bucks Stove & Range Co. Moreover, the Court has approved federal rulings requiring a State to support programs that compensate for past misdeeds, saying: "That the programs are also 'compensatory' in nature does not change the fact that they are part of a plan that operates *prospectively* to bring about the delayed benefits of a unitary school system. We therefore hold that such prospective relief is not barred by the Eleventh Amendment." Milliken v. Bradley, supra, at 290 (emphasis in original). The award of attorney's fees against a State disregarding a federal order stands on the same footing; like other enforcement powers, it is integral to the court's grant of prospective relief.

19. We do not understand the Attorney General to urge that the fees should have been awarded against the officers personally; that would be a remarkable way to treat individuals who have relied on the Attorney General to represent their interests throughout this litigation.

20. In Milliken v. Bradley, supra, we affirmed an order requiring a state treasurer to pay a substantial sum to another litigant, even though the District Court's opinion explicitly recognized that "this remedial decree will be paid for by the taxpayers of the City of Detroit and the State of Michigan," and even though the Court of Appeals, in affirming, stated that "the District Court ordered that the State and Detroit Board each pay one-half the costs" of relief. Bradley v. Milliken, 540 F.2d 229, 245 (CA6 1976).

might have been better form to omit the reference to the Department of Correction, the use of that language is surely not reversible error. . . .

Finally, the Attorney General argues that, even if attorney's fees may be awarded against a State, they should not be awarded in this case, because neither the State nor the Department is expressly named as a defendant. Although the Eleventh Amendment prevented respondents from suing the State by name, their injunctive suit against prison officials was, for all practical purposes, brought against the State. The actions of the Attorney General himself show that. His office has defended this action since it began. See *Holt I.* The State apparently paid earlier fee awards; and it was the State's lawyers who decided to bring this appeal, thereby risking another award.

Like the Attorney General, Congress recognized that suits brought against individual officers for injunctive relief are for all practical purposes suits against the State itself. The legislative history makes it clear that in such suits attorney's fee awards should generally be obtained "either directly from the official, in his official capacity, from funds of his agency or under his control, or from the State or local government (whether or not the agency or government is a named party)." S.Rep. No. 94–1011, p. 5 (1976). Awards against the official in his individual capacity, in contrast, were not to be affected by the statute; in injunctive suits they would continue to be awarded only "under the traditional bad faith standard recognized by the Supreme Court in *Alyeska.*" There is no indication in this case that the named defendants litigated in bad faith before the Court of Appeals. Consequently, the Department of Correction is the entity intended by Congress to bear the burden of the counsel fees award.

The judgment of the Court of Appeals is accordingly affirmed.

Justice REHNQUIST, dissenting.

The Court's affirmance of a District Court's injunction against a prison practice which has not been shown to violate the Constitution can only be considered an aberration in light of decisions as recently as last Term carefully defining the remedial discretion of the federal courts. Dayton Board of Education v. Brinkman, 433 U.S. 406 (1977); Milliken v. Bradley, 433 U.S. 267 (1977) (*Milliken II*). Nor are any of the several theories which the Court advances in support of its affirmance of the assessment of attorney's fees against the taxpayers of Arkansas sufficiently convincing to overcome the prohibition of the Eleventh Amendment. Accordingly, I dissent.

No person of ordinary feeling could fail to be moved by the Court's recitation of the conditions formerly prevailing in the Arkansas prison system. Yet I fear that the Court has allowed itself to be moved beyond the well-established bounds limiting the exercise of remedial authority by the federal district courts. The purpose and extent of that discretion in another context were carefully defined by the Court's opinion last Term in *Milliken II,* supra, at 280–281:

"In the first place, like other equitable remedies, the nature of the desegregation remedy is to be determined by the nature and scope of the constitutional violation. Swann v. Charlotte-Mecklenburg Board of Education, 402 U.S. [1] 16 [(1971)]. The remedy must therefore be related to 'the *condition* alleged to offend the Constitution . . . .' Milliken [v. Bradley], 418 U.S.

[717] 738 [(1974)]. Second, the decree must indeed be *remedial* in nature, that is, it must be designed as nearly as possible 'to restore the victims of discriminatory conduct to the position they would have occupied in the absence of such conduct.' Third, the federal courts in devising a remedy must take into account the interests of state and local authorities in managing their own affairs, consistent with the Constitution." (Footnotes omitted.)[1]

The District Court's order limiting the maximum period of punitive isolation to 30 days in no way relates to any condition found offensive to the Constitution. It is, when stripped of descriptive verbiage, a prophylactic rule, doubtless well designed to assure a more humane prison system in Arkansas, but not complying with the limitations set forth in *Milliken II,* supra. Petitioners do not dispute the District Court's conclusion that the overcrowded conditions and the inadequate diet provided for those prisoners in punitive isolation offended the Constitution, but the District Court has ordered a cessation of those practices. The District Court found that the confinement of two prisoners in a single cell on a restricted diet for 30 days did not violate the Eighth Amendment. While the Court today remarks that "the length of confinement cannot be ignored," it does not find that confinement under the conditions described by the District Court becomes unconstitutional on the 31st day. It must seek other justifications for its affirmance of that portion of the District Court's order.

Certainly the provision is not remedial in the sense that it "restore[s] the victims of discriminatory conduct to the position they would have occupied in the absence of such conduct." Milliken v. Bradley, 418 U.S. 717, 746 (1974) (*Milliken I*). The sole effect of the provision is to grant future offenders against prison discipline greater benefits than the Constitution requires; it does nothing to remedy the plight of past victims of conditions which may well have been unconstitutional. A prison is unlike a school system in which students in the later grades may receive special instruction to compensate for discrimination to which they were subjected in the earlier grades. *Milliken II,* supra, at 281–283. Nor has it been shown that petitioners' conduct had any collateral effect upon private actions for which the District Court may seek to compensate so as to eliminate the continuing effect of past unconstitutional conduct. See Swann v. Charlotte-Mecklenburg Board of Education, 402 U.S. 1, 28 (1971). Even where such remedial relief is justified, a district court may go no further than is necessary to eliminate the consequences of official unconstitutional conduct. *Dayton,* supra, at 419–420; Pasadena Board of Education v. Spangler; *Swann,* supra, at 31–32.

1. The court suggests that its holding is consistent with *Milliken II,* because it "was not remedying the present effects of a violation in the past. It was seeking to bring an ongoing violation to an immediate halt." This suggestion is wide of the mark. Whether exercising its authority to "remed[y] the present effects of a violation in the past," or "seeking to bring an ongoing violation to an immediate halt," the court's remedial authority remains circumscribed by the language quoted in the text from *Milliken II.* If anything, less ingenuity and discretion would appear to be required to "bring an ongoing violation to an immediate halt" than in "remedying the present effects of a violation in the past." The difficulty with the Court's position is that it quite properly refrains from characterizing solitary confinement for a period in excess of 30 days as a cruel and unusual punishment; but given this position, a "remedial" order that no such solitary confinement may take place is necessarily of a prophylactic nature, and not essential to "bring an ongoing violation to an immediate halt."

The Court's only asserted justification for its affirmance of the decree, despite its dissimilarity to remedial decrees in other contexts, is that it is "a mechanical—and therefore an easily enforced—method of minimizing overcrowding." This conclusion fails adequately to take into account the third consideration cited in *Milliken II*: "the interests of state and local authorities in managing their own affairs, consistent with the Constitution." 433 U.S., at 281. The prohibition against extended punitive isolation, a practice which has not been shown to be inconsistent with the Constitution, can only be defended because of the difficulty of policing the District Court's explicit injunction against the overcrowding and inadequate diet which have been found to be violative of the Constitution. But even if such an expansion of remedial authority could be justified in a case where the defendants had been repeatedly contumacious, this is not such a case. The District Court's dissatisfaction with petitioners' performance under its earlier direction to "make a substantial start," Holt v. Sarver, on alleviating unconstitutional conditions cannot support an inference that petitioners are prepared to defy the specific orders now laid down by the District Court and not challenged by the petitioners. A proper respect for "the interests of state and local authorities in managing their own affairs," *Milliken II*, 433 U.S., at 281, requires the opposite conclusion.[2]

The District Court's order enjoins a practice which has not been found inconsistent with the Constitution. The only ground for the injunction, therefore, is the prophylactic one of assuring that no unconstitutional conduct will occur in the future. In a unitary system of prison management there would be much to be said for such a rule, but neither this Court nor any other federal court is entrusted with such a management role under the Constitution. . . .

[Justice Rehnquist also dissented from the decision to grant attorney fees.]

---

1) Does the narrow character of the appeal distort the case in the Supreme Court? In which direction?

2) Try to formulate in your own words Justice Rehnquist's objection to the 30-day limitation on punitive isolation. Has Justice Stevens adequately responded to that objection? What basis is there for insisting on a time limitation that, according to Stevens, is not constitutionally required? Has Justice Stevens correctly characterized Judge Henley's theory for imposing the 30-day limitation? Or has he attempted to supply a new theory? Does his theory create its own problems?

3) Justice Rehnquist acknowledges that the 30-day limitation on punitive isolation might be justified to prevent confinements of excessive duration; but he insists that such a justification would place a federal court in a "man-

2. I reserve judgment on whether such a precautionary order would be justified where state officials have been shown to have violated previous remedial orders. I also note the similarity between this decree and the "no majority of any minority" requirement which was found impermissible in Pasadena Board of Education v. Spangler even though it too might have been defended on the theory that it was an easily enforceable mechanism for preventing future acts of official discrimination.

agement role" of a state agency that would be inconsistent with the Constitution. What does he mean by a "management role"? Isn't it simply an effort of a federal court to devise the most effective way of protecting federal constitutional rights against threats by the state? The so-called tailoring principle requires the remedy to fit the violation. Are prophylactic rules consistent with that principle?

4) Justice Stevens writes: "Finally, the exercise of discretion in this case is entitled to special deference because of the trial judge's years of experience with the problem at hand and his recognition of the limits on a federal court's authority in a case of this kind." But one should ask whether the factors mentioned warrant a "special deference." Might Judge Henley's long involvement be a source of special concern? Justice Stevens assesses Judge Henley's judicial temperament and speaks of Henley's recognition of the limits of his authority. Should that play any role in evaluating the remedy? Is Judge Henley's temperament a matter of the judicial record?

5) At various times Justice Stevens disagrees with the Arkansas Attorney General's interpretation of Judge Henley's opinion. Who read the opinion correctly? Would Justice Stevens have any reason to misread the opinion? Does he seem bent on affirmance? What might explain the difference between this case and the Court's general posture in the school desegregation cases cited by Justice Rehnquist?

6) The Supreme Court affirms the award of attorney's fees by the district court on the bad-faith exception theory. The opinion also states that the Arkansas Attorney General "does not question the accuracy of the finding" of bad faith, and there is "no reason to distinguish this award from any other penalty imposed to enforce a prospective injunction." Has the definition of bad faith changed somewhere between the district court and the Supreme Court? Why would the Attorney General have made the concession attributed to him? The district court disavowed the use of the contempt power and instead relied on its power to grant supplemental relief. Should the Supreme Court characterize the award as the functional equivalent of a "penalty" or "a remedial fine imposed for civil contempt"? Why did the Supreme Court not rely on the principal theory of the court of appeals?

The Arkansas prison litigation began to wind down after the Supreme Court's decision. The parties entered a comprehensive consent decree in October 1978, which included a Compliance Coordinator. In early 1981 "it became apparent that the cooperation of the parties necessary for continued progress within the framework of the Decree was no longer forthcoming." Finney v. Mabry, 534 F.Supp. 1026, 1088 (E.D.Ark.1982).

Chief District Judge Eisele, to whom the case was assigned, conducted about six weeks of hearings in 1981. He filed a reported opinion in late 1981. That opinion deals with administrative segregation, which is not intended to punish but to protect the prisoner or to maintain security. Judge Eisele discussed case precedent bearing on due process. The authorities suggested changes and were ordered to file a status report informing "the Court and the petitioners what action the Board has taken on the proposed changes." Plaintiffs were granted two weeks to comment. The Judge said that after receiving material from both sides he will enter a final order on "all issues relating to administrative segregation." 528 F.Supp. at 575. In 1982, Judge Eisele filed two other opinions, one on February 16, the second on August 20.

FINNEY v. MABRY

534 F.Supp. 1026 (E.D.Ark.1982).

EISELE, Chief Judge.

This case, which was orginally filed in April 1969, is a class action on behalf of all inmates confined in the Arkansas Department of Correction. The plaintiff class challenges the constitutionality of the conditions of confinement at the various institutions administered by the Arkansas Department of Correction. During the long history of the case numerous hearings have been held, and the Court has entered many orders determining the rights of the parties. In addition, the parties entered a Consent Decree in October 1978, which was made an order of this Court, setting forth certain minimum requirements that the respondents agreed to meet in the administration of the Arkansas Department of Correction. The Consent Decree set up a mechanism to monitor the degree of compliance by the respondents with the terms of the Decree, and allowed either party to petition the Court for dismissal of the case upon compliance with the terms of the Decree or upon the expiration of eighteen months from the date of the Decree, whichever, occurred first. The Arkansas Department of Correction operated under the Consent Decree until March 1981, when it became apparent that the cooperation of the parties, necessary for continued progress within the framework of the Decree, was no longer forthcoming. Upon the request of the plaintiff class, a hearing was scheduled for August 1981 to determine the extent of compliance by the Arkansas Department of Correction with the Constitution, the Consent Decree, and other prior orders of the Court in this case.

The plaintiff filed an amended petition setting forth approximately forty particular practices or conditions of the Arkansas Department of Correction which it alleged to be unlawful. The respondents denied that any conditions or practices of the Arkansas Department of Correction were unlawful, and requested that the case be dismissed. In addition, the respondents submitted at trial a list idenfitying approximately fifty additional issues which they contended were raised by the Consent Decree or prior orders of the Court, and therefore were in dispute at the hearing, although not included in the plaintiffs' petition. The plaintiffs agreed that the issues listed should be considered in dispute, so that the record could be made complete on the extent of compliance of the respondents. There were therefore pending approximately ninety matters upon which a determination was to be made concerning the extent of compliance of the Arkansas Department of Correction with the Constitution, the Consent Decree, and prior orders of the Court.

As would be expected, the degree of compliance demonstrated by respondents differed for the various issues in dispute. For many of the identified issues, the Court found that the respondents were in compliance, and in many cases had been in compliance for some time. In other areas, the Arkansas

Department of Correction had changed practices or policies shortly before or during the trial, or had adopted plans to do so, and the Court found that, with the implementation of those changes, the respondents would be in compliance. There were a few matters which were identified by the Court as still-existing problems in the Arkansas Department of Correction, and the respondents were held, with respect thereto, not to be in compliance with either the Constitution, prior orders of the Court, or the Consent Decree. . . .

Although this case was originally filed on behalf of all inmates of the Arkansas Department of Correction, housed in all institutions of the Department, it has become apparent that the problems remaining involve primarily the Cummins Unit, and, to a lesser extent, the Tucker Unit. The remaining institutions operated by the Department are essentially in compliance with respect to their "local" conditions of incarceration. The evidence presented at trial centered upon conditions at the Cummins Unit and the Tucker Unit, as did the arguments of counsel after the trial. The attorney for the plaintiff class conceded in a letter to the Court dated October 13, 1981, that "[s]ince the entry of the Consent Decree in this matter on October 15, 1978, the Department has achieved constitutional status at some of its institutions," but he did not specify any certain institutions. There is no question but that the conditions at the Women's Unit, which has been highly acclaimed by experts in the field, are sufficient to meet all the requirements of the Constitution and the prior orders of this Court. The Court also finds that the conditions at the Benton, Wrightsville, and the Diagnostic Units, and all of the separate work release units satisfy such requirements. It is therefore the opinion of the Court that these institutions will not require continuing supervision. Furthermore, the Cummins and Tucker Units will need only limited court controlled supervision during the "windup" period discussed below.

It should be noted that the Court is finding only that the conditions specific to the named institutions are being approved. As will be discussed in this opinion, there are several matters which apply to the entire Department, such as the provision of medical and mental health care, the grievance procedure and the affirmative action program, as to which a finding of total compliance cannot be made at this time. As to those services which are provided to all inmates of the Department on a system-wide basis, rather than on an institution by institution basis, the "release" of the specified institutions has no effect. The Department remains, of course, under an obligation to provide those services in a suitable manner to all inmates in all units, not just to those inmates at the Cummins and Tucker Units. As to all matters that are provided on a "local" rather than a "system-wide" basis, all units except Cummins and Tucker are in compliance.

It should also be noted that the release of these institutions does not mean that the Arkansas Department of Correction will necessarily be free of all future scrutiny concerning the conditions at them. The attorney for the plaintiff class opposed the release of any particular institutions or the dismissal of the suit as to any specific issues until the entire case was dismissed, apparently because of his concern that unless the entire department and all issues remained under the direct or indirect supervision of the Court until the Department is in compliance on all particulars, that the Department would "backslide" in those areas released from control in order to more easily bring those areas still under direct scrutiny into compliance. Although such a possibility does exist, the Court concludes that all deference should be given to the intentions of the respondents not to allow such "backsliding" to occur. The respondents are aware of their responsibilities to maintain the entire Department in a constitutional manner and have, indeed, made exceptional progress toward that goal. It is very doubtful that the success that they have worked so hard to achieve over the years would be forfeited easily through neglect or a lack of perseverance. Furthermore, the ruling of the Court is only that the institutions in question are in compliance with the requirements of the Constitution and the prior orders of the Court at this particular time. This decision would not preclude the inmates from raising the issue again in the future if conditions fall below the constitutional minimums. At some point, hopefully soon, jurisdiction over the Department must be relinquished completely by this Court and the respondents must be trusted with the responsibility to maintain conditions at the level that allowed dismissal of the case, without continual monitoring by the Court or a Court-approved third person. To relinquish active oversight in stages, and thereby to transfer greater responsibility back to the respondents in a somewhat gradual way, will increase the independence of the Department and will make this litigation more manageable for all concerned.

The remainder of this opinion will therefore deal with and resolve the disputes between the parties concerning the degree of compliance by the respondents within the requirements of the Constitution, the Consent Decree, and the prior orders of the Court in the various substantive areas, or issues, identified.

With respect to the largest group of issues identified, the Arkansas Department of Correction is in compliance, and had been in compliance for some time before the hearing. For many of these issues, which include such matters as the adequacy of and access to the law library, mail regulations and the opening of legal mail, and provision for religious requirements for Muslim inmates, the reports prepared by the Compliance Coordinator indicate that the Arkansas Department of Correction was in compliance at the time the report as to those matters was prepared. Although reluctant to concede any issue, the attorney for the plaintiff class did agree that further evidence beyond the reports of the Compliance Coordinator would not be required in order for the respondents to carry the burden of showing compliance. The Court accepts as true the uncontested findings of the Compliance Coordinator, and concludes that the Arkansas Department of Correction is in compliance with the Constitution, the Consent Decree, and other prior orders of this Court on all matters identified by the respondents in the list submitted which were not actively contested by the attorney for the plaintiff on the record during the trial of this case. These matters have been identified to the Court by the following abbreviated references which are known to the parties.

Use of force *policy* (emphasis supplied)

Running to and from work

Any punishment not authorized

Dental care

Two inmates in two-bunk punitive cell

Reporting requirement for exceptions

Privileges

Personal appearance

Discrimination against Muslims

Muslim diet

Muslim religious practices

Proper diet on punitive

Exercise on punitive

Legal advisor to inmates

Law libraries

Access to law libraries

Opening of legal mail

Mail regulations

Visiting regulations

Charging officer not on committee

No adjudication solely on informant

Informant's name and written statement must be before committee

Contraband must be presented to committee

Witness statement must be read into tape

Entire hearing must be tape recorded and kept three years

Hearing to be conducted weekdays between 6:00 a.m. and 6:00 p.m.

Written charges given to inmate 24 hours prior to hearing

Composition of committee: chairperson plus one security plus one treatment

Review of chief security officer prior to hearing

Charges/consequences fully explained

Charging officer excluded from hearing room

No supervision of inmate by charging officer during time of hearing

Written reason to inmate within 24 hours after hearing

Statement if no black on committee

No racial discrimination allowed in disciplinary proceedings

Minor discipline

It should also be noted that a few issues which were raised in the petition and amended petition by the plaintiff class were not actually disputed at trial. Specifically, the plaintiffs had alleged subversion by the respondents of the procedure for the investigation of complaints of excessive force, staff shortages resulting in curtailed time for recreation and inadequate supervision during recreation periods, and termination of the Compliance Coordinator as particular matters for which the respondents should be held to be not in compliance with the Constitution, the Consent Decree and prior orders of the Court. However, at times before and during the hearing these particular allegations were either abandoned by the plaintiffs or resolved after rulings by the Court. Except for the allegation of staff shortages for recreation, these allegations had raised new issues not addressed in the Consent Decree or court orders prior to the Consent Decree; therefore, the record is clear that they are not pending and no new or specific findings are required at this time. The problem of adequate supervision during recreation is part of the larger problem of inadequate staffing of the institutions at all times, and will be met through the plan for increased staffing as discussed herein below.

A second group of issues may be identified as to which the Arkansas Department of Correction was in compliance at the conclusion of the hearing and as to which it is not necessary to determine if the prior practices of the respondents would have been sufficient if still in effect. This group includes such matters as cleanliness in the East Building at Cummins, the grievance procedure, and provision of medical care for inmates. As to these matters the Court is satisfied that the recently adopted changes in practice meet the applicable standards, but does not, thereby, intend to sanction or condemn the prior practices of the respondents. It would be a waste of judicial resources to analyze carefully and technically each allegation about prior practices that have now been discarded in order to determine if they would be acceptable if still in effect. With respect to such issues the state of compliance of those policies or practices which were in place at the conclusion of the hearing will be examined without regard to the fact that the hearing itself may have been the catalyst for the changes in one or more of such areas.

As to most matters pertaining to conditions in the maximum security facility of the Cummins Unit, the Court found that the respondents are now in compliance, but will require that record-keeping procedures be established and that the newly adopted practices and procedures be monitored for a period of time to assure continuing compliance. The plan established by the respondents to rotate officers through the East Building on a regular basis, as required by the Consent Decree, is adequate if followed in practice. Similarly, the problem of maintaining minimum sanitation standards in the East Building has been accomplished recently through the efforts of Mr. Howard Smith, the maintenance director. As to both officer rotation and sanitation standards in the East Building of the Cummins Unit, the Court has concluded that the respondents are now in compliance with the Constitution, the Consent Decree and prior orders of the Court, but that continued compliance should be monitored before the Department is actually released on these issues.

The Court also concluded that the respondents are in compliance as to the repair of damaged facilities in the East Building and the periodic reevaluation of residents of the maximum security facility, except that further documentation will be required. The Arkansas Department of Correction has recently adopted a procedure to effectuate prompt repair of damage in the East Building, and has begun to keep an inventory of necessary supplies so that the time lapse before a repair or replacement can actually be made will be shortened. A new lighting system has also been installed in the maximum security facility and was reported by the attorney for the respondent to have become operational. Assuming that the procedures function as planned by Mr. Smith, the maintenance director, the Court is satisfied that repairs will be carried out in a satisfactory manner. However, because this, too, involves very recent changes in the procedures of the Department, some period of actual practice will be required before the Court may relinquish oversight. Furthermore, because incidents such as that involving Mr. Sherrod, which the Court believes to be the exception rather than the rule, are likely to occur if needed repairs are not reported and documented in a systematic fashion, an appropriate chain of paperwork must be established. The Court will require that a record report be made promptly of any needed repairs in the East Building by the person responsible for administration of that facility. The report must show the day that the fixture was damaged. After the report is sent to the maintenance department, the schedule for correction of the deficiency should be noted. Finally, after the repair has been completed, the date should be noted. Such a "paper-chase" will aid the Department in accomplishing the repairs promptly, and will enable later review of the problem by the Court if necessary.

As stated above, the Court also found that the respondents are now in compliance on the evaluation of residents of the East Building of the Cummins Unit and periodic reevaluation of those persons, but concluded that more complete records should be maintained. A record must be made of what the evaluation consisted of and should indicate the reasons that purportedly justify keeping the person in maximum. Any psychological counseling or testing, or other reference and the results thereof, should be noted. If no such reference is felt to be required, the reason should be noted. The maintenance of such records will cause the persons making these decisions to have to consider the problem thoroughly in all cases, and will document information for later reference within the institution, and by the Court if necessary.

The Court concluded that the respondents are now in compliance on the maintenance of constitutional conditions for those housed in punitive isolation. Very recent improvements have been made in programs for exercise and recreation, and in lighting and sanitation as discussed above, which are applicable to persons housed in punitive isolation. The major contested issue regarding punitive isolation was the policy of the Department of removing mattresses during daytime hours from the cells of those persons being held in punitive isolation. Without approving or disapproving the policy, the Court concludes that the removal of mattresses, and the denial of other privileges by the respondents as punishment, are matters fully within the discretion of the administrators of the prison. These are matters which reflect attitudes toward the use of punishment as a method of managing inmates within the context of a prison and do not rise to constitutional magnitude as presently enforced. The Court concludes that the conditions imposed on those persons being held in punitive isolation, as enforced at the conclusion of the hearing, are in compliance with the Constitution, the Consent Decree, and all prior orders of this Court.

The Court also concluded that with procedural changes recently adopted by the Department of Correction, and with the addition of a recording requirement now imposed by the Court, the disciplinary procedures followed by the respondents meet standards required by the Constitution, the Consent Decree, and prior orders of the Court. During the time the trial was being held, personnel of the Department finalized a new form to be completed by the disciplinary committee during the course of every disciplinary proceeding. A copy of the new form was made an exhibit during the closing arguments on this issue, and counsel for the respondents represented that the forms would actually be in use at the institution within a short time from that date (after they had been received from the printer). In addition, a new policy has been formulated concerning disciplinary procedures, and Mr. Battles and Mr. Dorsey testified on behalf of the Department of Correction that training sessions had been conducted to aid personnel in implementation of the new policy and forms. Counsel for the plaintiff class conceded, and the Court agrees, that if the new form is effectively used, many past problems that have been noted regarding the disciplinary procedures will be resolved. However, because the forms are so new, the forms and policy were not actually in effect in the Department at the time the hearing was recessed, some period of monitoring the new disciplinary procedures will be required. Furthermore, one problem with past disciplinaries that was not adequately dealt with by the new form is the requirement that medical personnel be consulted before a disciplinary is imposed for malingering when the inmate alleges a medical justification for refusing to work. The forms do state that such consultation is required. However, it is the opinion of the Court . . . that some record must be made of those who have checked the medical records and determined that the inmate has not been given an excusal from work for medical reasons. There must be a record made which identifies the person in the infirmary who is giving the information to the Disciplinary Committee. The notation may be written in the medical records, in the disciplinary records, or both, at the preference of the Department. Although the petitioners charged in the amended petition that the respondents' provision for counsel substitutes during disciplinary proceedings was inadequate, counsel for the petitioners agreed during the oral argument that recently implemented practices of the Department will satisfy constitutional requirements. Finally, the Court has concluded that the continuing use of multiple overlapping charges by the Department for a single incident does not create a problem as long as the practice of punishing for only a single infraction is continued. For example, the evidence showed that an inmate will often be charged with refusal to work, staying in living quarters, and refusal to follow the order of an officer for one incident in which he stayed in the barracks and refused to go to work. The evidence also demonstrated, however, that the same inmate would be given the same penalty as if he had been found to have violated only one rule. As long as multiple punishments are not imposed, charging the inmate with multiple infractions does not implicate constitutional standards. The conclusion of the Court was that the respondents would be in compliance if the new practices and procedures were implemented, as represented to the Court, and if records were made on the medical authority contacted on malingering charges, as required by the Court.

A new grievance procedure was also adopted during the course of the trial and modified following a discussion on the record concerning it. The Court approves the new procedure as modified, and finds that with the implementation of it the respondents will be in compliance on that issue. The implementation of the procedure is, however, an important and fairly complicated task that will require the training of numerous personnel at the institutions. Therefore, as with other recently adopted procedures and practices, the progress on the implementation and use of the grievance procedure must be monitored for a time. In this regard, the Court will require the Department to submit periodic self-evaluations for a short time on the progress that is made.

The Court has concluded also that the new classification system adopted by the Department, if implemented as described during the hearing, complies with the Constitution, the Consent Decree, and prior orders of the Court. It was planned that the new work classification system would be in effect at the institutions by the end of 1981 and that all manuals would be written and training completed concerning it by July 1982. Implementation of the new classification system is closely related to the medical contract and the intake unit procedures, both of which are also new. Therefore, progress toward implementation of the new medical classification system will be monitored. If it is put into effect in the way and according to the timetable planned, the respondents will be held to be in compliance.

An allegation by the petitioners, related to the classification system, was that the requirement that some inmates work in jobs that required long hours seven days a week, particularly jobs in the kitchen at Cummins, was unconstitutional. The evidence indicated that some jobs to which inmates were assigned did require significantly greater hours of work than did other jobs and that assignments to those jobs were often perceived as punishment by the prisoners, even if that were not the intention of those making the assignments. The Court concluded that, although it might be more equitable not to have such disparity in working hours among the inmates, and that it might be a good practice to rotate all or most inmates through those jobs, nevertheless these were matters within the administrative discretion of the management personnel of the prison and did not violate constitutional standards or any prior order of the Court.

The structure for the provision of medical services within the Department of Correction has been dramatically changed within the last several months. The Department had maintained a staff of medical personnel as its employees and had operated the medical facility directly. A contract for the provision of medical services has now been entered with a private company. Virtually all physicians in the Pine Bluff, Arkansas, area are to be involved on a limited basis in supplying medical care at the various institutions. The company will maintain a pharmacy service and emergency medical capability. All personnel of the medical facility will be employees of the independent company rather than personnel of the Department of Correction. Also, the use of inmate aids in the infirmary facility will be greatly reduced, and access by inmates to the medical files of other inmates will be more closely restricted and regulated. There are plans also, with the addition of new security personnel, to change the place of sick call to a more private area, and possibly to change the time of sick call.[2] Although the Court does not feel it is necessary to evaluate the medical services offered by the respondents prior to the contract, it does clearly appear that the services provided will be greatly im-

2. The Court has concluded, contrary to the allegations of the petitioners, that the time and place of sick call are administrative decisions within the discretion of prison management. The Court therefore finds no violation of a constitutional standard or of a prior order of this Court in the fact that the respondents have held sick call at 4:30 a.m.

proved as a result of the contract if implemented in accordance with the testimony. A trial period will be required to allow the contract system to become fully operational before its success may be adequately measured. The provision of medical services is, therefore, another area that must be monitored for a time before it may finally be said that the respondents are in full compliance. The Court will require periodic reports on the progress of the new medical services system and its capability to adequately meet the needs of the inmate population.

The Court has concluded that the respondents have supplied adequate amounts of clothing and sanitation supplies at the Cummins and Tucker Units. There was evidence that there were problems with such supplies during periods in the past. However, the Court is satisfied that those problems have been resolved and that, with the increase in maintenance staff, there is a more systematic approach that is expected to insure that such problems will not arise in the future. The respondents are, therefore, in compliance with the standards of the Constitution, the Consent Decree and prior orders of the Court on the provision of minimum supplies of clothing and sanitation items.

With recent improvements in the kitchen and planned improvements in the shower areas, it is also true that the respondents will have adequately met applicable sanitation standards at the Cummins Unit. Most evidence presented on the question of sanitation concerned conditions in the kitchen. Warden Sargent has now placed the kitchen under his direct supervision and impressed the Court that he recognizes the importance of the issue, and that he intends to use his best efforts to insure that the kitchen produces nutritionally adequate foods in a sanitary manner. A new boiler and a new scullery have been installed and will soon be operational, if they are not at this time. Examination reports by the state Health Department show that, although there have been some problems, for example with hot water, the kitchen has passed inspection. Mr. Smith, the maintenance director, explained the improvements that are being made in the shower areas at the institution and outlined the schedule for completion of those improvements. The Court concludes that the prior problems with sanitation that have existed have been largely resolved and that there are definite plans for improvements and a commitment to carry through with those plans. The completion of the planned improvements will be monitored, and the Court will require periodic status reports on the operation of the kitchen, particularly the availability and use of the new boiler and scullery. Therefore, considering those improvements, the Court will not find that the respondents are not in compliance in the maintenance of minimum sanitation standards.

The availability of notary service to inmates is another matter concerning which the Department of Correction recently implemented a new policy, and the Court may find that the new policy is adequate without the necessity of examining past practices of the Department. A new schedule for notary service was put into effect by the Department on May 21, 1981. . . . Counsel for the petitioners stated at the arguments that complaints about the lack of notary service had sharply decreased since the new schedule was adopted, and that it appeared to be adequate. The new schedule is so new, however, that it would not be proper for this Court to dismiss the issue without allowing some time to monitor the availability of notary service to determine if the new schedule is retained and if it will indeed be adequate to allow access by inmates to notary service as needed.

Similarly the Department has recently adopted a "System Six" as a method of evaluating youthful inmates that are transferred from the Tucker Unit to the Cummins Unit. Although little evidence was presented to the Court regarding how the process works, or how effective it is to accomplish the purpose, counsel for the petitioners indicated at the closing argument that it is adequate, if maintained at the present level. The Court will accept this evaluation and finds that the recently adopted process for the evaluation of youthful inmates transferred to the Cummins Unit complies with the requirements of the Constitution, the Consent Decree, and prior orders of the Court. Again, the operation of the system will be monitored until it has been actually in operation for a reasonable time before a final determination of compliance is made.

As to the matters just discussed, the Court concludes that if the respondents maintain conditions as they were at the time the hearing was concluded, or in some cases (as indicated above) complete planned improvements which were scheduled at the time the hearing ended, a final finding of compliance will be made. The Court will require that a final report be filed covering all outstanding issues sometime during the week of May 3, 1982, such report to reflect the factual developments concerning compliance and implementation that have occurred since the August 1981 hearings. The Court anticipates that the plaintiffs, with appropriate assistance as discussed below, will then have until June 14, 1982, to file any objections or exceptions to the report or to otherwise show cause why the respondents should not be found to be in compliance with the Constitution, the Consent Decree, this Opinion and Order, and all other prior orders of the Court, and why this proceeding should not be dismissed. If objections and exceptions are filed, the Court will give respondents until July 6, 1982, to respond. If a hearing is necessary, it will be scheduled for August 9, 1982.

There are two issues, the provision of mental health care and the use of inmate security, as to which the respondents made significant changes shortly before and during the hearing, which the Court finds will, if implemented, cure the defects in compliance, but as to which, nevertheless, the Court feels compelled to make a specific finding that the prior practices of the respondents were unconstitutional. The prior inmate mental health arrangements of the Department and the use of inmates in positions of power and control over other inmates, as reflected in the evidence, were unconstitutional, and continuation of those practices could not have been further tolerated. The respondents must understand that they may not revert to the old practices, regardless of lack of funds, or any other circumstance that might prompt a desire to do so. However, the new mental health facility and the new practices of the respondents bring them within compliance with the standards of the Constitution, the Consent Decree, and prior orders of the Court.

The Department of Correction has made drastic improvements during the history of the case in the mental health services available for inmates. The evidence indicates that personnel of the Department, who appear to have first been skeptical about the need for such services, now recognize the need and the assistance that can be provided by the mental health staff. When the case was originally filed, the Department had no mental health personnel. During the course of the most recent hearing, a separate facility with space for 44 inmates with the most severe needs became operational at the Diagnostic Unit as an interim facility to be used until the planned new permanent facility for mental health is completed. This progress shows the dedication of the Department to the long-term resolution of this serious problem. The Court was impressed with the testimony of Drs. Mobley and Powitzky concerning the needs for mental health programs and their efforts to meet those needs. These efforts are laudable and have brought the Department into a situation now where the Court can and does find, with the opening of the interim facility, that the respondents are in compliance.

The Court is equally convinced, however, that prior to the opening of the interim unit at the Diagnostic Center the situation of the Department in supplying mental health services was intolerable. As the evidence shows, the need is such an important one and the prior situation was so clearly inadequate that the Court is compelled to specifically state its conclusion that provision of a separate facility and treatment for the most severely mentally disturbed is constitutionally required. Persons who are severely sick simply cannot be held in custody unless they are provided with necessary medical services. Mental health treatment is clearly a necessary medical service in certain cases. Many inmates who have mental and emotional problems, and need temporary or "outpatient" type of treatment or counseling by psychiatrists or other mental health personnel, may, of course, remain in the general population; but there must be some manner of dealing with them while in the population. A facility such as had been provided in Barracks 16 may serve this purpose. However, in addition, there must be a permanent, separate facility so that those people who are most severely mentally disturbed may be removed, for their own protection and for the safety of others, from the correctional environment of the general population and provided with the treatment and services they need. Such a separate facility that is adequate for the present needs of the Department is now operational, and the respondents plan for a permanent facility to be built within the near future.

The Court also concludes that, if the institutions are staffed as planned, the respondents will be in compliance in providing for adequate security personnel to protect the lives of inmates. Nevertheless the Court feels it imperative to state specifically that the practice of using inmates as security personnel, with power over other inmates, is unconstitutional and may not be reverted to by the Department. The records of staffing introduced at trial demonstrate that the institutions, particularly the Cummins Unit, have been severely understaffed. The respondents have historically made up for the deficiency in free-world security personnel at the institutions by using trusted inmates in security positions. As the Court has discussed in prior opinions in this case, at one time the Cummins Unit was operated almost entirely by inmates with only a skeleton staff of free-world persons. The number of inmates in security positions has been reduced drastically over the years, as ordered by the Court. The transition from inmate to free-world control has been gradual, as it had to be. At the August 1981 hearing it was established that inmates were still being used as "turnkeys" and "floor walkers" [4] at the Cummins Unit. However, the respondents also introduced evidence at the hearing concerning a plan that has been adopted which calls for the Department to hire 128 new correctional officers over approximately a seven month period beginning in June 1981 and completed by February 1, 1982. Of the 128 new correctional officers, 116 are to be assigned to the Cummins Unit and eight to the Tucker Unit. With the addition of these free-world security personnel and the staffing plan that has been adopted, it will be possible for adequate security to be provided without the use of inmates as security personnel. Accordingly, the respondents represented a firm and fixed intention to phase out the use of inmates in positions of control entirely, including the positions of floor walkers and turnkeys as those jobs existed at the time of the hearing. Inmates will still be used as turnkeys on the riot gates, but only to mechanically open and close the gate under the direct supervision of a free-world guard. The turnkeys will exercise no inmate control discretion whatsoever. Under this plan, as represented to the Court during the hearing and arguments, the respondents will be in compliance on the issue of adequate inmate security staffing.

As stated on the record during the trial and the arguments, the respondents will not be allowed to return to the use of inmates in security positions at any of the institutions of the Arkansas Department of Correction. Inmates may not be placed in positions of authority over other inmates and may not be given power to exercise discretion in the control of other inmates in any way. The use of inmates in such control positions is unconstitutional. The respondents are to have phased out the use of all inmates in such positions on or before Monday, April 12, 1982. An injunction will be entered permanently prohibiting the respondents from placing inmates in positions of authority or discretion and control over other inmates after that date except in the most serious emergencies when absolutely no alternative for control is available and, even then, only for the minimum period necessary to bring the situation under the complete control of free-world authorities.

The respondents understand that the increases in staffing that are planned must be carried out. The number of free-world personnel working at the institutions has not been adequate to protect the safety of the inmates on a 24 hours basis as, indeed, respondents fully recognize. The Court is hesitant to require that a specific, rigid staffing pattern be maintained. Such matters are better left to the reasonable discretion of those whose job it is to manage the Department so that needed flexibility is available to adapt to changing circumstances. The Court is concerned, however, that minimum constitutional standards be met. The Court is satisfied that if the staffing plan is implemented as described during the hearing and the arguments those standards will be met. The Court is equally convinced that the past staffing of free-world personnel at the institutions has been inadequate. This deficiency in staffing has,

4. These terms are commonly used by the parties and were defined on the record at the hearing. Briefly, a "turnkey" is the person in charge of opening and closing the various barracks and corridor gates that control movement in the corridors and between the barracks. A "floor walker" is a person housed in a barracks who is responsible for maintaining peace and order within the barracks, reporting problems or infractions, and summoning help if necessary. There was much evidence of the abuses of the inmate control system and of its lack of effectiveness in protecting the safety of other inmates.

in turn, contributed to most of the problems of the system. The respondents have the responsibility to staff the institutions with free-world personnel in such numbers, of such professional quality, and in such manner as will adequately protect the safety of the persons incarcerated in those facilities. The new staffing plan will meet this responsibility if the correctional officers are hired, trained, motivated, and scheduled to work at the institutions as it was represented to the Court that they would be. No return to the *status quo ante* is constitutionally permissible.

There are several issues as to which the Court has concluded that the policies or practices of the respondents have not complied with the requirements of the Constitution, the Consent Decree or the prior orders of the Court, and as to which the respondents have not as yet adopted proposed changes that would comply. One such issue, involving the procedural requirements that must be followed before a person may be placed in administrative segregation and the conditions that may be imposed in administrative segregation, has been discussed in a separate order of this Court entered on December 15, 1981. Other matters as to which the respondents are not in compliance, specifically open barracks, overcrowding, affirmative action in the hiring of minorities, integration of the East Building and Barracks 14 and 16, and the use of racial slurs by officers in the presence of inmates, are discussed herein.

As previously noted by the Court, the problems of overcrowding and inadequate security are closely related in the context of this litigation. Although actual lack of space could be a constitutional deprivation resulting from overcrowded conditions in some circumstances, that is not the principal problem faced at this time by the Arkansas Department of Correction. The evidence indicated that, by the time of the hearing, the respondents had sufficiently reduced the number of inmates housed in the Cummins Unit so that overall population limitations had been met. As a result, in most parts of that institution the sheer number of inmates confined was not a major problem. The crowded conditions in certain barracks of the Cummins Unit, however, make it impossible for the inmates living therein to be adequately protected or supervised. For example, although a large number of inmates are housed in Barracks 19, the multiple use building, the barracks is arranged in such a way that adequate supervision is possible despite the large numbers, and security has not been a problem there. This is not true, however, in Barracks 5 through 12 at the Cummins Unit, the "100-man" or "open" barracks. In those eight barracks, the placement of double bunks along the walls and in the rear areas in the close proximity that is required makes it virtually impossible for a security guard to have an unobstructed view through the barracks from any angle. This inability to effectively monitor the barracks is made even worse by the practice of permitting [6] some inmates to drape blankets over the bunks to create some sense of privacy in the large and crowded room. The abilities of the guards to supervise the barracks is hampered also after lights have been turned out because the area of the barracks farthest from the hall (of which vision is greatly blocked by the bunks) is also the darkest area. The inadequate staffing of the Cummins Unit, as discussed ear-

6. Although the draping of blankets over the bunks in that way is against regulations, the respondents have not stopped the practice by the inmates, and therefore its effects must be considered as if the practice were officially permitted.

lier, has further complicated the problem. However, the increase in security personnel that is planned may not be enough to completely cure the problem.

The Court has attempted to interfere as little as possible with the daily administration of the Department of Correction throughout this litigation. It has been the practice of the Court to allow the respondents as much flexibility as possible in devising solutions to the various problems faced at the institutions, as long as minimum standards are established. It is the intention of the Court to maintain this practice for the resolution of this problem, if possible. With this objective in mind, the Court, by an order filed December 1, 1981, required the respondents to report to the Court in the following way:

"The respondents shall report . . . how they would implement an Order by the Court that the population in the eight barracks in question be reduced to 90 inmates within a period of four months and further reduced to 80 inmates within the following four months. The respondents should indicate how they would respond to such an order, what problems would be created by such an order, and how they would deal with the increased population problems that would result from that type of order. The respondents should also suggest alternatives which might make such an order unnecessary, such as internal patrols, or an adequate surveillance or communication system. The respondents should only suggest such alternatives that they consider feasible and which could be actually implemented within the institution by August, 1982."

The report of the respondents recounted briefly the history of the large open barracks and the reductions in population and improved conditions therein brought about by prior orders in this case. The respondents also provided statistical data concerning the number of inmates to be housed at Cummins, and the available bed space under existing arrangements in the barracks. In conclusion, the respondents stated that "[t]he bottom line of all of this is that the Department does not have available beds to absorb 80 or 160 inmates currently being housed in the open barracks at Cummins."

The respondents did not, however, state any specific new alternatives for solving the inmate safety problem without reducing the population in the open barracks. The respondents did point out the increases in security staff at the Cummins Unit that have occurred during and since the August 1981 hearing, and indicated their belief that the additional personnel should solve the safety problems in the open barracks cited by the Court. It was argued that the staffing patterns at the institution are now in place, as it was testified they would be during the hearing. "There is an officer present in the hall between each of the facing open barracks at all times. In addition to other officers periodically present in the barracks, there is a patrol officer whose only duty is to patrol the barracks." According to the testimony at the hearing and the description of the respondents, there are also other security personnel on duty in the institution performing certain tasks, such as the "shakedown detail," which should make the institution more secure throughout. The respondents also pointed out, as had been testified at the hearing, that the Department plans to place telephones in the hallways between each of the two facing open barracks for use by officers to obtain security assistance. Although the respondents were the ones, during the hearing, who originally suggested the use of cameras or sound equipment within the open barracks to allow limited numbers of security personnel to more effectively monitor each of the open barracks, they rejected such as an option in the Response because such fixed devices would be amenable to tampering or destruction by inmates. The respondents did suggest that the Department "has made a decision to purchase" a "Body Alert System" for use by security personnel throughout the Cummins Unit. As described by the respondents, in that "System" each officer would carry a small transmitter with which he could communicate with a person monitoring a receiver located at the telephone switchboard, a secure area. The respondents conceded, however, that this equipment is very expensive, the Department at this time does not have the funds to purchase the equipment, and it is not known when such funds might become available.

The position of the respondents was, basically, that improvements that have been made, or which are planned, in security at the Cummins Unit, as described at the August 1981 hearing, are sufficient to solve any security problems created by the overcrowding the Court found in the 100-man barracks, and therefore further measures should not be required. This position, however, reflects a misunderstanding of the Court's statements concerning the problem during the hearing and the intentions of the Court in the December 1, 1981 Order requiring a report from the respondents.

The Court has concluded that some additional measures are required to make the 100-man barracks reasonably safe. It is true that the problems of the number of security personnel on duty and the kind of equipment they have at their disposal, the use of inmate security personnel, the number of inmates housed at the institution, and many other factors are all related in determining the level of security and protection provided at the institution. Although the Court has ordered that the respondents will no longer be allowed to use inmates as security personnel with discretion over the actions of other inmates, it has attempted to provide the respondents with flexibility in how they will "juggle" the other factors to achieve the required result of a prison that is both secure and safe. The increases in security staff that the respondents have planned, and are implementing, were necessary and should be sufficient. However, the finding that the staffing patterns proposed for security personnel would be adequate did not mean that no other factors affecting security would have to be adjusted. Even with the increased personnel, the respondents are not able to adequately supervise the 100-man barracks as they are presently arranged. As discussed above, with bunk beds and blankets blocking the view, an officer in the hallway between the open barracks cannot monitor what is happening in all parts of the barracks. The situation is made worse at night when the lights are off. The fact of having so many persons in such close proximity only makes it more likely that incidents will occur, making adequate supervision that much more essential while it also makes it more difficult. Although having a security officer in the hall between the barracks is a great improvement over the situation as same existed before the hearing (with no free-world security even in the area for long periods of time), it is not sufficient. Additional measures, above those already planned by the respondents as testified at the August 1981 hearing, are required.

It should be noted also that the respondents' assertions that they cannot reduce the population in the barracks because they do not have enough additional beds elsewhere in the institution to accommodate the inmates that would be displaced are not a sufficient response to the problem. The Court is not unaware of the limited resources of the respondents; however, limited resources cannot be considered an excuse for not maintaining the institution according to at least minimum constitutional standards. If the State requires that certain persons be institutionalized, as it may, it has the corresponding obligation to meet their basic human needs, which includes some degree of protection, where necessary, from other persons that the State also requires to live in the institution. The goal of the Court in allowing flexibility to the respondents in how they meet these needs is to permit them to use the resources they have in the way they deem the most efficient and most desirable. But the obligation to meet those minimum standards in some way is unchanging.

The Court has concluded that resolution of this issue should remain open to allow the respondents another opportunity to devise a solution to the problems of security and safety in the open barracks. In the response filed on December 28, 1981, the respondents mentioned that as an experiment in Barracks 8 all double bunks had been removed. The respondents reported that the same number of inmates are housed in the barracks as were housed there before, but no details concerning the actual arrangement of the bunks was given. The results of the experiment were described as follows:

"[T]he elimination of double bunks has been well received by both inmates and officers. The technique has, quite frankly, been more helpful than was anticipated. A number of problems have decreased, most notably the hanging of sheets from the top bunk to hide activity of whatever nature from view. As problems decrease, so do tensions."

However, despite this promising report on a potential solution to the problem, the respondents did not provide the details to the Court of exactly what the "experiment" required, suggest it as an alternative for use in other barracks, or explain why the bunks in other barracks should not be similarly eliminated. In fact, it is not known to the Court if the "experiment" in Barracks 8 was temporary and the beds have again been stacked, or if the respondents considered it suitable to leave the beds at one level in that barracks. The potential of such a solution to the problem, however, restores the hesitancy of the Court to simply require that the population in the various barracks in question be reduced by a specific number. It is the desire of the Court to allow the respondents to develop a solution to the problem that is most acceptable to them, if that is possible.

Therefore, the Court will again direct that within 30 days of the date of this Order the respondents provide to the Court proposals that it would favor as methods of resolving the inmate safety problem in the open barracks at the Cummins Unit. The Court's Order of December 1, 1981, together with the discussion of that order herein, should serve as a guide to the respondents. This problem must be dealt with despite the additional security arrangements that have been placed in effect by respondents. The petitioners will then have an opportunity to respond to the report by the respondents. A hearing will be scheduled promptly thereafter, if necessary, to determine a final solution to the problem.

Another issue as to which a final solution cannot be ordered at this time is the provision for the full integration of the East Building and Barracks 14 and 16 at the Cummins Unit. As was discussed at the oral arguments following the August 1981 hearing, the level of racial integration of the institutions of the Department has been greatly increased since this litigation was commenced, and has been the subject of many prior discussions and orders by the Court. At present the Court finds that the institutions are satisfactorily integrated, except for the above named areas at the Cummins Unit.

The segregation in the East Building and Barracks 14 and 16 has been allowed by the respondents on the basis that such segregation was required to minimize the possibilities of violence at the institution. However, the allowance of segregation has been much broader than would, in the Court's opinion, be necessary to protect the safety of the inmates. Previous orders of the Court have recognized that there could be potential danger in individual situations in integrating two-person cells. The inmates at the Cummins Unit are convicted felons, and the possibility of violence cannot be dismissed lightly. It has been because of this possibility of violence that the Department of Correction has avoided integrating two-person cells in the maximum security units. . . .

[T]he respondents have not yet actually integrated the cells of the maximum security unit. The respondents did develop a questionnaire that is answered by all inmates upon entering the East Building. Respondents' exhibit 81–37. The integration questionnaire simply asks the inmate to indicate if he does or does not "have objections to being integrated in the East Building." Space is then provided to allow the inmate to indicate what his objections, if any, are. On the basis of responses on this questionnaire, the respondents have said that integration is not possible. However, the questionnaire seeks what amounts to a statement of preference. The focus is not on the real issue of when an inmate's safety might be involved. The form definitely creates the situation where, if the inmate says the right thing, he can avoid having a person of a different race in the cell with him. This does not meet the limited criteria set forth in the Court's earlier opinion, as quoted above.

The policy has been clearly stated and is still correct. Racial segregation cannot be allowed to continue. The attitude of the Department in general, and of the superior officers, seems to be consistent with that policy. However, the procedures employed have not accomplished that result in the East Building and Barracks 14 and 16. A better approach for identifying the few cases where safety is actually involved must be found. For those individuals as to which violence is a real threat, if celled with an individual of a different race, segregation for that reason is acceptable. The method devised for identifying such persons must be no broader than is necessary to accomplish that goal.

The respondents shall suggest to the Court within 30 days of this date proposals for accomplishing integration of the East Building and Barracks 14 and 16 of the Cummins Unit. A reasonable transition period to accomplish this integration shall be allowed. If the respondents contend that there are real hazards posed by integrating some individuals, the proposal should suggest as precise a method as possible for identifying those individuals. The petitioners will then be given an opportunity to respond to the proposal by the respondents, and a hearing will be scheduled promptly if necessary.

As to the final two matters of which the Court has found the respondents not to be in compliance, the use of racial slurs and the affirmative action program, the problem does not lie with the policy of the Department, but rather with the success of the Department in accomplishing the goals they have set. The Court does not doubt that the respondents have made efforts to attract black persons into upper level position and to stop the use of racial remarks by officers in speaking to and about inmates. However, the evidence was clear that the efforts have not been wholly successful in accomplishing those results.

The issue of the use of abusive language toward inmates has been the subject of several prior orders of the Court. See, e.g., Holt v. Hutto; Finney v. Hutto. The Consent Decree provides that no Department of Correction employee is to "verbally abuse, curse, or use racial slurs when addressing or talking with inmates." The Court is not now concerned with cursing in general by officers. The Court also is not concerned with language used by inmates. Although higher level officers should continue to discourage cursing, in efforts to promote the professionalism of the Department and the officers, it would not be realistic to hope to "sanitize" the language used in such an environment. However, the use of racial slurs toward inmates cannot be tolerated to any degree. The prior orders of the Court have been very explicit in this regard.

The problem has not been resolved, in the opinion of the Court, because the upper echelon personnel have not taken a sufficiently forceful position on the issue. It does not appear that the very high ranking officers actually use such language themselves. Also the written policies of the Department prohibit the use of racial slurs in addressing inmates, and this prohibition is most probably pointed out to newly hired officers during training. However, this warning accomplishes little when, as apparently has frequently been the case, the new officer goes to work and the low and mid-level officers then provide the example of the use of such language. Although there was some evidence that persons using racial epithets toward inmates have on occasion been reprimanded, there was also evidence from high level employees, including the Warden, that they knew such language was being used but passed it off as local custom. It is not a local custom, or a local problem; it is a national problem. The use of racial slurs in speaking to inmates is a direct violation of the orders of this Court, and such a violation of the law cannot be tolerated by supervisory personnel for any reason. The respondents must see that the use of racial slurs in addressing inmates is no longer allowed to continue at any level. It must be understood down the line of all supervisory personnel and correctional officers that not using such language in speaking to or about inmates is a condition of employment.

The implementation of the affirmative action program is a more complex issue with which to deal.[7] This is not an employment discrimination case

7. The plaintiffs attempted to raise as part of this issue possible discrimination by the respondents against blacks, both inmates and free-world personnel, in job assignment and benefits of employment. The particular questions raised concerned

where the court is interested in testing, and remedying if necessary, possible discrimination against blacks by the respondents in their hiring practices. The reason the affirmative action program is so important is not to benefit potential employees of the Department, although they are indirectly benefited. Rather, the importance is in obtaining a racial mix of the security personnel in order to alleviate feelings by black inmates, which are approximately half of the inmate population, that they are being discriminated against. The primary effort must be to hire qualified blacks and place them in positions of authority in all aspects of prison life.

The evidence demonstrated that the respondents have increased their efforts to recruit qualified black persons to work within the Department. Those efforts have been successful to the extent that blacks are well represented among the highest and the lowest ranking officers. In fact, it was shown that at the time of the hearing 53 percent of the correctional officers, the lowest level officers, were black. However, there have not been, and still are not, blacks in the middle management positions in significant numbers. This situation must be carefully monitored by respondents.

As discussed on the record during the oral arguments, the Court credits the testimony of Mr. Housewright that sincere efforts have been made to recruit blacks into middle positions, but such efforts have not been very successful. Several factors may be cited as contributing to that failure, the principal ones being an inability to pay competitive salaries and the rural location of the prisons. However, this failure cannot be used as an excuse for not continuing diligent efforts to recruit blacks who are already experienced in corrections work, and who could join the department at a middle or high level position. Recent improvements in the administration of the institutions and the working conditions for the officers, as discussed herein, should help to make the Department a more attractive place to work, and thereby aid in recruiting experienced personnel.

Furthermore, the respondents must intensify efforts to identify black correctional officers who are employed by the Department without prior correctional experience, but demonstrate potential that would qualify them for promotion within the Department. Efforts must be made to train such persons and promote them at a rate commensurate with their abilities, so that blacks will be better represented in the middle officer positions. The testimony was that the respondents have made efforts to train and promote from within, but have not achieved the success desired for various reasons. However, the Court finds it difficult to understand, with a pool of black persons for potential advancement as high as 50 percent of the relevant work force, why greater efforts at selection and training would not result in promotion and retention of a greater number of blacks.

the allegations that black officers rarely live on the "free line" and that "houseboys" for persons living on the free line are almost always black inmates. As noted on the record during the oral arguments following the August 1981 hearing, the Court does not perceive these as major issues in the case, and was not provided with sufficient evidence upon which to decide if the allegations of racial discrimination on these points are well taken. The Department was admonished only to avoid actual discrimination, of course, and also to avoid appearances of discrimination through stereotypes if possible.

A certain rigid percentage of black officers will not be established as a requirement for compliance. However, the respondents must know that blacks, as previously ordered, must be employed in reasonable numbers at *all* levels of free-world personnel.

It is the conclusion of the Court that a third party should not be appointed as a "monitor" to oversee the operations of the Arkansas Department of Correction as had been requested by the plaintiff class. The parties are well aware of the efforts by this Court to avoid court appointment of a monitor throughout the history of this litigation.[8] Such court involvement in the daily administration of the institutions should be undertaken only if absolutely necessary. The progress made by the respondents through their own efforts without a court-appointed monitor leads to the conclusion that no person need be now appointed to oversee the operation of the Department through the time of the final report by the respondents that is contemplated by the Court, as discussed herein.

The respondents will be required to file periodic reports on the progress being made in various areas in the next several months and a final report on all outstanding issues during the week of May 3, 1982, as discussed above. These reports shall be comprehensive, specific, and factual. Copies of the reports shall be served upon counsel for the plaintiff class at the time they are filed.

It is expected that counsel for the plaintiff class will require both financial assistance and additional personnel during the time period allowed for review of the respondents' final report. As discussed above, the attorney for the plaintiffs is to file any objections or exceptions he might have to the final report of the respondents on or before June 14, 1982. Some investigation and review of the facts presented by the respondents will be necessary in order to make such objections.

The parties shall jointly determine how the investigation and review by the plaintiffs contemplated by the schedule established by the Court shall be conducted. The primary financial obligation shall necessarily fall upon the respondents. After consultation with the respondents, counsel for the plaintiff class shall propose, on or before March 29, 1982, a plan for who shall conduct the investigation and review and what resources will be necessary. The respondents shall then notify the Court in writing on or before April 9, 1982, whether they agree with the proposal by the plaintiffs. If the respondents do not agree with the proposal by the plaintiffs, they shall state with specificity their objections thereto, and suggest to the Court an alternative proposal. The Court will thereafter enter an order resolving the issue, if necessary.

8. The parties agreed in the Consent Decree entered on October 5, 1978, that a person should be employed as Compliance Coordinator for the Arkansas Department of Correction, and Mr. Stephen LaPlante was so hired. The position of Compliance Coordinator was not created upon the order or suggestion of the Court, and the Court did not designate or appoint the person to serve in that position. Mr. LaPlante was selected jointly by the Commissioner of Correction, the Attorney General, and counsel for the plaintiffs, and his salary was paid by the respondents, as agreed upon in the Consent Decree. The powers and duties of the Compliance Coordinator were those agreed upon by the parties and set forth in the Consent Decree, and were not established by the Court.

The findings of the Court during the August 1981 hearing, as reflected on the record and discussed herein, demonstrate that the respondents have made great progress in improving conditions for inmates of the Arkansas Department of Correction. However, more progress must be made before this case can be dismissed. Vigilance by the respondents is required to assure, in areas in which the policies of the Department were found to be in compliance with the applicable standards, such as on the issue of excessive force, that those policies are actually practiced and followed by personnel at all levels. If a policy or regulation of the Department is constantly ignored, the effect is the same as if there were no such policy. Equal diligence will be required to put into effect various practices and policies, approved by the Court, in the way and according to the timetable that was presented to the Court. The findings of compliance are conditional upon the proper effectuation of the various programs. Therefore, the respondents must continue directly on the path they have charted to achieve success.

FINNEY v. MABRY

546 F.Supp. 628 (E.D.Ark.1982).

EISELE, J.

It now appears that after a long, and at times turbulent, history this case is ready for final disposition. The original complaint was filed in April 1969. The case has proceeded as a class action on behalf of all inmates of the Arkansas Department of Correction for the purpose of challenging the constitutionality of the conditions of confinement at the various units of the Department. Relatively early in the history of the case the Court determined that many conditions of confinement imposed by the respondents were unconstitutional. Efforts since that time have been directed toward improving the situation at the prison units to an acceptable level so that the case could be dismissed. Several hearings have been held to assess the progress being made. Numerous orders have been entered determining the rights of the parties and imposing specific requirements on the respondents in the operation of the Department of Correction. In addition, and most significantly, the parties voluntarily and as a result of their initiatives entered a Consent Decree in October 1978 in which the respondents agreed to meet certain minimum standards in the operation of the Department of Correction in accordance with a stipulated time schedule. Difficulties developed in meeting the schedule. Upon request of the plaintiff class, a hearing was held in August 1981 to determine the extent of compliance by the respondents with the Constitution, the Consent Decree and the prior orders of the Court. Following that hearing, and arguments by counsel, the Court made detailed findings concerning conditions at the prisons, and concluded that the performance of the respondents on a significant number of issues was sufficient to allow a finding of compliance; that in other areas the respondents would be found to be in compliance if certain procedures or facilities were implemented and provided as had been represented to the Court; and that on other issues the policies and practices of the respondents did not yet comply with the requirements of the Constitution, the Consent Decree, and the prior orders of the Court. A Memorandum Opinion was issued setting forth these findings and conclusions on February 16, 1982, and an Order was entered on March 2, 1982, imposing additional requirements on the respondents. Pursuant to that Order, periodic reports were submitted to the Court by the respondents describing their progress in implementing the various changes in facilities and procedures which had either been represented to the Court during the August 1981 hearing as projected or adopted, or had been required by the Court following the hearing. A final report on compliance was filed by the respondents on May 7, 1982.

It was, and is, the position of the respondents, as argued in the final report, that the requirements of the Constitution, the Consent Decree and all prior orders in this case have been complied with in all respects, and that the case should therefore be dismissed. The petitioners filed certain exceptions and objections to the final report, drawing into issue the conclusion stated therein that the Arkansas Department of Correction was in full compliance.

A short hearing was held on Monday, August 9, 1982, to hear evidence and arguments concerning the disputed issues in the case. At the end of that proceeding, the Court concluded, on the record, that the respondents were in compliance with the Consent Decree, the Constitution, and all prior orders of the Court. For the reasons stated on the record at that time, as explained and supplemented herein, it is with great satisfaction that the Court now concludes that jurisdiction over the Department of Correction must be finally relinquished and this case dismissed.

The dispute between the parties has been narrowed during the recent course of litigation to a few specific issues. As to many issues that were disputed up to the time of the final hearing, the petitioners have now agreed that the respondents are in compliance. For other issues, the dispute between the parties involves questions of law rather than questions of fact, and those matters are resolved by the Court herein. Each of the outstanding issues will be discussed independently.

As to certain matters, including the evaluation of transfers from the Tucker to the Cummins Unit; the provision of notary service for inmates; the maintenance of sanitation standards at the Cummins Unit, particularly the maximum security facility of that Unit; and the classification system, the Court determined at the conclusion of the hearing in August 1981 that the policies or practices of the respondents, either in effect at that time or planned to be put in effect in the very near future, would meet the requirements of the Constitution, the Consent Decree, and prior orders of the Court. As to these issues, the Court concluded that a final finding of compliance could not be entered at that time only because the particular policy or practice in question was very new, and in some instances not fully implemented so that the actual effects of the changed practice, or the ability of the respondents to carry it out as planned, could not be adequately measured. Therefore for these matters it was ordered that the practices of the respondents would be monitored for a period of time before a final decision concerning compliance would be made. The period for such monitoring ended with the submission of the final report by the respondents. As to each of these matters the petitioners have now agreed that the conduct of the respondents has remained satisfactory, and that a final finding of compliance may now be made. Therefore, no further inquiry is required, and the Court concludes that the respondents have conformed their practices in these areas to that represented to the Court during the August 1981 hearing, and are in compliance.

The Court also found in the February 1982 Memorandum Opinion that the respondents would be in compliance on the issues of an adequate grievance procedure for inmates and the provision of medical services for inmates if the programs that had been adopted shortly before and during the August 1981 hearing were implemented as planned. Again, the programs for the provision of these very important services were too new at that time to allow an evaluation of their effectiveness in actual practice. Therefore, it was required that the programs be monitored for a period of time, and also that the respondents submit reports to the Court and to the attorney for the plaintiff class at stated times describing progress made in implementing the new programs and evaluating their effectiveness. Such reports were made, and the petitioners have now agreed that the reports are accurate and that the programs as implemented meet the requirements of the Constitution, the Consent Decree, and prior orders of the Court. Indeed, the progress made in these two areas is exceptional. The medical services contract has met all expectations concerning its effectiveness and will very likely serve as a model for use in other institutional settings throughout the nation. For many years the Department of Correction had attempted to provide necessary medical services for inmates "in-house." However, the high cost of necessary basic medical supplies and equipment and difficulty in attracting qualified professionals to adequately staff the service made their efforts less than successful. The respondents have now contracted with a private company to provide essential medical services, and the results have proven that the decision to do so was well taken. The numbers of qualified trained medical personnel available and attending to the medical needs of the inmates have increased dramatically. Services are now being provided in a professional and efficient manner. Even the attorney for the petitioners praised the medical services program and its apparent success. Similarly, the grievance procedure has been administered professionally by the Department of Correction, and appears to have accomplished the desired result. The data collected by the respondents and provided to the Court in their periodic and final reports indicates that the grievance procedure continues to be well used by the inmates and that the planned time limitations for resolving grievances filed have been adhered to by ADC personnel. Based upon the reports submitted by the respondents, and the agreement thereto by the petitioners, the Court finds that the respondents are in compliance with the Constitution, the Consent Decree, and all prior orders of the Court on all matters concerning the provision of adequate medical services and a proper grievance procedure for the inmates of the Arkansas Department of Correction. . . .

The petitioners objected to the report of the respondents concerning evaluation of inmates on administrative segregation on several grounds. First, the petitioners argued that psychological reports should be prepared on all inmates in administrative segregation, rather than only on those inmates who voluntarily submit to the testing required to prepare those reports. The petitioners also objected to the stated attitude by the evaluation committee to give preference to knowledge concerning security risks perceived from the behavior of a particular inmate over information contained in a psychological report. The petitioners also made the allegation that the responses provided by the committee on the evaluation forms were "superficial," but offered no evidence in support of this allegation. The petitioners did not allege that the respondents were not conducting the evaluations in the time and manner that had been represented in the final report, or that the additional reporting requirement imposed by the Court had not been adopted or implemented as required. The Court has concluded that a finding of compliance may be made despite the objections of the petitioners. Actually, the accomplishments of the respondents in this regard are commendable. By increasing the frequency of the meetings of the review committee and demonstrating efforts to make the evaluation as thorough, meaningful and fair as possible, the respondents have actually gone beyond what was required by the last orders of the Court concerning this issue. To force inmates to submit to psychological evaluation would be counterproductive and wasteful of time and resources. Data obtained under such circumstances would be very questionable. Furthermore, making the final decision on housing an inmate based upon security considerations which are felt to override information contained in a psychological profile on the inmate is acceptable in the opinion of the Court. The evaluation committee is required to consider any information available concerning the psychological condition of the inmate or any such information reasonably obtainable which would be helpful in reaching a just decision. However, the committee members are not required to substitute the judgment of the mental health staff for their own judgment, and are free to come to a conclusion contrary to that stated in any psychological report. In a correctional institution security must be considered central to all other goals. Of course, to arbitrarily ignore psychological reports would defeat the requirement that such reports be prepared and be considered. However, the Court will not require that the reports be given any specific weight in the face of known behavior of the inmate. The ultimate decision must be left to the persons charged by the institution with the responsibility for such evaluations who must act in good faith, considering all appropriate criteria. The decision of the committee, and the basis for that decision, must be recorded by the committee in a meaningful way in accordance with standards previously established by the Court. There is no evidence before the Court that would indicate that the committee has not been operating in conformity with these requirements. Therefore, the Court has concluded that the respondents are in full compliance with the requirements of the Constitution, the Consent Decree, and all prior orders of the Court on the issue of evaluation and reevaluation of residents of the East Building of the Cummins Unit.

The procedure utilized by the Department of Correction for the discipline of inmates is another area where the dispute between the parties has narrowed to questions of law rather than fact. . . .

The respondents have proposed that the time limitation for the hearing of disciplinary charges be extended. The present policy requires that all disciplinaries be heard within 72 hours, excluding weekends and holidays. The proposed modification of the rule would allow that disciplinaries would not have to be dismissed unless not heard within five days in certain circumstances. . . . The idea of extending the "72 hour rule" was first suggested by the respondents during the oral arguments held in September 1981 following the August hearing. At that time the Court stated on the record that it was of the opinion that disciplinary charges should not have to be dismissed by the Department simply because they could not be timely heard due to the large number of such charges, despite diligent efforts to hear all disciplinaries within the allotted time, and therefore indicated that an extension was a reasonable proposal and would be considered. The attorney for the petitioners agreed at that time that an allowance for an extension to avoid this problem would be agreeable. However, the petitioners now argue that the rule change proposed would allow a blanket extension to five days in all cases, rather than in only those cases where it is necessary. The respondents argue that such a construction would be contrary to what is stated in the rule, and the Court agrees. The rule, as proposed, specifically states that the Disciplinary Committee is "expected" to hear all disciplinary charges within three days and that such is to be the "objective" of the Committee. The good faith of the Committee in operating according to the stated disciplinary policy must be assumed. To require a formal extension in each case would simply add greater paperwork. The proposed change in the rule is reasonable and adequately protects the interests of the inmates in having all charges heard promptly. Therefore, the proposed modification is approved by the Court and will not prevent a finding that the disciplinary procedures of the Department of Correction are in compliance with the Constitution, the Consent Decree, and all prior orders of the Court. . . .

As to three areas, the provision of mental health services, the use of inmates in security positions, and the staffing levels of free world personnel at the prison units, particularly the Cummins and Tucker Units, the Court found, following the 1981 hearings, that although the prior practices of the respondents had been inadequate, the respondents had presented to the Court newly adopted changes in those practices which, if implemented would be acceptable. For each issue the Court specifically ordered that the respondents were not to revert to the practice that had been in place prior to the August 1981 hearings, but no formal period for monitoring or reporting was actually imposed. The question now before the Court, therefore, as raised by the petitioners, is whether the respondents have complied with the orders of the Court to end the prior practices, and whether the new practices in each area have been implemented as planned and are adequate.

The respondents have been somewhat reluctant through the earlier course of this litigation to recognize the importance of providing mental health services for certain inmates. However, progress demonstrated both in the evidence presented at the August 1981 hearing and in the final report of the respondents filed May 7, 1982, shows that the respondents have now realized the necessity of providing such services and have fully accepted the responsibility for doing so. This capability is a key ingredient in a proper classification program and in establishing a system to protect both inmates and employees from inmates who are dangerous to themselves or others, or who themselves might be "victims" because of their mental condition, or who simply are mentally ill and in need of medical treatment.

. . . At the August 1981 hearing the respondents presented evidence indicating that a separate facility for the treatment of the most severely mentally ill inmates had been opened and was operational at the Diagnostic Unit as a temporary measure, and that a permanent facility for the custody and treatment of such inmates was planned. The Court specifically found that prior to the opening of this interim unit the level of mental health services provided by the Department was clearly inadequate, and ordered that from that point forward the respondents be required to "keep and maintain at all times a separate facility on a permanent basis for the housing and treatment of severely mentally disturbed inmates."

The final report of the respondents indicates that the requirements of the Court for the provision of mental health services have not only been met, but that plans are in progress to improve the program to an even greater degree by adding additional services and an intermediate care unit within one of the barracks at the Cummins Unit, and possibly by expanding the size of the planned permanent facility. . . . [N]o evidence concerning the mental health services provided by the Department was presented by the petitioners at the August 9, 1982, proceeding. The Court finds, therefore, that the program for the provision of mental health services, as described by the respondents in their final report to the Court, which is uncontested by the petitioners, is adequate . . . .

The use of inmates in security positions within the institution is another matter that has caused great problems throughout the long course of this litigation. . . . [A]t the time this action was commenced there were only a few free-world personnel employed by the Department of Correction, and almost all duties, including those of armed guards, were performed by inmate trusties. The practice of allowing some inmates to carry weapons was terminated some time ago. However, the evidence presented at the August 1981 hearing indicated that inmates were still employed in "turn-key" and "floor walker" positions in which they had power to exercise discretion over the movement and conditions of other inmates. The Court enjoined the continued employment of inmates in such positions except in serious emergency circumstances when no other alternative for control is available. The final report of the respondents indicated that the use of imates in such security positions had been phased out by the required date, and that inmates are no longer employed in positions allowing them to exercise the prohibited discretion. . . .

There is no question at this time but that the respondents are in compliance on the issue of increased staffing by free-world security personnel. The Court specifically found in the Memorandum Opinion filed February 17, 1982, that the prior staffing levels had been inadequate. Although no specific staffing pattern was imposed, the Court determined that if the plan to increase staffing was implemented as represented to the Court during the August 1981 hearing, the staffing level would be adequate. The final report of the respondents indicates that the staffing pattern was implemented as planned, and the petitioners have not contested this conclusion. Therefore, the Court concludes that the staffing of the prison units with free-world security personnel is adequate to meet the requirements of the Constitution, the Consent Decree, and all prior orders of the Court. This is a significant and major achievement because it directly and indirectly affects the ability of respondents to meet constitutional standards in many other areas.

It should be noted that the petitioners had requested that the Court enter an injunction requiring the respondents to maintain funding for the Department of Correction at not less than the present level so that continuation of the several newly implemented programs, particularly the staffing pattern, would be guaranteed. The Court denied this request on the record at the August 1982 hearing. The respondents are well aware of their responsibility to maintain conditions at the various units of the Department of Correction at an acceptable level. There is no question but that doing this will require continued employment of an adequate number of free-world personnel to maintain adequate security. In the same way there is no question but that maintaining compliance will require that the units not become overcrowded again, and therefore some solution for housing the anticipated increase in the inmate population must be devised. Providing such personnel and housing will certainly require that funding for the Department of Correction not only be maintained at present levels but probably increased as the inmate population increases. However, enjoining continued funding at any specific level would not be appropriate. Also, as a matter of comity, it is the opinion of the Court that such an order should be avoided as an unnecessary intrusion into the affairs of the State. The duty and responsibility of the State to adequately fund the prison system so that conditions remain in compliance will persist, regardless of the continued pendency of this action. The requested injunction is unnecessary and would be unwise. It will therefore be denied.

As to the remaining issues discussed in the Memorandum Opinion filed February 17, 1982, the Court concluded that the progress made by the respondents up to the time of the August 1981 hearing, or the changes planned by them up to that time, were not sufficient to bring the respondents into compliance with the requirements of the Constitution, the Consent Decree, and prior orders of the Court. These issues included the procedural requirements and conditions for administrative segregation, security in the open barracks of the Cummins Unit, integration of the East Building of the Cummins Unit, use of racial slurs in addressing or in the presence of inmates, and affirmative action in the hiring and promotion of personnel. Although the results accomplished since that time in some of these areas is not as great as might be hoped, the efforts of the respondents have been great, and for each area the results have at least been sufficient to allow a finding by the Court of compliance with the Constitution, the Consent Decree, and all prior orders of the Court.

The progress of the respondents in stopping the use of racial slurs in the presence of inmates, as documented in the final report submitted to the Court, is highly commendable. . . . [T]he use of such language has been a grave problem that detracted greatly from both the professionalism of the staff and the morale of the institution. Although the Department had long had a policy forbidding such language in addressing inmates, the evidence at the August 1981 hearing demonstrated that the policy had been to a considerable extent ignored. Racial epithets were used by both upper and lower echelon officers, and even those who did not use such language themselves often tolerated its use by others in their presence. The situation has now changed. The various memoranda and other documents attached to the respondents' final report on this issue show that the respondents have undertaken both to educate all officers that the use of such abusive language while at the institution will not be tolerated and could lead to termination of employment, and to periodically remind the officers of the importance of avoiding such language. The efforts of the respondents have apparently been greatly rewarded in that it appears that the use of racial slurs by employees in the presence of inmates has stopped rather abruptly. The respondents' Compliance Attorney reported that even the Inmate Council of the Cummins Unit agreed that the use of such language had been eliminated and was no longer a problem. A review of grievances filed since the institution of the grievance procedure also demonstrated that very few complained of the use of racial slurs. The petitioners stated in their Exceptions and Objections to the Final Report that they had no objections in this area and were satisfied with the report made to the Court by the respondents. The Court therefore accepts the final report of the respondents as true, and is very pleased with its contents. . . .

The procedural requirements that must be followed before placing an inmate in administrative segregation and the conditions that can be imposed on inmates in administrative segregation were matters for which the Court also found that the policy and practices of the Department of Correction were inadequate. A Memorandum Opinion dealing only with these issues was filed by the Court on December 15, 1981. That Memorandum Opinion contained specific directives concerning what would be required to bring the Department of Correction into compliance on these issues. The final report of the respondents indicates that all such requirements have been met. The petitioners have stated they have no objections to that report. Therefore, the Court concludes that the respondents are in compliance with the requirements of the Constitution, the Consent Decree, and all prior orders of the Court on procedures applicable to placing an inmate in administrative segregation and on the conditions of confinement in administrative segregation.

The results obtained in attempts by the respondents to integrate the East Building have not been as great as was hoped or expected, but the Court has determined that the remaining segregation is not the result of any objectionable policy or practice by the respondents. As was discussed at length in the Memorandum Opinion filed February 17, 1982, integration of the prison system has been a task to be accomplished during the integration of the East Building and Barracks 16 has remained a problem. The justification throughout the history of the case for the continued segregation of the inmates has been security. The areas of the institution that remain segregated are composed of two-man cells. The inmates housed in these areas are there either for punitive reasons, or because the administrators of the institution have perceived a security risk either for themselves or for others if they are housed in the general population. Therefore, threats of possible violence must be considered even more serious than if coming from an inmate in general population. However, the Court determined that the mechanism that had been employed by the respondents for screening to determine such possibilities of violence was much too broad. . . . The respondents did devise a new plan, which was presented to the Court and the attorney for the petitioner class at a conference concerning the matter on March 25, 1982. The efforts of the respondents according to the new plan have achieved limited results in that the portions of the institution in question remain mostly segregated. However, there have been many threats of violence or retaliation for attempted integration and some episodes of actual violence. Although the respondents have estimated that there would be only "limited to moderate violence of limited duration" if part of the cells were forcibly integrated, . . . the Court is hesitant to order such action due to the risks involved. The procedure now employed by the respondents, with diligent efforts by the personnel involved to promote integration to the extent possible without actually forcing it, should eventually cure the problem. Pressure among the inmates, either actual or perceived, to avoid integration must be alleviated to the extent possible. The fact that the desired results will take some time to accomplish should not prohibit a finding of compliance. . . . [T]he policy concerning integration has been established for some time and has been accepted by the Department. The procedure utilized to effectuate that policy is now more clearly directed at identifying those individual inmates who would indeed pose a bona fide threat to security or safety if required to cell with an inmate of another race. The policy and procedure of the Department to effectuate integration of the entire institution, and the attitude of the Department to achieve that goal as exhibited by the final report, are no longer objectionable. . . .

The affirmative action program for hiring and promoting women and minorities as free-world personnel, especially into mid-level management positions, is another area where the results accomplished have fallen somewhat short of expectations.[1] The efforts of the respondents have been greatly complicated by a hiring freeze in effect at the Department of Correction for part of the time since the last hearing in this case. The final report does indicate that some progress has been made. A special program, entitled the "Command Officers School" has just been started through which the Department plans to identify those lower level correctional officers, particularly blacks, who have demonstrated potential for advancement, and then to offer special training to those persons allowing them more rapid advancement. The Department has also created a new position in the Personnel Office with the responsibility to oversee compliance with the Department's Affirmative Action Plan. The respondents have stated in their pleadings their continued commitment to the Affirmative Action Program. It is the conclusion of the Court that the policy and attitude of the Department concerning the Affirmative Action Program, as reflected in the final report to the Court, are sufficient in the context of this case. A finding of full compliance on this issue is therefore warranted.

Another troublesome problem through[out] this litigation has been overcrowding of the various facilities operated by the Department of Correction. . . . [T]he problem of mere numbers of inmates has been resolved for some time. However, the greater security needs caused by crowded conditions have remained unsatisfied, particularly in the "open" or "100-man" barracks at the Cummins Unit. The recent increases in security staff at the unit have eased the situation somewhat, but have not been sufficient to solve

1. It must be noted here, as it has been in prior orders of the Court, that the concern of the Court in this case is not with the rights of potential minority and female employees of the Department, but rather with the rights of the inmate class to have an appropriate racial and sexual mix in the administrators of the system, especially those involved with security. This difference in focus greatly affects the standard for evaluating the affirmative action program of the Department. The Court has been informed that a suit to vindicate the rights of employees and potential employees of the Department of Correction pursuant to Title VII of the Civil Rights Act, 42 U.S.C. 2000e, et seq., has also been filed and is presently pending before the Honorable Oren Harris. Jones v. Hutto, No. PB–C–74–173.

the problem. The efforts of the Court have been to avoid imposing any specific solution which could cause a hardship for the Department, but rather to allow the respondents as much flexibility as possible to devise a solution, either by reducing the population in the barracks or by increasing security to an adequate level through other means. The position of the respondents has consistently been that forcing a reduction in the population of the barracks would only cause greater problems elsewhere in the system because of lack of adequate housing for the inmates that would be displaced by the population reduction. The alternative solution now devised by the respondents is adequate to bring the security in those open barracks to an acceptable level without requiring a population reduction. All of the beds in the barracks are now at floor level. No stacked double bunk beds remain. In addition, greater emphasis has been placed on prohibiting inmates from hanging or draping sheets, blankets or laundry from their beds. The combination of these factors has greatly increased the visibility through the barracks from points on the sides and front of the barracks, and has reduced tensions among inmates. Furthermore, lighting in the barracks has been increased, particularly in the commissary and picket areas which are farthest from the hallway. In the past these areas have been very dark, making it difficult for an officer outside the barracks to observe movement or activity in the barracks during sleeping hours. It was during this time period that many episodes of alleged violence among inmates were reported. The new lighting plan requires that the lights in the picket and commissary areas be left on during the night so that each large barracks is backlit, making continual visual supervision possible. A group of specially trained officers are also employed to "shake down" the various barracks on a random basis in order to curtail contraband. Finally, in addition to the officers that are always present in the hallways for visual surveillance of each barracks, a patrol officer enters the barracks on a random basis, inspecting each one at least once an hour at irregular times. This officer actually walks through the barracks checking activity among the inmates as well as locks, lights, latrines and the temperature. The Court has determined that these measures, if continued as represented to the Court, are sufficient to provide adequate safety and inmate security in the open barracks despite the numbers of inmates now housed there. Therefore, no order requiring a reduction of the population in those barracks will be entered. If the respondents continue the security measures as represented to the Court, they will be in compliance with the requirements of the Constitution, the Consent Decree, and all prior orders of the Court on the issue of inmate safety and overcrowding in the open barracks.

The petitioners have also raised other issues which were not discussed in the final report of the respondents. These are the use of excessive physical force against inmates, the housing of homosexual inmates and protective custody inmates in one barracks, and a lack of plans to adequately deal with projected increases in inmate population.

The parties agreed at the August 1981 hearing that the policy of the Department of Correction concerning the use of physical force in controlling inmates was acceptable and in compliance with the Constitution, the Consent Decree, and prior orders of the Court. The Department also has an established mechanism to investigate and resolve allegations by inmates of use of excessive force. The complaint of the petitioners at this time is that such allegations were not being investigated quickly enough and that the discipline meted out when excessive force was found was not strong enough to act as a deterrent against further such conduct by officers. The petitioners presented evidence concerning this allegation at the August 9, 1982, proceeding. The Court concluded on the record at that proceeding that the evidence produced would not justify a finding of non-compliance on this issue. It is undisputed that the policy of the Department prohibits the use of excessive force, and that that policy is enforced. No pattern or practice of excessive force was demonstrated. At most an isolated incident was proven.[2] Although any such abuse is not to be condoned, such isolated occurrences are not the proper subject for relief in this class action. It is probable, almost inevitable, that in the situation of any correctional institution occasional complaints of excessive force or abuse will arise. The individual inmates making such complaints retain their rights under 42 U.S.C. § 1983 as well as other possible remedies. There is no evidence before the Court which would indicate that the class of all inmates would be entitled to relief on the basis of a claim of excessive force. The policy and practice of the respondents are in compliance with the requirements of the Constitution, the Consent Decree, and prior orders of the Court, and therefore they may be dismissed on this issue despite the fact that individual allegations of excessive force still are made periodically, and are likely to be made in the future.

The housing plans for inmates is an administrative decision, and the plan for housing both homosexual and protective custody inmates in a single barracks does not violate the requirements of the Constitution or any prior order of the Court. Although the petitioners or the Court could disagree with the plan of grouping inmates in such a way, it is a matter of correctional policy within the discretion of the administrators of the institution. The petitioners have not demonstrated that the policy or plan has caused the violation of the rights of any inmate. Therefore, the allegation will not be held to require a finding of non-compliance.

Finally, speculation concerning projected increases in inmate population would not justify a finding by the Court that the respondents are not in compliance. The evidence presented in the August 1981 hearing shows both that the respondents agree with the petitioners that the populations of the Department of Correction are likely to increase greatly over the next few years and that plans are underway to meet the greater burdens placed on the Department by the increased population. To judge the plans as compared to the projected population increases at this time would be premature and based upon speculation. To enjoin a minimum level of funding for the Department would also be unwise for the reasons discussed earlier. As has been previously stated, the respondents are well aware of their obligation to maintain conditions at the various units of the Department of Correction at a constitutional and lawful level. This obligation will not end with the dismissal of this suit, but rather will continue for as long as the Department of Correction

2. As was stated on the record at the August 9, 1982 proceeding, no specific findings regarding the particular incident about which the petitioners submitted evidence will be made. The proof established would not support a finding of a pattern or practice of excessive force. Therefore, no basis for relief in this case has been shown even if all facts presented were considered as true, and specific findings concerning the incident are unnecessary.

is in operation. A similar suit could be filed tomorrow if the conditions are not so maintained or if there is a reversion to prior unacceptable policies and practices. Therefore, the projected population increases will not cause a finding of non-compliance at this time.

The conclusion of the Court is, therefore, that the respondents are in compliance with the requirements of the Constitution, the Consent Decree, and all prior orders of the Court on all issues concerning the conditions of confinement at the various units of the Arkansas Department of Correction. The Court has refused to enjoin affirmative future actions of the respondents, particularly minimum funding levels, as discussed herein. However, the Court notes that respondents have voluntarily agreed that reports on various issues will be made on a periodic basis which will then be available for inspection by the public. As pointed out above, the progress made in bringing many areas into compliance is a very recent achievement. Although the Court has concluded that the programs have been in effect for a long enough period that continued policing by the Court is not necessary, agreed internal monitoring by the Department for a period of time will help insure that the programs will be maintained at the present level and will underscore the importance of continued vigilance. The petitioners requested that reports be required on the issues of the time periods required for the hearing of disciplinary charges, the medical services contract, integration of the East Building of the Cummins Unit, inmate population increases, staffing levels and turnover, mental health services, and the classification system. . . . At the proceeding on August 9, 1982, the respondents agreed to undertake such a reporting obligation. In fact, the attorney for the respondents stressed the attitude of the respondents that no "backsliding" would be allowed on the results accomplished through the course of this litigation, and stated that plans had already been made for reports to be made, regardless of the requirements of the Court, and that such responsibility would be accepted enthusiastically. The reported intentions of the respondents were to make either monthly or quarterly reports to the Board of Corrections at their regular meetings. Such reports would then be a matter of public record and available for inspection by the press, the attorney for the inmate class, and any other members of the public. Such voluntary reports on a quarterly basis for the next year should be adequate to accomplish the purposes of the petitioners. Therefore, no mandatory injunction is required.

The services of the attorneys for the plaintiff class will no longer be needed. Messrs. Philip Kaplan, Jack Holt, Jr., and Phillip McMath were appointed by the Court to represent the class shortly after the case was filed in 1969. The amount of services required from Messrs. Holt and McMath have varied through the years of the litigation. The greatest load has been carried by Mr. Kaplan, who was the lead attorney and was active in the case the entire time. The role assumed by these gentlemen was both necessary and laudable, but also demanding and often publicly unpopular. The attorneys graciously accepted the appointment by the Court and worked diligently and professionally. It was their persistence, through the adversarial system, which helped to frame the issues and move the case forward to this final point. The Court hereby thanks them for their services to it and to the community, and finds that such services will no longer be needed and that they therefore may be released.

The Court cannot let pass without comment the significance of its finding that the respondents are operating the Arkansas prison system in compliance with the laws of this nation. This is obviously an important and significant achievement in the history of the Department of Correction and of the State of Arkansas. It attests to the vitality of our system of government that this prison system could be so transformed. That this result has been achieved, albeit through the process of litigation, without actual court intervention in the daily administration of the prison, is also significant. Although overseen by the Court, the changes were actually made by the duly constituted state officials who have come to recognize and accept their duty and responsibility to administer the system according to lawful and constitutional standards. *Their* duty, not the Court's.

The progress made cannot be overstated. In the early part of this century, the state prisoners were simply "sold" to the highest bidder as contract labor. Even after the State took on the operation of the prison system as a direct state function, it remained in concept a profit making venture. As late as the early 1960's there were but a handful of paid free-world people operating the entire prison system. Practically all of the jobs now filled by the approximately 1,000 free-world employees were then filled by inmates, including the jobs of keeping records and maintaining security in the institution. The conditions in effect at the time this case was filed caused Judge Henley to appropriately describe the institutional system as a "dark and evil world." [*Holt II*]. To bring the system to the point where it is today required disciplined planning, much physical and mental work, the expenditure of scarce financial and other resources on an unpopular cause, and the simple determination to do one's lawful duty. It is not possible to mention all of those who have played a role in achieving the result. But such a list would include a succession of governors and state legislators, past and present. It would include a succession of directors and staff members of the Department. It would include the attorneys on both sides and the Compliance Coordinator under the Consent Decree. Importantly, it would include the lowest echelons of the staff and their immediate superiors, who most constantly interface directly with the inmates and who have come to understand the importance of their work and to appreciate the dignity and professional status that comes from the fair and even-handed performance of their most difficult duties. Finally, and most importantly, that list must include the heavily burdened taxpayers of Arkansas.

The Court is genuinely pleased that the facts and circumstances mandate its relinquishment of further jurisdiction in this case.

It is therefore further Ordered that the attorneys appointed by the Court to represent the plaintiff class be, and they are hereby, relieved of all further obligations herein.

Finally, it is Ordered that this case be, and it is hereby, dismissed with prejudice.

---

1) Is the finale worthy of the play?

2) Does the relinquishment of jurisdiction reflect a radical improvement in defendant's behavior? a new prognosis for the future? a lessening of the

standards either of the law or of the presiding judge? a sense of exhaustion? Is Judge Eisele's action consistent with the action the Eighth Circuit took when Judge Henley tried to relinquish jurisdiction in *Holt III*? Would Judge Henley have relinquished jurisdiction in 1982? Does Judge Eisele's entry into the case signal a wholly new judicial posture, premised on "comity" and the desire to avoid "unnecessary intrusion into the affairs of the state"?

3) Judge Eisele discharges the lawyers representing plaintiffs and "dismisses the case with prejudice." What does that mean? See Rule 41(a)(2). Has he dissolved all the previous decrees? Suppose the defendants engage in some flagrant acts of racial discrimination. Would that violate the earlier decrees? Could Mr. Kaplan initiate contempt proceedings? Would he have to commence a new lawsuit? If so, what significance will be attributed to the record from the last decade of litigation?

4) The court says that the defendants' commitment to submit "voluntary reports" to the State Board for the next year is a way of ensuring against "backsliding." These reports are to be made public, but the court does not establish a way to evaluate these reports and to take appropriate action. Why did the judge dismiss the attorneys for the inmates?

Further Excerpts from Harris & Spiller Report

A. *THE EXTENT OF COMPLIANCE WITH ORDERS AND SUGGESTIONS*
[as of 1975]

Evaluating the extent of compliance with Holt v. Sarver was complicated by certain characteristics of the orders issued by the district court. As a rule, the orders were broad, general and often ambiguous. Specific compliance duties were not clearly identified. There was thus no objective standard with which the extent of compliance could be compared. The absence of substantive definition in the court orders was somewhat offset by numerous suggestions that appeared in the orders and the court's written opinions. The suggestions outlined goals the court expected the defendants to achieve and proposed methods to attain those goals, but they omitted mention of intricate details. Although they imposed no legally enforceable duties, it was clear that the court's suggestions were not to be taken lightly. There was an unmistakable inference that many suggestions were mandatory, whether enforceable or not. A representative opinion was expressed by Commissioner of Correction Terrell Don Hutto, who stated that all suggestions were regarded by the defendants as if they were orders. Judge Henley acknowledged that the suggestions were not "hard and fast orders," but he related that the defendants were expected to take positive action that was compatible with the suggestions. . . .

The Extent of Compliance

The field research for the study was primarily conducted from June through September, 1975, and compliance that subsequently occurred has been excluded from these findings. . . . [I]t was concluded on the basis of interview and documentary information that substantial compliance was achieved. Nevertheless, there was neither total compliance nor total noncompliance with duties imposed by the district court. There was compliance with some duties and noncompliance with others. There was at least partial compliance with most court-imposed duties.

a. Elimination of the Trusty Guard System

Guidelines issued by the district court in 1970 required elimination of trusty guards from the Arkansas prison system. There was general agreement during the field research that trusty guards had been completely eliminated. . . .

Despite the fact that armed trusties were eliminated, inmates were officially involved in the safety of other inmates. Unarmed inmates called "floorwalkers" were stationed inside the barracks and shared responsibility with civilian personnel for preventing violence and detecting and removing contraband (including weapons) from the dormitories. Commissioner Hutto contended that floorwalkers had no authority over other inmates. They could neither issue orders nor write disciplinary reports. He rationalized the existence of the floorwalker system by stating that floorwalkers were more effective than civilians in breaking up violent episodes and removing contraband from the barracks. According to the commissioner, inmate fights were less intense when inmate floorwalkers intervened and inmates were more cooperative with floorwalkers than with civilians in the removal of contraband. An attorney for the plaintiffs complained that the floorwalker system was a dangerous throwback to the old trusty guard system, but the district court believed otherwise. The court saw a substantial difference between the trusty guard system and the use of inmate floorwalkers. In Finney v. Hutto the court found that unlike trusty guards, floorwalkers were unarmed and had no sanctioned authority over inmates. Although it doubted that floorwalkers offered much protection, they presented no threat to inmate security.

b. Inmate Safety

There was a definite consensus among the principals that inmate safety had substantially improved since *Holt I* was filed. In its opinion of March 19, 1976, the district court expressed the doubt that any prison was "safe," but found that the Arkansas Department of Correction met the constitutional standard of "ordinary" care for the majority of inmates. From that standpoint, it could be stated that compliance was achieved with the court's expectations regarding inmate safety.

Improved inmate safety was attributed principally to two factors. The first was an increased number of free world personnel. The second factor was an increase in the number and an improvement in the quality of the searches—called "shakedowns"—of inmates and their living quarters. Commissioner Hutto reported that inmates were subjected to a "pat-down" search and scanned by metal detectors whenever they returned to living areas from their job assignments. "Strip-searches" were required of inmates returning from contact visits and those entering the maximum security confinement areas.

Other explanations were advanced for the improvement in inmate safety. An assistant attorney general stated that the 1969 legislative enactment of a "good-time" law, by which an inmate's release date depended upon institutional conduct, provided an incentive for inmates to refrain from violence. A mid-level prison manager attributed improved safety to the elimination of trusty guards. Another mid-level prison manager reported that several elements combined to cause a decrease in violence. One was the replacement of metallic inmate currency (which could be clustered inside a sock and used as a club-like weapon) with paper currency. Another factor was the construction of a new maximum security building which made it possible to further restrict the freedom of violent inmates and isolate them from the general population. A final factor that was mentioned was the use of inmate floorwalkers to maintain peace in the barracks.

That the district court found provisions for inmate safety constitutionally adequate carried no implication that the prisons were safe. The court documented the danger that still existed in the prisons by reporting that during August, 1975, two inmates were killed by other inmates. An attorney for the plaintiffs expressed the opinion that provisions for inmate safety were inadequate. According to him, severe overcrowding, administrative use of inmate informants and floorwalkers, and the presence of psychotic prisoners in the general population, jeopardized the safety of all inmates.

c. Brutality and Reprisals

Throughout the Holt v. Sarver litigation, the district court expressed concern over brutal treatment of inmates and reprisals against inmates for having sought judicial relief for their prison grievances or for having testified in judicial proceedings. In the opinion of March 19, 1976, the court found that neither brutality nor reprisals were officially allowed by the Department of Correction. According to the court, both were ". . . strictly forbidden by the prison rules . . . ." Nevertheless, it could not be stated that brutality and reprisals were eliminated from the Arkansas prison system. There was a general expression of resignation that episodes of both continued to occur despite official disapproval. The district court attributed instances of brutality to a lack of professionalism among employees.

It was clear that there were instances in which prison personnel used force against inmates. Corrections personnel typically characterized those instances as either justified or provoked by inmates. Prison brutality was described as both physical brutality and "mental harassment." It was reported by some inmates and certain employees that physical brutality took the form of beatings, making inmates run to and from work, fostering competition between inmates at work, and employees riding horses over inmates. Mental harassment was described by several individuals, who claimed that it took various different forms. According to them, civilian guards treated inmates as either "something less than human," or like children. They contended that inmates were "yelled at" and "browbeaten." One correctional officer reported that mental harassment took the form of favoritism and the arbitrary administration of prison disciplinary sanctions.

Although a few individuals reported that there was no longer any retaliation against inmates for petitioning the courts or for testifying against the prison administration, Commissioner Hutto stated that there was "very little retaliation" and several other individuals reported that inmates were still victims of administrative retaliation because of their litigation-related activities. These individuals explained that retaliation was subtle. It frequently assumed the form of inmate demotions in status, institutional disciplinary action based upon counterfeit charges, loss of job status, and harassment by free world guards.

d. Overcrowding in the Prison System

Attorneys for the plaintiffs characterized overcrowding as the "most pernicious problem" facing the prisons. In both *Holt I* and *II* the district court found Tucker and Cummins overcrowded. According to the court, in 1970 the population of Cummins prison was less than 1000, by 1973 it had increased to 1200, and during the district court hearings in the summer of 1975, the population was 1518. Commissioner Hutto reported in September, 1975, that the total population of the Arkansas prisons was 2300—an increase of 1600 inmates in approximately 18 months.

The Cummins barracks were seriously overcrowded. Inmates were housed in facilities that were not intended to serve as living quarters—such as the gymnasium and the infirmary—and the maximum security areas were especially overcrowded. The court found that, in the maximum security areas, single-person cells, equipped with a single washbasin and toilet, frequently held three or four inmates and that ". . . when one of the cells [was] used to house more than two people, one or more of them [had] to sleep on the floor."

e. Racial Segregation and Discrimination

Racial segregation and discrimination in the Arkansas prison system subdivided into two interrelated facets: that affecting inmates and that affecting employees. In the opinion of March 19, 1976, the district court found that although discriminaton was specifically prohibited by departmental regulations and there was no evidence of overt racial discrimination, ". . . in instances racial discrimination that [was] covert and perhaps even unconscious [was] still going on . . . ." The court acknowledged that the situation had "improved somewhat," but found it essentially the same as the court of appeals had described in Finney v. Arkansas Board of Correction: . . .

It was admitted without reservation that the maximum security and punitive segregation units at Cummins were racially segregated.

The district court found that race relations had "improved somewhat" but were still poor. It attributed poor race relations in part to the fact that few black employees held positions ". . . of authority that [were] meaningful to inmates in their day to day prison life . . . ." Among the department's efforts to improve race relations was an affirmative action personnel policy that was initiated in March, 1974. The thrust of the plan was to hire and promote employees regardless of race, thereby increasing the number of black employees and promoting larger numbers of those already employed. The court found that from March through August, 1974, 32.32% of the employee promotions went to blacks. The number of black employees in the department increased by 2.4% between August 30, 1973 and June 30, 1974 and it increased by 5.1% between March, 1974 and May, 1975. The district court found the affirmative action plan commendable but stated that it did not reach the problem involved. According to the court, the question ". . . [was] not whether the Department [was] discriminating against blacks in matters of hiring, promotions, or discharges, but whether the recruitment and promotional policies of the Department [were] designed to correct or alleviate the racial imbalance of the Department's staff . . . ." The court announced its dissatisfaction with departmental efforts to correct racial imbalance by hiring more black employees. Similarly, it termed inadequate departmental efforts to involve black employees in classification and discipline, and to assign blacks to positions that involved counselling and supervising inmates. . . .

B. *FACTORS THAT AFFECTED COMPLIANCE WITH THE COURT ORDERS*

Several broad factors apparently played important roles in determining the level of compliance and the speed with which compliance was achieved. Those factors were: the social and political climate, attitudes of the court and certain defendants, particular features of the court orders, considerations regarding management of the prisons, and monitoring mechanisms used in the case. Holt v. Sarver was notable for the complete absence of formal enforcement mechanisms. Considerations regarding the management of the prison system and attitudes of the court and certain defendants appeared to be especially important because to a large degree they influenced the role played by the other factors in the compliance process. There was, however, such overlapping and interaction among the various compliance factors that none of them could be separately analyzed without reference to each of the others.

1. *The Social and Political Climate*

An important factor that affected compliance from the outset of the Holt v. Sarver litigation was the social and political climate that existed during the compliance phase of the litigation. Loosely defined, the social and political climate was the prevailing mood or temper of the populace toward various social and political issues. The climate was important because it influenced values, perceptions and judgments of key figures and consequently affected their compliance efforts. Holt v. Sarver was born into a climate ripening for political and social change. The case was a product of the times, but it also asserted a powerful influence over the climate into which it was born.

Viewed expansively, the political and social climate in the state of Arkansas during the mid-1960's through the mid-1970's was jointly shaped by the awakening national recognition of human and civil rights and by events that occurred and conditions that existed within the state. Holt v. Sarver was undeniably a part of the incipient movement for reform of social institutions that was sweeping the country during the 1960's. The case was both a contributor to and a product of the civil rights movement. Circumstances within the state, however, played a more direct role in shaping the climate. Public disclosure of abhorrent conditions within the prison system contributed immeasurably to the socio-political climate. Nevertheless, the role that the civil rights movement played should not be overlooked because, along with the reaction of public figures, it helped determine that the ultimate public response to the disclosures would favor prison reform.

The Arkansas prisons were reportedly closed to public and court scrutiny before 1965 and the public was unaware until then of existing prison conditions and practices. Several individuals stated that the prison system had theretofore enjoyed general public approval. The public was believed reluctant to allow expenditures for normal prison operations, let alone prison improvement. Public opinion against prison reform was apparently perceived rather clearly by the Arkansas legislature, which was described as adamantly opposed to appropriating money for prison operations during the period preceding Holt v. Sarver.

Public opinion and the legislative attitude toward corrections were significantly affected by a chain of events that began unfolding in 1965. Those events were the disclosures contained in the State Police Report on conditions in Tucker prison, disclosures in the early federal litigation about conditions in the prisons, publication of the Study Commission Report with its disclosures of prison deficiencies and recommendations for improvement, and disclosures in the Holt v. Sarver litigation.

A number of individuals expressed the opinion that extensive news media coverage of the background events that preceded and led to the filing of the Holt v. Sarver case, and the facts that were revealed during the course of the litigation concerning conditions within the prison, contributed heavily to the creation of a political climate that was conducive to prison reform. The news media provided extensive coverage of the prison conditions. They reported court proceedings, the contents of reports issued by the Arkansas State Police and the Study Commission, made independent investigations into conditions in the prisons, and frequently commented editorially about the necessity for prison improvement. One investigation, inspired by the news media and assisted by Cummins superintendent Thomas Murton, resulted in the discovery of human skeletal remains buried on the Cummins prison grounds.

Principals to the litigation characterized news media coverage as generally fair, accurate, and in favor of prison reform. It was widely acknowledged that news coverage made the public aware that the Arkansas prison system suffered from serious deficiencies. Public reaction to the disclosures about prison conditions was described as "embarrassed," "horrified," "angry," and "resentful." According to a state senator, primarily as a result of extensive publicity, public opinion shifted from acceptance to a belief that the prison system was "philosophically wrong" and needed to be changed. Judge Henley explained that news coverage helped to fix public attitudes in favor of prison improvement. Attorneys for the plaintiffs expressed the belief that the news coverage caused the public to conclude that Arkansas had the most archaic, evil prison system in the country and influenced the public to favor prison reform.

Those interviewed generally agreed that news media coverage had a positive effect upon compliance. Commissioner Hutto said that although the legislature may have resented the widespread publicity generated by the litigation, news coverage was a factor that influenced the legislature to adopt a progressive attitude toward corrections. Commissioner Sarver, however, expressed the belief that news coverage had no effect upon compliance and two prison administrators said that news coverage had a negative effect upon compliance. News coverage helped shape the political climate in favor of prison reform. Yet, although several individuals acknowledged the importance of the news media, there apparently was no concerted effort to influence news coverage as a strategy for gaining compliance.

Despite the generally favorable depiction of news media coverage, there were several complaints. Commissioner Hutto complained that the national press presented a sensationalized and distorted picture of the prison system. Two mid-level prison administrators stated that the news media was biased against the department of correction and inaccurate in its reporting. Each of the principals contended that news media reports of the discovery of skeletal remains at Cummins was both inflammatory and distorted. According to them, the investigation had unearthed an old, unmarked graveyard and, contrary to media insinuation, was not evidence that inmates had been secretly murdered and buried at the prison.

Several individuals were instrumental in creating a climate that was conducive to change in the prison system. Because of positions they adopted, actions they took, and statements they made in reference to the prisons, public opinion became receptive to prison reform. Those persons were identified as Winthrop Rockefeller, governor of the state of Arkansas from 1966 to 1970; Daniel Stephens and Thomas Murton, both of whom served as superintendents of Cummins prison during the 1960's; and Robert Sarver, the first Commissioner of Correction for Arkansas.

According to several individuals, Governor Rockefeller was extremely concerned about improving the prison system. He caused the State Police Report to be published and, after publication, he made prison reform a top priority of his administration. Superintendent Stephens was referred to by some as the person most responsible for prison reform in Arkansas, because he was the first prison official to allow prisoners to send their complaints to the courts. Superintendent Murton was described as a crusading prison reformer who, although a poor administrator, had little regard for political considerations and shaped public opinion by publicly decrying abuses in the prison system. Commissioner Sarver's contribution to the shaping of the climate for reform was found in the assistance he provided inmates in filing the initial complaint in Holt v. Sarver, the fact that he neither denied the allegations contained in the complaints nor defended the conditions and practices in the prison system, and his recognition of the humanity of inmates and espousal of progressive principles to guide the reform of the system.

Although there was widespread agreement that the political and social climate was ripened for change, it was impossible to determine with precision the effect that ripening had upon the extent of compliance. The principal effect probably lay with the legislative response.

The Arkansas legislature reportedly felt the brunt of pressure from events surrounding the prison. Although there were no extravagant claims that public opinion aroused a fervor for prison reform, the lengthening chain of events was thought to have influenced the legislature to accept the notion that reform would inevitably come to the prison system and that the legislature would eventually have to appropriate money to operate the prison system. Describing the effect of the changed public opinion upon the Arkansas legislature, an assistant attorney general commented that none of the legislators wanted the public to perceive them as "condoning barbarism" in the prisons. An attorney for the plaintiffs reported his observation that public pressure generated by news media coverage made it easier for legislators to appropriate money and pass legislation that was necessary to remedy prison conditions. The public did not, however, clamor for prison reform—it tolerated reform.

2. *Attitudes of Key Participants in the Litigation*

The district court, administrators of the department of correction, and the Arkansas legislature were the key participants in the litigation during the compliance phase of Holt v. Sarver. Although the plaintiffs were important throughout the litigation, their role was peripheral during the compliance phase. They affected compliance primarily through actions of the district court. Because of the important role played by the court, corrections administrators, and the legislature, their attitudes regarding the prison system and the litigation were critical to the extent of compliance.

Attitudes of the key participants, along with situational realities in the litigation, largely determined the style and content of the orders that were issued, the nature of the monitoring and enforcement mechanisms that were employed, and, ultimately, the effect of the other compliance factors. As used herein, "attitudes" refers to the postures that the key figures assumed during the course of the litigation. Those postures were assumed in response to developments within the framework of the litigation and in response to occurrences outside the sphere of the litigation. They reflected the values, perceptions, and expectations of the protagonists.

The district court envisioned only a limited judicial role in state correctional reform; consequently, it attempted to minimize judicial intrusion into the management of the prison system. The court nevertheless demanded compliance with the requirements contained in its orders. Correctional administrators favored reform of the prison system from the outset of the litigation. They acknowledged respect for the role the court played in correctional reform and fear of the court's power to impose sanctions. During later stages of the litigation, they expressed misgivings over the court's continued presence in the operations of the prison system. The legislature resented the court's intrusion into the internal affairs of the department of correction and initially opposed state expenditures for the prison system. Eventually, legislators realized that the state would have to provide adequate financial support for the prison system. But, like prison administrators, the legislature resented the district court's retention of jurisdiction over Holt v. Sarver.

a. Attitudes of the District Court

The district court's attitude concerning its role in correctional reform and the court's expectations concerning compliance were both affected and reflected by the court's approach to compliance in Holt v. Sarver. The approach that the court adopted was clearly a factor that affected the level of compliance achieved. It was perhaps the most important factor.

Judge Henley's perception of the appropriate role of the federal court in remedying problems in state correctional facilities sharply changed following the opinion of the court of appeals in Jackson v. Bishop. The judge explained that Jackson v. Bishop signalled the end of the "hands-off" doctrine and caused him to reassess the role of the court. He decided after reassessment that the court could assume a more active role in the solution of prison problems. Despite that conclusion, he recognized constraints upon the court's power to intervene in the operations of the state prison system. The court's approach to the compliance phase of *Holt* reflected the judge's consideration for the attitudes of the Arkansas populace and state officials.

According to Judge Henley, a receptive attitude by the public and public administrators toward judicial decrees was critical to compliance. He expressed reservations about a federal court's ability to change state social institutions. According to him, the court's most important contribution in such cases was to bring the problems to the attention of the public and let public administrators do their jobs. The court could view complaints after the fact, adjudicate the rights involved and dictate policy limited to constitutionally required minimal standards, but it could not administer a state prison. It was better for the court to lead and direct compliance than to attempt to force unwilling administrators to comply. In the final analysis, the state had to reform its own institutions.

The judge related his belief that in cases involving social change the court's ideal role should be to advise public administrators and direct their attention to certain areas that needed improvement, rather than issuing direct, specific orders. He advocated flexibility rather than rigidity in the judicial approach to social problems and stated that while the courts should not be slow to declare the public interest, lack of haste in effecting remedies was often a sound judicial approach. Nevertheless, he acknowledged that the nature of individual cases might dictate different approaches. In his opinion, lawsuits that involved extremely bad conditions demanded swift remedial action. Similarly, if prison administrators resisted court-ordered changes, the court would be forced to issue highly specific orders.

The judge's attitude toward court intervention in state correctional problems and his perception of limitations upon the power of the federal courts affected his handling of the litigation in several ways. His orders did not stray far from the content of the pleadings before the court; the orders allowed great administrative flexibility; and the orders treated correctional problems in the sequence in which they arose during the lawsuit.

The problems considered most serious—usually the ones that prisoners complained about first—were given first priority. Rather than issuing a single extensive order at the outset that covered all phases of prison operations, the court issued a series of orders over an extended period that eventually affected all aspects of prison life. Judge Henley described this approach as beneficial to compliance because it dispelled resentment that the prison administrators might have felt had they initially faced orders that were overly broad in scope. He speculated that, if the initial decree had been too broad, the administration might have despaired of ever achieving compliance.

Orders that were issued in the litigation conformed to the court's attitude in other ways as well. They generally lacked specificity and depended upon the defendants to supply implementation details through reports and plans that they prepared for the court. Such an approach represented a judicial effort to minimize antagonism. The judge explained that, if the defendants took an active part in formulating compliance plans, the plans they formulated would correspond with their ability to comply. Therefore, rather than directly ordering changes, he frequently suggested changes through the use of dicta contained in the court's orders and opinions and through informal conferences. Although the court frequently promulgated its relief through recommendations and suggestions rather than orders, it was clear that, if no action had been taken in furtherance of the suggestions and recommendations, the defendants would have been "in trouble."

The content of the various orders reflected the judge's judicial philosophy just as did their format. He described his approach to the content of orders as a "practical, common sense" approach. He did not accept the notion that the solution to correctional problems required expertise and, indeed, he doubted that anyone in the country qualified as a correctional expert in the early stages of the *Holt* litigation. He recognized, however, that the solution of particular prison problems occasionally required expertise, and he acquired that expertise primarily through the in-court testimony of expert witnesses on particular points. Skepticism about the necessity for correctional expertise and a firm desire to minimize defendant resentment toward the court's role in prison reform were the primary reasons that the court refrained from appointing outside experts to either formulate relief or monitor compliance in Holt v. Sarver.

The district court's theory of achieving compliance by persuasion rather than force was clearly illustrated in the manner by which the court approached the Arkansas legislature. Several individuals described Judge Henley as an "astute politician" who was aware both of the indispensability to compliance of increased legislative appropriations and of the legislature's early opposition to appropriating funds for the prison system. An attorney for the plaintiffs stated that during litigation of the initial phase of Holt v. Sarver, Judge Henley commented that he expected the legislature to appropriate the funds necessary to operate a constitutional prison system. Although the assertion was unconfirmed, the plaintiffs' attorneys and Commissioner Sarver related their belief that the judge deliberately held court proceedings during times when the legislature was in session. They described the timing of the hearings as a method of awakening legislators to the reality that prison conditions were deplorable and as a method of impressing them with the necessity for adequately funding the system.

Perhaps most critical to compliance was the district court's expectation that the defendants would comply with all of the court orders. Judge Henley acknowledged that, at the time the Holt v. Sarver litigation began, he did not know what to expect about the extent and speed of compliance that could be achieved. Accordingly, his compliance goals at the outset were rather modest. He anticipated achieving the elimination of trusty guards from the system and vastly improving environmental conditions existing in the system, but he admitted having the expectation that it would take a substantial amount of time to achieve those broad goals. At the time of the field research, the judge stated that, although the defendants had done a remarkably good job in complying, he was not satisfied with the level of compliance. He explained that, in a case involving the unconstitutionality of conditions in a prison facility, a court could never be satisfied with the level of compliance. He expressed satisfaction with the speed with which capital improvements had been made, but he was surprised and displeased with the time it had taken to employ additional numbers of qualified prison personnel.

Despite the district court's preference for persuasive rather than forceful methods of achieving compliance, it repeatedly made clear to the defendants that it demanded compliance with all court orders. The court's determination to achieve compliance was communicated on more than one occasion. In *Holt II*, the district court recognized that certain aspects of compliance might be beyond the authority or ability of the defendants to perform. Nevertheless, the court assured the defendants that they would be expected to comply with constitutional requirements for operating the prison system, regardless of the actions of other political entities. The court simultaneously issued to political entities not parties to the litigation an implied threat that, unless they assisted the defendants in achieving compliance, the prison system would be closed. The court wrote:

"Let there be no mistake in the matter; the obligation of the respondents to eliminate existing unconstitutionalities does not depend upon what the Legislature may do, or upon what the Governor may do, or, indeed, upon what Respondents may actually be able to accomplish. If Arkansas is going to operate a Penitentiary System, it is going to have to be a system that is countenanced by the Constitution of the United States."

Judge Henley threatened the imposition of sanctions (in the form of dismissing correctional employees, imposition of contempt penalties and closure of prison facilities) for failure to comply with court orders. In Holt v. Sarver, he threatened to find the defendants in contempt of court if they took reprisals against inmates for testifying, and, in the same opinion, reminded the defendants of various other sanctions that were at the court's disposal if the defendants failed to comply:

"The Court does not now foresee that circumstances will arise which would require the Court to impose the ultimate sanction available to it, that of closing one or both of the prisons or enjoining the further reception of inmates at one or both institutions. Less rigorous, but effective, sanctions are available. The Court can direct the discharge of offending employees; the Court can punish for contempt, and it can award attorney's fees and expenses of litigation. So far, the Court has avoided the imposition of sanctions and hopes that it will not have to impose any in the future; but the sanctions are at hand, if needed."

The district court's chosen methods for remedying the problems of the Arkansas prison system and avoiding unnecessary antagonism toward the court were apparently successful. The defendants openly admitted sensitivity to the possibility that the court would apply sanctions if they did not comply with its orders. They took the court's threat of sanctions seriously. While making the defendants aware of the need for compliance, the actions of the court simultaneously defused hostility toward its role in the affairs of the prison. Public resentment of the court's intrusion into prison affairs did not materialize, none of the individuals who were interviewed objected to the manner in which the district court dealt with the problems of the prison system, and prison officials expressed great respect for the court's handling of the case—which was characterized "reasonable," "fair," and "practical." Several of the prison administrators claimed admiration for the expertise that the judge acquired during the course of the litigation. Commissioner Sarver commented that, when the *Holt* litigation began, the judge's knowledge of prisons and prison life was "unsophisticated." The growth of his knowledge about corrections was illustrated by the comments of Commissioner Hutto and his staff that the judge understood correctional problems, was familiar with correctional terminology, and that his orders, suggestions, and recommendations were consistent with sound correctional policies.

b. Attitudes of Prison Administrators and the Legislature

Attitudes of prison administrators and the Arkansas legislature were important throughout the litigation. The administration favored prison improvement from the very outset, although administrators sometimes differed from the court in their opinion of the dimensions that improvement should assume. Except for the most recent phases of the case, administrators generally accepted court intervention without resentment. Unlike prison administrators, the legislature was openly hostile to both court intervention and prison reform during the early stages of Holt v. Sarver. During a middle period between 1971 and 1974, legislators became quietly tolerant of court intervention and were apparently resigned to the reality that prison reform was inevitable. However, during the latter stages of the case, the legislature grew resentful of the judicial presence in corrections.

Attitudes of the high level prison administrators were a positive factor throughout most of the litigation. Both Commissioner Sarver and Commissioner Hutto were strongly in favor of improving the Arkansas prison system. Their plans for the prison system responded to and were generally consistent with the court's orders. Both respected the power and authority of the court. Both found the court orders compatible with principles of sound correctional management. Both attempted to use the litigation as a catalyst for additional funding. Both expressed a resolve to do whatever was within their power to comply with the court orders. There were, however, dissimilarities between the attitudes of the two administrators. Whereas Commissioner Sarver openly welcomed the lawsuit, Commissioner Hutto was guarded in his opinion of the litigation. Whereas Commissioner Sarver did not defend the prison system, Commissioner Hutto presented a strong evidentiary defense at each hearing. Toward the latter stages of the litigation, particularly after the court of appeals opinion in Finney v. Arkansas Board of Correction, Commissioner Hutto expressed resentment toward the court's continued intervention in affairs of the prison system. His attitude toward court intervention was perceived by the district court as a factor that hindered compliance.

Several individuals reported that during Robert Sarver's tenure, the Arkansas Department of Correction strongly favored reforming the prison system. Commissioner Sarver was a self-described prison reformer. It was reported that he welcomed court intrusion into the affairs of the prisons and he looked upon court intervention as a potential tool that could be used politically to improve the system. According to Commissioner Sarver, he assisted the presentation of the plaintiffs' case in the initial Holt v. Sarver trial by helping to draft the inmate complaints, by protecting inmate complainants and witnesses from retaliation by free world guards and other inmates, and by helping the plaintiffs' attorneys document deficiencies in the prisons. It was his position that the conditions in the system were indefensible and he took no steps to defend them. He presented only a token defense to the litigation. The district judge affirmed that during the earliest stages of the litigation there was no dispute about the underlying facts and no evidentiary defense was presented.

The administration of the department of correction under both Commissioner Sarver and Commissioner Hutto showed deep respect for the district court. Throughout the litigation the defendants took the court's orders seriously. According to several of the key participants in the litigation, the district judge earned the respect of the defendants by his stern demeanor and his reputation as a "tough" judge. The defendants were aware that in a case involving conditions in the Pulaski County, Arkansas, penal farm, the judge had found county officials in contempt of court and had closed the facility because of noncompliance with court orders.

There were attitudinal differences between the Hutto and Sarver administrations, but there was little evidence that those differences significantly affected compliance. Commissioner Hutto and several of his staff members expressed the opinion that the court should relinquish its jurisdiction over the *Holt* litigation. Resentment was reported within the correction department toward the court of appeals decision in Finney v. Arkansas Board of Correction. Several individuals predicted that no additional prison improvement would result from the decision. It was clear that during the latter stages of the litigation, judicial intervention was no longer welcomed as a tool for improving the prisons. It could be speculated that the Hutto administration would have responded differently if conditions in the prison had remained as they were in 1969, but there could be no argument that after 1973 the Hutto administration staunchly defended practices and conditions in the prison. Several persons related that prison administrators believed the system was in constitutional compliance. Hence, administrators felt that judicially ordered change was unjustified and they expressed resentment that inmates looked to the court for the solution of their prison-related problems. In its opinion of March 19, 1976, the district court observed that ". . . with the passage of time . . . and with improvements in prison conditions being made, there has been some hardening of Departmental attitudes and an unwillingness on the part of the prison administrators to go much, if any farther than they have gone . . . ."

The current administration's attitude that the prison system was constitutionally acceptable and needed no further improvement was tempered by the administration's respect for the court. Because of their respect for the court and court orders, the Hutto administration followed the letter of the orders. However, there appeared to be no attempt to go beyond the mandate of the court orders. The district court implicitly questioned whether the department really favored prison improvement. It pointed out that ". . . at practically every stage of the litigation evidence has brought to light practices of which those in higher positions of authority were ignorant and which they eliminated when the facts were disclosed." The court conjectured that

". . . the prison authorities should have discovered at least some of those conditions and practices for themselves . . . " and remarked that the defendants should have ". . . corrected them without waiting for them to be developed in the course of evidentiary hearings in . . . [the] lawsuit." The findings of the district court contrasted with assertions that the defendants desired to improve conditions for the inmates. Those findings paralleled the observation of a plaintiffs' attorney that the defendants were not interested in further improving conditions for prisoners.

The Arkansas legislature was indispensable to compliance even though it was not a defendant in the litigation. Compliance efforts were contingent upon a greatly increased funding level and the legislature had exclusive authority to appropriate funds with which to operate the department of correction. It was reported that during the early compliance phase of the litigation, immediately following the district court's initial decision in Holt v. Sarver, the legislature was angry about the decision and openly hostile toward court intervention. Commissioner Sarver confirmed that the legislature was furious about the first decision in *Holt.* An attorney for the plaintiffs remarked that several legislators objected that the court was attempting to convert the prisons into country clubs. During that period, several legislators made speeches denouncing court intervention in prison administration. One legislator described the litigation as a "thorn in the side" of the legislature and a "political move to disgrace the people of Arkansas and the people involved in the prison system."

Several individuals explained that the Arkansas legislature reacted negatively to the decision because Commissioner Sarver had assumed a favorable posture to the litigation and failed to defend the prison. They stated that while Robert Sarver remained commissioner of the department of correction, the legislature refused to appropriate the funds necessary to comply with the court orders. This theory attributed the negative legislative attitude as much to the actions of Commissioner Sarver as to the orders of the district court. Whether the legislative attitude was produced by the lawsuit or by Commissioner Sarver's reaction to the lawsuit, that attitude clearly had an adverse effect upon compliance. It placed definite limitations upon the ability of the commissioner to comply with the court order.

It was generally agreed among principals to the litigation that, from the time Robert Sarver was removed as commissioner until the court of appeals opinion in Finney v. Arkansas Board of Correction, the level of legislative appropriations for operating the department of correction facilitated compliance. During that time frame, legislators did not actively oppose either judicial intervention or prison reform. One legislator stated that the legislature realized that substantial amounts of money would have to be appropriated to operate the prisons. Whether grudgingly or willingly, a sufficient level of funding was reportedly appropriated.

Some individuals observed that during the period between 1971 and 1974 the legislature developed a sense of pride in the improvements that had been made in the prison system. However, several persons contended that after the appellate court decision in Finney v. Arkansas Board of Correction, the legislature lost interest in prison improvement. An assistant attorney general speculated that, as a result of the decision, the legislature might not authorize future appropriations for capital improvements in the prisons without a court order. Whether a negative legislative reaction would adversely affect compliance with future court orders remained to be seen.

3. *The Court Orders*

The court orders in Holt v. Sarver reflected Judge Henley's attitude toward the court's proper role in correctional reform. The orders were general, restrained, and limited in scope. They prescribed results to be reached, not steps to be taken en route. They fixed priorities and established a framework for compliance but left the details of implementation to the administrative discretion of the defendants. The orders apparently accomplished what the court hoped they would accomplish. They brought prison deficiencies to the attention of administrators and provided impetus for change. The court's approach minimized resistance to the orders. From that standpoint, the orders were independent factors that for the most part had a positive effect upon compliance.

The orders were, almost without exception, general in form. Seldom did the orders require specific compliance action. It was reported that the defendants frequently found it necessary to consult the court's opinion for "suggestions" or "recommendations" about precisely what the court expected of them. Further clarification was gained through informal conferences held between the district judge, attorneys for the litigants and, occasionally, correctional administrators. An assistant attorney general stated that the judge worked informally with the defendants regarding the administrative feasibility of reform in certain areas. He explained that the department of correction often checked with the judge to confirm whether anticipated departmental changes would be constitutionally acceptable. An attorney for the plaintiffs agreed that, as a matter of judicial style, Judge Henley operated in a relatively informal fashion, making suggestions and recommendations rather than issuing direct orders. According to this attorney, the judge frequently advised the defendants in his chambers that a certain practice should be eliminated or that another practice should be initiated. The defendants would subsequently appear at a court hearing and announce initiation or discontinuance of the practice in question.

The lack of specificity and rigidity was considered by many persons to be a factor that helped avoid the appearance that the court was unduly interfering with the internal affairs of the prison. It served to defuse hostility that might have developed toward judicial intervention. Moreover, the ongoing communication between the defendants and the court supplied definition to the orders and helped clarify the duties that were imposed. An indirect result of the communication was that departmental administrators frequently changed policies and practices in anticipation of later court orders.

Commissioner Hutto and Commissioner Sarver commented that the orders allowed the department wide operational leeway and contributed to an attitude of increased respect for the court. Commissioner Sarver observed that the court orders gave him freedom to move the prison system in directions he felt it should take and allowed him to make reforms that went beyond the strict requirements of the orders. He complained, however, that while the orders required him to institute needed reforms and allowed compliance leeway, they provided little political protection. According to him, the orders were subject to various interpretations and stimulated controversy over the actions necessary to satisfy the judicially established requirements. He said that legislators interpreted the orders narrowly, while he interpreted them expansively. When he tried to justify certain reforms by declaring that the federal court had ordered them, legislators argued that the proposed reforms exceeded the requirements of the orders. Several individuals attributed Commissioner Sarver's conflict with the legislature to his expansive interpretation of the orders.

There was a related consequence of the lack of specificity in the court orders. Attorneys for the plaintiffs expressed the opinion that the orders were so ambiguous that they were virtually unenforceable. Commissioner Sarver pointed out a danger with general and nonspecific orders, stating that such orders made it possible for unwilling defendants to evade compliance.

There, were, however, certain exceptions to the "general" nature of the orders. During later stages of the litigation the court issued specific orders in those areas in which there was a failure to achieve compliance. While the later orders pointed out compliance failures, several persons observed that they contributed to an attitude of resentment that the court had become enmeshed in the administrative affairs of the prison system.

No comprehensive orders were issued in the *Holt* litigation. Instead, the orders paralleled the development of the litigation. They were promulgated in a piecemeal fashion. The issues that were apparently of greatest urgency were dealt with first and those of lesser importance were dealt with subsequently. As improvement was made in one area of concern, the court's attention focused upon a different area and its orders reflected that shift. None of the principals attached significance to the sequential approach to prison problems and it could not be described as an intentional strategy. Nevertheless, Judge Henley expressed the belief that although inadvertent, the piecemeal promulgation of the orders probably had a positive effect upon compliance. He commented that, if orders affecting the whole range of issues dealt with in the *Holt* litigation had been issued simultaneously, the defendants might have been overwhelmed by the enormity of the task they faced.

The orders reportedly contained very little with which the defendants disagreed. Almost without exception, those interviewed avoided the criticism that any order harmed the prisons, inmates or employees. Commissioner Hutto related his belief that although some of the orders were based upon the incorrect interpretation of evidence before the court, practically everything that the court had ordered was consistent with sound correctional policies. Nevertheless, several individuals implied that the court lacked expertise in prison management, and that its orders bore the potential for harming inmates. Commissioner Hutto warned that there was a danger that the court might order actions taken to quickly alleviate a perceived correctional problem that could negatively affect an entire department of correction for many years. He stated that if a court were not careful, one single court order could send a corrections department in the wrong direction, with potentially disastrous consequences.

Agreement that the orders were consistent with good correctional practice probably resulted as much from the operational leeway that the orders permitted as the substantive content of the orders. Judge Henley stated that remediation of correctional problems required the application of common sense, not expertise in corrections. The orders that he issued reflected his belief. They established broad constitutional goals and generally allowed correctional administrators wide discretion in achieving those goals. Nevertheless, in certain areas, such as the medical program, the court required the defendants to cause studies undertaken that would result in specific recommendations for improvements and it ordered the defendants to implement the recommendations that eventually resulted. This approach was compatible with the court's philosophy of allowing administrative discretion and involving experts in the reform of the prison system only when expertise was essential.

4. *Management of the Prison System*

Management of the Arkansas prison system was an important compliance factor that assumed special importance because the court orders allowed substantial compliance leeway. The orders presumed that administrators were competent and dedicated to improving the prison system. Only in areas where noncompliance resulted from administrative failures did the court attempt to prescribe specific remedies that related to management. Because compliance depended heavily upon the undirected action of prison administrators, there was a tendency to overlook accomplishments and dwell upon failings. The level of compliance achieved was very high and, considering the dismal conditions that existed in the prison system when the litigation began, the improvement was remarkable. Credit should be given to the prison management for compliance with the court orders and improvement in the prison. By the same token, most compliance failures could also be attributed to management failures.

a. The Management Structure

The Arkansas Department of Correction and the Arkansas Board of Correction shared responsibility for the operations and management of the prison system, while the Arkansas legislature was responsible for financing the system. Both the department of correction and the board of correction were defendants in the Holt v. Sarver litigation but the legislature was not made a party to the litigation for tactical reasons.[356]

The division of responsibility for the prison system presented a potential for conflict between clashing governmental priorities. The prison system required increased financial support, but was not assigned a high priority by the legislature. Throughout the litigation the division of responsibility was an obstacle to compliance. At certain periods correctional administrators were able to secure funds for compliance, while at other periods they were not. Even though such funds were available, securing an adequate funding level was an administrative problem.

356. . . . Philip Kaplan explained that, if the legislature had been made a party to the suit, the litigation would have been unmanageable.

Tension existed throughout the litigation between the legislature and the department of correction over adequate funding for the prison system. The department required additional funds to improve the system and operate the prisons at a level comporting with human dignity but the legislature did not assign the prisons a high priority. The early stages of Holt v. Sarver best illustrated the tension between the legislature and the department. Several individuals reported that at the time Holt v. Sarver was filed, there was widespread acceptance by the general public and the legislature of the proposition that the prison system should be self-supporting. According to these individuals, the system of financing prison operations through prison-generated revenues had to be revamped before meaningful improvement could take place.

The task of simultaneously upgrading conditions in the prison system and abolishing its self-supporting nature—a delicate and politically controversial undertaking—initially fell to Commissioner Sarver. The commissioner clearly failed to abolish the prison's self-supporting nature. Nevertheless, his attempts to raise the funding level of the prison system ultimately contributed to the accomplishment of his purpose. Several individuals reported that Commissioner Sarver welcomed the *Holt* litigation, offered no evidentiary defense, and publicly blamed dismal prison conditions upon the legislative failure to adequately finance the system. The result of his action was predictable—legislative support for his administration eroded. Commissioner Sarver noted that his relationship with the legislature deteriorated to such an extent that in March, 1971, the legislature refused to pass an important $6,000,000 prison appropriation bill until the commissioner was removed from office. Upon Commissioner Sarver's refusal to resign, Governor Dale Bumpers fired him and the appropriation bill was reportedly enacted the following day.

Several reasons were advanced to explain the poor relationship that existed between Commissioner Sarver and the legislature. One state legislator characterized the commissioner as a reformer who possessed noble intentions but lacked administrative skills. The legislator acknowledged that reformers were necessary to initiate needed change, but he emphasized that sound fiscal management was critical to the change process. According to him and Commissioner Sarver, the legislature lost confidence in the commissioner's administrative ability. Despite contentions that Commissioner Sarver's lack of administrative skill led to his dismissal, it was admitted that the legislative loss of confidence was related to adverse news media publicity encouraged by the commissioner. Several individuals attributed Commissioner Sarver's conflict with the legislature to his favorable reaction to the litigation.

A final reason that was advanced as explanation for the difficulty that Commissioner Sarver had in extracting legislative appropriations related to his political affiliation. Commissioner Sarver was appointed to his position by Governor Winthrop Rockefeller. Both he and the governor were Republicans in a state government dominated by Democrats. Several individuals observed that the commissioner's inability to raise the level of prison funding typified a problem throughout the Rockefeller administration. It was reported that the Rockefeller administration had serious difficulties extracting funds from the legislature. This problem contrasted sharply with the administration of Governor Bumpers, who could apparently secure funds "as if by magic."

Conflict between the Arkansas legislature and the department of correction was virtually eliminated after the appointment of Terrell Don Hutto as commissioner of correction in May, 1971. Several individuals reported that Commissioner Hutto established a rapport with the legislature. The commissioner commented that he was initially well received by the legislature and that he had succeeded in maintaining strong legislative support throughout his tenure. He attributed the relationship to several factors—he avoided publicity, shunned the "reformer" image, and only requested expenditures that were absolutely necessary. He added that he found the legislature genuinely eager to improve the prison system. The result of the improved relations with the legislature was the legislative approval of every appropriation bill that the commissioner proposed.

Commissioner Hutto acknowledged the importance of legislative support to prison reform. He commented that ordering a correctional administrator to improve a prison system would be futile without legislative cooperation. That was especially true in Arkansas because the scale of needed improvement was tremendous. The nature of reform in the Arkansas system required large sums of money and a great deal of time. Legislative support was indispensable for that purpose. The commissioner stated that he attempted to cultivate a healthy working relationship with those legislators who had the greatest interest in and influence over legislation involving corrections. He explained that administrators cannot win fights with the legislature. Accordingly, he took particular care to avoid controversiality in his administration. The commissioner emphasized the importance of a public official maintaining a conservative political image, saying that it was "acceptable to talk conservatively and act liberally, but never the other way around in Arkansas."

Although the relationship between the department of correction and the Arkansas legislature improved markedly after March, 1971, there was no change in the management structure of the prison system. The department remained totally dependent on the cooperation of the legislature for adequate financing of its operations. That cooperation depended, in its turn, upon the political ability of the individual who held the position of commissioner of correction. There was no assurance that another impasse would not develop in the future between the department of correction and the legislature.

b. Administration of the Prisons

Toward later stages of the litigation, the district court found that top level prison administrators were qualified for their positions and commended administrative efforts to improve the system. According to the court, high level administrators were ". . . trying to do good jobs and to run an efficient, reasonably humane, constitutional prison." The court nevertheless characterized their efforts as somewhat less than successful and attributed noncompliance to deficiencies in prison administration. The court wrote in 1973 that it was not confronted ". . . so much with an unconstitutional prison system as a poorly administered one."

The court's finding that prison administration was deficient related principally to the hiring, training and supervision of correctional officers. Correctional officers were described as "unprofessional." The district court found that they were recruited from small rural towns near the prisons, were young, quick-tempered, poorly paid, poorly educated, poorly trained and had little general experience. . . .

According to Judge Henley, one of the most serious impediments to compliance was the failure of the administration's recruitment program. The problem had two facets—hiring qualified individuals and increasing the number of black employees. It was widely acknowledged that the task of hiring qualified individuals to fill positions as correctional officers was extremely difficult. The difficulty was ascribed to a number of considerations: the rural location of the prisons; the low salary and long working hours; the undesirable nature of the job; the unsavory reputation that the Arkansas prison system had acquired; and, the fact that blacks sympathized deeply with the plight of inmates and felt uncomfortable in the role of correctional officer. Clearly the hiring of personnel to work in the correctional system presented a serious problem. However, the district court found that prison administrators had not made a satisfactory attempt to overcome the obstacles to employing qualified personnel. . . .

In addition to administrative deficiencies in the area of employment, the district court found that prison administrators were lax in the supervision and training of personnel. Certain administrative shortcomings were of particular concern to the court. Before the Finney v. Arkansas Board of Correction decision, the administration did not routinely inform departmental employees of the substance of the orders issued by the court. Nor did it explain the way in which those orders affected the employees' daily job performance. Moreover, the department failed to impress employees with the realization that they were individually bound by the court orders and it failed to enforce departmental regulations issued through memoranda—particularly those prohibiting racial discrimination and brutality. The court found that these failures contributed significantly to noncompliance.

5. *Retention of Jurisdiction Over the Case*

Opinions varied about the effectiveness of the retention of jurisdiction as a compliance factor. It appeared that the retention of jurisdiction primarily affected compliance by facilitating the use of techniques and procedures for monitoring compliance progress. Nevertheless, certain individuals maintained that the court's continued jurisdiction had an independent effect upon compliance by the pressure that it imposed upon the defendants.

Except for the period from August 13, 1973 until November 18, 1974, (between the district court opinion in Holt v. Hutto and the court of appeals opinion in Finney v. Arkansas Board of Correction), the district court maintained jurisdiction over Holt v. Sarver from its inception. There were no projections about how much longer the court would retain jurisdiction, but Judge Henley expressed a desire to relinquish jurisdiction.

The district judge conceded that the "open" status of the litigation served as a reminder to the defendants of their compliance duties. Nevertheless, he voiced the opinion that the retention of jurisdiction had no effect upon compliance. He looked upon the retention of jurisdiction as an administrative headache for the court and contended that any enforcement mechanisms that were utilized could have been replicated in the absence of jurisdiction.

Several persons disagreed with the judge. Three of the principals to the litigation claimed that the retention of jurisdiction created pressure for compliance. An attorney for the plaintiffs considered the retention of jurisdiction essential for compliance. He conjectured that without the court's continued jurisdiction, there would have been no compliance. Commissioner Sarver stated that the most important result of the retention of jurisdiction was its effect upon the legislature. He explained that the court's presence prevented the legislature from "backing off" from prison improvement. An assistant attorney general observed that the continued judicial presence had two separate effects that contributed to attaining compliance. According to him, retention of jurisdiction made the defendants aware of their compliance obligations and it allowed the court to monitor compliance by informal methods.

There were indications that retention of jurisdiction had negative as well as positive effects upon compliance. Several individuals warned that the appellate court opinion in Finney v. Arkansas Board of Correction, ordering the district court to retain jurisdiction until the prison system was in full constitutional compliance, had evoked a negative response from the legislature that could hinder further compliance. An assistant attorney general claimed that the failure of the court of appeals to recognize the improvements that had been made in the prison system was a political mistake that could cause a legislative backlash. He stated that it was important for the court to recognize the positive strides made in the Arkansas correctional system. Commissioner Hutto agreed with that opinion. He stated that the Finney v. Arkansas Board of Correction opinion contributed to a general mood throughout the state that efforts to improve the prison system were futile. The commissioner acknowledged that the court had to retain jurisdiction for a sufficient length of time to assure that compliance progress was being made, but he asserted that, after such a determination had been made, the court should relinquish jurisdiction. He warned that excessive retention of jurisdiction would engender resentment toward the court; he left the impression that such a point had been reached in the *Holt* case. Commissioner Hutto added that, in addition to the resentment engendered by excessive retention of jurisdiction, it caused prison personnel to lose their creativity. He hypothesized that personnel could become trapped into attempting only to comply with court orders and the prison system could lose its internal drive to make improvements beyond the scope of the litigation.

6. *Monitoring and Enforcement Mechanisms*

Monitoring mechanisms are techniques and instruments, both formal and informal, that are used by courts to keep informed about the defendants' compliance progress. Compliance reports, persons appointed to monitor compliance, inmate petitions and letters, and compliance hearings are typical monitoring devices. Enforcement mechanisms are requirements and procedures that are designed to hasten or impel compliance that would apparently not otherwise be voluntarily achieved. The court's use of its contempt power, placing an institution in receivership, and compliance deadlines are typical enforcement mechanisms. Despite the suggestion implicit in this analysis that the distinction between monitoring and enforcement mechanisms is clear, that is not always the case. Monitoring mechanisms often serve to enforce compliance and enforcement mechanisms are often used to monitor compliance.

There was a conspicuous absence of enforcement mechanisms throughout most of the Holt v. Sarver litigation. The district court periodically imposed deadlines during the litigation, but those deadlines related to the filing of compliance reports and were not true enforcement deadlines. The court finally imposed a compliance deadline in an order issued on February 19, 1976, after field research for this study was completed. The court also treated a *pro se* inmate complaint as a motion to cite the defendants for contempt, but dismissed the motion without a hearing.

In contrast to the absence of enforcement mechanisms, the district court relied upon several different mechanisms to monitor compliance. The court ordered the defendants to file compliance reports on seven separate occasions. It held four separate compliance hearings. It inspected the prisons on at least three occasions. It relied upon a combination of inmate correspondence and petitions and the independent monitoring performed by the plaintiffs' attorneys. The monitoring mechanisms employed by the court appeared to be highly effective both in apprising the court of the defendants' compliance progress and as a positive factor contributing to the level of compliance that was achieved.

The basic monitoring mechanism employed by the district court was the duty that it imposed upon the defendants to file periodic compliance reports. Court orders issued on June 20, 1969, February 18, 1970, April 15, 1970, June 16, 1970, February 4, 1971, September 8, 1972 and February 19, 1976, required the defendants to file reports describing what steps they had taken and what steps they planned to bring the prison system up to minimal constitutional standards. Each order imposed a deadline for filing the reports. The court docket sheet revealed that the defendants filed compliance reports within each of the deadlines. Besides the compliance reports that were formally ordered, several of the principals reported that Judge Henley periodically made informal requests for compliance reports concerning relatively minor prison matters that were often brought to his attention by correspondence from inmates. According to several individuals, formal compliance reports were comprehensive and accurate, and kept the court advised of compliance progress. Attorneys for the plaintiffs complained, however, that in certain instances, especially regarding improvements in prison health services, the reports lacked detail. They conceded that the reports enabled them to ascertain the extent of compliance in areas that were obvious, such as capital improvements.

Inmate communications in the form of correspondence and formal complaints, directed to the district court and to counsel for the plaintiffs, provided a supplementary source of information that enabled the court to monitor conditions and practices within the prison system. The court responded to inmate communications in a number of different ways. It often informally required the defendants to investigate the cause of an inmate complaint and to file informal letter reports regarding their findings. Inmate communications were frequently forwarded to the plaintiffs' attorneys with a suggestion that the source of the complaint be investigated.

On four separate occasions the court held compliance hearings based upon inmate communications. Such hearings were convened by the court on its own motion. Compliance hearings were held over periods of several days, weeks, and even months, beginning on August 5, 1970, November 16, 1971, November 13, 1972 and March 25, 1975. The compliance hearings subjected the prison system to intensive scrutiny. The hearings focused upon compliance with earlier orders but, because the hearings also related to the broad mandate to bring conditions in the prison system up to constitutional standards, each hearing expanded the scope of the litigation.

There was general agreement among the principals that the monitoring devices kept the court and counsel apprised of compliance progress and contributed to the achievement of compliance. None of the various monitoring mechanisms was singled out as being less efficacious than the others. The enforcement value of the monitoring mechanisms included three distinctly separate effects. Referring to both the reports and the hearings, principals to the litigation reported that monitoring devices reminded the defendants of their compliance duties, required them to thoroughly examine conditions and practices in the prison system, and assisted them in finding practical solutions to some of the administrative problems that the prison system presented. Several individuals expressed the belief that the compliance reports placed pressure upon the defendants to comply. However, Commissioner Hutto disputed that contention. He explained that pressure for compliance was created by the existence of the district court's mandate, backed by the court's willingness to enforce that mandate with appropriate sanctions if necessary.

Most of the principals described the court's use of monitoring mechanisms in positive terms. Each believed that although the monitoring devices employed by the court caused a disruption inside the prison system, monitoring was vital to compliance. However, Commissioner Hutto stated that monitoring compliance through lengthy hearings had adverse effects. Such hearings involved enormous amounts of administrator and staff time that could have been used in substantive compliance duties. He stated that before each hearing, thousands of hours were devoted to preparation. In his view, the hearings actually slowed the rate of compliance. An attorney for the plaintiffs commented that the compliance hearings were costly in terms of court and attorneys' time. He suggested that the appointment of a master to monitor compliance would have achieved the same results at less cost.

C. *THE IMPACT OF THE LITIGATION*

Discussion of the impact of Holt v. Sarver must be prefaced with a note of caution concerning the validity of conclusions reached. The strongest conclusion regarding impact that can be drawn from this research is that the *Holt* litigation contributed to certain effects. It is conjectural whether the same effects would have occurred in the absence of the litigation. Conclusions regarding causality were especially tentative because of the close relationship between the litigation and the background events that took place during the period preceding *Holt.* The "State Police Report," the "Study Commission Report," and the early litigation that affected the prison system contributed immeasurably to the impact of Holt v. Sarver. The *Holt* litigation was itself a product of the background events. It would distort reality to overlook the background events in relating the impact of the litigation. Consequently, no attempt has been made to distinguish effects attributable solely to the *Holt* litigation from those attributable solely to the background events.

Court orders and efforts to comply with those orders marked the starting point and suggested the primary focus of the suit's impact, but the effects of the litigation extended beyond the ambit of compliance. Viewed from a broad perspective, the litigation touched several areas both within and outside the prison system. It caused a reassessment of governmental priorities and changed basic ideas about corrections. It caused an improvement in the management of the prison system while simultaneously creating administrative headaches. It led to the construction of new buildings. It improved the overall quality of life for inmates. The worst abuses in the prison system were eliminated. Yet, despite all of the changes and improvements, after ten years of nearly continuous litigation, the Arkansas prison system was somewhat less than ideal when examined in the summer of 1975. The impact of Holt v. Sarver was broad and profound, but it had definite limitations. Some limitations were built into the judicial response and others resulted from defendant noncompliance.

The *Holt* litigation was widely recognized as a catalyst for prison change and improvement. Opinions of several key figures in the litigation established that the litigation performed two separate functions that were vital to improvement within the prison system. It educated the public and public administrators about defects in the prison system and it provided a momentum for change. According to Commissioner Hutto, the litigation provided the basic impetus for reform of the prison system. An attorney for the plaintiffs expressed the same belief in different terms when he stated that the litigation created a climate for change. The litigation, particularly in its early stages, was generally believed indispensable to reform. Commissioner Hutto explained that court involvement focused public attention upon the prison system—which he said was a healthy development. He observed that the litigation awakened the public to the need for change and, by depicting the court as a scapegoat, prison administrators were able to make necessary improvements in the prison system that the public might not otherwise have tolerated.

Although not all of the changes in the prison system that occurred after Holt v. Sarver was filed could be directly attributed to the *Holt* litigation, the litigation provided impetus and established direction for the change that followed. It could thus be stated that changes made in the prison system from 1965 until 1976 derived at least indirectly from the litigation.

Improved management of the prison system was a significant result of the litigation. The presiding district judge commented that the *Holt* litigation highlighted the fact that poor management was partially responsible for the prison's problems. He believed that a major result of the litigation was improved prison management. Improvement could be traced to four separate elements: a unified department of correction was created where none had existed before; well-qualified individuals were appointed to administer the correction department; the prison system was adequately financed; and the trusty guard system was abolished.

Before the *Holt* case was filed, each of the correctional facilities was an independent entity. There was simply no correctional system in Arkansas. The Study Commission identified the absence of a correctional system as a major contributor to the chaos existing in the state's prisons. It recommended creation of a unified department of correction directed by a capable administrator. A unified department of correction was created before Holt v. Sarver was filed, but creation of the department was directly related to the background events that gave rise to *Holt.* Thus, in a broad sense, Holt v. Sarver provided the impetus for adopting the commission's recommendation. Robert Sarver was appointed the first commissioner of correction for the State of Arkansas and both he and his successor, Terrell Don Hutto, were described by Judge Henley as well qualified for the position.

Commissioner Hutto and Commissioner Sarver both expressed the opinion that the most significant result of the litigation was that it caused the prison system to be placed on a sound financial footing. According to both, all improvements in the prison system resulted from increased funding. The system of limiting prison expenditures to prison-generated revenues, historically engrained in the Arkansas prison system, was abrogated as a result of the litigation. Before Holt v. Sarver, the prison system literally cost the state treasury nothing. The change to a system directly financed from the state treasury was dramatic. One middle echelon prison administrator stated that the litigation helped convince the Arkansas legislature and the people of the state of the necessity to appropriate large sums of money for the prisons. Commissioner Hutto reported that in 1971, the legislature authorized the expenditure of $1 million (from revenues derived through the sale of prison industries) to run the entire department. The department budget subsequently increased substantially. The commissioner estimated that current total annual financial support for the department was approximately $9 million. According to him, legislative support for prison operations averaged $6 million per year; outlays for capital improvements averaged $2 million or $3 million each year, and, in addition to state appropriations, the Law Enforcement Assistance Administration reportedly contributed an average of $1,250,000 per year.

Management problems were considerably lessened by the elimination of inmate trusty guards pursuant to orders of the district court. Elimination of this guard system was closely related to increased appropriations for prison operations. It was reported that converting the prison system from a system run by inmates to a system run by free personnel was accomplished by increasing the number of free employees from 23 to over 500. The elimination of trusty guards from the prison system was widely considered one of the most important effects of the litigation and contributed critically to an improved quality of life for the inmate.

Despite significant improvements in the management of the prison, a number of individuals expressed the belief that the *Holt* litigation created major problems for the prison administration. The court hearings constituted a "major disruption" in the correctional system, inmates were allegedly more difficult to control as a result of the litigation, and the effect of the litigation upon employee morale was described as devastating.

Although the Holt v. Sarver litigation substantially improved the prison system, several individuals reported that the litigation had reached a point of diminishing returns. The resources that went into the litigation were allegedly greater than the benefits that could be derived from it. Several persons reported that correctional administrators and key prison personnel spent a substantial amount of time implementing court orders, compiling records to document compliance, and preparing for and participating in court hearings. Commissioner Hutto estimated that during the district court hearings in Finney v. Hutto, Cummins prison operated at 50% of its normal staff level. According to his rough estimate, based chiefly upon the cost involved in diverting staff and employee time to preparation for court proceedings, the hearings would ultimately cost the state between $200,000 and $500,000. It was stated that the time correctional administrators and employees spent preparing for court proceedings, documenting compliance efforts, and appearing in court diverted scarce administrative resources from direct inmate service.

The assertion that Holt v. Sarver diminished the human resources that would otherwise have been available to inmates had apparent validity. Proper recognition should be accorded the fact that litigation can be a highly disruptive intrusion into prison operations, depending upon the scope of the individual lawsuit, the nature of required change, the number and character of enforcement and monitoring devices employed, and the resources that prison administrators use to defend conditions and practices. Such a disruption could create administrative headaches and could easily lead to temporarily diminished services for inmates. There was ample evidence that the *Holt* litigation had such an effect. However, logic would suggest that such a diminution should be only temporary. Such a diminution does not support a conclusion that additional litigation would not be beneficial to inmates however, it suggests that careful consideration be given to the method employed for determining whether a system was in compliance with constitutional requirements. The disruptive potential of particular monitoring mechanisms is one important consideration.

Correctional personnel and lawyers for the defendants reported that inmates became more difficult to control as a result of the litigation. It was said that inmates had lost respect for authority, were "testy and belligerent," and that, rather than "just doing time," they "hassled the administration." A few individuals expressed the belief that administrative difficulties in controlling inmates were a result of correctional litigation that could be expected. They explained that prison litigation by its very nature places inmates and administrators in an adversarial, combative posture. Several individuals attributed disciplinary problems to the district court's sensitivity to misinterpretations by inmates and employees of the court orders. Inmates were said to have interpreted the orders to mean that they had greater "freedom" than was actually the case, while correctional officers were said to believe that the court orders prohibited them from disciplining inmates or from exercising reasonable force to maintain order.

The final reported administrative problem that resulted from the litigation was the demoralizing effect that inmate complaints to the federal court had upon personnel. Several individuals expressed the belief that inmates filed complaints as a method of harassing prison personnel. Commissioner Hutto stated that because of the district court's insistence that inmate complaints not be censored in any way, inmates were frequently able to file false, outlandish, obscene and scandalous complaints that were nevertheless widely publicized. According to the commissioner, a number of correctional officers had resigned because of the pressure created by slanderous allegations contained in inmate complaints. Several persons protested that the adverse publicity surrounding inmate complaints contributed to low correctional officer morale.

A great many improvements in the prison system related to the environment of the prisons and the quality of life enjoyed by the inmates. Those improvements largely responded directly to requirements established by the court orders . . . . They were clearly attributable to the litigation.

Several capital improvements were made in the prison system during the course of the *Holt* litigation. Inmate safety improved drastically as a result of the litigation. Incidents of brutality and reprisals against inmates decreased dramatically. There was a slight improvement in race relations and a reduction in incidents of racial discrimination. The number of black employees increased. Inmate health care services improved greatly. Conditions in the secure confinement building at Cummins improved. Fewer restrictions were placed upon inmate correspondence. Greater tolerance was allowed Black Muslim religious practices. Procedural regularity was introduced into prison disciplinary proceedings. Educational and rehabilitative services were made available to inmates.

The changes in the prison system were more than cosmetic; they were broad and profound. The system bore little, if any, resemblance in 1976 to the system that existed before 1969. Every aspect of prison life was improved by the litigation. Nevertheless, the quality of life inside the prison remained less than ideal. An attorney for the plaintiffs best summarized the difference between expectations and reality when he stated that "the litigation succeeded in bringing the Arkansas prison system into the twentieth century," but he was uncertain whether the system had been brought very far into the twentieth century. There was some agreement that, while the physical environment surrounding inmates had improved considerably as a result of the litigation, the emotional atmosphere in the prison had not improved and may have deteriorated.

The impact of the litigation upon the quality of life in the prison system was both limited and diluted. Impact was limited by restrictions on the power of the court and it was diluted by noncompliance with the court orders. Judge Henley explained that the principal limitations upon the court's ability to deal with problems in the corrections system related to substantive remedies. According to him, the court could only order changes that raised the conditions to a constitutional level of minimally acceptable standards. The court was powerless to order changes that brought living conditions up to standards that were ideal or which even amounted to sound correctional goals if those changes exceeded minimal acceptability. Thus the court was unable to order changes that were innovative.

A former member of the penitentiary board articulated the belief that although the *Holt* litigation was vital to prison improvement in Arkansas, it caused too rapid a rate of change in the penal system. There was such haste in complying with court orders that the changes in the prison system were along traditional lines. He expressed the opinion that new directions were needed for the correctional system and that the *Holt* litigation had provided an opportunity for innovation. Instead, the penal system responded to the litigation in a fairly traditional fashion so that, although it improved, it was neither better nor worse than other prison systems. Both he and Commissioner Hutto observed that the court's continued presence institutionalized the change that was made but it diminished the prospect of innovative change within the system.

Dilution of the litigation's impact upon the quality of life in the prison system corresponded directly to noncompliance with the court orders that was reported at length in Section III. None of the persons interviewed claimed that the quality of life in the prison was good. Inmate safety was improved, but the prisons were not safe and violent episodes were not infrequent. Incidents of brutality and retaliation were reported by inmates and acknowledged by administrators. The prisons were seriously overcrowded. Racial discrimination was still practiced and relations between the races remained poor. Medical and health care was deficient in several respects. The level of sanitation and cleanliness was improved but deficiencies remained. Conditions in the secure confinement areas were less than satisfactory. The Arkansas prison system had improved tremendously as a result of Holt v. Sarver, and there were indications that improvement would continue. Yet, despite the substantial contribution of the litigation, when the field research was completed, the Arkansas prison system was far from ideal. It left much to be desired.

II. An Alternative Perspective: Meanwhile Over in the Neighboring State of Texas

RUIZ v. ESTELLE

679 F.2d 1115 (5th Cir. 1982).

Before CLARK, Chief Judge, RUBIN and TATE, Circuit Judges.

ALVIN B. RUBIN, Circuit Judge:

"There is no iron curtain drawn between the Constitution and the prisons of this country." [1] When the remedial powers of a federal court are invoked to protect the constitutional rights of inmates, the court may not take a "hands-off" approach.

The duty to protect inmates' constitutional rights, however, does not confer the power to manage prisons, for which courts are ill-equipped, or the capacity to second-guess prison administrators. Federal courts should not, "in the name of the Constitution, become . . . enmeshed in the minutiae of prison operations." [5] Our task is limited to enforcing constitutional standards and does not embrace superintending prison administration.

This class action on behalf of more than 33,000 inmates confined in the various institutions operated by the Texas Department of Corrections

1. Wolff v. McDonnell, 418 U.S. 539, 555–56 (1974).

5. Bell v. Wolfish, 441 U.S. 520, 562 (1979).

("TDC") challenges the conditions of their confinement as cruel and unusual punishment and a denial of due process of law in violation of the eighth and fourteenth amendments to the Constitution. We are required to determine whether the district court correctly found that the conditions of confinement in TDC violate the Constitution and, if so, whether the remedy imposed went beyond the correction of constitutional deficiencies and intruded unduly on the state's management of its prison system or enmeshed the court in the details of prison management.

We affirm the district court's finding that TDC imposes cruel and unusual punishment on inmates in its custody as a result of the totality of conditions in its prisons. We also affirm the district court's finding that some of TDC's practices deny inmates due process of law. We affirm its conclusion that remedial measures are necessary. Concluding, however, that the district court inappropriately considered state law claims not raised by the parties, we reverse its order that TDC conform its practices to state statutory requirements. We also conclude that some of the remedial measures ordered are not demonstrably required to protect constitutional rights and intrude unduly on matters of state concern and we, therefore, narrow the scope of the relief ordered. . . .

The Texas state prison system, operated by TDC, is the largest in the United States. Its inmates, now numbering more than 33,000 are confined in cells or dormitories located in twenty-two separate units, almost all of which have maximum security. Most of the approximately 10,000 cells measure nine feet by five feet, but some are as large as sixty-six square feet. Most of the dormitories house large numbers of inmates and are crowded. After the consolidation of eight separate actions by individual inmates against W.J. Estelle, the Director of TDC, challenging the conditions of their confinement, the district court certified the case as a class action and permitted the United States to intervene as a plaintiff.

The trial began in Houston on October 2, 1978, and, after 159 days of trial, bridging a three-month recess, was completed on September 20, 1979. Three hundred forty-nine witnesses testified and 1,565 exhibits were received into evidence. The district court issued a 118-page memorandum opinion on December 12, 1980, indicating generally the relief it proposed to grant, and gave the parties an opportunity to agree on a proposed judgment. The parties later filed a proposed consent decree disposing of many of the issues.[11] The district court approved this consent decree, entered a decree granting equitable relief and a declaratory judgment on the issues not disposed of by the consent decree, appointed a special master to monitor implementation of the relief ordered, and denied TDC's motion for a stay. TDC then applied to this court for a stay, which we granted in part and denied in

11. The parties agreed on provisions concerning (a) health care, except for the continued use of the Huntsville Unit Hospital; (b) the conditions of confinement of mentally retarded and physically handicapped inmates; (c) the conditions of solitary confinement; (d) the rules concerning the use on inmates of chemical agents such as Mace and tear gas; (e) work safety and hygiene in TDC inmate work operations, except for the applicability of Texas state regulatory laws; and (f) procedures for administrative segregation of inmates. This consent decree, which the district court approved on March 3, 1981, is the first of two consent decrees that were approved in this case. It is reproduced as Appendix A to this opinion. In this opinion it is referred to as "the first consent decree."

part. TDC later sought a supplemental stay, which, again, we granted in part and denied in part. The parties then agreed to a second consent decree that modified parts of the district court's decree, and we remanded the case to enable the district court to hold a class action hearing on the proposed modifications. After that hearing, the district court approved the second consent decree and, in accordance with its terms, TDC moved under Fed.R.App.P. 42(b) for voluntary dismissal of its appeal of the provisions of the district court's decree that were superseded by the second consent decree. The case has also been before us on interlocutory appeals; this marks its seventh appearance in our court.[18]

We turn first to the pervasive issues still contested: TDC's attack on the fairness of the trial, the sufficiency of the district court's findings of fact, the intervention by the United States, and the joinder of the Texas Board of Corrections and individual members of the Board as parties defendant.

TDC contends that the district judge made many errors in his rulings concerning the conduct of the trial and the admissibility of evidence, the cumulative effect of which was so prejudicial as to deny TDC its right to a fair trial. The impugnment is more than a challenge to specific rulings, however, for it includes assertions that "the entire record is permeated with favoritism" toward the plaintiffs and "unrelenting unfairness" toward TDC and is infected both by "evident prejudgment" of the case in the plaintiffs' favor and by judicial bias.

The constitutional guarantee of due process of law ordains a fair trial. The trial judge must not become "personally embroiled" in the proceedings. He must not assume the role of prosecutor or defender. He must avoid even the appearance of favoring one side. However, "[o]nly when the judge's conduct strays from neutrality is a defendant thereby denied a fair trial as required by the Constitution." Moreover, even if the trial judge does commit error, it is presumed harmless until shown to be prejudicial. The

18. The prior proceedings were:

"1. TDC's petition for a writ of mandamus to bar the United States from participating in this action. We denied the petition. In re Estelle, 516 F.2d 480 (5th Cir. 1975) (*Ruiz I*), cert. denied, 426 U.S. 925 (1976) (Rehnquist, J., joined by Burger, C.J., & Powell, J., dissenting).

"2. TDC's appeal from parts of a preliminary injunction relating to the appearance of counsel substitute at disciplinary hearings involving the plaintiffs and to provision of adequate food to the plaintiffs to prevent weight loss while they were in solitary confinement. We affirmed, concluding that the plaintiffs had been subjected to 'threats, intimidation, coercion, punishment, and discrimination, all in the face of protective orders to the contrary by the district court.' Ruiz v. Estelle, 550 F.2d 238, 239 (5th Cir. 1977) (per curiam) (*Ruiz II*).

"3. TDC's application for a writ of prohibition preventing the transfer of the final portion of the trial from Houston to Tyler. In an unreported order we granted the application. Ruiz v. Estelle, No. — (5th Cir. Feb. 16, 1979) (*Ruiz III*). These proceedings resulted in a three-month break in the middle of the trial. See 503 F.Supp. at 1276 & n. 5.

"4. TDC's appeal from a district court order granting interim attorney's fees. We dismissed the appeal. Ruiz v. Estelle, 609 F.2d 118 (5th Cir. 1980) (*Ruiz IV*). TDC has not appealed from this order as part of its appeal from the final judgment.

"5. TDC's application for a stay of portions of the district court's decree, which we granted in part and denied in part. Ruiz v. Estelle, 650 F.2d 555 (5th Cir. 1981) (per curiam) (*Ruiz V*).

"6. TDC's second application for a stay of portions of the district court's decree, which we granted in part and denied in part. Ruiz v. Estelle, 666 F.2d 854 (5th Cir. 1982) (*Ruiz VI*)."

complaining party must prove that the error was substantial and that it prejudiced his case.

Though the trial judge must be neutral, he should not be a passive spectator. "He is a common law judge having that authority historically exercised by judges in the common law process," and not simply come but to say, "sustained," or "overruled." He may, when in his sound discretion he deems it advisable, comment on the evidence, question witnesses, elicit facts not yet adduced or clarify those previously presented, and maintain the pace of the trial by interrupting or setting time limits on counsel. He must not usurp the role of counsel, but he may manage the trial's course to achieve a "just, speedy, and inexpensive determination" of the action. Fed.R.Civ.P. 1. Obviously he has greater latitude in conducting a bench trial, for then it is his duty to determine the facts, and his conduct cannot influence jurors. In complex and protracted trials like this one, the trial judge must assume even greater responsibility for the direction of the trial than he undertakes in short and simple ones.

Pretrial discovery in this case was exhaustive, the district judge required complete pretrial disclosure of expected testimony, and he limited to some degree the length of cross-examination of a number of witnesses. The trial nevertheless lasted almost a full year. After the plaintiffs had presented all of their witnesses and the United States, as plaintiff-intervenor, had presented most of its witnesses, there was a three-month recess, ample time for TDC to prepare refutation and rebuttal.[31] All of these factors, together with the fact that the judge was the factfinder, must be considered in evaluating TDC's contentions.

The conduct of the district judge is attacked with a barrage of charges. TDC contends that his pretrial orders were more exacting of TDC than of the other parties,[32] and that during pretrial proceedings he was partial to the plaintiffs in many respects. TDC also contends that he excluded much of TDC's evidence,[33] treated TDC's witnesses unfairly in comparison with the treatment accorded the plaintiffs' witnesses, and improperly limited TDC's cross-examinations and rebuttals.[35] TDC contends generally that the record is "permeated with favoritism."

31. TDC also sought and obtained a six-month postponement of the initial trial date.

32. The district court required TDC not only to answer with great specificity the interrogatories put to it by the other parties but also to present pretrial outlines of the testimony TDC expected to elicit from each witness. TDC contends that the burdens imposed on it were "far more onerous than the mere guidelines imposed on the United States." In support of this contention, it does not compare what the district judge exacted of each of these parties, but rather contrasts TDC's "Trial Outline and Supplemental summaries of defense witness testimony" with a compendium of trial outlines furnished by the United States. However, the United States also furnished additional material, permitting TDC to photocopy the United States' witness files, some 30,000 pages.

33. To support its contention, TDC points to one instance in which, over the United States' claim of "surprise," the district judge admitted TDC's evidence and said he would give it minimal weight, and also to four times when he excluded TDC's proffered evidence on the ground of surprise. TDC points with suspicion to the district judge's praise of the United States for opening its files to TDC, and to five instances in which the district judge was presumably partial to the United States because he permitted the United States' witness to testify after only fragmentary pretrial disclosure of his expected testimony.

35. On a number of occasions the district judge informed TDC's cousel that he

Considering the full record of the lengthy trial, we find little probative value in the excluded evidence, and no prejudice in the district judge's rulings. TDC has not pointed to a single instance of the exclusion of defense testimony that was not either repetitive or insignificant in probative value. Error cannot be predicated on an evidentiary ruling unless a substantial right of the objecting party is affected. Fed.R.Evid. 103(a).[36] The district judge was required to make literally thousands of decisions on evidentiary issues, usually without advance notice, memoranda from counsel, or opportunity for independent research. In deciding such matters, trial judges are not expected to be either infallible or clairvoyant. The rules of evidence exact only the attainable, the avoidance of error that is prejudicial and affects a substantial right. This standard was fully met.

One time the district judge showed plaintiffs' counsel how to lay a foundation for testimony and four times he relieved a plaintiffs' lawyer who was having difficulty laying a predicate by asking the necessary questions himself. Doubtless the floundering lawyer eventually could have satisfied the formalities of each objection. Doubtless the need to conform to proper procedure gave the lawyer good, albeit embarrassing, experience. We see no reason, however, why the district judge should have further protracted the trial by requiring the lawyer eventually to master each difficulty alone, for there was no jury to be affected, and the judge himself could deftly cut what was only a technical knot and expedite the trial.

The district judge did credit the testimony of the plaintiffs' witnesses more frequently than that of TDC's witnesses, but in a bench trial the assessment of witness credibility is inherently his province. We are especially reluctant to set aside findings that are based upon a trial judge's determination of the credibility of witnesses giving contradictory accounts.

Neither any one episode pointed out in the briefs nor the weight of all of them cumulatively demonstrates that the trial was unfair. At the outset, the trial judge granted TDC's motion for a six-month postponement of the trial date. At TDC's motion, and for TDC's convenience, he changed the venue of the trial. After the plaintiffs and the United States had rested, he gave TDC three months to prepare its defense. He struck the testimony of the plaintiffs' witness who was shown to have violated the nondiscussion rule.

It is beyond either human capacity or the demands of justice that the trial judge decide correctly every issue arising in the trial. What is required is not a perfect score, but fairness, probity, and the avoidance of substantial prejudice.

considered the TDC's cross-examination of witnesses called by plaintiffs or the United States excessively detailed and lengthy. TDC's brief notes that several times the district judge terminated cross-examination when it lasted longer than he considered appropriate. We note, however, that in each case he did this only after first warning counsel, in some instances repeatedly, that the duration of cross-examination was far exceeding the amount of time taken on direct examination. The cross-examination was protracted. Much time was spent on minor detail. The rebuttal time allowed TDC was virtually unlimited.

36. "Absent a showing that substantial rights of the party were adversely affected, reversal for an erroneous ruling on evidence is not warranted. The burden of demonstrating that such substantial rights were affected is on the party who asserts an error . . . ." Crumpton v. Confederation Life Ins. Co., 672 F.2d 1248, 1253 (5th Cir. 1982). . . .

The first and second consent decrees settled many of the controverted issues, to which much of the trial testimony was devoted. On the matters covered by the consent decrees, their provisions were substantially the same as the remedies outlined by the district judge in his opinion. In addition, TDC does not contest many of the provisions of the district court's decree. Although this acquiescence is in no sense fatal to TDC's claims, it does indicate that TDC in effect concedes the correctness of many provisions in the district court's judgment.

The district judge's rulings appear to have been based only on what he learned from his seat on the bench and his perception of the evidence. Any adverse attitudes that he evinced were based on his performance of his judicial duties. The remarks of some lawyers during the trial carry notes of testiness and personal involvement that go beyond mere diligent representation of a client's interests, but the district judge never became personally embroiled in the proceedings and he presided over them patiently and fairly. We find neither abuse of discretion nor prejudicial error in his conduct of the trial. . . .

The district court, acting sua sponte, on April 12, 1974, "determined that the public interest will be served by the participation of the United States" and ordered the United States to appear as amicus curiae and to participate in this case "with the full rights of a party." W.J. Estelle, the Director of TDC, was then the only defendant. After appearing as amicus curiae, the United States moved in December 1974 to intervene as a party plaintiff under Fed. R.Civ.P. 24(b)(2), and also sought leave to file a complaint in intervention adding new causes of action, and adding the Texas Board of Corrections and its individual members as additional defendants. The United States relied upon "the inherent authority of the United States, through its Attorney General, to sue to remedy severe and widespread deprivations of constitutional rights." The motion was granted ex parte and TDC's later motion to dismiss the United States both as plaintiff-intervenor and as amicus curiae was denied.[51]

Whether or not the United States had inherent or implied authority to sue or to intervene in suits to protect the constitutional rights of individual citizens at the time the intervention was filed, Congress has since enacted the Civil Rights of Institutionalized Persons Act, 42 U.S.C.A. §§ 1997–1997j (West 1981) ("the Act"), which became law on May 23, 1980. The Act authorizes the Attorney General to initiate, id. §§ 1997a–1997b, or intervene in, id. § 1997c, civil actions on behalf of persons confined in specified state institutions, including jails, prisons, and other correctional facilities.

An appellate court must apply the law in effect at the time it renders its decision unless there is statutory language or legislative history to the contrary, or unless doing so would cause manifest injustice. It must apply that law "even where [the statute] does not explicitly recite that it is to be applied to pending cases." The "law" at issue in this case is the Act, particularly § 1997c, which deals with intervention by the United States. . . .

For these reasons, we affirm the district court's order permitting intervention.

51. In re Estelle, 516 F.2d 480 (5th Cir. 1975) (*Ruiz I*), cert. denied, 426 U.S. 925 (1976) (Rehnquist, J., joined by Burger, C.J., & Powell, J., dissenting).

In the original suits filed by individual inmates, only W.J. Estelle, the Director of TDC, was named as defendant. In its complaint in intervention, however, the United States also named as defendants the Texas Board of Corrections and its individual members. Texas law charges the Board of Corrections "with the exclusive management and control of" TDC.

This action was initiated under 42 U.S.C. § 1983, which provides that "[e]very person" who, under color of law, subjects a citizen to deprivation of his federal rights shall be liable to that citizen. The states' eleventh amendment sovereign immunity bars an action in federal court against a state or a state agency unless the state has consented to suit. Congress, in enacting § 1983, did not intend "to override the traditional sovereign immunity of the states." Thus neither states nor state agencies are "persons" within the meaning of § 1983.

The Board of Corrections is merely an agency of the state. It is, therefore, neither a "person" nor, consequently, a proper party defendant. As the United States now concedes, the district court's judgment must be reversed insofar as it casts the Board as a defendant, and the Board, as an entity, must be dismissed from this case.

The individual members of the Board, however, are of course persons. Although the Texas statute vests management of the prison system in the Board, the Board members are responsible as individuals, in the same manner as the Director of TDC, for any violation of constitutional rights caused by their management.[79]

TDC contends that the Board members are superfluous defendants because the Director of TDC is also a defendant and can respond to any court orders. The mere fact that one defendant can pay a judgment or effectuate a court order has never been deemed reason to dismiss other persons who are legally responsible to the plaintiff, and TDC cites no authority for the proposition that one amenable defendant suffices. Accordingly, the joinder of the individual members of the Board was proper.

Before reviewing the findings of fact relative to the charge of cruel and unusual punishment, we set out the legal precepts that we must follow. In Rhodes v. Chapman, 452 U.S. 337 (1981), which was decided after the district court had rendered its opinion and its orders in this case,[80] the Supreme Court considered for the first time the limitation that the eighth amendment, which is applicable to the states through the fourteenth amendment, "imposes upon the conditions in which a State may confine those convicted of crimes." After reviewing "the Eighth Amendment precedents for the general principles that are relevant to a State's authority to impose punishment for criminal conduct," the Court noted that the amendment "prohibits punishments which, although not physically barbarous, 'involve the unnecessary and wan-

79. Gay Student Servs. v. Texas A & M Univ., 612 F.2d 160, 164, 165 (5th Cir.), cert. denied, 449 U.S. 1034 (1980); see Alabama v. Pugh, 438 U.S. 781 (1978) (per curiam); Sessions v. Rusk State Hosp., 648 F.2d at 1069; Spicer v. Hilton, 618 F.2d 232, 236–37 (3d Cir. 1980).

80. The district court entered its original decree granting equitable relief and a declaratory judgment on April 20, 1981, and entered an amended version of this decree on May 1, 1981. It entered its order of reference, appointing the special master and outlining his powers and responsibilities, on April 20, 1981, and entered an amended version of the order of reference on July 24, 1981. *Rhodes* was decided on June 15, 1981.

ton infliction of pain.' " Thus the eighth amendment prohibits inflictions of pain that are " 'totally without penological justification.' "

"No static 'test' can exist by which courts determine whether conditions of confinement are cruel and unusual, for the Eighth Amendment 'must draw its meaning from the evolving standards of decency that mark the progress of a maturing society.' " These " 'judgments should not be, or appear to be, merely the subjective views of individual [judges].' " The judgments instead " 'should be informed by objective factors to the maximum possible extent.' "

The same "principles apply when the conditions of confinement compose the punishment at issue." "[C]onditions that cannot be said to be cruel and unusual under contemporary standards are not unconstitutional. To the extent that such conditions are restrictive and even harsh, they are part of the penalty that criminal offenders pay for their offenses against society."

Applying these precepts, the *Rhodes* Court held that confining two inmates to one cell, called double-celling, at an Ohio maximum security prison was not cruel and unusual punishment. Double-celling was made necessary by an unanticipated increase in prison population. It did not lead to deprivations of essential food, medical care, or sanitation. It did not "increase violence among inmates or create other conditions intolerable for prison confinement." It diminished job and educational opportunities only "marginally."

The Court had previously noted other facts. The cells measured sixty-three square feet. Each had a cabinet-type night stand and other furnishings. Double-celling had not reduced significantly the availability of space in the day rooms or visitation rooms, nor had it rendered the library or school facilities inadequate. There had been no increase in the rate of violence. The ratio of guards to inmates "satisfied the standard of acceptability" offered by the inmates' expert witness.

This review of the opinion makes it evident that Rhodes v. Chapman does not reject the "totality of conditions" test that we applied in Jones v. Diamond, 636 F.2d 1364, 1368 (5th Cir. 1981) (en banc). Like Justice Brennan in his concurring opinion, we read the majority opinion in Rhodes v. Chapman as adopting that test, just as another panel of this court recently did in Stewart v. Winter, 669 F.2d 328, 335–36 & n. 17 (5th Cir. 1982).[96] This interpretation is based not only on the opinion's precise and carefully chosen words but on its factual recitals. Were it necessary to decide only that confining two inmates in a single cell is not cruel and unusual punishment, there would have been no need to describe the general conditions in the prison. *Rhodes* holds that the confinement of two persons in one cell is not per se cruel and unusual when, all prison conditions having been considered "alone or in combination," inmates are not deprived of the "minimal civilized measure of life's necessities." This is also the reading that other courts have given to *Rhodes*. *Rhodes* does, however, hold that the totality of the conditions of confinement does not offend the Constitution unless prison conditions are cruel and unusual, and not merely harsh or restrictive.

96. The *Stewart* panel referred to *Rhodes* and the "totality of the circumstances" test while discussing whether a district judge had properly denied class certification in a lawsuit challenging conditions of confinement in several county jails. That panel did not actually apply the test, as we now do.

These precepts provide the illumination by which we examine those provisions of the district court's decree based on the eighth amendment.

At the time of trial, TDC confined over 26,000 inmates. (The inmate population has since increased to over 33,000.) About 1,000 were sleeping on floors. (None are now on floors but many are confined in tents.) In cells measuring forty-five square feet, originally designed for one occupant, TDC confined two to four inmates. The district court found that assault or molestation by fellow inmates was a continual threat. It found that the population density of inmates confined in dormitories was "shocking."

This overcrowding "exercises a malignant effect on all aspects of inmate life." [101] Day rooms designed for recreational purposes must serve double and even triple the number of inmates for which they were planned. Access to gymnasiums, outdoor playing fields, craft shops, and libraries is even more limited. Dining rooms are nearly always crowded.

Although TDC contends that, because of TDC's "work ethic," inmates spend little of their time in cells or dormitory sleeping areas, in fact inmates spend much of their time in their living quarters. Because of a shortage of civilian guards who can be assigned to supervise inmates working in agricultural programs, the full complement of inmates assigned to work on TDC's farms cannot safely be employed on any given day. "Therefore, at many units, the inmates work on a rotating basis. As many as one-half to three-fourths of the inmate agricultural force will remain idle in the living quarters on a specific day." In view of the "unprecedented surge" in prison population, new facilities being constructed will not eliminate the overcrowding. The district judge emphasized the threat to the inmates' safety, the lack of privacy for inmates, the increase in stress and tension, and the possible spread of disease, all caused by overcrowding.

TDC's prisons are severely understaffed. During the summer of 1979, TDC employed one guard for every 12.45 inmates, one of the worst guard-inmate ratios in the nation; [106] the average nationally is one guard for every five inmates. TDC's argument that its system requires fewer guards than others was rejected by the district court after a detailed analysis of staffing patterns.

Overcrowding, combined with the relatively small number of security guards, results in a "constant threat to the inmates' personal safety." Escapes are virtually unheard of and homicides are uncommon, but there is excessive nonhomicidal violence. "[V]irtually all inmates are exposed to, and many are victimized by, the concomitants of unguarded, overcrowded cells and dormitories—the ever-present risk of assaults, rapes and other violence—for every day of their incarceration at TDC." "TDC inmates are routinely sub-

101. [A]ccord, e.g., Worthington v. Fauver, 88 N.J. 183, 188–189, 440 A.2d 1128, 1130 (1982):

"It is commonly acknowledged that overcrowding in prisons causes grave problems. Rehabilitative programs and recreation become disrupted or nonexistent. As crowding increases, frustration and anger emerge, causing tempers to flare and fights to erupt. Lack of space makes it difficult if not impossible to segregate prisoners for disciplinary and other purposes. Overcrowding can contribute to riots."

106. With the help of additional legislative appropriations, by the time this appeal was heard, there was one guard for every 10.4 inmates. *Ruiz VI,* 666 F.2d at 860.

jected to brutality, extortion, and rape" by their cellmates. "Inmates who live in dormitories are exposed to the same threats of violence endemic to the cells." The threat to inmates in dormitories may be even greater because "[p]otentially assaultive inmates are present in great numbers in every dormitory" and the dormitories are "practically unsupervised." "Numerous examples of the inability of TDC staff to protect inmates' personal safety were graphically presented by credible testimony at the trial."

These conditions result from having too few civilian guards to supervise inmate activities adequately, from inadequate training for new guards, and from a high turnover rate that "results in virtually perpetual vacancies in low-level guard positions."

TDC officials have the power, the district judge found, to reduce TDC's inmate population quickly by increasing "good time" credit, and restoring forfeited good time. Inmates receive incentive ("PIP") points for good performance in work, education, and personal improvement programs. The Board of Pardons and Paroles declines to interview any inmate who has less than a specified number of PIP points, who has suffered a forfeiture of good time that has not been restored, or who is in Class III status. By awarding more PIP points, restoring lost good time, classifying more inmates in Class I status, and preparing favorable "institutional adjustment" reports, TDC officials could increase the number of inmates likely to receive parole. Moreover, TDC has failed to implement in more than a "half-hearted and unimaginative" fashion the work release program authorized by Texas law.

The web of conditions is not seamless. The findings of fact concerning various conditions at TDC are discrete. Moreover, the injunctive relief ordered by the district court includes provisions patently and properly directed at specific conditions. We now consider TDC's challenges to those findings that determine the totality of conditions caused by overcrowding in the presence of the other conditions discussed, particularly the size of the security staff.

The district judge's conclusion that TDC's prisons are seriously overcrowded is virtually conceded. TDC questions only whether this overcrowding constitutes cruel and unusual punishment, whether the remedies ordered are appropriate, and whether specific provisions of the decree are "ill-considered and unwise." TDC challenges the findings concerning the inadequacy of prison security and the existence of staff brutality as being clearly erroneous.

The district judge's findings concerning the specific episodes mentioned in his opinion turn entirely on the credibility of witnesses. On this, as on virtually every other aspect of the case, there was conflicting testimony. There was substantial evidence on the record to support the district judge's findings, and we have been given no reason to overturn them, save the inadequate reason that the testimony of others conflicts. We do not sit to reassess that testimony. This is neither our function as appellate judges nor within our power.

Based on these specific findings, the district judge made other, more general factual findings. He found that the life of the typical inmate within TDC is characterized by a constant threat of violence and that TDC staff members engage in "widespread" brutality of inmates. These findings necessarily are partly conclusory; their accuracy depends on inferences from the specific facts established.

Considering that TDC houses more than 33,000 inmates, it is proper to ask the question that this court put to counsel before oral argument: how many episodes of inmate assault must be shown to warrant the conclusion that there is a constant threat of violence? Patently the trial should not and cannot consist of a review either of every assault over a five-year period or of a day in the life of each of the inmates. The statistics presented are inconclusive. The homicide rate at TDC is less than in many cities. The assault rate is less than the rate reported in other prison cases, but this means only that other prisons are worse. The guard-inmate ratio is among the lowest in the nation. Considering the record as a whole, we are not left with that impression requisite to rejecting the district judge's findings, "the definite and firm conviction" that he was mistaken. . . .

Maximum Population: Effective November 1, 1981.

By November 1, 1981, TDC had to reduce its overall inmate population to a figure equal to twice the number of general population cells, plus the number of inmates who could be housed in dormitories that afford forty square feet (excluding bathing, toilet, and activity areas) per inmate. TDC may not thereafter, until further order of the court, accept any inmate whose confinement would cause the inmate population to exceed that figure.

By November 1, 1982, TDC must reduce its overall inmate population to a figure equal to 1.5 times the number of general population cells, plus the number of inmates who can be housed in dormitories that afford sixty square feet (excluding bathing, toilet, and activity areas) per inmate. TDC may not thereafter, until further order of the court, accept any inmate whose confinement would cause the inmate population to exceed that figure.

By November 1, 1983, TDC must reduce its overall inmate population to a number equal to the number of general population cells, plus the number of inmates who can be housed in dormitories that afford sixty square feet (excluding bathing, toilet, and activity areas) per inmate. TDC may not thereafter, until further order of the court, accept any inmate whose confinement would cause the inmate population to exceed that figure.

By August 1, 1982, no more than 50% of TDC's inmate population housed in cells may be assigned to cells of sixty square feet or less holding two inmates. By August 1, 1983, no inmate may be assigned with another inmate to a cell containing sixty square feet or less.

Beginning November 1, 1981, TDC could not confine any inmate to a dormitory providing less than forty square feet (excluding bathing, toilet, and activity areas) per inmate. By November 1, 1982, TDC may not confine any inmate to a dormitory providing less than sixty square feet (excluding bathing, toilet, and activity areas) per inmate.

To alleviate overcrowding, TDC is required to make maximum use of its authority to house inmates outside of TDC units on the work furlough program as authorized by Tex.Rev.Civ.Stat.Ann. art. 6166x–3 (Vernon 1970 & Cum.Supp.1982). By November 1, 1981, TDC was to have at least 300 inmates on work furlough; by May 1, 1982, TDC was to have at least 1,200 inmates on work furlough; and by November 1, 1982, and thereafter until further order of the court, TDC must at all times have at least 2,500 inmates on work furlough.

TDC must expand its temporary inmate furlough program as authorized by Tex.Rev.Civ.Stat.Ann. art. 6184n(2) (Vernon Cum.Supp.1982). By November 1, 1981, TDC was to have at least 300 inmates on this furlough program; by May 1, 1982, TDC was to have at least 600 inmates on furlough; and by November 1, 1982, and thereafter until further order of the court, TDC must at all times have at least 1,000 inmates on furlough.

TDC must expand its role in community corrections and establish minimum security institutions, honor farms, halfway houses, urban work or educational release centers, community treatment centers, and the like. These facilities must be located in areas near population centers of sufficient size to provide the services needed by inmates at the facilities. By November 1, 1981, TDC was to have filed with the court a plan for the establishment of such facilities with or without the participation of other state or local agencies.

TDC must not make a final selection of a site for, or undertake the construction of, any new units for housing inmates unless it has filed a report with the court demonstrating that specified conditions are met. These conditions require, *inter alia,* that the population of each new TDC unit or sub-unit not exceed 500 inmates, and each new TDC unit must be located within fifty miles of a Standard Metropolitan Statistical Area with a population exceeding 200,000 people.

TDC is prohibited from undertaking construction of any new facilities for the housing of inmates at existing correctional units unless it has filed a report with the court demonstrating, *inter alia,* that the space requirements in Part I of the decree will be met, and that it will be able to recruit and maintain adequate numbers of the employees needed to run the facilities.

TDC must submit a plan providing for the reorganization and decentralization of the management of each TDC unit housing more than 500 inmates, and ensuring that the affected units will be subdivided into units of no more than 500 inmates each.

By August 1, 1981, TDC was required to file with the court a plan and timetable for the training of new security officers and the retraining of existing security officers.

So long as TDC confines more than one inmate to a cell of sixty square feet or less, or to a dormitory, TDC must maintain a classification system that ensures that abuses of inmates by those with whom they live will be minimized. TDC was required, by August 1, 1981, to file with the court a plan setting forth an adequate classification system and a timetable for its implementation.

Although a district court has wide discretion in tailoring a remedial injunction, that discretion is not unconfined. As we have pointed out, the constitutional mandate against cruel and unusual punishment is not a warranty of pleasant prison conditions. Reparative injunctive relief must be targeted at elimination of the unconstitutional conditions. "[T]he nature of the violation determines the scope of the remedy." [139] Therefore, a court can order only relief sufficient to correct the violation found. We have neither commission nor competence to prescribe the purposes of confinement.

As a matter of respect for the state's role and for the allocation of functions in our federal system, as well as comity toward the state, the relief ordered by federal courts must be "consistent with the policy of minimum intrusion into the affairs of state prison administration that the Supreme Court has articulated for the federal courts." *Ruiz V.* "[T]he principles of federalism which play such an important part in governing the relationship between federal courts and state governments" are applicable "where injunctive relief is sought . . . against those in charge of an executive branch of an agency of state" government.[142] We should, therefore, fashion "the least intrusive remedy that will still be effective." [143] In shaping that remedy, we must also, as a matter of judicial administration, regard the essential nature of federal courts in an adversary system. Our remedial powers are inherently judicial, not administrative.

The experienced district judge gave lengthy and careful attention both to the trial of this case and to the fashioning of the reparative injunction. In many respects the decree he shaped is focused directly on steps to remedy the aspects of confinement that together make it cruel and unusual. In other respects the decree is, as the district court's order of reference to the special master recites, "infinitely broader than that encountered in any other example of correctional litigation." Considering both the constitutional violations to be excised and the scope of the therapy directed, we are left with the conviction that, without the guidance now provided by Rhodes v. Chapman, the district court adopted some remedies that are not essential for the elimination of unconstitutional prison conditions. Taken as a whole, the district court's decree administers a massive curative dose when it is not yet demonstrable that a lesser therapeutic measure would not suffice. Conservative treatment is essential because it is more readily administered, less costly to the state, and not irreversible. Therefore, the remedy should begin with what is absolutely necessary. If these measures later prove ineffective, more stringent ones should be considered. We turn now to the specifics.

Neither the number of inmates in one cell nor the amount of space provided for an inmate in a dormitory alone determines whether confinement is cruel and unusual. See *Ruiz VI.* If an inmate uses his living quarters only for sleeping, and is not threatened with violence, a single bunk space, eighteen or twenty square feet, may be adequate. The district judge found that the crowding of persons, the consequent effect on prison services and facilities, and the lack of security are specific conditions that combine to make confinement at TDC uncivilized and inhumane. However, we cannot know

139. Swann v. Charlotte-Mecklenburg Bd. of Educ., 402 U.S. 1, 16 (1971).

142. Rizzo v. Goode, 423 U.S. 362, 380 (1976).

143. Special Project, supra, 78 Colum. L.Rev. at 869; accord, Resident Advisory Bd. v. Rizzo ("federal equitable relief must be carefully tailored to be no more intrusive than is necessary to remedy proved constitutional violations"); see Dayton Bd. of Educ. v. Brinkman, 433 U.S. at 419–20; Hills v. Gautreaux, 425 U.S. 284, 293–94 (1976); Morgan v. Kerrigan, 530 F.2d 401, 429 (1st Cir.) ("the most reliable and least intrusive method"), cert. denied 426 U.S. 935 (1976).

whether the provision of additional guards and the consequent increase both in inmate security and in work opportunities, the diminished role of building tenders, and the various other remedial measures either incorporated in the consent decrees or approved by us elsewhere in this opinion will sufficiently relieve the conditions that combined to make double-celling cruel and unusual, with the result that confinement of two inmates to one forty-five-foot cell will be only the harshness sanctioned by *Rhodes,* or whether it will still be cruel and unusual. Current estimates for maximum security prison cells suggest that their cost ranges from $30,000 to $60,000 apiece. Approximately 10,000 additional cells would be required to house in a single cell every person now in a double cell less than sixty square feet in area. These additional cells, therefore, could cost at least $300,000,000 and require three to four years or more to build. Prisons once built cannot be readily adapted to other governmental uses.

Constitutional rights are not, of course, confined to those available at modest cost.[147] The very concept of federalism, the division of powers among the branches of the federal government, and the nature of the safeguards imposed by the Bill of Rights and the fourteenth amendment levy costs impossible for an accountant to calculate, but esteemed by us because they are literally priceless.

Yet in considering remedies for unconstitutional deprivation, the cost of one proposed remedy in comparison with the cost of others and the demonstrable need for the remedy should both be considered.[148] A remedy imposing great cost on a state should not be ordered unless its constitutional need has been demonstrated. Although we recognize the great discretion accorded a trial judge in fashioning remedies, the district judge here lacked the guidance of Rhodes v. Chapman and failed to consider the cost of the remedial measures ordered as well as the possibility of achieving constitutional conditions without requiring single-celling.

We turn to the dormitory space limitation. Neither sixty square feet, nor forty square feet, nor any other measure is constitutionally ordained. Yet the facts found serve as adequate basis to require more space for inmates confined in dormitories, not only to ameliorate living conditions but, more important, to enhance security and reduce violence. An inmate in a cell with one other person is exposed to assault only by that person; an inmate in an overcrowded dormitory having an inadequate security staff may be victimized by many. Moreover, a forty-square-feet-per-inmate dormitory space requirement will not occasion vast expense. At present, TDC is, by use of tents, providing forty square feet for most dormitory inmates. Only 128 inmates are confined in dormitories that house more than they would if there were forty square feet per inmate.

147. Todaro v. Ward, 565 F.2d 48, 54 n. 8 (2d Cir. 1977); Finney v. Arkansas Bd. of Correction. . . .

148. See Wright v. Rushen, 642 F.2d 1129, 1134 (9th Cir. 1981); Battle v. Anderson, 594 F.2d 786, 792 (10th Cir. 1979); Campbell v. McGruder, 580 F.2d 521, 540 (D.C.Cir. 1978); McMurry v. Phelps, 533 F.Supp. 742, 769 (W.D.La.1982); cf. Scott v. Illinois, 440 U.S. 367, 373 (1979) (appointment of counsel); Bounds v. Smith, 430 U.S. 817, 825 (1977) (access to courts). See generally Weinberger v. Romero-Barcelo ("In exercising their sound discretion, courts of equity should pay particular regard for the public consequences in employing the extraordinary remedy of injunction.").

The requirement of sixty square feet per inmate, however, would necessitate the construction of facilities for 2,831 additional inmates. If it costs only $10,000 per inmate to construct a dormitory instead of the $30,000 amount used to estimate the cost of constructing cells, the construction of dormitories for these additional inmates would cost almost $30,000,000.

It has not been demonstrated that provision of additional security guards and the other measures required by the district court's decree and the two consent decrees will not remedy the constitutional deficiency. It appears desirable, therefore, first to undertake measures that will not be both costly and irreversible. If these measures do not work, then additional ones may be necessary. This "wait and see" approach ensures that the intrusion into state processes will be no greater than that required to achieve compliance with the Constitution.

Accordingly, we affirm the provisions of the district court's decree that restrict TDC's acceptance of inmates to be housed in dormitories to those inmates who can be accommodated with a space of at least forty square feet. We vacate the provisions of the decree that require (1) single-celling and (2) sixty square feet per inmate in dormitories. This is without prejudice to the right of plaintiffs and plaintiff-intervenor to move for a further hearing, to be held one year after our order becomes effective, to determine whether, despite changes in prison conditions wrought as a result of it, compliance with constitutional requirements requires additional restrictions on inmate capacity. This is also without prejudice to the correlative right of TDC to seek a relaxation of the decree if TDC can demonstrate that the Constitution does not compel continuance of the decree.

The mandate that TDC must use good time, parole, and furlough programs to relieve overcrowding unnecessarily invades the management responsibility of state officials. Moreover, it requires detailed supervision of programs that relate only indirectly to the conditions of confinement. Directing state officials to achieve specific results should suffice; how they will achieve those results must be left to them unless and until it can be demonstrated judicial intervention is necessary. They may elect to balance prison population and physical facilities by parole, furloughs, pardons, confinement in county institutions, use of minimum security institutions for some inmates, changes in sentencing policies, or in other ways.

However inefficient the management of large prisons may be when compared with the administration of smaller ones, and however desirable it may be to locate prisons near large communities, the failure to do either does not cause confinement to be cruel and unusual. Palaces may be erected in the wilderness. Large prisons may be impersonal but they are not necessarily inhumane. There is of course some relationship between the new-facilities provisions of the district court's decree and the amelioration of prison conditions, but the measure of therapeutic effect is patently small. The effect of these remedial measures does not appear to us sufficient to warrant their economic cost, their intrusion on state decisionmaking, or the supervisory burden that their administration would impose on a federal court. . . .

The decree specifies how correctional officers will be schooled. If correctional officers are hired and trained, we must assume, until the contrary is shown, that they will be both trained and utilized with some minimal degree of wisdom. If, after they are employed, it is demonstrated that TDC officials are still violating inmates' constitutional rights, additional steps can then be taken. Here again, we deem the "wait and see" policy, rather than radical surgery, more in keeping with the constitutionally reparative function of the injunction.

Accordingly, we vacate [the pertinent section] of the district court's decree. This is without prejudice to the right of plaintiffs and plaintiff-intervenor to move for a further hearing, to be held one year from the date our order becomes effective, seeking further relief, or the correlative right of TDC to seek relaxation of the decree.

The decree requires only the filing of a plan. We affirm this provision of the decree without prejudice to the right of any party to object to the plan or to any court order adopted after the plan is submitted.[153]

The first consent decree disposes of all issues pertaining to medical care except the provision in the district court's decree restricting the use of Huntsville Unit Hospital ("HUH") to infirmary purposes, prohibiting treatment at HUH of inmates from any unit other than Huntsville, and requiring TDC to provide inmates with adequate hospital facilities meeting the Standards of the Texas Hospital Association ("THA") or the Joint Commission on Accreditation of Hospitals ("JCAH"). We, therefore, consider only conditions at HUH.

The state has an "obligation to provide medical care for those whom it is punishing by incarceration." "[A]cts or omissions sufficiently harmful to evidence deliberate indifference to serious medical needs" of inmates constitute cruel and unusual punishment. Neither inadvertent failure to provide adequate medical care, nor carelessness, nor even deliberate failure to conform to the standards suggested by experts is cruel and unusual punishment. The Constitution does not command that inmates be given the kind of medical attention that judges would wish to have for themselves, nor the therapy that Medicare and Medicaid provide for the aged or the needy. It prohibits only "deliberate indifference to serious medical needs."

HUH is not an accredited hospital. It is outmoded and inadequate. There was testimony that the effects of inadequate physical facilities are aggravated by deficiencies in sanitation and infection control; the number of physicians is inadequate; and TDC improperly relies on inmate medical assistants, who lack adequate training, for medical care. Inmate assistants have amputated fingers, set bones, applied casts, sutured wounds, repaired Achilles' tendons, given injections, administered medications, and kept records. Inmates, in many instances lacking adequate training, also serve as laboratory technicians, X-ray technicians, physical therapists, respiratory therapists, first aid attendants, and medical records clerks. Many of the inmates assigned to these tasks are uneducated and some are illiterate. The district court found "numerous" instances of "[g]rievous neglect of the personal care of patients at the HUH," but nothing in the findings indicates either that these are immanent in the hospital or that they are not remediable by a larger and better-trained staff.

153. Cf. Rhodes v. Chapman, 452 U.S. at 344 n. 9 (district court rejected five plans filed by defendants, then ordered defendants to implement court's plan).

JCAH standards are applied to hospitals in Texas by THA. Although HUH does not meet these standards, the record establishes that no prison hospital in any other state does. Some Federal Bureau of Prisons hospitals meet them but others do not. Of the 7,000 private hospitals in the United States, only 3,000 meet JCAH standards adequately for full accreditation and an additional 1,000 are on probation or one-year accreditation; the other 3,000 are not accredited because they do not meet the standards. Literally millions of persons receiving private medical care are being treated in hospitals that do not meet the requirements imposed by the district court's decree.

Expert standards are a useful guide but they are not a constitutional measure. Restricting use of HUH to Huntsville inmates and permitting it to render only infirmary care do not solve the medical care problem. Moreover, there have been additional developments since the district court issued its decree. By orders dated October 19, 1981, and November 5, 1981, the district court stayed the provision of its decree pertaining to HUH. In its October 19 order, the district court directed TDC to file a formal response to particular suggestions made by the plaintiffs concerning HUH. TDC filed this response. In the court's November 5 order, TDC's response is described as exhibiting "a commendable air of conciliation." That order further directs the parties to meet and discuss possible agreement on continued operation of HUH.

Accordingly, we vacate the provision of the district court's decree pertaining to the HUH and remand that issue to the district court for further proceedings consistent with this opinion after the district court has received a report concerning the results of the discussion it has ordered. Should the district court consider injunctive relief still necessary, its order shall not command the closing of HUH or restrict its use solely to Huntsville inmates. The order should instead be limited to requiring that TDC provide the minimum level of hospital care required by the Constitution. . . .

Ready access to the courts is a "fundamental constitutional right." Regulations and practices that unjustifiably obstruct such access are invalid. Access to courts entails not only freedom to file pleadings but also freedom to employ, without retaliation or harassment, those accessories without which legal claims cannot be effectively asserted: a law library containing basic legal materials; legal assistance both from lawyers and from other inmates; and the ability to communicate with courts, attorneys, and public officials.

The district court found "a persistent pattern of TDC interference with attempts by inmates to pursue legal actions." Although the disruption is not uniform throughout TDC, "[p]ractices and policies at the various units significantly restrict the times and places inmates may work on legal matters, severely inhibit communication among inmates about legal matters, encumber inmate efforts to have legal papers notarized, encourage the discriminatory harassment of inmates who take their grievances to court, and intrude on the communications between attorneys and their inmate clients." At some units, inmates were forbidden to work on legal matters during their free time in their cells or even to keep any legal papers there; at others, inmates were permitted to do legal work only in their cells, where they were crowded, lacked a desk or other firm writing surface, and often lacked books. The district court found that space limitations in TDC's libraries do not justify

TDC's restrictive access rules as applied, for there were frequently empty seats in the libraries. The court held that strip searches of inmates entering or leaving the library were unwarranted harassment.

TDC argues that the district court was "apparently willing to listen to only one side of the story" on this issue. It contends also that the practices condemned by the district court were not "adopted and enforced by the official defendants." This argument, however, is but a comment on the court's evaluation of credibility; for, although TDC officials testified to the contrary, there was ample evidence to support the district court's conclusions.

Although systemwide injunctive relief may not be predicated on individual misconduct that "is not part of a pattern of persistent and deliberate official policy," an institutional practice may be sufficiently prevalent to warrant such relief even though it is not embodied in regulations or imposed by official fiat. Executives have a duty to control their subordinates.

The evidence was sufficient to warrant the inference drawn by the district court that, although the disruptive policies he found were not formally sanctioned, they occurred so frequently and were so pervasive that they reflected a pattern of misconduct. While the case was pending, the district judge issued five separate protective orders to minimize what he found to be TDC harassment of the plaintiffs and witnesses in this case. On the record before us, we cannot conclude that the district court's findings were clearly erroneous.

The district court's decree enjoins TDC from unlawfully interfering with inmates' access to courts, counsel, and public officials. The decree prohibits censorship of attorney-client mail, ensures confidential attorney-client interviews, prohibits retaliation against inmates who complain of prison conditions or official misconduct, and requires that inmates have access to services and materials that would help them process their legal matters. TDC does not contend that any of these provisions of the decree exceeds the district court's authority. Because TDC has failed to eliminate these prevalent practices, which it contends it has never condoned, these provisions were appropriate.

TDC contends that, after our decision in Corpus v. Estelle, 551 F.2d 68 (5th Cir. 1977), TDC's practice of prohibiting inmates from giving or receiving actual legal assistance to or from each other was terminated. Whether or not all vestiges of this practice have been eliminated, the injunction that we affirmed in *Corpus* provides an adequate remedy for it. The decree in this case, therefore, must be modified to eliminate the duplication. We do not find the district court's remedy in other respects either disproportionate to the conditions found or unduly intrusive on the state. Therefore, we affirm Part V of the district court's decree, except for Part V(J), which we vacate.

The district court found a number of violations of inmates' right to due process in the administration of prison discipline. Some of these violations have been remedied by the first consent decree; others are addressed in Part IV of the district court's decree. In this appeal, apart from the provisions dealing with administrative segregation, TDC objects only to a prophylactic provision that requires it to tape record or in some other way make a verbatim record of all disciplinary hearings, preserve the recordings for at least one year, and follow prescribed procedures for making the recordings available to inmates or their legal representatives.[200]

TDC correctly points out that Wolff v. McDonnell holds that the Constitution requires only "a 'written statement by the factfinders as to the evidence relied on and reasons' for the disciplinary action." It does not require tape recordings. TDC argues that the possibility that a recording would be released might inhibit the willingness of inmates to testify against other inmates. It also argues that the existence of recordings creates the possibility of inadvertent disclosure of confidential information by counsel or a TDC employee.

The district court found that TDC had not maintained adequate written records of its disciplinary proceedings. Its decree is aimed directly at preventing any recurrence of that constitutional lapse.[203] Nothing in the decree forbids TDC to take measures to ensure the confidentiality of the recordings. Indeed the district court took account of security concerns by permitting TDC to exclude from release to an inmate any portion of a recording containing material that was recorded while the inmate "was excluded from the hearing for security reasons."

It is well-settled that, under the fourteenth amendment, a court may require remedial measures that the Constitution does not of its own force initially require.[204] Injunctive relief need not be confined to an order to cease an illegal practice. Once a constitutional violation has been proved, the court may, if necessary, exert its equitable power to prevent repetition of the violation, not only by the force of the contempt sanction but also by commanding measures that safeguard against recurrence.[205] The tape recording provision imposes little expense or inconvenience on TDC, does not change the manner in which state officials discharge their duties, is narrowly focused to prevent repetition of a proved constitutional violation, and is not unnecessarily intrusive on state functions. The district court did not, therefore, abuse its discretion by imposing this requirement. . . .

The district court's order of reference appoints a special master and provides for the appointment of "several monitors" to help the special master. It imposes on the special master the responsibility of seeing that the district court's decree is implemented, and empowers him to hold hearings, find

200. The district court explained the rationale behind this provision:

"Given TDC's failure to observe the requirements of due process, as well as its own written rules, in conducting disciplinary hearings, all such hearings which it conducts in the future must be recorded by tape recorder or by an equally efficient method."

203. Cf. Hutto v. Finney ("[T]aking the long and unhappy history of the litigation into account, the court was justified in entering a comprehensive order to insure against the risk of inadequate compliance."); Hoptowit v. Ray, 682 F.2d at 1247 ("a record of past constitutional violations and violations of past court orders").

204. See, e.g., North Carolina State Bd. of Educ. v. Swann, 402 U.S. 43, 46 (1971); Swann v. Charlotte-Mecklenburg Bd. of Educ., 402 U.S. at 15–16. "To prevent further constitutional deprivations, a court may order forms of relief not normally required by the Constitution but nevertheless necessary given the circumstances if the court's efforts are to be successful." Smith v. Sullivan, 611 F.2d 1039, 1044 (5th Cir. 1980).

205. See Smith v. Sullivan, 611 F.2d at 1044 ("[T]he federal courts have the power, and the duty, to make their intervention effective.").

facts, and make recommendations to the district court concerning TDC's compliance with the decree. As authority for the appointment the district court invoked both Fed.R.Civ.P. 53 [233] and its inherent power as a court of equity.

TDC contends that the appointment of a special master was improper because the district court failed to comply with rule 53, which, according to TDC, codifies and limits a court's authority to appoint a special master.[234] Rule 53(b) states that a district court may appoint a special master "only upon a showing that some exceptional condition requires" the appointment.[235]

The district court stated several reasons for its decision to make the appointment: the difficulty of superintending the implementation of "a comprehensive, detailed plan for the elimination of the unconstitutional conditions found to exist in the Texas prison system"; TDC's "record of intransigence toward previous court orders requiring changes in TDC's practices and conditions"; the "strained" working relations between TDC's lawyers and the plaintiffs' lawyers; TDC's failure to acknowledge even "completely evident" constitutional violations; and TDC's failure to conform its actual practices to its written policies and procedures. The district court did not, as TDC implies, simply rely on the "mere complexity" of the case.[238] Moreover, the court was not required to await the failure or refusal of TDC to comply with the decree before appointing an agent to implement it. Noncompliance may constitute one "exceptional condition" under rule 53, but it is not exclusive.

Furthermore, rule 53 does not terminate or modify the district court's inherent equitable power to appoint a person, whatever be his title, to assist it in administering a remedy.[240] The power of a federal court to appoint an

233. Rule 53 [is in the Appendix].

234. We reject TDC's suggestion that rule 53 does not permit the post-decretal appointment of a special master. Although rule 53 is concerned primarily with the appointment of a special master "as a factfinder *in advance of* the court's remedial decree or as an expert to recommend the amount of damages or other remedial relief after a finding of liability," Nathan, The Use of Masters in Institutional Reform Litigation, 10 Tol.L. Rev. 419, 428 (1979) (emphasis added), we have implicitly ratified reliance on rule 53 as authority for post-decretal appointment of a special master. Gary W. v. Louisiana, 601 F.2d 240, 243–45 (5th Cir. 1979); accord, Palmigiano v. Garrahy, 443 F.Supp. 956, 986, 989 (D.R.I.1977).

235. One article argues that rule 53's "exceptional conditions" requirement, as interpreted in La Buy v. Howes Leather Co., 352 U.S. 249 (1957), does not even apply in cases like this one. "The *La Buy* restrictions do not . . . bar the use of expert special masters in institutional reform cases. The policy considerations that support *La Buy's* interpretation of rule 53 are absent when resort is had to expert masters after the violations of the defendant institution have been determined." Special Project, supra, 78 Colum.L.Rev. at 807. This article does, however, state that "the use of masters in such cases must nonetheless meet the general rule 53[(b)] requirement that references to masters be the exception and not the rule." Id. at 808; cf. Gary W. v. Louisiana, 601 F.2d at 244 (quoting district court's recitation of facts justifying the "exception[al]" act of appointing a special master).

238. We note, however, that the sheer size of the Texas prison system could be found to pose special difficulties in implementing a remedial decree. As TDC says in its brief: "TDC administers the largest prison system in the United States. With an inmate population of over 29,000 [now with 33,000], TDC is larger even than the Federal Bureau of Prisons, which maintains facilities in every state in the Union." The plaintiffs' brief says that "about one of every ten American prisoners is confined in [TDC] units."

240. "Beyond the provisions of [Fed. R.Civ.P. 53] for appointing and making references to Masters, a Federal District Court has 'the inherent power to supply itself with this instrument for the administration of justice when deemed by it es-

agent to supervise the implementation of its decrees has long been established.[241] Such court-appointed agents have been identified by "a confusing plethora of titles: 'receiver,' 'Master,' 'Special Master,' 'master hearing officer,' 'monitor,' 'human rights committee,' 'Ombudsman,'" and others. The function is clear, whatever the title.

The district court's opinion stated the reasons for the appointment of the special master and his monitors. As it noted, we have previously approved the appointment of such agents to oversee compliance with continuing court orders.[244] Insofar as the special master is to report on TDC's compliance with the district court's decree and to help implement the decree, he assumes one of the plaintiffs' traditional roles, except that, because he is the court's agent, he can and should perform his duties objectively.

In its order of reference, the district court describes the special master's duties as entailing "enormous responsibilities." The decree affects twenty-two TDC units, with a staff of more than 3,000 and housing more than 33,000 inmates. The scope and complexity of the decree and the importance as well as the difficulty of ensuring compliance gave the court adequate reason to invoke its implied authority as a court of equity. Therefore we affirm the district court's decision to appoint the special master and his monitors to observe and report on TDC's compliance.

The special master is also given powers that are quasijudicial. He is permitted to hold hearings and is directed to find facts "concerning the defendants' compliance with the provisions of the Court's Orders and the need, if

sential.'" Schwimmer v. United States, 232 F.2d 855, 865 (8th Cir.) (quoting In re Peterson, 253 U.S. 300, 311 (1920), cert. denied, 352 U.S. 833 (1956); accord, Veneri v. Draper, 22 F.2d 33, 35 (4th Cir. 1927) ("the power is inherent in the federal courts independently of any statute"), cert. denied, 276 U.S. 633 (1928); Kaufman, Masters in the Federal Courts: Rule 53, 58 Colum.L.Rev. 452, 462 (1958) ("Over and above the authority contained in rule 53 to direct a reference, there has always existed in the federal courts an inherent authority to appoint masters as a natural concomitant of their judicial power."); see Reed v. Cleveland Bd. of Educ., 607 F.2d 737, 746 (6th Cir. 1979); Powell v. Ward, 487 F.Supp. 917, 935 (S.D.N.Y.1980), aff'd per curiam as modified, 643 F.2d 924 (2d Cir.), cert. denied, 454 U.S. 832 (1981); Jordan v. Wolke, 75 F.R.D. 696, 701 (E.D.Wis.1977); Connecticut Importing Co. v. Frankfort Distilleries, Inc., 42 F.Supp. 225, 227 (D.Conn. 1940). Compare Arthur Murray, Inc. v. Oliver, 364 F.2d 28, 32 (8th Cir. 1966) with Nathan, supra, 10 Tol.L.Rev. at 426–33. See generally Note, Force and Will: An Exploration of the Use of Special Masters To Implement Judicial Decrees, 52 U.Colo.L.Rev. 105, 109–11 (1980).

241. See In re Peterson, 253 U.S. at 312–14; Newman v. Alabama, 559 F.2d at 290 (appointment of master and several monitors suggested as "appropriate steps to ensure compliance with [district court's] decree"); Sun Theatre Corp. v. RKO Radio Pictures, Inc., 213 F.2d 284, 293 (7th Cir. 1954); Kroese v. General Steel Castings Corp., 179 F.2d 760, 764 (3d Cir.), cert. denied, 339 U.S. 983 (1950); Special Project, supra, 78 Colum.L.Rev. at 831.

244. 503 F.Supp. at 1390 (citing Gates v. Collier, 501 F.2d at 1321); see Miller v. Carson, 401 F.Supp. 835, 841 (M.D.Fla. 1975), aff'd in part, modified in part, and remanded, 563 F.2d 741, 752–53 (5th Cir. 1977); Newman v. Alabama, 559 F.2d at 290; Gary W. v. Louisiana, 601 F.2d at 244–45. TDC's reliance on United States v. City of Parma, supra, is misplaced. In that case, the district court appointed a special master "upon its own motion," and there was "no support . . . in the record" for the district court's conclusion that a special master was necessary for the orderly resolution of the case. 661 F.2d at 578. Moreover, the court noted that the appointment of a special master was "antithetical to the recommendations of" the plaintiff's own chief witness on remedy. Id. None of these circumstances is present in this case.

any, for supplemental remedial action." The order also establishes rules of procedure: the monitors are to make reports of factual observations and to submit them to the special master and the parties. If any party objects, the special master is to hold a hearing, then make his report to the district court. No objection may be filed to the special master's report that could have been filed to the monitor's report preceding it. The special master's findings of fact are to be accepted by the court unless clearly erroneous. In addition, the special master may hold hearings sua sponte without a preliminary monitor's report; and in such instances factual findings in his reports are to be credited unless clearly erroneous. He may, moreover, submit reports based on his own observations and investigations without conducting a hearing. The order of reference does not distinguish between the credit to be given such reports and those submitted after hearings and accompanied by an evidentiary record.

To fulfill his responsibilities, the special master is given sweeping powers, including "unlimited access" to TDC premises and records as well as the power to conduct "confidential interviews" with TDC staff members and inmates, and to require written reports from any TDC staff member. These powers are unconfined save by the following instructions: he is not to intervene in the administrative management of either TDC or any of its units and he is not to direct the defendants or any of their subordinates to take or to refrain from taking any specific action to achieve compliance.

The order of reference does not make clear that, in conducting investigations and hearings, the special master and the monitors are not to consider matters that go beyond superintending compliance with the district court's decree. Such an express constraint is appropriate because of the danger that the special master or the monitors may entertain inmate complaints that convert the remedial process into a surrogate forum for new § 1983 actions. In the interests both of prison administration and sound judicial procedure, it should be made clear to the plaintiffs, the special master, the monitors, and the TDC staff that the special master is not an inmate advocate or a roving federal district court. . . . [T]he powers of the court's appointed agent should not intrude to an unnecessary extent on prison administration.

In one respect, the order of reference is too sweeping. It permits the special master to submit to the district court "reports based upon his own observations and investigations in the absence of a formal hearing before him." This not only transcends the powers traditionally given masters by courts of equity, but denies the parties due process.

Accordingly, the order of reference shall be amended as follows: (1) it should be made clear that the special master and the monitors do not have the authority to hear matters that should appropriately be the subject of separate judicial proceedings, such as actions under § 1983, and that their duties are restricted to those set forth in the order of reference; and (2) unless based on hearings conducted on the record after proper notice, the reports, findings, and conclusions of the special master are not to be accorded any presumption of correctness and the "clearly erroneous" rule will not apply to them.

Finally, the reduction in the scope of the district court's decree directed by this opinion should occasion further inquiry by the district court to determine whether or not there is a continuing need for a staff of six monitors to assist the special master.

The Federal Constitution is a charter for all officials, federal and state. All those who wield the power of the sovereign must be equally obedient to its commands and faithful in ensuring its protections. They take the same oath we do—to uphold and to defend it.

The judicial determination has been made. The reparative injunction will require time, skill, and intensive effort. The district court and its special master must respect the right of the state to administer its own affairs so long as it does not violate the Constitution. The state must equally recognize the duty of the district court and the special master as its agent to ensure the restoration of constitutional conditions of confinement in TDC. The implemention of the district court's decree can become a ceaseless guerrilla war, with endless hearings, opinions, and appeals, and incalculable costs. But it is instead to be hoped that, if the state adopts the policy that inmates must be accorded their constitutional rights and that prison officials will not be permitted to indulge in petty practices designed to deny those rights, the period of judicial supervision can more speedily be concluded. To this end, it may not be inappropriate to include the exhortation that constitutional peace is the consummation devoutly to be wished as a result of *Ruiz VII*. . . .

APPENDIX A

UNITED STATES DISTRICT COURT
SOUTHERN DISTRICT OF TEXAS
HOUSTON DIVISION

DAVID RUIZ, ET AL., Plaintiffs, UNITED STATES OF AMERICA, Plaintiff-Intervenor v. W.J. ESTELLE, JR., ET AL., Defendants.	CIVIL ACTION NO. H–78–987

CONSENT DECREE

Pursuant to the Order of the Court of December 12, 1980, the parties to this cause have met and agreed, through counsel, as hereafter set out, on the provisions of an injunctive Order to be entered regarding the areas covered by their agreement. The Defendants have entered into such agreement with the express understanding that their agreement is not an admission of liability in any sense, and particularly is not an admission of bad faith. Further, Defendants expressly make it known that in their view the agreement hereafter set out in some respects goes beyond minimal, constitutional requirements, but they have entered into said agreement in a good faith effort to terminate this litigation in the areas covered by the agreement and to preclude the need for appeal as to such areas. Defendants, however, in executing this agreement expressly reserve the right to withdraw their consent thereto as to any part of this agreement which is not incorporated in the form hereafter set out in the final Order of the Court to be entered for the purpose of effectuating said agreement.

The major areas covered by this Decree are in full and complete compromise and settlement of any and all claims regarding such areas and, if Defendants fully comply with the provisions of this Decree, Plaintiffs and Plaintiff-Intervenor agree that neither will request any further relief from the Court on any of these areas except (1) as to the status of the Huntsville Hospital facility and conditions of administrative segregation confinement (extent of recreation; number of prisoners in administrative segregation cells and prohibition of routine use of administrative segregation pending disciplinary hearings) and (2) past, present and future individual claims of class members. Plaintiffs and Plaintiff-Intervenor agree that enforcement of this Decree will be limited to appropriate motions to effectuate the provisions of this Decree. No additional requirements beyond those expressly stated in the Decree will be requested of the Court except to the extent necessary to enforce the provisions of this Decree. Construction of the Decree will be governed by the ordinary and reasonable interpretation of the language therein so as to preclude any strained interpretation, the effect of which is to incorporate standards or relief beyond that agreed to in the Decree.

Accordingly, upon the Stipulation of the parties, dated as of February 10, 1981, Defendants, their successors, agents and employees (referred to collectively as "Defendants") are hereby ENJOINED as follows:

I. *HEALTH CARE*

A. Based on a survey of the medical, dental, and psychiatric needs of the Texas Department of Corrections (TDC) population, Defendants will by June 1, 1981, prepare and file with the Court a plan which will assure that prisoners receive necessary medical, dental and psychiatric care from the moment of their arrival in TDC. The plan shall include provision for:

"1. prompt identification of immediate needs for medical, dental and psychiatric care;

"2. compliance with American Medical Association (AMA) Standards for Health Services in Prison (July 1979), including a plan for implementation;

"3. development of standards for architectural, engineering, or equipment needs of prison health care facilities to the extent they are not addressed by the AMA Standards;

"4. accreditation by the Joint Commission on Accreditation of Hospitals (JCAH) of the TDC–UTMB Hospital (expected to be operational by May 30, 1982);

"5. adequate inpatient and outpatient psychiatric and other psychological care, including the provision of appropriate facilities for that purpose;

"6. a system to assure that no prisoner is assigned to do work that is contraindicated for his medical condition; and

"7. full access to health care for all prisoners, regardless of segregation status."

B. Defendants shall assure that no nonmedical staff may countermand any medical order regarding a prisoner's treatment, work or other related circumstances.

C. No prisoner shall be denied access to work, recreation, education or other programs or opportunities because of health status unless required for medical reasons as determined by a licensed physician.

D. No prisoner who arrives with medication and a prescription therefor will be deprived of that medication until a licensed physician has examined him and made a medical determination regarding continuation of that medication.

E. Subject to the review of the Court to assure compliance with AMA standards, Defendants shall:

"1. Initiate a program of accreditation by the AMA through an initial evaluation by the AMA pursuant to the AMA Standards, supra, to begin April 1, 1981 and to be completed by August 1, 1981. The results of that evaluation will be reported in writing to the Court by November 15, 1981. The report will identify areas of compliance and noncompliance and will recommend means of complying.

"2. Defendants will then prepare a plan for making TDC health care services and facilities accreditable, including a schedule for implementation. The plan will be filed with the Court on or before February 1, 1982. Every four months thereafter, until TDC health services and facilities are first accredited, Defendants will report progress in implementing the plan to the Court.

"3. As per paragraph A, 3, supra, to the extent the AMA Standards may not address architectural, engineering, or equipment needs of prison health care facilities, Defendants will obtain the services of the Texas Hospital Association in developing standards for facilities and equipment. Defendants will file such standards with the Court by January 2, 1982. Thereafter, all TDC medical facilities will be equipped consistent with the standards and all new health care facility construction will be consistent with the standards."

F. By September 1, 1981, Defendants will file with the Court a plan for the development of new or alternative facilities for housing inmates in need of chronic care or acute psychological and psychiatric care.

II. *SPECIAL NEEDS PRISONERS*

Special needs prisoners shall be defined as those who are mentally retarded, physically handicapped, developmentally disabled or require psychological or psychiatric care. Defendants will provide all special needs prisoners with adequate medical care, adequate living facilities and working conditions (if appropriate), fair discipline, and protection from other prisoners. By September 1, 1981, Defendants will file with the Court a plan which includes provision for:

"1. a system for adequately identifying special needs prisoners and for evaluating their needs;

"2. individualized treatment and placement plans appropriate for such prisoners' needs and assurances for their implementation;

"3. architectural modifications of portions of existing facilities to permit, insofar as possible, physically handicapped prisoners access to programs and activities; and

"4. compliance with the procedural requirements of Vitek v. Jones, 445 U.S. 480 (1980), for transfers of mentally disturbed prisoners to mental institutions.

III. *SOLITARY CONFINEMENT*

A. *Term of Solitary Confinement*

Defendants shall not confine any prisoner to more than one fifteen-day term in solitary confinement without holding a hearing conforming to the requirements of due process procedures which are applicable to prison disciplinary proceedings for each term in solitary confinement beyond the initial term. Consecutive disciplinary punishments are permitted only for violations arising from totally separate incidents.

B. *Health Precautions*

Defendants shall scrupulously follow Rules 4.3.4.2.4 and 4.3.4.2.7 of the Rules and Regulations and Grievance Procedures of TDC (1975) requiring physical examinations of all prisoners entering solitary confinement and monitoring of the physical and mental health of prisoners confined to solitary.

C. *Solitary Diet*

Prisoners held in solitary confinement will be fed the same daily full rations as the general inmate population during all the time that they are held in solitary.

IV. *USE OF CHEMICAL AGENTS*

By April 1, 1981, Defendants shall develop and file clear, concise written standards governing use of chemical agents, including (1) the filing of written reports on each use of chemical agents by TDC personnel and prompt and effective discipline of TDC personnel who violate the standards for use of chemical agents; (2) prompt examination, necessary treatment and necessary decontamination by medical personnel of all prisoners exposed to chemical agents and ventilation of the area in which the agents were used unless additional decontamination is required by the circumstances; (3) where reasonably feasible, review of the medical records of a prisoner prior to the use of chemical agents on him to ascertain whether the use of chemical agents is medically contraindicated; and (4) prohibition of use of chemical agents on prisoners confined to cells or other similar enclosures who do not present an imminent threat of injury to other persons. Further, the standards shall limit the use of chemical agents to the minimum necessary to prevent escape or imminent serious personal injury or property damage.

V. *WORK SAFETY AND HYGIENE*

By September 1, 1981, Defendants shall file with the Court a proposed work safety and hygiene plan prepared with the assistance of personnel from the United States Bureau of Prisons. The plan shall cover all TDC prisoner work operations and shall include the following elements: employment and necessary training of work safety and hygiene professionals, or other personnel, with authority to require security and administrative personnel to comply with their recommendations when circumstances are found to exist which pose an imminent or serious threat to health and safety, subject to review of such action at the earliest possible time by the Director of TDC or his designate; adequate record keeping; and safety and hygiene inspections by safety and hygiene professionals or other trained personnel.

VI. *ADMINISTRATIVE SEGREGATION*

By September 1, 1981, Defendants shall file with the Court a plan setting forth:

"1. the circumstances under which prisoners may be confined to administrative segregation;

"2. the procedures conforming to the requirements of Wolff v. McDonnell, 418 U.S. 539 (1974) and Wright v. Enomoto, 462 F.Supp. 397 (N.D.Cal. 1976), aff'd 434 U.S. 1052 (1978); and

"3. regular and frequent review of prisoners confined to administrative segregation, including the standards for such review.

VII. *DEVELOPMENT AND FILING OF PLANS: SPECIAL MASTER*

As required by the Court's Order of December 12, 1980, in developing the plans required by this Decree, Defendants shall address the relevant facts and conclusions contained in the Court's Memorandum Opinion of December 12, 1980. The parties understand that, by entering into the Consent Decree, there has been no agreement whether a Special Master will be appointed, or as to the role of a Special Master, including whether the agreements in this Consent Decree will be part of the reference to a Special Master.

SIGNED and ENTERED this 3rd day of March, 1981.

(s) Wm. Wayne Justice
Chief Judge
United States District Court
Eastern District of Texas
Judge Presiding

APPENDIX B

IN THE UNITED STATES DISTRICT COURT
FOR THE SOUTHERN DISTRICT OF TEXAS
HOUSTON DIVISION

DAVID RUIZ, et al., Plaintiffs UNITED STATES OF AMERICA Plaintiff-Intervenor vs. W.J. ESTELLE, JR., et al., Defendants	Civil Action No. H–78–987

AMENDED ORDER OF REFERENCE

The Court, having discovered an error in the text of the Order entered on June 18, 1981, modifying its earlier Order of April 20, 1981, appointing a Special Master in this cause, hereby issues this Amended Order of Reference which shall supersede the aforementioned previous Orders.

In a Memorandum Opinion filed on December 10, 1980, the Court announced its intention to appoint one or more Special Masters in this cause. Subsequently, the Court received nominations from all parties and reviewed at length the qualifications of those persons whose names were submitted for consideration. For the reasons set forth in its earlier opinion, the Court hereby appoints Vincent M. Nathan to serve as Special Master for the Court in this cause.

Mr. Nathan was nominated both by the plaintiffs and by the United States of America. A native Texan, he graduated from the University of Oklahoma College of Law in 1959. He was a member of the faculty of the College of Law of the University of Toledo for 16 years, during the last 10 of which he served as a Professor of Law. He is now engaged in the practice of law in Toledo, Ohio.

Mr. Nathan was appointed in December of 1975 by the United States District Court for the Northern District of Ohio to serve as Special Master in Taylor v. Perini, litigation involving the Marion Correctional Institution in Marion, Ohio. In January of 1977, Mr. Nathan was appointed by the same court to serve as Special Master in Jones v. Wittenburg [440 F.Supp. 60], litigation involving the Lucas County Jail in Toledo, Ohio.[1] In June of 1979 Mr. Nathan was appointed by the United States District Court for the Southern District of Georgia to serve as Special Monitor in Guthrie v. Evans, litiga-

1. Mr. Nathan's reports in *Taylor* were confirmed by the district court and published at 413 F.Supp. 198 (1976), 421 F.Supp. [740] 742 (1976), 431 F.Supp. [566] 570 (1977), 446 F.Supp. [1184] 1186 (1977), 455 F.Supp. [1241] 1255 (1978), and 477 F.Supp. 1289 (1978). His report in *Jones*, which was also confirmed by the district court, was published at 440 F.Supp. 60 (1977). *Taylor* is a rare example of prison conditions litigation which has come to an end, a fact which commends Mr. Nathan's appointment by this Court.

tion involving the Georgia State Prison in Reidsville, Georgia. He continues to serve that court as special monitor at this time.

Mr. Nathan is the author of The Use of Masters in Institutional Reform Litigation, 10 Tol.L.Rev. 419 (1979), which was republished and distributed by the Federal Judicial Center. He has served and continues to serve as a consultant for the National Institute of Corrections and is an acknowledged expert in the field of implementation of judicial decrees in a correctional setting. In view of his extensive experience and impressive credentials, Mr. Nathan is fully qualified to assume the enormous responsibilities of monitoring compliance with the Court's order in this cause. Because the scope of application of the Court's remedial orders in this case will be infinitely broader than that encountered in any other example of correctional litigation, it is essential that the Special Master be a person with extensive experience and an established record of success.

In addition, the Court will appoint several monitors to assist the Special Master. These monitors will be persons of high professional qualification who are nominated by the Special Master. The Special Master shall supervise the activities of such monitors in accordance with the guidelines announced in Newman v. Alabama, 559 F.2d 283, 290 (5th Cir. 1977), cert. denied [438 U.S. 915] (1978).[2]

The Court grounds its appointment of a Special Master in this case upon two independent sources of authority. First, it relies upon its inherent power to make such an appointment:

"Courts have (at least in the absence of legislation to the contrary) inherent power to provide themselves with appropriate instruments required for the performance of their duties . . . This power includes authority to appoint persons unconnected with the court to aid judges in the performance of specific judicial duties, as they may arise in the progress of a cause. From the commencement of our Government, it has been exercised by the federal courts, when sitting in equity, by appointing, either with or without the consent of the parties, special masters, auditors, examiners and commissioners."

Ex parte Peterson, 253 U.S. 300 (1920). The enforcement of its remedial order is a judicial duty which rests with this Court, and it has the inherent power to appoint a Special Master to provide assistance toward this end.

Second, the Court relies upon Rule 53 of the Federal Rules of Civil Procedure in making this reference. In its Memorandum Opinion of December 10, 1980, referred to above, the Court has demonstrated that the appointment of a Master is both necessary and appropriate in accordance with the provisions of Rule 53. The formal fact finding role contemplated by the Rule will be particularly relevant to the Special Master in this case to the extent that he may hold hearings and make factual findings as a result of those hearings for review by the Court.

2. The Court does not contemplate the appointment of a separate monitor for each prison in Texas as the Court in *Newman* suggested would be appropriate. The appointment of a separate and qualified monitor for each of Texas' 16 prisons would result in an enormous expenditure of public funds. Rather, the Court contemplates that the Special Master will be able to utilize a staff of perhaps 6 full-time monitors to monitor compliance throughout the Texas system. Such a model will achieve the minimal level of intrusiveness sought by the Court in *Newman*.

Pursuant to these bases of authority, the Special Master shall assist the Court by monitoring compliance with the Court's orders in this cause. All actions of the Special Master and any monitors or members of the Special Master's staff will be under the direct control and supervision of the Court. In particular, the Special Master and other persons operating on the Court's behalf shall not intervene in the administrative management of the Texas Department of Corrections or any of its institutions. In addition, the Special Master, his staff and any monitors who are appointed shall not be empowered to direct the defendants or any of their subordinates to take or to refrain from taking any specific action to achieve compliance. The sole power to direct compliance and to punish noncompliance remains with this Court. The duties of the Special Master, then, will be to observe, monitor, find facts, report or testify as to his findings, and make recommendations to the Court concerning steps which should be taken to achieve compliance. The Special Master may and should assist the defendants in every possible way, and to this end he may and should confer informally with the defendants and their subordinates on matters affecting compliance. In order to accomplish these objectives, the Special Master shall have the following powers:

"1. The Special Master shall have unlimited access to any facilities, buildings, or premises under the jurisdiction or control of the Texas Department of Corrections, and no advance notice of any visit or inspection shall be required.

"2. The Special Master shall have unlimited access to the records, files and papers maintained by the Texas Department of Corrections to the extent that such access is related to the performance of the Special Master's duties of monitoring compliance. Such access shall include all Departmental, institutional, and inmate records, including but not limited to medical records. The Special Master may obtain copies of all such relevant records, files and papers.

"3. The Special Master may conduct confidential interviews with all staff members and employees of the Texas Department of Corrections. In addition, he may engage in informal conferences with such staff members and employees, and such persons shall cooperate with the Special Master and respond to all inquiries and requests related to compliance with the Court's orders in this case. The Special Master may require compilation and communication of oral or written information relevant to such compliance.

"4. The Special Master may conduct confidential interviews and meetings at the institution to which they are confined with any prisoner or group of prisoners under the jurisdiction of the Texas Department of Corrections.

"5. The Special Master may attend any formal institutional meetings or proceedings at any institution under the jurisdiction of the Texas Department of Corrections.

"6. The Special Master may require written reports from any staff member or employee of the Texas Department of Corrections with respect to compliance with this Court's orders.

"7. The Special Master shall have the full power to order and conduct hearings with respect to the defendants' compliance with this Court's orders.

To this end he shall have the power to require the attendance of witnesses, including both prisoners and employees of the Texas Department of Corrections, and he shall exercise all other powers described in subsection (c) of Rule 53 of the Federal Rules of Civil Procedure.

"8. The Special Master may select and employ necessary administrative, clerical, and support staff. All such persons as well as the nature of their compensation shall be approved by the Court in advance of their employment. In addition, with advance permission of the Court, the Special Master may hire independent specialists and experts to assist him in fulfilling the responsibilities assigned to him by this Order.

"9. In exercising the powers enumerated in paragraphs 1 through 6 above, the Special Master may act by himself, or through monitors appointed by the Court. All actions of such monitors, however, shall be supervised and coordinated by the Special Master in order to accomplish the objectives of this Reference."

The Special Master shall, as he deems necessary or as required by the Court, file reports with the Court in which he shall make findings concerning the defendants' compliance with the provisions of the Court's Orders and the need, if any, for supplemental remedial action. In general, the Special Master's reports to the Court will be based upon reports prepared by individual monitors appointed by the Court as follows:

"1. Reports of their factual observations shall be prepared by the monitors appointed by the Court and shall be submitted to the parties and to the Special Master. Any objections to such a report shall be the subject of a hearing before the Special Master upon request of any party. After the parties have had an opportunity to respond or object to a monitor's report, with or without a hearing, the Special Master shall file his report with the Court, including his findings of fact based upon the monitor's report, the record of any hearing, or both.

"2. No objection may be filed to the Special Master's report which could have been filed to the monitor's report preceding it. Otherwise, any party may file written objections to the Special Master's report within fifteen days of the filing thereof with the Court. The objecting party shall note each particular finding or recommendation to which objection is made, shall provide proposed alternative findings, and may request a hearing or oral argument before the Court.

"3. Any request for a hearing before the Court must include a list of witnesses and documents to be presented to the Court. A copy of the objections, proposed findings, and any request for a rehearing shall be served on all parties.

"4. The Special Master's findings of fact shall be accepted by the Court unless shown to be clearly erroneous. Any evidence not previously presented to the Special Master in the course of the formal hearing preceding his report will be admitted at a hearing before the Court only upon a showing that the party offering it lacked a reasonable opportunity to present the evidence to the Special Master."

In addition, the Special Master may submit reports based upon hearings held by him in the absence of preliminary reports by monitors, and in such instances the Special Master's reports and findings shall be treated in accordance with the provisions of Rule 53 of the Federal Rules of Civil Procedure. The Special Master may also submit reports based upon his own observations and investigations in the absence of a formal hearing before him. In any event, however, the Special Master's findings must be based upon evidence which is made part of the record before the Court.

The Special Master shall be compensated at the rate of Ninety-Five Dollars ($95.00) per hour for services performed in accordance with this Order. Appropriate compensation for members of the Special Master's staff as well as that of monitors shall be established by the Court upon the recommendation of the Special Master and after notice to all parties. All reasonable expenses incurred by the Special Master in the course of the performance of his duties, including but not limited to the rental of office space and equipment in Texas, salaries of staff, long distance telephone, photocopying, printing, travel, data processing, and postage, shall be reimbursed.

The cost of the mastership shall be borne by the defendants as costs in this action. The Special Master shall submit to the Court periodic statements of his time and expenses for review and approval by the Court.

THE DEFENDANTS ARE HEREBY ORDERED to deposit the sum of One Hundred Fifty Thousand Dollars ($150,000.00) with the Clerk of this Court as interim payment of costs, and payments to the Special Master and to monitors shall be made by order of the Court out of such funds. As payments are made by the Clerk, the defendants shall deposit additional sums with the Clerk as the Court may order and direct.

The Special Master may cause copies of this Order of Reference or portions thereof to be posted in any facility under the jurisdiction of the Texas Department of Corrections and may cause such copies to be distributed to inmates within such facilities and to employees of the Texas Department of Corrections.

SO ORDERED this 24th day of July, 1981.

(s) Wm. Wayne Justice
William Wayne Justice
Chief Judge
United States District Court
Eastern District of Texas
Judge Presiding

APPENDIX C
IN THE UNITED STATES DISTRICT COURT FOR THE SOUTHERN DISTRICT OF TEXAS HOUSTON DIVISION

DAVID RUIZ, ET AL.,
Plaintiffs,
UNITED STATES OF AMERICA,
Plaintiff-Intervenor,
v.
W.J. ESTELLE, JR., ET AL.,
Defendants.

NO. H–78–987–CA

ORDER

On April 14, 1982, the Special Master in the above-styled civil action announced that the parties to the action had agreed to a stipulated modification of Sections II(A) and II(D) of the Amended Decree Granting Equitable Relief and Declaratory Judgment, entered May 1, 1981. Plainly, any alteration of a court's remedial order, suggested by the parties, is subject to approval by the court. Moreover, since this action is a class action, the notice provisions of Rule 23(e), F.R.Civ.P., requires that all class members be notified of the proposed settlement, and that they be given an opportunity to object to its terms. At the close of the hearing on April 14, 1982, the proposed settlement was accepted for review by the court; additionally, the parties were directed to submit to the court a jointly prepared form of notice to the class, and a proposal as to how such notice should be published.

In an order entered April 21, 1982, preliminary approval was given to the settlement. The terms of the modification are fair and reasonable, and protect, in all respects, the rights of the plaintiff class. As indicated in the order of April 21, a just settlement of the issues involved in the stipulated modification is in the best interests of all parties to this action, not only with respect to these particular issues, but more generally regarding the entire remedial phase of the case.

The order of April 21 also approved a form of notice to the class, as well as a proposed method of publication. Under the terms of this notice, the members were thoroughly apprised of the content of the settlement, and were given an opportunity to challenge its terms, by means of written objections. Class members were directed to file their objections with the clerk of the court, and provide copies to counsel for all parties, and to the Special Master. A hearing was held on June 1, 1982, in Houston, Texas, for the purpose of considering any objections to the proposed settlement filed by members of the plaintiff class.

Numerous inmates filed objections to the stipulated modification of Sections II(A) and II(D) of the Amended Decree. The objections raise serious concerns which merit close attention. With one notable exception, the central thread of the objections is skepticism about defendants' willingness to comply with the terms of the settlement. In view of the history of this litigation, this skepticism is fully understandable. However, as with all portions of the injunctive order in this action, defendants' compliance with the terms of the stipulation will be closely monitored. The Stipulated Modification contains elaborate provisions for ensuring enforcement of its terms. The court is satisfied that this procedure adequately protects the rights of the plaintiff class. Should evidence of noncompliance with the terms of the stipulation be called to the attention of the court, appropriate remedial action will be taken.

One objection filed by a member of the plaintiff class deserves special comment. Originally, notice of the proposed settlement was provided to plaintiff class only in English. Consequently, Spanish-speaking inmates were severely limited in their ability to review and comment on the terms of the settlement. To cure this shortcoming, the parties were directed to arrange for publication of notice in Spanish. Such arrangements were made forthwith, and the court is satisfied that all inmates of the Texas Department of Corrections have been adequately notified of the settlement. Giving consideration to the highly acute and sophisticated objections previously made by many of the members of the plaintiff class, it appears extremely unlikely that any meritorious objections not previously raised will be advanced. Thus, on the basis of the arguments and evidence adduced at the hearing, it appears that the stipulated modification of Section II(A) and II(D) of the Amended Decree should be finally approved.

This action has been remanded temporarily to the district court from the Court of Appeals for the Fifth Circuit, to permit a hearing as to the approval and entry of the stipulated modification of the Amended Decree *vel non.* It appears from the order of remand that entry of final approval will automatically re-vest jurisdiction over the appeal in the Court of Appeals. Nevertheless, the parties are directed to notify the Clerk of the Court of Appeals for the Fifth Circuit that the present order has been entered and to furnish him with a complete record in this matter, including all pleadings and orders relating thereto. The parties are further directed to take any action necessary to insure this action is reinstated in that court. Finally, defendants are directed, in accordance with Section XIV.A of the Stipulated Modifiation, to file in the Court of Appeals a motion for voluntary dismissal of the portion of their appeal relating to Sections II(A) and II(D) of the Amended Decree.

It is so ORDERED.

SIGNED and ENTERED this 1st day of June, 1982.

(s) Wm. Wayne Justice
Chief Judge
United States District Court
Eastern District of Texas
Judge Presiding

IN THE UNITED STATES DISTRICT COURT
FOR THE SOUTHERN DISTRICT OF TEXAS
HOUSTON DIVISION

DAVID RUIZ, et al., Plaintiffs, UNITED STATES OF AMERICA, Plaintiff-Intervenor, vs. W. J. ESTELLE, JR., et al., Defendants	Civil Action No. H–78–987 STIPULATED MODIFICATION OF SECTION II.D AND SECTION II.A OF AMENDED DECREE

Pursuant to the Court's order of March 29, 1982, the parties have met and discussed Section II,A of the Amended Decree of May 1, 1981, and the matters at issue in the current hearing concerning defendants' compliance with Section II,D of that decree. They stipulate, subject to the Court's approval, that Section II,D and Section II,A of the Amended Decree shall be superseded by the following provisions:

I. *DEFINITIONS*

A. *Support Service Inmate*

A Support Service Inmate is an Orderly, a Clerk, a Field Service Worker, or a Turnkey, as those positions are defined herein. Such positions shall be referred to herein collectively as Support Service jobs.

B. *Orderly*

An Orderly is an inmate who is assigned to provide building support services in a housing unit, hallway, infirmary, or in other areas of the institution.

C. *Clerk*

A Clerk is an inmate who is assigned to perform a variety of tasks related to the routine maintenance of nonsensitive unit records. He may provide typing, filing and other related services for staff members to the extent permitted herein.

D. *Field Service Worker*

A Field Service Worker is an inmate who has been assigned to agricultural work in a support capacity.

E. *Turnkey*

A Turnkey is an inmate whose job assignment requires him to open and close doors, gates or similar barriers upon direction and instruction of a staff member.

F. *Staff Member*

A Staff Member is a current or future civilian or uniformed employee of the Texas Department of Corrections.

G. *Sensitive Materials*

A document, record, or information relating to a particular inmate is sensitive if it

"(1) relates to his medical, psychiatric, or psychological condition or treatment; provided, however, that the mere designation of an inmate's medical classification (I, II, III, IV or V) is not sensitive information; or

"(2) relates to his criminal history, current offense, educational attainment, intelligence quotient, trust fund account, social history, known enemies, disciplinary record, next of kin, or home address."

Otherwise it is nonsensitive.

An inmate's medical, psychiatric and psychological files, and all documents filed therein, an inmate's unit and departmental files, and all documents typically filed therein, travel cards, disciplinary reports, incident reports, use of force reports and grievances are sensitive.

H. *Direct Supervision*

"(1) With respect to Orderlies, Field Service Workers, and Turnkeys, direct supervision consists of the performance of a function with the conscious awareness and acquiescence of and within the sight and sound of a staff member.

"(2) With respect to Clerks, direct supervision consists of the performance of a function under the circumstances described in Paragraph H(1), supra. In addition, with respect to documents typed by a Clerk, all such documents shall be typed verbatim from written information prepared by a staff member or from records. All documents typed by a Clerk must be reviewed and approved (by signature or initials) by a staff member.

I. *Indirect Supervision*

Indirect supervision shall consist of the following:

"(1) The existence of a standing order expressly given by a staff member; or

"(2) The existence of general directions delivered by a staff member.

"In either case, there shall be regular and periodic observation by a staff member of the performance of the task(s)."

J. *Bona fide Emergency*

A bona fide emergency is an event which constitutes an immediate and direct threat to the life, health, or safety of one or more individuals caused by natural disasters, medical conditions, fires and similar occurrences, but excluding riots, fights and other inmate disturbances.

K. *Full Compliance*

Full compliance with this Stipulation means a determination by the Court that the defendants are in compliance with all the terms of this Stipulation, either on a particular unit or system-wide, as the case may be.

II. *PROHIBITION AGAINST THE POSSESSION OR EXERCISE OF SUPERVISORY OR ADMINISTRATIVE AUTHORITY BY INMATES*

No inmate shall act in a supervisory or administrative capacity or exercise supervisory or administrative authority over other inmates; nor shall any inmate administer disciplinary action against another inmate. Further, no inmate shall be given a position that entails, or authorizes him expressly or impliedly to exercise, such authority.

III. *ORDERLY FUNCTIONS*

An inmate assigned to serve as an Orderly may perform only the following functions:

A. Perform general clean-up duties, such as mopping, sweeping, dusting, polishing, emptying trash, and washing windows;

B. Assist in preparing areas for special programs;

C. Operate windows;

D. Report needed maintenance;

E. Perform routine maintenance functions;

F. Distribute toiletry items, *e.g.*, soap, tooth powder and toilet paper;

G. Provide water to inmates locked in their cells;

H. Carry, inventory, sort, and distribute wearing apparel, laundry, or linens in his assigned housing unit;

I. Under the direct supervision of a staff member, assist in distributing meals to inmates in lock-up status;

J. Assist in loading and unloading of freight or other items;

K. Under direct supervision of a staff member, assist in the distribution of goods in the commissary room, but no inmate shall have access to another inmate's commissary withdrawal sheet or trust fund account report;

L. After a staff member has approved ingress to or egress from a housing unit, record (e.g., on a count board) prisoner movements permitted or ordered by a staff member; provided, however, that a staff member shall initiate and direct all movement in and out of all cells, cellblocks, dayrooms, dormitories and other areas of the unit; and provided further that no inmate may be required to inform another inmate of his destination until after the staff member has authorized his movement; and

M. Perform other tasks at the direction of a staff member, so long as such tasks are consistent with the provisions of Sections II and VII of this Stipulation.

Except for those functions described above that must be performed under the direct supervision of a staff member, all functions of an Orderly must be performed under the direct or indirect supervision of a staff member.

IV. *CLERK FUNCTIONS*

An inmate assigned to serve as a Clerk may perform only the following functions:

A. Update trusty and line force logs, farm reports, slips listing state property, stencils, forms, and similar reports;

B. Update the housing and job assignment board at each unit; provided, however, that all housing and job assignments must originate with and be made directly by a staff member, and a staff member shall fill out all cell assignments;

C. Fill out forms designed or designated by a staff member for ordering supplies and other materials;

D. Under the direct supervision of a staff member, type and file nonsensitive records and documents; and

E. Occasionally perform routine janitorial tasks as described in Sections III A through III E, supra, in the immediate area of his assignment and perform other tasks at the direction of a staff member so long as such tasks are consistent with the provisions of Sections I G, II, and VII of this Stipulation.

Except for those functions described above that must be performed under the direct supervision of a staff member, all functions of a Clerk must be performed under the direct or indirect supervision of a staff member.

V. *FIELD SERVICE WORKER FUNCTIONS*

Inmates assigned to serve as Field Service Workers may perform only the following functions:

A. Provide water to officers and to inmates;

B. Hook up trailers;

C. Maintain tools and equipment;

D. Perform agricultural work that is performed by other inmates;

E. Under the direct supervision of a staff member,

"(1) Act as a starting point for the work squad;

"(2) Act as last man in the work squad, counting off rows or distances; and

"(3) Work at the pace set by a staff member;

"provided, however, that no Field Service Worker may issue any order or instruction to another inmate or be responsible for reporting the pace or quality of another inmate's work; and"

F. Perform other tasks at the direction of a staff member so long as such tasks are consistent with the provisions of Sections II and VII of this Stipulation.

Except for those functions described above that must be performed under the direct supervision of a staff member, all functions of a Field Service Worker must be performed under the direct or indirect supervision of a staff member.

VI. *TURNKEY FUNCTIONS*

A. Under the direct supervision of a staff member, Turnkeys may possess keys and operate doors and gates for a period of time not to exceed sixty (60) days from the parties' signing of this Stipulation. Thereafter, until a unit comes into full compliance with the terms of this Stipulation pursuant to Section XIII, supra, Turnkeys at that unit may operate gates and doors at that unit only as follows:

"(1) Under the direct supervision of a staff member, a Turnkey may operate a door or gate if he is handed the key thereto by a staff member each time the door or gate is opened, and he returns the key to the staff member immediately after locking the door or gate;

"(2) Under the direct supervision of a staff member, a Turnkey may operate a door or gate to the extent that his only function is to push open and/or close (and thus lock) said door or gate after it is unlocked mechanically by a staff member."

B. No Turnkey may open or close a cell door except in the East Building of the Huntsville Unit, and then only under the direct supervision of a staff member; provided, however, that an inmate may, under the direct supervision of a staff member, operate any gate or door only for the purpose of maintenance or repair of locking mechanisms.

C. To the extent that Turnkeys are permitted to have keys in their possession while performing their duties, these keys may not be attached to thongs, straps, or other similar devices; such keys shall be checked out at the beginning and checked in at the end of each shift by the Turnkey with the officer on duty. A key count shall be made at the end of each day by a staff member. No Turnkey shall be allowed to keep any key in his cell or permanently in his possession.

D. From the time a unit is required by this Stipulation to be in full compliance pursuant to Section XIII, infra, Turnkeys may not operate gates or doors that have been determined under Section XII, infra, to be primary security points. Primary security points are those points which require the presence and actions of a staff member. All such primary security points will be controlled by a staff member, either with a key or through a locking device which he operates. All gates or doors determined under Section XII, infra, not to be primary security points may be operated by a Turnkey under direct supervision.

E. No Turnkey shall authorize or deny ingress or egress to or from any area of a unit without a direct and immediate order or signal from a staff member, and a staff member shall initiate and direct all movement in and out of cells, cellblocks, dayrooms, dormitories, and other areas of the unit.

F. Inmates assigned to serve as Turnkeys may also perform the following routine functions:

"(1) Load or unload freight or other supplies;

"(2) Perform routine janitorial tasks as permitted by Sections III A–E, supra, in the immediate area of his assignment; and

"(3) Perform other tasks at the direction of a staff member, so long as such tasks are consistent with the provisions of Sections II and VII of this Stipulation."

Turnkeys shall perform the routine functions described in Section VI D only under the direct or indirect supervision of a staff member.

G. On a permanent basis, under the indirect supervision of a staff member, a Turnkey may operate doors and gates through which inmates do not normally pass, which are also not primary security points.

VII. *IMPERMISSIBLE CONDUCT AND PRIVILEGES*

A. Forthwith, the defendants shall promulgate and enforce rules to ensure that:

"(1) No inmate possesses any weapons;

"(2) No inmate abuses other inmates whether physically or otherwise;

"(3) No inmate administers any punishment or other form of discipline to other inmates;

"(4) No inmate grants or denies another inmate access to any benefit or activity;

"(5) No inmate controls the movement or activities of other inmates, except as provided herein;

"(6) No inmate, except when on duty and as necessary to perform his legitimate job functions, has any greater access to areas of the unit than does any other inmate;

"(7) No inmate escorts another inmate from one place to another, with or without a staff member, except as required by a bona fide emergency;

"(8) All inmates are disciplined without regard to job assignment;

"(9) All inmates are treated the same regarding the search of their living quarters except as required by Section XI E, infra, and no inmate is exempt from a search of his property or his living quarters;

"(10) No inmate inventories another inmate's property or searches another inmate, his living area, or his property, and no inmate participates or accompanies a staff member in inventorying or searching another inmate or his property;

"(11) No inmate has access to confiscated weapons, alcohol, drugs, or other forms of contraband, and all contraband is disposed of in accordance with TDC policies;

"(12) No inmate keeps in his cell or living area any item prohibited in any other general population cell or living area on that unit;

"(13) No inmate gives or is required to give his commissary withdrawal slip or scrip book to another inmate;

"(14) No inmate enters or leaves a housing unit without direction from a staff member, who shall personally tally all such movements;

"(15) No inmate possesses handcuffs, other forms of restraints, or keys thereto;

"(16) No inmate mails or distributes another inmate's correspondence;

"(17) No inmate receives money, commissary goods, or services in exchange for any service, apart from payments approved by formal TDC policy;

"(18) No inmate has access to sensitive information, and all sensitive materials are kept inaccessible;

"(19) Like other assigned inmates, support service inmates are assigned to work a specific shift in a particular, limited location; provided, however, that like other assigned inmates, support service inmates may occasionally be assigned to work different shifts in other particular, limited locations;

"(20) Only an inmate formally assigned as an Orderly, Clerk, Turnkey, or Field Service Worker regularly performs the functions of that specific position;

"(21) No inmate is assigned to or, other than in exceptional circumstances, performs more than one Support Service job;

"(22) No inmate participates in the taking of any count; provided, however, that a Clerk may record the line turn-out for the field officer;

"(23) No inmate enforces departmental or institutional rules or regulations;

"(24) It is not a formal or informal part of any inmate's job to

'(a) report to staff members any information about inmates or events, including but not limited to rule violations, work performance, fights, and other disturbances;

'(b) break up a fight, come to the aid of staff members or inmates in the case of a confrontation, or maintain order or quiet in any area of a unit;

'(c) report any inmate's activities relating to grievances, legal actions, or any attempt to contact public officials, lawyers, or courts;

'(d) enforce or monitor work performance standards;

'(e) accompany a staff member on his rounds or movements throughout the unit;

'(f) determine or exercise influence over his or another inmate's living or work assignment;

'(g) assign or delegate work to another inmate;

'(h) relay notice of appointments, wake-ups, lay-ins, visits, or arrival of mail; provided, however, that no inmate receiving such notice(s) from any inmate shall be charged with a disciplinary offense or otherwise disadvantaged by failing to respond thereto; and provided further that a non-Support Service inmate may be assigned to give notice of early wake up to other inmates in his housing unit who work the same shift.

'(i) relay requests and information to a staff member; provided, moreover, that no inmate shall be required to communicate with a staff member through other inmates;

'(j) accompany staff members to the scene of a fight or disturbance; or

'(k) take votes on television programs and operate television sets. Television programming shall be selected by a majority of the inmates present to observe. The channel shall be set according to the vote of the majority. Allegations that the vote of the majority was not followed may be brought to the attention of the officer in charge by any inmate, and the officer shall resolve the problem.' "

B. No Support Service Inmate, by virtue of his assignment to a Support Service job, shall be afforded privileges not afforded to general population inmates. Specifically,

"(1) such inmates shall be treated like all other general population inmates with respect to whether and when their cell doors are opened and closed;

"(2) such inmates shall not be permitted to wear special jackets, or special or extra clothing that general population prisoners are not provided with or permitted to wear, or be excused from or allowed any special treatment with regard to clothing or TDC dress requirements, except as necessary for the performance of legitimate job functions;

"(3) such inmates shall not be permitted to have pets, possessions, hobbies, hobbycraft, or cell furnishings not available to all TDC prisoners;

"(4) such inmates shall not be permitted to operate any "store," gambling pool or racket, loan business, or other "business" that general population inmates are not permitted to operate; and

"(5) such inmates shall not be provided with any special access to extra food or, except as required by the performance of their legitimate job functions, special meal times."

VIII. *THE REASSIGNMENT OF CURRENT SUPPORT SERVICE INMATES*

The following shall govern the initial removal of certain inmates occupying (on or about the date of the Court's approval of this Stipulation) positions described in Section II, D of the Amended Decree. For the purpose of this Section only, these positions shall be referred to as "SSI jobs."

A. Within sixty (60) days of the Court's approval of this Stipulation, all inmates assigned to SSI jobs shall be reviewed by the State Classification Committee and removed to the extent required herein. This review shall encompass, at a minimum, the inmate's central file and his unit file. Such inmates may be retained as Support Service Inmates or permitted to perform Support Service jobs only under the following conditions:

"(1) They have not abused their position in SSI jobs;

"(2) They meet all criteria for selection of support service inmates contained in Section IX, infra, of this Stipulation; and

"(3) They would not be disqualified from serving as support service inmates by any of the criteria contained in Section X B, infra, of this Stipulation, other than Section X B (2), infra, but not Section VII of this Stipulation.

Through this review TDC shall select and remove not less than ten per cent (10%) of the inmates assigned to SSI jobs on each unit of the Texas Department of Corrections.

B. In addition, within sixty (60) days of the Court's approval of this Stipulation, the Special Master may require the removal of no more than twenty-five per cent (25%) of the inmates who occupied SSI jobs and performed the functions of housing unit orderlies or similar functions as described in Section

II, D of the Amended Decree, major's office count boys or bookkeepers, or countroom count boys or bookkeepers at the following units: Coffield, Darrington, Eastham, Ellis, Ramsey I, Ramsey II, and Retrieve. However, at any particular unit the Special Master may designate for removal no more than fifty per cent (50%) of the inmates assigned to any one of the three job groupings listed above. If the number of inmates so removed exceeds twenty-five per cent (25%) of the total number of inmates employed in a particular job grouping at a particular unit, one-half of the number designated for removal shall be removed within sixty (60) days, and all inmates designated for removal pursuant to this Subsection must be removed within one hundred twenty (120) days.

In designating inmates for removal pursuant to this subsection, the Special Master need not state any reason for such designation. However, the Special Master may recommend that a particular inmate be removed for cause as defined in Subsection A, supra, and state the basis for such recommendation. In the event such a recommendation is made by the Special Master, TDC shall make a good faith investigation into the conduct of said inmate to determine whether removal under the provisions of Subsection A is appropriate.

C. At any time the Special Master may make a recommendation to TDC that an inmate holding an SSI or Support Service job be removed for cause as defined in Sections VIII A, supra. Such recommendation shall be non-binding. In the event such a recommendation is made by the Special Master, TDC shall make a good faith investigation into the conduct of said inmate to determine whether removal under the provisions of Subsection A is appropriate.

D. In addition to the removals required by Subsections A and B, supra, within one (1) year of the Court's approval of this Stipulation TDC shall transfer an additional twenty-five per cent (25%) of all inmates assigned to SSI jobs and holding positions as or performing tasks similar to housing unit orderlies, countroom count boys or bookkeepers, and major's office count boys or bookkeepers at each of the following units: Coffield, Darrington, Eastham, Ellis, Ramsey I, Ramsey II, and Retrieve. An inmate transferred pursuant to this Subsection D may be immediately assigned to a support service job at his unit of reassignment.

E. An inmate whose removal by TDC for a cause defined in Subsection A, supra, is occasioned in whole or in part by possession of a weapon, violence, extortion or aggressive homosexual behavior may not be reassigned to or permitted to perform any function of a Support Service job for five (5) years following his removal. Any other inmate removed under the provisions of Subsections A or B, supra, may be assigned to a Support Service job at any unit other than Coffield, Darrington, Eastham, Ellis, Ramsey I, Ramsey II and Retrieve one (1) year after his removal; provided, however, such an inmate may not be reassigned to a Support Service job at any of the named units until one year after full compliance with the terms of this Stipulation is achieved at that unit.

IX. *CRITERIA FOR SELECTION OF SUPPORT SERVICE INMATES*

A. All assignments to Support Service jobs shall be approved by the State Classification Committee, and the appropriateness of any such assignment shall be documented in the inmate's central file. Copies of any such file and of the inmate's unit file shall be made available upon request to the Special Master and to counsel for plaintiffs and the United States. Inmates shall be selected for Support Service jobs only after a determination, based on their institutional file and behavior, that they are likely to perform their assigned tasks conscientiously and reliably, that they are not likely to abuse or attempt to abuse other inmates, and that they are not likely to exercise or attempt to exercise authority over other inmates.

B. No inmate shall be assigned to a Support Service job if he has been convicted in a court of law or in a prison disciplinary hearing within the immediately previous twelve (12) months of engaging in any of the following conduct while incarcerated in TDC:

"(1) Extortion, gaming, acts of assault, theft of personal property, or possession of a weapon;

"(2) Use, possession, or buying or selling of narcotics, marijuana, alcohol, other intoxicants, or other drugs;

"(3) Escape, attempt to escape, helping another inmate escape or attempt to escape; or

"(4) Aggressive sexual behavior."

C. The provisions of this Section IX shall apply only until the full compliance of this Stipulation. Thereafter, defendants shall not use any special selection procedure for assignment to Support Service jobs except as provided in this Stipulation.

X. *CRITERIA FOR REMOVAL OF INMATES FROM SUPPORT SERVICE ASSIGNMENTS*

A. Until full compliance with the terms of this Stipulation is achieved at a particular unit, all inmates holding turnkey positions at that unit shall be reviewed quarterly by the Warden or his delegate to determine their continued suitability to hold such jobs.

B. An inmate shall be removed from any Support Service job immediately

"(1) upon conviction by a disciplinary committee of an offense resulting in loss of good time or reduction in class; or

"(2) upon any determination, by disciplinary conviction or otherwise, that the inmate has abused his position or engaged in any conduct prohibited by Section VII, supra, or been convicted of a major violation involving conduct listed in Section IX B, supra."

An inmate removed under the provisions of Section X B(1) or X B(2) shall be ineligible for any Support Service job within TDC for five years to the extent that his removal was occasioned in whole or in part by possession of a weapon, violence, extortion, or aggressive homosexual behavior, and his records shall be annotated accordingly. An inmate removed pursuant to this Subsection for reasons other than those set out in the immediately preceding sentence shall become eligible for assignment to a Support Service job one year after his removal.

C. An inmate may be removed from a Support Service job at any time

"(1) for a job related infraction;

"(2) for unacceptable job performance; or

"(3) at the discretion of the Warden or Assistant Warden."

An inmate removed pursuant to this Subsection C shall be ineligible for reassignment to a Support Service job for a period of time to be determined by the Warden.

XI. *IMPLEMENTATION AND MONITORING PROCEDURES*

A. Within thirty days of the Court's approval of this Stipulation, a full job description of each Support Service job shall be prominently displayed in each unit in places accessible to all inmates and shall be reasonably protected from destruction. Such job descriptions shall include the place of work, the duties to be performed, shift assignment, the supervision required, the extent to which the job entails variances from normal institutional routines and practices (e.g. clothing, meal times, open cell door, etc.), and any particular instructions or proscriptions related to the performance of the job. This job description shall be explained by a staff member to each job holder. In addition, a written roster of all inmates assigned to Support Service jobs, by job title, shall be maintained in each unit.

B. Forthwith, the Director of the Texas Department of Corrections shall maintain a system, apart from the current grievance system, for staff members and inmates to report violations of this Stipulation or harassment or retaliation resulting from any such report. The system shall, at a minimum, provide for the following:

"(1) All such reports shall go directly to the Director or his designee without interception by unit staff;

"(2) All such reports shall be kept confidential except as provided in Subsection (4), infra;

"(3) All such reports shall be fairly investigated. All such investigations must be made by personnel from the central office who are separate and apart from unit staff. No unit staff may participate in the investigation except as witnesses. All findings shall be reported to the Director or his designee, who shall make a disposition report of what actions, if any, were taken, state the reasons for taking or failing to take any action, and personally sign the report; and

"(4) Copies of all staff or inmate reports, together with the disposition report, shall be provided on a current basis to the Special Master and to counsel for the plaintiffs and the United States at their request."

C. Within thirty days of the Court's approval of this Stipulation, specific inmate and employee disciplinary rules shall be promulgated setting out penalties for inmates and employees who violate the provisions of this Stipulation. Prompt and effective disciplinary action shall be taken against all staff members and inmates who violate or are responsible for violations of the provisions of this Stipulation.

D. Any regular grievance, disposition of any complaint under Section XI B, supra, disciplinary report, or disciplinary conviction regarding a Support Service Inmate will be promptly investigated, and the results of the investigation will be reviewed by the unit Warden for the purpose of determining whether the inmate should remain in a Support Service job.

E. Forthwith and until full compliance with the terms of this Stipulation is achieved at a particular unit, there shall be frequent and regular searches of all cells, dormitories, and other housing areas of Support Service Inmates in that unit. These searches shall be unannounced. Any staff member found to have intentionally given advance notice of any such search or to have aided in the hiding of weapons shall be discharged; any inmate guilty of such actions shall be appropriately disciplined.

F. Forthwith, the Director, Assistant Director or other personnel designated by the Director, shall make regular and periodic unannounced inspections of the units to ensure compliance with all aspects of this Stipulation. A written record of the findings of such inspections shall be maintained in the Director's office.

G. Forthwith, the Director shall issue a memorandum to all staff members and inmates declaring the Department's commitment to abide by and enforce the terms of this Stipulation, and making it clear that all staff members and inmates who do not conform to those requirements will be disciplined.

H. Within thirty days of the Court's approval of this Stipulation, a copy thereof shall be published in *The Echo* and distributed individually to all staff members.

XII. *STAFFING INCREASES*

All parties agree that the full implementation of this Stipulation will require a substantial increase in the number of uniformed officers and other staff employed by TDC. They agree that the minimum level of security staffing necessary to achieve full compliance with the terms of this Stipulation will be determined as follows:

"(1) By June 1, 1982, TDC will perform a security staffing needs analysis to determine the number of additional staff members it must have at each unit to fill each staff position on each shift so that staff members perform all of the functions, including manning gates and doors, that must under this Stipulation be performed by staff members and not by inmates, and to identify primary and secondary security points.

"(2) In addition, and by June 1, 1982, a similar analysis, which will include and reflect consideration of any relevant information submitted by any party, shall be performed by correctional experts selected by the Director of the National Institute of Corrections.

"(3) By June 1, 1982 TDC will perform a study of the feasibility and cost of installing locking and unlocking mechanisms at all security gates and doors through TDC.

"(4) The results of the two analyses referred to in (1) and (2) above shall be served on all parties and the Special Master, and compared, and an effort shall be made by the parties to resolve informally any differences between them. By July 1, 1982 the agreed upon staffing level and agreed upon primary and secondary security points shall be submitted to the Court for approval and entry of an appropriate order. They shall also be recommended to the Legislature and the Governor.

"(5) Failing agreement by the parties, the staffing number and the delineation of primary and secondary security points shall be determined as follows:

'(a) By July 15, 1982, plaintiffs shall select one person, and the defendants shall select one person. These two persons shall, by August 1, 1982, select a third person, who shall be experienced in corrections;

'(b) Full opportunity shall be provided to the parties to present their views on the different analyses. The process shall be carried out within the principles of sound mediation and under such rules and procedures as are established by the persons charged with making the decision;

'(c) The three persons shall meet, confer, and, by September 1, 1982, determine a staffing number and a delineation of primary and secondary security points based on the two analyses. All parties agree to submit that staffing number and the delineation of primary and secondary security points to the Court for approval and entry of an appropriate order. They shall also be recommended to the Legislature and the Governor.' "

XIII. *COMPLIANCE TIMETABLE*

A. All terms of this Stipulation for which no specific deadline is provided above shall be fully implemented and maintained at the Ramsey I Unit, the Ellis Unit, and the Eastham Unit as quickly as possible and not later than January 1, 1983; at the Coffield, Ramsey II, Retrieve and Darrington Units as quickly as possible and not later than January 1, 1984; and at all remaining units as quickly as possible and not later than January 1, 1985. Actions to achieve implementation may include priority assignment of new staff to these units, reassignment of existing staff from other units, internal reassignment of staff within each of the aforementioned units, and reclassification and reassignment of inmates.

B. On or before January 1, 1983, and on at least a quarterly basis thereafter until full compliance is achieved, the defendants shall submit a report to the Court detailing their progress toward compliance with all the terms of this Stipulation. If any such report reflects that full compliance cannot be achieved in accordance with the timetable established in Section XIII A of this Stipulation, the defendants may apply to the Court pursuant to the *Federal Rules of Civil Procedure* for an extension of time in which to achieve full compliance.

C. The provisions of this Stipulation shall apply to all new units and future additions to existing units except as indicated below:

"Security staffing at new units or additions to existing units shall be consistent with the staffing patterns established at comparable units pursuant to Section XII, supra; and inmates assigned to new units or additions to existing units will not be permitted to perform functions proscribed by this Stipulation."

XIV. *PROCEDURAL MATTERS*

A. The provisions of this Stipulation supersede those of paragraphs II,A and II,D of the Amended Decree entered on May 1, 1981. Within ten days following the approval of this Stipulation by the District Court, the defendants shall file in the United States Court of Appeals for the Fifth Circuit a motion pursuant to Rule 42(b), *F.R.App.P.* for voluntary dismissal of that portion of their pending appeal relating to paragraphs II,A and II,D of the Amended Decree, without prejudice to other portions of their appeal.

B. Any violation of this Stipulation shall be immediately reported to the Special Master, and the party found to be in violation shall be given a reasonable opportunity to correct any deficiency.

C. All prisoner witnesses for the hearing which began March 15, 1982, who were listed by the Special Master shall be given an election to be transferred to the Huntsville Unit, the Diagnostic Unit, the Wynne Unit or the Goree Unit, under the terms set forth in the Stipulation for the Protection of Witnesses as amended. Once an inmate witness elects such a transfer, he shall be entitled to remain at one of those units until the full implementation of this Stipulation is achieved. Any inmate not making such an election within fifteen days after the Court's approval of this Stipulation shall be deemed to have elected not to transfer.

D. This Stipulation shall be submitted to the Court for its approval pursuant to F.R.Civ.P. 23(e).

Dated:	4–20–82	/s/ Richard E. Gray, III
		/s/ Brian S. Greig
		Attorneys for Defendants
		/s/ Steven L. Winter
Dated:	4/14/82	/s/ D. Brorby
		Attorneys for Plaintiffs
Dated:	4–20–82	/s/ Jim D. Wiginton, by permission
Dated:	4/20/82	/s/ W.P. Clements, Jr.
		William P. Clements, Jr.
		Governor of the State of Texas
Dated:	4/18/82	/s/ W. Bradford Reynolds
		/s/ Patricia G. Littlefield
		Attorneys for Plaintiff-Intervenor

So Ordered this ______ day of ______, 1982.

____

Chief Judge
United States District Court
Eastern District of Texas
Judge Presiding

______

ON PETITION FOR REHEARING
688 F.2d 266 (5th Cir. 1982)

Before CLARK, Chief Judge, RUBIN and TATE, Circuit Judges. [September 16, 1982]

PER CURIAM:

After an opinion was rendered in this case, Ruiz v. Estelle, counsel for the plaintiffs-appellees, a class comprising the inmates confined in the various institutions operated by the Texas Department of Corrections ("TDC"), filed a petition for rehearing. It tells us, for the first time, that the parties disposed of one of the issues after it was briefed, argued, and submitted, and before the court issued its opinion. The petition also seeks reconsideration of other issues. We consider these points separately.

The parties resolved the Huntsville Unit Hospital issue several months before we issued our opinion in this case. In accordance with the request made by the inmate class and acquiesced in by the defendants, we vacate Parts of the panel opinion, which treat that issue.

The plaintiffs assert that the parties have agreed to a TDC fire safety plan that has been tentatively approved by the district court. Nothing contained in our opinion intimates that this agreement, never previously called to our attention, should be set aside, whether or not the fire safety provisions of the prior district court decree are affirmed. Accordingly, without setting aside our prior determination on this issue, we state expressly that the parties are not precluded from obtaining the district court's approval of a remedial order that grants additional relief. Cf. United States v. City of Miami, 664 F.2d 435, 447 (5th Cir. 1981) (en banc) (plurality opinion) ("[T]he parties to litigation are not to be deprived of the opportunity to compose their differences . . . .").

Our ruling that double-celling of inmates in administrative segregation does not constitute cruel and unusual punishment was based only on the record before us. It was not intended to preclude either party from seeking further relief. Accordingly, our opinion is amended so that Part IV(C)(3) of the district court's decree is vacated without prejudice.

We adhere to our holding that the direction to TDC to use good time, parole, and furlough programs was unduly intrusive. We fail to perceive how, under the district court's decree, even as modified by us, TDC will again become so overcrowded as to warrant such intrusion, for the decree contains specific provisions that limit prison population. TDC's problem will be whether there are facilities permitting the admission of inmates, not the method of discharging inmates. However, should TDC fail to comply with the district court's decree, and the inmate population be increased beyond the number authorized by the space requirements of the decree, and should TDC fail to remedy the situation, our order shall not preclude the direction of specific remedies.

Sua sponte, we clarify the references in our opinion to the time within which either party may seek changes in the district court's decree. Application for such changes may be filed after the decree, as modified by us, has been in force for one year, and the hearing shall be held in due course thereafter.

In all other respects the petition for rehearing is denied.

On November 17, 1982, Judge Justice awarded inmates' attorneys a reasonable fee: $1,662,683. Judge Justice's remark that "well over $1,000,000,000 will be required to repair the constitutional deficiencies demonstrated by measures that were not reversed on appeal" supplies some perspective. Ruiz v. Estelle, 553 F.Supp. 567, 593, 598 (S.D.Tex.1982).

---

1) Is "constitutional peace" more likely in Texas or Arkansas? What might account for the difference? Consider the size of the prison system, the attitude of the correction officials, the political climate, the lawyers, the posture and strategies of the trial judges, the design of the decree, and the role of the appellate court.

2) How do you characterize Judge Wayne Justice's role and style, as compared to Judge Henley's and Judge Eisele's? Which style is more likely to be effective? Which comports more nearly to your model of appropriate judicial behavior?

3) In *Ruiz,* the United States was invited by Judge Justice, a former U.S. attorney, to participate in the litigation as a "litigating amicus," that is an amicus with "full rights as a party." Should Judge Henley have extended a similar invitation? Why do you think he did not? What impact might an intervention by the United States have had on the Arkansas case? See United States v. City of Philadelphia, p. 36.

4) *Ruiz* involves ancillary personnel including a full-fledged special master. The Arkansas litigation largely proceeded with the judge alone, although a Compliance Coordinator helped administer the 1978 consent decree. What would have been gained or lost if a special master had been used in the Arkansas case?

5) Compare the standard of review used by the Fifth Circuit and that used by the Eighth Circuit (especially in *Holt III*). Which is more consistent with the proper allocation of power and responsibilities between trial and appellate courts in the federal judicial system? Is the Fifth Circuit whittling down substantive rights by limiting the remedy in several respects? Judge Rubin speaks of a "reparative injunction," rather than a "structural injunction," to describe the decree Judge Justice entered. Is he suggesting that the function of the decree was to place plaintiffs where they would have been but for the violations, rather than to remove the present threat to plaintiffs' rights? On the nomenclature, see O. Fiss, The Civil Rights Injunction (1978).

6) Both the Arkansas and the Texas lawsuits involve negotiated structural consent decrees. May negotiated remedies frustrate the substantive law? Are negotiated consent decrees in structural reform consensual in the same way that the negotiated price of a residence is consensual? Are negotiations and plan submission necessary a) To utilize the parties' expertise? b) To give the parties a feeling that they participated and to lend the result legitimacy? Is the adjudicatory format inconsistent with the give and take necessary to accomplish successful structural reform? Are masters or receivers surreptitious agents of brokered, secret, political deals? Is adjudication, on the other hand, simply a continuation of politics at another stage by other means? See Berger, Away From the Court House and Into the Field: The Odyssey of a Special Master, 78 Colum.L.Rev. 707 (1978); Chayes, The Role of the Judge in Public Law Litigation, 89 Harv.L.Rev. 1281 (1976); Fiss, The Su-

preme Court, 1978 Term—Foreword: The Forms of Justice, 93 Harv.L.Rev. 1, 44–58 (1979); Kirp, Legalism and Politics in School Desegregation, 1981 Wis.L.Rev. 924; Starr, Accommodation and Accountability: A Strategy for Judicial Enforcement of Institutional Reform Decrees, 32 Ala.L.Rev. 399 (1981).

7) Reconsider the party structure. The conflict in school lawsuits between idealists who favor racial balance achieved through busing and parents who subordinate balance to quality education is well documented. Bell, The Dialectics of School Desegregation, 32 Ala.L.Rev. 281, 283–85, 287, 294–95 (1981). Does allowing those affected to intervene solve the problem satisfactorily? See Rule 24(a); Wilton, Functional Interest Advocacy in Modern Complex Litigation, 1982 Wash.U.L.Q. 37, 58–61 (1982). What about dividing the Rule 23(b)(2) plaintiff class into subclasses? Rule 23(c)(4). See 23(d)(2). How can we be sure the plaintiffs' attorneys represent inarticulate members of a plaintiff class? Should the judge establish human rights committees and monitors and have them report to him directly? Should the judge visit the institution? Drake, Judicial Implementation and Wyatt v. Stickney, 32 Ala.L.Rev. 299, 307–08 (1981).

8) Who are the true defendants when a plaintiff class sues a state or local government facility: the named defendants, the legislature, or the taxpayers? What if the professional managers seize the opportunity of a lawsuit to negotiate a decree that requires them to spend a great deal more money than they have been receiving? After Judge Eisele dismissed the Arkansas litigation, the Arkansas Gazette reported that Robert Sarver, who was Correction Commissioner in 1969 when the suit was filed, "drew up some of the papers against himself." "I wrote out the writs on a yellow pad and gave them to the inmates, who typed them up and signed them," Sarver said, noting that he wrote only two of the more than 20 writs that were consolidated into the suit. "I raised the issue of the trusty system—frankly that was the only issue I thought we could get into court—and medical care." Wells, 'Dark and Evil World' Is Banished, Changed by Inmate Complaints, Arkansas Gazette, Aug. 15, 1982 at A1, col. 8. (discussed at p. 575 above). May the judge join as defendants people who did not violate plaintiffs' substantive rights but who are necessary for relief? The legislatures of Arkansas and Texas fund the states' prisons. What if they refuse to vote the necessary wherewithal to run the prisons as the judge ordered?

9) The Montgomery, Alabama city government decided that rather than run desegregated constitutional parks, it would get out of the park business. Gilmore v. City of Montgomery, 176 F.Supp. 776 (M.D.Ala. 1959), affirmed as modified, 277 F.2d 364 (5th Cir. 1960). States are unlikely to abandon the prison business. What if, however, instead of providing a constitutional prison, the authorities allow prisoners to remain in worse local jails in a holding pattern? May the judge order the state to release prisoners to relieve overcrowding? Tell the legislature to provide sufficient funds to construct new prisons? See Newman v. Alabama, 683 F.2d 1312 (11th Cir. 1982).

In the Willowbrook litigation, following protracted hearings, the parties agreed to a Consent Judgment. It provided for community placement of persons confined to an institution for the mentally retarded and established a seven-person Review Panel. Governor Carey requested that the state legislature appropriate $342,000 to finance the Review Panel, but that appropriation specifically failed to meet approval. Judge Bartels joined the state Comptroller as a defendant and held that unless funds were provided for the Review Panel in five days, the Governor and the Comptroller were in contempt. Judge Bartels was "unconvinced" that the Governor "has done all within his powers" to secure the funding. The court of appeals stayed and reversed the contempt. The Governor could not obey the federal judge's order except by violating state law; the court concluded that the Governor's dilemma was too cruel to approve. Plaintiffs argued that the Governor must provide funds on the ground that the state was forbidden from impeding the enjoyment of rights protected under the federal constitution. The court of appeals held that the district judge could not force the expenditure of state funds for a purpose the legislature "expressly disallowed," particularly where the court was unready to assume that refusal to pay for the Review Panel violated the constitution. The court said that, because the Consent Decree compelled the Governor to employ his "lawful authority," he had not violated it; it remitted plaintiffs to the legislature to seek the appropriation previously refused. The cavalry arrived on a petition for rehearing; the federal government allowed the Governor to use, "at his discretion," federal money to pay the Review Panel. New York State Association for Retarded Children, Inc. v. Carey, 631 F.2d 162 (2d Cir. 1980).

The Pennhurst case raised similar issues. Judge Broderick there dealt with the Commonwealth defendants' failure to pay for a Special Master and Hearing Master to implement a structural decree also reorganizing an institution for the mentally retarded. In July of 1981, defendants "advised the Court that it did not intend to comply with the Court's Orders" that they pay the masters. After Secretary of the Department of Public Welfare O'Bannon told a legislative appropriations committee that they were "not defendants to the suit" and that "I think the whole masters office is a redundant, ridiculous piece of bureaucracy," the legislature cut the Masters' appropriation from $900,000 to $35,000 and registered disapproval of the Masters' offices. Halderman v. Pennhurst State School and Hospital, 533 F.Supp. 631, 635 (E.D.Pa. 1981). Judge Broderick found that defendants thwarted the appropriation, and he imposed a $10,000 per day coercive contempt fine on them. Defendants paid the fine to the Court's Registry for 30 days. The judge then applied a portion of the coercive contempt fines, $100,000, to the expenses of the Masters' offices. Halderman v. Pennhurst State School and Hospital, 526 F.Supp. 423, 427 (E.D.Pa. 1981). He justified this action:

"The action of the Legislature of this Commonwealth in refusing to appropriate funds for the Masters and in expressing an intention that no other funds of the Commonwealth be used for the Masters cannot abrogate the Order of this Court based upon the right of the retarded residents of Pennhurst to such education, training, and care as will better enable them to cope with life as effectively as their capacities will permit. As heretofore pointed out, the Masters are an integral part of the remedy prescribed by the Court to make certain that the Commonwealth provides minimally adequate habilitation to the retarded residents of Pennhurst.

"It is clear that a '[s]tate-law prohibition against compliance with the District Court's decree cannot survive the command of the Supremacy Clause of the United States Constitution.' Washington v. Washington State Commercial Passenger Fishing Vessel Association, 443 U.S. 658, 695 (1979)." 533 F.Supp. at 638–639 (E.D.Pa. 1981).

What would have occurred if the Pennhurst defendants had refused to pay the $10,000 per day coercive exaction into the federal court's registry? Did Judge Broderick's solution allow the defendants to effect compliance while saving face? Did Judge Broderick find a way for the federal judiciary to allocate state tax revenues?

Earlier courts were more forceful, as revealed by the often cited decision In re Nevitt, 117 F. 448 (8th Cir. 1902). The St. Clair County, Missouri court judges refused to pay judgments on certain county bonds. The federal court issued a mandamus directing them to "levy a tax to make a partial payment" and imprisoned them "until such time as they shall comply." The reported opinion addressed the question whether to stay the coercive imprisonment while the contemnors sought a pardon from the executive. The circuit court of appeals settled the matter by holding that the president lacked authority to pardon coercive imprisonment. The opinion contains the frequently quoted metaphoric sentences that describe the indeterminate nature of coercive contempt. "They are imprisoned only until they comply with the orders of the court, and this they may do at any time. They carry the keys of their prison in their own pockets." 117 F. at 1461. See also Griffin v. County School Board, 377 U.S. 218 (1964) (schools opened by order of the Court).

Delaware Valley Citizens' Council for Clean Air v. Commonwealth of Pennsylvania, 678 F.2d 470 (3d Cir. 1982), involved a new twist: the court deprived the violator of funds. The Commonwealth entered into a consent decree agreeing to comply with the federal Clean Air Act. The General Assembly prohibited the state executive from spending funds to implement the program. The trial judge held the state executive branch defendants in civil contempt and ordered the federal government to refrain from funding the appropriate programs pending the Commonwealth's compliance. The court of appeals approved with a bold theory. a) "[I]njunctive relief against nonparties may be appropriate if necessary to afford full relief." 678 F.2d at 478 n. 17. b) The entire government of Pennsylvania was bound by the consent decree. Thus "the argument of inability to comply rings hollow." 678 F.2d at 475. c) The court forbade members of the legislature from intervening, in part because "their interests were adequately represented by the Commonwealth defendants." 678 F.2d at 474.

III. The Debate Over Legitimacy

Fuller, THE FORMS AND LIMITS OF ADJUDICATION

(copyright 1978 Harvard Law Review)
92 Harv.L.Rev. 353, 365–71, 381–404 (1978).

. . . Adjudication and Rationality

. . . It may be said that the essence of adjudication lies not in the manner in which the affected party participates in the decision but in the office of judge. If there is a judge and a chance to appear before him, it is a matter of indifference whether the litigant chooses to present proofs or reasoned arguments. He may, if he sees fit, offer no argument at all, or pitch his appeal entirely on an emotional level, or even indicate his willingness that the judge decide the case by a throw of the dice. It might seem, then, that our analysis should take as its point of departure the office of judge. From this office certain requirements might be deduced, for example, that of impartiality, since a judge to be "truly" such must be impartial. Then, as the next step, if he is to be impartial he must be willing to hear both sides, etc.

The trouble with this is that there are people who are called "judges" holding official positions and expected to be impartial who nevertheless do not participate in an adjudication in any sense directly relevant to the subject of this paper. Judges at an agricultural fair or an art exhibition may serve as examples. Again, a baseball umpire, though he is not called a judge, is expected to make impartial rulings. What distinguishes these functionaries is not that they do not hold governmental office, for the duties of a judge at a livestock fair would scarcely be changed if he were an official of the Department of Agriculture. What distinguishes them from courts, administrative tribunals, and boards of arbitration is that their decisions are not reached within an institutional framework that is intended to assure to the disputants an opportunity for the presentation of proofs and reasoned arguments. The judge of livestock may or may not permit such a presentation; it is not an integral part of his office to permit and to attend to it . . . .

It may be objected at this point that "reasoned argument" is, after all, not a monopoly of forensic proceedings. A political speech may take the form of a reasoned appeal to the electorate; to be sure, it often takes other forms, but the same thing may be said of speeches in court. This objection fails to take account of a conception that underlies the whole analysis being presented here the conception, namely, of a form of participating in a decision that is institutionally defined and assured.

When I am entering a contract with another person I may present proofs and arguments to him, but there is generally no formal assurance that I will be given this opportunity or that he will listen to my arguments if I make them . . . . During an election I may actively campaign for one side and may present what I consider to be "reasoned arguments" to the electorate. If I am an effective campaigner this participation in the decision ultimately reached may greatly outweigh in importance the casting of my own single vote. At the same time, it is only the latter form of participation that is the subject of an affirmative institutional guarantee. The protection accorded my right to present arguments to the electorate is almost entirely indirect and negative. The way will be held clear for me, but I shall have to pave it myself. Even if I am given an affirmative right (for example, under the "equal time" rule of the FCC) I am given no formal assurance that anyone will listen to my appeal. The voter who goes to sleep before his television set is surely not subject to the same condemnation as the judge who sleeps through the arguments of counsel.

Adjudication is, then, a device which gives formal and institutional expression to the influence of reasoned argument in human affairs. As such it assumes a burden of rationality not borne by any other form of social ordering. A decision which is the product of reasoned argument must be prepared itself to meet the test of reason. We demand of an adjudicative decision a kind of rationality we do not expect of the results of contract or of voting. This higher responsibility toward rationality is at once the strength *and the weakness* of adjudication as a form of social ordering.

In entering contracts, men are of course in some measure guided by rational considerations. The subsistence farmer who has a surfeit of potatoes and only a handful of onions acts reasonably when he trades potatoes for onions. But there is no test of rationality that can be applied to the result of the trade considered in abstraction from the interests of the parties. Indeed, the trade of potatoes for onions, which is a rational act by one trader, might be considered irrational if indulged in by his opposite number, who has a storehouse full of onions and only a bushel of potatoes. If we asked one party to the contract, "Can you defend that contract?" he might answer, "Why, yes. It was good for me and it was good for him." If we then said, "But that is not what we meant. We meant, can you defend it on general grounds?" he might well reply that he did not know what we were talking about. Yet this is precisely the kind of question we normally direct toward the decision of a judge or arbitrator. The results that emerge from adjudication are subject, then, to a standard of rationality that is different from that imposed on the results of an exchange.

I believe that the same observation holds true when adjudication is compared with elections. The key to the difference lies again in the mode in which the affected party participates in a decision. If, as in adjudication, the only mode of participation consists in the opportunity to present proofs and arguments, the purpose of this participation is frustrated, and the whole proceeding becomes a farce, should the decision that emerges make no pretense whatever to rationality. The same cannot be said of the mode of participation called voting. We may assume that the preferences of voters are ultimately emotional, inarticulate, and not subject to rational defense. At the same time there is a need for social order, and it may be assumed that this need is best met when order rests on the broadest possible base of popular support. On this ground, a negative defense of democracy is possible; the will of the majority controls, not because it is right, but—well, because it *is* the will of the majority. This is surely an impoverished conception of democracy, but it expresses at least one ingredient of any philosophy of democracy, and it suggests a reason why we demand of adjudication a kind of rationality that we do not expect of elections . . . .

Now if we ask ourselves what kinds of questions are commonly decided by judges and arbitrators, the answer may well be, "Claims of right." Indeed, in the older literature (including notably John Chipman Gray's The Nature and Sources of the Law (1909)) courts were often distinguished from administrative or executive agencies on the ground that it is the function of courts to "declare rights." If, then, we seek to define "the limits of adjudication," a tempting answer would be that the proper province of courts is limited to cases where rights are asserted. On reflection we might enlarge this to include cases where fault or guilt is charged (broadly, "the trial of accusations"), since in many cases it is artificial to treat the accuser (who may be the district attorney) as claiming a right. Though it is not particularly artificial to view the lawbreaker as violating "a right" of the state, to say that when the state indicts the lawbreaker it is claiming a remedial "right" against him does seem to reflect a misguided impulse toward forcing a symmetry between civil and criminal remedies. To avoid any such manipulations of natural modes of thought, let us then amend the suggested criterion to read as follows: The proper province of adjudication is to make an authoritative determination of questions raised by claims of right and accusations of guilt.

Is this a significant way of describing "the limits of adjudication?" I do not think so. In fact, what purports here to be a distinct assertion is merely an implication of the fact that adjudication is a form of decision that defines the affected party's participation as that of offering proofs and reasoned arguments. It is not so much that adjudicators decide only issues presented by claims of right or accusations. The point is rather that *whatever* they decide, or *whatever* is submitted to them for decision, tends to be converted into a claim of right or an accusation of fault or guilt. This conversion is effected by the institutional framework within which both the litigant and the adjudicator function.

Let me spell out rather painstakingly the steps of an argument that will show why this should be so. (1) Adjudication is a process of decision that grants to the affected party a form of participation that consists in the opportunity to present proofs and reasoned arguments. (2) The litigant must therefore, if his participation is to be meaningful, assert some principle or principles by which his arguments are sound and his proofs relevant. (3) A naked demand is distinguished from a claim of right by the fact that the latter is a demand supported by a principle; likewise, a mere expression of displeasure or resentment is distinguished from an accusation by the fact that the latter rests upon some principle. Hence, (4) issues tried before an adjudicator tend to become claims of right or accusations of fault.

We may see this process of conversion in the case of an employee who desires an increase in pay. If he asks his boss for a raise, he may, of course, claim "a right" to the raise. He may argue the fairness of the principle of equal treatment and call attention to the fact that Joe, who is no better than he, recently got a raise. But he does not have to rest his plea on any ground of this sort. He may merely beg for generosity, urging the needs of his family. Or he may propose an exchange, offering to take on extra duties if he gets the raise. If, however, he takes his case to an arbitrator he cannot, explicitly at least, support his case by an appeal to charity or by proposing a bargain. He will have to support his demand by a principle of some kind, and a demand supported by principle is the same thing as a claim of right. So, when he asks his boss for a raise, he may or may not make a claim of right; when he presents his demand to an arbitrator he *must* make a claim of right. . . .

If the analysis presented here is correct, three aspects of adjudication that seem to present distinct qualities are in fact all expressions of a single quality: (1) the peculiar mode by which the affected party participates in the decision; (2) the peculiarly urgent demand of rationality that the adjudicative process must be prepared to meet; and (3) the fact that adjudication finds its normal and "natural" province in judging claims of right and accusations of fault. So, when we say that a party entering a contract, or voting in an election, has no "right" to any particular outcome, we are describing the same fundamental fact that we allude to when we say that adjudication has to meet a test of rationality or of "principle" that is not applied to contracts and elections. . . .

I have suggested that it is not a significant description of the limits of adjudication to say that its proper province lies where rights are asserted or accusations of fault are made, for such a statement involves a circle of reasoning. If, however, we regard a formal definition of rights and wrongs as a nearly inevitable product of the adjudicative process, we can arrive at what is perhaps the most significant of all limitations on the proper province of adjudication. Adjudication is not a proper form of social ordering in those areas where the effectiveness of human association would be destroyed if it were organized about formally defined "rights" and "wrongs." Courts have, for example, rather regularly refused to enforce agreements between husband and wife affecting the internal organization of family life. There are other and wider areas where the intrusion of "the machinery of the law" is equally inappropriate. An adjudicative board might well undertake to allocate one thousand tons of coal among three claimants; it could hardly conduct even the simplest coal-mining enterprise by the forms of adjudication. Wherever successful human association depends upon spontaneous and informal collaboration, shifting its forms with the task at hand, there adjudication is out of place except as it may declare certain ground rules applicable to a wide variety of activities.

These are vague and perhaps trite observations. I shall attempt to bring them into sharper focus in a later part of this paper, particularly in a discussion of the relative incapacity of adjudication to solve "polycentric" problems. Meanwhile the point I should like to stress is that the incapacity of a given area of human activity to endure a pervasive delimitation of rights and wrongs is also a measure of its incapacity to respond to a too exigent rationality, a rationality that demands an immediate and explicit reason for every step taken. Back of both of these incapacities lies the fundamental truth that certain kinds of human relations are not appropriate raw material for a process of decision that is institutionally committed to acting on the basis of reasoned argument. . . .

The Forms of Adjudication

. . . [The reader] should not [be] misled into thinking that this paper condemns all departures of adjudication from a state of pristine purity. Certain mixed forms are valuable and almost indispensable, though their use is often attended by certain dangers.

In determining whether a deviant or mixed form impairs the integrity of adjudication the test throughout will be that already stressed repeatedly: Does it affect adversely the meaning of the affected party's participation in the decision by proofs and reasoned arguments? . . .

May the Arbiter Act on His Own Motion in Initiating the Case?

. . . [I]n most of the practical manifestations of adjudication the arbiter's function has to be "promoted" by the litigant and is not initiated by itself. But is this coy quality of waiting to be asked an essential part of adjudication?

It would seem that it is not. Suppose, for example, the collision of two ships under circumstances that suggest that one or both masters were at fault. Suppose a board is given authority to initiate hearings in such a case and to make a determination of fault. Such a board might conduct its hearings after the pattern of court proceedings. Both masters might be accorded counsel and a full opportunity for cross-examination. There would be no impairment of the affected parties' full participation by proofs and reasoned argument; the integrity of adjudication seems to be preserved.

Yet I think that most of us would consider such a case exceptional and would not be deterred by it from persisting in the belief that the adjudicative process should normally not be initiated by the tribunal itself. There are, I believe, sound reasons for adhering to that belief.

Certainly it is clear that the integrity of adjudication is impaired if the arbiter not only initiates the proceedings but also, in advance of the public hearing, forms theories about what happened and conducts his own factual inquiries. In such a case the arbiter cannot bring to the public hearing an uncommitted mind; the effectiveness of participation through proofs and reasoned arguments is accordingly reduced. Now it is probably true that under most circumstances the mere initiation of proceedings carries with it a certain commitment and often a theory of what occurred. The case of the collision at sea is exceptional because there the facts themselves speak eloquently for the need of some kind of inquiry, so that the initiation of the proceedings implies nothing more than a recognition of this need. In most situations the initiation of proceedings could not have the same neutral quality, as, for example, where the occasion consists simply in the fact that a corporation had gone two years without declaring a dividend.

. . . [To take a more central example, it] seems clear that a regime of contract (more broadly a regime of reciprocity) implies that the determination whether to assert a claim must be left to the interested party.

A contrary suggestion is advanced by Karl Llewellyn in The Cheyenne Way [written with E.A. Hoebel in 1941]. In answer to the question "Why do we leave it to the affected party whether to assert his claim for breach of contract?" he gives the startling explanation that this is because as a matter of actual experience the motive of self-interest has proved sufficient to maintain a regime of contract. He suggests that if in the future this motive were to suffer a serious decline, then the state might find itself compelled to intervene to strengthen the regime of contract. This curious conception is symptomatic of a general tendency of our times to obscure the role of reciprocity as an organizing principle and to convert everything into "social policy," which is another way of saying that all organization is by common aims (or by the aims that in the mind of the "policymaker" ought to be common).

. . . To enforce a contract for a party who is willing to leave it unenforced is just as absurd as making the contract for him in the first place. (I realize, of course, that there are contracts required by law, but this is obviously a derivative phenomenon which would lose all meaning if every human relation were imposed by the state and were called a "contract.")

The belief that it is not normal for the arbiter himself to initiate the adjudicative process has, then, a twofold basis. *First,* it is generally impossible to keep even the bare initiation of proceedings untainted by preconceptions about what happened and what its consequences should be. In this sense, initiation of the proceedings by the arbiter impairs the integrity of adjudication by reducing the effectiveness of the litigant's participation through proofs and arguments. *Second,* the great bulk of claims submitted to adjudication are founded directly or indirectly on relationships of reciprocity. In this case, unless the affected party is deceived or ignorant of his rights, the very foundations of the claim asserted dictate that the processes of adjudication must be invoked by the claimant.

Must the Decision Be Accompanied by a Statement of the Reasons for It?

We tend to think of the judge or arbitrator as one who decides and who gives reasons for his decision. Does the integrity of adjudication require that reasons be given for the decision rendered? I think the answer is, not necessarily. In some fields of labor arbitration (chiefly, I believe, where arbitration is a facility made available without charge by the state) it is the practice to render "blind" awards. The reasons for this practice probably include a belief that reasoned awards are often misinterpreted and "stir up trouble," as well as the circumstance that the arbitrator is so busy he has no time to write opinions. Under the procedures of the American Arbitration Association awards in commercial cases are rendered usually without opinion. (Written opinions are, however, usual in *labor* cases.) . . .

By and large it seems clear that the fairness and effectiveness of adjudication are promoted by reasoned opinions. Without such opinions the parties have to take it on faith that their participation in the decision has been real, that the arbiter has in fact understood and taken into account their proofs and arguments. A less obvious point is that, where a decision enters into some continuing relationship, if no reasons are given the parties will almost inevitably guess at reasons and act accordingly. Here the effectiveness of adjudication is impaired, not only because the results achieved may not be those intended by the arbiter, but also because his freedom of decision in future cases may be curtailed by the growth of practices based on a misinterpretation of decisions previously rendered.

May the Arbiter Rest His Decision on Grounds Not Argued by the Parties?

Obviously the bond of participation by the litigant is most secure when the arbiter rests his decision wholly on the proofs and argument actually presented to him by the parties. In practice, however, it is not always possible to realize this ideal. Even where all of the considerations on which the decision rests were touched on by the parties' arguments, the emphasis may be very different. An issue dealt with only in passing by one of the parties, or perhaps by both, may become the headstone of the arbiter's decision. This may mean not only that, had they foreseen this outcome, the parties would have presented different arguments, but that they might also have introduced evidence on very different factual issues.

If the ideal of a perfect congruence between the arbiter's view of the issues and that of the parties is unattainable, this is no excuse for a failure to work toward an achievement of the closest approximation of it. We need to remind ourselves that if this congruence is utterly absent—if the grounds for the decision fall completely outside the framework of the argument, making all that was discussed or proved at the hearing irrelevant—then the adjudicative process has become a sham, for the parties' participation in the decision has lost all meaning. We need to analyze what factors influence the desired congruence and what measures may be taken to promote it.

One circumstance of capital importance is the extent to which a particular process of adjudication takes place in a context of established rules. In branches of the law where the rules have become fairly settled and certain, it may be possible for lawyers to reach agreement easily in defining the crucial issues presented by a particular case. In such an area the risk is slight that the decision will fall outside the frame of reference set by the proofs and arguments. On the other hand in areas of uncertainty, this risk is greatly increased. There are, to be sure, dangers in a premature crystallization of standards. On the other hand, one of the less obvious dangers of a too long delayed formulation of doctrine lies in the inevitable impairment of the integrity of adjudication that is entailed, for the reality of the parties' participation is reduced when it is impossible to foretell what issues will become relevant in the ultimate disposition of the case.

These are considerations often overlooked in criticisms of the conduct of administrative agencies and labor arbitrators. Ex parte posthearing conferences with the parties are often motivated by a well-intentioned desire to preserve the reality of the parties' participation in the decision. Where the standards of decision are vague and fluctuating, when the time comes for final disposition of the case it may be apparent that most of what was argued and proved at the public hearing has become irrelevant. A desire to give a litigant a meaningful "day in court" may, paradoxically, lead to giving him a lunchhour out of court. In many cases this conduct should be characterized as inept, rather than wicked.

Those inexperienced in legal procedures often do not know of devices which have been developed by courts that will eliminate much of the need for such practices. In particular, requests for a reargument and the device of the tentative decree, with something like an order to show cause why it should not be made final, could often be used with advantage by labor arbitrators and administrative tribunals. This is not to say that these expedients will solve all problems. An arbitrator paid on a per diem basis by the parties may hesitate to run up his bill by requesting a second argument. In some situations a tentative decree may arouse expectations of such an intensity that a later modification becomes very difficult. The fundamental point made here, however, is that before we demand of lay arbiters that they act like judges, we must place them in a context, and arm them with procedures, that will make it possible for them to do their job properly and still act throughout like judges. . . .

Qualifications and Disqualifications of the Arbiter

. . . I shall merely suggest that the problem of securing a properly qualified and impartial arbiter be tried by the same touchstone that has been used throughout—what will preserve the efficacy and meaning of the affected party's participation through proofs and arguments? Obviously, a strong emotional attachment by the arbiter to one of the interests involved in the dispute, is destructive of that participation. In practice, however, another kind of "partiality" is much more dangerous. I refer to the situation where the arbiter's experience of life has not embraced the area of the dispute, or, worse still, where he has always viewed that area from some single vantage point. Here a blind spot of which he is quite unconscious may prevent him from getting the point of testimony or argument. By and large, I think the decisions of our courts in commercial cases do not represent adjudication at its highest level. The reason is a lack of judicial "feel" for the problems involved.

A sailor was once brought before a three-judge German court for violation of a provision of the criminal code which made it a serious offense to threaten another with bodily harm. Uncontradicted testimony proved that the prisoner had been heard to say, "I'll stick a knife in your guts and turn it around three times." Two judges, who had spent their lives in genteel surroundings far from the waterfront, were with great difficulty persuaded by the third to acquit.

Must the Decision Be Retrospective?

In practice both the decisions of courts and the awards of arbitrators are retrospective, both as to their effect on the litigants' rights and their effect as precedents for the decisions of other cases. A paradox is sometimes squeezed from this traditional way of acting, to the effect that courts, in order to avoid the appearance of legislating, cast their legislative enactments in the harshest possible form, making them ex post facto.

The philosophy underlying the retrospective effect of the judicial decision can be stated somewhat as follows: It is not the function of courts to create new aims for society or to impose on society new basic directives. The courts for various reasons analyzed previously are unsuited for this sort of task. Perhaps the most compelling objection to an assumption of any such function lies in the limited participation in the decision by the litigants who (1) represent generally only themselves and (2) participate in the decision only by proofs and arguments addressed to the arbiter. On the other hand, with respect to the generally shared aims and the authoritative directives of a society, the courts do have an important function to perform, that of developing (or even "discovering") case by case what these aims or directives demand for their realization in particular situations of fact. In the discharge of this function, at times the result is so obvious that no one thinks of a "retroactive effect." Theoretically, a court might distinguish between such decisions and those which announce a rule or standard that seems "new," even though it may represent a reasoned conclusion from familiar premises. But if an attempt were made to apply such a distinction pervasively, so that some decisions would be retrospective, some prospective only, the resulting confusion might be much less bearable than the situation that now obtains.

Generally the same considerations apply also to arbitration awards. It is not a matter of "concealing" the legislative nature of the arbitrator's award which makes him give it a retrospective effect. It is rather a conservative philosophy about the proper functions of adjudication, a philosophy which seeks to keep meaningful the adversary presentation, the particiation of litigants only through appeals to reason, etc.

How is Adjudication Affected by the Source of the Arbiter's Power?

The power to adjudicate may represent a delegated power of government, as in the case of a judge, or it may derive from the consent of the litigants, as in most forms of arbitration. Are these two basically different "forms" of adjudication? Obviously it has been a tacit assumption of this paper that they are not.

On the other hand, this does not mean that the discharge of the arbiter's function is wholly unaffected by the source of his power. In a summary way we may say that the possible advantages of adjudication supported by governmental authority are: (1) The judge is under less temptation to "compromise" than is the contractually appointed arbitrator. (2) The acceptability of the judge's decision may be enhanced by the fact that he seems to play a subservient role, as one who merely applies rules which he himself did not make.

Among the possible advantages of adjudication which derives its power from a contract of the parties are the following: (1) Being unbacked by state power (or insufficiently backed by it in the case of an ineffective legal sanction), the arbitrator must concern himself directly with the acceptability of his award. He may be at greater pains than a judge to get his facts straight, to state accurately the arguments of the parties, and generally to display in his award a full understanding of the case. (2) Being relatively free from technical rules of procedure, the wise and conscientious arbitrator can shape his procedures upon what he perceives to be the intrinsic demands of effective adjudication. Thus, the "due process" which animates his conduct of the hearing may appear to the parties as something real and not something that has to be taken on faith, as allegedly inhering in technical rules that seem quite arbitrary to the layman.

As a special quality of contractually authorized arbitration, which cannot unequivocally be called either an "advantage" or "disadvantage," we may note that the contract to arbitrate may contain explicit or implicit limits upon the adjudicative process itself. The arbitrator often comes to the hearing with a feeling that he must conduct himself in a way that conforms generally to the expectations of the parties and that this restriction is implicit in the contract of submission. Thus, if both parties desire and expect a more "literal" interpretation than the arbitrator himself would prefer, he may feel obligated to adopt an attitude of interpretation that he finds intellectually uncongenial.

The Limits of Adjudication

Attention is now directed to the question, What kinds of tasks are inherently unsuited to adjudication? The test here will be that used throughout. If a given task is assignd to adjudicative treatment, will it be possible to preserve the meaning of the affected party's participation through proofs and arguments?

[For purposes of addressing the question of limits, this] section introduces a concept—that of the "polycentric task"— which has been derived from Michael Polanyi's book The Logic of Liberty [(1951)]. In approaching that concept it will be well to begin with a few examples.

Some months ago a wealthy lady by the name of Timken died in New York leaving a valuable, but somewhat miscellaneous, collection of paintings to the Metropolitan Museum and the National Gallery "in equal shares," her will indicating no particular apportionment. When the will was probated the judge remarked something to the effect that the parties seemed to be confronted with a real problem. The attorney for one of the museums spoke up and said, "We are good friends. We will work it out somehow or other." What makes this problem of effecting an equal division of the paintings a polycentric task? It lies in the fact that the disposition of any single painting has implications for the proper disposition of every other painting. If it gets the Renoir, the Gallery may be less eager for the Cezanne but all the more eager for the Bellows, etc. If the proper apportionment were set for argument, there would be no clear issue to which either side could direct its proofs and contentions. Any judge assigned to hear such an argument would be tempted to assume the role of mediator or to adopt the classical solution: Let the older brother (here the Metropolitan) divide the estate into what he regards as equal shares, let the younger brother (the National Gallery) take his pick.

As a second illustration suppose in a socialist regime it were decided to have all wages and prices set by courts which would proceed after the usual forms of adjudication. It is, I assume, obvious that here is a task that could not successfully be undertaken by the adjudicative method. The point that comes first to mind is that courts move too slowly to keep up with a rapidly changing economic scene. The more fundamental point is that the forms of adjudication cannot encompass and take into account the complex repercussions that may result from any change in prices or wages. A rise in the price of aluminum may affect in varying degrees the demand for, and therefore the proper price of, thirty kinds of steel, twenty kinds of plastics, an infinitude of woods, other metals, etc. Each of these separate effects may have its own complex repercussions in the economy. In such a case it is simply impossible to afford each affected party a meaningful participation through proofs and arguments. It is a matter of capital importance to note that it is not merely a question of the huge number of possibly affected parties, significant as that aspect of the thing may be. A more fundamental point is that each of the various forms that award might take (say, a three-cent increase per pound, a four-cent increase, a five-cent increase, etc.) would have a different set of repercussions and might require in each instance a redefinition of the "parties affected."

We may visualize this kind of situation by thinking of a spider web. A pull on one strand will distribute tensions after a complicated pattern throughout the web as a whole. Doubling the original pull will, in all likelihood, not simply double each of the resulting tensions but will rather create a different complicated pattern of tensions. This would certainly occur, for example, if the doubled pull caused one or more of the weaker strands to snap. This is a "polycentric" situation because it is "many centered"—each crossing of strands is a distinct center for distributing tensions. . . .

It should be carefully noted that a multiplicity of affected persons is not an invariable characteristic of polycentric problems. This is sufficiently illustrated in the case of Mrs. Timken's will. That case also illustrated the fact that rapid changes with time are not an invariable characteristic of such problems. On the other hand, in practice polycentric problems of possible concern to adjudication will normally involve many affected parties and a somewhat fluid state of affairs. Indeed, the last characteristic follows from the simple fact that the more interacting centers there are, the more the likelihood that one of them will be affected by a change in circumstances, and, if the situation is polycentric, this change will communicate itself after a complex pattern to other centers. . . .

Now, if it is important to see clearly what a polycentric problem is, it is equally important to realize that the distinction involved is often a matter of degree. There are polycentric elements in almost all problems submitted to adjudication. A decision may act as a precedent, often an awkward one, in some situation not foreseen by the arbiter. Again, suppose a court in a suit between one litigant and a railway holds that it is an act of negligence for the railway not to construct an underpass at a particular crossing. There may be nothing to distinguish this crossing from other crossings on the line. As a matter of statistical probability it may be clear that constructing underpasses along the whole line would cost more lives (through accidents in blasting, for example) than would be lost if the only safety measure were the familiar "Stop, Look & Listen" sign. If so, then what seems to be a decision simply declaring the rights and duties of two parties is in fact an inept solution for a polycentric problem, some elements of which cannot be brought before the court in a simple suit by one injured party against a defendant railway. In lesser measure, concealed polycentric elements are probably present in almost all problems resolved by adjudication. It is not, then, a question of distinguishing black from white. It is a question of knowing when the polycentric elements have become so significant and predominant that the proper limits of adjudication have been reached. . . .

The final question to be addressed is this: When an attempt is made to deal by adjudicative forms with a problem that is essentially polycentric, what happens? As I see it, three things can happen, sometimes all at once. *First,* the adjudicative solution may fail. Unexpected repercussions make the decision unworkable; it is ignored, withdrawn, or modified, sometimes repeatedly. *Second,* the purported arbiter ignores judicial proprieties—he "tries out" various solutions in posthearing conferences, consults parties not represented at the hearings, guesses at facts not proved and not properly matters for anything like judicial notice. *Third,* instead of accommodating his procedures to the nature of the problem he confronts, he may reformulate the problem so as to make it amenable to solution through adjudicative procedures.

Only the last of these needs illustration. Suppose it is agreed that an employer's control over promotions shall be subject to review through arbitration. Now obviously an arbitrator cannot decide whether when Jones was made a Machinist Class A there was someone else more deserving in the plant, or whether, in view of Jones' age, it would have been better to put him in another job with comparable pay. This is the kind of allocative problem for which adjudication is utterly unsuited. There are, however, two ways of obtaining a workable control over promotions through arbitration. One of these is through the posting of jobs; when a job is vacant, interested parties may apply for promotion into it. At the hearing, only those who have made application are entitled to be considered, and of course only the posted job is in issue. Here the problem is simplified in advance to the point where it can be arbitrated, though not without difficulty, particularly in the form of endless arguments as to whether there was in fact a vacancy that ought to have been posted, and whether a claimant filed his application on time and in the proper form, etc. The other way of accommodating the problem to arbitration is for the arbitrator to determine not who should be promoted but who *has* been promoted. That is, the contract contains certain "job descriptions" with the appropriate rate for each; the claimant asserts that he is in fact doing the work of a Machinist A, though he is still assigned the pay and title of a Machinist B. The controversy has two parties—the company and the claimant as represented by the union—and a single factual issue, Is the claimant in fact doing the work of a Machinist A?

In practice the procedure of applying for appointment to posted jobs will normally be prescribed in the contract itself, so that the terms of the agreement keep the arbitrator's function with respect to promotions within manageable limits. The other method of making feasible a control of promotions through arbitration will normally result from the arbitrator's own perception of the limitations of his role. The contract may simply contain a schedule of job rates and job classifications and a general clause stating that "discharges, promotions, and layoffs shall be subject to the grievance procedure." If the arbitrator were to construe such a contract to give him a general supervision over promotions, he would embark himself upon managerial tasks wholly unsuited to solution by any arbitrative procedure. An instinct toward preserving the integrity of his role will move him, therefore, to construe the contract in the manner already indicated, so that he avoids any responsibility with respect to the assignment of duties and merely decides whether the duties actually assigned make appropriate the classification assigned by the company to the complaining employee. . . .

In closing this discussion of polycentricity, it will be well to caution against two possible misunderstandings. The suggestion that polycentric problems are often solved by a kind of "managerial intuition" should not be taken to imply that it is an invariable characteristic of polycentric problems that they resist rational solution. There are rational principles for building bridges of structural steel. But there is no rational principle which states, for example, that the angle between girder *A* and girder *B* must always be 45 degrees. This depends on the bridge as a whole. One cannot construct a bridge by conducting successive separate arguments concerning the proper angle for every pair of intersecting girders. One must deal with the whole structure.

Finally, the fact that an adjudicative decision affects and enters into a polycentric relationship does not of itself mean that the adjudicative tribunal is moving out of its proper sphere. On the contrary, there is no better illustration of a polycentric relationship than an economic market, and yet the laying down of rules that will make a market function properly is one for which adjudication is generally well suited. The working out of our common law of contracts case by case has proceeded through adjudication, yet the basic principle underlying the rules thus developed is that they should promote the free exchange of goods in a polycentric market. The court gets into difficulty, not when it lays down rules about contracting, but when it attempts to write contracts. . . .

Is Fuller's account of adjudication consistent with the way Judge Henley conducted the Arkansas prison cases? If not, which view do you prefer?

Fiss, THE FORMS OF JUSTICE

93 Harv.L.Rev. 1, 28–48 (1979).

I doubt whether dispute resolution is an adequate description of the social function of courts. To my mind courts exist to give meaning to our public values, not to resolve disputes. Constitutional adjudication is the most vivid manifestation of this function, but it also seems true of most civil and criminal cases certainly now and perhaps for most of our history as well.

Most accounts of the judicial function begin with the same story: two people in the state of nature are squabbling over a piece of property, they come to an impasse, and, rather than resorting to force, turn to a third party, a stranger, for a decision. Courts are but an institutionalization of the stranger. This story, much like the story of the social contract, operates in the ill-defined land between the normative and descriptive. It does not purport to be an accurate portrayal of social history, of how courts actually came into being, but nevertheless is supposed to capture or express the underlying "social logic" of courts, even though no attempt is made to reconcile this story with the underlying social reality. It seems to me, however, that once full account is taken of the role of courts in modern society, in ordinary criminal, constitutional, and statutory cases (e.g., antitrust, environmental, or securities law), and perhaps also in the traditional common law cases, it becomes clear that the familiar story fundamentally misleads. It does not capture the "social logic" of courts, and might well be replaced by another story: the sovereign sends out his officers throughout the realm to speak the law and to see that it is obeyed.

Disputation has a pervasive role in litigation. Disputes may arise as to the meaning of a public value or as to the existence of a norm, and thus provide the *occasions* for judicial intervention. Also, courts may rely on the antagonistic relationship between various individuals or agencies for the presentation of the law and facts. The judge hopes that the desire of each to win provides a motivating force. Disputation can thus be viewed as a *mode of judicial operation.* I will also concede that the judge's decision may bring an end to the dispute; dispute resolution may be one *consequence* of the judicial decision. But as pervasive a role as disputation may play in litigation, it is equally important to recognize that the *function* of the judge—a statement of social purpose and a definition of role—is not to resolve disputes, but to give the proper meaning to our public values. Typically, he does this by enforcing and thus safeguarding the integrity of the existing public norms or by supplying new norms. These norms may protect the fruits of one's bargains or labors; they may regulate the use of automobiles or determine responsibility for compensation; they may preserve the integrity of markets by curbing fraud or monopolization; or they may impose limits on the use of state power. In the structural suit, the judge reorganizes the institution as a way of discharging this very same function.

Of course, some disputes may not threaten or otherwise implicate a public value. All the disputants may, for example, acknowledge the norms and confine their dispute to the interpretation of the words of the contract or the price of a bumper. Such disputes may wind their way into court, and judges may spend time on these purely private disputes—private because only the interests and behavior of the immediate parties to the dispute are at issue. That seems, however, an extravagant use of public resources, and thus it seems quite appropriate for those disputes to be handled not by courts, but by arbitrators (though courts may have to act as background institutions enforcing or maybe even creating obligations to arbitrate). . . . The function of the arbitrator is to resolve a dispute. The function of the judge, on the other hand, must be understood in wholly different terms: he is a public officer; paid for by public funds; chosen not by the parties but by the public or its representatives; and empowered by the political agencies to enforce and create society-wide norms, and perhaps even to restructure institutions, as a way, I suggest, of giving meaning to our public values.

I may have overstated the position, and have drawn too sharp a distinction between arbitration and adjudication. I may have a too grandiose view of what people expect from judges as opposed to arbitrators. But it must be remembered that wholly apart from the question of whether dispute resolution has *any* claim on judicial resources, the question still remains whether it has a normatively *prior* claim on the office of the judge. The ultimate issue is whether dispute resolution is the ideal against which structural reform is to be judged. How might that priority be established? Three different tacks have been taken—one is instrumental, another is historical, and the third is axiomatic.

The instrumental critique, most strongly suggested by Donald Horowitz in a recent book, *The Courts and Social Policy,* emphasizes the high risk of error in structural reform as opposed to dispute resolution. The argument is that the judge should be limited to doing what he does best—dispute resolution. Under the instrumental critique, dispute resolution becomes the ideal simply because it is what courts can do best.

Some of the empirical premises underlying this position seem plausible enough. The task of structural reform is fraught with danger, not just in defining the rights, but also in implementing them within the operation of the state bureaucracy. It may also be true—note I only say "may"—that the risk of judicial error in dispute resolution is not nearly as great as it is in structural reform: in many instances there is virtually nothing to the remedial phase in dispute resolution, simply declaring whether plaintiff or defendant wins, nothing to compare to the difficulties inherent in the reorganization of an ongoing social institution, a public school system, a welfare department, or worse yet, an institution we know the least about, a prison. All of this may be safely conceded without, I am certain, accepting the normative conclusion that idealizes dispute resolution.

In the first place it is not clear why any social institution should be devoted to one and only one task, even the one it does best. Traditional separation of powers doctrine assumes a differentiation of judicial power from that of the executive and legislative branches, but it does not require that the differentiation be along *formal* as opposed to *functional* lines, nor does it require that any branch be devoted to one function alone. (Legislators, for example, spend considerable time on constituent services.) Each of the three great divisions of powers may have several different functions. The performance of one function may interfere with another, failures in one domain impair its capacity to perform in others, but there is no reason to believe that the relationship between the structural and dispute-resolution modes of discharging the judicial function is one of interference, that involvement in the structural litigation will compromise the judiciary's capacity to resolve disputes. The functions may well be independent, or maybe even complementary.

Furthermore, even if a choice must be made between the two functions, the instrumental critique assumes too narrow a criterion of choice in insisting that we preserve that function the institution performs best. Success rate is important in evaluating institutions, but two further factors must be introduced into the analysis: the value of a successful performance, and the success rate of alternative institutions performing comparable tasks. On either criterion, structural reform fares quite well.

The hypothesized low success rate of structural reform is amply compensated by the promise of greater social returns. If the choice be between resolving a dispute between two individuals, such as a dispute between a citizen and a policeman over some alleged incident of wrongdoing, or on the other hand, trying to eradicate conditions of lawlessness through a reorganization of the police department, the claim that the first is more likely to be "successful" clearly does not make it the more socially worthwhile enterprise, in terms of either the breadth of the corrective action or its durability. Success may come more rarely or less perfectly in a structural case, but a structural success, even if it is only partial, may well dwarf all the successes of dispute resolution; it may greatly reduce the need for dispute resolution by eliminating the conditions that give rise to incidents of wrongdoing; and it may even compensate for all its own failures.

The instrumental critique might have more appeal if it were clear that there were alternative institutions that could better perform this worthwhile but perilous activity. But just the opposite is true. Dispute resolution might be diverted to arbitration, but obviously such a diversion is not available for structural reform. It is among the most public of all forms of adjudication, involving constitutional values and the state bureaucracies. Some have suggested administrative agencies as the alternative, on the theory that these agencies might have some special expertise in the reorganization of ongoing social institutions not otherwise available to courts. But this suggestion also seems without basis. Before explaining why, let me emphasize that my intent is not to deny a role for administrative agencies in the constitutional domain, in the effort to give meaning to our constitutional values through structural reform, but only to suggest that their claim of special competency is not so strong as to altogether oust the courts, to justify transferring structural reform from the courts to administrative agencies, leaving the courts to do nothing more than resolve disputes. The instrumental critique must make a claim as strong as that in order to idealize dispute resolution as the judicial function and to accuse courts of acting illegitimately whenever they undertake structural reform.

The claim for diversion is largely predicated on the view that these administrative agencies possess some expert knowledge, and yet I for one fail to see the evidence to support that position. The instrumental critic in essence makes a comparative argument, one about the superiority of administrative agencies, but only attempts to document one-half of that argument. He typically points to "failures" of the courts, but never considers the "failures" of the administrative agencies, of which there are many. The literature is filled with the evidence of administrative failures, and teaches us to be wary of the claim of administrative expertise, also voiced at earlier times by the Progressives. Admittedly, structural reform is a perilous and arduous activity, but the problem is largely one of knowledge, knowing how large-scale organizations operate, not the distribution of that knowledge among various agencies. I doubt whether there is some special body of knowledge relevant for such a remedial undertaking, but even if there were, it still remains to be seen why it could not be made available to the judge, either through expert witnesses, or through auxiliary structures such as special masters. The evidentiary process of the administrative agency has long promised to be more open, broader, and freewheeling than that available to the judiciary, but it is not clear to me that this promise has ever been fulfilled, that such a liberated process would be consistent with rudimentary notions of due process, or even that such a process is needed for structural reform. The focus of a structural suit is necessarily broad, concerned with social conditions and organizational dynamics, not discrete and particularized incidents of wrongdoing; but the judicial process is capable of that breadth. Some might, I realize, emphasize the insight that comes from accumulated experience, rather than a body of knowledge that could be communicated to a decisionmaker; yet it is hard to see how this reformulation of the claim of expertise advances the cause. Some judges have been engaged in the reconstructive enterprise over a long period of time, say a decade, and though, as we will see, this involvement creates its own problems, it probably dwarfs all the experience presently possessed by administrative agencies on how to reconstruct ongoing social institutions.

The argument for diversion to administrative agencies thus seems to rest on exaggerated claims of expertise, a recurrence of a myth of Progressivism, but even more fundamentally it reflects a misunderstanding of why courts are involved in the first place. Courts are not entrusted with the reconstructive task on the theory that they possess some expertise (either in the form of knowledge or experience) on how best to perform that task. In the domain of instrumentalism, of means-end rationality, courts have no special claim to competency. Their special competency lies elsewhere, in the domain of constitutional values, a special kind of substantive rationality, and that expertise is derived from the special quality of the judicial process—dialogue and independence. The reconstructive endeavor, calling for instrumental judgments, should be seen . . . as but a necessary incident of that meaning-giving enterprise, as an attempt by the judge to give meaning to constitutional values in practical reality. Thus, even if one were to assume, as the instrumental critique would have us do, that administrative agencies possess an expertise in the domain of instrumental rationality, the diversion argument would still be deeply problematic because administrative agencies lack any special competency in this particular domain of substantive rationality. They lack the independence that is so essential for giving expression to our constitutional values.

The specialized jurisdictions of administrative agencies may lend support to the claim of expertise, but it also poses a threat to the independence of the agency: the regulators become too closely identified with the regulated. More fundamentally, administrative agencies are, as the Progressives well-realized, more tied to majoritarian politics than are courts, both because of ideology (they are sometimes allowed to make their judgments on the basis of the preferences of the body politic) and institutional arrangements (appointment for short terms, subject to removal when administrations change). The so-called independent regulatory agencies of the federal system might be seen as standing somewhere between the courts, on the one hand, and Congress and the Executive, on the other, but surely their relationship to the majoritarian branches is close enough as to make us wary of any claim, such as that embodied in the instrumental critique, that would make them the exclusive or even the primary agencies for giving meaning to our constitutional values. The truth of this assertion would be, I venture to say, conceded in most contexts. It seems no less true—maybe even more so—when the threat to those values is posed by the bureaucracies of the modern state and when structural reform is needed to remove that threat.

A second method for establishing the priority of the dispute-resolution model is historical—dispute resolution is "traditional," and structural reform "new." Support for this position comes from Abram Chayes, who in an important, recent article[75] identified a mode of adjudication that is quite similar to the structural one (though he attributes its formal characteristics to the "public" character of the rights, while I see them more linked to the organizational setting—all rights enforced by courts are public). He celebrates the "new" model, but, rather than centrally dealing with the questions of legitimacy, he emphasizes the positivistic or descriptive dimensions of his enter-

75. Chayes, The Role of the Judge in Public Law Litigation, 89 Harv.L.Rev. 1281 (1976). . . .

prise. He presents himself as a "biologist" describing the "evolution" of a "new" form of adjudication, which will, he adds secondarily, legitimate itself by winning the assent of the people, provided it is given chance to work.

I have my doubts as to whether the historical claim is wholly accurate as a purely descriptive matter. To my mind, what has evolved has been the *form* of adjudication, but not the *function.* The function of adjudication, whether in the nineteenth century or twentieth century, torts or criminal law, contract or antitrust, McCulloch v. Maryland or Brown v. Board of Education, has not been to resolve disputes between individuals, but rather to give meaning to our public values. What has changed is social structure, the emergence of a society dominated by the operation of large-scale organizations, and it is these changes in social structure that account for the changes over time in adjudicatory *forms.* Such changes should hardly be a cause for concern. What would, in fact, provoke a genuine crisis of legitimacy would be to insist on procedural modes shaped in a different social setting, to assume that adjudicatory forms created centuries ago should control today.

But, even assuming for a moment that the dispute-resolution model has a claim to historical priority, it remains to be seen what that has to do with legitimacy, which is essentially a normative judgment. One response to this puzzlement may try to link dispute resolution with the "case or controversy" requirement of article III, but this claim is without foundation. There is nothing in the text of article III—in the rather incidental use of the words "cases" or "controversies"—that constitutionally constricts the federal courts to dispute resolution. The late eighteenth century was the heyday for the common law, and, though that litigation may inform the construction of the words "cases" and "controversies," the function of courts under the common law was paradigmatically not dispute resolution, but to give meaning to public values through the enforcement and creation of public norms, such as those embodied in the criminal law and the rules regarding property, contracts, and torts. The courts created our law. They were the central law-making institutions. The judicial function implied by contemporary constitutional litigation, of which structural reform is part, is continuous with and maybe even identical to that of the common law. The issues have changed, and so has the social setting; that has required a change in the form of adjudication, though not its function.

Alternatively, it may be thought that the historical critique derives its normative power not from article III, but from the application of a theory that sees the people's "consent" as the basis of legitimacy. This argument equates "implied consent" with "actual consent," interprets the people's acceptance of the status quo as implying a consent to the existing institutional arrangements, and then locates the dispute-resolution model—but not the structural one—in the status quo. Such an argument might seem capable of transforming a historical priority into a normative priority, but in truth the argument fails, on a number of grounds.

First, one can wonder about this interpretation of the status quo, which reads dispute resolution in and structural reform out. Some historians . . . find antecedents for contemporary institutional litigation in the nineteenth century equity and receivership cases or the anti-trust and bankruptcy cases of the early twentieth century. Indeed, following this line of thought one might also argue that the very existence of the structural mode in constitutional litigation for the past decade or so is sufficient to place it within the status quo—it, too, implicitly has received the people's consent.

A second response, primarily exemplified by Chayes, is to table the question of legitimacy, to suggest that it has arisen prematurely. Assent by the people need not be given prospectively, in the way that might be suggested by the social contract metaphor: all the people come together at one historic moment and decide whether they wish to have a particular social institution. Consent can also be *earned.* But that takes time and thus structural reform should be given a chance to operate—a so-called trial run (assuming the past decade has not been sufficient). If it survives, it will then be given the same claim to legitimacy as the so-called traditional model: the institution will have legitimated itself.

A third response—and the one that seems most appealing to me—is to question consent theory itself. In part, the problem with the theory is one of ambiguity. What is it that one consents to when one "accepts" the status quo in adjudication? Is it the form? Or the function? Or is it the substantive results? Consent theory fails to answer these questions, or even to suggest a procedure for working toward answers, and as a consequence transforms the historical argument into an endorsement of the status quo. It might well work a colossal collapse of "is" and "ought." Beyond that, however, one can question the very premise upon which this critique of structural reform rests—the identification of consent with legitimacy. Institutions can seek their justifications in domains other than consent, even in a democracy.

A democratic political system is one ultimately dependent upon the consent of the people, but each and every institution need not be founded on consent. Consent goes to the system, not the particular institution; it operates on the whole rather than each part. The legitimacy of particular institutions, such as courts, depends not on the consent—implied or otherwise—of the people, but rather on their *competence,* on the special contribution they make to the quality of our social life. Legitimacy depends on the capacity of the institution to perform a function within the political system and its willingness to respect the limitations on that function. Legitimacy does not depend on popular approval of the institution's performance, and even less on popular approval of the processes through which that performance is rendered. It is the legitimacy of the political system as a whole that depends on the people's approval, and that is the source of its democratic character.

The people have the power to express their disapproval of how courts are discharging their function. Presumably, they can pass statutes to curb procedural innovations, or they can adopt constitutional amendments for overturning particular outcomes. Some might argue that the failure of the people to exercise this power is "implied approval" of all that the courts are doing today, but such an argument would be mistaken (this is surely a situation when inaction is not tantamount to action), and more importantly, it is unnecessary. The existence of the power of the people to express disapproval should be understood as the means by which institutions such as courts can be integrated into a system ultimately founded on the people's consent. Some institutions—the legislature, the school board, the police chief—may have a tighter, more direct connection to consent: particular incumbents serve at the pleasure of the people. To insist upon a similar consensual connection for the judiciary would, however, impair its independence and thus destroy its capacity to discharge its constitutional function within our political system.

For these reasons it seems impossible to ground the historical critique either on article III or on consent theory, and thus it, like the instrumental critique, fails to give dispute-resolution a normative priority. There is one further strategy to be considered, the one I called axiomatic. It postulates some formal attribute of a social process as a morally necessary attribute, on the basis of which the structural and dispute-resolution modes are to be evaluated. As it turns out, that attribute—individual participation, present in dispute resolution, absent in the structural mode—also implicates consent theory and shares many of its difficulties. It places adjudication on a moral plane with two other activities exalted by consent theory, voting and bargaining, and then tries to construct an ideal form of adjudication that preserves this connection with consensual activity, now in a highly individualized form, though it still fails to explain why consent is the touchstone of legitimacy of all institutions.

The most sustained effort to build a case for dispute resolution on the basis of moral axioms is Lon Fuller's essay, *The Forms and Limits of Adjudication.* This essay was written in the late 1950's, shortly before the heyday of structural reform. It was published in 1978, shortly after Professor Fuller's death, but was not updated to account, either as a descriptive or normative matter, for the intervening twenty years, the civil rights era. It is as though the period never occurred—an erasure of some portion of the history of procedure. The essay is nevertheless important for our purposes, for it seems largely motivated by a desire to establish the limits of adjudication, and the one limit Fuller in fact develops is clearly at war with the notion of structural reform. Borrowing an idea of Michael Polanyi, interestingly enough also introduced in the 1950's, Fuller insists that courts cannot perform "polycentric" tasks.

Fuller does not give any single, straightforward definition of polycentrism. It seems to refer to a type of dispute or problem which is many centered, much like, he says, a spider web, in the sense that a resolution of a polycentric dispute would necessarily have broad and never-ending repercussions. These disputes are to Fuller inappropriate for adjudication. Fuller explains why through an analysis of a series of examples. One example, appearing near the end of the essay, seems, remarkably enough, to address the problem of structural reform:

"The suggestion that polycentric problems are often solved by a kind of 'managerial intuition' should not be taken to imply that it is an invariable characteristic of polycentric problems that they resist rational solution. There are rational principles for building bridges of structural steel. But there is no rational principle which states, for example, that the angle between girder *A* and girder *B* must always be 45 degrees. This depends on the bridge as a whole. One cannot construct a bridge by conducting successive separate arguments concerning the proper angle for every pair of intersecting girders. One must deal with the whole structure."

One is left to wonder why adjudication must proceed on the basis Fuller suggests—angle by angle. Certainly that is not required by rationality; reason, even that of the judge, is not binary; it need not proceed angle by angle, but can encompass whole structures. The explanation seems much more concrete, it has to do with the enormous number of people affected by whole structures—by the construction of the bridge. It is simply impossible, Fuller explains, to have everyone affected participate in the lawsuit in a meaningful way.

At the core then of Fuller's conception of the limits of adjudication and his objection to having courts resolve polycentric problems is the individual's right to participate in a proceeding that might adversely affect him. This right might be preserved in a representative suit that accords with the traditional law of agency, where there is a true consensual bond between representative (agent) and principal, but it should be recognized that this right, taken in its highly individualistic cast, is denied, indeed seriously compromised, by the kind of representation lying at the heart of a structural suit—the representation of interests by spokesmen for groups and offices rather than identifiable individuals. Just imagine the kind of representation implicit in the famed Arkansas prison litigation, in which the court's conclusion—for example, that the trusty system at Cummins Farm was a form of cruel and unusual punishment—must necessarily affect a never-ending spiral of persons, officers, and interests: inmates, guards, administrators, legislators, taxpayers, indeed all the citizens of the state—present and future. The reconstruction of a prison, or for that matter the reconstruction of a school system, a welfare agency, a hospital, or any bureaucracy, is as polycentric as the construction of a bridge. All require the court to deal with whole structures. The judge must be certain that the full range of interests is vigorously represented, but he need not turn his back on the constitutional claim or deny an effective remedy because each and every individual affected will not or cannot meaningfully participate in the suit.

My conception of adjudication starts from the top—the office of the judge—and works down. I place adjudication on a moral plane with legislative and executive action. I start with the conception of state power embodied in the judge, treat courts as a coordinate source of government power, and see the form of adjudication shaped by function and social setting. Fuller rejects such an approach. He starts from the bottom and works up. Fuller starts with the individual, rather than the judge. He places adjudication on a moral plane with elections and contracts, analyzes these two social processes in terms of how the individual participates in each, through voting and bargaining, and then seeks to distinguish adjudication from these social processes. The distinguishing feature of adjudication, naturally enough, is also cast in individualistic terms, more precisely, in terms of how the individual participates in that process as opposed to elections and contracts—through proof and reasoned arguments. He then treats this right of the individual to participate in the proceeding—the moral equivalent of the right to vote and the right to bargain—as the master idea of adjudication. For Fuller, it explains and justifies certain formal features of adjudication, for example, party structure and the passivity of the judge. It also sets limits on adjudication. The right of individual participation is violated only at a distinct moral risk—the process is deemed not a form of adjudication, or at best a mixed or hybrid form of adjudication, "parasitic" upon the ideal.

At various points Fuller speaks as though he is being merely descriptive. What distinguishes adjudication from other social processes, he says, is the "institutional commitment" of adjudication to a particular mode of individual participation. On a purely descriptive level there is not much to his claim. It is not supported by a presentation of the evidence and it is contradicted by a great deal of the reality or experience that we would consider to be adjudication. Moreover, a purely descriptive account could never yield the normative judgments implicit in his conclusion as to what might constitute "parasitic" adjudication. Fuller's essay should be recognized for what it is: a postulation that the standard for judging the legitimacy of a process that purports to be adjudication is the affected individual's right to participate. I say "postulation," for although much of the essay rightly celebrates the role of reason in human affairs, and sees the important connection between reason and adjudication, there is no explanation of why reason requires the kind of individual participation that Fuller insists upon. In structural reform reason enters the process, not through the arguments of each and every individual affected, but through the arguments of the spokesmen for all the interests represented and through the decision of the judge. Reason is used to give meaning to our constitutional values.

How might an axiom such as Fuller's, proclaiming the sacredness of the individual right of participation, be judged? I realize that it may not be appropriate to demand justification of an axiom, for it is offered as a starting point, a proposition that you cannot look behind. Yet there must be more that can be said about it. Acceptance of an axiom must turn on something more than a momentary flash of intuition. In my judgment, the axiom can be assessed in terms of its consequences and its underlying social vision. An axiom might at first glance seem attractive enough, but its appeal may decline radically once its full implications are understood.

In assessing the consequences of the individual participation axiom it should first be understood that the issue is not whether there should be social processes that can further the participatory right—whether dispute resolution should exist—but whether a form of adjudication that violates that right—structural reform—is legitimate (or permissible). Fuller treats the participation axiom as a necessary condition, and that is the source of the problem. As a necessary condition, the axiom would render structural reform illegitimate, true enough, but more importantly, it would render illegitimate almost all adjudication—both of the common law and the constitutional variety—in which the courts were creating public norms. It would reduce courts to the function of norm enforcement, and reduce adjudication to a high-class (but subsidized) form of arbitration. It is no mere happenstance that Fuller spent a great deal of his professional life as an arbitrator; throughout the essay he refers to the judge as an "arbiter."

Virtually all public norm creation is polycentric. It affects as many people as structural reform, and equally impairs the capacity of each of the affected individuals to participate in the process. More often than not, there is a myriad of possible rules or solutions that could be formulated in each case. Consider the fellow-servant rule, the stop-look-and-listen doctrine, strict liability, the consideration requirement, the rules respecting offer and acceptance, the norms of the Marshall Court regarding the commerce clause, those of the

Warren Court regarding free speech, racial equality, civil and criminal procedure. The list could go on and on. It would probably include all judge-made law, and the doctrine of precedent itself. The list surely includes many "mistakes" or "wrong decisions," but that is not the issue: the issue is whether all these acts of norm creation represent a misuse of the judicial power, an incorrect appropriation of the concept of "adjudication." This is a conclusion that most of us—or maybe even all of us—would reject and yet it is a conclusion that would seem to follow from Fuller's axiom.

It should also be recognized that this axiom—like the liberty-of-contract doctrine of an earlier age—would be but a formal triumph of individualism. The axiom seems to celebrate the individual, but would leave the individual at the mercy of large aggregations of power—in Lochner [v. New York] the corporation; here, the state bureaucracies. Deprived of the opportunity to use the courts to protect himself, to have the full use of these centers of government power that stand apart from the state bureaucracies, the individual is thrown back to those social processes that are supposed to respect his participatory right—dispute resolution, voting, and bargaining. Each of these processes has important roles to play in our social life, but it is hard to believe that any of them enhance the *real* or *effective*—as opposed to the formal—power of those individuals who are abused by the large-scale organizations of the modern state, the school system, the hospital, the welfare department, or, even worse, the prison.

In truth, the individual participation axiom is rooted in a world that no longer exists. It is rooted in a horizontal world, in which people related to one another on individual terms and on terms of approximate equality. It is rooted in a world that viewed the law of contracts as The Law—not so incidentally, Fuller's substantive field of law. Our world, however, is a vertical one; the market has been replaced by the hierarchy, the individual entrepreneur by the bureau. In this social setting, what is needed to protect the individual is the establishment of power centers equal in strength and equal in resources to the dominant social actors; what is needed is countervailing power. A conception of adjudication that strictly honors the right of each affected individual to participate in the process seems to proclaim the importance of the individual, but actually leaves the individual without the institutional support necessary to realize his true self. In fact, the individual participation axiom would do little more than throw down an impassable bar—polycentrism—to the one social process that has emerged with promise for preserving our constitutional values and the ideal of individualism in the face of the modern bureaucratic state—structural reform.

IV. A Bibliography on the Structural Injunction

Aronow, The Special Master in School Desegregation Cases, 7 Hastings Const.L.Q. 739 (1980).

Bell, The Dialectics of School Desegregation, 32 Ala.L.Rev. 281 (1981).

Berger, Away from the Court House and into the Field: The Odyssey of a Special Master, 78 Colum.L.Rev. 707 (1978).

Brakel, Special Masters in Institutional Litigation, 1979 Am.B.Found. Research J. 543.

Chayes, The Role of the Judge in Public Law Litigation, 89 Harv.L.Rev. 1281 (1976).

Chayes, Public Law Litigation and the Burger Court, 96 Harv.L.Rev. 4 (1982).

Coffin, The Frontier of Remedies: A Call for Exploration, 67 Calif.L.Rev. 983 (1979).

Cover and Fiss, The Structure of Procedure (1979).

Diver, The Judge as Political Powerbroker: Superintending Structural Change in Public Institutions, 65 Va.L.Rev. 43 (1979).

Drake, Judicial Implementation and Wyatt v. Stickney, 32 Ala.L.Rev. 299 (1981).

Eisenberg and Yeazell, The Ordinary and the Extraordinary in Institutional Litigation, 93 Harv.L.Rev. 465 (1980).

Fiss, The Civil Rights Injunction (1978).

Fiss, Dombrowski, 86 Yale L.J. 1103 (1977).

Fiss, The Forms of Justice, 93 Harv.L.Rev. 1 (1979).

Fiss, The Social and Political Foundations of Adjudication, 6 Law & Human Behav. 121 (1982).

Fletcher, The Discretionary Constitution: Institutional Remedies and Judicial Legitimacy, 91 Yale L.J. 635 (1982).

Frug, The Judicial Power of the Purse, 126 U.Pa.L.Rev. 715 (1978).

Gaskins, Second Thoughts on "Law as an Instrument of Social Change," 6 Law & Human Behav. 153 (1982).

Gewirtz, Remedies and Resistance, 92 Yale L.J. 585 (1983).

Glazer, Should Judges Administer Social Services?, 50 Pub. Interest 64 (1978).

Goldstein, A *Swann* Song for Remedies: Equitable Relief in the Burger Court, 13 Harv.C.R.-C.L.L.Rev. 1 (1978).

Harris, The Title VII Administrator: A Case Study in Judicial Flexibility, 60 Cornell L.Rev. 53 (1974).

Henderson and Pearson, Implementing Federal Environmental Policies: The Limits of Aspirational Commands, 78 Colum.L.Rev. 1429 (1978).

Hinkle, Appellate Supervision of Remedies in Public Law Adjudication, 4 Fla.St.U.L.Rev. 411 (1976).

Horowitz, The Courts and Social Policy (1977).

Horowitz, The Judiciary: Umpire or Empire? 6 Law & Human Behav. 129 (1982).

Jennings, The Chancellor's Foot Begins to Kick: Judicial Remedies in Public Law Cases and the Need for Procedural Reforms, 83 Dick.L.Rev. 217 (1979).

Johnson, The Alabama Punting Syndrome, 18 Judges 4 (Spring 1979).

Johnson, The Constitution and the Federal District Judge, 54 Tex.L.Rev. 903 (1976).

Johnson, The Role of the Federal Courts in Institutional Litigation, 32 Ala.L. Rev. 271 (1981).

Kaufman, Masters in the Federal Courts: Rule 53, 58 Colum.L.Rev. 452 (1958).

Kirp, Legalism and Politics in School Desegregation, 1981 Wis.L.Rev. 924.

Kirp and Babcock, Judge and Company: Court-Appointed Masters, School Desegregation, and Institutional Reform, 32 Ala.L.Rev. 313 (1981).

Lottman, Enforcement of Judicial Decrees: Now Comes the Hard Part, I Mental Disability L.Rep. 69 (1976).

Mishkin, Federal Courts as State Reformers, 35 Wash. & Lee L.Rev. 949 (1978).

Nagel, Separation of Powers and the Scope of Federal Equitable Remedies, 30 Stan.L.Rev. 661 (1978).

Nathan, The Use of Masters in Institutional Reform Litigation, 10 U.Tol.L. Rev. 419 (1979).

Reynolds, The Mechanics of Institutional Reform Litigation, 8 Fordham Urb. L.J. 695 (1979–80).

Robbins and Buser, Punitive Conditions of Prison Confinement: An Analysis of Pugh v. Locke and Federal Court Supervision of State Penal Administration Under the Eighth Amendment, 29 Stan.L.Rev. 893 (1977).

Roberts, The Extent of Federal Judicial Equitable Power: Receivership of South Boston High School, 12 New Eng. L.Rev. 55 (1976).

Rothman, The Courts and Social Reform: A Postprogressive Outlook, 6 Law & Human Behav. 113 (1982).

Schuck, Suing Government (1983).

Smithson, The Special Master in Correctional Cases: A Preliminary Survey, 9 Clearinghouse Rev. 15 (1975).

Starr, Accommodation and Accountability: A Strategy for Judicial Enforcement of Institutional Reform Decrees, 32 Ala.L.Rev. 399 (1981).

Stone, Large Organizations and the Law at the Pass: Toward a General Theory of Compliance Strategy, 1981 Wis.L.Rev. 861.

Weinberg, The Bureaucratic Judiciary: The Future of Court-Ordered Change, 6 Law & Human Behav. 169 (1982).

Weinberg, The Courts as Social Reformers, 6 Law & Human Behav. 97 (1982).

Weinstein, The Effect of Austerity on Institutional Litigation, 6 Law & Human Behav. 145 (1982).

Yarborough, Judge Frank Johnson and Human Rights in Alabama (1981).

Yudof, Implementation Theories and Desegregation Penalties, 32 Ala.L.Rev. 441 (1981).

Special Project—The Remedial Process in Institutional Reform Litigation, 78 Colum.L.Rev. 784 (1978).

Developments in the Law—Class Actions, 89 Harv.L.Rev. 1318 (1976).

Developments in the Law—Section 1983 and Federalism, 90 Harv.L.Rev. 1133 (1977).

Note, Complex Enforcement: Unconstitutional Prison Conditions, 94 Harv. L.Rev. 626 (1981).

Note, Force and Will: An Exploration of the Use of Special Masters to Implement Judicial Decisions, 52 U.Colo.L.Rev. 105 (1980).

Note, Implementation Problems in Institutional Reform Litigation, 91 Harv.L.Rev. 428 (1977).

Note, Judicial Intervention and Organization Theory: Changing Bureaucratic Behavior and Policy, 89 Yale L.J. 513 (1980).

Note, "Mastering" Intervention in Prisons, 88 Yale L.J. 1062 (1979).

Note, Receivership as a Remedy in Civil Rights Cases, 24 Rutgers L.Rev. 115 (1969).

Note, The *Wyatt* Case: Implementation of a Judicial Decree Ordering Institutional Change, 84 Yale L.J. 1338 (1975).

Comment, Equitable Remedies: An Analysis of Judicial Utilization of Neoreceiverships to Implement Large Scale Institutional Change, 1976 Wis.L. Rev. 1161.

Chapter Ten

COMMON THEMES OF CONTEMPT

I. The Civil-Criminal Distinction

GOMPERS v. BUCKS STOVE & RANGE CO.

221 U.S. 418, 31 S.Ct. 492, 55 L.Ed. 797 (1911).

Justice LAMAR delivered the opinion of the Court.

. . . The defendants, Samuel Gompers, John Mitchell and Frank Morrison, were found guilty of contempt of court in making certain publications prohibited by an injunction from the Supreme Court of the District of Columbia. They were sentenced to imprisonment for twelve, nine and six months respectively, and this proceeding is prosecuted to reverse that judgment.

The order alleged to have been violated was granted in the equity suit of the "Bucks Stove & Range Company v. The American Federation of Labor and others," in which the court issued an injunction restraining all the defendants from boycotting the complainant, or from publishing or otherwise making any statement that the Bucks Stove & Range Company was, or had been, on the "Unfair" or "We don't patronize" lists. Some months later the complainant filed a petition in the cause, alleging that the three defendants above-named, parties to the original cause, in contempt of court and in violation of its order, had disobeyed the injunction by publishing statements which either directly or indirectly called attention to the fact that the Bucks Stove & Range Company was on the "Unfair" list, and that they had thereby continued the boycott which had been enjoined. . . .

But in making such investigation [as to whether the defendants disobeyed the injunction] it is . . . insisted that this is a proceeding at law for criminal contempt, where the findings of fact by the trial judge must be treated as conclusive, and that our investigation must be limited solely to the question whether, as a matter of law, the acts of alleged disobedience set out in the finding constitute contempt of court.

This contention, on the part of the Bucks Stove & Range Company, prevents a consideration of the case on its merits, and makes it necessary to enter into a discussion of questions more or less technical, as to whether this was a proceeding in equity or at law. Where results so controlling depend upon proper classification, it becomes necessary carefully to consider whether this was a case at law for criminal contempt where the evidence could not be examined for want of a bill of exceptions; or a case in equity for civil contempt, where the whole record may be examined on appeal and a proper decree entered.

Contempts are neither wholly civil nor altogether criminal. And "it may not always be easy to classify a particular act as belonging to either one of these two classes. It may partake of the characteristics of both." Bessette v. Conkey, 194 U.S. 329. But in either event, and whether the proceedings be civil or criminal, there must be an allegation that in contempt of court the defendant has disobeyed the order, and a prayer that he be attached and punished therefor. It is not the fact of punishment but rather its character and purpose that often serve to distinguish between the two classes of cases. If it is for civil contempt the punishment is remedial, and for benefit of the complainant. But if it is for criminal contempt the sentence is punitive, to vindicate the authority of the court. It is true that punishment by imprisonment may be remedial, as well as punitive, and many civil contempt proceedings have resulted not only in the imposition of a fine, payable to the complainant, but also in committing the defendant to prison. But imprisonment for civil contempt is ordered where the defendant has refused to do an affirmative act required by the provisions of an order which, either in form or substance, was mandatory in its character. Imprisonment in such cases is not inflicted as a punishment, but is intended to be remedial by coercing the defendant to do what he had refused to do. The decree in such cases is that the defendant stand committed unless and until he performs the affirmative act required by the court's order.

For example: If a defendant should refuse to pay alimony, or to surrender property ordered to be turned over to a receiver, or to make a conveyance required by a decree for specific performance, he could be committed until he complied with the order. Unless these were special elements of contumacy, the refusal to pay or to comply with the order is treated as being rather in resistance to the opposite party than in contempt of the court. The order for imprisonment in this class of cases, therefore, is not to vindicate the authority of the law, but is remedial and is intended to coerce the defendant to do the thing required by the order for the benefit of the complainant. If imprisoned, as aptly said in In re Nevitt, 117 Fed.Rep. 451, "he carries the keys of his prison in his own pocket." He can end the sentence and discharge himself at any moment by doing what he had previously refused to do.

On the other hand, if the defendant does that which he has been commanded not to do, the disobedience is a thing accomplished. Imprisonment cannot undo or remedy what has been done nor afford any compensation for the pecuniary injury caused by the disobedience. If the sentence is limited to imprisonment for a definite period, the defendant is furnished no key, and he cannot shorten the term by promising not to repeat the offense. Such imprisonment operates, not as a remedy coercive in its nature, but solely as punishment for the completed act of disobedience.

It is true that either form of imprisonment has also an incidental effect. For if the case is civil and the punishment is purely remedial, there is also a vindication of the court's authority. On the other hand, if the proceeding is for criminal contempt and the imprisonment is solely punitive, to vindicate the authority of the law, the complainant may also derive some incidental benefit from the fact that such punishment tends to prevent a repetition of the disobedience. But such indirect consequences will not change imprisonment which is merely coercive and remedial, into that which is solely punitive in character, or *vice versa.* . . .

The distinction between refusing to do an act commanded,—remedied by imprisonment until the party performs the required act; and doing an act forbidden,—punished by imprisonment for a definite term; is sound in principle, and generally, if not universally, affords a test by which to determine the character of the punishment.

In this case the alleged contempt did not consist in the defendant's refusing to do any affirmative act required, but rather in doing that which had been prohibited. The only possible remedial relief for such disobedience would have been to impose a fine for the use of complainant, measured in some degree by the pecuniary injury caused by the act of disobedience. . . .

But when the court found that the defendants had done what the injunction prohibited, and thereupon sentenced them to jail for fixed terms of six, nine and twelve months, no relief whatever was granted to the complainant, and the Bucks Stove & Range Company took nothing by that decree.

If then, as the Court of Appeals correctly held, the sentence was wholly punitive, it could have been properly imposed only in a proceeding instituted and tried as for criminal contempt. The question as to the character of such proceedings has generally been raised, in the appellate court, to determine whether the case could be reviewed by writ of error or on appeal. Bessette v. Conkey, 194 U.S. 324. But it may involve much more than mere matters of practice. For, notwithstanding the many elements of similarity in procedure and in punishment, there are some differences between the two classes of proceedings which involve substantial rights and constitutional privileges. Without deciding what may be the rule in civil contempt, it is certain that in proceedings for criminal contempt the defendant is presumed to be innocent, he must be proved to be guilty beyond a reasonable doubt, and cannot be compelled to testify against himself. . . .

There is another important difference. Proceedings for civil contempt are between the original parties and are instituted and tried as a part of the main cause. But on the other hand, proceedings at law for criminal contempt are between the public and the defendant, and are not a part of the original cause. The Court of Appeals recognizing this difference held that this was not a part of the equity cause of the Bucks Stove & Range Company v. The American Federation of Labor et al., and said that: "The order finding the defendants guilty of contempt was not an interlocutory order in the injunction proceedings. It was in a separate action, one personal to the defendants, with the defendants on one side and the court vindicating its authority on the other."

In this view we cannot concur. We find nothing in the record indicating that this was a proceeding with the court, or, more properly, the Government, on one side and the defendants on the other. On the contrary, the contempt proceedings were instituted, entitled, tried, and up to the moment of sentence treated as a part of the original cause in equity. The Bucks Stove & Range Company was not only the nominal, but the actual party on the one side, with the defendants on the other. The Bucks Stove Company acted throughout as complainant in charge of the litigation. As such and through its counsel, acting in its name, it made consents, waivers and stipulations only proper on the theory that it was proceeding in its own right in an equity cause, and not as a representative of the United States, prosecuting a case of criminal contempt. It appears here also as the sole party in opposition to the defendants; and its counsel, in its name, have filed briefs and made arguments in this court in favoring affirmance of the judgment of the court below.

. . .

In the first place the petition was not entitled "United States v. Samuel Gompers, et al." or "In re Samuel Gompers, et al.," as would have been proper, and according to some decisions necessary, if the proceedings had been at law for criminal contempt. This is not a mere matter of form, for manifestly every citizen, however unlearned in the law, by a mere inspection of the papers in contempt proceedings ought to be able to see whether it was instituted for private litigation or for public prosecution, whether it sought to benefit the complainant or vindicate the court's authority. He should not be left in doubt as to whether relief or punishment was the object in view. He is not only entitled to be informed of the nature of the charge against him, but to know that it is a charge and not a suit. . . .

Inasmuch, therefore, as proceedings for civil contempt are a part of the original cause, the weight of authority is to the effect that they should be entitled therein. But the practice has hitherto been so unsettled in this respect that we do not now treat it as controlling, but only as a fact to be considered along with others . . . in determining a similar question. Thus considering it we find that the petition instituting the contempt proceeding was entitled in the main cause "Bucks Stove & Range Company, plaintiff, v. The American Federation of Labor, et al., defendants, No. 27,305, Equity," and that the answers of the defendants, every report by the examiner in chancery, every deposition, motion and stipulation, every order—including the final decree and the amended decree, were all uniformly entitled in the equity cause. Not only the pleadings in the original cause but all the testimony, oral and written, was, by reference in the petition, made a part of the contempt proceedings. The trial judge quoted largely from this oral testimony thus introduced in bulk, and the severity and character of the sentence indicate that he was largely influenced by this evidence which disclosed the great damage done to the complainant's business by the boycott before the injunction issued.

It is argued the defendants' answers concluded with a statement that as questions of criminal and quasi-criminal intent were involved, a jury was better qualified to pass on the issues than a judge, and in the event he should be of opinion that the charges had not been sworn away, they moved that issues of fact should be framed and submitted to a jury. Such a motion was not inconsistent with the theory that this was a proceeding for civil contempt in equity, but was in strict accord with the practice under which questions of fact may be referred by the chancellor to a jury for determination.

In proceedings for civil contempt the complainant, if successful, is entitled to costs. . . . And evidently on the theory that this was a civil proceeding and to be governed by the rules applicable to an equity cause, the Bucks Stove & Range Company moved the court to amend the decree so as to award to it "its costs." After argument by solicitors for both parties, the motion was granted, and the court adjudged that the complainant do recover against the defendants its costs in said contempt proceeding. This ruling was no doubt correct as this was a civil case, but could not have been granted in a proceeding for criminal contempt, where costs are not usually imposed in addition to the imprisonment. Where they are awarded they go to the Government, for the use of its officers . . . .

In another most important particular the parties clearly indicated that they regarded this as a civil proceeding. The complainant made each of the defendants a witness for the company, and, as such, each was required to testify against himself—a thing that most likely would not have been done, or suffered, if either party had regarded this as a proceeding at law for criminal contempt—because the provision of the Constitution that "no person shall be compelled in any criminal case to be a witness against himself" is applicable, not only to crimes, but also to quasi-criminal and penal proceedings. . . .

. . . We have already shown that in both classes of cases there must be allegation and proof that the defendant was guilty of contempt, and a prayer that he be punished. The classification then depends upon the question as to whether the punishment is punitive, in vindication of the court's authority, or whether it is remedial by way of a coercive imprisonment, or a compensatory fine payable to the complainant. Bearing these distinctions in mind, the prayer of the petition is significant and determinative. After setting out in detail the acts of alleged disobedience, the petition closes with the following prayers: (1) "that the defendants show cause why they should not be adjudged in contempt of court and be punished for the same," and (2) "that petitioner may have such other and further relief as the nature of its case may require."

"Its case,"—not the Government's case. "That petitioner may have relief"—not that the court's authority may be vindicated. The Bucks Stove & Range Company was not asserting the rights of the public, but seeking "such other and further relief as the nature of its case may require." If it had asked that the defendants be forced to pay a fine to the Government, or be punished by confinement in jail, there could have been no doubt that punishment pure and simple was sought.

On the other hand, if it had prayed that the court impose a fine payable to the Bucks Stove & Range Company, the language would have left no doubt that remedial punishment was sought. It is not different in principle, if, instead of praying specifically for a fine payable to itself, it asks generally for "such relief as the nature of its case may require." In either event such a prayer was appropriate to a civil proceeding, and under it the court could have granted that form of relief to which the petitioner was entitled. But as the act of disobedience consisted not in refusing to do what had been ordered, but in doing what had been prohibited by the injunction, there could be no coercive imprisonment, and therefore the only relief, if any, which "the nature of petitioners' case" admitted, was the imposition of a fine payable to the Bucks Stove & Range Company.

There was therefore a departure—a variance between the procedure adopted and the punishment imposed, when, in answer to a prayer for remedial relief, in the equity cause, the court imposed a punitive sentence appropriate only to a proceeding at law for criminal contempt. The result was as fundamentally erroneous as if in an action of "A. vs. B. for assault and battery," the judgment entered had been that the defendant be confined in prison for twelve months.

If then this sentence for criminal contempt was erroneously entered in a proceeding which was a part of the equity cause, it would be necessary to set aside the order of imprisonment, examine the testimony and thereupon make such decree as was proper, according to the practice in equity causes on appeal. And, if upon the examination of the record it should appear that the defendants were in fact and in law guilty of the contempt charged, there could be no more important duty than to render such a decree as would serve to vindicate the jurisdiction and authority of courts to enforce orders and to punish acts of disobedience. For while it is sparingly to be used, yet the power of courts to punish for contempts is a necessary and integral part of the independence of the judiciary, and is absolutely essential to the performance of the duties imposed on them by law. Without it they are mere boards of arbitration whose judgments and decrees would be only advisory.

If a party can make himself a judge of the validity of orders which have been issued, and by his own act of disobedience set them aside, then are the courts impotent, and what the Constitution now fittingly calls the "judicial power of the United States" would be a mere mockery.

This power "has been uniformly held to be necessary to the protection of the court from insults and oppressions while in the ordinary exercise of its duties, and to enable it to enforce its judgments and orders necessary to the due administration of law and the protection of the rights of suitors." Bessette v. Conkey, 194 U.S. 324, 333.

There has been general recognition of the fact that the courts are clothed with this power and must be authorized to exercise it without referring the issues of fact or law to another tribunal or to a jury in the same tribunal. For if there was no such authority in the first instance there would be no power to enforce its orders if they were disregarded in such independent investigation. Without authority to act promptly and independently the courts could not administer public justice or enforce the rights of private litigants. . . .

Congress in recognition of the necessity of the case has also declared [in 18 U.S.C. § 401] that the courts of the United States "shall have power to punish by fine or imprisonment contempts of their authority . . . " including "disobedience . . . by any party to any lawful order . . . of the said courts." But the very amplitude of the power is a warning to use it with discretion, and a command never to exert it where it is not necessary or proper. For that reason we can proceed no further in this case because it is both unnecessary and improper to make any decree in this contempt proceeding.

For on the hearing of the appeal and cross appeal in the original cause in which the injunction was issued, it appeared from the statement of counsel in open court that there had been a complete settlement of all matters involved in the case of Bucks Stove & Range Company v. The American Federation of Labor et al. This court therefore declined to further consider the case, which had become moot, and those two appeals were dismissed. 219 U.S. 581. When the main case was settled, every proceeding which was dependent on it, or a part of it, was also necessarily settled—of course without prejudice to the power and right of the court to punish for contempt by proper proceedings. . . . If this had been a separate and independent proceeding at law for criminal contempt, to vindicate the authority of the court, with the public on one side and the defendants on the other, it could not, in any way, have been affected by any settlement which the parties to the equity cause made in their private litigation.

But, as we have shown, this was a proceeding in equity for civil contempt where the only remedial relief possible was a fine payable to the complainant. The company prayed "for such relief as the nature of its case may require," and when the main cause was terminated by a settlement of all differences between the parties, the complainant did not require and was not entitled to any compensation or relief of any other character. The present proceeding necessarily ended with the settlement of the main cause of which it is a part. . . . The criminal sentences imposed in the civil case, therefore, should be set aside.

The judgment of the Court of Appeals is reversed, and the case remanded with directions to reverse the judgment of the Supreme Court of the District of Columbia and remand the case to that court with direction that the contempt proceedings instituted by the Bucks Stove & Range Company be dismissed, but without prejudice to the power and right of the Supreme Court of the District of Columbia to punish by a proper proceeding, contempt, if any, committed against it.

---

1) Judges interpose the inadequacy prerequisite between plaintiffs and injunctions. Injunctions occur when plaintiff's injury will be difficult to value, the subject matter of the dispute is unique, or plaintiff's right is too important to allow defendant to violate it and pay damages. Enforcement factors also militate against equitable relief. Recalcitrants gum up the works, and judges must wield contempt to effect compliance. Before enjoining, the judge must decide that he treasures plaintiff's interest so much that he is willing to coerce defendant to allow plaintiff to enjoy it.

Equity's unique method of enforcement is coercive contempt, used to persuade defendant to allow plaintiff to enjoy the substantive right. The judge keeps the promise he made when he first said that plaintiff's money remedy was inadequate; he tells defendant to go to jail or to pay a fine until he complies. Coercive contempt resembles a Sword of Damocles, a second injunction with the sanction specified and hanging by a thread. Contemnor may comply and avoid the sword.

The judge has two other forms of contempt, compensatory and criminal; both confess failure and provide mere substitutes. If defendant disobeys the injunction, the judge may order him to pay plaintiff what plaintiff lost because of the breach as compensatory contempt. The judge gives plaintiff the money previously rejected as an inadequate remedy. Like compensatory contempt, criminal contempt occurs after defendant disobeys the injunction. Judges wield criminal contempt to punish contemnor's disrespect and to set an example, not to benefit plaintiff. Compensatory and criminal contempt are used when it is too late to coerce defendant. We should distinguish between prospective or coercive contempt, on the one hand, and compensatory and criminal or retrospective contempt, on the other. Perhaps, because of the inadequacy prerequisite, this is the basic distinction.

The usual distinction, however, is between a) civil contempt composed of compensatory and coercive, and b) criminal contempt. Civil contempt benefits a private litigant and follows civil procedure. Criminal contempt vindicates the public's interest in law obedience, imposes the stigma of a criminal conviction, and follows criminal procedure.

The procedure and consequences of criminal and civil contempt differ, but the tools are the same. The judge takes contemnor's money or freedom. Participants and observers have trouble telling the difference between the criminal and civil varieties of contempt. The *Gompers* test uses benefit to distinguish and focuses on the primary benefit; it ignores the "incidental" benefit. Further it employs definitiveness as a test despite the definitiveness of a compensatory contempt award. Criminal fines and sentences seldom turn out to be very definite. Trial judges continue to err in the same way the trial judge in *Gompers* did. See, e.g., United Steelworkers of America, Local 8417 v. Newport News Shipbuilding and Dry Dock Co., 220 Va. 547, 260 S.E.2d 222 (1979). Professor Dobbs provides some helpful guidance. Contempt of Court: A Survey, 56 Cornell L.Rev. 183, 235–49 (1971). See also Moskovitz, Contempt of Injunctions, Civil and Criminal, 43 Colum.L.Rev. 780 (1943).

2) The varieties of contempt may be commingled as both *Gompers* and the next decision, *Mine Workers*, indicate. Seven possibilities of contempt with each variety alone and in combination emerge. What possibilities existed in Walker v. City of Birmingham, p. 286? Moreover, contempt may be transformed in the course of the judicial process. The trial judge may think it civil, but the appellate court holds it criminal and reverses because of improper procedure. In *Mine Workers,* the Supreme Court transformed part of a criminal penalty into coercive contempt. Be alert for more sophisticated transformations. Ask, as you read further, whether *Gompers* posits too simple a world. Is *Gompers* an archaic remnant of the mechanical legal thinking characteristic of the late 19th and early 20th centuries?

3) The *Gompers* Court reversed because of a variance between the procedure and the remedy. It did not bar criminal contempt under proper procedure. This technical decision failed to end the controversy between Bucks Stove and Gompers. E. Lieberman, Unions Before the Bar 71–83 (1960). A committee was appointed to prepare and prosecute criminal contempt. The committee recommended that, although the three AFL officers were guilty of contempt, they be afforded an opportunity to "purge" themselves of contempt by confessing guilt, apologizing, and promising to obey in the future. Gompers, Morrison, and Mitchell refused to purge the contempt. They were tried for contempt, convicted, and received identical sentences. When those judgments reached the Supreme Court again, it reversed. Justice Holmes looked at similar offenses to find a statute of limitations for criminal contempt, concluded that a three-year statute governed, and ordered the contemnors released. Gompers v. United States, 233 U.S. 604 (1914).

4) Did the *Gompers* injunction limit free speech unconstitutionally? One of the Justices called the Federationist's column a "verbal act," 221 U.S. at

436–37, 439. Would a contemporary court strike down the injunction as a prior restraint? Rabban, The First Amendment in Its Forgotten Years, 90 Yale L.J. 514, 532 (1981). Would the Norris-LaGuardia Act (reprinted in the Appendix) bar the injunction?

UNITED STATES v. UNITED MINE WORKERS

330 U.S. 258, 67 S.Ct. 677, 91 L.Ed. 884 (1947).

Chief Justice VINSON delivered the opinion of the Court.

In October, 1946, the United States was in possession of, and operating, the major portion of the country's bituminous coal mines.[1] Terms and conditions of employment were controlled "for the period of Government possession" by an agreement entered into on May 29, 1946, between Secretary of the Interior Krug, as Coal Mines Administrator, and John L. Lewis, as President of the United Mine Workers of America. The Krug-Lewis agreement embodied far-reaching changes favorable to the miners; and, except as amended and supplemented therein, the agreement carried forward the terms and conditions of the National Bituminous Coal Wage Agreement of April 11, 1945.

On October 21, 1946, the defendant Lewis directed a letter to Secretary Krug and presented issues which led directly to the present controversy. According to the defendant Lewis, the Krug-Lewis agreement carried forward § 15 of the National Bituminous Coal Wage Agreement of April 11, 1945. Under that section either party to the contract was privileged to give ten days' notice in writing of a desire for a negotiating conference which the other party was required to attend; fifteen days after the beginning of the conference either party might give notice in writing of the termination of the agreement, effective five days after receipt of such notice. Asserting authority under this clause, the defendant Lewis in his letter of October 21 requested that a conference begin November 1 for the purpose of negotiating new arrangements concerning wages, hours, practices, and other pertinent matters appertaining to the bituminous coal industry.

Captain N.H. Collisson, then Coal Mines Administrator, answered for Secretary Krug. Any contractual basis for requiring negotiations for revision of the Krug-Lewis agreement was denied. In the opinion of the Government, § 15 of the 1945 agreement had not been preserved by the Krug-Lewis agreement; indeed, § 15 had been expressly nullified by the clause of the latter contract providing that the terms contained therein were to cover the period of Government possession. Although suggesting that any negotiations looking toward a new agreement be carried on with the mine owners,

1. The United States had taken possession of the mines pursuant to Executive Order 9728 of May 21, 1946, in which the President, after determining that labor disturbances were interrupting the production of bituminous coal necessary for the operation of the national economy during the transition from war to peace, directed the Secretary of the Interior to take possession of and operate the mines and to negotiate with representatives of the miners concerning the terms and conditions of employment. . . . [The private managers of the mines had been retained by the Government in the role of operating managers; earnings were for the account of the private owners.]

the Government expressed willingness to discuss matters affecting the operation of the mines under the terms of the Krug-Lewis agreement.

Conferences were scheduled and began in Washington on November 1, both the union and the Government adhering to their opposing views regarding the right of either party to terminate the contract. At the fifth meeting, held on November 11, the union for the first time offered specific proposals for changes in wages and other conditions of employment. On November 13 Secretary Krug requested the union to negotiate with the mine owners. This suggestion was rejected. On November 15 the union, by John L. Lewis, notified Secretary Krug that "Fifteen days having now elapsed since the beginning of said conference, the United Mine Workers of America, exercising its option hereby terminates said Krug-Lewis Agreement as of 12:00 o'clock P.M., Midnight, Wednesday, November 20, 1946."

Secretary Krug again notified the defendant Lewis that he had no power under the Krug-Lewis agreement or under the law to terminate the contract by unilateral declaration. The President of the United States announced his strong support of the Government's position and requested reconsideration by the union in order to avoid a national crisis. However, the defendant Lewis, as union president, circulated to the mine workers copies of the November 15 letter to Secretary Krug. This communication was for the "official information" of union members.

The United States on November 18 filed a complaint in the District Court for the District of Columbia against the United Mine Workers of America and John L. Lewis, individually and as president of the union. The suit was brought under the Declaratory Judgment Act and sought judgment to the effect that the defendants had no power unilaterally to terminate the Krug-Lewis agreement. And, alleging that the November 15 notice was in reality a strike notice, the United States, pending the final determination of the cause, requested a temporary restraining order and preliminary injunctive relief.

The court, immediately and without notice to the defendants, issued a temporary order restraining the defendants from continuing in effect the notice of November 15, from encouraging the mine workers to interfere with the operation of the mines by strike or cessation of work, and from taking any action which would interfere with the court's jurisdiction and its determination of the case. The order by its terms was to expire at 3:00 p.m. on November 27 unless extended for good cause shown. A hearing on the preliminary injunction was set for 10:00 a.m. on the same date. The order and complaint were served on the defendants on November 18.

A gradual walkout by the miners commenced on November 18, and, by midnight of November 20, consistent with the miners' "no contract, no work" policy, a full-blown strike was in progress. Mines furnishing the major part of the nation's bituminous coal production were idle.

. . . At the conclusion of the trial on December 3, the court found that the defendants had permitted the November 15 notice to remain outstanding, had encouraged the miners to interfere by a strike with the operation of the mines and with the performance of governmental functions, and had interfered with the jurisdiction of the court. Both defendants were found guilty beyond reasonable doubt of both criminal and civil contempt dating from November 18. The court entered judgment on December 4, fining the defendant Lewis $10,000, and the defendant union $3,500,000. On the same day a preliminary injunction, effective until a final determination of the case, was issued in terms similar to those of the restraining order.

. . .

[In section I of its opinion the Court addressed itself to the contention that the temporary restraining order and preliminary injunction were issued in violation of § 20 of the Clayton Act and § 4 of the Norris-La Guardia Act. The language of both statutes supported the contention. Section 20 of the Clayton Act provided that "no such restraining order or injunction shall prohibit any person or persons . . . from recommending, advising, or persuading others to strike." Similarly, the Norris-LaGuardia Act provided that "[n]o court of the United States shall have jurisdiction to issue any restricting order or . . . injunction in any case involving or growing out of a labor dispute to prohibit any person . . . from . . . advising, urging or otherwise causing or inducing without fraud or violence" other persons to strike. [Codified, 29 U.S.C. § 104, in the Appendix.] But the Court held that these statutes were aimed at the private employer and not intended to deprive the United States, as an employer, of the injunctive remedy. Then, in section II of its opinion, the Court gave an alternative ground for supporting the contempt convictions—that the District Court had jurisdiction to determine its jurisdiction, a section of the opinion reproduced and analyzed on p. 247.]

III.

The defendants have pressed upon us the procedural aspects of their trial and allege error so prejudicial as to require reversal of the judgments for civil and criminal contempt. But we have not been persuaded.

The question is whether the proceedings will support judgments for both criminal and civil contempt; and our attention is directed to Rule 42(b) of the Rules of Criminal Procedure. [The text of Criminal Rule 42 is in the Appendix.] The rule requires criminal contempt to be prosecuted on notice stating the essential facts constituting the contempt charged. In this respect, there was compliance with the rule here. Notice was given by a rule to show cause served upon defendants together with the Government's petition and supporting affidavit. The pleadings rested only upon information and belief, but Rule 42(b) was not designed to cast doubt upon the propriety of instituting criminal contempt proceedings in this manner. The petition itself charged a violation of the outstanding restraining order, and the affidavit alleged in detail a failure to withdraw the notice of November 15, the cessation of work in the mines, and the consequent interference with governmental functions and the jurisdiction of the court. The defendants were fairly and completely apprised of the events and conduct constituting the contempt charged.

However, Rule 42(b) requires that the notice issuing to the defendants describe the criminal contempt charged as such. The defendants urge a failure to comply with this rule. The petition alleged a willful violation of the restraining order, and both the petition and the rule to show cause inquired as to why the defendants should not be "punished as and for a contempt" of court. But nowhere was the contempt described as criminal as required by the rule.

Nevertheless, the defendants were quite aware that a criminal contempt was charged.[64] In their motion to discharge and vacate the rule to show cause, the contempt charged was referred to as criminal. And in argument on the motion the defendants stated and were expressly informed that a criminal contempt was to be tried. Yet it is now urged that the omission of the words "criminal contempt" from the petition and rule to show cause was prejudicial error. Rule 42(b) requires no such rigorous application, for it was designed to insure a realization by contemnors that a prosecution for criminal contempt is contemplated. Its purpose was sufficiently fulfilled here, for this failure to observe the rule in all respects has not resulted in substantial prejudice to the defendants.

Not only were the defendants fully informed that a criminal contempt was charged, but we think they enjoyed during the trial itself all the enhanced protections accorded defendants in criminal contempt proceedings. We need not treat these at length, for defendants, in this respect, urge only their right to a jury trial as provided in § 11 of the Norris-LaGuardia Act. But § 11 is not operative here, for it applies only to cases "arising under this Act," and we have already held that the restriction upon injunctions imposed by the Act do not govern this case. The defendants, we think, were properly tried by the court without a jury.

If the defendants were thus accorded all the rights and privileges owing to defendants in criminal contempt cases, they are put in no better position to complain because their trial included a proceeding in civil contempt and was carried on in the main equity suit. Common sense would recognize that conduct can amount to both civil and criminal contempt. The same acts may justify a court in resorting to coercive and to punitive measures. Disposing of both aspects of the contempt in a single proceeding would seem at least a convenient practice. . . . Rule 42(b), while demanding fair notice and recognition of the criminal aspects of the case, contains nothing precluding a simultaneous disposition of the remedial aspects of the contempt tried. Even if it be the better practice to try criminal contempt alone and so avoid obscuring the defendant's privileges in any manner, a mingling of civil and criminal contempt proceedings must nevertheless be shown to result in substantial prejudice before a reversal will be required.[73] That the contempt proceeding

64. It could be well argued that the use of the word "punished" in the petition and rule to show cause was in itself adequate notice, for "punishment" has been said to be the magic word indicating a proceeding in criminal, rather than civil, contempt. Moskovitz, Contempt of Injunctions, Civil and Criminal, 43 Col.L. Rev. 780, 789–90 (1943). But "punishment" as used in contempt cases is ambiguous. "It is not the fact of punishment but rather its character and purpose . . . ." Gompers v. Bucks Stove & Range Co.

Noteworthy also is the allegation in the affidavit that the defendants' violation of the restraining order had "interfered with this Court's jurisdiction." And the charge in the petition of "wilfully . . . and deliberately" disobeying the restraining order indicates an intention to prosecute criminal contempt.

73. We are not impressed with defendants' attack on the pleadings as insufficient to support a judgment for civil contempt. The petition, affidavit, and rule to show cause did not expressly mention civil contempt or remedial relief, but the affidavit contained allegations of interference with the operation of the mines and with governmental functions. These claims do not negative remedial or coercive relief. More significantly, the affidavit charged disobedience of the re-carried the number and name of the equity suit does not alter this conclusion, especially where, as here, the United States would have been the complaining party in whatever suit the contempt was tried. In so far as the criminal nature of the double proceeding dominates and in so far as the defendants' rights in the criminal trial are not diluted by the mixing of civil with criminal contempt, to that extent is prejudice avoided. Here, as we have indicated, all rights and privileges of the defendants were fully respected, and there has been no showing of substantial prejudice flowing from the formal peculiarities of defendants' trial. . . .

IV.

Apart from their contentions concerning the formal aspects of the proceedings below, defendants insist upon the inability of the United States to secure relief by way of civil contempt in this case, and would limit the right to proceed by civil contempt to situations in which the United States is enforcing a statute expressly allowing resort to the courts for enforcement of statutory orders. McCrone v. United States, 307 U.S. 61 (1939), however, rests upon no such narrow ground, for the Court there said that "Article 3, § 2, of the Constitution, expressly contemplates the United States as a party to civil proceedings by extending the jurisdiction of the federal judiciary 'to Controversies to which the United States shall be a Party.'" The United States was fully entitled to bring the present suit and to benefit from orders entered in its behalf. We will not reduce the practical value of the relief granted by limiting the United States, when the orders have been disobeyed, to a proceeding in criminal contempt, and by denying to the Government the civil remedies enjoyed by other litigants, including the opportunity to demonstrate that disobedience has occasioned loss.

V.

It is urged that, in any event, the amount of the fine of $10,000 imposed on the defendant Lewis and of the fine of $3,500,000 imposed on the defendant Union were arbitrary, excessive, and in no way related to the evidence adduced at the hearing.

Sentences for criminal contempt are punitive in their nature and are imposed for the purpose of vindicating the authority of the court. Gompers v. Bucks Stove & Range Co. The interests of orderly government demand that respect and compliance be given to orders issued by courts possessed of jurisdiction of persons and subject matter. One who defies the public authority and willfully refuses his obedience, does so at his peril. In imposing a fine for criminal contempt, the trial judge may properly take into consideration the extent of the willful and deliberate defiance of the court's order, the seriousness of the consequences of the contumacious behavior, the necessity of

straining order by failing to withdraw the notice of Nov. 15. We will not assume that the defendants were not instantly aware that a usual remedy in such a situation is to impose coercive sanctions until the act is performed. This is a function of civil contempt. . . . Furthermore, defendants' counsel, in argument on the motion to vacate, remarked that the United States was proceeding upon the theory of civil contempt, and attempted only to demonstrate the inability of the United States to seek this relief. And when the Government's suggestions for fines were before the court, defendants' counsel argued the excessiveness of the fines for either civil or criminal contempt.

effectively terminating the defendant's defiance as required by the public interest, and the importance of deterring such acts in the future. Because of the nature of these standards, great reliance must be placed upon the discretion of the trial judge.

The trial court properly found the defendants guilty of criminal contempt. Such contempt had continued for 15 days from the issuance of the restraining order until the finding of guilty. Its willfulness had not been qualified by any concurrent attempt on defendants' part to challenge the order by motion to vacate or other appropriate procedures. Immediately following the finding of guilty, defendant Lewis stated openly in court that defendants would adhere to their policy of defiance. This policy, as the evidence showed, was the germ center of an economic paralysis which was rapidly extending itself from the bituminous coal mines into practically every other major industry of the United States. It was an attempt to repudiate and override the instrument of lawful government in the very situation in which governmental action was indispensable.

The trial court also properly found the defendants guilty of civil contempt. Judicial sanctions in civil contempt proceedings may, in a proper case, be employed for either or both of two purposes: to coerce the defendant into compliance with the court's order, and to compensate the complainant for losses sustained. Gompers v. Bucks Stove & Range Co. Where compensation is intended, a fine is imposed, payable to the complainant. Such fine must of course be based upon evidence of complainant's actual loss, and his right, as a civil litigant, to the compensatory fine is dependent upon the outcome of the basic controversy.

But where the purpose is to make the defendant comply, the court's discretion is otherwise exercised. It must then consider the character and magnitude of the harm threatened by continued contumacy, and the probable effectiveness of any suggested sanction in bringing about the result desired.

It is a corollary of the above principles that a court which has returned a conviction for contempt must, in fixing the amount of a fine to be imposed as a punishment or as a means of securing future compliance, consider the amount of defendant's financial resources and the consequent seriousness of the burden to that particular defendant.

In the light of these principles, we think the record clearly warrants a fine of $10,000 against defendant Lewis for criminal contempt. A majority of the Court, however, does not think that it warrants the unconditional imposition of a fine of $3,500,000 against the defendant union. A majority feels that, if the court below had assessed a fine of $700,000 against the defendant union, this, under the circumstances, would not be excessive as punishment for the criminal contempt theretofore committed; and feels that, in order to coerce the defendant union into a future compliance with the court's order, it would have been effective to make the other $2,800,000 of the fine conditional on the defendant's failure to purge itself within a reasonable time. Accordingly, the judgment against the defendant union is held to be excessive. It will be modified so as to require the defendant union to pay a fine of $700,000, and further, to pay an additional fine of $2,800,000 unless the defendant union, within five days after the issuance of the mandate herein, shows that it has fully complied with the temporary restraining order issued November 18,

1946, and the preliminary injunction issued December 4, 1946. The defendant union can effect full compliance only by withdrawing unconditionally the notice given by it, signed John L. Lewis, President, on November 15, 1946, to J.A. Krug, Secretary of the Interior, terminating the Krug-Lewis agreement as of twelve o'clock midnight, Wednesday, November 20, 1946, and by notifying, at the same time, its members of such withdrawal in substantially the same manner as the members of the defendant union were notified of the notice to the Secretary of the Interior above-mentioned; and by withdrawing and similarly instructing the members of the defendant union of the withdrawal of any other notice to the effect that the Krug-Lewis agreement is not in full force and effect until the final determination of the basic issues arising under the said agreement.

We well realize the serious proportions of the fines here imposed upon the defendant union. But a majority feels that the course taken by the union carried with it such a serious threat to orderly constitutional government, and to the economic and social welfare of the nation, that a fine of substantial size is required in order to emphasize the gravity of the offense of which the union was found guilty. The defendant Lewis, it is true, was the aggressive leader in the studied and deliberate non-compliance with the order of the District Court; but, as the record shows, he stated in open court prior to imposition of the fines that "the representatives of the United Mine Workers determined that the so-called Krug-Lewis Agreement was breached," and that it was the union's "representatives" who "notified the Secretary of the Interior that the contract was terminated as of November 20th." And certainly it was the members of the defendant union who executed the nationwide strike. Loyalty in responding to the orders of their leader may, in some minds, minimize the gravity of the miners' conduct; but we cannot ignore the effect of their action upon the rights of other citizens, or the effect of their action upon our system of government. The gains, social and economic, which the miners and other citizens have realized in the past are ultimately due to the fact that they enjoy the rights of free men under our system of government. Upon the maintenance of that system depends all future progress to which they may justly aspire. In our complex society, there is a great variety of limited loyalties, but the overriding loyalty of all is to our country and to the institutions under which a particular interest may be pursued.

We are aware that the defendants may have sincerely believed that the restraining order was ineffective and would finally be vacated. However, the Government had sought a declaration of its contractual rights under the Krug-Lewis agreement, effective since May 29, 1946, and solemnly subscribed by the Government and the defendant union. The restraining order sought to preserve conditions until the cause could be determined, and obedience by the defendants would have secured this result. They had full opportunity to comply with the order of the District Court, but they deliberately refused obedience and determined for themselves the validity of the order. When the rule to show cause was issued, provision was made for a hearing as to whether or not the alleged contempt was sufficiently purged. At that hearing the defendants stated to the court that their position remained then in the status which existed at the time of the issuance of the restraining order. Their conduct showed a total lack of respect for the judicial process. Punishment in this case is for that which the defendants had done prior to imposition of the judgment in the District Court, coupled with a coercive imposition upon the defendant union to compel obedience with the court's outstanding order. . . .

Justice BLACK and Justice DOUGLAS, concurring in part and dissenting in part. . . .

We agree that the court had power summarily to coerce obedience to those orders and to subject defendants to such conditional sanctions as were necessary to compel obedience. And we agree that in such civil contempt proceedings to compel obedience, it was not necessary for the court to abide by all the procedural safeguards which surround trials for crime. Without such coercive powers, courts could not settle the cases and controversies before them. Courts could not administer justice if persons were left free pending adjudication to engage in conduct which would either immediately interrupt the judicial proceedings or so change the *status quo* of the subject matter of a controversey that no effective judgment could be rendered. Disorder in the courtroom, or so near to it as to interrupt a trial, and disobedience of an affirmative court order, are typical examples of offenses which must necessarily be dealt with summarily. To remove such imminent interference with orderly judicial proceedings, courts must have power to act immediately. In recognition of this fact, the contempt power came into existence. This power is of ancient lineage, has always been exercised by our courts, and has the express recognition of Congress under the name of contempt. . . . Where the court exercises such coercive power, however, for the purpose of compelling future obedience, those imprisoned "carry the keys of their prison in their own pockets," In re Nevitt, 117 F. 448, 461; by obedience to the court's valid order, they can end their confinement; and the court's coercive power in such a "civil contempt" proceeding ends when its order has been obeyed. . . . The District Court did not enter a conditional decree here. But this Court has modified the District Court's decree to provide as part of the judgment such a coercive sanction in the form of a conditional fine. We agree with the Court's decision in this respect.

The *Gompers* decision and many others have pointed out that the object of such coercive contempt proceedings is not to punish for an offense against the public, but to compel obedience to valid court orders. Yet the decision of this Court also approves unconditional fines as criminal punishment for past disobedience. We cannot agree to this aspect of the Court's judgment. At a very early date this Court declared, and recently it has reiterated, that in contempt proceedings courts should never exercise more than "the least possible power adequate to the end proposed." Anderson v. Dunn, 6 Wheat. 204, 231. . . .

In certain circumstances criminal contempt culminating in unconditional punishment for past disobedience may well constitute an exercise of "the least possible power adequate to the end proposed." Thus in situations which would warrant only a use of coercive sanctions in the first instance, criminal punishment might be appropriate at a later stage if the defendant should persist in disobeying the order of the court. Without considering the constitutional requisites of such criminal punishment, we believe the application of it inappropriate and improper here. The imposition of criminal punishment here was an exercise of far more than "the least possible power adequate to the end proposed." For here the great and legitimate "end proposed" was affirmative action by the defendants to prevent interruption of coal production pending final adjudication of the controversy. Coercive sanctions sufficient to accomplish this end were justified. From the record we have no doubt but that a conditional civil sanction would bring about at least as prompt and unequivocal obedience to the court's order as would criminal punishment for past disobedience. And this would accomplish a vindication of the District Court's authority against a continuing defiance. Consequently, we do not believe that the accomplishment of the justifiable "end proposed" called for summary criminal punishment which is designed to deter others from disobedience to court orders or to avenge a public wrong, rather than the imposition of a coercive sanction. And for the reasons stated by Mr. Justice Rutledge, we think that the flat $700,000 criminal fine against the defendant union is excessive by constitutional and statutory standards.

In determining whether criminal punishment or coercive sanction should be employed in these proceedings, the question of intent—the motivation of the contumacy—becomes relevant. Difficult questions of law were presented by this case. It is plain that the defendants acted willfully for they knew that they were disobeying the court's order. But they appear to have believed in good faith, though erroneously, that they were acting within their legal rights. Many lawyers would have so advised them. This does not excuse their conduct; the whole situation emphasized the duty of testing the restraining order by orderly appeal instead of disobedience and open defiance. However, as this Court said in Cooke v. United States, 267 U.S. 517, 538, "the intention with which acts of contempt have been committed must necessarily and properly have an important bearing on the degree of guilt and the penalty which should be imposed."

We think it significant that the conduct which was prohibited by the restraining order for violation of which these defendants have been punished for contempt is also punishable under the War Labor Disputes Act. That Act provides a maximum punishment of $5,000 fine and one year imprisonment for those who interfere with the operation of mines taken over by the United States. Had the defendants been tried under that statute, their punishment would have been limited thereby and in their trial they would have enjoyed all the constitutional safeguards of the Bill of Rights. Whatever constitutional safeguards are required in a summary contempt proceeding, whether it be for criminal punishment, or for the imposition of coercive sanction, we must be ever mindful of the danger of permitting punishment by contempt to be imposed for conduct which is identical with an offense defined and made punishable by statute. . . .

The situation of grave emergency facing the country when the District Court acted called for the strongest measures—measures designed to produce quick and unqualified obedience of the court's order. If the $10,000 fine on defendant Lewis and the $3,500,000 fine on the defendant union be treated as coercive fines, they would not necessarily be excessive. For they would then be payable only if the defendants continued to disobey the court's order. Defendants could then avoid payment by purging themselves. The price of continued disobedience would be the amount of the fines. . . . The fines would be fixed so as to produce the greatest likelihood that they would compel obedience.

We should modify the District Court's decrees by making the entire amount of the fines payable conditionally. On December 7, 1946, Mr. Lewis directed the mine workers to return to work until midnight, March 31, 1947. But, so far as we are aware, the notice which purported to terminate the contract has not been withdrawn. Thus, there has been, at most, only a partial compliance with the temporary injunction.

Hence our judgment should provide that the defendants pay their respective fines only in the event that full and unconditional obedience to the temporary injunction, including withdrawal of the notice which purported to terminate the contract, is not had on or before a day certain.

Justice RUTLEDGE, dissenting. . . .

The issues concerning the manner in which the contempt proceeding was conducted are in themselves of great moment, apart from the foregoing conclusions which I think are dispositive of the controversy. And the Court's rulings upon them are of such a character that I cannot accede by silence.

At times in our system the way in which courts perform their function becomes as important as what they do in the result. In some respects matters of procedure constitute the very essence of ordered liberty under the Constitution. For this reason, especially in the Bill of Rights, specific guaranties have been put around the manner in which various legal proceedings shall be conducted. They differentiate sharply between the procedures to be followed in criminal proceedings and in civil ones. These differences mark one of the great constitutional divides. They separate the zone of punishment for crime, with all its odious consequences, from that of giving civil relief, where no such consequences attend, not partially but completely.

In any other context than one of contempt, the idea that a criminal prosecution and a civil suit for damages or equitable relief could be hashed together in a single criminal-civil hodgepodge would be shocking to every American lawyer and to most citizens. True, the same act may give rise to all these varied legal consequences. But we have never adopted, rather our Constitution has totally rejected, the continental system of compounding criminal proceedings with civil adjudications. Our tradition is exactly the contrary and few would maintain that this has had no part in bringing about the difference existing today for individual freedom here and in Europe.

I do not think the Constitution contemplated that there should be in any case an admixture of civil and criminal proceedings in one. Such an idea is altogether foreign to its spirit. There can be no question that contempt power was conferred adequate to sustain the judicial function, in both civil and criminal forms. But it does not follow that the Constitution permits lumping the two together or discarding for the criminal one all of the procedural safeguards so carefully provided for every other such proceeding.

The founders did not command the impossible. They could not have conceived that procedures so irreconcilably inconsistent in many ways [30]

30. Upon the authorities, the following procedural provisions of the Bill of Rights, at least, would seem to apply to criminal contempt: The provision against double jeopardy, see In re Bradley, 318 U.S. 50; the provision against self-incrim-

could be applied simultaneously. Nor was their purpose to create any part of judicial power, even in contempt, wholly at large, free from any constitutional limitation or to pick and choose between the conflicting civil and criminal procedures and remedies at will. Much less was it to allow mixing civil remedies and criminal punishments in one lumped form of relief, indistinguishably compounding them and thus putting both in unlimited judicial discretion, with no possibility of applying any standard of measurement on review.

If this can be done in any case, it can be done in others. And that being true, if it can be done at all, not simply a loophole but a very large breach has been left in the wall of procedural protections thrown around the citizen's punishment for crime. For it is to be recalled that under the Court's ruling here upon the *Shipp* doctrine not merely the violation of valid judicial orders, but also the disobedience of invalid orders issued in excess of any court's jurisdiction becomes a crime and punishable as such by summary proceedings in criminal contempt, although the substantive rights involved in the litigation are wholly civil ones. The vastly expanded area of criminal conduct under this conception would afford equally wide room for dispensing with the criminal procedural protections under the unrestricted scope, otherwise than by "judicial discretion," which the present ruling concerning criminal or criminal-civil proceedings in contempt affords.

In my opinion, our system does not comprehend a power so unconfined anywhere within its broad borders, and it is time the large confusion about this were swept away. It is not necessary in this case to ask or decide whether all of the Constitution's criminal procedural protections thrown about all other criminal prosecutions, without suggestion of explicit exception, apply to criminal contempt proceedings. It is enough that we are sure some of them apply, as this Court has ruled repeatedly. It does not matter that some of those which incontestably are applicable may not have been put in issue or preserved for review in this case. The question cuts more deeply than the application of any specific guaranty. It affects the right to insist upon or have the benefit of any.

This case is characteristic of the long-existing confusion concerning contempts and the manner of their trial, among other things, in that most frequently the question of the nature and character of the proceeding, whether civil or criminal, is determined at its end in the state of review rather than, as it should be and as in my opinion it must be, at the beginning. . . . And this fact in itself illustrates the complete jeopardy in which rights are placed

ination, Gompers v. Buck's Stove & R. Co.; the provision for due process insofar as it necessitates "suitable notice and adequate opportunity to appear and to be heard," Blackmer v. United States, 284 U.S. 421, 440; and, although the Sixth Amendment protections have been said not to apply as such to criminal contempts, Myers v. United States, 264 U.S. 95, 104–105; Blackmer v. United States, 284 U.S. at 440, but see text infra, doubtless at least the provisions for "a speedy and public trial," for "compulsory process" and for the assistance of counsel, see Cooke v. United States, 267 U.S. 517, 537, are implied in the due process provision of the Fifth Amendment. And it has been said that the protection against cruel and unusual punishments in the Eighth Amendment applies to criminal contempt. United States ex rel. Brown v. Lederer, 140 F.2d 136, 139.

There are also protections not expressly included in the Bill of Rights which apply in criminal contempt, e.g., that the defendant is presumed to be innocent and must be proved guilty beyond a reasonable doubt. Gompers v. Bucks Stove & R. Co. . . .

when the nature of the proceeding remains unknown and unascertainable until the final action on review.

Not only is one thus placed in continuing dilemma throughout the proceedings in the trial court concerning which set of procedural rights he is entitled to stand upon, whether upon the criminal safeguards or only on the civil. He also does not and cannot know until it is too late, that is, until the appellate phase is ended, whether one group or the other of appellate jurisdictional and procedural rules applies. Indeed he may find that his right of review has been taken either prematurely or too late depending entirely on whether the appellate court finally concludes that the proceeding has been civil or criminal in character.

. . . What is most important . . . is that the person charged is entitled to know from the beginning, not merely at the end or some intermediate stage, in which sort of proceeding he is involved.

This rule has now been incorporated also in Rule 42(b) of the Federal Rules of Criminal Procedure, and was applicable in this case. By the terms of that rule the charge of criminal contempt was required to be "prosecuted on notice" and it was further commanded that the notice state "the essential facts constituting the criminal contempt charged *and describe it as such,*" which was not done here. The rule was adopted to outlaw "the frequent confusion between civil and criminal contempt proceedings," following immediately a suggestion made in McCann v. New York Stock Exchange, 80 F.2d 211.[45] . . . But it flatly incorporates the effect of the decision in the *Gompers* case . . . .

The language used by the Court was language of the Constitution . . . Careful as it was about expressly overruling prior decisions where the Sixth Amendment's requirement had not been observed, there can be no doubt that the Court was announcing for the future that the constitutional requirement must be complied with. And the result in the case itself accorded with what this view required.

One who does not know until the end of litigation what his procedural rights in trial are, or may have been, has no such rights. He is denied all by a hide-and-seek game between those that are criminal and those that are civil. The view which would seem to be the only one consistent with the whole spirit of the Constitution, and with the nature of our free institutions, is that all of the constitutional guaranties applicable to trials for crime should apply to such trials for contempt, excepting only those which may be wholly inconsistent with the nature and execution of the function the court must perform.

45. Judge L. Hand's opinion in the *McCann* case reads in part as follows:

". . . the respondent will often find it hard to tell whether the prosecution is not a remedial move in the suit, undertaken on behalf of the client. This can be made plain if the judge enters an order in limine, directing the attorney to prosecute the respondent criminally on behalf of the court, and if the papers supporting the process contain a copy of this order or allege its contents correctly. We think that *unless this is done the prosecution must be deemed to be civil and will support no other than a remedial punishment.* Nothing of the sort was done here, and the order must be reversed. . . . " (Emphasis added.) 80 F.2d 211, 214–215.

The possibilities of confusion are multiplied when the contempt is instituted in a suit in which the United States is a party, since the United States may bring civil as well as criminal contempt proceedings. McCrone v. United States, 307 U.S. 61.

As has been said, courts in performing this function are not above the Constitution; rather they are empowered to perform it in order to make the Constitution itself operative. Accordingly, not the least but the greatest possible application of it to this phase of their work is the only rule consistent with their place in the constitutional scheme. . . .

Hence, whatever may be true of indictment and jury trials, I see no compelling reason whatever for not applying the other limitations of the Sixth Amendment. None of them is inconsistent with the due and proper performance of the court's function in criminal contempt. Some at the least are applicable by virtue of the due process guaranty of the Fifth Amendment. "Due process of law, therefore, in the prosecution of contempt, except of that committed in open court, requires that the accused should be advised of the charges and have a reasonable opportunity to meet them by way of defense or explanation. We think this includes the assistance of counsel, if requested, and the right to call witnesses to give testimony, relevant either to the issue of complete exculpation or in extenuation of the offense and in mitigation of the penalty to be imposed." Cooke v. United States, 267 U.S. 517, 537. . . . Whether or not that case was a departure from our long established tradition that in criminal proceedings the defendant is entitled to be confronted with the witnesses against him, other departures should not be made.

Surely the rights to a speedy and public trial, to have compulsory process for obtaining witness in his favor, to have the assistance of counsel for his defense, and, as the *Gompers* case held, to be informed of the *nature* as well as the cause of the accusation, cannot be denied in our system to any person charged with crime, with the single exception of contempts committed in the immediate presence of the court by way of interference with the proceedings. Those guaranties are in no way inconsistent with the court's proper and complete discharge of its function in contempt. And they would seem to be essential to any conception of a fair trial as the Fifth Amendment's due process clause comprehends this.

When the assertion and securing of all other rights depends upon one, that one is the core of all. Here the right "to know that it was a charge, and not a suit" comprehended all other procedural rights in the trial and appellate courts. Without this, none could be asserted or maintained. The denial of that right, deferring it until the decision here is handed down, is in my opinion not only a denial of all. It is a violation both of the Constitution and of Rule 42(b).

But we are told that this, and all that followed or may have followed from it, make no difference because there was no prejudice. There are at least two answers. This Court has held that the denial of constitutional guaranties in trials for crime is in itself prejudice. . . . The other, there was prejudice and in the most important thing beyond knowing the nature of the proceeding in advance of trial, namely, in the penalty itself.

Not only was the penalty against the union excessive, as the Court holds. Vice infected both "fines" more deeply. As the proceeding itself is said to have been both civil and criminal, so are the two "fines." Each was imposed in a single lump sum, with no allocation of specific portions as among civil damages, civil coercion and criminal punishment. The Government concedes that some part of each "fine" was laid for each purpose. But the trial court did not state, and the Government has refused to speculate, how much was imposed in either instance for each of those distinct remedial functions.

This was in the teeth of the *Gompers* and other previous decisions here. The law has fixed standards for each remedy, and they are neither identical nor congealable. They are, for damages in civil contempt, the amount of injury proven and no more, Gompers v. Bucks Stove & R. Co.; for coercion, what may be required to bring obedience and not more, whether by way of imprisonment or fine; for punishment, what is not cruel and unusual or, in the case of a fine, excessive within the Eighth Amendment's prohibition. And for determining excessiveness of criminal fines there are analogies from legislative action which in my opinion are controlling.

The Government concedes that the Eighth Amendment's limitation applies to penalties in criminal contempt; and that in civil contempt the damages awarded cannot exceed the proven amount of injury. It also concedes, as I understand, that purely coercive relief can be no greater than is necessary to secure obedience. But in its view there was no necessity here for allocation of specific amounts in order to comply with these distinct standards. Rather punishment and damages may be lumped with a third undefined amount for civil coercion; and the whole mass sustained, without reference to the constituent elements or any of the established standards for measuring them, other than by over-all application of the Eighth Amendment's limitation to the mass. And in this view it maintains neither "fine" is excessive.

Obviously, however, when all these distinct types and functions of relief are lumped together, in a single so-called "fine," none of the long-established bases for measurement can be applied, for there is nothing to which they can apply. We can only speculate upon what portion of each "fine" may have been laid to compensate for damages, what for punishment, and what, if any,[54] for civil coercion. Moreover, the District Court made no findings whatever concerning the amount of civil damages sustained, even if it could be assumed that there was evidence to sustain such findings.[55] And on the record none of the "fine" was made contingent, affording an opportunity for compurgation, as is required for coercive penalties.[56]

54. The fines in this case were flat fines imposed absolutely, without contingency for compurgation or otherwise. The court acted on the Government's recommendation, which as to the union was made on the basis of $250,000 a day for the fourteen days elapsed after the restraining orders issued and the violations occurred. No part of the fine was laid contingently upon future conduct. Both penalties therefore would seem to be strictly criminal, or criminal combined with civil damages for past conduct, not coercive in the sense of coercive relief as contemplated in the decisions, . . . although the amounts fixed for each fine gave it "incidental" coercive effect in the popular sense. . . .

55. The Government's asserted loss in revenues, chiefly relied on for this purpose, was not only highly speculative rather than proven in amount. It was injury which would have followed from the strike had it arisen before or after seizure. Such damages may result from any strike whether the Government or another is "employer," and would seem to be both speculative and indirect within the rule forbidding the award of such damages. Hadley v. Baxendale, 9 Exch. 341.

56. . . . The order for coercive fines reads, by analogy to the order for coercive imprisonment that, unless there is obedience to the order of the court, the fine shall be paid on or before a day certain, in default of which the defendant shall be imprisoned until it is paid. See Doyle v. London Guarantee Co., 204 U.S. 599, 602. In the case of corporations or unincorporated associations, the default provision is either that the responsible of-

. . . When hybrid proceedings can produce hybrid penalties, concealing what is for punishment and what remedial, what criminal and what civil, and in the process can discard constitutional procedural protections against just such consequences, as convenience or other wholly discretionary impulse may command, then indeed to the extent we allow this will we have adopted the continental tradition of the civilians and rejected our own. No case in this Court heretofore has ever sustained such conglomerate proceedings and penalties.

That the Government is complainant here, both as "employer" seeking remedial relief and in sovereign capacity seeking to vindicate the court's authority by criminal penalty, does not nullify all these long-established limitations or put the courts wholly at large, limited by nothing except their unconfined discretion as to the scope and character of the relief allowable. Power there is to take adequate measures when violation is clearly shown and adequate proof is made to sustain them. For proven violation, criminal penalty within the Eighth Amendment's limits as we would measure similar impositions placed by Congress, at the most; for damages proven and found, civil award commensurate with the finding; and for coercion, civil relief by way of imprisonment or "fine," but in either case contingent only, not final, giving opportunity for compurgation and for termination, on its being made, of further penalty for the future.

These are the limitations the law has prescribed. They apply equally when the Government is complainant, and whether in one capacity or the other, or both, as when others are.[59] They cannot be dispensed with, separately or by conglomerating all into a single indiscriminate lump, at the suit of the Government or another, in this case or for others. To permit this would be to throw overboard the limitations prescribed by law and make the courts purely discretionary arbitrators of controversies. That cannot be done in our system.

The Court seemingly recognizes this, in part, in the revision it makes of the District Court's penalties. Lewis' fine is affirmed in amount but wholly changed in character. Instead of composite relief as the District Court made it, the Court makes that fine wholly a criminal penalty, thus in effect increasing the amount of his criminal imposition. The union's fine, though held excessive and "reduced," by what standard is not apparent, is replaced by a flat criminal fine of $700,000 plus a contingent penalty of $2,800,000 said to be entirely for civil coercion, although the strike was ended in December. Any award for civil damages allegedly sustained apparently is eliminated.

The Court thus purports to make separate the distinct items of relief commingled in the District Court's action. But in doing so, in my opinion, it wholly disregards the established standard for measuring criminal fines and its own as well as the District Court's function relating to them. If Lewis and

ficers be imprisoned, Parker v. United States, 126 F.2d 370, 379, or perhaps that execution issue against the contemnor's property. See United States v. Ridgewood Garment Co., 44 F.Supp. 435, 436. . . .

59. The limitations upon criminal contempt, procedural and remedial, always apply to the Government, for it alone can bring that proceeding. It cannot defeat them by mingling that proceeding and relief with civil ones, merely by virtue of being also the complaining civil litigant.

the union had been convicted on indictment and jury trial in a proceeding surrounded by all the constitutional and other safeguards of criminal prosecution for violating the War Labor Disputes Act, the maximum fines which could be applied by that Act's terms would be $5,000 for each. In addition, Lewis could have been imprisoned for a year.

In my opinion, when Congress prescribes a maximum penalty for criminal violation of a statute, that penalty fixes the maximum which can be imposed whether the conviction is in a criminal proceeding as such for its violation or is for contempt for violating an order of court to observe it temporarily. Gompers v. United States. If the fine or other penalty in such a case can be multiplied twice or any other number of times, merely by bringing a civil suit, securing a temporary restraining order and then convicting the person who violates it of criminal contempt, regardless of the order's validity and of any of the usual restraints of criminal procedure, the way will have been found to dispense with substantially all of those protections relating not only to the course of the proceedings but to the penalty itself.

But it is in relation to the flat criminal fine of $700,000 against the union that the Court's disregard of the constitutional and other standards is most apparent. By what measuring rod this sum has been arrived at as the appropriate and lawful amount, I am unable to say, unless indeed it is simply by a rough estimate of what the union should be forced to pay on all counts. Never has a criminal fine of such magnitude been heretofore laid and sustained, so far as I am able to discover. And only for treason, with one other possible exception, has Congress authorized one so large. Moreover, the Court's enumeration of factors to be taken into account indicates expressly, as I read the opinion, that one is the coercive effect of the imposition for the future, though it is thoroughly settled that in contempt criminal punishment is to be laid only for past conduct. . . .

Thus, the Court in effect imposes double coercive penalties, in view of the additional contingent award of $2,800,000 for that specific and sole purpose. I think the criminal fine of $700,000 not only constitutionally excessive, far beyond any heretofore sustained for violation of any statute or order of court. It is also an unlawful commingling of civil coercive and criminal penalties, without the essential contingent feature in the coercive phase, under our prior decisions.

Moreover, it is the District Court's function, not ours, in the first instance to fix the amounts of criminal fines. In equity proceedings for coercive relief, appellate courts including this one have power to revise and fix awards for such purposes, and if damages also are sought to review amounts awarded for this purpose for consistency with the proof. . . . But in a criminal proceeding, which is at law even in contempt, . . . our function is not in the first instance to fix the fines ourselves. That function is the District Court's. . . . We can only determine whether those imposed by it are excessive under the Eighth Amendment.

In its revision of the penalties therefore the Court in my opinion not only fails to unscramble the coercive and criminal elements, as the prior decisions here require to be done. It imposes grossly excessive criminal penalties, determined in amount by wholly arbitrary estimate related to no previously established standard legislatively or judicially fixed. And in doing so, it usurps the District Court's function. All this flows in part at least from its basic error, which is its failure to follow the rule of the *Gompers* and other cases that not only civil and criminal penalties, but also civil and criminal proceedings are altogether different and separate things, and under the Constitution must be kept so. . . .

No right is absolute. Nor is any power, governmental or other, in our system. There can be no question that it provides power to meet the greatest crises. Equally certain is it that under "a government of laws and not of men" such as we possess, power must be exercised according to law; and government, including the courts, as well as the governed, must move within its limitations. . . .

Justice MURPHY joins in this opinion.

---

1) Is a money payment to a government plaintiff the hardest form of contempt to classify as compensatory, coercive, or criminal? Would it be more difficult to classify the contempt if, after this opinion, the union disobeys again and the plaintiff asks for the $2,800,000?

2) Is the majority's view of whether the notice was adequate consistent with *Gompers?* with Rule 42(b)?

3) Should the distinctions between civil and criminal contempt be scuttled? California, for example, has a single set of statutes for coercive and criminal contempt; litigants who seek compensatory relief for breaches must proceed by an action at law: "The available judgments under the California procedure are limited to punishment for failure to obey a decree in the form of a fine not exceeding $500 or imprisonment not exceeding five days, or both, and to imprisonment until performance of the act, the failure to perform which constitutes the contempt, provided that performance is still in the power of the person imprisoned. There is no provision for a conditional fine, and there is no provision for the assessment of a fine payable to the private litigant by way of compensation for damages suffered. Under the California approach, it seems that any compensatory award to the injured party depends upon an ordinary action at law. . . ." Wright, Byrne, Haakh, Westbrook, and Wheat, Civil and Criminal Contempt in the Federal Courts, 17 F.R.D. 167, 180 (1955).

INTERNATIONAL BUSINESS MACHINE CORP. v. UNITED STATES

493 F.2d 112 (2d Cir. 1973).

Before MULLIGAN, OAKES and TIMBERS, Circuit Judges.

OAKES, Circuit Judge:

These appeals are by International Business Machines Corporation (IBM) and Cravath, Swaine & Moore (Cravath), a law firm which has represented IBM throughout the proceedings involved in this Government civil antitrust suit. In No. 73–2126 IBM seeks review of an adjudication of civil contempt against it for failure to comply with the very pretrial discovery order which IBM unsuccessfully sought to appeal or have vacated through a petition for an extraordinary writ in International Business Machines Corp. v. United

States, 480 F.2d 293 (2d Cir. 1973) (en banc), petition for cert. filed, 42 U.S.L.W. 3033 (U.S. June 11, 1973). In that case the appeal and petition for mandamus were dismissed on the basis of a lack of jurisdiction under the Expediting Act (15 U.S.C. § 29) and it was held that in no event was there any basis to review the trial court's interlocutory order either by appeal or mandamus. On petition of the Government filed June 25, 1973, Chief Judge Edelstein, after a hearing, entered an opinion, findings and order imposing a contingent, coercive fine of $150,000 per day until IBM complies with his discovery order, Pretrial Order No. 5. This order directed IBM to produce for the Government certain documents which IBM had previously delivered to a third party, Control Data Corporation, in the course of discovery in a civil antitrust action in the United States District Court for the District of Minnesota. IBM's claim both in the prior appeal and in this one is that the documents were protected from discovery by the attorney-client and work-product privileges. The trial judge, however, had ruled that, for purposes of the Government's antitrust suit, IBM had waived its claims of privilege by delivering the documents to Control Data in the Minnesota suit.

In No. 73–2127, IBM and Cravath assert that the district court has erroneously denied Cravath's petition to intervene in its own behalf as a party in the civil contempt hearing, for the purpose of asserting an attorney's work-product privilege against production of some of the documents and to require the district court to impose civil contempt sanctions upon Cravath or its partner, Mr. Bromley, so that it can obtain appellate review of the district court's rulings in connection with Pretrial Order No. 5.

Nos. 73–2145–6 is a petition for an extraordinary writ pursuant to 28 U.S.C. § 1651 and Fed.R.App.P. 21 in which IBM asks us to direct Chief Judge Edelstein to vacate the contempt order.

It should be noted that a direct appeal from the district court to the Supreme Court under the Expediting Act, 15 U.S.C. § 29, challenging the validity of Pretrial Order No. 5 is presently pending. There is also pending before the Supreme Court an extraordinary writ to review the district court's pretrial order . . ., and a petition for a writ of certiorari to review International Business Machines Corp. v. United States, supra.

Character of the Contempt Order

An order finding a party in criminal contempt is appealable. This is true because, in the language of the Supreme Court in Bloom v. Illinois, "[c]riminal contempt is a crime in the ordinary sense; it is a violation of the law, a public wrong which is punishable by fine or imprisonment or both." See Gompers v. United States, 233 U.S. 604, 610 (1914); Gompers v. Bucks Stove & Range Co. Hence an order punishing one criminally for contempt is a final judgment and review may immediately be obtained. Union Tool Co. v. Wilson, 259 U.S. 107, 111 (1922); Bessette v. W.B. Conkey Co., 194 U.S. 324, 336–338 (1904). The procedure in relation to criminal contempts is prescribed by 18 U.S.C. §§ 401 and 402 and Fed.R.Crim.P. 42. Appeals from criminal contempt orders are governed by Fed.R.Crim.P. 37. See generally Dobbs, Contempt of Court: A Survey, 56 Cornell L.Rev. 183, 235–45 (1971).

Generally speaking, however, an order of civil contempt is interlocutory and may not be challenged on an appeal until the entry of final judgment. Fox v. Capital Co., 299 U.S. 105, 107 (1936) (supplementary proceedings; contempt for failure to disclose assets); Doyle v. London Guarantee Co., 204 U.S. 599, 608 (1907). See also Mulligan, J., dissenting in International Business Machines Corp. v. United States, 471 F.2d 507, 519 n. 3 (2d Cir. 1972) (panel decision reversed en banc).[1]

Appellant IBM argues first that Judge Edelstein's contempt order, although styled as a "civil" order, is in reality a criminal contempt order and is hence appealable. This argument has three underlying premises: (1) vindication of a court's authority is a characteristic of criminal, not civil, contempt and such was the purpose of the order here; (2) if the order were civil, it could not be entered without consideration of "the character and magnitude of the harm threatened by continued contumacy," United States v. UMW; and (3) the severity of the penalties imposed here, i.e., $150,000 per day for noncompliance, is so great that necessarily the contempt order is criminal.

None of these premises are correct. The hallmark of civil contempt is that the sanction imposed is only contingent and coercive. Shillitani v. United States, 384 U.S. 364, 370 (1966); Penfield Co. v. SEC, 330 U.S. 585, 590 (1947); United States v. UMW; Gompers v. Bucks Stove & Range Co. Civil contempt, moreover, has a remedial purpose—compelling obedience to an order of the court for the purpose of enforcing the other party's rights, or obtaining other relief for the opposing party. Nye v. United States, 313 U.S. 33 (1941); McCrone v. United States, 307 U.S. 61, 64 (1939); Gompers v. Bucks Stove & Range Co. The distinction between civil and criminal contempt is, in short, "usually based on the purpose for which the contempt sentence is meted out." Dobbs, 56 Cornell L.Rev. at 235.

The district court did not leave in doubt the purpose which the contempt citation here was to serve. The order, dated August 1, 1973, makes it clear that the fine is for each day that IBM "fails to comply with Pretrial Order No. 5" and that IBM is "entitled to purge itself of this contempt at any time" by compliance with the discovery order. The order of July 10, 1973, requiring that the hearing proceed in respect to the possibility of contempt, clearly states that the hearing is to be "on the issue of a coercive fine . . . ." Thus the order was both coercive and contingent, indicating a civil rather than criminal contempt.

In regard to the amount of the coercive fine it was proper for the court to take into account the contemnor's resources and ability to pay. This it did, noting in the contempt order that its 1972 annual report showed earnings for that year in excess of $1,279,000,000 as against $1,078,000,000 in 1971 and

1. Exceptions to this rule are rare, but where they occur it is because the interlocutory nature of the order is no longer present. Hence, civil contempts against non-parties are immediately appealable because the appeal does not interfere with the orderly progress of the main case. See United States v. Fried, 386 F.2d 691, 694 (2d Cir. 1967). Where the main case is effectively terminated, the contempt order may no longer be interlocutory. New York Telephone Co. v. Communications Workers, 445 F.2d 39 (2d Cir. 1971). Finally, where the contempt proceeding is the sole court proceeding involved, as is the case where administrative agencies attempt to enforce orders, the civil contempt is not interlocutory in any sense. Cf. O'Connor v. O'Connell, 253 F.2d 365, 366 (1st Cir. 1958).

that the stockholders' equity as of December 31, 1972, was reported at $7,565,000,000. While $150,000 a day is a substantial sum, in reference to IBM's financial resources and the consequent seriousness of the burden to IBM, the sum represents only 5 per cent of any given day's earnings.[2] In any case, we fail to see how the magnitude of such a sum can turn a civil contempt into a criminal one, any more than the sending of an individual to jail turns a civil contempt into criminal contempt. . . . In neither case does the severity of the penalty change the nature of the contempt. See Gompers v. Bucks Stove & Range Co. It is not as if there were any punitive aspect in this contingent fine. Indeed, this is a classic case of using the court's power to afford "full remedial relief," McComb v. Jacksonville Paper Co., so as to enforce the right of the opposing party—here the right to discover certain documents.

IBM also claims that language in United States v. UMW compels a finding of criminal contempt here. There the Court said that a court imposing a civil, coercive fine "must . . . consider the character and magnitude of the harm threatened by continued contumacy . . . ." Several independent reasons militate against our concluding that the district court's failure explicitly to weigh this consideration turns what would otherwise be civil contempt into a criminal contempt. First, it must be noted that the Government in the July 16, 1973, hearing attempted to offer evidence of the harm to it by continued refusal by IBM to comply with the court's order. IBM objected to the introduction of that evidence, and the objection was sustained. Thus, even if IBM had a right to consideration by the court of the harm to the Government, it waived that right by objecting to the evidence of it.[3] Second, there is no reason to believe that a contempt order which is styled civil by the judge imposing it, which has a clearly civil purpose and which was imposed only after consideration of questions relevant only to civil contempt, would become criminal by failure to find explicitly with reference to one of the civil considerations. In other words, were we to read the language in the *UMW* case to require an explicit finding as to harm in all coercive, civil contempts, we still would not treat a failure to make such a finding as converting the civil contempt to a criminal contempt, which is essentially what IBM would have us do here. Third, in any case, we do not so read the language in the *UMW* case. The so-called requirement—that a court consider the harm of continued contempt—first appeared in United States v. UMW, and there it was propounded without explanation or citation. No case is cited to us where a civil, coercive contempt was voided for failure to meet this "requirement,"[4] nor do civil, coercive contempts always involve such findings. . . . We read this language in *UMW* as requiring that the coercive fine be reasonably set in relation to the facts, that it not be arbitrary. Judge Edel-

2. While in absolute terms IBM's fine may seem large, the same percentage of earnings fine against one with a salary of $50,000 would be less than $7 per day.

3. Apparently Judge Edelstein's exclusion of the Government's evidence arose from a confusion between the question of harm to the Government in determining the appropriate amount of the coercive fine and the question of actual damages suffered by the Government as a result of the delay for which a compensatory fine might be granted, the latter of which Judge Edelstein had postponed to a later hearing. Civil contempts may also include a compensatory fine based on the complainant's actual loss. See United States v. UMW.

4. The cases cited by IBM supporting the need for an inquiry into harm all relate to compensatory fines, not coercive fines. . . .

stein's memorandum is evidence that his decision was reasoned and that he gave consideration to the various factors which led to this particular fine—the ability of IBM to meet these payments without undue hardship and the imposition of a fine stiff enough to bring about expeditious compliance. Indeed, unlike the violation of a labor injunction, it is impossible to determine what harm is being suffered here by failure to provide this material for discovery. It may be worthless, or, more likely in view of the Government's offer of proof, it may be relevant and worthwhile, but to expect a finding of the "character and magnitude of the harm" involved in withholding essentially unknown documents would be to expect miracles of the court—indeed, would involve a prejudgment of the case on the merits. Fourth, and finally, the court's failure to make such a finding at worst would only go the amount of the coercive fine, not to the merits of the civil contempt itself. In light of IBM's often stated intention that it will comply with a definitive ruling on the Pretrial Order, rather than stand in contempt, no matter how nominal the fine, there would be little point in delaying the process by remanding for reconsideration of the amount of the fine.

Appealability of a Civil Contempt Order

IBM argues next that even if the contempt here were civil in nature, it would be appealable under a decision of this court, New York Telephone Co. v. Communications Workers, 445 F.2d 39 (2d Cir. 1971) . . . . In *New York Telephone Co.*, however, the court specifically noted that, even though the union was adjudged in civil contempt, the main action in which the order had been issued had effectively been terminated, so that the civil contempt adjudication being appealed from was no longer interlocutory. The court said: " . . . we doubt that anything further remains of the main action unless the district court grants leave to replead. Accordingly, our intervention by way of appeal runs no risk of disrupting the orderly course of proceedings below." Fox v. Capital Co. and Doyle v. London Guarantee Co. both involved orders to produce books and records in civil proceedings and resulted in civil contempts. These were held to be interlocutory only and not appealable. . . .

Reisman v. Kaplan, [375 U.S. 440 (1964)] is simply not applicable to this case. There the claim was that the IRS's summons machinery should be enjoined as to plaintiff because the summons sought material which incriminated him and also unlawfully appropriated the attorney's work product. The Supreme Court denied the injunction, because there was already adequate judicial review of the IRS's summons in a contempt proceeding, which was the only means to enforce the summons. Indeed, *Reisman* is contrary to IBM's case, because it stands for the adequacy of the judicial review in a contempt proceeding itself. In passing, the Court noted that a finding of civil or criminal contempt enforcing the summons would be appealable. This is so, and not surprisingly, because it would not be interlocutory. It would be the final order of the only proceeding before the court, which is certainly not the case here.[6]

6. Hickman v. Taylor, 329 U.S. 495 (1947), also relied upon by IBM, did, to be sure, relate to the disobedience of an attorney in connection with documents prepared by him in anticipation of litigation. But as a reading of that case below discloses, there was an adjudication there of criminal, not civil, contempt. See 153

The rule of Fox v. Capital Co. and Doyle v. London Guarantee Co. is not affected by the authorities cited to us and this is as it should be, because discovery orders at the pretrial stages of litigation are especially inappropriate for interlocutory appeals, as this court has recognized. . . . IBM makes a very emotional and rather heartwarming appeal relating to the sanctity of the attorney-client privilege and of the attorney's work-product and how—absent appealability in a civil contempt proceeding—they would be subject to invasion in the district court.[7] This emotional appeal, however, must be recognized for what it is—an attempt to provide a right of appeal of all discovery orders, for the same legal arguments IBM makes here with respect to its perhaps unique factual situation apply equally to the run-of-the-mill objections to discovery orders. And, indeed, attorney-client privilege and work-product are among the more common grounds of objection. . . . In short, the conclusion is and has been that, barring certain extraordinary circumstances, the possibility of abuse and injustice would actually be increased by opening wide the gates of review to discovery orders, than by leaving the determination to the wise discretion of experienced trial judges.

It is not as if we leave IBM without any possible remedy. As noted above, it has an appeal and two petitions before the Supreme Court at this time, and, finally, it may comply with the order and later appeal any final judgment to have its documents returned, or it may pay the fine and after final judgment or settlement appeal for the return of its money.

The Government's Change of Position

IBM also suggests an argument that because the Government has at various times before this court or in the Supreme Court specifically stated that the only way to obtain review of Pretrial Order No. 5 before the end of the case was for IBM or its representative to risk contempt, and thereby demonstrate its good faith and a solid basis of objections, the Government should be foreclosed from asserting nonappealability here. While we do not approve of the Government's attempt to mislead IBM, if that is what it was, appellate jurisdiction cannot be conferred on a court of appeals by consent. . . .

Procedure Below

Finally, IBM argues that manifest error and deprivation of due process in the proceedings below require us to direct the court below to vacate the contempt order under this court's All Writs Act power. This error, it is claimed, included a refusal to hold a hearing requested and required under Local Civil Rule 14 regarding the "alleged misconduct" involved, as well as the omission to hold the hearing required by Rule 42(b). The argument is that we have

F.2d 212, 214 (3d Cir.). The issue of appealability was not even discussed in the Supreme Court opinion affirming the judgment of the court of appeals. 329 U.S. 495.

7. The hardship involved is not a new one, nor has it been overlooked by courts.

"It may be true, as said in argument, that . . . if the order cannot be reviewed until after final decree it may come too late to be of any benefit to the party aggrieved. But the power to punish for contempt is inherent in the authority of courts, and is necessary to the administration of justice and part of the inconvenience to which a citizen is subject in a community governed by law regulated by orderly judicial procedure."

Doyle v. London Guarantee Co., 204 U.S. 599, 607 (1907).

jurisdiction under the All Writs Act, 28 U.S.C. § 1651, to correct these abuses, it being urged that a pre-enforcement challenge will speed the action as in Abbott Laboratories v. Gardner, 387 U.S. 136 (1967). These claims border on the frivolous. IBM received ample notice of the claim against it. It was given a full opportunity to present evidence, which it declined. In any case, Local Rule 14(b) provides that only "If the alleged contemnor *puts in issue his alleged misconduct* . . . he shall upon demand therefor, be entitled to have oral evidence taken thereon . . . ." (emphasis added). Here IBM admitted all of the facts necessary for the determination of contempt, namely, that it had failed to produce the documents required by Pretrial Order No. 5, and that it was not beyond its power to produce them. The record is replete with references to IBM's willingness to produce the documents if there were a final determination that it should produce them. The trial court, in separating the issue of a coercive fine from the Government's claim of damages, and refusing to hear the latter or to take evidence thereon or to conduct discovery in connection therewith, did not harm IBM in any manner, shape or form. At no point has IBM denied its failure to comply with the pretrial order, even though it has claimed that legally the court should not impose a sanction against it. But even if we are wrong, there is no jurisdiction for us to issue an all-purpose writ under International Business Machines Corp. v. United States in its construction of the Expediting Act. And, of course, in no event was the judge required to hold the hearing required in the case of criminal contempt by Fed.R.Crim.P. 42(b).

Intervention by Cravath

We agree with the Government that Cravath's attempted intervention in the contempt proceeding is not properly before this court. The application for intervention was never determined by the court below, because the application was not filed until the morning of the hearing on July 16, 1973. The intervention motion attempted to substitute the Cravath firm for IBM apparently on the ground that it was Cravath's decision rather than IBM's which led to the noncompliance with Pretrial Order No. 5. We feel, however, as was repeatedly stated, that the true purpose was to permit the lawyers to be adjudged in token contempt to provide an appellate vehicle and thereby escape the thrust of International Business Machines Corp. v. United States . . . .

We dismiss the appeal and deny the petition for mandamus.

TIMBERS, Circuit Judge (dissenting):

IBM has been ordered to pay to the United States a continuing fine in excess of $1,000,000 per week for alleged contempt.

Its alleged contempt is for having respectfully declined to produce for the government's inspection some 1200 documents which concededly are attorney-client communications. IBM's claim of privilege was rejected out of hand by the district court—without an opinion, without findings of fact, without any examination whatsoever of the documents in question. IBM's claim of privilege with respect to those documents has never been judicially reviewed, despite its repeated assurances of willingness to comply with an appellate determination of its claim of privilege. Indeed, the contempt adjudication below was sought by IBM itself for the express purpose of obtaining precisely that judicial review of its claim of privilege which the government on at least four occasions had advised the Supreme Court and our Court was the only way that IBM in good faith could obtain such review before the end of the case.[1]

The narrow question presently before us is whether the district court's contempt adjudication was civil or criminal. All agree that if it was criminal, the contempt adjudication is appealable to our Court now, since it is a final judgment in a proceeding separate from the antitrust action. The majority, by adopting its own reading of United States v. UMW, would ignore the Supreme Court's requirement that a district court in imposing a civil, coercive fine "must . . . consider the character and magnitude of the harm threatened by continued contumacy . . . ." In the instant case, the district court's contempt order was not based upon any such consideration whatsoever. The majority so concedes. But the majority also blinks at the district court's omission of this indispensable requirement for a civil contempt adjudication on the ground, among others, as the majority puts it, that the Supreme Court's "so-called requirement—that a court consider the harm of continued contempt—first appeared in United States v. UMW, and there it was propounded without explanation or citation." I think this is an exceedingly slender reed upon which to deny appellate review of a contempt order which imposes a continuing fine of a million dollars per week.

In light of the undisputed underlying facts which led to the district court order which is the basis for the contempt adjudication below, I would hold the contempt order to be criminal in nature and as such reviewable now by our Court. Since IBM has never waived its attorney-client privilege with respect to the documents in question, I would vacate the production order and remand the case to the district court with instructions to rule on the yet-to-be-ruled-on claim of privilege. . . .

After a hearing and oral arguments on May 12, 1972 and September 26, 1972—but without any findings of fact, without any written opinion and without any examination of the documents in question—Chief Judge Edelstein on September 26, 1972 in the Southern District action entered Pretrial Order No. 5 (hereinafter "the production order"). This production order, which has provided the basis for all subsequent proceedings, directed that:

"IBM immediately deliver to plaintiff, in the form provided to Control Data Corporation, a copy of each document withheld and excised by it from the said microfilm, all such documents purportedly being identified and described by Charles M. Waygood, attorney for defendant, in a letter addressed to plaintiff's counsel, dated April 4, 1972, a copy of said letter being attached to and made a part of this order."

It is for violation of this production order that IBM has been held in contempt.

1. See, e.g., the government's Motion To Dismiss Or Affirm, filed in the Supreme Court in June 1973 in IBM v. United States, No. 72–1173:

"If IBM is unwilling to await final judgment, it may refuse to comply with Pretrial Order No. 5 and risk sanctions under Rule 37(b)(2), Fed.R.Civ.P., including contempt. In the event of such a sanction against it, or its representative, IBM may be able to obtain judicial review before final judgment."

Despite repeated efforts, IBM has not been able to obtain judicial review of this production order.[5] The closest it has come to obtaining such review was by the original panel of this Court in IBM v. United States, which held that IBM had not waived its attorney-client privilege and directed that a new discovery order be entered providing for a judicial determination of the claim of privilege with respect to the documents withheld.[6]

Hence, in the present posture of this case, the underlying issues of whether the 1200 documents in question are privileged and whether IBM has knowingly and voluntarily waived its privilege as to them have not been judicially determined. There has been no determination whether the district court abused its discretion in compelling production of privileged documents which were expressly protected by the discovery order of Judge Neville. See IBM v. United States. Moreover, not even the majority denies that the practical effect of the production order of September 26, 1972 is to deprive IBM of the right to assert its attorney-client privilege or voluntarily to waive it. Bluntly, IBM is being coerced into either sacrificing its attorney-client privilege—a privilege it has zealously guarded—or being held in contempt and

5. IBM appealed to this Court from the production order pursuant to 28 U.S.C. § 1291 (1970). Concurrently it filed a petition for a writ of mandamus in this Court pursuant to 28 U.S.C. § 1651 (1970). Initially, a divided panel of this Court held that it had jurisdiction over both the appeal and the petition, and ordered that the production order be vacated. IBM v. United States, 471 F.2d 507.

On petition by the United States, this Court granted a rehearing en banc and reversed the panel decision. In a 4–2 decision, we held that the Expediting Act, 15 U.S.C. § 29 (1970), requires that appellate review of the production order be had, if at all, in the Supreme Court. Accordingly, we dismissed both the appeal and the petition for writ of mandamus. IBM v. United States, 480 F.2d 293. IBM on June 11, 1973 filed a petition for certiorari seeking review of our en banc decision. 41 U.S.L.W. 3658 (U.S. June 19, 1973) (No. 72–1662).

While the above proceedings were pending in this Court, IBM on November 24, 1972 filed a protective notice of appeal to the Supreme Court from the district court's production order of September 26, 1972. That appeal was docketed in the Supreme Court on February 24, 1973. 41 U.S.L.W. 3477 (U.S. March 6, 1973) (No. 72–1173).

On June 11, 1973, together with its petition for certiorari, IBM also filed in the Supreme Court a petition for mandamus to review the production order. 41 U.S.L.W. 3658 (U.S. June 19, 1973) (No. 72–1661).

On May 21, 1973, IBM moved in the district court for a further stay of the production order. The district court granted the stay until June 4.

On June 1, an application for a continuation of the stay was made to Mr. Justice Marshall who, after hearing argument on June 4, granted a temporary stay subject to further order of the full Court. On June 13, the Supreme Court entered an order denying a stay of the production order and the mandate of this Court.

On petition by the government filed June 25, 1973, the district court on August 1 entered the order presently before us holding IBM in contempt and directing it to pay a continuing fine of $150,000 per day. The district court refused to stay its contempt order and fine even for a single day.

On August 2, upon application by counsel for IBM and by counsel for Cravath, Swaine & Moore, we stayed the district court's contempt order and production order until the argument of the instant appeals. We also expedited the appeals and heard them on August 8. At the conclusion of the arguments on August 8, we continued the stays until determination of the instant appeals.

6. Although this 2–1 panel decision later was vacated by a 4–2 en banc decision of our Court, IBM v. United States, the en banc decision was limited to the holding that "we have no jurisdiction to review the discovery order below either by appeal or by mandamus." The en banc Court did not purport to rule on the validity of the production order, including the refusal of the district court to make a judicial determination of the claim of privilege.

required to pay a fine which has no relation either to the character of its alleged contumacious conduct or to the damage allegedly caused by its refusal to turn over the documents.

It is difficult to conceive of a more glaring instance of a wrong for which the law should provide a remedy—unless that first lesson that some of us learned under the New Haven elms is to be totally discarded.

CRIMINAL CONTEMPT ADJUDICATION BELOW

In my view, the contempt adjudication below was criminal in nature and as such is reviewable now by this Court.

True, the district court, in what strikes me as a transparent attempt to avoid appellate review, has larded its contempt order with all the civil contempt boilerplate—including a coercive recital and a purge provision. Styling the order as civil does not make it such.

Viewed realistically, the clear purpose and effect of the order is criminal in nature. Gompers v. Bucks Stove & Range Co. . . . The purpose of the order is punitive—to vindicate the authority of the court. By completely excluding the issue of damages in straining to frame a civil remedy, the district court first ignored the law of this Circuit, United States v. Aberbach, 165 F.2d 713, 715 (2 Cir. 1948) (Chase, J.), that a fine for civil contempt "which bears some reasonable relation to the amount of this damage [to the government] might lawfully be imposed." The court further ignored the requirement of United States v. UMW, that in assessing a civil fine in order to assure compliance the court "must . . . consider the character and magnitude of the harm threatened by continued contumacy, and the probable effectiveness of any suggested sanction in bringing about the result desired."

Moreover, the record is crystal clear that the district court's failure to comply with either of these indispensable requirements for a civil contempt adjudication was deliberate and not inadvertent. In its order of July 3, 1973 scheduling a hearing for July 16 "limited to the issues of the fine and damages to be assessed against [IBM] for its alleged contempt," the court excluded any consideration of the "character and magnitude" of the threatened harm and the "effectiveness" of any suggested sanction. Moreover, by its order of July 10, the court excluded from the July 16 hearing any consideration of the "question of damages" caused by IBM's alleged contumacious conduct. Thus, the only evidence before the court was IBM's balance sheet.

The continuing fine imposed of more than a million dollars per week can be ascribed to nothing other than the court's arbitrary assessment of IBM's will power. The fine is wholly unrelated to any actual harm sustained by the government, to the character and magnitude of any harm threatened by continued contumacy, or to the probable effectiveness of any lesser sanction coupled with the option of a subsequent increase in the fine if compliance were not forthcoming.

To avoid what to me is the inescapable conclusion that IBM has been held in criminal contempt, the majority states that the district court "did not leave in doubt the purpose which the contempt citation here was to serve." They say that "the order was both coercive and contingent, indicating a civil rather than criminal contempt." With deference, the majority ignores both the district court's decision of July 10, 1973 emphasizing "the desire of the court to insure that its [production order] be promptly obeyed," and the fact that the purpose to be accomplished by the order was not to remedy any harm sustained by the government.[7] The record before us is totally barren of any proof or any finding of harm. The remedy of a million dollar per week fine clearly demonstrates that its chief purpose was to vindicate the court's authority and to punish IBM if it failed to bow to the court's power.

The majority's suggestion that the district court's failure to "consider the character and magnitude of the harm threatened by continued contumacy," United States v. UMW, is of no importance, strikes me as a side-stepping of what I had thought, prior to today's majority opinion, to be a decision of the Supreme Court binding upon our Court. The majority says that the district court's refusal to weigh this consideration does not transform "what would otherwise be civil contempt into a criminal contempt." This ignores the stated purpose of the district court in holding IBM in contempt, and of the government in seeking to have it held in contempt. With due respect, I must say that the majority's strained reading of *UMW* as requiring merely "that the coercive fine be reasonably set in relation to the facts, that it not be arbitrary," utterly emasculates that landmark decision of the late Chief Justice Vinson. How can a contempt fine be reasonably or non-arbitrarily set if the "facts"—i.e. the harm caused by the contumacious conduct, as well as the character and magnitude of that conduct—are not even explored? It would have been no more impossible to determine the harm sustained in the instant case than it was to determine the harm caused by the nationwide coal miners' strike in *UMW*.[8] Furthermore the district court's failure to consider this issue affects not merely the *amount* of the fine, as the majority suggests; it goes directly to the *nature of the contempt adjudication.* United States v. UMW.

Assuming *arguendo* that part of the district court's contempt order could be construed as civil in nature, the fact that *any part* of it was criminal in nature makes the entire order immediately appealable. Union Tool Co. v. Wilson, 259 U.S. 107, 110 (1922); In re Merchants' Stock and Grain Co.,

7. The majority further ignores the purpose for which the government argued that the contempt order should issue. At the July 16, 1973 hearing, government counsel argued that IBM should be held in contempt because of the necessity "to have a precedent in this Court that IBM will obey the Court's orders and will obey them promptly and will obey them as they are directed to obey them and not on the basis of whether they want to or don't want to." The government's purpose in seeking contempt clearly was to punish past conduct and to deter future conduct. This is a criminal sanction. . . .

8. In United States v. UMW, 70 F.Supp. 42 (D.D.C.1946), modified and affirmed, 330 U.S. 258 (1947), although the severity of the harm caused by a nationwide coal miners' strike would appear to have been obvious, the government produced eight witnesses and substantial documentary evidence to justify the magnitude of the contempt adjudication and fine. The district court made findings of fact concerning the size of the existing stockpile of coal, the amount by which the rate of production decreased due to UMW's contempt, and the normal rate of consumption. In addition, the court received evidence and made detailed findings concerning the characteristics of the economy and of particular sectors thereof to establish exactly how the stoppage of coal production would cause damage and to what extent. Finally, the court made quantitative estimates as to the actual decline in national income and tax revenues which would result.

This is a far cry from the total absence in the instant case of any evidence or finding in the district court of "the character and magnitude of the harm threatened by continued contumacy." United States v. UMW, supra, 330 U.S. at 304.

223 U.S. 639, 642 (1912); In re Christensen Engineering Co., 194 U.S. 458, 461 (1904). The mere fact that the district court labeled the order as civil and adopted formal civil contempt boilerplate does not foreclose this Court from determining that at least part of the order was criminal in nature. The contempt adjudication below, even accepting *arguendo* the majority's criteria, surely was partially criminal because it cannot be gainsaid that it was not "wholly remedial" but rather was intended, at least in part, "as a deterrent to offenses against the public." McCrone v. United States. The court having excluded evidence relating to whether the contumacy was injurious to the government, it is simply impossible to say that the order was wholly civil. Since the court did not consider the "character and magnitude of the harm threatened," its order surely cannot be said to be "wholly remedial." And the court's statement in its Memorandum of Decision of July 10 that it wanted "to insure that its [production order] be promptly obeyed," indicates at the very least a purpose to deter offenses committed against the court and the public.

In short, for this Court to deny appellate review of the district court's crushing million dollar per week fine imposed on IBM, and to do so in reliance upon the district court's specious characterization of the contempt order as civil in nature, represents in my view a grave perversion of long established principles of civil contempt. Although carefully labeled to forestall appellate review, the contempt order in every real sense was punitive and was intended to vindicate the authority of the court. Gompers v. Bucks Stove & Range Co. I would hold the contempt order to be criminal and immediately appealable to our Court.

---

1) Courts use contempt in several ways: discovery sanctions, injunction violations, and in-court cut-ups, for example. Do these separate categories call for separate treatment? Or should all contempt be governed by a unified contempt doctrine?

2) The difference between civil and criminal contempt is most contested in determining trial court procedure, *Gompers,* and in deciding whether to allow an appeal, *IBM.* A major contempt issue is by how much to dilute the trial judge's power; appealability is worth examining both for its own sake and to explore that broad issue. Professor André concludes that the criminal-civil distinction is irrational, unresponsive to appealability policies, and insensitive to hardship created by delayed review. He argues that courts should allow contemnors to appeal coercive sanctions because of unnecessary hardship. André, The Final Judgment Rule and Party Appeals of Civil Contempt Orders: Time for a Change, 55 N.Y.U.L.Rev. 1041 (1980).

3) Is denying interlocutory appeals in coercive contempt a civil contempt equivalent of the collateral bar rule? It enforces respect for the trial judge and orderly process at the cost of perpetuating some injustice. Does delaying contemnors' appeals protect plaintiffs' rights to enjoy promptly what the substantive law says they should enjoy in fact? Is criminal contempt distinguishable because of the severe collateral consequences and the absence of an importunate private litigant?

4) Does Judge Timbers confuse compensatory and coercive contempt? Shouldn't coercive contempt always depend on the way the judge assesses contemnor's "will power"? If anything, wasn't $150,000 per day far too low to coerce IBM? A judge may imprison a person to coerce. What amount of coercive exaction would be the equivalent to prison for IBM? If after the Supreme Court's opinion in *Mine Workers,* the UMW had violated the injunction and the court had moved to collect the $2,800,000, could the union have appealed? Do fines partake of both criminal and civil contempt? Is the court's dilemma like that of the hypothetical railroad ticket agent trying to decide whether a centaur should ride with people in the passenger car or with livestock in a separate car?

Should criminal-civil classification for one purpose be classification for all purposes? Contempt in *IBM* is civil to prevent the delay and disruption of interlocutory appeals. If someone were civilly imprisoned to coerce would it be correct to classify the contempt as civil coercive and deny contemnor an appointed attorney? Should courts classify in light of purpose and policy aside from the variety of contempt?

5) The United States dismissed the underlying action in January, 1982. So while Cravath and IBM may have lost this skirmish, they won the war. The lack of amity and concord between the IBM team and Judge Edelstein reemerged in IBM's efforts to stop the judge from presiding over the hearings on whether the dismissal was consistent with the Tunney Act. United States v. IBM, 539 F.Supp. 473 (E.D.N.Y.1982). The court of appeals, however, held that the Tunney Act applied only to settlements, not dismissals; and it told Judge Edelstein to proceed no further. In re IBM, 687 F.2d 591 (2d Cir. 1982).

II. Equity Acts in Personam

W.W. Cook, THE POWERS OF COURTS OF EQUITY

15 Colum.L.Rev. 37, 106 (1915).

. . . When it is said that the law acts *in rem* while equity acts only *in personam,* it seems that what is in the mind of the person making the statement is the difference between the methods used by the law courts and by the courts of equity in enforcing their judgments and decrees respectively.

If a judgment *in personam* is entered at law for damages for a tort or breach of contract, the most usual method of enforcing the judgment, if it be not paid, is to issue execution against the defendant's property, and enough is sold to satisfy the plaintiff's claim. By virtue of such a proceeding the title to the property thus sold passes to the execution purchaser, and the defendant is deprived of his interest in it. Consistently with our use of the phrase in classifying actions, we may call this "procedure *in rem.*" The action and judgment however, are *in personam,* since the object of the action was, not to get at any specific *res* which defendant owned, but merely to enforce a personal liability, and so to obtain a personal judgment. Having pointed out this method of enforcing common law judgments, our writers now proceed to explain action *in personam* by discussing a bill for specific performance brought by vendee against vendor, in the case of a contract for sale of land. They point out that the chancellor, having ordered the defendant to convey to the plaintiff the title to the land in question, proceeds to punish him for contempt if he does not obey. Without a statute the chancellor cannot act *in rem* on the title so as to deprive defendant of it and vest it in the plaintiff. All this, of course, is elementary learning. Here, it is said, is the fundamental difference between law and equity. In the making of this comparison, however, there is involved a confusion of thought. In speaking of the court of equity, reference is had both to the character of the decree and also to the method of enforcing it. The decree is *in personam,* and the method of enforcing it is also *in personam.* In the case of the judgment at law, the reference is entirely to the method of enforcing it, but obviously in the case put the judgment is purely *in personam.* Legal judgment and equitable decree are alike *in personam,* in the sense that neither has the direct effect, independently of what is done under it, of depriving defendant of an interest in a piece of property. There is a difference in form, to be sure, in that the law court adjudges that plaintiff recover a certain sum to which it regards him to be entitled, while the chancellor orders defendant to do his duty; and this emphasis on duty rather than right has doubtless had its influence upon the character of equitable doctrines. The real difference, however, if there be any, lies in the character of the means used to enforce the judgment and decree respectively. The law court, say these writers, in enforcing its judgment, proceeds or acts *in rem,* while the chancellor in enforcing his decree proceeds only *in personam.*

. . . That there is a difference between acting *in rem* and acting *in personam,* where the judgment or decree is *in personam,* is clear. To levy on a man's property, sell it, pass title to it to a purchaser, and pay the proceeds to the plaintiff who holds the judgment *in personam,* is very obviously to do a fundamentally different thing from ordering the defendant to do an act and putting him in jail for contempt if he does not obey; and the phrases *in rem* and *in personam* probably express this as well as any others. . . . [T]he phrase *in personam* now acquires a shade of meaning somewhat different from any we have thus far given it. It now means merely that, as a punishment for not doing something and for the purpose of persuading him to do it, the court deals directly with the physical person of the defendant, as distinguished from dealing with his property. . . .

Let us begin by comparing what happens in the case of a bill in equity, the object of which is to obtain a decree solely for the payment of a sum of money, with the corresponding proceedings in an action in a court of law, the object of which is to obtain a money judgment. For example, in an ordinary bilateral contract for the purchase and sale of real estate, the vendor asks specific performance. Under the English and many American authorities he is entitled to this, and this is here assumed. The decree being duly entered, what happens? How does it differ from what happens under a judgment at law where the unpaid vendor (who has conveyed the property) obtains judgment for the purchase price? In both cases the primary right is *in personam;* the actions, the judgment and the decree are all *in personam.* Not until we reach the procedure to enforce judgment and decree respectively do we find any difference. [Professor Cook then describes the historical methods of enforcement.]

The judgment at law reads that plaintiff recover so much money; the decree in equity, that defendant is ordered to pay the sum. The traditional chancery procedure of course was, in the first instance, to commit the defendant to jail for contempt. Before discussing this let us follow the common law procedure on the judgment. Execution is issued either against the person or property of the defendant. In speaking of execution against the person, Blackstone says: "The intent of it [the writ of *capias ad satisfaciendum*] is to imprison the body of the debtor till satisfaction be made for the debts, costs and damages. . . . The writ is directed to the sheriff, commanding him to take the body of the defendant and have him at Westminster on a day therein named, to make the plaintiff satisfaction for his demands, and if he does not then make satisfaction, *he must remain in custody till he does.* . . . When a man is once taken in execution upon this writ, no other process can be sued out against his land or goods." This form of execution might be had upon almost every species of complaint, though in the early days this was not true. If the plaintiff gave the defendant, when in execution, permission to go at large, the judgment was discharged, irrespective of the intention of the plaintiff. This seems to have been a consequence of the rule which forbade the suing out of other process after taking defendant on a *capias.* The mere imprisonment itself, however long, (unless for life), apparently never had the effect at common law of discharging the judgment. If the judgment creditor chose, instead of taking defendant on a *capias* he could sue out a writ of *fieri facias* against the defendant's goods and chattels; or a writ of *levari facias* against his goods and the profits of his lands; or a writ of *elegit* against his goods and the possession of his lands. It is to the proceedings upon the writ of *fi. fa.* that attention is usually directed by writers who are comparing law and equity. Here of course the law proceeds *in rem,* the sheriff selling the goods and chattels (including chattels real) until he has raised enough to satisfy the judgment. Under the writ of *levari facias* in addition to seizing and selling the goods, the sheriff could receive the rents and profits of defendant's lands and apply them on the judgment. Under the writ of *elegit* the goods and chattels of the defendant were not sold, but appraised and delivered to the plaintiff at the appraised price, in whole or part satisfaction of his debt. If the goods were insufficient, then a moiety of lands which defendant had at the time of the judgment was also delivered to the plaintiff, to hold till out of the rents and profits thereof the balance of the debt was satisfied or defendant's interest expired.

Let us now return to the chancery proceedings. Suppose that, after the defendant had been put in jail for non-payment, he still remained obdurate: What happened? If proper proceedings were taken, a writ of sequestration was issued. The sequestrators under the sequestration could take all the goods and chattels in the possession of the defendant, or which they could come at without suit or action. The writ of sequestration also authorized the sequestrators to enter upon all "messuages, lands, tenements and real estates" of defendant, and to "collect, take and get into their hands the rents and profits thereof." Where the sequestration was for non-performance of a decree (for the payment of money) a sale of goods and chattels thus acquired could be ordered and the proceeds were applicable to the payment of the plaintiff's demand. This was done only on application to the court by the party in whose favor the decree was entered. Under this proceeding "it seems that the court will direct the sale not only of perishable commodities, but also of goods, such as rents paid in kind, or the natural produce of a farm, or household goods and furniture. The court will not sell terms of years, or leasehold estates, or any subject which passes by title and not by delivery, although it will direct the profits to be applied; because sequestrators can give no warranty for title, the property not being vested in them." Leases of land also were granted by the sequestrators under authority of the court and the rent applied to the plaintiff's demand. We are now in a position to see to what extent these methods of procedure really differ. In practical effect there is some but only a little difference. In both cases the defendant may be imprisoned until he pays the sum due. Is the object of imprisonment in both tribunals to compel the defendant to pay the amount of the plaintiff's claim? The common law court did not in form order the defendant to pay, and it was Professor Langdell's idea that the court was not trying to make him do so. He says:

> "A court of common law never lays a command upon a litigant, nor seeks to secure obedience from him. . . . Even when the defendant is subject to arrest, his arrest and imprisonment are not regarded by the law as a means of compelling him to pay the judgment; but his body is taken (as his property is) in satisfaction of the judgment."

It seems difficult to reconcile this view with what common law writers like Blackstone say, and also with what the court did. Defendant could be kept in jail until he paid. This rule is hard to understand if imprisonment were really regarded as satisfying the judgment, for one would expect (as under some modern statutes) an imprisonment for a definite time, depending perhaps on the amount of plaintiff's claim. The fact that the judgment was discharged if the plaintiff gave the defendant permission to go at large after arresting him on a *capias* seems to be a necessary result of the other rule that the common law would not permit plaintiff to adopt any other method of execution if he chose to arrest the defendant on a *capias.* However, assuming for the moment that Professor Langdell's theory is correct, the fact remains that the common law court put the same personal pressure on the defendant that the chancellor did. In whatever sense we use *in rem* as applied to procedure to enforce judgments and decrees, the common law court when it imprisoned the defendant was not acting *in rem.* If acting *in personam* means merely dealing with a defendant's physical person by imprisoning him, the law does act *in personam.* If, however, we say that a court is not acting *in personam* unless the object of the imprisonment is to induce the defendant to pay, the law court, if we accept Mr. Langdell's views as to the object of the imprisonment, is not acting *in personam,* but equity is. That, however, the object of the imprisonment of the defendant at law and equity is the same, *viz.,* to induce him to pay the plaintiff's claim, seems very clear, both from what is said about it in the books and also from certain rules which are identically the same in both courts. [Professor Cook then quoted Blackstone, describing a common law procedure, and Daniell, describing equity procedure—to show the similarity.]

. . . The common law, as we have seen, restricted the plaintiff to this procedure *in personam* if he chose it, but did not require him to use it, and did not permit it in all actions. Equity, on the other hand, doubtless because its decree was in the form of an order to the defendant to do his duty, required plaintiff to proceed *in personam* in the first instance, and refused to allow him to get at the defendant's property until it appeared that procedure against the person of the defendant had been unsuccessful in bringing him to terms. When the procedure *in personam* had failed, equity permitted in addition the use of procedure against the property of the defendant. If the plaintiff at common law used execution against property, he could get at defendant's goods and chattels (including chattels real) and the rents and profits of his land, and also get possession of a moiety of the land in order to get the rents and profits of the same. The title to goods and chattels passed either to the execution purchaser if they were sold, or to the plaintiff if they went to him under an *elegit;* and the same was true of the rents and profits. Interests in land (other than chattels real) could not be got at, i.e., there was no procedure *in rem* in the common law court (the judgment being *in personam*) to transfer title to land. Under the sequestration in equity, the result was very much the same. Goods and chattels and rents and profits of land could be got at, but not interests in land.[21] Can we say that equity was still acting *merely in personam* while the law court was acting *in rem?* In speaking of writs of sequestration, Professor Langdell maintained that "after all these are scarcely exceptions to the rule that the chancellor has no jurisdiction *in rem.* . . . The power of creating and extinguishing titles the chancellor never had nor claimed to have, except when it was given to him by statute." [22] Now it must be noted that Daniell assumes that the purchaser under the sale by the sequestrators got title, and it seems that the chancellor did make just this assumption. No decision of a common law court has been found in any modern time—that is, after sequestration became the regularly accepted order of things,—settling the question. In view of all the evidence, the assertion that title to chattels did not pass under the sequestration sale seems to be not proved. It seems to be based upon a very wide generalization derived from the well-known fact that the chancellor never claimed to have (in the absence of a statute) the power to pass complete title to interests in real estate. When we recall that the common law court did not possess this power in most actions, this does not seem to warrant so sweeping a generalization.

. . .

In view of all the evidence is it not probable that the correct statement is: Originally the chancellor could not act *in rem* in the sense of passing the legal title to property of any kind; but, in the development of our judicial system, he asserted successfully the power to do this in the case of chattels, by means of a sale under a writ of sequestration? Even if this be denied, it by no

21. Apparently not even chattels real, though there seems to be no good reason why this limitation was adopted. . . .

22. Langdell, Summary of Equity Pleading (2nd ed.) 35, note 4. Note that the learned writer uses "jurisdiction *in rem*" to mean "power to pass title." Whether procedure *in rem* includes more than this will be discussed later; assuming, for the moment, this restricted use to be correct, it follows that the law court when it imprisons defendant on a *ca. sa.* is not acting *in rem.* If it is not acting *in personam,* (as I think it is), it must be doing some third thing for which we have no name. The learned writer had, in the text to which this note was appended, said: "To some extent the Chancellor has asserted and maintained the right to proceed *in rem.*" He then describes writs of sequestration and assistance, and adds the note quoted from, thus seeming to maintain that in proceeding by sequestration and writ of assistance the chancellor was still acting *in personam.*

means follows that equity acts only *in personam.* If we recall that *in personam* means, in reference to procedure, nothing but bringing pressure to bear upon the defendant's physical person, it is clear that equity has done something which goes far beyond that. It has given the purchaser from the sequestrator: (1) full "equitable title" to the chattels; (2) possession of the chattels; (3) the right to use all the powers of the court of equity to protect the possession and "equitable title." As a consequence of the possession, the purchaser thus becomes, according to the common law, owner as against all the world except the defendant. On the other hand, the plaintiff, having received money, has, and may of course transfer, an indefeasible title to it, and is as well off as the judgment creditor in the legal action.[25]

May we not say, then, that in the fully developed system judgment at law and decree in equity for the recovery of a sum of money were, in spite of differences in their form, enforced in ways which were equally effective practically and between which there was very likely no fundamental difference in legal theory? This is not to say that the differences which did exist were not of importance, for they most certainly were. Procedure *in rem* may be regarded as the normal mode of enforcing a money judgment at law; procedure *in personam* the normal mode, historically, of enforcing a decree in equity for money. But at law procedure *in personam,* (or at least not *in rem*) could be and was used in many cases; and in equity procedure not *in personam* (and which very likely really was *in rem*) could be used whenever the normal procedure *in personam* failed. At any rate, we must say that if the common law did not at times act *in personam* in enforcing money judgments, it is hard to say what *in personam* means; [27] and that if the chancellor did not at times act *in rem* in enforcing decrees for money, he gave so good an imitation of it that it can with difficulty be distinguished from the genuine article.

Today of course it is generally provided by statute or rule of court that on equitable decrees for money, execution shall issue as in similar cases at common law. . . .

With this change has come another: the abolition of imprisonment for debt. Express constitutional provisions of this kind exist in most of our States. All modifications, conditions and restrictions upon imprisonment for debt provided by the laws of any State are by act of Congress applicable to process issuing from federal courts to be executed therein. The effect of these provisions upon equitable decrees for the payment of money thus becomes a question, more especially in States in which execution may issue upon such decrees, but also in those still using sequestration. For example, if a particular provision be held to apply to an action for breach of contract at law, will it also apply to an equitable decree for money based upon the same contract? If the vendor (who has conveyed) in a suit at law for the purchase price cannot have execution against the person, can he (if he has not con-

25. If, as Professor Ames suggested [Lectures on Legal History], the court of law in detinue, when it sends the sheriff after property which is already the plaintiff's, is acting *in rem,* it seems that the court of equity does the same thing under sequestration, even if the purchaser does not get a legal title as against the defendant.

27. In the entire comparison of law with equity, I have ignored entirely the extraordinary writs, such as mandamus, prohibition, habeas corpus, etc., in which, of course, the court of law acted *in personam* in every sense of the word.

veyed) get it by bringing a bill for specific performance? No attempt can be made to answer this question in detail here. It must suffice to point out that it seems to be commonly held that these provisions apply not only to legal but to corresponding equitable actions.[33] To quote from the Pennsylvania court's opinion in the case cited in the last note: "The main object of the statute . . . was to relieve from imprisonment in all cases where no offense appears, except that of omitting to pay money due on a contract. . . . The power to imprison for the purpose of enforcing a decree for the payment of money due on a contract no longer exists." We have thus the interesting result, in States taking this view, that judgment at law and decree in equity for the payment of money, where the action is one falling within the scope of these provisions, are both enforceable only by procedure *in rem.* . . .

D. E. C. Yale, LORD NOTTINGHAM'S 'MANUAL OF CHANCERY PRACTICE' AND 'PROLEGOMENA OF CHANCERY AND EQUITY' (1965)

In his introductory essay Professor Yale makes generally the same point as Walter Wheeler Cook: the primary sense of the maxim that equity acts *in personam* is in the realm of enforcement and that the maxim is a useful starting point but not totally accurate. Professor Yale's interest, however, is largely historical—not simply to show that there are *in rem* elements in the enforcement of injunctions but to explain how these elements came into being. He writes:

". . . The predominating characteristic of Equity procedure and process was thus personal constraint of the defendant: it was the mainspring, indeed, the sole machinery which the Chancellor had originally to command. This was in early times well adapted, and usually adequate, to support the kind of litigation which ordinarily occupied the Court in the fifteenth century, namely petitions for relief against force and fraud and the violent removal of a neighbour's landmark or even the neighbour himself. The failure of the common law to maintain order and to enforce its orders was partly due to the self-imposed restriction to pecuniary compensation, and partly to the curious fact that the Courts of law exercised no direct control over the execution of their decisions, which were often in effect as in form merely declaratory of right. The Chancery as a secretariat of State was always more adequately equipped with officers, and a Serjeant-at-arms was certainly more amenable to judicial control than an undersheriff. The organization was less diffuse and more concentrated than that of the common-law jurisdictions [which often had to rely on the unreliable sheriff in the country].

"Towards the end of the sixteenth century there are signs that the Chancellors were finding the imprisonment of a recalcitrant defendant a not altogether satisfactory way of enforcing obedience to their decrees. Additional pressure is brought to bear upon the defendant through fines and added rigours in the Fleet. . . . Straiter imprisonment than the ordinarily pretty

33. Ex rel. Scott v. The Jailer (Pa. 1855) 1 Grant, 237; Blake v. State (1875) 80 Ill. 11; Herrington v. Cassem (1898) 82 Ill.App. 594; Barclay v. Barclay (1900) 184 Ill. 375; People v. Spier (N.Y.1877) 12 Hun. 70.

lenient conditions in the Fleet was a frequent method in Elizabeth's time and the more severe judges like Ellesmere would put into irons a prisoner who refused to obey an order and inflict fines upon him. But these severities would scarcely help the mesne process . . . , and even by way of prosecuting a decree, if there was enough at stake, they might fail to coerce a strong-willed defendant."

While Cook speaks almost exclusively about writs of sequestration, Professor Yale describes the movement away from the exclusive reliance on the *in personam* process in terms of two writs—the writ of assistance and the writ of sequestration. This is his account of the rise of the writ of assistance:

". . . At the beginning of the seventeenth century, however, a significant practice appears in issuing writs of assistance [which called upon the sheriff to assist]. It had been the earlier practice where the decree directed the defendant to deliver possession of land to award to local commissioners, who were ordinarily justices of the peace together with the sheriff, a commission to enforce the decree and maintain the plaintiff in possession. The writ of assistance first appears as an additional method of attaining this end, e.g. in the event of resistance to the decree, but by the Restoration it was established as an independent process after an injunction to deliver possession. The writ recites default in obeying the Court's order 'in manifest contempt of us and our said court,' and unlike the common-law writ of possession directs the sheriff to maintain the plaintiff in possession.

"There was thus a note sounding *in personam* in the form of the writ: but it was obtainable without first imprisoning the defendant. It was enough to have a writ of execution, attachment, and injunction served; during the eighteenth century it was settled that where the plaintiff had obtained a decree and desired possession he might not imprison the defendant. The earlier forms, therefore, became ineffective except to maintain the cost of litigation and the writ of assistance in course of time ceases to be auxiliary and in appropriate cases becomes the substance of the process. This supersession of earlier, more personal, modes of enforcement carries with it as a matter of implication the increase of real property litigation in the Court and so the necessity to frame rules of law and limit the scope of discretion. Eventually the original attitude of the Court towards process suffered a complete reversal. In 1828 when the change in equity is virtually complete, counsel address the Vice-Chancellor in these terms:

'The principle of the Court is never to interfere with the personal liberty of the subject, where there are other means within its power for obtaining that which it seeks . . . Where the object has been to put a party in possession of property, if the Court can obtain that by its own proceedings, there is no authority for putting the person in prison. The Court cannot proceed in both ways at the same time.'

The process upon this writ offers an instance of the advance of Chancery jurisdiction."

Then Professor Yale gives this account of the writ of sequestration:

"Equally, if not more, striking as an illustration of this trend is the growth of sequestrations. This process designed to impound the defendant's goods and profits derived from land appears towards the end of the sixteenth century. Roger North in his biography of his brother, the Lord Keeper, gives an entertaining account of an early example in the time of Lord Keeper Coventry (1625–40):

" 'when Sir John Reed lay in the Fleet (with £10,000 in an iron cash chest in his chamber) for disobedience of a decree, and would not submit and pay the duty. This being presented to the Lord Keeper as a great contempt and affront upon the Court, he authorised men to go and break up his iron chest and pay the duty and costs and leave the rest to him and discharge his commitment. From thence came sequestrations which are now so established as the run of course after all other process fails, but is in nature of a grand distress, the best process at common law after a summons, such as a subpoena is: what need all that grievance and delay of the intervening process?'

But it is not quite true that, as is suggested in this tale, sequestrations were not heard of till Coventry's time, for they were regulated by Bacon's ordinances and appear to have their roots in the previous century. It is true that sequestrations as a part of mesne process may be rather later . . . .

"The sequestrators were commissioners acting independently of the sheriff, though a writ of assistance might be required to help them to possession. The writ of sequestration was available whether the defendant were already in the Fleet or not, but it cannot be said that the jurisdiction was on a safe basis until it was decided in 1641 [Perryman v. Dinham, 1 Ch.Rep. 152] by the Lord Keeper, with the concurrence of the Judges, that to award the writ against a defendant already committed did not amount to a double process—though by that date such a decision perhaps only ratified an accepted practice. But it was not inevitable that the Judges should have concurred in this determination. During the earlier part of the century the use of the writ had been developed in a significant manner. Lord Nottingham states the position in this way:

'Lord Bacon's rules restrain sequestrations to the thing in demand and exclude all other leases, lands or goods in question not contained in the suits. Bacon, 29. But if the thing in demand be a rent or sum of money charged upon land, there a sequestration of the same lands being in the defendant's hands may be granted. Bacon, 30. By these rules one would think that sequestrations were then in their infancy, for they are very much grown since, and are extended to things not in demand, as to lands, nay, copyhold lands where the suit is for a personal debt, and indeed were so long before: Hil. 37 Eliz., Wheatly v. St. John, a sequestration for money; but chiefly about 13 and 16 Jac.; which it seems my Lord Bacon meant to reform and to reduce it to the thing in demand which is undoubtedly ancient; 43 Eliz., Rumny v. Hall and 2 Mary in the county palatine of Chester.'

"Practice no doubt fluctuated, but it seems that to levy sequestrations on property not the subject matter of the suit was not at all common till after the Restoration when they became a frequent feature in process. Indeed in one special class of case [process against those possessing parliamentary privilege] they became the primary process. Generally, however, the object was to supplement the personal compulsion of the defendant, though in the course of time many of the earlier stages in process became mere formal preliminaries to laying the hand of the plaintiff on the defendant's property which was in many instances his sole object."

Professor Yale also points out that Chancery's movement away from the *in personam* maxim and the writ of sequestration aroused vigorous opposition among the common-law judges—what Lord Nottingham termed "bloody and desperate resolutions." These resolutions are described in one of Nottingham's famous opinions, Coulston v. Gardner (79 Selden Society 869). Professor Yale summarizes Lord Nottingham's evidence of the opposition:

"Elizabethan Courts provide early examples. In Brograve v. Watts it was pleaded in detinue that a sequestrator authorized by the Court of Requests had seized the goods in question; the plea was overruled, the Court declaring 'if a man be sued in a Court of conscience and will not stay, his body is to be imprisoned and no commission ought to be awarded for the taking of his goods.' The same was later said of a similar plea in trover.

"Even more striking is the decision which Heneage Finch roundly calls 'a bloody opinion,' noting that at the same time Bishop Williams was Lord Keeper—perhaps inferring he was indirectly responsible. This opinion was that upon an indictment for murder of a sequestrator he was probably 'no such legal officer that it should be malice implied to kill him.' On so controversial a matter, however, the prisoner seems to have been wise enough to obtain a pardon. And it is not reported that the common-law judges did in fact pronounce a decision on this ground which would in effect have been an incitement to what everyone else would have called murder."

Professor Yale says that after the Restoration the conflict between the jurisdictions was lessened and that sequestrations became an indispensable part of the process of chancery. It was also settled that sequestrations were available even to cover personal duties where the sequestered property was not itself directly involved. But there were limits.

". . . It is sometimes said that the process is not one *in rem* but rather that sequestered property is *in custodia legis.* Both these propositions, however, may be true. The latter phrase merely points the truth that the sequestrators had not by virtue of their commission any power to enter in upon an unwilling defendant. If force were needed a writ of assistance had to go to the sheriff. Nor was the court disposed to extend the effect of the process too far. To do so might injure purchasers. Sequestrations did not pass title. They had, therefore, to give way to innocent titles acquired in the manner approved by Equity. Lord Nottingham's opinion was that

'a sequestration will reach a purchaser who comes in *pendente lite* if he be a purchaser of the thing in demand but not otherwise, else there can be no dealing with any man who hath a suit in Chancery. A purchaser of the thing not in demand whether it be land or goods is also bound by the sequestration if his purchase were after the *teste* of the commission for sequestration or after the date of the order for that commission.' "

In this historical account Professor Yale points out that the common-law judges were eager to emphasize the restrictive or negative aspects of the *in personam* maxim, their challenge to innovations such as the writ of sequestration being based on the charge that the writ was inconsistent with the maxim.

Professor Yale also suggests that this opposition—which ultimately failed—should not obscure the positive effect of the maxim:

". . . [T]he enabling aspect of the maxim that Equity acts *in personam* is usually exemplified by the leading case of Penn v. Lord Baltimore. The principle involved is the well-known one that if the defendant is within the jurisdiction, the Court is ready to search his conscience even concerning matters involving property outside the jurisdiction and to decree the defendant to conduct himself, and even to convey the property, in a manner agreeable to good conscience."

The in rem/in personam distinction forces us to compare enforcement of injunctions with money judgments. The law, ancient lore told us, enforces in rem; equity acts only in personam. The dogma separated the in rem/in personam enforcement distinction from the distinction made in jurisdiction and judgments; thus a common transitory action will be based on in personam jurisdiction over the defendant and lead to an in personam judgment yet be enforced in rem.

A judgment at law still says "defendant owes plaintiff $64,000." See Federal Form 31. In rem enforcement means that the authorities collect the judgment impersonally without involving the defendant. The clerk first issues execution to the sheriff. The sheriff levies on the defendant's nonexempt property, takes the property, sells it to a buyer who takes title, and pays the money to the plaintiff. Garnishment is similar except that the sheriff realizes on a debt that a third person owes the defendant. The docketed judgment also creates a lien on defendant's local real property. Plaintiff enforces this lien as he would foreclose on a mortgage: the authorities sell the property, the buyer takes effective title, and the proceeds are applied to the judgment. In rem enforcement, in short, proceeds without compulsion against the defendant.

The in rem/in personam distinctions often break down. Collecting a money judgment may become in personam. State codes contain procedures called creditors' bills or supplementary procedure for plaintiffs to employ when execution, garnishment, and judgment liens prove ineffective. The court summons the defendant to answer questions. The defendant must appear and answer. If the plaintiff discovers property, defendant must convey it. If the defendant refuses to appear, answer or convey, then the judge issues personal orders to obey in the form of coercive contempt.

Before the wave of humanitarian reform that swept the nation in the 19th century, plaintiffs could use a capias to lock up the defendant in debtors' prison until the judgment was paid. We no longer have generally available debt imprisonment. When available, the plaintiff cannot imprison the defendant for failing to pay money he doesn't have. But defendant may be imprisoned for contempt if he fails to appear, answer, or convey. This contempt is coercive: contemnor "has the jail house keys in his pocket" and may cooperate to achieve release. If coercive contempt fails, the judge may order a decretal transfer. Federal Rule 70 and state equivalents allow an official to make an effective recordable deed.

Equity, in contrast, still acts in personam. The equity action ends with an order addressed to defendant's conscience defining defendant's duty. The judge may use contempt to alter a hesitant defendant's incentive to comply. An equity judge with in personam jurisdiction over defendant may order him to convey land out of the jurisdiction, enjoin infringement out of state, and forbid litigation in another forum. If the defendant demurs, the judge may quicken his conscience with contempt.

An equity action, on the other hand, may end with a money decree, perhaps expressed as a personal order to pay the clerk or plaintiff. Under appropriate statutes the plaintiff may employ all legal devices—execution, judgment lien, or garnishment—to collect an equity decree for money. The prohibition against imprisonment for debt prevents the plaintiff from seeking coercive contempt to collect a money decree. An order to defendant to "go to jail until you pay" imprisons for a civil debt. It also frustrates the policy of the exemption statutes because the defendant may sell property exempt from execution to secure release. Moreover, coercive imprisonment may lead friends and relatives to pay defendant's debt to get him out.

A judge at a supplemental proceeding to collect a money judgment may imprison defendant to coerce him to appear, to answer, or to convey property. Similarly an equity judge may coerce a defendant to turn over things, including money, he has and is able to turn over. Coercing a contemnor to perform an act he is able to perform is not imprisonment for debt. The result is the same at equity and law; the judge may jail a defendant-debtor who has the ability to pay but refuses to pay.

The preceding discussion of in rem/in personam enforcement is painted with a broad brush. Contempt is post-judgment procedure, and equity litigants need to know legal enforcement. Refinements not herein indicated will be encountered. Interested readers may pursue the subject in C. Huston, The Enforcement of Decrees in Equity (1915). Helpful contemporary sources are S. Riesenfeld, Creditors' Remedies and Debtors' Protection 1–465 (3d ed. 1979); Note, Body Attachment and Body Execution: Forgotten but Not Gone, 17 Wm. & Mary L.Rev. 543 (1976).

MYERS v. UNITED STATES

264 U.S. 95, 44 S.Ct. 272, 68 L.Ed. 577 (1924).

Mr. Justice McREYNOLDS delivered the opinion of the Court.

Plaintiffs in error challenged the jurisdiction of the court below—United States District Court, Western Division of the Western District of Missouri—to try and punish them for disobeying its order, upon the ground that the contumacious acts occurred in another division of the district. Only the question of jurisdiction is here.

An information charged that plaintiffs in error wilfully disobeyed the injunction lawfully issued in equity cause, St. Louis, San Francisco Railway Company, Complainant, v. International Association of Machinists, et al., Defendants, pending in the Western Division of the Western District of Missouri, by attempting, within the Southwestern Division of the same district, to prevent certain railroad employees from continuing at work. The order ran against men on strike, and the cause is treated as one within the purview of the Clayton Act . . . . [These provisions are essentially codified in 18 U.S.C.A. § 402, set out in the Appendix.]

Counsel for plaintiffs in error maintain that ordinary contempts punishable by courts of equity without trial by jury differ radically from the "statutory contempt" here disclosed, which, under the Clayton Act, must be dealt with as a criminal offense. And they insist that §§ 51, 52 and 53, Judicial Code, control the venue when such "statutory contempt" is alleged.

Section 51 provides that, with certain exceptions, "no person shall be arrested in one district for trial in another, in any civil action before a district court." . . . Section 52. "When a State contains more than one district, every suit not of a local nature, in the district court thereof, against a single defendant, inhabitant of such State, must be brought in the district where he resides; but if there are two or more defendants, residing in different districts of the State, it may be brought in either district, and a duplicate writ may be issued against the defendants, directed to the marshal of any other district in which any defendant resides." . . . Section 53. "When a district contains more than one division, every suit not of a local nature against a single defendant must be brought in the division where he resides; but if there are two or more defendants residing in different divisions of the district it may be brought in either division. . . . All prosecutions for crimes or offenses shall be had within the division of such districts where the same were committed, unless the court, or the judge thereof, upon the application of the defendant, shall order the cause to be transferred for prosecution to another division of the district."

None of the cited Code sections makes specific reference to contempt proceedings. These are *sui generis*—neither civil actions nor prosecutions for offenses, within the ordinary meaning of those terms—and exertions of the power inherent in all courts to enforce obedience, something they must possess in order properly to perform their functions. . . .

To disobey a judicial order is not declared criminal by the Clayton Act. It recognizes that such disobedience may be contempt and, having prescribed limitations, leaves the court to deal with the offender. While it gives the right to trial by jury and restricts the punishment, it also clearly recognizes the distinction between "proceeding for contempt" and "criminal prosecution." "No proceeding for contempt shall be instituted against any person unless begun within one year from the date of the act complained of; nor shall any such proceeding be a bar to any criminal prosecution for the same act or acts." [Section 25.]

The Clayton Act says nothing about venue in contempt proceedings; leaves it as theretofore. The power of the court below to issue the enjoining order is not questioned. By disobeying the order, plaintiffs in error defied an authority which that tribunal was required to vindicate. It followed established practice, as modified by the statute; and we think the objections to its jurisdiction are unsubstantial. . . .

Gompers v. United States does not support the claim that the challenged contempt proceedings amounted to prosecution for a criminal offense within the intendment of § 53, Judicial Code. While contempt may be an offense against the law and subject to appropriate punishment, certain it is that since the foundation of our government proceedings to punish such offenses have been regarded as *sui generis* and not "criminal prosecutions" within the Sixth Amendment or common understanding.

STILLER v. HARDMAN

324 F.2d 626 (2d Cir. 1963).

Before WATERMAN, HAYS and MARSHALL, Circuit Judges.

HAYS, Circuit Judge. Stiller sought to register in the Southern and Eastern districts of New York a judgment recovered against Squeez-A-Purse Corporation in a patent infringement suit in the Northern District of Ohio. The judgment sought to be registered and enforced in these proceedings held Stiller's patent valid and infringed and awarded him damages in the amount of $47,000 and an injunction enjoining Squeez-A-Purse Corporation, its officers, agents and privies from further infringement. The New York district courts permitted registration of the entire judgment but refused enforcement of the injunctive portion thereof. The parties cross appealed from the orders entered by the district courts. By stipulation the two cases were consolidated on appeal. We affirm the orders from which the parties have appealed.

Stiller moved in the Ohio district court to hold in contempt certain alleged privies of Squeez-A-Purse, to wit, Nathan Silverman, principal stockholder of Squeez-A-Purse, John P. Hardman and John P. Hardman, Inc., sole suppliers of Squeez-A-Purse, and Flex-A-Purse Corporation, a newly organized corporation controlled by Silverman. The Ohio district court held that it was without jurisdiction over the alleged privies.

The registration statute, 28 U.S.C. § 1963 (1958), authorizes the registration only of "[a] judgment in an action for the recovery of money or property." The insertion of the critical phrase "for the recovery of money or property" was explained in the Reviser's Note as intended "to exclude judgments in divorce actions, and any other actions, the registration of which would serve no useful purpose." Note on Legislative History following 28 U.S.C. § 1963 (1958).

Defendants urge that the judgment should have been denied registration. They argue that Section 1963 authorizes registration only if the original proceeding was an action for money or property. Since the Ohio action was one for a declaratory judgment of noninfringement, the argument continues, registration of the judgment awarded the patentee on his counterclaim should have been refused. . . . The fault of the argument lies in a devotion to too literal a reading of the statute, a reading which ignores the purpose of the legislation. We have no doubt that the term "action" in Section 1963 is meant to embrace legal proceedings instituted by way of counterclaim as well as through the filing of a complaint. To hold otherwise would be to attribute to Congress the adoption of a distinction which is wholly without justification. And we cannot read the statute to make registration under Section 1963 depend upon the form in which the action is brought rather than upon the nature of the judgment. . . .

The patentee, Stiller, argues that, in spite of the limited language of Section 1963, a judgment for an injunction can be registered and, after registration, can be enforced. He takes the further position that even if an injunction alone cannot be registered, a judgment which includes not only an injunction but an award for the recovery of money or property, is registrable and such a judgment is enforceable in its entirety. This interpretation is clearly contrary to the intent of the draftsmen since it would practically eliminate the exclusionary effect of the limiting phrase—permitting, for example, the registration of a divorce decree that also provided for alimony. Stiller also contends that the injunction is a decree for the recovery of property—the exclusive use of his patent. To adopt this point of view would completely emasculate the limiting provision and would not accord with the ordinary meaning of the phrase "recovery of property." . . .

Aside from the limiting language of the statute itself, a consideration of the necessities which led to the enactment of Section 1963 reveals a significant difference between money judgments and injunction orders which may well account for the omission of injunctions from the privilege of registration.

In the absence of a statute providing for the registration or summary enforcement of foreign judgment, see Uniform Enforcement of Foreign Judgments Act, it is usually necessary to bring an action of debt on a foreign money judgment and to obtain a new judgment of the forum before execution will issue. . . . This procedure created particular difficulties for claimants who had originally grounded federal jurisdiction on the existence of a federal question; for a suit on a judgment does not involve a federal question, however important federal questions may have been to the resolution of the original controversy. 2 Moore, Federal Practice ¶ 1.04[2], at 28 n. 20 (2d ed. 1962). Section 1963, which was adopted in 1948 during the revision of the Judicial Code, eliminates this jurisdictional problem, as well as providing a speedier and more efficient mechanism for the enforcement of federal judgments.

The situation with respect to injunctions is quite different. The mandate of an injunction issued by a federal district court runs throughout the United States. Leman v. Krentler-Arnold Co., 284 U.S. 448 (1932). Violation of an injunctive order is cognizable in the court which issued the injunction, regardless of where the violation occurred. . . . In the present case, for example, the Ohio district court had power to punish a violative infringement though the infringement took place in New York. There is therefore no such need for registration of injunction orders as there is for registration of the money judgment.

Thus, if the Ohio court had only issued an injunction order its judgment order would not have been registrable, but inasmuch as the Ohio judgment contained, together with an injunction order, an award for damages, the entire Ohio judgment is nominally registrable but the injunctive portion thereof is not enforceable.

In view of our interpretation of Section 1963 we affirm the decisions below upholding registration of the entire Ohio judgment, permitting enforcement of the award for damages and denying enforcement of the injunctive portion of the judgment.

1) The *Leman* Court's reasoning is contained in the following passage (284 U.S. at 451):

". . . The question of jurisdiction turns upon the nature and effect of the decree in the infringement suit and the relation to that suit of the contempt proceeding. When the respondent brought the suit in the Federal District Court for the District of Massachusetts, it submitted itself to the jurisdiction of the court with respect to all the issues embraced in the suit, including those pertaining to the counterclaim of the defendants, petitioners here. . . . The decree upon the counterclaim bound the respondent personally. It was a decree which operated continuously and perpetually upon the respondent in relation to the prohibited conduct. The decree was binding upon the respondent, not simply within the District of Massachusetts, but throughout the United States. . . . The respondent could not escape the decree by removing from, or staying without, the District of Massachusetts. Wherever it might conduct its affairs, it would carry with it the prohibition. Disobedience constituted contempt of the court which rendered the decree, and was none the less contempt because the act was committed outside the district, as the contempt lay in the fact, not in the place, of the disobedience to the requirement."

2) Stiller lacks jurisdiction over the apparent infringer in both the Rule 65(d) sense and the Rule 4 sense. Where did Stiller go wrong? Should he have sued both the entity and the people in Ohio? If Stiller files a new action in New York, would the New York defendants be sufficiently related to the Ohio litigation to be precluded by res judicata from litigating some of the issues litigated in Ohio?

3) The related trademark and copyright areas have statutory provisions addressed to this problem. Section 34 of the Trademark Act of 1946, 15 U.S.C. § 1116, provides:

". . . Any such injunction granted upon hearing, after notice to the defendant, by any district court of the United States, may be served on the parties against whom such injunction is granted anywhere in the United States where they may be found, and shall be operative and may be enforced by proceedings to punish for contempt, or otherwise, by the court by which such injunction was granted, or by any other United States district court in whose jurisdiction the defendant may be found.

"The said courts shall have jurisdiction to enforce said injunction, as herein provided [in this chapter], as fully as if the injunction had been granted by the district court in which it is sought to be enforced. The clerk of the court or judge granting the injunction shall, when required to do so by the court before which application to enforce said injunction is made, transfer without delay to said court a certified copy of all papers on file in his office upon which said injunction was granted."

Section 502(b) of the Copyright Act, 17 U.S.C. § 502(b), provides:

"(b) Any such injunction may be served anywhere in the United States on the person enjoined; it shall be operative throughout the United States and shall be enforceable, by proceedings in contempt or otherwise, by any United States court having jurisdiction of that person. The clerk of the court in granting the injunction shall, when requested by any other court in which enforcement of the injunction is sought, transmit promptly to the other court a certified copy of all the papers in the case on file in such clerk's office.

4) In New Jersey Communications Corporation v. American Telephone and Telegraph Co., 1968 Trade Cas. (CCH) ¶ 72,455 at 85,455 (S.D.N.Y. 1967), plaintiffs were not parties in the government's antitrust action in New Jersey that led to a final consent judgment. Plaintiffs sued in New York asking the court to construe the New Jersey injunction, to declare that defendants had violated it, to enforce it with contempt, and to enter a New York injunction. The district judge in New York dismissed the action. Plaintiffs, he said, might have a) intervened in the New Jersey action or b) filed a separate action. "We hold that this action must be dismissed for lack of jurisdiction over the subject matter. For this Court to undertake to decide whether a defendant named in an action filed in another District Court was guilty of a violation of the provisions of a final judgment entered in that action, and if found to be guilty, to undertake to fix and impose just punitive measures, would be an impertinent and unjustifiable intrusion on the jurisdiction of the other Court. Such a course, if pursued, would lead to confusion as to the construction to be placed upon the final judgment, a multitude of independent proceedings in numerous jurisdictions, and would defeat the very purposes of the final judgment." The Court added: "Quite aside from the dismissal of this action, we find total absence of a showing to support the granting of the injunctive relief sought by plaintiffs . . . ."

Does the court's statement that it lacks subject matter jurisdiction overstate the rule? If the case occurred today, could plaintiff preclude defendant from relitigating certain issues under Parklane Hosiery Co. v. Shore, 439 U.S. 322 (1979)?

5) Professor Reese discussed the type of action a plaintiff should file to enforce another state's equity decree. Then he wrote: "[T]he plaintiff could presumably seek a declaratory judgment to determine the extent of his rights under the foreign equity decree and at the same time ask for such supplemental relief as was necessary to give him the full enjoyment of these rights. As a last resort, he could sue on the original cause of action. In such a suit, the forum would clearly be compelled by the normal command of full faith and credit to accept the rendering court's findings of facts. Would it also be compelled to give the same relief? It has been suggested that this is not the case, since equitable relief is extraordinary relief and the forum should be permitted to use its own discretion in determining what form of relief to allow the plaintiff. This suggestion, however, finds no support in the language of the full faith and credit clause and its implementing statute. Furthermore, equitable relief has now become so common that it can hardly be considered more extraordinary than relief at law. It is therefore concluded that, subject to two possible exceptions, the forum should, generally at least, be required to give the same relief as that granted by the original court. The first exception covers the rare situation where the relief is of a kind which the forum does not grant; here the forum would presumably not be required to manufacture for the occasion something which hitherto has been unknown to it. The second possible exception is where the forum is asked to duplicate an order of the rendering court that the defendant should either do, or refrain from doing, a given act, and there would be no way of enforcing such an

order except by imprisoning, or otherwise punishing, the defendant. Here it may be that full faith and credit will not always require the forum to issue such an order and thus in effect assume the burden of enforcing defendant's obedience to the rendering court's decree. This is particularly likely to be true where the rendering court still has jurisdiction over either the defendant's person or his property and thus has means at its disposal of enforcing its own decree." Reese, Full Faith and Credit to Foreign Equity Decrees, 42 Iowa L.Rev. 183, 190–91 (1957).

6) A judge may grant an injunction that is effective outside his court's territorial jurisdiction; if defendant violates it, the judge may use domestic sanctions to enforce it. The in personam theory is more nettlesome when the substantive law differs between the injunction jurisdiction, I, and the jurisdiction where the injunction affects conduct, C. Three general questions arise: 1) whether an I court should enjoin conduct in C in the first place. See Seattle Totems Hockey Club, Inc. v. National Hockey League, 652 F.2d 852 (9th Cir. 1981); 2) whether an I court should enforce an I injunction when that affects conduct in C; 3) how much credence C should accord to the I injunction.

History provides little help. Earlier courts have dealt with decrees affecting foreign land, family support and custody orders, and injunctions against foreign suits. Policies assist only a little. Conduct in C may threaten I's values as expressed in I statutes and common law. Expanding I's law to conduct in C may meddle in C's internal affairs, interfere with C's law, and undercut C's policy. This sets the nationalizing force of full faith and credit against the parochial idea that each state may maintain its own legal system. Other nations respect United States law only because of comity. Full faith and credit tells one state to enforce the money judgment of another state even when the judgment is based on policy repugnant to the enforcement state. Fauntleroy v. Lum, 210 U.S. 230 (1908). Full faith and credit only tells states that domestic res judicata operates on interstate orders; neither res judicata nor full faith and credit applies fully to injunctions. Courts in C, the conduct state, shrink from contempt on two grounds. Contempt, it is asserted, is penal and beyond full faith and credit. R. Leflar, American Conflicts Law § 75 (1977). (This fails to explain reluctance to utilize compensatory or coercive contempt.) Moreover, injunctions are discretionary: courts may enforce the substantive right differently. Reese, 42 Iowa L.Rev. 183. (Discretion must, however, yield on occasion to finality.) The literature includes Feinberg, Economic Coercion and Economic Sanctions: The Expansion of United States Extraterritorial Jurisdiction, 30 Am.U.L.Rev. 323 (1981); White, Enforcement of Foreign Judgments in Equity, 9 Sydney L.Rev. 630 (1982); Developments in the Law-Injunctions, 78 Harv.L.Rev. 994, 1033–45 (1965). The following problems show the difficulty of accommodating federalism with unity and finality:

a) Summerland is a licensee of Billy Bob, fabulously successful country and western singing star. As part of its campaign to extirpate bootleg merchandise at Billy Bob's concerts, Summerland sued a New York silk-screening group, Marbles. Judge Paruzyski of New York's federal district court held that Marbles's T-shirts violated Summerland's and Billy Bob's right to publicity plus section 43(a) of the Lanham Act. She enjoined Marbles and all the people involved from, among other things, selling T-shirts that infringed Summerland's license. See Winterland Concessions Co. v. Sileo, 528 F.Supp. 1201 (N.D.Ill.1981).

At Billy Bob's concert in Elm City, California, a security guard apprehends Hi Cupola, a Marbles insider, with a van full of "I sang with Billy Bob in Elm City" T-shirts. Cupola was supplying T-shirts to a sales force, collecting money from them, and paying them commissions. May Summerland, a California concern, maintain compensatory contempt in California federal district court to recover Cupola's Elm City profits? May the California judge appoint Summerland's Los Angeles attorney to prosecute criminal contempt?

Under normal choice of law rules, remedies are determined by the law of the forum. Halstead v. United States, 535 F.Supp. 782, 794 (D.Conn. 1982). Hughes v. Fetter, 341 U.S. 609 (1951), and Broderick v. Rosner, 294 U.S. 629 (1935), may tell the California court to apply New York law to compensate. If the enforcement state lacks compensatory contempt, as California does, may it decline the suit or remit Summerland to a fresh action? Cf. "[F]ull faith and credit does not automatically compel a forum state to subordinate its own statutory policy to a conflicting public act of another state. . . . " Hughes v. Fetter, 341 U.S. 609, 611 (1951). "Whenever F2 disagrees seriously with the policies underlying F1's injunction, F2 should refuse recognition to avoid the peculiar position of having to coerce a defendant to obey an order that contravenes the state's public policy." Developments in the Law-Injunctions, 78 Harv.L.Rev. at 1044.

If Summerland pursues compensatory contempt in the California federal court which does not recognize compensatory contempt, should the federal judge follow federal or state practice? The answer appears to be federal, although clear decisions are scarce. See Guaranty Trust Co. v. York, 326 U.S. 99, 106 (1945); Folk v. Wallace Business Forms, Inc., 394 F.2d 240 (4th Cir. 1969); Sunbeam Corp. v. Golden Rule Appliance Co., Inc., 252 F.2d 467, 470 (2d Cir. 1958); Berry v. Midtown Service Corp., 104 F.2d 107, 109 (2d Cir. 1939).

b) A tort action for alienation of affections is brought by a plaintiff against a defendant who has "alienated" the affections of plaintiff's loved one. About half the states allow and half forbid the cause of action. A few jurisdictions including Alabama, Henley v. Rockett, 243 Ala. 172, 8 So.2d 852 (1942), grant injunctions to prevent a defendant from persisting in alienating conduct. Washington's Supreme Court recently abolished the action. Wyman v. Wallace, 94 Wash.2d 99, 615 P.2d 452 (1980).

Supporters of the alienation of affections cause of action argue that it vindicates the wronged spouse and society by preventing outsiders from tampering with the relationship. Many state legislatures, however, have passed "Anti-Heart Balm Statutes" to abolish the tort. The Washington court gave several reasons for abolition: Alienation of affections fails to preserve marital harmony. It leads to opportunities for blackmail and vicious settlements to avoid trials. Standards to assess damages are lacking, and successful plaintiffs appear to compel a forced sale of the spouse's affections.

Lucinda and Harrison Tyler Buchanan, III were married in Opelika, Alabama, but Harrison's passions soon dulled and he became as one with Earleen Pattingale. Lucinda sued Earleen for alienating Harrison's affections, and the Lee County circuit judge enjoined Earleen "from further consorting with said H. Tyler Buchanan III or alienating his affections from his aforesaid spouse." Earleen is a student at the University of Washington dental school. Apparently responding to a call or letter, Harrison left Lucinda and Opelika; he moved to Seattle where he has taken up residence with Earleen. Harrison wrote Lucinda that he plans to divorce her and marry Earleen. Is Earleen's behavior in Washington contempt of the Alabama injunction? If Earleen returns to Opelika, may the Lee County circuit judge punish her for criminal contempt? Impose a compensatory contempt award equal to tort damages? Coerce her with fines or imprisonment?

c) Bob Caitlin filed bankruptcy in United States bankruptcy court and discharged several debts including $8000 he owed to Nancy Grossman for welshing on a loan. All former creditors, including Grossman, received a discharge injunction which banned "the commencement or continuation of an action" to collect discharged debts. Caitlin's new ceramics business prospered after he opened a branch store in Hamburg, Germany. Grossman hired a German lawyer, sued Caitlin in Hamburg, obtained a German judgment for the mark equivalent of $8,000, and collected the judgment by realizing on the branch store's assets.

Germany denies domestic effect to a foreign bankruptcy discharge. May either the appropriate federal district judge or the United States bankruptcy court (as provided 28 U.S.C. § 1481) that discharged Caitlin and enjoined Grossman 1) punish Grossman for criminal contempt for violation of the discharge injunction by fining her $10,000? 2) order Grossman to drop the German action and restore the branch store's assets? 3) award Caitlin $8,000 to be collected from Grossman's assets in the United States? See Honsberger, Conflict of Laws and the Bankruptcy Reform Act of 1978, 30 Case W.Res.L.Rev. 631, 664–666 (1980).

Compare Societe Internationale v. Rogers, 357 U.S. 197 (1958), and In re Westinghouse Electric Corp. Uranium Contract Proceedings, 563 F.2d 992 (10th Cir. 1977). In each, an American court sought to force a discovered party to produce documents that could not be disclosed under the law of the country where the documents were located. The American courts declined to hold the discovered parties in contempt. "Unless an enjoining state's interest is overwhelming, considerations of fairness, and possibly due process, should prohibit subjecting someone either to a command to do an act contrary to the laws of another state or to a contempt charge for refusing to do the unlawful act." Developments in the Law-Injunctions 78 Harv. L.Rev. at 1033.

d) Three-year-old Thad suffers from acute lymphocytic leukemia. Thad's parents have treated his condition with laetrile. The state health authorities sought and received a order for "care and protection." Judge Schleider ordered that Thad receive chemotherapy, that his parents cease administering laetrile, and that their custody be restricted to assure proper medical supervision of Thad. See Custody of a Minor, 378 Mass. 732, 393 N.E.2d 836 (1979). The parents took Thad to Mexico, resumed laetrile therapy, and ceased chemotherapy. Laetrile therapy is legal in Mexico. Should Judge Schleider punish Thad's parents for criminal contempt?

The parents in the actual Massachusetts decision above did flee to Mexico with the child. After the little boy died, they returned; the judge found them guilty of contempt but freed them on the ground that they had suffered enough. The legal-medical debate about laetrile is summarized in Comment, The Uncertain Application of the Right of Privacy in Personal Medical Decisions: The Laetrile Cases, 42 Ohio St.L.J. 523 (1981).

e) The right of publicity litigation concerning the ability to maintain and exploit the late Elvis Presley's fame and mystique provides the basis for this problem. Some courts have held that the right is personal and dies with the "owner." See, e.g., Memphis Development Foundation v. Factors Etc., Inc., 616 F.2d 956 (6th Cir. 1980), followed in Factors Etc., Inc. v. Pro Arts, Inc., 652 F.2d 278 (2d Cir. 1981). Other jurisdictions call the right property and allow it to be exploited by a decedent celebrity's estate. See, e.g., Groucho Marx Productions, Inc. v. Day & Night Co., Inc., 523 F.Supp. 485 (S.D. N.Y.1981); and Estate of Presley v. Russen, 513 F.Supp. 1339 (D.N.J. 1981). The latter group has won in the law reviews. Felcher & Rubin, The Descendibility of the Right of Publicity: Is There Commercial Life After Death?, 89 Yale L.J. 1125 (1980).

Aletha Armsted died a tragic death in a crash on the highway at the peak of her career as a soul singer. Following her death, several imitators began to record "her" songs and to seek concert appearances. Aletha's executor sought an injunction against Milly Rains who billed her act as "Memories of Aletha." The executor sued in New James, a state that held the right descendible. Several questions emerge: Should Judge Rublee in New James enjoin Ms. Rains's imitations of Aletha outside of New James? Should she enjoin the imitations only in the states that recognize the right? If she enjoins the imitations everywhere, and Ms. Rains performs in a state that rejects the right, could the court impose compensatory or criminal contempt? Could she enjoin imitations everywhere and force Ms. Rains to post a bond to be forfeited upon violation? Should a court in a state that rejects the right give full faith and credit or comity to the New James injunction? Ms. Rains's record "Natural Aletha" is rising on the charts. If the company that recorded it is in a state that rejects the right, can Judge Rublee do anything to suppress it? At a minimum can she enjoin sales in New James? See Estate of Presley v. Russen, 513 F.2d 1339 (D.N.J.1981); Factors Etc., Inc. v. Pro Arts, Inc., 652 F.2d 278 (2d Cir. 1981).

Diversity jurisdiction and pendant claims in federal jurisdiction actions generate an additional layer of confusion where the states lack discernible law on the subject. This confusion raises the question whether a uniform or national approach is merited. Comment, Circuit Court of Appeals Must Accord Conclusive Deference to Another Circuit's Determination of the Law of A State Within the Other Circuit: Factors Etc., Inc. v. Pro Arts, Inc., 67 Cornell L.Rev. 415 (1982).

f) H. Grady Dobie is a crook. He has operated a Ponzi scheme in Maryland and the District of Columbia and defrauded the public of millions. Through several sham corporations Dobie borrowed money at 25% interest under the pretense of importing cocoa and coffee from Africa. Human gullibility and cupidity led to huge loans, many renewed several times and a steadily growing capitalization. But Dobie was always hopelessly insolvent. The more people loaned him, the more insolvent he became; because in fact, he imported nothing. Instead he used recent loans to pay back earlier ones. When Dobie learned that the Internal Revenue Service was investigating his affairs, he removed $3,000,000 of negotiable stock certificates from his office safe and sent them to an employee in Nassau, Bahamas.

The IRS filed a jeopardy assessment plus a tax lien and sued Dobie for an injunction. It asked a Maryland federal judge to appoint a receiver. The judge enjoined Dobie, agents, and confederates from "any selling, transferring, pledging, removing or dealing with his assets wherever located." He ordered Dobie to assign and deliver all assets, business records and "stock certificates" to a receiver. Except for $30,000 in a checking account, the stock in Nassau was the only "liquid" asset Dobie had. Dobie surreptitiously flew to Nassau, picked up the share certificates, returned to Atlanta, pledged the stock at First Dixie Bank for a loan of $2,400,000, and departed with a suitcase full of money for Libratia, a country without an extradition treaty with the United States. Including his debt to the IRS, there are $24,000,000 in outstanding claims against Dobie. See United States v. McNulty, 446 F.Supp. 90 (N.D.Cal.1978); United States v. Ross, 166 F.Supp. 243 (S.D. N.Y.1961). U.C.C. §§ 8–309, 8–317, 8–321 (1977).

First Dixie was blissfully ignorant of the lawsuit, the receiver, the injunction, and the tax lien. It wonders whether it may sell the pledged shares to repay its loan to Dobie. The IRS wonders whether the receiver is entitled to the stock. If First Dixie retains the stock, is the IRS eligible for a compensatory contempt award against Dobie? What good would that do? Gretchen Lamb had loaned $800,000 to Dobie Enterprises Inc. three days before Dobie skipped. What are Ms. Lamb's remedies? Finally, is Dobie in contempt of the injunction? What practical value does the injunction have? The order to assign to the receiver?

g) In wrestling with these problems, are you helped by the maxim that equity acts in personam?

Chapter Eleven

CRIMINAL CONTEMPT

The criminal law, Professor Frank Allen reminds us, is society's "heavy artillery." Governments employ the criminal law to deprive citizens of liberty and property. Criminal sanctions condemn morally and affix a stigma. The twentieth century teaches us, moreover, that tyrants misuse penal sanctions to ravage liberal institutions. "The very weight of criminal sanctions requires societies valuing individual volition to erect principles of containment in order that powers of government employed in law enforcement may be prevented from overreaching their bounds and destroying or impairing basic political values." Allen, The Morality of Means: Three Problems in Criminal Sanctions, 42 U.Pitt.L.Rev. 737, 738–9 (1981). The criminal law should not intervene when that will be unwise or counterproductive. Criminal sanctions are not ends but means to accomplish social goals; and when the means cost more than they achieve, we should abandon them. Allen, 42 U.Pitt.L.Rev. 737. The conduct the law interdicts, the means of evaluating that conduct, and the measures the law imposes cannot be divorced from political and ethical values. The problem stated more generally is how to achieve "the objectives of public order through the use of power so regulated as to preserve and nourish basic political values." F. Allen, The Borderland of Criminal Justice viii (1964).

Equity has expanded far beyond protecting property interests. The chancellor regulates business, protects the environment, and oversees some of the relations between races and genders; in particular he stands ready to safeguard constitutional values of the highest order. Equity's expansion has occurred at the same time the criminal law has moved from protecting persons and property to a vast range of disparate goals. Policymakers have endorsed this dual expansion without much thought to the criminal-equitable division of labor.

When a defendant breaches an injunction, the judge may move from the civil or equitable to the criminal domain because of the criminal contempt power. [The judge must consider contempt, civil and criminal. The two retrospective forms of contempt are compensatory and criminal.] Such a movement transforms the injunction into a criminal statute. Professor Allen's considerations become relevant at this point; the judge's role resembles both a legislature's, deciding whether to pass a criminal statute, and a prosecuting attorney's, determining how to exercise prosecutorial discretion.

The defendant has violated the interest that the injunction protected. What distinguishes a breach that will lead to criminal contempt from one that will be remedied with compensatory contempt alone? The judge considers the following things in deciding whether to pursue criminal contempt. First wilfullness, a form of mens rea, is an element of criminal but not civil contempt. Second, statutory crimes often involve violence or the threat of violence. People fear physical harm or threat of harm; they feel that pain and fear are noncompensable. Third, criminals often avoid detection. If the perpetrator discounts society's response by the chance that it will be imposed, the judge should increase society's response to reflect the risk that the perpetrator will evade apprehension. Fourth, crime is a business with high overhead; criminals are seldom able to pay damages to victims. If the perpetrator lacks property to compensate, the judge may take some of his or her liberty as a rough way of restoring the balance without compensating the victim. Kronman, Specific Performance, 45 U.Chi.L.Rev. 351, 375 n. 76 (1978).

This chapter begins by looking at the elements of criminal contempt and then focuses on the criminal contempt process by examining the relation between the judiciary and other governmental institutions. We ask how to divide the contempt power between the judge and, on the other hand, the legislature, the executive, the jury, and the plaintiff. Two views of contempt compete for prominence. They are the "sui generis-inherent" view and the "due process" view. In Mechanic v. Gruensfelder, the court said "a proceeding for criminal contempt is sui generis, and as such is controlled by its own rules—not the rules of the criminal law." 461 S.W.2d 298, 309 (Mo. App.1970). This approach provides celerity, efficiency, respect, practicality, flexibility, and autonomy for the trial judge. In contrast, the second paragraph of Justice Rutledge's dissent in *Mine Workers,* p. 848 states the due process view of contempt; it essentially assimilates criminal contempt to an ordinary crime. Clearly the majority and dissent in *Mine Workers* express this difference on the issues of mingling criminal and civil as well as the form of notice. The *Griffin* majority and dissent, p. 264 divide between the sui generis and due process models of civil contempt.

These two views of criminal contempt reflect basic notions about separation of powers. We fear concentrated power, and we divide power among the branches of government hoping to preserve individual liberty from abuse. The usual separations are absent in criminal contempt. Efficiency, celerity, practicality, flexibility, and respect argue for an arrangement that concentrates power. Yet the trial judge exercises an awesome and perhaps unparalleled concentration of power. A major theme in contempt is how much to dilute that power by allowing the legislature, a prosecutor, a grand jury, a petit jury, an appellate court, or the executive to share it. Ask yourself the following questions while reading this material. Are the arguments for concentrated power defeated by its potential for abuse? Is the concentrated power justified by the injunction's special mission in developing and preserving the public order?

I. Elements

Think through a criminal contempt for breach of an injunction from both sides. What documents must the prosecution prepare? How specific must they be? What are the elements of the offense that the prosecution must prove? Must the prosecution prove anything more than that contemnor knew of the injunction and violated it? See *Cape May,* p. 261, *Walker,* p. 286. What documents may the defense prepare? In addition to insisting that proper procedure is followed and refuting the elements, what defenses may the contemnor interpose?

THE UNITED MINE WORKERS CASE—THE PENSION FUND DISPUTE

77 F.Supp. 563 (D.D.C.1948), affirmed 177 F.2d 29 (D.C.Cir. 1949).

The Supreme Court handed down its decision in the *United Mine Workers* case in March 1947. See pp. 274, 839. An agreement was entered by July, but another dispute immediately flared up—this time over the welfare and retirement fund. That fund, to be composed of payments by the employers, was to be operated by three trustees—one appointed by the employers, another by the union (who was John L. Lewis), and the third—a neutral—selected by the other two. The trustees could not agree on the pension plan (Lewis wanted miners who had been employed for twenty years and were sixty years old to have a pension of $100 a month regardless of whether they were presently employed). By January, 1948, the neutral trustee resigned.

On March 12, Lewis, president of the International, wrote to the officers and members of the local unions. He described the dispute and added:

"Your representative Trustee, and all other representatives of the United Mine Workers of America, during this eight months' period have worked constantly and diligently to resolve with the Coal Operators and with the Trustees the several questions involved. These efforts have been without avail. The Coal Operators and their Trustee continue gleefully to violate the contract, and count each day a success when they can prevent expenditure of this money designed to alleviate the human misery in the coal industry. The destitution of the aged, the extremity of the sick and injured and the poverty of orphans and widows are things which concern them not. Nineteen forty-seven was the most financially profitable year in the history of the coal industry, and yet the millionaire coal operators of this country, with the aid of Robert Taft and his Slave Statute, are successfully preventing the distribution of this ten cents a ton Fund, which is designed only to abate human misery.

"During the past year and throughout the hard winter which has afflicted the nation, our membership have continued loyally and with a sense of public duty to break all records in the production of coal. This service increased the profits of the coal companies and should have won their respect for contract and some consideration for human values; but instead has made them contemptuous of their contractual and moral obligations.

"The winter is now gone. This office proposes to go forward in requiring the coal operators to honor their agreement. Your ears will soon be assailed by their outcries and wails of anguish. To relieve themselves, they need only to comply with the provisions of the Agreement which they solemnly executed in this office on July 8, 1947.

"Please discuss this matter in your local unions so that our membership may be fully advised. You will later hear more from this office on this subject."

A work stoppage immediately followed—which a Presidential board of inquiry claimed had "precipitated a crisis in the industry and in the nation as a whole." The next critical date was April 3, a Saturday, on which two things occurred. First, Lewis wrote to the officers and members of all the local units:

"Subsequent to my circular to you of March 12, the Press, many officials in government and the coal operators, individually and collectively, have repeatedly charged that I, by the message of March 12, authorized or directed or suggested or indirectly requested or recommended a stoppage of work, or as some have called it 'a strike' in protest to the dishonoring of the contract (as we saw it) by the coal operators.

"It is well known to you that I have not in connection with the present dispute, either by the circular of March 12, or by any other circular or document, or at any other time authorized, directed, suggested, requested or recommended any stoppage of work or any continuation of any stoppage and I do not now do so.

"Your actions in this regard in the original instance were your own, individually determined by you. I asked you on March 12 'to discuss the matter in your local union so that our membership may be fully advised.' Such discussions as may have been held, or which you may hereafter desire, have been and will continue to be, on your own initiative. As far as I know it is still the inherent right and privilege of American citizens to continue to exercise the right of free speech and freedom of assembly.

"Any action or decision which you may now care to take continues to be entirely for your own determination without direction of any character from me or from any of your International Officers.

"I, therefore, now repeat that you are not now under, and have never been under, any orders, directions or suggestions, expressed or implied from me, or any of the Union officers, to cease work or to continue to cease work in protest to the present dishonoring (as we see it) of the 1947 contract. I now report factually the events which have occurred and the situation as it presently exists."

Also, on the same day, April 3, the Attorney General commenced an injunctive proceeding. At 7:30 p.m. the District Court issued the following temporary restraining order, which by its terms would expire in ten days, on April 13:

"Now, therefore, it is by the Court this 3rd day of April 1948,

"Ordered that the defendant, International Union, United Mine Workers of America, hereinafter sometimes referred to as the Union, and its officers, agents, servants and employees, and all persons in active concert or participation with them, be and they are hereby restrained pending further order of this Court from continuing the strike now in existence at bituminous coal mines throughout the United States of America owned or operated by coal operators and associations signatory to the National Bituminous Coal Wage Agreement of 1947, executed at Washington, D.C., July 8, 1947, hereinafter referred to as the Agreement, and that the said defendant, International Union, United Mine Workers of America, and its officers, agents, servants and employees, and all persons in active concert or participation with them, be and they are hereby restrained pending further order of this Court from in any manner engaging in, permitting or encouraging the said strike or its continuation;

"And it is further ordered that the said Union, acting through its president and other appropriate officers, agents, servants and employees, forthwith instruct all members of the said Union employed in the bituminous coal mines covered by the Agreement to cease the said strike and immediately to return to their employment and that the said Union, acting through the said officers, agents, servants and employees, cease, desist and refrain from ordering, encouraging, recommending, instructing, inducing or in any wise permitting the said strike to continue;

"And it is further ordered that the defendants and each of them and their officers, agents, servants and employees, and all persons in active concert or participation with them, be and they are hereby restrained pending further order of this Court from encouraging, causing or engaging in a strike or lockout at any bituminous coal mines covered by the agreement, or from in any manner interfering with or affecting the orderly continuance of work at the said coal mines, and from taking any action which would interfere with the Court's jurisdiction . . . ."

The defendants were not formally served with the injunction until Monday morning, April 5. On April 7, Lewis moved to vacate the TRO. But, on that day, the Attorney General asked that Lewis and the union be ordered to show cause as to why they should not be held in contempt; and the District Court issued the order, returnable on April 12. On April 10 a new neutral trustee was appointed—Senator H. Styles Bridges. Meetings were immediately held and, by the morning of April 12, a pension plan had been adopted. Immediately, two telegrams were dispatched. One was sent to each District President and to the members of the Executive Board of the International. It read:

"This message is for your official information and for immediate transmission to all members of the Union. The Trustee vacancy in the 1947 Welfare Fund has now been filled by the selection of The Honorable H. Styles Bridges who has accepted the appointment. An early resolution of the questions at issue may now be expected. Your voluntary cessation of work should now be terminated and your protest ended. It is the belief of the International Union and your officers that the production of coal should be resumed forthwith. It is to your best interests and those of our Union and the public welfare that this be done. Therefore, you are now officially advised that you should return to your usual employment immediately upon receipt of this telegram. This message is sent in behalf of the International Union as well as in my official capacity as President.

"John L. Lewis

"President, United Mine Workers of America."

The other was sent to the local unions. It read simply: "Pensions granted. The agreement is now honored."

Lewis's attorney appeared in court on April 12, in response to the April 7th order to show cause. He reported what had transpired, and the court ordered that the alleged contempts be set down for trial. The court subsequently found Lewis and the union in criminal contempt and imposed a fine of $1,400,000 against the union and $20,000 against Lewis (though the court indicated—77 F.Supp. at 573—that if it "were to use its individual judgment, it would impose a prison sentence"). The District Court perceived this to be the issue (77 F.Supp. at 566–67):

"But the defendants' contention is this: That the First and the Thirteenth Amendments were violated because, as a matter of fact, no strike was called, no strike existed. These men, it is contended, did, as individuals, what they had a right to do, work or not to work, and they decided not to work.

"Now, we have to consider the validity of that claim objectively. If a nod or a wink or a code was used in place of the word 'strike,' there was just as much a strike called as if the word 'strike' had been used. . . .

". . . Now in the letter of March 12th, they say:

" 'The winter is now gone; this office proposes to go forward in requiring the coal operators to honor their agreement.'

"Go forward in what way? Any other way except strike?

" 'Your ears will soon be assailed by their outcries and wails of anguish. To relieve themselves they need only to comply with the provisions of the Agreement which they solemnly executed in this office on July 8, 1947.'

"Does that constitute a nod, or a wink, or the use of a code in order to call a strike? Is there any other reasonable interpretation? . . .

"The Court thinks the principle is this: that as long as a union is functioning as a union it must be held responsible for the mass action of its members. It is perfectly obvious not only in objective reasoning but because of experience that men don't act collectively without leadership. The idea of suggesting that from 350,000 to 450,000 men would all get the same idea at once, independently of leadership, and walk out of the mines, is of course simply ridiculous. . . .

"So that the rule of law which I have announced is the only rule which will preserve the unions, because if the plan is adopted throughout the country of trying to use a wink, a nod, a code, instead of the word 'strike', and if that sort of a maneuver is recognized as valid by the Courts, then you will have among the unions lawlessness, chaos, and ultimate anarchy. And then the unions will have to be socialized. In other words, they will have to be destroyed.

"So when the Court says that the Union must be held responsible, as long as it is functioning, for the mass action of its members, the Court is announcing a principle for the salvation of the unions themselves and their preservation, and the only rule that will save them from destruction.

"Of course, if a union comes in and says 'We have lost our hold on our members; they have gone; John Smith has executed a coup; he has taken them away from us,' and if they can show the Court by legitimate testimony that that is true, they are not guilty of contempt. But that is not the situation here.

"The Union and its President make no such claim. They don't contend for one instant that this Union isn't operating and functioning as a union, and that its members are not controlled from headquarters."

The Court of Appeals affirmed, but took a narrower view of the issue (177 F.2d, at 35):

". . . When Lewis sent his message of March 12th, the miners stopped work. When he sent the messages of April 12th, the miners returned to work. No word of any sort was sent by the Union or by Lewis to the miners between April 5th, when the court order was issued, and April 12th, when the dispute concerning the welfare fund was settled. In the long wire of the latter date, Lewis said, 'Therefore, you are now officially advised that you should return to your usual employment immediately upon receipt of this telegram.' It is difficult to disassociate that language from the inference that control of the stoppage lay in Lewis's hands. In their brief to us, the Union and Lewis refer to the telegrams of April 12th as orders or directions; they say 'the dispute was settled and the men had been ordered to return to work'; that the 'miners had been instructed to resume their employment'; twice they say that appellants 'had not only directed the miners to resume production," etc. And again they say that the telegrams 'sought to accomplish—and did accomplish—precisely what Government undertook in institution of its action.'

"Apart from the statements just quoted from their brief, the Union and Lewis contend that the existence of the dispute over the welfare fund caused the miners, individually, to walk out, and that the solution of the dispute caused them to resume work; in other words, that the status of the dispute, and not the Lewis communications, was the cause of the cessation and also of the resumption of work.

"Appellants were not convicted for causing the walk-out. They were convicted because they deliberately failed to comply with the court's order of April 3d. That was a temporary order. It sought the resumption of mining, for the protection of the national health and safety, until the court could consider the contentions of the parties relative to a further injunction. It was not even a preliminary injunction, which would continue until the basic dispute had been determined. It was limited to a few days until the petitions for preliminary injunction could be heard. The Union and Lewis ignored the order until the basic dispute was settled. The evidence supports their claim that they endeavored to settle the basic dispute, but it also shows conclusively that pending the settlement of that dispute they made no attempt to restore normal production.

"It seems plain enough that if Lewis had sent on April 5th telegrams of a directory or advisory nature, similar to those he sent on April 12th, neither he nor the Union would have been guilty of contempt of the court's order. When the basic objective was achieved, Lewis 'officially advised' the miners to return to work. He could have officially advised them on April 5th that in view of the court's order they should return to work pending further action of the court. That is what the court ordered him to do. That is what he did not do." [The Supreme Court denied certiorari, 338 U.S. 871 (1948).]

---

1) An injunction under Rule 65(d) must be specific enough to provide fair notice of the forbidden conduct. If defendants cannot understand enough to comply, an injunction cannot be the basis for contempt. "The

judicial contempt power is a potent weapon. When it is founded upon a decree too vague to be understood, it can be a deadly one. Congress responded to that danger by requiring that a federal court frame its orders so that those who must obey them will know what the court intends to require and what it means to forbid." International Longshoremen's Association, Local 1291 v. Philadelphia Marine Trade Association, 389 U.S. 64, 76 (1967). See also Swift & Co. v. United States, 196 U.S. 375, 401 (1905).

Is an injunction analogous to a criminal statute? Note, Criminal Contempt: Violations of Injunctions in the Federal Courts, 32 Ind.L.J. 514, 515 (1957). Should courts read injunctions like penal statutes? "It is the policy of this state to construe a penal statute as favorably to the defendant as its language and the circumstances of its application may reasonably permit; just as in the case of a question of fact, the defendant is entitled to the benefit of every reasonable doubt as to the true interpretation of words or the construction of language used in a statute." Keeler v. Superior Court, 2 Cal.3d 619, 631, 87 Cal.Rptr. 481, 488, 470 P.2d 617, 624 (1970). Todd, Vagueness Doctrine in the Federal Courts, 26 Stan.L.Rev. 855, 857–60 (1974).

2) If Lewis had sent the telegram below on April 5th and the "strike" had continued, would the court of appeals have affirmed contempt? "This office is compelled by a court order issued April 3 without notice to it to inform the members of the union to discontinue the work stoppage and to instruct all members to return to work. We order you to do that. This work stoppage was begun by miners in response to the coal operators' stubborn refusal to obey the contract and deal fairly with the miners' pensions. This office will continue to negotiate with the operators in the absence of a work stoppage ordered by the officers of the International Union until the operators have retreated from their heartless disobedience."

3) Identify the issue in the *Pension Fund Dispute.* Is it whether contemnors owed a duty to obey? Whether contemnors violated the injunction? Does anything but a strict and simple duty to obey or to effect compliance frustrate the administration of the substantive law? Does the standard for violation vary from criminal to compensatory and coercive contempt?

II. The Legislature's Domain

UNITED STATES v. HUDSON

11 U.S. (7 Cranch) 32, 33 L.Ed. 259 (1812).

This was a case certified from the Circuit Court for the District of Connecticut, in which, upon argument of a general demurrer to an *indictment* for a libel on the President and Congress of the United States, contained in the Connecticut Courant, of the 7th of May, 1806, charging them with having in secret voted two millions of dollars as a present to Bonaparte for leave to make a treaty with Spain, the judges of that Court were divided in opinion upon the question, *whether the Circuit Court of the United States had a common law jurisdiction in cases of libel.* . . .

[Opinion by JOHNSON, J.:]

The only question which this case presents is, whether the Circuit Courts of the United States can exercise a common law jurisdiction in criminal cases. We state it thus broadly because a decision on a case of libel will apply to every case in which jurisdiction is not vested in those courts by statute.

. . . For, the power which Congress possess to create Courts of inferior jurisdiction, necessarily implies the power to limit the jurisdiction of those Courts to particular objects; and when a Court is created, and its operations confined to certain specific objects, with what propriety can it assume to itself a jurisdiction—much more extended—in its nature very indefinite—applicable to a great variety of subjects—varying in every State in the Union—and with regard to which there exists no definite criterion of distribution between the district and Circuit Courts of the same district?

The only ground on which it has ever been contended that this jurisdiction could be maintained is, that, upon the formation of any political body, an implied power to preserve its own existence and promote the end and object of its creation, necessarily results to it. But, without examining how far this consideration is applicable to the peculiar character of our constitution, it may be remarked that it is a principle by no means peculiar to the common law. It is coeval, probably, with the first formation of a limited Government; belongs to a system of universal law, and may as well support the assumption of many other powers as those more peculiarly acknowledged by the common law of England.

But if admitted as applicable to the state of things in this country, the consequence would not result from it which is here contended for. If it may communicate certain implied powers to the general Government, it would not follow that the Courts of that Government are vested with jurisdiction over any particular act done by an individual in supposed violation of the peace and dignity of the sovereign power. The legislative authority of the Union must first make an act a crime, affix a punishment to it, and declare the Court that shall have jurisdiction of the offence.

Certain implied powers must necessarily result to our Courts of justice from the nature of their institution. But jurisdiction of crimes against the state is not among those powers. To fine for contempt—imprison for contumacy—enforce the observance of order, &c. are powers which cannot be dispensed with in a Court, because they are necessary to the exercise of all others: and so far our Courts no doubt possess powers not immediately derived from statute; but all exercise of criminal law cases we are of opinion is not within their implied powers.

---

1) *Hudson* serves two purposes. It protects citizens from a capricious and oppressive government. More specifically, it protects critics from retaliation. Is *Pentagon Papers*, p. 217 an equivalent curb on the executive's equitable initiative?

2) Should the Court have distinguished contempt from other crimes? In United States v. Dickinson, 465 F.2d 496, 513 (5th Cir. 1972), Judge Brown said: "Indeed, contempt may well be the last vestige of the so-called 'common law crimes,' insofar as a determination that particular conduct should be

punished as a contempt depends not so much on specific prohibited acts having occurred as on the Judge's subjective determination that the conduct was culpable, blameworthy, and deserving of punishment."

3) At the time United States v. Hudson was decided, a statute governed contempts, the Act of September 24, 1789, 1 Stat. 73, 83. It provided in Section 17:

> That all the said courts of the United States shall have power to . . . punish by fine or imprisonment, at the discretion of said courts, all contempts of authority in any cause or hearing before the same. . . .

Has Congress delegated its power to define criminal conduct to judges?

Judicial power to punish for contempt under § 17 was not questioned until 1830, and the courts regarded almost anything as contempt. Judge Peck punished one Lawless, a lawyer, for publishing an article criticizing one of Judge Peck's decisions. Lawless persuaded Congress to initiate impeachment proceedings against Peck for oppression. Peck was acquitted by a tie vote after a year of hearings. After the acquittal, James Buchanan presented a bill to Congress that became law and evolved into the present 18 U.S.C. § 401. (See Appendix) How does § 401 limit the contempt power that existed under the statute it replaced? Does § 401 meet the objection that in a limited government courts are also limited? Does it meet the objections to common law crimes? Does it pass the tests that proscribe vagueness and overbreadth? Do the checks of appeal, pardon, and impeachment rehabilitate it?

4) A series of Supreme Court decisions deal with state contempt convictions for critical comment on the judicial process. The later decisions apply a clear and present danger standard to reverse the contempts. Wood v. Georgia, 370 U.S. 375 (1962); Craig v. Harney, 331 U.S. 367 (1947); Pennekamp v. Florida, 328 U.S. 331 (1946); Bridges v. California, 314 U.S. 252 (1941); Patterson v. Colorado, 205 U.S. 454 (1907). Nye v. United States, 313 U.S. 33 (1941), overruled Toledo Newspaper Co. v. United States, 247 U.S. 402 (1918), and construed § 401 to eliminate federal judges' power to punish out of court publication absent an order. See Frankfurter and Landis, Power of Congress Over Procedure in Criminal Contempts in "Inferior" Federal Courts, 37 Harv.L.Rev. 1010 (1924); Nelles and King, Contempt by Publication in the United States, 28 Colum.L.Rev. 401 (1928); Schmidt, Nebraska Press Association: An Expansion of Freedom and Contraction of Theory, 29 Stan.L.Rev. 431, 433–36 (1977).

STATE EX REL. OREGON STATE BAR v. LENSKE

243 Ore. 477, 486, 405 P.2d 510, 407 P.2d 250 (1965).

[Lenske was convicted of federal income tax evasion. Before the conviction was reviewed on appeal, the Oregon State Bar filed a certified copy of the judgment of conviction with the Supreme Court of the State, which had previously adopted a rule providing that upon conviction of a crime involving moral turpitude a member of the bar could be summarily suspended. The Court then summarily entered an order suspending the defendant. A copy of the order was sent to both the Oregon State Bar and the defendant. Subsequently, the State Bar initiated contempt proceedings in the Oregon Supreme Court. The State Bar charged Lenske with having violated the Court's order of suspension by continuing to practice law and holding himself out to the public and members of the bar as eligible to practice law. The only instance detailed in the Court's opinion was when Lenske attempted to negotiate the settlement of a case he tried before the suspension. The Court concluded this was the practice of law, and that Lenske's belief that his tax evasion conviction would be reversed on appeal was no defense.]

HOLMAN, J. . . . This brings into question the extent of the court's power to punish for contempt. ORS 33.020(1) provides as follows:

". . . when the contempt is not one of those mentioned in paragraphs (a) and (b) of subsection (1) of ORS 33.010, or in subsection (1) of ORS 1.240, it must appear that the right or remedy of a party to an action, suit or proceeding was defeated or prejudiced thereby before the contempt can be punished otherwise than by a fine not exceeding $100."

Paragraphs (a) and (b) of subsection (1) of ORS 33.010 are as follows:

"(a) Disorderly, contemptuous or insolent behavior toward the judge, while holding the court, tending to impair its authority or to interrupt the due course of a trial or other judicial proceeding.

"(b) A breach of the peace, boisterous conduct or violent disturbance, tending to interrupt the due course of a trial or other judicial proceeding."

Subsection (1) of ORS 1.240 is as follows:

"(1) To preserve and enforce order in his immediate presence, and in the proceedings before him, when he is performing a duty imposed upon him by statute."

It is obvious that paragraphs (a) and (b) of subsection (1) of ORS 33.010 and subsection (1) of ORS 1.240 pertain to direct contempts in the presence of the court and have no application. It is also apparent that no right or remedy of a party was defeated by the defendant's action. Thus, under ORS 33.020(1), the imposition of a $100 fine is the maximum punishment for indirect contempts authorized by the legislature. . . .

The contempt power is the product of the early rule of English kings. It was the vehicle for assuring the efficiency, dignity of, and respect for the sovereign. As society became more diverse and extensive, the king found it necessary to have some aspects of his power exercised by representatives. The courts acted for the king and their exercise of the power arose from the presumed contempt of the king's authority. Gradually this basis shifted from a power of the courts as adjuncts of the king to one inherent in the courts themselves. It was one of the steps in the rise of the power of the courts in England.

This assumption of power was further enhanced in this country when the American colonies separated from England by revolution. The American system of government was based upon the constitutional separation of powers of the three established branches of government: the executive, the legislative, and the judicial. This reflected the early Americans' fear of the potential tyranny of concentrated power and was their effort to establish a system of checks and balances. See Goldfarb, The Contempt Power, ch. 1 (1963).

The separation of governmental powers is demonstrated in Article III, Section 1, Oregon Constitution, which is as follows:

"The powers of the Government shall be divided into three separate departments, the Legislative, the Executive, including the administrative, and the Judicial; and no person charged wtih official duties under one of these departments, shall exercise any of the functions of another, except as in this Constitution expressly provided."

Referring to the power of the court to punish for contempt, it was stated in Ex Parte Robinson, 86 U.S. (19 Wall.) 505, 510 (1873):

"The power to punish for contempts is inherent in all courts; its existence is essential to the preservation of order in judicial proceedings, and to the enforcement of the judgments, orders, and writs of the courts, and consequently to the due administration of justice. . . ."

It therefore follows that the legislature cannot unreasonably abridge or destroy the judicial power to punish for contempt because the legislature cannot take away a power which it does not give. . . . It may follow that the legislature has the authority to limit the court's power to punish for contempt where the court is a creature of the legislature and not constitutionally established. This question, however, does not have to be decided now as this is a constitutionally established court. Article VII, Section 1, Oregon Constitution.

. . . Many jurisdictions refuse to allow the legislature to abridge unreasonably a constitutionally established court's power to punish for contempt. [A Washington and a Michigan case were cited.] This is not the universal rule. The constitutions of five states (Arkansas, Georgia, Louisiana, Oklahoma, Virginia) specifically grant the legislature authority to regulate the judicial contempt power. Other courts concede the legislature this power. . . .

In most jurisdictions where the legislature is prohibited from unreasonably abridging or limiting the inherent judicial contempt power of the courts, it is nevertheless recognized that the legislature may make reasonable regulations covering the exercise of the power so long as the regulations do not substantially impair or destroy it. This prevents abuse of the court's power. . . .

We hold that the power of a constitutionally established court to punish for contempt may be regulated within reasonable bounds by the legislature but not to the extent that the court's power is substantially impaired or destroyed. The provision of ORS 33.020(1) limiting this court's power to punish for an indirect contempt to a fine of $100 except where the right or remedy of a party was prejudiced is an unreasonable limitation upon this court's inherent powers. It is therefore unconstitutional as applied to the facts here as it violates Article III, Section 1, of the Oregon Constitution in that it substantially destroys this court's power to enforce its lawful orders and decrees and is an attempted exercise of a judicial function by the legislative branch of government.

We realize that this is contrary to the following language in State v. Brownell [79 Ore. 123, 154 P. 428 (1916)]:

"It has been urged that, since constitutional courts have inherent power to punish for contempt, the Legislature has no power to limit their action in this respect. We do not regard section 671, L.O.L. [ORS 33.020(1)], as limiting their power to punish for contempt, but merely as prescribing the procedure for exercising such power. . . ."

This case was decided in 1916. At that time it might have been possible to consider a $100 fine as merely prescribing the procedure for exercising the contempt power. This is almost fifty years later, and what was then considered not to be a limitation upon the court's power most certainly is such a limitation now. The dollar has been devalued. . . .

This court therefore enters judgment of conviction against the defendant and sentences him to pay a fine in the sum of $500, payable to the Clerk of this Court within 20 days of the entry of the mandate. Upon the failure of the defendant to pay said fine within the allotted time, the Clerk is directed to issue a warrant for the arrest of the defendant and to direct the arresting officers to deliver him to the Sheriff of Multnomah County for incarceration in the county jail of said county to serve out said fine in accordance with the laws of this state relative to serving time for the nonpayment of fines in criminal matters.

---

1) A legislative limit on punishment checks judicial autonomy. Compare the Alabama statute in *Walker,* p. 286 to sections 401 and 402. A federal judge cannot, because of the "or" in § 401, sentence a criminal contemnor to both a fine and imprisonment. United States v. Barnette, 546 F.2d 187, 193 (5th Cir. 1977). Federal appellate courts review contempt sentences by asking whether the sentencing judge abused discretion, and appellate panels often reduce excessive criminal contempt sentences. Cheff v. Schnackenberg, 384 U.S. 373, 380 (1966); United States v. Green, 356 U.S. 165, 188 (1958); United States v. Green, 630 F.2d 566, 568–69 (8th Cir. 1980); United States v. Bukowski, p. 960. This contrasts sharply with their reticence in regular criminal appeals. Remember from *Mine Workers,* p. 839 that the Court converted criminal to coercive contempt. Does appellate vigilance substitute for a statutory limit on punishment?

2) The Kentucky court struck down, as an unconstitutional legislative infringement on the contempt power, a statute that limited the criminal penalty for refusing to testify to 24 hours imprisonment and a fine of $30. Arnett v. Meade, 462 S.W.2d 940 (Ky.1971).

IN RE MORRIS

194 Cal. 63, 227 P. 914 (1924).

MYERS, C. J. This matter comes before us on a writ of *habeas corpus.* The petitioner was charged, tried, and convicted in the police court of the city of Los Angeles, was sentenced to pay a fine of $250, and, in default of payment, to suffer ninety days' imprisonment in the city jail. He was charged with a misdemeanor under section 166, subdivision 4, of the Penal Code, which is as follows:

"Every person guilty of any contempt of court . . . of the following kinds is guilty of a misdemeanor: . . .

"4. Willful disobedience of any process or order lawfully issued by any court; . . ."

He was specifically charged with the willful disobedience of an order and injunction issued out of the superior court in and for the county of Sacramento in an action wherein the people of the State of California on the relation of the attorney-general was plaintiff against the Industrial Workers of the World . . .

. . . Summary proceedings for the punishment of contempt upon a rule or citation have always been recognized as *sui generis,* frequently arising in connection with civil actions, often partaking somewhat of the character of civil remedies, and always partaking largely of the character of criminal prosecutions. . . . These proceedings at the common law were spoken of as "criminal contempts" when they were directed primarily to the maintenance of the dignity and authority of the court, and as "civil contempts" when their primary object was the protection of the private rights of parties litigant. . . . Both of these classes of contempts are contemplated by and provided for in the provisions of our Code of Civil Procedure [sections 1209 to 1222] and are to be investigated and punished in the same manner and in accordance with the same rules. It is the plain intent of section 166 of the Penal Code, however, to give another and different aspect to the contempts there enumerated and to expressly attach to each of them the definite quality of a criminal offense. This intent is made certain when we refer to other sections of the same code. Section 11 thereof provides that, "This code does not affect any power conferred by law upon . . . any public body, tribunal or officer to impose or inflict punishment for a contempt." Section 657 provides, "A criminal act is not the less punishable as a crime because it is also declared to be punishable as a contempt." Section 658, "When it appears, at the time of passing sentence upon a person convicted upon indictment, that such person has already paid a fine or suffered an imprisonment for the act of which he stands convicted, under an order adjudging it a contempt, the court authorized to pass sentence may mitigate the punishment to be imposed, in its discretion."

. . . [Petitioner's argument] is . . . that the power to punish for contempt of its authority inheres in every court of record as an essential element of the jurisdiction vested in it by the constitution, without which it could not adequately function as a court; that by reason of the fundamental nature and purpose of this power it must be vested in each instance in that particular court whose order or authority has been contemned; that the legislature has no authority to take from the courts this essential power, that the attempt of the legislature to confer upon a police court the jurisdiction to punish a contempt consisting in the violation of an order of the superior court is in effect an attempt to take from the superior court an essential portion of its constitutional authority and is therefore void. From these premises petitioner deduces the conclusion that the jurisdiction to punish as a contempt the violation of an order issued by the superior court of Sacramento County is vested solely and exclusively in that court. If we were to regard petitioner's act solely as an offense against the dignity and authority of that court, we would agree with this conclusion . . . . But these cases do not hold that when an act which is a contempt of court is at the same time a specific criminal offense, denounced as such in the Penal Code, it will not be punishable as such. It was the plain intent of the legislature expressed in the cited code sections to give a double aspect to the wrongful acts there enumerated. In one aspect they are to be regarded as offenses against the dignity and authority of the court, remediable in accordance with the rules prescribed in the Code of Civil Procedure. In the other aspect they are to be regarded as offenses against the peace and dignity of the people of the state of California, and remediable as such in accordance with the rules prescribed in the Penal Code. It is apparent upon reflection that the same act may at the same time take on a third aspect in which it is to be regarded as an offense against private rights, and remediable as such by an ordinary action at law. Plainly the legislature did not intend to take away from the court contemned the power to punish a violator of its orders, but intended rather to provide an additional remedy which should be in a sense cumulative, and which should be available in the courts possessing the appropriate criminal jurisdiction. These remedies were not intended to be concurrent, but rather cumulative in character, though not strictly so, because each remedy is for a different offense, though the two offenses arise out of the same act.

Petitioner asserts that, regardless of the legislative intent, if we hold that jurisdiction herein was vested in the police court, the inevitable effect thereof will be to deprive the superior court of the power to punish its own contemners. He asserts that he, having been placed on trial in the police court, if thereafter haled before the superior court at Sacramento to answer for the same act as a contempt of that court, could then interpose a plea of once in jeopardy as a complete defense to that proceeding. He argues that the effect thereof would be to deprive the superior court of the power to punish for a violation of its own orders, because the violator, by the simple expedient of procuring himself to be charged in a police court or justice's court and there assessed a small penalty, could render himself immune to punishment by the court which he had contemned. The reasoning is sound, but it rests upon a false premise. The defense of once in jeopardy would not lie in such case because the two offenses are distinct and different, even though the act out of which they arise be the same. . . . In People v. Mead, 92 N.Y. 415, the defendant was indicted in one court upon a misdemeanor charge of contempt, consisting in the willful disobedience of an order which had been issued by another court. The indictment was based on section 143 of the New York Penal Code, which is identical with our section 166. All of our Penal Code sections bearing on the questions here under consideration were borrowed from the corresponding sections of the New York Penal Code, based on Field's draft. That case is therefore on all-fours with the one at bar. The court of appeals held that the defendant was subject to prosecution in that manner, saying:

"It was not necessary to the validity of the indictment that the accused should have been adjudged in contempt by the court whose process he disobeyed. The two proceedings are wholly independent of each other. One who disobeys the lawful order of a court not only offends against the dignity of the particular tribunal, but also against the public law. The particular court may pass over the contempt and suffer its order to be spurned, but the offense against the public remains. Their authority has been contemned, the administration of public justice assailed, and its power despised. For such an offense the guilty party may be punished by indictment, although the court whose order has been disobeyed may take the indignity in silence. The statute has made such disobedience, when willful in its character, an offense against the people, and not left it dependent upon the action or nonaction of the specific judge or court. The statute contemplates that both remedies or either may be pursued." . . .

We conclude that section 166 of the Penal Code is a remedial statute; that the remedy thus provided is intended to be cumulative or, rather, in addition to the remedies provided by the title of the Code of Civil Procedure on contempts; that the offenses denounced in the former code provision are separate and distinct from those denounced in the latter, and the question of "once in jeopardy" does not arise thereunder.

---

1) Would *Morris* survive contemporary double jeopardy standards? In Blockburger v. United States, 284 U.S. 299, 304 (1932), the Supreme Court stated in a noncontempt context: "The applicable rule is that where the same act or transaction constitutes a violation of two distinct statutory provisions, the test to be applied to determine whether there are two offenses or only one is whether each provision requires proof of a fact which the other does not." Mr. Justice Brennan, in his separate opinion in Abbate v. United States, 359 U.S. 187, 197 (1959), argued for an even stricter standard when the two offenses are prosecuted separately, rather than in one proceeding: "[S]uccessive federal prosecutions of the same person based on the same acts are prohibited by the Fifth Amendment even though brought under federal statutes requiring different evidence and protecting different federal interests." These standards govern federal prosecutions, but account must be taken of them in evaluating *Morris* because in Benton v. Maryland, 395 U.S. 784 (1969), the Supreme Court held the double jeopardy guarantee of the Fifth Amendment applicable to the States under the Fourteenth Amendment.

In Waller v. Florida, 397 U.S. 387 (1970), the Court precluded a second state court trial for an offense based on the same facts that supported conviction in an earlier municipal court trial. But in Bartkus v. Illinois, 359 U.S. 121 (1959), due process did not bar a state prosecution for violation of a state criminal statute after an acquittal for a federal offense involving the same evidence. Finally in Ashe v. Swenson, 397 U.S. 436 (1970), the Court held that in light of Benton v. Maryland, collateral estoppel "is embodied in the Fifth Amendment guarantee against double jeopardy." 397 U.S. at 445. Thus "when an issue of ultimate fact has once been determined by a valid and final judgment, that issue cannot be litigated between the same parties in any future lawsuit." 397 U.S. at 443.

In State v. Warren, 186 N.J.Super. 35, 451 A.2d 197 (1982), defendants refused to testify, were summarily convicted of contempt, and were sentenced to six-month terms. They were indicted for hindering the prosecution of another; they argued that the prosecutions were barred by the prohibition against double jeopardy. The court denied their motions to dismiss; but the court carefully distinguished contempt which occurred out of court, the kind we are studying.

Consider how these doctrines affect the four possibilities: a) contempt after a criminal conviction; b) contempt after a criminal acquittal; c) a criminal prosecution after a contempt conviction; d) a criminal prosecution after a contempt acquittal.

2) "[T]he Wisconsin Judicial Council concluded that as a matter of policy a person should not be punished twice for the same act. The policy behind the punitive sanction is the same as that behind a criminal sentence—a punishment imposed by the state upon antisocial conduct for the purpose of preventing similar conduct in the future by the person punished and by others. The state should be forced to choose which penalty—the punitive sanction or the criminal sentence—it thinks is most appropriate and pursue it. It should not be able to impose both, or failing to attain one be able to seek the other." Martineau, Contempt of Court: Eliminating the Confusion Between Civil and Criminal Contempt, 50 U.Cin.L.Rev. 677, 698 (1981). Thus the new Wisconsin contempt statute omitted a provision from the prior statute that a "person convicted of criminal contempt also could be convicted of any other criminal offense that the contumacious act might constitute." Should this affect the judge's power to employ coercive or compensatory orders? Suppose Witness refuses to testify and the judge orders her imprisoned to coerce testimony. The trial ends without Witness's testimony. The judge releases her. May the authorities then prosecute her either for criminal contempt or for a statutory crime, such as hindering prosecution? Suppose the judge enjoins Defendant from abusing his former spouse. He beats her. The judge sentences Defendant to six months for criminal contempt. May the former spouse seek a compensatory contempt award?

3) *Morris* was part of larger campaign. See also In re Wood, 194 Cal. 49, 227 P. 908 (1924), which contains the text of an injunction under the California criminal syndicalism law. Professor Murphy suggests that equitable antisyndicalism was part of the same trend as the equitable defamation struck down in *Near*, p. 189. Murphy, Near v. Minnesota in the Context of Historical Developments, 66 Minn.L.Rev. 95, 143 (1981). Brandenburg v. Ohio, 395 U.S. 444 (1969), probably completed the demise of syndicalism statutes and injunctions based on them.

4) *Morris* illustrates parts of the relationship between the criminal code and criminal contempt. Compare the federal statutes 18 U.S.C. §§ 402, 1509, 3691. May the legislature repeal § 401 or its equivalent and rely on a separate criminal offense such as § 1509 or the Field code statute discussed in *Morris*? Would the Executive's discretion to decline to prosecute interfere excessively with judicial independence? The next case addresses that problem. It grew out of the voting registration crises featured in United States v. Lynd litigation, p. 427 above. See J. Bass, Unlikely Heroes 164–68, 270 (1981); F. Read and L. McGough, Let Them Be Judged: The Judicial Integration of the Deep South 411–12 (1978).

III. Discretion to Prosecute

UNITED STATES v. COX

342 F.2d 167 (5th Cir. 1965).

Before TUTTLE, Chief Judge, and RIVES, JONES, BROWN, WISDOM, GEWIN and BELL, Circuit Judges.

JONES, Circuit Judge: On October 22, 1964, an order of the United States District Court for the Southern District of Mississippi, signed by Harold Cox, a judge of that Court, was entered. The order, with caption and formal closing omitted, is as follows:

"THE GRAND JURY, duly elected, impaneled and organized, for the Southern District of Mississippi, reconvened on order of the Court at 9:00 A.M., October 21, 1964, in Court Room Number 2 in Jackson, Mississippi, for the general dispatch of its business. The grand jury was fully instructed as to their duties, powers and responsibilities and retired to the grand jury room number 538 in the Federal Building at Jackson to do its work. The United States Attorney (and one of his assistants) sat with the grand jury throughout the day on October 21 and explained in detail to the grand jury the perjury laws and the Court's construction of such laws for their information. The grand jury heard witnesses throughout the day on October 21, 1964. On the morning of October 22, 1964, the grand jury, through its foreman, made known to the Court in open court that they had requested Robert E. Hauberg, United States Attorney, to prepare certain indictments which they desired to bring against some of the persons under consideration and about which they had heard testimony, and the United States Attorney refused to draft or sign any such indictments on instructions of the Acting Attorney General of the United States; whereupon the Court ordered and directed said United States Attorney to draft such true bills or no bills as the grand jury may have duly voted and desired to report and to sign such instruments as required by law under penalty of contempt. The United States Attorney was afforded one hour within which to decide as to whether or not he would abide by the instructions and order of the Court in such respect. At the end of such time, the Court re-convened and the United States Attorney was specifically asked in open court as to whether or not he intended to conform with the order and direction of the Court in said respects whereupon the United States Attorney answered that he respectfully declined to do so on instructions from Nicholas deB. Katzenbach, Acting Attorney General. He was thereupon duly adjudged by the Court to be in civil contempt of the Court and was afforded an opportunity to make any statement which he desired to make to the Court before sentence; whereupon the United States Attorney reiterated his inability to comply with the order of the Court upon express and direct instructions from Nicholas deB. Katzenbach, Acting Attorney General of the United States.

"WHEREFORE, IT IS ORDERED AND ADJUDGED by the Court that Robert E. Hauberg, United States Attorney, is guilty of civil contempt of this Court and in the presence of the Court for his said refusal to obey its said order and he is ordered into custody of the United States Marshal to be confined by him in the Hinds County, Mississippi, jail, there to remain until he purges himself of this contempt by agreeing to conform to said order by performing his official duty for the grand jury as requested in the several (about five) pending cases before them on October 21 and October 22, 1964.

"IT IS FURTHER ORDERED by the Court that a citation issue to Nicholas deB. Katzenbach, Acting Attorney General of the United States, directing him to appear before this Court and show cause why he should not be adjudged guilty of contempt of this Court for his instructions and directions to the United States Attorney to disregard and disobey the orders of this Court in the respects stated.

"The United States Attorney requested a stay of enforcement of this order and further proceedings herein for five days after this date to enable him to apply to the United States Court of Appeals for the Fifth Circuit for a writ of prohibition and such request is granted; and these proceedings and enforcement of this order in its entirety is stayed for five days, subject to the further orders of the United States Court of Appeals on said application; and for the enforcement of all of which, let proper process issue."

The United States Attorney, Robert E. Hauberg, and the Acting Attorney General, Nicholas deB. Katzenbach, have appealed from the order and they, joined by the United States, seek a writ of prohibition against the District Judge from enforcing the Court's order, and from asserting jurisdiction to require the Attorney General or the United States Attorney "to institute criminal prosecutions or to take any steps in regard thereto." The facts recited in the order are uncontroverted. . . . Although the issues here presented arose, in part at least, as an incident of a civil rights matter, no civil rights questions are involved in the rather broad inquiry which we are called upon to make.

The constitutional requirement of an indictment or presentment as a predicate to a prosecution for capital or infamous crimes has for its primary purpose the protection of the individual from jeopardy except on a finding of probable cause by a group of his fellow citizens, and is designed to afford a safeguard against oppressive actions of the prosecutor or a court. The constitutional provision is not to be read as conferring on or preserving to the grand jury, as such, any rights or prerogatives. The constitutional provision is, as has been said, for the benefit of the accused. The constitutional provision is not to be read as precluding, as essential to the validity of an indictment, the inclusion of requisites which did not exist at common law.

Traditionally, the Attorney for the United States had the power to enter a nolle prosequi of a criminal charge at any time after indictment and before trial, and this he could have done without the approval of the court or the consent of the accused. It may be doubted whether, before the adoption of the Federal Rules of Criminal Procedure, he had any authority to prevent the return of an indictment by a grand jury. There would be no constitutional barrier to a requirement that the signature of a United States Attorney upon an indictment is essential to its validity.

It is now provided by the Federal Rules of Criminal Procedure that the Attorney General or the United States Attorney may by leave of court file a dismissal of an indictment. Rule 48(a) Fed.Rules Crim.Proc. 18 U.S.C.A. In the absence of the Rule, leave of court would not have been required.

The purpose of the Rule is to prevent harassment of a defendant by charging, dismissing and re-charging without placing a defendant in jeopardy. . . . Rule 7 eliminates the necessity for the inclusion in an indictment of many of the technical and prolix averments which were required at common law, by providing that the indictment shall be a plain, concise and definite written statement of the essential facts constituting the offense charged. The Rule also provides that "It shall be signed by the attorney for the government." Rule 7(c) Fed.Rules Crim.Proc. 18 U.S.C.A.

The judicial power of the United States is vested in the federal courts, and extends to prosecutions for violations of the criminal laws of the United States. The executive power is vested in the President of the United States, who is required to take care that the laws be faithfully executed. The Attorney General is the hand of the President in taking care that the laws of the United States in legal proceedings and in the prosecution of offenses, be faithfully executed. The role of the grand jury is restricted to a finding as to whether or not there is probable cause to believe that an offense has been committed. The discretionary power of the attorney for the United States in determining whether a prosecution shall be commenced or maintained may well depend upon matters of policy wholly apart from any question of probable cause. Although as a member of the bar, the attorney for the United States is an officer of the court, he is nevertheless an executive official of the Government, and it is as an officer of the executive department that he exercises a discretion as to whether or not there shall be a prosecution in a particular case. It follows, as an incident of the constitutional separation of powers, that the courts are not to interfere with the free exercise of the discretionary powers of the attorneys of the United States in their control over criminal prosecutions. The provision of Rule 7, requiring the signing of the indictment by the attorney for the Government, is a recognition of the power of Government counsel to permit or not to permit the bringing of an indictment. If the attorney refuses to sign, as he has the discretionary power of doing, we conclude that there is no valid indictment. It is not to be supposed that the signature of counsel is merely an attestation of the act of the grand jury. The signature of the foreman performs that function. It is not to be supposed that the signature of counsel is a certificate that the indictment is in proper form to charge an offense. The sufficiency of the indictment may be tested before the court. Rather, we think, the requirement of the signature is for the purpose of evidencing the joinder of the attorney for the United States with the grand jury in instituting a criminal proceeding in the Court. Without the signature there can be no criminal proceeding brought upon an indictment. Substantial compliance rather than technical exactness meets the requirement of the rule. There seems to be no authority for the statement that the absence of a signature is not fatal. . . .

If it were not for the discretionary power given to the United States Attorney to prevent an indictment by withholding his signature, there might be doubt as to the constitutionality of the requirement of Rule 48 for leave of court for a dismissal of a pending prosecution.[9]

9. Consideration of the constitutionality of the rule is not necessary for the disposition of the matters before us.

Because, as we conclude, the signature of the Government attorney is necessary to the validity of the indictment and the affixing or withholding of the signature is a matter of executive discretion which cannot be coerced or reviewed by the courts, the contempt order must be reversed. It seems that, since the United States Attorney cannot be required to give validity to an indictment by affixing his signature, he should not be required to indulge in an exercise of futility by the preparation of the form of an indictment which he is unwilling to vitalize with his signature. Therefore he should not be required to prepare indictments which he is unwilling and under no duty to sign.

Judges Tuttle, Jones, Brown and Wisdom join in the conclusion that the signature of the United States Attorney is essential to the validity of an indictment. Judge Brown, as appears in his separate opinion, is of the view that the United States Attorney is required, upon the request of the grand jury, to draft forms of indictments in accordance with its desires. The order before us for review is in the conjunctive; it requires the United States Attorney to prepare and sign. A majority of the court having decided that the direction to sign is erroneous, the order on appeal will be reversed. . . .

Cox states the Executive's discretion to initiate criminal prosecution. In contempt, prosecutorial discretion is lodged in the court. Judges initiate criminal contempt. *Barnett,* the next decision, takes up the contempt equivalent of *Cox:* the decision to decline or to cease to prosecute. The *Cox* court is deeply concerned with the limits of judicial power. Does the *Barnett* court exercise its discretion consistently with a proper conception of the limits of the judicial power? V. Navasky, Kennedy Justice, Chapter 4 (1971); Chapters 9 and 13 of J. Bass's Unlikely Heroes (1981); and F. Read and L. McGough, Let Them Be Judged: The Judicial Integration of the Deep South 194–265 (1978), deal with other aspects of *Barnett.* While reading *Barnett,* ask yourself also whether the extraordinary quality of the events dilute its precedential value.

UNITED STATES v. BARNETT

1) Court of Appeals Decision of April 9, 1963—330 F.2d 369 (5th Cir.).

Before TUTTLE, Chief Judge, RIVES, CAMERON, JONES, BROWN, WISDOM, GEWIN and BELL, Circuit Judges.

PER CURIAM. The above members of the Court of Appeals for the Fifth Circuit, sitting en banc, being evenly divided in their opinion as to the correct answer to a question of law arising in this cause, and the Court, desiring instruction concerning it for the proper decision of the cause which is now pending before the Court, hereby certifies the following question to the United States Supreme Court:

Where charges of criminal contempt have been initiated in this Court of Appeals against two individuals, asserting that such individuals willfully disobeyed a temporary restraining order of the Court, which order was entered at the request of the United States, acting as amicus curiae pursuant to its appointment by an order of the Court which granted to it, among other rights, the right to initiate proceedings for injunctive relief, and the acts charged as constituting the alleged disobedience were of a character as to constitute also a criminal offense under an Act of Congress, are such persons entitled, upon their demand, to trial by jury for the criminal contempt with which they are charged?

A statement of the nature of this cause and of the facts on which the certified question arises, as required by Supreme Court Rules 28–29 follows:

1. The case presents the certified question of law relating to criminal contempt arising out of the case of Meredith, et al. v. Fair, et al., 5 Cir., 313 F.2d 534. This Court in the opinion of June 25, 1962, in Meredith v. Fair, 5 Cir., 1962, 305 F.2d 343, cert. denied, 1962, 371 U.S. 828, reversed the decision of the District Court and remanded it with directions.[1]

Thereafter on July 27, 1962, this Court by opinion and order at 306 F.2d 374, took further action. After setting aside a stay of execution of this Court's mandate pursuant to 28 U.S.C.A. § 2101(f) by one of the Judges of this Court, the Court then directed that its mandate be recalled and amended in order to make "explicit the meaning that was implicit in this Court's conclusions as expressed throughout its opinion in this cause, dated June 25, 1962." 306 F.2d 374, 378. The opinion then prescribed the terms of the amended mandate and order. The case was reversed and remanded with directions to the District Court "to grant all relief prayed for . . . and to issue forthwith a permanent injunction against each and all of the defendants-appellees . . . enjoining and compelling each and all of them to admit . . . Meredith, to the University of Mississippi . . . . Such injunction shall in terms prevent and prohibit said defendants-appellees, or any of the classes of persons referred to from excluding the plaintiff-appellant from admission to continued attendance at the Univeristy of Mississippi. . . ." This Court then said it would order its own injunction in these terms:

"Pending such time as the District Court has issued and enforced the orders herein required and until such time as there has been full and actual compliance in good faith with each and all of said orders by the actual admission of plaintiff-appellant to, and the continued attendance thereafter at the University of Mississippi, this Court herewith issues its own preliminary injunction enjoining and compelling each and all of said parties to admit plaintiff-appellant to, and allow his continual attendance at the University of Mississippi, further prohibiting and preventing said parties or any of them from excluding said plaintiff-appellant from attendance to and continued attendance thereafter on the same basis as other students at the University of Mississippi." 306 F.2d 374, 378.

2. On July 28, 1962, a formal order was entered by this Court in like terms to effectuate the amended mandate and orders to the District Court and providing for the preliminary injunction issued by this Court. This or-

1. On January 12, 1962, this Court at 298 F.2d 696 affirmed the denial of the preliminary injunction by the District Court and issued the Court's mandate forthwith to permit an early trial on the merits. On February 12, 1962, at 305 F.2d 341, the Court denied Meredith's application for a preliminary injunction pending appeal from the denial of injunctive relief by the District Court following trial on the merits.

der was also stayed, but on August 4, 1962, this Court vacated the stay or stays granted on July 28 and July 31, 1962.

This order likewise being stayed, the matter was presented by Meredith to Mr. Justice Black, Circuit Justice, who on September 10, 1962, vacated all of these stays with the further order "that the judgment and mandate of the Court of Appeals shall be effective immediately" and "pending final action by this Court on the petition for writ of certiorari" the "respondents be, and they are hereby enjoined from taking any steps to prevent enforcement of the United States Court of Appeals' judgment and mandate."[3] . . .

3. On September 18, 1962, this Court (Judges Brown, Wisdom and Bell), after first ascertaining from the District Court that it declined to enter an order in this form, entered its order allowing the United States to appear in the case. The order recited "It appearing from the application of the United States, filed this day, that the interests of the United States in the due administration of justice and the integrity of the processes of its courts should be presented in these proceedings . . ."; the order then prescribed:

"It is ordered that the United States be designated and authorized to appear and participate as amicus curiae in all proceedings in this action before this Court and by reason of the mandates and orders of this Court of July 27, 28, 1962, and subsequently thereto, also before the District Court for the Southern District of Mississippi to accord each court the benefit of its views and recommendations, with the right to submit pleadings, evidence, arguments and briefs and to initiate such further proceedings, including proceedings for injunctive relief and proceedings for contempt of court, as may be appropriate in order to maintain and preserve the due administration of justice and the integrity of the judicial processes of the United States."

4. On September 20, 1962, the United States filed an application for further injunctive orders. This verified petition brought to the attention of this Court the fact that on September 19, 1962, in Meadors et al v. James Meredith et al, the Chancery Court, Second District, Jones County, Mississippi, Cause No. 19365, had issued its injunction against Meredith, the Board of Trustees, various University officials, the United States Department of Justice, the Federal Bureau of Investigation, the Office of the Attorney General of the United States, and all United States Marshals and Deputy Marshals. The order of the State Court enjoined and prohibited such persons "from doing anything or performing any act, the execution of which is intended to enroll and register the Negro, James Meredith, as a student in the University of Mississippi . . . ."

The Government's application also advised the Court of the enactment by the Mississippi Legislature approved by the Governor of Mississippi, Senate Bill No. 1501, the effect of which made it a criminal offense for a person against whom any "criminal proceeding is pending" to ". . . attempt

3. On September 13, 1962, the District Court entered its injunction reciting that "This matter is now before this Court by virtue of the mandate of the United States Court of Appeals for the Fifth Circuit and the mandate of Mr. Justice Black of September 10, 1962, setting aside all stays . . . and putting into effect the mandates of the Court of Appeals for the Fifth Circuit . . . of July 17, 1962, July 27, 1962 and . . . its final order of August 4, 1962 . . . ." Race Relations Law Reporter p. 746.

. . . to enroll in any of the institutions" of higher learning specified in the Act. The application likewise informed the Court of the action of the Justice of the Peace Court in Jackson, Mississippi, on September 20, 1962.

On September 20, 1962, this Court (Circuit Judges Brown, Wisdom and Bell) entered its further injunctive order. It recited that "This matter is now before this Court on Petitions for Orders supplementing this Court's Order of July 28, 1962, to (1) restrain the enforcement of S.B. 1501 . . . ; (2) restrain any compliance with or enforcement of the injunction issued by the Chancery Court of Jones County, Mississippi, dated September 19, 1962 . . . ; (3) restrain the arrest of James Meredith on a conviction had in the Justice of the Peace Court in Jackson, Mississippi, on September 20, 1962 . . . ." The Court further recited that it "appearing that S.B. 1501, the aforesaid injunction issued by the State Court, and the conviction of James Meredith each constitute an interference with and obstruction of this Court's injunction of July 28, 1962." This Court thereupon ordered "that the appellees-respondents, their agents, employees and persons acting in concert with them or persons having actual notice of this order, including law enforcement and public officials in Mississippi, State, County and Municipal . . . " were enjoined and restrained from "(1) enforcing . . . the provisions of S.B. 1501 against James Meredith, or any other persons . . . ; (2) taking any steps to effectuate the conviction and sentence on September 20, 1962, in the Justice of the Peace Court in Jackson, Mississippi . . . , or arresting him or any other persons including federal officials or taking . . . any other action which has the purpose or effect of interfering with the enrollment of James Meredith . . . ; (3) taking or refraining from taking any action to comply with or to enforce the injunction issued by the Chancery Court of Jones County, Mississippi, on September 19, 1962 . . . ." The order concluded with this paragraph: "(4) This order is not intended to limit the authority of the District Court to proceed with respect to the matters referred to in paragraphs (1) and (2) of this order."

5. On September 21, 1962, the United States, amicus curiae, filed an application seeking an order to show cause why the Board of Trustees and certain administrative officials of the University should not be held in civil contempt.

This Court (Circuit Judges Brown, Wisdom and Bell) on September 21, 1962, entered its show cause order. The order recited that it "appearing from the application of the United States, amicus curiae, filed this day, that each of the defendants above named has failed and refused to comply with the terms of this Court's order of July 28, 1962, and are presently persisting in such failure and refusal . . . ." Thereupon the Court ordered that the named trustees "appear personally before this Court on September 24, 1962, at 11 a.m. o'clock in the Courtroom of the United States Court of Appeals for the Fifth Circuit in New Orleans, Louisiana, to show cause, if any they have, why they should not be held in civil contempt." The order went on to provide, however, that since the Court was advised that the District Court had ordered the named University administrative officials to show cause and that a hearing on the alleged contempt was then fixed for hearing in the District

Court for that day (September 21, 1962), the application to that extent was denied.[8]

6. On September 22, 1962, this Court (Circuit Judges Brown, Wisdom and Bell) entered its further show cause order. The order recited that it ". . . appearing from the verified petition of the United States of America, that [the named administrative officials of the University of Mississippi] together with the other respondents named in this Court's order of September 21, 1962, have failed and refused, and are now failing and refusing, to comply with this Court's order of July 28, 1962, . . . by failing and refusing to enroll and register, and admit to continued attendance at the University of Mississippi, James Howard Meredith . . . ." The Court thereupon ordered the named administrative officials "be made additional respondents to the show cause order of this Court of September 21, 1962, and that they show cause, if any they have, on September 24, 1962 . . ." at New Orleans why they should "not be held in civil contempt by reason of their failure and refusal to obey the order of this Court of July 28, 1962, and the other orders of this Court requiring the respondents to register and enroll and admit to continued attendance at the University of Mississippi James Howard Meredith."

7. By a majority vote of all of the active Judges, this Court convened (Judge Cameron absent on account of illness) en banc for the hearing of September 24, 1962, at New Orleans. On that hearing the Court heard extensive testimony bearing upon actions of the Board of Trustees, the administrative officials of the University, Governor Ross Barnett and other governmental officials showing that up to that time Meredith, although he had presented himself for admission, had not been admitted to the University as previously ordered by this Court. This evidence included the fact of the Board of Trustees' resolution of September 20, 1962, by which the Board invested Governor Barnett "with the full power, authority, right and discretion of this Board to act upon all matters pertaining to or concerned with the registration or non-registration, admission or non-admission and/or attendance or non-attendance of James H. Meredith . . . and that a certified copy of this Resolution together with copies of the conflicting injunctions of Honorable S. C. Mize dated September 13, 1962, and Chancellor L. B. Porter dated September 19, 1962 previously served upon the members of this Board, be furnished to the Governor . . . for such course of action as the Governor shall deem legal, fit and proper in the premises." The evidence also included the Governor's published television speech to the people of Mississippi which included the following statement:

". . . Therefore, in obedience to legislative and constitutional sanction, I interpose the rights of the Sovereign State of Mississippi to enforce its laws and regulate its internal affairs without interference on the part of the Federal Government or its officers and, in my official capacity as Governor of the State of Mississippi, I hereby make this proclamation:

"—Whereas, the United States of America consists of fifty Sovereign States bound together basically for their common welfare; and

8. The District Court on September 21, 1962, after hearing found each of the University officials not guilty and discharged the contempt proceedings. 7 Race Relations Law Reporter 754.

"—Whereas, the Constitution of the United States of America provides that each state is sovereign with respect to certain rights and powers; and

"—Whereas, pursuant to the 10th Amendment to the Constitution of the United States, the powers not specifically delegated to the Federal Government are reserved to the several states; and

"—Whereas, the operation of the public school system is one of the powers which was not delegated to the Federal Government, but which was reserved to the respective states pursuant to the terms of the 10th Amendment; and

"—Whereas, we are now face to face with the direct usurpation of this power by the Federal Government through the illegal use of the judicial decree:

"Now, therefore, I, Ross R. Barnett, as Governor of the Sovereign State of Mississippi, by authority vested in me, do hereby proclaim that the operation of the public schools, universities and colleges of the State of Mississippi is vested in the duly-elected and appointed officials of the State of Mississippi and I hereby direct each of said officials to uphold and enforce the laws duly and legally enacted by the Legislature of the State of Mississippi, regardless of this unwarranted and illegal and arbitrary usurpation of power; and to interpose the State Sovereignty and themselves between the people of the state and any body-politic seeking to usurp such power."

In the course of that hearing the President of the Board of Trustees of Higher Learning announced in open court on behalf of himself and the 12 members of the Board "that the Board was now ready and willing to fully perform all things ordered and directed by the former orders of this Court . . . ." Likewise, the Registrar of the University of Mississippi "announced in open court that he would be available in Jackson, Mississippi, not later than 1:00 p.m. on September 25, 1962, for the purpose of registering and admitting as a student . . . James H. Meredith in accordance with the orders of this Court . . . ."

8. At the conclusion of the hearing, the Court en banc entered its order of September 24, 1962.

After reciting the statements by the President of the Board of Trustees and the Registrar quoted in the preceding paragraph, the Court ordered the respondents to "fully and completely comply with all of the terms of the order of this Court dated July 28, 1962, including, but not limited to . . ." specific actions described in subparagraphs a, b, c, d, e. Subparagraph (b) required that the Board "revoke and rescind the action of the Board taken on September 20, 1962, appointing Ross R. Barnett, . . . as the agent of the Board to act upon all matters pertaining to the registration and admission of James H. Meredith." Subparagraph (d) required the Board to instruct the University officials "to register and receive James H. Meredith for actual admission . . ." and attendance at the University. Subparagraph (e) required that the Registrar "be available at Jackson, Mississippi, at the office of the . . . Board of Trustees, at the hours therein specified on September 25, 1962, for the purpose of the registration of the said James H. Meredith and his actual admission to, and the continued attendance thereafter at, the University. The order required counsel for the respondents to advise the Court by 6:00 p.m., September 25, 1962, as to the actions taken to comply with this order.

9. On the evening of September 24, 1962, the Government presented to this Court an application for a temporary restraining order against the State of Mississippi, Ross R. Barnett, Governor, the Attorney General, the Commissioner of Public Safety, two District Attorneys, various Sheriffs, Chiefs of Police, and all Sheriffs of the Counties of Mississippi. At 8:30 o'clock a.m., September 25, 1962, this Court (Chief Judge Tuttle, Circuit Judges Rives and Wisdom) entered its temporary restraining order. That order recites that it appeared "from the verified petition of the United States, amicus curiae . . . that the State of Mississippi, Ross R. Barnett, Governor [and the others mentioned] . . . threatened to implement and enforce, unless restrained by order of this Court, the provisions of a Resolution of Interposition . . . , the provisions of § 4065.3 of the Mississippi Code, and a proclamation of Ross R. Barnett invoking the doctrine of Interposition . . . ; that Paul G. Alexander has instituted two criminal prosecutions against . . . Meredith on account of the efforts of . . . Meredith to enroll in the University . . . pursuant to the orders of this Court; that A. L. Meador, Sr. . . . on September 19, 1962, instituted in the Chancery Court of the Second Judicial District of Jones County, Mississippi, a civil action against . . . Meredith to prevent him from attending the University . . . ; that on September 20, 1962, James Howard Meredith, while seeking to enroll at the University . . . in Oxford, Mississippi, pursuant to the orders of this Court, was served with a writ of injunction issued by the Chancery Court of Lafayette County, Mississippi at the instance of Ross R. Barnett, enjoining James Howard Meredith from applying to or attending the University of Mississippi; that on September 20, 1962, the State of Mississippi enacted Senate Bill 1501, the effect of which is to punish James Howard Meredith should he seek enrollment in the University . . . ." The Court proceeded to find that "the effect of the conduct of the defendants herein named in implementing the policy of the State of Mississippi as proclaimed by Ross R. Barnett will necessarily be to prevent the carrying out of the orders of this Court and of the District Court for the Southern District of Mississippi; and that the acts and conduct of the defendants named in the petition will cause immediate and irreparable injury to the United States consisting of the impairment of the integrity of its judicial processes, the obstruction of the due administration of justice, and the deprivation of rights under the Constitution and laws of the United States . . . ." On the basis of this, the Court entered its temporary restraining order as to the State of Mississippi, Ross R. Barnett, the Attorney General and others restraining them from:

"1. Arresting, attempting to arrest, prosecuting or instituting any prosecution against James Howard Meredith under any statute, ordinance, rule or regulation whatever, on account of his attending, or seeking to attend, the University of Mississippi;

"2. Instituting or proceeding further in any civil action against James Howard Meredith or any other persons on account of James Howard Meredith's enrolling or seeking to enroll, or attending the University of Mississippi;

"3. Injuring, harassing, threatening or intimidating James Howard Meredith in any other way or by any other means on account of his attending or seeking to attend the University of Mississippi;

"4. Interfering with or obstructing by any means or in any manner the performance of obligations or the enjoyment of rights under this Court's order of July 28, 1962 and the order of the United States District Court for the Southern District of Mississippi entered September 13, 1962, in this action, and

"5. Interfering with or obstructing, by force, threat, arrest or otherwise, any officer or agent of the United States in the performance of duties in connection with the enforcement of, and the prevention of obstruction to, the orders entered by this Court and the District Court for the Southern District of Mississippi relating to the enrollment and attendance of James Howard Meredith at the University of Mississippi; or arresting, prosecuting or punishing such officer or agent on account of his performing or seeking to perform such duty.

"IT IS FURTHER ORDERED that Paul G. Alexander and J. Robert Gilfoy be temporarily restrained from proceeding further, serving or enforcing any process or judgment, or arresting James Howard Meredith in connection with the criminal actions against him in the Justice of the Peace Court of Hinds County, Mississippi.

"IT IS FURTHER ORDERED that A. L. Meador, Sr., be temporarily restrained from taking any further action or seeking to enforce any judgments entered in the case of A. L. Meador, Sr., v. James Meredith, et al.

"IT IS FURTHER ORDERED that Ross R. Barnett be temporarily restrained from enforcing or seeking to enforce against James Howard Meredith, any process or judgment in the case of State of Mississippi, Ex Rel. Ross Barnett, Governor v. James H. Meredith."

10. Later that same night, September 25, 1962, this Court (Circuit Judges Rives, Wisdom and Gewin) entered an order requiring Ross R. Barnett to appear "personally before this Court on September 28, 1962, at 10:00 o'clock in the Courtroom of the United States Court of Appeals for the Fifth Circuit, . . . New Orleans, Louisiana, to show cause, if any he has, why he should not be held in civil contempt of the temporary restraining order entered by the Court this day."

This order recited the matters occurring in open court on September 24, and the orders heretofore described issued to the Board of Trustees and the administrative officials of the University and the issuance earlier that day of the temporary restraining order. The order then recited that it "appearing from the verified application of the United States, amicus curiae herein, that on the afternoon of this day Ross R. Barnett, having been served with a copy of the temporary restraining order . . . having actual knowledge of the terms of that order, deliberately prevented James H. Meredith from entering the office of the Board of Trustees in Jackson, Mississippi at a time when James H. Meredith was seeking to appear before Robert B. Ellis in order to register . . . and that by such conduct Ross R. Barnett did willfully interfere with and obstruct James H. Meredith in the enjoyment of his rights under this Court's order of July 28, 1962, and did willfully interfere with and obstruct Robert B. Ellis in the performance of his obligations under this

Court's order of July 28, 1962, all in violation of the terms of the temporary restraining order entered by the Court this day." . . .

[A similar order was entered against Lt. Gov. Paul Johnson on September 26.]

12. On September 28, 1962, this Court sitting en banc (Judge Cameron not sitting) heard the order to show cause as to Ross R. Barnett. It heard witnesses in open court including documentary evidence consisting of moving picture newsreel pictures of the occurrences by Ross R. Barnett during the efforts of James H. Meredith to enter the offices of the University of Mississippi at Jackson, Mississippi, for the purpose of registering and attending the University. This evidence included a copy of the terms of the Governor's proclamation addressed to James H. Meredith on September 25, 1962. It proclaimed:

"I, Ross R. Barnett, Governor of the State of Mississippi, having heretofore by proclamation, acting under the police powers of the State of Mississippi, interposed the sovereignty of this State on September 20, 1962, denied to you, James H. Meredith, admission to the University of Mississippi under such proclamation and for such reasons, do hereby finally deny you admission to the University of Mississippi."

At the conclusion of these hearings on September 28, the Court entered its order, findings of fact and conclusions of law and judgment of civil contempt.

The order recited that though required to appear in person, Ross R. Barnett failed to appear or respond in person or by counsel, but that upon hearing the evidence, it made its findings of fact based thereon, as follows:

1. Since this Court entered its order of July 28, 1962, and the District Court for the Southern District of Mississippi entered its order on September 13, 1962, requiring the admission of James H. Meredith to the University of Mississippi, Ross R. Barnett, as Governor of the State of Mississippi, has issued a series of proclamations calling upon all officials of the state to prevent and obstruct the carrying out of the Court's orders with respect to the admission of James H. Meredith to the University. Two of these proclamations were issued by Ross R. Barnett on September 24 and September 25, 1962.

2. On September 25, 1962, this Court entered its temporary restraining orders restraining Ross R. Barnett from interfering with or obstructing in any manner or by any means the enjoyment of rights or the performance of obligations under this Court's order of July 28, 1962 and the order of the District Court of September 13, 1962.

3. At approximately 4:30 P.M. on September 25, 1962, Ross R. Barnett, having full knowledge of the existence and terms of this Court's temporary restraining orders, went to the office of the Board of Trustees of Institutions of Higher Learning to Jackson, Mississippi at a time when James H. Meredith was due to appear at the office to be enrolled as a student in the University of Mississippi, pursuant to the order of this Court. When James H. Meredith arrived at the office and sought to enter for the purpose of enrolling, Ross R. Barnett deliberately prevented him from entering and told him that his application for enrollment was denied by Ross R. Barnett.

4. On September 26, 1962, James H. Meredith sought to enter the campus of the University of Mississipi in Oxford, Mississippi. He was prevented

from entering by Paul B. Johnson, Jr., Lieutenant Governor of the State of Mississippi, acting pursuant to the instructions and under the authorization of Ross R. Barnett.

5. The conduct of Ross R. Barnett in preventing James H. Meredith from enrolling as a student in the University of Mississippi has been with the deliberate and announced purpose of preventing compliance with the orders of this and other federal courts.

On the basis of these findings, this Court concluded that "Ross R. Barnett is in contempt of the temporary restraining orders entered by this Court on September 25, 1962," and it thereupon "ordered, adjudged and decreed that: Ross R. Barnett is in civil contempt . . . ; that such contempt is continuing; . . . " and thereafter civil sanctions were imposed in the following terms:

" . . . Ross R. Barnett shall be committed to and remain in the custody of the Attorney General of the United States and shall pay a fine to the United States of $10,000 per day unless on or before Tuesday, October 2nd, 1962 at 11:00 A.M. he shows to this Court that he [is] fully complying with the terms of the restraining orders, and that he has notified all law enforcement officers and all other officers under his jurisdiction or command:

"(a) To cease forthwith all resistance to and interference with the orders of this Court and the District Court for the Southern District of Mississippi;

"(b) To maintain law and order at and around the University and to cooperate with the officers and agents of this Court and of the United States in the execution of the orders of this Court and of the District Court for the Southern District of Mississippi to the end that James H. Meredith be permitted to register and remain as a student at the University of Mississippi under the same conditions as apply to all other students."

Judges Jones, Gewin and Bell dissented from that part of the judgment imposing a fine upon Governor Barnett. . . .

14. On October 2, 1962, pursuant to the time fixed in the contempt order of September 28, 1962, Governor Ross R. Barnett appeared before this Court through his counsel. In answer to questions from the Court, counsel stated that Governor Barnett was in full compliance with the Court's orders and would fully comply with the orders of the Court in the future to the extent to which he was able to do so. Upon this representation being made, the matter was continued until October 12, 1962, for further hearing before the Court en banc.

15. On October 12 in New Orleans the Court en banc (Judges Hutcheson and Cameron not sitting) held a further hearing on whether Governor Ross R. Barnett and Paul B. Johnson, Jr. had purged themselves. Submitted also was the motion filed by the State of Mississippi to dissolve the temporary restraining order and to dismiss the pending contempt proceedings. In connection with the question of whether he had purged himself of the civil contempt as previously adjudged, Respondent Barnett did not appear in person on October 12, but again he appeared by counsel. Counsel offered no proof, either by affidavit, oral testimony, or otherwise, bearing on the conduct of respondent following the contempt judgment. However, on that date counsel for Governor Barnett retracted their statements that Governor

Barnett intended in the future fully to comply so far as he was able with the orders of the Court. Moreover, on October 19th Governor Barnett filed a response through his counsel to which he attached a statement which he had publicly delivered on October 17. The substance and effect of this statement, and thus the substance and effect of Respondent's posture before this Court, is that Governor Barnett will, and must, reserve the right to determine whether compliance with, and enforcement of, this Court's orders are consistent with his duties, rights and obligations as Governor of the State of Mississippi. [The full text of this statement is set out in note 2 of Judge Wisdom's dissent below.]

However, the record shows that he did, in fact, between the contempt order of the Court on September 28, 1962, and the hearing on October 2, 1962, cease the physical resistance to the order of the Court directing the admission of James H. Meredith as a student at the University, which he had previously interposed personally and through other state officials. On the 30th day of September, 1962, the President of the United States issued a proclamation in the following language:

"Whereas the Governor of the State of Mississippi and certain law enforcement officers and other officials of that State, and other persons, individually and in unlawful assemblies, combinations and conspiracies, have been and are willfully opposing and obstructing the enforcement of orders entered by the United States District Court for the Southern District of Mississippi and the United States Court of Appeals for the Fifth Circuit; and

"Whereas such unlawful assemblies, combinations and conspiracies oppose and obstruct the execution of the laws of the United States, impede the course of justice under those laws and make it impracticable to enforce those laws in the State of Mississippi by the ordinary course of judicial proceedings; and

"Whereas I have expressly called the attention of the Governor of Mississippi to the perilous situation that exists and to his duties in the premises, and have requested but have not received from him adequate assurances that the orders of the courts of the United States will be obeyed and that law and order will be maintained;

"Now, therefore, I, John F. Kennedy, President of the United States, under and by virtue of the authority vested in me by the Constitution and laws of the United States, including Chapter 15 of Title 10 of the United States Code, particularly sections 332, 333 and 334 thereof, do command all persons engaged in such obstructions of justice to cease and desist therefrom and to disperse and retire peacefully forthwith.

"In witness whereof, I have hereunto set my hand and caused the seal of the United States of America to be affixed.

"Done at the city of Washington this 30th day of September in the year of our Lord Nineteen Hundred and Sixty-Two, and of the independence of the United States of America the One Hundred and Eighty-Seventh.

"/s/ JOHN F. KENNEDY"

The President also issued an executive order as a result of which a large force of United States Marshals and a part of the Army and Air Forces of the United States were employed for the enforcement of our orders.

16. At that hearing the Court also considered the motion to dissolve the temporary restraining order and the motions of the United States to enter a preliminary injunction. The Court again heard and received all of the evidence that had previously been offered at the hearing of September 28 and 29.

17. On October 19, 1962, a majority of this Court en banc (Judges Hutcheson and Cameron not sitting and Judges Gewin and Bell stating that they thought the matter should be remanded to the District Court for further proceedings) entered its preliminary injunction. The seven members of the Court unanimously concluded:

"The posture of this case at the time this motion for temporary injunction and the accompanying motion for temporary restraining order were filed, is that this Court had issued its injunction, above referred to, prohibiting the officials of the University and the Trustees of the Institutions of Higher Learning of the State of Mississippi from interfering with the admission of James H. Meredith and his continuance as a student in the University of Mississippi, and also prohibiting certain of the defendants now before the Court from further prosecuting criminal proceedings against the said Meredith; whereupon, it was alleged in this petition, the State of Mississippi, through its official state policy, pursuant to actions of its Legislature, and through the actions of its Governor by proclamation, and all of the other respondents, were then engaged in actively frustrating the execution of this Court's injunction against the officials of the University. This proceeding, therefore, is purely ancillary to the original lawsuit, and this Court has ample power to proceed against any party, including the State of Mississippi, which is shown to be engaged in a wilful, intentional effort to frustrate this Court's injunction.

"The motion to dissolve the restraining order and the motion to dismiss the contempt proceedings by the State of Mississippi are, therefore, denied.

"The ruling just stated equally disposes of the contention made by the respondents that this Court is now powerless to issue the temporary injunction. We, therefore, hold that the Court has the power to issue the injunction against the persons not previously named as defendants in a main suit to prevent their active interference with this Court's injunction. . . ."

18. Thereafter this Court (Judges Hutcheson and Cameron not sitting) entered its order of November 15, 1962, which ordered that "The Attorney General of the United States and such Attorneys in the Department of Justice as he may designate, be and they hereby are appointed by the Court to institute and to prosecute criminal contempt proceedings against the said Ross R. Barnett and Paul B. Johnson, Jr., pursuant to Rule 42b of the Federal Rules of Criminal Procedure and the order of this Court of September 18, 1962."

. . .

19. Thereafter the United States through the Attorney General filed on December 21, 1962, its application for an order requiring Ross R. Barnett and Paul B. Johnson, Jr. to show cause why they should not be held in criminal contempt. . . .

20. On January 3, 1963, the Court entered an order constituting the Court en banc for the consideration of all matters relating to criminal con-

tempt proceedings against Ross R. Barnett and Paul B. Johnson, Jr. (Judge Hutcheson "is excused from participating in the hearings and decisions of this Court by reason of conditions of his health").

21. Thereafter this Court en banc (Judges Cameron and Gewin dissenting) entered its order to show cause on January 4, 1963. The show cause order contained the following charges and order:

"Probable cause has been made to appear from the application of the Attorney General filed December 21, 1962, in the name of and on behalf of the United States that on September 25, 1962, Ross R. Barnett, having been served with and having actual notice of this Court's temporary restraining order of September 25, 1962, wilfully prevented James H. Meredith from entering the offices of the Board of Trustees of the University of Mississippi in Jackson, Mississippi, and thereby deliberately prevented James H. Meredith from enrolling as a student in the University pursuant to this Court's order of July 28, 1962; . . . that on September 27, 1962, Ross R. Barnett and Paul B. Johnson, Jr. wilfully failed to take such measures as were necessary to maintain law and order upon the campus of the University of Mississippi and did, instead, direct and encourage certain members of the Mississippi Highway Safety Patrol, Sheriffs and deputy Sheriffs and other officials of the State of Mississippi to obstruct and prevent the entry of James H. Meredith upon the campus of the University that day; that on September 30, 1962, Ross R. Barnett, knowing of the planned entry of James H. Meredith upon the campus of the University of Mississippi, knowing that disorders and disturbances had attended and would attend such entry, and knowing that any failure of the Mississippi Highway Patrol to take all possible measures for the maintenance of peace and order upon the campus could and would result in interferences with and obstructions to the carrying out of the Court's order of July 28, 1962, wilfully failed to exercise his responsibility, authority, and influence as Governor to maintain law and order upon the campus of the University of Mississippi; and that all of said acts, omissions and conduct of Ross R. Barnett and Paul B. Johnson, Jr., were for the purpose of preventing compliance with this Court's order of July 28, 1962, and of the similar order of the United States District Court for the Southern District of Mississippi, entered on September 13, 1962, and were in wilful disobedience and defiance of the temporary restraining order of this Court entered on September 25, 1962.

"IT IS ORDERED that Ross R. Barnett and Paul B. Johnson Jr., appear before this Court in the courtroom of the United States Court of Appeals for the Fifth Circuit in New Orleans, Louisiana, on February 8, 1963, at 9:30 o'clock a.m., to show cause, if any they have, why they should not be held in criminal contempt, and should either of them at said time and place show such cause, either by pleading not guilty to the charges contained in the application of the United States, or by other means, he shall thereafter appear before this Court for hearing upon said charges at a time and place to be fixed by the Court."

The Chief Judge of this Court then directed the Clerk, for convenience in handling all matters relating to the criminal contempt proceedings to assign a new number, No. 20,240, and a new caption, "United States v. Ross R. Barnett and Paul B. Johnson, Jr.," to the case.

Pursuant to notice from the Court, respondents filed nine motions and the State of Mississippi filed one motion to be considered at the hearing. These motions may be briefly described as follows:

1. Motion and plea of the State of Mississippi to dismiss the proceedings as being in violation of the Tenth and Eleventh Amendments to the Constitution.

2. Motions of Barnett and Johnson to dismiss all proceedings in original Action No. 20,240 for lack of process.

3. First alternative motions of Barnett and Johnson to dismiss original proceedings in cause No. 20,240 and all contempt proceedings in cause No. 19,475 based on improper and insufficient application.

4. Second alternative motions of Barnett and Johnson to dismiss original proceedings in cause No. 20,240 for lack of venue or jurisdiction.

5. Third alternative motions of Barnett and Johnson to dismiss all pending proceedings in Criminal Contempt for lack of Grand Jury presentment or indictment.

6. Demands of Barnett and Johnson for trial by jury.

7. Fourth alternative motions of Barnett and Johnson to dismiss all proceedings in original Action No. 20,240 for lack of jurisdiction to summons a constitutional jury.

8. Motions of Barnett and Johnson for severance.

9. Motion of Johnson to strike the third charge contained in the order to show cause of date January 4, 1963.

10. Motion of Barnett to strike the third and fourth charges contained in the order to show cause of date January 4, 1963.

After oral argument a majority of the members of the Court, as indicated on the order of the Court filed this date, sustained the motion of the United States to strike the motion, and plea numbered 1, overruled or denied motions numbered 2, 3, 4, 5, and 7, decided to certify the question raised by the motion numbered 6, and the motions numbered 8, 9 and 10 are not now passed on. . . .

TUTTLE, Chief Judge, and RIVES, WISDOM, and BROWN, Circuit Judges. . . . Two main contentions seem to run throughout the several opinions though stated in various ways. The first is, as Judge Bell succinctly phrases it, "in short, we must abide the statutes applicable to the district court when we act as a district court."

This is apparently based on the fact that in the orders of July 27–28 and again in the restraining order of September 25, this Court issued its own injunction. From this it is presumably argued that since district courts ordinarily issue injunctions, our essential nature changes from an appellate to a trial court when we issue an order with traditional *nisi prius* characteristics. In other words, the character of a court is fixed, not by the organic statute establishing it, but by the nature of the order issued at any given time.

This ignores at least two things. First, and paramount, is the fact that Congress has specifically clothed this Court in the disposition of cases before it with the express power to issue whatever orders are appropriate. 28 U.S.

C.A. § 2106.[6] Second, this court, as have most others, has not felt itself bound as a matter of power to the mechanism of a direction to the district court. Ordinarily this will be done. But frequently in run-of-the-mill cases, we have reversed and *rendered* decisions for one of the parties. If it may be done for a money judgment, it may likewise be done as to equitable relief. The statute and the practice reflect the flexible standard of that which is *appropriate.* What is *needed* is assuredly encompassed in what is appropriate. And it is now way too late to urge that injunctive orders of this Court were not needed to effectuate the holding in this Court's opinion of June 25 in the Meredith case,[7] 305 F.2d 343.

The second main theme is closely akin to the first. The argument is made that the Government chose this Court rather than the District Court as the forum in which to assert its interest. From that it is argued that while §§ 402 and 3691 each speak in terms of "any district court of the United States," we must read this as though Congress expressly specified a Court of Appeals as well. This is so because otherwise the Government, by artful, purposeful choice, could defeat a statutory right accorded contempt defendants had it gone into the District Court instead. Of course at the bottom of this argument is the assertion made at many times and in many ways that there was no need for this Court to have issued its injunctive orders of July 27–28 in the continuing terms employed, and that there was no need for it to enter its temporary restraining orders of September 25–26. A branch of that contention apparently is that once the District Court entered its injunction on September 13, our interest came to an end.

But our order was a continuing one until, in effect, Meredith should be admitted to and continued as a student on the same basis as any other student. The facts of record in this Court show without contradiction that until Sunday, September 30, 1962, Meredith was not admitted to the University, and indeed, he was prevented from admission by direct personal interposition of the Governor and Lieutenant Governor. During all of the events which occurred between September 13 and September 30, it was this Court's orders which were being wilfully disobeyed. While these actions amounted to disobedience of the District Court's injunction as well, this Court was hardly so powerless that to secure obedience to its own orders it would have to refer the matter to the District Court. At the time of the issuance of the temporary restraining orders of September 25–26, Meredith was not yet in the Uni-

6. "§ 2106. Determination. The Supreme Court or any other court of appellate jurisdiction may affirm, modify, vacate, set aside or reverse any judgment, decree, or order of a court lawfully brought before it for review, and may remand the cause and direct the entry of such appropriate judgment, decree, or order, or require such further proceedings to be had as may be just under the circumstances."

To this must be added the all writs statute, 28 U.S.C.A. § 1651.

7. With the successive stays of Judge Cameron (vacated by our several orders), the District Court either was, or thought itself, unable to take action. Unless this Court's decision of June 25 was to be frustrated, affirmative action was needed then and there. It had to come from and *through* this Court, and this Court alone. Hence the injunctive orders of July 27–28 were imperatively required.

Similarly this Court en banc unanimously on October 19, 1962, entered its preliminary injunction (Judges Bell and Gewin dissenting on one limited phase). In most unmistakable terms, it reaffirmed that the temporary injunctive orders of September 25 and 26 against the Governor and Lieutenant Governor, respectively, were each appropriate and essential.

versity. By the terms of this Court's order, the injunction issued by it continued at least until Meredith was admitted. It was this Court, then, whose orders were being frustrated.

While the Government took the initiative in seeking leave to enter the case as so-called amicus curiae with the specified powers, this Court must assume the full responsibility for the Government's presence thereafter. For only by the entry of the order of September 18 could the United States have participated. This was in effect a recognition that the sovereign's presence was needed by this Court to effectuate its decrees and to maintain and uphold the rule of law. All of this became doubly clear when in the course of hearings on the various civil contempt matters, it became evident that injunctive orders ancillary to the main case had to be entered against the Governor and Lieutenant Governor. And what was then understood to be a necessity calling for temporary relief was reaffirmed when the Court en banc on October 19, 1962, reaffirmed that action by the issuance of its preliminary injunction which is still in force and effect.

It was this Court which made its ruling of June 25. It was this Court which made its orders of July 27–28. It was this Court whose orders were being disobeyed. It was this Court which needed the assistance of the sovereign and called upon it to take appropriate steps for the execution of the decrees of this Court. The rights of these Defendants are not then to be measured by what might have been claimed had these asserted acts of defiance taken place as to the District Court alone.

Moreover, this Court had ancillary jurisdiction to effectuate its own decrees. To that end it was certainly appropriate that the Court in effect call on the sovereign's law officer to initiate and prosecute the necessary proceedings. . . . And, of course, this Court continued to have jurisdiction even after its mandate of July 28. By the terms of its affirmative injunction, it reserved jurisdiction, and even without express reservation the Court retained power to conduct further proceedings to protect its decrees after its mandate had issued. . . .

Since the Court had this power the argument expressed or implied, particularly in the opinions of Judges Cameron and Gewin, as to the amicus status of the Government does not detract from the validity of the Court's orders. The argument seems to be that the Government cannot be an amicus because it has taken, and continues to take, a partisan position. But a Court empowered to take ancillary action to effectuate its decree is hardly to be left to the assistance of one having the neutral position of a traditional amicus. Within its sound discretion it is for the Court to determine whether the presence of the United States having the status of a quasi-party is needed. Here, the Court on September 18 recognized that the United States was needed not only to "accord each Court the benefit of its views" but more important "to initiate such further proceedings, including proceedings for injunctive relief and proceedings for contempt of court, as may be appropriate in order to maintain and preserve the due administration of justice and the integrity of the judicial processes of the United States." This was not, as some of the opinions suggested (see, e.g., Judge Bell's opinion, Part V), the Government obtaining through a permissive court order that which it is asserted Congress has declined to allow. This was not the Government instituting a suit or intervening on behalf of private litigants to vindicate the civil rights of private suitors. It was the sovereign intervening in the sovereign's court to uphold and maintain the sovereign's rule of law. Congress never meant to withhold that power. If the effect of that is to make the United States a party then at least one problem arises, and one consequence flows from it.

The problem is whether the Government could become a party in this manner. The Federal Rules of Civil Procedure are not generally applicable to the Court of Appeals. F.R.Civ.P. 1. Hence, failure to follow F.R.Civ.P. 24 and 6(d) does not imperil either the order of September 18 or the temporary restraining orders of September 25. It is then only a question of assuring the parties thereby affected—here, Governor Barnett and Lieutenant Governor Johnson—of procedural due process by according them a fair opportunity to challenge the right of the Government to come into the case and the power or propriety of the Court's allowing the Government to do so. These defendants have repeatedly challenged these actions, and the Court—as it did en banc as recently as October 19—has rejected their contentions.

Once it is established or assumed that the Government is a "party" and procedural fairness has been accorded, as was the case here, the consequence is to add further weight to the proposition that a jury trial is not available since the alleged contempt is for violation of an order "entered in an action brought or prosecuted in the name of, or on behalf of, the United States." [18 U.S.C. § 402] . . .

CAMERON, Circuit Judge. Before us stand the highest two executive officers of a Sovereign State of this Union, charged, by direction of this Court, with the criminal offense of contumacious violation of its injunctive order. Never before has such a charge been brought by or in a Court of Appeals since its establishment by Congress in 1891, against either a state officer or a private citizen. . . .

Getting back to the mainstream of the debate on the question before us, it is clear to me that this Court is, and has been from the time it sought to recall its mandate, acting wholly beyond the jurisdiction vested in it by Congress. Professor Moore, in his Commentary on the United States Judicial Code, gives a detailed account of the history and jurisdiction of the Court of Appeals, § 0–03 (51), pp. 455, et seq. Having stated that the Evarts Act of 1891 created a Circuit Court of Appeals for each of the nine circuits into which the United States was divided, and pointed out that this number had increased to eleven, he states (p. 456) the following:

"Courts of Appeals have only appellate jurisdiction.

"Since the courts of appeals are created by Congress and not by the Constitution, Congress could confer original jurisdiction upon them, but it has not done so. They have an exclusively appellate jurisdiction. . . ."

. . . This Court, in my opinion, exhausted its jurisdiction when it reversed the decision of the District Court and remanded the case of James H. Meredith to that court with instructions to enter an injunction as prayed for. Meredith had filed his civil action asking for injunctive relief, and the District Court had denied the relief prayed for; Meredith appealed to this Court; this Court reversed and remanded the case with instructions as to the order which should be entered. There its jurisdiction ceased.

It could not, in my opinion, as an appellate court take hold of the case and essay to exercise the jurisdiction vested only in district courts. When it attempted to do so, the weaving of the tangled web began, and the Court has, in my opinion, been in a state of confusion ever since. Of course, the web had been woven when the Court in banc took hold. In my judgment the moves made and the actions taken leading up to and including the issuance of the citation against the defendants charging the offense of criminal contempt have been beyond the power and jurisdiction of the Court.

Assuming that all I have written is in error and that what the Court has been doing has been in an effort to enforce its legal order in fulfillment of its appellate jurisdiction, its power extended, in my opinion, no further, in any event, than the issuance and enforcement of civil contempt proceedings. Much of what the courts have said and the textwriters have repeated has been in justification of the right of a court to protect itself, and certainly I do not have a word to say against that right. But the right is limited to direct contempts and to enforcement of its orders rendered in the execution of its appellate jurisdiction. Moreover, even if it had the right to enforce by civil sanctions its orders in this case, certainly it has done so in a very adequate way. It did not enforce its imposition of the large fines and the sentencing of the defendants to imprisonment, apparently because the things the Court was trying to accomplish had already been satisfactorily performed. But the punishment for criminal contempt is entirely another matter and one not, in my opinion, of which this Court has jurisdiction. . . .

The opposition takes the position that the stays granted by me, particularly the first one of July 18th, had the effect of frustrating the will of the panel which had ordered the District Court to enter the injunction Meredith had prayed for. The position is further taken that this Court was left helpless unless it adopted the novel and unprecedented procedures embraced in the panel's orders of June 27–28. I do not believe that this position, taken first by the original panel of Judges Brown, Wisdom and DeVane and now adopted by the opposition, is justified.

The fact is that the record does not disclose that the District Court ever refused to carry out the original mandate, or ever took any step indicating that it would not faithfully obey any legal mandate the panel might issue. On July 20, two days after the original mandate had been received by the District Court and had been stayed by my order of July 18, the panel caused telegrams to be sent to the litigants requesting five-day briefs on whether the mandate should be recalled and other steps taken in this Court, thus holding in abeyance any action on the mandate by the District Court. Nine days after the District Court received the mandate the panel issued its order of July 27th the exact effect of which, as I see it, no one has ever explained. It seemed to place this Court in the driver's seat astride the District Court, leaving the District Court with no specific instructions and in effect with no discretion to act except specifically as the panel should direct. The District Court was then faced with successive stays issued immediately after new orders were issued by the panel. The final order of August 4th made it clear that the whole matter was to be subjected to some appellate procedure. It would have been a very unusual and presumptuous act if the District Court had essayed to enter any order under the existing circumstances. . . .

I revert now to the opposition's claim that the panel had no alternative except taking the extreme action represented by the unprecedented proceedings of July 27–28. [He then refers to footnote 7 of the opinion of Tuttle, Rives, Wisdom, and Brown, p. 923].

The decision of June 25th, 305 F.2d 343 at 361, required only that "the district court issue the injunction as prayed for in the complaint, the district court to retain jurisdiction." If the stays were without legal basis, and the District Court had refused to follow the panel's mandate, the panel had the simple and traditional power to enforce its decision by mandamus: . . .

The opposition, in its addendum, makes an interesting, but to me unconvincing, argument that this Court is empowered to fashion its own rules of procedure unsupported by any authority at all as far as I can discover. This, I think, may not be done. The effort is made to blaze an entirely new trail in the carefully guarded realm of criminal contempts. A surveyor attempting to establish a line in an unknown region must first find a monument, an established point of beginning. He must then find his bearings by two readings from the North Star. These requirements are a *sine qua non* of his ability to blaze a new trail. No court can, I think, invest itself with the right to take the liberties or the property of a citizen without a monument and bearings. There are none, as far as I can find, in the opposition's opinion. . . .

Judge BELL. Two brief comments appear to be in order following the formulation of the certified question, and the additional comments of the four members of the court who would deny jury trial.

First, the limited dissent of Judges Gewin and Bell referred to in Footnote 7 of their opinion with respect to the preliminary injunction entered October 19, 1962 should by no means be deemed insignificant. That dissent went to the heart of what has been the problem in this case since it was taken over by this court through the July 28, 1962 order. We dissented, not from the entry of the injunction, but because the court would not thereafter return the case to the District Court where it should have been all along; there to be handled, subject, of course, to the traditional mandamus procedure.

Under our court system the District Court speaks to litigants, while a Court of Appeals speaks, or should speak, to the District Court. This historical mode lends itself to the maintenance of judicial dignity and decorum, engenders and preserves respect for the law, and avoids an unseemly type of judicial scurrying about that results when there are no rules to follow.

I regret that the court will not also certify the following additional question, deemed by me at least to be of the utmost importance in the event of jury trial, so as to eliminate more makeshift procedures:

"If Respondents are entitled to trial by jury for the criminal contempt with which they are charged, may the order to show cause charging them be referred to the District Court where the alleged acts of contempt were committed for trial?"

---

2) Supreme Court Opinion—376 U.S. 681 (1964).

[The Supreme Court held that the governor and lieutenant-governor were not entitled to trial by jury. Justice Clark wrote for the Court:]

Governor Barnett and Lieutenant Governor Johnson first contend that the record clearly shows that the United States invoked the proceedings taken by the Court of Appeals and sought that court out as a source of orders, duplicating the orders obtained by the real party in interest in the District Court, solely for the purpose of by-passing the District Court and depriving them of their right to a jury. We find no evidence of this. Indeed, the Court of Appeals granted injunctive relief only after it had jurisdiction over Meredith's appeal, after it had acted upon that appeal and after its order was being frustrated. . . .

Excerpt from the dissenting opinion of Justice BLACK (joined by Justice DOUGLAS):

For many reasons I cannot agree with the Court's opinion. In the first place, Congress has never expressly given the Federal Courts of Appeals jurisdiction to try and punish people for criminal contempt of court, and I am unwilling to hold that such a power exists in these courts in the absence of a clear and unequivocal congressional grant. The business of trial courts is to try cases. That of appellate courts is to review the records of cases coming from trial courts below. In my judgment it is bad for appellate courts to be compelled to interrupt and delay their pressing appellate duties in order to hear and adjudicate cases which trial courts have been specially created to handle as a part of their daily work. And in particular, I believe that it is highly disruptive and downright injurious to appellate courts for them to attempt to take over and try criminal contempt cases, surcharged as these cases almost always are with highly emotional quarrels. . . . Appellate courts are too useful a part of our judicial system to be subjected to such unnecessary ordeals. I say unnecessary because trial courts are as qualified and capable to try criminal contempt cases as they are to try others.

Assuming, however, that a United States Court of Appeals does have jurisdiction to try criminal contempt cases, I agree for the reasons set out in Part A of my Brother Goldberg's dissenting opinion that Congress has commanded that defendants in those cases be accorded a right to trial by jury. His powerful arguments on this point stand unanswered by the Court. Even in construing statutes and rules governing civil cases we have taken pains, as Congress commanded, to resolve all doubts in favor of trial by jury as guaranteed by the Seventh Amendment. We should certainly be equally alert to construe statutes governing trials for criminal contempt so as to protect the right of jury trial guaranteed for the "Trial of all crimes" by section 2, cl. 3 of Article III of the original Constitution and for "all criminal prosecutions" by the Sixth Amendment.

Excerpt from the dissenting opinion of Justice GOLDBERG (joined by the CHIEF JUSTICE and Justice DOUGLAS): Defendants claim that 18 U.S.C. § 3691, entitles them to a jury trial in this case. That statute provides in relevant part that "the accused, upon demand therefor, shall be entitled to trial by a jury" whenever the alleged contempt "shall consist in willful disobedience of any lawful writ, process, order, rule, decree, or command of any district court of the United States by doing or omitting any act or thing in violation thereof, and the act or thing done or omitted also constitutes a criminal offense under any Act of Congress . . . ," except if the alleged contempt is "committed in disobedience of any lawful writ, process, order, rule, decree, or command entered in any suit or action brought or prosecuted in the name of, or on behalf of, the United States." The statutory right to a jury trial thus turns on three essential factors: (1) the source of the order; (2) the nature of the alleged violation; and (3) the character of the party that "brought or prosecuted" the "suit or action." I conclude for the reasons stated below that the District Court was the source of the basic order in this case; that the nature of the alleged violation would make it a criminal offense under 18 U.S.C. (Supp. IV) § 1509; and that the "suit or action" in the case was brought and prosecuted not by the United States, but by James Meredith, a private party. It follows that defendants have a statutory right to be tried for their alleged contempt by a jury of their peers.

---

3) Court of Appeals Decision of May 5, 1965—346 F.2d 99 (5th Cir.).

Before TUTTLE, Chief Judge, and RIVES, JONES, BROWN, WISDOM, GEWIN, and BELL, Circuit Judges.

RIVES, JONES, GEWIN and BELL, Circuit Judges:

CIVIL CONTEMPT

This Court, in September 1962, entered its findings of fact, conclusions of law, and judgments of civil contempt adjudging Ross R. Barnett and Paul B. Johnson, Jr., in civil contempt of the temporary restraining orders of this Court entered September 25, 1962. There has since been substantial compliance with this Court's orders. It therefore appears that no further proceedings in civil contempt are needed, and that it is appropriate to enter an order formally terminating the civil contempt proceedings.

CRIMINAL CONTEMPT

Criminal contempt is a *sui generis* proceeding for the protection of the integrity of the Court. The criminal contempt proceedings against Ross R. Barnett and Paul B. Johnson, Jr., were instituted pursuant to the order and direction of this Court of November 15, 1962. (J. Gewin dissenting). Those proceedings are, therefore, within the control of the Court and the Court has the power and authority to order them dismissed.

At the present time no sufficient reasons exist for the further prosecution of the proceedings against Barnett and Johnson. In the light of substantial compliance with the Court's orders, considerations of respect for the Court do not require the further prosecution of the criminal contempt proceedings. Nor does such further prosecution appear necessary for the purpose of deterring others from committing offenses like or similar to the alleged acts of contempt. The Civil Rights Act of 1964 has been generally recognized as creating a status under which the "law of the land" is now beyond question. Indeed there has been widespread, voluntary compliance with the provisions of said Act. It is highly improbable that other persons will hereafter commit acts similar to those herein charged.

The lapse of time since this Court ordered the criminal contempt proceedings to be instituted, and the changed circumstances and conditions have rendered the further prosecution of criminal contempt proceedings unnecessary. The rationale at least in part of Hamm v. City of Rock Hill, 1964, 379 U.S.

306, 315, 317, where the Civil Rights Act of 1964 was applied retroactively to abate state sit-in prosecutions, was based on the purpose of the Act "to obliterate the effect of a distressing chapter of our history." It was held that no public interest was to be served in continuing the prosecution. And so it is here. In what we consider an appropriate application of restraint to judicial power, we close out another part of the same chapter.

It is fortunate that we can so conclude because there may be no fair alternative course. Jury trial as a matter of right has been ruled out by the Supreme Court. For reasons which need not be stated, jury trial as a matter of discretion would not be granted by majority vote of this Court. For the same acts for which they stand charged with criminal contempt, the defendants have already been tried and adjudged by this Court to be in civil contempt.[2] This Court has already found against them on all of the elements of criminal contempt, excepting only that of intent, willfulness. That state of mind must be determined by inference from evidence, most if not all of which has been introduced and considered by the Court in the civil contempt proceedings. While we know that every judge of this Court would do his conscientious best to try the criminal contempt proceedings fairly and impartially, we are doubtful, to say the least, whether we and the other judges may not have formed a fixed opinion that the defendants are guilty. Thus some, or all of the present membership of this Court may be disqualified from sitting on a trial on the merits of these criminal contempt charges.[4] The statute [5] makes no provision for any replacement judge to sit on this en banc court and we doubt whether one can properly be devised by judicial invention. It follows that a fair trial on the merits is the subject of doubt, and dismissal of the criminal proceeding is the only course open that is clearly consistent with fundamental fairness.

The civil contempt judgements will stand but no sanctions will be imposed. The criminal proceeding is dismissed for the reasons stated above.

TUTTLE, Chief Judge (dissenting):

With deference, I dissent. This Court, on January 4, 1963 commenced criminal contempt proceedings against Ross Barnett and Paul Johnson, Jr.,

. . .

As the Court believed then I believe now: the charges were sufficiently grave to require a trial. The gravity of the charges was enhanced, not lessened, by the fact that they were against a governor and lieutenant governor of a state.

I agree that the Court now has full power to continue the prosecution or to dismiss it without more. I fully respect the judgment of those who believe the public interest, including the integrity of the judicial system, calls now for

2. This statement contemplates granting the motion of the government to dismiss Counts 3 and 4. These counts relate to the failure of defendants to maintain law and order at the university. The remaining two counts involve the frustration of the registration of Meredith by the defendants.

4. Compare the provision of Rule 42(b), F.R.Crim.P. that, "if the contempt charged involves disrespect to or criticism of a judge, that judge is disqualified from presiding at the trial or hearing except with the defendant's consent."

5. Section 46(c) of Title 28, U.S.Code, providing in part, "A court in banc shall consist of all circuit judges in regular active service."

a dismissal. I do not share that judgment. As I believed then, I believe now, that the public interest requires that a trial be held and that the guilt or innocence of these two respondents be determined.

JOHN R. BROWN, Circuit Judge (dissenting):

This Court, almost if not quite unanimously, has recently declared [in *Cox*] that the Executive has the uncontrolled discretion to determine whether a prosecution once commenced must go forward. That principle, by way of analogy, is pertinent here. Criminal contempt, as the cases often and just recently point out, partakes much of a criminal proceeding. A major distinction, however, is the identity of the *initiating* agency—for traditional criminal proceedings, the Executive; for criminal contempt, the Court. Despite some fundamental differences, I think the parallel is close, and I therefore agree with the Court that a Court initiating a charge of criminal contempt must have the power to determine whether the proceeding once commenced must inevitably go forward to trial and resulting conviction or acquittal. The Judiciary clothed in this particular instance with awesome powers comparable to those of the Executive in criminal proceedings has the right, and probably the unreviewable duty, to determine whether the public interest will best be served by a discontinuance short of trial. My difference, therefore, is in the assessment of the public interest and how it will be furthered or hindered by this action.

In concluding that the public interest requires that we continue on with the trial of the remaining charges we set in motion, I would emphasize, as does Judge Wisdom in Part V of his dissent, that I neither intimate guilt nor prejudge the outcome. Our dissents merely reiterate as echoes what our earlier order declared—there is probable cause and reasonable need for instituting and trying the charges. To conclude that we should adhere is no more a prejudgment than the entry of the order initiating the charges. Surely, the act of the Court in assaying the case and the public interest in its further continuance cannot transmute the dissenters' voice of difference into a prejudgment on the merits.

The Court, without demonstrating any factual support for its conclusion that all should halt now, dismisses the proceedings. Within the Court's announced opinion, I find no support for this generalized conclusion, nor can I find any when I examine all possible reasons.

We are dealing here with conduct of the State's highest officer. That conduct—whatever might be its legal sufficiency to supply the essential ingredient of *willfulness*—was and was intended by Governor Barnett to be a physical obstruction of this Court's decree that Meredith be admitted to the University. The conflict, on Governor Barnett's own words, was the State of Mississippi versus The United States of America. Consequently, as articulated by Judge Wisdom in Part IV of his dissent, this is more than contempt of this Court. The "contempt charge" is "the contempt of a governor of a state against the Nation."

Governor Barnett, for reasons officially proclaimed undertook physically to prevent Meredith's admission, the very thing specifically ordered by this Court. He was, in short, marshaling the whole force of Mississippi in opposing, not upholding, compliance with the Court's orders. . . .

Precisely because his duty was so high the likely consequences of his interposition so devastating, the responsibilities of moral leadership in the maintenance of law and order in the face of unpopular situations so awesome, it is important that Governor Barnett be held accountable for his actions which he would be the first to minimize in importance. To be held accountable is not to forecast the outcome. To be held accountable is not to speak in terms of punishment or even the certainty of it. To be held accountable is merely to require that through an orderly, fair trial,[4] it be determined whether the conduct of this high officer was or was not legally justifiable, was or was not a willful disobedience to a lawful order of this Court.

Now no one will ever know. The public—whose interest is at stake as we try to make constitutional federalism work—will know only that a governor successfully interposed himself to prevent compliance. It will know only that, save for skirmishes on procedural problems over the course of three years, such Governor never had to answer to the charges[5] which this Court thought serious enough to warrant their being brought and substantial enough to occupy its attention and that of the Nation's highest tribunal on several occasions, one of which concerned an issue of constitutional proportions closer in its 5-to-4 outcome than the 4-to-3 vote here. The chapter, with its death and violence, is indeed a regrettable one. But it is so not because a Court order was issued. Rather, it is because the Court order was not affirmatively, actively enforced by those now charged with obstruction of it. In the supremacy of the Constitution, in the supremacy of the rule of law, much suffers when a governor can do the things here charged without ever facing up to either the consequences[7] or even a judicial determination of legality or illegality.

WISDOM, Circuit Judge (dissenting): I respectfully dissent. To my mind, the Court's decision represents the exercise of judicial license, not of judicial restraint.

4. Although discussed candidly by Government counsel on its own motion in the briefs precipitated by the pretrial hearing held in the fall of 1964, none of the briefs (numbering in the hundreds of pages) filed by the highly skilled, energetic and responsible counsel for Governor Barnett even remotely hint at the disqualification of any one or more or all of the members of this Court to sit on this case because the order charged to be violated was ours, or that we initiated the show cause order and the order charging criminal contempt. On the contrary, they have assiduously refrained from replying to, or discussing, Government counsel's comments on this aspect or suggesting that we should recuse ourselves. To be sure, a jury trial, either mandatory or discretionary, either before this Court or upon a reference to the two District Courts in Mississippi, is earnestly sought. But if it is to be tried by Judges, no complaint is uttered that it falls to our lot, rather than imported, certified Judges, to assume the responsibility.

5. During all of this jousting, Governor Barnett has not yet had to face up to a formal plea of guilty or not guilty and, for that matter, he has yet to appear before this Court (save by counsel) though repeatedly ordered in person to do so.

7. I agree with what Judge Wisdom says in Part IV of his dissent about interposition, the likely consequences of Governor Barnett's acknowledged actions, and the necessity that all state officials from Governor to the constable "must know that they cannot with impunity flout federal law." Likewise, I concur in Part VI which points out so clearly an unquestioned liability for accrued civil sanctions and the inescapable fact that Meredith was admitted, not by reason of the Governor's "substantial compliance" with our decree, but by the superior force of military arms.

I do not complain of Ross Barnett's escaping punishment. I complain of a governor's escaping the risk of punishment an ordinary citizen or, perhaps, a registrar of voters runs if he is indicted for criminal contempt.

Sunday, September 30, 1962, was a climactic day for James Meredith. On three occasions before that day, the Governor and Lieutenant-Governor of Mississippi, with state highway troopers, sheriffs, and local police officers, had formed a wall barring Meredith's way into the University of Mississippi. No one will ever know whether the Governor of Mississippi could have made that Sunday a day to be remembered as marking the Deep South's turn toward a peaceful solution of its racial problems. What we do know is that the rioting and insurrection in Oxford on September 30, 1962, was the worst of many bad days in the Deep South marked by bloodshed, bombings, and church burnings. If the indictment may be dismissed in the interest of the public, that interest should be tested by the significance to the public of Governor Barnett's actions on September 30, 1962. On that day in Oxford, Mississippi, the Governor of the State flouted explicit orders of this Court, struck a blow against American federalism, and defied the Nation.

The Court does not purport to base its holding on any principle of law. The Court bases its holding on its confidence in a prescient majority's knowledge of what is best for the public. Working with what Dr. Gallup would consider a statistically small number for a reliable poll, the Court dismisses the indictments because its 4/3 poll indicates that the public reaction would be adverse to a trial of the defendants at this time.

The Court is not sitting in equity; the defendants are accused of *criminal* contempt. In order, therefore, to dismiss this case, the Court had to start with the assumption that criminal contempt proceedings, although a prosecution for a public wrong, are so unlike other criminal proceedings that the case may be dismissed, after indictment and before trial, whenever the Court concludes that dismissal is in the public interest. Two years ago, however, this case was enough like other criminal prosecutions for the Court to divide evenly on the question whether the defendants are entitled to a jury trial under Article III and the sixth amendment.

In arriving at its value judgment as to whether further prosecution would be in the public interest, the Court gave weight to the high state office Governor Barnett once held and Governor Johnson now holds, the assumed adverse effect a trial might have on federal-state relations, the defendants' "substantial compliance" with the orders of the Court (a reversal of the Court's thinking that will come as a surprise to the defendants), and the degree of felt necessity for prosecution since it is "highly improbable that other persons might hereafter commit" similar acts. *But this Court weighed all of these considerations no less than four times.* November 15, 1962, long after Meredith had registered at the University of Mississippi, the Court, with only one judge dissenting, directed the Department of Justice to file criminal contempt proceedings against Ross R. Barnett and Paul B. Johnson, Jr. December 21, 1962, the Court re-weighed these considerations when it issued the show cause order for criminal contempt. No matter, the majority says, there have been changes in "conditions" since 1962. Turning inward for calipers, the majority has measured the effect of these changes on the general attitude of the public, the reaction of public officials, and the probabilities of high state officials' interfering in the future with federal court orders.

Since there have been several occasions since 1962 when publication of such an opinion coincident with certain unpredictable events in this circuit might have raised questions as to the ability of the majority to measure public reaction and foresee the future, timing is everything. The majority finds that the Supreme Court's general amnesty decree for sit-in trespassers in Hamm v. City of Rock Hill makes its appropriate *now* to "close a chapter." I doubt whether we have reached the close of the chapter. But I know that we are a long, long way from the end of the book.

It is evident that the decisional process of the majority requires a precision in crystal-gazing and clairvoyant timing that permits no latitude for cloud or haze on the crystal ball. I speak seriously, not facetiously. I say that if the rightness of this decision teeters on the ability of the majority to read not only the collective mind of the Public but the minds of past, present, and future high state officials, and the extent to which lesser officials follow executive leadership, there is something wrong with basing this decision on the majority's appreciation of what is in the public interest.

As every judge knows, there is a certain amount of policy-making in decision-making. This process is especially apparent in cases involving the due process, equal protection, and interstate commerce clauses and other broad concepts that are part of the Constitution as a living organism. Here, however, the Court is not following a prescribed course requiring it to interpret the Constitution or statutes, and is not fact-finding after a hearing. The Court is acting on its own, contrary to a course of action the Court itself chose after careful consideration of all of the factors now before us.

The Court is less like a court than it is like St. Louis. The good French king used to sit under a spreading oak tree, not presiding even-handedly as a judge at a trial, but dispensing justice subjectively, arbitrarily, hit-or-miss, according to his fancy of the moment as to what was best for his subjects and when it was best for him to tell them about it. Coming closer home, the law in the Court's decision is like the Law West of the Pecos.

Hamm v. City of Rock Hill, 1964, 379 U.S. 306, lends no support to the Court's action. In that case the Supreme Court abated pending trespass convictions "in accordance with the long-established rule" that "convictions on direct review at the time the conduct in question is rendered no longer unlawful by statute" may be abated. There was a serious question as to the application of the principle of abatement because the convictions were in state courts and the abating statute was a federal statute, the Civil Rights Act of 1964. The majority of the Court overcame this difficulty by resorting to the Supremacy Clause; it was clear that the convictions, if federal, would abate. The comment on "policy" and the "public interest" refers to the declaration of policy in the Civil Rights Act of 1964. As the Court pointed out, "the public policy of the country is to prohibit discrimination in public accommodations as therein defined, [and therefore] there is no public interest to be served in the further prosecution of the petitioners." There is not the remotest implication in the Supreme Court's opinion that anyone on the Court entertained the notion that the sit-in cases should or could be dismissed on the majority's guess that there would be an adverse public reaction to further prosecution of the trespassers. Whether one agrees or disagrees with Hamm v. City of Rock Hill, it is a principled decision resting on an analysis of prior decisions, legal reasoning, and accepted judicial methodology. It is a typical example of the decisional process. It does not rest on the vagaries of a transcient majority's benevolent excursion into the Public Mind. . . .

. . . This Court speaks of a contempt case as "a sui generis proceeding for the protection of the integrity of the Court." So it is. And there is no doubt that a contempt proceeding has play in the joints. The Court holds, therefore, that in "light of the substantial compliance with the orders of the Court, it would appear that considerations of respect for the Court do not require the further prosecution of the criminal contempt proceedings." But this case involves more than considerations of respect for this Court.

The offense occurred at a time calling for moral leadership of the highest order. No great clairvoyance was needed to foresee death and disorder resulting from the confrontation of two armed forces. No one can say that the rioting and insurrection that took place September 30, 1962, in Oxford, Mississippi, and the death and disorder that have occurred in many other places in the South since that insurrection, were not due, at least in part, to the imprimatur the Governor of Mississippi placed on lawless defiance of the federal courts.

The judges in the majority have greater confidence in their ability to read the future than I. I cannot say as the Court says, *"[i]t is highly improbable that other persons will hereafter commit acts similar to those herein charged."* I say that a person who commits the acts with which Barnett is charged must be called to account. If he should be found guilty and punished, that punishment may deter others from committing similar acts. That at least is the theory on which criminal penalties rest.

This action is cast in the form of contempt of this Court. But the significance of the case for the public lies in the fact that within the setting framing the action the contempt charged was, in effect, *the contempt of a Governor of a State against the Nation—against American federalism, as established in the Constitution and as defined by the federal courts.* The serious threat Governor Barnett posed was to the constitutional relationship of the States to the National Government. A public wrong of such enormity carries with it a corresponding and unshirkable duty on the federal court to vindicate the rights of the Nation by bringing the alleged contemnor to trial.

The confrontation should have been a duel with drawn pencils between the Governor of Mississippi and the United States Attorney General in the Mississippi Law Journal. Or it should have started and stopped in the courts, as well it might have, when the University's Board of Trustees, with dignity and grace, agreed in open court to accept Meredith at the University. Unfortunately, Governor Barnett insisted upon a confrontation in the streets of Oxford and on the campus of the University. There was more at issue, therefore, than an affront to this Court's dignity when Ross Barnett, as the head of the State of Mississippi, mobilized sheriffs, highway troopers, and local police officers *and by force of arms overcame United States marshals enforcing the law.*

The Governor of Mississippi, trained in the law, knew or should have known that the Supremacy Clause makes hash of the so-called Doctrine of

Interposition. All informed persons know that this political poppycock has never been recognized in a court of law. But the uninformed, the uneducated, the very persons likely to resort to violence, were certain to be misled when their chief executive "interposed" himself between the United States and the University of Mississippi.

Ross Barnett happened to be Governor of Mississippi at an unfortunate time. It would be a mistake to overestimate his place as an obstructionist in the long-run solution of the complex problem of national social adjustment to the changing relationship of the races. What cannot be overestimated, however, in a short-run or long-run solution, is the importance of federal courts' standing fast in protecting federally guaranteed rights of individuals. To avoid further violence and bloodshed, all state officials, including the governor, must know that they cannot with impunity flout federal law.

The Civil Rights Act of 1964 cuts deep into customs that have regulated lives from cradle to coffin. But this law has not been in effect long enough to have had any wide and severe impact. The country is at the threshold of voluntary compliance with this law. If Congress should adopt the proposed Voting Rights Act of 1965, that law too will change many local customs and further exacerbate state-federal frictions. Southern governors and federal courts may be in for many, many long hot summers.

I cannot see into the unknown. But the dark realities of the past militate against the Court's taking a rosy, relaxed view of the future.

I have concentrated on Governor Barnett because at most of the critical times he preempted the center of the stage. In spite of my strong feeling that he should be tried, I do not intimate that he is guilty of *criminal* contempt. "Wilfulness" is an essential element of the offense distinguishing it from civil contempt. In the absence of proof of his wilful contempt, in a fair trial before the Court, Barnett is entitled to the benefit of the presumption of innocence.

An action involving indirect criminal contempt is like any other criminal proceeding in that vindication of the Court's power need not be immediate. But it must be as certain as death and taxes. In 1962 this Court concluded that the effectiveness of federal courts and the proper functioning of the federal system depend on the governor's being treated as an ordinary citizen when he flouts federal judicial decrees. The lapse of time only increases the urgency for prompt vindication of federal authority.

I see no justification whatever for relieving Barnett of his obligation to comply with the judgment against him for civil contempt. On September 28, 1962, this Court found Barnett in civil contempt of its order of September 25, 1962. We imposed a fine of $10,000 a day unless, before October 2, 1962, he had shown the Court that he was fully complying with the order and had notified all of the officers under his jurisdiction to cease interfering with the orders of the courts and to cooperate in the admission of Meredith to the University of Mississippi. Barnett made no pretense of complying with this order of September 28. On October 2, he compounded his contempt by failing to appear before the Court, after having been summoned, and instructed his attorney to advise the Court that he had *not* purged himself of contempt.[2]

Meredith registered at the University of Mississippi October 1, 1962. To win this battle, the United States Army had more soldiers under arms at Oxford, Mississippi, or held close by in reserve, than George Washington in the Revolutionary War ever commanded at one time. . . .

There is an unedifying moral to be drawn from this case of *The Man in High Office Who Defied the Nation:* The mills of the law grind slowly—but not inexorably. If they grind slowly enough, they may even come, unaccountably, to a gradual stop, short of the trial and judgment an ordinary citizen expects when accused of criminal contempt. There is just one compensating thought: Hubris is grist for other mills, which grind exceeding small and sure.

---

2. October 2, 1962, counsel for Governor Barnett, in answer to questions from the Court, stated that Governor Barnett was in full compliance with the Court's orders and would fully comply with the orders of the Court in the future. October 12, 1962, counsel for Governor Barnett, in open court, retracted their statements that Governor Barnett intended in the future to comply with the orders of the Court. October 19, 1962, Governor Barnett, through his counsel, filed a response to which was attached the following statement:

"*I have never taken the position that I have purged myself, nor have I authorized anyone to take such a position on my behalf.* My position is that I have upheld the law and am not in contempt of any Court.

"It is my position that my first obligation, as the Governor of Mississippi, is to my oath of office to uphold the Constitution and Laws of Mississippi and the Constitution of the United States, and to preserve law and order. The people of Mississippi built this University and their schools at great sacrifice. These properties and their control belong to the State, and the Supreme Court of the United States has expressly so ruled in Waugh v. University of Mississippi, 237 U.S. 589.

"All of the actions that I have taken were taken because of my duty to obey my oath as Governor, and as long as I am the Governor of this State, all actions that I will take in the future will be in obedience of this oath.

"I conscientiously believe that it is my duty, as Governor, deliberately, solemnly, and fully, and free from the control or interference of anyone to exercise, according to my own judgment and my own discretion, the duties the people have entrusted to me as their Governor, I would not be faithful to my oath of office, should I surrender to any Federal or other Courts the rights to exercise those discretionary powers the law has placed in me, to maintain law and order, to prevent a breach of the peace, violence or bloodshed, and my discretion must remain free. I shall ever and eternally stand for the exercise of my own discretion in my own right, and shall repudiate the right of anyone to take that discretion away from me and exercise it in my behalf. The Constitutions of the United States and the State of Mississippi provide for the separation of the Judicial, Executive and Legislative functions. The people have never given any right to any one of these departments to act for the other.

"If any act that I have done as Governor or any act I shall do as Governor in the future causes any person to believe that I have violated his right, the Courts are open to challenge me again in a proper court proceeding. Mississippi has not yet had her day in Court.

"My position is based upon the Constitution of the United States and the Constitution and Laws of the State of Mississippi. My every decision in this matter has been formed after careful and deliberate consideration of what I believe to be the law. *I have not changed my position in the slightest degree. I shall never apologize for anything I have said or done in this regard because I have acted in good faith in discharging the duties entrusted to me.* My conscience is clear. I am moved only by deep and abiding affection for the welfare of all the people of Mississippi. I shall ever keep the faith that the people of Mississippi have entrusted to me as their Governor." (Emphasis supplied.)

1) Why did the court of appeals in July 1962 both enter an appellate injunction and order a district court injunction? Why did the appellate injunction survive the September 13 district court injunction? Why did Judge Tuttle insist that an appellate court response was imperative? Why did the court of appeals join the United States two weeks before school started? Would "invited intervenor" be a more appropriate name for the government than "amicus"? Was the civil contempt really a second injunction with the penalty for violation specified?

2) Why did the court change the focus of contempt from a triggered coercive fine to criminal? Criminal contempt added wilfullness as an element, proof beyond a reasonable doubt, and the possibility of a jury trial. Why didn't the court simply levy the accumulated coercive fines? Did the court of appeals fear Mississippi jurors more than the Mississippi district judges? Did the court of appeals a) let the federal executive off the hook? b) frustrate the contemnor's efforts to become a martyr? Navasky quotes an attorney who worked on the contempt: "The fact that Governor Barnett defied the court and the Attorney General and the President and got away with it made inevitable Governor Wallace's stand in the schoolhouse door. No [Southern] Governor worth his salt could do less." V. Navasky, Kennedy Justice 238 (1971).

3) If you concluded that the court of appeals entered an appellate injunction to take charge and to get tough, how do you explain the amnesty? Evaluate the arguments for and against dropping the contempt in light of Professor Davis's statement that "Prosecutions are often withheld, sometimes on the basis of political, personal, or other ulterior influence, without guiding rules as to what will or will not be prosecuted, without meaningful standards stemming from either legislative bodies or from prosecutors themselves, through decisions secretly made and free from criticism, without supporting findings of fact, unexplained by reasoned opinions, and free from any requirement that the decisions be related to precedents." K. Davis, Discretionary Justice 224 (1969). Does Judge Wisdom's comparison of the court to St. Louis refer to the *Barnett* decision or to the allocation of prosecutorial power altogether? Would the court be acting less like St. Louis if it proceeded with criminal contempt?

4) Professor Kuhns argued that the executive should control the initiation of all criminal contempts. Kuhns, Limiting the Criminal Contempt Power: New Roles for the Prosecutor and the Grand Jury, 73 Mich.L.Rev. 484 (1975). His argument is directed to in-court contempts. Would executive instead of judicial discretion have cured any of the maladies you perceived in *Barnett?* Would prosecutors generally display much enthusiasm for prosecuting violations of civil injunctions? Would executive discretion interfere excessively with judicial prerogative?

5) Prosecutorial discretion is often exercised to prosecute only ringleaders. See *Debs,* p. 1 and *Walker,* p. 286. In United States v. Phillips, 525 F.Supp. 1 (N.D.Ill.1981), the government prosecuted only union officers who were named defendants and received the injunction by personal or abode service. The contemnors moved to dismiss for selective prosecution. The prosecuting attorney successfully asserted that selectivity is the only way to assure proof of knowledge and wilfullness beyond a reasonable doubt.

Does this apparent policy dilute the draconian effect of the *Cape May* rule, p. 261? or shorten the chapter on who owes a duty to obey an injunction?

6) Afterword: As we were preparing this edition, the University of Mississippi was celebrating the 20th anniversary of James Meredith's registration. Ole Miss had over 700 black students, 8% of the student body, as well as over 700 black alumni. The big controversy in Oxford in the fall of 1982 centered upon the first black Rebel cheerleader who was refusing to hoist the Confederate flag at Ole Miss home games. His view prevailed. In the spring of 1983, Ole Miss ceased to use the Confederate flag as an official symbol.

7) Common-garden variety federal criminal contempt proceeds under Criminal Rule 42. The government may, however, summon a grand jury and indict criminal contemnors. United States v. Petito, 671 F.2d 68 (2d Cir. 1982); United States v. Mensik, 440 F.2d 1232 (4th Cir. 1971); United States v. Sternman, 415 F.2d 1165, 1168 (6th Cir. 1969), certiorari denied 397 U.S. 907 (1970). The judge or the court as in *Barnett* normally possesses the initiative and the discretion. In re Brown, 454 F.2d 999 (D.C.Cir. 1971). The court cannot both present and try criminal contempt, so the court often asks the prosecuting attorney to prosecute. See, e.g., Frank v. United States, 384 F.2d 276, 278 (10th Cir. 1967), affirmed 395 U.S. 147 (1969). The court may, however, ask a party's attorney to prosecute. The court of appeals in Musidor v. Great American Screen, 658 F.2d 60, 64–65 (2d Cir. 1981), rejected the contemnor's argument that appointment of the civil plaintiffs' counsel to prosecute criminal contempt denied due process. In United States ex rel. Vuitton et Fils S.A. v. McNally, 519 F.Supp. 185 (E.D.N.Y.1981), the court balanced the civil plaintiff's expertise against other factors and requested that the government prosecute. Absent an appointment, the civil plaintiff lacks "standing" to maintain criminal contempt. In re Hartford Textile Corp., 648 F.2d 812 (2d Cir. 1981); In re Lahm Industries, Inc., 609 F.2d 567 (1st Cir. 1979); Kienle v. Jewel Tea Co., 222 F.2d 98 (7th Cir. 1955).

IV. Can Plaintiff Promise Amnesty?

Negotiation and settlement may enter the injunctive process at at least three different points: (a) before the judge issues the injunction; (b) after the injunction is issued, but before the defendant violates it; and (c) following issuance and violation, but before contempt. In *Boomer*, p. 79, we considered post-injunction negotiations. Now we consider post-violation negotiation. Can the plaintiffs promise the contemnor amnesty to acquire future quiescence? Can plaintiff bind the court? Should the court honor the settlement? Negotiation saves time and energy of all involved; it avoids the conflict that would arise in the contempt hearing and that might distort the parties' future dealings; and a negotiated settlement is likely to identify the parties' true interests with greater accuracy. What are the dangers? See Note, Injunction Negotiations: An Economic, Moral and Legal Analysis, 27 Stan.L.Rev. 1563 (1975).

We depart from amity and concord when we deal with post-violation negotiation in public employee strikes. When judges enjoin these strikes, strikers often defy, openly and massively. They may assume that contempt is a hollow threat, and that contempt, if commenced, will simply be settled. Amnesty from contempt becomes one of the terms of settlement. Should the judge participate in these negotiations? Should the plaintiff promise amnesty? Can the plaintiff deliver on the promise of amnesty? May the judge initiate criminal contempt when the parties agree not to proceed?

The Wall Street Journal quoted Professor Bernard Meltzer about a judge's role: "Amnesty today for defiance of an injunction against an illegal strike not only invites a repetition of those offenses tomorrow, but weakens the community's capacity to deal with them when they erupt. Thus a judge's successes as a mediator may compromise his own future capacity and that of all judges to discharge their unique responsibility—upholding the rule of law. And if a judge fails as a mediator, he may also compromise at least the appearance of objectivity if he finds it appropriate to sentence someone for criminal contempt.

"Failure of the judiciary to discharge its unique responsibility for the integrity of its own processes poses grave threats to order, to equity, and to peace itself.

"Public employees, even if they wage 'successful' strikes and then secure amnesty, will not in the end escape such chaos. For, as the rule of law erodes, so will the wealth, as well as the already scarce civility, of our cities; and blocs of employees will fight with each other and taxpayers for a piece of a smaller and smaller pie in cities that are less and less congenial." Notable & Quotable, Wall St. J., July 29, 1980, at 26, col. 4. Do you agree?

After defendant breaches, plaintiff may press for any type of contempt. What did *Gompers,* p. 831 say about whether a privately negotiated settlement ends plaintiff's right to compensatory contempt? In *Barnett,* p. 909 we studied prosecutorial discretion as a form of amnesty. *Alsbury* addresses a related issue: whether private settlement should affect the judge's decision to commence criminal contempt. Ask yourself: What distinguishes criminal from civil contempt? Will the judge's interference with the private settlement reduce the amount defendants will pay plaintiff to settle?

CANADIAN TRANSPORT (U. K.) LIMITED v. ALSBURY

[1953] 1 D.L.R. 385 (B.C.Ct.App., 1952), affirmed 105 Can.Crim.Cas. 311 (1953).

SIDNEY SMITH, J. A.: This appeal is by one, Poje, and fourteen others against an order of Chief Justice Farris . . . which found them all guilty of contempt in disobeying an injunction previously granted by Clyne, J.; Poje was fined $3,000 and committed to jail for 3 months; the others were each fined $300. . . .

On July 15th the plaintiff company obtained from Clyne, J. an *ex parte* injunction, enjoining the defendants, their servants and agents from picketing the ship, M.S. "Vedby," then docked at Nanaimo. . . .

. . . The direct object of the picketing was to prevent longshoremen from loading lumber that was there on the wharf near the "Vedby." This object was attained until after July 22nd. The injunction was served by the Sheriff at Nanaimo and his evidence, given later, showed that he served Poje personally, and as an officer of the Local Union, on July 15th. On July 16th there were something like 190 pickets in the vicinity of the wharf; the Sheriff read them the injunction and advised them to disperse, which they would not do. Following this reading, some longshoremen drove up in a car and asked Poje whether they were to load, to which he answered—"No, sir, no sir." They obeyed him. On July 18th the Sheriff served many other pickets at the wharf. On July 22nd there were 60 to 70 pickets on hand, including all the defendants, and the Sheriff read the injunction to them, and advised them to disperse. They made no move, and were still there when the Sheriff left half an hour later. Poje, who was the business agent of the Local Union, was directing the pickets both on July 16th and 22nd.

On July 22nd the defendants, who had all appeared by the same solicitor, filed notice of motion returnable on the 24th, to vacate the injunction. . . . On July 23rd the plaintiff company moved to attach or commit a number of defendants for their contempt in disobeying the injunction. Those moved against did not include any of the appellants except Poje. This motion was by special leave also made returnable on July 24th.

These motions both came before Farris C. J. in Chambers on the 24th (brought back from vacation by his fellow Judges to deal with the matter as head of his Court), and counsel for both the plaintiff and defendants appeared and produced a memorandum of settlement, by which the picketing was to be called off and the lumber loaded, the plaintiffs were to discontinue the action, withdraw the injunction, and drop further proceedings. The Chief Justice indicated his disapproval of this withdrawal of the motion to commit, and said that injunctions were not granted for bargaining purposes. He also indicated that he might proceed *mero motu* if, on further inquiry, a defiance of the Court was shown, as the affidavits already filed indicated. He further said that he would adjourn the motion until September 8th, and in the meantime obtain a report from the Sheriff on disobedience to the injunction. The Sheriff made a long report on August 4th, which was in substance repeated in his later oral evidence.

On September 8th counsel who had appeared on July 24th again appeared, stating he represented the defendant Alsbury and another, but he later stated that his instructions came from Poje. The Chief Justice then called on the Sheriff from Nanaimo, who took the stand and testified as to service of the injunction and the appellants' disregard of it. On conclusion of the evidence the Chief Justice told counsel retained by Poje that a *prima facie* case of contempt was made out, and he would issue writs of attachment against the appellants to bring them before him on September 15th. This was done; appellants were all brought in and gave bail. . . .

On September 15th the appellants appeared in Court, and the same counsel appeared for all of them. The Chief Justice, after making it clear that he was acting on his own motion, then had the Sheriff of Nanaimo sworn, who repeated the evidence he had given on the 8th, as to service of and disobedience to the injunction. Appellants did not cross-examine or call any evidence in answer except on a collateral point, not relevant here. Their counsel stated that he wished to argue three legal objections to the injunction, which made it a nullity; but as soon as he outlined what they were, the Chief Justice said that he overruled them. Just previous to that the Chief Justice said that counsel could leave with him a brief he had prepared on the law, and that he would hear argument as to extenuating circumstances. In closing the hearing, the Chief Justice said he would give judgment next day, and appellants' counsel left his brief to be handed in. Next day the Chief Justice handed down judgment finding that all the appellants had wilfully disobeyed the injunction; and he inflicted the penalties I have mentioned. The formal judgment pronounced the appellants all guilty of "gross contempt of Court" but did not specify it further. . . .

In reading text-writers' ideas on what should be classed as criminal contempts and what civil or procedural contempts, it seems to me they show a curious want of proportion. To say, firstly, that it is a criminal contempt to libel a party to a pending action, to insult a witness or juror, or a solicitor out of Court, or to advertise for witnesses; but that secondly, breach of an injunction cannot amount to anything but a civil wrong, does not carry conviction. The former offences are treated as criminal because it is said that they "interfere with the administration of justice." The inference is that breach of an injunction cannot interfere with the administration of justice. But does it not? The Courts are solicitous to ensure that the parties get a fair trial; that can only be with a view to getting them the judgment they are entitled to. But can the Courts say: "Our only concern is to see you get your judgment; we are indifferent as to whether you can enforce it." If disobeying an interim injunction is not interfering with justice, disobeying a final judgment must be equally pardonable. I cannot see how it is rational to treat one interference with justice differently from the other. In fact it would seem to me far more serious to flout express prohibitions of the Court than merely to infringe general principles covering litigation.

. . . Applying them to this case, I have no doubt that there was intentional disobedience to this injunction, and other conduct that the state was even more concerned with; a point that I will dwell on further, presently. There can be no doubt that the Chief Justice dealt with this conduct as an affront to the state; and there can be no doubt that contempt proceedings carried on by him were meant to impose punishment and not meant as anything like execution. Disobedience to the order was in the past, the plaintiff company had agreed to withdraw it; and there was no reason to apprehend repetition of the picketing enjoined. The committal order was thus clearly punitive, or "penal." . . .

Next appellants argued that the Chief Justice did not purport to and could not intervene and take contempt proceedings of his own motion *mero motu,* where the plaintiff company had retired. The record leaves no doubt that he purported so to act. No authority was cited against his power so to do; but appellants relied on the absence of authority for such power and also, as I understood, claimed that any contempt proceedings on an injunction were civil in their nature, and that this prevented the Chief Justice's acting except at the instance of a party. . . .

. . . I must say that that seems to me entirely good reasoning, when the contempt affects not only the party, but the dignity and prestige of the Court. Then it seems the only significance of the party's intervention is that, without it, ordinarily the Court would not be apprised of the contempt. When it is apprised (and anyone may bring contempt to its notice . . .) it seems to me the attitude of the moving party ceases to be relevant if the Court wishes to act as its own defender. Personally I see no reason whatever why the Court should not be entirely the initiator of proceedings in such a case, regardless of whether the contempt proceedings are to be classed as criminal, quasi-criminal or civil. Any other conclusion could lead to impossible situations, and seems to me would involve ideas entirely at variance with the general principles behind the whole conception of contempt proceedings. Not only do the very early cases, like R. v. Almon (1765), Wilm. 243, 97 E.R. 94, emphasize that contempt proceedings are necessary to preserve that respect for Courts without which they could not function, but the host of cases holding it criminal contempt to interfere with the administration of justice point the same way. Many of these deal with only the most indirect interference . . . ; and the contempts seem to have only a tenuous connection with the Court itself. But there seems to be no doubt that the real objection is that the acts committed, by weakening the efficiency of curial processes, take away from the repute of the Courts and the general respect for them. And I cannot doubt that any other conduct that will have similar effect can be similarly dealt with. Nor can I doubt that the Court can always act of its own motion, if this is necessary for its own protection. Why should the Court be defenceless merely because the party who might complain is too supine to do so, or has lost its incentive through making a settlement? I feel unable to accept any such doctrine.

Even in the case of contempts that are more commonly recognized as "criminal," in the vast majority the party moves even though it is the Court that may be the real sufferer. But there is no doubt that the Court itself can move, if the party does not, and I cannot believe that there is any distinction between one contempt and another, so long as the Court's prestige and repute are affected. And although disobedience to an injunction is commonly an injury to the party who obtained it, in most cases I think it is more. The injunction is one of a Court's mightiest weapons, and there must be few cases in which the Court does not suffer if it allows this weapon to be ignored. That must be so even without special circumstances. But there can be disobedience and disobedience: the circumstances can make all the difference. For centuries back distinction has been drawn between negligent or accidental contempts and contumacious contempts, though few of the reports deal with injunction cases. Disobedience can easily take forms that are a covert or even an open challenge to the Courts. This present case is, in the view I take, a case of that kind. Are we to be told that after a party has defied a Court, the Court can still do nothing because the other party is willing to swallow the contempt? Nothing short of the clearest authority would convince me that that is the law; and there is no such authority; and no such law.

Whether the Court in so protecting itself exercises civil or criminal powers is probably unnecessary to decide, though I have already indicated my views. I am satisfied that the power exists. If so, I cannot doubt that occasion had arisen here for its exercise. The way the injunction was received was a direct challenge to the Court's powers. After it had been served on the Union's officer, Poje, he continued not only to picket, but to picket with numbers that are very suggestive; in fact they can only be given a sinister interpretation. The primary object was undoubtedly to overawe the longshoremen, but even for that they were extravagantly excessive. On one occasion there were something like 190, on another between 60 and 70, on another more than 50. This clearly points to an attempt to impress the public with the power of the Union and the size of its resources. A threat of force was inherent in the very numbers. It was a challenge. Then Poje, after having been personally served, continued to direct the pickets in defiance of the injunction. Right after the injunction had been read in his presence on July 22nd, he openly told the longshoremen not to load. The pickets, who included the other appellants, when the Sheriff read the injunction to them, received it with levity and made no move though advised to disperse. Perhaps we can infer that they were expecting the injunction and had been instructed to ignore it. The Chief Justice was therefore justified in finding a contumacious contempt that called for his interference *mero muto.* Had he done nothing the public might easily have inferred that the Union had shown itself too much for the Court. . . .

[Excerpt from dissenting opinion of O'HALLORAN, J. A. (at 393):]

It is not sufficient, in my judgment, to commit people for breach of an *ex parte* injunction before trial for conduct, outside the Court, simply because of their non-compliance with that order, and because a Judge may personally feel strongly that it amounts to a contempt of Court. Not infrequently the decisions show, that conduct outside a Court which a Judge of first instance may have been misled into thinking to be a contempt of Court, is not so regarded by a higher Court which has a wider perspective and is well removed from the dust of the arena. . . .

In my judgment there was sufficient doubt in this case, to warn a Judge of first instance to leave it for the Attorney-General to proceed upon information or invoke s. 165 * of the Cr.Code. How cautious a Judge must be in himself initiating contempt proceedings and carrying them on himself (he becomes Attorney-General, prosecutor, jury and Judge) is illustrated even in the case of a contempt in open Court . . . .

Where a Judge takes it upon himself to initiate contempt proceedings in relation to something that has occurred outside Court he may place himself in an awkward position and embarrass the higher Courts by becoming a party in the appeal, . . . I think it must be generally accepted that it would be far from an edifying spectacle to have a high-ranking Superior Court Judge as a party before an Appellate Court in respect to a Court order he has made. Such a thing would do a great deal to undermine the dignity and prestige of a Superior Court of first instance in the eyes of the public.

As a matter of fact in this case the notice of motion for stay of committal was spoken to *ex parte* in this Court on September 18th. On being questioned as to service upon an opposite party, counsel for appellants . . . tentatively suggested service upon the Chief Justice of the Supreme Court who made the committal order. As presiding Judge on the appeal I felt there

* [That section provided: Everyone is guilty of an indictable offence and liable to one year's imprisonment who, without lawful excuse, disobeys any lawful order, other than for the payment of money, made by any court of justice, or by any person or body of persons authorized by any statute to make or give such order, unless some penalty is imposed, or other mode of proceeding is expressly provided, by law. Can.Rev.Stat. c. 36, s. 165 (1927).]

would be impropriety in such a course, and intimated to appellant's counsel that the Court of Appeal was in need of the aid of the Attorney-General and the motion was adjourned. The intimation was acted on, and the Attorney-General was served, appeared as intervenor and argued the motion and appeal in proper course (counsel for the plaintiff having obtained leave for his client to withdraw).

---

1) MacNeil v. United States, 236 F.2d 149 (1st Cir. 1956), certiorari denied 352 U.S. 912, is a comparable but less colorful decision. It holds that the trial judge may initiate criminal but not civil contempt. Would the *Alsbury* court allow the trial judge to initiate coercive fines or imprisonment to achieve compliance?

2) Does In re Murchison, 349 U.S. 133 (1955), bear on *Alsbury?* Justice Black wrote for the Court at 136–137: "A fair trial in a fair tribunal is a basic requirement of due process. Fairness, of course, requires an absence of actual bias in the trial of cases. But our system of law has always endeavored to prevent even the probability of unfairness. To this end no man can be a judge in his own case and no man is permitted to try cases where he has an interest in the outcome. . . . Fair trials are too important a part of our free society to let prosecuting judges be trial judges of the charges they prefer."

3) The power to punish direct or in-court contempt seems to play a significant role in *Alsbury.* Some later limitations of direct contempt might affect the persuasiveness of the opinions. In Mayberry v. Pennsylvania, 400 U.S. 455 (1971), a defendant vilified and slandered a judge in the course of his state criminal trial; and at the end of the trial, the trial judge pronounced him in contempt and sentenced him to 11 to 22 years' imprisonment. The Supreme Court held that it was a denial of due process to have this judge try the contempt charge: "[A] judge, vilified as was this Pennsylvania judge, necessarily becomes embroiled in a running bitter controversy. No one so cruelly slandered is likely to maintain the calm detachment necessary for fair adjudication." 400 U.S. at 465.

If the power of the court in *Alsbury* to proceed is premised on the view that Poje's conduct was an affront to the dignity and integrity of the court, could the trial judges be expected to be impartial—or any more impartial than the judge in *Mayberry?* Or does the *Mayberry* rule require vilification? See also In re Little, 404 U.S. 553, 554 (1972), which held it impermissible to hold defendant in contempt, when in summation the defendant, who was defending himself, said the court was biased and that he was a political prisoner—even though the trial court concluded that the statements "reflected on the integrity of the court and tendered to subvert and prevent justice."

Are *Mayberry* and *Little* distinguishable from *Alsbury* because the contemptuous conduct occurred in the courtroom? Was the *Alsbury* trial judge too personally involved to be and appear to be impartial? Does *mero motu* contempt concentrate power too much? Did the judge confuse judicial power to regulate conduct in the courtroom with power to punish violations of injunctions? Does the *Alsbury* opinion express the notion that disrespect is contempt? Does advancing the policy of punishing disrespect frustrate the adversary system and the idea that private parties maintain lawsuits?

4) Does *Alsbury* reveal that prosecutorial initiative is misplaced in contempt? In Board of Junior College District No. 508 v. Cook County College Teachers Union, Local 1600, 126 Ill.App.2d 418, 262 N.E.2d 125 (1970), certiorari denied 402 U.S. 998 (1971), a strike was enjoined but nevertheless continued. The strike was then settled. The board's attorney moved to dissolve the temporary injunction. The trial judge refused to dissolve; instead, he ordered the board's attorney to prepare a show cause order against violators. The board's attorney declined. The trial judge asked the State's Attorney to begin contempt proceedings. That office also declined. The trial judge appointed a member of the Illinois bar as amicus curiae to prosecute. Amicus recommended contempt, presented the evidence leading to conviction, and successfully argued the appeal. "Under no theory can a party that obtains an injunction bind the issuing court with condonation of contemptuous or illegal acts of those who violate the court's order. To give effect to such a theory would usurp the highest function of our courts." 262 N.E.2d at 129–130. Should contempt procedure be reformed to remove the power to initiate contempt from judges and to lodge it exclusively with the executive's prosecuting officials? Kuhns, Limiting the Criminal Contempt Power: A New Role for the Prosecutor and the Grand Jury, 73 Mich.L.Rev. 484 (1975).

5) If the injunction judge declines to press contempt, may a prosecuting attorney charge defendants under a criminal statute like the one in *Morris* or § 1509? Consider what your answer implies for separation of powers.

6) Compromise between the victim and the wrongdoer often ends criminal prosecutions. The victim may cease cooperating with the authorities or ask to drop the charges. An Arizona statute makes compromise formal in misdemeanor prosecutions: "If the party injured appears before the court in which the action is pending at any time before trial, and acknowledges that he has received satisfaction for the injury, the court may, on payment of the costs incurred, order the prosecution dismissed, and the defendant discharged. The reasons for the order shall be set forth and entered of record on the minutes and the order shall be a bar to another prosecution for the same offense." Ariz.Rev.Stat.Ann. § 13–3981(B) (1956). The Model Penal Code lets judges withhold imprisonment when a convicted criminal defendant "has compensated or will compensate the victim of his criminal conduct for the damage or injury that he sustained." Model Penal Code § 7.01(f) (Proposed Official Draft 1962).

7) The amnesty problem is part of a larger one: "How can one commit himself in advance to an act that he would in fact prefer not to carry out in the event, in order that his commitment may deter the other party?" T. Schelling, The Strategy of Conflict 36 (1960). Maximum threats "leave as little room as possible for judgment or discretion in carrying out the threat." Strategy of Conflict at 40. People with power employ the threat of sanctions to alter the recipient's incentives to behave in the future. A successful threat is one that averts enforcement. This benefits both parties. When a threat fails, both parties may seek to undo it. "The purpose of the threat is gone, its deterrence value is zero, and only the commitment exists to motivate ful-

fillment." Strategy of Conflict at 39. Once someone ignores a threat, imposing a sanction disproportionately larger than the harm caused by breach may create a dead weight loss. After a violation, it may be in both parties' interest to forget the sanction. The sanction also may be incompatible with other values such as a mutual need to work together afterwards and humane repugnance at unnecessary suffering. Put yourself in the position of a parent who has said "If you're in *one* minute after midnight, you are grounded for six months," or a head of state who has said, "If *one* soldier crosses this frontier, it's war." In both, the threatener's reputation and credibility for keeping promises may not be worth the consequences of keeping this particular one. Strategy of Conflict at 35–43, 119–61. Are the parental and international analogies relevant to injunctions where violation threatens respect for judicial orders and the rule of law?

8) Imprisonment is not a tactic assured to develop warm and cordial relations between employers and employees. Prohibiting public employee strikes failed to prevent strikes, injunctions, and negotiated amnesty. Legislatures have developed various ways of binding public employers to the mast to assure that they will not be tempted to amnesty strikers. Under New York's Taylor Law, public employees "automatically" lose two days' pay for each day they strike and the unions lose dues check-off. Two articles describe the administration of this statute in the 1979 prison guard strike. Zimmer and Jacobs, Challenging the Taylor Law: Prison Guards on Strike, 34 Indus. & Lab.Rel.Rev. 531 (1981); Peterson, Deterring Strikes By Public Employees: New York's Two-For-One Salary Penalty and the 1979 Prison Guard Strike, 34 Indus. & Lab.Rel.Rev. 545 (1981). Would you expect discretion and amnesty to creep back into this process to advance amiable employee relations as well as to prevent hardship and punishment? See Zimmer and Jacobs, 34 Indus. & Lab.Rel.Rev. at 539 n. 37, 541; Peterson, 34 Indus. & Lab.Rel.Rev. at 554–60.

9) Congress has forbidden federal employees from striking by a statute that forbids employment of any person who has engaged in a work stoppage against the government. 5 U.S.C. § 7311 (1976). A felony statute provides for fines or imprisonment. 18 U.S.C. § 1918 (1976). Unions that authorize or support strikes forfeit recognition rights, and participating employees lose their employee status. 5 U.S.C. §§ 7116(b)(7), 7120(f) (Supp. IV 1980). When the Professional Air Traffic Controllers Organization disobeyed an injunction and struck in August 1981, the government terminated the employees and decertified the union. Judge Green refused to impose coercive contempt fines for striking for any days after the employees were terminated or the union was decertified. United States v. PATCO, 524 F.Supp. 160, 164 (D.D.C.1981). Judge Green said: "[O]nce the government declared that the air traffic controllers would not be permitted to return to work, the obligations of defendants under the back-to-work provisions of the injunctive orders of the court ceased." But the possibility of criminal contempt remains. United States v. Phillips, 525 F.Supp. 1 (N.D.Ill.1981) (allegations of selective criminal prosecution rebutted; union officers' motion to dismiss show cause denied). The controllers' union filed for bankruptcy reorganization. Has the new day in public employee labor relations that dawned with the PATCO strike mooted the question of amnesty?

V. Petit and Grand Juries

BLOOM v. ILLINOIS

391 U.S. 194, 88 S.Ct. 1477, 20 L.Ed.2d 522 (1968).

Justice WHITE delivered the opinion of the Court.

Petitioner was convicted in an Illinois state court of criminal contempt and sentenced to imprisonment for 24 months for willfully petitioning to admit to probate a will falsely prepared and executed after the death of the putative testator. Petitioner made a timely demand for jury trial which was refused. Since in Duncan v. Louisiana [391 U.S. 145 (1968)], the Constitution was held to guarantee the right to jury trial in serious criminal cases in state courts, we must now decide whether it also guarantees the right to jury trial for a criminal contempt punished by a two-year prison term.

I.

Whether federal and state courts may try criminal contempt cases without a jury has been a recurring question in this Court. Article III, § 2, of the Constitution provides that "[t]he Trial of all Crimes, except in Cases of Impeachment, shall be by Jury . . . ." The Sixth Amendment states that "[i]n all criminal prosecutions, the accused shall enjoy the right to a speedy and public trial, by an impartial jury . . . ." The Fifth and Fourteenth Amendments forbid both the Federal Government and the States from depriving any person of "life, liberty, or property, without due process of law." Notwithstanding these provisions, until United States v. Barnett, the Court consistently upheld the constitutional power of the state and federal courts to punish any criminal contempt without a jury trial. . . . In re Debs; Gompers v. United States; Green v. United States, 356 U.S. 165, 183–187 (1958).[1] These cases construed the Due Process Clause and the otherwise inclusive language of Article III and the Sixth Amendment as permitting summary trials in contempt cases because at common law contempt was tried without a jury and because the power of courts to punish for contempt without the intervention of any other agency was considered essential to the proper and effective functioning of the courts and to the administration of justice.

United States v. Barnett signaled a possible change of view. The Court of Appeals for the Fifth Circuit certified to this Court the question whether there was a right to jury trial in an impending contempt proceeding. Following prior cases, a five-man majority held that there was no constitutional right to jury trial in all contempt cases. Criminal contempt, intrinsically and aside from the particular penalty imposed, was not deemed a serious offense requir-

1. Many more cases have supported the rule that courts may punish criminal contempt summarily, or accepted that rule without question. See cases collected in Green v. United States, 356 U.S. 165, 191, n. 2 (1958) (concurring opinion); United States v. Barnett. The list of the Justices of this Court who have apparently subscribed to this view is long. See Green v. United States.

The argument that the power to punish contempt was an inherent power of the courts not subject to regulation by Congress was rejected in Michaelson v. United States ex rel. Chicago, St. P., M. & O. R. Co., 266 U.S. 42, 65–67 (1924), which upheld the maximum sentence and jury trial provisions of the Clayton Act. . . .

ing the protection of the constitutional guarantees of the right to jury trial. However, the Court put aside as not raised in the certification or firmly settled by prior cases, the issue whether a severe punishment would itself trigger the right to jury trial and indicated, without explication, that some members of the Court were of the view that the Constitution limited the punishment which could be imposed where the contempt was tried without a jury. . . .

Two years later, in Cheff v. Schnackenberg, 384 U.S. 373 (1966), which involved a prison term of six months for contempt of a federal court, the Court rejected the claim that the Constitution guaranteed a right to jury trial in all criminal contempt cases. Contempt did not "of itself" warrant treatment as other than a petty offense; the six months' punishment imposed permitted dealing with the case as a prosecution for "a petty offense, which under our decisions does not require a jury trial." . . . It was not necessary in *Cheff* to consider whether the constitutional guarantees of the right to jury trial applied to a prosecution for a serious contempt. Now, however, because of our holding in Duncan v. Louisiana . . . that the right to jury trial extends to the States, and because of Bloom's demand for a jury in this case, we must once again confront the broad rule that all criminal contempts can be constitutionally tried without a jury. *Barnett* presaged a re-examination of this doctrine at some later time; that time has now arrived.

In proceeding with this task, we are acutely aware of the responsibility we assume in entertaining challenges to a constitutional principle which is firmly entrenched and which has behind it weighty and ancient authority. Our deliberations have convinced us, however, that serious contempts are so nearly like other serious crimes that they are subject to the jury trial provisions of the Constitution, now binding on the States, and that the traditional rule is constitutionally infirm insofar as it permits other than petty contempts to be tried without honoring a demand for a jury trial. We accept the judgment of *Barnett* and *Cheff* that criminal contempt is a petty offense unless the punishment makes it a serious one; but, in our view, dispensing with the jury in the trial of contempts subjected to severe punishment represents an unacceptable construction of the Constitution. . . . The rule of our prior cases has strong, though sharply challenged, historical support;[2] but neither this cir-

2. Blackstone's description of the common-law practice in contempt cases appears in 4 Commentaries on the Laws of England 286–287:

"The process of attachment for these and the like contempts must necessarily be as ancient as the laws themselves; for laws without a competent authority to secure their administration from disobedience and contempt would be vain and nugatory. A power, therefore, in the supreme courts of justice, to suppress such contempts by an immediate attachment of the offender results from the first principles of judicial establishments, and must be an inseparable attendant upon every superior tribunal.

"If the contempt be committed in the face of the court, the offender may be instantly apprehended and imprisoned, at the discretion of the judges, without any further proof or examination. But in matters that arise at a distance, and of which the court cannot have so perfect a knowledge, unless by the confession of the party or the testimony of others, if the judges upon *affidavit* see sufficient ground to suspect that a contempt has been committed, they either make a rule on the suspected party to show cause why an attachment should not issue against him, or, in very flagrant instances of contempt, the attachment issues in the first instance; as it also does if no sufficient cause be shown to discharge; and thereupon the court confirms and makes absolute the original rule." A similar account is contained in

cumstance nor the considerations of necessity and efficiency normally offered in defense of the established rule, justify denying a jury trial in serious criminal contempt cases. The Constitution guarantees the right to jury trial in state court prosecutions for contempt just as it does for other crimes.

Criminal contempt is a crime in the ordinary sense; it is a violation of the law, a public wrong which is punishable by fine or imprisonment or both. . . . Criminally contemptuous conduct may violate other provisions of the criminal law; but even when this is not the case convictions for criminal con-

2 W. Hawkins, A Treatise of the Pleas of the Crown 4, 141 (2d ed. 1724).

Of course, "Blackstone's Commentaries are accepted as the most satisfactory exposition of the common law of England. . . . [U]ndoubtedly the framers of the Constitution were familiar with it." Schick v. United States, 195 U.S. 65, 69 (1904).

Blackstone, however, was acutely aware that this practice was a significant departure from ordinary principles: "It cannot have escaped the attention of the reader that this method of making the defendant answer upon oath to a criminal charge is not agreeable to the genius of the common law in any other instance . . . ." 4 Blackstone, supra, at 287.

The unalloyed doctrine that by "immemorial usage" all criminal contempts could be tried summarily seems to derive from Mr. Justice (later Chief Justice) Wilmot's undelivered opinion in The King v. Almon (1765), first brought to public light by the posthumous publication of his papers, Wilmot, Notes 243 (1802), reprinted in 97 Eng.Rep. 94. Wilmot's opinion appears to have been the source of Blackstone's view, but did not become an authoritative part of the law of England until Rex v. Clement, 4 Barn. & Ald. 218, 233, 106 Eng.Rep. 918, 923 (K.B.1821). . . . The historical authenticity of this view has been vigorously challenged, initially by Solly-Flood, The Story of Prince Henry of Monmouth and Chief-Justice Gascoign, 3 Transactions of the Royal Historical Society (N.S.) 47, 61–64, 147–150 (1886). This led to the massive reappraisal of the contempt power undertaken by Sir John Fox: The King v. Almon, Pts. 1 & 2, 24 L.Q. Rev. 184, 266 (1908); The Summary Process to Punish Contempt, Pts. 1 & 2, 25 L.Q.Rev. 238, 354 (1909); Eccentricities of the Law of Contempt of Court, 36 L.Q. Rev. 394 (1920); The Nature of Contempt of Court, 37 L.Q.Rev. 191 (1921); The Practice in Contempt of Court Cases, 38 L.Q.Rev. 185 (1922); The Writ of Attachment, 40 L.Q.Rev. 43 (1924); J. Fox, The History of Contempt of Court (1927). On contempt generally, see R. Goldfarb, The Contempt Power (1963).

Learned writers have interpreted Fox's work as showing that until the late 17th or early 18th centuries, apart from the extraordinary proceedings of the Star Chamber, English courts neither had, nor claimed, power to punish contempts, whether in or out of court, by summary process. Frankfurter & Landis, Power of Congress over Procedure in Criminal Contempts in "Inferior" Federal Courts—A Study in Separation of Powers, 37 Harv.L.Rev. 1010, 1042–1052 (1924). Cf. J. Oswald, Contempt of Court 3, n. (g) (Robertson ed., 1910). Fox's own appraisal of the evidence, however, seems to have been that prior to the 18th century there probably was no valid basis for summary punishment of a libel on the court by a stranger to the proceedings, but that summary punishment for contempts outside the court consisting in resistance to a lawful process or order of the court, or contumacious behavior by an officer of the court, was probably permissible. J. Fox, The History of Contempt of Court 4, 49–50, 98–100, 108–110, 208–209 (1927); Fox, The Summary Process to Punish Contempt, Pt. 1, 25 L.Q. Rev. 238, 244–246 (1909). Although jury trials had been provided in some instances of contempt in the face of the court, Fox does not seem to have questioned that such contempts could be punished summarily. J. Fox, The History of Contempt of Court 50 (1927).

We do not find the history of criminal contempt sufficiently simple or unambiguous to rest rejection of our prior decisions entirely on historical grounds, particularly since the Court has been aware of Solly-Flood's and Fox's work for many years. See Gompers v. United States; Michaelson v. United States ex rel. Chicago, St. P., M. & O. R. Co., 266 U.S. 42, 66–67 (1924); Green v. United States, 356 U.S. 165, 185, n. 18 (1958). In any event, the ultimate question is not whether the traditional doctrine is historically correct but whether the rule that criminal contempts are never entitled to a jury trial is a necessary or an acceptable construction of the Constitution. . . .

tempt are indistinguishable from ordinary criminal convictions, for their impact on the individual defendant is the same. Indeed, the role of criminal contempt and that of many ordinary criminal laws seem identical—protection of the institutions of our government and enforcement of their mandates.

Given that criminal contempt is a crime in every fundamental respect, the question is whether it is a crime to which the jury trial provisions of the Constitution apply. We hold that it is, primarily because in terms of those considerations which make the right to jury trial fundamental in criminal cases, there is no substantial difference between serious contempts and other serious crimes. Indeed, in contempt cases an even more compelling argument can be made for providing a right to jury trial as a protection against the arbitrary exercise of official power. Contemptuous conduct, though a public wrong, often strikes at the most vulnerable and human qualities of a judge's temperament. Even when the contempt is not a direct insult to the court or the judge, it frequently represents a rejection of judicial authority, or an interference with the judicial process or with the duties of officers of the court. . . .

These apprehensions about the unbridled power to punish summarily for contempt are reflected in the march of events in both Congress and the courts since our Constitution was adopted. The federal courts were established by the Judiciary Act of 1789; § 17 of the Act provided that those courts "shall have power to . . . punish by fine or imprisonment, at the discretion of said courts, all contempts of authority in any cause or hearing before the same . . . ." 1 Stat. 83. . . . This open-ended authority to deal with contempt, limited only as to mode of punishment, proved unsatisfactory to Congress. Abuses under the 1789 Act culminated in the unsuccessful impeachment proceedings against James Peck, a federal district judge who had imprisoned and disbarred one Lawless for publishing a criticism of one of Peck's opinions in a case which was on appeal. The result was drastic curtailment of the contempt power in the Act of 1831, 4 Stat. 487. . . . That Act limited the contempt power to misbehavior in the presence of the court or so near thereto as to obstruct justice; misbehavior of court officers in their official transactions; and disobedience of or resistance to the lawful writ, process, order, or decree of the court. This major revision of the contempt power in the federal sphere, which "narrowly confined" and "substantially curtailed" the authority to punish contempt summarily, Nye v. United States, 313 U.S. 33, 47–48 (1941), has continued to the present day as the basis for the general power to punish criminal contempt.[6] 18 U.S.C. § 401.

6. At a later date, when passing the Clayton Act, Congress focused its attention on conduct which was not only criminally contemptuous but which also constituted other crimes under federal or state law. Contempts of this nature, unless committed in the presence of the court or so near thereto as to obstruct justice, or unless they involved disobedience to a court writ, process, order, or decree in a case brought by the United States, were required to be tried to a jury, and the possible punishment was limited to six months, a fine of $1,000, or both. 18 U.S.C. § 402. Circumscription of the contempt power was carried further in the Norris-LaGuardia Act, which extended the right to jury trial to contempt cases arising out of injunctions issued in labor disputes. 18 U.S.C. § 3692. The Civil Rights Act of 1957, 42 U.S.C. § 1995, provides a right to a *de novo* trial by jury to all criminal contemnors convicted in cases arising under the Act who are fined in excess of $300 or sentenced to imprisonment for more than 45 days, exception being made for contempts committed in the presence of the court or so near thereto as to obstruct justice, and misbehavior, misconduct, or disobedience

The courts also proved sensitive to the potential for abuse which resides in the summary power to punish contempt. Before the 19th century was out, a distinction had been carefully drawn between contempts occurring within the view of the court, for which a hearing and formal presentation of evidence were dispensed with, and all other contempts where more normal adversary procedures were required. Ex parte Terry, 128 U.S. 289 (1888); In re Savin, 131 U.S. 267 (1889). Later, the Court could say "it is certain that in proceedings for criminal contempt the defendant is presumed to be innocent, he must be proved to be guilty beyond a reasonable doubt, and cannot be compelled to testify against himself." Gompers v. Bucks Stove & Range Co., 221 U.S. 418, 444 (1911). . . . Chief Justice Taft speaking for a unanimous Court in Cooke v. United States, 267 U.S. 517, 537 (1925), said:

"Due process of law, therefore, in the prosecution of contempt, except of that committed in open court, requires that the accused should be advised of the charges and have a reasonable opportunity to meet them by way of defense or explanation. We think this includes the assistance of counsel, if requested, and the right to call witnesses to give testimony, relevant either to the issue of complete exculpation or in extenuation of the offense and in mitigation of the penalty to be imposed."

. . . It has also been recognized that the defendant in criminal contempt proceedings is entitled to a public trial before an unbiased judge, In re Oliver, 333 U.S. 257 (1948) . . . . In the federal system many of the procedural protections available to criminal contemnors are set forth in Fed.Rule Crim.Proc. 42.

Judicial concern has not been limited to procedure. In Toledo Newspaper Co. v. United States, 247 U.S. 402 (1918), the Court endorsed a broad construction of the language of the Act of 1831 permitting summary trial of contempts "so near [to the court] as to obstruct the administration of justice." It required only that the conduct have a "tendency to prevent and obstruct the discharge of judicial duty . . . ." This view proved aberrational and was overruled in Nye v. United States, 313 U.S. 33, 47–52 (1941), which narrowly limited the conduct proscribed by the 1831 Act to "misbehavior in the vicinity of the court disrupting to quiet and order or actually interrupting the court in the conduct of its business." The congressional purpose to fence in the power of the federal courts to punish contempt summarily was further implemented in Cammer v. United States, 350 U.S. 399, 407–408 (1956). A lawyer, the Court held, "is not the kind of 'officer' who can be summarily tried for contempt under 18 U.S.C. § 401(2)." In another development, the First Amendment was invoked to ban punishment for a broad category of arguably contemptuous out-of-court conduct. Bridges v. California, 314 U.S. 252 (1941); Pennekamp v. Florida, 328 U.S. 331 (1946); Craig v. Harney, 331 U.S. 367 (1947). Finally, over the years in the federal system there has been a recurring necessity to set aside punishments for criminal contempt as

of any officer of the court. The Civil Rights Act of 1964, § 1101, 42 U.S.C. § 2000h, provides a right to jury trial in all proceedings for criminal contempt arising under the Act, and limits punishment to a fine of $1,000 or imprisonment for six months. Again exception is made for contempts committed in the presence of the court, or so near thereto as to obstruct justice, and for the misbehavior, misconduct, or disobedience of court officers. Proof of criminal *mens rea* is specifically required. See Goldfarb & Kurzman, Civil Rights v. Civil Liberties: The Jury Trial Issue, 12 U.C.L.A.L.Rev. 486, 496–506 (1965).

either unauthorized by statute or too harsh. E.g., Ex parte Robinson, 19 Wall. 505 (1874); United States v. United Mine Workers; Yates v. United States, 355 U.S. 66 (1957).[8]

This course of events demonstrates the unwisdom of vesting the judiciary with completely untrammeled power to punish contempt, and makes clear the need for effective safeguards against that power's abuse. Prosecutions for contempt play a significant role in the proper functioning of our judicial system; but despite the important values which the contempt power protects, courts and legislatures have gradually eroded the power of judges to try contempts of their own authority. In modern times, procedures in criminal contempt cases have come to mirror those used in ordinary criminal cases. Our experience teaches that convictions for criminal contempt, not infrequently resulting in extremely serious penalties, . . . are indistinguishable from those obtained under ordinary criminal laws. If the right to jury trial is a fundamental matter in other criminal cases, which we think it is, it must also be extended to criminal contempt cases.

Nor are there compelling reasons for a contrary result. As we read the earlier cases in this Court upholding the power to try contempts without a jury, it was not doubted that the summary power was subject to abuse or that the right to jury trial would be an effective check. Rather, it seems to have been thought that summary power was necessary to preserve the dignity, independence, and effectiveness of the judicial process—"To submit the question of disobedience to another tribunal, be it a jury or another court, would operate to deprive the proceeding of half its efficiency." In re Debs, 158 U.S. 564, 595 (1895). It is at this point that we do not agree: in our judgment, when serious punishment for contempt is contemplated, rejecting a demand for jury trial cannot be squared with the Constitution or justified by considerations of efficiency or the desirability of vindicating the authority of the court.

We cannot say that the need to further respect for judges and courts is entitled to more consideration than the interest of the individual not to be

8. Limitations on the maximum penalties for criminal contempt are common in the States. According to Note, Constitutional Law: The Supreme Court Constructs a Limited Right to Trial by Jury for Federal Criminal Contemnors, 1967 Duke L.J. 632, 654, n. 84, in 26 States the maximum penalty that can be imposed in the absence of a jury trial is six months or less, in three States a jury trial must be provided upon demand of the defendant, in three other States the maximum penalty cannot exceed one year (this group of States includes Illinois, however, which, as the present case demonstrates, has no such limitation), in 15 States there is either no limitation upon the maximum penalty which may be imposed, or else that maximum exceeds one year, and finally, in three States, while there are statutes relating to particular kinds of contempt, there are no general contempt provisions. Independent examination suggests that the available materials concerning the law of contempt in some States are such that precise computation is difficult. It is clear, however, that punishment for contempt is limited to one year or less in over half the States.

Most other Western countries seem to be highly restrictive of the latitude given judges to try their own contempts without a jury. See Jann, Contempt of Court in Western Germany, 8 Am.U.L.Rev. 34 (1959); Bigelow, Contempt of Court, 1 Crim.L.Q. 475 (1959); Pekelis, Legal Techniques and Political Ideologies: A Comparative Study, 41 Mich.L.Rev. 665 (1943). By contrast, there was no right of appeal against a conviction for criminal contempt in England until the Administration of Justice Act, 1960, 8 & 9 Eliz. 2, c. 65. See Harnon, Civil and Criminal Contempts of Court, 25 Mod.L.Rev. 179 (1962).

subjected to serious criminal punishment without the benefit of all the procedural protections worked out carefully over the years and deemed fundamental to our system of justice. Genuine respect, which alone can lend true dignity to our judicial establishment, will be engendered, not by the fear of unlimited authority, but by the firm administration of the law through those institutionalized procedures which have been worked out over the centuries.

We place little credence in the notion that the independence of the judiciary hangs on the power to try contempts summarily and are not persuaded that the additional time and expense possibly involved in submitting serious contempts to juries will seriously handicap the effective functioning of the courts. We do not deny that serious punishment must sometimes be imposed for contempt, but we reject the contention that such punishment must be imposed without the right to jury trial. The goals of dispatch, economy, and efficiency are important, but they are amply served by preserving the power to commit for civil contempt and by recognizing that many contempts are not serious crimes but petty offenses not within the jury trial provisions of the Constitution. When a serious contempt is at issue, considerations of efficiency must give way to the more fundamental interest of ensuring the even-handed exercise of judicial power. In isolated instances recalcitrant or irrational juries may acquit rather than apply the law to the case before them. Our system has wrestled with this problem for hundreds of years, however, and important safeguards have been devised to minimize miscarriages of justice through the malfunctioning of the jury system. Perhaps to some extent we sacrifice efficiency, expedition, and economy, but the choice in favor of jury trial has been made, and retained, in the Constitution. We see no sound reason in logic or policy not to apply it in the area of criminal contempt.

Some special mention of contempts in the presence of the judge is warranted. Rule 42(a) of the Federal Rules of Criminal Procedure provides that "[a] criminal contempt may be punished summarily if the judge certifies that he saw or heard the conduct constituting the contempt and that it was committed in the actual presence of the court." This rule reflects the common-law rule which is widely if not uniformly followed in the States. Although Rule 42(a) is based in part on the premise that it is not necessary specially to present the facts of a contempt which occurred in the very presence of the judge, it also rests on the need to maintain order and a deliberative atmosphere in the courtroom. The power of a judge to quell disturbance cannot attend upon the impaneling of a jury. There is, therefore, a strong temptation to make an exception to the rule we establish today for disorders in the courtroom. We are convinced, however, that no such special rule is needed. It is old law that the guarantees of jury trial found in Article III and the Sixth Amendment do not apply to petty offenses. Only today we have reaffirmed that position. Duncan v. Louisiana . . . . By deciding to treat criminal contempt like other crimes insofar as the right to jury trial is concerned, we similarly place it under the rule that petty crimes need not be tried to a jury.

Petitioner Bloom was held in contempt of court for filing a spurious will for probate. At his trial it was established that the putative testator died on July 6, 1964, and that after that date Pauline Owens, a practical nurse for the decedent, engaged Bloom to draw and execute a will in the decedent's name. The will was dated June 21, 1964. Bloom knew the will was false when he presented it for admission in the Probate Division of the Circuit Court of Cook County. The State's Attorney of that county filed a complaint charging Bloom with contempt of court. At trial petitioner's timely motion for a jury trial was denied. Petitioner was found guilty of criminal contempt and sentenced to imprisonment for 24 months. On direct appeal to the Illinois Supreme Court, his conviction was affirmed. That court held that neither state law nor the Federal Constitution provided a right to jury trial in criminal contempt proceedings. . . .

Petitioner Bloom contends that the conduct for which he was convicted of criminal contempt constituted the crime of forgery under Ill.Rev.Stat., c. 38, § 17–3. Defendants tried under that statute enjoy a right to jury trial and face a possible sentence of one to 14 years, a fine not to exceed $1,000, or both. Petitioner was not tried under this statute, but rather was convicted of criminal contempt. Under Illinois law no maximum punishment is provided for convictions for criminal contempt. . . . In *Duncan* we have said that we need not settle "the exact location of the line between petty offenses and serious crimes" but that "a crime punishable by two years in prison is . . . a serious crime and not a petty offense." Supra, at 161, 162. Bloom was sentenced to imprisonment for two years. Our analysis of *Barnett* and Cheff v. Schnackenberg, 384 U.S. 373, makes it clear that criminal contempt is not a crime of the sort that requires the right to jury trial regardless of the penalty involved. Under the rule in *Cheff*, when the legislature has not expressed a judgment as to the seriousness of an offense by fixing a maximum penalty which may be imposed, we are to look to the penalty actually imposed as the best evidence of the seriousness of the offense. See *Duncan*, supra, at 162, n. 35.* Under this rule it is clear that Bloom was entitled to the right to trial by jury, and it was constitutional error to deny him that right. Accordingly, we reverse and remand for proceedings not inconsistent with this opinion.

---

1) Is *Bloom* part of a steady movement to assimilate contempt to an ordinary crime, to impose due process on contempt, and to favor protection for individuals over efficiency and respect?

2) Perhaps *Barnett*, p. 909, offers a better perspective from which to consider whether a criminal contemnor is entitled to a jury trial. Solicitor General Archibald Cox argued to the Supreme Court "The problem that faced

* [The footnote referred to reads:

"35. It is argued that Cheff v. Schnackenberg, 384 U.S. 373 (1966), interpreted the Sixth Amendment as meaning that to the extent that the length of punishment is a relevant criterion in distinguishing between serious crimes and petty offenses, the critical factor is not the length of the sentence authorized but the length of the penalty actually imposed. In our view that case does not reach the situation where a legislative judgment as to the seriousness of the crime is imbedded in the statute in the form of an express authorization to impose a heavy penalty for the crime in question. *Cheff* involved criminal contempt, an offense applied to a wide range of conduct including conduct not so serious as to require jury trial absent a long sentence. In addition criminal contempt is unique in that legislative bodies frequently authorize punishment without stating the extent of the penalty which can be imposed. The contempt statute under which Cheff was prosecuted, 18 U.S.C. § 401, treated the extent of punishment as a matter to be determined by the forum court. It is therefore understandable that this Court in *Cheff* seized upon the penalty actually imposed as the best evidence of the seriousness of the offense for which Cheff was tried."]

the Court of Appeals . . . was essentially one of restoring the principle of government according to law." On the specific point of a jury trial, he asserted, "Our Constitution guarantees the rights of unpopular minorities. The courts, rightly, jealously protect them. But the judicial protection may often prove hollow if the vindication of the court's decree can be prevented by the whim of a single juror sympathetic to a lawless mob or a lawless state official." J. Bass, Unlikely Heroes 249 (1981). If the Court had accepted Cox's argument, would that decision have encouraged the executive to employ injunctions and contempt instead of criminal prosecutions to enforce unpopular policy? How did the *Debs* Court respond to the contemnor's argument that a criminal prosecution was an adequate remedy at law? See p. 12.

3) Since § 401 contains no limit on punishment, the sentence actually imposed determines whether the contempt is serious or petty. Should the test be the possible sanction? See also §§ 402, 3691. Refinements have occurred. In Frank v. United States, 395 U.S. 147 (1969), the judge imposed three years probation for contempt without a jury; when contemnor violated the probation terms, jail was limited to six months because there was no jury. In Codispoti v. Pennsylvania, 418 U.S. 506 (1974), the judge found at the end of a trial that a criminal defendant had committed seven contempts and imposed consecutive contempt sentences of six months for six contempts and three months for the seventh contempt; but the Court held that if such a sentence aggregates more than six months, contemnor may summon a jury. If defendant breaches an injunction once a week for seven weeks, could the judge view these as discrete contempts and impose seven consecutive six-month sentences?

4) Should courts wield contempt against perjurors and filers of false documents? The United States Supreme Court had held earlier that a contempt conviction for perjury was improper under an earlier version of 18 U.S.C. § 401. In re Michael, 326 U.S. 224 (1945). Federal authorities are remitted to a criminal prosecution for perjury. Why? Did the *Michael* Court fear that 1) trial judges will abuse summary contempt procedure? 2) if the witness in fact told the truth, civil coercive imprisonment might be indefinite? Do cross-examination and criminal prosecutions suffice for a lying witness? Are forged documents distinguishable from invented perjured testimony? Dobbs, Contempt of Court: A Survey, 56 Cornell L.Rev. 183, 194–200 (1971). The *Michael* Court focused on the absence of a jury in contempt. Does *Bloom* repudiate *Michael?* Or was the Court unwilling to define substantive contempt for Illinois?

5) Does *Bloom* show the absurdity of treating everything called "contempt" the same way? Are there differences between the reticent grand jury witness, the filer of forged documents, the in-court cut-up, the suspended attorney, and the injunction violator? Are courts behaving like the government official who treated all trunks the same: tree, steamer, elephant, and bathing?

MUNIZ v. HOFFMAN

422 U.S. 454, 95 S.Ct. 2178, 45 L.Ed.2d 319 (1975).

Justice WHITE delivered the opinion of the Court.

The issues in this case are whether a labor union or an individual, when charged with criminal contempt for violating an injunction issued pursuant to § 10(*l*) of the Labor Management Relations Act, as added, 61 Stat. 149, and as amended, 29 U.S.C. § 160(*l*), has a right to a jury trial under 18 U.S.C. § 3692, and whether the union has a right to a jury trial under the Constitution when charged with such a violation and a fine of as much as $10,000 is to be imposed.

Early in 1970, Local 21 of the San Francisco Typographical Union commenced picketing a publishing plant of a daily newspaper in San Rafael, Cal. Shortly thereafter, the newspaper filed an unfair labor practice charge against this union activity, and the Regional Director of the National Labor Relations Board, in response to that filing, petitioned the District Court pursuant to § 10(*l*) for a temporary injunction against those activities pending final disposition of the charge by the Board. The District Court, after a hearing, granted the requested relief and, more than two months later, granted a second petition for a temporary injunction filed by the Regional Director in response to other union activities related to the original dispute. On June 24, 1970, Local 21 and certain of its officials were found to be in civil contempt of the latter injunction. After the entry of this contempt order, the tempo of illegal activities in violation of both injunctions increased, with other locals, including Local 70, participating. Various unions and their officers, including petitioners, were subsequently ordered to show cause why they should not be held in civil and criminal contempt of the injunctions. After proceedings in the criminal contempt case had been severed from the civil contempt proceedings, petitioners demanded a jury trial in the criminal case; this request was denied and petitioners were adjudged guilty of criminal contempt after appropriate proceedings. The District Court suspended the sentencing of petitioner Muniz and placed him on probation for one year; the court imposed a fine on petitioner Local 70 which, for purposes of this case, was $10,000.[1] On appeal of that judgment to the Court of Appeals, petitioners argued, *inter alia*, that they had a statutory right to a jury trial of any disputed issues of fact, relying on 18 U.S.C. § 3692; petitioners also argued that they had a right to a jury trial under Art. III, § 2, of the Constitution, and the Sixth Amendment. The Court of Appeals rejected these and other claims made by petitioners, 492 F.2d 929 (CA9 1974) who then petitioned this Court for a writ of certiorari. The writ was granted, 419 U.S. 992 (1974), limited to the questions whether petitioners had a statutory right to a jury trial and whether petitioner Local 70 had a constitutional right to jury trial in this case. . . .

[The Court rejected contemnors' argument that § 3692 required a jury trial.]

1. A fine of $25,000 was imposed initially, but $15,000 of that fine was subsequently remitted by the District Court based on Local 70's obedience of the injunctions subsequent to the adjudication of contempt.

We also agree with the Court of Appeals that the union petitioner had no right to a jury trial under Art. III, § 2, and the Sixth Amendment. Green v. United States, 356 U.S. 165 (1958), reaffirmed the historic rule that state and federal courts have the constitutional power to punish any criminal contempt without a jury trial. United States v. Barnett and Cheff v. Schnackenberg, 384 U.S. 373 (1966), presaged a change in this rule. The constitutional doctrine which emerged from later decisions such as Bloom v. Illinois; Frank v. United States, 395 U.S. 147 (1969); Baldwin v. New York, 399 U.S. 66 (1970); Taylor v. Hayes, 418 U.S. 488 (1974); and Codispoti v. Pennsylvania, 418 U.S. 506 (1974), may be capsuled as follows: (1) Like other minor crimes, "petty" contempts may be tried without a jury, but contemnors in serious contempt cases in the federal system have a Sixth Amendment right to a jury trial; (2) criminal contempt, in and of itself and without regard to the punishment imposed, is not a serious offense absent legislative declaration to the contrary; (3) lacking legislative authorization of more serious punishment, a sentence of as much as six months in prison, plus normal periods of probation, may be imposed without a jury trial; (4) but imprisonment for longer than six months is constitutionally impermissible unless the contemnor has been given the opportunity for a jury trial.

This Court has as yet not addressed the question whether and in what circumstances, if at all, the imposition of a fine for criminal contempt, unaccompanied by imprisonment, may require a jury trial if demanded by the defendant. This case presents the question whether a fine of $10,000 against an unincorporated labor union found guilty of criminal contempt may be imposed after denying the union's claim that it was entitled to a jury trial under the Sixth Amendment. Local 70 insists that where a fine of this magnitude is imposed, a contempt cannot be considered a petty offense within the meaning of 18 U.S.C. § 1(3), and that its demand for a jury trial was therefore erroneously denied.

We cannot agree. In determining the boundary between petty and serious contempts for purposes of applying the Sixth Amendment's jury trial guarantee, and in holding that a punishment of more than six months in prison could not be ordered without making a jury trial available to the defendant, the Court has referred to the relevant rules and practices followed by the federal and state regimes, including the definition of petty offenses under 18 U.S.C. § 1(3). Under that section, petty offenses are defined as those crimes "the penalty for which does not exceed imprisonment for a period of six months or a fine of not more than $500, or both." But in referring to that definition, the Court accorded it no talismanic significance; and we cannot accept the proposition that a contempt must be considered a serious crime under all circumstances where the punishment is a fine of more than $500, unaccompanied by imprisonment. It is one thing to hold that deprivation of an individual's liberty beyond a six-month term should not be imposed without the protections of a jury trial, but it is quite another to suggest that, regardless of the circumstances, a jury is required where any fine greater than $500 is contemplated. From the standpoint of determining the seriousness of the risk and the extent of the possible deprivation faced by a contemnor, imprisonment and fines are intrinsically different. It is not difficult to grasp the proposition that six months in jail is a serious matter for any individual, but it is not tenable to argue that the possibility of a $501 fine would be considered a serious risk to a large corporation or labor union. Indeed, although we do not reach or decide the issue tendered by the respondent—that there is no constitutional right to a jury trial in any criminal contempt case where only a fine is imposed on a corporation or labor union, we cannot say that the fine of $10,000 imposed on Local 70 in this case was a deprivation of such magnitude that a jury should have been interposed to guard against bias or mistake. This union, the respondent suggests, collects dues from some 13,000 persons; and although the fine is not insubstantial, it is not of such magnitude that the union was deprived of whatever right to jury trial it might have under the Sixth Amendment. We thus affirm the judgment of the Court of Appeals.

Justice DOUGLAS, dissenting. . . .

I would reverse the judgment against Local 70 on constitutional grounds. Article III, § 2, of the Constitution provides that "[t]he Trial of all Crimes, except in Cases of Impeachment, shall be by Jury . . . ." And the Sixth Amendment provides in pertinent part:

"In *all* criminal prosecutions, the accused shall enjoy the right to a speedy and public trial, by an impartial jury of the State and district wherein the crime shall have been committed . . . ." (Emphasis added.)

The Court fails to give effect to this language when it declares that a $10,000 fine is not "of such magnitude that a jury should have been interposed to guard against bias or mistake." I have previously protested this Court's refusal to recognize a right to jury trial in cases where it deems an offense to be "petty." But even the "petty offense" exception cannot justify today's result, for it is impossible fairly to characterize either the offense or its penalty as "petty."[6] Disobedience of an injunction obtained by the Board is hardly a transgression trivial by its nature; and the imposition of a $10,000 fine is not a matter most locals would take lightly. In any event, the Constitution deprives us of the power to grant or withhold trial by jury depending upon our assessment of the substantiality of the penalty. To the argument that the Framers could not have intended to provide trial by jury in cases involving only "small" fines and imprisonment, the response of Justices McReynolds and Butler in District of Columbia v. Clawans, 300 U.S. 617, 633–634 (1937) (separate opinion), is apt:

"In a suit at common law to recover above $20.00, a jury trial is assured. And to us, it seems improbable that while providing for this protection in such a trifling matter the framers of the Constitution intended that it might be denied where imprisonment for a considerable time or liability for fifteen times $20.00 confronts the accused."

I would follow the clear command of Art. III and the Sixth Amendment and reverse the judgment as to Local 70.

6. As noted in my dissenting opinion in Cheff v. Schnackenberg, 384 U.S. 373, 386–391 (1966), the "petty offense" doctrine began as an effort to identify offenses that were by their nature "petty," and the punishment prescribed or imposed was one factor to be considered in characterizing the offense. Under the Court's current formulation, the penalty is of controlling significance. See Codispoti v. Pennsylvania, 418 U.S. 506, 512 (1974).

[Justice Stewart's dissenting opinion joined by Justices Marshall and Powell is omitted. It argued that § 3692 compelled a jury trial.]

---

1) 18 U.S.C. § 1(3) defines a petty offense as one where the penalty does not exceed six months or $500 or both. Does *Muniz* inject further uncertainty into the contempt process? If the contemnor is an individual, is a fine limited to $500 unless the judge affords the contemnor an opportunity to summon a jury? Compare United States v. Hamdan, 552 F.2d 276, 280 (9th Cir. 1977); Douglass v. First National Realty Corp., 543 F.2d 894, 902 (D.C.Cir.1976) (*Muniz* limited to organizations), with Girard v. Goins, 575 F.2d 160, 163–65 (8th Cir. 1978) ($500 not necessarily the cap, but $2,500 to $10,000 nonpetty).

2) Contempt fines can be high. In United States v. Greyhound Corp., 508 F.2d 529 (7th Cir. 1974), the court of appeals affirmed a $600,000 criminal contempt fine imposed after a bench trial for violation of a court order. This is the contempt that led to the shareholders' derivative action that triggered Shaffer v. Heitner, 433 U.S. 186, 190 n. 3 (1977). Compare Judge Edelstein's $150,000 per day fine in IBM v. United States, p. 855.

UNITED STATES v. BUKOWSKI

435 F.2d 1094 (7th Cir. 1970), certiorari denied 401 U.S. 911 (1971).

Before SWYGERT, Chief Judge, FAIRCHILD and CUMMINGS, Circuit Judges.

CUMMINGS, Circuit Judge. Respondent appeals from a 3-year sentence for criminal contempt allegedly committed by him while a juror in the case of United States v. Durovic, et al. No. 64 CR 668 (N.D.Ill.1966).

On April 27, 1965, respondent and the other members of the trial jury were sworn for examination upon the voir dire. Between April 28, 1965, and the conclusion of the trial on January 31, 1966, Bukowski and his fellow jurors were ordered and directed by the trial judge to avoid discussing, reading or hearing about the case, either intentionally or inadvertently. The instructions directed them not to converse among themselves concerning the case, or with outsiders. They were expressly directed to avoid reading newspaper or magazine articles, and were warned concerning radio and television broadcasts. The district judge also admonished any juror obtaining outside information to report that fact to the court immediately. These instructions were given the jury every day, four times a day, during the entire duration of the trial until January 31, 1966.

The *Durovic* trial concerned allegedly fraudulent practices connected with the sale of the "anti-cancer" drug Krebiozen. During the course of the trial, an article by Dr. Andrew C. Ivy, a defendant, appeared in the July-August 1965 issue of the "Butcher Workman" magazine published by the Amalgamated Meatcutters and Butcher Workmen of North America. The article was entitled "The Truth That Won't Stay Buried," and the same edition contained an editorial on Krebiozen. Respondent, a member of the executive board of the Chicago Joint Board Amalgamated Meatcutters and Butcher

Workers, Fur, Leather and Luggage Division of the publishing organization, allegedly read these items and discussed them with other members of the jury. Similarly, respondent allegedly read and discussed subsequent articles on Krebiozen in the October 1965, November-December 1965, and January 1966 issues of "The Butcher Workman."

In addition to these improprieties, respondent was also charged with attending a convention of the Amalgamated Meatcutters in Springfield, Illinois, during the course of the trial. The minutes of the convention reveal that a speaker favorable to Krebiozen addressed the members, and subsequently a film on the same subject was shown. The members of the union at that convention entered a resolution calling for a "fair and impartial clinical test of Krebiozen." Respondent allegedly engaged in these activities in contravention of the court's order. At no time did Bukowski report any such activities to the trial judge as instructed.

On December 29, 1967, the United States Attorney for the Northern District of Illinois initiated contempt proceedings against respondent by filing a verified Notice and Petition For Rule to Show Cause with the district judge. The judge issued the Rule to Show Cause to respondent why he should not be held in criminal contempt under 18 U.S.C. § 401(3) for violating judicial orders regarding publicity and conduct of jurors during the Durovic trial.

Respondent filed motions to discharge the Rule to Show Cause in March 1968 which were denied on April 5. Subsequently, respondent unsuccessfully attempted to obtain recusation of the judge [Judge Julius Hoffman]. On January 7, 1969, the judge designated the offense as serious and denied a Supplemental Motion to Discharge the Rule to Show Cause. On January 16, 1969, after a jury trial, respondent was found guilty, and the judge sentenced him to imprisonment for three years. Respondent appeals from his conviction and sentence.

Respondent first objects to the manner in which criminal contempt proceedings were instituted against him. The procedures followed in intitiating this prosecution complied with the specifications of Rule 42(b) of the Federal Rules of Criminal Procedure relating to the disposition of contempts occurring out of the presence of the judge. The processes outlined by that rule include notice and specification of charges. Despite prior approval of the Rule's procedures (United States v. United Mine Workers of America), . . . respondent asserts their insufficiency.

Specifically, respondent contends that the Constitution prohibits imposition of the 3-year sentence without an indictment or presentment of a grand jury. He argues that the Fifth Amendment bars the Government from holding persons "to answer for a capital or otherwise infamous crime, unless on a presentment or indictment of a grand jury . . . ." A crime is "infamous" for purposes of this protection when it is punishable by imprisonment in a penitentiary. Mackin v. United States, 117 U.S. 348. Punishment of contempt by the 3-year sentence subjecting respondent to imprisonment in a penitentiary under 18 U.S.C. § 4083 purportedly establishes the conviction as an "infamous crime."

The identical argument was categorically rejected by the Supreme Court in Green v. United States, 356 U.S. 165, 183–187. The Court refused to interject any independent body into the criminal contempt process which might interfere with or impede judicial disposition of such matters. The majority rested its rejection of the requirements for either grand or petit jury action because of the *sui generis* "general status of contempts under the Constitution, whether subject to 'infamous' punishment or not." The traditionally summary nature of these proceedings led the Court to conclude:

"We do not write upon a clean slate. The principle that criminal contempts of court are not required to be tried by a jury under Article III or the Sixth Amendment is firmly rooted in our traditions. Indeed, the petitioners themselves have not contended that they were entitled to a jury trial. By the same token it is clear that criminal contempts, although subject, as we have held, to sentences of imprisonment exceeding one year, need not be prosecuted by indictment under the Fifth Amendment. In various respects, such as the absence of a statutory limitation of the amount of a fine or the length of a prison sentence which may be imposed for their commission, criminal contempts have always differed from the usual statutory crime under federal law. As to trial by jury and indictment by grand jury, they possess a unique character under the Constitution."

Respondent nevertheless asks this Court to depart from that ruling on the basis of more recent decisions of the Supreme Court. Criticism and continued attacks eroded the conclusion of *Green* that jury trials need never be afforded defendants in even serious criminal contempt cases. After forecasting possible reconsideration of the right to jury trial in United States v. Barnett . . . the Court exercised its supervisory powers over federal courts to require jury trials of serious contempts. Cheff v. Schnackenberg, 384 U.S. 373, 380. . . . Finally, in Bloom v. Illinois, . . . the Court reconsidered and repudiated the rule exempting criminal contempts from constitutional requirements of a jury trial in state cases as well. . . .

Though a fundamental departure from prior law, neither *Bloom* nor subsequent decisions of the Supreme Court dealing with serious contempts have expressly overruled the holding of *Green* excepting grand jury indictments in criminal contempts. Moreover, our reading of those decisions fails to disclose inconsistencies or implicit disapproval of that holding which would warrant reconsideration of *Green* by this Court.

No decision has indicated a rejection of the engrained conceptual framework of criminal contempts relied upon by the Court in *Green* as the basis for its ruling. These actions have traditionally been considered a unique, quasi-criminal sanction. . . . This constitutional distinction between the status of statutorily defined offenses and the judicial power to punish disobedience of court orders has been the doctrinal premise from which analysis of procedural safeguards has proceeded. Consequently, these constitutional "non-crimes" have been tested by the standards of due process rather than under the Fifth and Sixth Amendments' specific strictures governing federal criminal trials of statutory offenses. . . . The procedural protections which have gradually surrounded imposition of criminal contempt penalties thus represent the accretions of "fundamental fairness" rather than application of provisions of the Bill of Rights to contempt prosecutions as "crimes." . . .

We cannot, therefore, construe the extension of the right to jury trial in serious contempts as signalling the abandonment of the doctrine attributing special constitutional status to such proceedings. The Supreme Court has long recognized the function and practical impact of criminal contempts as well as the formal nature of the distinction between contempts and constitutionally defined "crimes." Still its decisions have uniformly adhered to that analytical construct. We may not depart from it at our choosing.

Nor does the reasoning of the cases relied upon by respondent otherwise persuade us that the holding of *Green* has been impliedly disapproved. The Court in *Bloom* balanced, on the one hand, the fundamental right of the accused to a jury trial as an independent check on arbitrary punishment, against the interests of the judiciary in independent, swift, and economic powers over disobedience.

In this case, indictment by grand jury would provide an additional check by another independent body of men, not against abusive imposition of punishment by an arbitrary judge, but against an undue trial. . . . Though substantial, this right has repeatedly been held outside the ambit of "due process of law." Hurtado v. California, 110 U.S. 516 . . . . The recent inclusion of jury trial within the Fourteenth Amendment's Due Process Clause in Duncan v. Louisiana, 391 U.S. 145 hardly suggests the necessity of reaching the same conclusion with respect to the right to indictment by grand jury. The two specific procedural institutions, their functions, and the interests which they serve, while related, are nonetheless capable of distinction. We can see no basis for anticipating possible re-examination of the status of the grand jury in the constitutional scheme. . . .

The extension of constitutional right to jury trial in serious contempts does not, moreover, indicate a rejection of the importance of considerations of judicial independence, efficiency and speed. Rather, in *Bloom* the Court recognized the importance of those factors, yet found them outweighed by the fundamental right sought and the otherwise unprotected interests guarded by an independent jury . . . . Provision for trial by jury largely nullifies the need for additional checks upon judicial power to punish contempt. The countervailing values need not be further sacrificed in order to protect the less compelling demand for protection against unfair trial.

Under these circumstances, we adhere to the holding of Green v. United States, 356 U.S. 165, that indictment by grand jury is not required in criminal contempt proceedings. We are mindful that obedience to the decisions of the Supreme Court may command cautious departure from narrow rulings. Here, however, neither the holding of *Green* nor the reasoning of that decision has been sufficiently eroded to warrant our independent consideration of the merits of respondent's constitutional claim.

Respondent next urges that the Notice and Rule to Show Cause did not adequately inform him of the "nature and cause of the accusation" as constitutionally required. See Cooke v. United States, 267 U.S. 517, 537. . . .

Specifically, respondent asserts that the Notice was insufficient because it failed to specify the grade of the offense charged. . . . Strictly speaking, the nature of contempt defies ready classification in terms of "grades" of offenses. Since Cheff v. Schnackenberg, . . . however, gradations of criminal contempt have developed as a consequence of the distinctions between "serious" and "petty" offenses drawn for purposes of determining the right to a jury trial. . . . An accused could not, therefore, be subject to serious punishment for criminal contempt without adequate prior information with which to exercise or waive his right to jury trial. Although there was no specification in the Notice or Rule to Show Cause concerning the "seriousness" of this contempt proceeding, the court designated the offense as "serious" and provided a jury trial upon respondent's request. Consequently, we can see no prejudice to respondent's fundamental rights, and no basis for invalidating his trial on that ground. . . .

Having reviewed the determination of respondent's guilt, we turn to consider the propriety of the 3-year sentence imposed by the district judge. Punishment of criminal contempt should reflect the "least possible power adequate to the end proposed." Anderson v. Dunn, 19 U.S. (6 Wheat.) 204, 231. Appellate courts bear "special responsibility" for preventing abuse of the contempt power, and this Court has the power in appropriate circumstances to revise sentences inflicted upon contemnors whether trial has been by judge or jury. . . .

The range of conduct set forth in the Petition for Rule to Show Cause certainly stated flagrant disregard of repeated judicial orders regarding most sensitive and important matters which would warrant harsh punishment. On the other hand, we conclude that imprisonment for 18 months adequately punishes such conduct and that a greater sentence would be excessive. . . .

The judgment of conviction is affirmed as modified.

---

1) Remember that the authorities may indict. See Note 2 following *Barnett*, p. 938. Why indict rather than use Rule 42(b) notice?

2) Does *Bukowski* reject *Bloom*'s underlying theory?

3) In United States v. Nunn, 622 F.2d 802 (5th Cir. 1980), defendant breached an injunction ordering him to turn in his pilot's certificate. "The matter was then presented before a grand jury that failed to indict Nunn." The government "proceeded through an application for contempt under F.R. Crim.Proc. 42(b)." 622 F.2d at 802. The court of appeals affirmed a contempt conviction, rejecting Nunn's argument that an indictment by a grand jury is a prerequisite for criminal contempt. Does *Nunn* reveal the need for a lay grand jury in contempt as a bulwark to insulate citizens from arbitrary and oppressive executive and judicial tactics?

4) Consider Professor Kuhns's argument that we should treat criminal contempts as ordinary criminal prosecutions, in particular that the prosecutor's office should initiate criminal contempt through the usual channels which may include indictment. This would, he asserts, be fairer, appear to be fairer, and eliminate confusion between criminal and civil contempt without interfering unnecessarily with any necessary judicial prerogatives. Kuhns, Limiting the Criminal Contempt Power: New Roles for the Prosecutor and the Grand Jury, 73 Mich.L.Rev. 484 (1975). Is the proposal wise? Is it constitutional? Kuhns limits his argument to recalcitrant witnesses. Is his argument even more cogent for injunction violators?

VI. The Executive: Pardons

EX PARTE GROSSMAN

267 U.S. 87, 45 S.Ct. 332, 69 L.Ed. 527 (1925).

Chief Justice TAFT delivered the opinion of the Court.

This is an original petition in this Court for a writ of *habeas corpus* by Philip Grossman against Ritchie V. Graham, Superintendent of the Chicago House of Correction, Cook County, Illinois. . . .

On November 24, 1920, the United States filed a bill in equity against Philip Grossman in the District Court of the United States for the Northern District of Illinois, under Section 22 of the National Prohibition Act . . . , averring that Grossman was maintaining a nuisance at his place of business in Chicago by sales of liquor in violation of the Act and asking an injunction to abate the same. Two days later the District Judge granted a temporary order. January 11, 1921, an information was filed against Grossman, charging that, after the restraining order had been served on him, he had sold to several persons liquor to be drunk on his premises. He was arrested, tried, found guilty of contempt and sentenced to imprisonment in the Chicago House of Correction for one year and to pay a fine of $1,000 to the United States and costs. The decree was affirmed by the Circuit Court of Appeals. In December, 1923, the President issued a pardon in which he commuted the sentence of Grossman to the fine of $1,000 on condition that the fine be paid. The pardon was accepted, the fine was paid and the defendant was released. In May, 1924, however, the District Court committed Grossman to the Chicago House of Correction to serve the sentence notwithstanding the pardon. The only question raised by the pleadings herein is that of the power of the President to grant the pardon.

Special counsel, employed by the Department of Justice, appear for the respondent to uphold the legality of the detention. The Attorney General of the United States, as amicus curiae, maintains the validity and effectiveness of the President's action. . . .

Article II, Section 2, clause one, of the Constitution, dealing with the powers and duties of the President, closes with these words:

". . . and he shall have power to grant Reprieves and Pardons for Offences against the United States, except in Cases of Impeachment."

The argument for the respondent is that the President's power extends only to offenses against the United States and a contempt of Court is not such an offense, that offenses against the United States are not common law offenses but can only be created by legislative act, that the President's pardoning power is more limited than that of the King of England at common law, which was a broad prerogative and included contempts against his courts chiefly because the judges thereof were his agents and acted in his name; that the context of the Constitution shows that the word "offences" is used in that instrument only to include crimes and misdemeanors triable by jury and not contempts of the dignity and authority of the federal courts, and that to construe the pardon clause to include contempts of court would be to violate the fundamental principle of the Constitution in the division of powers between the Legislative, Executive and Judicial branches, and to take from the federal courts their independence and the essential means of protecting their dignity and authority.

The language of the Constitution cannot be interpreted safely except by reference to the common law and to British institutions as they were when the instrument was framed and adopted. The statesmen and lawyers of the Convention who submitted it to the ratification of the Conventions of the thirteen States, were born and brought up in the atmosphere of the common law, and thought and spoke in its vocabulary. They were familiar with other forms of government, recent and ancient, and indicated in their discussions earnest study and consideration of many of them, but when they came to put their conclusions into the form of fundamental law in a compact draft, they expressed them in terms of the common law, confident that they could be shortly and easily understood.

In a case presenting the question whether a pardon should be pleaded in bar to be effective, Chief Justice Marshall said of the power of pardon (United States v. Wilson, 7 Peters, 150, 160):

"As this power had been exercised, from time immemorial, by the executive of that nation whose language is our language, and to whose judicial institutions ours bear a close resemblance; we adopt their principles respecting the operation and effect of a pardon, and look into their books for the rules prescribing the manner in which it is to be used by the person who would avail himself of it." . . .

The King of England before our Revolution, in the exercise of his prerogative, had always exercised the power to pardon contempts of court, just as he did ordinary crimes and misdemeanors and as he has done to the present day. In the mind of a common law lawyer of the eighteenth century the word pardon included within its scope the ending by the King's grace of the punishment of such derelictions, whether it was imposed by the court without a jury or upon indictment, for both forms of trial for contempts were had. [Citations to English cases omitted.]

These cases also show that, long before our Constitution, a distinction had been recognized at common law between the effect of the King's pardon to wipe out the effect of a sentence for contempt in so far as it had been imposed to punish the contemnor for violating the dignity of the court and the King, in the public interest, and its inefficacy to halt or interfere with the remedial part of the court's order necessary to secure the rights of the injured suitor. Blackstone IV, 285, 397, 398; Hawkins Pleas of the Crown, 6th Ed. (1787), Vol. 2, 553. The same distinction, nowadays referred to as the difference between civil and criminal contempts, is still maintained in English law. . . .

In our own law the same distinction clearly appears. . . . In the *Gompers Case* this Court points out that it is not the fact of punishment but rather its character and purpose that makes the difference between the two kinds of contempts. For civil contempts, the punishment is remedial and for the benefit of the complainant, and a pardon cannot stop it. For criminal contempts the sentence is punitive in the public interest to vindicate the authority of the court and to deter other like derelictions.

With this authoritative background of the common law and English history before the American Revolution to show that criminal contempts were within the understood scope of the pardoning power of the Executive, we come now to the history of the clause in the Constitutional Convention of 1787. The proceedings of the Convention from June 19, 1787 to July 23rd, were by resolution referred to a Committee on Detail for report of the Constitution (II Farrand's Records of Constitutional Convention, 128, 129) and contained the following (II Farrand, 146): "The power of pardoning vested in the Executive (which) his pardon shall not, however, be pleadable to an impeachment." On August 6th, Mr. Rutledge of the Committee on Detail (II Farrand, 185) reported the provision as follows: "He shall have power to grant reprieves and pardons; but his pardon shall not be pleadable in bar of impeachment." This is exactly what the King's pardon was at common law with the same limitation. IV Blackstone, 399. On August 25th (II Farrand, 411), the words "except in cases of impeachment" were added after "pardons" and the succeeding words were stricken out. On Saturday, September 8th (II Farrand, 547), a committee of five to revise the style of and arrange the articles was agreed to by the House. As referred to the Committee on Style, the clause read (II Farrand, 575): "He shall have power to grant reprieves and pardons except in cases of impeachment." The Committee on Style reported this clause as it now is: "and he shall have power to grant reprieves and pardons for offences against the United States except in cases of impeachment." There seems to have been no discussion over the substance of the clause save that a motion to except cases of treason was referred to the Committee on Style, September 10th (II Farrand, 564) was not approved by the Committee and after discussion was defeated in the Convention September 15th (II Farrand, 626, 627).

We have given the history of the clause to show that the words "for offences against the United States" were inserted by a Committee on Style, presumably to make clear that the pardon of the President was to operate upon offenses against the United States as distinguished from offenses against the States. It can not be supposed that the Committee on Revision by adding these words, or the Convention by accepting them, intended *sub silentio* to narrow the scope of a pardon from one at common law or to confer any different power in this regard on our Executive from that which the members of the Convention had seen exercised before the Revolution.

Nor is there any substance in the contention that there is any substantial difference in this matter between the executive power of pardon in our Government and the King's prerogative. The courts of Great Britain were called the King's Courts, as indeed they were; but for years before our Constitution they were as independent of the King's interference as they are today. The extent of the King's pardon was clearly circumscribed by law and the British Constitution, as the cases cited above show. The framers of our Constitution had in mind no necessity for curtailing this feature of the King's prerogative in transplanting it into the American governmental structures, save by excepting cases of impeachment; and even in that regard, as already pointed out, the common law forbade the pleading a pardon in bar to an impeachment.

. . .

Nothing in the ordinary meaning of the words "offences against the United States" excludes criminal contempts. That which violates the dignity and authority of federal courts such as an intentional effort to defeat their decrees justifying punishment violates a law of the United States (In re Neagle, 135 U.S. 1, 59, et seq.), and so must be an offense against the United States. Moreover, this Court has held that the general statute of limitation which forbids prosecutions "for any offense unless instituted within three years next after such offense shall have been committed," applies to criminal contempts. Gompers v. United States. In that case this Court said:

"It is urged in the first place that contempts can not be crimes, because, although punishable by imprisonment and therefore, if crimes, infamous, they are not within the protection of the Constitution and the amendments giving a right to trial by jury &c. to persons charged with such crimes. But the provisions of the Constitution are not mathematical formulas having their essence in their form; they are organic living institutions transplanted from English soil. Their significance is vital not formal; it is to be gathered not simply by taking the words and a dictionary, but by considering their origin and the line of their growth. . . . It does not follow that contempts of the class under consideration are not crimes, or rather, in the language of the statute, offenses, because trial by jury as it has been gradually worked out and fought out has been thought not to extend to them as a matter of constitutional right. These contempts are infractions of the law, visited with punishment as such. If such acts are not criminal, we are in error as to the most fundamental characteristic of crimes as that word has been understood in English speech. . . . "

It is said, however, that whatever may be the scope of the word "offenses" in the particular statute construed in the *Gompers Case*, its association in the Constitution is such as to show a narrower meaning. The word "offences" is only used twice in the original Constitution, once in the pardon clause, and once in Article I, Section 8, among the powers of Congress "to define and punish Piracies and Felonies committed on the high seas and offences against the Law of Nations." In the amendments, "offence" occurs but once and that in the Fifth Amendment in the clause forbidding double jeopardy. We do not see how these other two uses of the word can be said to limit the meaning of "offences" in the pardon clause.

The argument is that the word "offences" is used in the Constitution interchangeably with *crimes* and *criminal prosecutions.* But as has been pointed out in Shick v. United States, 195 U.S. 65, the term "offences" is used in the Constitution in a more comprehensive sense than are the terms "crimes" and "criminal prosecutions." . . . Contempt proceedings are *sui generis* because they are not hedged about with all the safeguards provided in the bill of rights for protecting one accused of ordinary crime from the danger of unjust conviction. This is due, of course, to the fact that for years before the American Constitution, courts had been held to be inherently empowered to protect themselves and the function they perform by summary proceeding without a jury to punish disobedience of their orders and disturbance of their hearings. So it is clear to us that the language of the Fifth and Sixth Amendments and of other cited parts of the Constitution are not of significance in determining the scope of pardons of "offences against the United States" in

Article II, Section 2, clause 1, of the enumerated powers of the President. We think the arguments drawn from the common law, from the power of the King under the British Constitution, which plainly was the prototype of this clause, from the legislative history of the clause in the Convention, and from the ordinary meaning of its words, are much more relevant and convincing.

Moreover, criminal contempts of a federal court have been pardoned for eighty-five years. In that time the power has been exercised twenty-seven times. . . . Such long practice under the pardoning power and acquiescence in it strongly sustains the construction it is based on. . . .

Finally, it is urged that criminal contempts should not be held within the pardoning power because it will tend to destroy the independence of the judiciary and violate the primary constitutional principle of a separation of the legislative, executive and judicial powers. . . .

The Federal Constitution nowhere expressly declares that the three branches of the Government shall be kept separate and independent. All legislative powers are vested in a Congress. The executive power is vested in a President. The judicial power is vested in one Supreme Court and in such inferior courts as Congress may from time to time establish. The Judges are given life tenure and a compensation that may not be diminished during their continuance in office, with the evident purpose of securing them and their courts an independence of Congress and the Executive. Complete independence and separation between the three branches, however, are not attained, or intended, as other provisions of the Constitution and the normal operation of government under it easily demonstrate. By affirmative action through the veto power, the Executive and one more than one-third of either House may defeat all legislation. One-half of the House and two-thirds of the Senate may impeach and remove the members of the Judiciary. The Executive can reprieve or pardon all offenses after their commission, either before trial, during trial or after trial, by individuals, or by classes, conditionally or absolutely, and this without modification or regulation by Congress. . . . Negatively, one House of Congress can withhold all appropriations and stop the operations of Government. The Senate can hold up all appointments, confirmation of which either the Constitution or a statute requires, and thus deprive the President of the necessary agents with which he is to take care that the laws be faithfully executed.

These are some instances of positive and negative restraints possibly available under the Constitution to each branch of the government in defeat of the action of the other. They show that the independence of each of the others is qualified and is so subject to exception as not to constitute a broadly positive injunction or a necessarily controlling rule of construction. The fact is that the Judiciary, quite as much as Congress and the Executive, is dependent on the coöperation of the other two, that government may go on. Indeed, while the Constitution has made the Judiciary as independent of the other branches as is practicable, it is, as often remarked, the weakest of the three. It must look for a continuity of necessary coöperation, in the possible reluctance of either of the other branches, to the force of public opinion.

Executive clemency exists to afford relief from undue harshness or evident mistake in the operation or enforcement of the criminal law. The administration of justice by the courts is not necessarily always wise or certainly considerate of circumstances which may properly mitigate guilt. To afford a remedy, it has always been thought essential in popular governments, as well as in monarchies, to vest in some other authority than the courts power to ameliorate or avoid particular criminal judgments. It is a check entrusted to the executive for special cases. To exercise it to the extent of destroying the deterrent effect of judicial punishment would be to pervert it; but whoever is to make it useful must have full discretion to exercise it. Our Constitution confers this discretion on the highest officer in the nation in confidence that he will not abuse it. An abuse in pardoning contempts would certainly embarrass courts, but it is questionable how much more it would lessen their effectiveness than a wholesale pardon of other offenses. If we could conjure up in our minds a President willing to paralyze courts by pardoning all criminal contempts, why not a President ordering a general jail delivery? A pardon can only be granted for a contempt fully completed. Neither in this country nor in England can it interfere with the use of coercive measures to enforce a suitor's right. The detrimental effect of excessive pardons of completed contempts would be in the loss of the deterrent influence upon future contempts. It is of the same character as that of the excessive pardons of other offenses. The difference does not justify our reading criminal contempts out of the pardon clause by departing from its ordinary meaning confirmed by its common law origin and long years of practice and acquiescence.

If it be said that the President, by successive pardons of constantly recurring contempts in particular litigation, might deprive a court of power to enforce its orders in a recalcitrant neighborhood, it is enough to observe that such a course is so improbable as to furnish but little basis for argument. Exceptional cases like this, if to be imagined at all, would suggest a resort to impeachment rather than to a narrow and strained construction of the general powers of the President.

The power of a court to protect itself and its usefulness by punishing contemnors is of course necessary, but it is one exercised without the restraining influence of a jury and without many of the guaranties which the bill of rights offers to protect the individual against unjust conviction. Is it unreasonable to provide for the possibility that the personal element may sometimes enter into a summary judgment pronounced by a judge who thinks his authority is flouted or denied? May it not be fairly said that in order to avoid possible mistake, undue prejudice or needless severity, the chance of pardon should exist at least as much in favor of a person convicted by a judge without a jury as in favor of one convicted in a jury trial? The pardoning by the President of criminal contempts has been practiced more than three-quarters of a century, and no abuses during all that time developed sufficiently to invoke a test in the federal courts of its validity.

It goes without saying that nowhere is there a more earnest will to maintain the independence of federal courts and the preservation of every legitimate safeguard of their effectiveness afforded by the Constitution than in this Court. But the qualified independence which they fortunately enjoy is not likely to be permanently strengthened by ignoring precedent and practice and minimizing the importance of the coördinating checks and balances of the Constitution.

1) Are the arguments for the pardon power more compelling for the criminal contemnor than for the criminal defendant? In Laing v. Commonwealth, p. 1028, the judge ordered Jim Laing to turn in his dog, Rickey. Laing failed to comply; the judge ordered Laing imprisoned for contempt; and the governor pardoned Laing. In considering whether to pardon Laing, was it dispositive that Rickey was not at large? Was it relevant? If Laing had been imprisoned "until you tell us where Rickey is," what does *Grossman* teach us about whether the governor could have pardoned him? In re Nevitt, 117 F. 448 (8th Cir. 1902), held that the executive lacked power to pardon civil imprisonment for the benefit of private parties. *Nevitt* is a product of the unreconstructed view that the contempt power is inherent and sui generis. Does it concentrate too much power in the trial judge? Should it be reconsidered in light of *Bloom*, p. 948?

2) How many people exercise discretion on whether to punish a person for contempt? In Chapter 3 we studied whether the judge has discretion to withhold an injunction. If we tamper with that discretion, isn't the lesson of this chapter that it will emerge in a different form in the contempt process?

Chapter Twelve

COMPENSATORY CONTEMPT

I. Maintaining Compensatory Contempt

LEVAN v. THIRD DISTRICT COURT

4 Idaho 667, 43 P. 574 (1896).

The petitioner was cited to appear before the court for contempt in disobeying the order of the court. He pleaded not guilty. An investigation was thereupon had, and evidence taken, with the result that the petitioner was found guilty of contempt of court. It was further found that in committing said contempt the petitioner had stopped or delayed the survey of mining property which had been ordered by the court; that in so doing he had damaged the party making the survey, namely, John Ranson et al., plaintiffs in the suit of John Ranson et al. v. D. B. Levan et al., as follows, namely:

Services of surveyor	$ 20 00
" " chainmen	12 00
" " flagmen	7 00
For meals	4 25
Services of two witnesses	5 00
Fees of attorneys	250 00
Total	$298 25

The said district court thereupon proceeded to assess a fine of $25 upon the petitioner, D. B. Levan, and entered the following judgment, to wit: "Now, therefore, in consideration of the premises, it is ordered and adjudged by the court that the said defendant, D. B. Levan, be fined in the sum of twenty-five ($25) dollars penalty, and the costs and disbursements of plaintiffs above mentioned herein, amounting in the aggregate to the sum of two hundred ninety-eight dollars and twenty-five cents ($298.25)" . . . . The defendant in said contempt proceedings presents the case to this court for review. . . .

MORGAN, C. J. (after stating the facts). The petitioner makes no objections to the action of the court in the assessment of the fine of $25 and costs of the contempt proceedings, but alleges that that portion of the judgment proposing to assess damages in the sum of $298.25 is wholly void, and that the court had no jurisdiction to render any such judgment; in other words, that the sole power of the court in contempt proceedings is defined by our statute, and is limited to a fine and imprisonment. . . . Section 5164 of our statute is as follows: "Upon the answer and evidence taken, the court must determine whether the person proceeded against is guilty of the contempt charged, and if it be adjudged that he is guilty of the contempt, a fine may be imposed upon him not exceeding five hundred ($500) dollars, or he may be imprisoned not exceeding five (5) days, or both." This is precisely the same as the statute of California relating to the same subject-matter. With reference to that statute, the supreme court of California, in the case of Galland v. Galland, 44 Cal. 478, says: "In this state the power of courts to punish for contempt has been regulated by statute. It is provided that, when one is adjudged guilty of contempt, he may be punished by 'a fine of not exceeding five hundred ($500) dollars, and by imprisonment for not exceeding five (5) days, except,' etc. Prac. Act, §§ 488, 489. This is a limitation upon the power formerly exercised by courts to punish for contempt."

In the case of Kirk v. Manufacturing Co., 26 Fed. 501, the court says: "The sole power of the federal courts to punish for contempt of their authority, both at law and in equity, is derived from section 725 of the Revised Statutes; and they cannot impose penalties, under the state statute, in the form of pecuniary indemnity to the party injured." The above was a case on appeal from the United States circuit court for Wisconsin. In that state the statute provides that, if any actual loss or injury has been produced to any party by the misconduct alleged, the court shall order a sufficient sum to be paid by the defendant to such party to indemnify him, and to satisfy his costs and expenses, instead of imposing a fine upon said defendant. Rev.St.Wis. § 3490. We have no such statute as the one quoted above, and therefore the district court, in contempt proceedings in this state, has no authority, under the statute, to proceed to assess any damages against the party for the loss or injury that may have been suffered by the party in the cause in which the contempt was committed. In Maxwell v. Rives, 11 Nev. 214, the court says, "The statute concerning contempts is a penal statute, and must be strictly construed in favor of those accused of violating its provisions." . . . In the case Ex parte Robinson, 19 Wall. 512, the court says, "The law happily prescribes the assessment which the court can impose for contempt. The seventeenth section of the judiciary act of 1789 [referring to the Revised Statutes of the United States] declares that the courts should have power to punish contempts of their authority, in any case or hearing, by a fine or imprisonment, at their discretion. The enactment is a limitation upon the manner in which the power shall be exercised, and must be held to be a negation of all other modes of punishment. The judgment of the court disbarring the petitioner, treated as a punishment for the contempt, was therefore unauthorized and void." So with our statute; Rev.St. § 5164 prescribes the punishment that may be inflicted by the court upon the person guilty of contempt, and must be held to be a limitation of the power of the court to punish the party so found guilty, and must also be held to be a negation of all other modes of punishment. It will be seen, therefore, that that part of the judgment assessing the damages to the injured party in the sum of $298.25 is wholly beyond the jurisdiction of the court, and is therefore void. So much of said judgment, therefore, must be set aside, and held to be of no effect. The proceedings of the district court in the assessment of the fine are approved. Costs awarded to the plaintiff.

SULLIVAN and HUSTON, JJ., concur.

---

1) The first question about compensatory contempt is whether to have it at all. Several states reject compensatory contempt, though most allow it. Does allowing compensatory contempt in the face of legislative silence illustrate the idea that judges may make contempt up as they go along?

2) Compensatory contempt may threaten the right to a jury trial. "To allow compensatory damages in the contempt proceeding would have the effect of turning it into an action for damages. In an action for damages, the parties are ordinarily entitled to a trial by jury . . . ." H.J. Heinz Co. v. Superior Court, 42 Cal.2d 164, 175, 266 P.2d 5, 12 (1954). The Alabama Supreme Court, instead of insisting on a separate action, allowed compensatory contempt in an ancillary proceeding in the injunction action and said that either party could call for a jury. Lightsey v. Kensington Mortgage & Finance Co., 294 Ala. 281, 315 So.2d 431 (1975). Do the courts that reject compensatory contempt adhere to the premise: "If money is involved, there must be a jury"? Have the courts that allowed compensatory contempt rejected this premise? Is a jury for compensatory contempt inconsistent with the original decision that plaintiff's remedy in a damage action was inadequate? Are compensatory contempt juries anachronisms from the era of separate law and equity courts? Rendleman, Compensatory Contempt: Plaintiff's Remedy When a Defendant Violates an Injunction, 1980 U.Ill.L.F. 971 discusses the legislative and jury issues at pp. 982–85.

Your editors lack unanimity on whether a jury should find facts in compensatory contempt. Professor Fiss thinks that a jury could but that it is unlikely. Civil Rights Injunction 54–55 (1978). Professor Rendleman thinks that the argument for a jury is misguided. Compensatory Contempt, 1980 U.Ill.L.F. at 982–85.

3) Assume a federal court in Idaho in a diversity action enjoined the defendant. Defendant ignores the injunction and plaintiff suffers money damage. Would the federal judge allow juryless compensatory contempt in the injunction action? "[A] federal court may afford an equitable remedy for a substantive right recognized by a State even though a State court cannot give it." Guaranty Trust Co. v. York, 326 U.S. 99, 106 (1945). See also *Sunbeam* below p. 993.

4) In evaluating compensatory contempt, compare it to the parallel legal remedy for money damages. Should compensatory contempt be procedurally as smooth and financially as remunerative as the legal remedy? Compensatory contempt is ironic because the judge must use money despite the earlier holding that money was an inadequate remedy. How can the judge award money in the face of his earlier decision that money is inadequate?

McCOMB v. JACKSONVILLE PAPER CO.

336 U.S. 187, 69 S.Ct. 497, 93 L.Ed. 599 (1949).

Justice DOUGLAS delivered the opinion of the Court.

This is a civil contempt proceeding arising out of Walling v. Jacksonville Paper Co., 317 U.S. 564, which we decided January 18, 1943. The District Court had held that none of respondents' employees in specified classes were covered by the Fair Labor Standards Act. . . . We sustained a judgment of the United States Court of Appeals which reversed the District Court, modifying it slightly to include a larger class of employees than the United States Court of Appeals had held to be covered.

On remand the District Court, without a further hearing entered a decree enjoining respondents from violating the Act in any of the following particulars: (1) by paying the designated classes of employees less than 30¢ an hour from the date of the judgment to October 24, 1945, or less than 40¢ an hour thereafter . . . ; (2) by employing such employees for a workweek longer than 40 hours unless they receive compensation for employment in excess of 40 hours in the workweek at a rate not less than one and one-half times the regular rate at which they are employed; and (3) by failing to keep and preserve records as prescribed by the Administrator, particularly records of the hours worked each workday and each workweek by each of the employees and of the total wages paid to each for each workweek.

Respondent took no appeal from this order. This was in 1943. In 1946 the Administrator instituted this contempt proceeding alleging that respondents had not complied with the minimum wage, overtime, and recordkeeping provisions of the judgment in many specified respects. He prayed that respondents be required to terminate their continuing violations and in order to purge themselves of their contempts to make payment of the amounts of unpaid wages due the affected employees. The District Court found violations of the provisions of the decree. It found that (1) respondents had set up a completely false and fictitious method of computing compensation without regard to the hours actually worked which were unlawful under the Act; (2) respondents had adopted a plan which gave the employees a wage increase in the guise of a bonus and yet excluded that increase from the regular rate of pay for the purpose of computing overtime; (3) respondents had classified some employees as executive or administrative employees in plain violation of the regulations of the Administrator adopted under § 13(a)(1) of the Act; and (4) one of the respondents had employed pieceworkers in excess of the maximum workweek without paying them overtime compensation.

The District Court held that a civil contempt required a "wilful" violation of a decree; and that there was in this case no showing of any "wilful" violation of any "specific" provision of the former decree "prohibiting the doing of any specific thing." The District Court further held that it had no power on the application of the Administrator to enforce compliance with its former decree by ordering the payment of unpaid statutory wages. It accordingly considered the application of the Administrator as an amended complaint seeking a broadening of the previous decree and entered such an injunction.

All parties appealed. The United States Court of Appeals affirmed the judgment. It ruled that respondents had violated the provisions of the decree couched in terms of the Act in the respects found by the District Court. It also held that the District Court was warranted in concluding that there was no "wilful contempt" since neither the law nor the injunction specifically referred to or condemned the practices which were found to violate the Act.

. . .

First. The absence of wilfulness does not relieve from civil contempt. Civil as distinguished from criminal contempt is a sanction to enforce compliance with an order of the court or to compensate for losses or damages sustained by reason of noncompliance. . . . Since the purpose is remedial, it matters not with what intent the defendant did the prohibited act. The decree was not fashioned so as to grant or withhold its benefits dependent on the state of mind of respondents. It laid on them a duty to obey specified provisions of the statute. An act does not cease to be a violation of a law and of a decree merely because it may have been done innocently. The force and vitality of judicial decrees derive from more robust sanctions. And the grant or withholding of remedial relief is not wholly discretionary with the judge, as Mr. Justice Brandeis wrote for a unanimous Court in Union Tool Co. v. Wilson, 259 U.S. 107, 111–112. The private or public rights that the decree sought to protect are an important measure of the remedy.

Second. As we have noted, the decree directed respondents to obey the provisions of the Act dealing with minimum wages, overtime, and the keeping of records. There was no appeal from it. By its terms it enjoined any practices which were violations of those statutory provisions. Decrees of that generality are often necessary to prevent further violations where a proclivity for unlawful conduct has been shown. . . . Respondents' record of continuing and persistent violations of the Act would indicate that that kind of a decree was wholly warranted in this case. Yet if there were extenuating circumstances or if the decree was too burdensome in operation, there was a method of relief apart from an appeal. Respondents could have petitioned the District Court for a modification, clarification or construction of the order. . . . But respondents did not take that course either. They undertook to make their own determination of what the decree meant. They knew they acted at their peril. For they were alerted by the decree against any violation of specified provisions of the Act.

It does not lie in their mouths to say that they have an immunity from civil contempt because the plan or scheme which they adopted was not specifically enjoined. Such a rule would give tremendous impetus to the program of experimentation with disobedience of the law . . . . The instant case is an excellent illustration of how it could operate to prevent accountability for persistent contumacy. Civil contempt is avoided today by showing that the specific plan adopted by respondents was not enjoined. Hence a new decree is entered enjoining that particular plan. Thereafter the defendants work out a plan that was not specifically enjoined. Immunity is once more obtained because the new plan was not specifically enjoined. And so a whole series of wrongs is perpetrated and a decree of enforcement goes for naught.

That result not only proclaims the necessity of decrees that are not so narrow as to invite easy evasion; it also emphasizes the danger in the attitude expressed by the courts below that the remedial benefits of a decree will be withheld where the precise arrangement worked out to discharge the duty to pay, which both the statute and the decree imposed was not specifically enjoined.

We need not impeach the findings of the lower courts that respondents had no purpose to evade the decree, in order to hold that their violations of it warrant the imposition of sanctions. They took a calculated risk when under the threat of contempt they adopted measures designed to avoid the legal consequences of the Act. Respondents are not unwitting victims of the law. Having been caught in its toils, they were endeavoring to extricate themselves. They knew full well the risk of crossing the forbidden line. Accordingly where as here the aim is remedial and not punitive, there can be no complaint that the burden of any uncertainty in the decree is on respondents' shoulders.

Third. We have no doubts concerning the power of the District Court to order respondents, in order to purge themselves of contempt, to pay the damages caused by their violations of the decree. We can lay to one side the question whether the Administrator, when suing to restrain violations of the Act, is entitled to a decree of restitution for unpaid wages. Cf. Porter v. Warner Holding Co., 328 U.S. 395. We are dealing here with the power of a court to grant the relief that is necessary to effect compliance with its decree. The measure of the court's power in civil contempt proceedings is determined by the requirements of full remedial relief. . . .

The decree that was violated in the present case relates to the payment of wages and overtime pay required by §§ 6 and 7 of the Act. It does not, however, compute the weekly and monthly amount that is due each employee under the correct construction of the Act. Nor does it contain the names of the payees. But it provides the formula by which the amounts can be simply computed. If it had gone one step further and made the computation, listing the amounts due each employee, the case would then be on all fours with the alimony cases. Yet the circumstance that changing payrolls and fluctuating rates of pay make that impractical in this type of case does not mark a material difference.

The direction of the court was that respondents make payments of wages to their employees pursuant to a prescribed formula. If the court is powerless to require the prescribed payments to be made, it has lost the most effective sanction for its decree and a premium has been placed on violations. The fact that another suit might be brought to collect the payments[3] is, of course, immaterial. For the court need not sit supinely by waiting for some litigant to take the initiative. Vindication of its authority through enforcement of its decree does not depend on such whimsical or fortuitous circumstances. The fact that the Administrator is the complainant[4] and that the back wages go to the employees is not material. It is the power of the court with which we are dealing—the power of the court to enforce compliance

3. Section 16(b) authorizes suits by employees to recover wages and overtime unlawfully withheld.

4. It is the Administrator who is directed and authorized by § 11(a) of the Act to bring actions to restrain violations of the Act of the character involved here. . . .

with the injunction which the Act authorizes, which the court has issued, and which respondents have long disobeyed.

Justice RUTLEDGE concurs in the result.

Justice FRANKFURTER, with whom Justice JACKSON concurs, dissenting.

Obedience must of course be secured for the command of a court. To secure such obedience is the function of a proceeding for contempt. But courts should be explicit and precise in their commands and should only then be strict in exacting compliance. To be both strict and indefinite is a kind of judicial tyranny.

In such a case as this, only after an administrative order has been formulated and a court has adjudicated that the order is within the administrator's statutory authority does the command of a court come into existence, disobedience of which may be punished as contempt. For violation of the Fair Labor Standards Act as such, one may be made to suffer civil penalties or imprisonment, but the latter only after conviction by a jury. For violation of the command of an injunction issued under the Act, however, he may not only be exposed to more severe civil penalties than the Act by its own terms imposes, but made to suffer imprisonment without benefit of jury trial. It is for such reasons that this Court has indicated again and again that a statute cannot properly be made the basis of contempt proceedings merely by incorporating a reference to its broad terms into a court order. . . . These considerations become increasingly important as there is increasing use of injunctions for the enforcement of administrative orders and statutory duties.

. . . [B]oth [lower] courts found no contempt. They did so because there was lacking that clearness of command in the court's order which warranted a finding of its disobedience, if due regard were paid to the proper construction of the injunction as the starting point of the contempt proceedings. At the least, such was a warrantable interpretation of the circumstances of this case, and we are disentitled to set our interpretation against theirs.

In reversing the conclusion of the two lower courts that there was no contempt because there was no disobedience of the injunction, the Court is rendering a decision of far-reaching import to the law of injunctions. Today's ruling happens to concern an injunction against an employer. Tomorrow it may be an injunction against employees, as it was yesterday and too often in the past. One of the grievances which led to the Norris-LaGuardia Act was the generality of the terms of labor injunctions. Ambiguity lurks in generality and may thus become an instrument of severity. Behind the vague inclusiveness of an injunction like the one before us is the hazard of retrospective interpretation as the basis of punishment through contempt proceedings. The two lower courts, in finding that generally to enjoin obedience to a law is too vague a foundation for proceedings in contempt, were avoiding the very evil with which labor injunctions were justly charged. And of course it is not to be assumed that the allowable vagueness of an injunction varies with the use to which the injunction is put. This Court ought not to encourage injunctions couched in such indefinite terms by setting aside the findings of the courts below that the injunction did not forbid with explicitness sufficient to justify a finding of contempt.

NORTHSIDE REALTY ASSOCIATES, INC. v. UNITED STATES

605 F.2d 1348 (5th Cir. 1979).

Before BROWN, Chief Judge, COLEMAN and TJOFLAT, Circuit Judges.

JOHN R. BROWN, Chief Judge:

[The government had obtained an injunction under a federal statute, 42 U.S.C. § 3613 (1976), barring Northside from racial discrimination in the sale of real estate. Violations were proved. The court of appeals sustained the finding of a violation and then addressed the contempt issue:] . . .

A Free Ride For Nonparties On Attorney General's Coattail?

We cannot . . . end our discussion by affirming the District Court's order of contempt. We must also consider what remedial measures could, or should, have been awarded by the District Court. It is the Government's contention that the District Court should have awarded compensatory damages to nonparty victims of Northside's discriminatory practices. Conceding that such relief is unavailable in an original § 3613 action brought by the Attorney General, the Government argues that compensatory damages for nonparty discriminatees may nonetheless be awarded in this civil contempt action.

The District Court rejected this contention, stating that in a civil contempt action compensatory damages may be awarded only to a party to the proceedings. See Clark v. Boynton, 5 Cir., 1966, 362 F.2d 992, 997–98.

While we need not foreclose altogether the possibility of third party compensatory relief in civil contempt cases, we agree with the District Court that compensatory damages for nonparties ought not to be granted here as part of the Government's remedy in a civil contempt proceeding brought by the Attorney General to enforce a § 3613 injunction.

In the first place, such a remedy appears to exceed the scope of a contempt proceeding. As courts have frequently stated, the purposes of a civil contempt proceeding are two-fold: to compensate the prevailing party [22] for losses or damages caused by the other's noncompliance and to coerce the

22. The cases make it clear that the "prevailing" party (or "complainant") to whom compensatory damages may be awarded is the party litigant who won the original injunction. See, e.g., Hutto v. Finney ("Civil contempt may . . . be punished by a remedial fine, which compensates the party who won the injunction . . . ."); United States v. United Mine Workers ("Where compensation is intended, a fine is imposed, payable to the complainant. Such fine must of course be based upon evidence of complainant's actual loss . . . ."); see also Gompers v. Bucks Stove & Range Co. ("Proceedings for civil contempt are between the original parties, and are instituted and tried as part of the main cause."). Although the Government has cited cases in which equitable relief has been awarded to nonparties (primarily in the context of suits for back pay under the labor laws or Title VII of the Civil Rights Act), the Government has cited *no* case in which compensatory relief has been actually awarded to a person not a party to the proceedings.

derelict party into compliance with the original injunction. McComb v. Jacksonville Paper Co.; United States v. United Mine Workers; Southern Railway Co. v. Lanham, 5 Cir., 1968, 403 F.2d 119, 124 ("Civil contempt is 'wholly remedial' serves only the purpose of a party litigant, and is intended to coerce compliance with an order of the court or to compensate for losses or damages caused by noncompliance.").

An award of legal damages to nonparties goes beyond these purposes. Most obviously, the award would not compensate the complaining party—the Government in this case—who has already been appropriately compensated through the District Court's award of costs and attorneys' fees.[23] However, "Ordinarily, of course, the civil contempt fine 'must not exceed the actual loss to the complainant caused by respondent's violation of the decree in the main cause plus complainant's reasonable expenses in the proceedings necessitated in presenting the contempt for the judgment of the court.' " Clark v. Boynton, 362 F.2d at 998, quoting Parker v. United States, 1 Cir., 1946, 153 F.2d 66, 71. Moreover, such an award would have at best a tangential effect in coercing future compliance with the Court's decree. The sort of relief sought by the Government here, monetary damages for individual housing discriminatees, is a purely legal remedy, Curtis v. Loether, 1974, 415 U.S. 189, which compensates for past wrongs. The enforcement purpose of a contempt order is much better served by ordering, as was done here, the payment of a daily fine in the event of noncompliance with the Court's order. Cf. United States v. United Mine Workers (recognizing the coercive effect of a conditional fine in civil contempt cases).[24]

It must also be remembered that "[p]roceedings for civil contempt are between the original parties, and are instituted and tried as a part of the main cause." Gompers v. Bucks Stove & Range Co. Accordingly, we would be reluctant to allow this civil contempt proceeding to be used, as the Government would have us do, to enlarge upon the original injunctive action by bringing in new parties with new issues in what would most likely be a new proceeding.[25] The relief sought by the Government here cannot be charac-

23. Regardless of whether an award of attorneys' fees to the Government would be appropriate in an original § 3613 proceeding, such an award may be made, in the Trial Court's discretion, in a civil contempt action. . . .

24. The Government claims that Hutto v. Finney supports its contention that an award of compensatory damages to nonparties would serve a coercive purpose. Although there is dicta in *Hutto* suggesting that an award compensating a prevailing party for losses sustained as a result of a contemnor's disobedience would not constitute retroactive monetary relief for Eleventh Amendment purposes, we do not consider the Supreme Court's remarks to be dispositive of the issue before us—that of the *propriety* of awarding compensatory relief to *nonparties* in a civil contempt proceeding brought to enforce a § 3613 injunction. The relief sought here is not the sort mentioned by the Supreme Court, and the award of damages to *nonparties* involves entirely different considerations than does an award to parties.

25. The Government has given us no indication of how the amount of compensatory awards is to be determined. The record certainly gives little indication of the amounts of damages suffered by those individuals whom the Court found to be victims of Northside's discrimination. Indeed, it is unclear exactly who these victims are. They are apparently the witnesses specifically found by the Court to have been the objects of racial discrimination and also certain of Northside's sales agents who lost sales as a consequence of Northside's wrongful acts. Presumably a hearing would be required to ascertain the amount of damages suffered by each of these individuals at the hands of Northside.

terized as merely an incidental part of the main cause. It is an altogether new and different matter.

Even were we confident that third party compensatory relief might be a proper remedy in some civil contempt cases, a number of considerations make us ill-disposed to allow such relief in this case. Without elaboration, we mention several difficult legal questions that come to mind. By allowing the relief requested by the Government, we would in effect transform the civil contempt proceeding into a representative class action, with the Government as the representative party. This would take the action far beyond the scope of an ordinary contempt proceeding and would raise all the "class action problems"—such as certification, notice and fair representation—that such a proceeding entails. Questions would arise concerning the Government's standing to sue for damages on behalf of third parties and concerning the Court's power to award legal relief to persons not before the Court. Difficult Seventh Amendment issues would also have to be resolved, as well as problems regarding what, if any, limitations period should be applied in considering an individual's damages claim. Additionally, there would be difficult questions concerning the collateral estoppel or res judicata effect to be given to findings made by the Court in the contempt proceeding and in any subsequent proceeding or proceedings that might be had to determine the amount of damages to be awarded an individual discriminatee.

Finally, we point out that there is no compelling need for the relief sought by the Government. Congress has authorized a private Title VIII cause of action whereby private parties may obtain injunctive relief, compensatory damages, and attorneys' fees. 42 U.S.C.A. § 3612. In this case, several of the witnesses testified that, at the time of their dealings with Northside, they felt that they had been discriminated against. These individuals appeared to be intelligent people, presumably able to make their own determinations about whether or not to seek legal redress. For those witnesses who may not have been aware of any discrimination at the time, they may yet have a cause of action. See Reeb v. Economic Opportunity Atlanta, Inc., 5 Cir., 1975, 516 F.2d 924 (Title VII case). Since Congress has authorized an adequate remedy for individual victims of housing discrimination, we see no reason to imply another one.

We have considered all the arguments on this issue, and we now hold that here the Government may not be awarded compensatory damages for nonparties in a civil contempt action brought to enforce a § 3613 injunction. The problems are substantial. The need is not. Absent express congressional mandate, this Court will not aid the building of such a house of cards.

---

1) Are the legal questions the *Northside* court identifies really so difficult? Is a class action the only type of representative suit? Do both *Northside* and *McComb* turn on the statutes involved? Do the dissent in *McComb* and the court in *Northside* ignore the compensatory nature of the proceedings? Can *Northside* and *McComb* be reconciled? See Compensatory Contempt, 1980 U.Ill.L.F. at 976–78.

2) Who may enforce an injunction? This question is more acute in civil than in criminal contempt, probably because of the judge's prosecutorial func-

tion in the latter. The antitrust division resolves about 75% of its business by consent decree; without admitting wrongdoing, the defendant agrees to comply in the future. Some argue that Justice fails to compel defendants to adhere to the decrees. Third parties lack "standing" to enforce these decrees. Sullivan, Enforcement of Government Antitrust Decrees by Private Parties: Third Party Beneficiary Rights and Intervenor Status, 123 U.Pa.L. Rev. 822, 873–92 (1975), discusses post-judgment intervention and United States v. Western Electric, 1968 Trade Cas. (CCH) ¶ 72,415 (N.D.N.J. 1968), affirmed mem. sub nom. Clark Walter & Sons, Inc. v. United States, 392 U.S. 659. See also, Golden v. National Finance Adjusters, 555 F.Supp. 42, 46 (E.D.Mich.1982).

In class actions like Lucy v. Adams, p. 1029, class-member nonparties to the original injunction may take advantage of it. The nonparty in Lasky v. Quinlan, 558 F.2d 1133 (2d Cir. 1977), was less fortunate. In 1973, five jail inmates obtained an injunction which provided for improvements in jail conditions. The judge did not certify a plaintiff class. Contempt consisting primarily of attorneys' fees and disbursements was reversed because the action was moot. None of the named plaintiffs were in custody; no party had an interest in enforcing the decree. "In the absence of a class certification, the plaintiffs cannot prosecute the action on behalf of the present inmates . . . While Rule 71 [see Appendix] may support a separate action by a present inmate to enforce the order obtained by the plaintiffs, it cannot be used by a party to enforce an order in an action in which he no longer has standing to sue." The court said that civil contempt is remedial to serve the plaintiff, intended neither to deter nor to vindicate the court's authority. 558 F.2d at 1137.

Should courts discuss the issue in terms of standing? Should nonparties file separate actions against enjoined defendants and move for offensive issue preclusion? See Parklane Hosiery Co., Inc. v. Shore, 439 U.S. 322 (1979). See generally Compensatory Contempt, 1980 U.Ill.L.F. at 976–77.

PACIFIC GAMBLE ROBINSON CO. v. MINNEAPOLIS & ST. LOUIS RAILWAY CO.

92 F.Supp. 352 (D.Minn.1950).

NORDBYE, Chief Judge. This proceeding first came before this Court on April 16, 1949, upon plaintiff's motion for a temporary mandatory injunction requiring defendant, a common carrier by rail, to furnish railroad refrigerator cars to plaintiff company, which is engaged in the wholesale distribution and sale of perishable fresh fruits, vegetables and groceries in Minneapolis. An order granting that relief was filed by this Court on April 27, 1949, after an extended hearing, and a temporary mandatory injunction was issued. Pacific Gamble Robinson Co. v. M. & St. L. R. Co., D.C., 83 F.Supp. 860. The defendant appealed from that order, and on May 12, 1950, the Court of Appeals dismissed the appeal . . . upon the ground that the question presented on appeal—the propriety of the temporary mandatory injunction—was moot because defendant had begun to furnish the refrigerator cars required by plaintiff on or about June 20, 1949. At that time, the plaintiff's employees had ended their strike, which defendant contended prevented service to plaintiff, and defendant's employees again were willing to serve the plaintiff's plant as instructed by the defendant because, as they contended, they no longer felt concerned over their physical safety when doing so.

The trial of the main action, which seeks a permanent mandatory injunction, has been continued in this Court pending the decision of the Court of Appeals on the appeal from the granting of the temporary injunction. Plaintiff now admits that no permanent injunction is necessary in order for it to obtain from defendant the refrigerator cars which it now needs, and no other relief is requested in the complaint. Plaintiff objects to the dismissal, however, upon the ground that a civil contempt proceeding, which it now has pending against defendant seeking a fine for its benefit in the sum of $205,118.64 by reason of damages sustained for alleged violation of the temporary injunction, has not been disposed of. Plaintiff alleges, and defendant apparently does not deny for the purpose of this motion, that defendant failed and refused to furnish refrigerator cars to plaintiff after this Court issued the temporary mandatory injunction and until the strike of plaintiff's employees ended. . . .

The nature of a civil contempt proceeding must be recognized. It is a part of the main action, and if sound it may result in a fine for the benefit of the plaintiff as damages suffered as a result of the contempt. If, however, the main action is dismissed or is unsustainable, any civil contempt proceeding must fall. Gompers v. Bucks Stove & Range Co. . . . The vitality of a temporary injunction is derived from the pendency of the main action. It is ancillary thereto. And its ultimate and basic validity, as well as any contempt orders predicated thereon, necessarily depends upon the outcome of the main action. Obviously, if the entire controversy were not now moot and the trial on the merits disclosed that plaintiff was not entitled to a permanent injunction, then the temporary injunction would necessarily fall, together with any and all rights to enforce civil contempt for any disobedience. Circumstances have now arisen which prevent this Court from finally determining whether or not the temporary injunction was providently granted. A decision at this time on the merits would be a determination of an abstract question. The merits of the controversy between the parties has not and cannot be determined by reason of the happening of the events which have terminated the dispute which invoked the equitable jurisdiction of this Court. Such a termination divests the Court of any equitable grounds to proceed further, either to enforce any interlocutory orders or to enter a final decree. And without a final decree, a civil contempt order cannot have any finality. . . .

It must be emphasized that the primary purpose of a civil contempt proceeding is to enforce obedience to the Court's order. . . . The purpose is remedial. In issuing a mandatory injunction, the Court in event of disobedience may place the violator in custody until he obeys the Court's order. But such disposition would not be by way of punishment, but rather as a means to enforce the Court's decree. Any assessment of a fine in a civil contempt proceeding against a defendant for a violation of the temporary mandatory injunction would likewise be imposed primarily as a remedial measure with incidental benefit to the plaintiff, in that the fine may be determined for his use in light of the injury to him. But, in the instant controversy, there is now no need for any proceeding in civil contempt to assess damages for plaintiff's benefit in order to coerce defendant to comply with the Court's order. . . . Certainly, where no remedial relief is necessary by reason of the termination of the controversy, the arm of a court of equity cannot be utilized in a civil contempt proceeding to punish past wrongs. Whether the contempt proceedings should be permitted to continue is not the question. Rather, the question is whether it exists so it can be continued. . . .

Although plaintiff points out that the *Gompers* case involved a settlement of the action and the instant case did not, that distinction does not appear important. The Supreme Court appears to have based its decision upon termination of the action, not upon the cause of termination. For it cites Worden v. Searls [121 U.S. 14 (1887)], which did not involve termination of an action by settlement, but because the patent which the court there enjoined the defendant from violating was held to be a nullity. The fact of termination without need of further equitable relief, not the cause of termination, seems to be the basis for the *Gompers* decision. And certainly the instant case is terminated, in so far as injunctive relief is concerned, just as effectively as was the *Gompers* case. For here, as plaintiff also recognizes, a permanent injunction is not necessary. Defendant is doing that which plaintiff requests. No danger of defendant's failure to comply with the temporary injunction in the future is shown. The strike of plaintiff's employees which was the alleged reason for defendant's failure to serve plaintiff no longer exists. No need for either a temporary or permanent injunction appears. Defendant is now producing and furnishing the service which plaintiff in this action demanded and required. There is no fundamental distinction between the settlement of a controversy as in the *Gompers* case, a trial on the merits adverse to plaintiff as in Worden v. Searls, . . . or the mootness of the controversy between the parties hereto, which deprives a court of equity of any jurisdiction to proceed further in determining the question of injunctive relief. . . .

Under all the circumstances, therefore, defendant is entitled to a dismissal of the main action including the civil contempt proceeding, without prejudice, however, to the Court's right to act on any criminal contempt which may have existed. . . . Moreover, the dismissal will be without prejudice to plaintiff's right to proceed against the defendant in a court of competent jurisdiction for damages allegedly sustained by plaintiff as the result of defendant's failure to provide the switching service to plaintiff at the times and in the manner alleged herein. . . .

---

1) Does *Pacific Gamble Robinson* impair the judge's ability to use an interlocutory injunction to preserve a dispute in order to decide it? Does it allow plaintiff to profit from a later victory? Should plaintiff recover compensatory contempt for defendant's violations occurring between the injunction and eventual compliance? See Backo v. Local 281, United Brotherhood of Carpenters and Joiners, 438 F.2d 176 (2d Cir. 1970); Getka v. Lader, 71 Wis.2d 237, 238 N.W.2d 87 (1976). Are *Gompers* and *Worden* distinguishable? Does the collateral bar rule insulate the substantive part of the injunc-

tion from scrutiny in compensatory contempt? See *United Mine Workers*, p. 274, (no); Matter of Carter, 691 F.2d 390 (8th Cir. 1982) (yes).

2) Does defendant's unilateral cessation differ from bilateral settlement? Note, Injunction Negotiations: An Economic, Moral and Legal Analysis, 27 Stan.L.Rev. 1563, 1588–89 (1975). Does the idea that plaintiff should recover no compensation when defendant violates an incorrect injunction govern where defendant obeys a correct injunction? Did the court neglect compensatory to concentrate on coercive contempt? criminal contempt? both coercive and criminal contempt? Finally, should plaintiff be entitled to a permanent injunction even though defendant ceased "voluntarily"? See Compensatory Contempt, 1980 U.Ill.L.F. at 974–75 n. 13.

NEW JERSEY ZINC CO. v. LOCAL 890 OF INTERNATIONAL UNION OF MINE, MILL & SMELTER WORKERS

57 N.M. 617, 261 P.2d 648 (1953).

SEYMOUR, Justice. This is an appeal from a decree of the district court of Grant County, adjudging the defendants, appellants, in contempt of court for violating a permanent injunction issued by the court on July 9, 1951. . . . [T]he relevant portion of [the injunction] reads as follows:

"1. That defendants and each of them, and their wives, mothers, sisters and children as their agents, be and they are hereby permanently enjoined and restrained from trespassing upon plaintiff's property and blocking the roads and other entrances to the property of plaintiff in such manner as to restrain, coerce or prevent the employees of plaintiff from returning to work, or from illegally attempting to keep said employees from continuing in their employment with plaintiff."

On December 18, 1951, appellee filed its motion for order to show cause seeking to have appellants held in contempt for violation of the permanent injunction, the alleged violations occurring December 6 through December 18, inclusive, 1951. Hearing was had February 28 and 29, 1952. Decision of the trial court was rendered March 10, 1952 finding appellants guilty of contempt and levying specific fines in varying amounts, totalling $5,720, in part against the unions and in part against the individual appellants, to be paid to the clerk of the court for the use and benefit of appellee as compensation for its losses and damages by reason of the violation of the permanent injunction.

The matter is now here on appeal from the contempt decree . . . .

It is undisputed that the strike mentioned in . . . the equity complaint [one starting on October 19, 1950] was settled in late January of 1952 and that the picket line was withdrawn and ceased to exist.

The question for determination is whether or not the settlement of the strike and the withdrawal of the picket line terminated the jurisdiction of the lower court to continue the trial of and make disposition of the civil contempt proceedings commenced a month before such settlement and withdrawal. . . .

It is one contention of appellee that the original suit in equity did not seek an injunction against the strike but against certain picketing activities, and the termination of the strike was therefore irrelevant as regards "the settlement of the main cause." This would seem unsound in view of the case of Pacific Gamble Robinson Co. v. Minneapolis & St. L. Ry. Co., D.C. . . . .

This case of Pacific Gamble Robinson Co. v. Minneapolis & St. L. Ry. Co. convinces us of the relevancy of the ending of the strike and the withdrawal of picket lines in trying to determine whether there has been a settlement of the main cause within the meaning of the *Gompers* case. It is further to be noted that this case dealt with a fine, such as here involved, as distinguished from the imprisonment involved in the *Gompers* case.

. . . . In the instant case, the permanent injunction was entered, the appeal period expired, and that, too, remains on the records today; but, with the conclusion of the strike and the withdrawal of the picket lines, the permanent injunction became a matter of history. If appellee takes the position that an order should have been entered in the original equity case dissolving the permanent injunction, we cannot follow it that far—such an order is simply a piece of paper and has nothing to do with reality. . . .

Appellee further contends for the principle of equity jurisprudence that a court of equity, having assumed jurisdiction for one purpose will entertain it for all purposes, legal or equitable, connected with the principal controversy. Ample authority in our own decisions is cited. We find no merit in this contention; the situation might be different if appellee had sought damages in and as a part of its original action in equity. In such event, the equity court, absent appellee's consent to settlement, would have retained jurisdiction for the purpose of assessing damages. However, there was no such claim and the damages here involved, having the fundamental purpose of coercion in a civil contempt action, are not involved in the general equitable principle advanced by appellee.

Finally, in urging the validity of this contempt decree, great emphasis has been placed by appellee on the necessity of sustaining the dignity and authority of the courts. Much has been written on this subject in impressive and penetrating language. It cannot be stated better than it is by Mr. Justice Lamar in the *Gompers* case. In that regard, this Court feels impelled to say only this: That the activities of the appellants as revealed by the record indicate a violent and inexcusable contempt for the trial court and its orders; nevertheless, the theory of our government and our history leave no question as to the strength and vitality of the power vested in the judiciary. If that power lives in fear of its derogation, it is a dangerous thing. The dominating idea must be the responsibility of the judiciary to exercise that power wisely and always within its limitations. . . .

The contempt decree of March 10, 1952 is vacated and set aside without prejudice, however, to the trial court's right to act on any criminal contempt which may have been committed, and without prejudice to appellee's right to proceed against appellants in a court of competent jurisdiction for damages allegedly sustained by appellee as a result of appellants' acts.

---

1) Should the court have considered how the compensatory contempt figured into the way the parties settled the conflict? Did the court confuse compensatory with coercive contempt? criminal contempt? both coercive and criminal contempt? *Pacific Gamble Robinson* and *Local 890* send the plaintiff to a separate action for damages. If plaintiff must receive the money damages previously found inadequate, should plaintiff have access to the procedural advantages of compensatory contempt? Would your response to the decisions differ in jurisdictions that remit all requests for damages for breach of injunctions to separate actions? See Compensatory Contempt, 1980 U.Ill. L.F. at 981.

2) Reconsider the last paragraph of the *McComb* majority opinion in light of *Pacific Gamble Robinson* and *Local 890.* If defendant violates, may the judge begin compensatory contempt? Or must the judge "sit supinely by waiting for some litigant to take the initiative"? How does compensatory contempt differ from the criminal contempt in *Alsbury,* p. 940?

II. Allocating Responsibility for the Violation

In several decisions in Chapter 14 below on who must obey an injunction, the court considers whether an injunction against a principal compels subordinates to obey. The courts determine the duties of those at the bottom by the conduct of those at the top. *Telling* shows that conduct at the bottom may determine liability at the top.

TELLING v. BELLOWS-CLAUDE NEON CO.

77 F.2d 584 (6th Cir. 1935).

Before HICKS, SIMONS, and ALLEN, Circuit Judges.

SIMONS, Circuit Judge. The appeal is from a decree imposing penalties and costs upon the appellants as officers and directors in control of a corporation for civil contempt in the violation of an injunction restraining patent infringement. The patent was held valid and infringed by this court . . . . Pursuant to our mandate, decree was entered in the District Court for injunction and accounting against the Sun Ray Gas Corporation and certain of its officers, not including the present appellants. Upon the date the injunction issued, the assets of the enjoined company were transferred to the Sun Ray Products, Inc., which assumed its predecessor's liabilities. Infringement continuing, contempt proceedings were instituted against the new corporation, resulting in [a] decree for damages. Subsequently the present appellants were brought into the case by supplemental bill, and, from a decree adjudging them guilty of contempt and imposing penalties, the appeal is taken. . . .

The Sun Ray Gas Corporation was in the business of manufacturing, selling, leasing, and servicing luminous signs. Its signs were in the main equipped with electrodes held by us to infringe Claude patent, No. 1,125,476, for a "system of illuminating by luminescent tubes." Injunction issued September 30, 1929, of broad scope, restraining not only manufacture and sale of infringing signs, but their leasing and servicing. After the service of the injunctional order no infringing signs were manufactured or sold, either by Sun Ray Gas Corporation or its successor, Sun Ray Products, Inc. It is, however, clearly established by the evidence that many infringing signs continued under lease and were serviced by the latter corporation. The defense is that Telling and Curtis, having caused to be issued to their subordinates written orders that all infringing electrodes be replaced by noninfringing electrodes, and being told and in good faith believing that this was done, are not guilty of contempt.

Telling, Curtis, and Woolrich were the controlling stockholders and directors of Sun Ray Products, Inc. Curtis was also for a time its president. Woolrich made no contest and has not appealed. We are concerned, therefore, with the decree only as it applies to Telling and Curtis. Notwithstanding the written orders to subordinates to replace infringing electrodes, infringing signs continued in use and were serviced. The master found that Woolrich had falsified the records, making it appear that all signs had been changed over from the infringing type. Meanwhile, Telling had been loaning large sums of money to the corporation, and had taken as security liens on the company's signs leased to customers. On October 22, 1929, arrangements were made at a board of directors' meeting, Telling and Curtis participating, for a large loan to be made by Telling to the company, to be used partly to defray the expense of changing infringing electrodes. The master found from this that appellants knew at that time that infringing electrodes were in use between September 30, 1929, and the date of the directors' meeting. In March of 1930, Telling instructed T.J. Keller to check up and report to him on the number of signs that were still infringing, and upon receipt of Keller's report gave instructions to replace the infringing electrodes, whereupon a twenty-four hour a day shift was employed, which continued for three weeks at a weekly pay roll of $5,000 per week. Nevertheless, as late as February, 1931, many signs were found in Cleveland and other cities still equipped with the infringing device. In December, 1930, Telling and Curtis resigned as directors. On January 28, 1931, Telling took judgment on his notes, had a receiver appointed, who advertised and sold the mortgaged signs, which Telling bid in and later sold. Of these, forty were identified as equipped at least in part with infringing electrodes. In addition, Telling had upon his residence an infringing sign, claimed to be used for the purpose of advertising the corporation's business. It is urged and not disputed that neither Telling nor Curtis were practical men in the organization; that they did not themselves install or service signs; that it would have been impossible for them to inspect all signs being serviced, and doubtful whether even upon inspection they could have determined whether or not the infringing device had been replaced.

These circumstances . . . bring us to a consideration of the problem of appellants' liability. That the injunctional order was disobeyed by the corporation, and that it is liable, is not in dispute. That the decree was directed not only to the corporation, but to its officers and agents, and that Telling and Curtis knew its terms, is also not in controversy. It is urged, however, that lack of knowledge on the part of Telling and Curtis that their orders had been disobeyed and their records falsified, and the failure of the evidence to show any willful or contumacious acts upon their part in defiance of the injunction, absolves them from liability. We do not understand, however, that in cases of corporate infringement knowledge of the director or officer charged with infringing that the article manufactured or sold (or leased or serviced) did infringe, is material. . . . Nor is either willfulness or contumaciousness an essential element in civil contempt, however indispensable it may be to a finding of criminal contempt. . . .

Inquiry suggests itself as to the duty of the controlling directors or officers of a corporation when a mandatory injunction of which they have knowledge issues, directing them to refrain from infringement. The corporation being an abstraction can act only through its officers or agents. Clearly something must be done about it, and certainly in a case where, as here, infringement will automatically continue unless affirmative action is taken to stop it. We may concede without deciding that where an injunctional order requires something to be done forthwith, which it is humanly impossible to do instantaneously, reasonable interpretation must be given to the court's command, and that compliance therewith within such time as under all of the circumstances would appear to be reasonable may be substantial compliance with the order. It may also be conceded, again without deciding, that where the injunction is addressed to directors not active in the mechanical activities of their business, and obedience to which requires mechanical activity, that the order is substantially complied with when the officers or directors take such steps as are under all of the circumstances reasonably appropriate to secure prompt obedience to the court order. Granting also that the written instructions issued by the corporation to its service department to replace infringing electrodes were reasonably calculated to secure obedience to the injunction, and certainly steps in compliance with a court order cannot be interpreted as in defiance thereof, nevertheless, when it was brought home to Telling and Curtis on October 22, 1929, that infringement was still continuing, and to Telling again in March of 1930 that many infringing electrodes had not yet been replaced and neither did anything further than to repeat instructions previously given and disregarded, then we think it cannot be said in any view of the case that the steps taken to insure compliance with the injunctional order, were reasonably appropriate to that end. Just what should have been done we do not feel obliged to indicate, though the appellees suggest that it would have been a simple matter to have turned off the offending signs. We are, however, constrained to hold that in the light of all circumstances there was clear and convincing evidence to sustain the findings and conclusions of the master that the appellants were guilty of contempt.

We are not unaware that there are holdings . . . which lend support to the contention that it is misfeasance and not mere nonfeasance that imposes upon officers of a corporation liability for its torts. Defiance of a mandatory injunction, however, transcends in importance and sinister consequence the commission of a mere tort, and the court in the above case was concerned with a question of accounting for damages after injunction rather than with a contempt proceeding. . . . We are not unmindful also that the rule we here apply may in instances prove harsh in placing officers of a corporation endeavoring in good faith to comply with court decree at the mercy of dishonest employees who violate instructions. Safety, however, lies in diligence, and the court is primarily concerned with preserving for the owner his adjudicated patent monopoly and for the courts a proper respect for their decrees.

In conclusion it must be added to what we have said of the duty of officers and directors to insure compliance with the orders of the court, that Telling, in loaning money upon the security of infringing devices, foreclosing his liens thereon, buying in and selling the pledged property, and in the maintaining at his own residence an infringing sign, acted solely in his individual capacity, and not as an officer and director of the corporation, and in these acts was guilty of contempt without regard to other considerations herein discussed, and as to such acts it is immaterial whether he knew or was ignorant that the property involved infringed the patent. . . .

---

1) What is plaintiff's burden of proof in compensatory contempt? The court says that plaintiff's proof must be clear and convincing. But does this stringent standard encourage plaintiffs to file separate actions for breach of the substantive standard instead of pursuing compensation for breach of the injunction? Is it faithful to the inadequacy prerequisite? See Compensatory Contempt, 1980 U.Ill.L.F. at 980–81.

2) What is defendant's duty to comply or to assure compliance? Does defendant have more of a duty to obey an injunction than to avoid a tort? A breach of contract? Compare *McComb* p. 975. Is lack of wilfullness a defense? Lack of negligence? Why? See Compensatory Contempt, 1980 U.Ill.L.F. at 979. Is *Telling* palatable because plaintiff could file a separate action and recover comparable damages? Should judges tolerate more injunctive vagueness in compensatory than criminal contempt? Does the standard for violation vary from criminal to civil contempt?

3) Rule 65(d) tells judges to grant "specific" injunctions. Is the issue in *McComb* whether the government may use a form injunction? Developments in the Law—Injunctions, 78 Harv.L.Rev. 994, 1064–67 (1965), discusses vagueness-specificity and narrowness-breadth. The interplay between a) contemnor's state of mind, b) vagueness-specificity, c) narrowness-breadth, d) burden of proof, and e) criminal and civil contempt has produced a baffling array of decisions. See Note 1), p. 895.

"Since an injunction prohibits conduct under threat of judicial punishment, basic fairness requires that those enjoined receive explicit notice of precisely what conduct is outlawed." Schmidt v. Lessard, 414 U.S. 473, 476 (1974). See also International Longshoremen's Association, Local 1291 v. Philadelphia Marine Trade Association, 389 U.S. 64, 76 (1967); Marshall v. Local Union No. 639, International Brotherhood of Teamsters, Chauffeurs, Warehousemen and Helpers of America, Inc., 593 F.2d 1297, 1302–03 (D.C.Cir.1979); Sekaquaptewa v. MacDonald, 544 F.2d 396, 406–07 (9th Cir. 1976); Palmigiano v. Garrahy, 448 F.Supp. 659, 670–71 (D.R.I.1978); International Society for Krishna Consciousness of Western Pennsylvania, Inc. v. Griffin, 437 F.Supp. 666 (W.D.Pa.1977); Pliscou v. Holtville Unified School District, 411 F.Supp. 842 (S.D.Cal.1976); Sweetarts v. Sunline, Inc., 299 F.Supp. 572 (E.D.Mo.1969); Lyon v. Bloomfield, 355 Mass. 738, 247 N.E.2d 555 (1969); United States Time Corp. v. G.E.M. of Boston, Inc., 345 Mass. 279, 186 N.E.2d 920 (1963). See generally Note, Criminal Contempt: Violations of Injunctions in the Federal Courts, 32 Ind.L.J. 514, 516–20 (1957).

4) Does the judge retain equitable discretion to withhold a compensatory award? "The argument is that where the court of whose authority contempt is charged either finds that there was no contempt or purges the offender, a judicial power has been exercised which is discretionary and is not subject to review. But the fact that a remedial order was entered in a contempt proceeding is not in itself a reason why it should not be subject to correction by an appellate court. . . . In the determination of the question whether an injunction has been violated and, if so, whether compensation shall be made to the injured party, there may be occasion for the exercise of judicial discretion; but the order to be entered in such a proceeding is not exclusively or necessarily a discretionary one. . . . Moreover, legal discretion in such a case does not extend to a refusal to apply well-settled principles of law to a conceded state of facts. . . . " Union Tool Co. v. Wilson, 259 U.S. 107, 112 (1922).

III. The Measure of Compensatory Contempt

How much should plaintiff recover when defendant breaches an injunction? Before enjoining, the judge decided that money was inadequate; a money remedy for compensatory contempt must reflect that decision. How? The Court in *Mine Workers* and the court in *Northside Realty* said plaintiff should recover "actual loss," but there is more than one way to measure money recovery.

LEMAN v. KRENTLER-ARNOLD HINGE LAST CO.

284 U.S. 448, 52 S.Ct. 238, 76 L.Ed. 389 (1932).

Chief Justice HUGHES delivered the opinion of the Court.

This is a contempt proceeding against the respondent, Krentler-Arnold Hinge Last Company, for violation of a permanent injunction granted in an infringement suit.

. . . Upon hearing, the District Court held the respondent to be guilty of "civil contempt" for deliberate violation of the injunction and ordered a reference to a master to take an account of the profits made by the respondent through such violation and to ascertain the petitioners' costs and expenses in the contempt proceeding. On the master's report, the District Court entered a decree for the recovery by the petitioners of $39,576.26 as profits, together with counsel fees, expenses and interest, making a total of $49,292.89. . . .

The Circuit Court of Appeals refused recovery of profits upon the ground that in a proceeding for civil contempt the relief should be based upon the "pecuniary injury or damage" which the act of disobedience caused the complaining party, including such reasonable expenses as were incurred in the bringing of the proceeding. There is no question here that the respondent had made profits through the infringing sales in violation of the injunction, and the amount of the profits was ascertained, but the appellate court held that the petitioners were limited to the damages caused by such sales and that no damages had been shown. We think that the court erred in imposing this limitation. The fact that a proceeding for civil contempt is for the purpose of compensating the injured party, and not, as in criminal contempt, to redress the public wrong, does not require so narrow a view of what should be embraced in an adequate remedial award.

While the distinction is clear between damages, in the sense of actual pecuniary loss, and profits, the latter may none the less be included in the concept of compensatory relief. In a suit in equity against an infringer, profits are recoverable not by way of punishment but to insure full compensation to the party injured. As this Court said in Mowry v. Whitney, 14 Wall. 620, 653: "The profits which are recoverable against an infringer of a patent are in fact a compensation for the injury the patentee has sustained from the invasion of his right." The court of equity in such cases applies familiar principle in "converting the infringer into a trustee for the patentee as regards the profits thus made." Packet Co. v. Sickles, 19 Wall. 611, 617. This is not to say that there is an actual fiduciary relation which would give the right to an accounting for profits regardless of the existence of a basic claim to equitable relief. Root v. Railway Co., 105 U.S. 189, 214, 215. Referring to the case last cited, this Court succinctly stated the controlling principle in its opinion in Tilghman v. Proctor, 125 U.S. 136, 148, as follows: "But, as has been recently declared by this court, upon an elaborate review of the cases in this country and in England, it is more strictly accurate to say, that a court of equity, which has acquired, upon some equitable ground, jurisdiction of a suit for the infringement of a patent, will not send the plaintiff to a court of law to recover damages, but will administer full relief, by awarding, as an equivalent or a substitute for legal damages, a compensation computed and measured by the same rule that courts of equity apply to the case of a trustee who has wrongfully used the trust property for his own advantage." Profits are thus allowed "as an equitable measure of compensation." Hamilton Shoe Co. v. Wolf Brothers, 240 U.S. 251, 259. . . . In view of the principles governing the broader relief obtainable in equity, as contrasted with those applicable in courts of law, it is apparent that there is no necessary exclusion of profits from the idea of compensation in a remedial proceeding.

The respondent insists that this contempt proceeding is not a suit in equity, but, as we have seen, the proceeding is a part of the main cause in equity and is for the enforcement of the decree, and there is no reason why in such a proceeding equitable principles should not control the measure of relief to be accorded to the injured party. It is also urged that an award of profits involves a discovery and accounting from a party charged with a penal liability. This argument is also based on a misconception of the nature of the proceeding, which is not penal but remedial, and the remedy should be complete. Accordingly it has been repeatedly assumed that, in a proceeding for civil contempt for disobedience to an injunction granted in an infringement suit, the profits derived from the violation of the injunction are recoverable. . . .

We are of the opinion that the District Court properly allowed the profits in question, and, in this respect, the decree of the Circuit Court of Appeals modifying the decree of the District Court is reversed and that of the District Court affirmed.

The patent infringement statute in effect when the Court decided *Leman* provided that the patentee should recover "profits." In 1946, Congress changed the standard to provide for "damages . . . in no event less than a reasonable royalty." 35 U.S.C. § 284 (1976). If Congress intended to eliminate the "profits" approach to patent infringement, should a judge award a patentee the contemnor's profits in compensatory contempt for violation of an injunction against infringement?

SUNBEAM CORP. v. GOLDEN RULE APPLIANCE CO.

252 F.2d 467 (2d Cir. 1958).

Before HAND, HINCKS and LUMBARD, Circuit Judges.

HINCKS, Circuit Judge. This is an appeal from a judgment holding the appellant, Golden Rule Appliance Co., Inc., in civil contempt for violation of a consent decree entered in an injunction action brought by Sunbeam Corporation to enforce a claim of unfair competition under the New York Fair Trade Law, N.Y. General Business Law § 369–a et seq. Among other terms, the consent decree forbade Golden Rule from advertising or selling any price-fixed Sunbeam product below the list price set by Sunbeam pursuant to the New York Fair Trade Law.

The judgment below has three main provisions: (1) Golden Rule is to pay Sunbeam $1,000 as a "fine"; (2) Golden Rule is to pay Sunbeam $2,500 as reimbursement for all costs of this litigation including counsel fees; (3) Golden Rule is to pay Sunbeam a $2,500 fine for every future sale of a Sunbeam product in violation of the consent decree.

Golden Rule is a "discount house" located in New York City which sold, among other products, electrical appliances, including some of Sunbeam's. The discount operation is based upon large volume with a comparatively low profit margin upon the individual items. This type of operation, as are other retail operations, is subject to the New York Fair Trade Law, which permits manufacturers of trademarked products in open competition to maintain a desired price level in the state. Sunbeam took advantage of the statute's provisions and duly established minimum prices for the resale of its products in the State of New York. Its conduct in so doing was saved from conflict with the Antitrust Laws of the United States by the Miller-Tydings Act, 15 U.S.C.A. § 1, as supplemented by the McGuire Act, 15 U.S.C.A. § 45.

In June 1954, Sunbeam commenced suit against Golden Rule for alleged violations of Sunbeam's established prices. The consent decree, referred to above, was filed on August 1, 1956. The present proceeding, commenced in January 1957 by the issuance of a show-cause order, is based upon sales made by the defendant in November and December, 1956, at prices below the established resale price. At the hearing several professional shoppers testified to such sales. . . .

The appellant's main attack is directed against [these] three pecuniary provisions of the [contempt order]. It contends that these, because punitive and confiscatory, have no proper place in a decree for civil contempt. . . .

The first pecuniary provision of the decree requires Golden Rule to pay Sunbeam $1,000 as compensation for past violations of the injunction. I agree with Judge Hand that the order for the $1,000 fine cannot stand. I think I should say, however, that I reach the result he indicates by a somewhat difference approach. In a Fair Trade case such as this, in which the defendant's violation, without depriving the plaintiff of any sales which it might otherwise have made, has only caused some injury to the plaintiff's good will, I find it difficult to view the defendant's profits as included in the concept of compensation to the plaintiff. In such cases the relationship between the defendant's profits and "compensation" to the plaintiff seems substantially more remote than in patent infringement cases such as Leman v. Krentler-Arnold Hinge Last Co., . . . which Judge Hand cites, in which it is plausible to infer that sales of the patented article made by the defendant would have been made by the plaintiff but for the defendant's wrongful conduct. Restatement, Torts, § 747.

The problem now presented to us is whether, in a contempt proceeding arising from violation of the decree of a federal court in a Fair Trade case, an award of the defendant's profits to the plaintiff may be viewed as "compensatory" relief within the well established federal rule that only compensatory relief may be awarded in civil contempt proceedings. United States v. United Mine Workers; Gompers v. Bucks Stove & Range Co. In the federal contempt cases I find no intimation that the notion of "compensatory relief" differs from that applied by the federal courts in shaping the recovery in patent infringement cases. Leman v. Krentler-Arnold Hinge Last Co. And since our immediate problem relates to the power of a federal court to enforce its decree, even in a diversity case such as this a remedy provided by a State contempt statute is not applicable: we may not give effect to § 773 of the New York Judiciary Law which provides that the plaintiff may recover $250 for each violation of a civil contempt decree even absent proof of damages. Guaranty Trust Co. v. New York, 326 U.S. 99.

However, it now seems established that in trade-mark cases, in which as in Fair Trade cases the plaintiff has suffered injury to his good will, the infringer, like the patent infringer, is held to the accountability of a trustee for profits derived from property illegally dealt with. . . . In both types of cases the crucial injury is one to the plaintiff's good will; in both the plaintiff may recover the defendant's profits. I think that in the one type as in the other the recovery may be classified as compensatory, rather than punitive, within the meaning of the federal rule limiting awards in civil contempt cases to those which are compensatory. An award in such cases surely cannot be characterized as "punitive." For its effect goes no further than to give to the plaintiff the profits derived by the defendant's wrongful conduct: it does not take from the defendant assets not related to its wrongful conduct. As noted in the Blue Bell Co. case, [213 F.2d 354, 362–63 (10th Cir. 1954)], such a recovery rests "upon the equitable principle of unjust enrichment" which is the antithesis of punishment. Restatement, Restitution, § 1.

For these reasons I think it would have been proper here to impose a fine, payable to the plaintiff, in the amount of the defendant's profits. However, for the reasons stated by Judge Hand, I agree with him that on the record here the proofs were not sufficient to make even a *prima facie* showing of the profits made by the defendant.

The second provision of the judgment ordered Golden Rule to pay Sunbeam $2,500 to cover expenses of the litigation including counsel fees. In this we find no error. Such expenses may be estimated and appraised by the court without proof of exact expenditures. . . . See . . . Moskovitz, Contempt of Injunctions, Civil and Criminal, 43 Colum.L.Rev. 780, 806–7, where it is stated that an

". . . award for counsel fees, and other expenses of suit, need not be based on evidence of actual cost. This failure to require evidence seems proper since the courts should be expert in assessing the value of legal services and the costs of bringing suit. The award should be limited to what is reasonable, actual expenditure not being the test, . . . inasmuch as plaintiff controls the amount of such expense."

The third provision of the judgment orders that Golden Rule pay Sunbeam $2,500 for each future violation of the consent decree.

This provision we affirm for the reasons stated in Judge Hand's opinion.

Affirmed, except as to the $1,000 fine which is reversed.

HAND, Circuit Judge (concurring). . . .

First, as to the "fine" of $1,000. The Supreme Court in Leman v. Krentler-Arnold Hinge Last Co., held that in a civil contempt proceeding for violation of a judgment forbidding infringement of a patent, the court might award to the patentee the infringer's profits upon his sales, even though the patentee proved no damages. It is true that the Third Circuit *in banco* decided by a vote of five to two that this was not what the Supreme Court meant, and that the plaintiff must show "that the contemptuous conduct did, in fact, have substantial injurious effect upon his economic interest" (National Drying Machinery Co. v. Ackoff, 245 F.2d 192, 194). However, I find it impossible to reconcile this holding with the language used in Leman v. Krentler-Arnold Hinge Last Co. This doctrine is equally applicable to the case at bar. The defendant acquired articles in question subject to a lawful condition that it should not sell them below the Fair Trade price. In selling them below that price it received the proceeds as illegally as the infringer receives the proceeds of whatever infringing articles he may manufacture and sell.

However, difficulty arises in ascertaining what in fact were the defendant's profits. These consisted of the difference between the prices at which it sold and those at which it bought from the plaintiff, or from the plaintiff's middlemen. It is true that by destroying all the documents showing the prices at which it had bought or sold, the presumption arose *contra spoliatorem,* and justified the conclusion that the contents of the documents of purchase and sale if produced would have shown that it did realize profits. . . . That however, does not fix the amount of the profits unless there be a maximum beyond which the profits could not have gone. . . . Although it might be proper to take as the maximum for the minuend the Fair Trade prices, there is no way to find the proper subtrahend: i.e., the prices at which the defendant bought. And most important of all, there is no way to ascertain how many and what articles the defendant sold at less than Fair Trade prices. . . . Much as we should like to find a way by which to compute the profits, we cannot do so, and for that reason I concur with Judge Hincks in holding that the "fine" for past disobedience may not stand. Had the plaintiff sought to punish the defendant criminally for disobedience of the judgment, as it could have done, this lamentable result could have been avoided, but the proceeding was in no sense for criminal contempt.

We also hold that what I have called the "fine" *in terrorem* should be affirmed. For support of this conclusion we rely upon United States v. United Mine Workers, . . . which imposed a "fine" as part of the civil remedy, conditioned upon the defendant union's continuing an existing strike. . . . The "fine" that the court imposed upon the union in that case was of two kinds: $700,000 as damages for the injury already done by the strike and $2,800,000 *in terrorem* to secure its discontinuance. The Court agreed that in fixing the amount of the second "fine" the court should "consider the amount of the defendant's financial resources and the consequent seriousness of the burden to that particular defendant" . . . ; but the "fine" was only "a means of securing future compliance" with the decree and was not measured by any damage that the plaintiff might suffer from future disobedience. In both that case and here this "fine" was imposed only conditionally and depended upon the contemnor's future conduct. The only distinction is that there the future conduct forbidden was continuing a strike already in existence, and here it is future sales of the plaintiff's goods below the Fair Trade prices. We can see no relevant difference between ceasing to strike against an employer and ceasing to sell goods one has procured below their fixed price. . . . [T]his does not mean that we have no control whatever over the amount of a "fine" *in terrorem;* but there is no ground for disturbing the discretion of the District Court in this case.

We therefore reverse the "fine" of $1,000, but otherwise affirm the judgment.

LUMBARD, Circuit Judge (concurring in part and dissenting in part).

I would affirm the judgment in all respects.

I agree with Judge Hand and Judge Hincks in what they say about the award of $2,500 as reimbursement for costs and expenses and the award of $2,500 for each future violation.

As to the fine of $1,000 for past disobedience, it seems to me that the District Court had the power to impose a fine which would approximate the probable damages. Although it is impossible in cases such as this to say what the loss to the plaintiff has been, the authorities seem to support the view that it is enough to show the profits which the contemnor made and to award such amount. Leman v. Krentler-Arnold Hinge Last Co.

Here there is a further difficulty because the defendant by its own calculated and deliberate action of systematically destroying all records relating to these prohibited sales made it virtually impossible for the plaintiff to produce any proof of the extent of defendant's profits from such sales. The goods were purchased from various wholesalers of the plaintiff. So far as appears from the record the only way in which the plaintiff could have secured any evidence of defendant's sales would have been to conduct an examination of the accounts of scores of its wholesale customers in the New York area. To require such effort and expense merely because the defendant has destroyed the evidence would place a wholly disproportionate burden on the plaintiff.

As it is we do have proof that on five separate occasions during November and December 1956, buyers employed by the plaintiff did purchase articles from defendant at prices more than 20% off retail list, and therefore in violation of the law. We also know that the gross profit to Golden Rule on one of the sales was in excess of four dollars. In view of the fact that the defendant was a discount house operating on the basis of volume selling, it is not unreasonable to conclude that hundreds of such sales were made. Thus the award of $1,000 seems to me, in the circumstances, to be a reasonable estimate.

Moreover, it is clear that the defendant counted on having to pay fines and awards as the necessary and expected expense of running a business which was constantly in contempt of judicial admonitions. Obviously the fact that Golden Rule might be required to pay $250 for each violation under the New York law was no deterrent but merely reduced by that much the profit which it made. Nor did the fact that Golden Rule had previously been adjudged in contempt eighteen times, presumably an expensive procedure entailing not only court costs but attorney's fees, deter the defendant from a continuance of these activities. A business which can assume such costs and expenses and yet continue merrily on its campaign of calculated contempt cannot be heard to complain that a federal court is without power to assess damages of $1,000 when it has deliberately destroyed the only reasonable means of arriving at a more exact assessment. . . .

For these reasons I would affirm the District Court award of $1,000.

---

1) Should compensatory contempt judges employ the measurement formula that would have been employed in a separate damage action? Does measuring damage by the wrongdoer's gain advance some substantive policies better than measuring by plaintiff's loss? Does it advance the initial decision to enjoin? Compensatory Contempt, 1980 U.Ill.L.F. at 986–89.

2) *Sunbeam* focuses our attention on legally recognized injuries not susceptible to compensation. See Compensatory Contempt, 1980 U.Ill.L.F. at 1008 n. 186. When defendant violated the injunction, what interest did it affect? How was this interest compensated? Is the remedy more bounty than compensation? In a Virginia case, the court awarded only attorney fees. Arvin, Inc. v. Sony Corp. of America, 215 Va. 704, 213 S.E.2d 753 (1975).

3) Was New York correct to provide minimum damage every time defendant disobeys an injunction? Compare statutory damages in the Copyright Act, 17 U.S.C. § 504(c)(1) (1976). Is the $250 a bounty, a fine, punitive damage, or "compensation" for the uncompensable margin of injury that led the court to enjoin?

4) Try to develop an intelligible damage measure for *Sunbeam.* Sunbeam made all its accustomed profit when the wholesalers bought the items. If the Fair Trade price is magic, the lower Golden Rule's markup, the more Sunbeam is injured. The larger the injury, the lower the damage. Is the preceding irrelevant to the goal of taking the profit out of wrongdoing? The court finds an injury to goodwill. Is that a disingenuous fiction? Congress

repealed the legislation that allowed Fair Trade and mooted the raging controversy. Pub.L. No. 94–145, 89 Stat. 801 (1975).

5) Is Golden Rule's behavior the sort that calls for criminal sanctions? Where defendant's conduct is outrageous and plaintiff's injury is impalpable, courts often award punitive damages. In a case like *Sunbeam,* should a compensatory contempt judge award punitive damages? Should a judge substitute punitive damages for a criminal contempt fine? Will punitive damages advance the policies that initially led the judge to enjoin? Compensatory Contempt, 1980 U.Ill.L.F. at 992–95. Will allowing a private litigant to sue for punitive contempt turn the criminal process over to a private litigant?

6) *Gompers,* p. 831 teaches us that criminal punishment must follow criminal procedure. Should courts retain the "actual loss" measure because it prevents the contempt judge from punishing contemnor under the guise of compensating plaintiff? Does measuring by contemnor's gain and adding punitive damages violate *Gompers*'s policy? See Compensatory Contempt, 1980 U.Ill.L.F. at 995–97.

7) Compensatory contempt awards usually include attorney fees as part of plaintiff's cost of enforcing the injunction. See Compensatory Contempt, 1980 U.Ill.L.F. at 998–1002. Rendleman argues that the judge uses the damage part of the compensatory contempt award to advance the substantive standard and the cost-to-enforce part including attorney fees to advance the inadequacy prerequisite. What justifies this departure from the usual American rule denying attorney fees absent statute? Should the judge possess discretion to deny attorney fees? Should recovery turn on whether defendant violated wilfully? The *Sunbeam* court allowed attorney fees without proof based on judicial expertise. This approach is fading; contemporary courts tend to insist on proof. See, e.g., Cook v. Ochsner Foundation Hospital, 559 F.2d 270, 273 (5th Cir. 1977).

IV. The Borderline of Compensatory Contempt: Civil Fines

FEDERAL TRADE COMMISSION v. A. McLEAN & SON

94 F.2d 802 (7th Cir. 1938).

Before EVANS and SPARKS, Circuit Judges, and LINDLEY, District Judge.

SPARKS, Circuit Judge. The Federal Trade Commission has filed a petition for a rule against McLean and Son, a corporation, and one against M. J. Holloway and Company, a corporation, to show cause why each should not be adjudged in contempt of this court for violation of a decree entered by this court July 1, 1936. That decree was entered pursuant to application of the Commission for enforcement of its order against both respondents to cease and desist from certain practices theretofore found by the Commission to constitute unfair and forbidden methods of competition. . . .

The petition presented in each case was filed under the same title and number as the original proceeding, and was filed as a part of that proceeding. The prayer of each petition is as follows:

"Wherefore, Federal Trade Commission prays that said (respondent) be ordered to show cause why it should not be adjudged in contempt of this Court, in having so disobeyed said decree of this Court so made and entered on the first day of July, 1936."

Respondents filed answers in the nature of motions to dismiss the petitions for rule to show cause on the grounds that:

1. The object of the petitions for contempt is necessarily punitive and not compensatory, and accordingly should have been presented as an independent petition and not as supplemental proceedings in the original cause.

. . .

In reply to respondents' motions to dismiss, petitioner, the Commission, stated that its proceeding was one for civil contempt, and that it was a part of a proceeding based upon section 5 of the Federal Trade Commission Act, 15 U.S.C.A. § 45, which provides for a civil proceeding only and for a decree in the nature of an injunction; that it was not punitive; that it was wholly remedial, being prosecuted in the public interest; and that it was ancillary to the main case and in aid of the enforcement of the decree of this court. It further urged that the assessment of a fine would not indicate that the proceeding was criminal since a fine is as much an incident of civil contempt as of criminal, the difference between the two being that in civil contempt the fine must bear a relation to the injury sustained by the complaining party. In its petitions for rules to show cause, the Commission made no allegation of injury to itself and no request for fines payable to it in compensation for expense incurred as a result of respondents' alleged contempts. However, in its brief in opposition to the motions to dismiss, to show that it was entitled to such fines, it made the following statement:

"The Government, under the decree of this Court, represents the interests of the Government and of the public. The Government has borne the expense of a nationwide investigation to ascertain the facts which constitute the company's violations of the decree herein, and it pays all salaries and other expenses incident to the prosecution of this proceeding. The public is, as a matter of law, injured by such violations. The Government is entitled to a fine which bears a reasonable relation to all these injuries. The amount may not be calculated with accuracy, but the Court may reasonably approximate it in fixing a fine in a substantial sum.

"The cash outlay required of the Government in its investigations and in the prosecution of the pending petition may not be ascertained with certainty; but it manifestly is a substantial sum.

"That violations of the decree injure the public may not be doubted or denied. Respondent's total sales are so great that such injuries to the public, when expressed in dollars, must be a substantial sum. A proceeding in civil contempt is ancillary to the case in which the decree was entered. It depends upon and is co-existent with the right to enforce such decree."

The Commission thus asserted its right, as a party injured by violation of a decree in its favor, to the remedy or relief afforded by means of civil contempt proceedings. . . . [W]e concluded that the Commission was not entitled to the relief sought, by the means sought. It appeared that the question of the right of an administrative board, an agency of the Government, created principally for the purpose of regulating competition, to invoke rights customarily accorded to private litigants, had not previously been raised nor settled. . . . Having found that the protection of private rights was emphasized throughout the cases relating to civil contempt proceedings as their principal purpose, we became convinced that the Commission, an agency of the Government, representing no private interest of its own, but acting solely in the public interest, had no such standing as a private party that it could utilize procedure intended to safeguard the rights and interests of private parties. That the Commission does act in the public interest alone we think there can be no question. . . .

The Commission now appears to acquiesce in the conclusion that civil contempt proceedings are not appropriate to the proceeding here involved, as indicated by a supplemental brief filed herein, seventeen days after hearing of the cause, wherein it urges its right to prosecute proceedings for criminal contempt in its own name. It now states: "Counsel for the Commission respectfully submit that the petition herein presents an element of civil contempt, although it also presents a larger and more important element of criminal contempt—a criminal element that goes to the inherent power of this Court to vindicate its own dignity and rightful power . . . . The only practical change will be that the fine will be punitive, and there may be fine or imprisonment, or both, with no limits except the sound discretion of this Court." . . .

We think that not only the respondent, but also the court is entitled to know from the original petition and briefs in support thereof just what theory the petitioner relies upon for the relief sought in his petition. . . . . We are convinced that the Commission has no right now to demand permission to continue prosecution of the proceedings as in criminal contempt. Nor do the facts disclosed by the petitions for rule to show cause, and the suggestions filed in opposition thereto, show such deliberate intent to violate the order of the court that we feel impelled to prosecute a proceeding on our own motion to punish respondents for contempt of our order. . . .

---

1) Is McLean's argument based on the same premise as the decisions refusing to grant compensatory contempt? See *Levan*, p. 972 above. Does this premise persist because the vocabulary is inadequate to comprehend the interests in contempt? As note 64 of *Mine Workers*, p. 842 says, punishment is an ambiguous word. Are the $2,800,000 in *Mine Workers* and the $2,500 in *Sunbeam* either fines or punishments? Does each threaten to fine or punish later? Was the $700,000 in *Mine Workers* criminal or compensatory? See Judge Hand's concurring opinion in *Sunbeam*. Do both *Sunbeam* and *McLean* reveal that using the word "fine" to describe compensatory contempt either misleads or confuses? Should compensatory recovery for breach of an injunction be called something with less opprobrious connotations than contempt?

2) Section 19 of the FTC Act was enacted in 1975. It authorizes the agency to apply for consumer redress where it has found a § 5 violation.

The court may, upon finding dishonesty or fraud, rescind or reform contracts, refund money, return property, award damages, or notify the public. Section 13(b) authorizes the agency to seek injunctive relief against lawbreakers. 15 U.S.C. §§ 53(b), 57b(b) (1976). Do these amendments cure the regulatory maladies revealed by *McLean?* See also Cohan & Hayes, Contempt Proceedings: Another Dimension to Consumer Protection, 14 Suffolk U.L.Rev. 1 (1980).

3) Does the FTC lose compensatory contempt because it failed to record the time it spent? Does the court's decision to forbid the FTC from amending to prosecute criminal contempt survive *Mine Workers,* p. 839? Should the court grant the FTC leave to amend to seek punitive damages? Should the court allow the government to recover for the public loss to strip the ill gotten gains from contemnor? *Leman,* p. 991; *Northside Realty Assoc.,* p. 979; Compensatory Contempt, 1980 U.Ill.L.F. at 977–78.

UNITED STATES v. BROTHERHOOD OF RAILROAD TRAINMEN

95 F.Supp. 1019 (D.D.C.1951).

TAMM, District Judge. The defendant unincorporated association, the Brotherhood of Railroad Trainmen, is before the Court for sentencing in a case in which the defendant union has pleaded guilty to charges of civil and criminal contempt for violating the temporary restraining order issued by this Court December 14, 1950.

The Court, in imposing sentence upon the defendant, will impose a separate punishment for the criminal contempt and for the civil contempt, although it appears from at least one recent Supreme Court decision that the Courts have the authority to impose a so-called lump sum fine in this type of case, without breaking it up as to the part of the fine which is to be apportioned to the civil contempt and to the criminal contempt. United States v. United Mine Workers of America. This Court is of the opinion that the better practice is to identify the sentence by specific amounts. Cf. Rutledge, J., dissenting in United States v. United Mine Workers. . . .

The Court is of the opinion from the facts in this case that it is necessary for the Court to vindicate its authority by what the Court considers a substantial fine. Obviously a fine is the only proper punishment that the Court can impose upon an unincorporated association.

This case presents to the Court a unique situation. The Court has not heretofore encountered a case in which a union entered a plea of guilty to an offense of this kind. This fact—that the union pleaded guilty—has considerable social import apart from the proceedings in this case. Unions must accept their obligations and responsibilities, as well as their rights, if they are to continue to grow and prosper. The Court sees in this proceeding a recognition on the part of the union of its obligations and responsibilities for the conduct of its members, or a portion of its members, and certainly such recognition bespeaks continued progress in the ranks of union organization.

Upon the plea of guilty to the criminal contempt charge, it is the sentence of the Court that the defendant, Brotherhood of Railroad Trainmen, pay a fine of $50,000. The Court in imposing this fine recognizes that the acts constituting the contempt were not participated in by the entire membership of this union, and the Court observes that the union is accepting the responsibility as a union for the contempt of what represents a very small percentage of its members—that is, about 10 per cent.

Passing to the civil contempt, the Court points out that judicial sanctions in civil contempt proceedings may be employed for either one or both of the following purposes: first, to coerce the defendant into compliance with the Court order; and second, to compensate the complainant for the damages he has suffered. United States v. United Mine Workers. Under the circumstances in which this case comes before the Court, the utilization of punishment for the purpose of coercion is not necessary. In other words, the Court in imposing its fine for civil contempt under the facts of this case must do so on the fundamental basis that its purpose is either to compensate the complainant for the loss it has sustained or for the expense to which it has gone in bringing these proceedings.

It is well to note once again that the conduct which is the basis of this action was participated in by a very limited number of the union's members. However, the Court is unable with any degree of fairness or accuracy to estimate the loss that the complainant—which fundamentally is the people of the United States of America—has suffered as a result of this misconduct. It is impossible for the Court accurately to measure the inconvenience of the thousands or tens or hundreds of thousands of travelers who suffered from delayed schedules, missed connections, and other discomforts and inconveniences, as a result of this walkout on the part of some of these men. It is impossible for the Court to estimate in financial terms, in dollars and cents, the loss that has been suffered by the people of the United States as a result of the embargo on the mail, as a result of the delay of shipment of munitions of warfare, and possibly the transportation of troops to the Korean War. If the Court attempted to measure the compensation in those terms, it would require using the services of a firm of accountants who would have to devote several years to trying to estimate what the loss to the people of the United States was.

Under the circumstances, the Court believes that a proper measure of civil damages in this case would be a reasonable representation of the cost to the Government of bringing these proceedings. Because the Court has no other figures upon which to go, the Court will accept the statement of the United States Attorney for the District of Columbia that the cost to the Government was approximately $25,000 and will utilize this figure in imposing its punishment on the defendants for civil contempt.

In the civil contempt proceedings and upon the plea of guilty to those charges, it is the sentence of the Court that the defendant, the Brotherhood of Railroad Trainmen, pay a fine of $25,000.

---

1) When a plaintiff with a strong substantive interest proves damages as specifically as the situation will permit, should the judge allow recovery that

might be denied to another plaintiff? D. Dobbs, Handbook on the Law of Remedies 151–53 (1973). Should a plaintiff who proves that the defendant violated the injunction recover attorney fees even though she cannot prove any other damage? Does granting only attorney fees advance the inadequacy prerequisite? Compensatory Contempt, 1980 U.Ill.L.F. at 1001. Does the court's inability to vindicate plaintiff's interest with compensatory damages in *Brotherhood of Railroad Trainmen* and in *Sunbeam,* p. 993 reveal the need for punitive damages? coercive contempt? criminal contempt?

2) Several combinations of contempt have emerged. Criminal and compensatory are both retrospective and easy to combine as in *Brotherhood of Railroad Trainmen.* Criminal contempt may hamper a plaintiff seeking a compensatory award. The self-incrimination privilege might retard discovery and, in any event, prevents plaintiff from summoning contemnor. The plaintiff must prove that contemnor's conduct was wilfull; the criminal burden of proof is beyond a reasonable doubt. Thus the judge may impose a compensatory award but exonerate the contemnor of criminal contempt. See Norman Bridge Drug Co. v. Banner, 529 F.2d 822, 829–30 (5th Cir. 1976).

3) The rule that damages be proved under a recognized remedial theory distinguishes criminal from compensatory contempt and prevents courts from punishing defendants and granting private windfalls after mere civil procedure. In G. & C. Merriam Co. v. Webster Dictionary Co., the court of appeals considered the trial judge's remedy, a $50,000 fine payable to Merriam. The trial judge had failed to articulate the purpose of the fine. Plaintiff argued that a compensatory award could compensate and vindicate the court's authority over a refractory contemnor. Defendant argued that the $50,000 was either a procedurally defective criminal fine or an arbitrary, unproved damage award. The court of appeals remanded for the trial judge, among other things, to hold a hearing on a proper compensatory award. G. & C. Merriam Co. v. Webster Dictionary Co., Inc., 639 F.2d 29, 40–41 (1st Cir. 1980).

4) Before enjoining, the judge held that money was inadequate. The defendant breached. The defendant has reduced plaintiff to the inadequate remedy; it is too late for plaintiff to enjoy the substantive right. The judge might have imprisoned contemnor as coercive contempt before the breach to enforce the personal order and to ensure that plaintiff enjoyed the interest. After the breach and the compensatory award, should the judge imprison the contemnor to ensure payment of the inadequate remedy to plaintiff? Should inability to pay be a defense? O'Leary v. Moyer's Landfill, Inc., 536 F.Supp. 218 (E.D.Pa.1982); Compensatory Contempt, 1980 U.Ill.L.F. at 1003–07. Should contemnor's bankruptcy discharge a compensatory contempt award? Parker v. United States, 153 F.2d 66 (1st Cir. 1946); 11 U.S.C. § 523(a)(6), (7) (Supp.IV 1980); Rendleman, Liquidation Bankruptcy Under the '78 Code, 21 Wm. and Mary L.Rev. 575, 690–91 (1980).

Chapter Thirteen

COERCIVE CONTEMPT

"It is because men are sinners that justice can be achieved only by a certain degree of coercion on the one hand, and by resistance to coercion and tryanny on the other." Niebuhr, Love, Justice, Sin and Force, in War and the Christian Conscience 137 (A. Marrin ed. 1971).

I. Coercion as Negotiation

Contempt makes injunctions work. Criminal and compensatory contempt are retrospective and deal with past violations. The threat of criminal and compensatory contempt deters. On the other hand, coercive contempt is prospective and operates directly. Judges coerce defendants to secure for plaintiffs the interest protected by the substantive law. Coercive contempt is the method a judge uses to keep the promises he made when he said that the remedy at law was inadequate. Compensatory contempt gives plaintiff that inadequate remedy; criminal contempt gives plaintiff nothing at all. Coercive contempt is equity's writ of execution. Coercive contempt involves a conditional order. The judge tells contemnor to either allow plaintiff to enjoy her rights or to suffer the consequences for failure to do so. The usual sequence of coercive contempt follows: defendant is enjoined; defendant violates; judge imposes coercive contempt by telling defendant-contemnor to comply "or else"; contemnor fails to obey; judge exacts the previously imposed "else"; the coercive tactic persists until contemnor complies. Thus the order we call coercive contempt looks a lot like a second injunction, the first injunction repeated with the penalty for breach specified. Human nature and the course of events cause judges and contemnors to deviate from this traditional pattern, but you should attempt to find the pattern in the decisions that follow.

Helpful articles about coercive contempt include: Fink, Basic Issues in Civil Contempt, 8 N.M.L.Rev. 55 (1977); Kuhns, The Summary Contempt Power: A Critique and a New Perspective, 88 Yale L.J. 39 (1978); Moskovitz, Contempt of Injunctions, Civil and Criminal, 43 Colum.L.Rev. 780 (1943); Note, Standards of Punishment in Contempt Cases, 39 Calif.L.Rev. 552 (1951); Note, Coercive Contempt and the Federal Grand Jury, 79 Colum.L.Rev. 735 (1979); Note, Procedures for Trying Contempts in the Federal Courts, 73 Harv.L.Rev. 353 (1959); Note, The Coercive Function of Civil Contempt, 33 U.Chi.L.Rev. 120 (1965); Note, Civil and Criminal Contempt in the Federal Courts, 57 Yale L.J. 83 (1947). The granddaddy of them all is Beale, Contempt of Court, Criminal and Civil, 21 Harv.L.Rev. 161 (1908).

We must approach the problem of coercion from a perspective that allows for the exceptional. Most of us march to the beat of the law written in the books or announced by a legislature or judge. Contemnors hear their own drummer. Webber v. Gray, 228 Ark. 289, 307 S.W.2d 80 (1957), may be an extreme case. Defendant considered herself a woman scorned, and she harassed plaintiff unmercifully to "force her attentions upon him." She approached him in person on the street, communicated with him through the mail 200 times a year, and often called his family, co-workers, and associates on the telephone. She had a wedding announcement published; later she applied for a marriage license. The trial court enjoined this conduct in 1949. Between then and December 1956, plaintiff charged contempt five times. At each hearing, the judge found that defendant had violated the order. At the first three hearings, the judge postponed judgment on contempt, expressing doubts about defendant's mental condition; at the fourth, the judge sentenced her to 30 days, to begin "when directed by this Court"; at the fifth, six years later, the judge reenjoined her, found her guilty of contempt, and imposed a six-month suspended sentence conditioned upon a bond to secure compliance. Defendant appealed.

The Arkansas Supreme Court affirmed the injunction without mentioning the contempt. Plaintiff, the court opined, should be able to "pursue his lawful daily occupation and family activities unhampered by . . . protracted molestations." The court approved injunctions when that relief "can be applied with practical success and without imposing an impossible burden on the court or bringing its processes into disrepute." The appellate court sent the controversy back to the trial court. Did the trial judge's earlier experience in administering the injunction belie the appellate court's optimism about employing injunctions enforced with contempt? The Arkansas court said that defendant's acts "are not criminal and might be classed as trivial if they had been merely sporadic or of short duration." 307 S.W.2d at 84.

A society committed to individual liberty encounters difficulties in dealing with conduct which has passed out of the realm of the pixilated, excentric, or barmy and into the realm of nuisance or crankiness to others, but which has not become objectively dangerous to either defendant or others. Are ambivalence and bewilderment the proper responses to this conduct? Do criminal penalties and involuntary civil commitment offer alternatives to contempt? Do procedural differences affect your answer? Should the trial judge, after enjoining, fine or imprison defendant even though loss of money and liberty apparently affect her only marginally?

An earlier chancellor would have turned the Arkansas plaintiff out, chanting the maxim "Equity protects property rights, not personal rights." This redoubt has fallen, a victim of direct attack and attrition; prospective relief has erected its triumphant banner on the precept's wreckage. Moskovitz, Civil Liberties and Injunctive Protection, 39 Ill.L.Rev. 144 (1944); Developments in the Law-Injunctions, 78 Harv.L.Rev. 994, 997–1021 (1965). The maxim may, however, express a wise policy. Administration of equitable relief is a burden at best. Positive incentives alter conduct better than negative ones. Human cussedness sometimes raises intractable barriers to enforcement.

One reason to prefer a money remedy is that enforcement with coercive contempt may be expensive, protracted, and psychologically burdensome.

Coercive imprisonment raises the cost of legal and factual error. Obdurate contemnors who would rather rot in jail than comply cause excruciating problems. Edward Gibbon wrote of the late Roman Empire and the Christians, "It is incumbent on the authors of persecution previously to reflect whether they are determined to support it in the last extreme. They excite the flame which they strive to extinguish; and it soon becomes necessary to chastise the contumacy, as well as the crime of the offender." E. Gibbon, The History of the Decline and Fall of the Roman Empire 373–74 (Modern Library ed.). Should the judge consider before enjoining whether defendant will comply? Will that inquiry leave plaintiff's substantive rights hostage to defendant's refractory spirit? See Rendleman, The Inadequate Remedy at Law Prerequisite for an Injunction, 33 U.Fla.L.Rev. 346, 355–57 (1981).

Coercive contempt may be viewed as a threat, a negotiating tactic that rests somewhere between words and conduct. Our legal system limits the threats a judge may make. The judge possesses power to fine or imprison; he should manipulate these variables to alter contemnor's incentives to comply. He says, in effect, "I will see to it that it is less painful for you to obey than it is to breach. Make it easy on yourself." How should judges calculate the hardship of noncompliance? The Court in *United Mine Workers* told trial judges setting coercive contempt to consider "the character and magnitude of the harm threatened by continued contumacy, and the probable effectiveness of any suggested sanction in bringing about the result desired," plus the contemnor's resources and the burden the sanction will create. 330 U.S. 258, 304 (1946). Money damages were previously found to be inadequate; plaintiff is entitled to enjoy the right in fact, not a cash substitute. The threatened coercion should be more onerous to the contemnor than the economic and noneconomic value of the enjoined conduct to the plaintiff plus the cost of substituting a judicial, for a private transaction. R. Posner, Economic Analysis of Law § 7.2 (2d ed. 1977).

Courts distinguish coercive from compensatory contempt. Compensatory awards are measured to reimburse and are reviewed on that standard. Perfect Fit Industries, Inc. v. Acme Quilting Co., 673 F.2d 53, 56–7 (2d Cir. 1982). Coercive contempt should "make it more economical for [contemnor] to comply than to continue its contempt." The mental quality of the breach bears on what measures will suffice. Moreover the trial judge "has broad discretion to design a remedy that will bring about compliance." The court of appeals will review coercion by asking whether the judge's measures were reasonable and not arbitrary.

Reconsider whether $150,000 per day was enough to coerce IBM to produce the documents, p. 885. Should a conditional coercive threat to prevent a wrong or to achieve proper conduct in the future exceed the criminal sentence that may be imposed retrospectively later to punish a consummated wrong?

The judge's coercive tools are blunt. We will use Rickey, Jim Laing's sheep-killing dog from below, p. 1028 to illustrate. The judge ordered Jim Laing to turn Rickey in because the dog had been killing sheep. The order failed to produce Rickey. First, the judge, after unsuccessfully ordering Laing to bring Rickey in, may impose tangible measures at once or after passage of a period to comply: "Bring Rickey in today or else" differs from "Bring Rickey in within 10 days or else." Second, the tangible measures may take the form of money, jail, or perhaps both: "I fine you $100 per day, until we have Rickey" or "We will hold you in jail until you turn Rickey in." Our legal system subordinates plaintiff's substantive interests to humanitarian impulses. We neither torture, starve, nor brainwash contemnors. We do not wire contemnors to a Tucker telephone or feed them "grue" to extract information or to encourage compliance. Instead the most severe coercion consists of sitting in the local jail without income, affection or decent food. Third, coercion may be definite or indefinite. The amount of coercion depends on contemnor who can end the measures by complying. Contemnor, the judge may quote, has the jailhouse keys in his pocket. The coercive process must accommodate to the person who will not cooperate. Theoretically the judge could imprison a recalcitrant contemnor forever; the humanitarian impulse intervenes, however. Section 1826 of the United States Code (in the Appendix) limits federal coercive imprisonment for witnesses to 18 months. The new Wisconsin contempt statute limits coercive imprisonment to six months and coercive fines to $2,000 per day. Wis.Stat.Ann. § 785.04(1) (West 1981). Judges usually find a way to release a terminally stubborn contemnor. Finally, the judge may state the coercion as conditional or unconditional: "Go to jail until you comply" *or* "If you don't comply, I will sentence you to six months in jail." The judge may combine retrospective with prospective contempt; he may punish past contempt and compensate for earlier wrongs while attempting to coerce future behavior.

A rude continuum of coercive contempt follows: it begins with lenient and moves to severe. (a) "You are in contempt. I expect you to obey." (b) "I forbade you from striking but you have struck. You are in contempt and forbidden from striking tomorrow." (c) "You must purge your violation by agreeing not to violate again." (d) "You must obey within five days or I will fine you $500." See United States v. United Mine Workers, 330 U.S. 258, 305 (1947); "Dismiss the prohibited lawsuit against defendant now or pay a fine. Your fine will be $5 per day until you comply." See Scott v. Hunt Oil Co., 398 F.2d 810, 811 (5th Cir. 1968). (e) "Put it back the way it was or else." See Bell v. Southwell, p. 176; United States v. Kirkland, 518 F.Supp. 65, 66 (S.D.Fla.1981). (f) "Go to jail for eighteen months or until you testify." See In re Liberatore, 574 F.2d 78, 81 (2d Cir. 1978); United States v. Carroll, 567 F.2d 955, 957 (10th Cir. 1977). (g) "Go to jail until you comply." See Uphaus v. Wyman, 360 U.S. 72, 81 (1959); In re Nevitt, 117 F. 448, 459 (8th Cir. 1902).

Coercive contempt varies from almost innocuous to most severe. Stages (a) through (e) of "contempt" or enforcement are difficult to distinguish from enjoining. Contemnor may hold any coercive contempt losses to zero by simply complying. Most threateners would rather achieve the desired conduct than carry out the threat. How can the judge employ the variables we have discussed to achieve cooperation from those who lack a sense of urgency about complying with abstract law? How can we make things work when trust and good faith are absent? Readers who wish to pursue the matter further may see T. Schelling, The Strategy of Conflict (1960), which inspired much of the material that follows.

We begin with the substantive law expressed in an injunction and explore the limits on the judge's ability to enforce those norms. Our inquiry compares the strength of plaintiff's substantive interest with the coercion necessary to achieve. We ask whether and when to subordinate the substantive interest to other policies. Negotiation blends into coercion because talk is cheap. Our society lacks a "cross my heart and hope to die" promise that shows an irrevocable commitment. Acting under legal constraints, the judge seeks to persuade the contemnor that disobedience will cost more than it gains.

The judge's and the contemnor's decisionmaking are perforce interdependent: the acts of each depend on the course of action each anticipates the other will pursue. People calculate to advance their values; victory means that the winner advances his values, not that the adversary is destroyed. The least wasteful way for the judge to solve the problem is to achieve plaintiff's entitlement from defendant without injuring defendant. The judge should exploit the potential application of coercion to achieve a mutually advantageous, less destructive result. Since this conflict is bargaining on another plane, the judge cannot advance the plaintiff's values unless contemnor cooperates in some fashion. Lengthy coercion that fails to achieve the desired result is the mutually destructive, worst solution because plaintiff's substantive entitlement is frustrated and defendant suffers whatever loss coercion entails.

We must assume a rational adversary. People who fail to understand threats are not susceptible to them. The judge cannot control a madman with threats. Irrationality may be a short-run tactic that some people employ, recognizing that careless, self-destructive, short-fused, "crazy like a fox" people are more likely than cool and rational people to get their own way. Schelling reminds us that "If a man knocks at a door and says that he will stab himself on the porch unless given $10, he is more likely to get the $10 if his eyes are bloodshot." The Strategy of Conflict 22. Perhaps the Arkansas courts ignored this precept in deciding Webber v. Gray.

From the judge's perspective, a threat must be believable. Fining the teachers' union $5 per day, suspended, until it stops the strike is simply a sham. Similarly, a threat so enormous that the threatener would shrink from carrying it out is impotent. In the movie Raiders of the Lost Ark, Indiana Jones threatens to blow up the captured ark with a bazooka shell unless the Nazis release Marion. Belloq, however, realizes that Jones treasures the ark; he calls Jones's bluff. Jones retires cravenly. "We have learned that a threat has to be credible to be efficacious, and that its credibility may depend on the costs and risks associated with fulfillment for the party making the threat." The Strategy of Conflict 6. So the threatener who really doesn't mean it may blunder dramatically. Credibility imposes an upper limit on coercion.

Sometimes, however, as the following story of Captain Hornsby and the sultan illustrates, a bluff accomplishes its purpose:

"In the 1880s, when England was still an empire and Lord Salisbury was prime minister, a sultan somewhere in Africa committed an unspeakable offense against the canons of civilized behavior and the sovereignty of the British crown. Lord Salisbury summoned Capt. Hornsby of the Royal Navy, instructing him to to sail up the heathen river and deliver to the sultan a stern remonstrance. Either the sultan ceased and desisted or her majesty's government would take important action. The captain asked what he was to do if the sultan refused to accede to the ultimatum. Lord Salisbury considered the question, and then, mumbling in the approved diplomatic manner, said: 'Well, yes, of course . . . well, you'll have to steam away, won't you?'

"The captain took his gunboat to Africa and proceeded upriver to the sultan's compound. Knowing that if the sultan resorted to a test of arms he had no hope of victory, the captain made a show of noisily running out his guns. He went ashore with as much pomp as he could muster, attended by flags, drums and smartly dressed marines. The sultan listened politely to the sermon from London. 'And what happens, captain,' he said, 'if I reject this singularly insolent communication?'

"The captain bowed and unobtrusively placed his hand on the hilt of his sword. 'Although I assure your highness that I would do so with profound regret, I would have no choice but to carry out the second part of my instructions.'

"The sultan . . . promptly capitulated to the British demand. Upon his return to England, Capt. Hornsby was promoted to the rank of admiral."

Lapham, Tragedy to Farce to Tragedy, Washington Post, April 10, 1982 at A15, col. 5.

Fines and imprisonment hurt a contemnor who values money and liberty. A fine transfers money to the judge. Carrying out the threat, however, may hurt the threatener. Society loses when contemnor is imprisoned: society loses contemnor's enterprise, whatever that is worth, and the taxpayers must board, room, and guard contemnor. At this stage the judge, as society's agent, and the contemnor share an interest in avoiding destruction and wasted resources.

The judge seeks to influence contemnor by communicating to him that their behavior is interdependent. An unconditional threat creates no incentive to cooperate. Neither does a bluff perceived as such. To succeed, the judge must bring the nonbluff aspect of the threat home to the contemnor. Lacking a way to undertake an irrevocable commitment, the judge has no verbal way to do this. So the threat must be pregnant with concrete measures.

Moreover, after the threat has failed, carrying it out (in particular by imprisonment) will harm contemnor without directly benefiting anyone. Few enjoy torturing others, and people can always find "humanitarian" reasons not to enforce a threat. Contemnor's unobliging conduct has changed the world. The judge may view this new world and react in three ways. First, the judge may keep his word and impose the threat. Second, the judge may have intended the threat as a bluff, and never expected to carry it out. Finally, he may change his mind, "chicken out" if you like. Striking public employees may ignore an injunction because they anticipate "amnesty." See *Alsbury*, p. 940.

A threatened person will consider the judge's three possible reactions, and he will compare the value advanced by disobedience with the severity of the threat, discounted by the probability that the judge will carry it out. The judge controls the last two variables in contemnor's calculation. The only threat that is too severe is the threat that is so enormous that it is ridiculous, for instance, Jones's threat to blow up the ark. The threatener may rationally threaten to do things that would be irrational to do. While inherent incredibility limits threats, a sensible threatener may commit himself to action that he or others might prefer not to take.

After violation, what incentives does the judge have to fulfill the threat? All of us seek to preserve our credibility and reputations for keeping our word. If the contemnor believes the threat, it makes little difference that carrying it out will injure the judge too. Moreover, the judge's hand may be stengthened if he is, or is believed to be, firm. The judge, in short, seeks to advance the plaintiff's substantive interest and to preserve his own credibility. Do Walker v. Birmingham, p. 286 and *Alsbury,* p. 940 express this policy?

The judge may control the probability that the threat will be carried out by relinquishing the initiative: "The trip wire will automatically set off a bomb if your troops advance. It's in your hands." The tort doctrine of last clear chance is an analogy. The judge strives to create a situation where he is helpless to control events, but where the contemnor has a last clear chance to turn aside or stop. The Strategy of Conflict at 137–39. This tactic suffers the defects of all threats. Words will rarely suffice; conduct is necessary to affirm the commitment. For example, an army may burn the bridges behind it to leave itself no retreat and to send a message to the enemy: "We have no choice except to stand and fight." The judge may publicly commit honor, reputation, and credibility. The message is simple: "You are in inextricable peril. Only you can prevent the damage." How can the judge use the tools available to convey that message?

Relinquishing the initiative is a sound tactic only when it achieves the desired conduct from contemnor. Is the judge confident that he can define the goal, predict the measures to be taken, and control coercion? Ambiguity, human psychology, and personal chemistry lurk in every communication. Things seldom work out precisely as planned, usually worse, Murphy's law says. Did the threat define precisely and communicate effectively the issue, the goal, the satisfactory behavior, and that the judge will accept no less? Does the contemnor know precisely what the judge will do and what will happen after that and after that?

Interdependent decisionmaking may go awry. Coercion and resistance develop a dynamic separate from the judge's goal. Coercion gets out of hand and may become savagery. Steps, actions, threats, reactions and countermeasures generate a sense of showdown. Are there accidental, unintended, or petty violations that do not trigger the threat? Will an escape valve be needed if the threat demands the impossible? Should the judge determine in advance whether the contemnor is crazy or hotheaded? What if the contemnor turns out to prefer to suffer the consequences of noncompliance rather than perform desired conduct and symbolically throws the keys out the jail house window? May the judge seek a graceful way to undo the commitment? If a safety valve exists, should the judge communicate it with the threat? Crisis, in short, is dangerous and difficult to manage.

If the judge strives reasonably for amity and concord, however, this effort will often lead the contemnor to sneak, probe, and erode. The contemnor will exploit the ambiguity of language, the unpredictability of events, and the judge's ambivalence. He will seek loopholes and will disobey by inches.

Although a judge's reputation for being short-fused or unpredictable may help to prevent incremental tactics, the reasonable judge eschews such a reputation.

Observers find it difficult to distinguish coercion from punishment. The numerous appellate decisions on whether a particular contempt is coercive or criminal illustrate this. As *Gompers,* p. 831 and common sense remind us, punitive imprisonment benefits plaintiff by coercing future compliance because "punishment tends to prevent a repetition of the disobedience." Similarly, compensatory awards alter contemnors' incentives to comply in the future. Coercion starts as a threat, a more concrete negotiating technique. Once coercion leaves the verbal stage, it becomes tangible measures—fine or imprisonment—plus a threat of more. The measures lend credibility to the threat, and the threat of more measures alters incentives. When does negotiation by threats and measures fail to achieve accommodation but instead degenerate into bitter-end conflict? Events may transform coercive into criminal contempt. When does coercive contempt become criminal? The last section of this chapter treats the art of diagnosing and curing coercive contempt that has undergone the metamorphosis into criminal contempt.

If coercion is a specialized form of negotiation, some forms of coercion are more like negotiation than others. Coercing testimony from a criminal may involve barter, but in the end the threat will be to invoke the sovereign's power to take assets or to imprison. In many forms of injunctive litigation, the question of right and wrong is less stark, and counterpolicies further muddle coercive techniques. Another principle applies to some disputes. When people must live and work together after the dispute, decisionmakers should avoid Carthaginian solutions that destroy or humiliate one disputant. Maintaining interpersonal harmony and smooth relations may be more important in the long term than the way any single dispute is settled. Eisenberg, Private Ordering Through Negotiation: Dispute-Settlement and Rulemaking, 89 Harv.L.Rev. 637, 645 (1976). Decisions can often be explained in no other way. All the participants will be working with one another for the foreseeable future. Certain tactics are eschewed. Someone will counsel rational persuasion, compromise, patience, and even dissimulation. A skeptic may ask whether this desire for harmony may, in Eisenberg's words, "lead to outcomes based on compromise without regard to principle, merely for the sake of peace"? 89 Harv.L.Rev. at 646.

We may expect the sort of mild coercion discussed above where the parties to the injunction are locked into an ongoing relationship. Many structural injunctions are negotiated under the shadow of coercion by the parties, aided by the judge, and administered over several years. Chayes, The Role of the Judge in Public Law Litigation, 89 Harv.L.Rev. 1281, 1292–96, 1298–1302 (1976). School children, institutional patients, or prisoners will depend on the defendant for many things over a long period. The defendant may nullify plaintiffs' victory by literal but begrudging and unsatisfactory compliance. Eisenberg, 89 Harv.L.Rev. at 676. The "winner" of a lawsuit may prefer remedial compromise to an all-or-nothing solution. Contempt in structural injunctions is often parley and compromise, another form of accommodation between mutually dependent groups. The parties simply continue the process of negotiation that began with the injunction and its administration. Kirp, Legalism and Politics in School Desegregation, 1981 Wis.L.Rev. 924. The federal bench has articulated and administered important and legitimate values without resorting to draconian enforcement tactics.

The defendant who violates a structural injunction breaks the tacit understanding of graduated progress. The judge is an outside decisionmaker. He stands for the integrity of the substantive rules and the need to respect authority. He may view interpersonal relationships as less important than do the disputants. We may expect some sort of visibly coercive or punitive response. The judge's institutional interest in the integrity of the substantive rules and respect for orders may retard an amicable solution. Is this what happened in *Alsbury,* p. 940?

II. The Range of Coercive Contempt

PENFIELD CO. v. SECURITIES & EXCHANGE COMMISSION

330 U.S. 585, 67 S.Ct. 918, 91 L.Ed. 1117 (1947).

Justice DOUGLAS delivered the opinion of the Court.

The Securities and Exchange Commission, acting pursuant to its authority under § 20(a) of the Securities Act of 1933, . . . issued orders directing an investigation to determine whether Penfield Company had violated the Act in the sale of stock or other securities. In the course of that investigation it directed a subpoena *duces tecum* to Young, as an officer of Penfield, requiring him to produce certain books of the corporation covering a four year period ending in April, 1943. See § 19(b) of the Act. Upon Young's refusal to appear and produce the books and records, the Commission filed an application with the District Court for an order enforcing the subpoena.[1] After a hearing, the court ordered Young, as an officer of Penfield, to produce them, [and that order was affirmed by the Court of Appeals]. Young persisted in his non-compliance. The Commission then applied to the District Court for a rule to show cause why Young should not be adjudged in contempt—a proceeding which, as we shall see, was one for civil contempt. The District Court delayed action on the motion until after disposition of a criminal case involving Young, Penfield, and others. When that case was concluded, the court, after hearing, adjudged Young to be in contempt. It refused, however, to grant any coercive relief designed to force Young to produce the documents but instead imposed on him a flat, unconditional fine of $50.00 which he paid.

That was on July 2, 1945. On September 24, 1945, the Commission filed a notice of appeal in the District Court and subsequently a statement of

1. Sec. 22(b) provides:

"In case of contumacy or refusal to obey a subpoena issued to any person, any of the said United States courts, within the jurisdiction of which said person guilty of contumacy or refusal to obey is found or resides, upon application by the Commission may issue to such person an order requiring such person to appear before the Commission, or one of its examiners designated by it, there to produce documentary evidence if so ordered, or to give evidence touching the matter in question; and any failure to obey such order of the court may be punished by said court as a contempt thereof."

points challenging as error the action of the District Court in imposing the $50.00 fine instead of a remedial penalty calculated to make Young produce the documents. The Circuit Court of Appeals reversed, holding that the District Court erred in imposing the fine and directing that Young be ordered imprisoned until he produced the documents. 157 F.2d 65 . . .

The question on the merits is two-fold: (1) whether the Circuit Court of Appeals erred in granting the Commission remedial relief by directing that Young be required to produce the documents; and (2) whether that court exceeded its authority in reversing the judgment which imposed the fine and in substituting a term of imprisonment conditioned on continuance of the contempt.

As we have already noted, the Act requires the production of documents demanded pursuant to lawful orders of the Commission and lends judicial aid to obtain them. There is no basis in the record before us for saying that the demand of the Commission exceeded lawful limits. There is, however, a suggestion that the District Court was warranted in denying remedial relief since the contempt hearing came after a criminal trial of petitioners in another case, during the course of which many of Penfield's books and records were examined. The thought apparently is that the Commission had probed enough into Penfield's affairs. But the District Court did not hold that the Commission's request had become moot, that the documents produced satisfied its legitimate needs, or that the additional ones sought were irrelevant to its statutory functions. We agree with the Circuit Court of Appeals that at least in absence of such a finding, the refusal of the District Court to grant the full remedial relief which the Act places behind the orders of the Commission was an abuse of discretion. The records might well disclose other offenses against the Securities Act of 1933 which the Commission administers. The history of this case reveals a long, persistent effort to defeat the investigation. The fact that Young paid the fine and did not appeal indicates that the judgment of contempt may have been an easy victory for him. On the other hand, the dilatory tactics employed suggest that if justice was to be done, coercive sanctions were necessary.

When the Circuit Court of Appeals substituted imprisonment for the fine, it put a civil remedy in the place of a criminal punishment. For the imprisonment authorized would be suffered only if the documents were not produced or would continue only so long as Young was recalcitrant. On the other hand, the fine imposed by the District Court . . . was unconditional and not relief of a coercive nature such as the Commission sought. It was solely and exclusively punitive in character. . . .

As already noted, Young did not appeal from the order holding him in contempt and subjecting him to a fine. Young maintains, however, that once the fine was imposed and paid, the jurisdiction of the court was exhausted; that the Circuit Court of Appeals was without authority to substitute another penalty or to add to the one already imposed and satisfied. That argument rests on the statute granting federal courts the power to punish contempts for their authority [now 28 U.S.C. § 401]. . . . The statute gives the federal courts power "to punish, by fine or imprisonment, at the discretion of the court, contempts of their authority," including violations of their lawful orders. At least in a criminal contempt proceeding both fine and imprisonment may not be imposed since the statute provides alternative penalties. In re Bradley, 318 U.S. 50. Hence if a fine is imposed on a contemnor and he pays it, the sentence may not thereafter be amended so as to provide for imprisonment. The argument here is that after a fine for criminal contempt is paid, imprisonment may not be added to, or substituted for the fine, as a coercive sanction in a civil contempt proceeding. If that position is sound, then the statutory limitation of "fine or imprisonment" would preclude a court from imposing a fine as a punitive measure and imprisoment as a remedial measure, or *vice versa*. . . .

We assume, *arguendo*, that the statute allowing fine or imprisonment governs civil as well as criminal contempt proceedings. If the statute is so construed, we find in it no barrier to the imposition of both a fine as a punitive exaction and imprisonment as a coercive sanction, or *vice versa*. That practice has been approved. . . . When the court imposes a fine as a penalty, it is punishing yesterday's contemptuous conduct. When it adds the coercive sanction of imprisonment, it is announcing the consequences of tomorrow's contumacious conduct. At least in that situation the offenses are not the same. And the most that the statute forbids is the imposition of both fine and imprisonment for the same offense. . . .

There is a difference of view among us whether the portion of the order of the Circuit Court of Appeals which set aside the unconditional fine of $50 imposed on Young is here for review. But if we assume that it is, a majority of the Court is of the opinion that the Circuit Court of Appeals was correct in setting it aside, since the fine was imposed in a civil contempt proceeding. . . .

Justice RUTLEDGE, concurring.

. . . [T]he action of the Circuit Court of Appeals was exactly in accordance with the ruling in the *Gompers* case and was required by it. In both cases the proceedings were wholly civil in character. In both a criminal penalty was imposed. And in both the judgment laying it was reversed and the cause was remanded to the trial court for further proceedings looking only to the giving of civil relief.

The only difference is that in the *Gompers* case the contemnors had not entered upon the service of the void criminal sentence of imprisonment but appealed from it, while here Young paid the fine and did not appeal. That action on his part, however, cannot oust the Commission of its statutory right of appeal and review or of its right to civil relief. If the contempt proceeding were criminal in character, a different question might be presented. But compliance with a void criminal penalty, void because imposed in a wholly civil proceeding, cannot make it valid or oust either the courts of their civil jurisdiction in matters of relief or opposing parties of their rights in that respect.

Since I am in agreement with the Court's view that the *Gompers* ruling and others in accord with it are controlling in this case, I think the judgment of the Circuit Court of Appeals should be affirmed, though with modification in one respect [namely, that the character and scope of relief should be left, in the first instance, for the District Court, rather than the Court of Appeals]. I find it difficult, however, to reconcile the action taken here with what was done in the *Mine Workers* decision. A majority there held, as I thought contrary to the *Gompers* ruling, that civil and criminal contempt could be prosecuted in a single contempt proceeding conducted according to the rules of procedure applicable in equity causes, and that both types of relief, civil and criminal, could be imposed in such a mixed proceeding. It was also held that on review the appellate court is free to substitute its own judgment concerning the nature and extent of both types of relief for that of the trial court, and therefore that in remanding the cause for further proceedings there was no necessity to leave room for the further exercise of the trial court's discretion in relation to either type of relief.

If in that case a single mixed proceeding could suffice without regard to the requirements of Rule 42(b) and the *Gompers* line of decisions concerning procedures to be followed in instituting and conducting contempt proceedings, for the imposition of both civil and criminal penalties, I see no valid reason why the same thing could not be done in this cause or why both the criminal fine imposed by the District Court and the civil relief given by the Circuit Court of Appeals should not be allowed to stand.

It is true that if the proceeding is to be taken as having been both civil and criminal a serious question would be presented on the terms of [18 U.S.C.A. § 401] whether imposition and payment of the fine here did not exhaust judicial power to deal further with the proceeding, more especially in its criminal phase. But that question too, I take it, necessarily would be settled if the *Mine Workers* ruling were to govern here.

It is also true that in this case the United States was not a party by that name, as it was in the *Mine Workers* case, to the civil litigation in which the contempt proceeding arose or to the contempt proceeding itself. But the Commission was the moving party in both, representative as such of the public interest . . . . And, in view of the vast liberality allowed by the *Mine Workers* decision concerning matters of procedure and relief in contempt proceedings, it hardly can be a solid ground for distinguishing the cases that in one the public interest was represented, as to the criminal phase, *eo nomine* United States, in the other under the name of the Securities and Exchange Commission. Cf. In re Bradley, 318 U.S. 50. Indeed the record shows that in the present case the United States Attorney and the Assistant United States Attorney participated in the contempt proceeding in the District Court.

Notwithstanding these difficulties, since the Court rests the decision in this cause upon the *Gompers* rule, which in my opinion represents the settled law, I join in the affirmance of the judgment of the Circuit Court of Appeals, both insofar as it reversed the District Court's judgment because of the denial of coercive relief and in relation to its reversal of the criminal penalty imposed by the District Court. . . .

Justice FRANKFURTER, with whom concurs Justice JACKSON, dissenting.

Beginning with the Interstate Commerce Act in 1887, it became a conventional feature of Congressional regulatory legislation to give administrative agencies authority to issue subpoenas for relevant information. Congress has never attempted, however, to confer upon an administrative agency itself the power to compel obedience to such a subpoena. . . .

Instead of authorizing agencies to enforce their subpoenas, Congress has required them to resort to the courts for enforcement. In the discharge of that duty courts act as courts and not as administrative adjuncts. The power of Congress to impose on courts the duty of enforcing obedience to an administrative subpoena was sustained precisely because courts were not to be automata carrying out the wishes of the administrative [agency]. They were discharging judicial power with all the implications of the judicial function in our constitutional scheme. . . .

The judgment immediately before us is that of the Circuit Court of Appeals setting aside the fine imposed by the District Court and reversing its refusal to issue a coercive order. The ultimate question is the correctness of what the District Court did and what it refused to do. It is essential therefore to focus attention on the precise circumstances in which the District Court acted as it did. This is what the record tells us:

"Mr. Cuthbertson: So far as the punishment which the Court might see fit to impose, that is up to the Court. We are still anxious to get a look at these books and records, so I suggest to the Court, if he be so disposed, whatever punishment the Court might see fit to impose would be in connection with or so long as he refused to produce his books and records for our inspection.

"The Court: I don't think that I am going to be disposed to do anything like that. I sat here for six weeks and listened to books and records. The Government produced people from all over the United States in connection with the Penfield matter.

"Mr. Cuthbertson: I might say, your Honor, that we have in mind that these books and records may disclose certain acts other than those charged in the indictment. We don't propose to go over the same matter that the Court went over in connection with the criminal case.

"The Court: The Court can take judicial notice of its own books and records, and in that trial the evidence was clear and definite and positive from all of the Government's witnesses, that during one period of time this defendant had nothing whatsoever to do with the Penfield Company. Whether that period of time is covered by what the Securities and Exchange Commission seeks or not, I don't know.

"The judgment and sentence of the Court is that the defendant pay a fine of $50, and stand committed until paid."

Bearing in mind that the District Court was not an automaton which must unquestioningly compel obedience to a subpoena simply because the Commission had issued it, we must consider whether the District Court had abused the fair limits of judicial discretion. If a district court believes that howsoever relevant a demand for documents may have been at the time it was made, circumstances had rendered the subpoena obsolete, it is entitled to consider the merits of the subpoena as of the time that its enforcement is sought and not as of the time that it was issued. The above colloquy means nothing unless it means that Judge Hall was of the view that events had apparently rendered needless the call from Young for the documents. He may have been wrong in that belief. At all events it was the view of a judge who had presided for six weeks over a trial in which these matters were canvassed. The Circuit Court of Appeals did not have before it, nor have we, the knowledge or the basis for knowledge that Judge Hall had, and so neither court can say with any confidence that he did not have ground for thinking that the change in circumstances revealed in the course of the trial obviated the need for the demand that was made upon Young. We surely ought not to reverse the action of the district judge on the abstract assumption that papers ordered to be produced as relevant to an inquiry at the time the subpoena issued continued relevant several months later. We ought not to assume that a subpoena was proper months later when a proceeding lasting more than six weeks before the judge who had approved the subpoena in the first instance persuaded him that the circumstances no longer called for carrying out the terms of the subpoena. When the trial judge stated his understanding that the intervening circumstances had rendered inappropriate the use of his coercive powers, counsel for the Government did not gainsay the judge's view. The failure of Government counsel to contradict the interpretation of facts by the Court does not present any technical ground of not allowing a point to be raised on appeal to which no exception was taken. The significance of counsel's silence is its confirmation of the judge's interpretation of the circumstances. At least in the absence of contradiction, the interpretation of the facts by the trial judge was a proper basis for the exercise of his judicial discretion.

On the record before us, Judge Hall exercised allowable discretion in finding that the subpoena had spent its force, and in concluding not to compel obedience to it. At the same time, he was justified in finding that because Young had disobeyed the subpoena while it was still alive, he should be fined and made to feel that one cannot flout a court's authority with impunity.

The question, then, is whether the Court could impose what constituted a fine for criminal contempt, that is, to vindicate the law as such, without a formal pleading charging Young with such disobedience. We do not think Judge Hall had to direct the clerk to issue an attachment against Young to inform him of that which he obviously knew and which the proceedings had made abundantly clear to him. The true significance of our opinion in United States v. United Mine Workers . . . , as we understand it, is that contempt proceedings are *sui generis* and should be treated as such in their practical incidence. They are not to be circumscribed by procedural formalities, or by traditional limitations of what are ordinarily called crimes, except insofar as due process of law and the other standards of decency and fairness in the administration of federal justice may require. On this record we find not the faintest denial of any safeguard or of appropriate procedural protection.

---

1) Following the notion that the judge should use the least severe measures first, the Court told trial judges to use criminal sanctions only when civil contempt is inappropriate. Shillitani v. United States, 384 U.S. 364, 371 n. 9 (1966). Are there escalating degrees of contempt with criminal the most severe? In Haney v. Woodward & Lothrop, Inc., 330 F.2d 940 (4th Cir. 1964), the court of appeals said that a $100 suspended criminal fine for failure to allow discovery "did not give the plaintiff his whole entitlement," 330 F.2d at 945. Did the trial judges in *Penfield* and *Haney* illustrate an unsteady adherence to protecting plaintiffs' substantive interests?

2) Does *Penfield* impose an obligation on judges to coerce? Professor Chambers's empirical study teaches us that coercive imprisonment works. Michigan counties imprison tardy family support debtors to quicken their consciences to pay. Jail and believable threats of jail, coupled with an organized, self-starting public enforcement system, increase the amount of money collected. D. Chambers, Making Fathers Pay (1979). If the judge finds the plaintiff's interest significant enough to merit injunctive protection, shouldn't coercion follow breach as night follows day? Will hard-nosed coercion pacify society generally?

3) Could the trial judge reverse the order of contempts—impose coercive first and then criminal? Witness is granted immunity and testifies before the grand jury. The grand jury indicts Defendant. Then, at trial, Witness refuses to repeat her grand jury testimony. The judge may imprison her to persuade her to testify. Suppose Witness remains obdurate and the criminal prosecution against Defendant fails. After Defendant and the jury are dismissed, may the judge conduct a criminal contempt hearing before a jury and sentence Witness to three years? See United States v. Brummitt, 665 F.2d 521 (5th Cir. 1981) (five years); Danning v. Lavine, 572 F.2d 1386, 1389–1390 (9th Cir. 1977); United States v. Petito, 519 F.Supp. 838 (E.D. N.Y.1981); Watkins v. Howard, 441 F.Supp. 486 (E.D.Wis.1977).

4) May a federal judge combine fines and imprisonment in order to coerce? In United States v. Pilcher, 672 F.2d 875 (11th Cir. 1982), the court approved imprisonment and a $500 per day fine to coerce a tax protester. See also In re Dinnan, 625 F.2d 1146 (5th Cir. 1980). Did the Court in *Penfield* err when it assumed "arguendo" that § 401 applied to coercive contempt?

5) Coercive contempt may combine with both criminal and compensatory contempt. Judge Woodbridge finds that Beverly Tucker has converted Jerry Kupka's heirloom Studebaker and orders her to return it. When she refuses, Judge Woodbridge may award plaintiff Kupka damages for lost use, fine defendant Tucker $1,000 for violating the court order, and impose a coercive fine of $100 on Tucker for each day Kupka remains carless.

LANCE v. PLUMMER

353 F.2d 585 (5th Cir. 1965), certiorari denied 384 U.S. 929 (1966).

Before TUTTLE, Chief Judge, THORNBERRY, Circuit Judge, and CARSWELL, District Judge.

TUTTLE, Chief Judge: This is an appeal from an injunction forbidding the appellant to interfere with the compliance by certain St. Augustine restaurants and motels with Title II of the Civil Rights Act, and from a judgment of civil contempt against appellant for violation of the order of injunction. The two appeals have been consolidated in this Court, so that the validity of the injunctive order and the order adjudging Lance in civil contempt are both before the Court for consideration.

On July 20, 1964, Lucille Plummer and seven other named individuals filed suit against James E. Brock and twenty other named individuals and corporations (designated as Class I defendants), who were owners, managers or operators of certain restaurants or motels in St. Augustine, Florida, and against Holsted R. Manucy and seventeen other named individuals, Ancient City Hunting Club or Ancient City Gun Club, and U. S. Klans, Knights of the Ku Klux Klan, Inc. (designated as Class II defendants). . . .

On July 28, 29 and 30, 1964, the district court received evidence on the plaintiffs' application for preliminary injunction with respect to Class I defendants. A subsequent hearing was scheduled on plaintiffs' application for preliminary injunction with respect to Class II defendants, but was not held, because on July 30, 1964, counsel for certain of the named Class II defendants, in a stipulation entered into in open court, consented to the entry of a temporary restraining order enjoining his clients, until further order of the court, from committing any of the acts charged in the complaint to have been theretofore committed by them, without admitting that such acts had in fact been committed.

On August 5, 1964, the district court entered findings of fact and conclusions of law, in which it was found that one or more named plaintiffs had on some occasion subsequent to July 2, 1964, been refused service in each of the named Class I defendants, "solely on the ground of race or color," and the court concluded that preliminary injunction should issue. The injunction, issued to be effective August 8, 1964, forbade the Class I defendants, their agents, servants, employees, attorneys, and all persons in active concert or participation with them from further violation of Title II.

With respect to the Class II defendants, the injunction order further provided:

"3. Effective immediately, and without the posting or filing of injunctive bond by Plaintiffs, it is further ORDERED that Holsted Richard Manucy, Gene Manucy, Holsted David Manucy, Herbert R. Manucy, Alonzo H. Manucy, Jr., Buddy Cooper, M. E. Cooper, Bobby Lee Bacon, Melvin E. Manucy, Pat Winston Howard, and Holsted Richard Manucy as President of Ancient City Hunting Club and/or Ancient City Gun Club, an unincorporated and unchartered voluntary association of individuals, and each member of said association or organization, *and any other persons to whom notice or knowledge of this Order may come,* shall not in any way interfere with, molest, threaten, intimidate or coerce any person of the Negro race with the purpose of interfering with such person's right to seek, use and enjoy the goods, services, facilities, privileges, advantages and accommodations of any, all or either of the places of public accommodation identified by name and address in Paragraph 1 hereof, nor attempt to so interfere with, molest, threaten, intimidate or coerce any person of the Negro race for such purpose, nor punish or attempt to punish any person of the Negro race for exercising, having exercised or attempting to exercise any right of privilege granted hereunder.

"4. Effective immediately, and without the posting or filing of injunctive bond by Plaintiffs, it is further ORDERED that none of the persons specifically identified in Paragraph 3 hereinabove, *nor any other person to whom notice or knowledge of this Order may come*, shall in any way interfere with, molest, threaten, intimidate or coerce any, all or either of the several Class I Defendants identified by name, establishment and address in numbered Paragraph 1 hereof, with the purpose of causing him, her, it or them to deny, abridge, withhold, condition, limit or otherwise interfere with Negro persons in their securing food, beverages, service and accommodations at and in their admission to and use and enjoyment of the goods, services, facilities, privileges, advantages and accommodations, of any, all or either of the said establishments identified in Paragraph 1 hereof." (Emphasis supplied.)

On August 11, 1964, Arthur Funderberk, and two other Negroes, none of whom was a named plaintiff in the case, sought and received service in the Pancake House, a restaurant operated by William Chew, one of the named Class I defendants. The appellant, Charles Lance, Jr., who was a volunteer, unsalaried, deputy sheriff[2] who said he had been instructed by the sheriff of St. Johns County to protect Negroes testing the Civil Rights Law, was in the restaurant at the time. As Funderberk and his companions left the restaurant, they were followed by two white teenagers. The trial court found that Lance cursed the three Negroes who testified they heard the words, "black bastards." Lance testified that he said, "You know I have to protect these black sons of bitches."

On the following day, Funderberk and a companion unsuccessfully sought to register for a room in the Palms Congress Inn motel, adjoining the Pancake House and a part of the same establishment owned by Empire Inns, Inc., and managed by William Chew. At this juncture Lance, who had driven up to the motel right behind Chew entered the motel, and upon receiving what the court could find to be a "signal" from Mrs. Chew, proceeded to follow the Negroes, after they left the motel in a car at a time when the trial court found they neither needed nor asked for any protection from the sheriff's office; nor were they informed by Lance at this time or any other time that he had any such purpose in following them.

On August 14, 1964, a sworn petition was filed in the main cause, referring to the injunction order of August 5 and charging that Chew and Empire Inns, Inc., had violated the order and should be ordered to show cause why they should not be held in civil contempt. In addition, an affidavit was sworn to, stating that "Upon information and belief . . . Charlie Lance . . . is a member of the Ancient City Hunting Club, and as such . . . a Class II Defendant herein." On August 14, the trial court issued an order directing "the defendants William Chew, . . . Empire Inns, Inc., and Charles Lance Jr.," to appear before him on August 17 to show cause "why they should not be adjudged to be in civil contempt . . . by their wilful disobedience of the Order for Interlocutory Injunction entered . . . on August 5, 1964." Before the show cause order was served upon Lance, on the evening of August 14, Funderberk drove up to the adjoining motel and let two white men out of his car. At this time, appellant Lance was having dinner with his family in the Pancake House; whereupon he left his family and again followed Funderberk for a considerable distance.

2. The Florida statute permits a sheriff of a county to name any number of deputies, with or without salary, each of whom is apparently bonded but many of whom apparently are uncompensated and are appointed solely at their request. St. Johns County apparently had a great number of these so that, in fact, the trial court found that its sheriff appointed most everyone who asked and that he actually did not know all of his own deputies by name.

On August 15, the show cause order was served upon Lance and a hearing was had resulting in findings near the close of the hearings including the following:

"With respect to the respondent, Charles Lance, Jr., the Court finds that, first of all, he had actual knowledge and notice of the entry of the injunction and, in general, of its terms; that on August 11, 12 and 14, he violated the terms of the Injunctive Order by cursing these three men, Funderberk, McBride and Lawton, as they were leaving the premises of the Palms Congress Restaurant, the Pancake House, I guess it's called; that he further violated the terms of paragraphs 3 and 4 of the Injunctive Order by intimidating, molesting, threatening, or attempting to do these things, to Arthur Funderberk on August 12 and August 14 by following him away from the Palms Congress Motel and Restaurant."

Subsequently, on August 20, the trial court entered the following order:

"That by virtue of the findings herein, Charles Lance, Jr., is hereby added as a named Class II defendant in the interlocutory injunction of August 5, 1964, and further, that the respondent, Charles Lance, Jr., having been found to have actual notice of the interlocutory injunction dated August 5, 1964, and to have violated the terms of paragraphs 3 and 4 thereof is hereby found to be guilty of civil contempt. The respondent, Charles Lance, Jr., is hereby ordered to obey all terms of the interlocutory injunction issued herein. Within twenty days of this order, he shall submit a verified report to this Court that he has resigned his position as deputy sheriff of St. Johns County, Florida, and surrendered his badge and other incidents of office and of police equipment to his superiors; and that he shall no longer act under any color, guise, or pretense as a law enforcement or peace officer. That the respondent, Charles Lance, Jr., is ordered to pay to Tobias Simon, as attorney for plaintiffs, two hundred dollars as his fee in this matter and that proof of payment be included in said report. It shall be further understood that the Court, in directing the respondent, Charles Lance, Jr., to resign from his position as an honorary deputy sheriff of St. Johns County, Florida, does not intend to interfere with or restrict in any way the powers and authority of the sheriff to administer his office and to appoint deputies or employ other persons in his department. This sanction has been imposed by the Court in these specific circumstances only in view of the particular findings made as to this respondent's conduct herein, and that he was an unsalaried deputy working primarily on a voluntary basis without regular assignment or hours of duty."

Later, the trial court filed additional findings of fact which outlined factors influencing its decision to require Lance's resignation as a deputy sheriff. This latter requirement was stayed pending appeal by an order of this court entered on September 17, 1964. On September 14, 1964, the cases for permanent injunction were finally heard before the district court; all parties rested upon evidence already adduced at the hearing on the petition for interlocutory injunction. The district court then entered a permanent injunction on September 19, 1964. The appeal to this Court is taken from both the permanent injunction and the district court order of August 20, holding Lance in contempt. The cases have been consolidated for the purposes of appeal.

Upon this appeal, Lance makes several contentions attacking both the injunction order and his being treated as being subject to it and also the scope and validity of the contempt order itself.

Initially, appellant contends that the class action filed by the named plaintiffs was not an adequate vehicle upon which the trial court could enjoin conduct by the named defendants, and those in active concert with them, from denying rights to all Negro citizens. It is Lance's contention that the complaint could claim and actually achieve protection only for the named plaintiffs and could afford no protection to the particular movant, Funderberk, who sought and obtained the show cause order on the contempt proceedings. This contention is based upon the argument that § 204(a) of Title II of the Civil Rights Act of 1964 authorizes a civil action to be brought for preventive relief to "the person aggrieved" by the offender; the Act further provides a public remedy, available to the Attorney General, whenever he has reasonable cause to believe that a pattern of resistance to the full enjoyment of any of the rights secured by the Act exists. From the existence of these two remedies, plus the Act's statement in § 207(b) that "The remedies provided in this title shall be the exclusive means of enforcing the rights based on this title," appellant asks the Court to conclude that the district court had no jurisdiction to entertain a class action for the enforcement of rights based on Title II of the Act.

We do not find this argument persuasive, especially in light of the further language in § 207(b) which says, "but nothing in this title shall preclude any individual . . . from pursuing any remedy, civil or criminal, which may be available for the vindication or enforcement of such right," and in light of the fact that other civil rights statutes containing somewhat similar wording have not in the past been so construed. See, for instance, 42 U.S.C.A. § 1983 which says, "Every person . . . shall be liable to the party injured in an action at law . . . or other proper proceeding for redress." The limitation of the authority to bring an action in that section "to the party injured" has not been held to prevent proceedings by class suits. See Sharp v. Lucky, 5 Cir., 252 F.2d 910. We conclude that Congress did not intend to do away with the right of named persons to proceed by a class action for enforcement of the rights contained in Title II of the Civil Rights Act.

Appellant's next complaint is that he was improperly required to respond to a show cause order when he was not a named defendant, and there was no proof to the effect that he was a member of one of the Class II organizations. He contends that the court had no power to bind him simply because notice or knowledge of the order came to his attention.

It is certainly true that Rule 65(d) of Federal Rules of Civil Procedure provides that "Every order granting an injunction and every restraining order . . . is binding only upon the parties to the action, their officers, agents, servants, employees, and attorneys, and upon those persons in active concert or participation with them who receive actual notice of the order by personal service or otherwise." The court's order here complained of sought to bind all persons receiving actual notice whether or not they fell within the class of "parties to the action, etc." However, the court's findings clearly showed that its order adding Lance as a Class II defendant was justified from the court's determination (1) that his conduct was "in active concert or participation" with the named defendant William Chew and his wife, and (2) that he was doing the acts alleged in the complaint as being carried on by the named Class II defendants. There was nothing to prevent the court's adding any other named member of the second class of defendants for, as alleged in the original complaint, "Each class of defendants is in addition, representative of a larger class more fully described in the Amended Complaint." While this could, of course, not bind any person who did not fall within the ambit of the Federal Rules, it did permit the addition of any named person as a Class II defendant to conform to the proof as to conduct which would justify the court's considering him as an actor in the manner outlined in the original complaint.

The admitted nexus between Lance and Chew during the period when Lance committed the acts in question, clearly warranted the trial court's determination that Lance was subject to the terms of the injunction as being in active participation with Chew. His conduct, having been properly found by the trial court to be such as was expressly prohibited by the injunctive order affecting the Class II defendants, also warranted the trial court's adding him as an added named defendant of the second class. It is true that the trial court stated that no evidence had been introduced to show that Lance was a member of one of the organizations named in Class II. This, however, did not prevent him from being named as an individual member of the class.

The next question raised by appellant tests the validity of that part of the contempt order that required him to resign his position as deputy sheriff, ordering that he "shall no longer act under any color, guise, or pretense as a law enforcement or peace officer." Appellant contends that this is in the nature of punishment rather than in the nature of a sanction applied to cause Lance to comply with the court's injunctive order. The trial court concluded that the order depriving Lance of the right to serve as sheriff did not in any material way interfere with the functions of the State of Florida or of St. Johns County in any substantial manner. The court stated, "I conclude that if persons are appointed special or auxiliary deputies, without investigation, simply upon application, that it approaches the ludicrous to assert that the conduct by the Sheriff of his office is being interfered with in any meaningful way when one of such volunteers is required to divest himself of his authority by being required to resign as deputy."

The parties are not in disagreement as to the nature of sanctions that can be imposed when a civil contempt violation occurs. Only remedial or coercive sanctions may be imposed in civil contempt proceedings, such as are designed to compensate the complainant for losses sustained and coerce obedience for the benefit of the complainant. . . . If the trial court, as it found here, determines that a voluntary unpaid auxiliary or extra deputy sheriff is "riding his badge," that is, using his badge for the very purpose of violating an injunctive order of the court by intimidating those whose duty, if any, it is to protect in the exercise of their rights, we think there can be no doubt about the power of the court to require him to give up his badge and cease his functions as a peace officer so long as he continues in such conduct. However, since sanctions imposed in civil contempt proceedings must always give to the alleged contemnor the opportunity to bring himself into compliance, the sanction cannot be one that does not come to an end when he repents his past conduct and purges himself. Thus, while the court here had the power to require Lance to surrender his badge and to remain off of the sheriff's list of auxiliary deputies so long as he continued to violate the terms of the injunctive order against the Class II defendants, such prohibition could not extend beyond such term. The prohibition, therefore, that Lance should "no longer act under any color, guise, or pretense as a law enforcement or peace officer" should be modified by expressly stating that such prohibition should last only until Lance should satisfy the trial court that he was no longer in violation of the injunctive order and that he would in good faith thereafter comply with the terms of the order. . . .

We share with counsel for appellant his expressed opinion that it is desirable that the unhappy incidents that plagued the community here involved may now be a matter of the past. In order that we may hasten the time when it can be ascertained whether this is truly so, we affirm the judgment of the trial court in each of the appeals before us after modifying the order in . . . the appeal from the contempt citation, by adding the following sentence to paragraph numbered 3 of the order dated August 20, 1964:

"The sanction affecting respondent's power to act as a law enforcement or peace officer shall continue until the said Charles Lance shall purge himself by satisfying the court that he is no longer engaging in any of the acts prohibited by paragraphs 3 and 4 of the Injunction dated August 5, 1964."

The stay heretofore entered by this Court is now vacated and the mandate of this Court shall issue forthwith.

[Certiorari was subsequently denied by the Supreme Court, 384 U.S. 929, accompanied by the following opinions of Justices Black and Harlan:]

Justice BLACK, dissenting from the denial of certiorari.

Now and then the Court refuses to review a case which raises issues of such great importance that I feel constrained to record my own belief that the case should be heard. This is one of those cases. . . .

Lance first contends that the District Judge exceeded his authority in attempting to make his injunction binding not only on the named defendants who were parties to the lawsuit but also on all persons who had notice of the order. . . . Rule 65(d), Fed.Rule Civ.Proc. would seem to bar such an order. The summary contempt power of courts is a very limited one and the apparent conflict between what the court did here and what this Court in *Chase National Bank* said a district court could not do, is too important to liberty to leave this judgment standing without review.

The significance of this case, however, does not lie merely in the District Court's questionable assumption of jurisdiction to bind Lance by its injunction; but the manner in which the courts below exercised the power to punish for contempt also makes the case peculiarly appropriate for review here. The question of the punishment here is even more important because it is imposed not after a full trial with all the constitutional Bill of Rights' guarantees but after a summary contempt proceeding in which a single judge lays down the law, prosecutes those who disobey it, passes judgment on the alleged violations, and finally imposes punishment as he sees fit. . . .

By ordering this state officer to surrender his badge and resign from his state office, the District Judge below assumed for the federal judiciary a new, unprecedented, and, I believe, highly dangerous power. To give federal judges such authority not only seems completely out of place in our federal form of government but also comes perilously close to violating the constitutional obligation of the Federal Government to guarantee to every State a republican form of government. Subjecting a state official's tenure of office to the discretion of the federal judiciary makes state officers responsible not to the people of the State but instead to federal judges who, according to the holding here, may oust them from their state office without even so much as a simple notice to the State whose officers they are. I cannot help but believe that the legislators who passed the Civil Rights Act of 1964 will be greatly surprised if not shocked to learn that by passage of that law they empowered federal judges to remove state officers without even giving these impeached officers a trial by jury. Federal courts have heretofore been reluctant to exercise equity powers to interfere with a State's governmental operations. See, e.g., Douglas v. Jeannette, 319 U.S. 157 (refusal to enjoin criminal prosecutions); Walton v. House of Representatives, 265 U.S. 487 (refusal to enjoin the removal of state official from office). No reason is given by the courts below for not respecting the authority of a State to conduct its governmental operations by agents responsible to the people of the State. There is no suggestion that the traditional remedies for contempt are inadequate in this case. And no one claims that this new federal-judge power to remove state officers is necessary to enforce the salutary provisions of the Civil Rights Act of 1964. It is clear that the judge's order here provides complete protection to the plaintiff's rights without that part compelling the State's deputy sheriff to hold his job at the pleasure of United States judges.

I regret that the Court refuses to review this case in order to make it clear to all the people just how far this new contempt power of federal judges goes. Here it is only an appointed deputy sheriff that is removed from office, but if this new contempt enforcement power is legal I can think of no reason why it cannot be used against more important state officials whether elected or appointed. If federal judges can remove deputy sheriffs why not sheriffs, members of the state legislatures, state judges, and why not even state governors? In considering the importance of this power to remove state officers, it is highly relevant that this new power jeopardizes not merely officers in a few States, but threatens every state officer in every State from Florida to Alaska, from Maine to California and Hawaii. In order to protect the rights of citizens to vote in state elections this Court recently announced the constitutional principle of "one person, one vote." It seems a little early to graft onto that principle a new one giving United States judges the power to remove state officials chosen by the people in strict accordance with the "one person, one vote" principle.

Justice HARLAN.

This is one of those rare instances in which I feel justified in noting my dissent to the action of the Court on a petition for certiorari, not involving an adjudication on the merits. I fully share my Brother Black's view that the issues in this case are important and that certiorari should be granted.

1) Is *Lance* the same as *Debs*, p. 1? Both judges tried to enjoin a mob, an undefinable class of nonparties, who may have interfered with relief. F. Read and L. McGough, Let Them Be Judged 231 (1978), describes the explosive situation in St. Augustine at this time. Evaluate the judge's other options: a) add Lance to the injunction as a named defendant; b) request that Lance be prosecuted under § 1509; and c) conduct a criminal contempt trial and sentence Lance to 60 days. Could Funderberk have recovered compensatory contempt damages for mental anguish? The court of appeals's dilemma was that Lance's misconduct was a past act, and the only appropriate sanction was retrospective—criminal or compensatory—contempt; however, the trial judge had followed civil procedure, and no one proved any compensatory damages. Would you feel differently about sentencing Lance to a six-month criminal term? Does the ultimate mild sanction obviate the procedural deficiencies?

2) *Lance* tested the limits of the coercive imagination. Was the district judge's response to Lance's conduct criminal or civil contempt? Does § 401 provide for that? Was the court of appeals's solution criminal? coercive? compensatory? Does § 401 apply? How will Lance "satisfy the court"? Apologize? Behave for six months? Does "purge" mean a) promise to be good, or b) stop doing something you are doing?

3) Is coercing an apology really a mild sanction? Could the judge tell Lance to write an apology letter to Funderberk? In Miami Herald Publishing Co. v. Tornillo, 418 U.S. 241 (1974), the Court forbade the government from compelling a newspaper editor, by a threat of criminal punishment, to publish a reply. The compelled right of reply violated the first amendment because it infringed on editorial judgment and decisionmaking and absorbed the newspaper's time, cost, and space. See Van Alstyne, The Mobius Strip of the First Amendment: Perspectives on Red Lion, 29 S.C.L.Rev. 539 (1978). Walter Schaefer argues, however, that a judge should be able to force a defamation defendant to "direct the publication of an appropriate retraction." Schaefer, Defamation and the First Amendment, 52 U.Colo.L.Rev. 1, 18 (1980).

In Birnbaum v. United States, 588 F.2d 319 (2d Cir. 1978), a Tort Claims Act case, the government had opened plaintiffs' mail. The trial judge told the government to pay each plaintiff $1000 and to supply an apology letter. The court of appeals upset the latter remedy becuse it was not "money damages," the only form of relief 28 U.S.C. § 1346(b) allows. See also Cruikshank v. United States, 467 F.Supp. 539, 543–544 (D.Hawaii 1979). Does the judge's in personam or equity power over Lance distinguish him from the judge in *Birnbaum?* "The measure of the court's power in civil contempt proceedings is determined by the requirements of full remedial relief. They may entail the doing of various acts . . . ." McComb v. Jacksonville Paper Co, 336 U.S. 187, 193 (1949).

4) In "Thieving Buggers" and "Stupid Sluts": Insults and Popular Culture in New France, 36 Wm. & Mary Q. 524 (1979), Professor Moogk tells about an eighteenth century remedy, the "amende honorable." A person "whose crime offended public morality or threatened the social order" was "ordered 'to declare in a loud and clear voice that he repented, and to beg forgiveness from God, the King, and justice.'" 36 Wm. & Mary Q. at 525.

Closer to home, baseball fans will remember that in the summer of 1981 the St. Louis Cardinals' Gary Templeton was suspended indefinitely without pay until he apologized for making a rude and undignified gesture at the hometown fans.

Consider the municipal court judge who sentences first offenders to write a "confessional" letter to the local paper. National Law Journal, May 3, 1982 p. 55. Should judges sentence a) drunk drivers to lecture high school classes on drinking and driving? b) price fixers to lecture Chambers of Commerce on competition?

Is enforced penitence inconsistent with the spirit of a free society? "If there is any fixed star in our constitutional constellation, it is that no official, high or petty, can prescribe what shall be orthodox in politics, nationalism, religion, or other matters of opinion or force citizens to confess by word or act their faith therein." West Virginia State Board of Education v. Barnette, 319 U.S. 624, 642 (1943).

5) The Minnesota Department of Human Rights found that a policeman had handled a youth roughly and uttered a racial epithet. The statute allowed the Department to order "affirmative action" to effectuate the anti-discrimination statute. The Department told the city and the police chief to write a letter of apology. The Minnesota Supreme Court reversed on the ground that the statute did not authorize the remedy. Such a letter, the court said, debases and humiliates the writer. The next result will be resentment, hardly calculated to advance human rights. True apologies communicate remorse, but government agencies lack the power to order an emotion. Only a tyranny would empower the government to either coerce a lie from one willing to lie or to hold in contempt one without remorse who refuses to lie. City of Minneapolis v. Richardson, 307 Minn. 80, 239 N.W.2d 197 (1976). See also Alto-Reste Park Cemetery Association v. Pennsylvania Human Relations Commission, 7 Pa.Cmwlth. 203, 298 A.2d 619 (1972), modified on other grounds 453 Pa. 124, 306 A.2d 881 (1973). Do these considerations apply to *Lance?* Is the federal judge limited by statute to fine or imprisonment? Should a courtroom be used to train thespians? Would a public apology be a degredation ceremony?

6) Could the judge have ordered Lance imprisoned until he purged himself of contempt by promising not to interfere with anyone's civil rights? Consider Anne Marie Davies: After "various legal proceedings, which were altogether ineffectual" to establish that she owned some houses, Anne Marie Davies, "under the fixed impression that wrong had been done her, . . . attempted to take forcible possession." Restrained from "further molesting the owner," she nevertheless persisted in her attempts. Two judges sent her to prison for contempt after telling her "that she would be released upon her promising to give up her idle and vexatious claim, and undertaking to abstain from further attempts to enter upon the property." The notion that "she would speedily apply for her release, and give the undertaking required of her" proved chimeral. She stayed in prison 18 months refusing steadfastly "to acknowledge that she is in the wrong." In re Davies, 21 Q.B.D. 236, 237 (1888).

Did the judges who imprisoned Davies leave their reputations hostage to an obdurate contemnor? What were the judges' options after 18 months?

Was their dilemma to release Davies and appear timid or to keep her and appear harsh? T.W. Chitty, for plaintiff, agreed to an order continuing the injunction, allowing certain measures to enlist the police to enforce the injunction, and forbidding Davies from filing judicial documents without leave of court. She was discharged. Did Chitty capitulate? Mathew, J., commented: "I desire to express the opinion that in cases where the contempt for which punishment is inflicted is the doing of an act prohibited by the order of the court—where what has been done by the offender cannot be undone—it is not advisable that an order for committal should be so framed as to permit the possibility of the lamentable consequences to the prisoner which have followed upon the sentence in this case. . . . The offence of Mrs. Davies, annoying and vexatious as it undoubtedly was, cannot be considered as of a serious nature or one meriting a long incarceration. I regret that a form of order similar to that which we now make was not adopted in the first instance. Recourse ought not to be had to process of contempt in aid of a civil remedy where there is any other method of doing justice." 21 Q.B.D. at 238–39.

Lord Coleridge wrote: "I assent to the proposed order, but I do so distinctly on the ground that it is assented to on behalf of the plaintiff in the action as affording him adequate protection. Where the court has given its decision, and the person against whom the court has decided defies the court, ignores its decision, and persists in persecuting the person in whose favour the court has decided, with groundless claims and vexatious actions, however, reluctant the court may be to do so, it has, in my opinion, no choice but to enforce its judgment by the imprisonment of the contumacious person. There is nothing to the contrary, as it appears to me, in the authorities which have been cited by my learned brother. Happily in this case a method has been found of protecting the person whom the court is bound to protect, and under these circumstances I agree that the prisoner should be discharged from custody." 21 Q.B.D. at 240. Did Davies impale each judge on one horn of the dilemma? Do their predicaments illustrate the wisdom of the inadequacy prerequisite?

III. The Coercive-Criminal Conundrum

LAING v. COMMONWEALTH OF VIRGINIA

205 Va. 511, 137 S.E.2d 896 (1964).

I'ANSON, J., delivered the opinion of the court.

Jim Laing was held to be in contempt for his willful disobedience of an order of the Circuit Court of Giles County, entered on May 25, 1963, ordering him to deliver or cause to be delivered to the sheriff of the county a certain German shepherd dog, known as "Rickey," and his punishment was fixed at four months in jail and a fine of $1,000. We granted Laing a writ of error.

Laing contends that (1) the court below was without jurisdiction to order him to deliver the dog; (2) the evidence adduced at trial shows it was impossible to comply with the court's order; and (3) the evidence was insufficient to hold him in contempt.

Laing concedes that the amount of punishment imposed was within the discretion of the trial judge, and that is not an issue here.

The present contempt proceedings arose out of a judgment entered in the court below on July 28, 1961, wherein it was found that Rickey was a sheep-killing dog and he was ordered to be killed by the sheriff of the county, but a stay of execution was granted in order to allow Laing to apply for an appeal to this Court. We affirmed the judgment of the trial court. Laing v. Commonwealth, 203 Va. 682, 127 S.E.2d 142, rehearing denied October 8, 1962; cert. denied by the Supreme Court of the United States January 14, 1963, and petition for rehearing denied on February 18, 1963.

Subsequent to the appellate proceedings the circuit court entered an order directing the sheriff to proceed to execute its judgment of July 28, 1961, but Rickey could not be found in the county.

On April 17, 1963, Laing filed a petition in the court below praying that the dog's life be spared and that he be permitted to keep and maintain "his dog and pet," properly kenneled, at his residence in Giles county. After a hearing, on May 25, 1963, the prayer of the petition was denied, and the court found that Laing had removed the dog from the jurisdiction of the court and had secreted it, and ordered that he forthwith deliver, or cause to be delivered, the dog to the sheriff so that the order of the court of July 28, 1961, might be carried into effect. There were no objections made or exceptions taken to this order.

Laing having failed to comply with the order of May 25, the court issued a rule on June 6, 1963, directing him to appear and show cause why he should not be held in contempt.

At the hearing on the rule, on June 21, 1963, Laing testified that he did not have possession of the dog on May 25, 1963, when he was ordered to produce it; that he had given Rickey to another person; and that he had not seen the dog for approximately a year and a half or two years prior to the institution of this contempt proceeding. He further testified that he did not know the whereabouts of Rickey but that he would bring him back if he were permitted to kennel him safely at his home. When asked by the court if he had made any effort to comply with the court's order, he stated that he had not.

The trial court, after hearing this evidence and observing the demeanor of the witness, concluded that Laing had made no effort to comply with its order and had no intention to do so. Thus he was adjudged to be in contempt, but he was given an opportunity to purge himself of contempt by delivering Rickey to the sheriff on or before July 1, 1963. However, he did not avail himself of this privilege and the court entered the final contempt judgment, which is now before us.

Laing concedes that the trial court had jurisdiction over him as a person, but he says that by reason of the failure of an "officer of the law" to take the dog into *custodia legis,* as required by § 29–197, Code of 1950, the circuit court had no jurisdiction of the subject matter and thus his conviction of contempt is void.

The Commonwealth readily concedes that the disobedience of a void order is not contempt. . . . But it says that the order here was not void and Laing was under a legal duty to comply with it, however erroneous he may have believed the mandate to be. We agree with the Commonwealth's contention.

Code § 29–197 provides in part:

". . . Any warden or other person who has reason to believe that any dog is killing livestock . . . shall apply to a justice of the peace of the county, city or town wherein such dog may be who shall issue a warrant requiring the owner . . . to appear before the trial justice [county court] . . . ."

Code § 29–175 provides that "County and municipal courts and circuit courts shall have concurrent jurisdiction for the trial of offenses against game, inland fish, and dog laws of the state."

The quoted language from § 29–197 relates to the place where the warrant may be issued and confers jurisdiction of the subject matter on the county court of the county wherein the dog may be. There is no language in the entire statute which requires the dog to be in the physical possession or control of the game warden or other person when applying for a warrant requiring the owner of the dog to appear. Nor does the statute require that the court have the actual custody or possession of the dog at the time of the hearing. The purpose of the above quoted portion of the statute is for the court to determine if the dog is a killer of livestock, and the warrant is designed to require the owner or custodian, if known, to appear and make his defense in behalf of the dog, if he is so disposed. See Laing v. Commonwealth, supra, 203 Va. at p. 684, 127 S.E.2d p. 144.

The jurisdiction of the circuit court was invoked by Laing on appeal from the county court and again through his petition filed after he had exhausted his remedies in defense of Rickey in this Court and the Supreme Court of the United States.

The record shows that Rickey killed certain sheep in Giles county; that the warrant directing Laing, the dog's owner, to appear before the court was issued on the day the offense occurred; that Laing resided in Giles county, and that the dog was kenneled there except for a short time when he was taken into an adjoining county to be treated for gunshot wounds inflicted by an officer of the law at the time he was seen killing the sheep. Thus proper venue was laid in Giles county and the circuit court had jurisdiction over both the dog and Laing under Code §§ 29–175 and 29–197, and upon it being invoked by Laing on appeal. Moreover, it is axiomatic that when a court acquires jurisdiction of the subject matter and the person, it retains jurisdiction until the matter before it has been fully adjudicated.

Under the agreed statement of facts it was stipulated that Laing was permitted to retain custody of the dog during the pendency of the proceedings. While Laing's actions have shown that taking custody of the dog may be the better course, there is no jurisdictional requirement that this be done under § 29–197.

Laing next says that even if the court had jurisdiction to determine the matter, it is impossible for him to comply with the order as he no longer has the dog, having given up possession of it before the May 25, 1963, order was entered. There is no merit in this contention.

It is true that the inability of an alleged contemner, without fault on his part, to render obedience to an order of court, is a good defense to a charge of contempt. But where an alleged contemner has voluntarily and contumaciously brought on himself disability to obey an order, he cannot avail himself of a plea of inability to obey as a defense to the charge of contempt.

When one shows by his conduct a deliberate and studied effort to disobey a valid order of a court, he subjects himself to punishment for contempt.

Laing's testimony shows that he had maintained sufficient control over the dog to make it possible for him to obey the court's order; that he could have returned it to the jurisdiction of the circuit court if he so desired; and that he had no intention of returning the dog to Giles county unless he was given assurance by the court that its order directing the sheriff of the county to kill the dog would be nullified and he be permitted to keep it unharmed. The very fact that, before these contempt proceedings, Laing filed his petition asking that he be allowed to keep "his dog," shows that if he received a favorable decision on his petition he would have been able to bring it back it Giles county. Having the means to return the dog, it was Laing's duty to deliver it when ordered to do so by the court. But even if it was impossible for Laing to deliver Rickey to the sheriff (and the evidence shows otherwise) this was brought about by his own acts in an effort to prevent the execution of the orders of the circuit court of July 28, 1961, and May 25, 1963, and is not a valid defense to the contempt proceedings founded upon his failure to comply with the court's May 25, 1963, order.

There is ample evidence in this record to support the court's finding that Laing willfully and deliberately refused to obey the court's order of May 25, 1963. The record reveals that the court below was patient with Laing and acted fairly and impartially toward him throughout the contempt proceedings by giving him an opportunity to purge himself of contempt, but he refused to do so. Thus, Laing's conviction for contempt was proper and necessary to uphold the dignity and power of the court.

For the reasons stated, the judgment of the lower court is affirmed.

---

1) Several features combine to make it difficult to distinguish coercive from criminal contempt. First, the environment often reeks with hostility. Does anyone think that Circuit Judge Sexton only wanted Rickey when he imposed the "or else" order on Jim Laing? Second, the judge's tools, money and time, are the same for both forms of contempt. The policies of coercion and punishment are sufficiently imprecise that confusion inevitably occurs.

2) Is the exaction of the "or else" for violation of a coercive order criminal contempt? Must it follow criminal procedural safeguards?

3) Classification is important for more than procedural reasons. The Giles County files show two things not revealed in the appellate report. On August 19, 1964, about three weeks before the appellate opinion, the Dog Warden reported that he "took possession of said dog on August 8, 1964, and performed the duty of killing said dog by cremation. . . ." After the

appellate opinion, Jim Laing surrendered to the authorities. Did Laing have to serve the sentence and pay the fine?

Laing did begin to serve the sentence, but on November 9, 1964, effective on the 12th, the Governor pardoned Laing, who had paid the fine. Moreover, the pardon, carefully phrased, said "there has been full compliance with the orders of the Circuit Court of Giles County. The honor of the court and the dignity of its orders have thus been vindicated and preserved. In view of the foregoing and in consideration of the advanced age and poor health of the subject and his wife it appears to the Executive that he is a fit subject for clemency." Did the Governor think he was pardoning coercive contempt? Did the Sheriff have to honor the pardon? For years, substantial Giles County sentiment held that the "cremated" dog was not Rickey. If the Sheriff had been convinced that the Dog Warden had erred, would refusal to release Laing have been proper? If Rickey had remained at large, would the Governor's pardon of Laing have been proper? In re Nevitt, pp. 804, 917.

4) Consider the way the *Laing* pattern concentrates coercion. The judge says or hints "you have 10 days to comply, and failing compliance you will serve 4 months." Does this coerce more effectively than "You will serve 4 months or until you comply"? Which form of coercion should a judge employ to compel testimony in an ongoing trial? Two recent articles argue for the *Laing* form of contempt. Kuhns, The Summary Contempt Power: A Critique and a New Perspective, 88 Yale L.J. 39, 113–18 (1978). Professor Kuhns names this "an explicitly conditional criminal contempt sentence." What does he mean? Note, Coercive Contempt and the Federal Grand Jury, 79 Colum.L.Rev. 735, 772 (1979), also calls for "hybrid" sanctions.

JENCKS v. GOFORTH

57 N.M. 627, 261 P.2d 655 (1953).

SEYMOUR, Justice. This litigation arose out of a strike on the part of the members of the International Union of Mine, Mill and Smelter Workers against their employer, The New Jersey Zinc Company. The strike was of long duration. . . .

The basic litigation . . . [was] filed June 12, 1951 in the District Court of Grant County, New Mexico, by The New Jersey Zinc Company, a corporation, plaintiff, v. Local 890 of International Union of Mine, Mill and Smelter Workers, its officers, agents and members, and International Union of Mine, Mill and Smelter Workers, its officers, agents and employees, defendants. . . .

On the same day, June 12, 1951, the trial court issued the temporary restraining order and set hearing upon the temporary injunction for June 20, 1951. Hearing on application for permanent injunction was set for the same time and place. The relevant portion of the temporary restraining order reads as follows:

"It is, therefore, by the Court, considered, ordered and adjudged that defendants and each of them be, and they are hereby enjoined and restrained, until the further order of this Court, from trespassing upon plaintiff's property and blocking the roads and other entrances to the property of plaintiff in such manner as to restrain or coerce the employees of plaintiff from returning to work."

Hearing was had June 21, 1951 through June 26, 1951 and, on June 30, 1951, the trial court, in letter form, gave its decision that the temporary restraining order should be made permanent and directed counsel to submit findings of fact, conclusions of law and a formal order.

On July 9, 1951 there were filed the findings of fact and conclusions of law of the trial court, and the order of the court granting permanent injunction, the relevant portion of which reads as follows:

"1. That defendants and each of them, and their wives, mothers, sisters and children as their agents, be and they are hereby permanently enjoined and restrained from trespassing upon plaintiff's property and blocking the roads and other entrances to the property of plaintiff in such manner as to restrain, coerce or prevent the employees of plaintiff from returning to work, or from illegally attempting to keep said employees from continuing in their employment with plaintiff."

No appeal was taken from nor was any attack made upon the decision in the trial court in this basic cause of action in equity. . . .

On July 11, 1951, two days after the permanent injunction, plaintiff filed its motion for an order to show cause, seeking to have defendants held in contempt for violation of the temporary restraining order; the order was issued and hearing set for July 20, 1951. After hearing, and on July 23, 1951, the trial court gave its memorandum decision and entered its decree finding both the Local 890 and the International Union, and six individual defendants guilty of contempt, levying fines of $4,000 each against the two unions and sentencing the individuals to ninety days in jail. It was further provided that one-half of each fine was to be remitted provided defendants refrained from blocking the road, and jail sentences to be suspended provided the individuals refrained from the forbidden activities for one year commencing July 25, 1951. The relevant portion of the decree is as follows:

"3. That there be and hereby is assessed against defendant International Union of Mine, Mill and Smelter Workers a fine in the sum of Four Thousand ($4,000.00) Dollars to be paid to the Clerk of this Court; one-half of this fine will be remitted provided this defendant, its Officers, Agents and Employees refrain from blocking or causing to be blocked the road which is involved in this case that goes off the new Santa Rita highway west of the railroad through the premises of the plaintiff to Fierro, and refrain from otherwise violating the provisions of the Permanent Injunction of July 9, 1951, for a period of one year commencing July 25, 1951.

"4. That the defendants Clinton E. Jencks, Cipriano Montoya, Ernest Velasquez, Vincente Becerra, Pablo Montoya and Fred Barreras do each of them receive and they are hereby given a sentence of ninety (90) days in the common jail of Grant County, New Mexico; this sentence will be suspended provided said defendants and each of them cause the road which is involved in this case that goes off the new Santa Rita highway west of the railroad through the premises of the plaintiff up to Fierro to be opened to unobstructed travel by the general public and the officials and employees of plaintiff going to and returning from work, and otherwise cause the provisions of the Permanent Injunction of July 9, 1951 to be complied with by the members of said Local 890, its members and agents, for a period of one year commencing July 25, 1951." . . .

[In 1952 the Supreme Court of New Mexico affirmed the contempt decree of July 23, 1951. 56 N.M. 447, 245 P.2d 156 (1952).] [U]pon the filing of the mandate, the trial court appointed three attorneys amici curiae, and issued an order requiring applicants to show cause, on September 5, 1952, why the order suspending their sentences should not be revoked for violation of the suspension order. Applicants first challenged the power of the court to inflict criminal punishment in a civil suit in equity. Upon an adverse ruling, hearing was had at which applicants took the stand and categorically denied the violations. The trial court then made an order revoking the suspension and sentencing each of the applicants to ninety days in the Grant County jail. Motion for an appeal to the Supreme Court was denied and, on this writ of habeas corpus, applicants challenge the validity of both the original decree of contempt of July 23, 1951, and the judgment revoking the suspension. Their petition for the writ was filed in this Court September 30, 1952, and the writ issued from this Court on the same date, releasing the applicants, subject to the further order of this Court and subject to further imprisonment, should this Court so direct.

. . . Was the particular contempt order of July 23, 1951 simply irregular and improvident, or was it so in excess of the power of the court as to result in a failure of jurisdiction? The law is settled on the principle that irregularity or improvidence in the judgment of a lower court must be raised by appeal, and failure to do so ends the matter; there can be no collateral attack. It is equally well settled that a failure of jurisdiction can be raised at any time and in any proceedings. And whether the matter ended in the trial court or in a court of last appeal, lack of jurisdiction in the original cause is subject to collateral attack. . . .

It is conceded that the contempt proceedings which resulted in the order of July 23, 1951, was a civil contempt action as distinguished from a criminal contempt action. Paragraphs 3 and 4 of this order . . . involve a fine against the defendant unions payable to the clerk of the court, one-half to be remitted on certain conditions, and ninety-day jail sentences against individual defendants, suspended on certain conditions. Only the matter of imprisonment is here involved.

Since this is admittedly a civil contempt proceedings, the first question is whether the "sentence" was a proper one and, second, if improper, to what extent: Was it simply error to be corrected on appeal, or was it so defective as to constitute a complete failure in jurisdiction? . . .

The *Gompers* case . . . has been taken to say that a civil contempt proceeding cannot result in an imprisonment for a definite period of time. If this is literally true, then the sentence here involved, which will now result in imprisonment for ninety days, was necessarily in error. The theory in support of this contention is, of course, that the imprisonment can be only punishment for a past act and, therefore, improper in civil contempt. The argument is logical and the language of the *Gompers* case supports it.

In our judgment, however, the *Gompers* case does not pass upon the question before us. . . .

. . . Mr. Justice Lamar was dealing with a civil contempt decree in which the trial court, having found a violation of its order, *then and there* sentenced three individuals to imprisonment for twelve, nine and six months respectively. We agree that this could be punishment only for a past act and was, therefore, erroneous.

Such is not the case before us. The picturesque phrase, "he carries the keys of his prison in his own pocket," while expressing effectively a general principle of law, will not serve to determine all of the vast number of cases arising in the field of civil contempt. It is intended to express the idea that in a civil contempt action coercion must be the primary motive of the court's action and the contemnor must be in a position to purge himself. This we believe to have been the case in the situation before us.

. . . As of the day this particular decree was entered, and it is that day which controls, the decree was truly coercive; as to the imprisonment for ninety days, there was no single one of the defendants unable to purge himself by obedience to the court's order. This we believe to be literally true and further believe it to satisfy the ancient test of "having the keys to the prison." A phrase such as this must implement the law, not control it.

In taking this position, this Court finds full authority in the case of United States v. United Mine Workers . . . .

In this decision, the Supreme Court of the United States has used a conditional fine as a proper civil contempt sentence. Obviously, in the event of the failure of the union to obey and purge itself, the fine of $2,800,000 would become final and payment be enforced. At that time, the moment at which this penalty becomes final, it is primarily punitive; no one will contend, however, that for this reason the Supreme Court was in error in its decision and unable to enforce the fine in the event of *continued* disobedience. Mr. Justice Lamar in the *Gompers* case, in speaking of imprisonment and the incidental coercive or punitive effects thereof, stated:

". . . But such indirect consequences will not change imprisonment which is merely coercive and remedial, into that which is solely punitive in character, or vice versa."

All will admit that in a proper case either a fine or imprisonment may properly flow from a civil contempt action. In the instant case, we do not have the suspended or conditional fine of the *Mine Workers* case, but we do have the equivalent thereof, namely, a suspended term of imprisonment, in each case, at the time of pronouncement, the primary purpose was coercive; in each case, the capacity to purge was equally available. To find any difference in the cases is to submit to the force of language and phrases having no true relevance. There is no substantial difference between a conditional fine for a sum certain and a conditional prison sentence for a time certain.

. . . In the instant case, the record reveals that these individuals flagrantly violated the specific terms of the court's order here involved; it is difficult to imagine a more open and complete disrespect and disregard for the orders of a trial court. Since the trial court has not exceeded its power, its decree should be enforced.

It is the direction of this Court that the writ of habeas corpus filed in this Court September 30, 1952, be discharged, and that the defendants and each of them be forthwith remanded to the custody of the Sheriff of Grant County, New Mexico.

---

1) *Jencks* and the two *Local 890* opinions at p. 985 and p. 1045 grew out of the same famous strike as the movie "Salt of the Earth." Clinton Jencks, the organizer, and many of the strikers played themselves. Herbert Biberman, the director of the movie, had earlier been imprisoned for contempt after he refused to cooperate with the House Un-American Activities Committee; the CIO had expelled Local 890 for alleged Communist affiliations; and union projectionists refused to put the pro-union picture on the screen. In the film, the issues in the strike were Mexican-American civil rights, improved mine safety, indoor plumbing in company houses, and eventually, sexual equality. The wives joined the campaign for indoor plumbing. When the men were enjoined, they switched roles with their spouses. The men reluctantly tackled the household chores while the women faced picket line harassment and, under the injunction in the opinion, imprisonment. In the end, the mine operators came around and the men accepted their wives as equals.

2) Law review comments on the decisions include: Comment, Contempt—Punishment for Contempt—Civil Safeguards Sufficient When Contemnor Imprisoned for a Term Dependent on Further Violation of Injunction, 67 Harv.L.Rev. 889 (1954); Comment, Civil Contempt—Injunctions—Punishment of Violations Through the Revocation of Determinate Suspended Sentences, 39 Minn.L.Rev. 447 (1955); Comment, Equity Procedure: Civil Contempt: Use of Suspended Sentence to Enforce Prohibitory Injunction, 1 U.C.L.A.L.Rev. 220 (1954);

3) Does the criminal characterization have burdens as well as benefits? Following *Jencks,* would Laing have had to go to jail after Rickey's "cremation"?

N.L.R.B. v. TRUCK DRIVERS & HELPERS, LOCAL UNION 676

450 F.2d 413 (3d Cir. 1971).

Before HASTIE, Chief Judge, FREEDMAN, Circuit Judge, and WEBER, District Judge.

HASTIE, Circuit Judge. Underlying the present proceeding, initiated by the National Labor Relations Board to obtain an adjudication in civil contempt against Truck Drivers and Helpers, Local 676, International Brotherhood of Teamsters, is a 1965 decree of this court enjoining the union from engaging in or encouraging employees to engage in secondary boycotting in violation of section 8(b)(4)(B) of the National Labor Relations Act. On March 25, 1969, this court found the union in contempt of our 1965 decree and entered a purgation decree that again enjoined it from secondary boycotting and, in addition, provided as follows:

"FURTHER ORDERED that upon the failure of the respondent, its officers, agents, successors and assigns, to comply with any of the purgation provisions hereinabove provided by this order, this Court will deal further with the matter by imposing a fine of $5,000 on the respondent, and an additional fine of $500 per day so long as such non-compliance of this order or of the decree continues, and by such other means as the Court shall determine, including the issuance of body attachment upon any officer or agent responsible for such non-compliance. The fine provisions of this paragraph shall apply for a period of three years from the date of this order, if there are no further violations of this order during such period. This limitation shall not be construed to otherwise affect the duration of this order or of the Court's decree of March 30, 1965, or the Board's power to seek any additional relief from this Court with respect to any future violations of the order or decree."

Now, the Board, alleging more recent misconduct in willful violation of our 1969 decree is asking that we assess a $5,500 fine against the union and specify prospective fines in larger amounts to deter future contumacy. . . .

The charge of contempt is based upon events that occurred in June 1970 at a Salem, New Jersey job site, where a nuclear power generating station was being constructed under the management of United Engineers and Constructors, Inc. United Engineers employed about 1000 persons in various trades on the project. In addition, two other contractors M.J. Doyle, Inc. and William C. Reppenhagen, Inc. were actively engaged in work at the job site. Each of the three above named employers had a collective bargaining agreement with Teamsters Local 676.

It has been stipulated that in June 1970 Fred Powell was the "Chief Union Shop Steward on the Salem, New Jersey project, and as such steward investigated and presented grievances to United Engineers, collected union dues, and transmitted messages and information originating with the union." . . . The President of Local 676 and its principal administrative and executive officer was John P. Greeley. He had authority to call strikes and work stoppages.

Trap Rock Industries supplied stone to United Engineers for and at the project. On June 22 and 23, the days of the occurrences now in question, there existed a labor dispute between Local 676 and Trap Rock. No dispute existed between the union and United Engineers, Doyle or Reppenhagen.

Early on the morning of June 22, some 24 loaded trucks stood on the access road outside of the sole gate to the project area waiting to deliver crushed stone that had been quarried by Trap Rock.

Fred Powell, the chief union shop steward on the Salem project, admitted in his testimony before this court that he prevented these trucks from entering the job site. We also find that during the morning of June 22, Powell threatened Roger Gimbernat, the Assistant Project Superintendent of United Engineers, that, if the trucks delivered the Trap Rock stone all the Teamsters would walk off the job. . . .

Later during the morning, John Greeley, President of Local 676, arrived at the job site and engaged in discussions about the problem of Trap Rock deliveries. In a conversation with Stanley Clewett, Project Superintendent for United Engineers, President Greeley solicited the cooperation of United Engineers in keeping trucks carrying material from Trap Rock away from the project and predicted that otherwise there would be "trouble." Although Greeley refused to state what "trouble" would ensue, the union's answer to this contempt citation admits that Greeley told Clewett that "our people get annoyed about the situation and might walk off the job." . . .

During the afternoon of June 22, union members under the leadership of Powell placed equipment near the gate in position to block trucks from entering. The Trap Rock trucks departed without unloading their stone.

On June 23, the union put into effect an area-wide strike against Trap Rock. Throughout that day there was work stoppage by union truck drivers employed by the neutral contractors at the Salem job site, with only two of more than 50 union drivers reporting to work. Two small groups of employees who belonged to the union but were not truck drivers did work. In addition, Powell admitted telling "my drivers" late during the afternoon of June 22: "Well fellows, I am going to take a personal holiday tomorrow, a holiday, and you fellows do what you want to do." He also admitted that the following day he came to the job site, stayed outside the gate and said: "Fellows, I am going home. I am taking a holiday." He did not identify the audience to whom he spoke. . . .

Finally, Powell testified that he was not disciplined by the union for his conduct, but that he was criticized informally for taking too much on himself.

We conclude that on June 22 and 23, 1970 the union, acting through its President and the shop stewards on the Salem job site, willfully violated and acted in contempt of this court's purgation order of March 26, 1969, by threatening neutral employers with work stoppages by their employees and subsequently causing such work stoppages in furtherance of its labor dispute with another employer at a time when no labor dispute existed between it and the neutral employers. Because the assessment of a prospective fine of $5,000 for each future act of this kind has proved an inadequate deterrent, it is now appropriate not only that a fine of $5,500 in addition to the costs of this proceeding be assessed for the violations of June 22 and 23, 1970, but also that, as a more substantial deterrent, a prospective fine of $20,000 for each future violation, and an additional $2,000 for each day that the violation shall continue, now be predetermined and announced.

---

1) Coercion uses two kinds of threats: a) "We will coerce *until* you act," and b) "We will coerce *if* you act." "Coercion-until" obviates much of the risk that the contemnor will view the threat as a bluff. By undertaking to coerce, converting words to action, the judge is committed to continue coercion. "Coercion-if," on the other hand, may be a bluff. The contemnor may not believe that the threat is real until the judge commences coercive measures. By then the damage may be done; nothing may remain to be coerced.

We distinguish between coercion-if, which deters, stops, or prevents undesired conduct and coercion-until, which compels and creates desired conduct. To deter with coercion-if, the judge sets the trip wire and waits. To compel with coercion-until, the judge initiates measures that will cease when compliance occurs. "Do nothing" is easier to administer than "Cooperate." Deterrent threats are less ambiguous to contemnor because the consequences of abstaining are clearer. Compelling threats that must be administered in the future contain troublesome assurances that are hard to demonstrate. The judge may be tempted to reexamine and change aims. In short, the judge may not compel to the end because he may reconsider or lose his nerve. Actions speak louder and more clearly than inaction. Obedience to coercion-until is more obvious than obedience to coercion-if. It is less conspicuous to forbear in response to coercion-if than to perform in response to coercion-until, and the judge may make a special allowance for a contemnor who is backed down and humiliated.

Coercion-if deters by being passive and defensive. Coercion-until compels by being active and offensive. The judge who employs coercion-if will be tempted to make the deterrent credible by wielding it, perhaps by developing graduated deterrence. The conduct the judge seeks to deter by coercion-if may be once-and-for-all; when it occurs, the judge's failure to deter is complete and final. Examples are the marches on Good Friday and Easter in *Walker* p. 286. What about violations in *Jencks?*

Can measures taken afterward be anything but reprisal and punishment, in short, criminal contempt? Can specific measures for past conduct ever be coercive contempt? Once the event the judge sought to prevent occurs inextricably, keeping the threat advances no one's immediate interest. The judge seeks to preserve his long-term reputation for keeping his word, but that is removed from the immediate conflict. If, as in *Jencks*, keeping the threat cannot lead to relief for the plaintiff, can the measures be coercive? Graduated deterrence may occur where coercion-if has been threatened, the contemnor breaches, and the breach is susceptible to repetition. For example, the judge tells the infringer, "Your coercive contempt fine will start in one week and will be $100 each day you infringe." Passive deterrence, the trip wire, may fail. Exacting the fine may communicate the reality of the threat by fulfilling it progressively. Coercion will work after the fine starts. Even if you conclude that the jail sentence in *Jencks* was criminal contempt, would this fine be coercive because the judge intends it to alter contemnor's future behavior? Or have we adroitly substituted coercion-until in the guise of coercion-if?

2) Assume you are the judge coercing Jill McGurth, a judgment debtor, to tell where the inventory from her insolvent camera business is. You order her to tell where the cameras are. When she refuses, you hold her in contempt and order her to jail until she tells. Is that coercive contempt? Suppose alternatively you conclude that an indefinite sentence is potentially too severe and that McGurth will comply after a little time passes and reason is restored. So you tell her that she is in contempt and sentenced to one year in jail suspended on condition that, within a week, she tell where the cameras are. Do the contemnors in *Jencks* argue that the judge's lenience in delaying and limiting the jailing converts coercive contempt to criminal?

3) Is the critical question really whether the jail term is determinate? Does that question confuse a threat with reality? Is the right question whether the judge imposed it to change future conduct or to punish past conduct? Is it whether the contemnor may comply with the order during imprisonment and end the contempt?

How does *Jencks* differ from finding the cameras? If the judge imprisons Jencks and the other strikers, does that effect compliance? Does the New Mexico court misuse the term "purge"? Does "purge" mean 1) stop disobeying a negative order, or 2) obey a positive order? Judge Sexton declared Jim Laing in contempt and allowed him nine days to deliver Rickey; he imposed the fine and imprisonment only after the nine days passed. Does that differ from either *Jencks* or the case of Jill McGurth?

4) The issue in *Jencks* is whether the contempt was civil or criminal. How did the courts in *Laing* and *Local 676* address that issue? Are the decisions inconsistent? Which is correct? The judge may combine coercive and criminal contempt in several ways. First, he may conduct a criminal contempt trial, impose the opportunity to purge, and after that fails, sentence criminally. Is this *Laing?* Does the contempt remain coercive until the judge imposes the criminal sentence? French v. Town of Clintwood, 203 Va. 562, 125 S.E.2d 798 (1961), certiorari denied 371 U.S. 962 (1963). Second, he may conduct a criminal trial and impose the criminal sentence to begin only after a coercive opportunity to purge elapses. In Doyle v. London Guarantee, 204 U.S. 599 (1907), the judge gave the contemnor time to comply to be followed by a definite sentence failing compliance. The Court held that this was civil and thus not appealable. If the contemnor had waited and appealed from the definite sentence after the time ran, then would the result differ? Third, the judge may conduct a civil hearing, impose a period to purge, conduct a criminal hearing, and sentence criminally. People v. Superior Court, 28 Cal.App.3d 600, 104 Cal.Rptr. 876 (1972). Does the final paragraph of *Local 676* combine compensatory, criminal, and coercive features?

5) In Cliett v. Hammonds, 305 F.2d 565 (5th Cir. 1962), the trial judge enjoined contemnor from asserting that she owned certain land. After finding her in contempt for remaining in possession and threatening armed resistance, the judge said that unless contemnor obeyed within 30 days, she would be jailed for 90 days and that if she did not purge herself during the 90 day confinement, she would be punished for each day thereafter she remained in contempt. Criminal safeguards were not followed. How do you think the court of appeals responded to the 90-day sentence? Would it have been civil if it had been indefinite, to end upon compliance? Should the appellate court focus on the 90 days or the 30 days that precede it? Comment, Contempt: Civil Contempt Order May Not Include Absolute Sentence, 47 Minn. L.Rev. 907 (1963). The contemnor had persisted in her belief through 25 years and protracted litigation. Was 90 days too short? Does the criminal-civil procedural distinction make it difficult for trial judges to manipulate their limited tools to coerce most effectively?

6) Does the governor's pardon in *Laing* reveal that no criminal sentence is truly determinate? Compare Federal Rule of Criminal Procedure 35(b) (in the Appendix). When does a judge cease to serve plaintiff's interest, throw contemnor's keys out the window, and vindicate the social interest in obedience? The Supreme Court of Washington found that contemnors could purge contempt for "the breach of a prohibited act that cannot be undone." Purging may be inferred from contemnor's contrition. "In such a situation," the court said, "it must be left to the considered discretion of the trial court

to decide whether the contemnor has purged himself of contempt by his subsequent conduct and attitude." Keller v. Keller, 52 Wash.2d 84, 91, 323 P.2d 231, 235 (1958). See also Comment, 47 Minn.L.Rev. at 911–12. Compare Lance v. Plummer above, p. 1018.

7) Consider a triggered fine. Does prison differ from a fine in social stigma, coerciveness, or interference with personal affairs in a way that courts should recognize procedurally? Remember that the best coercion is the coercion that is adroitly displayed but never employed. In *United Mine Workers*, the majority modified the criminal $3,500,000 fine to $700,000 criminal with $2,800,000 coercive conditioned on compliance with the injunction within 5 days. Would the $2,800,000 have been coercive if the strike had continued into the 6th day? Does the absolute, all-at-once penalty in *Mine Workers* distinguish it from the daily fines in *Local 676?* Does an absolute penalty resemble a determinate sentence and a daily fine an indeterminate sentence? Why did the *Local 676* court find wilfullness? In *Local 676*, must the judge follow criminal procedure to trigger the $5,000 fine? Set future fines at $20,000?

In Hoffman v. Beer Drivers and Salesmen's Local 888, 536 F.2d 1268 (9th Cir. 1976), the United States court of appeals agreed that contemnors had lacked an opportunity to "purge" fines after the judge imposed them. But it also said: "Wherever a compliance fine is assessed and an opportunity given to purge, the failure to purge will bring about a due date. The due date occurs because the actor has failed to use the key to the jail which the court provided. . . . The occurrence of the due date does not transform civil proceedings, whose sole aim is to secure compliance, into a criminal proceeding. Were it otherwise, compliance with laws or orders could never be brought about by fines in civil contempt proceedings. Always the final order requiring payment will follow the act or omission which constitutes the failure to purge." 536 F.2d at 1273. See also NLRB v. Blevins Popcorn Co., 659 F.2d 1173, 1183–1186 (D.C.Cir.1981).

8) The daily fine may be coercive at dawn, determinate at dusk. Dobbs, Contempt of Court: A Survey, 56 Cornell L.Rev. 183, 276 (1971). Unlike the jail sentence which is a dead-weight loss to society, the money has to go somewhere. This truism opens potentially creative ways to use the money. May the plaintiff also carve a compensatory award out of the coercive fine? In part of the *Pennhurst* structural litigation, Judge Broderick ordered the defendants to pay for a Master in the institution. When defendants refused, he imposed a $10,000 per day coercive fine. After defendants had paid $300,000, Judge Broderick applied $100,000 of the accrued coercive fine to pay accrued costs of the Master's office. "Civil contempt fines, such as those imposed in this case, were intended by this court to accomplish two purposes—to coerce compliance with the Court's Orders and to compensate for harm sustained by the disobedience of this Court's Orders." Halderman v. Pennhurst State School and Hospital, 526 F.Supp. 423, 427 (E.D.Pa.1981). See above, p. 803. See also Cabrera v. Municipality of Bayamon, 622 F.2d 4 (1st Cir. 1980); Harthman v. Witty, 480 F.2d 337, 340 (3d Cir. 1973); Palmigiano v. Garrahy, 443 F.Supp. 956, 984–990 (D.R.I.1977). In Mobile County Jail Inmates v. Purvis, 551 F.Supp. 92 (S.D.Ala.1982), however, Judge Pittman refused to designate coercive fines to benefit the inmates.

9) Reconsider the way judges set coercive fines. Is a coercive fine that is equal to plaintiff's potential money damage faithful to the original decision to enjoin defendant? Remember that plaintiff's money remedy is inadequate. May a coercive fine equal to plaintiff's damage encourage a defendant, under some circumstances, to violate the injunction? R. Posner, Economic Analysis of Law §§ 4.9, 7.2 (2d ed. 1977). If defendant disobeys an injunction despite a coercive fine large enough to "assure" compliance, should the plaintiff receive compensation and the government the balance?

IV. Coercive Procedure

A. Initiation, Settlement, Mootness

SECOR v. SINGLETON

35 F. 376 (E.D.Mo.1888).

THAYER, J. 1. The motion to adjudge respondents guilty of contempt notwithstanding the return to the citation, like a demurrer, admits all the facts stated in the return. Complainants, as non-resident stockholders of the Missouri, Iowa & Nebraska Railway Company, on May 10, 1882, obtained a final decree against the then county judges of Scotland county and the county collector, enjoining them and their successors in office "from levying or attempting to levy, collecting or in any manner attempting to collect, from or of the Missouri, Iowa & Nebraska Railway Company, any taxes whatever, state, county, school, or municipal, . . . until the expiration of the period of exemption from taxation limited in the charter of said railway company, to-wit, until December 1, 1892." The interest which complainants have in the property that had been exempted from taxation was that of stockholders in the railroad company that then owned the exempt property, and it was on the strength of such interest that they were allowed to maintain the bill for an injunction, and eventually secured the decree above mentioned. The respondents' return alleges, among other things, that all the property of the Missouri, Iowa & Nebraska Railway Company to which the exemption from taxation applies, was sold under a decree of foreclosure on August 18, 1886, and that on December 3, 1886, it was delivered to and became vested in a corporation known as the "Keokuk & Western Railroad Company," "and that the complainants have no longer any interest whatsoever in said . . . property, or in the question of the taxation thereof, or in the matter of collecting taxes thereon." . . . The question accordingly arises whether, in the face of the admission that the complainants had lost all interest whatsoever in the maintenance of the injunction when the information herein was filed, the court ought to entertain their application to punish the respondents for a contempt. This question must be answered in the negative. When an injunction has been granted, as in this instance, in a suit between individuals to protect one of the parties in the enjoyment of some private right, immunity, or franchise, it seems to be the rule that no one can complain of a violation of the same, unless it be some one who has a present interest in maintaining the injunction, nor unless he was a party to the suit in which the order was obtained, or for some reason stands in privity with one who was a party to the litigation. In cases where an injunction has been granted to enforce or maintain a merely private right a proceeding instituted to punish a party for violating the order is very generally regarded as a proceeding to redress a private injury in which the public have no concern, and for that reason the prosecutor or person filing the information must have an interest in the proceeding differing from that of the general public; otherwise the courts will not entertain the information. . . . The cases show that a party in whose favor an injunction has been awarded may by express agreement, or by his conduct, release the injunction, or at least waive his right to have particular acts done in violation of the restraining order adjudged to be a contempt. . . . It would seem to follow that an injunction obtained to protect a merely private right, is so far within the control of the party obtaining it, and is so far a matter of individual concern, that only those persons who have a present interest in the right to be protected, can be heard to complain of its violation. If a person in whose favor an injunction has been granted complains of its violation, a presumption should no doubt be indulged that he still has an interest in the subject-matter to which the injunction relates, without any averment to that effect; and if such interest is called in question by the respondent, the court ought not to inquire very particularly as to the extent of the prosecutor's interest, further than to assure itself that the prosecutor is not a mere intermeddler. If the present complainants are now stockholders of the Keokuk & Western Railroad, which has become the owner of the exempt property, I am inclined to the view that that gives them a sufficient interest to maintain this prosecution, assuming for the purposes of the case that the property in the hands of the Keokuk & Western Railroad is still exempt from taxation. Nevertheless it is essential that the person who sets on foot a prosecution for contempt should have some present interest in enforcing obedience to the order which has been violated. When it is admitted, as in the present case, that no such interest exists, the court cannot properly entertain the proceeding.

2. What has been said disposes of the motion; but as the action of the court in overruling the motion on the ground above stated does not necessarily end the proceeding, and as some other questions have been discussed, they will be decided. First in order of importance is the plea that the court ought not to punish the respondents for the alleged contempt, because the Keokuk & Western Railroad Company has for a long period acquiesced in the acts constituting the alleged contempt. That there has been such acquiescence admits of no controversy on the facts recited in the return. In March, 1886, William Y. Wyne, as collector of Scotland county, intervened in a suit brought to foreclose a mortgage on the property of the Missouri, Iowa & Nebraska Railway for the purpose of collecting taxes for the year 1885, levied by the county court of Scotland county on what is claimed to have been property that was exempt from taxation according to the decree of this court and the decision of the supreme court of Missouri, in Scotland Co. v. Railway Co., 65 Mo. 123. Subsequently, in the year 1887, he brought suit against the Keokuk & Western Railroad Company, in the circuit court of Scotland county, to recover taxes for the year 1886, assessed against the same property. The present county judges of Scotland county, who are made respondents, did not levy the taxes for 1885 and 1886 so sued for, such levy having been made, it seems, by their predecessors in office. They made an appro-

priation, however, of certain money to prosecute the intervention in the foreclosure proceeding for the taxes of 1885. These are the several acts constituting the alleged contempt. In each of those suits the Keokuk & Western Railroad joined issue and went to trial long before the present information was filed by the complainants to punish the respondents for contempt in bringing the suits. In one of the cases judgment had already been recovered for the taxes of 1886 before the information was filed. In the other case it seems that the Keokuk & Western Railroad was instrumental in causing the same to be set for trial and heard, although the respondents had taken no action in that direction. That case, however, is as yet undecided. After these acts, after the Keokuk & Western Railroad Company has participated for months in litigation that was carried on apparently in open violation of a decree of this court, and after it had been defeated in one of the suits, the present information was filed on March 16, 1888, and it is now insisted that the court shall commit the respondents for contempt unless they release the judgment already obtained, and dismiss the intervention which is still pending and undetermined. On the face of the transaction it looks very much as though the Keokuk & Western Railroad Company is the real prosecutor, and as though its object was to defeat the suits above mentioned, which it has not succeeded in doing in the courts before whom the same are pending. If such be the fact, the right to insist that the respondents shall be punished for contempt because the suits were brought, and that they shall be compelled to dismiss the same, must be denied. The parties have acquiesced too long in the right asserted by the respondents to maintain those actions, to now insist, so far, at least, as those particular suits are concerned, that they have all the time been prosecuted in violation of the orders of this court. . . . If such was their view of the effect of the injunction, they should have asked this court to interpose its authority to arrest the prosecution of the suits at an earlier day. As a purchaser from the Missouri, Iowa & Nebraska Railway of the property to which the exemption attached, no reason is perceived why the Keokuk & Western Railroad Company might not have lodged an information complaining of the alleged violation of the decree of May 10, 1882. It did not choose to pursue that course. It made its election to defend the suits as though rightfully brought, and took the chances of making a successful defense. Having adopted that course, (if the facts be as stated in this return,) the court will not, at the instance of the Keokuk & Western Railroad Company, adjudge the prosecution of those particular suits to be a contempt, nor will it interfere with the further prosecution of the same in the respective courts in which they are now pending. If it be true that the complainants filed the present information of their own volition, to protect their own interests, and that they did not file it at the solicitation of the Keokuk & Western Railroad Company, the conclusion already announced would not be changed. It is obvious that complainants can have no personal interest in the subject-matter of the controversy, except as stockholders of the Keokuk & Western Railroad Company, which now owns the exempt property. Though the taxes for the years 1885 and 1886 were assessed against the Missouri, Iowa & Nebraska Railroad, yet, under the law, they can only be enforced against the property on which they were levied, and that has long since passed into the possession of the Keokuk & Western Railroad. Both the state and the county of Scotland must look to property now belonging to the Keokuk & Western Railroad for payment of the tax-bills, even if it be conceded that the assessments were lawful. Assuming the matters stated in the return to be true, it is not possible to conceive how the Missouri, Iowa & Nebraska Railway can at the present day be in anywise interested in the pending controversy. That being the case, and inasmuch as complainants derive whatever interest they have in maintaining the injunction from their connection with the Keokuk & Western Railroad Company, it follows that if the railroad company has waived or forfeited its right to have respondents punished for contempt because of the acts alleged in the information and return, then the complainants are equally without right to maintain such prosecution. . . .

---

1) Does *Secor* stand for the idea that civil contempt must be pressed by an aggrieved person with a present grievance? Does it forbid contempt to vindicate an abstract interest in seeing that everyone obeys the law? Was plaintiff guilty of excessive inactivity? Does *Secor* recognize that the parties may settle informally as evidenced by acquiescence in violations? Does the *Secor* court apply the doctrine of real party in interest, standing, laches, or estoppel?

2) Reconsider the question of whether an outsider to litigation may pursue contempt. Should any person injured by a violation be able to recover compensatory contempt damages? to seek coercive sanctions to achieve future compliance? See *Northside Realty,* p. 979 above and the Notes following it. Can plaintiffs trust the government to be the watchdog and press criminal contempt?

LOCAL 890 OF INTERNATIONAL UNION OF MINE, MILL & SMELTER WORKERS v. NEW JERSEY ZINC CO.

58 N.M. 416, 272 P.2d 322 (1954).

SEYMOUR, Justice. . . .

Point II of plaintiffs in error reads as follows:

"The trial court erred in proceeding with civil contempt proceedings on September 5, 1952, which proceedings sought to invoke the suspended sentence imposed by the judgment of July 23, 1951 for the following reasons:

"A. That in the month of January, 1952, long before the hearing on September 5, 1952, the strike was settled, the picket line removed, and the dispute between the parties fully terminated. . . .

"C. The court erred in its judgment and order following a hearing on September 5 in invoking the suspended prison sentences imposed upon the plaintiffs in error by the judgment of July 23, 1951, for the reason that such sentences could not have a coercive or remedial effect upon defendants since the entire controversy between the parties had terminated in January, 1952. The coercive purpose of the judgment on July 23, 1951 had ended, and there was no act which the defendants could do or perform to purge themselves of said prison sentences of definite duration." . . .

Point II, sub-paragraphs A and C, seeks to have us apply in the instant case the principle found determinative by this Court in New Jersey Zinc Co. v. Local 890 of International Union of Mine, Mill & Smelter Workers, [p. 985]. In that case we determined that the trial court was without jurisdiction to proceed with civil contempt proceedings when, pending the trial thereof, the strike, which was the basis of the original complaint, was settled and the dispute betwen the parties terminated. In that case the hearing upon charges of contempt was had subsequent to the settlement of the strike and the fines then imposed. As of the time of the hearing, the fines imposed could not have a coercive effect because the strike was over and the picket lines gone.

The foregoing situation differs from the instant case in that the hearing on the contempt charges in the instant case was in late July, 1951, and the suspended sentences imposed long prior to the termination of the strike. As of that time the suspended sentences were well calculated to have a coercive effect upon the defendants as distinguished from the fine imposed in the New Jersey Zinc Co. case last above cited, which was imposed at a contempt hearing subsequent to the termination of the strike.

The real essence of the position of plaintiffs in error lies in their view that the contempt hearing in the instant case was held, not in late July, 1951, but on September 5, 1952. In this view we consider plaintiffs in error to be mistaken, and in this difference of viewpoint appears the answer to the balance of their contentions. . . .

It remains our view [set forth in Jencks v. Goforth, p. 1032] that the contempt hearing in the instant case was had in late July, 1951, at which time a suspended sentence for a definite term was assessed in a civil contempt proceeding. What then was the character of the hearing on September 5, 1952? Since a suspended sentence is commonly a creature of the criminal law, it is there that the applicable principles are found. This does not mean that the sentences here involved are criminal; we have found that they are not, Jencks v. Goforth, supra; we feel free, however, in contempt proceedings to draw both from criminal and civil law for the principles controlling our decision. . . .

. . . [W]e must deny the contention of the plaintiffs in error that the coerciveness of the suspended sentences is to be evaluated as of the hearing on September 5, 1952, long after the strike had ended . . . .

Judgment of the trial court is affirmed and it is the direction of this Court that the defendants and each of them be forthwith remanded to the custody of the Sheriff of Grant county.

UNITED STATES v. PROFESSIONAL AIR TRAFFIC CONTROLLERS ORGANIZATION

525 F.Supp. 820 (E.D.Mich.1981).

COHN, District Judge.

On August 10, 1981, this Court entered an order determining civil contempt fines against the Professional Air Traffic Controllers Organization (PATCO) Local 321 in the amount of $100,000 and against six PATCO Local 321 members . . . each in the amount of $1,000 for failure to purge a judgment of civil contempt entered on August 4, 1981. The Court stayed enforcement to enable defendants to more fully develop their argument that the Court was without authority to enter the order. Briefs and a hearing followed. The propriety of the August 10, 1981 order is therefore properly reviewable.

More particularly, on August 3, 1981 plaintiff United States of America obtained a temporary restraining order against a strike by PATCO, PATCO Local 321, certain named individuals who were either officers, directors or members of PATCO and the general membership of PATCO. On August 4 the Court entered an order to show cause why a judgment of contempt should not be entered and after a hearing later that day entered a judgment of civil contempt against certain defendants. The judgment provided for conditional daily fines of $100,000 against PATCO Local 321 and $1,000 against certain named individuals for each day the strike was not terminated; the fines were to begin accruing at 7:00 a.m. on August 5.

The August 10 order determining civil contempt fines imposed fines for the first day; since the strike was continuing at 7:00 a.m. on August 5 the contempt had not been purged. As of 3:00 p.m. on August 5, however, plaintiff made it clear that it would not allow striking members of PATCO to return to work and thus it was no longer possible for defendants to purge the contempt. The "no return to work" position has been reiterated by plaintiff a number of times since.

The temporary restraining order was entered on August 3 upon a showing by plaintiff that the PATCO strike was illegal, 5 U.S.C. § 7311, that it threatened to significantly interfere with the normal flow of air traffic and operation of the air traffic control system and that its continuance would result in immediate and irreparable injury to plaintiff and the citizens of the United States. The conditional fines imposed on August 4 were clearly intended to coerce an end to the strike; plaintiff disclaimed any interest in compensatory or punitive fines.

Now before the Court is the question of its right to assess the fines on August 10 in light of the firing of PATCO members at 3:00 p.m. on August 5, and whether it was appropriate to impose the fines in light of all of the circumstances.

Defendants have filed a motion to vacate the judgment of civil contempt and the order determining the fines, asserting (1) the firing of all air traffic controllers who had not reported for work by 3:00 p.m. on August 5, which includes the individual defendants, rendered the dispute which gave rise to the judgment and order moot; (2) the firing resulted in a material change in circumstances which requires that the order be vacated; (3) in light of the August 5 firing, assessment of fines on August 10 was punitive rather than coercive; (4) the assessment of fines on August 10 did not serve the purposes intended by the conditional assessment of fines in the judgment of August 4; and (5) the Court failed to take into account defendants' ability to pay the fines when they were assessed.

In short, defendants argue that the firing rendered the dispute between plaintiff and defendants moot and therefore removed the Court's power to assess fines, or in the exercise of its discretion the Court should vacate the fines because by its own actions plaintiff made it impossible for defendants to return to work and purge themselves of contempt even if they had so desired.

Plaintiff's response, expressing commendable candor, acknowledges the Court has discretion to vacate or reduce the fines based on rational considerations. It urges the Court not to do so, however, because of the illegal nature of the strike and the fact that because of the strike the air traffic system is considerably overburdened and the public is still suffering costs and inconvenience.

At the Court's request plaintiff has filed a status report on similar cases pending in other districts. Of the approximately ninety civil actions instituted by plaintiff in an effort to halt the strike, only five, including the one at bar, apparently have resulted in judgments of civil contempt. In the District of Columbia, fines imposed by Judge Harold Greene have not yet been reduced to judgment pending resolution of the question of subject matter jurisdiction. In the Central District of Illinois and the District of Colorado the fines have apparently been reduced to judgment, while in the District of Hawaii plaintiff's motion to reduce the fines to judgment is still pending.

No useful purpose would be served by any extended discussion of the law of civil contempt in a dispute such as the one before the Court. The law, as well as the differences between civil and criminal contempt and the consequences which flow from a finding of one or the other, have been fully discussed in Gompers v. Buck's Stove & Range Company, and United States v. United Mine Workers.

These cases make clear that the Court on August 10 gave inadequate consideration to the defenses available to defendants to avoid imposition of the fines, notwithstanding their failure to purge themselves of the contempt by 7:00 a.m. on August 5. First, the Court should have given greater recognition to the fact that because of the firing of the air traffic controllers at 3:00 p.m. on August 5, it was no longer possible for defendants to return to work. Plaintiff, after initially seeking the coercive fines on August 4, by its own actions effectively precluded the fine schedule contained in the August 4 judgment of civil contempt from having any effect. Plaintiff's initiative, which made it impossible for defendants to purge themselves of contempt, was followed by its willingness to allow the temporary restraining order to lapse and its failure to proceed with the request for preliminary injunction. In essence, "the main case was settled." *Gompers.*

The Court on August 10 also should have given greater attention to the rule of United States v. United Mine Workers, that it is necessary in fixing the amount of a coercive fine to consider the defendants' financial resources and consequent burden the fines place on the particular defendants. Finally, the Court did not fully appreciate that in determining the amount of a fine it may proceed on a basis it deems just and is not locked into the specific amount initially imposed. NLRB v. Construction and General Laborers' Union Local 1140, 577 F.2d 16 (8th Cir. 1978). In so doing it has very wide discretion. G & C Merriam Co. v. Webster Dictionary Co., Inc.

The parties should of course be mindful that the considerations the Court now deems pertinent were not called to its attention on August 10.

While there is authority that a conditional jail sentence designed to secure compliance with an injunction in a labor dispute (analogous to the conditional fines here) may be imposed after the strike has been settled, Jencks v. Goforth, and Local 890 of International Union of Mine, Mill and Smelter Workers v. New Jersey Zinc Co., such an approach has been properly criticized on the ground that when the jail sentence commences it stands as punishment rather than coercion. See Casenote, 39 Minn.L.R. 447 (1955). It can be perceived in no other way.

So in this case, assessment of the fines on August 10, after plaintiff by its own acts made it impossible for defendants to return to work, could only be punitive.[2] Whatever coercive force existed in the August 4 judgment of civil contempt has been removed by plaintiff. Moreover, no inquiry was made on August 10 into the financial condition of any of the defendants or their ability to pay the fines assessed. Finally, the fact that in only three of the approximately ninety cases commenced across the country do air traffic controllers who did not return to work face fines suggest an inappropriate unevenness of treatment by this Court.

For all of the considerations mentioned above and in exercise of the broad discretion the law allows in these matters, the Court rationally concludes the order determining civil contempt fines of August 10, 1981 should be vacated. See In re Cueto.[3] [p. 1097 below.]

It should be perfectly clear that in vacating the fines the Court expresses no opinion on the underlying dispute regarding the air traffic controllers' strike and does not intend to denigrate the undoubted authority of a court to impose criminal sanctions for violation of its orders. See Labor Relations Commission v. Fall River Educators' Association, 416 N.E.2d 1340, 1351 (1981). Nor is the Court overlooking the considerable disrespect shown by defendants in their refusal to obey the restraining order issued on August 3. What must be emphasized is what the Court has already noted: the sole purpose of the conditional fines imposed on August 4 was to coerce the defendants into returning to work. Plaintiff did not seek an order of punishment for the disobedience nor did it ask for compensation for any injury it suffered. When by its own actions it made it impossible for the coercive purpose of the fines to be effected before entry of an enforceable order allowing their collection, it mooted the process it set in motion with the filing of the complaint. Once defendants were fired, further judicial action was simply inappropriate.

---

1) In Keller v. Keller, 52 Wash.2d 84, 323 P.2d 231 (1958), the trial judge adjudged contemnor in contempt and sentenced him to jail for six months; confinement was suspended on condition that contemnor not molest his spouse, pay her support, and move out. Contemnor disobeyed. The spouse signed an affidavit to support a motion to revoke the suspension of the jail sentence, but she later recanted "and expressed the wish that [contemnor]

2. If the fines were to stand, payment would be made to plaintiff, not as defendants' employer but rather as sovereign. Winner Corporation v. H.A. Caesar & Co., Inc., 511 F.2d 1010 (6th Cir. 1975).

3. Since defendants were in contempt of the Court's August 3 restraining order when the judgment of civil contempt was entered on August 4, the Court declines to vacate the judgment.

not be committed to jail." The court affirmed the trial judge's order revoking the suspension. Contemnor's "noncompliance with the order of July 5, 1956, not only prejudiced [the spouse's] rights (which she may elect to waive), but also constituted contemptuous conduct toward the court (which is not within her right to waive). The court could have cited [contemnor] for contempt on its own motion." 323 P.2d at 235. The contempt was and remained civil coercive because contemnor "may purge himself of contempt during the fixed period of his confinement, or he may elect to serve out the fixed term." 323 P.2d at 235. Contemnor could purge the failure to pay support by performance. What about contemnor's misconduct that consisted of "the breach of a prohibited act that cannot be undone"? "It must be left to the considered discretion of the trial court to decide whether contemnor has purged himself of contempt by his subsequent conduct and attitude." 323 P.2d at 235.

2) If you objected to the court of appeals's contempt order in Lance v. Plummer, p. 1018, do you find the *Keller* court's order worse? Does the *Keller* court allow the coercive tail to wag the criminal dog? Courts may convict violators of criminal contempt if the procedure and proof are proper. Does *Keller* punish under the guise of coercing and frustrate contemnor's right to criminal procedure before punishment? Should the procedure accorded contemnor turn on the dominant purpose of the particular contempt proceeding?

B. Procedural Safeguards

Wright, Byrne, Haakh, Westbrook, Jr., and Wheat, CIVIL AND CRIMINAL CONTEMPT IN THE FEDERAL COURTS

17 F.R.D. 167, 180–81 (1955).

. . . It is apparent that the value of [abolishing the distinction between civil and criminal contempt] depends upon the procedural safeguards which surround the proceeding. On the one hand, there is the consideration that whether the judgment of the court be punitive or coercive in nature, the court is always relying (except in those cases involving a compensatory fine) upon a sanction which is traditionally regarded as criminal in nature. On the other hand, if such procedural safeguards as the requirement of proof beyond a reasonable doubt and the privilege against self-incrimination are invoked, the rights of a private litigant seeking to obtain compliance with an injunction may be seriously jeopardized. Thus, in the last analysis, the question of the need for classifying contempt proceedings into criminal and civil categories depends upon a determination of the degree of protection to be given the contempt defendant and the further determination whether this same protection is to be extended to him where the sanctions of fine or imprisonment or both are used conditionally as a means of coercing compliance with the court's decree.

It is the opinion of the committee that a balance of these considerations indicates the desirability of preserving the distinction between civil and criminal contempt proceedings. Certainly in the case of criminal contempt proceedings, it would be unwise in the extreme to remove any of the traditional safeguards accorded the contempt defendant. On the other hand, where the purpose of the contempt proceeding is remedial as in the case of the private litigant seeking to obtain compliance with injunctive relief accorded him by the court, these traditional safeguards are not necessary since regardless of the character of the relief the contempt defendant will respond either by way of a compensatory fine or compliance with a conditional order. Justice to the private litigant under these circumstances would seem to require that his burden be no greater than in the civil proceeding which gave rise to his right to relief in the first instance.

Having reached this conclusion, the question remains as to the bases upon which the distinction between civil and criminal contempt proceedings shall be drawn. Little difficulty should be encountered in this regard since the work of the advisory committee on the criminal rules has already pointed the way. The purpose of the proceeding should be the controlling factor, and a requirement that the papers initiating the contempt proceeding state the relief sought and characterize the proceeding as civil or criminal would be a simple and effective method of implementing this distinction. . . .

Note, PROCEDURES FOR TRYING CONTEMPTS IN THE FEDERAL COURTS

73 Harv.L.Rev. 353, 354–357 (1959).

. . . [P]roceedings which may result in the imposition of coercive or deterrent civil contempt remedies seem to be distinguishable in several respects from ordinary civil proceedings. Doubtless all such proceedings, no matter what type of sanction is made available, have a common "civil" nature in that the purpose of the proceedings and the sanctions which ensue is to aid a private litigant. Thus it appears sound to resort to general civil practice as a matrix for civil contempt procedures. Yet some aspects of the presently operative and prospective civil remedies suggest that they should be invoked only after a proceeding which incorporates certain safeguards which have perhaps been more commonly associated with criminal procedure.

These sanctions employ the traditional methods of punishing criminals—imprisonment and fine payable to the state. Since they are imposed as the consequence of an encroachment upon state authority, the stigma of antisocial conduct will in some cases attend their imposition. The verbal civil-criminal distinction may not mitigate this effect of a contempt order to any appreciable extent, but it may be tempered by the fact that the civil sanctions can result only at the behest of a private party. Neither the presently operative nor the prospective civil sanctions will be imposed in the event of compliance by the contemnor. This circumstance—often expressed in the observation that the defendant "carries the keys to his own prison"—has been advanced as a reason why procedure is not of substantial concern to civil contempt defendants. It should not be overlooked, however, that the defendant's dilemma immediately following the issuance of a contempt order can be very serious. Thus, the procedure whereby this situation may be produced seems of major importance. This is especially likely to be the case in the common instance of a defendant's asserted testimonial privilege. Furthermore, it should be recognized that, while the operation of the sanction may be prospective or conditional, the matter at issue is not the defendant's future activity but his past conduct. A court is without power to impose a contempt sanction unless a violation has already occurred. Thus a civil contempt order, like a criminal conviction, embodies a condemnation of the defendant's past conduct. Especially in view of the breadth and complexity of injunctive decrees which may issue out of modern economic regulation, a defendant's contention that his conduct has not violated an injunction may raise serious questions of fact and law. Accordingly, a court's imposition of a contempt sanction may seem more like an original determination of the unlawfulness of a course of conduct of crucial importance to the defendant and in which he has engaged in good faith, than like a simple compulsion to obey the law in the future. Under such circumstances the contention that the defendant has no substantial interest in the procedure afforded him to dispute an assertion that his conduct violated the injunction is unconvincing.

There is no necessary correlation between the severity of the burden imposed on the defendant by a coercive or deterrent civil contempt sanction and the cost of making the complainant whole; nor is there any assurance that the imposition of such a sanction will inure to the complainant's benefit. Rather, the term of a coercive imprisonment or per diem fine is inherently tied to the exigencies of compelling obedience. Likewise, if the contempt order provides that a fine of a fixed sum be paid if compliance is not forthcoming by a certain date or levies a fixed fine for each future violation, the amount of the fine will be determined not by the cost of repairing the complainant's injury, but by reference to the necessities of coercion or deterence, to be assessed in the judge's discretion. Such an order is analogous to a penal statute in that it attempts to evaluate the quantum of state power necessary to coerce obedience to or deter disobedience of the law, and thus requires the exercise of a legislative judgment. It appears then that these sanctions are designed to protect the interest of the state in vindicating its authority as well as that of the complainant in obtaining redress. This consideration, taken together with the possibility of stigma which may result from the imposition of sanctions similar in form to criminal punishment, suggests that ordinary civil practice should not necessarily be determinative of the procedures afforded in cases of civil contempt. . . .

---

1) Should a coerced contemnor be entitled to the same procedural safeguards as a criminal contemnor? Should these procedural safeguards be available in *all* civil contempt proceedings? The Harvard Note struggles for an element of moderation: "A possible solution is to demand of trial judges that they resort to criminal procedures unless civil procedures are clearly appropriate, making abuse of such discretion grounds for reversal at the appellate level." Note, 73 Harv.L.Rev. at 369. Is this a satisfactory rule of law?

2) Persons accused of crimes are accorded extensive procedural protection: There must be an official decision to prosecute. In the federal system and many of the states, serious prosecutions must be preceded by grand jury indictments. The accused is entitled to detailed information about the nature and cause of the accusation. An indigent defendant is entitled to appointed counsel in felony prosecutions and in misdemeanors where incarceration is

given. The charge and trial must be where the alleged crime occurred. The accused is entitled to bail. The trial must be speedy, public, and before a jury where the possible sentence exceeds six months. The defendant is entitled to compel testimony, to confront accusers, and to cross-examine witnesses. The accused may claim the privilege against self-incrimination. Unreasonable searches and seizures are forbidden; wrongfully obtained evidence, including illegal confessions, will be excluded. The accused is entitled to be tried before an impartial factfinder and to be acquitted unless the prosecution proves all elements of the offense beyond a reasonable doubt. Defendants may not be held twice in jeopardy, nor may cruel and unusual punishment be inflicted. How many of these protections do you think apply to coercive contempt? Should courts require the same procedure for all coercive contempts?

3) The trend is to blend criminal into coercive procedure especially where imprisonment may be contemplated. Contemnor will be entitled to appointed counsel and Criminal Rule 42(b)'s procedural amenities. The judge cannot close the entire contempt proceeding but may only close to protect grand jury secrecy. In re Bongiorno, 694 F.2d 917 (2d Cir.1982); In re Rosahn, 671 F.2d 690 (2d Cir.1982).

SIDNEY v. MacDONALD

536 F.Supp. 420 (D.Ariz.1982).

CARROLL, District Judge.

On July 23, 1981, then Chairman of the Hopi Tribe, Abbott Sekaquaptewa, acting in his representative capacity for and on behalf of the Hopi Tribe, filed a Motion For Order To Show Cause Re: Contempt, against Defendants Peter MacDonald, acting in his representative capacity as the Navajo Tribal Chairman, the Navajo Tribe and individual members of the Navajo Tribe. Ivan L. Sidney, current Hopi Tribal Chairman, has been substituted as Plaintiff. An evidentiary hearing on this matter was held on December 2 and 3, 1981. . . .

Plaintiff's motion was amended prior to hearing to drop the allegations of contempt levied against the individual members of the Navajo Tribe. The amended complaint makes four requests. First, Plaintiff seeks an order of contempt against Defendants Peter MacDonald and the Navajo Tribe for failing to comply with the September 11, 1980, Court order in that such Defendants have not caused to be disassembled and removed certain structures found to have been unlawfully constructed on Hopi partitioned lands ("old-new construction") in violation of Paragraph (A), of the September 11, 1980, order. . . . Third, the Plaintiff moves that a mandatory injunction be issued directing defendants Peter MacDonald and the Navajo Tribe to disassemble and remove such "old-new construction" . . . . Fourth, Plaintiff seeks an award of costs and attorneys' fees.

Following the presentation of evidence, the Court took this matter under advisement. The Court has considered the Plaintiff's motion for contempt and all matters relevant thereto and enters the following Memorandum Opinion and Order:

On February 10, 1977, the Court entered a Judgment of Partition with respect to the Hopi-Navajo Joint Use Area. The Judgment of Partition, at paragraph 7(b), provided that "no new construction in the area hereby partitioned to the Hopi Tribe shall hereafter be commenced or continued by the Navajo Tribe, or any member thereof, without the written authorization of the Hopi Tribe."

On September 14, 1979, Plaintiff filed its Second Motion For Order To Show Cause And Preliminary Injunction. Plaintiff alleged that the Navajo Tribe and/or certain members thereof had engaged in unlawful new construction on Hopi lands in violation of Paragraph 7(b) of the Court's February 10, 1977, Judgment of Partition. An order to show cause was obtained and served upon Defendant Peter MacDonald and the Navajo Tribe, requiring them to appear and show cause why a contempt order and a mandatory injunction should not issue against them and why costs and attorneys' fees should not be assessed.

Following an evidentiary hearing on the show cause matter, the Court entered its Findings of Fact, Conclusions of Law, and Order on September 11, 1980. The order provided in pertinent part as follows:

"(A) Defendant Peter MacDonald and the Navajo Tribe on behalf of the members of the Navajo Tribe, shall, within ninety (90) days, cause the buildings found to be 'new construction' under the Court's Order of February 10, 1977, and described in Findings of Fact Nos. 9, 10, 12, 13, 14, 16, 17, 23, 24, 25, 27, 28, and 30, to be disassembled and removed from their present location to a place outside the Hopi Reservation. . . .

"(C) The provisions of Paragraph 7(b) of the Judgment of Partition continue to be in full force and effect and binding upon the Navajo Tribe, the Tribal officers, and the individual tribal members, villages, and clans."

Plaintiff contends that Defendants have failed to comply in certain instances with either of these provisions. Accordingly, this motion for an order of contempt and mandatory injunction was filed.

In a civil contempt proceeding the burden of persuasion is on the movant to establish by clear and convincing evidence proof of contempt. United States v. Rylander, 656 F.2d 1313 (9th Cir.1981). In such proceedings the *prima facie* showing consists of proof that the "defendant has failed to comply with a valid Court order." Once a *prima facie* showing has been made, the defendant must provide an explanation for the failure to comply. . . .

Here, Defendants Peter MacDonald and the Navajo Tribe have provided the Court with two explanations for their failure to comply with the September 11, 1980, order. First, Defendants argue that they cannot be held in contempt for the conduct of individual Navajo Tribal members over whom they have no control. Defendants urge that such inability to comply is an absolute defense. Second, Defendants argue that the evidence demonstrates that they have taken all reasonable steps within their power to secure compliance and have thus discharged the duty imposed by the September 11, 1980, order.

The Hopi contend that Defendants Peter MacDonald and the Navajo Tribe have failed to comply with Paragraph (A) of the September 11, 1980, order with respect to Findings of Fact Nos. 9, 10, 12, 23, 24 and 28 which describe the following structures:

"9. In July through October, 1979, Violet Ashkey, a member of the Navajo Tribe, without Hopi permission, engaged in the construction of a new home within the Hopi partitioned area, being the partially constructed building near the blueroofed hogan.

"10. Between September 5, 1979, and October 18, 1979, Guy and Esther Sosi, members of the Navajo Tribe, without Hopi permission, engaged in the construction of a hogan located south of the Low Mountain area within the Hopi partitioned area. . . .

"12. Tommy White, a member of the Navajo Tribe, engaged in the construction of a shed near the site of the house, located on Hopi land, without Hopi permission, in May-June of 1979. . . .

"23. During the summer of 1979, Mr. Stutterer, without Hopi permission, built a hogan within the Hopi partitioned area.

"24. During the Fall of 1979, members of the Navajo Tribe, without Hopi permission, engaged in construction of a hogan belonging to Nellie Begay. The hogan is located within the Hopi partitioned area. . . .

"28. The home belonging to Ruth Benally is new and was constructed within the Hopi partitioned area, without Hopi permission, after this Court had entered its February 10, 1977, order."

In order to make a *prima facie* showing of a violation regarding this "old-new construction," Plaintiff must show that (a) the challenged structures were declared by the September 11, 1980, order to be in violation of the February 10, 1977, order and (b) such structures had not been entirely dismantled and removed as contemplated by the September 11, 1980, order.

Here, the Court finds that in all cases such *prima facie* showing has been made by way of stipulation or uncontroverted evidence. Accordingly, absent any recognizable defense to the contrary, a contempt citation must issue . . . .

The Ninth Circuit has recently reaffirmed its position regarding the burden on respondent with respect to the defense of inability to comply. Quoting from N. L. R. B. v. Trans Ocean Export Packing, Inc., 473 F.2d 612, 616 (9th Cir. 1973), the Court states as follows:

". . . although inability to comply with a judicial decree constitutes a defense to a charge of civil contempt, the federal rule is that one petitioning for an adjudication of civil contempt does not have the burden of showing that the respondent has the capacity to comply. The contrary burden is upon the respondent. To satisfy this burden the respondent must show 'categorically and in detail' why he is unable to comply."

United States v. Rylander, 656 F.2d 1313, 1316 (9th Cir. 1981).

Defendants Peter MacDonald and the Navajo Tribe argue, as they have in prior proceedings, that they are unable to comply with the September 11, 1980, order because they are without jurisdiction over individual Navajos living on the Hopi partition of the former Joint Use Area. This argument is premised upon the Navajo Tribe's inability to enter Hopi lands for purposes of effectuating the order themselves. The Defendants do not argue that they lack the power to impose Navajo laws on individual tribal members residing on Hopi land. Thus, Defendants seek to establish their inability to comply with the Court's order merely by proving that the contemptuous conduct results from the individual-isolated activities of certain tribal members. As in prior proceedings, the Court finds this argument to be without merit for the reasons which follow.

It is clear that the Court has the power to enter orders against either tribe which directly affect the rights and interests of that tribe's membership. Sekaquaptewa v. MacDonald, 591 F.2d 1289 (9th Cir. 1979). In *Sekaquaptewa* the Ninth Circuit settled the issue relating to the identity of proper parties in actions seeking a resolution of intertribal disputes. The Court held that while either tribe, acting through its chairman may bring an action against the other, individual tribal members are "barred from participating." Id. at 1291. Such prohibition applies even if the dispute involves or affects the rights of individual tribal members. The rationale is that Congress intended that there be "quick and fair resolution" of such disputes. If individual persons were allowed to participate, such intent would be quickly frustrated. Thus, the Circuit Court concluded that each tribe, acting through its chairman, was the proper representative party for its respective membership.

Extrapolating from this principle to the next logical step, it is clear that if the tribe adequately represents the interests of its membership, then a Court may properly enter an order directing them to cause their members to take certain actions.

Here, the Navajo argue that they "lack jurisdiction" over those individual Navajos residing on Hopi partitioned lands. However, the Navajo have failed to demonstrate that these persons are no longer subject to Navajo tribal authority. In the absence of such proof the claimed defense of inability to comply based upon "lack of jurisdiction" cannot stand.

The Plaintiff's Response To Defendants' Post-Hearing Memorandum In Opposition To Plaintiff's Second Order To Show Cause, filed March 19, 1980, sets forth an illustrative list of reasonable actions which the Hopi claimed the Navajo Tribe has the power to impose on individual Navajos residing on Hopi partitioned land. Such actions include:

"1. Withholding of tribal benefits

"2. Imposing administrative requirements

"3. Monitoring the acquisition of construction materials by the individual Navajos residing on Hopi partitioned lands."

In Plaintiff's Response . . ., Plaintiff asserted that as a result of the partition order, the Navajo Tribe need not resort to adopting regulations for the purpose of compelling the compliance of its membership. The Hopi argued that presently the Navajo officials need only to seek enforcement of the Court's prohibition by bringing offenders directly to the attention of the Court."

In this case, the Navajo Defendants failed to demonstrate that they have attempted to do any of the above.

Defendants have offered no adequate legal explanation as to why they are unable to comply with the order. Accordingly, the Court finds that the Defendants have not shown "categorically and in detail" why compliance is impossible and thus, have not met their burden of proof with respect to this defense. Therefore, whether Defendants are to be excused for their noncompliance depends upon whether good faith efforts have been made to take all reasonable steps within their power to secure compliance.

The situation presented is similar to certain union-management disputes which frequently arise during a wildcat labor strike. In such situations, it is well settled that while the union's responsibility for the continued illegal strike activities of its membership is not absolute, such organization may nevertheless find itself in contempt of court if it has not engaged in good faith efforts to secure the compliance of its membership with the cease and desist order. United States v. International Union, United Mine Workers of America. . . . Thus, a labor organization does not establish its inability to comply with a cease and desist order merely by proving that the contemptuous conduct results from the stray activities of its membership. Similarly, the Navajo Tribe cannot establish its inability to comply with the September 1980, order merely by proving that contravention of such order occurs because of the stray activities of individual Navajos.

Mr. Percy Deal, Director of the Navajo-Hopi Land Dispute Office, testified to the various efforts taken by Defendants to comply with the September 11, 1980, court order. The Court has carefully reviewed this testimony and has concluded that the Navajo Tribe has not taken all reasonable steps within their power to secure the compliance of the Tribe and its membership.

First, there is no evidence that the Navajo Tribe ever sought to actively compel the compliance of the individual Navajos affected by the order. The Tribe has not passed regulations directed at this issue, nor have tribal sanctions been imposed. In the absence of such efforts or justification for failing to have done so, it cannot be said that all reasonable steps have been taken.

Secondly, the efforts that were taken consist in large part of simply communicating the requirements of the order to the individuals involved and their Chapter leaders.[2] The Court finds that merely advising those involved of their responsibilities under a court order is not enough. The law commands more than lip service to discharge one's duties imposed by a judicial decree.

Accordingly, the Court finds that Plaintiff has established a *prima facie* showing of contempt, and Defendants have failed to establish a cognizable defense. The Court concludes that a contempt citation for the continued violation of the September 11, 1980, order of this Court is proper.

As the order which follows set forth in detail, the Court has determined it necessary to (a) grant the requested injunctive relief, (b) impose fines and (c) provide built-in monitoring devices.

2. Some of the "good faith efforts" undertaken by the Navajo include letters sent by Mr. Deal to the individual Navajos in alleged non-compliance with the September 1980 order. These advisory letters were sent to such individuals on August 5, 1981, two full weeks after the Hopi Tribe filed the present motion for contempt. Such efforts come too little and too late to have any present credibility or relevance.

The Court notes that Defendants' arguments concerning the equities involved with respect to the disassembly and removal of persons' homes are all irrelevant considering the present posture of this matter. Such arguments are properly raised in a motion to modify order or on appeal. The September 1980 order clearly required Defendants to cause the disassembly and removal of certain enumerated structures. The only issue now before this Court was whether such structures had been removed and, if not, whether the Defendants were otherwise excused. Defendants did not at any time seek to modify or amend the September 1980 order. . . .

IT IS ORDERED that Defendants Peter MacDonald and the Navajo Tribe are in contempt of this Court as a result of their violations of Paragraph 7(b), of the February 10, 1977, and Paragraph (a), of the September 11, 1980, order, with respect to Findings of Fact Nos. 9, 10, 12, 23, 24, and 28, as set forth in the September 11, 1980, order.

IT IS FURTHER ORDERED that as a result of such conduct, the Defendants Peter MacDonald and the Navajo Tribe shall, on or before May 31, 1982:

1. Cause the structures identified in Findings of Fact Nos. 9, 10, 12, 23, 24, and 28, in the September 11, 1980, order to be disassembled and removed to a location outside the Hopi partitioned lands.

2. Take appropriate steps to insure the restoration of the Hopi land to its original state prior to such construction.

3. Cease and desist from providing construction assistance in any form, i.e., labor or materials, to Navajos residing on Hopi partitioned lands without first ascertaining whether the requesting individual has obtained the necessary prior written Hopi consent.

IT IS FURTHER ORDERED that the Defendants shall pay a $500.00 fine for every day after April 16, 1982, that any of the specified structures remain in any form on Hopi partitioned lands. . . .

IT IS FURTHER ORDERED that a status hearing is set for Monday, April 26, 1982, at 11:00 a.m. in Courtroom No. 6, United States Courthouse and Federal Building, Phoenix, Arizona, for purposes of discussing the status of the Defendants' compliance with this order.

IT IS FURTHER ORDERED that Plaintiff may file and serve upon Defendants a verified statement of costs and request for reasonable attorneys' fees. Responses shall be filed in accordance with Rule 11, Local Rules of Practice. An evidentiary hearing shall be noticed by the Court, if necessary.

---

1) *Sidney* combines coercive with compensatory contempt. Like United Mine Workers—The Pension Fund Dispute, p. 891 and *Telling*, p. 987, *Sidney* places responsibility on a leader when someone at the bottom of the hierarchy disobeys. All three decisions raise the issue of whether contemnor violated the injunction or what contemnor's duty to effect compliance is. Do you accept *Sidney's* liberality on this issue because the contempt resembles a second injunction with the penalty specified? Would a six-month criminal sanction be palatable? A damage award for mesne profits? See D. Dobbs, Handbook on the Law of Remedies § 5.8 (1973).

2) Is contemnor's mental state irrelevant? Does the judge retain equitable discretion to refuse to coerce a recusant defendant? In the issuance stage, plaintiff prevails by showing a preponderance of evidence. Does the clear and convincing standard in the contempt stage qualify plaintiff's right to defendant's conduct? Does it break the promise the judge made when he found plaintiff's remedy at law inadequate?

3) The way courts allocate proof in coercive contempt can be complex. Matter of Battaglia, 653 F.2d 419 (9th Cir. 1981), dealt with a contemnor who claimed a memory loss. The proponent of coercive contempt must prove "the contempt" by clear and convincing evidence. The witness may explain failure to comply, for example, inability to obey; if contemnor fails to meet this burden to produce evidence, the proponent's prima facie case supports contempt, as in *Sidney*. If the witness testifies that he does not remember, he meets this burden to produce. The proponent may, however, prove by clear and convincing evidence that the witness *did* remember and thereby establish contempt. Do rules allocating the burden and setting the quantum of proof help decide disputes tried to judges without juries?

4) Assume that after the *Sidney* decision a) contemnors breach by not removing the structures and the district judge imposes a $500 fine; b) contemnors appeal challenging the injunction; and c) the court of appeals holds that the injunction is incorrect. Does the collateral bar rule mean that contemnors must pay the $500 fine? The Court said in *United Mine Workers* that "The right to remedial relief falls with an injunction which events prove was erroneously issued," p. 276. Should the collateral bar rule and the overarching respect policy turn on the elusive civil-criminal distinction? Unlike a compensatory award, a triggered fine is paid to the public treasury. Would plaintiff profit from an order to which he was not entitled? The fine is a definite response to past conduct. Contrast Latrobe Steel Co. v. United Steelworkers of America, 545 F.2d 1336, 1342 (3d Cir. 1976), and United States v. Spector Foods Corp., 544 F.2d 1175, 1182 (3d Cir. 1976), with AMF Inc. v. International Fiberglass Co., Inc., 469 F.2d 1063, 1065 (lst Cir. 1972). Should courts approve coercive contempt fines but not compensatory awards to preserve respect for the court and court orders? Inland Steel Co. v. Local Union No. 1545, UMW, 505 F.2d 293, 296-298 (7th Cir. 1974); Brotherhood of Locomotive Firemen and Enginemen v. Bangor and Aroostook Railway Co., 420 F.2d 72 (D.C.Cir. 1969), certiorari denied 397 U.S. 1024 (1970). If the collateral bar rule does not apply to civil contempt, is the injunction protected by res judicata or law of the case in contempt? Siebring v. Hansen, 346 F.2d 474, 477 (8th Cir. 1965); World's Finest Chocolate, Inc. v. World Candies, Inc., 409 F.Supp. 840, 844-845 (N.D.Ill. 1976); Schlegel Manufacturing Co. v. King Aluminum Corp., 381 F.Supp. 649 (S.D. Ohio 1974).

JOHANSEN v. STATE

491 P.2d 759 (Alaska 1971).

DIMOND, Justice.

Appellant's wife divorced him in May 1966. The divorce decree required appellant to pay $100 a month for the support of his two children.

Between the date of the divorce and April 1970, appellant paid only $148 in child support. A bench warrant was issued by the superior court, and appellant was arrested and brought before the court to show cause why he should not be held in contempt of court for failure to pay child support as required by the divorce decree.

Following the hearing in May 1970, the superior court entered an order finding that appellant was in arrears in his child support obligation in the amount of $4,876. The court further found appellant in "civil contempt" and sentenced him to serve 60 days in jail. Commencement of the sentence was deferred until October 1, 1970. The court also provided that the sentence "may be further deferred if a payment on child support obligation herein is made by Daniel Johansen commensurate with his income or if, at that time, it can be shown that Daniel Johansen has no money to pay child support through no fault of his own."

From this contempt order an appeal has been taken. Appellant argues (1) that the contempt proceeding, although denominated as civil in nature, was in reality criminal, and that he was denied the constitutional safeguards guaranteed to him by the Alaska Constitution in criminal proceedings; [and] (2) that there was no evidence before the superior court upon which to base a finding of contempt . . . . The case raises two additional points which we shall pass upon. They concern the possibility that this appeal has been rendered moot by events occurring after the entry of judgment in the superior court and the procedure to be utilized by a court to bring a similarly situated defendant before it.

Mootness

The circumstances which might be thought to render this case moot arose after the briefs were filed. Hence, appellee's failure to raise the issue will not preclude our consideration of it. Courts have the power, as a matter of sound judicial policy, to dismiss moot appeals. . . . This rule should apply even when the mootness issue is not raised by the appellee, if the reason is because the events causing the appeal to be mooted occur after the briefs were filed.

The appellant was not imprisoned on October 1, 1970, or at any time thereafter as a result of the order quoted above. Further, on October 6, 1970, the appellant made a payment of $750 to the court trustee. The court trustee has taken no further action in connection with this case. Under these circumstances, it may be thought that the appellant has satisfied the decree and the case is moot.

We decline to reach this result . . . . [A] careful reading of the lower court's order indicates that the events described above have not necessarily relieved the defendant of the threat of incarceration based on the order itself.

The key clause says only that "commencement of said sentence *may* be further deferred if a payment on child support obligation herein is made by Daniel Johansen commensurate with his income." (emphasis added.) That appellant's sentence apparently has been deferred to this date does not necessarily mean that at some future time the appellant might not be incarcerated on the basis of this order alone. . . .

Procedural Safeguards in Contempt Proceedings in Nonsupport Cases

Appellant argued at trial that the proceedings contained criminal elements and that he was entitled to various criminal procedural safeguards. The court ruled that the proceedings were for civil contempt and therefore the criminal rules were inapplicable. The issue presented—whether a contempt hearing to compel compliance with the child support order is a civil or criminal proceeding—is one of first impression in this state.

Recourse to statutory law is helpful but not dispositive of the issue.[1] However, the statutes do furnish some guidance. AS 09.50.010 speaks of the acts or omissions which constitute contempt. Subdivision (5) of that section, with which we are concerned here, provides that it is a contempt of the authority of the court to disobey a lawful judgment, order, or process of the court. AS 09.50.030 further provides:

> "A person who is charged with contempt of court not committed in the presence of the court, where the act or thing so charged as a contempt is of such nature as to constitute also a criminal offense under a statute of the United States or a law of this state, has a right to jury trial."

AS 11.35.010 makes wilful failure without lawful excuse to support a child a crime. Thus, it is clear that, for purposes of the right to a jury trial, our statutes classify indirect contempts for nonsupport, such as that alleged in the case at bar, as a crime and a jury trial is available. Appellant was not afforded the right to jury trial in the case at bar. On this basis alone, the superior court's order of contempt must be reversed.

Our conclusion concerning appellant's right to a jury trial, however, does not dispose of this appeal, for here appellant seeks the full panoply of criminal procedural protections, and we must decide whether he and others in his position should receive them. Our statutes speak no further on this subject. It is necessary, therefore, to consider in some detail the contours of contempt doctrine to determine the proper scope of courts' powers and defendants' rights in contempt proceedings for nonsupport.

As we noted recently in State v. Browder, contempt was originally regarded as a crime, punishable by criminal sanctions. Whether this was because "[t]he original law of contempt embraced only what is now known of as criminal contempt," or because every contempt inevitably contains an element of disrespect for the authority of government (one of the hallmarks of criminal contempt) is not clear. It is certain, however, that "the genesis of modern day contempt was a crime." [486 P.2d 925, 933 (Alaska 1971).]

1. Even the location of the contempt laws in the state statutes permits ambiguous inferences. The contempt provisions are found in AS 09.50.010-09.50.060, part of the Code of Civil Procedure, but these sections are specifically made applicable to "criminal actions" by AS 12.80.010, part of the Code of Criminal Procedure.

The common law soon began to categorize contempts, and one of the earliest distinctions was between criminal and civil contempt. The exact development of the distinction is not clear, although it has been traced at least as far back as the 18th century. Significantly, the earliest explications of civil contempt evidence little agreement as to exactly what distinguished it from criminal contempt.

"Halsbury reported that older English law distinguished criminal contempts by their procedural implementation as much as by any innate substantive differences which might have existed between them and other offenses." [Goldfarb, The Contempt Power 49 (1963).]

Nonetheless, that there is a distinction between civil and criminal contempt appears to have become firmly established, both in England and in this country, by the late 19th century. It now remains to explore what that distinction is, and whether it is based on sound reasoning.

The leading case is Gompers v. Buck's Stove & Range Company, where the United States Supreme Court held:

"It is not the fact of punishment, but rather its character and purpose, that often serve to distinguish between the two classes of cases. If it is for civil contempt the punishment is remedial, and for the benefit of the complainant. But if it is for criminal contempt the sentence is punitive, to vindicate the authority of the court."

These polar concepts—"remedial" (or "coercive") v. "punitive"—seem clear enough, and, indeed, this distinction has been widely accepted. Yet even *Gompers* noted that the distinction was far from absolute:

"Contempts are neither wholly civil nor altogether criminal. . . . It is true that punishment by imprisonment may be remedial as well as punitive . . . .

"It is true that either form of imprisonment has also an incidental effect. For if the case is civil and the punishment is purely remedial, there is also a vindication of the court's authority. On the other hand, if the proceeding is for criminal contempt and the imprisonment is solely punitive, to vindicate the authority of the law, the complainant may also derive some incidental benefit from the fact that such punishment tends to prevent repetition of the disobedience."

Despite this weakness, the main test remains that suggested by the *Gompers* case: The character and purpose of the punishment serve to distinguish civil from criminal contempt. This remedial-punitive distinction is not perfectly sharp. We must now decide whether, whatever its faults, the remedial-punitive distinction is sharp enough to justify complete procedural cleavage between civil and criminal contempt.

Elements of punitive as well as remedial punishment are almost invariably present in every civil contempt. If coercive imprisonment is imposed in order to effectuate compliance with a court order and thus aid a private litigant (remedial punishment), it nonetheless also has the effect of deterring contemptuous conduct in the future and of punishing the contemnor for his act of noncompliance—both of which are clearly attributes of criminal sanctions. This overlapping is tolerable if in civil contempt cases the court provides that imprisonment is conditional upon the defendant's continued refusal to comply with the court's order. This step, which insures that the defendant indeed does "carry the keys of [his] prison in [his] own pockets," [In re Nevitt, 117 F. 448, 461 (8th Cir. 1902)], assuming he has the ability to comply, would be sufficient to establish the coercive aspect of the imprisonment as its dominant one. Theoretically, once confronted with the reality and imminence of a stay in jail as a result of his noncompliance, the contemnor could immediately purge himself and avoid incarceration completely. If he did this, punishment would not be present at all, and deterrence would not be nearly as significant as the coercive (hence remedial) aspects of the proceedings. Under these circumstances, the characterization of the action as civil is not doctrinally objectionable, and the civil criminal distinction is reasonably clear.[22]

There is a more serious problem inherent in the civil contempt doctrine. Although imprisonment—indeed potentially unlimited incarceration—is at stake, the civil contempt defendant is afforded no more procedural protection than the ordinary civil litigant. This is because of the belief that civil contemnors do not need criminal procedural safeguards since they are not placed under the criminal sanction of a fixed sentence; that is, they "carry the keys of their prison in their own pockets." However, this may not be true:

"Both compliance and inability to comply are complete defenses to coercive imprisonment proceedings. The contemnor may have already complied or be incapable of doing so, *yet the determination of these facts is made without criminal safeguards even though imprisonment hinges on the outcome of that determination.*" [Comment, The Coercive Function of Civil Contempt, 33 U.Chi.L. Rev 120, 125 (1965).]

A better rationale for denying procedural safeguards rests on the position of the plaintiff. In criminal contempt, where the government initiates the action, the granting of procedural safeguards does not conflict with the rights of any individual. "But granting additional safeguards to the defendant in a civil contempt proceeding is directly opposed to the interests of the complainant to whom the defendant owes a duty by reason of a prior judicial decree." [117 F. at 461] If this is so, where should the balance be struck?

The competing interests are strong in the instant case. Defendant, faced with incarceration, has an interest in receiving those procedural protections which insure that he has been accorded a fair trial. Defendant's children have an interest in receiving support for the sustenance of life. Defendant's former wife, now charged with the responsibility of raising the children, needs contributions from the children's father in order to meet her responsi-

22. There are two disadvantages to the character-of-the punishment test which affect primarily the trial courts and to which we call attention here. The first is that punishment is not determined until the end of the proceeding, whereas the need for classification exists from the beginning. Trial courts may overcome this in most instances by announcing at the outset the goal of the contempt action, specifying whether the action is designed primarily to vindicate the court's authority or to coerce compliance with one of its orders for the benefit of a third party. The second is that the alleged contemnor, at the time of his wrongful act, has no way of knowing whether he has committed a civil or criminal contempt or what his sanction will be. Goldfarb, [The Contempt Power (1963)] at 66. We deem this disadvantage outweighed by the benefits of an otherwise workable classificatory scheme and mitigated, for purposes of due process notice requirements, by the trial court's announcement, at the beginning of the proceedings, of the purpose of any punishment imposed.

bility. Further, the interests of both children and wife are heightened in that they seek enforcement of a prior judicial decree. The state has an interest in the welfare of the children as the ultimate source of their support in the event that their parents fail them.

In these circumstances we find it appropriate to delineate the rights of the parties in such a way that all legitimate interests will be protected as fully as possible, departing from traditional contempt doctrine in those areas where we have found it to be deficient or where strict adherence to it would not lead to the soundest rule of law in terms of all the parties' interests.

The purpose of contempt proceedings for nonpayment of child support decrees is to coerce the defendant to pay money. It is not to punish him for his past failure to pay.[27] What we are dealing with here is the question of imprisonment to compel performance of an act. In this regard AS 09.50.050 states:

"When the contempt consists of the omission or refusal to perform an act which is yet in the power of the defendant to perform, he may be imprisoned until he has performed it."

Thus, it is necessary to determine whether defendant has the resources with which to satisfy the court order, that is, whether he has the ability to comply with an order of support. Should this determination be made without all criminal safeguards—with the exception of jury trial—even though incarceration hangs on the outcome? We believe that it should, subject to the following guidelines, because of the relative positions of the parties. At the outset, it should be determined by the trial judge whether the alleged contemnor contests the assertion that he has the ability to comply with the court's order of child support. In the event the defendant makes no issue of his ability to comply, then the defendant can be imprisoned in order to compel compliance without the intervention of a jury trial. On the other hand, if the defendant asserts that he lacks the ability to comply with the court's order of child support, then he is entitled to a jury trial on this issue.

At the contempt trial, the burden of proving noncompliance, by a preponderance of the evidence, with the court's order should be on the plaintiff, who initiates the action. Since all payments in child support cases in Alaska are made through the office of the court trustee, . . . proof of noncompliance should be a simple matter. In almost all child support contempt cases, the crucial issue will concern the defendant's *ability to comply*. This was the situation in the instant case. The burden of proof in this respect should remain with the defendant.[28] This is where it presently rests, in this state and in other jurisdictions; such allocation of the burden of proof is appropriate. Defendant is already under a court order to pay a certain amount of money; presumably the prior adjudication was based on evidence that the amount

27. Of course, the prosecuting authority can always seek conviction for violation of AS 11.35.010, or initiate proceedings for criminal contempt under AS 09.50.010(5) for past wilful flouting of the court's authority, but either of these occurrences would initiate a criminal proceeding in which defendant would have to be afforded full criminal procedural safeguards. This distinction should be made clear at the outset of the contempt nonsupport proceedings.

28. That is, defendant must prove his inability to comply with the court order. Put in procedural terms, inability to comply is an affirmative defense.

fixed was fair and in proportion to defendant's ability to pay.[31] Further, putting the burden on the plaintiff (of proving defendant's ability to pay) seems unfair. Defendant, as a father, is under a general duty to support his children. AS 11.35.010. He is further under a specific obligation to pay a certain sum by virtue of the court order. By the time these cases reach trial stage, the father usually has failed to fulfill these obligations for a considerable period of time. He should be required to present the reasons, if there are any, for his failure to meet his legal obligation to support his children. Further, the particular facts regarding his inability to pay will be known to him, whereas his former wife and his children generally will know little of his financial situation or earning capacity.

The shifting of the burden of proof entails a partial change of the ordinary standard employed in criminal cases. But this is still advantageous to both parties. The defendant's protection increases as the burden of proof is shifted. He needs only to show by a preponderance of the evidence that he is unable to pay. Once he has met this burden, incarceration, as a coercive method, serves no useful purpose. At the same time the interest of the complainants in receiving money which defendant is able to pay, is protected under this approach.

It is now evident that traditional contempt doctrine cannot satisfactorily answer whether child support contempt hearings are "criminal" or "civil" in nature. We have, instead, looked to a balancing of the parties' interests to determine what procedure should be followed in such cases. We have drawn from both sides of the law. We have found a jury trial not only mandated by our statutes but warranted as a procedural protection to the defendant facing incarceration. On the other hand, we have left inability to comply as an affirmative defense, thereby keeping the burden of proof on the central issue on defendant. Doubtless, further procedural questions will arise in future cases. We shall continue to weigh the interests as we have done here. All we do today is attempt to delineate the procedural aspects of contempt proceedings in nonsupport cases where the purpose is to coerce the defendant's performance of his obligation.

AS 09.50.010(5) provides that it is a contempt of the authority of the court to disobey a lawful judgment, order, or process of the court. Under this statute, the purpose of the contempt proceeding in this case and a resulting sentence of imprisonment was either to coerce the appellant into paying support money for his children or to punish him for his past failure to pay, or both. The question is whether the evidence was sufficient to justify finding appellant in contempt and sentencing him to a term of imprisonment.

Disobedience of a lawful order of the court connotes more than the mere failure to comply with such order. The word "disobey" has the connotation of wilfully failing to comply, without some lawful or reasonable excuse for not complying.[33] If such an excuse does exist and it is established, there can be no contempt of the authority of the court.

31. It is no answer that the prior adjudication was then or is now incorrect. Defendant has already had one day in court on this issue; that he did not contest the divorce or the amount of support requested cannot be charged against his children. Further, he can always seek modification of the support order. AS 09.55.220.

33. This is not unlike the situation in a criminal case where we have held that

Appellant is an Alaskan Native born in the Native village of Ekuk and raised in the nearby Native fishing village of Dillingham. In appellant's brief, it is stated that he is uneducated. Appellant's experience is sharply limited. His whole life, with the exception of four years in the military, has been spent in the village. His only occupation has been fishing, except for some very limited experience as a waiter in Dillingham working a few nights a month as work was available. He has been trained for no other occupation but fishing.

Appellant's last good fishing season, when he cleared $3,200, was in 1965, before his divorce. Since that time he has cleared no more than $700 in any year because of poor fishing conditions. Appellant has been and is heavily in debt to a local cannery in Dillingham. In addition to other sums owed the cannery, appellant owes about $7,200 on his fishing vessel.

Appellant has made attempts to find other employment. But he was unsuccessful, principally, it appears, because prospective employers would not hire fishermen. Appellant testified that he could not quit fishing because he owes so much money to the cannery. He did not know of any way of making more money than as operator of a fishing vessel. In the 1969 fishing season, the year prior to the hearing on this matter, appellant testified that he had gone "in the red." In that year he went deeper in debt to the cannery. Appellant testified that he might have gotten a full time job with Wien Consolidated Airlines in Dillingham if he had given up fishing as his occupation, but that he could not be certain of this. From his testimony, it appears that appellant was continuing his occupation as a fisherman while waiting for a good fishing season to make up his losses and make a profit.

At the conclusion of the hearing, the judge stated that he could not contemplate issuing a judgment which would in effect order the appellant to go somewhere else to live and work at another job. But then the judge reversed his position by stating that appellant had remained in a depressed area year after year hoping for the big strike that had never come, that he ought not to stay in Dillingham, and that he was in contempt of court. The question here is whether one may be required to change his place of residence as a condition of not being held in contempt in a case of this type.

In these circumstances, we cannot agree with the trial judge's suggestion that appellant leave his home in Dillingham and seek employment in an urban community, such as the city of Anchorage. There is no indication from the record that such a move would hold a promise of success within appellant's inherent but unexercised capabilities. Rather, it seems that it would be a gamble, based on little more than hope, that an untrained person could earn more in an urban environment doing an undetermined job than he could in his home locality at his life-long occupation. . . .

We hesitate now to adopt a rule allowing a superior court to force a man to move from one community to another, in the process renouncing his life-long occupation to seek an undetermined one, on the penalty of being found in contempt for failure to do so. In short, leaving Dillingham to seek em-

conduct cannot be criminal unless it is shown that the one charged with criminal conduct had criminal intent, that is, an awareness or consciousness of some wrongdoing. Speidel v. State, 460 P.2d 77, 78, 80 (Alaska 1969).

ployment elsewhere would be outside the reasonable effort we require of a father in such cases.

We are remanding this case for a trial before a jury. We recognize it is within the function of the jury to make a factual determination as to whether appellant has presented a sufficient excuse for not complying with the order of child support. But we are determining as a matter of law, rather than leaving the question to the jury, that in the circumstances of this case, it is not contempt for a father to refuse to leave his village and seek more promising work in the city.

On the other hand, we hold there is a jury question as to the existence of a lawful excuse for non-compliance with the child support order while the appellant resides in Dillingham. In Houger v. Houger we spoke of a father's primary and continuing obligation to support his children and of the fact that the inability of a father to engage in his chosen trade may not excuse him from that obligation. We said:

"But there may be other kinds of work which appellee could engage in despite any disability he may have. He should be required to seek such other work with respect to his obligation to support his children even though such work may not appeal to him, because there is no room for professional or occupational pride where the duty of child support is involved." [449 P.2d 766, 770 (Alaska 1969).]

We adhere to *Houger* and hold that in a contempt action such as we have here, the father will not be permitted to succeed on the defense of having a legitimate reason or excuse for not complying with an order of child support where he has not made a reasonable effort to employ his earning capacity in directions other than the one he has chosen as his chief means of livelihood.

In this situation a jury question is involved. Considering the evidence of appellant's life-long vocation of being a fisherman, his indebtedness to the local cannery, the existence of other type of employment in Dillingham, and his attempts to seek other such employment, we find there can be a difference of opinion among reasonable men as to whether appellant did establish by preponderance of the evidence a legitimate and reasonable excuse for failure to comply with the order of child support.

The present action was initiated by the court trustee who, after notifying Johansen of his noncompliance, obtained simultaneously a show cause order and a bench warrant for appellant's arrest. While such methods may have been appropriate at the time the court trustee acted, we note that recent amendments to the Criminal Rules would preclude the use of bench warrant and arrest as a means of bringing child support contempt defendants into court, absent a showing that they have refused to appear and answer.

Civil Rule 90(b), which deals with indirect contempts, provides that upon a proper showing by ex parte motion supported by affidavits, "the court shall *either* order the accused party to show cause at some reasonable time . . . why he should not be punished for the alleged contempt, *or* shall issue a bench warrant for the arrest of such party." (emphasis added.) In determining which of these approaches should be used, Criminal Rule 4 [41] is helpful. Subdivision (1) of Criminal Rule 4(a) now provides in part:

"(a) . . . a warrant for the arrest of the defendant shall issue . . . if the person taking the complaint has reason to believe that the defendant will not appear in response to a summons."

And Rule 4(a)(2) specifies that

"(a) summons instead of a warrant should issue if the person taking the complaint has reason to believe that the defendant will appear in response thereto . . . ."

This specific criminal rule controls the court's authority under Civil Rule 90(b) to use either a show cause order or a bench warrant, and, moreover, makes it clear that Civil Rule 90(b) authorizes the use of a bench warrant for contempt only if there is a reason to believe that the defendant will not appear in response to the show cause order.

The judgment of contempt is reversed and the case is remanded to the superior court for further proceedings not inconsistent with this opinion.

---

1) Did the authorities resort to equity instead of criminal nonsupport because they feared that a criminal jury would acquit Johansen? Should a jury express the community's moral sentiment before the government locks anyone up? Will interposing a jury insulate Johansen from overreaching and prevent oppression? Do you think the legislature intended the statute the court cited to apply to coercive contempt? Compare the Alaska statute to 18 U.S.C. § 3691 in the Appendix.

2) Will the *Johansen* decision hamper the enforcement of plaintiffs' substantive interests? Will the enforcement process become too formal, cumbersome, and protracted?

3) Should courts classify a contempt as either criminal or civil and allow every consequence to flow from that decison? Or should they analyze the purpose and environment of a particular decison and decide what procedure should be followed and what consequences should flow?

4) *Johansen* has attracted no following out of Alaska. Later Alaska decisions reveal some implications of the Alaska court's approach. Gwynn v. Gwynn, 530 P.2d 1311 (Alaska 1975), grew out of a child custody dispute. The judge awarded custody of two children to Robert, their father. The children importuned Joan, their mother, with reports of mistreatment; she sent them money to fly to her home in Anchorage. Charged with contempt for disobeying the custody order, Joan requested a jury trial. The trial judge classified the contempt as civil, denied her request, found her in contempt, and imposed a $200 fine plus a 30-day jail sentence suspended on condition of future obedience. The Alaska Supreme Court reversed for a jury trial. Joan's conduct "constitutes an offense with a possible jail sentence." A judge may not, the court ruled, "summarily convict and imprison for a past violation (as opposed to a continuing violation) of an order of his own creation."

41. The criminal rules are applicable here for a number of reasons. A criminal sanction, incarceration, is a possible outcome of these proceedings. A criminal procedural device, arrest, is being used. See generally discussion at 766-767 supra.

At the hearing "no remedial action to correct her conduct remained available to the court." The suspended feature failed to obviate the sentence's punitive nature and justification. The dissenter made several points. Aside from the contempt, Joan committed "no act which would constitute an independent crime." Joan's defense to contempt was that her conduct lacked a wilful component: unlike Johansen, she did not argue that she was unable to obey. Joan's suspended sentence would be effective "to forestall a repetition of this conduct"; but if his defense were true, jailing Johansen could achieve no support from him.

Continental Insurance v. Bayless & Roberts, Inc., 548 P.2d 398 (Alaska 1976), grew out of a $10,000 contempt fine against a corporation for failure to comply with a discovery order. The Alaska court classified the contempt as criminal and required criminal contempt notice. Because corporations cannot be imprisoned and failure to answer interrogatories is not a crime, the court refused to require a jury trial.

E.L.L. v. State, 572 P.2d 786 (Alaska 1977), resulted from an attempt to coerce testimony. Contemnor argued that the contempt was criminal and that she was entitled to a jury trial. The court replied: "It is clear that the superior court's dominant purpose in remanding petitioner to custody was to force compliance with its order that she testify before the grand jury. It is equally clear that petitioner has the ability to comply, but simply chooses not to do so. Her imprisonment is conditioned solely on her continued refusal to testify, in defiance of that order. Thus, she indeed carries the key to her freedom in her own pocket. Until such time as she agrees to testify or the grand jury is discharged, petitioner may properly be confined for her refusal to comply with the superior court's order." 572 P.2d at 789. Note, Imprisonment for Civil Contempt of Court: The Alaska Constitutional Jury Trial Requirement, 8 U.C.L.A.-Alaska L.Rev. 139, 144–56 (1979), argues that all imprisonment for civil contempt is punitive and that therefore these contemnors are entitled to a jury trial.

Justice Connor asked in his dissent in Gwynn v. Gwynn, 530 P.2d 1311, 1316 (Alaska 1975), whether a jury impeded coercive contempt's goal:

"Coercive force is one of the primary criteria by which law, properly so-called, is distinguished from mere social obligation and rules of prudence not having the force of law. Without the availability of civil contempt, the law as between private parties loses its coercive quality, and for all practical purposes becomes mere voluntarism rather than law. The ability of one party to invoke the remedy of civil contempt is vital to the functioning of the legal order, as well as the effectuation of the particular rights which that party seeks to enforce.

"To be effective, the remedy of civil contempt must be expeditious, relatively certain, and of such a nature that it will, by the exertion of increasingly onerous pressures, compel ultimate compliance with the established right of the other party to require either action, or forebearance from action, by the party who has committed the civil contempt. A requirement of jury trial can, in some instances, lead to a flaunting of civil process by an unreasonable party to a civil action. For example, imposing punishment for past acts is of no avail if no deterrent exists against future contumacy. But civil contempt by its nature looks to the future. Its purpose is to compel future conduct in conformity with a valid judicial order.

"Furthermore, a jury trial not only makes the civil contempt remedy cumbersome, it permits a recalcitrant party to argue and persuade a jury that his conduct was not sufficiently wilful to constitute a crime. Yet the purpose of civil contempt is not to determine whether a person is a criminal, but merely to assure that a person, whether or not he possessed a criminal intent, will comply with a valid order of the court."

5) Family support is crucial to the creditors, and the state may end up supporting the creditors if the debtor fails. Special rules apply to family support and not to other civil debts. The creditor usually has access to all the usual collection devices. Vehko, Enforcement of Family Support Obligations in Virginia, 21 Wm. & Mary L.Rev. 881 (1980). Family support obligations are not discharged in bankruptcy. 11 U.S.C. § 523(a)(5) (Supp. IV 1980). The debtor's exemptions are limited. Contempt is not barred by state prohibitions against debt imprisonment. Inability to comply is a defense, but judges often take as hard-nosed a view of it as the trial judge in *Johansen*.

In Elzey v. Elzey, 291 Md. 369, 435 A.2d 445 (1981), the 75-year old defendant had stopped $125.00 a week alimony payments to his ex-wife after he retired from his plumbing business. The trial judge held him in contempt and sentenced him to serve 90 days or until he "purged himself by paying the arrearage." 435 A.2d at 446. He served 90 days. Later that year defendant again was held in contempt; his ex-wife levied on his pickup truck and mobile home and had them sold. Two years later, at a third hearing, defendant testified that he was in poor health, lived in his present wife's home, and received social security benefits which could not discharge his alimony obligation. The circuit court found that because defendant's "financial inability resulted from his own decision to retire," 435 A.2d at 448, he was able to pay and could be held in contempt. Defendant was sentenced to 120 days or until he paid back support payments. The appellate court ended the trial judge's sport; it reversed, saying that there was no finding of defendant's bad faith in retiring or of his ability to continue to pay $125.00 a week to his ex-wife. Rather, the finding of financial inability to pay made the imprisonment improper.

6) Professor David Chambers analyzed the Michigan Friend of the Court system which resembles the Alaska system applied in *Johansen*. He learned that if the enforcement system is tough, organized, visible, and willing to jail slow payers, then a significant amount of family support will be collected. D. Chambers, Making Fathers Pay (1979); Chambers, Men Who Know They Are Watched: Some Benefits and Costs of Jailing for Nonpayment of Support, 75 Mich.L.Rev. 900 (1977). In individual cases, however, jail is costly. People in jail earn nothing. Employers may discharge them, and they may lose the opportunity to earn anything once out.

Chambers's empirical study about imprisonment to coerce payment of family support teaches us quite a bit about coercive contempt generally. Credible threats of coercive measures cause people to cooperate. Warnings alone do not change conduct unless real measures are possible. Many of the fathers who went to jail paid more after they got out. Making Fathers Pay at 101. Few groups "pay as well as they are able without threat," and "there are few groups so unable to pay that the threat of jail does not produce substantial additional payments." Making Fathers Pay 118–19. Witness the effect of the "deferred" sentence on Johansen who at the time of trial "has cleared no more than $700 in any year."

Chambers, on apparent "humanitarian" grounds, shrinks back from liberal jailing to collect family support; he suggests wage assignments/garnishments. Chambers, 75 Mich.L.Rev. at 933–36. Professor Mnookin disagrees. Mnookin, Review: Using Jail for Child Support Enforcements, 48 U.Chi.L.Rev. 338 (1981). "[M]aking fathers pay is a nasty but often necessary task . . . . Bentham and Hobbes may be right that the systematic application of force, and the threat to use it, can change conduct for the better." Mnookin, 48 U.Chi.L.Rev. at 369, 370.

7) Would a contemnor who interposes the defense of inability to comply with a family support order be entitled to an appointed attorney? The Michigan Supreme Court rejected assigned counsel in Sword v. Sword, 399 Mich. 367, 249 N.W.2d 88 (1976). The contemnor is jailed to coerce and has the keys in his pocket. The government must strive to obtain the support; assigned lawyers would run up the cost and delay the proceedings. See also Jolly v. Wright, 300 N.C. 83, 265 S.E.2d 135 (1980). However, jail is harsh, and a lawyer may assist the factfinder in deciding the inability issue correctly. Other decisions find a right to counsel. Mastin v. Fellerhoff, 526 F.Supp. 969 (S.D. Ohio 1981); McNabb v. Osmundson, 315 N.W.2d 9 (Iowa 1982). Should a civil characterization be decisive where coercion may deprive contemnor of liberty? See Note, The Indigent Defendant's Right to Court-Appointed Counsel in Civil Contempt Proceedings for Nonpayment of Child Support, 50 U.Chi.L.Rev. 326 (1983); Note, Due Process in the Civil Nonsupport Proceeding: The Right to Counsel and Alternatives to Incarceration, 61 Tex.L.Rev. 291 (1982).

UNITED STATES v. WILSON

421 U.S. 309, 95 S.Ct. 1802, 44 L.Ed.2d 186 (1975).

Chief Justice BURGER delivered the opinion of the Court.

We granted certiorari to decide whether a district court may impose summary contempt punishment under Fed.Rule Crim.Proc. 42(a) when a witness who has been granted immunity, refuses on Fifth Amendment grounds to testify. The Court of Appeals held that in such circumstances a judge cannot dispose of the contempt summarily, but must proceed under Rule 42(b), which calls for disposition only after notice and hearing, and "a reasonable time for the preparation of the defense."

Respondents Wilson and Bryan, along with one Robert Anderson, were charged in separate indictments with separate bank robberies. Respondent Wilson, and Anderson, were charged with armed robbery of a bank in Tuxedo, N.Y. Respondent Bryan, and Anderson, were charged with armed robbery of a bank in Mount Ivy, N.Y. Prior to Anderson's trial both respondents pleaded guilty to charges against them, but neither was immediately given a final sentence. Sentencing of Wilson was deferred, and, pending a presentence report, Bryan was given a provisional 25-year sentence, as required by 18 U.S.C. § 4208(b), (c).

At Anderson's trial for the two robberies, respondents were summoned as witnesses for the prosecution. When questioned, however, each refused to testify, contending that his answers might incriminate him. The judge then granted them immunity, 18 U.S.C. §§ 6002–6003, and, relying on Goldberg v. United States, 472 F.2d 513 (CA2 1973), ordered them to answer forthwith. He informed them that as long as they did not lie under oath they could not be prosecuted by reason of any testimony, but that if they continued to refuse to answer he would hold them in contempt. Respondents nevertheless persisted in their refusals, and the judge summarily held them in contempt. . . .

Both respondents were then sentenced to six months' imprisonment, consecutive to any sentences imposed for the bank robberies. The judge made it clear that he would consider reducing the contempt sentences, or eliminating them completely, if respondents decided to testify. When counsel pointed out that a presentence study was being prepared on Bryan the judge responded: "I am going to impose the maximum . . . with the deliberate intention of revising that sentence to what might be appropriate in light of the very study that is going to be made."

The trial proceeded, but without Bryan's testimony the evidence against Anderson on the Mount Ivy robbery was such that at the end of the Government's case the judge granted Anderson's motion for acquittal. The jury was unable to reach a verdict on the Tuxedo robbery. At a later trial Anderson was convicted of that robbery.

Respondents appealed their contempt convictions. The Court of Appeals rejected the claim that their Fifth Amendment rights would have been violated by compelling them to testify after they had been granted immunity, but it accepted their contention that use of the summary contempt power was improper, and it remanded for proceedings under Rule 42(b). 488 F.2d 1231 (CA2 1973). The court reasoned that "[i]f . . . counsel had been given 'a reasonable time for the preparation of the defense,' Fed.R.Crim.P. Rule 42(b), she might have marshalled and presented facts in mitigation of the charge."

In requiring Rule 42(b) disposition the Court of Appeals considered itself bound by its own previous decisions, and by this Court's decision in Harris v. United States, 382 U.S. 162 (1965). In a previous case the Court of Appeals had held:

"Summary disposition is thus available only when immediate punishment is necessary to put an end to acts disrupting the proceedings, such as threats to the judge, disturbances in the courtroom or insolence before the court. It is not a remedy to be used in a case like this where the contempt consists of no more than orderly refusal in the absence of the jury to answer a question on Fifth Amendment grounds . . . ." United States v. Pace, 371 F.2d 810, 811 (CA2 1967).

In another case the Court of Appeals had interpreted the language of our *Harris* decision to require that "[a]bsent . . . disruptive conduct, which affronts the dignity for the court, a hearing pursuant to Rule 42(b) is required to explore possible exculpatory or mitigating circumstances." United States v. Marra, 482 F.2d 1196, 1200 (CA2 1973). In the Court of Appeals' view only a disorderly or obstreperous interference with court proceedings provides an occasion for use of the summary contempt power. . . .

Respondents' refusal to answer, although not delivered disrespectfully, plainly falls within the express language of Rule 42(a), and constitute contemptuous conduct. Rule 42(a) was never intended to be limited to situations where a witness uses scurrilous language, or threatens or creates overt physical disorder and thereby disrupts a trial. All that is necessary is that the judge certify that he "saw or heard the conduct constituting the contempt and that it was committed in the actual presence of the court." Respondents do not contest that these requirements are met here. Indeed, here each refusal was in the context of a face-to-face encounter between the judge and respondents. See Illinois v. Allen, 397 U.S. 337 (1970); Cooke v. United States, 267 U.S. 517 (1925).

The refusals were contemptuous of judicial authority because they were intentional obstructions [7] of court proceedings that literally disrupted the progress of the trial and hence the orderly administration of justice. Yates v. United States, 227 F.2d 844 (CA9 1955). Respondents' contumacious silence, after a valid grant of immunity followed by an explicit, unambiguous order to testify, impeded the due course of Anderson's trial perhaps more so than violent conduct in the courtroom. Violent disruptions can be cured swiftly by bodily removing the offender from the courtroom, or by physical restraints, Illinois v. Allen, supra; see Ex parte Terry, 128 U.S. 289 (1888), and the trial may proceed. But as this case demonstrates, a contumacious refusal to answer not only frustrates the inquiry but can destroy a prosecution. Here it was a prosecution; the same kind of contumacious conduct could, in another setting, destroy a defendant's ability to establish a case.

The face-to-face refusal to comply with the court's order itself constituted an affront to the court, and when that kind of refusal disrupts and frustrates an ongoing proceeding, as it did here, summary contempt must be available to vindicate the authority of the court as well as to provide the recalcitrant witness with some incentive to testify. In re Chiles, 22 Wall. 157, 168 (1875). Whether such incentive is necessary in a particular case is a matter the Rule wisely leaves to the discretion of the trial court.[9]

7. The trial judge explained to respondents the protection accorded by the grant of immunity and that if they continued in their refusals he would hold them in contempt. He also offered them an opportunity to speak in their own behalf. Groppi v. Leslie, 404 U.S. 496, 501 (1972). Moreover, the judge made it clear that he would consider reducing the sentences if respondents did testify. In view of this their continued refusals to testify can only be termed intentional.

9. In Shillitani v. United States, 384 U.S. 364, 371 n. 9 (1966), we said:

"[T]he trial judge [should] first consider the feasibility of coercing testimony through the imposition of civil contempt. The judge should resort to criminal sanctions only after he determines, for good reason, that the civil remedy would be inappropriate."

Here, of course, that admonition carries little weight because at the time they acted contemptuously both respondents were incarcerated due to their own guilty pleas. Under the circumstances here the threat of immediate confinement for civil contempt would have provided little incentive for them to testify. Contrast, Anglin v. Johnston, 504 F.2d 1165 (CA7 1974), cert. denied, 420 U.S. 962 (1975). Nevertheless, the careful trial judge made it clear to respondents that if they relented and obeyed his order he would

Our conclusion that summary contempt is available under the circumstances here is supported by the fact that Rule 42 has consistently been recognized to be no more than a restatement of the law existing when the Rule was adopted, Bloom v. Illinois; Notes of the Advisory Committee on Rule 42(a), 18 U.S.C.App. p. 4513; Cooke v. United States, 267 U.S. 517 (1925), and the law at that time allowed summary punishment for refusals to testify, Hale v. Henkel, 201 U.S. 43 (1906). . . .

The Court of Appeals considered itself bound by language in Harris v. United States, 382 U.S. 162 (1965), to hold Rule 42(a) inapplicable to the facts here. The crucial difference between the cases, however, is that *Harris* did not deal with a refusal to testify which obstructed an ongoing trial. In *Harris* a witness before a grand jury had been granted immunity, and nevertheless refused to answer certain questions. The witness was then brought before a District Judge and asked the same questions again. When he still refused to answer, the court summarily held him in contempt. We held in that case that summary contempt was inappropriate because there was no compelling reason for an immediate remedy.

A grand jury ordinarily deals with many inquiries and cases at one time, and it can rather easily suspend action on any one, and turn to another while proceedings under Rule 42(b) are completed. We noted in *Harris* that "swiftness was not a prerequisite of justice . . . . Delay necessary for a hearing would not imperil the grand jury proceedings." 382 U.S., at 164. Trial courts, on the contrary, cannot be expected to dart from case to case on their calendars any time a witness who has been granted immunity decides not to answer questions. In a trial, the court, the parties, witnesses, and jurors are assembled in the expectation that it will proceed as scheduled. Here the District Judge pointed out this problem when defense counsel asked for a continuance; he said: "I think we cannot delay this trial. I cannot delay it. I have many other matters that are equally important to the people concerned in those cases which are following." Delay under Rule 42(b) may be substantial, and all essential participants in the trial may no longer be readily available when a trial reconvenes. In *Harris* this Court recognized these problems in noting that summary punishment may be necessary where a "refusal [is] . . . an open, serious threat to orderly procedure." 382 U.S., at 165. A refusal to testify during a trial may be such an open, serious threat, and here it plainly constituted a literal "breakdown" in the prosecution's case.

In an ongoing trial, with the judge, jurors, counsel, and witnesses all waiting, Rule 42(a) provides an appropriate remedial tool to discourage witnesses from contumacious refusals to comply with lawful orders essential to prevent a breakdown of the proceedings. Where time is not of the essence, however, the provisions of Rule 42(b) may be more appropriate to deal with contemptuous conduct. We adhere to the principle that only " '[t]he least possible power adequate to the end proposed' " should be used in contempt cases. Anderson v. Dunn, 6 Wheat. 204, 231 (1821). . . . As with all power, the authority under Rule 42(a) to punish summarily can be abused; the courts of appeals, however, can deal with abuses of discretion without restrict-

consider reducing their sentences; and he also explained that he would consider other factors in deciding whether to reduce the sentences.

ing the Rule in contradiction of its express terms, and without unduly limiting the power of the trial judge to act swiftly and firmly to prevent contumacious conduct from disrupting the orderly progress of a criminal trial.

Justice BLACKMUN, with whom Justice REHNQUIST joins, concurring.

In Brown v. United States, 359 U.S. 41 (1959), the petitioner had refused, on Fifth Amendment grounds, to answer questions put to him by a federal grand jury. He thereafter was immunized by the District Judge but, on returning to the grand jury room, persisted in his refusal to answer questions. He again was taken before the District Judge, who repeated the grand jury's questions and ordered the petitioner to answer. He again refused. The court then, pursuant to Fed.Rule Crim.Proc. 42(a), adjudged him guilty of criminal contempt. This Court, by a 5–4 vote, sustained the judgment, and expressly approved the use of summary proceedings; it did so on the ground that the refusal to answer before the District Judge was a contempt "committed in the actual presence of the court," within the meaning of Rule 42(a).

Less than seven years later, in Harris v. United States, 382 U.S. 162 (1965), the Court, with two new Justices, was confronted with a factual situation identical in all relevant respects to that in *Brown*. In *Harris*, however, the Court, again by a 5–4 vote, concluded that the witness' refusal to answer the questions before the District Judge was not a contempt "committed in the actual presence of the court." It reasoned:

"The real contempt, if such there was, was contempt before the grand jury—the refusal to answer to it when directed by the court. Swearing the witness and repeating the questions before the judge was an effort to have the refusal to testify 'committed in the actual presence of the court' for the purposes of Rule 42(a). It served no other purpose, for the witness had been adamant and had made his position known. The appearance before the District Court was not a new and different proceeding, unrelated to the other. It was ancillary to the grand jury hearing and designed as an aid to it."

The Court then expressly overruled *Brown*.

I was not on the Court when *Brown* and *Harris* were decided. Had I been, I would have joined the Court in *Brown* and the dissenters in *Harris*. Although I join the Court's opinion today, I write separately to express my conviction that *Harris*, at the most, now stands for nothing more than the proposition that a witness' refusal to answer grand jury questions is not conduct "in the actual presence of the court," even when the questions are restated by the district judge and the witness persists in his refusal to answer.[1]

Summary contempt, especially summary criminal contempt, as the Court indicates, is not a power lightly to be exercised.[2] Nevertheless, summary criminal contempt is a necessary and legitimate part of a court's arsenal of

1. The Solicitor General has invited the Court in this case to overrule *Harris*. Since the refusal to testify, involved here, occurred during the course of a trial rather than before a grand jury, I agree with the Court's tacit conclusion to save the question of overruling *Harris* for another day.

2. Although the use of civil contempt, as opposed to the more drastic criminal contempt, is usually to be preferred as a remedy, I am aware of no requirement that the less drastic sanction must be employed in all cases. Indeed, despite the fact that respondents were already incarcerated for substantive criminal offenses,

weapons to prevent obstruction, violent or otherwise, of its proceedings. It is not seriously disputed that a refusal to testify is punishable as a criminal contempt. So long as this Court holds, as it has, that the summary procedure of Rule 42(a) satisfies the requirements of due process, the Rule should be read to mean precisely what it says.

Justice BRENNAN, with whom Justice DOUGLAS and Justice MARSHALL join, dissenting.

The question for decision in this case is one of procedure: is the criminal contempt of nonviolently and respectfully refusing to testify at a criminal trial punishable summarily by the trial judge pursuant to Fed.Rule Crim.Proc. 42(a), or must the trial judge prosecute the contempt on notice pursuant to Rule 42(b), allowing a reasonable time for the preparation of the defense? A trial judge in the District Court for the Southern District of New York summarily punished respondents under subdivision (a) of Rule 42 for refusing to testify at a trial. The Court of Appeals for the Second Circuit reversed and remanded on the ground that Harris v. United States, 382 U.S. 162 (1965), and the Court of Appeals' own prior decision in United States v. Marra, 482 F.2d 1196 (1973), which had relied upon *Harris*, compelled the conclusion that the proper course was to prosecute on notice under subdivision (b) of the Rule. 488 F.2d 1231 (1973). I would affirm the judgment of the Court of Appeals. . . .

The Court today declines the Government's invitation to overrule Harris v. United States, supra, and in that circumstance *Harris* clearly compels affirmance of the judgment of the Court of Appeals. *Harris* interpreted subdivision (a) of Rule 42 as having a narrowly limited scope and expressly excluded its application to a nonviolent, respectful refusal to answer questions on the ground of self-incrimination. The Court emphasized that subdivision (a) reached a narrow category of situations and "was reserved 'for exceptional circumstances' . . . such as acts threatening the judge or disrupting a hearing or obstructing court proceedings." Such acts, the Court held, are not present in the case of a nonviolent, respectful refusal to answer questions on the ground of self-incrimination because in such a case "the dignity of the court was not being affronted: no disturbance had to be quelled; no insolent tactics had to be stopped."

The Court stated its rationale for the narrow interpretation of subdivision (a) as follows:

"We reach that conclusion in light of 'the concern long demonstrated by both Congress and this Court over the possible abuse of the contempt power' . . . and in light of the wording of the Rule. Summary contempt is for 'misbehavior' . . . in the 'actual presence of the court.' Then speedy punishment may be necessary in order to achieve 'summary vindication of the court's dignity and authority.' "

it appears to be clear that service of their sentences could have been interrupted to compel them to serve an intervening sentence for contempt. See, e. g., United States v. Liddy, 166 U.S.App.D.C. 289, 510 F.2d 669 (1974), cert. denied, 420 U.S. 980 (1975). . . .

The Court continued:

"Summary procedure, to use the words of Chief Justice Taft, was designed to fill 'the need for immediate penal vindication of the dignity of the court . . . ..' We start from the premise long ago stated in Anderson v. Dunn, 6 Wheat. 204, 231, that the limits of the power to punish for contempt are '[t]he least possible power adequate to the end proposed.' In the instant case, the dignity of the court was not being affronted: no disturbance had to be quelled; no insolent tactics had to be stopped. The contempt here committed was far outside the narrow category envisioned by Rule 42(a)."

Only last Term, the Court again emphasized that summary punishment for contempt " 'always and rightly, is regarded with disfavor' " in light of the "heightened potential for abuse posed by the contempt power," Taylor v. Hayes, 418 U.S. 488, 498, 500 (1974), and is to be resorted to only when necessary for " 'immediate penal vindication of the dignity of the court.' "

I see no escape from the application of *Harris* to this case based on the difference that respondents were witnesses at an ongoing trial while the witness in *Harris* was a grand jury witness, brought before the judge and asked the same questions he had not answered before the grand jury. The Court argues that while the delay necessitated by Rule 42(b) procedures would be unlikely seriously to disrupt grand jury proceedings it would have substantial disruptive effects in a trial. I doubt that compliance with Rule 42(b) procedures necessarily would have substantial disruptive effects in a trial [7] but in any event those effects are not the kind of obstruction of court proceedings, *Harris*, supra, at 164, that justify summary punishment under subdivision (a). For *Harris* limits application of that subdivision to conduct in the presence of the judge "where immediate corrective steps are needed to restore order and maintain the dignity and authority of the court." Johnson v. Mississippi, 403 U.S. 212, 214 (1971).[8] In the case of respondents' nonviolent, respectful refusal to answer questions on the ground of self-incrimination, "the dignity

7. In United States v. Marra, 482 F.2d 1196 (CA2 1973), the Court of Appeals rejected that argument, stating:

"In an uncomplicated case of the present type, where the facts are simple and a brief consultation between the witness and his retained or assigned counsel should be sufficient to enable him to prepare for a Rule 42(b) hearing, there appears to be no sound reason why the hearing could not be held within a day or two of the witness' refusal to obey the court's order. Since the hearing would in all likelihood require no more than an hour or two of the court's time, trial of the criminal case could be suspended with a minimum disruption to the judicial process. Such a procedure, furthermore, lessens the risk that the witness' contumacy is the result of fright, confusion, or misunderstanding. Indeed, with the advice of counsel, or faced with imposition of a criminal sentence, he may decide to cooperate." . . .

The Court of Appeals said of the situation in the instant case:

"If . . . counsel had been given 'a reasonable time for the preparation of the defense,' Fed.R.Crim.P. 42(b), she might have marshalled and presented facts in mitigation of the charge. Significantly, the record reveals the possibility of a psychiatric defense, at least for Wilson . . . .

"Finally, because of the posture of the case, the record is silent on other facts which may well exist in defense or mitigation of the charge against both appellants, and which could be properly developed at a plenary hearing."

The trial judge has broad discretion to specify the time for preparation of a defense to a charge of criminal contempt. See Nilva v. United States, 352 U.S. 385, 395 (1957).

8. "[Rule 42(b)] is controlling in any case of contempt occurring outside the

of the court was not being affronted," *Harris*, supra at 165, and the absence of that crucial element in respondents' refusal to answer questions foreclosed application of subdivision (a) by the trial judge.

---

1) The Court assumes a continuum of contempt from more lenient civil to more drastic criminal. Is this assumption accurate?

2) The Court also assumes that the judge's order was criminal contempt. In Shillitani v. United States, 384 U.S. 364, 369–370 (1966), however, the Court discussed a similar order: "Despite the fact that Shillitani and Pappadio were ordered imprisoned for a definite term, their sentences were clearly intended to operate in a prospective manner—to coerce, rather than punish. As such, they relate to civil contempt. While any imprisonment, of course, has punitive and deterrent effects, it must be viewed as remedial if the court conditions release upon the contemnor's willingness to testify." Professor Kuhns says the order in *Wilson* was not really coercive. The Summary Contempt Power: A Critique and a New Perspective, 88 Yale L.J. 39, 91–92 n. 316 (1978). How would you have advised Wilson right after the judge "made it clear that he would consider reducing the contempt sentences, or eliminating them completely, if [Wilson] decided to testify?" What would the judge have said if he had been asked, "Will you eliminate the sentence if they testify"?

3) Two barriers may have interfered with the coercive impact of imprisonment. First, Bryan and Wilson were about to begin long criminal sentences, and the judge could only coerce them for the duration of Anderson's trial. The trial judge might have suspended the federal criminal sentences while imprisoning Wilson and Bryan to coerce their testimony. Bruno v. Greenlee, 569 F.2d 775 (3d Cir. 1978); United States v. Liddy, 510 F.2d 669 (D.C.Cir.1974) (en banc), certiorari denied 420 U.S. 980 (1975). Why didn't he?

Second, coercion could last only as long as the criminal trial. A variation on the criminal/coercive remedy we saw above in Laing v. Commonwealth at p. 1028 has been suggested. Professor Kuhns calls it "conditional summary criminal contempt." 88 Yale L.J. at 118. A Note calls it a "hybrid civil-criminal form of sanction." Note, Coercive Contempt and the Federal Grand Jury, 79 Colum.L.Rev. 735, 772 (1979). The judge would tell the reticent witness, "You have one day to testify; and if you refuse, I'll sentence you to six months." Or "I sentence you to six months; but if you testify in this trial, I'll suspend the balance." This concentrates coercion in the period before the definite term begins, or in the second example, before the trial ends. Does it also increase confusion? When, if ever, would criminal procedure be necessary? Should the judge, at a minimum, have given contemnors overnight to think about testifying?

4) If Wilson's and Bryan's contempt is really coercive, does Rule 42 apply? Is Rule 42 designed for an in-court cut-up instead of a person who disobeys an injunction or a reticent witness? Consider the difference between Rules 42(a) and (b). Does a geographical test—whether contemnor's

actual presence of the court, but it applies too to most cases of contempt in the court's presence." 3 C. Wright, Federal Practice and Procedure 171–172 (1969).

conduct occurred in or out of the judge's presence—lead to proper analysis of how little or much procedure to accord? Professor Dobbs offers another test: "A better approach would not ask whether the contempt is direct, but whether there is any factual dispute that would require a hearing and whether, even in the absence of such a dispute, there is a demonstrated need for the use of summary contempt powers." Dobbs, Contempt of Court: A Survey, 56 Cornell L.Rev. 183, 229 (1971). Do you agree?

5) Has the Court in *Wilson* emphasized the respect policy and lost sight of other goals? Does the Court equate disobedience with disruption? Has the Court started punishing wrongdoers and stopped seeking the testimony?

6) Do we need a civil counterpart to Criminal Rule 42 to define compensatory and coercive contempt and to outline the procedure for each. The author of the Columbia Note suggests amendments to § 1826 providing for an adequate time to prepare through notice, a hearing, appointed counsel, and for other protections. 79 Colum.L.Rev. at 757-63.

Having enjoined without a jury, in part because plaintiff's right is too important to be frustrated by a jury, is it fair to the plaintiff for the judge to summon a jury to enforce the order? The inadequacy prerequisite prevented a jury from blunting the substantive law at trial. Will a jury at the enforcement stage reintroduce "jury equity" and nullify or dilute the substantive law at a later stage? Compare O. Fiss, The Civil Rights Injunction 53–54 (1978), with Rendleman, The Inadequate Remedy at Law Prerequisite for an Injunction, 33 U.Fla.L.Rev. 346, 353–56 (1981). See Note 1 after Bloom v. Illinois, p. 955; Note, Due Process in Civil Contempt Proceedings: A Comparison With Juvenile and Mental Incompetency Requirements, 44 Fordham L.Rev. 1029, 1038 (1976).

Coercive contempt is part of a process of negotiation and enforcement to obtain plaintiff's substantive rights. No clear breaks, no sharp corners tell an observer where enjoining ends and coercive enforcement begins. The process of enforcement involves negotiation and compromise. Will the additional formality of jury procedure and the relative inflexibility of a jury verdict hamper essential give and take? Will a jury introduce a potential for delay into a process that importunes for speed? Injunctive defendants, such as striking public employees, often possess an abiding interest in delay. Does the counter interest in prompt enforcement militate against allowing a defendant to continue to disobey while a jury is impanelled and sworn?

7) The enforcement process involves negotiation. Arguably *Wilson* attenuates the procedure in that process too much. Procedure should bring the parties face to face and encourage them to exchange information and concessions. The judge's role is crucial. He should remain impartial, facilitate the negotiation, and supply information about power. Kuhns, The Summary Contempt Power: A Critique and a New Perspective, 88 Yale L.J. 39, 82–83, 102–03 n.384 (1978); Leff, Injury, Ignorance and Spite—The Dynamics of Coercive Collection, 80 Yale L.J. 1, 43–44 (1970). The process should draw things out as much as is compatible with the plaintiff's interest to encourage negotiation. This will also reduce the appearance of unfairness, enhance the process's legitimacy, and allow everybody to cool off. The procedure should allow trips from the deposition or grand jury to the judge. The judge should admonish, warn, and let contemnor consult with counsel.

This will impress contemnor with the seriousness of the enterprise and avoid coercion based on misunderstanding. On-the-spot contempt as in *Wilson* prevents this process from occurring.

Power becomes explicit as the coercive process unfolds. Contemnor may persist in the face of coercion and deprive the plaintiff of substantive rights or delay to extract concessions. The judge may deprive contemnor of liberty or resources. If contemnor is an average person who prefers to stay at home, the untoward consequences of persistence will emerge. Many coercive contempts appear to be all or nothing. Neither statistical compromise, nor a reasonable amount between offer and counteroffer appears on the surface. Moreover, neither party trusts the other, and there may be no continuing relationships. The ritual of decision, however, should let the parties explain, explore alternatives, and get a feeling for the other side to learn whether their goals are really mutually exclusive. Chapter 4 of W. Fisher and M. Ury's Getting to Yes (1981) is entitled "Invent Options for Mutual Gain."

In the end, the judge may simply tell contemnor "Stubbornness will hurt you more than it will achieve for you." Contemnor may need to rationalize surrender. The role of contemnor's attorney alters when the judge says something like "Come back tomorrow and tell your client to bring her toothbrush." After zealously championing the client's cause, the attorney often plays a significant role in achieving compliance.

8) Negotiation takes time. Procedural safeguards sometimes provide that time. Even with safeguards and time, the process of coercion may fail. We will shift the scene back to Mississippi when James Meredith was trying to integrate Ole Miss to illustrate how negotiation continues between the contemnors and their attorneys. See United States v. Barnett, p. 909. Charles Clark and J. P. Coleman represented several Ole Miss trustee-defendants. Barnett had been telling the trustees that he had a plan, and the board had appointed him registrar. The Circuit Court sat en banc and threatened to hold the trustees in contempt. F. Read and L. McGough pick up the story as follows:

"Prior to the trip to New Orleans and while in New Orleans, Clark pleaded with the board to recognize that Governor Barnett had no plan but defiance. They could continue to refuse to obey the Court and face jail and confiscatory fines and still not block Meredith's enrollment. Clark argued,

'Just think of the chancellor who orders a man to convey real property. They're not going to let a man refuse to sign the deed and keep the land from being conveyed. They're going to appoint the Clerk of Court as a scrivener and he's going to write the deed himself and you've all seen that threatened and done. ('Well, yes we have.') Well, they're going to appoint the Clerk of Court or somebody similar as the Registrar of the University of Mississippi and write James Meredith into the University as a student and you'll be pining away in the cell wishing you had your property back.'

But Clark's logic did not remove the pressure from home. Charles Fair, the chairman of the board, remembers that while the board was in New Orleans, state legislators who had traveled to the Ole Miss campus sent a telegram to the board asking, 'Can we begin to dig trenches and build barricades?'

"The board finally faced reality on September 24, in that Fifth Circuit courtroom in New Orleans. Chief Judge Tuttle, addressing the Mississippi lawyers, emphasized that the time for the board to make its position definite could be postponed no longer:

'[Y]ou'd better be prepared before this hearing adjourns to tell this Court whether the clients that you represent, and who are all in court, and who, I express the hope, will not leave the court until the hearing is finally disposed of, will comply with any order touching on the admission of this man in the University, if such order is reasserted and made perfectly plain as a result of this hearing. I don't ask you to state that now, but before the Court adjourns I expressly state the hope that each of you will be prepared to state for your clients whether you will comply with any order the Court makes.'

Judge Brown was even more direct: 'Are the clients which you represent prepared not to obey [the Court's] order?' Judge Gewin continued the pressure: 'Are the men you represent ready to perform the mandates of the decree of this Court's order?' Judge Hutcheson joined the chorus: 'Counsel, excuse me. How can we avoid a finding that the Board had disobeyed our order? How can we avoid it? Suppose we wanted to avoid it. We could not, like I say, wash our hands of it.' Chief Judge Tuttle icily summed up: 'We haven't fixed it, but I will state to you that I think we have all agreed that, thus far, before this hearing is over we will get a commitment from every member of the Board that is present in the court as to whether he will comply with the order, if the order is made firm and definite on this matter.'

"After seeing in open court that the judges on the Fifth Circuit were on the brink of issuing contempt citations, the board members, sick at heart but still desiring above all to preserve the university, capitulated. Former Governor Coleman requested a short delay in the hearing; he realized he had to inform his clients that further resistance was impossible and that they had to agree to obey the Court. A twenty-minute recess was ordered by Chief Judge Tuttle and counsel were told to return with an answer from each trustee as to whether he was willing to comply with court orders. After the recess the members of the board returned and Chief Judge Tuttle informed them that the Court had concluded that they had 'willfully and intentionally violated the Court's order.' Judge Tuttle then said the Court would defer finding them guilty of contempt until they had a chance to report whether they now would obey the injunction. Ashen-faced, the members of the board announced that they were now willing to comply with all court orders.

"The Court then issued an order to the board to revoke the action of September 4, relieving university officials from their normal duties and placing authority to admit Meredith in the hands of the trustees. It ordered the board to nullify the action taken September 20 investing the Governor with the board's enrollment power, to prepare notification to all officials of the state that orders of the Court were to be fulfilled, and to instruct appropriate university officials to register Meredith and to permit his continued attendance. The Court also ordered the registrar of Ole Miss, the unfortunate Mr. Ellis, to be available at Jackson from 1 to 4 p.m. on September 25, at the offices of the board of trustees for the purpose of registering Meredith. Lastly, the Court ordered that it be notified by 4 p.m. on September 25, whether the order that Meredith be enrolled at the board of trustees' office in Jackson had been effectuated. The board, belatedly, had displayed courage and good sense." Let Them Be Judged 231–32 (1978). (Copyright 1978 F. Read and L. McGough).

J. Bass describes what apparently occurred during the twenty minute recess: "J. P. Coleman and Charles Clark privately explained the facts of life to the board members, who already were aware that Barnett had no plan. The board listened closely and finally one of them asked the lawyers, 'Are you telling me those judges can take my property and that boy will still get in Ole Miss?' When assured this was the case, he continued, 'And you're saying they can put me in jail and that boy will still get in?' As the facts sank in, he told his fellow board members, 'Shee-it! What are we here talking about?' Another board member, who had said to Barnett he would stick with him 'till hell freezes over,' subsequently told him, 'Well, governor, it froze over in a hurry.' " Unlikely Heroes 185. As Judge Wisdom, dissenting from the decision not to prosecute Barnett for contempt, said, "the University's Board of Trustees, with dignity and grace, agreed in open court to accept Meredith at the University," p. 935. Did the trustees' attorneys fulfill their duty to represent their clients zealously within the boundaries of the law?

The Ole Miss denouement reveals the dynamics of the attorney-contemnor relationship and the way procedural safeguards might facilitate compliance. It also introduces the next section of this chapter: What happens when coercive techniques fail? How can judges and plaintiffs prevent failure? Barnett, feeling betrayed, stood alone. Should the court have realized that negotiation was over and that defiance would lead to crisis? Could it have ordered the clerk of court to register Meredith? See Rule 70 in the Appendix; C. Huuston, The Enforcement of Decrees in Equity 15–16 (1915). Barnett physically blocked the door. Meredith arrived, accompanied by John Doar and Chief Marshall James McShane. "Now which one of you is James Meredith," Barnett said before turning Meredith and his escorts away.

Bass continues: "Barnett also met with John Satterfield, a prominent Mississippi lawyer, immediate past president of the American Bar Association, and an active promoter for the Citizens Councils in their early days of organizing. Satterfield would tell the Fifth Circuit, 'I discussed with the Governor the Order to Show Cause on Contempt, advised him it was void, the Court was without jurisdiction, there is no requirement to appear, and this Court has absolutely no power in the proceedings which are now before the Court, yes, sir.' " Unlikely Heroes 187. Contrast this advice with the advice the trustees received.

Coercive contempt is negotiation through threats, promises, and measures. Did the federal government fail to demonstrate to Barnett that it meant business? Did it neglect to search for a mutually acceptable way for Barnett to save face? Did it subordinate James Meredith's constitutional rights to avoiding the appearance of "heavy-handedness"? What did this do for the government's credibility as a negotiator with future defendants? Attorney General Robert Kennedy negotiated with Governor Barnett until the Ole Miss crisis ended. "Nowhere was this patience, this commitment to negotiation, this idea that reasonable men can work things out, this assumption that confrontation should always be avoided and that mediation rather than coercion is the proper way to achieve social change—nowhere were these attitudes more evident than in Robert Kennedy's incessant negotiations with Governor Ross Barnett of Mississippi in September 1962, when the Kennedys sought assurances from Barnett that he would protect James Meredith . . . ." V. Navasky, Kennedy Justice 164–65 (1977).

Chapter 4 of *Kennedy Justice* contains long excerpts from the transcripts of the conversations between Kennedy and Barnett. The issue between them was whether Barnett would keep order. Why should the Executive negotiate with a defendant to achieve something already mandated by a court order? Should the plaintiff let a defendant posture publicly while negotiating privately? Should Kennedy have realized that Barnett's primary reference group was the white South, that compromise was futile, and that concrete measures were imperative? Should the court have used formal procedure to bring the negotiation between the federal government and Barnett into the courtroom (and anterooms)?

9) Are there times when procedure, negotiation, and coercion are futile to solve the problem at hand? Beginning coercion or negotiation does not always ensure success. The contemnor may be self-disciplined and rational. The judge may communicate the threat. The contemnor may hear and appreciate the threat, be able to perform the desired act, and understand the judge's conviction that the threat will be carried out. Contemnor may prefer the alternatives over obedience. He may doubt the judge's resolve. The contemnor may act firm, and the plaintiff may back down. So the judge and plaintiff may have to play out a war of nerves, the topic of the section that follows. How can the judge and plaintiff tell whether coercion will fail? When should the judge subordinate his credibility, the plaintiff's substantive rights, and public respect for courts?

V. Ending Coercive Enforcement: Cassandra and Penelope

This section examines two problems. Assume first that the judge finds that contemnor is able to comply, but that the judge's factual assumptions are incorrect. What happens when the judge errs in finding the facts that lead to coercive imprisonment? Will contemnor be imprisoned forever to coerce him to do something that, in fact, is not within his power? Second, assume that the judge undertakes to coerce a contemnor who will not be coerced. How does the system handle a contemnor who refuses to cooperate under pressure? Will contemnor be imprisoned forever to coerce him to do something he, in fact, will never do?

Imprisonment is the most severe form of coercion. The judge's options are to imprison pending compliance or to imprison failing compliance, to end when a definite time passes. The federal recalcitrant witness statute, 28 U.S.C. § 1826 (1976), limits coercive imprisonment to eighteen months. The new Wisconsin statute limits coercive imprisonment to six months. Wis. Stat.Ann. § 785.04(1)(b). Are these limits wise? "[F]ixing a definite term of imprisonment might defeat the purpose intended, as the party might prefer to serve the specified term, rather than obey the order." Czarra v. Czarra, 124 Ill.App. 622, 624 (1906). Note, Coercive Contempt and the Federal Grand Jury, 79 Colum.L.Rev. 735, 765 (1979), lists the drawbacks of a definite term with an opportunity to comply: a) The contemnor "knows at the outset what his maximum loss of liberty will be and can make a calculated judgment as to whether he is willing to suffer a loss as the price of remaining silent . . . "; b) "[T]he coercive effect of the confinement diminishes as its termination approaches . . . "; and c) "[D]ecreasing the maximum possible length of incarceration diminishes the likelihood that the contemnor will give in during any fixed period." "This type of sentence," Justice Tom Clark observed, "would benefit an incorrigible witness." Shillitani v. United States, 384 U.S. 364, 370 n.6 (1966).

If 18 months seems too lenient, the alternative is to imprison pending compliance. Most states allow potentially indefinite coercive imprisonment. In the two problems we examine, that may turn into life imprisonment. Comment, Equity-Contempt-Duration of Imprisonment, 36 Mich.L.Rev. 1016, 1018 (1938). See Uphaus v. Wyman, 360 U.S. 72, 81–82 (1958); Penfield Co. v. SEC, 330 U.S. 585, 594 (1947); In re Nevitt, 117 F. 448, 449 (8th Cir. 1902); Culver City v. Superior Court, 38 Cal.2d 535, 241 P.2d 258 (1952); City of Vernon v. Superior Court, 38 Cal.2d 509, 241 P.2d 243 (1952); Moskovitz, Contempt of Injunctions, Civil and Criminal, 43 Colum.L.Rev. 780, 801–02 & n.95 (1943). We selected mythical figures to achieve universality for the two problems, but we realize that, like all analogies, these are imperfect, although evocative. The contemnors in the following decisions, Drake v. National Bank of Commerce and In re Cueto, stand in for the mythical figures. The Cassandra problem is the contemnor who speaks the truth and is disbelieved. "How can the prisoner being tortured for secrets that he really does not know persuade his captors that he does not know them?" T. Schelling, The Strategy of Conflict 115 (1960). Lloyd Drake is our Cassandra. Penelope prevailed through patience and outwaited her enemies, the suitors. Maria Cueto is our Penelope. She raises this question: Does the coerced contemnor have any sure way to convince her adversary that he cannot force her to comply?

Contempt opinions articulate an unbending view of the potential length of coercive imprisonment. As the Supreme Court opined in Uphaus v. Wyman, "If [contemnor] chooses to abide by the result of the adjudication and obey the order . . . , he need not face jail. If, however, he continues to disobey, we find on this record no constitutional objection to the exercise of the traditional remedy of contempt to secure compliance." 360 U.S. 72, 82 (1959). See also McCrone v. United States, 307 U.S. 61, 63 (1939); People ex rel. Valenti v. McCloskey, 6 N.Y.2d 390, 393, 189 N.Y.S.2d 898, 899, 160 N.E.2d 647, 650 (1959). "One who has been directed by a court to perform an act . . . may," New York's Appellate Division added, "be imprisoned until the act is performed," because contemnor "should not be allowed to bargain and barter with the court on the conditions of her compliance." People ex rel. Feldman v. Warden, 46 A.D.2d 256, 258–259, 362 N.Y.S.2d 171, 173–174 (1974), affirmed 36 N.Y.2d 846, 370 N.Y.S.2d 913, 331 N.E.2d 691 (1975).

The contemnor should be immured not for a finite but for a potentially unlimited period to dispel "the notion that a witness may choose to be silent for a price." Zicarelli v. New Jersey State Comm'n of Investigation, 55 N.J. 249, 272, 261 A.2d 129, 141 (1970). "The law will not bargain with anybody to let its courts be defied for a specific term of imprisonment. There are many persons who would gladly purchase the honors of martyrdom in a popular cause at almost any given price, while others are deterred by a mere show of punishment. Each is detained until he finds himself willing to conform. This is merciful to the submissive, and not too severe upon the refractory." Judge Black, quoted in In re Nevitt, 117 F. at 461. Coercive imprisonment lasts only one day at a time; each day "announc[es] the consequences of tomorrow's contumacious conduct." Penfield Co. v. SEC, 330 U.S. at 594. As quaintly stated, contemnors may comply at any time because "they carry the keys of their prison in their own pockets." In re Nevitt, 117 F. at 461. A student note discussing a contemnor in her fifth year of coercion said "it is evident that the purposes of justice will be served best by keeping such persons as defendant under lock and key. She may well spend her life in confinement, unless her attitude changes." Comment, 36 Mich.L.Rev. at 1018.

Coercive measures continue only so long as something exists to coerce. In United States v. PATCO, p. 1046, the coercive order to return to work lost its power to coerce when the strikers were fired. Coercion ended. Courts release imprisoned contemnors who are unable to comply. See Shillitani v. United States, 384 U.S. at 371; Elzey v. Elzey, 435 A.2d 455 (Md. 1981), p. 1070. Contemnors go free if no one needs their compliance, as when the grand jury's term expires, Shillitani v. United States, 384 U.S. at 365; Ex parte Jackson, 95 Tex.Crim. 200, 253 S.W. 287 (1923); Note, Coercive Contempt and the Federal Grand Jury, 79 Colum.L.Rev. at 765–66; or when the court enters judgment in the action, Danning v. Lavine, 572 F.2d 1386 (9th Cir. 1978). However, these contemnors may have to contend with a) another grand jury, Shillitani v. United States, 384 U.S. at 371 n.8 (dicta); In re Boyden, 675 F.2d 643, 644 (5th Cir. 1982); Ex parte Jackson, 253 S.W. at 289 (dicta); b) the same question during discovery in aid of execution, Danning v. Lavine, 572 F.2d at 1389–1390 (dicta); or c) criminal contempt, United States v. Morales, 566 F.2d 402, 409 (2d Cir. 1977); Watkins v. Howard, 441 F.Supp. 486 (E.D.Wis.1977). What about Cassandra, the contemnor whose story was merely unlikely but not untrue?

Civil contemnors may be released when time makes it apparent that the fact-finding process went awry. Coercive measures may be transformed into criminal sanctions after a certain amount of time passes. Courts must prevent coercive orders from becoming criminal; they must keep plaintiff from punishing contemnor under the guise of coercion and without criminal procedural protections. That is the way courts articulate releasing Penelope contemnors.

Assume John Randolph has Henry St. George's unique copy of Tucker's Blackstone. St. George wants the book back, but Randolph claims that it was a gift and that he lost it anyway. St. George sues to replevy. Three impartial witnesses plus St. George say that St. George loaned it to Randolph. If St. George subpoenas Randolph and he refuses to answer questions, may Judge Bolling imprison him to coerce him to testify?

Judge Bolling finds that the book is St. George's and that Randolph has it. He orders Randolph to return it. Will a decretal transfer under Rule 70 (in the Appendix) help St. George? Consider the following possibilities: 1) Randolph refuses to surrender the Blackstone. May Judge Bolling imprison him to secure compliance? Would this be imprisonment to collect a civil debt? 2) Judge Bolling enters an order for Randolph to pay St. George the value of the book. May he imprison him until St. George is paid? 3) Judge Bolling finds that Randolph, a constructive trustee, sold the book and buried the proceeds in his apple orchard. May the judge imprison Randolph until he tells where the money is buried? 4) Judge Bolling finds that Randolph has the Blackstone and he gives him three days to return it. Randolph then says "I burned it and threw the ashes in the river." May Judge Bolling imprison him without criminal procedure? 5) Judge Bolling awards St. George $800 compensatory contempt. Randolph refuses to pay. May he order Randolph imprisoned to coerce him to pay? Rendleman, Compensatory Contempt: Plaintiff's Remedy When Defendant Violates an Injunction, 1980 U.Ill.L.F. 971, 1003–07. Do you distinguish the imprisonments by saying that the judge may coerce to order a defendant to do something the defendant is capable of doing without imprisoning for debt?

A personal remedy raises the stakes of incorrect fact-finding. Suppose Randolph testifies, "I returned the book to St. George." May Judge Bolling disbelieve Randolph, find that he has it, and order him imprisoned until he remembers where it is? If Randolph's story was true, will Judge Bolling imprison him forever or until he does the impossible? After Randolph languishes in jail for six months, Judge Bolling concludes that he was wrong and that Randolph was telling the truth all along. Is there any graceful way for the judge to release the contemnor? If Judge Bolling had incorrectly disbelieved Randolph and entered a money judgment for $800, would the consequences of his incorrect fact-finding have been so serious? Does your answer support the stated preference for money damages whenever possible?

DRAKE v. NATIONAL BANK OF COMMERCE

168 Va. 230, 190 S.E. 302 (1937).

CAMPBELL, C. J., delivered the opinion of the court.

On the 31st day of January, 1936, the National Bank of Commerce of Norfolk filed in the Court of Law and Chancery of the City of Norfolk the following application for the appointment of a receiver for the Marine Equipment Company, Incorporated, a defunct corporation:

"Your petitoner, National Bank of Commerce of Norfolk, respectfully represents:

"1. That Marine Equipment Company, Incorporated, is a corporation duly chartered under the laws of the State of Virginia, February 9, 1927.

"2. That your petitioner is a creditor of said corporation in an amount exceeding $5,000.00 in excess of securities held by your petitioner.

"3. That the charter of said corporation was annulled on May 31, 1932, because of its failure to pay Registration Fees and Franchise Taxes for two preceding years, and that said corporation was thereby dissolved in the manner required by law.

"4. That the principal office of said corporation was in the City of Norfolk, Virginia.

"Wherefore, your petitioner makes application to this Honorable Court for the appointment of a Receiver or Receivers of and for such corporation, to take charge of the estate or effects thereof, and to collect the debts and property due and belonging to said corporation, with all of the powers and authority provided by law.

"And your petitioner will ever pray, etc."

On the same day an order was entered which sets forth that upon the application of National Bank of Commerce of Norfolk, upon notice accepted by Henry Bowden, Esq., counsel for the former officers and directors of the corporation, W. L. Parker was appointed receiver. The president of the corporation, at the date of its incorporation, was Lloyd S. Drake. . . .

On the 5th of February, 1936, W. L. Parker, receiver, filed his report, setting forth that due to loss by fire, there had been collected by Drake, from various insurance companies, the sum of $22,344; that Lloyd S. Drake had been president, treasurer and a director of the corporation; that he had made demand upon Drake that he deliver to him the sum of $22,000, and any other corporate property in his possession, and that said demand had been ignored.

Acting upon the recommendation of the receiver, this order was entered by the court:

"Adjudged, ordered and decreed that Lloyd S. Drake do appear before the Judge of this Court at 10 A. M. on the 13th day of February, 1936, and account to the Court for all assets of Marine Equipment Company, Incorporated, coming into his hands or under his control, and to show cause, if any he can, why he should not be adjudged in contempt of this Court for his failure to obey the order thereof entered in this cause on the 31st day of January, 1936;

"Further ordered that a copy hereof be duly served upon the said Lloyd S. Drake."

On the return day of the rule Drake appeared and filed a motion to dismiss the rule, on the grounds that the court was without jurisdiction to enter the order and that it nowhere appeared that Drake had in his possession any money or property belonging to the corporation. This motion was overruled and thereupon Drake filed his answer in the cause, which admitted the collection of the fire insurance money, but claimed that while out hunting he had lost the sum of $18,000.

After the introduction of evidence by the parties, the court entered an order adjudging Drake guilty of contempt of court, and he was ordered confined in jail until he paid to the receiver the sum of money set forth in his answer. . . .

The second assignment of error challenges the action of the court in finding Drake guilty of contempt and confining him in jail until the payment to the receiver of the sum of money collected by him.

In support of the contention that the court erred in adjudging Drake guilty of contempt, these conclusions are relied upon:

"(1) That this is a criminal or quasi criminal charge against Drake and is to be governed by the principles and is to be determined under the principles of criminal law and procedure.

"(2) That under criminal law and procedure, Drake, in this case, is presumed to be innocent until his guilt is established beyond a reasonable doubt.

"(3) That the burden is on the prosecution to show the guilt of Drake beyond all reasonable doubt.

"(4) That this burden never shifts but remains on the prosecution throughout the entire case.

"(5) That in determining the guilt of the prisoner, the court is not at liberty to indulge in surmise, supposition or conjecture and should not guess as to what are the facts when it comes to passing upon the liberty of a man."

This court, in numerous cases, has dealt with the question of contempt and the rule is well settled in Virginia that contempt proceedings are of two classes. The last case upon the subject is Roanoke Water etc. Co. v. Roanoke Glass Company, 151 Va. 229, 144 S.E. 460, 462. In that case Mr. Justice Holt said:

"Proceedings for contempt of court are of two classes—those prosecuted to preserve the power and to vindicate the dignity of the court, and those instituted to preserve and enforce the rights of private parties. The former are criminal and punitive in their nature; the latter are civil and remedial. In re Nevitt (C.C.A.) 117 F. 448; Gompers v. Buck's Stove & Range Co. . . .

The case at bar falls within the second class and by the weight of authority the burden of proof is on Drake to show his inability to comply with the order of the court. Cutting v. Van Fleet (C.C.A. 9th Cir.) 252 F. 100.

In the trial of the contempt proceeding this principle seems to have been recognized, since the record shows that Drake, who testified in his own behalf, was the first witness called to testify in the case. The evidence was taken *ore tenus* before the court, and therefore, the conclusion on the facts stands upon the same plane as the verdict of a jury. . . .

The case made out by Drake is fully stated in the answer filed by him and is as follows:

"(3) There had . . . come into the hands of this Respondent certain moneys under the following circumstances:

"The successors in business, Lloyd S. Drake and C. S. Phillips, of the corporation above mentioned, suffered a fire loss in said business on account of which certain insurance companies paid to them a net amount of $20,575.00, said payments being in the form of drafts.

"It was agreed between your Respondent and the said Phillips that he should collect the proceeds of said drafts in actual cash and hold the same without deposit, to be disposed of afterwards in liquidating the debts of said concern. When the greater portion of said drafts arrived, your Respondent was in New York City and he, while in said city, in compliance with his understanding with C. S. Phillips, collected said drafts in cash and took physical possession of said cash and kept the same in his person; $19,500.00 of said cash was in denominations of five hundred dollar bills, and $1,075.00 of said cash was in smaller bills of varying denominations. The $1,075.00 was kept in a separate parcel from the $19,500 which itself was in a parcel held together by a rubber band. On Saturday, the 18th day of January, 1936, Respondent returned to Norfolk, reaching here about 10:00 o'clock on that day. He went to his office and at once notified Phillips that he had returned and requested him to come to the office. At about 1:30 o'clock P. M. on that day, Phillips came to the office and was informed by this respondent that he had the cash derived from said drafts, on his person and made an engagement with him, it being then after banking hours, to meet him there Monday morning and go with him to the bank of the National Bank of Commerce of Norfolk, Virginia, for the purpose of adjusting and settling their indebtedness to said bank. On Monday morning, the 20th of January, 1936, Mr. Phillips met your Respondent at said office and to his surprise Respondent learned for the first time that the banks were closed that day on account of some legal holiday. The visit to the bank was therefore postponed to take place the next day. On the morning of that day, Monday, Respondent paid from the proceeds in his hands the following debts due by the business:

"To W. J. Callan, $500.00; to J. L. Spence, $500.00; to Thos. A. Bryan & Company, $475.00; to J. D. Apperson, $250.00; to the telephone company, $35.00, and to Gulf Refining Company, $15.00; to Henry Bowden, $100.00. In addition to that Respondent had paid out in expenses for various trips for the concern, $200.00, which he deducted from said money of the Respondent. Thinking and believing that after the liquidation of the debts of the concern there would be coming to him at least $500.00, Respondent deducted that much more from the moneys in his possession and devoted it to the payment of his personal bills and the bills of his family. This left in your Respondent's possession, $18,000.00 in one roll held together by a rubber band.

"On the afternoon of Monday, the 20th day of January, 1936, Respondent, accompanied by a friend, Anthony Reibaldi, of Portsmouth, Virginia, who had suggested the trip, went bird hunting in Norfolk County some few miles from Portsmouth, and the said Respondent having at the time in his possession and on his person for safe keeping the $18,000.00 in bills of five hundred denominations hereinabove last mentioned, at the time. At about dusk on that evening when Respondent and his companion were concluding their hunting and were returning to Respondent's automobile, Respondent missed from his pocket the $18,000.00 above mentioned and discovered that the same had disappeared. Respondent and his companion searched as best they could for said money that evening and returned the next morning at sunrise and devoted the rest of that day also to searching for said money as well as a part of Wednesday, the 22nd of January, 1936, the following day, having also enlisted the aid of other trustworthy persons in the neighborhood in said search. Said search, however, proved unavailing and your Respondent does not know what became of said money beyond the fact that the same was lost.

"Your Respondent also adopted other means in attempting to recover said money as will more fully appear from the evidence.

"On Wednesday Respondent notified his associate, Mr. S. C. Phillips, of the loss of said money and on Thursday notified the National Bank of Commerce."

Anthony Reibaldi, Drake's companion on the hunting trip, was introduced as a witness and testified in detail regarding the hunt, his evidence practically dovetailing that of Drake.

Several witnesses testified as to the good reputation of Drake for truth and veracity.

Counsel for Drake contend that he is an uncontradicted and unimpeached witness, and therefore, under the doctrine of Epperson v. De Jarnette, 164 Va. 482, 180 S.E. 412, 413, his evidence is conclusive of the matter. The rule laid down in the above case is as follows:

"While the jury is the judge of the weight of testimony and the credibility of witnesses, it cannot arbitrarily disregard the uncontradicted evidence of unimpeached witnesses which is not inherently incredible and not inconsistent with other facts and circumstances appearing in the record, even though such witnesses are interested in the results of the litigation."

In a technical sense Drake stands as an unimpeached witness, but in view of the evidence on behalf of the receiver (direct and circumstantial), it is going too far afield to say that he stands as an uncontradicted witness. All that the record shows as to the loss of the money is the statement of Drake that he lost it. Reibaldi merely repeats the self-serving declaration made by Drake when he claims to have discovered his loss. This is not corroboration. On the other hand, it clearly appears that after Drake collected the money in the manner stated by him, he was meticulous in his endeavor to show that he had this large sum of money on his person. He informed a Mr. Welton who occupied the drawing room with him on his return from New York to Norfolk, that he had a large sum of money upon his person. On the way to the hunting grounds he showed Reibaldi the package of money and permitted Reibaldi to handle it. He gave as his reason for showing the money to Reibaldi, that on a previous occasion Reibaldi had shown him a "roll" of money. His conduct was unusual and only one inference can be drawn from the display of such a large sum of money, and that inference is that Drake was paving the way to establish the fact of his possession, in the event the money was afterwards lost. Another pregnant fact is that, though Phillips was an alleged partner in the business and entitled to share in the proceeds, Drake did not notify him of the loss until two days after it occurred.

Phillips, when testifying as a witness, contradicted the statement of Drake that he agreed to the collection of the insurance money in cash and stated that the drafts were to be converted into "certified checks or cashiers' checks." Phillips further stated that when he first met Drake, after his (Drake's) return to Norfolk, this incident occurred:

"We sat down to have lunch and Drake then mentioned that he had this money in currency, and it worried me, any idea of an amount of that kind, and anything might happen, and I cautioned him to be extremely careful and mentioned the question of a safe deposit box. The answer came back that the banks were closed and I said, 'What can we do? You had better give it to me to take care of. I won't lose it.' I said, 'I won't feel satisfied until this thing is handled properly.' Then I said, 'What are you going to do this afternoon?' Then he said, 'I am going hunting,' I said 'Why don't you do something, at least give me a part of that money to take care of and I will find some place to put it where it will be safe?' but he would not agree to that, and then as far as seeing the money, I really saw just the edge of the bills."

If this statement of Phillips is true, and the court sitting as a jury has said it is true, it would indicate that Drake had constituted himself sole custodian of the money, instead of being willing to share the responsibility of its safety with Phillips.

Drake also was contradicted by the witness Whitehurst, vice-president of the Bank of Commerce, in regard to the requested assignment to the bank of the proceeds of the insurance to protect the bank's loan to the Marine Equipment Corporation.

Standing alone, the evidence of Drake that he lost the money in the manner detailed is apparently not inherently incredible, but when the record is further examined and the whole matter weighed, we are unable to say that the trial court erred in its view that the statement of Drake was unbelievable . . . .

We find no error in the judgment of the trial court, and it is therefore affirmed.

---

1) Even a disinterested bystander might conclude that Drake's bird-hunt story was a tissue of facile lies; that, if released, he would quickly "find" the money on his way out of town; and that a few weeks in the Sergeant's custody would jar his memory. Professor Dobbs observed that "the stories told on these occasions sometimes lack versimilitude . . . . Witnesses testified to Drake's good reputation for truth and veracity, but this reputation had no doubt been formed before Mr. Drake testified to the loss of $18,000 in cash while bird-hunting." Dobbs, Contempt of Court: A Survey, 56 Cornell L.Rev. 183, 220 n. 145 (1971).

2) Documents on file, however, show that Lloyd Drake spent more than eight months in jail before petitioning to be released. He argued that he was unable to pay and that "certain of his friends and acquaintances out of pity for [his] distressing plight" had contributed $1,500 to be paid to the receiver when Drake was released. The Chancellor found "the Court being of opinion that said Lloyd S. Drake has been sufficiently punished for his said contempt, and lacks the ability to comply with the order adjudicating him guilty of contempt except to the extent set forth in his said petition for release, it is Ordered that the said Lloyd S. Drake be and he is hereby released." The receiver accepted the $1,500 to reduce the debt and did not object. Drake was released. Did the judge think he was the governor pardoning criminal contempt? Compare Jim Laing's pardon quoted in Note 3 after *Laing*, p. 1032.

3) A cynic might admire Drake's resolution and speculate that Drake and his friends gathered later in the shade of a secluded tree to divide the $18,000 before going their separate ways. But it proved impossible to coerce Drake before the receiver was willing to exchange less than ten percent of the debt for Drake's release. Let us presume that Drake's story was mere-

ly unlikely but not untrue; in short, that Drake testified truthfully and that the courts erred in imprisoning him. What price did this error inflict?

4) Drake commenced an indefinite coercive sentence which, because he could not comply, was literally interminable. Such a sentence has four types of consequences. First, society's moral sense recoils at a court issuing an impossible order and punishing someone who is unable to obey. Maggio v. Zeitz, 333 U.S. 56, 72 (1948); J. Rawls, A Theory of Justice 237–39 (1971). Second, because nothing existed to coerce, the order was criminal contempt after civil procedure. In practical terms, the error let the receiver use in personam process to collect a civil debt, thus frustrating the prohibition against debt imprisonment. V. Countryman, Cases and Materials on Debtor and Creditor 83–84 (1974). Third, the contemnor owed a civil debt, but the law subordinates the creditor's interest in collecting to two humanitarian counterpolicies. Legislatures intend property exempt from execution to be a cushion to protect the debtor and the debtor's family from the depths of abject poverty. Vukowich, Debtors' Exemption Rights, 62 Geo.L.J. 779, 784–86 (1974). But a debtor in jail is likely to sell exempt property to secure release. Fourth, as appears to have occurred in *Drake,* orders imprisoning a judgment debtor "exert pressure on friends and relatives to ransom the accused party." Justice Jackson said this "would be a flagrant abuse of process." Maggio v. Zeitz, 333 U.S. at 64. For example, in Vail v. Quinlan, 406 F.Supp. 951, 957 (S.D.N.Y.1976), an indigent imprisoned for failure to pay a contempt fine was released after a relative loaned him money. The Supreme Court reversed on other grounds. Juidice v. Vail, 430 U.S. 327 (1977). An incorrect coercive order provides a plaintiff with considerable and effective collection leverage that the average creditor lacks.

5) What barriers should appellate courts erect to prevent the consequences that follow from interminable coercive sentences? Two Supreme Court opinions concerning turnover orders in bankruptcy consider burden of proof, presumption, and res judicata-preclusion as ways of preventing error and obviating its consequences. See Maggio v. Zeitz, 333 U.S. 56 (1948), and Oriel v. Russell, 278 U.S. 358 (1929). The Bankruptcy Act charges the trustee to collect the estate's property. The trustee is equivalent to the receiver in *Drake.* Bankruptcy courts developed nonstatutory turnover proceedings; the trustee invokes the court's power to order the stubborn bankrupt or others to produce or account for property. J. MacLachlan, Handbook of the Law of Bankruptcy § 191 (1956). The turnover proceeding results in an in personam order to surrender or account for the property. This "turnover" order resembles the trial judge's order to turn over in *Drake.* Professor Moore compares it to a mandatory injunction. Moore, Res Judicata and Collateral Estoppel in Bankruptcy, 68 Yale L.J. 1, 2 (1958). Bankruptcy courts employ coercive contempt to enforce turnover orders. They confront erroneous fact-finding. The judge conducts a hearing where the bankrupt disputes the trustee's evidence. Nevertheless the judge finds that the bankrupt has the estate property or knows where it is; he orders the bankrupt to produce or to tell. The bankrupt does not appeal. The order having failed to produce the property, the judge imposes coercive imprisonment on the bankrupt. The bankrupt appeals from contempt. Maggio v. Zeitz, 333 U.S. at 59; Oriel v. Russell, 278 U.S. at 361.

Maggio and *Oriel* face three issues: 1) the trustee's burden of proof, 2) whether to presume that the bankrupt-contemnor continues to possess the property, and 3) the preclusive effect in contempt of the turnover decision. In adjusting these procedural doctrines to protect contemnors, the court must consider plaintiff's substantive interest and expeditious and inexpensive collection and administration of bankruptcy estates.

The Supreme Court insists that the elements leading to a turnover order—the bankrupt possesses and refuses to deliver property—be proven by clear and convincing evidence. "Clear and convincing" is required for fraud; a turnover order is "equivalent to one of fraud." Oriel v. Russell, 278 U.S. at 362. Accord, Maggio v. Zeitz, 333 U.S. at 63, 64. In addition, because the order anticipates coercive imprisonment, putting liberty at issue, a high standard of proof is appropriate to reduce the risk of error. 278 U.S. at 363; McCormick, Handbook of the Law of Evidence § 341 (2d ed. 1972); R. Posner, Economic Analysis of Law § 21.3 (2d ed. 1977). Finally, the high standard focuses the adjudicator's judgment on the draconian finality of contempt and the deadly seriousness of the proceeding. It tells the judge to reject "questionable experiment[s] in coercion which will recoil to the discredit of the judicial process if time proves the adjudication to have been improvident and requires the courts to abandon its enforcement." 333 U.S. at 67.

The Court decided not to require proof beyond a reasonable doubt; however, Justice Black's separate opinion argued that proof beyond reasonable doubt is necessary in contempt. 333 U.S. at 78. Coercive contempt curtails liberty. But, as the majority saw it, coercive contempt "punishes" incidentally to enforcing the plaintiff's rights; it is designed to compel the contemnor to perform lawful duties. Error creates hardship, "but the conscience of judges in weighing the evidence under a clear perception of the consequences, together with the opportunity of appeal and review, if properly taken, will restrain the courts from recklessness of bankrupt's rights on the one hand and prevent the bankrupt from flouting the law on the other." 278 U.S. at 363, 364. To what burden of proof did the *Drake* court subscribe?

The Second Circuit developed a presumption: if the trustee shows the bankrupt possessed property, then the court will presume that this possession persisted until the bankrupt explained how and when it ceased. In re Luma Camera Service, Inc., 157 F.2d 951, 953 (2d Cir. 1946), reversed sub nom. Maggio v. Zeitz, 333 U.S. 56 (1948). Trustees argued for the Second Circuit's presumption because, while they carry the burden of proof, only the bankrupt has access to the evidence. The presumption smokes out the bankrupt's evidence, destroying the advantage of not disclosing. 333 U.S. at 60. In *Drake,* the court said that the burden of proof was on Drake to show inability to comply. Does this have the same effect as the Second Circuit's presumption?

In *Maggio*, Justice Jackson faced the Second Circuit's presumption packaged in an ingenious opinion by Judge Jerome Frank. In re Luma Camera Service, Inc., 157 F.2d 951. The Supreme Court had earlier refused to review the order to turn the property over. In the later contempt action, Judge Frank declined to overrule the presumption; yet, by overstating it, he invited the Supreme Court to repudiate it on the instant appeal from contempt. The trustee had shown an inventory shortage attributable to Maggio, the bankrupt. The trustee relied on the presumption to carry Maggio's possession of the inventory down to the contempt order. Affirming the contempt order, Judge Frank assumed that Maggio had exchanged the inventory for cash and dissipated the cash before the order. But if Maggio had denied the trustee's evidence of possession at the turnover hearing, he would have admitted issuing a false financial statement and invited a criminal prosecution. Schwartz, Turnover and Contempt Proceedings in the Light of the History of Maggio v. Zeitz, 5 U.C.L.A. L.Rev. 75, 78 (1958).

Thus, said Judge Frank, "Although we know that Maggio cannot comply with the order, we must keep a straight face and pretend that he can, and must thus affirm orders which first direct Maggio to do an impossibility and then punish him for refusal to perform it." In re Luma Camera Service, Inc., 157 F.2d at 955. Does this repeat the evils of *Drake*? Does it frustrate the exemption statutes, pressure relatives and friends to ransom the contemnor, and lead to something very close to debt imprisonment? Does it hamper the bankrupt's fresh start? Does it produce criminal punishment without a jury and proof beyond a reasonable doubt? 157 F.2d at 953.

The *Maggio* Court confronted the presumption directly. The Court felt that trial judges should not administer the presumption rigidly, mechanically, and unreasonably. They should consider many individual factors: How much time had passed? Is the property fungible, perishable, salable, or consumable? Is the bankrupt thrifty or a "fast-living adventurer"? 333 U.S. at 64–66.

The *Maggio* Court also dealt with the presumption indirectly; it discussed the turnover order's effect in contempt and the protections against debt imprisonment in turnover and contempt orders. To prevent delay, inconsistency and unnecessary expense the contempt judge will accord some credence to the earlier order to return the property. Judge Frank, in the *Maggio* contempt, gave the turnover order res judicata effect. He observed wryly that this perpetuated the error created by the presumption, under the ostensible theory that two wrongs make a right. In re Luma Camera Service, Inc., 157 F.2d at 954; see also Oriel v. Russell, 278 U.S. at 363. The turnover order adjudicates that the bankrupt can comply. What about bankrupts or other litigants who lied and were disbelieved? Or even worse, what about Cassandra, who told improbable truths and was disbelieved? The contempt hearing comes too late to recant or to repeat with emphasis. Contemnors may find themselves coercively imprisoned for failing to obey impossible orders. "This," the late Professor MacLachlan understated, "presents a problem." J. MacLachlan, Handbook of the Law of Bankruptcy § 192 (1956).

The Supreme Court, nevertheless, held in *Maggio* that the turnover order was res judicata and subject only to direct attack, and that the order was insulated from scrutiny in the contempt proceeding. 333 U.S. at 68–69. Ordinarily courts reserve full-fledged res judicata for final judgments, applying the more flexible law of the case doctrine to separate phases of the same lawsuit. Restatement (Second) of Judgments § 13 (1980); Vestal, Law of the Case: Single-Suit Preclusion, 1967 Utah L.Rev. 1. The Court in *United Mine Workers* said that courts should refuse to base civil contempt on an incorrect order: "The right to remedial relief falls with an injunction which events prove was erroneously issued." 330 U.S. at 294–95 (1947). See also Note 3 after Sidney v. McDonald, p. 1053. Should judges send someone into coercive imprisonment to vindicate an unsound order?

Justice Jackson said in *Maggio* that a turnover order must be phrased "primarily to get at property rather than to get at a debtor." 333 U.S. at 63. The object of the order is to obtain the specific property or "specifically identified" proceeds. The trustee must establish that the property or its proceeds exist at the date of the turnover proceeding, and that defendant possesses the property and is able to surrender it. 333 U.S. at 63–64. Does anything short of this rule potentially transform the turnover order into a money judgment and coercive contempt into imprisonment for debt? Does the rule dilute the res judicata effect of the turnover order?

What must the trustee or plaintiff prove in contempt? How may the bankrupt or other contemnor defend? The court of appeals appeared to feel that if the bankrupt had denied having the property at the turnover hearing and simply repeated this denial at the contempt hearing, then the contempt judge properly refused to give this testimony any credit. 333 U.S. at 71, 75. Erroneous fact-finding at the turnover hearing could therefore lead to perpetual imprisonment. Aside from res judicata, if the contempt judge presumes conclusively that the bankrupt possessed the property on the date of the turnover proceeding, would that be imprisonment for debt?

The Supreme Court provided a way out. The contempt judge must accept the turnover order and accord preclusive effect to the finding that the contemnor possessed the property on that date. But the contemnor may testify that he is unable to comply on the date of the contempt hearing. If the contemnor testifies that he does not currently possess the property, the contempt judge may choose to believe that testimony even though he disbelieved identical testimony at the turnover proceeding. 333 U.S. at 73–76 n. 6. Would denying the contemnor the defense of inability to comply on the date of contempt convert coercive into criminal contempt? 333 U.S. at 70–72.

The Supreme Court used present inability to comply to provide another safety valve for error. It may have indulged in sleight of hand to allow the contempt judge to correct an erroneous turnover order. Does *Maggio* also open an escape hatch for the stubborn contemnor? In dicta, the Court in both *Oriel* and *Maggio* discussed the ways contemnors may obtain release. The unpleasant "inconvenience of being restrained of his liberty" may produce the money "thus justifying the court's incredulity." But when confinement fails and "a reasonable interval of time has supplied the previous defect in the evidence, and has made sufficiently certain what was doubtful before, namely, the bankrupt's inability to obey the order, he has always been released . . . ." Epstein v. Steinfeld, 206 F. 568, 569–570 (E.D.Pa.1913), quoted in Maggio v. Zeitz, 333 U.S. at 72; Oriel v. Russell, 278 U.S. at 366. "The shadow of the prison gates" coupled with a believable denial that he can presently comply may "convince the court that his is not a wilful disobedience which will yield to coercion." 333 U.S. at 76.

The Court avoided saying that res judicata is too rigid a concept for an issue with a prospective effect on liberty. When the contemnor files habeas corpus, the judge is relieved from admitting error by saying, "Contempt was a good joke, but we carried it too far." Instead, the judge can believe that it is impossible for contemnor to comply at present, perhaps articulating it by saying that imprisonment has dissipated the presumption. In re Bar-Craft Dresses, Inc., 101 F.Supp. 921 (S.D.N.Y.1952). The contemnor need not account for the property or proceeds; instead the time in prison may strengthen his previous denial. Cf. In re Luma Camera Service, Inc., 84 F.Supp. 839 (S.D.N.Y.1949) (*Maggio* on remand). Under the guise of surreptitiously admitting that previous fact-finding went awry, may the judge allow the stubborn or lying contemnor to escape? Credible explanations are much in order, however, and judges retain their ability to disbelieve conclusory and fantastic stories. Cf. Maggio v. Zeitz, 333 U.S. at 75–76 (dicta); Lopiparo v. United States, 216 F.2d 87, 91 (8th Cir. 1954), certiorari denied 348 U.S. 916 (1955) (testimony at contempt hearing disbelieved); In re California Motors, Inc., 122 F.Supp. 885 (S.D.N.Y.1954); In re Sussman, 85 F.Supp. 570 (S.D.N.Y.1949).

6) Would the *Maggio-Oriel* analysis have affected the result in Lloyd Drake's contempt? If you were the judge who ordered Drake released, would you expect to experience nagging second thoughts that perhaps Drake had hoodwinked you, the receiver, and his friends after all?

7) If *Johansen,* p. 1060 had been governing precedent when Drake was tried, would Drake have been entitled to a jury? If you had represented Drake, would you have requested a jury? Compare *Johansen* with *Maggio* and *Drake* on the issues of quantum of proof and allocation of the burden of proof, as well as the preclusive effect of the prior determination.

8) What of Penelope, the silent contemnor who will deign not to provide even an evasive answer? The contemnor who "offers no evidence" or "stands mute" remains in jail under *Maggio.* 333 U.S. at 75. *Maggio* provides an escape hatch for only some of the stubborn. Consider intractable Daisy Tegtmeyer.

In the *Tegtmeyer* litigation, the judge found that Daisy Tegtmeyer was a trustee and had to account to plaintiff for trust funds and profits. The master ordered her to turn over the property or to tell where it was. She refused to answer. She was committed to county jail pending delivery or answers. After four years, she sought to be released; she argued that she had been punished enough, that she was imprisoned incorrectly for a money debt, and that her health was broken.

The appellate court in 1937 refused to release her. The court found that she was not imprisoned because she had failed to pay a general civil debt, but because she had refused to obey an order to turn over and because she had refused to answer questions about specific property. The trial court had found obedience within her capability. Moreover, she was not being punished at all, but merely coerced until she used the key in her pocket and complied with the orders. Tegtmeyer v. Tegtmeyer, 292 Ill.App. 434, 11 N.E.2d 657 (1937). The appellate court, identically constituted, sent similar messages in 1940 and 1942. Tegtmeyer v. Tegtmeyer, 314 Ill.App. 16, 40 N.E.2d 767 (1942); Tegtmeyer v. Tegtmeyer, 306 Ill.App. 169, 28 N.E.2d 303 (1940). We do not know how it all ended.

Tegtmeyer captures the courts' dilemma. Daisy Tegtmeyer never offered to plead that answers would tend to incriminate her. 28 N.E.2d at 307. Nor did she assert that she was unable to comply. 11 N.E.2d at 663.

Through seventeen years of litigation, including more than four of imprisonment, "she has never . . . offered to pay the whole or any part of the money she owes these plaintiffs." 40 N.E.2d at 770. She did tell the master "I am the only one that is being made to comply with the laws, and if others can break the laws, then so can I. . . . " 28 N.E.2d at 307. How should a court, which actively seeks to give plaintiffs what they are entitled to, respond to unremitting defiance? Will a humane judge stand idly by while a refractory contemnor spends the rest of her life in jail? The author of Michigan Law Review Note, quoted above p. 1085, thought so.

Does a coercive order lose its coercive force over time and become punitive? See Lambert v. Montana, 545 F.2d 87 (9th Cir. 1976); In re Farr, 36 Cal.App.3d 577, 111 Cal.Rptr. 649 (1974); Catena v. Seidl, 68 N.J. 224, 343 A.2d 744 (1975). See also Note, Due Process in Civil Contempt Proceedings: A Comparison with Juvenile and Mental Incompetency Requirements, 44 Fordham L.Rev. 1029 (1976); Comment, Contempt: Civil Contempt Order May Not Include Absolute Sentence, 47 Minn.L.Rev. 907, 913–14 (1963); Comment, Incarceration for Civil Contempt: An Asserted Eighth Amendment Challenge Faces a Semantical Defense, 11 San Diego L.Rev. 1026 (1974). Procedurally, the decisions deal with jailed contemnors' habeas corpus petitions. Most involve orders to testify. Contemnor refuses to answer, and the judge orders coercive imprisonment pending a satisfactory answer. Many claim some testimonial privilege and persist in adhering to the policy of the privilege even after the judge rejects it and orders contemnor to testify. In re Cueto, 443 F.Supp. 857, 860 (S.D.N.Y.1978). Two simply refused to answer. Lambert v. Montana, 545 F.2d at 88; Catena v. Seidl, 68 N.J. 224, 343 A.2d 744 (1975). Everybody knows that contemnor knows the answer. Lambert v. Montana, 545 F.2d at 88; Farr v. Superior Court, 99 Cal.Rptr. at 345. How should judges deal with the terminally stubborn contemnor? The order to produce property is comparatively easier. The judge may disbelieve contemnor's denial and imprison to coerce; then, under *Maggio*, he may believe contemnor's denial and end coercive imprisonment. *Maggio* allows the judge to say "At first I saw it (the property), but now I don't." The silent contemnor offers no similar solution.

IN RE CUETO

443 F.Supp. 857 (S.D.N.Y.1978).

ROBERT L. CARTER, District Judge.

Movants, Maria Cueto and Raisa Nemikin, were cited for civil contempt under 28 U.S.C. § 1826(a) for refusing to answer certain questions before a grand jury investigating the terrorist bombing activities of an organization called Fuerzas Armadas de Liberacion Nacional Puertorriquena ("FALN"). Pursuant to their contempt adjudications, they were ordered confined during the life of the grand jury or until they agreed to testify, and both have been held in confinement at the Metropolitan Correctional Center—Nemikin since March 1, and Cueto since March 8, 1977. The grand jury term expires on May 9, 1978. [This opinion is dated January 23, 1978].

Movants claim that their refusal to testify before the grand jury, being based upon moral and religious commitments, is irrevocable. Accordingly, they urge that since they will not betray their religious convictions by giving testimony, their incarceration has had and can have no coercive effect, and that their continued incarceration clearly has become punitive. Therefore, movants contend that the due process guarantees of the federal constitution mandate their release in that their continued confinement bears no reasonable relationship to the purposes for which they were committed.

A clearer understanding of the narrow issue raised in this motion requires a somewhat more detailed recapitulation of the history of this litigation than ordinarily would be warranted.

Cueto has been actively involved in the work of the Episcopal Church since 1966, and her activities have been concentrated largely on issues and programs affecting the Hispanic Community. She became a member of the National Commission on Hispanic Affairs ("Commission") which was organized as an arm of the Episcopal Church to aid the Church in performing its mission of helping to provide opportunities for improving the socio-economic status of the Hispanic Community in the United States. Cueto became a director of the Commission in 1972 and held that position at the time when the events which led to her present incarceration transpired.

Nemikin has been secretary to the Commission since 1972 and held that position when she refused to give testimony before the grand jury.

In 1974–75, a series of bombings occurred at a number of buildings in New York City where banks and corporate offices were housed. FALN claimed responsibility for these terrorist acts. A grand jury investigation of the bombings and FALN's relationship to them was initiated, and on November 9, 1976, a new grand jury was organized to continue the investigation. In due course, subpoenas were issued calling for the production of certain records of the Commission.

Movants were questioned by the FBI concerning Carlos Torres, a member of the Commission whom the FBI was trying to locate and question since the government had reason to believe that Torres was implicated in the planning and/or execution of the bombings. Thereafter, subpoenas were issued calling for movants to appear before the grand jury to testify. Movants sought to quash the subpoenas, but Judge Pierce denied that motion on February 4. See In re Wood, 430 F.Supp. 41 (S.D.N.Y.1977) (Pierce, J.).

Nemikin appeared before the grand jury on February 18, 1977, and was asked and refused to answer the following questions: When did you last speak to or otherwise communicate with Carlos Torres? Identify all funds of the Commission which were directed, openly or in secret, in whole or in part, to FALN or to any FALN member? Identify to the grand jury any person you know who was involved in or claimed responsibility for the dynamite bombing of Fraunces Tavern on January 24, 1975, resulting in the death of four persons?

Cueto appeared before the grand jury on March 4 and refused to answer the following questions: Do you know anything about the whereabouts of Carlos Torres? Did Torres play any part in the bombing of Fraunces Tavern in New York on January 24, 1975? This grand jury is trying to find out, among other things, who is responsible for the bombing of Fraunces Tavern that killed four people. Can you tell us the names of any person who participated in the bombing or do you have any information at all with respect to it?

Movants were taken before Judge Frankel of this court who advised them that they had no recognizable right to refuse to answer the questions put to them before the grand jury. Each persisted in her refusal, and each was adjudged in contempt by Judge Frankel—Nemikin on February 26 and Cueto on March 4. Each was ordered incarcerated for the life of the grand jury or until they agreed to testify pursuant to 28 U.S.C. § 1826(a) . . . .

Judge Frankel's adjudication of contempt was affirmed on appeal. In re Cueto, 554 F.2d 14 (2d Cir. 1977). Thereafter, on or about May 20, 1977, movants, making substantially the same argument being made here, sought relief before Judge Stewart of this court from incarceration or, in the alternative, for an order fixing their incarceration to a certain and definite term. Judge Stewart denied their motion as being premature, insofar as it asserted that their confinement no longer served a coercive function, in view of the short length of their incarceration—at the time, slightly in excess of 60 days.

Movants urge here that their refusal to testify is grounded in firmly held religious beliefs, and that their work with the Commission was a part of the mission of the Episcopal Church of the United States to millions of Spanish speaking people who have experienced a history of denial of basic human rights in this country. Movants claim that their function as lay ministers in the Church would be impaired if they testified, and they assert, in effect, that since they will never testify, the coercive objective of their confinement will not be realized and their continued confinement can only be punitive.

Movants' recalcitrance is supported by the Bishop and other dignitaries of the Episcopal Church of Puerto Rico, by the National Council of the Churches of Christ in the United States ("National Council"), by the Bishop of the Episcopal Diocese of New York and by the resigned Bishop of the Episcopal Diocese of Pennsylvania, as well as by other less eminent persons and bodies in the Church. The National Council and the various Bishops referred to have been allowed to appear as amici curiae. All assert that movants' defiance of the court's order to provide information to the grand jury is an exercise of the First Amendment right of freedom of religion, the matrix of religious and individual liberty in an open society. Amici also assert, although movants do not, that Cueto and Nemikin have no knowledge of FALN or of the bombings. While the Episcopal Church of the United States, under whose auspices the Commission was organized and functions, did not appear as amicus curiae, the government, in an exemplary demonstration of prosecutorial candor, advises that the Presiding Bishop of that body has met repeatedly with responsible government officials seeking movants' release. Thus, for whatever it is worth, a sizable segment of the officialdom of the Episcopal Church holds and has articulated a concern that tenets of religious freedom which are protected by the Constitution are being infringed by the government's insistence that these two women be required to respond to the grand jury inquiry, and movants' continued incarceration is viewed as wrongful governmental persecution.

While it is difficult for me to understand how that position can be seriously advanced by amici curiae in light of the particuarly innocuous questions put to Cueto and Nemikin before the grand jury, I need not face the religious issue frontally since Judge Pierce has conclusively demonstrated that no violations of the First Amendment's guarantee of religious freedom are even remotely involved in this case. Although movants concede that that issue is foreclosed, they argue that the fact that movants believe themselves compelled to continue in their stance of defiance because of their religious convictions and commitments—a position, as I have indicated, that is supported by a not insignificant segment of their Church's hierarchy—provides an articulated moral basis for their recalcitrance.

Cueto's and Nemikin's posture is surely wrongheaded and without support in law, but I accept what I conceive to be the real point of the argument, that is, that movants are acting in good faith. Good faith, however, may not justify refusal to perform a legal obligation. See United States v. Mine Workers. And the fact that their action, though misguided, is taken in good faith, is, as is often the case in real life, irrelevant.

As a threshold consideration, it must be remembered that movants have been held to be in civil contempt pursuant to 28 U.S.C. § 1826—a statute which, in 1970, codified a long standing civil contempt practice in the federal courts with respect to recalcitrant witnesses before a court or grand jury. . . .

We deal, therefore, with a judicial determination and practice expressly adopted and codified as legislative policy by the Congress. Under these circumstances, movants' situation cannot be equated or compared with open-ended and indeterminate incarceration for civil contempt which is possible under state law and practice, based on a doctrine of inherent judicial authority and not adopted and codified, as here, as legislative policy as well. Moreover, the developments in the cases on which movants rely have come about to supply a termination point to potentially life-long confinement pursuant to summary court proceedings and without a trial by jury.

For this reason, I believe that reliance on McNeil v. Director, Patuxent Institution, 407 U.S. 245 (1972); Jackson v. Indiana, 406 U.S. 715 (1972); Catena v. Seidl, 65 N.J. 257, 321 A.2d 225 (1974), or In re Farr, 36 Cal. App.3d 577, 111 Cal.Rptr. 649 (1974) is misplaced. Moreover, for different considerations, the determinations in In re Grumbles, Cr. No. 722–71 (D.N.J. Feb. 22, 1973), and In re the Special February 1975 Grand Jury, No. 76 GJ 1128 (N.D.Ill. Jan. 6, 1978), do not advance movants' cause.

In Jackson v. Indiana, petitioner, a deaf mute, had been charged in 1968 with the separate robberies of two women (total value of the stolen property involved was $9.00). After a competency hearing, the petitioner was found by the state court to lack sufficient comprehension to be able to stand trial and was committed to the Indiana Department of Mental Health until that agency should certify him as sane. The Court held that a person who is charged with a criminal offense and is committed solely by reason of an incapacity to stand trial cannot be held in custody for more than a reasonable time necessary to determine whether there is a substantial probability that he will attain that capacity in the foreseeable future. If it is found that no such substantial probability exists, the state must institute normal civil proceedings required for indefinite commitment of the mentally incompetent or grant immediate release. "At the least, due process requires that the nature and duration of commitment bear some reasonable relation to the purpose for which the individual is committed."

In McNeil v. Director, Patuxent Institution, the petitioner had been sentenced by a Maryland court to five years imprisonment. The trial court, thereafter, had committed petitioner to a state institution as a defective delinquent for observation for an indeterminate period. The period of observation had extended to six years by the time the case reached the Supreme Court—one year beyond the sentence imposed for the crime charged. The Court ordered petitioner's release, holding that due process considerations require that the nature and duration of incarceration must be reasonably related to the purpose the commitment is designed to serve.

Those cases are not controlling here. We are not dealing with a situation in which a judge imposes an open-ended sentence pursuant to which the incarceration could continue for all of the individual's life. Summary proceedings which result in sentences of potential life duration shock the conscience, and thus are regarded as an abberration in an open society committed to the rule of law, grounded in reason and fairness.

Similarly, the state cases, although relevant since they support and enunciate the legal thesis movants advance here, are inapposite. In the case at bar, unlike the state cases, there is no possibility of an open-ended, indeterminate or long term incarceration in that movants' confinement, when imposed, had to terminate on May 9, 1978.

In In re Farr a newspaper reporter, who had published information which counsel had been ordered not to make public and who refused to reveal to the trial court the source from which the forbidden data had been obtained, was adjudged in civil contempt and ordered incarcerated until he revealed the identities of the persons who had supplied him with the prohibited matter. The California Court of Appeals held that coercive incarceration to compel compliance with a court order "presents a special problem when disobedience . . . is based upon an established articulated moral principle." In such a situation, the court held, it becomes "necessary to determine the point at which commitment ceases to serve its coercive function and becomes punitive in character." When incarceration of the contemnor becomes penal, the length of the incarceration under California law must terminate in five days. The court held that in a proper proceeding "a determination may be made whether petitioner's continued incarceration will accomplish the purpose of the order requiring that he reveal the identity of the persons who had violated the trial court's order . . . . The ultimate fact to be determined by the trial court is the presence or absence of a substantial likelihood that petitioner's continued commitment will serve that purpose . . . ."

Similarly, in Catena v. Seidl the State Commission of Investigation called Girado Catena, "a suspected member of the hierarchy of organized crime," to testify before it. Catena appeared but refused to answer some 80 questions put to him. He was cited for civil contempt on March 4, 1970, by the New Jersey Superior Court and was incarcerated until such time as he would give the sought testimony. His various appeals failed, and on January 4, 1974, he applied to the trial court for release. The trial court, taking into account his age (72), his poor health and deteriorating physical condition, the length of his confinement, the substantial likelihood that his continued confinement would not result in his testifying before the State Commission and, therefore, that his confinement would possibly continue for the life of the Commission whose term had been extended to December 31, 1979, ordered his release on the grounds that his continued incarceration could no longer be deemed coercive. The New Jersey Supreme Court accepted the trial court's formulation as the proper test but held that its application did not warrant Catena's release at that time.

When the case reached the New Jersey Supreme Court again a year later, however, the majority agreed that the test as then applied to the facts mandated Catena's release. ("Catena II").

Again, the rationale of this case is to terminate a confinement which could conceivably keep a contemnor incarcerated for many years. While accepting the humane and equitable principles underlying the test adopted by the California and New Jersey courts, I agree with the dissent in *Catena II* that what the two courts have done is to "substitute [the contemnor's] dogma for the law duly adopted by society."

That seems to me to be a fatal weakness of the principle. Here we are being asked to accept movant's view that to force them to give what seems to be innocuous-enough testimony is to require them to breach their religious vows, when as Judge Pierce's decision makes clear, there are in actuality no religious principles at stake. Perhaps all that is being articulated and acted upon by the contemnors is a commonplace view among the "outs" in a social system—here the Hispanic poor among whom movants work—that one is being a traitor to one's group if she cooperates with law enforcement officials.

Movants may well continue in the erroneous belief that they are acting from religious conviction protected by the Constitution, particularly since they are being supported by some segments of their Church, and indeed may continue to refuse throughout the term of the grand jury to testify. Experience does indicate, however, that threats to refuse to testify are not always acted upon when the threats themselves fail. See United States v. Sanchez, 459 F.2d 100, 103 (2d Cir. 1972). In any event, the fact of their possible continued recalcitrance is an insufficient basis to justify release when they are facing incarceration only until a specific termination date, May 9, 1978.

There are two federal cases on which movants rely as applying the theory of law they urge be applied in this case. Those cases are In re Grumbles, Cr. 722–71 (D.N.J.1973), and In re The Special February 1975 Grand Jury. In the *Grumbles* case, Judge Williamson, who had ordered the incarceration for contempt, concluded that with only one month to go before the expiration of the grand jury "the order of the Court in holding these people in contempt has been brought forth to Patricia Grumbles and Donald Grumbles in no uncertain terms. I feel, however, now and at this point that the incarceration" has become punitive. . . . Accordingly, he ordered their release.

The Illinois case is less clear. One of the contemnors, Pedro Archuleta, had been adjudged in civil contempt by this court, as well as by the district court in Illinois. Archuleta had been confined under the order of the latter court since July 27, 1977. At a January 6, 1978 hearing Archuleta was asked whether he would change his mind and testify. Archuleta responded in the negative. Judge Parsons stated that he was satisfied that Archuleta would not change his mind, that the latter was sincere in his dedication to the cause he believed he served and ordered his release. The other parties who had been confined for shorter periods were not released.

While Judge Williamson and Judge Parsons paid at least lip service to movants' thesis, their action can be rationalized on a considerably firmer legal foundation. A district judge has wide latitude in a civil contempt situation in determining whether to order coercive incarceration at all, and if incarceration is deemed warranted, the length of incarceration imposed is within his sound discretion as long as it does not extend beyond the grand jury term. See In re Buonacoure, 412 F.Supp. 904, 907 (E.D.Pa.1976). In the absence of abuse of discretion, the judgment will not be disturbed on appeal. Cf. Keyes v. United States, 314 F.2d 123 (9th Cir. 1963). A "contempt citation is a matter in [the] discretion of the judge who gives it . . . ." United States v. Reide, 494 F.2d 644, 647 (2d Cir. 1974). Having ordered coercive incarceration for a certain period, surely the judge may in his discretion modify his judgment, based upon whatever rational considerations appeal to him, including ordering that the coercive incarceration be terminated short of the time originally fixed without the contemnor having complied with the court's order. As I see it, it is the exercise of that discretion afforded the district judges that is involved in the above cited federal cases. In sum I find no support for the application of the legal theory which movants urge in any situation in which a civil contempt citation has been made pursuant to Section 1826.

That does not end the matter, however. In most other jurisdictions movants could apply to the judge who cited them for contempt for a modification of the court's original judgment. Our court, however, pursuant to Rule 6 of our local Assignment and Calendar Rules, refers all matters relating to the grand jury to the Part I Judge. Rule 6 does not explicitly state that all matters relating to proceedings before the grand jury shall be heard by the Part I Judge, as is true in respect of Rule 5 of the Calendar Rules of the Eastern District, but through practice and usage Rule 6 has been so interpreted, or at least it has been so construed by the members of the court involved in the history of these Cueto-Nemikin proceedings.

Movants have appeared before at least five different judges of this court (Judges MacMahon, Pierce, Frankel, Stewart and now myself) because they raised an issue or made application at the time when the particular judge was on his tour of duty in Part I. While each of the preceding judges could have, if he wished, taken the case as his own and maintained jurisdiction over it, none chose to do so. After Judge Frankel cited movants for contempt, movants made their first application for release on May 12 to Judge Frankel. Judge Frankel advised them that the matter should be referred to Judge Stewart, then the Part I Judge.

There surely exists in this court the power to mitigate and lessen coercive incarceration once imposed. Our rules and practice would appear to consign that authority to the Part I Judge. Accordingly, as the Part I Judge to whom the matter was referred and before whom the matter has been *sub judice,* I must determine—apart from movants' rejected legal thesis—whether other considerations warrant movants' release from further coercive incarceration.

Movants are clearly misguided in their continued refusal to adhere to their legal obligation to testify before the grand jury since their defiance cannot be justified under any recognized or accepted First Amendment ground. See In re Wood. However, movants have now been held in coercive custody for more than 10 months. There has been no showing or indication in any of the papers presented to me that these women are other than what they appear to be—persons legitimately engaged in the work of their Church. There has been no showing that they are themselves involved in criminal activities or engaged in crime. There has been no indication that they belong to FALN, or condone or espouse its terrorists' views. All that has been shown is that one Carlos Torres was a one time member of the Commission and movants may have talked to him and may have had some knowledge as to his whereabouts.

In respect of the latter knowledge, however, it is clear that whatever they might have known about Torres' whereabouts last February and March has now become stale information and is unlikely to advance the grand jury investigation. Information as to whether funds of the Commission ever found their way to FALN can surely be ascertained, and more accurately, from other sources. Indeed, it seems unlikely that the Episcopal Church would allow one of its agencies to be corrupted away from its true mission of helping uplift and service the poor, to give financial assistance to murderers and terrorists. The Episcopal Church hierarchy continues to accept both these women as proper church officials duly engaged in the work of the Church. Under these circumstances it does not appear to me that any legitimate purpose is being furthered in keeping the women in custody. The sanctity of the law has been duly vindicated in a coercive incarceration of some ten months duration. Humane considerations require their release.

My preference, of course, would have been for movants to seek their release from Judge Frankel, who originally cited them for contempt, because I do not wish to be placed in a position of appearing even *sub silentio* to be critical of the adjudication Judge Frankel made. Indeed, I am satisfied that my conclusions are no different than those Judge Frankel would reach if faced with this problem at this time. At any rate, it does not appear to me that coercive incarceration beyond six months duration is justified in situations of this kind. Since that period has long passed, movants are ordered released from coercive confinement. The court will exercise authority granted under Rule 6 of our local rules and retain jurisdiction of this case for any future proceedings.

---

1) Terminal stubbornness takes us back to coercive negotiation as interdependent decision-making with conduct substituted for words. Both judge and contemnor leave the realm of threat. How does conduct allow each to coordinate predictions of the other's behavior? The minimax principle holds that each disputant will seek to minimize the other's maximum possible gain and to maximize his own minimum possible gain. How can each advance his interest in reaching a less mutually destructive solution?

2) "Chicken," Schelling tells us, "is a universal form of adversary engagement." T. Schelling, Arms and Influence 116 (1966). Chicken is a game of nerve to force the other to pull back or flinch and avert tragedy. Through willingness to encounter mutual or individual risk, one communicates to the other that the other has the last chance to prevent destruction. How can the

captured spy who is being tortured to reveal secrets he knows convince his captors that he will never break and thereby stop the torture? What tactics may Maria Cueto use to convince Judge Carter that she has relinquished the initiative to him? How can Judge Carter know that the next day of coercion will not suffice? What can he do to convince her that she alone controls her release? T. Schelling, The Strategy of Conflict 139 n. 17; Arms and Influence 42 n. 5.

3) Did things get out of control in *Tegtmeyer*, p. 1096? Is the result in *Tegtmeyer* the worst possible? Was Judge Carter in *Cueto* invited to play chicken? Did he decline? Or did he play and lose? Will the *Cueto* decision create a reputation for yielding that other contemnors will exploit in the future? Will Judge Carter respond in the same way to a surly gangster? Would a reputation for recklessness and unreasonableness help the contemnor? The judge? Two readable accounts of long-distance contemnors are G. Liddy, Will, The Autobiography of G. Gordon Liddy (1980), and R. Harris, Freedom Spent, Part 3, "Taking the Fifth" (1976).

4) Most economic problems involve divisible objects and compensable activities. Money incentives do not, however, animate long-distance contemnors. Silence is a principle. Once it is gone contemnor has no place to stop. Attention focuses on an all-or-nothing solution. The contemnors seek to demonstrate their obduracy.

May the coercing judge be performing a service for the members of some subcultures by allowing them a chance to demonstrate their loyalty? May contemnors simply be playing deaf and dumb because of "organized crime's oath of silence"? Catena v. Seidl, 343 A.2d at 740–747. May silence be rational because they, in Fred Schauer's words, prefer cement walls to cement boots? Is it sensible to prefer a life in prison to a risky liberty outside? Comment, 11 San Diego L.Rev. at 1033 n. 28, 1039 n. 65. May the authorities be taking advantage of these considerations to achieve criminal punishment without proving breach of the criminal law? Fear of retaliation is not a defense to coercive contempt; Note, The Dilemma of the Intimidated Witness in Federal Organized Crime Prosecutions: Choosing Among the Fear of Reprisals, the Contempt Powers of the Court, and the Witness Protection Program, 50 Fordham L.Rev. 582 (1982), argues that it should be. Do you agree?

5) May the reticence of some union leader and reporter contemnors be animated by self-interest? Might silence a) demonstrate militance, toughness, professionalism, and loyalty? b) create an immediate media hero and lead to previously unavailable resources and moral support? A principle is usually involved, albeit rejected by the judge: reporters' source anonymity, the first amendment in *Cueto,* love of a canine friend in *Laing,* not to mention adherence to even feebler causes. In the final analysis, was the *Barnett* majority, p. 909 correct to withhold martyrdom? "Sweet are the uses of adversity." W. Shakespeare, As You Like It, Act II, scene i, line 12.

6) Is there a strain of cussedness and stubbornness in human nature that seeks to resist authority and to preserve automomy? Does pressure get people's backs up? Do people who yield to pressure lose face? Do people receive credit after they are forced to do something? We remember the mar-

tyrs who preferred to die rather than live as apostates with more favor than the government officials who administered the Roman Empire.

7) Reread the statement Martin Luther King made at the press conference after the decision to disobey the Birmingham injunction, p. 292. Does his articulated basis for disobedience differ from Cueto's reasons to refuse to testify?

8) A coercive jail sentence consists of a series of consecutive small coercions to demonstrate the threat and make it plausible. The motion to be released on the ground that imprisonment has lost its coercive force is often called a *Grumbles* motion after the unreported decision discussed in *Cueto.* How should courts articulate the test that enough is enough? Is placing the burden of proof on contemnor to show that the contempt lacks coercive force simply sleight-of-hand? Is the holding in *Cueto* so narrow that it may never apply to another contemnor?

9) Should adherence to "an established moral principle" shorten a contemnor's stay? In re Farr, 111 Cal.Rptr. at 653 (1974) (citing R. Goldfarb, The Contempt Power 60 (1963)) said "yes." Is the New Jersey court correct in observing that the "moral principle" test is "incapable of practical application"? Catena v. Seidl, 343 A.2d at 747 n. 1 (1975). Why didn't Judge Carter adopt the "moral principle" criterion in *Cueto?* Or did he, without admitting it?

10) In Bloom v. Illinois, p. 948, the Court said that a judge without a jury may imprison for only six months. Would an Alaska contemnor be entitled to a jury on a *Cueto* or *Grumbles* motion, citing *Johansen,* p. 1060? Should judges release long-distance contemnors after six months? Wis.Stat. Ann. § 785.04(1)(b). Is § 1826's provision too long and out of touch with human nature? Note, 79 Colum.L.Rev. at 766–73. On the other hand, if the legislature has decided how long is long enough, should a judge ever release a contemnor before the statutory period has elapsed?

11) Is it intelligible to attempt to determine when contempt loses its coercive force and the metamorphosis into punishment occurs? Is the criminal contempt invalid because it is unlimited and therefore cruel and unusual? Because the judge imposed it after mere civil procedure? Would ten years of "coercive" contempt be permissible if the judge imposed it as a criminal sentence after criminal procedure and told contemnor that if she obeyed, he would grant a motion to reduce her sentence?

12) Could a judge end coercive confinement because imprisonment no longer coerced and then convict contemnor of criminal contempt for wilfull disobedience? See United States v. Morales, 566 F.2d 402, 408–409 (2d Cir. 1977); United States v. Berardelli, 565 F.2d 24 (2d Cir. 1977); United States v. De Simone, 267 F.2d 741, 747 (2d Cir. 1959), certiorari denied 361 U.S. 827; In re Farr, 64 Cal.App.3d 605, 614, 134 Cal.Rptr. 595, 600 (1976). May the judge conduct a criminal contempt proceeding and impose a coercive order to be followed by a criminal sentence if the coercive order fails? Compare Laing v. Commonwealth at p. 1028.

13) Which of the following do the terminally stubborn contemnor's tactics resemble? a) Stanley Kowalski in "A Streetcar Named Desire" standing outside in the street shouting "Hey Stella" until Stella, chagrined at the ruck-

us, relents and lets him back in the apartment? b) The mother who says, "There's no law that says children have to bring grandchildren to visit their grandmother on Thanksgiving instead of going to the mountains. I'll just tell my friends that you're too busy to see your mother"? c) The IRA hunger strikers in Dublin's Maze prison? d) Mahatma Gandhi? What moral premise helps these tactics work? Is it the same premise that allowed the lady of an earlier era to keep the key from the search party by placing it in her bosom?

14) Consider this footnote from T. Schelling, The Strategy of Conflict 127 n. 7 (1960): "Edward Banfield showed me this irresistible quotation about the Bhats and Charans of the west of India, revered as Bards. 'In Guzerat they carry large sums in bullion, through tracts where a strong escort would be insufficient to protect it. They are also guarantees of all agreements of chiefs among themselves, and even with the government.

" 'Their power is derived from the sanctity of their character and their desperate resolution. If a man carrying treasure is approached, he announces that he will commit traga, as it is called: or if an engagement is not complied with, he issues the same threat unless it is fulfilled. If he is not attended to, he proceeds to gash his limbs with a dagger, which, if all other means fail, he will plunge into his heart; or he will first strike off the head of his child; or different guarantees to the agreement will cast lots who is to be first beheaded by his companions. The disgrace of these proceedings, and the fear of having a bard's blood on their head, generally reduce the most obstinate to reason. Their fidelity is exemplary, and they never hesitate to sacrifice their lives to keep up an ascendency on which the importance of their cast depends.' (The Hon. Mountsuart Elphinstone, History of India [ed. 7; London, 1889] p. 211)."

Chapter Fourteen

WHO IS BOUND BY AN INJUNCTION

Who is bound by an injunction? The familiar proposition, powerfully articulated by L. Hand in *Alemite* below, p. 1124, is that only the parties are bound. This chapter evaluates that proposition, but first we will stress the ambiguity of the term "bound." We cannot determine who is bound by the decree unless we know what it means to be "bound." At least three possible meanings emerge:

(a) Lack of Freedom to Relitigate. A person may be bound by a decree in the sense that he is not free to relitigate any of the conclusions of law and findings of fact that underlie the injunction and are, in a sense, implicit in the decree. For example, the legality of the dual school system has not been open to relitigation following Brown v. Board of Education, and, in one sense, all school boards—regardless of whether they were a party in *Brown*—are "bound" by that determination. Courts will not let decided issues be relitigated either under stare decisis or res judicata.

Of course some people ignore precedent until a judge personalizes it in an injunction. Several years after Loving v. Virginia had declared anti-miscegenation statutes illegal, for example, a racially mixed couple applied to an Alabama official for a marriage license. An assistant attorney general backed the official decision to refuse the license. He said, "When the U.S. Supreme Court rules in a case it is just binding on people in that particular case. The Alabama law is still law until it is stricken down. They don't just wipe these laws off the books all over the United States because of one ruling." A second specific lawsuit was necessary. United States v. Brittain, 319 F.Supp. 1058 (N.D.Ala.1970). Farber, The Supreme Court and the Rule of Law: Cooper v. Aaron Revisited, 1982 U.Ill.L.Rev. 387, attacks this attitude toward the rule of law. We agree with Professor Farber; but we accept the dolorous reality of human cussedness.

(b) Amenable to Criminal Sanctions. The members of a school board might be bound by a decree in the sense that they are amenable to criminal sanctions for disobeying the decree. Aside from criminal contempt sanctions people risk other criminal sanctions, and thus we are entitled to use the word "bound." For example, suppose the federal court decree provides that the particular school board must allow black students to attend the formerly all-white school, the school board grants those requests, and then some members of a white-citizen group attack the black students who are attempting to exercise the rights of the decree. Even if the attackers cannot be punished for criminal contempt, they may be prosecuted under some criminal statute, such as 18 U.S.C. § 1509 (in the Appendix). If so, they can be said to be "bound" by the decree in the sense that they have a legal obligation not to interfere with the exercise of the rights provided by that decree. They are not free to relitigate the issues involved, and breach of this legal obligation will be punished criminally. Criminal statutes create duties for everyone, but we usually think of an injunction and criminal contempt as affecting only parties.

(c) Amenable to Civil Remedies. People might be bound by the injunction in the sense that, if they do what is forbidden or interfere with the exercise of rights under the decree, they will be confronted with civil contempt remedies. For example, if the school board refuses to honor the transfer requests of the blacks, a compensatory or coercive contempt order may be entered—the members may be required to pay for the injuries done, to reopen a choice period, or to pay a fine or remain in jail for each day of noncompliance. Similarly, other persons may be "bound" by the decree in the sense that they could almost automatically be named as additional parties (e.g., joinder under Federal Rule of Civil Procedure 20) or a new suit may be commenced against them. Such civil remedies protect the previous decree, and new defendants may be denied an opportunity to relitigate the question underlying the previous decree.

Federal Rule of Civil Procedure 65(d) was enacted in 1914 as part of the Clayton Act. It states the governing principles for the federal system: an injunction "is binding only upon the parties to the action, their officers, agents, servants, employees, and attorneys, and upon those persons in active concert or participation with them who receive actual notice of the order by personal service or otherwise." How does the rule use the word "binding"?

One of your editors published a long article about the topic of this chapter. He concluded that the state of the art was low indeed, and he suggested that courts should alter the way they analyze the question. See Rendleman, Beyond Contempt: Obligors to Injunctions, 53 Tex.L.Rev. 873 (1975). Useful articles may be found in Dobbyn, Contempt Power of the Equity Court over Outside Agitators, 8 St. Mary's L.J. 1 (1976); Note, Contempt Proceedings Against Persons Not Named in an Injunction, 46 Harv.L.Rev. 1311 (1933); Note, Binding Nonparties to Injunction Decrees, 49 Minn.L. Rev. 719 (1965); Comment, Community Resistance to School Desegregation: Enjoining the Undefinable Class, 44 U.Chi.L.Rev. 111 (1976). Four Notes, written in the 1950s before Congress passed 18 U.S.C. § 1509, deal with the problem of enforcing *Brown*: The Law, The Mob, and Desegregation, 47 Calif.L.Rev. 126 (1959); The Range of Federal Injunctions, 6 Utah L.Rev. 363 (1959); Contempt by Strangers to a Federal Court Decree, 43 Va.L.Rev. 1294 (1957); Legal Sanctions to Enforce Desegregation in the Public Schools: The Contempt Power and the Civil Rights Acts, 65 Yale L.J. 630 (1956).

I. Obstruction of Justice

SEAWARD v. PATERSON

[1897] 1 Ch. 545, 76 Law Times 215.

LINDLEY, L.J.— . . . On the 15th July 1896 North, J. granted an injunction in an action against a man named Paterson, to restrain him from infringing a certain covenant in a lease, which had been granted to Paterson. The real controversy at that time turned upon the fact that Paterson had got a boxing club, or something of the kind, on the first, second, and third floors of a house in Fetter-lane, and that was complained of by other people, and was an infringement of the covenant contained in the lease. North, J., having come to that conclusion, granted an order restraining Paterson, his under-tenants, agents, and servants, from doing or suffering to be done anything which might interfere with the full and quiet enjoyment by the plaintiff or his under-tenants of the premises adjoining or neighbouring to the first, second, and third floors of the messuage or tenement demised by the plaintiff to the defendant, or which should be or tend to grow to be an annoyance, nuisance, damage, inconvenience, disturbance, or injury to the plaintiff or his superior landlord, or his or their tenants, or from using the premises, or suffering the same to be used otherwise than for the purpose of a private club, without the written license of the plaintiff. The injunction, as is usual in such cases, follows the language of the covenant; but the real nuisance complained of was the noise and disturbance created by the boxing performances which were taking place. Now Murray was present in court, and heard a good deal of the proceedings which led to that injunction being granted. He says that he left the court shortly before the actual injunction was pronounced, or before judgment was given; but he knew the result. He says that he knew all about it. Notwithstanding that, what was done—I do not say by whom at present—was this: There were arrangements made for having these boxing performances in September and October, and on the 9th and 21st Oct. some more of these boxing performances took place, and upon that an application was made to North, J. to commit Paterson for that infringement of the injunction. Before that came on for hearing, it appears that Paterson turned round and said that Murray was the person who was really responsible for the nuisance. Thereupon, proceedings were taken to commit Murray. He was not a party to the action, either first or last. Now let us pause and consider upon what jurisdiction the court can proceed against Murray. There is no injunction against him—he is no more bound by that injunction than any other member of the public. He is, however, bound, like other members of the public, not to interfere with, and not to obstruct, the course of justice. And the case made against him must be this, if it be anything: not that he has technically infringed the injunction, which has not been granted against him in any sense of the word, but that he has been aiding and abetting others in setting the court at defiance, and deliberately treating the order of the court as unworthy of notice. If he has so conducted himself, it is perfectly idle to say that there is no jurisdiction to attach him for contempt, as distinguished from a breach of the injunction, which has a technical meaning. . . . Mr. Seward Brice has argued very strenuously that there is no such jurisdiction; and has founded his argument, and based it mainly, on a passage in Lord Eldon's judgment in Iveson v. Harris (7 Ves. 251, at p. 256). . . . Iveson v. Harris was a case of prohibition, and Lord Eldon, differing from a view taken by the Court of Exchequer with respect to proceedings on a bail bond not being a proceeding against a prohibition restraining the original action so as to incur a contempt, as to which I say nothing, says this: "I have no conception that it is competent to this court to hold a man bound by an injunction who is not a party in the cause for the purpose of the cause. The old practice was that he must be brought into court, so as according to the ancient laws and usages of the country to be made a subject of the writ. The jurisdiction in lunacy is quite distinct." That strikes me as perfectly right. Lord Eldon is addressing himself there to persons bound by the injunction; he is not considering those persons who assist others in setting the court at defiance; he does not deal with that class of persons at all. The law is there defined in a way which is familiar to anybody accustomed to the procedure in Chancery. A notice of motion to commit a man for breach of an injunction which is technically wrong unless he is bound by the injunction, and a notice of motion to commit a man for contempt of court, not because he is bound by the injunction by being a party to the cause or anything of that kind, but because he is conducting himself so as to obstruct the course of justice, are totally different things. The difference is very marked. In the one case the party who is bound by the injunction is proceeded against; the proceedings against him are for the purpose of enforcing the order of the court for the benefit of the person who got the order. In the other case the court will not allow its process to be set at nought, and treated with contempt. The consequence is this: that in the one case the person who is interested in enforcing the order is enforcing it for his own benefit; while, in the other case, if the order of the court has been contumaciously set at nought, he cannot settle it with the person so acting and save that person from the consequences of his act. The difference between the two kinds of contempt is perfectly well known, although in some cases there may be a little difficulty in saying on which side of the line they fall. . . . The facts, of course, are all important, and I agree at once that, if I can accept Murray's suggestion that he was present on the two occasions referred to simply as a spectator—if that were really true in substance—I cannot regard him as having done anything which justified the court in making an order against him. I should think that that was not anything like enough. But let us see. What is Murray? I will not allude now to his past career; I pass that over; it is quite unnecessary to go into that. What is his connection with the club? Murray and a friend of his called Coaney, alias Brown, give Paterson references; Murray introduces Paterson to Mr. Norris, his solicitor; Murray from first to last—I do not care how it is done exactly—finances Paterson. Paterson has not got any money; he wants 300*l*. or 400*l*. in course of time to get in and furnish the club, and get a billiard-table, and he gets all his money from Murray. . . . Then arises this very important matter: Just before the trial comes on there is a bill of sale, and just after the trial there is an agreement by Paterson to sell the whole of the concern to Murray—whether it is carried through or not I do not know. Murray is said to be an ordinary member of this club, and he evidently takes a very considerable interest in it. He is the man who has found the money, and, so far as I can draw the inference, he carries on the club. It is evident that Paterson was a mere tool of somebody. . . . The view taken by North, J. is this: "Now, looking at the history of Murray's connection with the club, I have not the least doubt as to the character in which he was present on the occasions in question. He was not there present as a mere spectator, but he was there as one of the persons interested. That, I consider, is proved by the statements which are really not in dispute between the parties, looking at the whole of the evidence." There is a little ambiguity about that expression, "He was there as one of the persons interested"; but I have not the slightest doubt that Murray was at the bottom of the whole thing. I give him credit for taking a view, which, if there was anything in it, might be of use to him. I dare say he thought that, if these boxing matches were not advertised, and the public were not invited to come, and so on, the thing would not matter. That was not, perhaps, within the objection, but he knew perfectly well that what was within the objection was creating a disturbance, under any circumstances, without having boxing matches. He did not do anything intentionally which he thought would get him into gaol—of course he did not; he was not so foolish as that. I have not the slightest doubt, therefore, that what was done was a gross breach of the injunction . . . .

THE REESE CASE

The theory of Seaward v. Paterson was soon picked by American courts. In re Reese, 107 F. 942 (8th Cir. 1901), an antistrike suit, relied on it. Reese was charged with coming into Kansas at the head of a column of about 300 men, called strikers, and interfering with the men and the plant of the party protected by the injunction. The decree ran against the named defendants and "all other persons who have or may combine, confederate, or conspire with said defendants or either of them." Reese was not a party; indeed, the court was of the view that "the complainant intentionally and studiously avoided making him a party." Id. at 947. The court also found that "he did the acts complained of without any relation to or connection with the defendants, as an independent exercise of his own will." Id. at 945. The trial court found him in contempt and ordered imprisonment for three months. The appellate court released Reese because he was tried on the theory that he violated the injunction, rather than that he obstructed justice. But the court went out of its way to subscribe to the Seaward v. Paterson theory (107 F. at 945):

". . . Now, it being conceded that he was not such a party, it is attempted to sustain the sentence of commitment on the broad ground that the petitioner, if not technically guilty of violating the injunctive order, was guilty of contemptuously obstructing the administration of justice by doing the things which other parties had been enjoined from doing, with knowledge of such injunctive order against him. In support of this contention we are directed to section 725, Rev.St.U.S. 1878 [now, with some modifications, 18 U.S.C. § 401], which is as follows:

" 'The said courts shall have power to impose and administer all necessary oaths, and to punish, by fine or imprisonment, at the discretion of the court, contempts of their authority: provided that such power to punish contempts shall not be construed to extend to any cases except the misbehavior of any person in their presence, or so near thereto as to obstruct the administration of justice, the misbehavior of any of the officers of said courts in their official transaction, and the disobedience or resistance of any such officer, or by any party, juror, witness, or other person, to any lawful writ, process, order, rule, decree, or command of the said courts.'

"This section undoubtedly confers ample power upon the court to punish any person for intentional resistance to any of its orders. The word 'disobedience' aptly applies to a party or other person against whom an order is made. The word 'resistance' manifestly is applicable to a party to the suit, and may be applicable to 'other persons' referred to in the section. It is entirely consonant with reason, and necessary to maintain the dignity, usefulness, and respect of a court, that any person, whether a party to a suit or not, having knowledge that a court of competent jurisdiction has ordered certain persons to do or to abstain from doing certain acts, cannot intentionally interfere to thwart the purposes of the court in making such order. Such an act, independent of its effect upon the rights of the suitors in the case, is a flagrant disrespect to the court which issues it, and an unwarrantable interference with and obstruction to the orderly and effective administration of justice, and as such is and ought to be treated as a contempt of the court which issued the order. Such contempts, however, are totally different offenses from those which the parties to the case commit when they disobey a direct order made in a case for the benefit of the complainant. The one is an offense against the majesty and dignity of the law. The other is a violation of the rights of a particular suitor, at whose instance and for whose protection the particular injunctive order disobeyed was issued by the court. The power to punish for contempt is not limited to cases of disobedience by parties to the suit of some express command or rule against them, but, subject to the limitations imposed by section 725, supra, is co-extensive with the necessity for maintaining the authority and dignity of the court. . . ."

---

1) Are both *Seaward* and *Reese* a lot of doctrinal sound and fury on behalf of plaintiffs who neglected to sue the correct defendants? Did Paterson's conduct differ from a defendant in a money action who converts nonexempt assets into exempt property to avoid paying plaintiff's judgment? Is *Seaward* based on the theory that judges use contempt sanctions against parties to coerce them to comply but use contempt against nonparties to punish disrespect? If a party violated an injunction in a way that destroyed the opportunity to comply, could the judge punish that party? Does *Reese* adopt that part of *Seaward*? Does *Reese* base criminal contempt on the policy of preserving respect? Does the *Reese* court subordinate contemnor's opportunity to litigate to the goal of punishing disrespect? Is that too high a procedural price to pay for respect?

2) The obstruction-of-justice theory may have continuing vitality in some state courts; but it is no longer available in the federal court system. This change is probably due to Federal Rule 65(d). Often the objection is cast in more generalized terms. Justice Brandeis described the obstruction of justice theory in Chase National Bank v. Norwalk, 291 U.S. 431, 437 (1934), as a violation of "established principles of equity jurisdiction and procedure." But in truth the needs that gave rise to the obstruction-of-justice concept are substantial; in order to evaluate the concept more fully, we must assess alternative methods of satisfying these needs. The questions are whether there are any real differences between the substitutes and the obstruction-of-justice concept, and whether these substitutes ameliorate the unfairness of the obstruction-of-justice concept.

(a) New Injunctive Proceedings

The plaintiffs' may commence a separate injunctive proceeding against nonparties who are preventing the parties from performing their obligations under the decree or who are interfering with the enjoyment of the rights granted by the decree. These ancillary proceedings would have to be started promptly, so plaintiff would probably resort to procedures for temporary restraining orders and preliminary injunctions. In any event, once the judge issues an injunction against obstruction, any subsequent obstruction would be amenable to the contempt power.

The obstruction issue is likely to arise where the initial injunction touches on deeply held feelings. The implementation of Brown v. Board of Education led to many anti-obstruction injunctions. The first occurred where the school board was not under a court order to desegregate, but instead instituted a desegregation plan on its own, Brewer v. Hoxie School District No. 46, 238 F.2d 91 (8th Cir. 1956). The board's attempt to desegregate was greeted with interference and obstruction instigated by persons who were not state officials. The board responded by commencing an injunctive suit in federal court against these persons. The claim for relief was primarily predicated on the power of the federal courts to safeguard "the right of members of the school board to be free from interference with the performance of a duty which the Constitution imposes on them." It is a right, the court of appeals said, that "derives directly from the Supremacy Clause and the related constitutional provision imposing upon the State officers an oath or affirmation to support the Constitution and it is a federal right." (at 95). The court found "additional support" for the anti-obstruction injunction in 42 U.S.C. § 1985(3). That statute provides a damage remedy for injuries arising from a conspiracy to prevent state officials from affording equal protection of the laws. The court held, in part relying on the all-writs statute, 28 U.S.C. § 1651, that the federal court could enjoin a conspiracy made actionable by § 1985(3), and that the school board, acting in loco parentis, could assert the rights of the school children.

Kasper v. Brittain, 245 F.2d 92, 97 (6th Cir. 1957), followed. Here the injunctive suit was brought by a public official, a public school principal,* alleging that Kasper, a rabble-rouser with no connection with any public officials, was making speeches that would inflame the public and make desegregation impossible or difficult. Compared with *Brewer* there were two differences: (1) The injunction against Kasper's obstruction was a temporary restraining order, issued ex parte; and (2) in *Kasper* the school desegregation was to take place under a federal court order. But the court viewed these differences as of no significance and, relying on *Brewer,* merely declared: "The Federal Court is always empowered to enforce its decrees by orderly process." For the *Kasper* court, the only real issue was whether the anti-obstruction injunction (the TRO) abridged Kasper's freedom of speech, and the court resolved this issue adversely to Kasper by invoking the clear-and-present-danger test and the *United Mine Workers* rule.

The next step occurred in Faubus v. United States, 254 F.2d 797 (8th Cir. 1958). The Governor had used the National Guard in Little Rock to prevent Negro children from entering what had traditionally been the white school. This obstruction prevented Negro students from enjoying certain rights, while in *Brewer* and *Kasper* the obstruction prevented school officials

* The United States appeared as amicus, but it was clear that it construed that role in the more traditional sense and thus, for the court, did not raise any *Debs*-type problem about statutory authorization.

from performing their duty. As Hohfield would have put it, these were just two sides of the same coin, and it was anticipated by the § 1985(3)-ground in *Brewer.* There were, however, other factual elements in *Faubus* of more substance: (1) Unlike *Brewer* or *Kasper,* the obstructor was a state official; (2) unlike *Brewer* or *Kasper,* the party seeking the injunctive relief against the obstruction was the United States; (3) like *Kasper* but unlike *Brewer,* the school desegregation was to take place under a court order.

The fact that the obstructors were state officials should have made it easier to grant relief: the obstruction itself—state officials denying blacks the opportunity to go to school with whites—could be viewed as a denial of equal protection of the laws, as a form of discriminatory conduct prohibited by the Fourteenth Amendment. However, the moving party was the United States, which made it difficult to rely on this equal-protection theory. If the court relied on this equal-protection theory, the *Debs* question may have been raised: Could the Department of Justice bring injunctive litigation on behalf of the United States to enforce the equal protection clause in the absence of statutory authorization? It is not clear that the Eighth Circuit would have answered that question in the affirmative, nor whether the Executive—in 1957—wanted an affirmative answer. This led the court, and presumably the Department to stress the third fact—that the rights being interfered with derived from a court order. Then the court of appeals was able to claim that what was at stake was "the due administration of justice" and that the anti-obstruction injunction was designed to protect "the integrity of the federal courts," the courts "belonging to the United States." True, there was no statutory authorization for the Department to institute injunctive litigation to protect those persons exercising rights under a federal court order, and thus some reliance had to be placed on the *Debs* theory. But this was a far more limited use of the *Debs* theory, and thus perhaps less questionable than one that viewed the obstructor's conduct as simply a denial of equal protection. And it should be emphasized that the court felt there was a need to bolster even this limited *Debs* theory by emphasizing, at the tail end of its discussion, that the plaintiffs in the original desegregation action were the "real parties in interest and they joined the Government in praying for the preliminary injunction" against the Governor and other obstructors.

The pertinent portion of the court's opinion reads:

"The second question for decision is whether the District Court had jurisdiction to make its order of September 9, 1957, inviting the Attorney General and the United States Attorney to appear as amici curiae, and authorizing them to submit pleadings, evidence, arguments and briefs, and to file a petition for injunctive relief to prevent obstructions to the carrying out of the court's orders. The appellants contend that the court was without authority to make the order, and that the Attorney General and the United States Attorney as amici curiae were without authority to file a petition for injunctive relief.

"The District Court in *Aaron,* as has already been stated, reserved, in its judgment and decree, jurisdiction 'for the entry of such other and further orders, as may be necessary to obtain the effectuation of the plan [of gradual school integration]' as contemplated and set forth in its opinion. When the court was informed that the effectuation of the plan which it had approved and ordered into effect was being prevented by the appellants' use of the National Guard, action was called for to vindicate the court's judgment and orders.

"It was proper for the court to do all that reasonably and lawfully could be done to protect and effectuate its orders and judgments and to prevent them from being thwarted by force or otherwise. The court could not, with propriety, employ private counsel to do the necessary investigative and legal work. It has, we think, always in the past been customary for a federal District Court to call upon the law officers of the United States for aid and advice, in comparable situations.

"As the Supreme Court said in Universal Oil Products Co. v. Root Refining Co., 328 U.S. 575, 581, 'After all, a federal court can always call on law officers of the United States to serve as amici . . . . Amici selected by the court to vindicate its honor ordinarily ought not to be in the service of those having private interests in the outcome.'

"In our opinion, the status of the Attorney General and the United States Attorney was something more than that of mere amici curiae in private litigation. They were acting under the authority and direction of the court to take such action as was necessary to prevent its orders and judgments from being frustrated and to represent the public interest in the due administration of justice.

"It seems to us unnecessary to labor the point, since the plaintiffs in the *Aaron* case were, at the time of the hearing on September 20, 1957, still real parties in interest and they joined the Government in praying for the preliminary injunction which was granted and which we do not doubt the court had power to grant." 254 F.2d, at 804–05.

As could be expected, *Faubus,* with its emphasis on the "due administration of justice," has not been confined to situations where the private plaintiff who obtained the original decree formally joined the United States application for injunctive relief against the obstructor. The operative assumption in the Department of Justice was that it could—on its own—seek injunctive relief against any person, public official or private person, who interferes with the exercise of rights or performance of duties arising from a federal court decree. Thus, in United States v. Farrar, 414 F.2d 936 (5th Cir. 1969), the Government obtained an injunction against those private individuals who "persuaded" Negroes to retract choices they exercised under a freedom-of-choice desegregation plan imposed by decree. That decree was entered in a suit brought by the Department of Justice under powers granted to it by Title IV of the Civil Rights Act of 1964; but the theory of the Department's complaint, which was accepted apparently without question by the opposing parties and the court of appeals, was not tied to this particular fact.

The pertinent portion of the court's opinion reads: "[T]he United States brought suit, pursuant to 28 U.S.C. §§ 1345 and 1651, to enjoin eleven white persons who were not parties to the original decree from interfering with the freedom of choice of Negro citizens in order 'to safeguard the due administration of justice in its courts and the integrity of its judicial process' and in order to secure relief 'from conduct of the [appellees] denying equal protection of the laws to citizens of the United States . . . .' " 414 F.2d, at 938.

What has emerged from this line of school desegregation cases is a doctrine that has several elements: (a) Nonparties can be enjoined from interfering with the exercise of rights or performance of duties arising from another decree. (b) These nonparties need not be public officials constrained by another law, such as the equal protection clause. (c) This ancillary injunctive proceeding could be brought by either (i) a party whose rights are being interfered with, (ii) a party who is being prevented by the obstructor from performing his duty, or (iii) the Department of Justice acting in the name of the United States. (d) Despite their absence from the original proceeding, the nonparties are not free to question the grant of the rights or the imposition of duties, to relitigate the findings of fact or conclusions of law underlying the original decree. This is clearly the case when, as is often true, the anti-obstruction injunction is ex parte (a TRO) and buttressed by the *United Mine Workers* rule. We think that the same result would follow if the anti-obstruction injunction took the form of a preliminary (*Faubus*) or permanent (*Farrar*) injunction.

United States v. Hall, discussed in the last section of this chapter confirms this doctrine. Does it mean that the obstruction-of-justice concept has emerged in a new form? True, this new doctrine requires the court to go through the formality of issuing a new prohibition specifically addressed to the alleged obstructor. But, given the high notice requirements of the obstruction-of-justice concept, as illustrated by another early federal case, Garrigan v. United States, 163 F. 16 (7th Cir. 1908), a doubt arises about the functional significance of this new anti-obstruction prohibition. Is it nothing more than a device or technique to give the obstructor a "second chance," not rooted in any deep sense of fairness. On the other hand, is a "second chance" better than no chance? Does the combination of ex parte procedure with the collateral bar rule justify the alternative of holding nonparties in contempt? Why should the plaintiff avoid individualizing the obstructor as a defendant and isolating his conduct? If people are named as parties and sued separately will they be more likely to comply? Beyond Contempt, 53 Tex.L. Rev. at 910.

(b) *Criminal Prosecutions*

The second alternative, a criminal prosecution against the obstructor, does not even afford a "second chance"; it seems even more similar to the allegedly defunct obstruction-of-justice concept.

The federal criminal code has a criminal statute that deals explicitly and directly with obstruction, 18 U.S.C. § 1509. It was enacted in response to the school desegregation crisis in Little Rock and has a saving clause for the *Faubus* theory for injunctive relief. It should be noted that, although the statute is confined to obstruction that involves "threats of force" and is done "willfully," the penalty, not more than a year in jail or a fine of $1000, is not severe.

The Department of Justice has also used 18 U.S.C. § 241—a felony statute—to punish an alleged obstructor. The first instance was the prosecution of the murderers of Mrs. Luizzo. She was killed while helping participants in the historic Selma-to-Montgomery march, a march that was conducted under the protection of a federal court order issued by Judge Johnson in Williams v. Wallace, 240 F.Supp. 100 (M.D.Ala.1965). The decree read:

"Ordered, adjudged and decreed that, pending further order of this Court, George C. Wallace, as Governor of the State of Alabama, Albert J. Lingo, as Director of Public Safety for the State of Alabama, and James G. Clark, Jr., as Sheriff of Dallas County, Alabama, their successors in office, agents, representatives, employees, and other persons in active concert and participation with them be and each is hereby restrained and enjoined from:

"(1) Arresting, harassing, threatening, or in any way interfering with the efforts to march or walk, or the marching or walking, by the plaintiffs, members of their class, and others who may join with them, along U. S. Highway 80 from Selma, Alabama, to Montgomery, Alabama, said march as presently approved by this Court, to commence in Selma, Alabama, not earlier than Friday, March 19, 1965, and not later than Monday, March 22, 1965, and to terminate in Montgomery, Alabama; and

"(2) Otherwise obstructing, impeding, or interfering with the peaceful non-violent efforts by said plaintiffs, members of their class, and others who may join with them, in protesting and demonstrating by assembling and by marching along U. S. Highway 80 from Selma, Alabama, to Montgomery, Alabama, as said march is proposed in plaintiffs' plan filed with this Court and served on the defendants on March 16, 1965, and to the extent that said plan is presently approved by this Court.

"It is further ordered, adjudged and decreed that, pending further order of this Court, the defendants George C. Wallace, as Governor of the State of Alabama, Albert J. Lingo, as Director of Public Safety for the State of Alabama, and James G. Clark, Jr., as Sheriff of Dallas County, Alabama, their successors in office, agents, representatives, employees, and all others acting in concert with them, be and each is hereby restrained and enjoined from failing to provide police protection for the plaintiffs, members of their class, and others who may join with them, in their march, as presently scheduled and presently approved by this court, to commence not earlier than Friday, March 19, 1965, and not later than Monday, March 22, 1965, along U. S. Highway 80 from Selma, Alabama, to Montgomery, Alabama."

Section 241 punishes conspiracies to interfere with the exercise of a "right . . . secured by the Constitution and laws of the United States." The prosecution's theory was that a right granted or protected by a federal court order was indeed a right secured by the laws of the United States and thus within the ambit of § 241. The Department did not harmonize this reading of § 241 with § 1509, the criminal statute that deals with such interferences in quite specific but significantly less severe terms. And the Court of Appeals avoided that problem, as well as others, by sustaining the convictions on the view that the right interfered with was, in the style of United States v. Cruikshank, 92 U.S. 542 (1875), a right "secured by the Constitution" (rather than the court order)—the right to petition and assemble in behalf of obtaining the right to vote in federal elections. Wilkins v. United States, 376 F.2d 552 (5th Cir. 1967). The court, through Judge Coleman, said at 561:

"The Selma to Montgomery march (assembly) was not in connection with any specifically impending federal election. The proceedings in Williams v.

Wallace . . . were expressly pleaded in the indictment, however, by title and number. Those proceedings directly concerned the denial of the right to register to vote in federal elections and with an assembly for the purpose of protesting that condition. Therefore, guided by . . . *Cruikshank,* we hold that any citizen of the United States participating in the march was exercising an attribute of national citizenship, guaranteed by the United States, and that a conspiracy against those participating would be a violation of 18 U.S.C. § 241.

"We thus find it unnecessary to pass upon the contention of the Government that the rights of the participants emanated from the Court Order, that the Court Order emanated from the Constitution and laws of the United States, and that such Court Order thus conferred a right within the ambit of § 241.

"In touching upon this point, however, we would point out that the Court Order was directed solely to state action and the Government admits that there was none here involved. Moreover, we are impressed with the consideration that if a right or privilege is secured by the Constitution or laws of the United States it requires no advance validation by a court order. Likewise, if not so secured it would be hard to see how a court order could do that which the Constitution or the federal laws had failed to do. The Court Order was, however, a very pertinent factor in the alleged offense in that it described times, places, and the nature of the federally guaranteed rights to be exercised. It thus fully informed the defendants of the offense charged against them and it limited the bounds within which the prosecution had to operate."

Since *Wilkins,* the Department has used § 241 in combination with § 1509 to deal with alleged obstructors of court-ordered school desegregation. See Rosecrans v. United States, 378 F.2d 561 (5th Cir. 1967) and United States v. Hayes, 444 F.2d 472 (5th Cir. 1971), where the defendants were not state officials, the obstruction took the form of bombing, and the Department successfully prosecuted under a two-count indictment. One count charged a violation of § 1509. The other charged a violation of § 241—but it is not clear whether, for purposes of § 241, the right interfered with was the right to go to a desegregated school or the right to enjoy the benefits of a federal court order. In *Rosecrans,* the Fifth Circuit, in summarizing the § 241 count, identifies the right as the "right to attend the . . . public schools in Duval County, Florida, pursuant to a permanent injunctive decree of the United States District Court for the Middle District of Florida." In *Hayes* the court identifies the right as the "right to attend school without regard to race or color." Neither appellate opinion contains any discussion as to the applicability of § 241, either alone or in conjunction with § 1509. In *Hayes,* however, a challenge to the statute was made in a subsequent collateral proceeding; the District Judge held that § 241 did reach the conduct alleged and that under the recent Supreme Court decision in Griffin v. Breckenridge, 403 U.S. 88 (1971), Section 2 of the Thirteenth Amendment would permit the application of § 241 to private conspiracies to interfere with the right to attend public schools without regard to race or color. Hayes v. United States, No. 5384 (E.D. Tex. November 18, 1971). This district court decision on § 241, which resolves one of the central issues that divided the Supreme Court in United States v. Guest, 383 U.S. 745

(1966), comes several years after Congress passed another statute to deal specifically with such conduct. That is Title I of the Civil Rights Act of 1968, now codified as 18 U.S.C. § 245 (b)(2)(1970). Why, then, did the Department use § 241?

II. Agency and "Privity"

The theory of compelling an agent to obey injunctions against the employer is that because the agent benefits the employer, the employer will represent the agent. Courts attempt to reconcile two policies. They seek to prevent named defendants from continuing the forbidden conduct through straws. They also attempt to avoid holding people in contempt unless they had a day in court personally or through a representative. Do the *Lennon* and *Alemite* decisions adopt the same theory of obligation as *Seaward*? Should the judge assume representation from agency? Examine the relationships to discern whether or not the principal's and agent's interests conflict.

Important political and legal background about the lawsuit that led to *Lennon* and the role of then Circuit Judge William Howard Taft is found in A. Paul, Conservative Crisis and the Rule of Law 111–16 (1960).

IN RE LENNON

166 U.S. 548, 17 S.Ct. 658, 41 L.Ed. 1110 (1897).

This was a petition for a writ of *habeas corpus* originally filed in the Circuit Court for the Northern District of Ohio.

The petitioner alleged that he was a citizen of the State of Ohio, and was unlawfully restrained of his liberty by the marshal, under an order of the Circuit Court of the United States, made in a case pending in that court, wherein the Toledo, Ann Arbor and North Michigan Railway Company, a corporation of the State of Michigan, was complainant, and several railway companies, citizens of Ohio, as well as the Michigan Central Railroad Company, a citizen of Michigan, were defendants.

The bill in that case . . . averred the complainant to be the owner of a line of railroad from Toledo, Ohio, northwesterly through the State of Michigan; that a large part of its business consisted in the transportation of freight cars from points in the States of Michigan, Minnesota and Wisconsin to points in Ohio and other States east thereof, and that it was engaged as a common carrier in a large amount of interstate commerce, which was regulated and controlled by the Interstate Commerce Act of Congress. The bill further averred that the defendants' lines of railroad connected with those of complainant at or near Toledo, and that a large and important part of its business consisted in the interchange of freight cars between the defendant and complainant companies, and was subject to the provisions of the Interstate Commerce Act; that it was the duty of the defendant companies to afford reasonable and equal facilities for the interchange of traffic, and to receive, forward and deliver freight cars in the ordinary transaction of business, without any discrimination; that the defendant companies, and their employés, had given out and threatened that they would refuse to receive from complainant cars billed over its road for transportation by complainant to their destination, for the reason that the complainant had employed as locomotive engineers in its service men who were not members of the Brotherhood of Locomotive Engineers, "an irresponsible voluntary association," and that the locomotive engineers in the employ of the defendant companies had refused to handle cars to be interchanged with the complainant's road; notwithstanding that they continued to afford the other railroad companies full and free facilities for the interchange of traffic, while refusing to transact such business with the complainant, thereby illegally discriminating against it.

Upon the filing of this bill, and upon the application of the complainant, the Circuit Court issued an injunction against the defendants, their officers, agents, servants and employés, enjoining them from refusing to afford and extend to the Toledo, Ann Arbor and North Michigan Railway Company the same facilities for an interchange of interstate business between the companies as were enjoyed by other railway companies, and from refusing to receive from the complainant company cars billed from points in one State to points in another State, which might be offered to the defendant companies by the complainant.

The injunction was served upon the Lake Shore and Michigan Southern Railway Company, one of the defendants, one of whose employés was the appellant, James Lennon, a locomotive engineer, who had received notice of the injunction, and, still continuing in the service of the company, had refused to obey it.

Thereupon the Lake Shore company applied to the court for an attachment against Lennon, and certain others of its engineers and firemen, setting forth that, with full knowledge of the injunction theretofore made, they had refused to obey the order of the court, and deserted their locomotives and engines in the yard of the company, for the reason that Ann Arbor cars of freight were in the trains of such company, and that they had refused to haul such cars and perform their service for that reason.

. . . The court found that Lennon was guilty of contempt in disobeying the order of injunction, and imposed a fine of fifty dollars and costs.

. . .

Justice BROWN, after stating the case, delivered the opinion of the court.

The only question which can properly be raised upon this writ is whether the Circuit Court exceeded its jurisdiction in holding the petitioner for a contempt and in imposing upon him a fine therefor. We are not at liberty to consider the testimony, or to inquire whether the facts, as they appeared upon the hearing, justified the action of the Circuit Court. It is only upon the theory that the proceedings and judgment of the court were nullities that we are authorized to reverse its action. It has been too frequently decided, to be now open to question, that a writ of *habeas corpus* cannot be made use of to perform the functions of a writ of error or an appeal. . . .

Acting upon this theory, the petitioner claims that the Circuit Court exceeded its jurisdiction in adjudging him guilty of contempt, for the reason that it had no jurisdiction of the original bill, because one of the defendants to such bill was a citizen of the same State with the complainant; because petitioner was not a party to the suit and was never served with a subpoena or the injunction; and, finally, because it was beyond the jurisdiction of a court of equity to compel the performance of a personal contract for service.

[The Court first decided that there was federal jurisdiction.] . . .

2. The facts that petitioner was not a party to such suit, nor served with process of subpoena, nor had notice of the application made by the complainant for the mandatory injunction, nor was served by the officers of the court with such injunction, are immaterial, so long as it was made to appear that he had notice of the issuing of an injunction by the court. To render a person amenable to an injunction it is neither necessary that he should have been a party to the suit in which the injunction was issued, nor to have been actually served with a copy of it, so long as he appears to have had actual notice. . . .

Conceding the question whether he had such notice in this case to be open to review here, we are of opinion that upon the facts appearing in this record this question must be answered, as it was answered in the court below, in the affirmative. . . .

It appears that, immediately after the injunction order was granted and served upon the Lake Shore company, the company had copies of the order printed, and attached thereto a notice, signed by its superintendent, calling the attention of employés to the injunction; that printed copies of the injunction and notice were posted on all the bulletin boards at roundhouses where engineers took their engines, and that it was the duty of engineers to examine all notices so posted before starting on their runs. That on the morning of the 18th of March, Lennon was upon his engine at Alexis, making a run with his train from Monroe to Toledo; that on his arrival at Alexis, and before he refused to receive and haul the Ann Arbor car, Mr. Chillcote, an agent of the Lake Shore company, handed to him (Lennon) a printed copy of said injunction order, and the notice signed by the general superintendent, and he received and examined them.

Mr. Chillcote says: "I handed him these papers and he said he had seen the order; that it was posted somewhere; I think at the roundhouse, I think at Detroit. I wouldn't say positive as to that; but he said he had seen a copy of it. . . . I simply handed it to him, and he said, 'We understand the order,' or 'We have seen the order,' or words to that effect." Chillcote further says: "He stated when I handed him the order, before he read it, that he understood it."

Mr. Keegan testified that he was present when the copy of the order was handed to Lennon, and that he said, "I have seen it before." This occurred about 10 o'clock A.M., and Lennon, after having the copy of the order delivered to him and admitting that he had seen it before and understood it, refused to receive the Ann Arbor car until after 2:30 P.M., when he received a telegram from Mr. Watson, an officer of the Brotherhood of Locomotive Engineers, saying, "you can come along and handle Ann Arbor cars," and he then at once proceeded with his train to Toledo, receiving and hauling the Ann Arbor car.

3. To the objection that it was beyond the jurisdiction of a court of equity to compel the performance of a personal contract for service, and to interfere by mandatory injunction with petitioner's contract with the railway com-

pany, it is sufficient to say that nothing of the kind was attempted. The petitioner, as one of the employés of the Lake Shore railway, was enjoined from refusing to extend to the Ann Arbor railway such facilities for the interchange of traffic on interstate commerce business between such railways as were enjoyed by other companies, and from refusing to receive from the Ann Arbor company cars billed from points in one State to points in other States. No attempt was made to interfere with petitioner's contract with his own company, or to compel a continuance of his service in such company. There could be no doubt of the power of the court to grant this injunction, which bore solely upon the relations of the railway companies to each other. It was alleged in the bill to have been a part of the regular business of the defendant roads to interchange traffic with the Ann Arbor road, and the injunction was sought to prevent an arbitrary discontinuance of this custom. Perhaps, to a certain extent, the injunction may be termed mandatory, although its object was to continue the existing state of things, and to prevent an arbitrary breaking off of the current business connections between the roads. But it was clearly not beyond the power of a court of equity, which is not always limited to the restraint of a contemplated or threatened action, but may even require affirmative action, where the circumstances of the case demand it. . . .

It appears from the testimony in this case that Lennon was on his run as engineer from Detroit, Michigan, to Air Line Junction, near Toledo, with a train of forty-five cars. Having reached an intermediate station called Alexis, he was ordered to take on an empty car from the Ann Arbor road. He refused to take the car into the train and held the train there for five hours, and then proceeded on his run after receiving a dispatch from the chairman of a committee of the Engineer Brotherhood instructing him to "come along and handle Ann Arbor cars." When he first received the order at Alexis to take the Ann Arbor car he refused, and said, "I quit," but afterwards agreed with the superintendent of the division to take the train to its destination if the order to take the boycotted car was countermanded. Though he claimed to have quit at Alexis at about 10 o'clock he brought his train to its destination, and when told what his next run would be gave no notice of having quit or intending to quit.

It is not necessary for us to decide whether an engineer may suddenly and without notice quit the service of a railway company at an intermediate station or between stations, though cases may be easily imagined where a sudden abandonment of a trainload of passengers in an unfrequented spot might imperil their safety and even their lives. It is sufficient, in the present case, to observe that the court found, upon the testimony, that the petitioner did not quit in good faith in the morning, but intended to continue in the company's service, and that his conduct was a trick and device to avoid obeying the order of the court.

The finding of the court in this particular is not open to review, and hence the question whether the court has power to compel the performance of a personal contract for service does not arise. It was a question for the court to determine whether the petitioner's action in delaying the train five hours at Alexis was taken in pursuance of a determination to abandon the service of the company, or for the purpose of disobeying the lawful injunction of the court. The finding of the court was against the petitioner upon that point.

ALEMITE MANUFACTURING CORP. v. STAFF

42 F.2d 832 (2d Cir. 1930).

Before MANTON, L. HAND, and CHASE, Circuit Judges.

L. HAND, Circuit Judge. The plaintiff sued Joseph Staff, the respondent, together with Louis A., John, and Samuel G. Staff, as partners, for infringement of its patent. It failed to serve Louis and Samuel; upon the trial John swore that the business was his alone, and the suit was therefore dismissed as to Joseph. A decree was entered against John, "his agents, employees, associates and confederates," enjoining them from infringing, or "aiding or abetting or in any way contributing to the infringement," and a writ followed in the same terms, which was served upon the counsel for both defendants. At the time of the suit Joseph was a salesman for John, but later, having left his employ, he set up in business for himself, and was proved to have infringed the patent. The plaintiff then began proceedings in the original suit to punish Joseph for contempt, asserting that he was bound by the decree, and that his new business was a violation of the writ. The District Judge found that John "had no connection or part whatever in the acts of contempt hereby adjudged against Joseph Staff," but that nevertheless Joseph was guilty, and fined him for contumacy. Thereupon he appealed.

We agree that a person who knowingly assists a defendant in violating an injunction subjects himself to civil as well as criminal proceedings for contempt. This is well settled law. Ex parte Lennon; Seaward v. Paterson. On the other hand no court can make a decree which will bind any one but a party; a court of equity is as much so limited as a court of law; it cannot lawfully enjoin the world at large, no matter how broadly it words its decree. If it assumes to do so, the decree is pro tanto brutum fulmen, and the persons enjoined are free to ignore it. It is not vested with sovereign powers to declare conduct unlawful; its jurisdiction is limited to those over whom it gets personal service, and who therefore can have their day in court. Thus, the only occasion when a person not a party may be punished, is when he has helped to bring about, not merely what the decree has forbidden, because it may have gone too far, but what it has power to forbid, an act of a party. This means that the respondent must either abet the defendant, or must be legally identified with him. Strictly, therefore, the addition of such words as the plaintiff here relies on, adds nothing to the decree. Without them any one is liable who knowingly does what the court has properly enjoined; with them nobody is liable who does not. So far as In re Reese may hold the contrary, we cannot agree.

Thus, if the defendant is not involved in the contempt, the employee cannot be; the decree has not been disobeyed, so far as it is valid. We may assume for argument that it is not necessary for the defendant expressly to authorize the act; that it is enough if the employee acts within the scope of his authority. But that does not affect the principle; rather it illustrates it, since the authority of an agent need never be express. . . .

The Supreme Court in Ex parte Lennon held in contempt an employee who refused to move cars of the defendant railway after a mandatory injunction had directed it to accept those of another road whose employees were on strike. Lennon was still in the defendant's employ, and this was the ground of the decision, for though the defendant had directed him to move the cars, his refusal was apparently imputed to it, since he was presumably acting within his authority, though contrary to his orders. He had brought to pass what the court had power to forbid, the defendant's neglect to move the cars. It was conceded that if he had not been in the defendant's employ, he would have escaped. We think that if his act had been without the scope of his authority, the same must be true, for it is not the act described which the decree may forbid, but only that act when the defendant does it.

This is far from being a formal distinction; it goes deep into the powers of a court of equity. Upon proceedings to punish for contempt, the propriety of the decree is not open, even though it be founded upon an unconditional statute. The respondent may only deny any knowledge of the decree, or that his act was within it. The unlawfulness of his conduct has been determined, and, if he has not been a party and has had no day in court, he is condemned without hearing. It is by ignoring such procedural limitations that the injunction of a court of equity may by slow steps be made to realize the worst fears of those who are jealous of its prerogative. The District Court had no more power in the case at bar to punish the respondent than a third party who had never heard of the suit.

---

1) *Alemite* is Learned Hand's major contribution to equity. It contains more than met your eye. Reread it. Is Judge Hand correct that *Lennon* can be distinguished? Who was more fully represented in the injunctive proceeding—Lennon or Joseph Staff? See Beyond Contempt, 53 Tex.L.Rev. at 892–900.

2) What bearing, if any, does Rule 65(d) have on the situation in *Alemite*? Must the person to be bound be an agent at the time of the injunctive suit? At the time of disobedience? At both times? Does *Alemite* require a narrow reading of Rule 65(d) to require that an agent violate in active concert or participation with named defendants?

3) What is *Alemite*'s lesson for a plaintiff about to choose defendants? Should plaintiff sue people or businesses? Does *Alemite* allow wrongdoers to sever their business connections and continue violating? Does *Alemite* prejudice plaintiff who still may sue former agents in a second action for violating the underlying substantive standard? Why did Alemite proceed against Joseph Staff for contempt instead of beginning a second patent infringement action against him? Should Alemite have moved to substitute Joseph as a defendant-successor in interest under Rule 25(c)? Compare Panther Pumps & Equipment Co. v. Hydrocraft, Inc., 566 F.2d 8, 22–25 (7th Cir. 1977). Many contemporary decisions that raise *Alemite* issues involve corporate or commercial succession, and they are discussed below.

BALTZ v. THE FAIR

178 F.Supp. 691 (N.D.Ill.1959).

LA BUY, District Judge.

On July 16, 1957, the trial court entered Findings of Fact, Conclusions of Law, and a Judgment Order adjudging the plaintiffs patent to be valid and infringed. The complaint was brought against The Fair, a seller, alleging the sale of devices embodying the invention of the patent in suit, "to wit—No. 281 and other Rich 'Bounce-A-Way' spring suspended hobby horses"; Rich Industries, the manufacturer thereof, became a party defendant by undertaking the defense and filing answer.

On February 18, 1959, plaintiffs filed a petition for an order adjudicating respondents in civil contempt for violating the decree and injunction. The petition alleges, that The Fair disobeyed and disregarded the injunction and sold and is selling spring-suspended hobby horses manufactured by The De Luxe Game Corporation, which devices are substantially identical and the full equivalent of those found to infringe the patent; that De Luxe Game Corporation, with full knowledge of the injunction, aided, abetted and induced The Fair to disregard the injunction by agreeing to indemnify it and save it harmless for any damages resulting from an action for patent infringement and to defend it in any action brought for infringement by virtue of the sale of its hobby horses; that The Fair sold and offered for sale hobby horses manufactured by The Gong Bell Manufacturing Company which are the full equivalent of and substantially identical to those found to infringe the patent; that The Gong Bell Manufacturing Company, with full knowledge of the injunction aided, abetted and induced The Fair to disobey the injunction by agreeing to indemnify it from any damages ensuing from the sale of its devices; that Montgomery Ward, subsequent to the entry of the judgment and injunction, acquired a majority of the capital stock of The Fair, and participated in these violations with The Fair, its subsidiary.

Only the respondent, The Fair, has filed answer to said petition in accordance with the order of this court. None of the other respondents has filed an answer. The Fair admits the entry of the injunction, alleges service of the writ upon it on or about August 28, 1958, denies disobedience with the terms thereof, denies the sale of hobby horses manufactured by The Gong Bell Manufacturing Company, denies De Luxe Game Corporation aided, abetted or induced The Fair to violate the injunction, admits the existence of the indemnity agreement between them, but avers it is in accord with regular business practice, admits that Montgomery Ward owns a majority of its capital stock and that it is a subsidiary thereof, but denies any privity with it for violation of said injunction.

The Fair has also filed a motion for summary judgment and for an order dismissing the petition for the reason (1) the only accused device in the above patent action was that manufactured by Rich Industries, who became a party to that action, and if The Fair has sold the device manufactured by said company, it could not have violated the injunction because Rich Industries is now plaintiffs' licensee; (2) by a stipulation between counsel in the patent action, which was not filed with the court, defendants understood and believed that the issues of the patent suit were limited and confined to the device manufactured by Rich Industries; and (3) there is pending a declaratory judgment suit brought by De Luxe Game Corporation against Wonder Products Company, one of the plaintiffs herein, for a declaration of non-infringement and invalidity of the patent.

The basic issue to be resolved is whether the respondents named in plaintiffs' petition are within the scope of the decree and injunction entered on July 15, 1957.

The Judgment Order recites as follows:

"That a perpetual injunction issue out of and under the Seal of this Court, directed to the defendants, Rich Industries, Inc. and The Fair, their associates, directors, officers, attorneys, clerks, agents, servants, workmen, representatives, confederates, privies, successors and all persons, firms, and corporations claiming by, through or under them, or in act of concert or participation with them, or under their authority, restraining and enjoining them and each of them, and they and each of them be and are hereby permanently enjoined and restrained from directly or indirectly making, using, selling or offering to sell, except under license from the plaintiffs, any spring-suspended hobby horses embodying the inventions disclosed and claimed in either claim 1 or 2 of said Letters Patent Re. 23,849 or in any other way infringing thereon." . . .

Any terms included in an injunction which go beyond the language of Rule 65(d) cannot enlarge the proper scope of the injunctive order. Regal Knitwear Co. v. N.L.R.B.

All persons who are in privity with parties to the litigation or who aid and abet such parties in disobeying the injunction are guilty of contempt of court if they have knowledge of the injunction although they are not named in the order granting the injunction or are not themselves parties to suit. Privity involves a person so identified in interest with another as to represent the same legal rights and who is therefore bound by the judgment adjudging such rights. Conversely, persons who are not parties to the injunction or in privity with them and whose rights have not been adjudicated therein are not bound by the decree in so far as it operates in personam and cannot be held liable for acts done contrary to its terms. Privity is not established merely because persons are interested in the same question or in proving the same set of facts or because the question litigated is one which might affect such other person's liability as a judicial precedent in a subsequent action.

The alleged indemnity agreements relating to the sale of another manufacturer's product does not make such other manufacturer a party nor in privity with the defendant manufacturer, Rich Industries, even though such product may be the full equivalent of the patented device unless the product was furnished by the defendant manufacturer. Of course, by virtue of the indemnity agreements there is a privity between such other manufacturer and The Fair, but the agreement does not relate to the same device or subject matter found to infringe the patent in suit, and there exists no such identity of subject matter so as to render the judgment binding upon such other manufacturer. The decree upon which plaintiffs rely does not prevent another manufacturer from making or using the same identical thing. An adjudication between plaintiffs and The Fair and Rich Industries does not constitute a final adjudication as to other infringers and such infringement should not be heard or decided in a contempt proceeding. The remedy of injunction is strictly in personam and, unless a statute so authorizes, is not directed against property. It is a fundamental doctrine of the law that a party to be affected by a personal judgment must have his day in court and an opportunity to be heard, and even a previous finding of validity of a patent does not foreclose subsequent re-examination thereof and also of the question of infringement by another.

It appears there exists no controversy as to any material issue of fact which relates to the status or relation of the named respondents to the named defendants in the patent action, and the only question to be decided is whether, on the uncontroverted facts and accepting the truth of the allegations of plaintiffs' petition and other documents, the named respondents are within the scope of the injunction. The court is of the opinion that the named respondents are not in privity with the defendants either by relationship or by behavior.

An order has this day been entered dismissing the Petition for Civil Contempt.

---

1) Did Judge La Buy have to think even for a minute to find that The Fair was obligated to obey the injunction? Did he unnecessarily narrow Rule 65(d) to mean that all defendants must violate in concert to be in contempt? Should plaintiff have filed a second infringement action instead of contempt? Was the civil contempt that plaintiff did file the practical equivalent of an infringement action? Beyond Contempt, 53 Tex.L.Rev. at 888–92.

2) In Ex parte Davis, 470 S.W.2d 647 (Tex.1971), contemnor's grantor had been forbidden from using the property "for any purpose other than residential use." Contemnor, knowing of the injunction, acted contrary to it. The court rejected the plaintiff's argument that contemnor was obligated to obey because he was "privy" to the original defendants; it exonerated contemnor because he was a nonparty not in active concert or participation with defendants. If plaintiffs had brought a second action, would contemnor-Davis have been bound by the judgment in his grantor's action? F. James & G. Hazard, Civil Procedure 592 (2d ed. 1977). Are terms like "successors" and "privity" less precise than the words in Rule 65(d)? Is "privity" the worst offender because judges might apply res judicata concepts to contempt? See Beyond Contempt, 53 Tex.L.Rev. at 879–81.

III. Successors

The judge seeks to protect plaintiff's substantive interest by granting an injunction; because money is inadequate, he hopes that plaintiff will enjoy the rights. Yet the illegal conduct continues or threatens to continue under another guise, in this instance by defendant's successors. When plaintiff charges contempt, the judge asks whether the relationship between the named defendant and contemnor guarantees that defendant adequately represented contemnor's interest.

A. Succession in Public Office

LUCY v. ADAMS

224 F.Supp. 79 (N.D.Ala.1963).

GROOMS, District Judge. This matter came on for hearing at this time upon the request of petitioner, Hubert E. Mate, in his capacity as Dean of Admissions of the University of Alabama, for construction of the present efficacy of the judgment rendered in this cause on July 1, 1955, wherein it was decreed as follows:

"1. That the defendant, William F. Adams, his servants, agents, assistants and employees, and those who might aid, abet, and act in concert with him, are hereby permanently enjoined and restrained from denying the plaintiffs and others similarly situated the right to enroll in the University of Alabama and pursue courses of study thereat, solely on account of their race or color."

William F. Adams, who was the Dean of Admissions of the University of Alabama, resigned effective February 3, 1961. Since the first day of October, 1961, petitioner, Hubert E. Mate, has occupied the position of Dean of Admissions of the University of Alabama. . . .

The question was directly decided by Judge Dawkins for the Supreme Court of Louisiana, in the case of Crucia v. Behrman, 147 La. 144, 84 So. 525. In that case, the Court had issued an injunction against the Mayor of New Orleans and the Police Inspector Mooney enjoining them from interfering with the plaintiff in holding musical performances in his restaurant. Mooney was succeeded by Inspector Boyle, who caused the plaintiff to be arrested for acts which had been covered by the injunction. Boyle was not connected with the police department when the writ was issued and had never been made a party to the suit. The Court discharged him from a rule for contempt. Upon review, the Supreme Court said:

". . . It cannot be, in granting injunctive relief in a matter of this sort, that it is necessary to make every member of the police department a party defendant, in order that they may be held responsible for a violation of such a writ. In such cases the writ runs against the office, and embraces all who are charged with the execution of its functions and the official acts sought to be prohibited, whether by the present incumbent or others who may succeed to such duties; and they are guilty of contempt if they have knowledge of the existence of such writ. High on Injunctions (4th Ed.) vol. 2, p. 1453, § 1443. Otherwise, by the mere changing or shifting of individuals, such writs could be violated with impunity and the court's orders rendered nugatory. The case is quite different from one in which private individuals have been enjoined from doing private acts, and in which it has been held that only those made parties defendant and served with process were liable for violation of a writ.

"The respondent inspector admits that he was informed by the counsel for plaintiff of the existence of the injunction, but says that he cannot take notice of such information, because if he did the work of his office would be seriously handicapped by the many assertions and contentions of counsel for accused persons with whom his department deals. This is doubtless true in ordinary cases. However, in the instant case the existence of *the writ*, held in force by the suspensive appeal, *was a matter of public record, which could easily have been verified by applying either to the civil district court or by communicating with the counsel for the city.*" (Emphasis supplied.) . . .

There appears to be no question as to petitioner's knowledge of the writ issued in this case. The Court is, therefore, of the opinion that the injunction issued on July 1, 1955, is binding upon petitioner herein, in his capacity as Dean of Admissions of the University of Alabama, and upon all of those connected with the University who have knowledge of such decree.

---

1) Footnote 1 of the opinion stated:

"The Annotator comments as follows respecting the amended rule [25(d)]: 'Where the successor does not intend to pursue the policy of his predecessor which gave rise to the lawsuit, it will be open to him, after substitution, as plaintiff to seek voluntary dismissal of the action, or as defendant to seek to have the action dismissed as moot or to take other appropriate steps to avert a judgment or decree. . . . Subdivision (d)(2). This provision, applicable in "official capacity" cases as described above, will encourage the use of the official title without any mention of the officer individually, thereby recognizing the intrinsic character of the action and helping to eliminate concern with the problem of substitution. If for any reason it seems desirable to add the individual's name, this may be done upon motion or on the court's initiative; thereafter the procedure of amended Rule 25(d)(1) will apply if the individual named ceases to hold office. . . . Where an action is brought by or against a board or agency with continuity of existence, it has been often decided that there is no need to name the individual members and substitution is unnecessary when the personnel changes. . . . The practice encouraged by amended Rule 25(d)(1) is similar.' "

The Supreme Court approved the amendment to Rule 25 on April 17, 1961, and authorized the transmittal of the amendment to Congress under 28 U.S.C. § 2072. Justice Douglas filed this dissenting statement:

"Most of the proposed changes in the Rules of Civil Procedure are picayune and harmless, yet hardly worth making apart from any over-all revision of the Rules. The change in Rule 25 of the Rules of Civil Procedure is, however, a major one; and it seems to me unwise. The policy that a cabinet officer under one administration pursues is often not the policy of the next administration. I would not make the contrary assumption, as does the proposed change. I think the ends served by Snyder v. Buck, 340 U.S. 15, are proper ones. The Rule in its present form leaves the burden on the claimant who challenges a particular government policy to re-establish that the controversy he had with a predecessor is a live one as respects the successor. The burden should rest there, not with the newcomer to office."

2) Vivian Malone and James Hood sought to be admitted to the University of Alabama for the 1963 summer session. Does this decision spare the 1963 applicants the necessity of relitigation because eight years earlier Autherine Lucy's lawyers sued for a plaintiff class? What advantages, procedural and otherwise, might the 1963 applicants have achieved by proceeding in the *Lucy* action instead of filing their own suit? May anyone in the plain-

tiff class benefit from Lucy's injunction? If so, and if Rule 25(d) automatically substitutes the successor as a party, do class injunctions against government officials ever expire? Beyond Contempt, 53 Tex.L.Rev. at 930 n. 282. Must the successor actually know about the injunction? Must the successor be in "active concert or participation"? Should a judge hold in contempt an official who lacked an opportunity to participate in formulating the rule he is accused of violating? Is Rule 25(d) consistent with Rule 65(d)?

3) Is *Lucy* palatable because the substantive issue was easy and the law had not changed? Assume the prior administration at the University had negotiated an affirmative action consent decree that turns out to be "improvident" because 1) the federal executive's policy changed, and 2) the "goals" prove to be "unrealistic." Would the judge deny the successor Dean an opportunity to contest that decree before enforcing it? Compare the *Pasadena* and *Holiday Inn* decisions under Rule 60(b)(5), p. 499 and p. 514.

4) Is *Lucy* consistent with the Eleventh Amendment, which has been read to prohibit suits against a state in the federal courts? In Ex parte Young, 209 U.S. 123 (1908), the Supreme Court decided that the Eleventh Amendment did not preclude federal court litigation to enjoin a state official from enforcing an unconstitutional state act. Apparent conflict with the Eleventh Amendment was resolved this way:

". . . The act to be enforced is alleged to be unconstitutional, and if it be so, the use of the name of the State to enforce an unconstitutional act to the injury of complainants is a proceeding without the authority of and one which does not affect the State in its sovereign or governmental capacity. It is simply an illegal act upon the part of a state official in attempting by the use of the name of the State to enforce a legislative enactment which is void because unconstitutional. If the act which the state Attorney General seeks to enforce be a violation of the Federal Constitution, the officer in proceeding under such enactment comes into conflict with the superior authority of that Constitution, and he is in that case stripped of his official or representative character and is subjected in his person to the consequences of his individual conduct." (at 159–160)

Can you reconcile *Young* with Federal Rule 25(d), which seems to make the injunction against a state official "binding" on the office, rather than on the officeholder? Should plaintiff sue the successor separately? Compare the view the court took of Rule 25(d) in note 9 of *Lankford*, p. 160. Is Ex parte Young oblivious to the real problem of how to tame an unruly bureaucracy? See Fiss, The Forms of Justice, 93 Harv.L.Rev. 1, 24 (1979).

SPOMER v. LITTLETON

414 U.S. 514, 94 S.Ct. 685, 38 L.Ed.2d 694 (1973).

Justice WHITE delivered the opinion of the Court.

This is a companion case to *O'Shea* v. *Littleton,* [414 U.S. 488 (1973)] involving claims which the respondents, 17 black and two white residents of Cairo, Illinois, individually and as representatives of the class they purport to represent, set forth in that portion of their amended civil rights complaint which alleged wrongful conduct on the part of Peyton Berbling, individually and in his capacity as State's Attorney for Alexander County, Illinois, the county in which the city of Cairo is located. . . . [T]he complaint alleged a broad range of racially discriminatory patterns and practices in the administration of the criminal justice system in Alexander County by the Police Commissioner of Cairo, Magistrate Michael O'Shea and Associate Judge Dorothy Spomer of the Alexander County Circuit Court, State's Attorney Berbling, and Earl Shepherd, an investigator for Berbling. Allegedly, a decade of active, but lawful, efforts to achieve racial equality for the black residents of Cairo had resulted in continuing intentional conduct on the part of those named as defendants in the complaint to deprive the plaintiff-respondents of the evenhanded protection of the criminal laws, in violation of various amendments to the Constitution and 42 U.S.C. §§ 1981, 1982, 1983, and 1985.

In particular, the complaint charged State's Attorney Berbling with purposeful racial discrimination, under color of state law, by neglecting to provide for respondents' safety though knowing of the possibility of racial disorders, by refusing to prosecute persons who threaten respondents' safety and property, and by refusing to permit respondents to give evidence against white persons who threaten them. It was alleged, with particular incidents recounted as to some charges, that "Berbling has denied and continues to deny" the constitutional rights of respondents and members of their class by following the practices of (a) refusing to initiate criminal proceedings and to hear criminal charges against white persons upon complaint by members of respondents' class, (b) submitting misdemeanor complaints which have been filed by black persons against whites to a grand jury, rather than proceeding by information or complaint, and then either interrogating witnesses and complainants before the grand jury with purposeful intent to racially discriminate, or failing to interrogate them at all, (c) inadequately prosecuting the few criminal proceedings instituted against whites at respondents' behest in order to lose the cases or settle them on terms more favorable than those brought against blacks, (d) recommending substantially greater bonds and sentences in cases involving respondents and members of their class than for cases involving whites, (e) charging respondents and members of their class with significantly more serious charges for conduct which would result in no charge or a minor charge against a white person, and (f) depriving respondents of their right to give evidence concerning the security of members of their class. Each of these practices was alleged to be willful, malicious, and carried out with intent to deprive respondents and members of their class of the benefits of the county criminal justice system and to deter them from peacefully boycotting or otherwise engaging in protected First Amendment activity. Since there was asserted to be no adequate remedy at law, respondents requested that Berbling be enjoined from continuing these practices, that he be required to "submit a monthly report to [the District Court] concerning the nature, status and disposition of any complaint brought to him by plaintiffs or members of their class, or by white persons against plaintiffs or members of their class," and that the District Court maintain continuing jurisdiction in this action.[5]

5. Damages were also sought against Berbling for these practices and for an alleged conspiracy with his investigator, Shepherd, to refuse to prosecute those

The District Court dismissed that portion of the complaint requesting injunctive relief against Berbling, as well as against Investigator Shepherd, Magistrate O'Shea, and Judge Dorothy Spomer, for want of jurisdiction to grant any such remedy, which was perceived as directed against discretionary acts on the part of these elected state officials. The Court of Appeals reversed, holding that whatever quasi-judicial immunity from injunctive proscription it had previously recognized was appropriate for a prosecutor, was not absolute, and since respondents' alternative remedies at law were thought to be inadequate, an injunctive remedy might be available if respondents could prove their claims of racial discrimination at trial.

The Court of Appeals rendered its decision on October 6, 1972. At the subsequent election in November of that year, petitioner W. C. Spomer was chosen by the voters to succeed Berbling as State's Attorney for Alexander County, and Spomer took office on December 4. In the petition for certiorari filed with this Court on January 3, 1973, seeking review of the Court of Appeals' approval of the possibility of some form of injunctive relief addressed to the State's Attorney in the course of his prosecutorial role, petitioner Spomer relied upon Supreme Court Rule 48(3), which provides that "[w]hen a public officer is a party to a proceeding here in his official capacity and during its pendency dies, resigns, or otherwise ceases to hold office, the action does not abate and his successor is automatically substituted as a party." Respondents did not oppose the substitution,[8] and we granted certiorari . . . .

It has become apparent, however, that there is nothing in the record upon which we may firmly base a conclusion that a concrete controversy between W. C. Spomer and the respondents is presented to this Court for resolution. No allegations in the complaint cited any conduct of W. C. Spomer as the basis for equitable or any other relief. Indeed, Spomer is not named as a defendant in the complaint at all, and, of course, he never appeared before either the District Court or the Court of Appeals. The injunctive relief requested against former State's Attorney Berbling, moreover, is based upon an alleged practice of willful and malicious racial discrimination evidenced by enumerated instances in which Berbling favored white persons and disfavored Negroes. The wrongful conduct charged in the complaint is personal to Berbling, despite the fact that he was also sued in his then capacity as

who threatened respondents' safety and to prevent them from giving evidence against whites concerning acts threatening their personal safety. . . . The Court of Appeals held that "insofar as defendant Berbling was acting within his prosecutorial function he has a quasi-judicial immunity from suit for damages under the Civil Rights Act," and remanded to allow respondents to amend the complaint and to have the District Court determine in the first instance whether some of the acts then alleged would be sufficiently removed from quasi-judicial activity "to warrant removing the cloak of immunity from them." Berbling's petition for certiorari questioning this aspect of the Court of Appeals' ruling was not timely filed in this Court and has been denied. No question concerning damage relief is involved in the case presently before us.

8. In their brief in opposition to the petition, p. 6, respondents stated that they "seek only equitable relief against petitioner W. C. Spomer. Because the amended complaint asks relief against Berbling in his individual as well as his official capacity, he remains a party in interest in this action." Of course, Spomer, not Berbling, filed for review of the Court of Appeals' decision respecting injunctive relief, and Berbling is not before the Court in this case. Nor did respondents ever seek relief of any kind against Spomer by their complaint.

State's Attorney.[9] No charge is made in the complaint that the policy of the office of State's Attorney is to follow the intentional practices alleged, apart from the allegation that Berbling, as the incumbent at the time, was then continuing the practices he had previously followed. Cf. Allen v. Regents of the University System of Georgia, 304 U.S. 439, 444–445 (1938). Nor have respondents ever attempted to substitute Spomer for Berbling after the Court of Appeals decision, so far as the record shows, or made any record allegations that Spomer intends to continue the asserted practices of Berbling of which they complain. The plain fact is that, on the record before us, respondents have never charged Spomer with anything and do not presently seek to enjoin him from doing anything.[10] Under these circumstances, recognizing that there may no longer be a controversy between respondents and any Alexander County State's Attorney concerning injunctive relief to be applied *in futuro*, . . . we remand to the Court of Appeals for a determination, in the first instance, of whether the former dispute regarding the availability of injunctive relief against the State's Attorney is now moot and whether respondents will want to, and should be permitted to, amend their complaint to include claims for relief against the petitioner. . . .

The judgment of the Court of Appeals is vacated and the case is remanded for further consideration and proceedings consistent with this opinion.

---

1) Compare *Spomer*'s view of succession with *Lankford*, p. 160, *Lucy*, and Justice Douglas's dissent to Rule 25(d). Which evaluates executive policy-making more accurately?

2) Is *Lucy* distinguishable on the ground that the change in office occurred after the injunction was issued? Is *Spomer* only a discrete application

9. This Court's Rule 48(3), governing automatic substitution of successor public officers when the predecessor was a party "in his official capacity," is based upon Fed.Rule Civ.Proc. 25(d), as amended in 1961. Prior to the 1961 amendment, substitution was not automatic. The history and application of former and present Rule 25(d) are sketched in 3B J. Moore, Federal Practice ¶ 25.09[1]–[3] (2d ed. 1969). Of particular relevance is the Advisory Committee Note on the 1961 "automatic substitution" amendment to Rule 25(d), which suggests that "[i]n general it will apply whenever effective relief would call for corrective behavior by the one then having official status and power, rather than one who has lost that status and power through ceasing to hold office." The question of whether corrective behavior is thought to be necessary is, of course, dependent on whether the dispute with the predecessor continues with the successor.

10. Despite the statement respondents made in their brief in opposition to the petition for certiorari, the record does not contain any indication that respondents have ever sought injunctive relief against Spomer in any proceedings in the District Court or the Court of Appeals. Nor would they have had reason to do so in the absence of knowledge that he would succeed Berbling. While Spomer did substitute himself in place of his predecessor, and his counsel made the somewhat extraordinary statement at oral argument that "there is nothing in this record, nor will there be on the part of my client, to indicate that he would change the policies which are alleged to have been exercised by his predecessor," to determine whether respondents have a live controversy with Spomer, we must look to the charges *they* press. Indeed, counsel for respondents observed at oral argument of this case that "in order for us to proceed against Mr. Spomer, it would be necessary for us to investigate the facts to see that the concession apparently made by the State's Attorney is true and amend our complaint." This merely serves to underscore our concern that we are being asked to render an opinion on the merits of what is now and may continue to be a hypothetical or abstract dispute. . . .

of the prematurity rules of Fletcher v. Bealey, p. 109 and *Reserve Mining,* p. 116?

3) Does the conduct of the prosecutor's office reflect the incumbent's personality? the structure of the office? the political and social context? Is there any reason to think that the election of Spomer would change things in Cairo? Who should carry the burden of proving the likelihood of change? See Fiss, Dombrowski, 86 Yale L.J. 1103, 1150–52 (1977).

4) Is the *Spomer* issue a matter of Article III case or controversy? Why might the Court have framed it as such? What might explain the unanimity of the *Spomer* Court?

B. Commercial Succession

---

1. In Rem Injunctions

SILVERS v. TRAVERSE

82 Iowa 52, 47 N.W. 888 (1891).

BECK, C. J. An information was filed in the district court of Wapello county charging the plaintiff in this case with violating an injunction restraining the sale of intoxicating liquors upon premises described in the decree . . . . The decree was introduced in evidence on the trial of the case. It enjoins and restrains all persons from using or occupying the premises for unlawful keeping or traffic in intoxicating liquors. The plaintiff herein was not a party to the injunction proceedings. He leased the premises from the defendant named in the injunction decree . . . . It was shown upon the hearing on the information for contempt, by sufficient evidence, that the plaintiff occupied and controlled the premises, and used them for the unlawful keeping and sale of intoxicating liquors. No evidence was introduced on the trial on behalf of the plaintiff. . . .

The . . . objections to the judgment in the contempt proceedings are based upon the ground that the plaintiff was not a party to the injunction proceedings. Code, section 1543, provides that "any person violating the terms of any injunction" to abate the nuisance existing in a place kept for the unlawful keeping or sale of intoxicating liquors shall be punished for contempt. It will be observed that this section declares that a place maintained for the unlawful keeping and sale of intoxicating liquors is a nuisance, which may be abated by injunction. There is no statute prescribing what persons shall be made defendants under this section. Doubtless, the person maintaining the place at the time is a proper party. The decree for abatement operates upon the property as well as upon the person of the defendant. It declares the sentence of the law that the nuisance shall be abated, and, by process issued thereunder, doubtless the order of abatement may be enforced. It is plain that the decree reaches further than the party named as a defendant. It enforces the mandate of the law for the abatement of the nuisance, and to that end reaches the property itself. One who used the property unlawfully for the sale of intoxicating liquors, in addition to being a violator of the law, violated the injunction resting upon the property, and, as such, may be punished for contempt, though he was not a party to the injunction proceedings.

It is insisted that the plaintiff was illegally found guilty of contempt, for the reason that it was not shown that he had knowledge of the injunction proceedings. The action for an injunction pertained to and affected real estate . . . This action is notice to all the world of the matter involved therein; and all persons dealing with the property, or acquiring an interest therein, after the proceedings were instituted, are charged with notice of the proceedings. . . . The decree was against plaintiff's lessor, who was the defendant in the suit. It affected his right and interest in the property; that is, it limited and cut off his power to use the property for the unlawful keeping and sale of intoxicating liquors. The decree was a restriction upon the use of the property which followed it as a burden, and, as it were, an incumbrance. Surely the plaintiff, in taking the property, took it subject to this restriction and burden. In our opinion, these conclusions are based upon familiar doctrines applicable to all actions and proceedings in the courts. If the rule we announce be not recognized, the attempt to enforce injunctions to abate nuisances of all kinds would be vain. The defendant perpetrating the nuisance could wholly defeat the law by leasing or transferring the property to one who had no notice thereof. He could begin anew the perpetration, and could only be enjoined by a new action, and when so enjoined he could in a like manner transfer the property and so on indefinitely, defeating the law, to the scandal of public justice, and the oppression of the people. In our opinion, the district court lawfully exercised its jurisdiction in the contempt proceeding.

---

1) The in rem injunction was prohibition's gift to equity. The liquor nuisance statutes were noncriminal methods to enforce various prohibition laws. See Black, The Expansion of Criminal Equity Under Prohibition, 5 Wis.L.Rev. 412 (1930). Why weren't the authorities satisfied to prosecute under the criminal statutes? The courts and legislatures responded to the problem of illegal businesses that die in the morning and are reborn in the evening. What happened to the idea that injunctions are in personam? Is the shortcut worth the chance of unfairness to a bona fide successor?

2) Would a title searcher find the injunction? See Federal Rules 54(a), 58, 77(d) and 79(b) plus their state counterparts. Plaintiffs who become judgment creditors normally file money judgments in the judgment docket to create judgment liens on defendant-judgment debtors' local real property and to provide constructive notice; buyers of real estate routinely examine the docket to learn whether judgment liens exist. Does *Silvers* elevate an injunction to a judgment lien? Would a lessee like this contemnor conduct a title search? Is the better analogy to covenants in deeds? or to lis pendens? Is *Silvers* a logical extention of *Cape May,* p. 261? See Beyond Contempt, 53 Tex.L.Rev. at 911–16.

3) Does Rule 65(d) allow in rem injunctions? When reading *Regal,* the next case, ask whether it destroys the basis for in rem injunctions against suc-

cessors. Dobbs, Contempt of Court: A Survey, 56 Cornell L.Rev. 183, 259 (1971); Beyond Contempt, 53 Tex.L.Rev. at 911–16.

2. THE UNCERTAIN IMPACT OF RULE 65(d)

REGAL KNITWEAR CO. v. NATIONAL LABOR RELATIONS BOARD

324 U.S. 9, 65 S.Ct. 478, 89 L.Ed. 661 (1945).

Justice JACKSON delivered the opinion of the Court.

The National Labor Relations Board, after appropriate proceedings, issued a cease and desist order against the petitioner, . . . and thereafter obtained from the Circuit Court of Appeals for the Second Circuit an order for its enforcement. . . . We granted certiorari, limited to a single question on which there was a conflict in practice between different circuits. The Board has followed the formula which orders not only a particular respondent, but also "its officers, agents, successors and assigns" to cease and desist. The question is whether enforcement will be granted without deleting "successors and assigns" from those enjoined. The Circuit Courts of Appeals for the First, Second, Third, Fourth, and Eighth Circuits, and the Court of Appeals for the District of Columbia have upheld the authority of the Board to include such a provision. In some of these cases change of ownership was shown to be probable and in other cases there was no such proof. The Second Circuit, in refusing to delete the provision, said: "In allowing these words to stand we wish to make it clear, however, that we do not hold that a 'successor' or an 'assign' will be in contempt of our order if it should (even after notice of the order, but without participating with the respondent in any disobedience by it) do exactly those things which the order forbids. In other words, we do not hold that those words impose any liability which would not exist without them." Labor Board v. Blackstone Mfg. Co., 123 F.2d 633, 635. . . . The Circuit Court of Appeals for the Seventh Circuit, on the other hand, consistently eliminates the provision as to successors and assigns from the order, but recognizes that successors or assigns under some circumstances are bound by the Board's order, even without the words.

When one court of appeals strikes out the provision but says its absence may in some circumstances have the same effect as if it were there, and another court of appeals approves the provision but says its presence may have no more effect than if it were out, there is more than a faint suggestion that the conflict is over semantics rather than over practical realities.

The formula that includes successors and assigns, among others, is one probably borrowed from the jargon of conveyancing. Doubtless these words often are used, not out of consideration of their appropriateness, but because of their familiarity. Courts of equity sometimes have used this formula in their decrees. . . . The National Labor Relations Board has employed this formula consistently since 1937, and some state labor boards have followed the example. Not only have circuit courts of appeals, except of the Seventh Circuit, generally enforced orders containing this provision, but this Court has several times done so. Southport Petroleum Co. v. Labor Board, 315 U.S. 100, 106, note 6.

The dearth of cases in which actual controversies have been precipitated by this more general than discriminating use of this ritual indicates that its significance both for good and ill is greater in anticipation than in retrospect.

Administrative agencies have considerable latitude to shape their remedies within the scope of their statutory authority and, where the infirmity is inadequacy of findings to show appropriateness of the choice made in the particular case, are ordinarily entitled to have the case remanded for further consideration. . . . The courts, nevertheless, may not grant an enforcement order or injunction so broad as to make punishable the conduct of persons who act independently and whose rights have not been adjudged according to law. Chase National Bank v. Norwalk, 291 U.S. 431 (1933); Alemite Mfg. Corp. v. Staff.

The Federal Rules of Civil Procedure provide that: "Every order granting an injunction and every restraining order . . . is binding only upon the parties to the action, their officers, agents, servants, employees, and attorneys, and upon those persons in active concert or participation with them who receive actual notice of the order by personal service or otherwise." This is derived from the common-law doctrine that a decree of injunction not only binds the parties defendant but also those identified with them in interest, in "privity" with them, represented by them or subject to their control. In essence it is that defendants may not nullify a decree by carrying out prohibited acts through aiders and abettors, although they were not parties to the original proceeding.

The term "successors and assigns" in an enforcement order of course may not enlarge its scope beyond that defined by the Federal Rules of Civil Procedure. Successors and assigns may, however, be instrumentalities through which defendant seeks to evade an order or may come within the description of persons in active concert or participation with them in the violation of an injunction. If they are, by that fact they are brought within scope of contempt proceedings by the rules of civil procedure. We have indicated that Labor Board orders are binding upon successors and assigns who operate as "merely a disguised continuance of the old employer." Southport Petroleum Co. v. Labor Board, 315 U.S. at 106. We have also said of an injunction to restrain violation of the Fair Labor Standards Act, which is somewhat analogous to Labor Board orders, that "Not only is such an injunction enforcible by contempt proceedings against the corporation, its agents and officers and those individuals associated with it in the conduct of its business, but it may also, in appropriate circumstances, be enforced against those to whom the business may have been transferred, whether as a means of evading the judgment or for other reasons." Walling v. Reuter Co., 321 U.S. 671, 674. In both of these cases the reference is not merely to succession, but to a relation between the defendant and the successor which might of itself establish liability within the terms of Rule 65.

We do not undertake to decide whether or under what circumstances any kind of successor or assign will be liable for violation of a Labor Board order. It is true that we have said that "Questions of construction had better be ironed out before enforcement orders issue than upon contempt proceedings." (J. I. Case Co. v. Labor Board, 321 U.S. 332, 341.) But it is apparent from Rule 65, and from the views of one circuit court of appeals as to the narrow effect of the words in the order and of another as to the broad effect of the order without the words, that whether one brings himself in contempt as a "successor or assign" depends on an appraisal of his relations and behavior and not upon mere construction of terms of the order. If defendants enter upon transactions which raise doubts as to the applicability of the injunction, they may petition the court granting it for a modification or construction of the order. . . . While such relief would be in the sound discretion of the court, we think courts would not be apt to withhold a clarification in the light of a concrete situation that left parties or "successors and assigns" in the dark as to their duty toward the court. Enforcement orders are issued to effectuate the purposes of the Act, not for the entrapment of parties, and courts no less than parties desire to avoid unwitting contempts as well as to punish deliberate ones.

No concrete case is before us. We have here an abstract controversy over the use of these words, and it is as sterile as abstract controversies usually are. The employer objects to the words of the order merely as words. They do not enlarge its own obligation, and if it complies with the order, little by way of obligation could be passed to a successor or assign by the order that is not in any event imposed by statute. The Board is not here attempting to reach or to hold anyone in contempt by virtue of such orders. No successor or assign appears before us complaining that these words put him in jeopardy. No one can be punished for contempt because of these words until after a judicial hearing, in which their operation could be determined on a concrete set of facts. All that is before us is the question whether we will hold abstractly that this provision is an illegal one to include in a cease and desist order of the Labor Board or an enforcement order of the Court.

Whether it is wise that an order attempt to define its own effect on others than parties to the action when the law has already done so is not for us to say. We cannot say that "successors and assigns" as well as "officers and agents" may not under some circumstances be among those reached by the order within the scope of Rule 65 and hence cannot say that it is not a permissible provision.

Chief Justice STONE, dissenting, with whom Justice ROBERTS and Justice REED concur.

An injunction is a continuing threat to those named as subject to it, of the pains of contempt proceedings if they disobey its provisions. The opinion of the Court recognizes that the present injunction running against the employer's "successors and assigns" purports to include within its sweep some who are not subject to its command and is thus a threat to those over whom the Court has no authority. The opinion also admits that the persons who are bound by the present decree would be as effectively bound if the decree were to omit the words "successors and assigns." See Walling v. Reuter Co., 321 U.S. 671, 674–675. . . .

It has long been deemed to be an abuse of power for a federal court to enjoin practices in which a defendant has not engaged and which are unrelated to those which may be properly enjoined. See Labor Board v. Express Publishing Co., 312 U.S. 426 . . . . To me it seems no less a misuse of authority for a court, as well as for the Labor Board itself, to threaten those who are not subject to its command. This is the more so where the tendency of the threat is to inflict an unauthorized penalty on the employer by deterring third persons from dealing with him to acquire his property and business, in circumstances in which that may lawfully be done.

That there have been numerous cases before this Court, where the Board's order has not been challenged in this respect, is significant only as showing how extensive the abuse has become and how ready employers and the lower courts have been to acquiesce in threatened wrong when the injury seemed not to be immediate. But these are not reasons for our acquiescence, when the question is brought to us for decision for the first time. It is no part of the function of the Board or of courts to make unwarranted threats against suitors or innocent third persons. Such misleading and unwarranted use of the phrase should be avoided, either by striking it from the decree or so qualifying it as to designate the class of "successors and assigns" to whom it may be lawfully applied. Cf. Southport Co. v. Labor Board, 315 U.S. 100, 107.

---

1) Does *Regal* destroy the basis for in rem injunctions by holding that successors may be held in contempt only if they act contrary to the order "in active concert or participation" with named defendants? Does *Regal* hold that the judge must find "that the successor was an instrumentality through which an enjoined party, and not merely the successor, sought to evade the injunction"? Merriam v. Webster Dictionary Co., p. 1146 below.

2) The Texas court freed a contemnor who had knowingly acted contrary to an injunction against his seller. He was neither a party nor in active concert or participation with a named party. Citing *Regal,* the court said "even when the injunction is worded to include 'successors and assigns' it is not effective as to non-party successors. . . . " Ex parte Davis, 470 S.W.2d 647 (Tex.1971).

UNITED STATES PIPE AND FOUNDRY CO. v. NATIONAL LABOR RELATIONS BOARD

398 F.2d 544 (5th Cir. 1968).

Before John R. BROWN, Chief Judge, and BELL, Circuit Judge, and HOOPER, District Judge.

GRIFFIN B. BELL, Circuit Judge: The novel question presented in this case turns on the breadth of the remedy which the Board may fashion under § 10(c) of the National Labor Relations Act. 29 U.S.C.A. § 160(c).[1]

1. [That statute reads] in pertinent part:

". . . If upon the preponderance of the testimony taken the Board shall be of the opinion that any person named in the complaint has engaged in or is engaging in any such unfair labor practice, then the Board shall state its findings of fact and shall issue and cause to be served on such person an order requiring such person to cease and desist from such unfair labor practice, and take such affirmative action including reinstatement of employees with or without back pay, as will effectuate the policies of this subchapter: *Provided,* That where an order directs reinstatement of an employee, back pay may be required of the employer or labor organization, as the case may be, responsible for the discrimination suffered by him . . . ."

United States Pipe and Foundry Company obligated itself to purchase the assets, including the manufacturing facilities of Perma Vinyl Corporation. Perma Vinyl was engaged in manufacturing plastic pipe in Florida. United States Pipe consummated the purchase and continued the manufacture of plastic pipe in the acquired facilities in the same manner and with substantially the same work force. [Perma Vinyl's name was changed to Dade Plastics.] The president of Perma Vinyl became its plant manager. United States Pipe was then ordered to remedy unfair labor practices committed by Perma Vinyl prior to the acquisition by reinstating four employees who had been discharged by Perma Vinyl.

The acquisition took place in December 1964. In May, 1964 Perma Vinyl was charged with violating the Act, a complaint was issued on the charges in July 1964, and the matter was heard before a Trial Examiner in September 1964. No decision had been rendered by the Trial Examiner when the Perma Vinyl assets were transferred to United States Pipe in December 1964.

It is undisputed that United States Pipe had notice of the pending unfair practice proceedings prior to the date of closing. It is contended, however, that this notice was not brought home to United States Pipe until after it had obligated itself in November 1964 to go forward with the purchase. There is evidence of record in the form of the testimony of the president of Perma Vinyl which supports the finding of the Board that United States Pipe had ample notice prior to becoming finally obligated to go forward. We thus consider the appeal on the basis of United States Pipe having acquired the assets with notice of the unfair practice proceedings.

The Board issued its order in April 1965 on the decision of the Trial Examiner holding against Perma Vinyl on the original charges. United States Pipe was in no way involved in that proceeding or in the unfair labor practices forming the subject matter of the proceeding. The Board order against Perma Vinyl was not contested and United States Pipe is not claiming the right to contest that decision on the merits. Its complaint arises out of the Board requiring it, as successor to Perma Vinyl, to remedy the derelictions of Perma Vinyl.

In July 1965 United States Pipe was served with notice which in effect required it to show cause why it should not be charged, as Perma Vinyl's successor, with remedying the unfair labor practices including the reinstatement of the four employees. The notice was in the form of a back pay specification hearing. The Trial Examiner, following prior Board decisions, ruled that United States Pipe was not so obligated. See Symns Grocer Co., 109 NLRB 346 (1954). The Board reversed, expressly overruling the *Symns* case.

United States Pipe petitioned to review and set aside that order of the Board and the Board has cross-petitioned for enforcement of its order. United States Pipe makes two assertions: First, it contends that the Board was without power to enter the order against it; and second, that it was denied due process of law by the Board. We reject both contentions and thereby deny the petition for review and enforce the order of the Board.

We will first consider the due process argument. As we have stated, United States Pipe had notice of the pending unfair practice proceedings against Perma Vinyl. After the entry of the Board order against Perma Vinyl a proceeding was instituted to settle the question of remedies due under that order. That proceeding was brought against United States Pipe and Dade Plastics Co. United States Pipe received notice of this proceeding and duly answered. A hearing was held before a Trial Examiner and United States Pipe appeared and participated without restriction at the hearing. There is no contention of a denial of due process by virtue of having been deprived of the right to defend the original charges, so that question is not before us. We hold that United States Pipe was not deprived of substantive or procedural due process in the premises. Whether the ruling against it on the merits was incorrect is another question and will be next considered. . . .

[T]he Board relied on John Wiley & Sons, Inc. v. Livingston, 1964, 376 U.S. 543. . . . One question in that case was whether an arbitration agreement was binding on a successor corporation. The court was of the view that the objectives of the national labor policy require that the right of owners to rearrange their businesses be balanced by some protection to the employees from a sudden change in the employment relationship. The court concluded that the arbitration agreement was binding upon a purchaser of the business whenever a "similarity and continuity of operation across the change of ownership" is shown. This ruling has been followed in other cases to hold that a collective bargaining agreement is binding on subsequent purchasers of a business. . . .

The case before us does not involve back pay. Perma Vinyl paid all sums due to the date of the transfer to United States Pipe. The Board sought no further sums from Perma Vinyl. No reason is given for this amnesty. The Board did not seek back pay from United States Pipe and this approach was in an apparent effort to give the change of position from the *Symns* case a type of prospective application.[4] The Board, however, takes the strong position that equity required United States Pipe to reinstate the four employees in the event they desire to be reinstated.

This contention rests on the fact that United States Pipe continued to operate the plant in the same manner and with the same jobs. The order does not require that jobs be created. . . .

The order simply seeks to effectuate the policy and purposes of the Act to the end of protecting the employees in question. We conclude that the Board had the power under § 10(c), based on the circumstances obtaining, to require United States Pipe to reinstate the employees involved. Only United States Pipe can reinstate the employees; it took the plant with notice that the employees were claiming their jobs; the jobs still exist; the exigencies of the situation are such that the policy of protecting the employees can only be afforded by United States Pipe. The Board has properly balanced the equities.

4. We thus do not reach the question whether United States Pipe might also be required to provide back pay to these employees. . . . Section 10(c), fn. (1), would seem to cast this burden on the wrongdoer, Perma Vinyl, but the back pay question remains for another day.

The Board changed its position after the purchase but that was a risk entailed in the purchase. United States Pipe was a bona fide purchaser as distinguished from an alter ego or a disguised continuance. It was not acting in concert or participation to evade the Board order. In any event, it purchased with notice of the unfair practice proceedings and continued the same operation even to the jobs in question. This was a sufficient basis for requiring it to offer reinstatement to the employees on the successorship theory. . . .

The petition to review is denied; the petition to enforce is granted.

Does *U.S. Pipe* depart from *Regal* by obligating a successor not "in active concert or participation" to obey an order? If so, what makes *U.S. Pipe* acceptable?

GOLDEN STATE BOTTLING CO., INC. v. NATIONAL LABOR RELATIONS BOARD

414 U.S. 168, 94 S.Ct. 414, 38 L.Ed.2d 388 (1973).

Justice BRENNAN delivered the opinion of the Court.

The principal question for decision in this case is whether the bona fide purchaser of a business, who acquires and continues the business with knowledge that his predecessor has committed an unfair labor practice in the discharge of an employee, may be ordered by the National Labor Relations Board to reinstate the employee with backpay.

Petitioners are Golden State Bottling Co., Inc. (Golden State), and All American Beverages, Inc. (All American). All American bought Golden State's soft drink bottling and distribution business after the National Labor Relations Board had ordered Golden State, "its officers, agents, successors, and assigns" to reinstate with back pay a driver-salesman, Kenneth L. Baker, whose discharge by Golden State was found by the Board to have been an unfair labor practice. In a subsequent backpay specification proceeding to which both Golden State and All American were parties, see 29 CFR §§ 102.52–102.59, the Board found that All American continued after the acquisition to carry on the business without interruption or substantial changes in method of operation, employee complement, or supervisory personnel. In that circumstance, although All American was a bona fide purchaser of the business, unconnected with Golden State, the Board found that All American, having acquired the business with knowledge of the outstanding Board order, was a "successor" for purposes of the National Labor Relations Act and liable for the reinstatement of Baker with backpay under the principles announced in Perma Vinyl Corp., 164 N.L.R.B. 968 (1967), enforced sub nom. United States Pipe & Foundry Co. v. NLRB. The Board therefore ordered that All American reinstate Baker and that Golden State and All American jointly or severally pay Baker a specified sum of net backpay. 187 N.L.R.B. 1017 (1971). The Court of Appeals for the Ninth Circuit, one judge dissenting, enforced the order. We granted certiorari. We affirm. . . .

[W]e cannot find fault with the Court of Appeals' conclusion that, on the record as a whole, substantial evidence supported the Board's finding that All American purchased the business with knowledge of the unfair labor practice litigation. Eugene Schilling, Golden State's secretary and manager of the bottling business, who had discharged Baker and then closely followed the progress of the litigation, continued with the enterprise under All American's ownership with the title of general manager and "president." . . .

We agree that the Board's remedial powers under § 10(c) include broad discretion to fashion and issue the order before us as relief adequate to achieve the ends, and effectuate the policies, of the Act. Early on, this Court recognized that § 10(c) does not limit the Board's remedial powers to the actual perpetrator of an unfair labor practice and thereby prevent the Board from issuing orders binding a successor who did not himself commit the unlawful act. We have said that a Board order that, as in this case, runs to the "officers, agents, successors, and assigns" of an offending employer, may be applied, not only to a new employer who is "merely a disguised continuance of the old employer," Southport Petroleum Co. v. NLRB, 315 U.S. 100, 106 (1942), but also " 'in appropriate circumstances . . . [to] those to whom the business may have been transferred, whether as a means of evading the judgment *or for other reasons.*' " Regal Knitwear Co. v. NLRB (emphasis added). . . . If the words "person named in the complaint has engaged in . . . any . . . unfair labor practice" in § 10(c) do not restrict Board authority to prevent orders running to the offending employer's successors and assigns who have acquired the business as a means of evading the Board order, we do not see how those words may be read to bar the Board from issuing reinstatement and backpay orders against bona fide successors when the Board has properly found such orders to be necessary to protect the public interest in effectuating the policies of the Act. The Board's orders run to the evader and the bona fide purchaser, not because the act of evasion or the bona fide purchase is an unfair labor practice, but because the Board is obligated to effectuate the policies of the Act. Construing § 10(c) thus to grant the Board remedial power to issue such orders results in a reading of the section, as it should be read, in the light of " 'the provisions of the whole law, and . . . its object and policy.' " Mastro Plastics Corp. v. NLRB, 350 U.S. 270, 285 (1956).

It is also argued, however, that Fed.Rule Civ.Proc. 65(d), in any event, is a bar to judicial enforcement of a Board order requiring that a bona fide successor reinstate with backpay an employee illegally discharged by its predecessor. We disagree.[4] Rule 65(d) provides that injunctions and restraining

4. A short answer to petitioners' argument might appear to be that, because the Board's supplemental order to All American required only reinstatement and backpay, and not that All American cease and desist from future unlawful activity, no injunctive relief was ordered, and therefore Rule 65(d) need not be considered. But we have previously found Rule 65(d) applicable to mandatory injunctions and have noted that the courts of appeals have applied it "not only to prohibitory injunctions but to enforcement orders and affirmative decrees as well." International Longshoremen's Assn. v. Philadelphia Marine Trade Assn., 389 U.S. 64, 75 and n. 14 (1967); see generally Developments in the Law—Injunctions, 78 Harv.L.Rev. 994, 1061–1063 (1965).

In not requiring the bona fide purchaser to cease and desist, the Board followed prior practice. . . . This approach seems consistent with the fact that the successor's obligations do not arise out of its own unfair labor practices.

orders shall be "binding only upon the parties to the action, their officers, agents, servants, employees, and attorneys, and upon those persons in active concert or participation with them who receive actual notice of the order by personal service or otherwise." See generally O. Fiss, Injunctions 691–700 (1972). We reject petitioners' contention that Regal Knitwear Co. v. NLRB, supports the argument that this Rule is a bar to judicial authority to enforce Board orders against bona fide successors. In *Regal Knitwear*, the Court refused the offending employer's application to strike the phrase "successors and assigns" from the Board's order, citing Walling v. James V. Reuter, Inc., 321 U.S. 671 (1944), which involved an injunction against violation of the Fair Labor Standards Act. . . .

Plainly then, *Regal Knitwear* recognizes that Rule 65(d) is not a bar to enforcement of all Board orders running to successors or assigns not themselves offending employers. The Court simply left open the question of whether the Rule precludes the enforcement of remedial orders running to a successor who is a bona fide purchaser. We answer that question today by holding that the Rule is not a bar to judicial enforcement of the Board order entered against the bona fide successor in this case.

Rule 65(d) "is derived from the common-law doctrine that a decree of injunction not only binds the parties defendant but also those identified with them in interest, in 'privity' with them, represented by them or subject to their control." *Regal Knitwear.* Persons acquiring an interest in property that is a subject of litigation are bound by, or entitled to the benefit of, a subsequent judgment, despite a lack of knowledge. Restatement of Judgments § 89, and comment *c* (1942); see 1 J. Story, Equity Jurisprudence § 536 (14th ed. 1918). This principle has not been limited to *in rem* or *quasi in rem* proceedings. Restatement of Judgments, supra, § 89, comment *d;* see ICC v. Western N. Y. & P. R. Co., 82 F. 192, 194 (WD Pa.1897). We apply that principle here in order to effectuate the public policies of the Act. "Courts of equity may, and frequently do, go much farther both to give and withhold relief in furtherance of the public interest than they are accustomed to go when only private interests are involved." Virginian R. Co. v. System Federation, 300 U.S. 515, 552 (1937); see Walling v. James V. Reuter, Inc., 321 U.S., at 674–675. We hold that a bona fide purchaser, acquiring, with knowledge that the wrong remains unremedied, the employing enterprise which was the locus of the unfair labor practice, may be considered in privity with its predecessor for purposes of Rule 65(d). Cf. United States v. Hall. [p. 1180].

Our holding in no way contravenes the policy underlying Rule 65(d), of not having "order[s] or injunction[s] so broad as to make punishable the conduct of persons who act independently and whose rights have not been adjudged according to law." Regal Knitwear; see Alemite Mfg. Corp. v. Staff. The tie between the offending employer and the bona fide purchaser of the business, supplied by a Board finding of a continuing business enterprise, establishes the requisite relationship of dependence. Moreover, procedures were announced in *Perma Vinyl* which provide the necessary procedural safeguards. There will be no adjudication of liability against a bona fide successor "without affording [it] a full opportunity at a hearing, after adequate notice, to present evidence on the question of whether it is a successor which is responsible for remedying a predecessor's unfair labor practices. The successor [will] also be entitled, of course, to be heard against the enforcement of any order issued against it." 164 N.L.R.B., at 969.

In this case, All American has no complaint that it was denied due notice and a fair hearing. It was made a party to the supplemental backpay specification proceeding, given notice of the hearing, and afforded full opportunity, with the assistance of counsel, to contest the question of its successorship for purposes of the Act and its knowledge of the pendency of the unfair labor practice litigation at the time of purchase. . . .

---

1) Is *Golden State* consistent with *Regal?* Does *Golden State* govern civil contempt proceedings? criminal contempt proceedings?

2) Is the issue in contempt whether a successor is in "active concert or participation"? Were the three successors in *Regal, U.S. Pipe,* or *Golden State* parties? Does Rule 65(d) analysis play a role in deciding whether party-successors are liable under substantive law? Is *Golden State* a variation on the analytical technique of Baltz v. The Fair, p. 1026? Beyond Contempt, 53 Tex.L.Rev. at 891–92.

3) After *Golden State,* may a judge enjoin a successor from conduct the successor has not engaged in? Must American obey the order against Golden State simply because the Labor Board sent it notice? If American later discharges an employee unfairly, would it be guilty of criminal contempt?

4) The successor doctrines combine with *Alemite* to create a multiple corporate shell game played in trademark, copyright, patent, and government regulation-consumer protection. While reading *Webster,* the next decision, ask how much the quality of the process that led to the injunction affected the reach that the court was willing to give it.

G. & C. MERRIAM CO. v. WEBSTER DICTIONARY CO., INC.

639 F.2d 29 (1st Cir. 1980).

Before COFFIN, Chief Judge, WYZANSKI, Senior District Judge, and KEETON, District Judge.

KEETON, District Judge.

By judgment dated February 7, 1980, appellants Webster Publishing Company, Ltd., Webster Home Mailing Service, Ltd., and Webster Home Mailing Service, Inc. (collectively, "Webster Publishing") and George W. Hoskins were held in contempt of court for violation of an injunction issued by the district court on October 27, 1977, and were assessed a fine, jointly and severally, in the amount of $50,000. They now appeal from that judgment, challenging the validity of the injunction and arguing that they did not violate it, that they were not bound by it, and that the fine cannot be sustained under theories of either civil or criminal contempt.

This action arose out of a trademark dispute involving advertisements for various "Webster" dictionaries placed by two brothers and their several closely-held corporations. In December, 1975, Plaintiff-Appellee G. & C. Merriam Co. ("Merriam") brought an action in the district court against Webster Dictionary Company, Inc., a/k/a John Hoskins Sales Agency ("Webster Dictionary Company"), alleging that certain advertisements for dictionaries placed by Webster Dictionary Company violated the Lanham Act, 15 U.S.C. § 1125(a), and Mass.Gen.Laws ch. 93A, and constituted unfair competition. Merriam charged that Webster Dictionary Company's advertisements contained false and deceptive statements deliberately calculated to mislead the public into believing that the dictionaries offered by defendants were Merriam's higher quality "Webster's Third New International Dictionary Unabridged" and that the advertisements violated Merriam's trademark rights. Merriam sought damages and injunctive relief.

On January 28, 1976, Merriam moved for a preliminary injunction to restrain Webster Dictionary Company from placing further advertisements suggesting that the dictionaries offered by Webster Dictionary Company were the Merriam dictionary. After a hearing, the district court by Memorandum and Order of May 19, 1976 denied Merriam's request for preliminary relief on the ground that "the defendant's voluntary amendment of the advertisement makes unnecessary the issuance of a preliminary injunction." [1]

Subsequently, Merriam attempted to conduct discovery through depositions, requests for documents, interrogatories, and requests for admissions. Webster Dictionary Company failed to respond to Merriam's discovery requests. On March 21, 1977 Webster Dictionary Company informed the district court by letter that it was discharging its attorneys by reason of its insolvency, and that Webster Dictionary Company "was willing to consent to the entry of an appropriate judgment against it." On April 25, 1977, the case was called for trial. Webster Dictionary Company failed to appear by counsel.

The district court, holding that Webster Dictionary Company had defaulted, proceeded with a hearing on damages. Merriam's counsel later submitted a proposed form of permanent injunction and judgment. On October 27, 1977, the district court issued findings of fact and entered a default judgment for Merriam against Webster Dictionary Company, granting the requested injunctive relief and awarding Merriam damages, costs and, attorneys' fees totaling $75,169.19. The injunction permanently enjoined Webster Dictionary Company [3] and its "officers, directors, principals, servants, employees, consultants, agents, attorneys, representatives, successors, and assigns, and others acting in association therewith, including, but not limited to, John P. Hoskins and Thomas H. Lucas" from, *inter alia,* "publishing, advertising, offering for sale or selling, or causing to be published, adver-

1. The district court in its memorandum also noted that "plaintiff does not have the exclusive right to refer to its product as 'Webster Dictionary.' G. & C. Merriam Company v. Syndicate Publishing Co., 237 U.S. 618, 622 (1915)," and that "[w]hile it may be a considerable overstatement to describe the defendant's dictionary as world-famous, these words do not suggest that the book being sold is the plaintiff's dictionary."

3. The district court's order named "Webster Reference Books, Inc. (formerly The Webster Dictionary Company, Inc.), John Hoskins Sales Agency, Ltd., ..."

tised, offered for sale or sold, any publication by means of any one or more of the following descriptions, titles, representations:" . . .

"(7) as to any publication or trade name described or identified by the word 'Webster' (or any variant thereof), any of the following descriptions or representations:

"(a) world-famous

"(b) authentic

"(c) original

"(d) genuine

"(e) renowned

"(f) any variant of (a)–(e) above

"(g) any other word or combination of words used to imply the meaning of one or more of (a)–(e) above. . . . "

Webster Dictionary Company failed to file a timely appeal from the district court's judgment.

On August 2, 1979, Merriam moved for the issuance of an order to show cause and for a contempt order, alleging in substance that George Hoskins and the three corporations referred to herein as Webster Publishing were bound by the district court's injunction of October 27, 1977, and that they had violated the injunction by the manner in which they had advertised various dictionaries, encyclopedias, and a home mailing service. In particular Merriam complained of appellants' use of an illustration of Noah Webster, captioned as "the inspiration for the founding of our company" the description of appellants' "Webster" dictionaries and encyclopedias as, *inter alia,* "authoritative," and the description of Webster Publishing as, *inter alia,* "world famous." The district court issued an order to show cause requiring John Hoskins, George Hoskins, and Webster Publishing to show why they should not be held in civil contempt for failure to comply with the injunction. Thomas H. Lucas was not named in the show cause order.

After some discovery, a hearing on Merriam's Motion for Contempt was held on October 11, 1979, at which appellants were represented by counsel. Merriam's Motion for Contempt was dismissed by agreement as to John Hoskins, formerly president of Webster Dictionary Company, because he had left Webster Dictionary Company in 1977 and was not associated with appellants or their alleged contempt. The court heard argument on whether appellants were bound by and had violated the injunction, and heard some evidence concerning Merriam's damages, but noted that if the court found appellants had violated the injunction an additional hearing on damages would probably be held. The court indicated that it intended to decide the question whether appellants were in contempt on the basis of the deposition of George Hoskins and documents offered in evidence by Merriam and stipulated to (except with respect to relevance) by appellants, consisting primarily of documents relating to incorporation and interests in Webster Publishing and copies of the challenged advertisements of Webster Publishing.

On January 25, 1980, the district court issued its Findings, Ruling and Order on Merriam's motion for contempt. The court found as facts that (1) appellants had been duly served; (2) appellants were "successors of the original defendant or persons acting in concert with it"; (3) George Hoskins was a "key employee" of Webster Dictionary Company and "the principal" of the corporate appellants, Webster Publishing; (4) George Hoskins had actual knowledge of the terms of the original injunction; and (5) appellants' use of the words "world-famous" and "authoritative" in their advertisements violated the injunction. Based on these findings, the court held that appellants were bound by the injunction issued against Webster Dictionary Company and that appellants were thus in contempt of court. On February 7, 1980, the district court entered a contempt judgment against appellants, including an order that they pay to Merriam a fine in the amount of $50,000, with interest from January 25, 1980. From that judgment they appeal.

Central to the determination of the legal questions presented by this case is an understanding of the relationship among John and George Hoskins, the two groups of closely-held reference book marketing companies (collectively referred to as Webster Dictionary Company and Webster Publishing, respectively), and the offending advertisements.[5] John Hoskins incorporated the original defendant, Webster Dictionary Company, in 1975, and was its president and sole shareholder until about March 1, 1977, at which time he left the reference book business. George Hoskins began working with his brother John for Webster Dictionary Company in 1975, as general sales manager. Webster Dictionary Company's business was to solicit mail-order sales of various dictionaries through advertisements in newspapers and periodicals in the United States and Canada, which orders were forwarded to the actual publishers, who shipped directly to the customer.

Although the record is not altogether clear on the point, it could be reasonably inferred that in Webster Dictionary Company's activities John Hoskins was in charge, that George Hoskins was the next most active person in the operation, and that corporate formalities were not rigorously observed.

Webster Dictionary Company operated out of the adjacent apartments of John and George Hoskins in Toronto, Canada. At most it had about six employees. George Hoskins, as general sales manager, was responsible for all aspects of Webster Dictionary Company's advertising and sales, including the design, preparation and placement of advertisements. Although there was no written agreement as to George's compensation, he received a "draw" that varied on occasion based on his personal needs, and he expected to share in the corporation's profits, an expectation based on George's "relationship with [his] brother." Nevertheless, no evidence was before the court to show that George was an "officer," director, or shareholder of Webster Dictionary Company.

Webster Dictionary Company never got off the ground financially, and it went out of business some time in late 1977. George Hoskins continued to be employed by Webster Dictionary Company until about May, 1977, and had continuing contacts with it thereafter.

At some time in mid-1976, George Hoskins, while still employed by Webster Dictionary Company, started Webster Publishing as a sole proprietorship. In March, 1977, George Hoskins incorporated three related corporations, collectively referred to herein as Webster Publishing. John Hoskins

5. Except for the uncertainties noted, the facts stated here, taken primarily from the deposition of George Hoskins, appear not to be in dispute.

apparently had nothing to do with Webster Publishing; George was clearly the principal operator of the business and he was sole incorporator, president and a director of each of the related corporations. His wife was sole shareholder.

Webster Publishing's business bears a striking resemblance to that of Webster Dictionary Company: mail order sales of reference books (dictionaries and encyclopedias) through advertisements placed in newspapers and periodicals. These advertisements, which were placed and either commissioned or designed by George Hoskins, used a number of the same types of "sales pitches" as those of Webster Dictionary Company (e.g., substantial advertised discounts attributed to "the recession," a photograph of Noah Webster, descriptions of Webster Publishing as "world famous," "authoritative," "America's foremost dictionary company," etc.). Webster Publishing's offending advertisements began to appear in late 1977, and continued through mid-1979. Thomas Lucas, who served as "legal consultant" to Webster Dictionary Company and was specifically named in the injunction, continued to serve in that capacity for Webster Publishing.

Ordinarily the validity and terms of an injunction are not reviewable in contempt proceedings. Alemite Mfg. Corp. v. Staff. They may be challenged only on appeal in the original proceeding and not by collateral attack. . . . But cf. 11 C. Wright & A. Miller, Federal Practice and Procedure § 2960, at 597 (1973) (suggesting that an exception should be made where "there was no opportunity for effective review of the order before it was violated").

In this case, the injunction was entered by default judgment, when Webster Dictionary Company did not appear at trial, after it had previously indicated it would consent to "an appropriate judgment against it." A judgment entered in these circumstances is a judgment on the merits and, in relation to liability as distinguished from damages,[7] ordinarily has the same legal effect between the parties and their privies as a judgment rendered after a fully-contested trial. Trans-World Airlines, Inc. v. Hughes, 449 F.2d 51, 63–64, 69 (2d Cir. 1971), rev'd on other grounds, 409 U.S. 363 (1973). Here, Webster Dictionary Company failed effectively to exercise its right of appeal. Thus, Webster Dictionary Company and its privies cannot now challenge the injunction on the merits.

The principles stated [above] constrain only those who are bound by an injunction. Persons beyond its scope *cannot* be held to have violated it because it does not apply to them. They are "free to ignore it." *Alemite.* Therefore, this case turns on whether appellants were properly held to be bound by the district court's injunction of October 27, 1977, even though they were not parties to the original action and were not named in the injunction. . . .

7. Although a default judgment conclusively establishes the defendant's liability, damages cannot be assessed without a hearing at which plaintiffs must "establish the extent of their damages resulting from defendant's violations." Eisler v. Stritzler, 535 F.2d 148, 153–54 (1st Cir. 1976). In the instant case, a hearing on Merriam's damages as against Webster Dictionary was held on April 25, 1977, which provided the basis for the district court's October 27, 1977 Findings of Fact.

To hold a nonparty bound by an injunction it is thus essential to prove either that the nonparty participated in the contumacious act of a party or that the nonparty was subject to the injunction because legally identified with a party.

Did appellants participate in the contumacious act of a party?

Proof of a relationship to the pre-injunction act of a party may be circumstantially suggestive, but a nonparty, if not legally identified with a party, can be found to be in contempt only if in active concert or participation with a party in postinjunction activity. Regal Knitwear Co. v. NLRB. Fed.R.Civ. P. 65(d). Thus, a key principle in cases binding a nonparty who is not legally identified with a party is that a person properly named in the injunction must have had a material role in the subsequent violation of that injunction.

The acts for which appellants were held in contempt occurred at a time after John Hoskins had withdrawn from all participation in Webster Dictionary Company. Also, if Webster Dictionary Company still existed when any of these acts occurred, there is no finding, and it is doubtful that the evidence most favorably viewed would support a finding, that Webster Dictionary Company was in any way involved in these acts. Thus, because no contumacious act of John Hoskins or Webster Dictionary Company has been found, appellants cannot be held on the basis of aiding or abetting them.

A more problematic issue is raised by the relationship between appellants and Thomas Lucas, the other individual named in the injunction. The evidence shows that he served as "legal consultant" to Webster Dictionary Company and served in the same capacity to Webster Publishing. Although named in the injunction, Lucas was not named in the show cause order or the adjudication of contempt. We do not consider whether there may be circumstances in which persons may be held in contempt for aiding and abetting a party who is not also held in contempt. In any event, the order now on appeal cannot be sustained on the theory that appellants aided and abetted Lucas in violation of the injunction. Appellee did not seek to develop the case on this theory, either before the district court or before this court, and the record is thus devoid of essential findings, even if the legal theory should be determined to be valid.

Was George Hoskins legally identified with one or more of the enjoined parties?

Fed.R.Civ.P. 65(d) provides in pertinent part that an order granting an injunction "is binding only upon the parties to the action, their officers, agents, servants, employees, and attorneys, and upon those persons in active concert or participation with them who receive actual notice of the order by personal service or otherwise." It might be argued that, in view of Rule 65(d), only "officers, agents, servants, employees, and attorneys" can now be determined to be within the group that *Alemite* referred to as "legally identified with" a party. Such a narrow reading of Rule 65(d) is inappropriate, however, in light of the fact that this rule is

"derived from the common-law doctrine that a decree of injunction not only binds the parties defendant but also those identified with them in interest, in 'privity' with them, or subject to their control. Its essence is that defendants may not nullify a decree by carrying out prohibited acts through aiders and abettors, although they were not parties to the original proceeding."

Regal Knitwear.

With respect to persons who may be legally identified with a party as "successors or assigns," the Court added:

"The term 'successors and assigns' in an enforcement order of course may not enlarge its scope beyond that defined by the Federal Rules of Civl Procedure. Successors and assigns may, however, be instrumentalities through which defendant seeks to evade an order or may come within the description of persons in active concert or participation with them in the violation of an injunction. If they are, by that fact they are brought within scope of contempt proceedings by the rules of civil procedure . . . "

In view of this passage it may be doubted that a "successor" can be within the permissible scope of contempt proceedings absent a finding that the successor was an instrumentality through which *an enjoined party,* and not merely the successor, sought to evade the injunction. We need not consider that question in the present case, just as the Supreme Court found it unnecessary in *Regal Knitwear* to "decide whether or under what circumstances any kind of successor or assign will be liable for violation of a Labor Board order." In any event, if any successor is subject to contempt proceedings *as successor,* rather than as a person "in active concert or participation with" an enjoined party, the successor must be one who has received a *transfer* of the business or some part of it *from the enjoined party.* See Herrlein v. Kankakis, 526 F.2d 252, 254–255 (7th Cir. 1975) (transfer of assets from one entity to the other after issuance of injunction was essential to finding the latter liable as a successor in interest). Cf. Golden State Bottling Co. v. NLRB (for purposes of Rule 65(d), transferee of business, as "bona fide successor," is in privity with predecessor and is bound by NLRB remedial order directed to predecessor). . . . Counsel have not called our attention to any case, nor have we found any, in which a second business entity was held to be a successor or in privity with an enjoined previously existing business entity, so as to subject the successor to contempt proceedings, in the absence of proof that the second entity acquired the business, or at least a relevant part of it *from the first entity.* It is not enough to prove that the first entity went out of existence and that the second entity entered into the enjoined type of business activity, knowing about the injunction but without having acquired the business, or a relevant part of it, from the first entity.

In the Findings, Ruling and Order of January 25, 1980, the district court found that appellants were "successors of the original defendant [Webster Dictionary Company] or persons acting in concert with it." We cannot affirm on the basis of this finding, however, because we are unable to determine whether this disjunctively phrased finding was meant to be an unconditional finding of successorship and, if so, whether this mixed determination of fact and law . . . may have been affected by an error of law with respect to the requirements for successorship. Even if the evidence before the district court were considered sufficient to support a circumstantial inference of successorship—an issue we do not decide—we cannot determine that the district court made a finding of successorship in the legally relevant sense.[9]

In *Regal Knitwear* the controversy over the permissible scope of contempt proceedings was focused on whether nonparties were legally identified with a party as "successors" or "assigns." We turn now to a materially different issue: Was George Hoskins within the permissible scope of contempt proceedings because he was "legally identified with" Webster Dictionary Company *when the injunction was issued* and for that reason continued to be subject to the injunction even after Webster Dictionary Company went out of existence? This is an issue that was not before the Court in *Regal Knitwear.*

[The evidence indicates] that, though not an officer, director, or shareholder of Webster Dictionary Company, George Hoskins was the next most active person in the operation of the corporation—John Hoskins being the most active. The evidence amply supported the district court's finding that George Hoskins was a "key employee" of Webster Dictionary Company as well as "the principal" of the corporate appellants. This alone, however, is insufficient to support the district court's conclusion that George Hoskins was bound by the injunction. The central reason that one who is not a party to the action in which the injunction was issued cannot be bound by it is that he has not had his day in court *with respect to the validity of the injunction.* Cf. *Alemite.* Absent an opportunity to contest liability, his knowledge of the injunction is not sufficient to bind him as an individual, id., as distinguished from prohibiting him from acting in the forbidden way on behalf of the enjoined party. Thus, the relevant inquiry is not merely whether (in addition to having knowledge of the injunction) George Hoskins was a "key employee" of Webster Dictionary Company but whether he had such a key role in the corporation's participation in the injunction proceedings that it can be fairly said that he has had his day in court in relation to the validity of the injunction. To meet this requirement, the evidence must go beyond proving merely that George Hoskins was a "key employee" of Webster Dictionary Company. We conclude that it does so.

The record before us, with respect to the hearing in January 1976, discloses that those present on behalf of Webster Dictionary Company included persons holding the positions of "general sales manager of the company, lawyer consultant and general counsel." Although George Hoskins was not identified by name in the record of that hearing, it is undisputed that he is the person who held the position of general sales manager of Webster Dictionary Company at that time. The presence of George Hoskins at these proceedings together with other circumstantial evidence in the record, would support the inference that George Hoskins participated in Webster Dictionary Company's decisionmaking with respect to its litigation position in the original injunction proceeding.

9. If not cured by a showing of George Hoskins' legal identification with Webster Dictionary Company in some way (as may be possible for reasons developed immediately infra), this defect is exacerbated in the present case by the fact that the original injunction was issued "by default." . . . In the present case the district court expressed doubts about the breadth of the injunction. "It goes pretty far. It may have gone too far." "[T]he injunction—which was actually entered after your withdrawing your appearance in the first case, and there was nobody here to represent the defendant—may [be] too broad, and I may want to modify it . . . ."

The fact that George Hoskins was not formally an "officer" of Webster Dictionary Company is not determinative of the question of legal identification with a party in the context of a close corporation operating out of the adjacent apartments of two brothers. The record supports an inference that his responsibilities were substantial, as was his expectation of remuneration if the venture was successful. In his position of "general sales manager," George was a principal actor with respect to the activities that were the occasion for invoking the judicial power of the district court. Advertisements designed, written, and placed by George Hoskins precipitated the injunction, and strikingly similar advertisements, for which he was again responsible, resulted in this contempt proceeding. The businesses were nearly identical—mail order sales of dictionaries and encyclopedias. Thomas Lucas served as "consultant" and "legal advisor" to both corporations. George Hoskins' tenure with Webster Dictionary Company and Webster Publishing overlapped substantially—he started Webster Publishing in mid-1976, but did not leave Webster Dictionary Company until May, 1977 and even thereafter had continuing contacts with Webster Dictionary Company.

In short, a factfinder, weighing the evidence, may find no material difference between George Hoskins' actions as a "key employee" of Webster Dictionary Company and actions in his "individual" capacity as principal of Webster Publishing. The evidence raises a fact issue as to whether this is a case of the same person continuing to do essentially the same thing with the same high degree of practical control, discretion and responsibility, before and after the injunction, with knowledge of the injunction, and after participating in the enjoined firm's corporate decisionmaking regarding its position in the injunction proceedings. If it is found that George Hoskins was legally identified with Webster Dictionary Company in this way, then he is bound by the injunction and the appellant corporations founded by him are also subject to it.

The record before us, however, is not such as to compel a factfinding that George Hoskins was legally identified with Webster Dictionary Company in this way. Evidence of his decisionmaking authority and influence over the corporate policy of Webster Dictionary Company, particularly in relationship to the injunction proceedings, is sparse. One reason for the paucity of evidence is that George Hoskins, though represented by counsel, did not appear in person at the show-cause hearing and his testimony came in only by a deposition that, by reason of the frequent intervention of his counsel left many questions unanswered. To the extent that the interrupted questions were objectionable, no adverse inference should be drawn. But, neither party having asked for a ruling by the court on interrupted questions and the deponent being a person cited to show cause and not having appeared in person as a witness at the hearing, if the court concludes that a question was proper and should have been answered, we think it appropriate for the factfinder to take these circumstances into account in assessing the significance of the sparsity of proof.

The deposition testimony of George Hoskins, moreover, could be interpreted as indicating that he believed the injunction applied to him in his activities through Webster Publishing, and that he altered his advertisements to avoid running afoul of it. In answer to the question whether he "violat[ed] any of the terms of the injunction," he answered,

"No, I wouldn't have done it if I thought I was in violation. The word world famous is not that important to me. If I'd have known it was . . . if I was that familiar with the injunction I just wouldn't have done it."

Appellants contend strenuously that, on the authority of the "nearly identical" *Alemite* case, George Hoskins cannot be bound. In *Alemite,* John Staff, his "agents, employees, associates and confederates" were enjoined from infringing or "aiding and abetting or in any way contributing to the infringement" of a patent. Joseph Staff, who at the time of the injunction was employed by John as a salesman, subsequently left John's employ, set up his own business, and infringed the patent. The court held that Joseph was not bound by the original injunction where John was not involved in Joseph's infringement.

Although there are definite factual similarities between *Alemite* and the instant case, the two are distinguishable. Joseph Staff was described merely as a "salesman" for his brother's corporation. No participation of Joseph in the planning and direction of the activities causing the original patent infringement is disclosed. In contrast, on the evidence in the record before us, George Hoskins may fairly be found to have been a "managing official." . . . Nor is there any indication that the successor firm in *Alemite* was so nearly identical to the original defendant in its business and mode of operation as is the case here, or of any overlap of Joseph Staff's service to the two companies. In short, the facts recited in *Alemite* disclosed none of the factors that, in this case, would support a finding that George Hoskins was legally identified with Webster Dictionary Company when the injunction was issued.

From another perspective, permitting a finding of legal identification of George Hoskins with Webster Dictionary Company, on the record before us, may be viewed as an instance of piercing corporate veils. We are aware of no case either supporting or opposing the application of this concept to the exercise of contempt power in the enforcement of an injunction. There are, of course, precedents for piercing a corporate veil in other contexts. See, e.g., Zubik v. Zubik, 384 F.2d 267 (3d Cir. 1967), cert. denied, 390 U.S. 988 (1968); My Bread Baking Co. v. Cumberland Farms, Inc., 353 Mass. 614, 233 N.E.2d 748 (1968). The analogy seems apt, and we conclude that it is appropriate from this perspective also for the present case to turn on a fact finding as to whether George Hoskins was legally identified with Webster Dictionary Company.

For the foregoing reasons we conclude that the evidence in the record before us is sufficient to raise a fact question as to whether George Hoskins was legally identified with Webster Dictionary Company in the sense relevant to his having had his day in court on the validity of the injunction. Because we cannot determine that the district court addressed this question and made the necessary findings, applying a legal standard consistent with the views expressed in this opinion, we must remand for further proceedings consistent with this opinion. In such further proceedings, it will be appropriate to afford all parties an opportunity to present further evidence.

If, on remand, the district court finds that George Hoskins was legally identified with Webster Dictionary Company in relation to the injunction proceedings, he and the Webster Publishing entities are subject to the injunction. A party and his privies cannot circumvent a court's injunction against the activities they had effectuated before the injunction, through one legal entity, by the creation of another entity through which they, or some of them, continue essentially the same activity. . . .

---

1) Does *Webster* unnecessarily prolong the life of a not too ingenuously disguised continuance? Did Merriam's attorneys fail to suggest a broad enough injunction or to properly draft their show-cause order? Why didn't Merriam file a second infringement action against George?

2) Does *Alemite* or *Regal* cause more problems for Merriam? *Alemite* limited the contempt inquiry in part because of the collateral bar rule. If Merriam seeks civil compensatory contempt and if, under *United Mine Workers,* p. 274 the collateral bar rule is inapplicable to civil contempt, then shouldn't anyone who violates plaintiff's substantive rights under the injunction pay compensatory contempt damages?

3) If no one had a "day in court" leading to the injunction, will the injunction be capable of supporting contempt? May infringers evade their legal obligations by defaulting? Does an opportunity to litigate suffice? If so, didn't George have that opportunity?

4) Additional successor decisions include Donovan v. Janitorial Services, Inc., 672 F.2d 528 (5th Cir. 1982); and Great Western Cities, Inc. v. Binstein, 536 F.Supp. 808 (N.D.Ill.1982). Knowledge or the absence of it is often a feature of successor cases. See NLRB v. Sequoia District Council of Carpenters, 568 F.2d 628 (9th Cir. 1977); Shakman v. Democratic Organization of Cook County, 533 F.2d 344 (7th Cir. 1976), certiorari denied 429 U.S. 858; Monroe v. Bombard, 422 F.Supp. 211 (S.D.N.Y.1976).

5) As *Webster* suggests, succession cases are also close to insolvency and bankruptcy practice. See SEC v. Wencke, 622 F.2d 1363 (9th Cir. 1980); Panther Pumps & Equipment Co., Inc. v. Hydrocraft, Inc., 566 F.2d 8 (7th Cir. 1977); Herrlein v. Kanakis, 526 F.2d 252 (7th Cir. 1975); Monroe v. Bombard, 422 F.Supp. 211 (S.D.N.Y.1976). In particular, the successor may have received something resembling a fraudulent conveyance; but the plaintiff may prefer pursuit of the assets under contempt in the injunction litigation over filing a separate fraudulent conveyance action, perhaps in state court. Compare Griffin v. Prince Edward County, p. 264 with Panther Pumps & Equipment Co., Inc. v. Hydrocraft, Inc., 566 F.2d 8, 22–25 (7th Cir. 1977); Herrlein v. Kanakis, 526 F.2d 252 (7th Cir. 1975); Monroe v. Bombard, 422 F.Supp. 211 (S.D.N.Y.1976).

6) The court's power to protect assets at stake in litigation with broad ex parte stays is also involved. This power may be expressed as in custodia legis, various receivership theories, or the bankruptcy court's automatic stay. See SEC v. Wencke, 622 F.2d 1363, 1368–1372 (9th Cir. 1980) (securities receivership); Kennedy, The Automatic Stay in Bankruptcy, 11 U.Mich.J.L. Ref. 175 (1978); Kennedy, Automatic Stays Under the New Bankruptcy Law, 12 U.Mich.J.L.Ref. 3 (1978). Environmental Defense Fund v. EPA, 485 F.2d 780, 784 n. 2 (D.C.Cir. 1973), affirmed sub nom. Fri v. Sierra

Club, 412 U.S. 541, states an expansive theory of obligation to halt a related action.

7) Mr. Dunbar distinguished limiting injunctions to parties from protecting property under judicial "custody" as follows: "The common practice upon appointing receivers of enjoining all persons from interfering with the property is not founded upon any doctrine inconsistent with the principles under consideration. By the appointment of a receiver the court takes into its custody all the property belonging to the defendant within its jurisdiction. Any interference will the property is an interference with the action of the court. All persons are bound at their peril to refrain from acts which may hinder the court or its officers in the execution of their duties. An act which constitutes such an interference or hindrance is a contempt, not because it violates an order of the court, but because it embarrasses the court in the performance of its functions. The contempt is committed, although no injunction or restraining order against the act done has been issued . . . and although the persons accused had no intention of interfering in any way with the operations of the court. . . . " Dunbar, Government By Injunction, 13 L.Q.Rev. 347, 365 (1897).

8) Problem: Billy Bob is a country and western singing star. His concert tours are marred with phantom tortfeasors who violate his right to publicity by peddling unlicensed and bootleg merchandise to the throngs that attend his concerts. The day before Billy Bob's concert in Hamden, Judge Abele enjoined various ABC companies and Does. The orders were posted about the concert hall. At the concert, Billy Bob's employees seized bootleg tapes and "Billy Bob" T-shirts from Crimdell and served the injunction on him. They called the judge and asked her to amend the complaint to add Crimdell as a defendant and to order Crimdell to show cause why he should not be held in contempt. Crimdell consults you the next morning with two questions: May Billy Bob keep the merchandise? Will the contempt charge stick? See Winterland Concessions Co. v. Geisel, 511 F.Supp. 310 (N.D.Ill. 1981); Joel v. Various John Does, 499 F.Supp. 791 (E.D.Wis.1980).

IV. Defendant Class Actions

This chapter considers who is "bound" by an injunction. So far the relationship between defendant and contemnor had an independent existence apart from the litigation. A real-world nexus between the parties and nonparties existed, and some courts thought that sufficient to "bind" the nonparties. But now, turning to the class action, we deal with a relationship between the party and contemnor that is created by the lawsuit and does not necessarily exist independently. The contemnor's only connection with the defendant may be that the plaintiff or the court thinks that he is a member of a class which is formally constituted for the lawsuit, represented by the defendant. One important question is whether this litigative relationship is sufficient to bind the "nonparty." To put it somewhat differently, can Rule 23 be harmonized with Rule 65(d).

Here we analyze the class action device from the defendant's perspective. That perspective is often overlooked in formulating the rules governing the class action device because the prime "contemporary function" of the class action is to aggregate a multitude of small damage claims to create sufficient economic incentive to be a plaintiff or a plaintiff's lawyer. What should the limits or contours of the class represented be? How can the court determine that contemnor was represented adequately? We must examine these questions against the background of the inherently suspect method of choosing the representative. With the plaintiff class action, it is self-appointment. However, with the defendant class action, it is even worse—appointment by the adversary. Read Rule 23 in the Appendix. Ask how it protects members of defendant classes. Is a plaintiff likely to select the "best" representative to oppose him? Are conscripted litigants ever adequate representatives? Who pays the cost of participation? See Note, Defendant Class Actions, 91 Harv.L.Rev. 630 (1978); and Note, Federal Rule of Civil Procedure 23: A Defendant Class Action with a Public Official as the Named Representative, 9 Val.U.L.Rev. 357 (1975).

THE HADNOTT v. AMOS LITIGATION

Hadnott v. Amos was a suit attempting to place certain National Democratic Party of Alabama (NDPA) candidates on the ballot in Alabama. The defendant class consisted of all the Judges of Probate of the State of Alabama. Each of Alabama's 67 counties has a probate judge. Under Alabama law the Probate Judge of each county is responsible for conducting elections in the county. Among other things, he must cause to be printed upon the ballot the names of all candidates who have been nominated and certified to him. Certificates of nomination for nominees in a single county are filed directly with the Probate Judge of the county. Certificates of nomination for all officers elected on a greater than countywide basis (referred to as a statewide basis), such as congressmen, Presidential electors, or state officials, are filed with the Secretary of State. The Secretary then certifies the appropriate names to the Probate Judges.

The chosen representative of this class is Edward A. Grouby, the Probate Judge of Autauga County. In addition to Grouby, some state officers are named as defendants—Albert Brewer, the Governor; MacDonald Gallion, the Attorney General; and Mabel S. Amos, the Secretary of State. It is not alleged that any of these have any control over the Probate Judge. No explanation is given in the complaint for the choice of Grouby, nor does one appear in any of the opinions. It might have been an alphabetical choice. The only mention of Autauga County occurs in the complaint. It is alleged that one of the named plaintiffs, Sallie Hadnott, a black who was a candidate for local office in Autauga County, had attempted to file the necessary papers with Judge Grouby; the complaint states that on one occasion she was rebuffed, on another she could not find the Judge, and then she placed the documents in the mail. The complaint invokes Federal Rule 23 and alleges that the prerequisites of subsections (a), (b)(1), (b)(2) and (b)(3) are satisfied. The language of those subsections is tracked, with the only further specifications being that the relief sought against defendant Edward Grouby as Judge of Probate of Autauga County, Alabama, is typical of the relief sought against all probate judges in Alabama.

The complaint was predicated principally on two claims. The first related to the state Corrupt Practices Law—under which some NDPA candidates were disqualified. That law, generally pertaining to campaign finances and expenditures, requires that within five days after the announcement of a candidacy, the candidate establish a finance committee. The plaintiffs claimed the law was invalid on its face. But their principal argument was one of "selective enforcement"—that the statutory disqualification sanction was imposed on the NDPA candidates because of their race or political views.

The second claim upon which the complaint rested related to the Garrett Law of the state. That law requires that candidates for office file a declaration of intention to run on or before March 1 of the year in which the general election is held. The plaintiffs had not complied with this requirement. Their principal argument here was that the early filing requirement was invalid on its face because it protected the May 1 regular Democratic primary. They also claimed that the law was invalid because it did not comply with the procedures of section I of the Voting Rights Act of 1965.

This lawsuit started late. The triggering event seemed to have been the September 10 decision of Secretary of State Amos to refuse to certify any (but two) of the NDPA candidates for statewide office. Suit was filed on September 13. On September 18 the three-judge district court that had been convened (consisting of Judges Godbold, Johnson and Pittman) issued what was denominated a Temporary Restraining Order. It sought to protect the rights of NDPA candidates by having ballots prepared for the November 5 election which would include the names of NDPA candidates, to be used in the eventuality that the plaintiffs won. The pertinent paragraph read:

"4. The Judge of Probate of each county using the voting machine process in whole or in part shall, to the extent applicable to the ballot in the particular county, include the aforesaid names as candidates in the printing of labels, programming of machines, and all other steps necessary to prepare such voting machine for the November, 1968, general election. The Judges of Probate shall make such preparations that upon receipt of later instructions from the Secretary of State or from this court they may block out said names and be prepared to take such other steps as would be necessary to eliminate said names from the voting machine ballot should the judgment of this court provide for no, other, or different action from that specified herein."

A hearing was held on September 30, and on October 11 a decision was rendered (295 F.Supp. 1003). That opinion had only one sentence on the class action aspects: "We hold that the plaintiffs properly bring this suit as a class action, and that the defendant Edward H. Grouby properly represents a class of defendants composed of the Judges of Probate of all counties in Alabama." On the merits, the court, over Judge Johnson's dissent, concluded that the statutes were not unconstitutional and, accordingly, dissolved the TRO. The District Court in Hadnott v. Amos did not believe the Garrett Act fell within the ambit of section 5 of the Voting Rights Act of 1965, which by its terms applies to statutes establishing a "voting qualification or prerequisite to voting" or to a "standard, practice or procedure with respect to voting." 42 U.S.C.A. § 1973c (1970). The District Court also held the Corrupt Practices Law not invalid.

After losing at the District Court level, the plaintiffs moved immediately to the Supreme Court. On October 14, 1968, the Monday following the issuance of the District Court opinion, an appeal to the Supreme Court was filed by plaintiffs. On the same day the appeal was filed, plaintiffs moved in the Supreme Court to accelerate the consideration of the cause so the effective relief could be granted for the November 5 election. Accompanying the motion for expedited consideration was a motion to reinstate the temporary restraining order entered by the District Court on September 18. Later on the same day, October 14, the Supreme Court set both of plaintiffs' preceding two motions down for oral argument on Friday, October 18, and reinstated the District Court's injunction of September 18, 1968, pending the determination of the motions. On Saturday, October 19, the Supreme Court entered the following order in Hadnott v. Amos (393 U.S. 904):

"The order entered October 14, 1968, restoring temporary relief is continued pending action upon the jurisdictional statement which has been filed.

"The motion to advance and expedite is denied."

Nothing further happened in the case until the election on November 5. Then the scene shifts to Greene County and Probate Judge James Dennis Herndon. The NDPA candidates for county offices in Greene County were not on the ballot. Only those NDPA candidates certified by Amos—that is, those running for statewide offices—were on the ballot. (The NDPA "straight ticket" received 1938 votes.) This article from the November 5 issue of the Birmingham News (an afternoon paper) captures the event:

"Greene County general election ballots distributed here today did not list the names of six National Democratic Party of Alabama candidates seeking county offices.

"Probate Judge James Dennis Herndon confirmed that the six local Negro candidates, whose names appeared on the county's official absentee ballot distributed recently, had been dropped after a temporary federal court injunction ordering their certification was dissolved Oct. 10.

"Herndon said the six were not covered by an appeal of the three-judge panel's majority decision, filed recently by the new, largely Negro party, and basis for ballot appearance of NDPA candidates for presidential elector.

" 'Don't ask me why this group didn't appeal. Maybe they didn't pay their lawyer; I don't know,' Herndon said.

"He added that, in compliance with pending appellate court litigation, names of all state-level NDPA candidates would appear on today's regular ballot, distributed early this morning to county polling places.

"The six local candidates dropped included: Vassle Knott, Harry C. Means, Levi Morrow Sr., and Frenchie Burton, NDPA candidates for County Commissioner posts; Robert Hines, candidate for County Board of Education post 1 and J. A. Posey Sr., candidate for post 2.

"According to Judge Herndon, none of the six qualified in person with his office or, in his words, 'said anything to me about running.' He said several of the six had been to his office on other matters, but never mentioned their candidacy."

There is no dispute that Judge Herndon was formally served (by certified mail) with copies of the District Court orders of September 18 and October 11; and also that he was not formally served with copies of the Supreme Court orders of October 14 and October 19. Nor did the attorneys for the defendants notify the probate judges.

In any event, right after the election, proceedings were set in motion in both the District Court and the Supreme Court. The plaintiffs moved in the Supreme Court—asking that Judge Herndon be held in contempt and that the election be set aside. And then, five days later, on November 20, the United States entered the case for the first time, but made its motions in the District Court. On November 21, the District Court entered orders: (1) designating the United States as an amicus curiae and a party in the case; (2) adding as a party defendant James Dennis Herndon; (3) directing the "Defendant, James Dennis Herndon, and others, to show cause, if any they have, why they should not be restrained pending a final determination of this action from giving effect to the results of the November 5, 1968, election in Greene County for local county offices." On December 20, 1968, the District Court issued its order, with the consent of Judge Herndon, enjoining and restraining him from giving effect to the results of the November 5, 1968, election in Greene County for local county offices.

Then, on March 25, 1969, the Supreme Court delivered these opinions:

HADNOTT v. AMOS

394 U.S. 358, 89 S.Ct. 1101, 22 L.Ed.2d 336 (1969).

Justice DOUGLAS delivered the opinion of the Court. . . .

NDPA candidates, mostly Negroes, were elected to various local offices in Etowah, Marengo, and Sumter Counties. But in Greene County the NDPA candidates for local office were left off the ballot except for absentee voters. In Greene County the only candidates appearing on the ballot were the regular Democratic Party nominees for local offices and they received between 1,699 and 1,709 votes each. It appears that NDPA candidates in Greene County would have won had they been on the ballot [1] for 1,938 ballots were marked for the NDPA "straight ticket."

. . . On the merits of the appeal, we reverse.

First. The Alabama Corrupt Practices Act requires each candidate within five days "after the announcement of his candidacy for any office" to file a statement showing "the name of not less than one nor more than five persons" chosen to receive, expend, audit, and disburse funds for his election. Ala.Code, Tit. 17, § 274 (1958).

The disqualification of the NDPA candidates for their alleged failure to satisfy this provision of the Alabama Act implicates Probate Judge Herndon, who was responsible for the preparation of the Greene County ballot which omitted their names.

1. NDPA ran mostly Negro candidates—60 out of 67. In Greene County, Negroes of voting age are in a numerical majority—5,001 Negro, 1,649 white, according to the 1960 census.

In this case the black candidates for Greene County offices designated finance committees in February 1968 prior to their entry in the Democratic primary. Appellees contend that it was sufficient to justify Judge Herndon's omission of the names and that the NDPA candidates did not file a second designation of financial committee after May 7, the date of the primary, and the date on which those candidates were nominated by the NDPA. Appellants contend that disqualification for that reason constituted discriminatory enforcement of the Corrupt Practices Act in violation of the Equal Protection Clause. Since the names of the white candidates who won the May 7 primary were placed on the ballot, although they also did not file a second designation after that date, appellees clearly have the burden of justifying the denial of ballot places to the black NDPA candidates. Appellees have failed to satisfy that burden.

Alabama law requires all candidates for local office, not selected in primaries, to be nominated by mass meeting on the first Tuesday in May of the election year. Ala.Code, Tit. 17, §§ 413, 414 (1958). The certificate of nomination sent to Judge Herndon, probate judge for Greene County, on September 4, stated that NDPA nominees had been selected pursuant to a mass meeting.

On September 18 the District Court temporarily restrained the omission from the ballot of NDPA candidates for state and local office. That restraint was dissolved on October 11. Meanwhile counsel for the white Green County candidates, who was the county solicitor, prompted Judge Herndon to file [as an appendix to the defendants' answer in the district court] an affidavit in which he stated that to the "best of my knowledge and belief" the NDPA held no local mass meeting on May 7 at which nominations were made, and further that none of the six NDPA candidates "filed or offered to file in my office" the designation of financial committee required by the Corrupt Practices Act. Yet when his deposition was taken on December 27, the judge conceded that the mass meeting might have been held without his hearing about it and admitted knowledge that the black candidates had filed designations of financial committee in February. He did not say why in these circumstances the February filing did not suffice for the general election; the designations refer to candidacies for the general election as well as the primary election. Nor did he offer any explanation why if the February filings by the white candidates sufficed for the general election, the filings of the black candidates should be treated differently. The record is therefore utterly devoid of any explanation adequate to satisfy appellees' burden. It is true that at oral argument in this Court counsel for appellees suggested that the Alabama courts might construe the statutory words—"[w]ithin five days after the announcement of his candidacy . . . each candidate for a county office . . . shall file [the designation statement] with the judge of probate"—to require a second filing by losers in a primary who stand at the general election as candidates of another party. But it was not urged, nor could it be on this record, that appellees' distinction between the black and white candidates was rested on that construction. . . .

When the Alabama Act is construed as appellants' opponents were allowed to construe it without suffering disqualification, we conclude that appellants met the same requirements. Unequal application of the same law to different racial groups has an especially invidious connotation.

Second. In 1967 Alabama passed the Garrett Act (L.1967, Act 243) barring from the ballot in a general election a candidate for a state, district, or federal office "who does not file a declaration of intention to become a candidate for such office with the Secretary of State on or before the first day of March of the year in which such general election is held." The Garrett Act also requires a declaration of the political party whose nomination the candidate seeks; or if he is not a party candidate that he will run as an independent. A like provision bars probate judges from printing on ballots the names of candidates for county offices unless they have filed a declaration of intention on or before the prior March 1. Accordingly, . . . Judge Herndon justifies his omission of those candidates from the Greene County ballot, on the ground that they did not comply with the Garrett Act. . . .

The question is whether the Garrett Act is affected by § 5 of the Voting Rights Act of 1965, 79 Stat. 439, 42 U.S.C. § 1973c (1964 ed., Supp. III), which provides that whenever States like Alabama seek to administer "any voting qualification or prerequisite to voting, or standard, practice, or procedure with respect to voting different from that in force or effect on November 1, 1964," the State may institute an action in the United States District Court for the District of Columbia for a declaratory judgment that "such qualification, prerequisite, standard, practice, or procedure does not have the purpose and will not have the effect of denying or abridging the right to vote on account of race or color." It is further provided in § 5 that unless and until the District of Columbia court enters such judgment "no person shall be denied the right to vote for failure to comply with such qualification, prerequisite, standard, practice, or procedure."

The Garrett Act is in respects material here on all fours with Whitley v. Williams, 393 U.S. 544 [decided on March 3, 1969], in which we held that a like provision added to the Mississippi Code could not be applied until it had been approved in one of the two ways provided in § 5 of the Voting Rights Act of 1965.

In the *Whitley* case we dealt with a new Mississippi law which, *inter alia,* changed the time for filing a petition as an independent candidate from 40 days before the *general* election to 60 days before the *primary* election.

We held that this new provision was subject to § 5 of the Voting Rights Act of 1965 as it was aimed "at increasing the difficulty for an independent candidate to gain a position on the general election ballot." Id., at 570. And we added that the change "might also undermine the effectiveness of voters who wish to elect independent candidates." Ibid. The increased barriers placed on independent candidates by Alabama's Garrett Act likewise bring it within the purview of § 5 of the Federal Act. The Alabama officials, therefore, acted unlawfully in disqualifying independent candidates in the 1968 election for failure to comply with the Garrett Act.

On the merits, we reverse the District Court and remand the cause with directions (1) to issue an appropriate order requiring the prevailing NDPA candidates in Etowah, Marengo, and Sumter Counties to be treated as duly elected to the offices for which they ran; and (2) to require the state and local officials promptly to conduct a new election in Greene County for the various county offices contested by NDPA candidates, at which election the NDPA candidates for those respective positions shall appear on the ballot.

The motion to hold Judge Herndon in contempt will be disposed of in a separate opinion.

[Justice Black did not participate. Justices White and Stewart dissented. They would remand the case to the three-judge court to determine whether the Corrupt Practices Act required a filing of committee designations after losing the Democratic primary.]

IN RE HERNDON

394 U.S. 399, 89 S.Ct. 1107, 22 L.Ed.2d 367 (1969).

PER CURIAM. The appeal in Hadnott v. Amos, . . . decided today, was argued with the motion filed by appellants on November 19, 1968, "for an order to show cause why Judge Herndon should not be held in contempt and for other relief." . . .

We conclude that decision on the motion should await timely initiation and completion of appropriate proceedings in the District Court to determine whether Judge Herndon's failure to place NDPA candidates on the ballot constituted contempt of the order of September 18 of the District Court. Decision on the motion is therefore postponed.

It is so ordered.

Justice BLACK took no part in the consideration or decision of this case.

Justice DOUGLAS, whom Justice HARLAN joins, dissenting.

This is a motion requesting that we initiate a proceeding against Herndon, Probate Judge in Greene County, Alabama, for disobedience of our order . . . . Our order, if obeyed, would have resulted in the black candidates, sponsored by the National Democratic Party of Alabama (NDPA), having been on the ballot for county offices in Greene County in the general election of November 1968. They were, it is alleged, left off the ballot due to the actions of Judge Herndon, as related in Hadnott v. Amos.

This motion, filed by appellants . . . , states they are informed and believe that Judge Herndon's failure to place these nominees on the ballot was done "wilfully and with actual knowledge of the order of this court." Judge Herndon filed his response to that motion, in which he denied that the omission of the NDPA candidates for county office was "willfully or contumaciously done with actual knowledge of the said orders of this court."

This motion was briefed and argued when [Hadnott v. Amos] was presented on the merits.

I have studied the record and read the briefs; and as presently advised I think there is probable cause to conclude that Judge Herndon knowingly and purposefully evaded our order. What the ultimate conclusion will be depends, of course, on a full hearing at which Judge Herndon receives that notice and that opportunity to be heard which is required by due process. But if what appears to be probable cause matures into full-fledged findings, we have a flagrant violation of our order, which involves a vital problem of civil rights, involving the command of the Fifteenth Amendment, that extends the ballot to the blacks.

In a case of far less consequence the Court, proceeding by contempt on an information filed by the Attorney General, United States v. Shipp, 214 U.S. 386, 439, held a sheriff and his deputies in contempt for silent cooperation with a mob in hanging a prisoner whose case was before this Court. That sheriff acted by merely turning his back and letting the mob run wild. In the present case, if the facts alleged are proven, Judge Herndon's affirmative acts unlawfully kept the NDPA candidates off the ballot.

Rule 42(a) of the Federal Rules of Criminal Procedure governs contempt in the presence of the court. Rule 42(b) covers the contempt alleged here, viz., disrespect or violation of this Court's order. . . .

I would issue the notice prescribed by Rule 42(b), designate an attorney to represent the Court, appoint a Master, and get on with the hearings.

Reservation of action on the motion implicates the Double Jeopardy Clause. Successive federal prosecutions of the same person based on the same acts are prohibited by the Fifth Amendment. See United States v. Lanza, 260 U.S. 377, 382; Abbate v. United States, 359 U.S. 187, 197 (opinion of Brennan, J.). It was held in Pereira v. United States, 347 U.S. 1, 9, that

"[A] defendant may be convicted of [two offenses] even though the charges arise from a single act or series of acts, so long as each requires the proof of a fact not essential to the other."

In the instant case, however, it is likely that the facts underlying both contempt charges will be identical. In fact, it may have been impossible for Judge Herndon to have violated one court order without violating the other.

For some time no further proceedings were had in the District Court on the issue of Judge Herndon's alleged contempt. It seemed as though the matter had been forgotten. Then, on October 3, 1970, on its own initiative (though not without a reminder by one of the plaintiffs' attorneys, who was appearing before the court on another matter and mentioned the pending contempt charges as almost an aside), the District Court entered a show-cause order against Judge Herndon. He was required to show why he was not to be held in contempt. The hearing was held in December 1970 and on January 7, 1971, the following contempt orders were issued by the court, signed by Judges Godbold, Johnson, and Pittman.

HADNOTT v. AMOS

325 F.Supp. 777 (M.D.Ala.1971).

PER CURIAM.

CIVIL CONTEMPT

This proceeding was initiated in September, 1968, by the plaintiffs, Negro and white electors of the National Democratic Party of Alabama, on behalf of themselves and others similarly situated, to require the defendants, including James Dennis Herndon in his capacity as Probate Judge of Greene County, Alabama, to place upon the official ballots for the 1968 general election the names of National Democratic Party of Alabama candidates for state and local elections. On September 18, 1968, this Court issued a temporary restraining order in this case, which order was renewed on September 28, 1968, and, after a hearing on the merits, renewed again on October 8, 1968. The temporary restraining order was dissolved on October 11, 1968; however, on October 14, 1968, the United States Supreme Court restored this Court's order of September 18, 1968, and, after a hearing on the merits, again restored, on October 19, 1968, this Court's September 18, 1968 order.

The evidence in this case reflects that James Dennis Herndon had actual knowledge of this Court's order of September 18, 1968, and had actual knowledge that, after this Court had dissolved its September 18, 1968 order, the Supreme Court of the United States on October 14, 1968, reinstated and restored said order and, further, had actual knowledge that, after a hearing conducted on October 18, 1968, the Supreme Court of the United States again restored and reinstated this Court's order of September 18, 1968. The evidence in this case further reflects that, notwithstanding this actual knowledge, James Dennis Herndon, in his capacity as Probate Judge of Greene County, Alabama, failed to list the names of the local National Democratic Party of Alabama candidates on the official ballot for Greene County, Alabama.

This Court finds that the evidence of knowledge and the failure and refusal of James Dennis Herndon to comply with this Court's order of September 18, 1968, as restored and reinstated by the Supreme Court on October 14, 1968, and on October 19, 1968, is clear and convincing. The disobedience of James Dennis Herndon to this Court's order of September 18, 1968, was to the damage of Frenchie Burton, Vassie Knott, Harry C. Means, Levi Morrow, Sr., Robert Hines and J. A. Posey, Sr., in that said individuals, who were members of the class that initiated this civil action, would have been elected to the Court of County Commissioners and the Board of Education of Greene County, Alabama, had their names been on the Greene County general election ballot of November 5, 1968. This Court further finds and concludes that it is appropriate to impose a fine to compensate said injured parties for their actual loss or damage suffered by reason of the disobedience of this Court's order by James Dennis Herndon. The evidence reflects that said injured parties suffered actual loss and financial damage as follows:

Name	Amount Lost
Frenchie Burton	$1,333.00
Vassie Knott	1,333.00
Harry C. Means	1,333.00
Levi Morrow, Sr.	1,333.00
Robert Hines	60.00
J. A. Posey, Sr.	60.00

This Court further finds and concludes from the evidence in this case that the other claims made by the plaintiffs for damage and loss are either not applicable because said damages were not sustained by parties to this action, or are too speculative; therefore, all claims other than those hereinabove listed will be denied.

Accordingly, it is the ORDER, JUDGMENT and DECREE of this Court that James Dennis Herndon be and he is hereby adjudged guilty of civil contempt of this Court for his failure and refusal to comply with this Court's order of September 18, 1968.

It is the further ORDER, JUDGMENT and DECREE of this Court that a judgment be and the same is hereby rendered against James Dennis Herndon in the total amount of $5,452; the judgment herein and hereby rendered represents the actual loss to Frenchie Burton in the amount of $1,333, Vassie Knott in the amount of $1,333, Harry C. Means in the amount of $1,333, Levi Morris, Sr., in the amount of $1,333, Robert Hines in the amount of $60, and J. A. Posey, Sr., in the amount of $60, caused by James Dennis Herndon's violation of this Court's order of September 18, 1968.

It is the further ORDER, JUDGMENT and DECREE of this Court that James Dennis Herndon pay to the Clerk of this Court the sum of $5,452 within ten days from the date of this order, which money will be distributed by the Clerk of this Court to the following individuals in the amounts specified:

Name	Amount
Frenchie Burton	$1,333.00
Vassie Knott	1,333.00
Harry C. Means	1,333.00
Levi Morrow, Sr.	1,333.00
Robert Hines	60.00
J. A. Posey, Sr.	60.00

It is the further ORDER, JUDGMENT and DECREE of this Court that the cost incurred in this civil contempt proceeding be and the same are hereby taxed against James Dennis Herndon, for which execution may issue.

IN RE HERNDON

325 F.Supp. 779 (M.D.Ala.1971).

PER CURIAM.

CRIMINAL CONTEMPT

This Court now concludes from the evidence presented in this case that James Dennis Herndon is guilty of criminal contempt of this Court. The basis for this conclusion is that on September 18, 1968, this Court issued a temporary restraining order in this case, which order was renewed on September 28, 1968, and again on October 8, 1968. While this temporary restraining order was dissolved by this Court on October 11, 1968, the United States Supreme Court on October 14, 1968, restored and reinstated this Court's temporary restraining order of September 18, 1968. After a hearing on October 18, 1968, the Supreme Court on October 19, 1968, again restored and reinstated this Court's order of September 18, 1968. The thrust of this order as entered by this Court on September 18, 1968, as the same pertained to Greene County, Alabama, was to order James Dennis Herndon, in his capacity as Probate Judge of Greene County, Alabama, to list the names of local National Democratic Party of Alabama candidates on the official ballot for the general election on November 5, 1968.

This Court finds from the evidence presented upon this question of criminal contempt that the failure of James Dennis Herndon to list local National Democratic Party of Alabama candidates on the ballot for Greene County, Alabama, for the November 5, 1968, general election was after the said James Dennis Herndon had actual knowledge of the temporary restraining order issued by this Court on September 18, 1968, and after the said James Dennis Herndon had actual knowledge that the Supreme Court of the United States had on October 14, 1968 and again on October 19, 1968, restored and reinstated this Court's order of September 18, 1968. The evidence in this case reflects, beyond a reasonable doubt, that James Dennis Herndon had actual knowledge of these orders. This Court further finds that the failure of James Dennis Herndon to list candidates Frenchie Burton, Vassie Knott, Harry C. Means, Levi Morrow, Sr., Robert Hines, and J. A. Posey, Sr., on the ballot for Greene County, Alabama, for the November 5, 1968, general election constituted a willful violation of the order of this Court of September 18, 1968, as restored and reinstated by the Supreme Court of the United States on October 14, 1968, and on October 19, 1968. This conduct on the part of Herndon, which was knowing and willful, constituted criminal contempt of this Court. Accordingly, it is the

ORDER, JUDGMENT and DECREE of this Court that James Dennis Herndon be and he is hereby adjudged guilty of criminal contempt of this Court for violating the order of this Court made and entered September 18, 1968, as restored and reinstated by the Supreme Court of the United States on October 14, 1968, and on October 19, 1968. It is the further

ORDER, JUDGMENT and DECREE of this Court that James Dennis Herndon be and he is hereby fined the sum of $300, which sum is to be paid to the Clerk of this Court within ten days from this date. It is the further

ORDER, JUDGMENT and DECREE of this Court that James Dennis Herndon be and he is hereby placed on probation for a period of one year from this date; this probationary sentence is subject to the general terms and conditions of probation on file in the Clerk's Office of this Court.

---

1) Some procedural arcana may be explained by remembering that *Hadnott* was brought before a three-judge court under a statute, 28 U.S.C. § 2281, that has been substantially revised. Sallie Hadnott was a clever name for a civil rights class plaintiff. Alabama also gave us the class actions of White v. Crook, 251 F.Supp. 401 (M.D.Ala.1966), and Washington v. Lee, 263 F.Supp. 327 (M.D.Ala.1966); probable jurisdiction noted 387 U.S. 928, affirmed per curiam 390 U.S. 333 (1967).

2) Reread Rule 23. Are the *Hadnott* plaintiff and defendant classes (b)(2) or (b)(3) classes? Does (b)(2) protect defendants better than (b)(3)? Do the arguably unconstitutional statutes create a sufficient nexus for a (b)(1)

defendant class? Perhaps plaintiffs were suing under the time-tested theory "sue everybody, God will know his own."

Why did plaintiffs' lawyers use a plaintiff class instead of just suing the "wrongdoers" with an individual plaintiff? Why not use a (b)(2) plaintiff class seeking an injunction to bind defendants, their agents, and successors. If plaintiffs omitted a plaintiff class, would Rule 65(d), issue preclusion-collateral estoppel, and Rule 25(d) protect them adequately? Remember the cost of notice to the class which might be required by either the rule or due process and the delay occasioned by the certification process. Might the plaintiff class facilitate enforcement? There are two answers. The plaintiff class costs nothing, and, who knows, it might help. It may be easier for a member of a plaintiff class to move for contempt. Should an unnamed class member have any greater rights to initiate contempt than any other citizen?

3) Could the trial judge decline to certify a defendant class of government officials on the ground that, while not technically bound, they will obey a decision that a local statute is unconstitutional? Is faith in precedent as a remedy touching but naive? Rendleman, Prospective Remedies in Constitutional Adjudication, 78 W.Va.L.Rev. 155, 155–61 (1976).

4) Afterword: The money for Herndon's fine was raised by subscription; the fines were paid within the ten days the court allowed. The NDPA candidates won the rerun election. George Wallace was inaugurated governor of Alabama on the same day in January 1971 as the circuit judge administered oaths to the NDPA victors in Greene County. This was a historic event in the seven-eighths black county that had been ruled exclusively by whites since reconstruction.

5) James Dennis Herndon was a University of Alabama Law School graduate. Should the Alabama Bar have taken any steps after these contempt decisions? Herndon moved from Eutaw, the Greene County seat, to Aliceville; later he became a vice president and trust officer of the City National Bank of Tuscaloosa, Alabama.

6) Rule 52(a) tells judges to find facts specially and state conclusions of law separately. This dictate forces decisionmakers to think about what they are doing and provides a basis to review what they did. Are the contempt opinions in *Herndon* adequate to fulfill Rule 52(a)'s policies? What was the evidence that Herndon actually knew about the operative order? Why didn't someone send Herndon notice by ordinary or registered mail? Should the plaintiffs have sent it? Defendants? The Supreme Court?

7) After the November election, could the NDPA candidates have sued Herndon for damages under 42 U.S.C. § 1983? Does the compensatory contempt award equal their damages in a separate action? What "other damage" did plaintiffs claim? Does criminal contempt trouble you more than civil? What shows that Herndon breached wilfully? Can the three-judge court try Herndon for breach of the Supreme Court's stay?

8) Did the nexus between Herndon and other defendants assure that he was adequately represented? How does Rule 23 protect unnamed defendant class members? Did the protections work?

V. Enjoining a Mob: *Debs* Revisited

MECHANIC v. GRUENSFELDER

461 S.W.2d 298 (Mo.App.1970).

PER CURIAM.

In this habeas corpus proceeding petitioners seek review of their convictions for contempt of court for violation of a temporary restraining order issued by the Circuit Court of St. Louis County. . . .

On March 24, 1970, Washington University filed its petition for injunction against seven individuals "individually and as representatives of an unnamed class of persons whose identities are unknown but who are participating in the acts referred to [t]herein." Petitioner Mechanic was one of the seven. The entire class was referred to as "defendants." The petition stated that on March 23, 1970, the named defendants and other defendants, numbering some 250, invaded certain premises belonging to plaintiff, namely South Brookings Hall and the Army Air Force Reserve Officers Training Corps facilities [hereinafter R.O.T.C.] without permission, and engaged in conduct which, stripped of its legal verbiage, constituted a riot. This conduct and its threatened continuation hampered and interfered with the conduct of the University's business, damaged and threatened damage to its property and that of others by which the University would be irreparably injured and for which it had no adequate remedy at law. The University prayed for issuance of a temporary restraining order, a temporary injunction and a permanent injunction against "all defendants (including all others who are members of the class aiding, abetting and assisting those defendants specifically named herein and all other individuals who may gain actual knowledge of such order) and each of them" from a broad range of activities which would interfere with the operation of the University, the activities of other persons using the University facilities, or would damage the property of the University or of others within or about the University premises.

On the same day, *ex parte,* the Court issued its temporary restraining order and order to show cause which is set forth in the margin.[1] Bond as called for

1. TEMPORARY RESTRAINING ORDER AND ORDER TO SHOW CAUSE

"This matter having come for hearing on the plaintiff's verified petition and motion and the Court having read the petition and motion and having heard the statement of counsel and being fully advised in the premises finds that plaintiff's petition states a claim for relief and that there will be irreparable damage unless this Order is issued.

"NOW THEREFORE, it is ordered, adjudged and decreed that defendants, and all persons acting in conjunction with them or on their behalf, and all others who are members of the class aiding, abetting and assisting those defendants specifically named herein and all other individuals who may gain actual knowledge of this Order, be and hereby are restrained and enjoined from:

"1. Engaging in assaulting others against the peace or to the terror or disturbance of others on or about plaintiff's property in St. Louis County, Missouri.

"2. Physically hindering, obstructing, interfering with, delaying, molesting or harassing other persons desiring to enter upon or to pass through or to go about plaintiff's property in St. Louis County, Missouri, for the purpose of conducting their business or for any other purpose.

"3. Unauthorized entering or occupying the inside of any buildings or edifices

in the Order was filed and upon application of the named defendants was ordered increased on two occasions, which was done. Additional parties, including petitioner Kogan, were added by motion. Of the seven petitioners before us, two—Kogan and Mechanic—were named parties to the original suit as amended and five were not named parties.

On the night of May 4, and the early morning of May 5, 1970, while the restraining order was in full effect, there occurred on the Washington University Campus the events giving rise to the contempt convictions now before us. At approximately 10:30 P.M. a "rally" began at the quadrangle, at which a large number of individuals gathered. Speeches were made, and the crowd left the quadrangle area and marched through the dormitory area of the campus to the R.O.T.C. facilities arriving there at approximately 11:45 P.M. The crowd at those facilities was large, estimated by various witnesses as 600 to 2000 persons.

Much shouting occurred, volleys of rocks were thrown at the R.O.T.C. facility breaking windows and otherwise damaging the building, the door was ripped off the building, the interior furniture and papers were strewn about and damaged, the building was set on fire, firemen attempting to fight the blaze were driven off by volleys of rocks and firecrackers, policemen and security guards of the University attempting to control the crowd and protect the building were subjected to additional volleys of rocks and firecrackers. The building was extensively damaged. Although euphemistically referred to as a "demonstration" by some of the witnesses, the activities of the night constituted a riot.

On May 5, plaintiff filed in the Circuit Court its "Motion for Issuance of Attachment for Contempt Pursuant to Rules 92.15 and 35.01 Revised Statutes of Missouri 1959" against petitioners.

The motion set forth the specific acts of each petitioner claimed to be in violation of the restraining order, alleged actual knowledge of the order by each petitioner, and prayed that the petitioners be brought before the Court to show cause why they should not be held in contempt and punished accord-

of plaintiff in St. Louis County, Missouri, or engaging therein, thereat or thereabout in any acts or conduct of whatsoever character which interferes with, intimidates, harasses or hinders plaintiff's employees or any other members of the University community, or the public at large having usual and customary access to plaintiff's property in St. Louis County, Missouri, or which in any way interferes with or hinders the proper and normal conduct of plaintiff's operations, or of others who are members of the University community.

"4. Molesting, converting, abusing or otherwise physically disturbing any personal or real property of plaintiff or under the care, custody or control of plaintiff or within or about plaintiff's premises in St. Louis County, Missouri. "This Order shall be effective as to all persons and bound thereby from and after receipt of it through service or otherwise and shall remain in effect until the further Order of the Court.

"It is further ordered that plaintiff give bond to be approved by the Court in the amount of $1,000, conditioned that all damages and costs of defendants be paid in the event the foregoing Order be dissolved without the issuance of a temporary injunction thereon.

"It is further ordered that defendants on the 9th day of April 1970, appear in Division No. 1 of the Circuit Court of the County of St. Louis, Missouri, sitting at Clayton, Missouri at 9:30 A.M., and then and there show cause, if any there be, why a temporary injunction should not be issued covering the matters in this restraining order described.

"Dated at Clayton, Missouri, this 24th day of March, 1970.

(signed) George E. Schaaf, Judge"

ingly. On the same day the Court issued its attachment for contempt and order to show cause and its writ of attachment to the sheriff of St. Louis County. Petitioners do not dispute that they received a copy of the motion for issuance of attachment and the writ of attachment.

Trial of petitioners for contempt began on May 25, 1970, and concluded on June 11, 1970. The Court filed its findings of fact, conclusions of law, decree, judgment and order of commitment as to each petitioner. The findings of fact were made "both on a preponderance of the evidence and beyond a reasonable doubt." As to each petitioner the Court found the specific act or acts constituting the contempt and made a finding that each petitioner had actual knowledge of the restraining order. Each petitioner was found guilty of criminal and civil contempt and sentenced to the county jail for periods ranging from three months to six months for the criminal contempt. Fines for criminal contempt were also imposed. Shorter jail sentences were imposed for the civil contempt subject to purging, which sentences run concurrently with the criminal sentences.[3] . . .

[W]e turn to the contention of petitioners Winkler, Murphy, Ryan, Bothwell and Achtenberg, that their convictions for contempt are fatally defective because: "(1) They were not parties bound by the proceedings (2) they were not properly within any purported class as required by law (3) there was no proof, as so found by the trial court, of any concerted activity by them in aid of other defendants."

We are cited by petitioners to Alemite Mfg. Corporation v. Staff, an opinion by Judge Learned Hand, holding that a third party to a patent infringement suit could not be punished for contempt.

Alemite involved a civil contempt case in which the winning litigant was attempting to extend the protections of its decree to third parties against whom no relief had been granted. To the extent the case discusses the law in civil contempt cases it is persuasive; to the extent it purports to address itself to criminal contempt it is *dicta.*

. . . We are unable . . . to find any elements of civil contempt in the punishment imposed in this proceeding. The relief sought by plaintiff in its original petition was restraint of activities which would interfere with the conduct of University operations, cause the destruction of University property, and allow the harassment of employees, students and the public on the University property. That was the nature of the restraints contained in the temporary restraining order. . . .

The contempt charged here and found by the trial court was the doing of acts forbidden by the restraining order. The conduct of May 4 and 5 completely thwarted the restraints imposed and the protection desired. Contempt proceedings could not restore the building, recall the rocks and firecrackers thrown or unbreak the windows. No enforcement of the order for the benefit of the University could be accomplished by civil contempt proceedings resulting in imprisonment nor could the petitioners purge their com-

3. The punishment for each petitioner was:

Name	Criminal	Civil
Lawrence Kogan	6 months and $500	30 days
Howard Mechanic	6 months and $500	30 days
Margaret Murphy	4 months and $150	20 days
William Bothwell	4 months and $250	15 days
Michael Ryan	3 months and $150	10 days
Dennis Winkler	3 months and $150	10 days
Joel Achtenberg	3 months and $150	10 days

pleted contempt. In such posture the imposition of jail sentences for civil contempt was improper as to all petitioners. Gompers v. Bucks Stove and Range Co.

Before turning to the above set-out contentions of petitioners as they pertain to criminal contempt it would be well to examine Walker v. City of Birmingham, affirming contempt convictions upheld by the Alabama Supreme Court, 279 Ala. 53, 181 So.2d 493. The *Walker* case bears striking similarity to the cases now before us. The City brought its bill of complaint seeking injunctive relief against 139 individuals and two organizations who were alleged to have sponsored, participated in, conspired to commit and encouraged "sit-in" and "kneel-in" demonstrations, mass street parades, trespasses on private property, congregating in mobs in public places, and unlawful picketing. These actions were expected to continue. The Circuit Court issued, *ex parte,* its restraining order prohibiting a wide range of conduct by respondents and others including "all persons having notice of such order."

Two days after the issuance of the Order a street parade was held in which the contemnors participated. The parade was unlawful in that a permit had not been obtained from the City. Certain of the contemnors were not parties to the suit brought by the City but did have actual knowledge of the restraining order. The Alabama Supreme Court in upholding the convictions of non-party contemnors stated: "The general rule is that one who violates an injunction is guilty of contempt, although he is not a party to the injunction suit, if he has notice or knowledge of the injunction order, and is *within the class of persons whose conduct is intended to be restrained,* or acts in concert with such a person." Walker v. City of Birmingham, 279 Ala. 53, 181 So.2d 493, 503 (emphasis supplied).

Although not discussing the above language, the United States Supreme Court did affirm the convictions of all contemnors, thus recognizing that being a party to the suit is not a requirement for a criminal contempt conviction. . . .

The court below had jurisdiction of the subject matter and equity powers, and issued its order on pleadings properly invoking its action. The contention of these five petitioners is, essentially, that they were not bound by the injunction and therefore could not be in contempt of it. We think this overlooks the essential difference between being bound by a court order (the essence of civil contempt) and deliberately interfering with the processes of a court (the essence of criminal contempt). Ex parte Clark, 208 Mo. 121, 106 S.W. 990. Criminal contempt is punishable because it constitutes an interference with the judicial system. If it occurs in the presence of the court it may be summarily punished; if it occurs outside the presence of the court it may be punished only after notice and hearing. Rule 35.01, V.A.M.R. This difference in procedure is based upon the availability of facts to the judge who must make the determination of contempt. Ex parte Clark, supra. But we do not understand that this difference in procedure also creates a difference in who may be found in contempt. Whether occurring within the presence of the court or without, it is the interference with the judicial system which is being punished. Certainly no argument can be advanced that a spectator in a courtroom who disrupts trial proceedings could escape punishment for contempt simply because he was a stranger to the litigation. Nor can one who deliberately and knowingly interferes with an order of the court which seeks to preserve the property of the plaintiff during the pendency of the litigation escape punishment for such interference simply because he is not a party to the litigation.

The restraining order was sought by plaintiff to prevent a repetition on its campus of disruptive activities causing damage to its property and interfering with the operation of the University. Such activities had already occurred and were threatened for the future. The participants were numerous, varying and hard to identify in full. They were not an organization or other readily identifiable group. Plaintiff's petition made clear that it sought the injunctive relief in order to terminate the disruptive riotous actions of a substantial group on its campus. The restraining order as entered sought also to meet this problem. Whether the restraints imposed were greater than necessary to cope with the problem or whether the order restrained activity not intended we need not decide. Its thrust was directed to all who might engage in riotous activity against the University property, employees, students or persons properly on the campus. It was intended to prevent exactly the conduct engaged in on May 4 and 5. As such, the persons whose conduct was intended to be restrained were those persons participating in riotous activities against University property, employees, students or persons properly on the campus. Any person so engaging was a member of the class intended to be restrained and if such person had knowledge of the order his conduct in violation of it was contemptuous.

We do not conclude, as petitioners do, that the class intended to be restrained must be a definable identifiable group of individuals who would under the class action rules be bound as parties if their representatives in the litigation had judgment rendered against them. We will not explore, and need not explore, the degree to which an amorphous group such as this could be individually bound *as a party* by a class action suit such as this. It is enough to say that participation in the activities of May 4 and 5 by persons having actual knowledge of the restraining order was an interference with the order of the court and was contemptuous. Walker v. City of Birmingham.

What we have heretofore said in regard to Walker v. City of Birmingham disposes of petitioners' contention that the temporary restraining order was void for vagueness. It was certainly clear enough that the conduct occurring on May 4 and 5 was prohibited by the restraining order. If portions of the order were too vague the way to attack those portions was through the judicial processes, not through willful disobedience of the clear restraints imposed. Walker v. City of Birmingham; Howat v. Kansas, 258 U.S. 181.

Those petitioners not named parties to the original suit claim they lacked any way of attacking the order through judicial channels. We cannot conclude that such fact, even if true, would authorize deliberate violation of the order, and we do not believe *Walker*, so holds. But if petitioners believed their rights were being infringed by the temporary restraining order they were free to attempt intervention to seek modification of the order or to have it set aside.

Petitioners' contention that no adequate reason was shown for excusing a hearing prior to issuance of the restraining order and therefore no contempt can be adjudged is a collateral attack on the order and without merit. The order was a valid and subsisting order of a court having jurisdiction and was to be obeyed. Temporary restraining orders may be issued without notice or hearing. . . . The circumstances of the issuance of the order might be pertinent in a proceeding to set it aside or modify it, but has no place in a contempt proceeding.

The restraining order did not become non-existent because no hearing on the request for temporary injunction was held prior to May 4. It is true that a temporary restraining order is just that—temporary—and that hearing on more permanent relief at which both sides have an opportunity to be heard should be held expeditiously. But no undue delay appears here. The hearing on the temporary injunction was continued on several occasions either to enable the Court to pass on various pre-hearing motions or to add parties and obtain service on them. This does not invalidate the temporary restraining order. United States v. United Mine Workers of America.

The contention that the bond was defective and the restraining order was therefore void is also without merit. In Curtis v. Tozer, Mo.App., 374 S.W.2d 557 [30], we held that the provisions of the statute requiring a bond are read into the bond. The bond in this case named as obligees the defendants named in the petition and that is all that Rule 92.09, V.A.M.R. requires. Upon the filing of the bond in compliance with the rule, the temporary restraining order became effective. Petitioners' objection to the bond is that it did not name them, either individually or as a group, as obligees. First of all, we do not believe the rule requires the plaintiff or the court to anticipate every person who might disobey the court's order and include them in the bond. Curtis v. Tozer, Mo.App., 374 S.W.2d 557 [28]. Secondly, the petition described "defendants" in broad language sufficient to include anyone with knowledge of any subsequent court order and the bond ran to "defendants." . . .

Ex parte Dillon, Mo.App., 96 S.W.2d 1095, relied on by petitioners was a civil contempt case. We can see some justification for the holding there that if the persons are bound by the injunction they should be named as obligees, either individually or by descriptive appellation. We do not, however, understand the requirement of a bond to be to protect people who deliberately and willfully interfere with the court processes. It is instead to protect parties who sustain damage as a result of compliance with a temporary restraining order later determined to have been illegally or improperly issued. . . .

Petitioners also attack the motion for attachment and the attachment itself as insufficient to comply with Rule 35.01(b). . . .

The motion for attachment also specifically sets forth the acts which each petitioner was alleged to have done in violation of the restraining order and the date and place of occurrence. In respect to petitioner Murphy, she was charged with unauthorized entry into the R.O.T.C. facility, the very ground upon which the court based its finding of contempt. In the case of the other petitioners the charge was contempt "by throwing bricks, stones, and other missiles in, upon and about said Reserve Officers Training Corps facilities," also the very acts for which they were found in contempt. All petitioners were charged with "engaging with others in said company of approximately

600 persons in chanting, loud, boisterous, tumultuous conduct resulting in the interference with, intimidation and harassment of plaintiff's employees and the normal conduct of the Washington University operations." The charges were sufficiently definite to advise the petitioners of the conduct claimed to be contemptuous and to allow them to prepare their defense.

. . .

We now reach the merits. In order to sustain the convictions here two findings beyond a reasonable doubt must be made as to each petitioner—actual knowledge of the restraining order and conduct in violation of the order. The restraining order by its express language restrained only specific persons, aiders and abettors, persons acting in conjunction with defendants and "all other individuals who may gain actual knowledge of this Order . . . " We deal first with knowledge. As to petitioners Kogan and Mechanic, no problem exists as both were parties to the original litigation and had been served with the restraining order. As to the remaining petitioners some discussion is required of the University's attempts to bring the restraining order to the attention of its students and others on its campus.

. . .

Margaret Murphy was not a student at the University. There was testimony, however, that she attended a meeting at Holmes Lounge on March 24, at which the temporary restraining order was discussed extensively. During the course of the discussion she spoke for approximately two minutes during which she referred to the restraining order as a "paper pig" and "another form of repression." Such evidence was sufficient to warrant the court's findings that she had actual knowledge of the restraining order.

Joel Achtenberg was employed by the University but was not a student. Captain Abernathy, the University security chief, testified that he knew Joel Achtenberg and had known him for some time prior to March 26. On March 26, in the R.O.T.C. area Captain Abernathy read twice that portion of the restraining order having to do with disturbing the property of the University over his bullhorn to a crowd of approximately 200 persons. He stated Joel Achtenberg was part of that crowd. Such evidence is sufficient to warrant the court's finding that Joel Achtenberg had actual knowledge of the restraining order. The Captain's subsequent statement that some attempt was made to shout him down does not prevent the conclusion that those persons in the crowd heard the amplified reading of a portion of the order, that portion Achtenberg was found guilty of violating.

As to petitioners Bothwell, Ryan and Winkler we are confronted with a different situation. In their brief here and on oral argument the special prosecutors appointed by the Court have admitted that actual knowledge of these petitioners must be based on the extensive publicity given to the order both by the University and the daily press. The prosecutors admit, and on the record before us we concur, that no evidence is present which directly shows these petitioners were aware of the order. The findings of fact of the trial court as to these three petitioners recited the extensive publicity and stated the petitioners had actual knowledge. This is in contrast to the specific findings as to the other petitioners of actual knowledge based upon factual findings heretofore set out as to those petitioners. We conclude the court's finding of actual knowledge as to Ryan, Winkler and Bothwell was based upon the extensive publicity given the restraining order by the University and the press. None of the three resided in dormitories; all lived off campus. Bothwell attended the Eden Farm campus at Pacific, Missouri, some distance from the main campus and there is no evidence that the documents circulated by the University ever reached Eden Farm campus. None of these three petitioners was identified at meetings where the order was discussed, none was placed at gatherings where the order or any part of it was read.

In view of the proceeding here where the essence of the contempt is the knowing violation of a court order we are unable to conclude that the essential element of notice or knowledge was established as to these three petitioners beyond a reasonable doubt. As indicated, circumstantial evidence may be used to establish this element. But such evidence must lead to the conclusion that in fact these petitioners had actual knowledge of the order. We do not believe it necessary for the prosecution to establish that in fact the petitioners read a copy of an order received by them. Nor is it necessary to establish that they listened to an order read to a gathering of which they were a part. Such proof would be very nearly impossible. But there must be some evidence of record to put the individual petitioner into a place or position where the existence of the order was called to his attention. Mere presence in a community or potential access to the information, no matter how widespread the publicity, cannot be held sufficient to confer actual knowledge in the absence of evidence showing the matter was brought to the individual's attention. In Curtis v. Tozer, supra, the evidence established the reading of the injunction in the presence of the petitioners. Such proof is sufficient to support a finding of knowledge. Here too the evidence placed petitioners Murphy and Achtenberg at places where the order was discussed or read, and we have held that sufficient.

We are not unaware of the substantial burden imposed by the law or of the difficulties the law imposes in enforcement of the order of a court in this type of situation. One who knowingly interferes with the orders of a court should be punished, but the threshold question is knowledge. That question must be determined by what the individual actually knew established by direct or circumstantial evidence, not what he should have known or could have known. . . .

The evidence in this case establishes only that these three petitioners should have known or could have known of the existence of the restraining order. That evidence does not establish that they did in fact know. The sentences and judgments of Bothwell, Ryan and Winkler must be set aside and their release ordered. . . .

It follows from what has been said herein that 1) the jail sentences imposed on all petitioners for civil contempt were illegal and are set aside; 2) petitioners Michael A. Ryan, William Bothwell and Dennis Winkler are illegally restrained in that the evidence does not support the finding that they had actual knowledge of the temporary restraining order and they are ordered discharged forthwith; and 3) petitioners Howard Mechanic, Joel Achtenberg, Margaret Murphy and Lawrence Kogan are not illegally restrained on their sentences for criminal contempt and as to those sentences our writ should be and is quashed and those petitioners are remanded to the custody of respondent.

WOLFE, P.J., and BRADY and DOWD, JJ., concur.

---

1) During the late 1960's and early 1970's, the turbulence of an earlier generation of students led many authorities to enjoin student protest. The literature includes G. Holmes, Student Protest and the Law 269–326 (1969); Herman, Injunctive Control of Disruptive Student Demonstrations, 56 Va.L. Rev. 215 (1970); Rosenthal, Injunctive Relief Against Campus Disorders, 118 U.Pa.L.Rev. 746 (1970); Note, Campus Confrontation: Resolution by Injunction, 6 Colum.J.L. & Soc.Probs. 1 (1970). The most thoughtful is Note, Equity on the Campus: The Limits of Injunctive Regulation of University Protest, 80 Yale L.J. 987 (1971); it also collects unreported opinions and lower court decisions. Will the exigencies that gave birth to the student protest injunction emerge again in another guise? See State of Missouri v. United States Bankruptcy Court, 647 F.2d 768 (8th Cir. 1981) (farmers occupy bankrupt grain elevator: injunction to remove blockade and clear the facility).

2) Did the university authorities seek injunctions because they thought injunctions were milder medicine than criminal prosecutions and more likely to succeed? Because of the mystique that injunctions acquired in the civil rights era? Because defendants may have been denied a jury trial?

3) Did these injunctions interfere with protected expression? Would *Carroll,* p. 328 compel notice? Will the authorities be able to name student demonstrators? Must they resort to "all persons" orders and the *Seaward* theory, p. 1109? Do the notice rules and the collateral bar rule allow the plaintiff to evade the adversary system's inconvenience?

4) Is the *Mechanic* court correct in limiting *Alemite*? Did *Alemite* involve civil contempt? Does the *Mechanic* court properly build a bridge between in-court and out-of-court contempt? Does the court, without saying so, adopt *Seaward's* distinction between civil and criminal contempt? From the idea that everyone must behave in the courtroom, does it follow that everyone must obey court orders? Compare § 401(1) with § 401(3). Does the collateral bar rule prevent nonparties from arguing in contempt that an ex parte injunction is erroneous? See Beyond Contempt, 53 Tex.L.Rev. at 882–84, 901–03, 920–21.

5) Washington v. Washington State Commercial Passenger Fishing Vessel Association, 443 U.S. 658 (1979), was a complex appeal that affirmed an injunction guaranteeing Indian tribes a specific share of the salmon and trout that passed through tribal areas in Washington State. The Court responded to an objection from the association of commercial fishers in a long footnote:

"The associations advance a third objection as well—that the District Court had no power to enjoin individual nontreaty fishermen, who were not parties to its decisions, from violating the allocations that it has ordered. The reason this issue has arisen is that state officials were either unwilling or unable to enforce the District Court's orders against nontreaty fishermen by way of state regulations and state law enforcement efforts. Accordingly, nontreaty fishermen were openly violating Indian fishing rights, and, in order to give federal law enforcement officials the power via contempt to end those violations, the District Court was forced to enjoin them. The commercial fishing organizations, on behalf of their individual members, argue that they should not be bound by these orders because they were not parties to (although the associations all did participate as *amici curiae* in) the proceedings that led to their issuance.

"If all state officials stand by the Attorney General's representations that the State will implement the decision of this Court, this issue will be rendered moot because the District Court no longer will be forced to enforce its own decisions. Nonetheless, the issue is still live since state implementation efforts are now at a standstill and the orders are still in effect. Accordingly, we must decide it.

"In our view, the commercial fishing associations and their members are probably subject to injunction under either the rule that nonparties who interfere with the implementation of court orders establishing public rights may be enjoined, e.g., United States v. Hall, cited approvingly in Golden State Bottling Co. v. NLRB, or the rule that a court possessed of the res in a proceeding *in rem,* such as one to apportion a fishery, may enjoin those who would interfere with that custody. See Vendo Co. v. Lektro–Vend Corp., 433 U.S. 623, 641. But in any case, these individuals and groups are citizens of the State of Washington, which was a party to the relevant proceedings, and 'they, in their common public rights as citizens of the State, were represented by the State in those proceedings, and, like it, were bound by the judgment.' Tacoma v. Taxpayers, 357 U.S. 320, 340–41. Moreover, a court clearly may order them to obey that judgment. See Golden State Bottling. . . ." 443 U.S. at 692 n. 32.

Dissenting Justice Powell responded: "In addition to the burdens placed upon non-Indian fishermen, the Court's decision is likely to prove difficult to enforce fairly and effectively. To date, the District Court has had to resort to the outer limits of its equitable powers in order to enforce its decree. This had included taking over supervision of all of the commercial fishing in the Puget Sound area, ordering the creation of a telephone 'hot line' that fishermen can use to determine when and where they may legally fish, and ordering United States Marshals to board fishing craft and inspect for violations of the court's preliminary injunction. Indeed, in his response to the petition for certiorari in the present case, the Solicitor General set forth in some detail the extraordinary difficulty the Government has had in enforcing the District Court's decrees, saying:

" '[T]he default of the state government has required the United States to concentrate a disporportionate amount of its limited fisheries enforcement personnel on what is essentially a local enforcement problem. Agents of the National Marine Fisheries Service, the United States Fish and Wildlife Service, the United States Marshals Service, and the Coast Guard have been diverted from their regular duties to assist the district court in implementing the Indians' treaty rights. This has resulted in a reduction in the federal fisheries services available for the rest of the country and for the enforcement of the ocean fisheries programs governed by the Fishery Conservation Management Act of 1976.' Brief of Respondent United States on Petition for Certiorari.

"These problems, it seems to me, will be exacerbated by a formula apportionment such as that ordered by the Court." 443 U.S. at 706 n. 9.

Contempt decisions in the fisheries conflict include: United States v. Baker, 641 F.2d 1311 (9th Cir. 1981) (non-party contemnor-fishers with actual notice in "privity" with party were held in criminal contempt); United States v. Olander, 584 F.2d 876 (9th Cir. 1978); Puget Sound Gillnetters Association v. United States District Court for the Western District of Washington, 573 F.2d 1123 (9th Cir. 1978); United States v. State of Washington, 459 F.Supp. 1020 (W.D.Wash.1978); United States v. Crookshanks, 441 F.Supp. 268 (D.Or.1977); Puget Sound Gillnetters Association v. Moos, 88 Wn.2d 677, 565 P.2d 1151 (1977); Washington State Commercial Passenger Fishing Vessel Association v. Tollefson, 89 Wash.2d 276, 571 P.2d 1373 (1977).

Is enforcing the fishing injunction a variation on the problem of the recalcitrant bureaucracy encountered in *Hecht*, p. 132, and *Lankford*, p. 160, and the prison litigation in Chapter 9? Why doesn't the federal judge in the fisheries litigation enjoin the state authorities to enforce the federal injunction and spare everyone a lot of grief?

UNITED STATES v. HALL

472 F.2d 261 (5th Cir. 1972).

Before WISDOM, THORNBERRY and GODBOLD, Circuit Judges.

WISDOM, Circuit Judge:

This case presents the question whether a district court has power to punish for criminal contempt a person who, though neither a party nor bearing any legal relationship to a party, violates a court order designed to protect the court's judgment in a school desegregation case. We uphold the district court's conclusion that in the circumstances of this case it had this power, and affirm the defendant's conviction for contempt.

On June 23, 1971, the district court entered a "Memorandum Opinion and Final Judgment" in the case of Mims v. Duval County School Board. The court required the Duval County [Jacksonville], Florida school board to complete its desegregation of Duval County schools, in accordance with the Supreme Court's decision in Swann v. Charlotte-Mecklenburg Board of Education, 1971, 402 U.S. 1, by pairing and clustering a number of schools which had theretofore been predominantly one-race schools. This order culminated litigation begun eleven years before, Braxton v. Board of Public Instruction. This Court affirmed the district court's order in Mims v. Duval County School Board, 5 Cir. 1971, 447 F.2d 1330. The district court retained jurisdiction to enter such orders as might be necessary in the future to effectuate its judgment.

Among the schools marked for desegregation under the plan approved by the district court was Ribault Senior High School, a predominantly white school. The plan directed pairing of Ribault with William E. Raines Senior High School, a predominantly black school, so that the black enrollment would be 59 percent at Raines and 57 percent at Ribault. After the desegregation order was put into effect racial unrest and violence developed at Ribault, necessitating on one occasion the temporary closing of the school. On March 5, 1972, the superintendent of schools and the sheriff of Jacksonville filed a petition for injunctive relief in the *Mims* case with the district court. This petition alleged that certain black adult "outsiders" had caused or abetted the unrest and violence by their activities both on and off the Ribault campus. The petition identified the appellant Eric Hall, allegedly a member of a militant organization known as the "Black Front," as one of several such outsiders who, in combination with black students and parents, were attempting to prevent the normal operation of Ribault through student boycotts and other activities. As relief the petitioners requested an order "restraining all Ribault Senior High School students and any person acting independently or in concert with them from interfering with the orderly operation of the school and the Duval County School system, and for such other relief as the court may deem just and proper."

At an ex parte session on March 5, 1972, the district court entered an order providing in part:

"1. All students of Ribault Senior High School, whether in good standing or under suspension, and other persons acting independently or in concert with them and having notice of this order are hereby enjoined and restrained from

"(a) Obstructing or preventing the attendance in classes of students and faculty members;

"(b) Harassing, threatening or intimidating any faculty, staff member or employee of Ribault Senior High School or the Duval County School Board;

"(c) Harassing, threatening or intimidating any student en route to and from school;

"(d) Destroying or attempting to destroy, defacing or attempting to deface any structure, buildings, materials or equipment of Ribault Senior High School or the Duval County School Board;

"(e) Committing any other act to disrupt the orderly operation of Ribault Senior High School or any other school of the Duval County School System;

"2. Until further order of this Court, no person shall enter any building of the Ribault Senior High School or go upon the school's grounds except the following:

"(a) Students of Ribault Senior High School while attending classes or official school functions;

"(b) The faculty, staff, and administration of Ribault Senior High School and other employees of the Duval County School Board having assigned duties at the school;

"(c) Persons having business obligations which require their presence on the school's premises;

"(d) Parents of Ribault Senior High School students or any other person who has the prior permission of the principal or his designee to be present on the school's premises;

"(e) Law enforcement officials of the City of Jacksonville, the State of Florida or the United States Government."

The order went on to provide that "[a]nyone having notice of this order who violates any of the terms thereof shall be subject to arrest, prosecution and punishment by imprisonment or fine, or both, for criminal contempt under the laws of the United States of America. . . . " The court ordered the sheriff to serve copies of the order on seven named persons, *including Eric*

Hall. Hall was neither a party plaintiff nor a party defendant in the *Mims* litigation, and in issuing this order the court did not join Hall or any of the other persons named in the order as parties.

On March 9, 1972, four days after the court issued its order, Hall violated that portion of the order restricting access to Ribault High School by appearing on the Ribault campus. When questioned by a deputy United States marshal as to the reasons for his presence, Hall replied that he was on the grounds of Ribault for the purpose of violating the March 5 order. The marshal then arrested Hall and took him into custody. After a nonjury trial, the district court found Hall guilty of the charge of criminal contempt and sentenced him to sixty days' imprisonment.

On this appeal Hall raises two related contentions. Both contentions depend on the fact that Hall was not a party to the *Mims* litigation and the fact that, in violating the court's order, he was apparently acting independently of the *Mims* parties. He first points to the common law rule that a nonparty who violates an injunction solely in pursuit of his own interests cannot be held in contempt. Not having been before the court as a party or as the surrogate of a party, he argues that in accordance with this common law rule he was not bound by the court's order. Second, he contends that Rule 65(d) of the Federal Rules of Civil Procedure prevents the court's order from binding him, since Rule 65(d) limits the binding effect of injunctive orders to "parties to the action, their officers, agents, servants, employees, and attorneys, and . . . those persons in active concert or participation with them who receive actual notice of the order by personal service or otherwise." We reject both contentions.

For his first contention, that a court of equity has no power to punish for contempt a nonparty acting solely in pursuit of his own interests, the appellant relies heavily on the two leading cases of Alemite Manufacturing Corp. v. Staff, and Chase National Bank v. City of Norwalk, 1934, 291 U.S. 431. In *Alemite* the district court had issued an injunction restraining the defendant and his agents, employees, associates, and confederates from infringing the plaintiff's patent. Subsequently a third person, not a party to the original suit and acting entirely on his own initiative, began infringing the plaintiff's patent and was held in contempt by the district court. The Second Circuit reversed in an opinion by Judge Learned Hand, stating that "it is not the act described which the decree may forbid, but only that act when the defendant does it." In *Chase National Bank* the plaintiff brought suit against the City of Norwalk to obtain an injunction forbidding the removal of poles, wires, and other electrical equipment belonging to the plaintiff. The district court issued a decree enjoining the City, its officers, agents, and employees, "and all persons whomsoever to whom notice of this order shall come" from removing the equipment or otherwise interfering with the operation of the plaintiff's power plant. The Supreme Court held that the district court had violated "established principles of equity jurisdiction and procedure" insofar as its order applied to persons who were not parties, associates, or confederates of parties, but who merely had notice of the order. See also Regal Knitwear Co. v. NLRB. . . .

This case is different. In *Alemite* and *Chase National Bank* the activities of third parties, however harmful they might have been to the plaintiffs' interests, would not have disturbed in any way the adjudication of rights and obligations as between the original plaintiffs and defendants. Infringement of the *Alemite* plaintiff's patent by a third party would not have upset the defendant's duty to refrain from infringing or rendered it more difficult for the defendant to perform that duty. Similarly, the defendant's duty in *Chase National Bank* to refrain from removing the plaintiff's equipment would remain undisturbed regardless of the activities of third parties, as would the plaintiff's right not to have its equipment removed by the defendant. The activities of Hall, however, threatened both the plaintiffs' right and the defendant's duty as adjudicated in the *Mims* litigation. In *Mims* the plaintiffs were found to have a constitutional right to attend an integrated school. The defendant school board had a corresponding constitutional obligation to provide them with integrated schools and a right to be free from interference with the performance of that duty. Disruption of the orderly operation of the school system, in the form of a racial dispute, would thus negate the plaintiffs' constitutional right and the defendant's constitutional duty. In short, the activities of persons contributing to racial disorder at Ribault imperiled the court's fundamental power to make a binding adjudication between the parties properly before it.

Courts of equity have inherent jurisdiction to preserve their ability to render judgment in a case such as this. This was the import of the holding in United States v. United Mine Workers of America. There the district court had issued a temporary restraining order forbidding a union from striking, though there was a substantial question of whether the Norris–LaGuardia Act had deprived the district court of jurisdiction to issue such an order. The Supreme Court upheld the defendants' contempt conviction for violation of this order. As an alternative holding the Court stated that the contempt conviction would have been upheld even if the district court had ultimately been found to be without jurisdiction. This holding affirmed the power of a court of equity to issue an order to preserve the status quo in order to protect its ability to render judgment in a case over which it might have jurisdiction. See Walker v. Birmingham (Brennan, J., dissenting).

The integrity of a court's power to render a binding judgment in a case over which it has jurisdiction is at stake in the present case. In *Mine Workers* disruptive conduct prior to the court's decision could have destroyed the court's power to settle a controversy at least potentially within its jurisdiction. Here the conduct of Hall and others, if unrestrained, could have upset the court's ability to bind the parties in *Mims,* a case in which it unquestionably had jurisdiction. Moreover, the court retained jurisdiction in *Mims* to enter such further orders as might be necessary to effectuate its judgment. Thus disruptive conduct would not only jeopardize the effect of the court's judgment already entered but would also undercut its power to enter binding desegregation orders in the future.

The principle that courts have jurisdiction to punish for contempt in order to protect their ability to render judgment is also found in the use of in rem injunctions. Federal courts have issued injunctions binding on all persons, regardless of notice, who come into contact with property which is the subject of a judicial decree. See United States v. Dean Rubber Manufacturing Co., 1946, W.D.Mo., 71 F.Supp. 96; Converse v. Highway Construction

Co., 6 Cir. 1939, 107 F.2d 127; Cherry v. Insull Utility Investments, Inc., 1932, N.D.Ill., 58 F.2d 1022, rev'd on other grounds sub nom. Guaranty Trust Co. v. Fentress, 7 Cir., 61 F.2d 329. A court entering a decree binding on a particular piece of property is necessarily faced with the danger that its judgment may be disrupted in the future by members of an undefinable class—those who may come into contact with the property. The in rem injunction protects the court's judgment. The district court here faced an analogous problem. The judgment in a school case, as in other civil rights actions, inures to the benefit of a large class of persons, regardless of whether the original action is cast in the form of a class action. At the same time court orders in school cases, affecting as they do large numbers of people, necessarily depend on the cooperation of the entire community for their implementation.

As this Court is well aware, school desegregation orders often strongly excite community passions. School orders are, like in rem orders, particularly vulnerable to disruption by an undefinable class of persons who are neither parties nor acting at the instigation of parties. In such cases, as in voting rights cases, courts must have the power to issue orders similar to that issued in this case, tailored to the exigencies of the situation and directed to protecting the court's judgment. The peculiar problems posed by school cases have required courts to exercise broad and flexible remedial powers. See Swann v. Charlotte-Mecklenburg Board of Education, 1971, 402 U.S. 1, 6, 15. Similarly broad applications of the power to punish for contempt may be necessary, as here, if courts are to protect their ability to design appropriate remedies and make their remedial orders effective.

The appellant also asserts that Rule 65(d) of the Federal Rules of Civil Procedure prevents the court's order from binding him. He points out that he was not a party to the original action nor an officer, agent, servant, employee, or attorney of a party, and denies that he was acting in "active concert or participation" with any party to the original action.[4]

In examining this contention we start with the proposition that Rule 65 was intended to embody "the common-law doctrine that a decree of injunction not only binds the parties defendant but also those identified with them in interest, in 'privity' with them, represented by them or subject to their

4. The government contends that Hall was acting "in active concert and participation" with parties to the action. In 1962, in an unreported order not made part of the record in the present case, the district court held that the *Braxton* suit was a class action pursuant to Rule 23(a)(3) of the Federal Rules of Civil Procedure. Consequently, the government argues, all minor black children were and are parties to the *Braxton–Mims* litigation. Therefore Hall, by engaging in disruptive activities with some black students, was acting in concert and participation with parties under Rule 65(d).

This argument fails because all minor black children were not parties to *Braxton* and *Mims.* Prior to the 1966 amendment of Rule 23, Rule 23(a)(3) provided for what was then known as a "spurious" class action. The spurious class action was essentially a permissive joinder device, in which the court's decision would bind only those persons actually before the court. . . . Those persons who did not actually join in the litigation in this case, therefore, were not parties and are not parties now. The district court has not, since 1962, made any further determination that the *Braxton–Mims* litigation could be maintained as a class action, as required by present Rule 23(c). There is no evidence or allegation that Hall was acting in active concert or participation with any of the persons who actually were parties to the suit.

control." Regal Knitwear Co. v. NLRB. Literally read, Rule 65(d) would forbid the issuance of in rem injunctions. Note, Binding Nonparties to Injunction Decrees, 49 Minn.L.Rev. 719, 736 (1965). But courts have continued to issue in rem injunctions notwithstanding Rule 65(d), since they possessed the power to do so at common law and since Rule 65(d) was intended to embody rather than to limit their common law powers. See United States v. Dean Rubber Manufacturing Co., 1946, W.D.Mo., 71 F.Supp. 96; In re Lustron Corp., 7 Cir. 1950, 184 F.2d 798, cert. denied, 1951, 340 U.S. 946; Converse v. Highway Construction Co., 6 Cir. 1939, 107 F.2d 127; Zeleznik v. Grand Riviera Theater Co., 6 Cir. 1942, 128 F.2d 533.

Similarly, we conclude that Rule 65(d), as a codification rather than a limitation of courts' common-law powers, cannot be read to restrict the inherent power of a court to protect its ability to render a binding judgment. See In re Williams, 1969, D.C.D.C., 306 F.Supp. 617. We hold that Hall's relationship to the *Mims* case fell within that contemplated by Rule 65(d). By deciding *Mims* and retaining jurisdiction the district court had, in effect, adjudicated the rights of the entire community with respect to the racial controversy surrounding the school system. Moreover, as we have noted, in the circumstances of this case third parties such as Hall were in a position to upset the court's adjudication. This was not a situation which could have been anticipated by the draftsmen of procedural rules. In meeting the situation as it did, the district court did not overstep its powers.

We do not hold that courts are free to issue permanent injunctions against all the world in school cases. Hall had notice of the court's order. Rather than challenge it by the orderly processes of law, he resorted to conscious, willful defiance. See Walker v. Birmingham.

It is true that this order was issued without a hearing, and that ordinarily injunctive relief cannot be granted without a hearing. See 7 J. Moore, Moore's Federal Practice ¶ 65.04[3] & n. 8a (1972). But we need not hold that this order has the effect of a preliminary or permanent injunction. Rather, the portion of the court's order here complained of may be characterized as a temporary restraining order, which under Rule 65(b) may be issued ex parte. The prohibition directed to restricting access to the school grounds nowhere purported to be an injunction. Moreover, Hall's violation occurred within four days of the issuance of the order, well within the ten-day limitation period for temporary restraining orders. The present case is therefore distinguishable from the situation presented in Harrington v. Colquitt County Board of Education, 5 Cir. 1971, 449 F.2d 161, a direct appeal from a permanent injunction, in which this Court struck language purporting to enjoin persons beyond the scope of Rule 65(d).

We hold, then, that the district court had the inherent power to protect its ability to render a binding judgment between the original parties to the *Mims* litigation by issuing an interim ex parte order against an undefinable class of persons. We further hold that willful violation of that order by one having notice of it constitutes criminal contempt. The judgment of the district court is affirmed.

1) Before focusing on *Hall*, reread Note 2 after *Reese*, p. 1113. Did the *Hall* court write an anti-obstruction injunction? Consider the alternatives available. The authorities could have commenced a state trespass prosecution against Hall. If they were uncomfortable with the state courts, the federal authorities might have considered § 1509. Finally, if they knew who the troublemakers were, they could have sought to enjoin the troublemakers as named defendants.

2) Two law journals favored us with helpful short notes on *Hall:* Note, Injunctions: Can They Bind Parties Not Mentioned in Rule 65(d)?, 35 U.Pitt.L.Rev. 483 (1973); and Note, Injunctions—Contempt Power—Citation Proper Against Nonparty Who Violates Court Order in School Desegregation Case, 26 Vand.L.Rev. 625 (1973). Two longer pieces were sharply critical: Beyond Contempt, 53 Tex.L.Rev. at 916–24; and Comment, Community Resistance to School Desegregation: Enjoining the Undefinable Class, 44 U.Chi.L.Rev. 111 (1976). Another article approved *Hall:* Dobbyn, Contempt Power of the Equity Court Over Outside Agitators, 8 St. Mary's L.J. 1 (1976).

As you may have already learned, one of your editors vigorously criticized United States v. Hall in his long article. The other editor, as is apparent from the first edition, takes a different view.

3) Does *Hall* represent the institutional posture of a court system accustomed to administering school desegregation? F. Read & L. McGough, Let Them Be Judged 510–21 (1978), discusses Jacksonville and Ribault during this period. Rule 65(d) is based on the Clayton Act; it was drafted in an environment characterized by antistrike injunctions. Should the *Hall* court assume that the drafters didn't foresee injunctions that affect the whole community and excite deep passions?

4) Does Rule 65(d) ban in rem injunctions? Reread Note 7, after *Webster*, p. 1157 above. Many of the decisions the *Hall* court cites concern interference with a bankruptcy court's assets. Today the Bankruptcy Reform Act has replaced the custody theories that led to these contempts with an automatic stay, 11 U.S.C. § 362; in any event, the contempt was normally of the civil coercive-second injunction variety to restore the property to the debtor or to the estate. Should the *Hall* court extend these decisions to criminal contempt for trespassing on school grounds?

5) Does Rule 65(d) only work in business cases? Has *Seaward* or obstruction of justice contempt triumphed elsewhere? Do courts create difficulties for themselves by undertaking injunctions to solve problems that exceed their institutional capabilities?

6) Was Hall accessible to be served with process before the court granted the injunction? How did the court achieve personal jurisdiction over Hall? When? Should the parties have made Hall a defendant and provided him an opportunity to defend? Do the reasons the Court gave for notice in *Carroll*, p. 328 apply to Hall? Was the "temporary restraining order" in *Hall* essentially final because it interdicted conduct the following day? After the authorities served the injunction on Hall, should he have moved to intervene or dissolve?

7) Does anyone who acts contrary to an injunction interfere with defendant's duty and frustrate plaintiff's right to relief? Does jurisdiction to determine jurisdiction assume personal jurisdiction and an opportunity to litigate? Does *Hall* "overrule" *Alemite*'s holding that a nonparty not "in active concert or participation" is beyond the ambit of contempt? Does the court's right-duty test restore *Seaward* contempt and allow the court to punish all knowing violators?

8) Assume an injunction limits picketing at a school to two pickets. Ribble, a nonparty who opposes pairing, comes along with his sign, sees two pro-pairing pickets in place, and joins them to dramatize his disagreement. The authorities charge Ribble with contempt for violating the injunction. Will the collateral bar rule prevent Ribble from arguing to defend contempt that the injunction violates the first amendment because it limits expression excessively?

9) The long-awaited Restatement (Second) of Judgments dealt with the issue of *Hall*:

> Duty Not to Obstruct Compliance with Judgment
>
> A person who is not precluded by the rules of res judicata from litigating a claim or issue determined by a judgment may nevertheless have a duty to refrain from obstructing compliance with the judgment.
>
> Illustration:
>
> 3. P obtains a judgment requiring that S, a school district reassign pupils to eliminate racial segregation. T, who was not a party to the suit, obstructs the movement of pupils under the reassignment plan. Even if T has standing to litigate the issues on which the judgment is based, and thereby obtain nullification or modification of the reassignment plan, under applicable law T may be liable for contempt of court for his obstructive conduct.

Restatement (Second) of Judgments § 63 (1980).

The American Law Institute based Illustration 3 on *Hall:* the Reporter's Note says that *Hall* is "a clearly correct result and helps to clarify the matter." Does the Restatement understand *Hall* correctly? Why did the Illustration fail to mention the injunction obtained by the United States? Did the drafters waffle by saying only that the person "may . . . have" a duty?

10) "The right to lay down general rules for the government of the community, to declare *ex cathedra*, in advance of any contentious proceeding in which the question arises, what may and what may not lawfully be done, to impose on the whole community a duty to refrain from doing a certain act, is in its nature a legislative right." Dunbar, Government By Injunction, 13 L.Q.Rev. 347, 362 (1897).

Mr. Dunbar responded to the *Debs* injunction: "It is no light matter that suspicion even should rest upon the judiciary of warping principles to meet the supposed exigencies of cases as to which the strongest passions of the community are aroused. . . . It should not be forgotten that no course is more dangerous than to justify the exercise of a doubtful power by the supposed necessities of a particular emergency. Courts must adhere to fixed principles, lest the departure justified to-day by a present emergency, itself justify tomorrow a departure inspired by some sinister motive." Government By Injunction, 13 L.Q.Rev. 347, 366–67 (1897). Do you agree?

Appendix

FEDERAL PROCEDURAL RULES AND FEDERAL STATUTES PERTAINING TO INJUNCTIVE LITIGATION

Table of Contents

1. FEDERAL RULES OF CIVIL PROCEDURE

2. FEDERAL RULES OF CRIMINAL PROCEDURE

3. FEDERAL RULES OF APPELLATE PROCEDURE

4. RULES OF THE SUPREME COURT

Rule
27. Stay Pending Review on Certiorari.
50. Applications to Individual Justices; Practice in Chambers.
51. Stays.

5. TITLE 18, UNITED STATES CODE

Sec.
241. Conspiracy Against Rights of Citizens.
242. Deprivation of Rights Under Color of Law.
401. Power of Court.
402. Contempts Constituting Crimes.
1509. Obstruction of Court Orders.
3691. Jury Trial of Criminal Contempts.
3692. Jury Trial for Contempt in Labor Dispute Cases.

6. TITLE 28, UNITED STATES CODE

1252. Direct Appeals From Decisions Invalidating Acts of Congress.
1254. Courts of Appeals; Certiorari; Appeal; Certified Questions.
1257. State Courts; Appeal; Certiorari.
1291. Final Decisions of District Courts.
1292. Interlocutory Decisions.
1331. Federal Question.
1343. Civil Rights and Elective Franchise.
1345. United States as Plaintiff.
1651. Writs.
1826. Recalcitrant Witnesses.
2101. Supreme Court; Time for Appeal or Certiorari; Docketing; Stay.
2201. Creation of [Declaratory Judgment] Remedy.
2202. Further Relief.
2283. Stay of State Court Proceedings.

7. TITLE 29, UNITED STATES CODE

101. Limitation on Issuance of Restraining Orders and Injunctions.
104. Enumeration of Specific Acts Not Subject to Restraining Orders or Injunctions.
107. Issuance of Injunctions in Labor Disputes; Hearing; Findings of Court; Notice to Affected Persons; Temporary Restraining Order; Undertakings.

8. TITLE 42, UNITED STATES CODE

1983. Civil Action for Deprivation of Rights.

1. FEDERAL RULES OF CIVIL PROCEDURE

Rule 23. Class Actions

(a) Prerequisites to a Class Action. One or more members of a class may sue or be sued as representative parties on behalf of all only if (1) the class is so numerous that joinder of all members is impracticable, (2) there are questions of law or fact common to the class, (3) the claims or defenses of the representative parties are typical of the claims or defenses of the class, and (4) the representative parties will fairly and adequately protect the interests of the class.

(b) Class Actions Maintainable. An action may be maintained as a class action if the prerequisites of subdivision (a) are satisfied, and in addition:

(1) the prosecution of separate actions by or against individual members of the class would create a risk of

(A) inconsistent or varying adjudications with respect to individual members of the class which would establish incompatible standards of conduct for the party opposing the class, or

(B) adjudications with respect to individual members of the class which would as a practical matter be dispositive of the interests of the other members not parties to the adjudications or substantially impair or impede their ability to protect their interests; or

(2) the party opposing the class has acted or refused to act on grounds generally applicable to the class, thereby making appropriate final injunctive relief or corresponding declaratory relief with respect to the class as a whole; or

(3) the court finds that the questions of law or fact common to the members of the class predominate over any questions affecting only individual members, and that a class action is superior to other available methods for the fair and efficient adjudication of the controversy. The matters pertinent to the findings include: (A) the interest of members of the class in individually controlling the prosecution or defense of separate actions; (B) the extent and nature of any litigation concerning the controversy already commenced by or against members of the class; (C) the desirability or undesirability of concentrating the litigation of the claims in the particular forum; (D) the difficulties likely to be encountered in the management of a class action.

(c) Determination by Order Whether Class Action to be Maintained; Notice; Judgment; Actions Conducted Partially as Class Actions.

(1) As soon as practicable after the commencement of an action brought as a class action, the court shall determine by order whether it is to be so maintained. An order under this subdivision may be conditional, and may be altered or amended before the decision on the merits.

(2) In any class action maintained under subdivision (b)(3), the court shall direct to the members of the class the best notice practicable under the circumstances, including individual notice to all members who can be identified through reasonable effort. The notice shall advise each member that (A) the court will exclude him from the class if he so requests by a specified date; (B) the judgment, whether favorable or not, will include all members

who do not request exclusion; and (C) any member who does not request exclusion may, if he desires, enter an appearance through his counsel.

(3) The judgment in an action maintained as a class action under subdivision (b)(1) or (b)(2), whether or not favorable to the class, shall include and describe those whom the court finds to be members of the class. The judgment in an action maintained as a class action under subdivision (b)(3), whether or not favorable to the class, shall include and specify or describe those to whom the notice provided in subdivision (c)(2) was directed, and who have not requested exclusion, and whom the court finds to be members of the class.

(4) When appropriate (A) an action may be brought or maintained as a class action with respect to particular issues, or (B) a class may be divided into subclasses and each subclass treated as a class, and the provisions of this rule shall then be construed and applied accordingly.

(d) Orders in Conduct of Actions. In the conduct of actions to which this rule applies, the court may make appropriate orders: (1) determining the course of proceedings or prescribing measures to prevent undue repetition or complication in the presentation of evidence or argument; (2) requiring, for the protection of the members of the class or otherwise for the fair conduct of the action, that notice be given in such manner as the court may direct to some or all of the members of any step in the action, or of the proposed extent of the judgment, or of the opportunity of members to signify whether they consider the representation fair and adequate, to intervene and present claims or defenses, or otherwise to come into the action; (3) imposing conditions on the representative parties or on intervenors; (4) requiring that the pleadings be amended to eliminate therefrom allegations as to representation of absent persons, and that the action proceed accordingly; (5) dealing with similar procedural matters. The orders may be combined with an order under Rule 16, and may be altered or amended as may be desirable from time to time.

(e) Dismissal or Compromise. A class action shall not be dismissed or compromised without the approval of the court, and notice of the proposed dismissal or compromise shall be given to all members of the class in such manner as thc court directs.

Rule 24. Intervention

(a) Intervention of Right. Upon timely application anyone shall be permitted to intervene in an action: (1) when a statute of the United States confers an unconditional right to intervene; or (2) when the applicant claims an interest relating to the property or transaction which is the subject of the action and he is so situated that the disposition of the action may as a practical matter impair or impede his ability to protect that interest, unless the applicant's interest is adequately represented by existing parties.

(b) Permissive Intervention. Upon timely application anyone may be permitted to intervene in an action: (1) when a statute of the United States confers a conditional right to intervene; or (2) when an applicant's claim or defense and the main action have a question of law or fact in common. When a party to an action relies for ground of claim or defense upon any

statute or executive order administered by a federal or state governmental officer or agency or upon any regulation, order, requirement or agreement issued or made pursuant to the statute or executive order, the officer or agency upon timely application may be permitted to intervene in the action. In exercising its discretion the court shall consider whether the intervention will unduly delay or prejudice the adjudication of the rights of the original parties.

(c) Procedure. A person desiring to intervene shall serve a motion to intervene upon the parties as provided in Rule 5. The motion shall state the grounds therefor and shall be accompanied by a pleading setting forth the claim or defense for which intervention is sought. The same procedure shall be followed when a statute of the United States gives a right to intervene. When the constitutionality of an act of Congress affecting the public interest is drawn in question in any action to which the United States or an officer, agency, or employee thereof is not a party, the court shall notify the Attorney General of the United States as provided in Title 28, U.S.C. § 2403.

Rule 25. Substitution of Parties

. . . *(d) Public Officers; Death or Separation from Office.*

(1) When a public officer is a party to an action in his official capacity and during its pendency dies, resigns, or otherwise ceases to hold office, the action does not abate and his successor is automatically substituted as a party. Proceedings following the substitution shall be in the name of the substituted party, but any misnomer not affecting the substantial rights of the parties shall be disregarded. An order of substitution may be entered at any time, but the omission to enter such an order shall not affect the substitution.

(2) When a public officer sues or is sued in his official capacity, he may be described as a party by his official title rather than by name; but the court may require his name to be added.

Rule 38. Jury Trial of Right

(a) Right Preserved. The right of trial by jury as declared by the Seventh Amendment to the Constitution or as given by a statute of the United States shall be preserved to the parties inviolate.

(b) Demand. Any party may demand a trial by jury of any issue triable of right by a jury by serving upon the other parties a demand therefor in writing at any time after the commencement of the action and not later than 10 days after the service of the last pleading directed to such issue. Such demand may be indorsed upon a pleading of the party.

(c) Same: Specification of Issues. In his demand a party may specify the issues which he wishes so tried; otherwise he shall be deemed to have demanded trial by jury for all the issues so triable. If he has demanded trial by jury for only some of the issues, any other party within 10 days after service of the demand or such lesser time as the court may order, may serve a demand for trial by jury of any other or all of the issues of fact in the action.

(d) Waiver. The failure of a party to serve a demand as required by this rule and to file it as required by Rule 5(d) constitutes a waiver by him of trial by jury. A demand for trial by jury made as herein provided may not be withdrawn without the consent of the parties. . . .

Rule 39. Trial by Jury or by the Court

(a) By Jury. When trial by jury has been demanded as provided in Rule 38, the action shall be designated upon the docket as a jury action. The trial of all issues so demanded shall be by jury, unless (1) the parties or their attorneys of record, by written stipulation filed with the court or by an oral stipulation made in open court and entered in the record, consent to trial by the court sitting without a jury or (2) the court upon motion or of its own initiative finds that a right of trial by jury of some or all of those issues does not exist under the Constitution or statutes of the United States.

(b) By the Court. Issues not demanded for trial by jury as provided in Rule 38 shall be tried by the court; but, notwithstanding the failure of a party to demand a jury in an action in which such a demand might have been made of right, the court in its discretion upon motion may order a trial by a jury of any or all issues.

(c) Advisory Jury and Trial by Consent. In all actions not triable of right by a jury the court upon motion or of its own initiative may try any issue with an advisory jury or, except in actions against the United States when a statute of the United States provides for trial without a jury, the court, with the consent of both parties, may order a trial with a jury whose verdict has the same effect as if trial by jury had been a matter of right.

Rule 52. Findings by the Court

(a) Effect. In all actions tried upon the facts without a jury or with an advisory jury, the court shall find the facts specially and state separately its conclusions of law thereon, and judgment shall be entered pursuant to Rule 58; and in granting or refusing interlocutory injunctions the court shall similarly set forth the findings of fact and conclusions of law which constitute the grounds of its action. Requests for findings are not necessary for purposes of review. Findings of fact shall not be set aside unless clearly erroneous, and due regard shall be given to the opportunity of the trial court to judge of the credibility of the witnesses. The findings of a master, to the extent that the court adopts them, shall be considered as the findings of the court. It will be sufficient if the findings of fact and conclusions of law are stated orally and recorded in open court following the close of the evidence or appear in an opinion or memorandum of decision filed by the court. Findings of fact and conclusions of law are unnecessary on decisions of motions under Rules 12 or 56 or any other motion except as provided in Rule 41(b).

. . .

Rule 53. Masters

(a) Appointment and Compensation. The court in which any action is pending may appoint a special master therein. As used in these rules the word

"master" includes a referee, an auditor, an examiner, and an assessor. The compensation to be allowed to a master shall be fixed by the court, and shall be charged upon such of the parties or paid out of any fund or subject matter of the action, which is in the custody and control of the court as the court may direct; provided that this provision for compensation shall not apply when a United States magistrate is designated to serve as a master pursuant to Title 28, U.S.C. § 636(b)(2). The master shall not retain his report as security for his compensation; but when the party ordered to pay the compensation allowed by the court does not pay it after notice and within the time prescribed by the court, the master is entitled to a writ of execution against the delinquent party.

(b) Reference. A reference to a master shall be the exception and not the rule. In actions to be tried by a jury, a reference shall be made only when the issues are complicated; in actions to be tried without a jury, save in matters of account and of difficult computation of damages, a reference shall be made only upon a showing that some exceptional condition requires it. Upon the consent of the parties, a magistrate may be designated to serve as a special master without regard to the provisions of this subdivision.

(c) Powers. The order of reference to the master may specify or limit his powers and may direct him to report only upon particular issues or to do or perform particular acts or to receive and report evidence only and may fix the time and place for beginning and closing the hearings and for the filing of the master's report. Subject to the specifications and limitations stated in the order, the master has and shall exercise the power to regulate all proceedings in every hearing before him and to do all acts and take all measures necessary or proper for the efficient performance of his duties under the order. He may require the production before him of evidence upon all matters embraced in the reference, including the production of all books, papers, vouchers, documents, and writings applicable thereto. He may rule upon the admissibility of evidence unless otherwise directed by the order of reference and has the authority to put witnesses on oath and may himself examine them and may call the parties to the action and examine them upon oath. When a party so requests, the master shall make a record of the evidence offered and excluded in the same manner and subject to the same limitations as provided in the Federal Rules of Evidence for a court sitting without a jury. . . .

(e) Report.

(1) *Contents and Filing.* The master shall prepare a report upon the matters submitted to him by the order of reference and, if required to make findings of fact and conclusions of law, he shall set them forth in the report. He shall file the report with the clerk of the court and in an action to be tried without a jury, unless otherwise directed by the order of reference, shall file with it a transcript of the proceedings and of the evidence and the original exhibits. The clerk shall forthwith mail to all parties notice of the filing.

(2) *In Non-Jury Actions.* In an action to be tried without a jury the court shall accept the master's findings of fact unless clearly erroneous. Within 10 days after being served with notice of the filing of the report any party may serve written objections thereto upon the other parties. Application to the court for action upon the report and upon objections thereto shall be by motion and upon notice as prescribed in Rule 6(d). The court after hearing

may adopt the report or may modify it or may reject it in whole or in part or may receive further evidence or may recommit it with instructions.

(3) *In Jury Actions.* In an action to be tried by a jury the master shall not be directed to report the evidence. His findings upon the issues submitted to him are admissible as evidence of the matters found and may be read to the jury, subject to the ruling of the court upon any objections in point of law which may be made to the report.

(4) *Stipulation as to Findings.* The effect of a master's report is the same whether or not the parties have consented to the reference; but, when the parties stipulate that a master's findings of fact shall be final, only questions of law arising upon the report shall thereafter be considered . . . .

(f) A magistrate is subject to this rule only when the order referring a matter to the magistrate expressly provides that the reference is made under this Rule.

Rule 54. Judgments; Costs

(a) Definition; Form. "Judgment" as used in these rules includes a decree and any order from which an appeal lies. A judgment shall not contain a recital of pleadings, the report of a master, or the record of prior proceedings.

(b) Judgment Upon Multiple Claims or Involving Multiple Parties. When more than one claim for relief is presented in an action, whether as a claim, counterclaim, cross-claim, or third-party claim, or when multiple parties are involved, the court may direct the entry of a final judgment as to one or more but fewer than all of the claims or parties only upon an express determination that there is no just reason for delay and upon an express direction for the entry of judgment. In the absence of such determination and direction, any order or other form of decision, however designated, which adjudicates fewer than all the claims or the rights and liabilities of fewer than all the parties shall not terminate the action as to any of the claims or parties, and the order or other form of decision is subject to revision at any time before the entry of judgment adjudicating all the claims and the rights and liabilities of all the parties.

(c) Demand for Judgment. A judgment by default shall not be different in kind from or exceed in amount that prayed for in the demand for judgment. Except as to a party against whom a judgment is entered by default, every final judgment shall grant the relief to which the party in whose favor it is rendered is entitled, even if the party has not demanded such relief in his pleadings.

(d) Costs. Except when express provision therefor is made either in a statute of the United States or in these rules, costs shall be allowed as of course to the prevailing party unless the court otherwise directs; but costs against the United States, its officers, and agencies shall be imposed only to the extent permitted by law. Costs may be taxed by the clerk on one day's notice. On motion served within 5 days thereafter, the action of the clerk may be reviewed by the court.

Rule 57. Declaratory Judgments

The procedure for obtaining a declaratory judgment pursuant to Title 28 U.S.C. § 2201, shall be in accordance with these rules, and the right to trial by jury may be demanded under the circumstances and in the manner provided in Rules 38 and 39. The existence of another adequate remedy does not preclude a judgment for declaratory relief in cases where it is appropriate. The court may order a speedy hearing of an action for a declaratory judgment and may advance it on the calendar.

Rule 62. Stay of Proceedings to Enforce a Judgment

(a) Automatic Stay; Exceptions—Injunctions, Receiverships, and Patent Accountings. Except as stated herein, no execution shall issue upon a judgment nor shall proceedings be taken for its enforcement until the expiration of 10 days after its entry. Unless otherwise ordered by the court, an interlocutory or final judgment in an action for an injunction or in a receivership action, or a judgment or order directing an accounting in an action for infringement of letters patent, shall not be stayed during the period after its entry and until an appeal is taken or during the pendency of an appeal. The provisions of subdivision (c) of this rule govern the suspending, modifying, restoring, or granting of an injunction during the pendency of an appeal. . . .

(c) Injunction Pending Appeal. When an appeal is taken from an interlocutory or final judgment granting, dissolving, or denying an injunction, the court in its discretion may suspend, modify, restore, or grant an injunction during the pendency of the appeal upon such terms as to bond or otherwise as it considers proper for the security of the rights of the adverse party. If the judgment appealed from is rendered by a district court of three judges specially constituted pursuant to a statute of the United States, no such order shall be made except (1) by such court sitting in open court or (2) by the assent of all the judges of such court evidenced by their signatures to the order.

(d) Stay Upon Appeal. When an appeal is taken the appellant by giving a supersedeas bond may obtain a stay subject to the exceptions contained in subdivision (a) of this rule. The bond may be given at or after the time of filing the notice of appeal or of procuring the order allowing the appeal, as the case may be. The stay is effective when the supersedeas bond is approved by the court.

(e) Stay in Favor of the United States or Agency Thereof. When an appeal is taken by the United States or an officer or agency thereof or by direction of any department of the Government of the United States and the operation or enforcement of the judgment is stayed, no bond, obligation, or other security shall be required from the appellant. . . .

(g) Power of Appellate Court Not Limited. The provisions in this rule do not limit any power of an appellate court or of a judge or justice thereof to stay proceedings during the pendency of an appeal or to suspend, modify, restore, or grant an injunction during the pendency of an appeal or to make any order appropriate to preserve the status quo or the effectiveness of the judgment subsequently to be entered.

(h) Stay of Judgment as to Multiple Claims or Multiple Parties. When a court has ordered a final judgment under the conditions stated in Rule 54(b), the court may stay enforcement of that judgment until the entering of a subsequent judgment or judgments and may prescribe such conditions as are necessary to secure the benefit thereof to the party in whose favor the judgment is entered.

Rule 65. Injunctions

(a) Preliminary Injunction.

(1) *Notice.* No preliminary injunction shall be issued without notice to the adverse party.

(2) *Consolidation of Hearing With Trial on Merits.* Before or after the commencement of the hearing of an application for a preliminary injunction, the court may order the trial of the action on the merits to be advanced and consolidated with the hearing of the application. Even when this consolidation is not ordered, any evidence received upon an application for a preliminary injunction which would be admissible upon the trial on the merits becomes part of the record on the trial and need not be repeated upon the trial. This subdivision (a)(2) shall be so construed and applied as to save to the parties any rights they may have to trial by jury.

(b) Temporary Restraining Order; Notice; Hearing; Duration. A temporary restraining order may be granted without written or oral notice to the adverse party or his attorney only if (1) it clearly appears from specific facts shown by affidavit or by the verified complaint that immediate and irreparable injury, loss, or damage will result to the applicant before the adverse party or his attorney can be heard in opposition, and (2) the applicant's attorney certifies to the court in writing the efforts, if any, which have been made to give the notice and the reasons supporting his claim that notice should not be required. Every temporary restraining order granted without notice shall be indorsed with the date and hour of issuance; shall be filed forthwith in the clerk's office and entered of record; shall define the injury and state why it is irreparable and why the order was granted without notice; and shall expire by its terms within such time after entry, not to exceed 10 days, as the court fixes, unless within the time so fixed the order, for good cause shown, is extended for a like period or unless the party against whom the order is directed consents that it may be extended for a longer period. The reasons for the extension shall be entered of record. In case a temporary restraining order is granted without notice, the motion for a preliminary injunction shall be set down for hearing at the earliest possible time and takes precedence of all matters except older matters of the same character; and when the motion comes on for hearing the party who obtained the temporary restraining order shall proceed with the application for a preliminary injunction and, if he does not do so, the court shall dissolve the temporary restraining order. On 2 days' notice to the party who obtained the temporary restraining order without notice or on such shorter notice to that party as the court may prescribe, the adverse party may appear and move its dissolution or modification and in that event the court shall proceed to hear and determine such motion as expeditiously as the ends of justice require.

(c) Security. No restraining order or preliminary injunction shall issue except upon the giving of security by the applicant, in such sum as the court deems proper, for the payment of such costs and damages as may be incurred or suffered by any party who is found to have been wrongfully enjoined or restrained. No such security shall be required of the United States or of an officer or agency thereof.

The provisions of Rule 65.1 apply to a surety upon a bond or undertaking under this rule.

(d) Form and Scope of Injunction or Restraining Order. Every order granting an injunction and every restraining order shall set forth the reasons for its issuance; shall be specific in terms; shall describe in reasonable detail, and not by reference to the complaint or other document, the act or acts sought to be restrained; and is binding only upon the parties to the action, their officers, agents, servants, employees, and attorneys, and upon those persons in active concert or participation with them who receive actual notice of the order by personal service or otherwise.

(e) Employer and Employee; Interpleader; Constitutional Cases. These rules do not modify any statute of the United States relating to temporary restraining orders and preliminary injunctions in actions affecting employer and employee; or the provisions of Title 28, U.S.C. § 2361, relating to preliminary injunctions in actions of interpleader or in the nature of interpleader; or Title 28, U.S.C. § 2284, relating to actions required by Act of Congress to be heard and determined by a district court of three judges.

Rule 65.1 Security: Proceedings Against Sureties

Whenever these rules, including the Supplemental Rules for Certain Admiralty and Maritime Claims, require or permit the giving of security by a party, and security is given in the form of a bond or stipulation or other undertaking with one or more sureties, each surety submits himself to the jurisdiction of the court and irrevocably appoints the clerk of the court as his agent upon whom any papers affecting his liability on the bond or undertaking may be served. His liability may be enforced on motion without the necessity of an independent action. The motion and such notice of the motion as the court prescribes may be served on the clerk of the court, who shall forthwith mail copies to the sureties if their addresses are known.

Rule 67. Deposit in Court

In an action in which any part of the relief sought is a judgment for a sum of money or the disposition of a sum of money or the disposition of any other thing capable of delivery, a party, upon notice to every other party, and by leave of court, may deposit with the court all or any part of such sum or thing, whether or not that party claims all or any part of the sum or thing. The party making the deposit shall serve the order permitting deposit on the clerk of the court. Money paid into court under this rule shall be deposited and withdrawn in accordance with the provisions of Title 28, U.S.C., §§ 2041, and 2042; the Act of June 26, 1934, c. 756, § 23, as amended (48 Stat. 1236, 58 Stat. 845), U.S.C., Title 31, § 725v; or any like statute.

The fund shall be deposited in an interest-bearing account or invested in an interest-bearing instrument approved by the court.

Rule 70. Judgment for Specific Acts; Vesting Title

If a judgment directs a party to execute a conveyance of land or to deliver deeds or other documents or to perform any other specific act and the party fails to comply within the time specified, the court may direct the act to be done at the cost of the disobedient party by some other person appointed by the court and the act when so done has like effect as if done by the party. On application of the party entitled to performance, the clerk shall issue a writ of attachment or sequestration against the property of the disobedient party to compel obedience to the judgment. The court may also in proper cases adjudge the party in contempt. If real or personal property is within the district, the court in lieu of directing a conveyance thereof may enter a judgment divesting the title of any party and vesting it in others and such judgment has the effect of a conveyance executed in due form of law. When any order or judgment is for the delivery of possession, the party in whose favor it is entered is entitled to a writ of execution or assistance upon application to the clerk.

Rule 71. Process in Behalf of and Against Persons Not Parties

When an order is made in favor of a person who is not a party to the action, he may enforce obedience to the order by the same process as if he were a party; and, when obedience to an order may be lawfully enforced against a person who is not a party, he is liable to the same process for enforcing obedience to the order as if he were a party.

Rule 72. Magistrates; Pretrial Matters

(a) Nondispositive Matters. A magistrate to whom a pretrial matter not dispositive of a claim or defense of a party is referred to hear and determine shall promptly conduct such proceedings as are required and when appropriate enter into the record a written order setting forth the disposition of the matter. The district judge to whom the case is assigned shall consider objections made by the parties, provided they are served and filed within 10 days after the entry of the order, and shall modify or set aside any portion of the magistrate's order found to be clearly erroneous or contrary to law.

(b) Dispositive Motions and Prisoner Petitions. A magistrate assigned without consent of the parties to hear a pretrial matter dispositive of a claim or defense of a party or a prisoner petition challenging the conditions of confinement shall promptly conduct such proceedings as are required. A record shall be made of all evidentiary proceedings before the magistrate, and a record may be made of such other proceedings as the magistrate deems necessary. The magistrate shall enter into the record a recommendation for disposition of the matter, including proposed findings of fact when appropriate. The clerk shall forthwith mail copies to all parties.

A party objecting to the recommended disposition of the matter shall promptly arrange for the transcription of the record, or portions of it as all parties may agree upon or the magistrate deems sufficient, unless the district judge otherwise directs. Within 10 days after being served with a copy of the recommended disposition, a party may serve and file specific, written objections to the proposed findings and recommendations. A party may respond to another party's objections within 10 days after being served with a copy thereof. The district judge to whom the case is assigned shall make a de novo determination upon the record, or after additional evidence, of any portion of the magistrate's disposition to which specific written objection has been made in accordance with this rule. The district judge may accept, reject, or modify the recommended decision, receive further evidence, or recommit the matter to the magistrate with instructions.

Rule 77. District Courts and Clerks

. . . *(d) Notice of Orders or Judgments.* Immediately upon the entry of an order or judgment the clerk shall serve a notice of the entry by mail in the manner provided for in Rule 5 upon each party who is not in default for failure to appear, and shall make a note in the docket of the mailing. Such mailing is sufficient notice for all purposes for which notice of the entry of an order is required by these rules; but any party may in addition serve a notice of such entry in the manner provided in Rule 5 for the service of papers. Lack of notice of the entry by the clerk does not affect the time to appeal or relieve or authorize the court to relieve a party for failure to appeal within the time allowed, except as permitted in Rule 4(a) of the Federal Rules of Appellate Procedure.

---

2. FEDERAL RULES OF CRIMINAL PROCEDURE

Rule 35. Correction or Reduction of Sentence

The court may correct an illegal sentence at any time and may correct a sentence imposed in an illegal manner within the time provided herein for the reduction of sentence. The court may reduce a sentence within 120 days after the sentence is imposed, or within 120 days after receipt by the court of a mandate issued upon affirmance of the judgment or dismissal of the appeal, or within 120 days after entry of any order or judgment of the Supreme Court denying review of, or having the effect of upholding a judgment of conviction. The court may also reduce a sentence upon revocation of probation as provided by law.

Rule 42. Criminal Contempt

(a) Summary Disposition. A criminal contempt may be punished summarily if the judge certifies that he saw or heard the conduct constituting the contempt and that it was committed in the actual presence of the court. The order of contempt shall recite the facts and shall be signed by the judge and entered of record.

(b) Disposition Upon Notice and Hearing. A criminal contempt except as provided in subdivision (a) of this rule shall be prosecuted on notice. The notice shall state the time and place of hearing, allowing a reasonable time for the preparation of the defense, and shall state the essential facts constituting the criminal contempt charged and describe it as such. The notice shall be given orally by the judge in open court in the presence of the defendant or, on application of the United States attorney or of an attorney appointed by the court for that purpose, by an order to show cause or an order of arrest. The defendant is entitled to a trial by jury in any case in which an act of Congress so provides. He is entitled to admission to bail as provided in these rules. If the contempt charged involves disrespect to or criticism of a judge, that judge is disqualified from presiding at the trial or hearing except with the defendant's consent. Upon a verdict or finding of guilt the court shall enter an order fixing the punishment.

3. FEDERAL RULES OF APPELLATE PROCEDURE

Rule 8. Stay or Injunction Pending Appeal

(a) Stay Must Ordinarily Be Sought in the First Instance in District Court; Motion for Stay in Court of Appeals. Application for a stay of the judgment or order of a district court pending appeal, or for approval of a supersedeas bond, or for an order suspending, modifying, restoring or granting an injunction during the pendency of an appeal must ordinarily be made in the first instance in the district court. A motion for such relief may be made to the court of appeals or to a judge thereof, but the motion shall show that application to the district court for the relief sought is not practicable, or that the district court has denied an application, or has failed to afford the relief which the applicant requested, with the reasons given by the district court for its action. The motion shall also show the reasons for the relief requested and the facts relied upon, and if the facts are subject to dispute the motion shall be supported by affidavits or other sworn statements or copies thereof. With the motion shall be filed such parts of the record as are relevant. Reasonable notice of the motion shall be given to all parties. The motion shall be filed with the clerk and normally will be considered by a panel or division of the court, but in exceptional cases where such procedure would be impracticable due to the requirements of time, the application may be made to and considered by a single judge of the court.

(b) Stay May Be Conditioned Upon Giving of Bond; Proceedings Against Sureties. Relief available in the court of appeals under this rule may be conditioned upon the filing of a bond or other appropriate security in the district court. If security is given in the form of a bond or stipulation or other undertaking with one or more sureties, each surety submits himself to the jurisdiction of the district court and irrevocably appoints the clerk of the district court as his agent upon whom any papers affecting his liability on the bond or undertaking may be served. His liability may be enforced on motion in the district court without the necessity of an independent action. The motion

and such notice of the motion as the district court prescribes may be served on the clerk of the district court, who shall forthwith mail copies to the sureties if their addresses are known. . . .

Rule 21. Writs of Mandamus and Prohibition Directed to a Judge or Judges and Other Extraordinary Writs

(a) Mandamus or Prohibition to a Judge or Judges; Petition for Writ; Service and Filing. Application for a writ of mandamus or of prohibition directed to a judge or judges shall be made by filing a petition therefor with the clerk of the court of appeals with proof of service on the respondent judge or judges and on all parties to the action in the trial court. The petition shall contain a statement of the facts necessary to an understanding of the issues presented by the application; a statement of the issues presented and of the relief sought; a statement of the reasons why the writ should issue; and copies of any order or opinion or parts of the record which may be essential to an understanding of the matters set forth in the petition. Upon receipt of the prescribed docket fee, the clerk shall docket the petition and submit it to the court.

(b) Denial; Order Directing Answer. If the court is of the opinion that the writ should not be granted, it shall deny the petition. Otherwise, it shall order that an answer to the petition be filed by the respondents within the time fixed by the order. The order shall be served by the clerk on the judge or judges named respondents and on all other parties to the action in the trial court. All parties below other than the petitioner shall also be deemed respondents for all purposes. Two or more respondents may answer jointly. If the judge or judges named respondents do not desire to appear in the proceeding, they may so advise the clerk and all parties by letter, but the petition shall not thereby be taken as admitted. The clerk shall advise the parties of the dates on which briefs are to be filed, if briefs are required, and of the date of oral argument. The proceeding shall be given preference over ordinary civil cases.

(c) Other Extraordinary Writs. Application for extraordinary writs other than those provided for in subdivisions (a) and (b) of this rule shall be made by petition filed with the clerk of the court of appeals with proof of service on the parties named as respondents. Proceedings on such application shall conform, so far as is practicable, to the procedure prescribed in subdivisions (a) and (b) of this rule.

(d) Form of Papers; Number of Copies. All papers may be typewritten. Three copies shall be filed with the original, but the court may direct that additional copies be furnished.

Rule 27. Motions

(a) Content of Motions; Response; Reply. Unless another form is elsewhere prescribed by these rules, an application for an order or other relief shall be made by filing a motion for such order or relief with proof of service on all other parties. The motion shall contain or be accompanied by any matter required by a specific provision of these rules governing such a motion, shall state with particularity the grounds on which it is based, and shall set forth the order or relief sought. If a motion is supported by briefs, affidavits or other papers, they shall be served and filed with the motion. Any party may file a response in opposition to a motion other than one for a procedural order [for which see subdivision (b)] within 7 days after service of the motion, but motions authorized by Rules 8, 9, 18 and 41 may be acted upon after reasonable notice, and the court may shorten or extend the time for responding to any motion.

(b) Determination of Motions for Procedural Orders. Notwithstanding the provisions of (a) of this Rule 27 as to motions generally, motions for procedural orders, including any motion under Rule 26(b), may be acted upon at any time, without awaiting a response thereto, and pursuant to rule or order of the court, motions for specified types of procedural orders may be disposed of by the clerk. Any party adversely affected by such action may by application to the court request consideration, vacation or modification of such action.

(c) Power of a Single Judge to Entertain Motions. In addition to the authority expressly conferred by these rules or by law, a single judge of a court of appeals may entertain and may grant or deny any request for relief which under these rules may properly be sought by motion, except that a single judge may not dismiss or otherwise determine an appeal or other proceeding, and except that a court of appeals may provide by order or rule that any motion or class of motions must be acted upon by the court. The action of a single judge may be reviewed by the court.

(d) Form of Papers; Number of Copies. All papers relating to motions may be typewritten. Three copies shall be filed with the original, but the court may require that additional copies be furnished.

Rule 36. Entry of Judgment

The notation of a judgment in the docket constitutes entry of the judgment. The clerk shall prepare, sign and enter the judgment following receipt of the opinion of the court unless the opinion directs settlement of the form of the judgment, in which event the clerk shall prepare, sign and enter the judgment following final settlement by the court. If a judgment is rendered without an opinion, the clerk shall prepare, sign and enter the judgment following instruction from the court. The clerk shall, on the date judgment is entered, mail to all parties a copy of the opinion, if any, or of the judgment if no opinion was written, and notice of the date of entry of the judgment.

Rule 43. Substitution of Parties

(c) Public Officers; Death or Separation from Office.

(1) When a public officer is a party to an appeal or other proceeding in the court of appeals in his official capacity and during its pendency dies, resigns or otherwise ceases to hold office, the action does not abate and his successor is automatically substituted as a party. Proceedings following the substitution shall be in the name of the substituted party, but any misnomer not affecting the substantial rights of the parties shall be disregarded. An

order of substitution may be entered at any time, but the omission to enter such an order shall not affect the substitution.

(2) When a public officer is a party to an appeal or other proceeding in his official capacity he may be described as a party by his official title rather than by name; but the court may require his name to be added.

Rule 44. Cases Involving Constitutional Questions Where United States is Not a Party

It shall be the duty of a party who draws in question the constitutionality of any Act of Congress in any proceeding in a court of appeals to which the United States or any agency thereof, or any officer or employee thereof, as such officer or employee, is not a party, upon the filing of the record, or as soon thereafter as the question is raised in the court of appeals, to give immediate notice in writing to the court of the existence of said question. The clerk shall thereupon certify such fact to the Attorney General.

---

4. RULES OF THE SUPREME COURT

Rule 18. Supersedeas on Appeal

1. Whenever an appellant entitled thereto desires a stay on appeal, he may present for approval to a judge of the court whose decision is sought to be reviewed, or to such court when action by that court is required by law, or, subject to paragraph 2 hereof, to a justice of this court, a motion to stay the enforcement of the judgment appealed from, with which, if the stay is to act as a supersedeas, shall be tendered a supersedeas bond which shall have such surety or sureties as said judge, court, or justice may require. . . .

2. Application hereunder to a justice of this court will normally not be entertained unless application therefor has been made to a judge of the court rendering the decision appealed from or to such court, or unless the security offered below has been disapproved by such judge or court. All such applications are governed by Rules 50 and 51.

Rule 27. Stay Pending Review on Certiorari

Applications pursuant to 28 U.S.C. § 2101(f) to a justice of this court will normally not be entertained unless application for a stay has first been made to a judge of the court rendering the decision sought to be reviewed, or to such court, or unless the security offered below has been disapproved by such judge or court. All such applications are governed by Rules 50 and 51.

Rule 50. Applications to Individual Justices; Practice in Chambers

1. All motions and applications addressed to individual justices shall normally be submitted to the clerk, who will promptly transmit them to the jus-

tice concerned. If oral argument on the application is desired, request therefor shall accompany the application.

2. All motions and applications addressed to individual justices shall be accompanied by proof of service on all other parties. In urgent cases, proof of telegraphic dispatch to such parties of notice that the motion, application, or request is being made will suffice.

3. The clerk will in due course advise all counsel concerned, by means as speedy as may be appropriate, of the time and place of the hearing, if any, or, if no hearing is requested or granted, of the disposition made of the motion or application.

4. During the term, applications will be addressed to the justice duly allotted to the circuit within which the case arises. The court or the chief justice will seasonably instruct the clerk as to the distribution of applications during vacation, and whenever a circuit justice is temporarily absent or disabled.

5. A justice denying an application made to him will note his denial thereon. Thereafter, unless action on such application is by law restricted to the circuit justice, or is out of time under Rule 34(3), the party making the application may renew the same to any other justice, subject to the provisions of this rule. Except where the denial has been without prejudice, such renewed applications are not favored.

6. Any justice to whom an application for a stay or for bail is submitted may refer the same to the court for determination.

Rule 51. Stays

1. Stays may be granted by a justice of this court as permitted by law; and writs of injunction may be granted by any justice in cases where they might be granted by the court. . . .

2. All applications for stays or injunctions made pursuant to this or any other rule must show whether application for the relief sought has first been made to the appropriate court or courts below, or to a judge or judges thereof, and shall be submitted as provided in Rule 50. . . .

5. TITLE 18, UNITED STATES CODE

§ 241. Conspiracy against rights of citizens

If two or more persons conspire to injure, oppress, threaten, or intimidate any citizen in the free exercise or enjoyment of any right or privilege secured to him by the Constituition or laws of the United States, or because of his having so exercised the same; or

If two or more persons go in disguise on the highway, or on the premises of another, with intent to prevent or hinder his free exercise or enjoyment of any right or privilege so secured—

They shall be fined not more than $10,000 or imprisoned not more than ten years, or both; and if death results, they shall be subject to imprisonment for any term of years or for life.

§ 242. Deprivation of rights under color of law

Whoever, under color of any law, statute, ordinance, regulation, or custom, willfully subjects any inhabitant of any State, Territory, or District to the deprivation of any rights, privileges, or immunities secured or protected by the Constitution or laws of the United States, or to different punishments, pains, or penalties, on account of such inhabitant being an alien, or by reason of his color, or race, than are prescribed for the punishment of citizens, shall be fined not more than $1,000 or imprisoned not more than one year, or both; and if death results shall be subject to imprisonment for any term of years or for life.

§ 401. Power of court

A court of the United States shall have power to punish by fine or imprisonment, at its discretion, such contempt of its authority, and none other, as—

(1) Misbehavior of any person in its presence or so near thereto as to obstruct the administration of justice;

(2) Misbehavior of any of its officers in their official transactions;

(3) Disobedience or resistance to its lawful writ, process, order, rule, decree, or command.

§ 402. Contempts constituting crimes

Any person, corporation or association willfully disobeying any lawful writ, process, order, rule, decree, or command of any district court of the United States or any court of the District of Columbia, by doing any act or thing therein, or thereby forbidden, if the act or thing so done be of such character as to constitute also a criminal offense under any statute of the United States or under the laws of any State in which the act was committed, shall be prosecuted for such contempt as provided in section 3691 of this title and shall be punished by fine or imprisonment, or both.

Such fine shall be paid to the United States or to the complainant or other party injured by the act constituting the contempt, or may, where more than one is so damaged, be divided or apportioned among them as the court may direct, but in no case shall the fine to be paid to the United States exceed, in case the accused is a natural person, the sum of $1,000, nor shall such imprisonment exceed the term of six months.

This section shall not be construed to relate to contempts committed in the presence of the court, or so near thereto as to obstruct the administration of justice, nor to contempts committed in disobedience of any lawful writ, process, order, rule, decree, or command entered in any suit or action brought or prosecuted in the name of, or on behalf of, the United States, but the same, and all other cases of contempt not specifically embraced in this section may be punished in conformity to the prevailing usages at law.

§ 1509. Obstruction of court orders

Whoever, by threats or force, willfully prevents, obstructs, impedes, or interferes with, or willfully attempts to prevent, obstruct, impede, or interfere with, the due exercise of rights or the performance of duties under any order, judgment, or decree of a court of the United States, shall be fined not more than $1,000 or imprisoned not more than one year, or both.

No injunctive or other civil relief against the conduct made criminal by this section shall be denied on the ground that such conduct is a crime.

§ 3691. Jury trial of criminal contempts

Whenever a contempt charged shall consist in willful disobedience of any lawful writ, process, order, rule, decree, or command of any district court of the United States by doing or omitting any act or thing in violation thereof, and the act or thing done or omitted also constitutes a criminal offense under any Act of Congress, or under the laws of any state in which it was done or omitted, the accused, upon demand therefor, shall be entitled to trial by a jury, which shall conform as near as may be to the practice in other criminal cases.

This section shall not apply to contempts committed in the presence of the court, or so near thereto as to obstruct the administration of justice, nor to contempts committed in disobedience of any lawful writ, process, order, rule, decree, or command entered in any suit or action brought or prosecuted in the name of, or on behalf of, the United States.

§ 3692. Jury trial for contempt in labor dispute cases

In all cases of contempt arising under the laws of the United States governing the issuance of injunctions or restraining orders in any case involving or growing out of a labor dispute, the accused shall enjoy the right to a speedy and public trial by an impartial jury of the State and district wherein the contempt shall have been committed.

This section shall not apply to contempts committed in the presence of the court or so near thereto as to interfere directly with the administration of justice nor to the misbehavior, misconduct, or disobedience of any officer of the court in respect to the writs, orders or process of the court.

---

6. TITLE 28, UNITED STATES CODE

---

§ 1252. Direct appeals from decisions invalidating Acts of Congress

Any party may appeal to the Supreme Court from an interlocutory or final judgment, decree or order of any court of the United States, the United States District Court for the District of the Canal Zone, the District Court of Guam and the District Court of the Virgin Islands and any court of record of

Puerto Rico, holding an Act of Congress unconstitutional in any civil action, suit, or proceeding to which the United States or any of its agencies, or any officer or employee thereof, as such officer or employee, is a party.

A party who has received notice of appeal under this section shall take any subsequent appeal or cross appeal to the Supreme Court. All appeals or cross appeals taken to other courts prior to such notice shall be treated as taken directly to the Supreme Court.

§ 1254. Court of appeals; certiorari; appeal; certified questions

Cases in the courts of appeals may be reviewed by the Supreme Court by the following methods:

(1) By writ of certiorari granted upon the petition of any party to any civil or criminal case, before or after rendition of judgment or decree;

(2) By appeal by a party relying on a State statute held by a court of appeals to be invalid as repugnant to the Constitution, treaties or laws of the United States, but such appeal shall preclude review by writ of certiorari at the instance of such appellant, and the review on appeal shall be restricted to the Federal questions presented;

(3) By certification at any time by a court of appeals of any question of law in any civil or criminal case as to which instructions are desired, and upon such certification the Supreme Court may give binding instructions or require the entire record to be sent up for decision of the entire matter in controversy.

§ 1257. State courts; appeal; certiorari

Final judgments or decrees rendered by the highest court of a State in which a decision could be had, may be reviewed by the Supreme Court as follows:

(1) By appeal, where is drawn in question the validity of a treaty or statute of the United States and the decision is against its validity.

(2) By appeal, where is drawn in question the validity of a statute of any state on the ground of its being repugnant to the Constitution, treaties or laws of the United States, and the decision is in favor of its validity.

(3) By writ of certiorari, where the validity of a treaty or statute of the United States is drawn in question or where the validity of a State statute is drawn in question on the ground of its being repugnant to the Constitution, treaties or laws of the United States, or where any title, right, privilege or immunity is specially set up or claimed under the Constitution, treaties or statutes of, or commission held or authority exercised under, the United States.

§ 1291. Final decisions of district courts

The courts of appeals shall have jurisdiction of appeals from all final decisions of the district courts of the United States, the United States District Court for the District of the Canal Zone, the District Court of Guam, and the

District Court of the Virgin Islands, except where a direct review may be had in the Supreme Court.

§ 1292. Interlocutory decisions

(a) The courts of appeals shall have jurisdiction of appeals from:

(1) Interlocutory orders of the district courts of the United States, the United States District Court for the District of the Canal Zone, the District Court of Guam, and the District Court of the Virgin Islands, or of the judges thereof, granting, continuing, modifying, refusing or dissolving injunctions, or refusing to dissolve or modify injunctions, except where a direct review may be had in the Supreme Court. . . .

(b) When a district judge, in making in a civil action an order not otherwise appealable under this section, shall be of the opinion that such order involves a controlling question of law as to which there is substantial ground for difference of opinion and that an immediate appeal from the order may materially advance the ultimate termination of the litigation, he shall so state in writing in such order. The Court of Appeals may thereupon, in its discretion, permit an appeal to be taken from such order, if application is made to it within ten days after the entry of the order: *Provided, however,* That application for an appeal hereunder shall not stay proceedings in the district court unless the district judge or the Court of Appeals or a judge thereof shall so order.

§ 1331. Federal question

The district courts shall have original jurisdiction of all civil actions arising under the Constitution, laws, or treaties of the United States.

§ 1343. Civil rights and elective franchise

The district courts shall have original jurisdiction of all civil action authorized by law to be commenced by any person:

. . . (3) To redress the deprivation, under color of any State law, statute, ordinance, regulation, custom or usage, of any right, privilege or immunity secured by the Constitution of the United States or by an Act of Congress providing for equal rights of citizens or of all persons within the jurisdiction of the United States.

(4) To recover damages or to secure equitable or other relief under any Act of Congress providing for the protection of civil rights, including the right to vote.

§ 1345. United States as plaintiff

Except as otherwise provided by Act of Congress, the district courts shall have original jurisdiction of all civil actions, suits or proceedings commenced by the United States, or by any agency or officer thereof expressly authorized to sue by Act of Congress. . . .

§ 1651. Writs

(a) The Supreme Court and all courts established by Act of Congress may issue all writs necessary or appropriate in aid of their respective jurisdictions and agreeable to the usages and principles of law.

(b) An alternative writ or rule nisi may be issued by a justice or judge of a court which has jurisdiction.

§ 1826. Recalcitrant witnesses

(a) Whenever a witness in any proceeding before or ancillary to any court or grand jury of the United States refuses without just cause shown to comply with an order of the court to testify or provide other information, including any book, paper, document, record, recording or other material, the court, upon such refusal, or when such refusal is duly brought to its attention, may summarily order his confinement at a suitable place until such time as the witness is willing to give such testimony or provide such information. No period of such confinement shall exceed the life of—

"(1) the court proceeding, or

"(2) the term of the grand jury including extensions, before which such refusal to comply with the court order occurred, but in no event shall such confinement exceed eighteen months."

(b) No person confined pursuant to subsection (a) of this section shall be admitted to bail pending the determination of an appeal taken by him from the order for his confinement if it appears that the appeal is frivolous or taken for delay. Any appeal from an order of confinement under this section shall be disposed of as soon as practicable, but not later than thirty days from the filing of such appeal.

§ 2101. Supreme Court; time for appeal or certiorari; docketing; stay

. . . (f) In any case in which the final judgment or decree of any court is subject to review by the Supreme Court on writ of certiorari, the execution and enforcement of such judgment or decree may be stayed for a reasonable time to enable the party aggrieved to obtain a writ of certiorari from the Supreme Court. The stay may be granted by a judge of the court rendering the judgment or decree or by a justice of the Supreme Court, and may be conditioned on the giving of security, approved by such judge or justice, that if the aggrieved party fails to make application for such writ within the period allotted therefor, or fails to obtain an order granting his application, or fails to make his plea good in the Supreme Court, he shall answer for all damages and costs which the other party may sustain by reason of the stay.

§ 2201. Creation of [declaratory judgment] remedy

In a case of actual controversy within its jurisdiction, except with respect to Federal taxes, any court of the United States, upon the filing of an appropriate pleading, may declare the rights and other legal relations of any interested party seeking such declaration, whether or not further relief is or could be sought. Any such declaration shall have the force and effect of a final judgment or decree and shall be reviewable as such.

§ 2202. Further relief

Further necessary or proper relief based on a declaratory judgment or decree may be granted, after reasonable notice and hearing, against any adverse party whose rights have been determined by such judgment.

§ 2283. Stay of State court proceedings

A court of the United States may not grant an injunction to stay proceedings in a State court except as expressly authorized by Act of Congress, or where necessary in aid of its jurisdiction, or to protect or effectuate its judgments.

---

7. TITLE 29, UNITED STATES CODE

---

§ 101. Limitation on issuance of restraining orders and injunctions

No court of the United States, as herein defined, shall have jurisdiction to issue any restraining order or temporary or permanent injunction in a case involving or growing out of a labor dispute, except in a strict conformity with the provisions of this Act [29 USCS §§ 101–110, 113–115]; nor shall any such restraining order or temporary or permanent injunction be issued contrary to the public policy declared in this Act [29 USCS §§ 101–110, 113–115].

§ 104. Enumeration of specific acts not subject to restraining orders or injunctions

No court of the United States shall have jurisdiction to issue any restraining order or temporary or permanent injunction in any case involving or growing out of any labor dispute to prohibit any person or persons participating or interested in such dispute (as these terms are herein defined) from doing, whether singly or in concert, any of the following acts:

(a) Ceasing or refusing to perform any work or to remain in any relation of employment;

(b) Becoming or remaining a member of any labor organization or of any employer organization, regardless of any such undertaking or promise as is described in section 103 of this title;

(c) Paying or giving to, or withholding from, any person participating or interested in such labor dispute, any strike or unemployment benefits or insurance, or other moneys or things of value;

(d) By all lawful means aiding any person participating or interested in any labor dispute who is being proceeded against in, or is prosecuting, any action or suit in any court of the United States or of any State;

(e) Giving publicity to the existence of, or the facts involved in, any labor dispute, whether by advertising, speaking, patrolling, or by any other method not involving fraud or violence;

(f) Assembling peaceably to act or to organize to act in promotion of their interests in a labor dispute;

(g) Advising or notifying any person of an intention to do any of the acts heretofore specified;

(h) Agreeing with other persons to do or not to do any of the acts heretofore specified; and

(i) Advising, urging, or otherwise causing or inducing without fraud or violence the acts heretofore specified, regardless of any such undertaking or promise as is described in section 103 of this title.

§ 107. Issuance of injunctions in labor disputes; hearing; findings of court; notice to affected persons; temporary restraining order; undertakings

No court of the United States shall have jurisdiction to issue a temporary or permanent injunction in any case involving or growing out of a labor dispute, as defined in this chapter, except after hearing the testimony of witnesses in open court (with opportunity for cross-examination) in support of the allegations of a complaint made under oath, and testimony in opposition thereto, if offered, and except after findings of fact by the court, to the effect—

(a) That unlawful acts have been threatened and will be committed unless restrained or have been committed and will be continued unless restrained, but no injunction or temporary restraining order shall be issued on account of any threat or unlawful act excepting against the person or persons, association, or organization making the threat or committing the unlawful act or actually authorizing or ratifying the same after actual knowledge thereof;

(b) That substantial and irreparable injury to complainant's property will follow;

(c) That as to each item of relief granted greater injury will be inflicted upon complainant by the denial of relief than will be inflicted upon defendants by the granting of relief;

(d) That complainant has no adequate remedy at law; and

(e) That the public officers charged with the duty to protect complainant's property are unable or unwilling to furnish adequate protection.

Such hearing shall be held after due and personal notice thereof has been given, in such manner as the court shall direct, to all known persons against whom relief is sought, and also to the chief of those public officials of the county and city within which the unlawful acts have been threatened or committed charged with the duty to protect complainant's property: *Provided, however,* That if a complainant shall also allege that, unless a temporary restraining order shall be issued without notice, a substantial and irreparable injury to complainant's property will be unavoidable, such a temporary restraining order may be issued upon testimony under oath, sufficient, if sustained, to justify the court in issuing a temporary injunction upon a hearing after notice. Such a temporary restraining order shall be effective for no longer than five days and shall become void at the expiration of said five days. No temporary restraining order or temporary injunction shall be issued except on condition that complainant shall first file an undertaking with adequate security in an amount to be fixed by the court sufficient to recompense those enjoined for any loss, expense, or damage caused by the improvident or erroneous issuance of such order or injunction, including all reasonable costs (together with a reasonable attorney's fee) and expense of defense against the order or against the granting of any injunctive relief sought in the same proceeding and subsequently denied by the court.

The undertaking mentioned in this section shall be understood to signify an agreement entered into by the complainant and the surety upon which a decree may be rendered in the same suit or proceeding against said complainant and surety, upon a hearing to assess damages of which hearing complainant and surety shall have reasonable notice, the said complainant and surety submitting themselves to the jurisdiction of the court for that purpose. But nothing in this section contained shall deprive any party having a claim or cause of action under or upon such undertaking from electing to pursue his ordinary remedy by suit at law or in equity.

8. TITLE 42, UNITED STATES CODE

§ 1983. Civil action for deprivation of rights

Every person who, under color of any statute, ordinance, regulation, custom, or usage, of any State or Territory, subjects, or causes to be subjected, any citizen of the United States or other person within the jurisdiction thereof to the deprivation of any rights, privileges, or immunities secured by the Constitution and laws, shall be liable to the party injured in an action at law, suit in equity, or other proper proceeding for redress.

TABLE OF CASES

The principal cases are in italic type. Cases cited or discussed are in roman type. References are to pages.

INDEX

References are to Pages

University Casebook Series

December, 1983

ACCOUNTING AND THE LAW, Fourth Edition (1978), with Problems Pamphlet (Successor to Dohr, Phillips, Thompson & Warren)

George C. Thompson, Professor, Columbia University Graduate School of Business.
Robert Whitman, Professor of Law, University of Connecticut.
Ellis L. Phillips, Jr., Member of the New York Bar.
William C. Warren, Professor of Law Emeritus, Columbia University.

ACCOUNTING FOR LAWYERS, MATERIALS ON (1980)

David R. Herwitz, Professor of Law, Harvard University.

ADMINISTRATIVE LAW, Seventh Edition (1979), with 1983 Problems Supplement (Supplement edited in association with Paul R. Verkuil, Dean and Professor of Law, Tulane University)

Walter Gellhorn, University Professor Emeritus, Columbia University.
Clark Byse, Professor of Law, Harvard University.
Peter L. Strauss, Professor of Law, Columbia University.

ADMIRALTY, Second Edition (1978), with Statute and Rule Supplement

Jo Desha Lucas, Professor of Law, University of Chicago.

ADVOCACY, see also Lawyering Process

AGENCY, see also Enterprise Organization

AGENCY—PARTNERSHIPS, Third Edition (1982)

Abridgement from Conard, Knauss & Siegel's Enterprise Organization, Third Edition.

ANTITRUST: FREE ENTERPRISE AND ECONOMIC ORGANIZATION, Sixth Edition (1983), with Problems in Antitrust Supplement

Louis B. Schwartz, Professor of Law, University of Pennsylvania.
John J. Flynn, Professor of Law, University of Utah.
Harry First, Professor of Law, New York University.

ANTITRUST SUPPLEMENT—SELECTED STATUTES AND RELATED MATERIALS (1977)

John J. Flynn, Professor of Law, University of Utah.

BUSINESS ORGANIZATION, see also Enterprise Organization

BUSINESS PLANNING (1966), with 1983 Supplement

David R. Herwitz, Professor of Law, Harvard University.

BUSINESS TORTS (1972)

Milton Handler, Professor of Law Emeritus, Columbia University.

CHILDREN IN THE LEGAL SYSTEM (1983)

Walter Wadlington, Professor of Law, University of Virginia.
Charles H. Whitebread, Professor of Law, University of Southern California.
Samuel Davis, Professor of Law, University of Georgia.

CIVIL PROCEDURE, see Procedure

CLINIC, see also Lawyering Process

COMMERCIAL LAW (1983)

Robert L. Jordan, Professor of Law, University of California, Los Angeles.
William D. Warren, Professor of Law, University of California, Los Angeles.

COMMERCIAL LAW, CASES & MATERIALS ON, Third Edition (1976), with 1982 Bankruptcy Supplement

E. Allan Farnsworth, Professor of Law, Columbia University.
John Honnold, Professor of Law, University of Pennsylvania.

COMMERCIAL PAPER, Second Edition (1976)

E. Allan Farnsworth, Professor of Law, Columbia University.

COMMERCIAL PAPER (1983) (Reprinted from COMMERCIAL LAW)

Robert L. Jordan, Professor of Law, University of California, Los Angeles.
William D. Warren, Professor of Law, University of California, Los Angeles.

COMMERCIAL PAPER AND BANK DEPOSITS AND COLLECTIONS (1967), with Statutory Supplement

William D. Hawkland, Professor of Law, University of Illinois.

COMMERCIAL TRANSACTIONS—Principles and Policies (1982)

Alan Schwartz, Professor of Law, University of Southern California.
Robert E. Scott, Professor of Law, University of Virginia.

COMPARATIVE LAW, Fourth Edition (1980)

Rudolf B. Schlesinger, Professor of Law, Hastings College of the Law.

COMPETITIVE PROCESS, LEGAL REGULATION OF THE, Second Edition (1979), with Statutory Supplement and 1982 Case Supplement

Edmund W. Kitch, Professor of Law, University of Chicago.
Harvey S. Perlman, Professor of Law, University of Virginia.

CONFLICT OF LAWS, Seventh Edition (1978), with 1982 Supplement

Willis L. M. Reese, Professor of Law, Columbia University,
Maurice Rosenberg, Professor of Law, Columbia University.

CONSTITUTIONAL LAW, Sixth Edition (1981), with 1983 Supplement

Edward L. Barrett, Jr., Professor of Law, University of California, Davis.
William Cohen, Professor of Law, Stanford University.

CONSTITUTIONAL LAW: THE STRUCTURE OF GOVERNMENT (Reprinted from CONSTITUTIONAL LAW, Sixth Edition), with 1983 Supplement

Edward L. Barrett, Jr., Professor of Law, University of California, Davis.
William Cohen, Professor of Law, Stanford University.

CONSTITUTIONAL LAW, CIVIL LIBERTY AND INDIVIDUAL RIGHTS, Second Edition (1982), with 1983 Supplement

William Cohen, Professor of Law, Stanford University.
John Kaplan, Professor of Law, Stanford University.

CONSTITUTIONAL LAW, Tenth Edition (1980), with 1983 Supplement (Supplement edited in association with Frederick F. Schauer, Professor of Law, College of William and Mary)

Gerald Gunther, Professor of Law, Stanford University.

CONSTITUTIONAL LAW, INDIVIDUAL RIGHTS IN, Third Edition (1981) (Reprinted from CONSTITUTIONAL LAW, Tenth Edition), with 1983 Supplement (Supplement edited in association with Frederick F. Schauer, Professor of Law, College of William and Mary)

Gerald Gunther, Professor of Law, Stanford University.

CONSUMER TRANSACTIONS (1983), with Selected Statutes and Regulations Supplement

Michael M. Greenfield, Professor of Law, Washington University.

CONTRACT LAW AND ITS APPLICATION, Third Edition (1983)

The late Addison Mueller, Professor of Law, University of California, Los Angeles.
Arthur I. Rosett, Professor of Law, University of California, Los Angeles.
Gerald P. Lopez, Professor of Law, University of California, Los Angeles.

CONTRACT LAW, STUDIES IN, Second Edition (1977)

Edward J. Murphy, Professor of Law, University of Notre Dame.
Richard E. Speidel, Professor of Law, University of Virginia.

CONTRACTS, Fourth Edition (1982)

John P. Dawson, Professor of Law Emeritus, Harvard University.
William Burnett Harvey, Professor of Law and Political Science, Boston University.
Stanley D. Henderson, Professor of Law, University of Virginia.

CONTRACTS, Third Edition (1980), with Statutory Supplement

E. Allan Farnsworth, Professor of Law, Columbia University.
William F. Young, Professor of Law, Columbia University.

CONTRACTS, Second Edition (1978), with Statutory and Administrative Law Supplement (1978)

Ian R. Macneil, Professor of Law, Cornell University.

COPYRIGHT, PATENTS AND TRADEMARKS, see also Competitive Process

COPYRIGHT, PATENT, TRADEMARK AND RELATED STATE DOCTRINES, Second Edition (1981), with Problem Supplement and Statutory Supplement

Paul Goldstein, Professor of Law, Stanford University.

COPYRIGHT, Unfair Competition, and Other Topics Bearing on the Protection of Literary, Musical, and Artistic Works, Third Edition (1978)

Benjamin Kaplan, Professor of Law Emeritus, Harvard University,
Ralph S. Brown, Jr., Professor of Law, Yale University.

CORPORATE FINANCE, Second Edition (1979), with 1982 New Developments Supplement

Victor Brudney, Professor of Law, Harvard University.
Marvin A. Chirelstein, Professor of Law, Yale University.

CORPORATE READJUSTMENTS AND REORGANIZATIONS (1976)

Walter J. Blum, Professor of Law, University of Chicago.
Stanley A. Kaplan, Professor of Law, University of Chicago.

CORPORATION LAW, BASIC, Second Edition (1979), with 1983 Case and Documentary Supplement

Detlev F. Vagts, Professor of Law, Harvard University.

CORPORATIONS, see also Enterprise Organization

CORPORATIONS, Fifth Edition—Unabridged (1980), with 1983 Supplement

The late William L. Cary, Professor of Law, Columbia University.
Melvin Aron Eisenberg, Professor of Law, University of California, Berkeley.

CORPORATIONS, Fifth Edition—Abridged (1980), with 1983 Supplement

The late William L. Cary, Professor of Law, Columbia University.
Melvin Aron Eisenberg, Professor of Law, University of California, Berkeley.

CORPORATIONS, Second Edition (1982), with 1982 Corporation and Partnership Statutes, Rules and Forms

Alfred F. Conard, Professor of Law, University of Michigan.
Robert N. Knauss, Dean of the Law School, University of Houston.
Stanley Siegel, Professor of Law, University of California, Los Angeles.

CORPORATIONS, THE LAW OF: WHAT CORPORATE LAWYERS DO (1976)

Jan G. Deutsch, Professor of Law, Yale University.
Joseph J. Bianco, Professor of Law, Yeshiva University.

CORPORATIONS COURSE GAME PLAN (1975)

David R. Herwitz, Professor of Law, Harvard University.

CORRECTIONS, SEE SENTENCING

CREDIT TRANSACTIONS AND CONSUMER PROTECTION (1976)

John Honnold, Professor of Law, University of Pennsylvania.

CREDITORS' RIGHTS, see also Debtor-Creditor Law

CRIMINAL JUSTICE, THE ADMINISTRATION OF, Second Edition (1969)

Francis C. Sullivan, Professor of Law, Louisiana State University.
Paul Hardin III, Professor of Law, Duke University.
John Huston, Professor of Law, University of Washington.
Frank R. Lacy, Professor of Law, University of Oregon.
Daniel E. Murray, Professor of Law, University of Miami.
George W. Pugh, Professor of Law, Louisiana State University.

CRIMINAL JUSTICE ADMINISTRATION, Second Edition (1982), with 1983 Supplement

Frank W. Miller, Professor of Law, Washington University.
Robert O. Dawson, Professor of Law, University of Texas.
George E. Dix, Professor of Law, University of Texas.
Raymond I. Parnas, Professor of Law, University of California, Davis.

CRIMINAL LAW, Third Edition (1983)

Fred E. Inbau, Professor of Law Emeritus, Northwestern University.
James R. Thompson, Professor of Law Emeritus, Northwestern University.
Andre A. Moenssens, Professor of Law, University of Richmond.

CRIMINAL LAW (1982), with 1983 Supplement

Peter W. Low, Professor of Law, University of Virginia.
John C. Jeffries, Jr., Professor of Law, University of Virginia.
Richard C. Bonnie, Professor of Law, University of Virginia.

CRIMINAL LAW, Third Edition (1980)

Lloyd L. Weinreb, Professor of Law, Harvard University.

CRIMINAL LAW AND PROCEDURE, Fifth Edition (1977)

Rollin M. Perkins, Professor of Law Emeritus, University of California, Hastings College of the Law.
Ronald N. Boyce, Professor of Law, University of Utah.

CRIMINAL PROCEDURE, Second Edition (1980), with 1983 Supplement

Fred E. Inbau, Professor of Law Emeritus, Northwestern University.
James R. Thompson, Professor of Law Emeritus, Northwestern University.
James B. Haddad, Professor of Law, Northwestern University.
James B. Zagel, Chief, Criminal Justice Division, Office of Attorney General of Illinois.
Gary L. Starkman, Assistant U. S. Attorney, Northern District of Illinois.

CRIMINAL PROCEDURE, CONSTITUTIONAL (1977), with 1980 Supplement

James E. Scarboro, Professor of Law, University of Colorado.
James B. White, Professor of Law, University of Chicago.

CRIMINAL PROCESS, Third Edition (1978), with 1983 Supplement

Lloyd L. Weinreb, Professor of Law, Harvard University.

DAMAGES, Second Edition (1952)

Charles T. McCormick, late Professor of Law, University of Texas.
William F. Fritz, late Professor of Law, University of Texas.

DEBTOR-CREDITOR LAW (1984)

Theodore Eisenberg, Professor of Law, Cornell University.

DEBTOR-CREDITOR LAW, Second Edition (1981), with Statutory Supplement

William D. Warren, Dean of the School of Law, University of California, Los Angeles.
William E. Hogan, Professor of Law, New York University.

DECEDENTS' ESTATES (1971)

Max Rheinstein, late Professor of Law Emeritus, University of Chicago.
Mary Ann Glendon, Professor of Law, Boston College.

DECEDENTS' ESTATES AND TRUSTS, Sixth Edition (1982)

John Ritchie, Emeritus Dean and Wigmore Professor of Law, Northwestern University.
Neill H. Alford, Jr., Professor of Law, University of Virginia.
Richard W. Effland, Professor of Law, Arizona State University.

DECEDENTS' ESTATES AND TRUSTS (1968)

Howard R. Williams, Professor of Law, Stanford University.

DOMESTIC RELATIONS, see also Family Law

DOMESTIC RELATIONS, Third Edition (1978), with 1980 Supplement

Walter Wadlington, Professor of Law, University of Virginia.
Monrad G. Paulsen, Dean of the Law School, Yeshiva University.

ELECTRONIC MASS MEDIA, Second Edition (1979)

William K. Jones, Professor of Law, Columbia University.

EMPLOYMENT DISCRIMINATION (1983)

Joel W. Friedman, Professor of Law, Tulane University.
George M. Strickler, Professor of Law, Tulane University.

ENERGY LAW (1983)

Donald N. Zillman, Professor of Law, University of Utah.
Laurence Lattman, Dean of Mines and Engineering, University of Utah.

ENTERPRISE ORGANIZATION, Third Edition (1982), with 1982 Corporation and Partnership Statutes, Rules and Forms Supplement

Alfred F. Conard, Professor of Law, University of Michigan.
Robert L. Knauss, Dean of the Law School, University of Houston.
Stanley Siegel, Professor of Law, University of California, Los Angeles.

ENVIRONMENTAL POLICY LAW (1982)

Thomas J. Schoenbaum, Professor of Law, Tulane University.

EQUITY, see also Remedies

EQUITY, RESTITUTION AND DAMAGES, Second Edition (1974)

Robert Childres, late Professor of Law, Northwestern University.
William F. Johnson, Jr., Professor of Law, New York University.

ESTATE PLANNING, Second Edition (1982), with Documentary Supplement

David Westfall, Professor of Law, Harvard University.

ETHICS, see Legal Profession, and Professional Responsibility

ETHICS AND PROFESSIONAL RESPONSIBILITY (1981) (Reprinted from THE LAWYERING PROCESS)

Gary Bellow, Professor of Law, Harvard University.
Bea Moulton, Legal Services Corporation.

EVIDENCE, Fourth Edition (1981)

David W. Louisell, late Professor of Law, University of California, Berkeley.
John Kaplan, Professor of Law, Stanford University.
Jon R. Waltz, Professor of Law, Northwestern University.

EVIDENCE (1968)

Francis C. Sullivan, Professor of Law, Louisiana State University.
Paul Hardin, III, Professor of Law, Duke University.

EVIDENCE, Seventh Edition (1983), with Rules and Statute Supplement (1984)

Jack B. Weinstein, Chief Judge, United States District Court.
John H. Mansfield, Professor of Law, Harvard University.
Norman Abrams, Professor of Law, University of California, Los Angeles.
Margaret Berger, Professor of Law, Brooklyn Law School.

FAMILY LAW, see also Domestic Relations

FAMILY LAW (1978), with 1983 Supplement

Judith C. Areen, Professor of Law, Georgetown University.

FAMILY LAW AND CHILDREN IN THE LEGAL SYSTEM, STATUTORY MATERIALS (1981)

Walter Wadlington, Professor of Law, University of Virginia.

FEDERAL COURTS, Seventh Edition (1982), with 1983 Supplement

Charles T. McCormick, late Professor of Law, University of Texas.
James H. Chadbourn, late Professor of Law, Harvard University.
Charles Alan Wright, Professor of Law, University of Texas.

FEDERAL COURTS AND THE FEDERAL SYSTEM, Hart and Wechsler's Second Edition (1973), with 1981 Supplement

Paul M. Bator, Professor of Law, Harvard University.
Paul J. Mishkin, Professor of Law, University of California, Berkeley.
David L. Shapiro, Professor of Law, Harvard University.
Herbert Wechsler, Professor of Law, Columbia University.

FEDERAL PUBLIC LAND AND RESOURCES LAW (1981), with 1983 Supplement

George C. Coggins, Professor of Law, University of Kansas.
Charles F. Wilkinson, Professor of Law, University of Oregon.

FEDERAL RULES OF CIVIL PROCEDURE, 1983 Edition

FEDERAL TAXATION, see Taxation

FOOD AND DRUG LAW (1980), with Statutory Supplement

Richard A. Merrill, Dean of the School of Law, University of Virginia.
Peter Barton Hutt, Esq.

FUTURE INTERESTS (1958)

Philip Mechem, late Professor of Law Emeritus, University of Pennsylvania.

FUTURE INTERESTS (1970)

Howard R. Williams, Professor of Law, Stanford University.

FUTURE INTERESTS AND ESTATE PLANNING (1961), with 1962 Supplement

W. Barton Leach, late Professor of Law, Harvard University.
James K. Logan, formerly Dean of the Law School, University of Kansas.

GOVERNMENT CONTRACTS, FEDERAL (1975), with 1980 Supplement

John W. Whelan, Professor of Law, Hastings College of the Law.
Robert S. Pasley, Professor of Law Emeritus, Cornell University.

INJUNCTIONS, Second Edition (1984)

Owen M. Fiss, Professor of Law, Yale University.
Doug Rendleman, Professor of Law, College of William and Mary.

INSTITUTIONAL INVESTORS, 1978

David L. Ratner, Professor of Law, Cornell University.

INSURANCE (1971)

William F. Young, Professor of Law, Columbia University.

INTERNATIONAL LAW, see also Transnational Legal Problems and United Nations Law

INTERNATIONAL LAW IN CONTEMPORARY PERSPECTIVE (1981), with Essay Supplement

Myres S. McDougal, Professor of Law, Yale University.
W. Michael Reisman, Professor of Law, Yale University.

INTERNATIONAL LEGAL SYSTEM, Second Edition (1981), with Documentary Supplement

Joseph Modeste Sweeney, Professor of Law, Tulane University.
Covey T. Oliver, Professor of Law, University of Pennsylvania.
Noyes E. Leech, Professor of Law, University of Pennsylvania.

INTRODUCTION TO LAW, see also Legal Method, On Law in Courts, and Dynamics of American Law

INTRODUCTION TO THE STUDY OF LAW (1970)

E. Wayne Thode, late Professor of Law, University of Utah.
Leon Lebowitz, Professor of Law, University of Texas.
Lester J. Mazor, Professor of Law, University of Utah.

JUDICIAL CODE and Rules of Procedure in the Federal Courts with Excerpts from the Criminal Code, 1984 Edition

Henry M. Hart, Jr., late Professor of Law, Harvard University.
Herbert Wechsler, Professor of Law, Columbia University.

JURISPRUDENCE (Temporary Edition Hardbound) (1949)

Lon L. Fuller, Professor of Law Emeritus, Harvard University.

JUVENILE, see also Children

JUVENILE JUSTICE PROCESS, Second Edition (1976), with 1980 Supplement

Frank W. Miller, Professor of Law, Washington University.
Robert O. Dawson, Professor of Law, University of Texas.
George E. Dix, Professor of Law, University of Texas.
Raymond I. Parnas, Professor of Law, University of California, Davis.

LABOR LAW, Ninth Edition (1981), with 1983 Case Supplement and 1977 Statutory Supplement

Archibald Cox, Professor of Law, Harvard University.
Derek C. Bok, President, Harvard University.
Robert A. Gorman, Professor of Law, University of Pennsylvania.

LABOR LAW, Second Edition (1982), with Statutory Supplement

Clyde W. Summers, Professor of Law, University of Pennsylvania.
Harry H. Wellington, Dean of the Law School, Yale University.
Alan Hyde, Professor of Law, Rutgers University.

LAND FINANCING, Second Edition (1977)

The late Norman Penney, Professor of Law, Cornell University.
Richard F. Broude, Member of the California Bar.

LAW AND MEDICINE (1980)

Walter Wadlington, Professor of Law and Professor of Legal Medicine, University of Virginia.
Jon R. Waltz, Professor of Law, Northwestern University.
Roger B. Dworkin, Professor of Law, Indiana University, and Professor of Biomedical History, University of Washington.

LAW, LANGUAGE AND ETHICS (1972)

William R. Bishin, Professor of Law, University of Southern California.
Christopher D. Stone, Professor of Law, University of Southern California.

LAWYERING PROCESS (1978), with Civil Problem Supplement and Criminal Problem Supplement

Gary Bellow, Professor of Law, Harvard University.
Bea Moulton, Professor of Law, Arizona State University.

LEGAL METHOD (1980)

Harry W. Jones, Professor of Law Emeritus, Columbia University.
John M. Kernochan, Professor of Law, Columbia University.
Arthur W. Murphy, Professor of Law, Columbia University.

LEGAL METHODS (1969)

Robert N. Covington, Professor of Law, Vanderbilt University.
E. Blythe Stason, late Professor of Law, Vanderbilt University.
John W. Wade, Professor of Law, Vanderbilt University.
Elliott E. Cheatham, late Professor of Law, Vanderbilt University.
Theodore A. Smedley, Professor of Law, Vanderbilt University.

LEGAL PROFESSION (1970)

Samuel D. Thurman, Dean of the College of Law, University of Utah.
Ellis L. Phillips, Jr., Professor of Law, Columbia University.
Elliott E. Cheatham, late Professor of Law, Vanderbilt University.

LEGISLATION, Fourth Edition (1982) (by Fordham)

Horace E. Read, late Vice President, Dalhousie University.
John W. MacDonald, Professor of Law Emeritus, Cornell Law School.
Jefferson B. Fordham, Professor of Law, University of Utah.
William J. Pierce, Professor of Law, University of Michigan.

LEGISLATIVE AND ADMINISTRATIVE PROCESSES, Second Edition (1981)

Hans A. Linde, Judge, Supreme Court of Oregon.
George Bunn, Professor of Law, University of Wisconsin.
Fredericka Paff, Professor of Law, University of Wisconsin.
W. Lawrence Church, Professor of Law, University of Wisconsin.

LOCAL GOVERNMENT LAW, Revised Edition (1975)

Jefferson B. Fordham, Professor of Law, University of Utah.

MASS MEDIA LAW, Second Edition (1982)

Marc A. Franklin, Professor of Law, Stanford University.

MENTAL HEALTH PROCESS, Second Edition (1976), with 1981 Supplement

Frank W. Miller, Professor of Law, Washington University.
Robert O. Dawson, Professor of Law, University of Texas.
George E. Dix, Professor of Law, University of Texas.
Raymond I. Parnas, Professor of Law, University of California, Davis.

MUNICIPAL CORPORATIONS, see Local Government Law

NEGOTIABLE INSTRUMENTS, see Commercial Paper

NEGOTIATION (1981) (Reprinted from THE LAWYERING PROCESS)

Gary Bellow, Professor of Law, Harvard Law School.
Bea Moulton, Legal Services Corporation.

NEW YORK PRACTICE, Fourth Edition (1978)

Herbert Peterfreund, Professor of Law, New York University.
Joseph M. McLaughlin, Dean of the Law School, Fordham University.

OIL AND GAS, Fourth Edition (1979)

Howard R. Williams, Professor of Law, Stanford University.
Richard C. Maxwell, Professor of Law, University of California, Los Angeles.
Charles J. Meyers, Dean of the Law School, Stanford University.

ON LAW IN COURTS (1965)

Paul J. Mishkin, Professor of Law, University of California, Berkeley.
Clarence Morris, Professor of Law Emeritus, University of Pennsylvania.

PATENTS AND ANTITRUST (Pamphlet) (1983)

Milton Handler, Professor of Law Emeritus, Columbia University.
Harlan M. Blake, Professor of Law, Columbia University.
Robert Pitofsky, Professor of Law, Georgetown University.
Harvey J. Goldschmid, Professor of Law, Columbia University.

PERSPECTIVES ON THE LAWYER AS PLANNER (Reprint of Chapters One through Five of Planning by Lawyers) (1978)

Louis M. Brown, Professor of Law, University of Southern California.
Edward A. Dauer, Professor of Law, Yale University.

PLANNING BY LAWYERS, MATERIALS ON A NONADVERSARIAL LEGAL PROCESS (1978)

Louis M. Brown, Professor of Law, University of Southern California.
Edward A. Dauer, Professor of Law, Yale University.

PLEADING AND PROCEDURE, see Procedure, Civil

POLICE FUNCTION, Third Edition (1982), with 1983 Supplement

Reprint of Chapters 1–10 of Miller, Dawson, Dix and Parnas's CRIMINAL JUSTICE ADMINISTRATION, Second Edition.

PREPARING AND PRESENTING THE CASE (1981) (Reprinted from THE LAWYERING PROCESS)

Gary Bellow, Professor of Law, Harvard Law School.
Bea Moulton, Legal Services Corporation.

PREVENTIVE LAW, see also Planning by Lawyers

PROCEDURE—CIVIL PROCEDURE, Second Edition (1974), with 1979 Supplement

The late James H. Chadbourn, Professor of Law, Harvard University.
A. Leo Levin, Professor of Law, University of Pennsylvania.
Philip Shuchman, Professor of Law, Cornell University.

PROCEDURE—CIVIL PROCEDURE, Fourth Edition (1978), with 1983 Supplement

Richard H. Field, late Professor of Law, Harvard University.
Benjamin Kaplan, Professor of Law Emeritus, Harvard University.
Kevin M. Clermont, Professor of Law, Cornell University.

PROCEDURE—CIVIL PROCEDURE, Third Edition (1976), with 1982 Supplement

Maurice Rosenberg, Professor of Law, Columbia University.
Jack B. Weinstein, Professor of Law, Columbia University.
Hans Smit, Professor of Law, Columbia University.
Harold L. Korn, Professor of Law, Columbia University.

PROCEDURE—PLEADING AND PROCEDURE: State and Federal, Fifth Edition (1983)

David W. Louisell, late Professor of Law, University of California, Berkeley.
Geoffrey C. Hazard, Jr., Professor of Law, Yale University.
Colin C. Tait, Professor of Law, University of Connecticut.

PROCEDURE—FEDERAL RULES OF CIVIL PROCEDURE, 1983 Edition

PRODUCTS LIABILITY (1980)

Marshall S. Shapo, Professor of Law, Northwestern University.

PRODUCTS LIABILITY AND SAFETY (1980), with 1983 Case and Documentary Supplement

W. Page Keeton, Professor of Law, University of Texas.
David G. Owen, Professor of Law, University of South Carolina.
John E. Montgomery, Professor of Law, University of South Carolina.

PROFESSIONAL RESPONSIBILITY, Second Edition (1981), with 1983 Selected National Standards Supplement

Thomas D. Morgan, Dean of the Law School, Emory University.
Ronald D. Rotunda, Professor of Law, University of Illinois.

PROPERTY, Fourth Edition (1978)

John E. Cribbet, Dean of the Law School, University of Illinois.
Corwin W. Johnson, Professor of Law, University of Texas.

PROPERTY—PERSONAL (1953)

S. Kenneth Skolfield, late Professor of Law Emeritus, Boston University.

PROPERTY—PERSONAL, Third Edition (1954)

Everett Fraser, late Dean of the Law School Emeritus, University of Minnesota.
Third Edition by Charles W. Taintor, late Professor of Law, University of Pittsburgh.

PROPERTY—INTRODUCTION, TO REAL PROPERTY, Third Edition (1954)

Everett Fraser, late Dean of the Law School Emeritus, University of Minnesota.

PROPERTY—REAL AND PERSONAL, Combined Edition (1954)

Everett Fraser, late Dean of the Law School Emeritus, University of Minnesota.
Third Edition of Personal Property by Charles W. Taintor, late Professor of Law, University of Pittsburgh.

PROPERTY—FUNDAMENTALS OF MODERN REAL PROPERTY, Second Edition (1982)

Edward H. Rabin, Professor of Law, University of California, Davis.

PROPERTY—PROBLEMS IN REAL PROPERTY (Pamphlet) (1969)

Edward H. Rabin, Professor of Law, University of California, Davis.

PROSECUTION AND ADJUDICATION, Second Edition (1982), with 1983 Supplement

Reprint of Chapters 11–26 of Miller, Dawson, Dix and Parnas's CRIMINAL JUSTICE ADMINISTRATION, Second Edition.

PUBLIC REGULATION OF DANGEROUS PRODUCTS (paperback) (1980)

Marshall S. Shapo, Professor of Law, Northwestern University.

PUBLIC UTILITY LAW, see Free Enterprise, also Regulated Industries

REAL ESTATE PLANNING (1980), with 1980 Problems, Statutes and New Materials Supplement

Norton L. Steuben, Professor of Law, University of Colorado.

REAL ESTATE TRANSACTIONS (1980), with Statute, Form and Problem Supplement

Paul Goldstein, Professor of Law, Stanford University.

RECEIVERSHIP AND CORPORATE REORGANIZATION, see Creditors' Rights

REGULATED INDUSTRIES, Second Edition, 1976

William K. Jones, Professor of Law, Columbia University.

REMEDIES (1982)

Edward D. Re, Chief Judge, U. S. Court of International Trade.

RESTITUTION, Second Edition (1966)

John W. Wade, Professor of Law, Vanderbilt University.

SALES (1980)

Marion W. Benfield, Jr., Professor of Law, University of Illinois.
William D. Hawkland, Chancellor, Louisiana State University Law Center.

SALES AND SALES FINANCING, Fourth Edition (1976), with 1982 Bankruptcy Supplement

John Honnold, Professor of Law, University of Pennsylvania.

SALES LAW AND THE CONTRACTING PROCESS (1982)

Reprint of Chapters 1–10 of Schwartz and Scott's Commercial Transactions.

SECURED INTERESTS IN PERSONAL PROPERTY (1984)

Douglas G. Baird, Professor of Law, University of Chicago.
Thomas H. Jackson, Professor of Law, Stanford University.

SECURED TRANSACTIONS IN PERSONAL PROPERTY (1983) (Reprinted from COMMERCIAL LAW)

Robert L. Jordan, Professor of Law, University of California, Los Angeles.
William D. Warren, Professor of Law, University of California, Los Angeles.

SECURITIES REGULATION, Fifth Edition (1982), with 1983 Cases and Releases Supplement and 1983 Selected Statutes, Rules and Forms Supplement

Richard W. Jennings, Professor of Law, University of California, Berkeley.
Harold Marsh, Jr., Member of the California Bar.

SECURITIES REGULATION (1982), with 1983 Supplement

Larry D. Soderquist, Professor of Law, Vanderbilt University.

SENTENCING AND THE CORRECTIONAL PROCESS, Second Edition (1976)

Frank W. Miller, Professor of Law, Washington University.
Robert O. Dawson, Professor of Law, University of Texas.
George E. Dix, Professor of Law, University of Texas.
Raymond I. Parnas, Professor of Law, University of California, Davis.

SOCIAL WELFARE AND THE INDIVIDUAL (1971)

Robert J. Levy, Professor of Law, University of Minnesota.
Thomas P. Lewis, Dean of the College of Law, University of Kentucky.
Peter W. Martin, Professor of Law, Cornell University.

TAX, POLICY ANALYSIS OF THE FEDERAL INCOME (1976)

William A. Klein, Professor of Law, University of California, Los Angeles.

TAXATION, FEDERAL INCOME (1976), with 1983 Supplement

Erwin N. Griswold, Dean Emeritus, Harvard Law School.
Michael J. Graetz, Professor of Law, University of Virginia.

TAXATION, FEDERAL INCOME, Fourth Edition (1982)

James J. Freeland, Professor of Law, University of Florida.
Stephen A. Lind, Professor of Law, University of Florida.
Richard B. Stephens, Professor of Law Emeritus, University of Florida.

TAXATION, FEDERAL INCOME, Volume I, Personal Income Taxation (1972), with 1983 Case Supplement; Volume II, Taxation of Partnerships and Corporations, Second Edition (1980), with 1983 Legislative Supplement

Stanley S. Surrey, Professor of Law, Harvard University.
William C. Warren, Professor of Law Emeritus, Columbia University.
Paul R. McDaniel, Professor of Law, Boston College Law School.
Hugh J. Ault, Professor of Law, Boston College Law School.

TAXATION, FEDERAL WEALTH TRANSFER, Second Edition (1982)

Stanley S. Surrey, Professor of Law, Harvard University.
William C. Warren, Professor of Law Emeritus, Columbia University.
Paul R. McDaniel, Professor of Law, Boston College Law School.
Harry L. Gutman, Instructor, Harvard Law School and Boston College Law School.

TAXATION OF INDIVIDUALS, PARTNERSHIPS AND CORPORATIONS, PROBLEMS in the (1978)

Norton L. Steuben, Professor of Law, University of Colorado.
William J. Turnier, Professor of Law, University of North Carolina.

TAXES AND FINANCE—STATE AND LOCAL (1974)

Oliver Oldman, Professor of Law, Harvard University.
Ferdinand P. Schoettle, Professor of Law, University of Minnesota.

TORT LAW AND ALTERNATIVES, Third Edition (1983)

Marc A. Franklin, Professor of Law, Stanford University.
Robert L. Rabin, Professor of Law, Stanford University.

TORTS, Seventh Edition (1982)

William L. Prosser, late Professor of Law, University of California, Hastings College.
John W. Wade, Professor of Law, Vanderbilt University.
Victor E. Schwartz, Professor of Law, American University.

TORTS, Third Edition (1976)

Harry Shulman, late Dean of the Law School, Yale University.
Fleming James, Jr., Professor of Law Emeritus, Yale University.
Oscar S. Gray, Professor of Law, University of Maryland.

TRADE REGULATION, Second Edition (1983)

Milton Handler, Professor of Law Emeritus, Columbia University.
Harlan M. Blake, Professor of Law, Columbia University.
Robert Pitofsky, Professor of Law, Georgetown University.
Harvey J. Goldschmid, Professor of Law, Columbia University.

TRADE REGULATION, see Antitrust

UNIVERSITY CASEBOOK SERIES—Continued

TRANSNATIONAL LEGAL PROBLEMS, Second Edition (1976) with 1982 Case and Documentary Supplement

Henry J. Steiner, Professor of Law, Harvard University.
Detlev F. Vagts, Professor of Law, Harvard University.

TRIAL, see also Evidence, Making the Record, Lawyering Process and Preparing and Presenting the Case

TRIAL ADVOCACY (1968)

A. Leo Levin, Professor of Law, University of Pennsylvania.
Harold Cramer, of the Pennsylvania Bar.
Maurice Rosenberg, Professor of Law, Columbia University, Consultant.

TRUSTS, Fifth Edition (1978)

George G. Bogert, late Professor of Law Emeritus, University of Chicago.
Dallin H. Oaks, President, Brigham Young University.

TRUSTS AND SUCCESSION (Palmer's), Fourth Edition (1983)

Richard V. Wellman, Professor of Law, University of Georgia.
Lawrence W. Waggoner, Professor of Law, University of Michigan.
Olin L. Browder, Jr., Professor of Law, University of Michigan.

UNFAIR COMPETITION, see Competitive Process and Business Torts

UNITED NATIONS IN ACTION (1968)

Louis B. Sohn, Professor of Law, Harvard University.

UNITED NATIONS LAW, Second Edition (1967), with Documentary Supplement (1968)

Louis B. Sohn, Professor of Law, Harvard University.

WATER RESOURCE MANAGEMENT, Second Edition (1980), with 1983 Supplement

Charles J. Meyers, Dean of the Law School, Stanford University.
A. Dan Tarlock, Professor of Law, Indiana Unversity.

WILLS AND ADMINISTRATION, Fifth Edition (1961)

Philip Mechem, late Professor of Law, University of Pennsylvania.
Thomas E. Atkinson, late Professor of Law, New York University.

WORLD LAW, see United Nations Law